YSTD

Who's

JUNIOR & SE

Biographical Titles Currently Published by Marquis Who's Who

Who's Who in America
Who's Who in America derivatives:
    Who's Who in America Junior & Senior High School Version
    Geographic/Professional Index
    Supplement to Who's Who in America
    Who's Who in America Classroom Project Book
Who Was Who in America
    Historical Volume (1607-1896)
    Volume I (1897-1942)
    Volume II (1943-1950)
    Volume III (1951-1960)
    Volume IV (1961-1968)
    Volume V (1969-1973)
    Volume VI (1974-1976)
    Volume VII (1977-1981)
    Volume VIII (1982-1985)
    Volume IX (1985-1989)
    Index Volume (1607-1989)
Who's Who in the World
Who's Who in the East
Who's Who in the Midwest
Who's Who in the South and Southwest
Who's Who in the West
Who's Who in Advertising
Who's Who in American Law
Who's Who of American Women
Who's Who of Emerging Leaders in America
Who's Who in Entertainment
Who's Who in Finance and Industry
Index to Who's Who Books
Directory of Medical Specialists
Supplement to Directory of Medical Specialists

Who'sWho in America ®
JUNIOR & SENIOR HIGH SCHOOL VERSION

VOLUME 1: SCIENCE & TECHNOLOGY
1989-1991

MARQUIS
Who'sWho

Macmillan Directory Division
3002 Glenview Road
Wilmette, Illinois 60091 U.S.A.

James J. Pfister—President
Paul E. Rose—Executive Vice President
Timothy J. Sullivan—Vice President, Finance
A. Robert Weicherding—Vice President, Publisher
Sandra S. Barnes—Group Vice President, Product Management
Jill E. Lazar—Product Manager
John L. Daniels—Product Manager
Frederick M. Marks—Manager, Biographical Research

WHO'S WHO IN AMERICA JUNIOR & SENIOR HIGH SCHOOL VERSION is a
registered trademark of Macmillan Information Company, Inc.

Library of Congress Catalog Card Number 04–16934
International Standard Book Number 0–8379–1250–4
Product Code Number 030615

Manufactured in the United States of America

Table of Contents

Preface

The editors of Marquis Who's Who are pleased to introduce
the premier edition of the *Who's Who in America Junior & Senior
High School Version*. This publication is specifically designed for
junior and senior high school students by focusing on subjects and
individuals of great interest to young people. Entries in the
Junior & Senior High School Version contain exactly the same
information found in *Who's Who in America*, but with two key
differences. First, the type size is more than twice as large. Second,
each biographical profile appears in an unabbreviated, full-text format.
These two features enhance the book's overall readability. The
Junior & Senior High School Version has approximately 6000 entries
and is organized in four, easy-to-reference volumes: Science and
Technology, Politics and Government, Sports, and Entertainment.

The *Who's Who in America Junior & Senior High School Version*
will help junior and senior high school students with social studies
research projects and assignments. Its large type size, full-text format,
and subject organization will make information more accessible.

The standards of admission are exactly the same as those used in
Who's Who in America. The research staff provided important
information on high profile individuals who failed to submit
addenda to their biographies on their own. Sketches compiled by
the researchers are denoted by an asterisk. As always, ultimate
selection for the *Junior & Senior High School Version* was based on
reference value. Individuals became eligible for listing by virtue of
their positions and/or noteworthy achievements that have proved to
be of significant value to society. An individual's desire to be listed
was not sufficient reason for inclusion, nor were wealth or social
position criteria. Purchase of the book was not a factor in the
selection of biographees.

The editors exercise the utmost care in preparing each sketch
for publication. Occasionally, however, errors do appear.
Students and school librarians who use the directory are encouraged
to draw to the attention of the publisher any errors found so that
corrections can be made in a subsequent edition.

Cultural Organization, 1972,
nguished Pub. Service award
nal Science Foundation, 1984.
w Am. Physical Society,
ogical Society Am., Mineralogical
ty Am., Geological Society
hington, Am. Acad. Arts and
nces; member Am. Nuclear
ety, Seismological Society Am.,
national Union Geological
nces (president 1972-76), Brit.
hem. Society, Brit. Mineralogical
ty, Am. Chemical Society, Am.
sophical Society, Society Am.
eriologists, Am. Geophysical
n (president 1972-74), Am.
ciation Petroleum Geologists,
hem. Society, Washington Acad.
nces, Biophys. Society,
sophical Society Washington, Phi
Kappa (senator-at-large 1972—),
a Xi, National Acad. Sciences,
nal Institute Medical (senior).
Cosmos (president 1972).
e: Resources for the Future
porated 1616 P St Northwest
hington District of Columbia
6

RNATHY, FREDERICK H.,
nanical engineering educator;
Denver, June 30, 1930; son of
y James and Irene Sarah
man) A.; married AnnaMaria
ert, June 18, 1961; children:
h, Marian, Pauline. Bachelor of
nce in Mechanical Engineering,
ark College Engineering, 1951;
graduate, Oak Ridge School
tor Tech., 1952; Master of
nce, Harvard University, 1954,
or of Philosophy, 1959. Gordon
ay professor mechanical
eering Harvard University,
bridge, Massachusetts, 1963-72,
(on leave); director engineering
National Science Foundation,
hington, 1972-73, director

energy-realted research; 1973-74;
director Textile/Clothing Tech. Corp.,
Cambridge. Fellow Am. Acad. Arts
and Sciences; member American
Society of Mechanical Engineers, Am.
Society Engineering Education, Am.
Physical Society. Home: 45 Islington
Road Auburndale Massachusetts
02166 Office: Harvard University
Pierce Hall Cambridge Massachusetts
02138

ABRAMS, RICHARD LEE, physicist;
born Cleveland, April 20, 1941; son of
Morris S. and Corinne (Tobias) A.;
married Jane Shack, August 12, 1962;
children: Elizabeth, Laura. Bachelor
Engineering Physics, Cornell
University, Ithaca, New York, 1964,
Doctor of Philosophy, 1968. Member
tech. staff Bell Telephone
Laboratories, Whippany, New Jersey,
1968-71; section head Hughes
Research Laboratories, Malibu,
California, 1971-75, department
manager; 1975-83; chief scientist
Space and Communications group
Hughes Aircraft Company, El
Segundo, California, 1983-89; chief
scientist Hughes Research
Laboratories, Malibu, California,
1989—; program co-chairman
Conference on Laser Engineering and
Applications, Washington, 1979;
chairman Conference on Lasers and
Electro-Optics, Phoenix, 1982.
Associate editor: Optics Letters, 1979-
82; patentee in field. Fellow Institute
of Electrical and Electronics
Engineers (associate editor Jour.
Quantum Electronics 1980-83,
centennial medal 1989), Optical
Society Am. (board directors 1982-85,
vice president 1988, pres.-elect 1989);
member Institute of Electrical and
Electronics Engineers Quantum
Electronics and Applications Society
(adminstrve. committee 1980-83, vice

Key to Information

[1] **GIBSON, OSCAR JULIUS,** [2] physician; [3] born Syracuse, New York, August 31, 1937; [4] son of Paul Oliver and Elizabeth H. (Thrun) G.; [5] married Judith S. Gonzalez, April 28, 1968; [6] children: Tom, Pat. [7] Bachelor of Arts, University of Pennsylvania, 1960; Doctor of Medicine, Harvard University, 1964. [8] Diplomate Am. Board Internal Medicine. [9] Intern Barnes Hospital, St. Louis, 1964-65, resident, 1965-66; clinical associate National Heart Institute, National Institute of Health, Bethesda, Maryland, 1966-68; chief resident medicine University Oklahoma Hospitals, 1968-69; vice president medical staff Baptist Medical Center, Oklahoma City, 1982-86, senior vice president 1986—; member Oklahoma Board Medicolegal Examiners, 1985—. [10] Contributor articles to professional journals. [11] Board directors Oklahoma Arthritis Foundation, 1982; trustee North Central Mental Health Center, 1985—. [12] Served with United States Army, 1955-56. [13] Recipient R.T. Chadwick award National Institute Health, 1988. [14] Fellow Association of Teachers Preventive Medicine; member Association of Medical Colleges, Sigma Xi. [15] Republican. [16] Roman Catholic. [17] Clubs: Harvard (Oklahoma City) Miami Country. [18] Lodge: Knights of Columbus. [19] Avocations: swimming, weight lifting, numismatics. [20] Home: 6060 North Ridge Avenue Oklahoma City Oklahoma 73126 [21] Office: Baptist Medical Center 1986 Cuba Highway Oklahoma City Oklahoma 73120

KEY

[1]   Name
[2]   Occupation
[3]   Vital Statistics
[4]   Parents
[5]   Marriage
[6]   Children
[7]   Education
[8]   Professional certifications
[9]   Career
[10] Writings and creative works
[11] Civic and political activities
[12] Military
[13] Awards and fellowships
[14] Professional and
     association memberships
[15] Political affiliation
[16] Religion
[17] Clubs
[18] Lodges
[19] Avocations
[20] Home address
[21] Office address

Table of Abbreviations

The following abbreviations were not expanded into full text because they have more than one meaning.

acad.–academy, academic

adj.–adjunct, adjutant

adv.–advocate, advisory

Am.–America, American

Brit.–British, Brittanica

Can.–Canada, Canadian

cert.–certificate, certification, certified

cons.–consultant, consultants

corp.–corporation, corporate

Corp.–Corporation, Corporate

corr.– correspondent, corresponding, correspondence

del.–delegate, delegation

Del.–Delaware, Delegate, Delegation

Dem.–Democrat, Democratic

denom.–denomination, denominational

devel.–development, developmental

div.–division, divinity, divorce

exam.–examination, examining

fin.–financial, finance

geog.–geographic, geographical

grad.–graduate, graduated

hon.–honorary, honorable

Ind.–Indiana, Independent

legis.–legislation, legislative

libr.–librarian, library

lic.–licensed, license

lit.–literary, literature

math.–mathematics, mathematical

micros.–microscopic, microscopical

mus.–museum, musical

NE–Nebraska, Northeast

PTO– Pacific Theatre of Operations, Parent Teacher Organization

pub.–publisher, publishing, published, public

rev.–review, revised

sci.–science, scientific

tech.–technical, technology

trans.–transaction, transferred

VA–Virginia, Veterans' Administration

vet.–veteran, veterinary

vol.–volunteer, volume

Who's Who in America
JUNIOR & SENIOR HIGH SCHOOL VERSION

ABELSON, PHILIP HAUGE, physicist; born Tacoma, April 27, 1913; son of Ole Andrew and Ellen (Hauge) A.; married Neva Martin, December 30, 1936; 1 child, Ellen Hauge Abelson Cherniavsky. Bachelor of Science, Washington State College, 1933, Master of Science, 1935; Doctor of Philosophy, University California, 1939; Doctor of Science, Yale University, 1964, Southern Methodist University, 1969, Tufts University, 1976; Doctor of Hebrew Literature, University Puget Sound, 1968. Assistant physicist Carnegie Institution of Washington, 1939-41, chairman biophysics section department terrestrial magnetism; 1946-53, director Geophysics Laboratory; 1953-71, president institution; 1971-78; trustee from 1978—; associate physicist Naval Research Lab, Washington, 1941-42, physicist; 1942-44, senior physicist; 1944-45, principal physicist; 1945; civilian in charge Naval Research Laboratory branch Navy Yard, Philadelphia, 1944-45; resident fellow Resources for the Future Incorporated, Washington, 1985—; Chairman committee on radiation cataracts National Research Council, 1949-57, sub-com. on shock, 1950-53, member plowshare adv. committee, 1959-63; general adv. committee Atomic Energy Commission, 1960-63; member biophysics and biophys. chemistry study section National Institute Arthritis and Metabolic Disease[...] Institutes of Health, 19[...] physical biology tr[...] committee 1958-60, [...] counselors, 1960-6[...] National Aeronautics [...] Administration, 1960[...] National Acad. Scie[...] Institute of Medicine, 1[...] Energy for Tomorrow, [...] of Pessimism, 1985; [...] board Jour National C[...] 1947-52; editor: R[...] Geochemistry, 1959, V[...] Energy: Use, Cons[...] Supply, 1974, F[...] Economics, Nutrition, [...] 1975; Materials; Re[...] Nonrenewable, 1976, E[...] Continuing Revolutio[...] editor Journal Geophys[...] 1959-65; editor Scier[...] 1962-85, dep. editor f[...] applied scis., 1985—[...] Distinguished Civilian [...] 1945, annual award [...] Washington Acad. [...] Distinguished Alum[...] Washington State Un[...] Hillebrand award Che[...] Washington, 1962, Mo[...] award, 1967, Mellon av[...] Mellon University, 1[...] Priestley award Dicki[...] 1973, Sci. Achieve[...] American Medical Asso[...] Hon. Scroll award Distri[...] Institute Chemists, 197[...] United Nations Educati[...]

president 1982, president 1983, board editors 1987-89), Tau Beta Pi, Phi Kappa Phi. Club: Riviera Country (Pacific Palisades, California). Home: 922 Enchanted Way Pacific Palisades California 90272

ACHESON, ALLEN MORROW, consulting engineer; born Tanta, Egypt, June 12, 1926; son of Samuel Irvine and Hazel Lenore (Welker) A.; married Mary Jean Baird, August 5, 1950 (divorced May 1978); children: Rebecca R., Jennifer E., Scott A., Jon M.; married Judith H. Buwalda, May 29, 1983. Bachelor of Science in Mechanical Engineering, Iowa State University, 1950; Doctor of Humane Letters, Tarkio College, 1985. Registered professional engineer, Missouri, Iowa, Michigan, Kansas, Alaska, Queensland, Australia. Station superintendent Iowa Pub. Service Company, Carroll, 1950-54; engineer Proctor & Gamble Company, 1954-55, Iowa-Ill. Gas & Electric Company, 1955-56; manager City Power & Light Company, Independence, Missouri, 1956-60; management adviser Yanhee Electricity Authority, Bangkok, Thailand, 1960-63; executive vice president Black & Veatch International, Kansas City, Missouri, 1964-73; president Black & Veatch International, 1973-88; general partner Black & Veatch, 1974-75, also chairman board of directors, executive ptnr; 1975—. Trustee Tarkio (Missouri) College, 1964-77, chairman, 1975-77; elder Trinity and Rolling Hills United Presbyterian Church With United States Naval Reserve, 1944-46. Recipient Professional Achievement citation College Engineering, Iowa State University, 1976. Fellow Am. Cons. Engineers Council (chairman

international engineering division); member American Society of Mechanical Engineers, National, Missouri Socs. Professional Engineers, Society Am. Military Engineers. Home: 224 W 124th St Kansas City Missouri 64145 Office: Black and Veatch International 1500 Meadow Lake Parkway Kansas City Missouri 64114

ADAIR, ROBERT KEMP, physicist, educator; born Fort Wayne, Indiana, August 14, 1924; son of Robert Cleland and Margaret (Wiegman) A.; married Eleanor Reed, June 21, 1952; children—Douglas McVeigh, Margaret Guthrie, James Cleland. Bachelor of Philosophy, University Wisconsin, 1947, Doctor of Philosophy, 1951. Instructor physics University Wisconsin, Madison, 1950-53; physicist Brookhaven (New York) National Laboratory, 1953-58; member faculty Yale University, New Haven, 1958—, professor physics; 1961-72, Eugene Higgins professor physics; 1972-88, Sterling professor physics; 1988—, chairman department physics; 1967-70, director div. physical sciences; 1977-80; associate director for high energy and nuclear physics Brookhaven National Laboratory, New Haven, 1987-88; physicist National Baseball League, 1987—. Author: (with Earle C. Fowler) Strange Particles, 1963; Concepts in Physics, 1969, The Great Design, 1987; associate editor Physical Rev., 1963-66; associate editor Physical Rev. Letters, 1974-76, editor, 1978-84. Served with infantry Army of the United States, 1943-46. Guggenheim fellow, 1954; Ford Foundation fellow, 1962-63; Sloane Foundation fellow, 1962-63. Fellow Am. Physical Society (chairman division particles and fields 1972-73); member National Acad.

Sciences (chairman physics section 1986—). Home: 50 Deepwood Dr Hamden Connecticut 06517 Office: Yale U J W Gibbs Lab New Haven Connecticut 06520

AGNEW, HAROLD MELVIN, physicist; born Denver, March 28, 1921; son of Sam E. and Augusta (Jacobs) A.; married Beverly Jackson, May 2, 1942; children: Nancy E. Agnew Owens, John S. Bachelor of Arts, University Denver, 1942; Master of Science, University Chicago, 1948, Doctor of Philosophy, 1949. With Los Alamos Sci. Laboratory, 1943-46, alternate div. leader; 1949-61, leader weapons div.; 1964-70, director; 1970-79; president GA Techs. Incorporated, San Diego, 1979-85, director; 1985—; director Blaws Corp., 1967-72; director DBA Systems, Incorporated; sci. adviser Supreme Allied Commander in Europe, Paris, France, 1961-64; Chairman Army Sci. Adv. Panel, 1965-70, member, 1970-74; member aircraft panel President's Sci. Adv. Committee, 1965-73; member United States Air Force Sci. Adv. Board, 1957-69, Def. Sci. Board, 1965-70, Governor New Mexico Radiation Adv. Council, 1959-61; secretary New Mexico Health and Social Services, 1971-73; chairman general adv. committee Arms Control and Disarmament Agency, 1974-77, member, 1977-81; member aerospace safety adv. panel National Aeronautics and Space Administration, 1964-70, 86—; member United States Army Sci. Board, 1978-80, White House Sci. Council, 1982-89; adj. professor University California, San Diego, 1988—. Member council engring. NRC, 1978-82; member Los Alamos Board Educational Trustees, 1950-55, president, 1955; trustee San Diego Mus. Art, 1983-87; member

Woodrow Wilson National Fellowship Foundation, 1973-80; New Mexico State senator, 1955-61; secretary New Mexico Legis. Council, 1957-61; chairman New Mexico Senate Corp. Commission, 1957-61; member Federal Emergency Agency, 1982-88; board of directors Federation Rocky Mountain States, Incorporated, 1975-77. Recipient Ernest Orlando Lawrence award Atomic Energy Commission, 1966; Enrico Fermi award Department Energy, 1978. Fellow Am. Physical Society, American Association for the Advancement of Science; member National Acad. Sciences, National Acad. Engineering, Council on Foreign Relations, Phi Beta Kappa, Sigma Xi, Omicron Delta Kappa. Home: 322 Punta Baja Solana Beach California 92075

ALBEE, ARDEN LEROY, educator, geologist; born Port Huron, Michigan, May 28, 1928; son of Emery A. and Mildred (Tool) A.; married Charleen H. Ettenheim, 1978; children: Janet, Margaret, Carol, Kathy, James, Ginger, Mary, George. Bachelor of Arts, Harvard, 1950, Master of Arts, 1951, Doctor of Philosophy, 1957. Geologist United States Geological Survey, 1950-59; professor geology California Institute Tech., 1959—; chief scientist Jet Propulsion Laboratory, 1978-84, dean grad. studies; 1984—; consultant in field, 1950; chairman lunar sci. rev. panel National Aeronautics and Space Administration, 1972-77, member space sci. adv. committee, 1976-84. Asso. editor: Journal Geophysical Research, 1976-82 , Annual Rev. Earth Space Scis, 1978—; contributor numerous articles to professional journals. Recipient Exceptional Sci. Achievement medal National

Aeronautics and Space Administration, 1976. Fellow Mineralogical Society Am. (associate editor Am. Mineralogist 1972-76), Geological Society Am. (associate editor bull. 1972—), Geochem. Society, Am. Geophysical Union. Home: 2040 Midlothian Dr Altadena California 91001

ALDRIN, EDWIN (BUZZ), JR., former astronaut, science consultant; born Montclair, New Jersey, January 20, 1930; children: James Michael, Janice Ross, Andrew John. Bachelor of Science, United States Military Academy, 1951; Doctor of Science in Astronautics, Massachusetts Institute of Technology, 1963; Doctor of Science (honorary), Gustavus Adolphus College, 1967, Clark University, 1969, University Portland, 1970, St. Peter's College, 1970; Doctor of Letters (honorary), Montclair State College, 1969; Doctor of Humanities (honorary), Seton Hall University, 1970. Commissioned officer United States Air Force, 1951, advanced through grades to colonel; served as fighter pilot in Korea; 1953; pilot Gemini XII orbital rendezvous space flight, November 11-15, 1966; lunar module pilot on first manned lunar landing Apollo XI; commander Aerospace Research Pilots School, Edwards Air Force Base, California, 1971-72; retired United States Air Force, 1972; now with Center for Aerospace Sciences University North Dakota, Grand Forks; sci. consultant Beverly Hills Oil Company, Inforex Computer Company, Laser Video Corp., Mutual of Omaha Insurance; founder Research and Engineering Cons., 1972. Author: Return to Earth, 1973; (with Malcolm McConnell) Men From Earth, 1989. Decorated Distinguished Service Medal, Legion of Merit, Distinguished Flying Cross with oak leaf cluster, Air medal with 2 oak leaf clusters; recipient numerous awards including Presidential medal of Freedom, 1969. Fellow American Institute of Aeronautics and Astronautics; member Society Experimental Test Pilots, Royal Aeronautical Society (hon.), Sea Space Symposium; charter International Acad. Astronautics (corr.), Sigma Xi, Tau Beta Pi. Club: Masons (33 degree). Established record over 7 hours and 52 minutes outside spacecraft in extravehicular activity. Office: Center for Aerospace Scis U North Dakota Box 8216 University Station Grand Forks North Dakota 58202

ALEXANDER, MARTIN, educator, researcher; born Newark, February 4, 1930; son of Meyer and Sarah (Rubinstein) A.; married Renee Rafaela Wulf, August 26, 1951; children: Miriam H., Stanley W. Bachelor of Science, Rutgers University, 1951; Master of Science, University Wisconsin, 1953, Doctor of Philosophy, 1955. Assistant professor agronomy Cornell University, Ithaca, New York, from 1955, now L.H. Bailey prof; advisor agys. federal government, Washington, 1965—, United Nations agys., Kenya, France, Italy, 1963—; member committees National Acad. Sci., Washington, 1971—; consultant. Author: Microbial Ecology, 1971, Introduction to Soil Microbiology, 1977; editor: Advances in Microbial Ecology, 5 volumes, 1977-81. Recipient Indsl. Research 100 award, 1968, Fisher award Am. Society Microbiology, 1980. Fellow Am. Acad. Microbiology, American Association for the Advancement of Science, Am. Society Agronomy (Soil Sci. award 1964). Home: 301

Winthrop Dr Ithaca New York 14853 Office: Cornell U Ithaca New York 14853

ALFVÉN, HANNES OLOF GOSTA, physicist; born May 30, 1908. Doctor of Philosophy, University Uppsala, 1934. Professor theory of electricity Royal Institute Tech., Stockholm, 1940-45, professor electronics; 1945-63, professor plasma physics; 1963-73; professor department applied physics and information sci. University California, San Diego, 1967—; member Swedish Sci. Adv. Council, 1963-67; past member Swedish Atomic Energy Commission; past governor Swedish Def. Research Institute, Swedish Atomic Energy Company; past sci. adv. Swedish Government; president Pugwash Confs. on Sci. and World Affairs, 1970-75; member panel on comets and asteroids National Aeronautics and Space Administration. Author: Cosmical Electrodynamics, 1950; On the Origin of the Solar System, 1954; Cosmical Electrodynamics: Fundamental Principles, 1963; Worlds-Antiworlds, 1966; The Tale of the Big Computer, 1968; Atom, Man and the Universe, 1969; Living on the Third Planet, 1972; Evolution of the Solar System, 1976; Cosmic Plasma, 1981. Recipient Nobel prize for physics, 1970; Lomonsov gold medal Union of Soviet Socialist Republics Acad. Sciences, 1971; Franklin medal, 1971, Bowie Gold medal Am. Geophysical Union, 1987. Fellow Royal Society (England); member Swedish Acad. Sciences, Akademia NAUK (Union of the Soviet Socialist Republics), National Academy of Sciences (foreign associate), others. also: Department Plasma Physics, Royal Institute Tech, S-100-44 Stockholm 70, Sweden

ALLEN, JOSEPH P., astronautical industry executive; born Crawfordsville, Indiana, June 27, 1937; son of Joseph P. and Harriet (Taylor) A.; married Bonnie Jo Darling, July 9, 1961. Bachelor of Arts (Rector scholar 1955-59), DePauw University, 1959; Bachelor of Arts Fulbright scholar, Christian Albrechts University, Kiel, Germany, 1959-60; Master of Science, Yale University, 1961, Doctor of Philosophy, 1965. Guest research associate Brookhaven National Laboratory, 1962-65; staff physicist Nuclear Structure Laboratory, Yale University, 1965; research associate University Washington, 1966; scientist-astronaut Lyndon B. Johnson Manned Spacecraft Center, National Aeronautics and Space Administration, Houston, 1967-75; assistant administrator for legis. affairs Lyndon B. Johnson Manned Spacecraft Center, National Aeronautics and Space Administration, Washington, 1975-78; on staff and astronaut Lyndon B. Johnson Space Center., 1978-85, astronaut, crew member 1st operational flight of Space Shuttle Columbia; 1982, crew member 1st Space salvage in history Space Shuttle Discovery; 1985; now president Space Industries, Incorporated, Houston. Author: Entering Space; also articles in field. Member Am. Physical Society, Am. Astronautical Society, Am. Astronomical Society, American Association for the Advancement of Science, Phi Beta Kappa, Sigma Xi, Beta Theta Pi, Phi Eta Sigma. Office: Space Industries Incorporated 711 W Bay Area Boulevard Houston Texas 77598

ALLEN, LEW, JR., laboratory executive, former air force officer;

born Miami, Florida, September 30, 1925; son of Lew and Zella (Holman) A.; married Barbara Frink Hatch, August 19, 1949; children: Barbara Allen Miller, Lew III, Marjorie Allen Dauster, Christie Allen Jameson, James Allen. Bachelor of Science, United States Military Academy, 1946; Master of Science, University Illinois, 1952, Doctor of Philosophy in Physics, 1954. Commissioned 2d lieutenant United States Army Air Force, 1946; advanced through grades to general United States Air Force, 1977, retired; 1982; physicist test div. Atomic Energy Commission, Los Alamos, New Mexico, 1954-57; sci. advisor Air Force Special Weapons Laboratory, Kirkland, New Mexico, 1957-61; with office of special tech. Secretary of Defense, Washington, 1961-65; from director special projects to deputy director adv. plans Air Force Space Program, 1965-72; director National Security Agency, Fort Meade, Maryland, 1973-77; commander Air Force Systems Command, 1977-78; vice chief of staff United States Air Force, Washington, 1978, chief of staff; 1978-82; director Jet Propulsion Laboratory, California Institute Tech., Pasadena, California, 1982—; chairman COSEPUP (National Acad. Sciences) panel on impact of national security controls on international tech. transfer, 1985-87. Decorated Distinguished Service Medal with 3 oak leaf clusters, Legion of Merit with 2 oak leaf clusters, Joint Service Commendation medal. Member Am. Physical Society, Am. Geophysical Union, National Acad. Engineering, Council on Foreign Relations, Sigma Xi. Republican. Episcopalian. Clubs: Sunset (Los Angeles); Alfalfa (Washington). Avocations: ballooning, rafting. Office: Jet Propulsion Lab California Institute Tech 4800 Oak Grove Dr Pasadena California 91109

ALLEN, WILLIAM FREDERICK, JR., mechanical engineer; born North Kingstown, Rhode Island, June 22, 1919; son of William Frederick and Anita Lucy (Freeman) A.; married Doris Evelyn Pendoley, September 6, 1952; children: William Frederick, Janet Anita, Thomas Joseph, Paul Norman. Bachelor of Science in Engineering, Brown University, 1941; Master of Science in Mechanical Engineering, Harvard University, 1947, postgraduate, 1947-48; Doctor Tech. (honorary), Wentworth Institute Tech., 1983. Registered professional engineer, 20 states and Ontario. Assistant in engineering Brown University, 1941-43, instructor; 1943-44; teaching fellow in mechanical engineering Harvard University, 1948; with Stone & Webster Engineering Corp., Boston, 1948—; engineering manager, vice president Stone & Webster Engineering Corp., 1968-71, senior vice president; 1971, president; 1972-78, chief executive officer; 1973—, chairman; 1978-86, also board of directors; 1969—; president, chief executive officer Stone & Webster Incorporated, 1986—, chairman, chief executive officer; 1988—; director Blue Cross of Massachusetts, vice chairman, 1983—. Trustee Thayer Acad., Braintree, Massachusetts, 1974-84, president, 1979-81; trustee Northeastern University, New England Aquarium; national board member Junior Achievement. Served with United States Naval Reserve, 1944-46. Fellow American Society of Mechanical Engineers (life); member National Acad. Engineering, Sigma Xi, Tau Beta Pi. Roman Catholic. Office:

Stone & Webster Incorporated 250 W 34th St New York New York 10119

AMBLER, ERNEST, government official; born Bradford, England, November 20, 1923; came to United States, 1953, naturalized, 1958; son of William and Sarah Alice (Binns) A.; married Alice Virginia Seiler, November 19, 1955; children: Christopher William, Jonathan Ernest. Bachelor of Arts, New College, Oxford University, 1945, Master of Arts, 1949, Doctor of Philosophy, 1953. With Armstrong Siddeley Motors, Limited, Coventry, England, 1944-48; Nuffield Research fellow Oxford University, 1953; with National Institute Standards and Tech. (formerly National Bureau Standards), Commerce Department, 1953-89; div. chief inorganic materials div. National Institute Standards and Tech. (formerly National Bureau Standards), Commerce Department, Washington, 1965-68, deputy director; 1973, acting director; 1975-78, director bureau; 1978-89; director Institute for Basic Standards, Washington, 1968-73; Liaison representative to div. physical sciences National Acad. Sci.-NRC, 1968-69; Sponsor's del. National Conference Standards Laboratory, 1968; United States representative International Committee on Weights and Measures, 1972—; acting under secretary for tech. United States Department Commerce. Patentee low temperature refrigeration apparatus. D.C. member board governors Israel/U.S. Binat. Industrial Research and Devel. Foundation; member Maryland High Tech. Roundtable. Recipient Arthur S. Flemming award Washington Junior Chamber of Commerce, 1961; John Simon Guggenheim Memorial Foundation fellow, 1963; recipient William A. Wildhack award in metrology, 1976, President's award for Distinguished Federal Civilian Service, 1977. Fellow American Association for the Advancement of Science; member Am. Physical Society (editor Rev. Modern Physics 1966-69), Washington Acad. Sciences. Home: 1600 N Oak St #626 Arlington Maryland 22209 Office: National Institute Standards & Tech Building 101 Route 270 Gaithersburg Maryland 20899

AMES, ADELBERT, III, neurophysiologist, educator; born Boston, February 25, 1921. Doctor of Medicine, Harvard University, 1945. Intern, then resident in internal medicine Presbyn. Hospital, 1945-52; research associate Medical School, Harvard University, Boston, 1955-69, professor physiology, department surgery; 1969—, Charles Anthony Pappas professor neurosci.; neurophysiologist in neurosurgery Massachusetts General Hospital, Boston, 1969—. Recipient Research Scientist award National Institute of Mental Health, 1968—. Member Am. Physiological Society, Am. Society Neurochemistry, Society Neurosci., International Society Neurochemistry. Office: Mass Gen Hosp 467 Warren Building Old Concord Road Lincoln Massachusetts 01773

AMES, BRUCE N(ATHAN), biochemist, geneticist; born New York City, December 16, 1928; son of Maurice U. and Dorothy (Andres) A.; married Giovanna Ferro-Luzzi, August 26, 1960; children: Sofia, Matteo. Bachelor of Arts, Cornell University, 1950; Doctor of Philosophy, California Institute Tech., 1953. Chief section microbial genetics National Institutes of Health, Bethesda, Maryland, 1953-68; professor biochemistry University

California, Berkeley, 1968—, chairman biochemistry department; 1983—; adv. board National Cancer Institute, 1976-82. Research, publications on bacterial molecular biology, histidine biosynthesis and its control, RNA and regulation, mutagenesis, detection of environ. mutagens and carcinogens, genetic toxicology, oxygen radicals and disease. Recipient Flemming award, 1966, Rosenstiel award, 1976, Federation Am. Society Exptl. Biology award, 1976, Felix Wankel award, 1978, John Scott medal, 1979, Corson medal, 1980, New Brunswick lectureship Am. Society Microbiology, 1980, Mott prize General Motors Research Foundation, 1983, Gairdner award, 1983, Tyler prize Environmental Achievement, 1985. Member Am. Society Biological Chemists, Am. Society Microbiology, Environmental Mutagen Society (award 1977), Genetics Society, Am. Association Cancer Research, Society Toxicology, Am. Chemical Society (Eli Lilly award 1964), Am. Acad. Arts and Sciences, National Acad. Sci. Home: 1324 Spruce St Berkeley California 94709 Office: U California Department Biochemistry Berkeley California 94720

ANDERS, WILLIAM ALISON, aerospace and diversified manufacturing company executive, former astronaut, former ambassador; born Hong Kong, October 17, 1933; son of Arthur Ferdinand and Muriel Florence (Adams) A.; married Valerie Elizabeth Hoard, June 26, 1955; children: Alan Frank, Glen Thomas, Gayle Alison, Gregory Michael, Eric William, Diana Elizabeth. Bachelor of Science, United States Naval Academy, Annapolis, 1955; Master of Science, United States Institute Tech., Wright-Patterson AFB, 1962. Commnd. 2d lieutenant United States Air Force, 1955, pilot, engineer; 1955-69; astronaut NASA-Johnson Space Center, Houston, 1963-69, Apollo 8, 1st lunar flight, 1968; executive secretary National Aeronautical and Space Council, Washington, 1963-72; commissioner Atomic Energy Commission, Washington, 1973-74; chairman Nuclear Regulatory Commission, Washington, 1975-76; United States Ambassador to Norway 1976-77; vice president, general manager nuclear energy products div. General Electric Company, 1977-80; vice president, general manager aircraft equipment div. General Electric Company, DeWitt, New York, 1980-84; senior executive, vice president operations Textron Incorporated, Providence, Rhode Island, 1984—; major-general United States Air Force Reserve, 1983-88, National Acad. Engineering. Decorated various mil. awards; recipient Wright, Collier, Goddard and Arnold flight awards; co-holder several world flight records. Member Society Experimental Test Pilots (holder several world speed and altitude records), Defense Sci. Board, Tau Beta Pi. Office: Textron Incorporated 40 Westminster St Providence Rhode Island 02903

ANDERSON, CARL DAVID, scientist; born New York City, September 3, 1905; son of Carl David and Emma Adolfina (Ajaxson) A.; married Lorraine Elvira Bergman; children—Marshall David, David Andrew. Bachelor of Science, California Institute of Tech., 1927, Doctor of Philosophy magna cum laude, 1930; honorary Doctor of Science, Colgate University, 1937, Gustavus Adolphus College, 1963;

Doctor of Laws (honorary), Temple University, 1948. Coffin research fellow California Institute Tech., 1927-28, teaching fellow in physics; 1928-30, research fellow in physics; 1930-33, assistant professor physics; 1933-37, associate professor; 1937-39, professor; 1939-76, professor emeritus; 1976—, chairman div. physics, math. and astronomy; 1962-70. Awarded gold medal Am. Institute of City of New York, 1935; Nobel prize in physics, 1936; Elliott Cresson medal of the Franklin Institute, 1937; John Ericsson medal Am. Society Swedish Engrs., 1960. Member Am. Physical Society, Am. Philosophical Society, National Acad. Sciences, Sigma Xi, Tau Beta Pi. Research on X-Ray photoelectrons, 1927-30; research on gamma rays and cosmic rays since 1930. Office: California Institute Tech Department Physics Pasadena California 91109

ANDERSON, DAVID PREWITT, university dean; born Twin Falls, Idaho, September 14, 1934; son of Robert Kyle and Margaret Elizabeth (Prewitt) A.; married Janice Gale Schmied, December 21, 1962; children: Kathryn Lynn, Christopher Kyle. Student, University Idaho, 1952-54; Bachelor of Science, Washington State University, 1959, Doctor of Veterinary Medicine, 1961; Master of Science, University Wisconsin, 1964, Doctor of Philosophy, 1965. Diplomate: Am. Coll. Vet. Microbiologists. National Institutes of Health trainee University Wisconsin, 1961-64, assistant professor vet. sci., assistant director biotron; 1965-69; professor medical microbiology, director Poultry Disease Research Center, University Georgia, 1969-71, associate dean research and grad. affairs College Vet. Medicine; 1971-73, dean; 1975—; member committee animal health National Acad. Sci., 1977-80; member animal health sci. research adv. board United States Department Agriculture, 1978-85; member adv. committee Center for Vet. Medicine, Food and Drug Administration, 1984—. Editor: Avian Diseases. Member American Veterinary Medical Association, Am. Association Avian Pathologists, Poultry Sci. Association, National Acads. Practice. Home: 190 Harris St Winterville Georgia 30683

ANDERSON, DON LYNN, educator, geophysicist; born Frederick, Maryland, March 5, 1933; son of Richard Andrew and Minola (Phares) A.; married Nancy Lois Ruth, September 15, 1956; children: Lynn Ellen, Lee Weston. Bachelor of Science, Rensselaer Polytechnic Institute, 1955; Master of Science, California Institute Tech., 1959, Doctor of Philosophy, 1962. With Chevron Oil Company, Montana, Wyoming, California, 1955-56; with Air Force Cambridge Research Center, Boston, 1956-58, Arctic Institute North America, Boston, 1958; member faculty California Institute Tech., Pasadena, 1962—, associate professor geophysics; 1964-68, professor; 1968—, director seismological laboratory; 1967—; principal investigator Viking Mars Seismic Experiment; member various committees National Aeronautics and Space Administration; chairman geophysics research forum National Acad. Sciences, also member various committees. Asso. editor: Journal Geophysical Research, 1965-67, Tectonophysics, 1974-77; editor: Physics of the Earth and Planetary Interiors. Recipient Exceptional Sci. Achievement award National

Aeronautics and Space Administration, 1977; Sloan Foundation fellow, 1965-67; Emil Wiechert Medal German Geophys. Society, 1986; Arthur L. Dey medal Geol. Society Am., 1987. Fellow Am. Geophysical Union (James B. Macelwane award, 1966, president tectonophysics section 1971-72, chairman Macelwane award committee 1975, Bowie Medal Committee 1985, president elect 1986-88, president 1988), Geological Society Am. (associate editor bull. 1971—, Penrose medal committee 1989), American Association for the Advancement of Science; member National Acad. Sci. (chairman seismology committee 1975, chairman Geophysics Research Forum 1984-86), Am. Acad. Arts and Sciences, Royal Astronomical Society (Gold medal 1988), Seismological Society Am., Sigma Xi. Home: 669 E Alameda St Altadena California 91001 Office: California Institute Tech Div Geology & Planetary Scis Pasadena California 91109

ANDERSON, DUWAYNE MARLO, earth and polar scientist, university administrator; born Lehi, Utah, September 9, 1927; son of Duwayne LeRoy and Fern Francell (Fagan) A.; married June B. Hodgin, April 2, 1980; children by previous marriage: Lynna Nadine, Christopher Kent, Lesleigh Leigh. Bachelor of Science, Brigham Young University, 1954; Doctor of Philosophy (Purdue Research Foundation fellow), Purdue University, 1958. Professor soil physics University Arizona, Tucson, 1958-63; research scientist, chief earth sciences branch (Cold Regions Research and Engineering Laboratory), Hanover, New Hampshire, 1963-76; chief scientist, div. polar programs National Science Foundation, Washington, 1976-78; member Viking sci. team National Aeronautics and Space Administration, 1969-76; dean faculty natural sciences and math. State University of New York Buffalo, 1978-84; associate provost for research and grad. studies Texas A&M University, College Station, 1984—; also councilor Texas A&M Research Foundation, 1984—; Pegrum lecturer State University of New York, 1980; consultant National Aeronautics and Space Administration, 1964, National Science Foundation, 1979-81, United States Army Cold Regions Research and Engineering Laboratory, Hanover, New Hampshire; senior United States representative, Antarctica, 1976, 77; board of directors, member executive committee Houston Area Research Center, 1984—; visiting professor, lecturer numerous universities. Editor: (with O.B. Andersland) Geotechnical Engineering for Cold Regions, 1978; Cons. editor: Soil Sci, 1965-81, (with O.B. Andersland) Cold Regions Science and Tech, 1978-82; Contributor numerous sci. and tech. articles to professional journals. Board of directors Ford K. Sayre Memorial Ski Council, Hanover, 1969-71; board of directors Grafton County Fish and Game Association, 1965-76, president, 1968-70; board of directors Hanover Conservation Council, 1970-76, vice president, 1970-73; board of directors Buffalo Mus. Sci., 1980-84, vice president, 1982-84. Served in United States Air Force, 1946-49. Recipient Sci. Achievement award Cold Regions Research and Engineering Laboratory, 1968; co-recipient Newcomb Cleveland award American Association for the Advancement of Science, 1976; Sec. of Army Research fellow, 1966.

Fellow Geological Society Am., Am. Society Agronomy; member International Glaciological Society, Am. Polar Society, Am. Geophysical Union (special task force on cold regions hydrology 1974-84), American Association for the Advancement of Science, Soil Sci. Society Am., Niagara Frontier Association Research and Devel. Directors (president 1983-84), Member Licensing Executives Society, Buffalo Mus. Sci. (board directors), National Aeronautics and Space Administration Teams (Viking, Skylab & Planetary Geology & Geophysics Working Group), Comet Rendevous/Asteroid Flyby Mission Team, Sigma Xi, Sigma Gamma Epsilon, Phi Kappa Phi. Republican. Home: 8720 Bent Tree Dr College Station Texas 77840 Office: Tex A&M U Associate Provost Research and Grad Studies 305 E Bizzell Hall College Station Texas 77843

ANDERSON, PHILIP WARREN, physicist; born Indianapolis, December 13, 1923; son of Harry W. and Elsie (Osborne) A.; married Joyce Gothwaite, July 31, 1947; 1 daughter, Susan Osborne. Bachelor of Science, Harvard University, 1943, Master of Arts, 1947, Doctor of Philosophy, 1949; Doctor of Science (honorary), University Illinois, 1979. Member staff Naval Research Laboratory, 1943-45; member tech. staff Bell Telephone Laboratories, Murray Hill, New Jersey, 1949-84; chairman theoretical physics department Bell Telephone Laboratories, 1959-60, assistant director physical research laboratory; 1974-76, consultant director; 1976-84; Fulbright lecturer University Tokyo, 1953-54; Loeb lecturer Harvard University, 1964; professor theoretical physics Cambridge (England) University, 1967-75; professor physics Princeton University, 1975—; Overseas fellow Churchill College, Cambridge University, 1961-62; fellow Jesus College, 1969-75, hon. fellow, 1978—; Bethe lecturer, 1984. Author: Concepts in Solids, 1963, Basic Notions of Condensed Matter Physics, 1984. Recipient Oliver E. Buckley prize Am. Physical Society, 1964; Dannie Heinemann prize Göttingen (Ger.) Acad. Sciences, 1975; Nobel prize in physics, 1977; Guthrie medal Institute of Physics, 1978; National Medal Sci., 1982. Fellow Am. Physical Society, Am. Acad. Arts and Sciences, American Association for the Advancement of Science; member National Acad. Sciences, Royal Society (foreign), Physical Society Japan, European Physical Society, Accademia Lincei. Research in quantum theory, especially theoretical physics of solids, spectral line broadening, magnetism, superconductivity. Office: Princeton U Department Physics Princeton New Jersey 08544

ANDERSON, THOMAS PATRICK, mechanical engineer, educator; born Chicago, October 22, 1934; son of Clarence Kenneth and Anne (Moran) A.; married Elizabeth Ann Toof, July 9, 1960; children—Patricia, James. Bachelor of Science in Mechanical Engineering, Northwestern University, 1956, Master of Science, 1958, Doctor of Philosophy, 1961. Registered professional engineer, Illinois, Iowa. Engineer Askania Regulator Company, Chicago, 1953-55; research engineer Cook Research Laboratories, Skokie, Illinois, summer, 1956, ARO Incorporated, Tullahoma, Tennessee, summers 1958, 59; assistant professor, then associate professor Northwestern University, 1960-66; professor mechanical engineering University Iowa, 1966-75, chairman department; 1966-70; program manager Office Systems Integration and Analysis, National Science Foundation, 1974-75, program manager div. intergovtl. sci. and pub. tech.; 1975-78, acting director industrial program; 1976-78; dean School Sci. and Engineering, Southern Illinois University, Edwardsville, 1978-83; professor School Engineering School Sci. and Engineering, Southern Illinois University, 1978—; consultant, associate deputy director interdeptl. energy study Office Sci. and Tech., 1963-65. Contributor numerous articles to professional journals. Named One of Ten Outstanding Young Men Chicago Junior Association Commerce and Industry, 1964. Fellow Iowa Acad. Sci.; member American Association of University Profs., Am. Geophysical Union, American Institute of Aeronautics and Astronautics, Am. Physical Society, Am. Society Engineering Education, American Society of Mechanical Engineers, New York Acad. Sciences, Sigma Xi.

ANDREWS, RICHARD VINCENT, physiologist, educator; born Arapahoe, Nebraska, January 9, 1932; son of Wilber Vincent and Fern (Clawson) A.; married Elizabeth Williams, June 1, 1954; children: Thomas, William, Robert, Catherine, James, John. Bachelor of Science, Creighton University, 1958, Master of Science, 1959; Doctor of Philosophy, University Iowa, 1963. Instructor biology Creighton University, Omaha, 1958-60; instructor physiology University Iowa, 1960-63; assistant professor Creighton University, 1963-65, associate professor, 1965-68, professor physiology, 1968—, assistant medical dean, 1972-75, dean grad. studies, 1975-85; visiting professor Naval Arctic Research Laboratory, 1963-72, University British Columbia, 1985-86; consultant Veteran's Administration, Omaha Pub. Power; plenary speaker Union of the Soviet Socialist Republics Symposium on Environment, 1970. Contributor articles to professional journals. Served with Medical Corps United States Army, 1951-54. National Science Foundation fellow, 1962-63; NSF-NIH-ONR-AINA grantee, 1963—. Fellow Explorers Club, Arctic Institute North America; member Am. Physiological Society, Am. Ecological Society, Am. Mammal Society, Endocrine Society, Society Experimental Biology and Medicine, Sigma Xi. Office: 2500 California St Omaha NE 68178

ANFINSEN, CHRISTIAN BOEHMER, biochemist; born Monessen, Pennsylvania, March 26, 1916; son of Christian Boehmer and Sophie (Rasmussen) A.; married Florence Bernice Kenenger, November 29, 1941 (divorced 1978); children: Carol Bernice, Margot Sophie, Christian Boehmer; married Libby Shulman Ely, 1979. Bachelor of Arts, Swarthmore College, 1937, Doctor of Science, 1965; Master of Science, University Pennsylvania, 1939; Doctor of Philosophy, Harvard, 1943; Doctor of Science (honorary), Georgetown University, 1967, New York Medical College, 1969, Gustavus Adolphus College, 1975, Brandeis University, 1977, Providence College, 1978; Doctor of Medicine (honorary), University Naples Medical School, 1980, Adelphi University, 1987.

Assistant professor biological chemistry Harvard Medical School, 1948-50, professor biochemistry; 1962-63; chief laboratory cellular physiology and metabolism National Heart Institute, Bethesda, Maryland, 1950-62; chief laboratory chemical biology National Institute Arthritis and Metabolic Diseases, Bethesda, 1963-82; professor biology Johns Hopkins University, Baltimore, 1982—; visiting professor Weizmann Institute Sci., Rehovot, Israel, 1981-82, board governors 1962. Author: The Molecular Basis of Evolution, 1959; contributor articles to professional journals. Am. Scandinavian fellow Carlsberg Laboratory, Copenhagen 1939; sr. cancer research fellow Nobel Institute, Stockholm, 1947; Markle scholar 1948; Guggenheim fellow Weizmann Institute, 1958; recipient Rockefeller Pub. Service award, 1954-55, Nobel prize in chemistry, 1972. Member Am. Society Biological Chemists (president 1971-72), Am. Acad. Arts and Sciences, National Acad. Sciences, Washington Acad. Sciences, Am. Philosophical Society, Federation Am. Scientists (treasurer 1958-59, vice chairman 1959-60, 73-76), Pontifical Acad. Sci. Home: 4 Tanner Court Baltimore Maryland 21208 Office: Johns Hopkins U Department Biology 34th & Charles St Baltimore Maryland 21218

ANGEL, JAMES ROGER PRIOR, astronomer; born St. Helens, England, February 7, 1941; came to United States, 1967; son of James Lee and Joan (Prior) A.; married Ellinor M. Goonan, August 21, 1965; children—Jennifer, James. Bachelor of Arts, Oxford (England) University, 1963, Doctor of Philosophy, 1967; Master of Science, California Institute Tech., 1966. From research associate to associate professor physics Columbia University, 1967-74; visiting associate professor astronomy University Texas, Austin, 1974; member faculty University Arizona, Tucson, 1974—; professor astronomy University Arizona, 1975—, professor optical sci.; 1984—. Sloan fellow, 1970-74. Member Am. Astronomical Society (Pierce prize 1976, vice president 1987—), Optical Society Am. Research on white dwarf stars, quasars, astron. instruments and telescopes. Office: Steward Obs University Ariz Tucson Arizona 85721

ANSELL, GEORGE STEPHEN, metallurgical engineering educator; born Akron, Ohio, April 1, 1934; son of Frederick Jesse and Fanny (Soletsky) A.; married Marjorie Boris, December 18, 1960; children: Frederick Stuart, Laura Ruth, Benjamin Jesse. Bachelor in Metallurgical Engineering, Rensselaer Polytechnic Institute, 1954, Master in Metallurgical Engineering, 1955, Doctor of Philosophy, 1960. Physical metallurgist United States Navy Research Laboratory, Washington, 1957-58; member faculty Rensselaer Polytechnic Institute, Troy, New York, 1960-84, Robert W. Hunt professor; 1965-84, chairman materials div.; 1969-74, dean engineering; 1974-84; president Colorado School Mines, Golden, 1984—; consultant in field; member adv. council to board of directors Adolph Coors Company, Golden; board of directors United Bank Denver. Editor books; patentee in field; contributor over 100 articles to professional journals. Served with United States Navy, 1955-58. Recipient Hardy Gold Medal American Institute of Mining, Metallurgy and Petroleum Engineers, 1961, Curtis W. McGraw award Am. Society

Engineering Education, 1971, Souzandrade Gold Medal of University Merit Federal University Maranhao, 1986. Fellow Metallurgical Society (president 1986-87), Am. Society Metals (Alfred H. Geisler award 1964, Bradley Stoughton award 1968); member NSPE, Am. Society Engineering Education (Curtis W. McGraw award 1971), Sigma Xi, Tau Beta Pi, Phi Lambda Upsilon. Club: Denver. Office: Colorado School of Mines 1500 Illinois St Golden Colorado 80401

ARBER, WERNER, microbiologist; born Gränichen, Switzerland, January 3, 1929; married; 2 children. Educated, Aargau (Switzerland) Gymnasium, Eidgenössische Technische Hochschule, Zurich. Assistant Laboratory Biophysics, University Geneva, 1953-58, docent, then extraordinary professor molecular genetics; 1962-70; research associate department microbiology University Southern California, 1958-59; visiting investigator department molecular biology University California, Berkeley, 1970-71; professor microbiology University Basel (Switzerland), 1971. Co-recipient Nobel prize for physiology or medicine, 1978. Member National Acad. Sciences (foreign associate). Office: Biozentrum der Universitat, U Basel, 70 Klingelbergstrasse, CH-4056 Basel Switzerland

ARCHIBALD, JAMES DAVID, biology educator, paleontologist; born Lawrence, Kansas, March 23, 1950; son of James R. and Donna L. (Accord) A. Bachelor of Science in Geology, Kent State University, 1972; Doctor of Philosophy in Paleontology, University California, Berkeley, 1977. Gibb's instructor department geology

Yale University, New Haven, 1977-79, assistant, then associate professor department biology; 1979-83; curator of mammals Peabody Mus. Natural Historical, New Haven, 1979-83; associate professor, then professor department biology San Diego State University, San Diego, 1983—; extensive field expeditions in Montana, Colorado, New Mexico, Pakistan, 1973—. Author: A Study of Mammalia and Geology Across the Cretaceous-Tertiary Boundary, 1982; contributor articles to professional journals. Scholar Yale University, San Diego State University; fellow Alcoa Foundation, University Calif.-Berkeley; grantee Sigma Xi, National Geog. Society, National Science Foundation, Petroleum Research Foundation, San Diego State University. Member Society Vertebrate Paleontology, Geological Society Am., Paleontological Society, Society Systematic Zoologists, Am. Society Mammalogists, Willi Hennig Society, Sigma Xi. Office: San Diego State U Department Biology San Diego California 92182

ARDEN, BRUCE WESLEY, computer science and electrical engineering educator; born Minneapolis, May 29, 1927; son of Wesley and Clare Montgomery (Newton) A.; married Patricia Ann Joy, August 25, 1951; children: Wayne Wesley, Michelle Joy. Student, University Delaware, 1944; Bachelor of Science in Electrical Engineering, Purdue University, 1949; postgraduate, University Chicago, 1949; Master of Arts, University Michigan, 1955, Doctor of Philosophy, 1965. Detail engineer Allison div. General Motors Corp., Indianapolis, 1950-51; assistant professor department computing and communication sciences University Michigan, Ann Arbor, 1965-67;

associate professor University Michigan, 1967-70, professor; 1970-73, chairman department; 1971-73, from research assistant to associate director Computing Facilities; 1951-73; professor, chairman department electrical engineering and computer sci. Princeton University, 1973-85, Arthur Le Grand Doty professor engineering; 1981-86; professor electrical engineering, computer sci., dean engineering and applied Sci. University Rochester, 1986—; visiting professor University Grenoble, France, 1971-72; guest professor Siemons Research, Munich, Germany, 1983, also consultant; consultant to General Motors Corp., Ford Corp., Westinghouse Company, Radio Corporation of America, Xerox Data Systems, International Business Machines Corporation.; Member sci. council Institute for Computer Applications in Sci. and Engineering, 1973-79; chairman committee on anti-ballistic missile data processing National Acad. Sci., 1966-71; member panel Institute Computer Sci. and Tech., 1980-86; member acad. adv. council Wang Institute, 1978-87; member study section National Institutes of Health, 1985-88. Author: An Introduction to Digital Computing, 1963; (with K. Astil) Numerical Algorithms: Their Origins and Applications, 1970; editor: What Can Be Automated?, 1980. Served with United States Naval Reserve, 1944-46, 49-50. Fellow American Association for the Advancement of Science; member Institute of Electrical and Electronics Engineers (senior), Association for Computing Machinery, Univs. Space Research Association (board directors 1982-88), Sigma Xi, Tau Beta Pi, Eta Kappa Nu. Office: U Rochester College Engring & Applied Service Rochester New York 14627

ARMSTRONG, JOHN ALLAN, business machine company research executive; born Schenectady, New York, July 1, 1934; son of Orlo Lucius and Mary Kathryn (Moffitt) A.; married Elizabeth Jean Saunders, September 20, 1958; children: Sarah Richardson, Jennifer Mary. Bachelor of Arts summa cum laude, Harvard University, 1956, Master of Science, Doctor of Philosophy, 1961. Research fellow in applied physics Harvard University, Cambridge, Massachusetts, 1961-63; with International Business Machines Corporation, 1963—; research staff member Yorktown Heights, New York, 1963-67, director physical sci.; 1976-80; member corp. tech. committee Armonk, New York, 1980-81; manager materials and tech. devel. East Fishkill, New York, 1981-83; vice president research div., logic and memory Yorktown Heights, 1983-86, director research; 1986-87, vice president, director research; 1987—; member National Adv. Committee on Semiconductors. Fellow American Association for the Advancement of Science, Optical Society Am., Am. Physical Society (Pake prize 1989); member National Acad. Engineering, Royal Swedish Acad. Engineering Sciences (foreign member). Office: International Business Machines Corporation Corp Post Office Box 218 Yorktown Heights New York 10598

ARMSTRONG, NEIL A., computer systems company executive, former astronaut; born Wapakoneta, Ohio, August 5, 1930; son of Stephen Armstrong; married Janet Shearon; children: Eric, Mark. Bachelor of Science In Aeronautical Engineering, Purdue University, 1955; Master of Science in Aeronautical Engineering,

University Southern California. With Lewis Flight Propulsion Laboratory, National Advisory Committee for Aeronautics, 1955; then aeronautical research pilot for National Advisory Committee for Aeronautics (later National Aeronautics and Space Administration, High Speed Flight Station), Edwards, California; astronaut Manned Spacecraft Center, National Aeronautics and Space Administration, Houston, 1962-70; command pilot Gemini 8; commander Apollo 11; deputy associate administrator for aeros. Office Advanced Research and Tech., Headquarters National Aeronautics and Space Administration, Washington, 1970-71; professor aerospace engineering University Cincinnati, 1971-79; chairman board Cardwell International, Limited, 1980-82; chairman CTA, Incorporated, 1982—; director Cincinnati Gas & Electric Company, Eaton Corp., Taft Broadcasting Company, Cincinnati Milacron, UAL Incorporated, USX Incorporated. Member President's Commission on Space Shuttle, 1986, National Commission on Space, 1985-86. Served as naval aviator United States Navy, 1949-52, Korea. Recipient numerous awards, including Octave Chanute award Institute Aeronautical Sciences, 1962, Presidential Medal for Freedom, 1969, Exceptional Service medal National Aeronautics and Space Administration, Hubbard Gold medal National Geog. Society, 1970, Kitty Hawk Memorial award, 1969, Pere Marquette medal, 1969, Arthur S. Fleming award, 1970, Congl. Space Medal of Honor, Explorers Club medal. Fellow American Institute of Aeronautics and Astronautics (hon., Astronautics award 1966), International Astronautical Federation (hon.),

Society Experimental Test Pilots; member National Acad. Engineering. Address: 31 N Broadway Lebanon Ohio 45036

ASIMOV, ISAAC, biochemist, author; born Petrovichi, Russia, January 2, 1920; came to United States, 1923; son of Judah and Anna Rachel (Berman) A.; married Gertrude Blugerman, 1942 (divorced 1973); children: David, Robyn Joan; married Janet Jeppson, 1973. Bachelor of Science, Columbia University, 1939, Master of Arts, 1941, Doctor of Philosophy, 1948; holder 14 honorary degrees. Faculty Boston University School Medicine, 1949—, associate professor biochemistry; 1955-79, professor; 1979—. Author 408 books including: Pebble in the Sky, 1950, I, Robot, 1950, The Stars, Like the Dust, 1951, Foundation, 1951, Foundation and Empire, 1952, Currents of Space, 1952, Second Foundation, 1953, Caves of Steel, 1954, End of Eternity, 1955, Races and People, 1955, The Naked Sun, 1957; textbook Biochemistry and Human Metabolism, rev. edit, 1957; World of Carbon, 1958, World of Nitrogen, 1958, Nine Tomorrows, 1959, The Words of Science, 1959, Realm of Numbers, 1959, The Living River, 1960, Kingdom of the Sun, 1960, Realm of Measure, 1960, Wellsprings of Life, 1960, Words from Myths, 1961, Realm of Algebra, 1961, Life and Energy, 1962, Words in Genesis, 1962, Fact and Fancy, 1962, Words on the Map, 1962, Search for the Elements, 1962, Words from the Exodus, 1963, The Human Body, 1963, The Genetic Code, 1963, Intelligent Man's Guide to Science, 1960, View from a Height, 1963, Kite that Won the Revolution, 1963, Human Brain, 1964, A Short History of Biology, 1964, Quick and

Easy Math, 1964, Adding a Dimension, 1964, A Short History of Chemistry, 1865, The Greeks, 1965, Of Time and Space and Other Things, 1965, The New Intelligent Man's Guide to Science, 1965, An Easy Introduction to the Slide Rule, 1965, Fantastic Voyage, 1966, The Noble Gases, 1966, The Neutrino, 1966, The Roman Republic, 1967, Understanding Physics, 1966, Is Anyone There?, 1967, To the Ends of the Universe, 1967, Mars, 1967, Egyptians, 1967, Asimov's Mysteries, 1968, Science, Numbers and I, 1968, Stars, 1968, Galaxies, 1968, A Whiff of Death, 1968, Near East, 1968, Asimov's Guide to the Bible, volume 1, 1968, volume 2, 1969, The Dark Ages, 1968, Words from History, 1968, Photosynthesis, 1969, The Shaping of England, 1969, Twentieth Century Discovery, 1969, Nightfall and Other Stories, 1969, Opus 100, 1969, ABC's of Space, 1969, Great Ideas of Science, 1969, Solar System and Back, 1970, Asimov's Guide to Shakespeare (2 volumes), 1970, Constantinople, 1970, ABC's of the Ocean, 1970, Light, 1970, The Stars in Their Courses, 1971, Where Do We Go from Here?, 1971, What Makes the Sun Shine?, 1971, The Sensuous Dirty Old Man, 1971, The Best New Thing, 1971, Isaac Asimov's Treasury of Humor, 1971, The Hugo Winners, Volume 2, 1971, The Land of Canaan, 1971, ABC's of the Earth, 1971, The Left Hand of the Electron, 1972, The Gods Themselves, 1972, Asimov's Guide to Science, 1972, More Words of Science, 1972, ABC's of Ecology, 1972, The Early Asimov, 1972, The Shaping of France, 1972, The Story of Ruth, 1972, Asimov's Annotated Don Juan, 1972, The Shaping of North America, 1973, Today and Tomorrow and, 1973, Jupiter, the Largest Planet, 1973, Please Explain, 1973, How Did We Find Out About Numbers, 1973, How Did We Find Out About Dinosaurs, 1973, The Tragedy of the Moon, 1973, Asimov on Astronomy, 1974, The Birth of the United States, 1974, Before the Golden Age, 1974, Our World in Space, 1974, How Did We Find Out About Germs, 1974, Asimov's Annotated Paradise Lost, 1974, Tales of the Black Widowers, 1974, Earth: Our Crowded Spaceship, 1974, Asimov on Chemistry, 1974, How Did We Find Out About Vitamins, 1974, Of Matters Great and Small, 1975, The Solar System, 1975, Our Federal Union, 1975, How Did We Find Out about Comets, 1975, Science Past—Science Future, 1975, Buy Jupiter and Other Stories, 1975, Eyes on the Universe, 1975, Lecherous Limericks, 1975, Heavenly Host, 1975, The Ends of the Earth, 1975, How Did We Find Out About Energy, 1975, Asimov on Physics, 1976, Murder at the ABA, 1976, How Did We Find Out About Atoms, 1976, The Planet That Wasn't, 1976, The Bicentennial Man and Other Stories, 1976, More Lecherous Limericks, 1976, More Tales of the Black Widowers, 1976, Alpha Centauri, The Nearest Star, 1976, How Did We Find Out About Nuclear Power, 1976, Familiar Poems Annotated, 1977, The Collapsing Universe, 1977, Asimov on Numbers, 1977, How Did We Find Out About Outer Space, 1977, Still More Lecherous Limericks, 1977, Hugo Winners, Volume II, 1977, The Beginning and the End, 1977, Mars, The Red Planet, 1977, The Golden Door, 1977, The Key Word and Other Mysteries, 1977, Asimov's Sherlockian Limericks, 1977, One Hundred Great Science Fiction Short Short Stories, 1978, Quasar, Quasar, Burning Bright, 1978, How Did We

Find Out About Earthquakes, 1978, Animals of the Bible, 1978, Life and Time, 1978, Limericks: Too Gross, 1978, How Did We Find Out About Black Holes?, 1978, Saturn and Beyond, 1979, In Memory Yet Green, 1979, Opus 200, 1979, Extraterrestrial Civilizations, 1979, How Did We Find Out About Our Human Roots?, 1979, The Road to Infinity, 1979, A Choice of Catastrophes, 1979, Isaac Asimov's Book of Facts, 1979, The Science Fictional Solar System, 1979, The Thirteen Crimes of Science Fiction, 1979, How Did We Find Out About Antarctica?, 1979, Casebook of the Black Widowers, 1980, How Did We Find Out About Oil?, 1980, In Joy Still Felt, 1980, Microcosmic Tales, 1980, Who Dun It?, 1980, Seven Deadly Sins of Science Fiction, 1980, The Annotated Gulliver's Travels, 1980, How Did We Find Out About Coal, 1980, In the Beginning, 1981, Asimov on Science Fiction, 1981, Venus: Near Neighbor of the Sun, 1981, How Did We Find Out About Solar Power?, 1981, How Did We Find Out About Volcanoes?, 1981, Views of the Universe, 1981, The Sun Shines Bright, 1981, Change, 1981, A Glossary of Limericks, 1982, How Did We Find Out About Life in the Deep Sea, 1982, The Complete Robot, 1982, Laughing Space, 1982, Exploring the Earth and the Cosmos, 1982, How Did We Find Out About the Beginning of Life, 1982, Foundations Edge, 1982, How Did We Find Out About the Universe, 1982, Counting the Eons, 1983, The Winds of Change and other Stories, 1983, The Roving Mind, 1983, The Measure of the Universe, 1983, The Union Club Mysteries, 1983, Norby, the Mixed-Up Robot, 1983, How Did We Find Out About Genes, 1983, The Robots of Dawn, 1983, others. X Stands for Unknown, 1984, Norby's Other Secret, 1984, How Did We Find Out About Computers, 1984, Opus 3000, 1984, Banquet of the Black Widowers, 1984, Limericks for Children, 1984, Asimov's New Guide to Science, 1984, How Did We Find Out About Robots, 1984, Asimov's Guide to Halley's Comet, 1985, Exploding Suns, 1985, Norby and the Lost Princess, 1985, How Did We Find Out About the Atmosphere, 1985, The Edge of Tomorrow, 1985, The Subatomic Monster, 1985, The Disappearing Man and Other Stories, 1985, Robots and Empire, 1985, Norby and The Invaders, 1985, How Did We Find Out About DNA?, 1985, The Alternate Asimovs, 1986, The Dangers of Intelligence, 1986, How Did We Find Out About the Speed of Light, 1986, Best Science Fiction of Isaac Asimov, 1986, Best Mysteries of Isaac Asimov, 1986, Foundation and Earth, 1986, Robot Dreams, 1986, Norby and the Queen's Necklace, 1986, Far as Human Eye Could See, 1987, How Did We Find Out About Blood, 1987, Past, Present and Future, 1987, How Did We Find Out About Sunshine?, 1987, How to Enjoy Writing, 1987, Norby Finds a Villain, 1987, Fantastic Voyage II, 1987, How did We Find Out About the Brain?, 1987, Did Comets Kill the Dinosaurs?, 1987, Beginnings, 1987, Asimov's Annotated Gilbert and Sullivan, 1988, How did We Find Out About Superconductivity?, 1988, Other Worlds of Isaac Asimov, 1988, Relativity of Wrong, 1988, Prelude to Foundation, 1988, Azazel, 1988, Norby Down to Earth, 1988, How Did We Find Out About Microwaves, 1989, Asimov's Galaxy, 1989. Served as corporal United States Army, 1945-46. Recipient James T. Grady award Am. Chemical Society, 1965, AAAS-

Westinghouse Sci. Writing award, 1967. Democrat. Avocation: a man's work is his play. Home and Office: 10 W 66th St Apartment 33A New York New York 10023

ATAL, BISHNU SAROOP, acoustics research executive; born Kanpur, Uttar Pradish, India, May 10, 1933; came to United States, 1961; son of Jagannath Prasad and Lakshmi Devi (Lakshmi) A.; married Kamla Atal, July 3, 1959; children: Aka, Namita. Bachelor of Science with honors, University Locknow, India, 1952; electrical engineering degree, Indian Institute Science, Bangalore, 1955; Doctor of Philosophy in Electrical Engineering, Polytechnic Institute Brooklyn, 1968. Senior research assistant Indian Institute Sci., Bangalore, 1955-56, lecturer; 1957-60; senior research fellow Central Electrical Engineering Research Institute, Pilani, Rajasthan, India, 1960-61; member tech. staff American Telephone and Telegraph Company Bell Laboratories, Murray Hill, New Jersey, 1961-85, head acoustics research; 1985—.
Contributor articles to various publications. Fellow Acoustical Society Am., Institute of Electrical and Electronics Engineers (Acoustics, Speech and Signal Processing Senior Tech. Achievement award 1975, ASSP Senior award 1980, Centennial medal 1984, Morris N. Liebman Memorial Field award 1975); member National Acad. Engineering. Office: AT&T Bell Labs 600 Mountain Avenue Room 2535 Murray Hill New Jersey 07974

ATANASOFF, JOHN VINCENT, physicist; born Hamilton, New York, October 4, 1903; son of John and Iva Lucina (Purdy) A.; married Lura Meeks, June, 1926 (divorced 1949); children—Elsie Whistler, Joanne Gathers, John Vincent; married Alice Crosby, June 17, 1949. Bachelor of Science in Electrical Engineering, University Florida, 1925, Doctor of Science (honorary), 1974; Master of Science, Iowa State University, 1926; Doctor of Philosophy, University Wisconsin, 1930; Doctor of Science (honorary), Moravian College, Bethleham, Pennsylvania, 1981; Doctor of Letters, Western Maryland College, 1984. From assistant professor to associate professor physics Iowa State University, Ames, 1930-42; chief acoustics div. Naval Ordnance Laboratory, White Oak, Maryland, 1942-49, director fuses; 1951-52; sci. advisor Chief Army Field Forces, Fort Monroe, Virginia, 1949-51; president Ordnance Engineering Corp., Frederick, Maryland, 1952-56; vice president Aerojet General Corp., Azusa, California, 1956-61; president Cybernetics Incorporated, Frederick, 1961—; consultant scientist Stewart-Warner Corp., Chicago, 1961-63, Honeywell Incorporated, Minneapolis, 1968-71, Control Data Corp., Washington, 1968-71. Contributor articles to acoustical, physical and seismol. journals; inventor 1st electronic digital computer, 1935, binary alphabet, 1943; patentee in field (32). Decorated Order of Cyril and Methodius 1st class (Bulgaria); recipient Distinguished Civilian Service award U.S. Navy, 1945; citation Seismol. Society, 1947, citation Bureau Ordinance, 1947; Distinguished Achievement award Iowa State University Alumni, 1983; Computing Appreciation award EDUCOM, 1985; named to Iowa Inventors Hall of Fame, 1978, Computer Pioneer medal Institute of Electrical and Electronic Engineers, 1984, Iowa Governor's Sci. medal,

1985, medal of Bulgaria, 1985, Holley medal American Society of Mechanical Engineers, 1985. Member Bulgarian Acad. Sci. (foreign member), Phi Beta Kappa, Pi Mu Epsilon, Tau Beta Pi. Democrat. Club: Cosmos (Washington). Home: 11928 E Baldwin Road Monrovia Maryland 21770

AUERBACH, STANLEY IRVING, ecologist, educator; born Chicago, May 0, 1921; son of Abraham and Carrie (Friedman) A.; married Dawn Patricia Davey, June 12, 1954; children: Andrew J., Anne E., Jonathan B., Alison M. Bachelor of Science, University Illinois, 1946, Master of Science, 1947; Doctor of Philosophy, Northwestern University, 1949. Instructor, then assistant professor Roosevelt University, Chicago, 1950-54; associate scientist, then scientist health physics div. Oak Ridge National Laboratory, 1954-59, senior scientist, section leader; 1959-70, director ecological sci. div.; 1970-72, director environmental sciences div.; 1972-86, senior research advisor; 1986—; adj. professor ecology University Tennessee, 1965—; adj. research professor radiation ecology University Georgia, 1964—; member United States executive committee International Biological Program, co-chairman program coordinating committee, director deciduous forest biome project, 1969-74; member executive committee Sci. Adv. Board, United States Environmental Protection Agency, 1986—; member National Acad. Sci. Adv. Committee on Research to Secretary Agriculture, 1969-70, National Academy of Engineering Power Plant Siting Program Commission, 1970-71, member board energy studies, 1974-77, chairman committee on energy and environmental, 1974-77, chairman environmental studies board, 1983-86, member committee on physical sciences, math. and resources, 1982-83, member committee on natural resources, 1979-82; chairman architectural rev. committee Oak Ridge National Laboratory, 1971-84; member aquatic biology committee ORSANCO; member ecological adv. board Bureau Reclamation; member National Acad. Sci.-NAE Board on Energy Studies, 1974-77; member Corps of Engineers board environmental consultant Tenn.-Tombigbee Waterway, 1975—; member ad hoc committee on transuranic burial Energy Research and Development Administration (Department Energy), 1976-78; member President's Special Committee on Health and Environmental Effects of Increasing Coal Utilization, 1977-78, Resources for the Future Research Adv. Committee, 1978—; member commission natural resources National Research Council, 1979—; member adv. council Water Resources Research Center, University Tennessee, 1980—; Member Tennessee Citizens Wilderness Planning, board of directors, 1968; trustee Institute Ecology, 1971-74. Ecology editor: Environment Internat, 1979—; adv. board: Environ. and Experimental Botany, 1967—; board editors: Radiation Research, 1975-77. Served to 2d lieutenant Army of the United States, 1942-44. Recipient U.S. Department Energy District Assoc. award, 1987. Fellow American Association for the Advancement of Science; member Am. Institute Biological Sciences (board govs.), Society Zoology (chairman ecology division), Am. Society Agronomy, Brit.

Ecological Society, Health Physics Society, Entomological Society Am., Society Systematic Biology, Ecological Society Am. (chairman committee radioecology 1963-65, secretary 1964-69, chairman fin. committee 1969, president 1971-72, Distinguished Service award 1985), Sigma Xi (president Oak Ridge branch 1972-73, chairman admissions 1980-82), Alpha Epsilon Pi. Spl. research ecology centipedes, radioecology and radioactive waste disposal, environ. behavior of radionuclides, ecosystem analysis. Home: 24 Wildwood Dr Oak Ridge Tennessee 37830 Office: Post Office Box X Oak Ridge Tennessee 37831

AXELROD, JULIUS, biochemist, pharmacologist; born New York City, May 30, 1912; son of Isadore and Molly (Leichtling) A.; married Sally Taub, August 30, 1938; children: Paul Mark, Alfred Nathan. Bachelor of Science, City College of New York, 1933; Master of Arts, New York University, 1941, Doctor of Science (honorary), 1971; Doctor of Philosophy, George Washington University, 1955, Doctor of Laws (honorary), 1971; Doctor of Science (honorary), University Chicago, 1965, Medical College Wisconsin, 1971, Medical College Pennsylvania, 1974, University Pennsylvania, 1986, Hahnemann University, 1987; Doctor of Laws (honorary), City College of New York, 1972; Doctor honoris causa, University Panama, 1972, University Paris (Sud), 1982, Ripon Coll, 1984, Tel Aviv University, 1984. Chemist Laboratory Industrial Hygiene, 1935-46; research associate 3d New York University research div. Goldwater Memorial Hospital, 1946-49; associate chemist section chemical pharmacology National Heart Institute, National Institutes of Health, 1949-50, chemist; 1950-53, senior chemist; 1953-55; acting chief section pharmacology Laboratory Clinical Sci. National Institute of Mental Health, 1955, chief section pharmacology; 1955-84; guest worker Laboratory Cell Biology National Institute of Mental Health, 1984—; Otto Loewi memorial lecturer New York University, 1963; Karl East Paschkis memorial lecturer Philadelphia Endocine Society, 1966; National Institutes of Health lecturer, 1967; Nathanson memorial lecturer University Southern California, 1968; James Parkinson lecturer Columbia University, 1971; Wartenberg lecturer Am. Acad. Neurology, 1971; Arnold D. Welch lecturer Yale University, 1971; Harold Carpenter Hodge distinguished lecturer toxicology University Rochester, 1971; Bennett lecturer Am. Neurological Association, 1971; Harvey lecturer, 1971; Mayer lecturer Massachusetts Institute Tech., 1971; distinguished professor sci. George Washington University, 1972; Salmon lecturer New York Acad. Medicine, 1972; Eli Lilly lecturer, 1972; Mike Hogg lecturer University Texas, 1972; Fred Schueler lecturer Tulane University, 1972; numerous other hon. lectures; visiting scholar Herbert Lehman College City University New York, 1973; professorial lecturer George Washington University, 1959—; panelist United States Board Civil Service Examiners, 1958-67; member research adv. committee United Cerebral Palsy Association, 1966-69; member psychopharmacology study section National Institute of Mental Health, 1970-74; member International Brain Research Organization; member research adv. committee National Foundation; visiting committee

Brookhaven National Laboratory, 1972-76; board overseers Jackson Laboratory, 1974-88. Member editorial board Journal Pharmacology and Experimental Therapeutics, 1956-72, Journal Medicinal Chemistry, 1962-67, Circulation Research, 1963-71, Currents in Modern Biology, 1966-72; member editorial adv. board Communication in Behavioral Biology, 1967-73, Journal Neurobiology, 1968-77, Journal Neurochemistry, 1969-77, Journal Neurovisceral Relation, 1969, Rassegna di Neurologia Vegetativa, 1969—, International Journal Psychobiology, 1970-75; hon. cons. editor Life Scis, 1961-69; co-author: The Pineal, 1968; contributor papers in biochem. actions and metabolism of drugs, hormones, action of pineal gland, enzymes, neurochem. transmission to professional journals. Recipient Meritorious Research award Association Research Nervous and Mental Diseases, 1965; Gairdner award distinguished research, 1967; Nobel prize in med. physiology, 1970; Alumni Distinguished Achievement award George Washington University, 1968; Superior Service award Department of Health, Education and Welfare, 1968; Distinguished Service award, 1970; Claude Bernard professorship and medal University Montreal, 1969; Distinguished Service award Modern Medicine magazine, 1970; Albert Einstein award Yeshiva University, 1971; medal Rudolf Virchow Medical Society, 1971; Myrtle Wreath award Hadassah, 1972; Leibniz medal Acad. Sci. East Germany, 1984; Salmon medal New York Acad. Medicine. Fellow Am. Acad. Arts and Sciences, Am. Society Neuropsychopharmacology; member German Pharmacol. Society (corr.), Am. Chemical Society, Am. Society Pharmacology and Experimental Therapeutics (Torald Sollmann award 1973), American Association for the Advancement of Science, National Acad. Sciences, Am. Neurological Association (hon.), Royal Society London (foreign), Institute Medicine (senior), Deutshe Academie Naturfoucher (East Germany) Sigma Xi, Am. Psychopathol. Association (hon.). Home: 10401 Grosvenor Place Rockville Maryland 20852 Office: NIH Department Health Edn & Welfare Building 36 Room 3A-15 Bethesda Maryland 20892

BABCOCK, HORACE WELCOME, astronomer; born Pasadena, California, September 13, 1912; son of Harold Delos and Mary Geddie (Henderson) B.; married 1940 (divorced 1958); children: Ann Lucille, Bruce Harold; married Elizabeth Mae Aubrey, 1958; 1 son, Kenneth L. Bachelor of Science, California Institute Tech., 1934; Doctor of Philosophy, University California, 1938; Doctor of Science (honorary), University Newcastle-upon-Tyne (England), 1965. Assistant Lick Observatory, Mount Hamilton, California, 1938-39; instructor Yerkes and McDonald Observatory, Williams Bay, Wisconsin, Fort Davis, Texas, 1939-41; with Radiation Laboratory, Massachusetts Institute of Technology, 1941-42, Rocket Project, California Institute Tech., 1942-45; staff member Mount Wilson and Palomar Observatory, Carnegie Institution of Washington, California Institute Tech., Pasadena, 1946—; director Mount Wilson and Palomar Observatory, 1964-78. Author sci. and tech. papers in professional journals. Recipient USN Bureau Ordnance Devel. award, 1946; Draper medal National Academy of Sciences, 1957; Eddington medal Royal Astronomical

Society, 1958; Gold medal, 1970; Bruce medal Astronomical Society Pacific, 1969. Member Royal Astronomical Society (associate), Societé Royale des Sciences de Liege (corr. member), Am. Philosophical Society, Am. Acad. Arts and Sciences, National Academy of Sciences (councilor 1973-76), Am. Astronomical Society (councilor 1956-58), Astronomical Society Pacific, International Astronomical Union, Tau Beta Pi. Home: 2189 N Altadena Dr Altadena California 91001 Office: Mt Wilson and Las Campanas Obs Carnegie Institute Washington 813 Santa Barbara St Pasadena California 91101

BACHRACH, HOWARD L., biochemist; born Faribault, Minnesota, May 21, 1920; son of Harry and Elizabeth (Panovitz) B.; married Shirley F. Lichterman, June 13, 1943; children: Eve E., Harrison J. Bachelor of Arts in Chemistry, University Minnesota, 1942, Doctor of Philosophy in Biochemistry, 1949. Research chemist synthetic rubber Jos. E. Seagram & Company, 1942; Research assistant explosives research laboratory National Defense Research Committee project Carnegie Institute Tech., Pittsburgh, 1942-45; research assistant University Minnesota, Minneapolis, 1945-49; biochemist foot-and-mouth disease mission United States Department Agriculture, Denmark, 1949-50; research biochemist virus laboratory University Calif-Berkeley, 1950-53; chief scientist, head biochem. and physical investigation Plum Island Animal Disease Center, Greenport, New York, 1953-80, research chemist, advisor to director; 1981-89, sci. collaborator; 1989—; charter member Senior Executive Service United States Government; member viral and rickettsial grants subcom. Walter Reed Army Institute Research, 1982-85; consultant Pan Am. Health Organization, Brazil, 1981, Cooper State Reserve Service, United States Department Agriculture, 1982-83, Report Rev. Committee National Academy of Sciences, 1984, Office Tech. Assessment United States Congress, 1984-85, 88-89, National Research Council, 1984, 86-88, National Cancer Institute, 1984—, Texas Agricultural and Mechanical University Institute Bioscis. & Techs., 1987—. Recipient Naval Ordnance Devel. award, 1945, Certificate of Merit USDA, 1960, Distinguished Service award U.S. Department Agr., 1982, Presidential citation, 1965, U.S. Senior Executive Service award, 1980, Newcomb Cleveland prize American Association for the Advancement of Science, 1982, National Award for Agrl. Excellence, 1983, Alexander von Humboldt award, 1983, National Medal Sci., 1983, ISI Citation Classic Publ., 1986; named to Agriculture Sci. Hall of Fame, 1987; New York Acad. Sciences fellow, 1982. Hon. member Am. College Veterinary Microbiologists; member Am. Chemical Society (Kenneth A. Spencer medal 1983), Am. Society Virology, Sigma Xi, Gamma Alpha, Phi Lambda Upsilon. Home: 295 Dayton Road Southold New York 11971

BACKUS, JOHN, computer scientist; born Philadelphia, December 3, 1924; son of Cecil Franklin and Elizabeth (Edsall) B.; married Una Stannard, 1968; children: Karen, Paula. Bachelor of Science, Columbia University, 1949, Master of Arts, 1950; Doctor of University (honorary), University York, England, 1985. Programmer International Business

Machines Corporation, New York City, 1950-53, manager programming research; 1954-59; staff member International Business Machines Corporation T.J. Watson Research Center, Yorktown Heights, New York, 1959-63; International Business Machines Corporation fellow International Business Machines Corporation Research, Yorktown Heights and San Jose, California, 1963—. Adv. board: New Generation Computing. Served with Army of the United States, 1943-46. Recipient W. Wallace McDowell award Institute of Electrical and Electronic Engineers, 1967; National medal of Sci., 1975; Harold Pender award Moore School Electrical Engineering, University Pennsylvania, 1983; Achievement award Indsl. Research Institute, Incorporated, 1983. Fellow Am. Acad. Arts and Sciences; member National Acad. Engineering, National Acad. Sciences, Association Computing Machinery (Turing award 1977), Am. Math. Society, European Association Theoretical Computer Sci. System designer IBM 704, Fortran programming lang., Backus-Naur Form Lang., function level programming; member design group ALGOL 60 lang. Home: 91 St Germain Avenue San Francisco California 94114 Office: International Business Machines Corporation Almaden Research Center 650 Harry Road San Jose California 95120

BAER, ERIC, science educator; born Nieder-Weisel, Germany, July 18, 1932; came to United States, 1947, naturalized, 1952; son of Arthur and Erna (Kraemer) B.; married Ana Golender, August 5, 1956; children: Lisa, Michelle. Master of Arts, Johns Hopkins, 1953, Doctor of Engineering, 1957. Research engineer,

polychems. department E.I. du Pont de Nemours & Company, Incorporated, 1957-60; assistant professor chemistry and chemical engineering University Illinois, 1960-62; associate professor engineering Case Institute Tech., 1962- 66; professor, head department polymer sci. Case Western Reserve University, 1966-78; dean Case Institute Tech., 1978-83, Leonard Case professor macromolecular sci.; 1984—; consultant to industry, 1961—, Edison Polymer Innovations Corp. Author articles in field.; Editor: Engineering Design for Plastics, 1963, Polymer Engineering and Science, 1967—. Recipient Curtis W. McGraw award ASEE, 1968. Member Am. Chemical Society (Borden award 1981), Am. Physical Society, Am. Institute Chemical Engineering, Society Plastics Engineering (international award 1980), Plastics Institute Am. (trustee). Home: 2 Mornington Lane Cleveland Heights Ohio 44106 Office: Case Western Reserve U Cleveland Ohio 44106

BAGBY, MARVIN ORVILLE, chemist; born Macomb, Illinois, September 27, 1932; son of Byron Orville and Geneva Floriene (Filbert) B.; married Mary Jean Jennings, August 31, 1957; children: Gary Lee, Gordon Eugene. Bachelor of Science, Master of Science, Western Illinois University, 1957. With Northern Regional Research Center, United States Department Agriculture Agricultural Research Service, Peoria, Illinois, 1957—, research leader fibrous products research unit; 1974-80; manager Northern Agricultural Energy Center, 1980-85, also research leader hydrocarbon plants and biomass research unit; 1980-82, leader oil chemical research; 1985—;

consultant numerous special assignments government projects. Contributor articles to professional journals. Served with Army of the United States, 1953-55. Member Am. Chemical Society, American Association for the Advancement of Science, Technical Association of the Pulp and Paper Industry, Am. Oil Chemists Society, New York Acad. Sci., Am. Society Agricultural Engineers. Methodist. Home: 209 S Louisiana St Morton Illinois 61550 Office: 1815 N University St Peoria Illinois 61604

BAILEY, LEONARD LEE, surgeon; born Takoma Park, Maryland, August 28, 1942; son of Nelson Hulburt and Catherine Effie (Long) B.; married Nancy Ann Schroeder, August 21, 1966; children: Jonathan Brooks, Charles Connor. Bachelor of Science, Columbia Union College, 1960-64; postgraduate, NIH, 1965; Doctor of Medicine, Loma Linda University, 1969. Diplomate Am. Board Surgery, Am. Board Thoracic Surgery. Intern Loma Linda University Medical Center, 1969-70, resident in surgery; 1970-73, resident in thoracic and cardiovascular surgery; 1973-74; resident in pediatric cardiovascular surgery Hospital for Sick Children, Toronto, Ontario, Can., 1974-75; resident in thoracic and cardiovascular surgery Loma Linda University Medical School, 1975-76, assistant professor surgery; 1976—, assistant professor pediatrics; 1978—, director pediatric cardiac surgery; 1976—. Member Am. College Cardiology, Society Thoracic Surgery, Am. Association Thoracic Surgery, Western Thoracic Surgical Association, Western Society Pediatric Research, Walter E. McPherson Society (clinical investigator of year 1976, 85). Democrat. Seventh-day Adventist. Office: Loma Linda U Med Center Loma Linda California 92350

BAKER, DONALD JAMES, oceanographer, administrator; born Long Beach, California, March 23, 1937; son of Donald James and Lillian Mae (Pund) B.; married Emily Lind Delman, September 7, 1968. Bachelor of Science, Stanford University, 1958; Doctor of Philosophy, Cornell University, 1962. Postdoctoral fellow Grad. School Oceanography, University Rhode Island, Kingston, 1962-63; National Institutes of Health fellow in chemical biodynamics Lawrence Radiation Laboratory, University California, Berkeley, 1963-64; research fellow, assistant professor, associate professor physical oceanography Harvard University, 1964-73; research professor department oceanography, senior oceanographer, applied physics laboratory University Washington, Seattle, 1973-77; senior fellow Joint Institute for Study Atmosphere and Ocean, 1977-86, professor department oceanography; 1979-86, chairman department oceanography; 1979-81; dean College Ocean and Fishery Sciences, 1981-83; group leader deep-sea physics group Pacific Marine Environmental Laboratory, National Oceanographic and Atmospheric Administration, Seattle, 1977-79; board governors Joint Oceanographic Institutions, Incorporated, 1979—, president, 1983—; distinguished visiting scientist Jet Propulsion Laboratory, California Institute Tech., 1982—; co-chairman executive committee International Southern Ocean Studies (National Science Foundation project), 1974-84; vice-chairman joint panel, global weather experiment National Acad. Sciences, 1976-81, member ocean sciences board, ocean sciences policy board, 1979—, member committee on atmospheric sciences, 1978-81, member climate research committee, 1979—; member space and earth sci. adv. committee National Aeronautics and Space Administration, 1982-86 , member space sci. board, 1984-87, chairman committee on earth sciences, 1984-87; member environmental panel Navy Research Adv. Committee, 1983-86, member National Aeronautics and Space Administration earth system sciences committee, 1983-86; officer Joint Sci. Committee for World Climate Research Program, 1987—; member United States national committee for international council sci. unions National Acad. Sciences, 1987—, committee on global change, 1987—; member United States Sci. Steering Committee for World Ocean Circulation Experiment, 1985—; chairman National Aeronautics and Space Administration Center Sci. Assessment Team, 1987-88; chairman International World Ocean Circulation Experiment Sci. Steering Group, 1988—; member earth sci. and applications adv. committee National Aeronautics and Space Administration, 1989—. Co-editor in chief: Dynamics of Atmospheres and Oceans Jour, 1975-79; Contributor sci. articles to professional journals. Fellow American Association for the Advancement of Science, Explorers Club; member Am. Geophysical Union, Am. Meteorological Society (council 1982—), The Oceanography Society (president 1988—), Marine Tech. Society , Sigma Xi. Patentee deep-sea pressure gauge. Home: 4531 28th St Northwest Washington District of Columbia 20008 Office: Joint Oceanographic Instns Incorporated 1755 Massachusetts Avenue Northwest Washington District of Columbia 20036

BAKER, JAMES PORTER, physician, educator; born Hallsboro, Virginia, November 21, 1931; son of William Howard and Alice Leigh (Dance) B.; married Patricia Ormand, April 11, 1975; children: David, Daniel, Steven. Bachelor of Science, Virginia Polytechnic Institute, 1954; Doctor of Medicine, Medical College Virginia, 1958. Diplomate: Am. Board Internal Medicine. Intern Massachusetts Memorial Hospital, Boston, 1958-59; resident United States Naval Hospital, Chelsea, Massachusetts, 1962-63; assistant resident Medical College Virginia, Richmond, 1964-65, cardiopulmonary research fellow; 1965-67, instructor Medicine; 1966-67, assistant professor; 1967-70, associate professor; 1970-75, advisor School Dentistry; 1972-75, medical director respiratory Intensive Care Unit; 1967-75; medical co-director respiratory therapy and pulmonary laboratories Medical College Virginia, 1967-75; medical director respiratory car services Medical Center Hospitals, Norfolk, Virginia, 1975; professor medicine Eastern Virginia Medical School, Norfolk, 1975—, chairman department internal medicine; 1978—, interim dean; 1983-84; director pulmonary div. medical service programs Eastern Virginia Medical Authority, Norfolk; consultant pulmonary diseases United States Naval Regional Medical Center, Portsmouth, Virginia, Veteran's Administration Medical Center, Hampton, Virginia; member staff Medical Centers Hospitals, Norfolk, DePaul Hospitals, Norfolk, Bayside Hospital, Virginia Beach. Contributor articles to professional journals. Served with Medical Corps United States Navy, 1959-64; served to captain United States Naval Reserve, 1964—. National Institutes of Health fellow, 1965-66; A.D. Williams fellow, 1966-67. Fellow Am. College Chest Physicians (sci. program committee 1974-75), American College of Physicians (governor Virginia chapter 1983-88); member Am. Thoracic Society (executive committee 1975-78, TB committee 1975-78), American Medical Association (joint rev. committee respiratory therapy education 1973-78), Am. Lung Association (respiratory disease consultation team 1974-78), Am. Association Respiratory Therapy (board med. advisors, chairman 1982-83), Alpha Omega Alpha. Home: 213 61st St Virginia Beach Virginia 23451 Office: 825 Fairfax Avenue Norfolk Virginia 23507

BAKER, LEE EDWARD, biomedical engineering educator; born Springfield, Missouri, August 31, 1924; son of Edward Fielding and Oneita Geneva (Patton) B.; married Jeanne Carolyn Ferbrache, June 20, 1948; children: Carson Phillips, Carolyn Patton. Bachelor of Electrical Engineering, University Kansas, 1945; Master of Electrical Engineering, Rice University, 1960; Doctor of Philosophy in Physiology, Baylor University, 1965. Registered professional engineer, Texas. Assistant professor electrical engineering Rice University, Houston, 1960-64; assistant professor physiology Baylor University College Medicine, Houston, 1965-69, associate professor; 1969-75; professor biomed. engineering University Texas, 1975-82; Robert L. Parker Senior Centennial Professor Engineering University Texas, Austin,

1982—. Co-author: Principles of Applied Biomedical Engineering, 1968, 3d edition, 1989; author, co-author scientific papers. Served to lieutenant United States Navy, 1943-46, PTO, 1951-53. Special research fellow National Institutes of Health, 1964-65. Member Institute of Electrical and Electronics Engineers (senior), Biomed. Engineering Society (senior), Association for Advancement Medical Instrumentation, Am. Physiological Society, New York Acad. Sciences. Episcopalian. Avocation: gardening. Office: University Tex Biomed Engring ENS 610 Austin Texas 78712

BAKER, WILLIAM OLIVER, research chemist; born Chestertown, Maryland, July 15, 1915; son of Harold May and Helen (Stokes) B.; married Frances Burrill, November 15, 1941; 1 son, Joseph Burrill. Bachelor of Science, Washington College, 1935, Doctor of Science, 1957; Doctor of Philosophy, Princeton University, 1938; Doctor of Science, Georgetown University, 1962, University Pittsburgh, 1963, Seton Hall University, 1965, University Akron, 1968, University Michigan, 1970, St. Peter's College, 1972, Polytechnic Institute New York, 1973, Trinity College, Dublin, Ireland, 1975, Northwestern University, 1976, University Notre Dame, 1978, Tufts University, 1981, New Jersey College Medicine and Dentistry, 1981, Clark University, 1983, Fairleigh Dickinson University, 1983; Doctor of Engineering, Stevens Institute Tech., 1962, New Jersey Institute Tech., 1978; Doctor of Laws (honorary), University Glasgow, 1965, University Pennsylvania, 1974, Kean College, New Jersey, 1976, Lehigh University, 1980, Drew University, 1981; Doctor of Humane Letters (honorary),

Monmouth College, 1973, Clarkson College Tech., 1974. With American Telephone and Telegraph Company Bell Laboratories, 1939-80, in charge polymer research and devel.; 1948-51, assistant director chemical and metallurgical research; 1951-54, director research, physical sciences; 1954-55, vice president research; 1955-73, president; 1973-79, chairman board; 1979-80; board of directors Summit Trust Company, General Am. Investors, Incorporated; visiting lecturer Northwestern University, Princeton University, Duke; Schmitt lecturer University Notre Dame, 1968; Harrelson lecturer North Carolina State University, 1971; Herbert Spencer lecturer University Pennsylvania, 1974; Charles M. Schwab Memorial lecturer Am. Iron and Steel Institute, 1976; National Institutes of Health lecturer, 1958, Metallurgical Society Am. Institute Mining Engrs./Am. Society Metals distinguished lecturer, 1976; Miles Conrad Memorial lecturer National Federation Abstracting and Indexing Services, 1977; Wulff lecturer Massachusetts Institute of Technology, 1979; Whitehead lecturer University Georgia, 1985; Lazerow lecturer University Pittsburgh, 1984; Taylor lecturer Pennsylvania State University, 1984; other lectureships; consultant Office Sci. and Tech., 1977-81; member Princeton Grad. Council, 1956-64; board visitors Tulane University, 1963-82; member commission sociotech. systems National Research Council, 1974-78, also chairman adv. board on military personnel supplies, 1964-78; member committee on physical chemistry of div. chemistry and chemical tech., 1963-70; also steering committee President's Food and Nutrition Study Commission International Relations National Acad. Scis.-NRC, 1975; member panel on physical chemistry Office Naval Research, 1948-51; past member President's Sci. Adv. Committee, 1957-60; national sci. board National Science Foundation, 1960-66; past chairman National Sci. Information Council, 1959-61; member sci. adv. board National Security Agency, 1959-76, consultant, 1976—; consultant Department Def., 1958-71, special assistant president for sci. and tech., 1963-73; consultant Panel of Operations Evaluation Group, United States Navy, 1960-62; member New Jersey Board Higher Education, 1967—, executive committee, 1970—, vice chairman, 1970-72, 82-84; member liaison committee for sci. and tech. Library of Congress, 1963-73; member President's Foreign Intelligence Adv. Board, 1959-77, 81—; chairman President's Adv. Group Anticipated Advances in Sci. and Tech., 1975-76; vice chairman President's Committee Sci. and Tech., 1976-77; board regents National Library Medicine, 1969-73; board visitors Air Force Systems Command, 1962-73; member management adv. council Oak Ridge National Laboratory, 1970-78; member National Commission on Libraries and Information Sciences, 1971-75, Commission on Critical Choices for Ams., 1973-75, National Cancer Adv. Board, 1974-80, National Commission on Excellence in Education, 1981-83, National Commission on Jobs and Small Business, 1985-87, National Commission on Role and Future State Colleges and Universities, 1985—; member, vice chairman Commission on Sci. and Tech. New Jersey 1985—; member Carnegie Forum on Education Sci. Tech. and The Economy, 1985—; co-chairman American Association for the

Advancement of Science program on teaching sci. and math., 1985—; member panel adv. Institute Materials Research, National Bureau Standards, 1966-69; member Council Trends and Perspectives, United States Chamber of Commerce, 1966-74; chairman tech. panels adv. to National Bureau Standards, National Acad. Scis.-NRC, 1969-78; member National Council Educational Research, 1973-75; member energy research and devel. adv. council Energy Policy Office, 1973-75; member Project Independence adv. committee Federal Energy Administration, 1974-75, Gov.'s Committee to Evaluate Capital Needs New Jersey, 1974-75; member governing board National Enquiry into Scholarly Communication, 1975-79; adv. council New Jersey Regional Medical Library, 1975—, Federal Emergency Management Adv. Board, 1980—, Gas Research Institute Adv. Board, 1978-85; member adv. board New Jersey Sci./Tech. Center, 1980-86; member sci. adv. board Robert A. Welch Foundation, 1968—; visiting committee for chemistry Harvard, 1959-72; member council Marconi Fellowships, 1978—; visiting committee, div. chemistry and chemical engineering California Institute Tech., 1969-72; visiting committee on sciences and math. Drew University, 1969—; associate in university seminar on tech. and social change Columbia, 1969-80; visiting committee, department materials sci. and engineering Massachusetts Institute of Technology, 1973-76; board overseers College Engineering and Applied Sci. University Pennsylvania, 1975—; board of directors Council on Library Resources, 1970—, Health Effects Institute, 1980—, Clinical Scholar

Program Robert Wood Johnson Foundation, 1973-76, Third Century Corp., 1973-76. Contributor: High Polymers, 1945, Symposium on Basic Research, AAAS, 1959, Rheology, Volume III, 1960, Technology and Social Change, 1964, Science: The Achievement and the Promise, 1968, Annual Rev. Materials Sci, 1976, Advancing Materials Research, 1987, various other books.; member editorial adv. board Journal Information Sci; past member adv. editorial board Chemical and Engring. News; hon. editorial adv. board Carbon; contributor numerous articles to tech. journals. Trustee Urban Studies, Incorporated, 1960-78, Aerospace Corp., 1961-76, Carnegie-Mellon University, 1967-87, now emeritus, Princeton, 1964-86, now emeritus, Fund New Jersey, 1974—, Harry Frank Guggenheim Foundation, 1976—, General Motors Cancer Research Foundation, 1978—, Charles Babbage Institute, 1978—, Newark Mus., 1979—; trustee Rockefeller University, 1960—, chairman, 1980—; trustee Andrew W. Mellon Foundation, 1965—, chairman, 1975—. Named 1 of 10 top scientists in U.S. industry, 1954; recipient Perkin medal, 1963; Honor scroll Am. Institute Chemist, 1962; award to execs. American Society for Testing and Materials, 1967; Edgar Marburg award, 1967; Indsl. Research Institute medal, 1970; Frederik Philips award Institute of Electrical and Electronic Engineers, 1972; Indsl. Research Man of Year award, 1973; Procter prize Sigma Xi, 1973; James Madison medal Princeton University, 1975; Mellon Institute award, 1975; Society Research Administrators award for distinguished contributions, 1976; von Hippel award Materials Research Society, 1978; Fahrney medal Franklin

Institute, 1977; New Jersey Sci/Tech. medal, 1980; Harvard University fellow, 1937-38; Procter fellow, 1938-39; recipient Jefferson medal New Jersey Patent Law Association, 1981; David Sarnoff prize AFCEA, 1981; Vannevar Bush prize National Sci. Board, 1981; National Security medal, 1983; Baker medal Security Affairs Support Association, 1984; National Medal Tech., 1985, Thomas Alva Edison Sci. medal State of New Jersey, 1987, National Materials Advancement award Federation Materials Socs., 1987. Fellow Am. Physical Society, Am. Institute Chemists (Gold medal 1975), Franklin Institute, Am. Acad. Arts and Sciences; member Directors of Industrial Research, Am. Chemical Society (past member committee national defense, cons., past member committee chemistry and pub. affairs, Priestley medal 1966, Parsons award 1976, Willard Gibbs award 1978, Madison Marshall award 1980), Am. Philosophical Society, National Acad. Sciences (council 1969-72, committee sci. and pub. policy 1966-69), National Acad. Engineering (Bueche prize 1986), Institute Medicine (council 1973-75), Industrial Research Institute (director 1960-63, medal 1970), Sigma Xi, Phi Lambda Upsilon, Omicron Delta Kappa. Clubs: Chemists of New York (honorary), Cosmos, Princeton of Northwestern New Jersey. Holder 13 patents. Office: AT&T Bell Telephone Labs 600 Mountain Avenue Murray Hill New Jersey 07974

BAKKEN, EARL ELMER, electrical engineer, bioengineering company executive; born Minneapolis, January 10, 1924; son of Osval Elmer and Florence (Hendricks) B.; married Constance L. Olson, September 11, 1948 (divorced May 1979); children: Wendy, Jeff, Brad, Pam; married Doris Jane Marshall, October 21, 1982. Bachelor of Electrical Engineering, University Minnesota, 1948, postgraduate in electrical engineering. Partner Medtronic, Incorporated, Minneapolis, 1949-57, president; 1957-74, chairman, chief executive officer; 1974-76, founder, senior chairman; 1976-85, senior chairman; 1985—. Contributor articles to professional journals; developer first wearable, external, battery-powered heart pacemaker. Chairman board of directors Bakken Library Electricity in Life, Minneapolis, 1975—, Archaeus Project, Minneapolis, 1985—; board of directors Children's Heart Fund, Minneapolis, 1977—. Served to staff sergeant United States Army Air Force, 1942-46. Recipient Minnesota Business Hall of Fame award, 1978, Outstanding Achievement award University Minnesota, Minneapolis, 1981, Med.-Tech. Outstanding Achievement award Wale Securities, 1984, Engineering for Gold award NSPE, 1984. Fellow Bakken Society, Instrument Society Am., Institute of Electrical and Electronics Engineers (Centennial medal 1984); member North America Society Pacing and Electrophysiology (associate, Distinguished Service award 1985), Association Advancement Medical Instrumentation, Am. Antiquarian Society, Minnesota Medical Alley Association (board directors 1985—). Republican. Lutheran. Avocations: history of med. elec. tech., future studies, ballroom dancing. Office: Medtronic Incorporated 7000 Central Avenue NE Minneapolis Minnesota 55432

BALLARD, ROBERT DUANE, marine scientist; born Wichita, Kansas, June

30, 1942; son of Chester Patrick and Harriet Nell (May) B.; married Marjorie C. Jacobsen, July 1, 1966; children: Todd, Doug. Bachelor of Science, University California, Santa Barbara, 1965; postgraduate, University Hawaii, 1965-66, University Southern California, 1966-67; Doctor of Philosophy in Marine Geology and Geophysics, University Rhode Island, 1974. Assistant scientist Woods Hole (Massachusetts) Oceanographic Institution, 1974-76, associate scientist; 1976-83, senior scientist; 1983—; private consultant Benthos, Incorporated, North Falmouth, Massachusetts, 1982-83; consultant deputy chief naval operations for submarine warfare, 1983—; visiting scholar Stanford University, 1979-80, consultant professor, 1980-81, director Deep Submergence Laboratory, 1983—; president Deep Ocean Search and Survey, 1983—. Author: Exploring Our Living Planet, 1983. With United States Army, 1965-67; with United States Navy, 1967-70. Recipient Sci. award Underwater Society Am., 1976, Newcomb Cleveland prize American Association for the Advancement of Science, 1981, Cutty Sark Sci. award, 1982, Centennial Awd., National Geog. Society, 1988. Member Geological Society Am., Marine Tech. Society (Compass Distinguished Achievement award 1977), Am. Geophysical Union, Explorers Club. Leader 1st expdn. to reach sunken Titanic. Office: Woods Hole Oceanographic Instn Woods Hole Massachusetts 02543 *

BALLHAUS, WILLIAM FRANCIS, JR., federal agency administrator, research scientist; born Los Angeles, January 28, 1945; son of William Francis Sr. and Edna A. (Dooley) B.; married Jane Kerber; children from previous marriage: William Louis, Michael Frederick; stepchildren: Benjamin Joel, Jennifer Angela. Bachelor of Science in Mechanical Engineering with honors, University California, Berkeley, 1967, Master of Science in Mechanical Engineering, 1968, Doctor of Philosophy in Engineering, 1971. Research scientist United States Army Aviation Research & Development, Ames Research Center, Moffett Field, California, 1971-79; chief applied computation aeronautics branch NASA-Ames Research Center, Moffett Field, 1979-80, director astronautics; 1980-84, director; 1984—; acting associate administrator National Aeronautics and Space Administration Headquarters, Washington, 1988-89. Contributor articles on computational fluid dynamics to professional journals. Member sci. and acad. adv. board University California, 1987—; member engring. adv. board University California, Berkeley and Davis, San Jose State University; chairman government and education div. United Way of Santa Clara County, California, 1987. Captain United States Army Reserve. Decorated Presidential Rank of Meritorious Executive, 1985, Distinguished Executive, 1988; recipient H. Julian Allen award NASA-Ames Rsch. Center, 1977, Arthur S. Flemming award Jaycees, Washington, 1980, Distinguished Professional Engineering Sci. and Tech. award NSPE, 1986, Distinguished Executive Service award Senior Executives Association, 1989. Fellow American Institute of Aeronautics and Astronautics (president 1988-89, Lawrence Sperry award 1980), Royal Aeronautical Society; member National Academy of

Engineering, International Acad. Astronautics, Tau Beta Pi (named Eminent Engineer Berkeley chapter). Roman Catholic. Office: NASA Ames Research Center Mail Stop 200-1 Moffett Field California 94035

BALTIMORE, DAVID, microbiologist, educator; born New York City, March 7, 1938; son of Richard I. and Gertrude (Lipschitz) B.; married Alice S. Huang, October 5, 1968; 1 daughter, Teak. Bachelor of Arts with high honors in Chemistry, Swarthmore College, 1960; postgraduate, Massachusetts Institute of Technology, 1960-61; Doctor of Philosophy, Rockefeller University, 1964. Research associate Salk Institute Biological Studies, La Jolla, California, 1965-68; associate professor microbiology Massachusetts Institute of Technology, Cambridge, 1968-72, professor biology; 1972—, Am. Cancer Society professor microbiology; 1973-83, director Whitehead Institute Biomed. Research; 1982—. Member editorial board: Journal Molecular Biology, 1971-73, Journal Virology, 1969—, Science, 1986—. Board governors Weizmann Institute Sci., Israel; board of directors Life Sci. Research Foundation; co-chairman Commission on a National Strategy of Acquired Immune Deficiency Syndrome; board mgrs. Swarthmore; ad hoc program adv. committee on complex genome, National Institute of Health. Recipient Gustav Stern award in virology, 1970; Warren Triennial prize Massachusetts General Hospital, 1971; Eli Lilly and Company award in microbiology and immunology, 1971; U.S. Steel Foundation award in molecular biology, 1974; Gairdner Foundation annual award, 1974; Nobel prize in physiology or medicine, 1975. Fellow American Association for the Advancement of Science, Am. Medical Writers Association (hon.); member National Acad. Sciences, Am. Acad. Arts and Sciences, Institute Medical, Pontifical Acad. Sciences, Royal Society (England) (foreign). Home: 26 Reservoir St Cambridge Massachusetts 02138 Office: Whitehead Institute Biomed Research 9 Cambridge Center Cambridge Massachusetts 02142

BARASH, PAUL GEORGE, anesthesiologist, educator; born Brooklyn, February 22, 1942; son of Abraham Malcolm and Rose (Shenker) B.; married Norma Ellen Bernard, August 19, 1967; children—David, Daniel, Jed. Bachelor of Arts, City College of New York, 1963; Doctor of Medicine, University Kentucky, 1967; Master of Arts (honorary), Yale University, 1982. Diplomate Am. Board Anesthesiology. Intern State University of New York Kings County Hospital, Brooklyn, 1967-68; resident Yale-New Haven Hospital, 1970-72, chief resident; 1972-73; assistant professor anesthesiology Yale University, New Haven, 1973-78, associate professor anesthesiology; 1978-82, professor anesthesiology; 1982—, chairman department anesthesiology; 1983—. Associate editor: Advances in Anesthesia, 1984; associate editor Journal Clin. Monitoring, 1984. Served to surgeon United States Public Health Service, 1968-70. Fellow Am. College Anesthesiology, Am. College Chest Physicians; member Society Cardiovascular Anesthesiologists (president 1984-86), Connecticut Society Anesthesiologists (president 1982-83), International Anesthesia Research Society, Am. Society Anesthesiologists (editor-in-chief Anesthesia Refresher Courses 1985—). Home: 867 Robert Treat Extension Orange Connecticut 06477 Office: Yale U School Medicine 333 Cedar St New Haven Connecticut 06510

BARDEEN, JOHN, physicist, emeritus educator; born Madison, Wisconsin, May 23, 1908; son of Charles Russell and Althea (Harmer) B.; married Jane Maxwell, July 18, 1938; children—James Maxwell, William Allen, Elizabeth Ann Bardeen Greytak. Bachelor of Science, University Wisconsin, 1928, Master of Science, 1929; Doctor of Philosophy, Princeton University, 1936. Geophysicist Gulf Research & Devel. Corp., Pittsburgh, 1930-33; member Society Fellows Harvard, 1935-38; assistant professor physics University Minnesota, 1938-41; with Naval Ordnance Laboratory, Washington, 1941-45; research physicist Bell Telephone Laboratories, Murray Hill, New Jersey, 1945-51; professor physics, electrical engineering University Illinois, 1951-75, emeritus; 1975—; member President's Sci. Adv. Committee, 1959-62. Recipient Ballantine medal Franklin Institute, 1952; John Scott medal Philadelphia, 1955; Fritz London award, 1962; Vincent Bendix award, 1964; National Medal Sci., 1966; Morley award, 1968; medal of honor Institute of Electrical and Electronic Engineers, 1971; Franklin medal, 1975; co-recipient Nobel prizes in physics, 1956, 72; Presidential medal of Freedom, 1977; Lomonosov medal Soviet Acad. Sciences, 1987. Fellow Am. Physical Society (Buckley prize 1954, president 1968-69); member Am. Acad. Arts and Sci., Institute of Electrical and Electronics Engineers (hon.), Am. Philosophical Society, Royal Society Great Britain (foreign member), Acad. Sci. Union of the Soviet Socialist Republics (foreign member), Indian National Sci. Acad. (foreign), Japan Acad. (hon.), Pakistan Acad. Sci. (foreign), Austrian Acad. Sci. (corr.), Hungarian Acad. Sci. (foreign). Office: U Illinois Department Physics Urbana Illinois 61801

BARNES, CHARLES D., physiologist, educator; born Carroll, Iowa, August 17, 1935; son of Jack Y. and Gladys R. (Beckwith) B.; married Leona Gladys Wohler, September 8, 1957; children: Tara Lee, Teagen Yale, Kalee Meion, Kyler Alen. Bachelor of Science, Montana State University, 1958; Master of Science, University Washington, 1961; Doctor of Philosophy, University Iowa, 1962. Assistant professor department anatomy and physiology Ind. University, Bloomington, 1964-68, associate professor; 1968-71; professor Ind. University, Terre Haute, 1971-75; professor, chairman department physiology Texas Tech. University Health Sciences Center, Lubbock, 1975-83; chairman department vet. and comparative anatomy, pharmacology and physiology Washington State University, Pullman, 1983—; visiting scientist Instituto di Fisiologia Umana della University di Pisa, Italy, 1968-69. Author: (with L. Eltherington) Drug Dosage in Laboratory Animals, 1964, 2d edition, 1973, (with C. Kircher) Readings in Neurophysiology, 1968, (with Davies) Regulation of Ventilation and Gas Exchange, 1978, (with Hughes) Neural Control of Circulation, 1980, (with Orem) Physiology in Sleep, 1980, (with Crass) Vascular Smooth Muscle, 1982, (with McGrath) Air Pollution-Physiologic Effects, 1982. Recipient National Institutes of Health

Career Devel. award, 1967-72. Member American Association for the Advancement of Science, Am. Institute Biological Sciences, Am. Physiological Society, Am. Society Pharmacology and Experimental Therapeutics, Association Chairman Departments Physiology, International Brain Research Organization, Radiation Research Society, Society Experimental Biology and Medicine, Society Neuroscis., Society General Physiologists, Sigma Xi. Office: Wash State U Department VCAPP Pullman Washington 99164-6520

BARR, IRWIN ROBERT, aeronautical engineer; born Newburgh, New York, May 16, 1920; son of Abraham Herman and Esther (Reibel) B.; married Florence Lenore Skliar, October 19, 1941 (deceased February 1957); children: Mary Barr Megee, Betty Barr Mackey, Joan Barr Blanco, Alan Howard; married Dorothy Friendly Weeks, September 20, 1958. Certificate aeronautical engineering, Institute Aeros. (formerly Casey Jones School Aeros.), 1940; postgraduate engineering management, University California, Los Angeles, 1967. Registered professional engineer, Maryland. Design group engineer Glenn L. Martin Company, Baltimore, 1940-50; chief ordnance engineer to president and chief executive officer AAI Corp. (formerly Aircraft Armaments, Incorporated), Hunt Valley, Maryland, 1950—; vice president United Industrial Corp., New York City, 1979. Author various papers and reports on weapons devel., economics of solar energy; patentee rocket stabilization and control systems, aircraft, weapons, ground vehicles, underwater weapons, wheels, suspensions, bearings, solar energy collectors. Served with United States Army Air Force, 1944-46. Named to Ordnance Hall of Fame, Aberdeen Proving Ground, Maryland, 1985. Member Am. Defense Preparedness Association (adv. council), American Society of Heating, Refrigeration and Air Conditioning Engineers, Association United States Army, National Security Industrial Association (trustee, executive committee), International Solar Energy Society. Home: 2020 Belfast Road Sparks Maryland 21152 Office: AAI Corp Post Office Box 126 Hunt Valley Maryland 21030

BARRATT, RAYMOND WILLIAM, educator, biologist; born Holyoke, Massachusetts, May 4, 1920; son of George A. and Elizabeth (Bretschneider) B.; married Helen Ruggles, July 1943 (divorced 1968); children: Marguerite E., William R.; married Barbara H. Kellerup, October 16, 1971. Bachelor of Science, Rutgers University, 1941; Master of Science, University New Hampshire, 1943; Doctor of Philosophy, Yale, 1948; Master of Arts (honorary), Dartmouth, 1958. Assistant plant pathology and horticulture University New Hampshire, 1943-44; research associate, assistant plant pathologist Connecticut Agricultural Experiment Station, 1944-45; research associate biology Stanford, 1948-53, research biologist, acting assistant professor; 1953-54; member faculty Dartmouth, 1954-70, professor botany; 1958-62, professor biology; 1962-70, chairman department; 1965-69; lecturer microbiology Dartmouth (Medical School), 1962-70; professor biology, dean of sci. Humboldt State University, 1970-84; member visiting staff Vermont Environmental Center, Ripton, summers 1970, 71. Member

Hanover School Board, 1964-68; Member Dresden (New Hampshire) School Board, 1964-68, chairman, 1968; Board of directors Fungal Genetics Stock Center, 1970-85. Member Genetics Society Am. (chairman committee maintenance genetic stocks 1964-68), Sigma Xi, Alpha Zeta, Phi Sigma, Kappa Sigma. Research microbial genetics. Home: 6949 Fickle Hill Road Arcata California 95521

BARTON, DEREK HAROLD RICHARD, chemist; born England, September 8, 1918; son of William Thomas and Maude Henrietta (Lukes) B.; married Jeanne Wilkins, December 20, 1944; 1 son, William Godfrey Lukes; married Christiane Cosnet, November 5, 1969. Bachelor of Science with 1st class honours, Imperial College, London, 1940, Doctor of Philosophy in Organic Chemistry (Hofmann prize), 1942; Doctor of Science, University London, 1949; Doctor of Science (honorary), University Montpelier, France, 1962, University Dublin, Ireland, 1964, University St. Andrews, Scotland, 1970, Columbia University, Scotland, 1970, University Coimbra, Portugal, 1971, Oxford University, 1972, Manchester University, 1972, University South Africa, 1973, University La Laguna, Tenerife, Spain, 1975, University Western Virginia, Tenerife, Spain, 1975, University Sydney, Australia, 1976; Doctor (h.c.), University Valencia, 1979, University Sheffield, 1979, University Western Ontario, 1979, University Metz, 1979, Weizmann Institute Science, 1979. Government research chemist 1942-44; research chemist Messrs. Albright & Wilson, Birmingham, 1944-45; assistant lecturer, then ICI research fellow Imperial College, 1945-49; visiting lecturer Harvard University, 1949-50; reader organic chemistry Birkbeck College, London, 1950-53, professor organic chemistry; 1953-55, fellow; 1970-85, emeritus professor; 1978; Regius professor chemistry Glasgow University, 1955; Max Tishler lecturer Harvard University, 1956; Aub lecturer Medical School, 1962; professor organic chemistry Imperial College, 1957-78; director Institute of Chemistry and Natural Substances, Gif-sur-Yvette, France, 1978-85; professor chemistry Texas Agricultural and Mechanical University, College Station, 1985—; Arthur D. Little professor Massachusetts Institute of Technology, 1958; Karl Folkers visiting professor universities Illinois and Wisconsin, 1959; Falk-Plaut lecturer Columbia University, 1961; Renaud lecturer Michigan State University, 1962; inaugural 3M's lecturer University Western Ontario (Canada), 1962; 3m's lecturer University Minnesota, 1963; Sandin lecturer University Alberta, 1969; Graham Young lecturer, Glasgow, 1970; Rose Endowment lecturer Bose Institute, Calcutta, 1972; Sieglitz lecturer University Chicago, 1974; Bachman lecturer University Michigan, 1975; Woodward lecturer Yale University, 1972; 1st Smissman lecturer University Kansas, 1976; Priestley lecturer Pennsylvania State University, 1977; Cecil H. and Ida Green visiting professor University British Columbia, 1977; Benjamin Rush lecturer University Pennsylvania, 1977; Firth visiting professor University Sheffield, 1978-79; Romanes lecturer, Edinburgh, 1979; member Council Sci. Policy United Kingdom, 1965—. Created knight bachelor, 1972; decorated Order Rising Sun 2d class (Japan), 1972;

chevalier Legion of Honor (France), officier, 1986, 1974; knight of Mark Twain, 1975; recipient Nobel prize in chemistry, 1969; Royal medal, 1972; British Columbia Law Gold medal Indian Association Cultivation Sciences, 1972; medal Society Cosmetic Chemistry Great Britain, 1972; medal Union Sci. Workers Bulgaria, 1978; medal University Sofia, 1978; medal Acad. Sciences Bulgaria. Fellow Chemical Society (1st Corday-Morgan medal 1951, Tilden lecturer 1952, 1st Simonsen memorial lecturer 1958, Hugo Muller lecturer 1963, Pedler lecturer 1967, Robert Robinson lecturer 1970, 1st award natural product chemistry, 1961, Longstaff medal 1972; president Perkin division 1971; national president 1973), Royal Society (Davy medal 1961), Royal Society Edinburgh; foreign fellow Am. Chemical Society (Fritzsche medal 1956, 1st Roger Adams medal 1959, 2d Centennial Priestly Chemistry award 1974), Indian National Sci. Acad.; foreign associate National Acad. Sciences; foreign hon. member Am. Acad. Arts and Sciences, Pharmaceutical Society Japan, Royal Acad. Sciences Spain; hon. fellow Deutsche Akademie der Naturforscher Leopoldina, Indian Chemical Society; hon. member Society Quimica de Mexican, Belgm Chemical Society, Chilean Chemical Society, Acad. Pharmaceutical Sciences United States, Danish Acad. Sciences and Letters, Nacional Acad. Exact, Physical and Natural Sciences Argentina, Hungarian Acad. Sciences, Society Italiana per il Progresso delle Scienze, Acad. Sciences France; corr. member Argentinian Chemical Society; foreign member Acad. des Ciencias da Lisboa, Acad. Nazionale dei Lincei; member Brit. Association Advancement Sci. (president Sect. B, 1969), International Union Pure and Applied Chemistry (president 1969). Office: Tex A&M U Chemistry Department College Station Texas 77843 also: Imperial College Sci & Tech, Prince Consort Road, S Kensington, London SW7, England

BASCOM, WILLARD NEWELL, scientist, engineer; born New York City, November 7, 1916; son of Willard Newell and Pearle (Boyd) B.; married Rhoda Nergaard, April 15, 1946; children: Willard, Anitra. Student, Colorado School Mines. Registered professional engineer, Florida, District of Columbia. Research engineer University California, Berkeley, 1945-50, Scripps Institute Oceanography, La Jolla, California, 1950-54; executive secretary National Acad. Sciences, Washington, 1954-62; president Ocean Sci. and Engineering, Incorporated, Washington, 1962-72; director Coastal Water Research Project, Long Beach, California, 1973-85; consultant to government and industry. Author: Waves and Beaches, 1964, A Hole in the Bottom of the Sea, 1961, Deep Water, Ancient Ships, 1976, The Crest of the Wave, 1988; over 100 articles; patentee deep ocean search/recovery system. Recipient Distinguished Achievement medal Colorado School Mines, 1979, Compass Distinguished Achievement award Marine Tech. Society, 1970. Clubs: Explorers (Explorers medal 1980), Adventurers.

BASOLO, FRED, chemistry educator; born Coello, Illinois, February 11, 1920; son of John and Catherine (Marino) B.; married Mary P. Nutley, June 14, 1947; children: Mary Catherine, Freddie, Margaret-Ann, Elizabeth Rose. Bachelor of Education, Southern Illinois University,

1940, Doctor of Science (honorary), 1984; Master of Science, University Illinois, 1942, Doctor of Philosophy in Inorganic Chemistry, 1943. Research chemist Rohm & Haas Chemical Company, Philadelphia, 1943-46; member faculty Northwestern University, Evanston, Illinois, 1946—, professor chemistry; 1958—, Morrison professor chemistry; 1980—, chairman department chemistry; 1969-72; guest lecturer National Science Foundation summer institutes; chairman board trustees Gordon Research Conference, 1976; president Inorganic Syntheses, Incorporated, 1979-81; member board chemical sciences and tech. NRC-Nat. Acad. Sciences; consultant in field; Riley lecturer Notre Dame University; Welch lecturer University Texas; Distinguished visiting lecturer University Iowa; Arthur D. Little lecturer Massachusetts Institute of Technology; Zuffanti lecturer Northwestern University; Krug lecturer University Illinois; hon. professor Lanzhou University, Peoples Republic of China. Author: (with R.G. Pearson) Mechanisms of Inorganic Reactions, 1958, (with R.C. Johnson) Coordination Chemistry, 1964; associate editor Chemical Revs., 1960-65, Inorganica Chemica Acta, 1967—, Inorganica Chemica Acta Letters, 1977—; editorial board Journal Inorganic and Nuclear Chemistry, 1959—, Journal Molecular Catalysis, Chemical Revs.; co-editor Catalysis, Transition Metal Chemistry; editor Inorganic Syntheses XVI; contributor articles to professional journals. Recipient Ballar medal, 1972, Southern Illinois University Alumni Achievement award, 1974, Dwyer medal, 1976, James Flack Norris award for Outstanding Achievement in Teaching of Chemistry, 1981, Oesper Memorial award, 1983; Guggenheim fellow, 1954-55; National Science Foundation fellow, 1961-62; NATO sr. scientist fellow Italy, 1981. Fellow National Acad. Sciences, American Association for the Advancement of Science (chairman chemistry section 1979), Am. Acad. Arts and Sciences; member Am. Chemical Society (assistant editor journal 1961-64, chairman division inorganic chemistry 1970, president 1983, board directors 1982-84, award for research in inorganic chemistry 1964, Distinguished Service award in inorganic chemistry 1975, N.E. regional award 1971), Chemical Society London, Italian Chemical Society (hon.), Acad. National dei Lincei (Italy), Sigma Xi, Phi Lambda Upsilon, Alpha Chi Sigma, Phi Kappa Phi, Kappa Delta Phi, Phi Lambda Theta (hon.). Office: Department Chemistry Northwestern U Evanston Illinois 60201

BASOV, NIKOLAI GENNADIEVICH, physicist; born Usman, near Voronezh, Union of Soviet Socialist Republics, December 14, 1922; son of Gennadiy Fedorovich and Zinaida Andreevna (Molchanova) B.; married Ksenia Tikhonovna, July 18, 1950; children: Gennadiy, Dmitriy. Graduate, Moscow Mechanical Institute, 1950, Cand. Physical Math. Science, 1953, Doctor Physical Math. Science, 1956; Doctor of Laws (honorary), Polish-Mil.-Tech. Academy, 1972, Jena University, 1974, Prague Polytechnic Institute, 1975, University Pavia, Italy, 1977, Madrid Polytechnic University, Italy, 1985. With P N Lebedev Physical Institute, Union of the Soviet Socialist Republics Acad. Sci., 1948—; vice director for sci. work P N Lebedev Physical Institute, Union of the Soviet Socialist Republics Acad.

Sci., 1958-73, head laboratory quantum radio physics; 1963—; professor solid state physics Moscow Institute Physical Engineers, 1963—; director P N Lebedev Physical Institute, 1973—. Author over 500 works. Research on principle of molecular generator, 1952, realized molecular generator on molecular beam of ammonia, 1955, 3-level system for receiving states with inversal population suggested, 1955, proposed use of semicondrs. for creation lasers, 1958, realized various types of semicondr. lasers with excitation through p-n junctions, electronic and optical pumping, 1960-65, research on obtaining short powerful pulses of coherent light; proposed thermal and chemical methods for laser pumping, 1962, gas dynamic lasers, 1966; research optical data processing, 1965—; proposed, 1961, realized thermonuclear reactions by using powerful lasers, 1968; inventor electron-beam pumped semicondr. laser projection TV, 1968; proposed, 1966, realized eximer lasers, 1970; realized stimulation of chemical reactions by infrared laser radiation, 1970; proposed and realized electro-ionization laser, 1971; chief editor Priroda, 1967—, Kvantovaya Elektronika, 1971—. Member Communist Party, 1951—; deputy Union of Soviet Socialist Republics Supreme Soviet, 1974—; member praesidium Supreme Soviet, 1982—; vice president executive council World Federation Sci. Workers, 1976—, vice president, 1983—; president All-Union Society Znanie, 1978—. Decorated Order Lenin (5), hero twice Socialist Labour; recipient Lenin prize, 1959; Nobel prize for fundamental research in quantum electronics resulting in creation of masers and lasers, 1964; Gold medal Czechoslovakian Acad. Sciences, 1975; A. Volta's gold medal, 1977; Order of Kirill and Mephodii (Bulgaria), 1981; E. Henkel gold medal German Dem. Republic, 1986; Commodor's cross of Order of Merit, Poland, 1986, Kalinga prize United Nations Educational Scientific and Cultural Organization, 1986. Fellow Optical Society Am., Indian National Sci. Acad.; member Union of the Soviet Socialist Republics Acad. Sciences (member presidium), Acad. Sciences German Dem. Republic, Polish, Czechoslovakian acads. scis., German Acad. Natural Sciences Leopoldina, Bulgarian Acad. Sciences, Royal Sweden Acad. Engineering Sciences. Office: PN Lebedew Physical Institute, 53 Leninsky Prospekt, Moscow Union of Soviet Socialist Republics

BATES, DAVID MARTIN, botanist, educator; born Everett, Massachusetts, May 31, 1934; son of Leslie Marriner and Ann Louise (Gustafson) B.; married Jane Sandra Schwarz, September 4, 1956; children: Jonathan David, Leslie Marriner. Bachelor of Science, Cornell University, 1959; Doctor of Philosophy, University of California at Los Angeles, 1963. Postdoctoral fellow Brit. Mus., 1962-63; assistant professor Cornell University, Ithaca, New York, 1963-69, associate professor; 1969-75, professor; 1975—, director L.M. Bailey Hortorium; 1969-83. Author: Hortus Third. With United States Army, 1954-56. National Science Foundation fellow; recipient Gold medal Garden Club Am. Member Botanical Society Am., Am. Society Plant Taxonomists (president 1983), International Association Plant Taxonomy, Society for Econ. Botany (president 1989), American Association for the

Advancement of Science, Societe de Biogeographie, International Palm Society, Association Systematic Collections (president 1976-78). Home: 140 Forest Home Dr Ithaca New York 14850 Office: Cornell U L H Bailey Hortorium 468 Mann Libr Ithaca New York 14853-4301

BATESON, MARY CATHERINE, anthropology educator; born New York City, December 8, 1939; daughter of Gregory and Margaret (Mead) B.; married J. Barkev Kassarjian, June 4, 1960; 1 child, Sevanne Margaret. Bachelor of Arts, Radcliffe College, 1960; Doctor of Philosophy, Harvard University, 1963. Instructor Arabic Harvard University, 1963-66; associate professor anthropology Ateneo de Manila University, 1966-68; senior research fellow psychology and philosophy Brandeis University, 1968-69; associate professor anthropology Northeastern University, Boston, 1969-71; researcher University Tehran, 1972-74; visiting professor Northeastern University, 1974-75; professor anthropology, dean grad. studies Damavand College, 1975-77; professor anthropology, dean social sci. and humanities University Northern Iran, 1977-79; visiting scholar Harvard University, 1979-80; dean faculty, professor anthropology Amherst College, 1980-87; Clarence Robinson professor anthropology and English George Mason University, 1987—; president Institute Intercultural Studies, from 1979. Author: Structural Continuity in Poetry: A Linguistic Study of Five Early Arabic Odes, 1970, Our Own Metaphor: A Personal Account of a Conference on Consciousness and Human Adaption, 1972, With a Daughter's Eye: A Memoir of Margaret Mead and Gregory Bateson, 1984, Composing a Life, 1989; co-author: Angels Fear: Towards an Epistemology of the Sacred, 1987, Thinking AIDS, 1988; co-editor: Approaches to Semiotics: Anthropology, Education, Linquistics, Psychiatry and Psychology, 1964. Fellow Ford Foundation, 1961-63, National Science Foundation, 1968-79, Guggenheim Foundation, 1987-88. Member Am. Anthropological Association, Society Iranian Studies, Lindisfarne Association, Phi Beta Kappa. Address: 172 Lexington Avenue Cambridge Massachusetts 02138

BATZEL, ROGER ELWOOD, chemist; born Weiser, Idaho, December 1, 1921; son of Walter George and Inez Ruth (Klinefelter) B.; married Edwina Lorraine Grindstaff, August 18, 1946; children: Stella Lynne, Roger Edward, Stacy Lorraine. Bachelor of Science, University Idaho, 1947; Doctor of Philosophy, University California at Berkeley, 1951. Member staff Lawrence Livermore (California) Laboratory, 1953—, head chemistry department; 1959-67, associate director for chemistry; 1961-71, associate director for testing; 1961-64, associate director for space reactors; 1966-68, associate director chemical and bio-med. research; 1969-71, director laboratory; 1971-88, associate director at large; 1988-89, director emeritus; 1989—. Served with United States Army Air Force, 1943-45. Named to Alumni Hall of Fame University Idaho, 1972; recipient distinguished assoc. award U.S. Department Energy, 1982. Fellow American Association for the Advancement of Science, Am. Physical Society; member Sigma Xi. Club: Commonwealth of California

(San Francisco). Office: Lawrence Livermore Lab Post Office Box 808 L-1 Livermore California 94550

BAUM, BERNARD RENE, biosystematist; born Paris, February 14, 1937; son of Kurt and Martha (Berl) B.; married Danielle Habib, May 24, 1961; 1 child, Anat. Bachelor of Science, Hebrew University, Jerusalem, 1963, Master of Science, 1963, Doctor of Philosophy, 1966. Research scientist Agriculture Can., Ottawa, Ontario, 1966-74, senior research scientist; 1974-80, principal research scientist; 1980—; chief vascular plants section Biosystematics Research Institute Agriculture Can., 1981—. Author: Oats: Wild and Cultivated, 1977, Monograph of Tamarix, 1978, World Registry of Avena Cultivars, 1972, World Registry of Barley Cultivars, 1985; associate editor Can. Journal Botany, 1986—, Euphytica, 1987—. Fellow Acad. Sci.-Royal Society Can.; member Can. Botanical Association (Lawson medal 1979), Botanical Society Am., Am. Society Plant Taxonomists, International Association Plant Taxonomists, Classification Society, Linnean Society London, Botanical Society Am., Organization Plant Taxonomy of the Mediterranean Area. Home: 15 Murray St, Suite 408, Ottawa, Ontario Canada K1M 9M5 Office: Biosystematics Research Center, Research Br, Cen Exptl Farm, Ottawa, Ontario Canada K1A 0C6

BAUMGARDT, BILLY RAY, university official, agriculturist; born Lafayette, Indiana, January 17, 1933; son of Raymond P. and Mildred L. (Cordray) B.; married D. Elaine Blain, June 8, 1952; children: Pamela K. Baumgardt Farley, Teresa Jo Baumgardt Adolfsen, Donald Ray. Bachelor of Science in Agr., Purdue University, 1955, Master of Science, 1956; Doctor of Philosophy, Rutgers University, 1959. From assistant to associate professor University Wisconsin, Madison, 1959-67; professor animal nutrition Pennsylvania State University, University Park, 1967-70, head department dairy and animal sci.; 1970-79, associate director agricultural experiment station; 1979-80; director agricultural research, associate dean Purdue University, West Lafayette, Ind., 1980—. Contributor chapters to books, articles to sci. journals. Recipient Wilkinson award Pennsylvania State University, 1979. Fellow American Association for the Advancement of Science; member Am. Dairy Sci. Association (Nutrition Research award 1966; president 1984-85), Am. Institute Nutrition, Am. Society Animal Sci., Rotary, Sigma Xi. Home: 812 Lazy Lane Lafayette Indiana 47904 Office: Purdue University W Lafayette Indiana 47907

BAUMGARTNER, JAMES EARL, mathematics educator; born Wichita, March 23, 1943; son of Earl Benjamin and Gertrude J. (Socolofsky) B.; married Yolanda Yen-Hsu Loo, January 29, 1966; children—Eric James, Jonathan David. Bachelor of Arts, University California, Berkeley, 1964, Doctor of Philosophy, 1970; Master of Arts (honorary), Dartmouth College, 1981. J W Young research instructor Dartmouth College, Hanover, New Hampshire, 1969-71, assistant professor math.; 1971-76, associate professor; 1976-80, professor; 1980-83, J.G. Kemeny professor math.; 1983—; visiting assistant professor California Institute Tech. Pasadena 1971-72. Cons. editor Journal Symbolic Logic, 1983—; editor: Axiomatic Set Theory,

1984; contributor articles to professional journals, chapters to books. Member Am. Math. Society (editor Transactions and Memoirs 1988—), Math. Association Am., Association Symbolic Logic. Home: Lindy Lane Hanover New Hampshire 03755 Office: Dartmouth College Department Math Hanover New Hampshire 03755

BEAN, ALAN LAVERN, space artist, retired astronaut; born Wheeler, Texas, March 15, 1932; son of Arnold H. B.; children: Clay, Amy. Bachelor of Science in Aeronautical Engineering, University Texas, 1955; graduate, United States Navy Test Pilot School; Doctor Science (honorary), Texas Wesleyan University, 1972, University Akron; student, St. Mary's College, 1962; private studies with various art tchrs. Commissioned ensign United States Navy, 1955; advanced through grades to captain; test pilot various aircraft United States Navy, Patuxent, Maryland, 1960-63; astronaut Manned Spacecraft Center, National Aeronautics and Space Administration, 1963—, lunar module pilot Apollo XII; 1969, retired; 1975; Member International Adv. Board Frederic Remington Art Mus., Ogdensburg, New York, 1986. Exhibited in group shows at Bryant Galleries, Houston, 1974, National Air and Space Mus., Smithsonian Institute, Washington, 1978-80; Astronaut/Cosmonaut art in LaGeode, Paris, 1985; Bus. in the Arts Awards, Hirshorn Mus. and Sculpture Garden, Washington, 1986; one man shows include Opera Association, Fort Worth, 1983, Meredith Long Gallery, Houston, 1984; represented in numerous pubs. including Aviation Space magazine, Time magazine, Art Gallery International magazine; host, narrator (video) The Safe and Succesful Use of Art Materials, 1986. Decorated Distinguished Service Medal with cluster, Navy Astronaut Wings; Navy Distinguished Service medal with cluster; recipient Man of Year award Texas Press Association, 1969, Rear Adm. William S. Parsons award, 1970, Distinguished Engineering Graduate award University Texas, 1970, Godfrey L. Cabot award, 1970, Special Trustees award National Acad. TV Arts and Sciences, 1970, Yuri Gagarin award American Institute of Aeronautics and Astronautics, 1974, Merit award New York Art Directors Club, 1985. Fellow Am. Astronomical Society; member Delta Kappa Epsilon. 4th man to walk on moon; comdr. 2d Skylab mission, set record 59 days in space; back-up comdr. Apollo-Soyuz Test Project in 1975; holds 10 world records in aeros. and astronautics. Home and Studio: 26 Sugarberry Circle Houston Texas 77024

BEATTIE, DONALD A., energy scientist, consultant; born New York City, October 30, 1929; son of James Francis and Evelyn Margaret (Hickey) B.; married Ann Mary Kean, March 27, 1973; children: Thomas James, Bruce Andrew. Bachelor of Arts, Columbia University, 1951; Master of Science, Colorado School Mines, 1958. Regional geologist Mobil Oil Company, 1958-63; Apollo lunar experiments program manager National Aeronautics and Space Administration, 1963-72; director National Aeronautics and Space Administration energy systems div. National Aeronautics and Space Administration, Washington, 1978-82; vice president Houston operations BDM Corp., 1983-84; consultant on energy and space tech. 1984—;

director advanced energy research and tech. National Science Foundation, 1973-75; deputy assistant administrator Energy Research and Development Administration, 1975-77; acting assistant secretary Department Energy, Washington, 1977-78; solar energy coordinator U.S./USSR Cooperative in Sci. and Tech.; United States representative Vienna Institute for Comparative Economic Studies Workshop on Energy; member engineering techs. adv. committee Montgomery College. Contributor numerous articles on lunar sci., energy to professional journals. Active Boy Scouts Am., 1958-71. Served with Air Corps United States Navy, 1951-56. Recipient Exceptional Service medal National Aeronautics and Space Administration, 1971, Senior Executive Service and Outstanding Performance award, 1980; Superior Achievement award Department Energy, 1978. Fellow American Association for the Advancement of Science, member Geological Society Am., Am. Astronomical Society, National Space Club. Office: 13831 Dowlais Dr Rockville Maryland 20853

BEAUFAIT, FREDERICK W(ILLIAM), civil engineering educator; born Vicksburg, Mississippi, November 28, 1936; son of Frank W. and Eleanor Chambliss (Haynes) B.; married Lois Mary Erdman, November 27, 1964; children: Paul Frederick, Nicole. Bachelor of Science, Mississippi State University, 1958; Master of Science, University Kentucky, 1961; Doctor of Philosophy, Virginia Polytechnic Institute, 1965. Engineer L E Gregg & Associates, Lexington, Kentucky, 1959-60; visiting lecturer civil engineering University Liverpool, England, 1960-61;

professor civil engineering Vanderbilt University, Nashville, 1965-79; professor, chairman department civil engineering West Virginia University, Morgantown, 1979-83, associate dean College Engineering; 1983-86; dean College Engineering Wayne State University, Detroit, 1986—; visiting professor civil and structural engineering University Wales-Cardiff, 1975-76; consultant in field. Co-author: Computer Methods of Structural Analysis, 1970; author: Basic Concepts in Structural Analysis, 1977. Vice chairman stewardship committee 1st Presbyterian Church, Morgantown, 1982, elder, 1983-85, member long-range planning committee, 1985-86; deacon Southminster Presbyterian Church, Nashville, 1968-69, elder, 1971-73, 78-79, clk. of session, 1971-73; board of directors Presbyterian Campus Ministry, Nashville, 1972-78, treasurer, 1972-75, president, 1976-78; member citizens adv. committee Metropolitan School System, Nashville, 1978-79. Member American Society of Civil Engineers, Am. Concrete Institute, Am. Society Engineering Education, Engineering Society Detroit, Engineering Accreditation Commission, Morgantown Chamber of Commerce (chairman county-wide sewerage committee), Chi Epsilon, Tau Beta Pi. Home: 63 Ridge Road Grosse Pointe Farms Michigan 48236 Office: Wayne State U College of Engring Detroit Michigan 48202

BECHER, WILLIAM DON, electrical engineering educator, corporate executive; born Bolivar, Ohio, November 26, 1929; son of William and Eva Vernette (Richardson) B.; married Helen Norma Hager, August 31, 1950; children: Eric Alan, Patricia

Lynn. Bachelor of Science in R.E, Tri-State University, 1950; Master of Science in Electrical Engineering, University Michigan, 1961, Doctor of Philosophy, 1968. Registered professional engineer, Michigan, New Jersey. Project engineer Bogue Electric, Paterson, New Jersey, 1950-53; senior devel. engineer Goodyear Aircraft Corp., Akron, Ohio, 1953-57; senior systems engineer Beckman Instruments, Fullerton, California, 1957-58; engineering supervisor Bendix Aerospace Systems, Ann Arbor, Michigan, 1958-63; research engineer University Michigan, Ann Arbor, 1963-68; adj. professor electrical engineering 1978-79, 81—; professor electrical engineering University Michigan, Dearborn, 1968-78; chairman 1971-76; engineering department manager Environmental Research Institute Michigan, Ann Arbor, 1977-79, associate director; 1981—; professor electrical engineering, dean College Engineering New Jersey Institute Tech., Newark, 1979-81; president Michigan Computers & Instrumentation, Incorporated, Ann Arbor, 1976—; engineering consultant, 1968—. Author: Courses in Continuing Education for Electronics Engineers, 1975, 76, Logical Design Using Integrated Circuits, 1977. Served with United States Army, 1953-55. General Electric Company fellow, 1962-63. Member Institute of Electrical and Electronics Engineers (senior), Am. Society Engineering Education, Machine Vision Association of Society Manufacturing Engineers, Order of Engineers, Sigma Xi, Alpha Sigma Lambda, Eta Kappa Nu, Phi Kappa Phi, Tau Beta Pi. Patentee in field. Home: 691 Spring Valley Ann Arbor Michigan 48105 Office: Environ Research Institute 3300 Plymouth Road Ann Arbor Michigan 48105

BECHTEL, STEPHEN DAVISON, JR., engineering company executive; born Oakland, California, May 10, 1925; son of Stephen Davison and Laura (Peart) B.; married Elizabeth Mead Hogan, June 5, 1946; 5 children. Student, University Colorado, 1943-44; Bachelor of Science, Purdue University, 1946, Doctor in Engineering (honorary), 1972; Master of Business Administration, Stanford University, 1948; Doctor of Science (honorary), University Colorado, 1981. Registered professional engineer, New York, Michigan, Alaska, California, Maryland, Hawaii, Ohio, District of Columbia, Virginia, Illinois. Engineering and management positions Bechtel Corp., San Francisco, 1941-60; president Bechtel Corp., 1960-73, chairman of companies in Bechtel group; 1973-80; chairman Bechtel Group, Incorporated, 1980—; board of directors International Business Machines Corporation; former chairman Business Council; life councillor, past chairman Conference Board; member policy committee Business Roundtable; member Labor-Mgmt. Group, National Action Council on Minorities in Engineering, from 1974. Trustee, member, past chairman bldg. and grounds committee California Institute Tech.; member president's council Purdue University; member adv. council Stanford University Grad. School Business. Served with United States Marine Corps, 1943-46. Decorated officer French Legion of Honor; recipient Distinguished Alumnus award Purdue University, 1964, Distinguished Alumnus award University Colorado, 1978; Ernest C.

Arbuckle Distinguished Alumnus award Stanford University Graduate School Business, 1974; Man of Year Engineering News-Record, 1974; Outstanding Achievement in Constrn. award Moles, 1977; Distinguished Engineering Alumnus award University Colorado, 1979; Herbert Hoover medal, 1980; Washington award Western Society Engrs., 1985, Chmn.'s award Am. Association Engineering Socs., 1982. Fellow American Society of Civil Engineers (Engineering Management award 1979, President award 1985), Institution Chemical Engineers (United Kingdom, hon.); member American Institute of Mining, Metallurgy and Petroleum Engineers, National Acad. Engineering (past chairman, chairman industry adv. board), California Acad. Sciences (hon. trustee), Am. Society French Legion of Honor (board directors), Fellowship of Engring (United Kingdom, foreign member), Chi Epsilon, Tau Beta Pi. Clubs: Pacific Union, Bohemian, San Francisco Golf (San Francisco); Claremont Country (Berkeley, California); Cypress Point (Monterey Peninsula, California); Thunderbird Country (Palm Springs, California); Vancouver (British Columbia); Ramada (Houston); Links, Blind Brook (New York City); Met. (Washington); Augusta (Georgia) National Golf; York (Toronto); Mount Royal (Montreal). Office: Bechtel Group Incorporated 50 Beale St Post Office Box 3965 San Francisco California 94119

BECK, STANLEY DWIGHT, entomology educator, researcher; born Portland, Oregon, October 17, 1919; son of Dwight William and Eunice (Dodd) B.; married Isabel Helene Stalker, August 29, 1943; children: Bruce Dwight, Diana Helene, Karen Christine, Marianne Elizabeth. Bachelor of Science, Washington State University, 1942; Master of Science, University Wisconsin, 1947, Doctor of Philosophy, 1950; Doctor of Science, Luther College, 1972. Assistant professor entomology University Wisconsin, Madison, 1950-57, associate professor; 1957-64, professor; 1964-69, W.A. Henry Distinguished professor; 1969—; chairman cotton study team National Acad. Sci., Washington, 1973-75; member editorial committee Annual Rev. Entomology, 1975-79. Editor, Wisconsin Acad. Scis., Arts and Leters, 1957-60; author: Simplicity of Science, 1959, Animal Photoperiodism, 1963, Insect Photoperiodism, 1968, (2d edition), 1980, Modern Science and Christian Life, 1970. Chairman Madison Lutheran Campus Ministry, Wisconsin, 1967-72; member Council of Southern Wisconsin District, Am. Lutheran Church, 1968-70 and member Task Force on Ethical Issues in Medicine, 1975-76; member Task Force on Church and Disabilities Wisconsin Conference Chs., 1980-82. Served to lieutenant United States Naval Reserve, 1942-45. American Association for the Advancement of Science fellow, 1964; recipient Founders Memorial award Entomol. Society Am., 1962, Distinguished Achievement award Washington State University Almuni Association, 1981. Member American Association for the Advancement of Science, Entomological Society Am. (president 1981-82), National Academy of Sciences, Am. Society Zoologists, Phi Beta Kappa. Lutheran. Home: 6100 Gateway Green Monona Wisconsin 53716 Office: Department Entomology U Wisconsin Madison Wisconsin 53706

BECKEN, BRADFORD ALBERT, engineering executive; born Providence, October 5, 1924; son of Albert R. and Ruth M. (Stephenson) B.; married Gaynelle M. Lane, November 30, 1946; children: Bradford Albert, Brian A., Christian L., Anne Tracey. Student, University Rhode Island, 1942-43; Bachelor of Science, United States Naval Academy, 1946; Bachelor of Science in Electronics, United States Naval Postgrad. School, 1952; Master of Science, University of California at Los Angeles, 1953, Doctor of Philosophy, 1961. Commissioned officer United States Navy, advanced through grades to commander; consultant Airtronics-Spl. Warfare Laboratory, 1967; manager systems engineering laboratory submarine signal div. Raytheon Company, Portsmouth, Rhode Island, 1967-70, manager engineering; 1970-82, director tech. Portsmouth Engineering Laboratory; 1982—. Author: Advances in Hydroscience, 1964. Trustee Newport Hospital, 1977, chairman board, 1979-84; chairman board of directors Newport Health Care Corp. Recipient Asst. Chief Bureau Ships award, 1963. Fellow Acoustical Society Am.; member Am. Defense Preparedness Association, Naval War College Foundation, United States Naval Institute, United States Naval Acad. Alumni Association. Episcopalian. Home: 260 Fischer Circle Portsmouth Rhode Island 02871 Office: Raytheon Company Submarine Signal Div 1847 W Main Road Portsmouth Rhode Island 02871

BECKMAN, ARNOLD ORVILLE, chemist, instrument manufacturing company executive; born Cullom, Illinois, April 10, 1900; son of George W. and Elizabeth E. (Jewkes) B.; married Mabel S. Meinzer, June 10, 1925; children: Gloria Patricia, Arnold Stone. Bachelor of Science, University Illinois, 1922, Master of Science, 1923; Doctor of Philosophy, California Institute Tech., 1928; Doctor of Science (honorary), Chapman College, 1965; Doctor of Laws (honorary), University California, Riverside, 1966, Loyola University, Los Angeles, 1969, Whittier College, 1971, University Illinois, 1982, Pepperdine University, 1977; Doctor of Hebrew Literature (honorary), California State University, 1984. Research associate Bell Tel. Laboratories, New York City, 1924-26; chemical staff California Institute Tech., 1926-39; vice president National Tech. Laboratory, Pasadena, California, 1935-39; president National Tech. Laboratory, 1939-40, Helipot Corp., 1944-58, Arnold O. Beckman, Incorporated, South Pasadena, California, 1946-58, Beckman Instruments, Incorporated, Fullerton, California, 1940-65; chairman board Beckman Instruments, Incorporated (sub. SmithKline Beckman Corp.), from 1965; vice chairman SmithKline Beckman Corp., 1984-86; bd.director Security Pacific National Bank, 1956-72, adv. director, 1972-75; board director Continental Airlines, 1956-71, adv. director, 1971-73. Author articles in field; inventor. Member President's Air Quality Board, 1970-74; chairman System Devel. Foundation, 1970-88; chairman board trustees emeritus California Institute Tech.; hon. trustee California Mus. Foundation; board overseers House Ear Institute, 1981—; trustee Scripps Clinic and Research Foundation, 1971-83, hon. trustee, 1983—; board of directors Hoag Memorial Hospital With United States Military Corps, 1918-19. Benjamin Franklin fellow

Royal Society Arts.; named to National Inventors Hall of Fame, 1987. Fellow Association Clinical Scientists; member Am. Acad. Arts and Sciences, Los Angeles Chamber of Commerce (board director 1954-58, president 1956), California Chamber of Commerce (director, president 1967-68), National Acad. Engineering (Founders Award, 1987), National Association of Manufacturers, Am. Institute Chemists, Instrument Society Am. (president 1952), Am. Chemical Society, American Association for the Advancement of Science, Social Sci. Research Council, Am. Association Clinical Chemistry (hon.), Newcomen Society, Sigma Xi, Delta Upsilon, Alpha Chi Sigma, Phi Lambda Upsilon. Clubs: Newport Harbor Yacht, Pacific.
Patentee in field. Home: 107 Shorecliff Road Corona del Mar California 92625 Office: 100 Academy Dr Irvine California 92715

BEDFORD, JOHN MICHAEL, medical educator, researcher; born Sheffield, England, May 21, 1932. Bachelor of Arts, Cambridge (England) University, 1955, Master of Arts, Vet. Bachelor of Medicine, 1958; Doctor of Philosophy, University London, 1965. Junior fellow surgery Bristol (England) University Vet. School, 1958-59; research associate physiology Worcester (Massachusetts) Foundation, 1959-61, scientist; 1966-67; assistant professor Royal Vet. College, University London, 1961-66; assistant professor to associate professor anatomy Columbia University, New York City, 1967-72; professor reproductive biology and anatomy Medical College, Cornell University, Ithaca, New York, 1972—, now Harold and Percy Uris professor reproductive biology in ob-gyn.; 1981—. Member Society Reprodn.,

Am. Association Anatomists, Endocrine Society, Brit. Society Study Fertility. Office: Cornell U Med College Department Ob-Gyn 525 E 68th St New York New York 10021

BEDNORZ, GEORG, physicist; born May 16, 1950. Graduate, University Munster, Federal Republic of Germany, 1976; Doctor of Philosophy, Swiss Federal Institute Tech., ETH Zurich, 1982. Researcher International Business Machines Corporation Zurich Research Laboratory, Ruschlikon, Switzerland, 1982—; lecturer Swiss Federal Institute Tech. and University Zurich, 1987—. Co-recipient Thirteenth Fritz London Memorial award, 1987, Nobel Prize in physics Royal Swedish Acad. Society, 1987; recipient Dannie Heineman prize Minna James Heineman Stiftung, Acad. Sciences Gottingen, West Germany, 1987, Robert Wichard Pohl prize German Physical Society, 1987, Hewlett-Packard Europhysics prize, 1988, Marcel-Benoist prize Marcel-Benoist Foundation, 1986, APS International prize for new materials research, 1988, Viktor Moritz Goldschmidt prize German Mineralogical Society, 1987, Otto-Klung prize Otto-Klung Foundation, 1987. Office: International Business Machines Corporation Zurich Research Lab, Saumerstrasse 4, CH-8803, Ruschlikon Switzerland

BELL, CHESTER GORDON, computer engineering company executive; born Kirksville, Missouri, August 19, 1934; son of Roy Chester and Lola Dolph (Gordon) B.; married Gwendolyn Kay Druyor, January 3, 1959; children: Brigham Roy, Laura Louise. Bachelor of Science in Electrical Engineering, Massachusetts Institute of Technology, 1956, Master of Science in Electrical Engineering, 1957. Engineer Speech Communication Laboratory, Massachusetts Institute of Technology, Cambridge, 1959-60; manager computer design Digital Equipment Corp., Maynard, Massachusetts, 1960-66, vice president engineering; 1972-83; professor computer sci. Carnegie-Mellon University, 1966-72; vice chairman Encore Computer Corp., Marlboro, Massachusetts, 1983-86; assistant director National Science Foundation, Washington, 1986—; vice president research and devel. Ardent Computer, Sunnyvale, California, 1987—; director Institute Research and Coordination Acoustic Music, 1976-81; trustee Computer Mus., 1982—. Author: (with Newell) Computer Structures, 1971, (with Grason, Newell) Designing Computers and Digital Systems, 1972, (with Mudge, McNamara) Computer Engineering, 1978, (with Siewiorek, Newell) Computer Structures, 1982. Recipient 6th Mellon Institute award, 1972. Fellow Institute of Electrical and Electronics Engineers (McDowell award 1975), (Eckert-Mauchly award 1982), American Association for the Advancement of Science; member National Acad. Engineering, Association Computing Machinery (editor Computer Structures section 1972-78), Eta Kappa Nu. Home: 85 E India Row Apartment 11E Boston Massachusetts 02110 Office: Ardent Computer Sunnyvale California 94086

BELL, STOUGHTON, computer scientist, mathematician, educator; born Waltham, Massachusetts, December 20, 1923; son of Conrad and Florence Emily (Ross) B.; married Mary Carroll O'Connell, February 26, 1949 (divorced 1960); children: Karen, Mark; married Laura Joan Bainbridge, May 24, 1963 (divorced 1979); children: Nathaniel Stoughton, Joshua Bainbridge. Student, Harvard University, 1946-49; Bachelor of Arts, University California, Berkeley, 1950, Master of Arts, 1953, Doctor of Philosophy, 1955. Member staff Sandia Corp., Albuquerque, 1955-66; div. supervisor Sandia Corp., 1964-66; visiting lecturer University New Mexico, 1957-66, director computing center; 1966-79, associate professor math.; 1966-71, professor math. and computer sci.; 1971—; visiting lecturer New Mexico Acad. Sciences, 1965—; national lecturer Association for Computing Machinery, 1972-74. Co-author: Linear Analysis and Generalized Functions, 1965, Introductory Calculus, 1966, Modern University Calculus, 1966. Served with Army of the United States, 1943-44. Member Association for Computing Machinery, Am. Math. Society, Math. Association Am., Society Industrial and Applied Math., Am. Statistical Association, Ops. Research Society Am. Office: Computer Sci Department U New Mexico Albuquerque New Mexico 87131

BENACERRAF, BARUJ, pathologist, educator; born Caracas, Venezuela, October 29, 1920; came to United States, 1939, naturalized, 1943; son of Abraham and Henriette (Lasry) B.; married Annette Dreyfus, March 24, 1943; 1 daughter, Beryl. Bachelor es L., Lycee Janson, 1940; Bachelor of Science, Columbia University, 1942; Doctor of Medicine, Medical School Virginia, 1945; Master of Arts, Harvard University, 1970; Doctor of Medicine (honorary), University Geneva, 1980; Doctor of Science (honorary), New York University, 1981, Virginia Commonwealth University, 1981,

Yeshiva University, 1982, University Aix-Marseille, 1982, Columbia University, 1985, Adelphi University, 1988. Intern Queens General Hospital, New York City, 1945-46; research fellow department microbiology Columbia University Medical School, 1948-50; charge de recherches Centre National de Recherche Scientique Hospital Broussais, Paris, 1950-56; assistant professor pathology New York University School Medicine, 1956-58, associate professor; 1958-60, professor; 1960-68; chief immunology National Institute Allergy and Infectious Diseases, National Institutes of Health, Bethesda, Maryland, 1968-70; Fabyan professor comparative pathology, chairman department Harvard Medical School, 1970—; president, chief executive officer Dana-Farber Cancer Institute, 1980; member immunology study section National Institutes of Health; president Federation Am. Societies Experimental Biology, 1974-75; chairman sci. adv. committee Centre d'Immunologie de Marseille. Editorial board: Journal Immunology. Trustee, member sci. adv. board Trudeau Foundation; member sci. adv. committee Children's Hospital Boston; board governors Weizmann Institute Medicine; member award committee General Motors Cancer Research Foundation, also chairman selection committee Sloan prize, 1980. Served to captain Medical Corps Army of the United States, 1946-48. Recipient T. Duckett Jones Memorial award Helen Hay Whitney Foundation, 1976; Rabbi Shai Shacknai lecturer and prize Hebrew University Jerusalem, 1974; Waterford award for biomed. scis., 1980; Nobel prize for medicine or physiology, 1980; Correspondant Emerite de l'Institut de la Santé et de la Recherche Scientifique. Fellow Am. Acad. Arts and Sciences; member National Acad. Sciences, National Institute Medicine, Am. Association Immunologists (president 1973-74), Am. Association Pathologists and Bacteriologists, Am. Society Experimental Pathology, Society Experimental Biology and Medicine, Brit. Association Immunology, French Society Biological Chemistry, Harvey Society, International Union Immunology Socs. (president 1980-83), Alpha Omega Alpha. Home: 111 Perkins St Boston Massachusetts 02130 Office: Dana-Farber Cancer Institute 44 Binney St Boston Massachusetts 02115

BENDIXEN, HENRIK HOLT, physician, educator, dean; born Fredriksberg, Denmark, December 2, 1923; came to United States, 1954, naturalized, 1960; son of Carl Julius and Borghild (Holt) B.; married Karen Skakke, December 20, 1947 (deceased 1984); children: Nils, Birgitte; married Lilo M. Laver, May 29, 1985. Cand. Phil., University Copenhagen, 1943, CM, CChir, 1951, Doctor of Medicine (honorary), 1987; Doctor of Medicine (honorary), Jagiellonian University, Krakow, Poland, 1985. Diplomate Am. Board Anesthesiologists. Intern Copenhagen County Hospital, 1951-52; cand. in surgery and anesthesia Denmark and Sweden, 1952-54; resident in anesthesia Massachusetts General Hospital, Boston, 1954-57, anesthetist; 1957-69; assistant clinical professor Harvard University, Boston, 1957-69; professor anesthesia, chief department University California, San Diego, 1969-73; medical director University Hospital, San Diego, 1971-72; professor anesthesiology Columbia University, New York City,

1973—, chairman department anesthesiology; 1973-85, acting provost College Physicians and Surgeons; 1980-81, alumni professor; 1984, vice president health sciences, dean faculty medicine; 1984—, E.M. Papper professor anesthesiology; 1985-86; director anesthesiology service Presbyn. Hospital, New York City, 1973-85; Wesley Bourne lecturer McGill University, 1969, Benjamin Howard Robbins memorial lecturer Vanderbilt University, 1975, John J. Bonica lecturer University Washington, Seattle, 1982; president Greater Boston Anesthesia Teaching Conference, 1965; member panel on drugs in anesthesia National Research Council, 1966, committee on shock, 1969, committee on anesthesia, 1970, chairman ad hoc committee on adverse reactions to anesthetic agents, 1971; member executive committee on research Massachusetts General Hospital, 1966, executive committee on teaching and education, 1967; chairman executive committee University Hospital, 1970; member executive committee medical board Presbyterian Hospital, 1973, 78-79, trustee, 1979, chairman committee on professional safety and liability, 1982-83, vice president medical board, 1982-83; chairman committee on honors and awards College Physicians and Surgeons, Columbia University, 1977, committee on business of research, 1981-82, policy committee on sci. and tech., 1982—, orthopedic search committee 1982—, member executive committee faculty council, 1979-80; consultant United States Naval Hospital, Chelsea, Massachusetts, 1957-69, San Diego, 1969-73, department anesthesia Vassar Brothers Hospital, Poughkeepsie, New York, 1977—.

Author: Respiratory Care, 1965; member editorial board Anesthesia & Analgesia, 1981-83; contributor numerous articles to professional journals. Member board visitors school medicine University Pittsburgh, 1985; trustee Mary Imogene Bassett Hospital, Cooperstown, New York, 1986—. Recipient Ralph Waters award, 1985. Fellow Am. College Anesthesiologists, American Association for the Advancement of Science, Fraction of Anesthetists, Royal College Surgeons England; member American Medical Association (editorial board Archives of Surgery 1971), Massachusetts Medical Society, Suffolk County Medical Society, California Medical Society, Am. Society Anesthesiologists (committee on cons. 1963, committee on econs. 1971), Massachusetts Society Anesthesiologists (president 1966), New England Society Anesthesiologists (Horace Wells orator 1979), California Society Anesthesiologists, International Anesthesia Research Society, Scandinavian Society Anesthesiologists, Association Am. Medical Colls. (council of education socs. 1967), American Association for the Advancement of Science, Am. Heart Association, California Thoracic Society (cons. in pulmonary disease 1972), Society Critical Care Medicine (president 1974, chairman committee on bylaws 1977), New York State Society Anesthesiologists (program chairman postgrad. assembly in anesthesiology 1980-82, general chairman 1983-86), New York State Medical Society, New York Countcal Society, Association University Anesthetists (council 1970), Am. Society Pharmacology and Experimental Therapeutics, Am. Physiological Society, Am. Society

Clinical Pharmacology and Therapeutics, New York Acad. Medicine, New York Acad. Sci., New York Medical and Surgical Society (secretary 1978), Minnesota Surgical Society (hon.), Belgian Society Anesthesiologists (hon.), National Institute Health (general med. research program project committee 1967, training committee on anesthesia 1971), National Academy of Sciences Institute Medicine (correspondent committee on human rights 1983), Scandinavian Society Anesthesiologists (hon.), Danish Society Anesthesiology (Husfeldt lecturer 1974), Omicron Kappa Upsilon. Clubs: Harvard (Boston); University, Century (New York City). Home: Daisy Lane Irvington New York 10533 Office: Columbia U College Physicians & Surgeons 630 W 168th St New York New York 10032

BENNETT, ALBERT FARRELL, biology educator; born Whittier, California, July 18, 1944; son of John C. and Edna R. (Lederer) Kidd; married Rudi C. Berkelhamer, May 14, 1977; children: Hilary J. Arnold, Laura K. Arnold, Mari J., Andrew M. Bachelor of Arts in Zoology, University California, Riverside, 1966; Doctor of Philosophy in Zoology, University Michigan, 1971. Miller postdoctoral fellow University California, Berkeley, 1971-73, acting assistant professor zoology; 1973-74; assistant professor biological sciences University California, Irvine, 1974-78, associate professor; 1978-83, professor; 1983—, chairman department developmental and cell biology; 1984-86, 1988—, acting dean School Biological Sciences; 1986-88; visiting research associate, associate professor anatomy University Chicago, 1981-82; visiting research

fellow zoology University Adelaide, South Australia, 1983-84; member population biology panel National Science Foundation, Washington, 1982-86. Contributor articles to professional journals. Recipient hon. fellowship Woodrow Wilson Foundation, 1966, Career Devel. award National Institutes of Health, 1978-83; grantee National Science Foundation, 1974—. Fellow American Association for the Advancement of Science; member Am. Physiological Society (member editorial board 1982—, chair comp. physiology section 1988—), Am. Society Naturalists, Ecological Society Am., Society Experimental Biology, Am. Society Zoology (member editorial board 1986—, chair membership committee 1988, president elect 1989)), Phi Beta Kappa. Home: 24 Perkins Court Irvine California 92715 Office: U Calif-Irvine School Biol Sci Irvine California 92717

BENZER, SEYMOUR, neurosciences educator; born New York City, October 15, 1921; son of Mayer and Eva (Naidorf) B.; married Dorothy Vlosky, January 10, 1942 (deceased 1978); children: Barbara Ann Benzer Freidin, Martha Jane Benzer Goldberg; married Carol A. Miller, May 11, 1980; 1 child, Alexander Robin. Bachelor of Arts, Brooklyn College, 1942; Master of Science, Purdue University, 1943, Doctor of Philosophy, 1947, Doctor of Science (honorary), 1968; Doctor of Science, Columbia University, 1974, Yale University, 1977, Brandeis University, 1978, City University of New York, 1978, University Paris, 1983. Member faculty Purdue University, 1945-67, professor biophysics; 1958-61, Stuart distinguished professor biology; 1961-67; professor biology California

Institute Tech., 1967-75, Boswell professor neurosci.; 1975—; biophysicist Oak Ridge National Laboratory, 1948-49; visiting associate California Institute Tech., Pasadena, 1965-67. Contributor articles to professional journals. Research fellow California Institute Tech., 1949-51; Fulbright research fellow Pasteur Institute, Paris, 1951-52; sr. National Science Foundation postdoctoral fellow Cambridge, England, 1957-58; recipient Award of Honor Brooklyn College, 1956; Sigma Xi research award Purdue University, 1957; Ricketts award University Chicago, 1961; Gold medal New York City College Chemistry Alumni Association, 1962; Gairdner award of merit, 1964; McCoy award Purdue University, 1965; Lasker award, 1971; T. Duckett Jones award, 1975; Prix Leopold Mayer French Acad. Sciences, 1975; Louisa Gross Horwitz award, 1976; Harvey award Israel, 1977; Warren Triennial prize Massachusetts General Hospital, 1977; Dickson award, 1978; Rosenstiel award, 1986; T.H. Morgan medal Genetics Society Am., 1986, Karl Spencer Lashley award, 1988. Fellow Indian Acad. Sciences (hon.); member National Acad. Sciences, Am. Acad. Arts and Sciences, Am. Philosophical Society (Lashley award 1988), Harvey Society, New York Acad. Sciences, American Association for the Advancement of Science, Royal Society London (foreign member), Indian Acad. Sci. (foreign member). Home: 2075 Robin Road San Marino California 91108

BERANEK, LEO LEROY, business and engineering consultant; born Solon, Iowa, September 15, 1914; son of Edward Fred and Beatrice (Stahle) B.; married Phyllis Knight, September 6, 1941 (deceased November 1982); children: James Knight, Thomas Haynes; married Gabriella Sohn, August 10, 1985. Bachelor of Arts, Cornell College, 1936, Doctor of Science (honorary), 1946; Master of Science, Harvard University, 1937, Doctor of Science, 1940; Doctor of Engineering (honorary), Worcester Polytechnic Institute, 1971; Doctor.Commercial Science (honorary), Suffolk University, 1979; Doctor of Laws (honorary), Emerson College, 1982; Doctor Pub. Service (honorary), Northeastern University, 1984. Instructor physics Harvard, 1940-41, assistant professor; 1941-43, director research on sound; 1941-45; director Electro-Acoustics and Systems Research Laboratories, 1945-46; associate professor communications engineering Massachusetts Institute of Technology, 1947-58, lecturer; 1958-81; tech. director Acoustics Laboratory, 1947-53; president, director, chief executive officer Bolt Beranek & Newman, Cambridge, Massachusetts, 1953-69; chief scientist Bolt Beranek & Newman, 1969-71, director; 1953-84; president, chief executive officer, director Boston Broadcasters, Incorporated, 1963-79, chairman board; 1980-83; part-owner WCVB-TV, Boston, 1972-82; chairman board Mueller-BBM GmbH, Munich, Germany, 1962-86; board of directors Tech. Integration and Devel. Group, Incorporated, Billerica, Massachusetts. Author: (with others) Principles of Sound Control in Airplanes, 1944, Acoustic Measurements, 1949, 2d edition, 1988, Acoustics, 1954, 2d edition, 1986, Music, Acoustics and Architecture, 1962; editor, contributor: (with others) Noise Reduction, 1960, Noise and Vibration Control, 1971, 2d edition, 1988; editor: (with others) Noise

Control mag, 1954-55; associate editor: (with others) Sound mag, 1961-63; member editorial board: (with others) Noise Control Engring, 1973-77; contributor (with others) articles on acoustics, audio and TV communications systems to tech. publications. Member Massachusetts Gov.'s Task Force on Coastal Resources, 1974-77; charter member board overseers Boston Symphony Orchestra, 1968-80, chairman, 1977-80, trustee, 1977-87, vice president, 1980-83, chairman board trustees, 1983-86, hon. chairman, 1987; member visiting committee Center Behavioral Scis., Harvard University, 1964-70, visiting committee biology and related research facilities, 1971-77, 86—, member visiting committee physics department, 1983—, now board overseers university; member advisory committee mgmt. devel. Harvard Business School, 1965-71; member council for arts Massachusetts Institute Tech., 1972—; president World Affairs Council Boston, 1975-78, vice chairman board, 1979-86; trustee Cornell College, 1955-71, Emerson College, 1973-79; board of directors Opera Company of Boston, president, 1961-63, hon. chairman, 1987—; board of directors Boston 200, 1975-77, United Way Massachusetts Bay, 1975-80, Flaschner Judicial Institute, 1977-81; member Massachusetts Commission on Judicial Conduct, 1986—; chairman Curtis-Saval International Center, Boston, 1987—. Guggenheim fellow, 1946-47; recipient Presidential certificate of merit, 1948; Cornell College Alumni Citation, 1953; 1st Silver medal le Groupement des Acousticiens de Langue Francaise Paris, 1966; Abe Lincoln TV award Southern Baptist Convention, 1975; Media award National Association for the Advancement of Colored People, 1975; named Station WCRB Person of the Year, 1987. Fellow Acoustical Society Am. (Biennial award 1944, executive council 1944-47, vice president 1949-50, president 1954-55, associate editor 1946-60, Wallace Clement Sabine Architectural Acoustics award 1961, Gold medal award 1975), National Acad. Engineering (director marine board, committee pub. engineering policy, aeros. and space engineering board), Am. Acad. Arts and Sciences, Am. Physical Society, American Association for the Advancement of Science, Audio Engineering Society (president 1967-68, Gold medal 1971, governor 1966-71), Institute of Electrical and Electronics Engineers (chairman professional group audio 1950-51); member Institute Noise Control Engineering (charter president 1971-73, director 1973-75), Am. Standards Association (chairman acoustical standards board 1956-68, director 1963-68), Massachusetts Broadcasters Association (director 1973-80, president 1978-79, Distinguished Service award 1980), Boston Community Media Council (treasurer 1973-76, vice president 1976-77), Cambridge Society Early Music (president 1963-71, director 1961-79), Acad. Distinguished Bostonians, Greater Boston Chamber of Commerce (director 1973-79, vice president 1976-79, Distinguished Community Service award 1980, 83), Phi Beta Kappa, Sigma Xi, Eta Kappa Nu. Episcopalian. Clubs: Massachusetts Inst. Tech. Faculty, St. Botolph, Harvard, City. Office: 975 Memorial Dr Suite 804 Cambridge Massachusetts 02138

BERG, PAUL, biochemist, educator; born New York City, June 30, 1926; son of Harry and Sarah (Brodsky) B.; married Mildred Levy, September 13, 1947; 1 son, John. Bachelor of Science, Pennsylvania State University, 1948; Doctor of Philosophy (NIH fellow 1950-52), Western Reserve University, 1952; Doctor of Science (honorary), University Rochester, 1978, Yale University, 1978, Washington University, St. Louis, 1986. Postdoctoral fellow Copenhagen (Denmark) University, 1952-53; postdoctoral fellow School Medicine, Washington University, St. Louis, 1953-54; Am. Cancer Society scholar cancer research department microbiology School Medicine, Washington University, 1954-57, from assistant to associate professor microbiology; 1955-59; professor biochemistry Stanford School Medicine, 1959—, Sam, Lula and Jack Willson professor biochemistry; 1970, chairman department; 1969-74; director Stanford University Beckman Center for Molecular and Genetic Medicine, 1985; non-resident fellow Salk Institute, 1973; adv. board National Institutes of Health, National Science Foundation, Massachusetts Institute of Technology; visiting committee department biochemistry and molecular biology Harvard University; board sci. advisors Jane Coffin Childs Foundation Medical Research, 1970-80; chairman sci. adv. committee Whitehead Institute, 1984; international adv. board Basel Institute Immunology. Contributor professional journals; Editor: Biochem. and Biophys. Research Communications, 1959-68; editorial board: Molecular Biology, 1966-69. Served to lieutenant (junior grade) United States Naval Reserve, 1943-46. Recipient Eli Lilly prize biochemistry, 1959; V.D. Mattia award Roche Institute Molecular Biology, 1972; Henry J. Kaiser award for excellence in teaching, 1972; Distinguished Alumnus award Pennsylvania State University, 1972; Sarasota Medical awards for achievement and excellence, 1979; Gairdner Foundation annual award, 1980; Lasker Foundation award, 1980; Nobel award in chemistry, 1980; New York Acad. Sci. award, 1980; Sci. Freedom and Responsibility award American Association for the Advancement of Science, 1982; National Medal of Sci., 1985; named California Scientist of Year California Museum Sci. and Industry, 1963; numerous special and distinguished lectureships including Harvey lecturer, 1972, Lynen lecturer, 1977, Priestly lectrs. Pennsylvania State University, 1978, Dreyfus Distinguished lectrs. Northwestern University, 1979, Lawrence Livermore Dir.'s Distinguished lecturer, 1983, W.H. Stein Memorial lecturer Rockefeller University, 1984, Charles E. Dohme Memorial lecturer Johns Hopkins University, 1984, Weizmann Institute Sci. Jubilee lecturer, 1984, University Houston Nobel Prize Winners Series, 1985. Member Institute Medicine, National Acad. Sciences, Am. Acad. Arts and Sciences, Am. Society Biological Chemists (president 1974-75), Am. Society Microbiology, Am. Philosophical Society, Japan Biochem. Society (elected foreign member 1978), French Acad. Sci. (elected foreign member 1981). Office: Stanford School Medicine 838 Santa Fe Avenue Stanford California 94305

BERGER, FRANK MILAN, scientist, former pharmaceutical company executive; born Pilsen, Czechoslovakia, June 25, 1913; came to United States, 1947, naturalized, 1953; son of Otto and Martha (Weigner) B.; married Bozena Jahodova, March 15, 1939 (deceased November 1972); children: Franklin Milan, Thomas Jan; married A. Christine Spade, May 21, 1975. Doctor of Medicine, University Prague, Czechoslovakia, 1937, State University of New York, 1948; Doctor of Science (honorary), Philadelphia College Science and Pharmacy, 1966. Research fellow physiology University Prague, 1934-36, research assistant bacteriology; 1936-38; bacteriologist Czechoslovak State Institute Health, 1938-39; senior resident Monsall Hospital Infectious Diseases, Manchester, England, 1941-43; chief pharmacologist Brit. Drug Houses, London, 1945-47; assistant professor pediatrics University Rochester, 1947-49; director research Carter-Wallace Incorporated, 1949-55, vice president; 1955-58; president Wallace Laboratories div. Carter-Wallace Incorporated, Cranbury, New Jersey, 1958-73; member adv. council department biology Princeton University, 1961-74, lecturer, professor; 1969-74; member sci. adv. committee Waksman Institute Microbiology, Rutgers University, 1960-67; consultant Surgeon General, Walter Reed Army Medical Center, Washington, 1974-80; president Mario Negri Institute Foundation for Biomed. Research, Incorporated, 1973—; professor psychiatry University Louisville Medical School, 1974—; hon. professor microbiology Waksman Institute Microbiology, Rutgers University, 1982—. Fellow New York Acad. Sciences, Am. Coll Neuropsychopharmacology, Royal Society Medicine, American Association for the Advancement of Science; member Am., Brit., Can. pharm. socs., Am. Bacteriol. Society, Society Experimental Biology and Medicine, American Medical Association, American Association of University Women, Am. Chemical Society, Biometric Society, Sigma Xi. Clubs: Cosmos (Washington); Nassau (Princeton); Princeton (New York City), New York Athletic (New York City). Discovered tranquilizer meprobamate, muscle-relaxant mephenesin, pain-reliever carisoprodol, also method purification penicillin. Office: 515 E 72d St New York New York 10021

BERGER, JAMES O., statistics educator. Bachelor of Arts, Cornell University, 1971, Doctor of Philosophy, 1974. Faculty department statistics Purdue University, 1974—, now Richard M. Brumfield distinguished professor statistics. Office: Purdue U Department of Stats West Lafayette Indiana 47907

BERGER, PHILIP ALAN, biological psychiatry educator and researcher; born Newark, June 7, 1943; son of Leo and Dorothy Ruth (Davidson) B.; married Deborah Jane Sanner, October 3, 1964 (divorced October 1980); children: Tamara Louis, Cynthia Maria; married Meredith JoAnn Dunn, December 6, 1980; children: Melissa Victoria, Jessica Michelle. Bachelor of Arts, Dartmouth College, 1965, Bachelor in Medical Scis., 1967; Doctor of Medicine, Harvard University, 1969. Diplomate Am. Board Psychiatry and Neurology. Intern in pediatrics University California Medical Center, San Francisco, 1969-70; chief resident Stanford (California) University School Medicine, 1970-73, assistant professor; 1974-80, associate professor; 1980-84, professor; 1984—, Kenneth T. Norris professor; 1985—; principal investigator Stanford Mental Health Research Center, 1977—; chairman rev. committee National Institute of Mental Health, Washington, 1980-84; secretary National Mental Health Adv. Council, Washington, 1984-87. Editor: Psychiatry for Primary Care Physicians, 1979, American Handbook Biology Psychiatry Volume III, 1986; contributor 230 articles to professional journals (A.E. Bennett award, 1977). Grantee National Institutes of Health, 1977, John T. and Catherine MacArthur Foundation, 1982. Fellow Am. Psychiat. Association, Am. College Neuropharmacology (program chairman 1986); member Biological Psychiatry (sec.-treas. 1986-87). Avocations: photography, astronomy, pvt. pilot. Home: 8 Franciscan Ridge Portola Valley California 94025 Office: Stanford U Department of Psychiatry Stanford California 94305

BERGGREN, WILLIAM ALFRED, geologist, research micropalentologist, educator; born New York City, January 15, 1931; son of Wilhelm Fritjof and Lilly Maria (Skog) B.; married Lois Albee, June 19, 1954 (divorced July 1981); children—Erik, Anna Lisa, Anders, Sara Maria; married Marie Pierre Aubry, June 19, 1982. Bachelor of Science, Dickinson College, 1952; Master of Science, University Houston, 1957; Doctor of Philosophy, University Stockholm, 1960, Doctor of Science, 1962. Research micropaleontologist Oasis Oil Company, Tripoli, Libya, 1962-65; assistant scientist Woods Hole Oceanographic Institute, Massachusetts, 1965-68; associate scientist Woods Hole Oceanographic Institute, 1968-71, senior scientist; 1971—; adj. professor Brown University,Providence, 1968—. Editor:(with others) Catastrophes and Earth History, 1984; contributor articles to sci. journals. Recipient Mary Clark Thompson medal National Acad. Sciences, 1982. Fellow Geological Society Am.; member Am. Association Petroleum Geologists, Society Econ. Paleontologists and Mineralogists, Paleontological Society Am. (co-editor journal 1980-84), Sigma Xi. Avocation: skiing. Office: Woods Hole Oceanographic Institute Water St Woods Hole Massachusetts 02543

BERGSTRÖM, K. SUNE D., biochemist; born Stockholm, January 10, 1916; son of Sverker B. and Wera (Wistrand) B.; married Maj Gernandt, July 30, 1943. Docent physiological chemistry, Doctor of Medicine, Karolinska Institute, Stockholm, 1944, Doctor Medical Science in Biochemistry, 1944; Doctor h.c., University Basel, Switzerland, 1960, University Chicago, 1960, Harvard University, 1976, Mount Sinai Medical School, 1976, Medical Academy Wroclaw, Poland, 1976, McMaster University, Hamilton, Can., 1988. Research fellow University London, 1938, Columbia University, New York City, 1940-41, Squibb Institute Medical Research, New Brunswick, New Jersey, 1941-42; assistant biochem. department Medical Nobel Institute, Karolinska Institute, Stockholm, 1944-47; research fellow University Basel, 1946-47; professor physiological chemistry University Lund, Sweden, 1947-58; professor chemistry Karolinska Institute, 1958-80, dean medical faculty; 1963-66, rector; 1969-77; chairman board of directors Nobel Foundation, Stockholm, 1975-87; president Royal Swedish Acad.

Sciences, 1983-85; chairman World Health Organization Adv. Committee Medical Research, Geneva, 1977-82; La Madonnina lecturer, Milan, Italy, 1972; Dunham Lecturer Harvard University, 1972; Dohme lecturer Johns Hopkins University, 1972-73; Merrimon lecturer University North Carolina, Chapel Hill, 1973; V.D. Mattia lecturer Roche Institute, 1974; Harvey lecturer Harvey Society, New York City, 1974; General Amir Chand orator All India Institute, New Delhi, 1978; Cairlton lecturer University Texas Health Sci. Center, Dallas, 1979; member Swedish Medical Research Council, 1952-58, 64-70, Swedish Natural Sci. Research Council, 1955-62. Contributor articles to sci. journals. Decorated Grand Officier de l'Ordre du Mérite, Paris, 1984; recipient Anders Jahre Medical prize, Oslo, 1972, Gairdner award University Toronto, 1972, Louisa Gross Horwitz prize Columbia University, 1975, Francis Amory prize Am. Acad. Arts and Sciences, 1975, Albert Lasker Basic Medical Rsch. award, New York City, 1977, Robert A. Welch award, Houston, 1980, Nobel prize, 1982. Member Royal Swedish Acad. Sciences, Swedish Acad. Engineering Sciences, Am. Acad. Arts and Sciences, Am. Philos Society (Benjamin Franklin medal 1988), Am. Society Biological Chemists, Acad. Sciences Union of the Soviet Socialist Republics, Academia Leopoldina (German Democratic Republic), Royal Society Edinburgh, Medical Acad. Union of the Soviet Socialist Republics, Finska Vetenskaps-Societeten, Swedish Society Medical Sciences, senior member Institute of Medicine, National Academy of Sciences, foreign associate National Academy of Sciences, Pontifical Acad. Sciences, Città del Vàticano.

Office: Karolinska Institutet, Nobelkansli Box 60250, 104 01 Stockholm Sweden

BERLINER, HANS JACK, computer scientist; born Berlin, Germany, January 27, 1929; came to United States, 1937, naturalized, 1943; son of Paul and Theodora (Lehfeld) B.; married Araxie Yacoubian, August 15, 1969. Bachelor of Arts, George Washington University, 1954; Doctor of Philosophy, Carnegie Mellon University, 1975. Systems analyst United States Naval Research Laboratory, 1954-58; group head systems analysis Martin Company, Denver, 1959-60; adv. systems analyst International Business Machines Corporation, Gaithersburg, Maryland, 1960-69; senior research scientist Carnegie-Mellon University, Pittsburgh, 1974—. Member editorial board Artificial Intelligence, 1976—, Pitman: Research Notes in Artificial Intelligence, 1984—. Served with Army of the United States, 1951-53. Awarded title International Grandmaster Corr. Chess, 1968. Member Association Computing Machinery, International Joint Conference Artificial Intelligence, United States Chess Federation, International Computer Chess Association. Among leading chess players United States, 1950—, New York State champion, 1953, Southwest Open champion, 1960, So. Open champion, 1949, United States Open Corr. Chess champion, 1955, 56, 59, World Corr. Chess champion, 1968-72. Developed 1st computer program to defeat a world champion at his own game (backgammon), 1979; developer world's strongest computer chess machine program, 1985—, among .5% of all registered tournament chess players; discovered Bx tree search algorithm, 1975, SNAC method of constructing polynomial evaluation functions, 1979. Home: 657 Ridgefield Avenue Pittsburgh Pennsylvania 15216

BERNSTEIN, RICHARD BARRY, chemistry educator, researcher; born New York City, October 31, 1923; son of Simon and Stella Ruth (Grossman) B.; married Norma Bianca Olivier, December 17, 1948; children: Neil David, Minda Dianne, Beth Anne, Julie Lynn. Bachelor of Arts, Columbia College, New York City, 1943, Master of Arts in Chemistry, 1946; Doctor of Philosophy in Chemistry, Columbia University, New York City, 1948; Doctor of Science (honorary), University Chicago, 1988. From assistant professor to associate professor chemistry Illinois Institute Tech., Chicago, 1948-53; from associate professor to professor University Michigan, Ann Arbor, 1953-63; professor University Wisconsin, Madison, 1963-67, Daniells professor chemistry; 1967-73; Doherty professor chemistry University Texas, Austin, 1973-77; Higgins professor natural sciences, department chemistry Columbia University, 1977-82; senior vice president Occidental Petroleum Research Corp., Irvine, California, 1982-83; professor chemistry University of California at Los Angeles, 1983—; researcher Manhattan Project, S.A.M. Laboratories, Columbia University, 1942-46; Hinshelwood lecturer Oxford (England) University, 1980 . Author: Chemical Dynamics Via Molecular Beams and Lasers, 1982, (with R.D. Levine) Molecular Reaction Dynamics, 1974, Molecular Reaction Dynamics and Chemical Reactivity, 1987; editor: Atom-Molecule Collision Theory, 1979, Chemical Physics Letters, 1978-81, 85—. Served with Corps of Engineers United States Army, 1944-46. Associated Press Sloan fellow, 1956-60, National Science Foundation fellow, 1960-61; Fairchild Distinguished scholar California Institute Tech., 1986; recipient R.A. Welch award in chemistry, 1988. Fellow American Association for the Advancement of Science, Am. Acad. Arts and Sciences, Am. Physical Society; member National Acad. Sciences (Chemical Sciences award 1985), Am. Chemical Society (Debye award, 1981, Langmuir, 1988). Office: University of California at Los Angeles Department of Chem 405 Hilgard Avenue Los Angeles California 90024

BERTIN, JOHN JOSEPH, engineering educator, researcher; born Milwaukee, October 13, 1938; son of Andrea and Yolanda G. (Pasquali) B.; married Ruth Easterbrook; children: Thomas Alexander, Randolph Scott, Elizabeth Anne, Michael Robert. Bachelor of Arts, Rice Institute, Houston, 1960; Master of Science, Rice Institute, 1962; Doctor of Philosophy, Rice Institute, Houston, 1966. Aerospace technologist National Aeronautics and Space Administration Johnson Space Center, Houston, 1962-66; professor University Texas, Austin, 1966—; consultant McGinnis, Lochridge & Kilgore, Austin, 1978-83, Sandia National Labs, Albuquerque, 1980—, BPD Difesa e Spazio, Rome, 1980-82; director Center Excellence for Hypersonic Training and Research; visiting professor United States Air Force Acad., Colorado Springs, 1988-89. Co-author: Aerodynamics for Engineers, 1979, Engineering Fluid Mechanics, 1984. President Western Hills Little League, Austin, 1975.

Recipient Dynamics Teaching award College Engineering, Austin, 1978, Texas Executive Teaching award Ex-Students Association University Texas, Austin, 1982, Tau Beta Pi Faculty award, 1986. Fellow American Institute of Aeronautics and Astronautics (director region IV 1983-86, distinguished lecturer); member New York Acad. Sciences. Office: Department Aerospace Engring U Tex Austin Texas 78712

BESCH, EVERETT DICKMAN, veterinarian, university dean; born Hammond, Indiana, May 4, 1924; son of Ernst Henry and Carolyn (Dieckmann) B.; married Mellie Darnell Brockman, April 3, 1946; children: Carolyn Darnell, Ceryl Lynn, Cynthia Lee, Charlotte Ann, Everett Dickman. Doctor of Veterinary Medicine, Texas Agricultural and Mechanical College, 1954; Master of Public Health, University Minnesota, 1956; Doctor of Philosophy, Oklahoma State University, 1963. Instructor University Minnesota, 1954-56; assistant professor Oklahoma State University, 1956-64, professor, head department vet. parasitology and pub. health; 1964-68; dean School Vet. Medicine, Louisiana State University, 1968—; secretary-treasurer Association Am. Vet. Medical Colleges, 1974-78, secretary council deans, 1976-80, chairman council deans, 1980-81; member National Adv. Council Health Professions Education, 1982-86. Author articles, chapter in book. Served with United States Navy, 1942-48. Member Association Teachers Veteran Pub. Health and Preventive Medicine (president 1968), Am., Louisiana vet. med. associations, Am. Society Parasitologists, Conference Pub. Health Veterinarians (president 1971-72), Am. Association Food Hygiene Veterinarians (president 1976-77), Am. Association Veteran Parasitologists, Helminthological Society, Washington, Conference Research Workers Animal Diseases. Research interests: arthropod vectors of disease, internal parasites of ruminants. Home: 1453 Ashland Dr Baton Rouge Louisiana 70806

BETHE, HANS ALBRECHT, physicist, educator; born Strassburg, Alsace-Lorraine, Germany, July 2, 1906; came to United States, 1935; son of Albrecht Theodore and Anna (Kuhn) B.; married Rose Ewald, 1939; children: Henry, Monica. Educated Goethe Gymnasium, Frankfurt on Main, University Frankfort; Doctor of Philosophy, University Munich, 1928; Doctor of Science, Brooklyn Polytechnic Institute, 1950, University Denver, 1952, University Chicago, 1953, University Birmingham, 1956, Harvard University, 1958. Instructor in theoretical physics universities of Frankfort, Stuttgart, Munich and Tubingen, 1928-33; lecturer universities of Manchester and Bristol, England, 1933-35; assistant professor Cornell University, 1935, professor; 1937-75, professor emeritus; 1975—; director theoretical physics div. Los Alamos Sci. Laboratory, 1943-46; Member Presdl. Study Disarmament, 1958; member President's Sci. Adv. Committee, 1956-60. Author: Mesons and Fields, 1953, Elementary Nuclear Theory, 1957, Quantum Mechanics of One-and Two-Electron Atoms, 1957, Intermediate Quantum Mechanics, 1964; Contributor to: Handbuch der Physik, 1933, Reviews of Modern Physics, 1936-37, Physical Rev. Recipient A. Cressy Morrison prize New York Acad. Sci., 1938-40; Presidential Medal of Merit, 1946; Max

Planck medal, 1953; Enrico Fermi award Atomic Energy Commission, 1961; Nobel Prize in physics, 1967; National Medal of Sci., 1976; Vannevar Bush award National Science Foundation, 1985. Foreign member Royal Society London; member Am. Philosophical Society, National Acad. Sciences (Henry Draper medal 1968), Am. Physical Society (president 1954), Am. Astronomical Society. Office: Cornell U Lab Nuclear Studies Ithaca New York 14853

BEVAN, DONALD EDWARD, marine scientist, university dean; born Seattle, February 23, 1921; son of Arther and Violette B.; married Tanya L. Potapova, September 8, 1971. Bachelor of Science, University Washington, 1948, Doctor of Philosophy, 1959; postdoctoral student, Moscow University, 1959-60. Senior fisheries biologist University Washington, Seattle, 1955-59; lecturer, research assistant professor University Washington, 1959-61, research associate prof; 1961-64, associate professor; 1964-66, professor; 1966-86, professor emeritus; 1986—, associate dean College Fisheries; 1965-69, dean; 1980-85, director University Computer Center; 1968-69, assistant vice president research; 1969-77, adj. professor Institute Marine Studies; 1973—, associate dean College Ocean and Fishery Sciences; 1984-86; president, director University Book Stores, 1977—, professor emeritus; 1986—; member US-USSR Pacific Fisheries Negotiations. Author articles and pamphlets in field. Served to captain, artillery United States Army, World War II. Decorated Purple Heart, Bronze Star. Member Pacific Region Fisheries Council (chairman sci. and statis. committee), N. Pacific Fisheries Council, Marine Tech. Society, Am. Institute Fishery Research Biologists, Pacific Fisheries Biologists, Sigma Xi, Phi Sigma. Home: 29801 NE Cherry Valley Road Duvall Washington 98019 Office: U Wash Henderson Hall HN15 Seattle Washington 98195

BEYSTER, JOHN ROBERT, engineering company executive; born Detroit, July 26, 1924; son of John Frederick and Lillian Edith (Jondro) B.; married Betty Jean Brock, September 8, 1955; children: James Frederick, Mark Daneil, Mary Ann. Bachelor of Science in Engineering, University Michigan, 1945, Master of Science, 1948, Doctor of Philosophy, 1950. Registered professional engineer, California. Member staff Los Alamos Sci. Laboratory, 1951-56; chairman department accel. physics Gulf General Atomic Company, San Diego, 1957-69; president, chairman board Sci. Applications, Incorporated, La Jolla, California, 1969—; member Joint Strategic Target Planning Staff, Sci. Adv. Group, Omaha, 1978—; panel member National Measurement Laboratory Evaluation panel for Radiation Research, Washington, 1983—; director Scripps Bancorp, La Jolla, 1983. Co-author: Slow Neutron Scattering and Thermalization, 1970. Served to lieutenant commander United States Navy, 1943-46. Fellow Am. Nuclear Society, Am. Physical Society. Republican. Roman Catholic. Office: Sci Applications International Corp 10260 Campus Point Dr San Diego California 92121

BICK, KATHERINE LIVINGSTONE, scientist, government official; born Charlottetown, Canada, May 3, 1932; came to United States, 1954; daughter of Spurgeon Arthur and Flora Hazel

(Murray) Livingstone; married James Harry Bick, August 20, 1955 (divorced); children: James A., Charles L.; married Ernst Freese, 1986. Bachelor of Science with honors, Acadia University, Can., 1951, Master of Science, 1952; Doctor of Philosophy, Brown University, 1957. Research pathologist University of California at Los Angeles Medical School, 1959-61; assistant professor California State University, Northridge, 1961-66; laboratory instructor Georgetown University, Washington, 1970-72, assistant professor; 1972-76; deputy director neurological disorder program National Institute Neurological and Communicative Disorders and Stroke, National Institutes of Health, Bethesda, Maryland, 1976-81, acting deputy director; 1981-83, deputy director; 1983-87; deputy director extramural research Office of Director National Institutes of Health, 1987—. Editor: Alzheimer's Disease: Senile Dementia and Related Disorders, 1978, Neurosecretion and Brain Peptides, Implications for Brain Functions and Neurol. Disease, 1981, The Early Story of Alzheimer's Disease, 1987; contributor articles to professional journals. President Woman's Club, McLean, Virginia, 1968-69; board of directors Fairfax County (Virginia) Young Women's Christian Association, 1969-70; president Emerson Unitarian Church, 1964-66, Bethesda Place Homeowner's Association, 1982. Recipient Can. National Research Council award Acadia University, 1951-52, fellow, 1951-52; Universal Match Foundation fellow Brown University, 1956-57; National Institutes of Health Dir.'s award, 1978; Federal Executive Institute Leadership fellow, 1980; Special Achievement award National Institutes of Health, 1981, 83; Superior Service award U.S. Public Health Service, 1986. Member Am. Neurological Association, Am. Acad. Neurology, American Association for the Advancement of Science, Am. Society Zoologists, Western Society Naturalists, Association for Research in Nervous and Mental Disease, International Brain Research Organization, World Federation Neurology Research Group on Dementias (executive secretary Am. region 1984-86, chairman 1986—). Office: NIH Department Health & Human Services 9000 Rockville Pike Bethesda Maryland 20892

BICKEL, PETER JOHN, statistician; born Bucharest, Roumania, September 21, 1940; came to United States, 1957, naturalized, 1964; son of Eliezer and P. Madeleine (Moscovici) B.; married Nancy Kramer, March 2, 1964; children: Amanda, Stephen. Bachelor of Arts, University California, Berkeley, 1960, Master of Arts, 1961, Doctor of Philosophy, 1963. Assistant professor statistics University California, Berkeley, 1964-67, associate professor; 1967-70, professor; 1970—, chairman department statistics; 1976-79, dean physical sciences; 1980-86; visiting lecturer math. Imperial College, London, 1965-66; fellow J S Guggenheim Memorial Foundation, 1970-71; North Atlantic Treaty Organization senior sci. fellow, 1974. Author: (with K. Doksum) Mathematical Statistics, 1976; Associate editor: Annals of Math. Statistics, 1968-76, 1986—; contributor articles to professional journals Fellow John D. and Catherine T. MacArthur Foundation, 1984. Fellow Institute Math. Statistics (president 1980), Am. Statistical

Association, American Association for the Advancement of Science; member Royal Statistical Society, International Statistical Institute, National Acad. Sci., Am. Acad. Arts Sciences. Office: U California Department Stats Evans Hall Berkeley California 94720

BIEDERMAN, RONALD R., engineer, educator; born Hartford, Connecticut, October 19, 1938. Bachelor of Science, University Connecticut, 1960, Master of Science, 1962, Doctor of Philosophy in Materials Science, 1968. Instructor metallurgy University Connecticut, 1962-68; professor mechanical engineering Worcester Polytechnic Institute, Massachusetts, 1968—, director electron microscope facility; 1975—, now George F. Fuller professor mechanical engineering. Member Am. Society Metals (Stanley P. Rockwell Memorial lecturer 1981), American Institute of Mining, Metallurgy and Petroleum Engineers. Office: Department Mech Engring Worcester Polytechnic Institute Worcester Massachusetts 01609

BILELLO, JOHN CHARLES, engineer, educator; born Brooklyn, October 15, 1938; son of Charles and Catherine (Buonadonna) B.; married Mary Josephine Gloria, August 1, 1959; children: Andrew Charles, Peter Angelo, Matthew Jonathan. Bachelor of Education, New York University, 1960, Master of Science, 1962; Doctor of Philosophy, University Illinois, 1965. Senior research engineer General Telephone & Electronics Laboratory, Bayside, New York, 1965-67; member faculty State University of New York, Stony Brook, 1967-87; assistant professor State University of New York, 1967-71, associate professor; 1971-75, professor engineering; 1975-87, dean; 1977-81; dean School Engring and Computer Sci. California State University, Fullerton, 1986—, professor mechanical engineering; 1986—; guest scientist Brookhaven National Laboratories, 1975—; visiting professor Polytechnic of Milan, 1973-74; visiting scholar King's College, London University, 1983; visiting North Atlantic Treaty Organization exchange scholar Oxford University, 1986; project director synchroton topography project University Consortium, 1981-86. Associate editor: Materials Letters, 1981—, Journal Materials Science and Engring., 1984—. NATO sr. faculty fellow Enrico Fermi Center, Milan, Italy, 1973. Member Am. Physical Society, Am. Society for Metals, Am.-Inst. Metallurgical Engineers, Materials Research Society. Office: California State U School Engring & Computer Sci Fullerton California 92634

BILLINGHAM, RUPERT EVERETT, zoologist, educator; born Warminster, England, October 15, 1921; son of Albert E. and Helen (Green) B.; married Jean Mary Morpeth, March 29, 1951; children—John David, Peter Jeremy, Elizabeth Anne. Bachelor of Arts, Oriel College, Oxford, England, 1943, Master of Arts, 1947, Doctor of Philosophy, 1950, Doctor of Science, 1957. Lecturer zoology University Birmingham, England, 1947-51; research fellow Brit. Empire Cancer Campaign; hon. research associate department zoology University College, London, 1951-57; member Wistar Institute; Wistar professor zoology University Pennsylvania, Philadelphia, 1957-65; professor, chairman department medical genetics, director Henry Phipps Institute, University Pennsylvania Medical School, 1965-71; professor, chairman department cell biology and anatomy University Texas Health Sci. Center at Dallas, 1971-86; member allergy and immunology study section National Institutes of Health, 1959-62; member transplantation immunology committee National Institute Allergy and Infectious Diseases, National Institutes of Health, 1968-70, 71-73, member council, 1980-83; member sci. adv. board St. Jude Children's Research Hospital, Memphis, 1965-70; member sci. adv. committee Massachusetts General Hospital, 1976-79. Contributor articles to professional journals; Editorial board: Transplantation, 1980-82; adv. editorial board: Placenta, 1980-85; asso. editor: Am. Journal Reproductive Immunology and Microbiology, 1981-86; adv. editor: Journal Experimental Medicine, 1963-84; asso. editor: Journal Immunology, 1964-72, Cellular Immunology, 1970-86, Journal Experimental Zoology, 1976-80; hon. editorial board: Developmental and Comparative Immunology, 1977-80. Served to lieutenant Royal Navy, 1942-46. Recipient Alvarenga prize College Physicians, Philadelphia, 1963; hon. award Society Plastic Surgeons, 1964; Fred Lyman Adair award Am. Gynecol. Society, 1971. Fellow Royal Society (London), New York Acad. Sciences, Am. Acad. Arts and Sciences; member Am. Association Immunologists, Transplantation Society (president 1974-76), Am. Association Transplant Surgeons (hon.), International Society Immunology of Reprodn. (president 1983-86). Home: Rt 2 102 B Vineyard Haven Massachusetts 02568

BINFORD, THOMAS ORIEL, computer scientist, educator; born Jefferson Twp., Pennsylvania, April 13, 1936; son of Robert J. and Ruth A. (Sandbach) B.; married Ione Gargioné

Junqueira, December 30, 1975. Bachelor of Science, Pennsylvania State University; Doctor of Philosophy, University Wisconsin. With Massachusetts Institute of Technology, Artificial Intelligence Laboratory, 1966-70; with Stanford (California) University Artificial Intelligence Laboratory, 1970—; professor computer sci. (research). Associate editor: Robotics Research. Office: Computer Sci Department Stanford U Stanford California 94305

BINNIG, GERD KARL, physicist, educator; born July 20, 1947; married Lore Binnig, 1969; 2 children. Diploma in Physics, Goethe University, Frankfurt, Federal Republic Germany, Doctor of Philosophy. Research staff member International Business Machines Corporation Zurich Research laboratory, 1978—, group leader; 1984—; group leader International Business Machines Corporation Almaden Research Center, San José, 1985-86; professor Physics University Munich, 1987—; visiting professor Stanford University, 1986. Co-recipient Nobel prize in Physics, 1986; recipient Physics prize, German Physical Society, 1982, Otto Klung prize, 1983, Joint King Faisal International prize for Sci. and Hewlett-Packard Europhysics prize, 1984, Elliot Cresson medal, Franklin Institute, Philadelphia, 1987, Grosses Verdienstkreuz mit Stern und Schulterband des Verdienstordens, 1987. Avocations: music, tennis, soccer, golf. Office: International Business Machines Corporation Research Physics Group, Schelling-strasse 4, Sektion Physic der Universitat, 8000 Munich 40, Federal Republic of Germany

BIRD, ROBERT BYRON, chemical engineering educator, author; born Bryan, Texas, February 5, 1924; son of Byron and Ethel (Antrim) B. Student, University Maryland, 1941-43; Bachelor of Science in Chemical Engineering, University Illinois, 1947; Doctor of Philosophy in Chemistry, University Wisconsin, 1950; postdoctoral fellow, University Amsterdam, 1950-51; Doctor of Engineering (honorary), Lehigh University, 1972, Washington University, 1973, Tech. University Delft, Holland, 1977, Colorado School Mines, 1986; Doctor of Science (honorary), Clarkson University, 1980. Assistant professor chemistry Cornell University, 1952-53, Debye lecturer; 1973, Julian C. Smith lecturer; 1988; research chemist DuPont Experimental Station, summer 1953; member faculty University Wisconsin, 1951-52, 53—, professor chemical engineering; 1957—, C.F. Burgess distinguished professor chemical engineering; 1968-72, John D. MacArthur professor; 1982—, Vilas research professor; 1972—, chairman department; 1964-68; visiting professor University California, Berkeley, 1977; D L Katz lecturer University Michigan, 1971; W N Lacey lecturer California Institute Tech., 1974; K. Wohl Memorial lecturer University Del., 1977; W K Lewis lecturer Massachusetts Institute of Technology, 1982; lecturer Lectures in Sci. Humble Oil Company, 1959, 61, 64, 66; lecture tour Am. Chemical Society, 1958, 75, Canadian Institute Chemistry, 1961, 65; consultant to industry, 1965—; member adv. panel engineering sci. div. National Science Foundation, 1961-64. Author: (with others) Molecular Theory of Gases and Liquids, 2d printing, 1964, Transport Phenomena, 40th printing, 1988, Spanish edition, 1965, Czech edition, 1966, Italian edition, 1970, Russian edition, 1974, Een Goed Begin: A Contemporary Dutch Reader, 1963, 2d edition, 1971, Comprehending Technical Japanese, 1975, Chinese edition, 1985, Dynamics of Polymeric Liquids, Volume 1, Fluid Mechanics, Volume 2, Kinetic Theory, 1977, 2d edition, 1987; Reading Dutch: Fifteen Annotated Stories from the Low Countries, 1985; also numerous research publications; Am. editor: (with others) Applied Science Research, 1969-86; adv. board Industrial and Engring. Chemistry, 1970-72; editorial board Journal Non-Newtonian Fluid Mechanics, 1975—. Served to 1st lieutenant Army of the United States, 1943-46. Decorated Bronze Star; Fulbright fellow Holland, 1950; Fulbright lecturer, 1958; Guggenheim fellow, 1958; Fulbright lecturer Japan, 1962-63; Fulbright lecturer Sarajevo, Yugoslavia, 1972; recipient Curtis McGraw award Am. Association Engineering Education, 1959, Westinghouse award, 1960, Corcoran award, 1987, National Medal of Sci., President Reagan, 1987. Fellow Am. Physical Society (Otto Laporte lecturer 1980), Am. Institute Chemical Engineers (William H. Walker award 1962, Professional Progress award 1965, Warren K. Lewis award 1974), Am. Acad. Arts and Sciences; member Am. Association Netherlandic Studies, Can. Association Netherlandic Studies, Am. Chemical Society (chairman Wisconsin section 1966, unrestricted research grant Petroleum Research Fund 1963), Society Rheology (Bingham award 1974), Am. Acad. Mechanics, Brit. Society Rheology, Dutch Physical Society, Royal Institute Engineers (Holland), National Acad. Engineering, New York

Acad. Sciences, Am. Acad. Arts and Sciences, Wisconsin Acad. Sciences, Arts and Letters, Royal Dutch Acad. Sciences (foreign), Phi Beta Kappa, Sigma Xi (vice president Wisconsin section 1959-60), Tau Beta Pi, Alpha Chi Sigma, Phi Kappa Phi, Omicron Delta Kappa, Sigma Tau. Office: Chem Engring Department 3004 Engring Building 1415 Johnson Dr U Wisconsin Madison Wisconsin 53706-1691

BLACK, SIR JAMES (WHYTE), pharmacologist; born June 14, 1924. Bachelor of Medicine, ChB, University St. Andrews. Assistant lecturer physiology University St. Andrews, 1946; lecturer physiology University Malaya, 1947-50; senior lecturer University Glasgow Vet. School, 1950-58; with ICI Pharms. Limited, 1958-64; head biological research, deputy research director Smith, Kline & French, Welwyn Garden City, 1964-73; professor, chairman department pharmacology University College, London, 1973-77; director therapeutic research Wellcome Research Laboratories, 1978-84; professor analytical pharmacology King's College Hospital Medical School, University London, 1984—. Created knight, 1981; recipient Nobel prize for medicine, 1988. Fellow Royal College Physicians, Royal Society (Mullard award 1978). Office: Rayne Institute Analytical Pharm, 123 Coldharbour Lane, London SE5 9NU, England *

BLACKBURN, JACK BAILEY, civil engineering educator; born Sterling, Oklahoma, October 19, 1922; son of Raymond Wasden and Vonnie Irene (Bailey) B.; married Janice Ann Keller, September 2, 1949; children—Judith Ann Blackburn Cameron, Jo Ann. Bachelor of Science, Oklahoma University, 1947; Master of Science, Purdue University, 1949, Doctor of Philosophy, 1955. Grad. assistant, research assistant, research engineer Joint Highway Research Project Purdue University, 1947-55; associate professor civil engineering, associate director Maryland Highway Research Program, University Maryland, 1955-58; transportation planning engineer Harland Bartholomew and Associates, St. Louis, then Memphis, 1958-60; professor civil engineering, director Arizona Transportation and Traffic Institute, University Arizona, Tucson, 1960-63; professor, head civil engineering department Kansas State University, Manhattan, 1963-72; professor engineering Arizona State University, 1972—; Member National Acad. Sci./Nat. Acad. Engineering building research adv. board, 1968-71.

Served with Army of the United States, 1943-46. Member American Society for Testing and Materials (chairman subcom. on evaluation of data of C-9 committee on concrete 1956-58), Engineers Council Professional Devel. (ad hoc visitors list 1964-69), American Society of Civil Engineers (chairman publs. committee, urban planning and devel. division 1971-75, chairman committee on career guidance 1972-75), Manhattan Chamber of Commerce (director 1968-71), National Society Professional Engineers (executive board engrs. in education practice section 1968-71, secretary 1971—, chairman 1972-73), Am. Arbitration Association. Home: 4343 N 84th Place Scottsdale Arizona 85251

BLEDSOE, WOODROW WILSON, mathematics and computer sciences educator; born Maysville, Oklahoma, November 12, 1921; son of Thomas Franklin and Eva (Matthews) B.;

married Virginia Norgaard, January 29, 1944; children: Gregory Kent, Pamela Nelson, Lance Woodrow. Bachelor of Science in Math., University Utah, 1948; Doctor of Philosophy in Math., University California, 1953. Lecturer in math. University Calif.-Berkeley, 1951-53; mathematician, staff member Sandia Corp., Albuquerque, 1953-60, head math. department; 1957-60; mathematician, researcher Panoramic Research Incorporated, Palo Alto, California, 1960-65, president; 1963-65; professor math. computer sci. University Texas, Austin, 1966—, acting chairman department math.; 1967-69, chairman department math.; 1973-75, Ashbel Smith professor math. and computer sci.; 1981—; on leave University Texas, 1984-87; vice president, director artificial intelligence Microelectronics and Computer Tech. Corp., Austin, 1984-87; general chairman International Joint Conference Artificial Intelligence, Massachusetts Institute of Technology, Cambridge, Massachusetts, 1975-77; trustee International Joint Conference on Artificial Intelligence, 1978-83; member subcom. for computer sci. Adv. Committee Math. and Computer Sci., National Science Foundation, 1979-82; visiting professor Massachusetts Institute of Technology, 1970-71, Carnegie-Mellon University, Pittsburgh, 1978. Editor: (with Donald Loveland) Automated Theorem Proving, 1984; board editors International Journal of Artificial Intelligence, 1972—, also rev. editor, 1973-77; author numerous tech. papers in refereed journals, confs. Vice-pres. Capitol Area council Boy Scouts Am., Austin, 1979-83. Served to captain United States Army, 1940-45, European Theatre of Operations. National Science Foundation research grantee, 1972—; National Institutes of Health research grantee, 1967-72. Member Am. Math. Society, Association Computing Machinery, Am. Association Artificial Intelligence (president 1984-85). Mormon. Office: Department Math U Tex Robert Lee Moore Hall 8 100 Austin Texas 78712

BLOBEL, GUNTER, cell biologist, educator; born Waltersdorf, Silesia, Germany, May 21, 1936. Doctor of Medicine, University Tubingen, Federal Republic of Germany, 1960; Doctor of Philosophy, University Wisconsin, 1967. Assistant professor cell biology Rockefeller University, New York City, 1969-73, associate professor; 1973-76, professor; 1976—. Contributor articles to professional journals and chapters to books. Recipient Gairdner Foundation award, 1982, Warburg medal German Biochem. Society, 1983, Wilson medal Am. Society Cell Biology, 1986, Louisa Gross Horwitz prize Columbia University, 1987. Member National Acad. Sciences (United States Steel award in molecular biology 1978, Richard Lounsberg award 1983), Am. Acad. Arts and Sciences, Japan Biochem. Society (hon.). Office: Rockefeller U Cell Biology Labs 1230 York Avenue New York New York 10021

BLOCH, ERICH, electrical engineer, science foundation executive; born Sulzburg, Germany, January 9, 1925; came to United States, 1948, naturalized, 1952; son of Joseph and Tony B.; married Renee Stern, March 4, 1948; 1 daughter, Rebecca Bloch Rosen. Student, Federal Polytechnic Institute, Zurich, Switzerland, 1945-48; Bachelor of Science in Electrical Engineering, University Buffalo, 1952; honorary degrees, University

Massachusetts, George Washington University, Colorado School Mines, State University of New York Buffalo, University Rochester, Oberlin College, University Notre Dame, Ohio State University. With International Business Machines Corporation, 1952-84; vice president general manager International Business Machines Corporation, East Fishkill, New York, 1975-80; vice president tech. personnel devel. International Business Machines Corporation, Armonk, New York, 1980-84; member committee computers in automated manufacturing National Research Council, 1980-84; director National Science Foundation, Washington, 1984—; Trustee Marist College, Poughkeepsie, New York, 1978-82. Author. Recipient U.S. medal of technology, 1985. Fellow Institute of Electrical and Electronics Engineers; member National Acad. Engineering, American Association for the Advancement of Science, Am. Society Manufacturing Engineers (hon.). Patentee in field. Office: National Sci Found 1800 G St Northwest Washington District of Columbia 20550

BLOCH, KONRAD EMIL, biochemist; born Neisse, Germany, January 12, 1912; came to United States, 1936, naturalized, 1944; son of Frederick D. and Hedwig (Steimer) B.; married Lore Teutsch, February 15, 1941; children—Peter, Susan. Chemical Engineer, Technische Hochschule, Munich, Germany, 1934; Doctor of Philosophy, Columbia University, 1938. Assistant professor biochemistry University Chicago, 1946-50, professor; 1950-54; Higgins professor biochemistry Harvard University, Cambridge, Massachusetts, 1954—. Recipient Nobel

prize in physiology and medicine, 1964, Ernest Guenther award in chemistry of essential oils and related products, 1965, National Medal of Sci., 1988. Fellow Am. Acad. Arts and Sciences; member National Acad. Sciences, Am. Philosophical Society. Office: Harvard U Department Biochemistry 12 Oxford St Cambridge Massachusetts 02138

BLOEMBERGEN, NICOLAAS, physicist, educator; born Dordrecht, The Netherlands, March 11, 1920; came to United States, 1952, naturalized, 1958; son of Auke and Sophia M. (Quint) B.; married Huberta D. Brink, June 26, 1950; children: Antonia, Brink, Juliana. Bachelor of Arts, Utrecht University, 1941, Master of Arts, 1943; Doctor of Philosophy, Leiden University, 1948; Master of Arts (honorary), Harvard, 1951. Teaching assistant Utrecht University, 1942-45; research fellow Leiden University, 1948; member Society Fellows Harvard, 1949-51, associate professor; 1951-57, Gordon McKay professor applied physics; 1957—, Rumford professor physics; 1974, Gerhard Gade university professor; 1980; visiting professor University Paris, 1957, University California, 1965, Collège de France, Paris, 1980; Lorentz guest professor University Leiden, 1973; Raman vis professor Bangalore, India, 1979; Fairchild distinguished scholar California Institute Tech., 1984. Author: Nuclear Magnetic Relaxation, 1948, Nonlinear Optics, 1965; also articles in professional journals. Recipient Buckley prize for solid state physics Am. Physical Society, 1958, Dirac medal University New South Wales (Australia), 1983; Stuart Ballantine medal Franklin Institute, 1961; Half Moon trophy Netherlands Club New

York, 1972; National medal of Sci., 1975; Lorentz medal Royal Dutch Acad., 1978; Frederic Ives medal Optical Society Am., 1979; von Humboldt sr. scientist award Munich, 1980; Nobel prize in Physics, 1981; Guggenheim fellow, 1957. Fellow Am. Physical Society, Am. Acad. Arts and Sciences, Institute of Electrical and Electronics Engineers (Morris Liebmann award 1959, Medal of Honor 1983); hon. fellow Indian Acad. Sciences; member Optical Society Am. (hon.), National, Royal Dutch acads. scis., National Acad. Engineering, Am. Philosophical Society, Deutsche Akademie der Naturforscher Leopoldina, Koninklyke Nederlandse Akademie von Wetenschappen (corr.), Paris Acad. Sciences (foreign associate). Office: Harvard U Department Physics Pierce Hall Cambridge Massachusetts 02138

BLOOM, FLOYD ELLIOTT, physician, research scientist; born Minneapolis, October 8, 1936; son of Jack Aaron and Frieda (Shochman) B.; married D'Nell Bingham, August 30, 1956 (deceased May 1973); children: Fl'Nell, Evan Russell; married Jody Patricia Corey, August 9, 1980. Bachelor of Arts cum laude, Southern Methodist University, 1956; Doctor of Medicine cum laude, Washington University, St. Louis, 1960; Doctor of Science (honorary), Southern Methodist University, 1983, Hahnemann University, 1985, University Rochester, 1985. Intern Barnes Hospital, St. Louis, 1960-61; resident internal medicine Barnes Hospital, 1961-62; research associate National Institute of Mental Health, Washington, 1962-64; fellow departments pharmacology, psychiatry and anatomy Yale School Medicine, 1964-66, assistant professor; 1966-67, associate professor; 1968; chief laboratory neuropharmacology National Institute of Mental Health, Washington, 1968-75; acting director div. special mental health National Institute of Mental Health, 1973-75; commissioned officer United States Public Health Service, 1974-75; director Arthur Vining Davis Center for Behavorial Neurobiology; professor Salk Institute, La Jolla, California, 1975-83; director div. preclin. neurosci. and endocrinology Research Institute of Scripps Clinic, La Jolla, 1983—; member Commission on Alcoholism, 1980-81, National Adv. Mental Health Council, 1976-80. Author: (with J.R. Cooper and R.H. Roth) Biochemical Basis of Neuropharmacology, 1971, 5th edition, 1987; (with Lazerson and Hofstadter) Brain, Mind, and Behavior, 1984, (with Lazerson) 2d edition, 1988; editor: Peptides: Integrators of Cell and Tissue Function, 1980; co-editor: Regulatory Peptides. Recipient A. Cressy Morrison award New York Acad. Sciences, 1971, A.E. Bennett award for basic research Society Biological Psychiatry, 1971, Arthur A. Fleming award Science magazine, 1973, Mathilde Solowey award, 1973, Biological Sci. award Washington Acad. Sciences, 1975, Alumni Achievement citation Washington University, 1980, McAlpin Research Achievement award Mental Health Association, 1980, Lectr.'s medal College de France, 1979, Steven Beering medal, 1985, Distinguished fellow Am. Psychiatric Association, 1986. Fellow American Association for the Advancement of Science (board dirs 1986—), Am. College Neuropsychopharmacology (member council 1976-78, chairman program committee 1987, president 1988—); member National Acad. Sci. (chairman section neurobiology 1979-83), Institute Medicine (member council 1986—), Am. Acad. Arts and Sciences, Society Neurosci. (secretary 1973-74, president 1976), Am. Society Pharmacology and Experimental Therapeutics, Am. Society Cell Biology, Am. Physiological Society, Am. Association Anatomists, Research Society Alcoholism (chairman program committee 1985-87). Home: 1145 Pacific Beach Dr Apartment B405 San Diego California 92109

BLUFORD, GUION STEWART, JR., astronaut, air force officer; born Philadelphia, November 22, 1942; son of Guion Stewart and Lolita Harriet (Brice) B.; married Linda M. Tull, April 7, 1964; children: Guion Stewart, James Trevor. Bachelor of Science in Aerospace Engineering, Pennsylvania State University, 1964; graduate, Squadron Officers School, 1971; Master of Science in Aerospace Engineering, Air Force Institute Tech., 1974, Doctor of Philosophy in Aerospace Engineering, 1978; Doctor of Science honorary, Florida Agricultural and Mechanical University, 1983; Master of Business Administration, University Houston, 1987; Doctor of Science (honorary), Texas Southern University, Virginia State University, Morgan State University, Baltimore, Stevens Institute Tech., Tuskeger University, Bowie (Maryland) State College, Thomas Jefferson University, Chicago State University, Georgian Ct. College. Commissioned 2d lieutenant United States Air Force, 1965, advanced through grades to colonel; 1983; F-4C fighter pilot 12 Tactical Fighter Wing United States Air Force, Cam Ranh Bay, Vietnam, 1966-67; T-38 instructor pilot 3630 Flying Training Wing United States Air Force, Sheppard Air Force Base, Wichita Falls, Texas, 1967-72; chief aerodynamics and airframe branch Air Force Flight Dynamics Laboratory, Wright-Patterson Air Force Base, Dayton, Ohio, 1975-78; National Aeronautics and Space Administration astronaut Johnson Space Center, Houston, 1978—. Decorated USAF Command Pilot Astronaut Wings; decorated Meritorious Service award, Commendation medal, Air medal with 9 oak leaf clusters, Cross of Gallantry with palm Vietnam; recipient Leadership award Phi Delta Kappa, 1962, Outstanding Flight Safety award Air Tng. Command, USAF, 1970, Mervin E. Gross award Air Force Force Institute Tech., 1974, Distinguished National Scientist award National Society Black Engrs., 1979, Group Achievement award National Aeronautics and Space Administration, 1980, Distinguished Alumni award Pennsylvania State University Alumni Association, 1983, 85, Space Flight medal National Aeronautics and Space Administration, 1983, Pennsylvania Distinguished Service medal, 1984. Fellow American Institute of Aeronautics and Astronautics (associate); member Air Force Association, Tau Beta Pi. Christian Scientist. Office: Johnson Space Center Astronaut Office CB Houston Texas 77058

BLUMBERG, BARUCH SAMUEL, research center executive; born New York City, July 28, 1925; son of Meyer and Ida (Simonoff) B.; married Jean Liebesman, April 4, 1954; children: Anne, George, Jane, Noah. Bachelor of Science, Union College, Schenectady, 1946; Doctor of Medicine, Columbia University, 1951; Doctor of Philosophy, Balliol College,

Oxford University, England, 1957; 16 honorary doctoral degrees. Intern, resident Columbia div. Bellevue Hospital, New York City, 1951-53; fellow in medicine Columbia-Presbyn. Medical Center, New York City, 1953-55; chief geog. medicine and genetics section National Institutes of Health, Bethesda, Maryland, 1957-64; associate director clinical research Fox Chase Cancer Center, Philadelphia, 1964-86, vice president population oncology; 1986—; University professor medicine and anthropology University Pennsylvania; George Eastman visiting professor Balliol College, Oxford University, 1983-84; Raman visiting professor, Bangalore, India, 1986; Ashland visiting professor University Kentucky, Lexington, 1986, 87. Contributor articles to professional journals.

Served to ensign United States Naval Reserve, 1943-46. Recipient Albion O. Berstein, M.D. award Medical Society State of New York, 1969, Grand Sci. award Phi Lambda Kappa, 1972, Annual award Eastern Pennsylvania br. Am. Society Microbiology, 1972, Passano award Williams & Wilkens Company, 1974, Modern Medicine Distinguished Achievement award, 1975, International award Gairdner Foundation, 1975, Karl Landsteiner Memorial award Am. Association Blood Banks, 1975, Nobel prize in physiology or medicine, 1976, Scopus award Am. Friends of Hebrew University, 1977, Strittmatter award Philadelphia County Medical Society, 1980, Distinguished Service award Pennsylvania Medical Society, 1982, Zubrow award Pennsylvania Hospital, 1986, Achievement award Sammy Davis Junior National Liver Institute, 1987, John P. McGovern award Am. Medical Writers Association, 1988.

Fellow American College of Physicians, Royal College Physicians; member National Acad. Sciences, Association Am. Physicians, Am. Society Clinical Investigation, Am. Society Human Genetics, Am. Association Physical Anthropologists, John Morgan Society, Chesapeake and Ohio Canal Society. Clubs: Provincetown Yacht, Atheneum. Discover causative agent hepatitis B and hepatitis B vaccine. Office: Fox Chase Cancer Center 7701 Burholme Avenue Philadelphia Pennsylvania 19111

BOBKO, KAROL J., astronaut; born New York City, December 23, 1937; son of Charles P. and Veronica (Sagatis) B.; married Frances Dianne Welsh, February 11, 1961; children: Michelle Ann, Paul Joseph. Bachelor of Science, United States Air Force Academy, 1959; graduate, United States Air Force Aerospece Research Pilot School, 1966; Master of Science, University Southern California, 1970. Commissioned officer United States Air Force, 1959, advanced through grades to colonel, pilot trainee; 1959-61, F-100 tactical fighter pilot; 1961-63, F-105 tactical fighter pilot; 1963-65, test pilot; 1965-67, astronaut; 1967—, member (pilot) 1st mission Space Shuttle Challenger; 1983; commander Space Shuttle Discovery Mission 51D, 1985; commander maiden voyage Space Shuttle Atlantis 51J, 1985. Office: NASA Johnson Space Center Houston Texas 77058

BOHMONT, DALE WENDELL, agricultural consultant; born Wheatland, Wyoming, June 7, 1922; son of J.E. and Mary (Armann) B.; married Marilyn J. Horn, March 7, 1969; children: Dennis E., Craig W. Bachelor of Science, University Wyoming, 1948, Master of Science,

1950; Doctor of Philosophy, University Nebraska, 1952; Master of Public Adminstration, Harvard University, 1959. Registered investment adv., Securities and Exchange Commn. Pub. school teacher Rock River, Wyoming, 1941-42; from research assistant to head plant sciences University Wyoming, 1946-60; associate director experiment station Colorado State University, 1961-63; dean, director agriculture University Nevada, Reno, 1963-82, dean, director emeritus; 1982—; president Bohmont Cons. Incorporated, 1982—; member Brucheum Group, Waynesboro, Virginia, 1984; consultant Devel. & Resources Corp., New York City, 1968—, Frederiksen, Kamine & Associates, Sacramento, 1976, Nevada Agricultural Foundation, 1986—; president Enide Corp., Reno, 1974-80, Thermal Dynamics International, 1983-87; co-chairman research planning (West Div. Agriculture Experiment Stations), 1975; member executive committee, council administrative heads agriculture National Association State University Land Grant Colleges, 1975. Contributor articles to professional journals; member editorial board: Crops and Soils, 1962—. Served with United States Army Air Force, 1942-45. Fellow American Association for the Advancement of Science, Agronomy Society; member Western Society Weed Sciences (hon.), Western Crop Sci. Society (president 1962-63), National Expt. Sta. Directors Association (chairman 1967-68), Am. Range Management Society, Farm House (director 1962—), Weed Society Am. (hon.), Sigma Xi, Gamma Sigma Delta (president 1964-66), Alpha Zeta, Alpha Tau Alpha, Phi Kappa Phi. Lodge: Lions (vice president 1985-86, president 1986-87

board dirs. 1985—). Home: 280 Island Avenue Reno Nevada 89501

BOHR, AAGE NIELS, physicist; born June 19, 1922; married Marietta Bettina Soffer (deceased 1978); 3 children: married Bente Meyer Scharff, 1981. Doctor of Philosophy, University Copenhagen, Denmark, 1954; Doctor honoris causa, Manchester University, 1961; honorary degrees, Oslo University, 1969, Heidelberg University, 1971, Trondheim University, 1972, Uppsala University, 1975. Junior sci. officer Department Sci. and Industrial Research, London, 1943-45; research associate Institute Theoretical Physics University Copenhagen, London, 1946—, professor physics; 1956—; director Niels Bohr Institute, 1962-70; member board Nordita, 1958-74, director, 1975-81. Author: Rotational States of Atomic Nuclei, 1954; (with Ben R. Mottelson) Nuclear Structure, Volume 1, 1969, Volume 2, 1975. Recipient Dannie Heineman prize, 1960; Pope Pius XI medal 1963; Atoms for Peace award, 1969; H.C. Ørsted medal, 1970; Rutherford medal, 1972; John Price Wetherill medal, 1974; Nobel prize in physics, 1975; Ole Römer medal, 1976. Member Danish, Norwegian, Yugoslavian, Polish, Swedish acads. scis., Royal Physiograph. Society Lund, Sweden, Am. Acad. Arts and Sciences, National Acad. Sciences (United States), Deutsche Akademie der Naturforscher Leopoldina, Am. Philosophical Society, Finska Vetenskaps-Societeten, Pontifical Acad. Research quantum physics; specialist nuclear physics. Office: Niels Bohr Institute, Blegdamsvej 15-17, DK-2100 Copenhagen Denmark

BOIS, PIERRE, medical research organization executive; born Oka,

Quebec, Canada, March 22, 1924; son of Henri and Ethier (Germaine) B.; married Joyce Casey, September 8, 1953; children: Monique, Marie, Louise. Doctor of Medicine, University Montreal, Quebec, 1953, Doctor of Philosophy, 1957; honorary doctorate, University Ottawa, Ontario, 1982, University Manitoba, 1985, University Sherbrooke, 1986. Research fellow pathology University Montreal, 1957-58, assistant associate professor department pharmacology; 1960-64, professor, head department anatomy; 1964-70, dean faculty medicine; 1970-81; president Medical Research Council of Can., 1981—; assistant professor histology, Ottawa, Ontario, Can., 1958-60. Contributor over 130 publications to professional journals. Recipient Distinguished Service award Can. Society Clinical Investigation, 1986, Francisco Hernandez award 1986. Fellow Royal Society Can., Royal College Physicians and Surgeons Can.; member Am., French Canadian associations anatomists, New York Acad. Sciences, American Association for the Advancement of Science, Can. Federation Biological Socs., Can. Society Clinical Investigation. Research and numerous publs. on morphological effects of hormones, histamine and mast cells in magnesium deficiency, muscular dystrophy, exptl. thymic tumors. Office: Med Research Council Can, 20th Floor Jeanne Mance Building, Tunney's Pasture, Ottawa, Ontario Canada K1A 0W9

BOLEY, BRUNO ADRIAN, engineering educator; born Gorizia, Italy, May 13, 1924; came to United States, 1939, naturalized, 1945; son of Orville F. and Rita (Luzzatto) B.; married Sara R. Kaufman, May 12, 1949 (deceased September 1983); children: Jacqueline, Daniel L. Bachelor of Civil Engineering, City College of New York, 1943, Doctor of Science honorary, 1982; Master in Aeronautical Engineering, Polytechnic Institute Brooklyn, 1945, Doctor of Science in Aeronautical Engineering, 1946. Assistant director structural research, aeronautical engineering department Polytechnic Institute Brooklyn, 1943-48; engineering specialist Goodyear Aircraft Corp., 1948-50; associate professor aeronautical engineering Ohio State University, 1950-52; associate professor civil engineering Columbia University, 1952-58, professor; 1958-68; Joseph P. Ripley professor engineering, chairman theoretical and applied mechanics Cornell University, Ithaca, New York, 1968-72; dean Technological Institute, Walter P. Murphy professor Northwestern University, Evanston, Illinois, 1973-86, dean emeritus, Walter P. Murphy professor emeritus; 1986—; professor civil engineering and engineering mechanics Columbia University, New York City, 1987—; member adv. committee George Washington University, Princeton University, Yale University, Cornell University, FAMU/FSU Institute Engineering, Duke University, National Cheng Kung University, Republic of China; chairman Midwest Program for Minorities in Engineering, 1975-82; board governors Argonne National Laboratory, 1983-86. Author: Theory of Thermal Stresses, 1960, High Temperature Structures and Materials, 1964, Thermoinelasticity, 1970, Crossfire in Professional Education, 1976; also articles, numerous tech. papers; editor-in-chief: Mechanics Research

Communications; board editors: Journal Thermal Stresses, Bulletin Mechanical Engring. Education, International Journal Computers and Structures, International Journal Engring. Science, International Journal Fracture Mechanics, International Journal Mechanical Engring. Scis., International Journal Solids and Structures, Journal Applied Mechanics, Journal Structural Mechanics Software, Letters in Applied and Engring. Science, Nuclear Engring. and Design. Recipient Distinguished Alumnus award Polytechnic Institute New York, 1974; Townsend Harris medal, 1981; NATO sr. sci. fellow, 1964-65. Fellow American Institute of Aeronautics and Astronautics, American Association for the Advancement of Science, Am. Acad. Mechanics (president 1974, Distinguished Service medal 1987); hon. member American Society of Mechanical Engineers (executive committee, president applied mechanics division 1975, board govs. 1984-86), National Acad. Engineering (chairman task force engineering education 1979-80, education adv. board 1982-86, editorial board The Bridge 1986—), Society Engineering Sciences (president 1975, Distinguished Service medal 1987), Association Chairmen Departments Mechanics (founder, president 1970-72), International Association Structural Mechanics in Reactor Tech. (chairman 1977, adv.-gen. 1979—), International Union Theoretical and Applied Mechanics (secretary Congress committee 1976-84, member bureau 1988—), Am. Society Engineering Education (project board 1987), New York Acad. Sciences (named Outstanding Educator of Am. 1971), United States National Committee Theoretical and Applied Math. (chairman 1975-79), Illinois Council Energy Research and Devel. (chairman 1979-84), England Foundation (conference committee 1986—). Office: Columbia U Department Civil Engring/Engring Mechanics 610 Mudd Building New York New York 10027

BOLLE, DONALD MARTIN, engineering educator; born Amsterdam, Netherlands, March 30, 1933; came to United States, 1955, naturalized, 1961; son of Maarten C. and Petronella (Kramer) B.; married Barbara June Girton, November 29, 1957; children—Alan Martin, Thomas Raymond, John Kenneth, Cornelis Adrianus. Bachelor of Science, Durham University, England, 1954; Doctor of Philosophy, Purdue University, 1961; Master of Arts (honorary), Brown University, 1966. Assistant professor electrical engineering Purdue University, 1961-62; National Science Foundation postdoctoral fellow department applied math. and theoretical physics Cambridge (England) University, 1962-63; assistant professor engineering Brown University, 1963-66, associate professor; 1966-70, professor; 1970-80; Chandler-Weaver chair electrical engineering Lehigh University, Bethlehem, Pennsylvania, 1980-81; dean Lehigh University (College Engineering and Applied Sci.), 1981-88; senior vice president acad. affairs Polytechnic University, Brooklyn, 1988—; Richard Merton visiting professor Technische Hochschule, Braunschweig, Germany, 1967; consultant in field. Fellow Institute of Electrical and Electronics Engineers, American Association for the Advancement of Science; member Am. Society Electrical Engineers, American Civil

Liberties Union, Sigma Xi, Tau Beta Pi, Eta Kappa Nu. Home: 769 Glen Cove Avenue Glen Head New York 11545 Office: Polytechnic University 333 Jay St Brooklyn New York 11201

BOLT, BRUCE ALAN, seismologist, educator; born Largs, Australia, February 15, 1930; son of Donald Frederick and Arlene (Stitt) B.; married Beverley Bentley, February 11, 1956; children: Gillian, Robert, Helen, Margaret. Bachelor of Science with honors, New England University College, 1952; Master of Science, University Sydney, Australia, 1954, Doctor of Philosophy, 1959, Doctor of Science (honorary), 1972. Math. master Sydney (Australia) Boys' High School, 1953; lecturer University Sydney, 1954-61, senior lecturer; 1961-62; research seismologist Columbia University, 1960; director seismographic stations University California, Berkeley, 1963-89, professor seismology; 1963—, chairman Grad. Council; 1980-82; Member committee on seismology National Acad. Sciences, 1966-72; member Day Fund committee National Acad. Sciences, 1974-76; also chairman national earthquake obs. committee 1979-81; member earthquake and wind forces committee Veteran's Administration, 1971-75; member California Seismic Safety Commission, 1978—, chairman, 1984-86; earthquake studies adv. panel United States Geological Survey, 1979-83, United States Geodynamics Committee, 1979-84. Author, editor textbooks on applied math., earthquakes, geological hazards and detection of underground nuclear explosions. Recipient H.O. Wood award in seismology, 1967, 72; Fulbright scholar, 1960; Churchill College Cambridge overseas fellow, 1980. Fellow Am. Geophysical Union (member geophys. monograph board 1971-78, chairman 1976-78), Geological Society Am., California Acad. Sciences (trustee 1981—, president 1982-85), Royal Astronomical Society (associate); member National Acad. Engineering, Seismological Society Am. (editor bull. 1965-70, director 1965-71, 73-76, president 1974-75), International Association Seismology and Physics Earth's Interior (executive committee 1964-67, vice president 1975-79, president 1980-83), Earthquake Engineering Research Institute, College Univs. Research Earthquake Engineering, (sec 1988—), Australian Math. Society, Sigma Xi. Clubs: University; Chit Chat. Research on dynamics, elastic waves, earthquakes, reduction geophysical observations; inferences on structure of earth's interior; consultant on seismic hazards. Home: 1491 Greenwood Terrace Berkeley California 94708

BOLT, RICHARD HENRY, science educator, business executive; born Peking, People's Republic of China, April 22, 1911; son of Richard Arthur and Beatrice (French) B.; married Katherine Mary Smith, June 24, 1933; children: Beatrice Bolt Scribner, Richard Eugene, Deborah Bolt Zieses. Bachelor of Arts in Architecture, University Calif.-Berkeley, 1933, Master of Arts in Physics, 1937, Doctor of Philosophy in Physics, 1939. Associate in physics University Illinois, 1940; National Research Council fellow in physics Massachusetts Institute of Technology, Cambridge, 1939-40; research associate Massachusetts Institute of Technology, 1941-43, associate professor physics; 1946-54, professor acoustics; 1954-64, adj. professor acoustics; 1983-85, lecturer political sci.; 1964-70, director acoustics laboratory; 1946-57; associate director National Science Foundation, 1960-63; principal consultant biophysics and biophys. chemistry study section National Institutes of Health, Bethesda, Maryland, 1957-59; chairman board Bolt, Beranek & Newman, Incorporated, Cambridge, 1953-76; chairman emeritus Bolt, Beranek & Newman, Incorporated, 1976—; visiting scientist Massachusetts State Legislature, 1977; guest lecturer Institute Acoustics, Academia Sinica, Peking and Xian, China, 1981; Sci. liaison officer Office of Scientific Research and Development, London, 1943-44; chief tech. aide National Def. Research Committee, 1944-45; member Armed Forces-Nat. Research Council chairman committee on hearing and bio-acoustics, 1953-55; president International Commission on Acoustics, 1951-57; chairman committee on sound spectrograms National Research Council, 1976-79; chairman adv. panel on White House tapes United States District Court District of Columbia, 1973-74. Author: (with other) Sonics, 1959; also numerous articles in sound, acoustics, noise control, sci. and public policy. Fellow Center for Advanced Study in Behavioral Sciences, Stanford, 1963-64; Phi Beta Kappa vis. scholar, 1979-80; New England award Engineering Socs. New England, 1980. Fellow Acoustical Society Am. (president 1949-50, Biennial award 1942, Gold medal 1979), Institute of Electrical and Electronics Engineers, Am. Acad. Arts and Sciences, American Association for the Advancement of Science (director 1969-77), Institute Noise Control Engineering, National Acad. Engineering, Acad. Applied Sciences, Massachusetts Engineers Council (chairman 1975-77), Am. Institute Physics (governor board 1957-63), Phi Beta Kappa, Sigma Xi, Eta Kappa Nu. Club: Cosmos (Washington). Home and Office: Tabor Hill Road Lincoln Massachusetts 01773

BOLZ, RAY EMIL, retired engineering educator; born Cleveland, October 24, 1918; son of William and Amelia Anne (Waechter) B.; married Jean Kathryn Hoeft, October 4, 1944; children: Elaine Kathryn, Nancy Jane, Patricia Lynn, Janet Gail. Bachelor of Science in Engineering, Case Institute Tech., 1940; Master of Science, Yale University, 1942, Doctor Engineering, 1949; Doctor Engineering, Worcester Polytechnic Institute, 1984. Research scientist National Advisory Committee for Aeronautics, 1942-46, head jet engine combustion section; 1944-46; assistant professor aeronautical engineering Rensselaer Polytechnic Institute, 1947-50; faculty Case Western Reserve University, 1950-73, professor aeronautical engineering, coordinator research; 1952-55, head department mechanical engineering; 1956-60, head engineering div.; 1960-67; dean Case Western Reserve University (School Engineering), 1967-73; vice president, dean faculty Worcester (Massachusetts) Polytechnic Institute, 1973-84, retired, 1984; Cons. to industry, 1950—; member adv. panel to engineering div. National Science Foundation, 1958-61, adv. panel to course content and improvement section, 1961-66; applied mechanics reviewer. Adv. committee Air Force Institute Tech., 1971-74. Trustee Worcester Craft Center, 1978—, president, 1983—. Recipient award for advancement basic and applied sci. Yale University, 1957; Outstanding Alumni award Case Western Res. University, 1968. Fellow American Society of Mechanical Engineers (vice president, chairman policy board education 1968-70); member Am. Society Engineering Education (member board engineering coll. council 1975-80), Am. Institute Aeronautical and Astronautics, Cleveland Engineering Society (board govs. 1972-73), Engineering Council Professional Devel. (chairman region II 1963-68), Sigma Xi. Unitarian (trustee 1964-68, president board trustees 1967-68). Home: 21 Lantern Lane Worcester Massachusetts 01609

BONICA, JOHN JOSEPH, physician; born Filicudi Messina, Italy, February 16, 1917; came to United States, 1927, naturalized, 1928; son of Antonino and Angela (Zagame) B.; married Emma Louise Baldetti, June 7, 1942; children: Angela, Charlotte, Linda, John. Student, Long Island University, 1934-37; Bachelor of Science, New York University, 1938; Doctor of Medicine, Marquette University, 1942; Doctor.Med.Scis. (honorary), University Siena, 1972; Doctor of Science (honorary), Medical College Wisconsin, 1977. Diplomate Am. Board Anesthesiology. Intern St. Vincent's Hospital, New York City, 1942-43; resident St. Vincent's Hospital, 1943-44; practice medicine specializing in anesthesiology; chairman anesthesiology University Washington Medical Center, Seattle, 1960-77; director department anesthesiology Tacoma General Hospital, 1947-63, Pierce County Hospital, 1947-60; clinical associate department anatomy University Washington, Seattle, 1948-60; professor University Washington, 1960—, chairman department anesthesiology; 1960-77; director Pain Clinic, Medical Center and affiliated hospitals, 1961-79, Anesthesia Research Center, 1968-77, Pain Center, University Washington, Seattle, 1980-83; visiting professor and lecturer various Am., European, Latin Am., Australian, New Zealand, Asiatic, Near Eastern, South African universities; senior consultant anesthesiology Madigan Army Hospital, Fort Lewis, Washington, 1947-77, Veteran's Administration Hospital, Seattle, 1960—; member anesthesia training committee National Institutes of Health, 1965-69, chairman general medical research program-project committee, 1970-72, chairman ad hoc committee on acupuncture, 1972-75; consultant ministries of health, Argentina, 1955, Brazil, 1959, Italy, 1954, 60, Sweden, 1969; consultant ministries of health Ministry Education Japan, 1969, Ministry Education and Health Venezuela, 1966, 69; member adv. committee Committee on Scholarly Communication with People's Republic of China, National Acad. Sciences, 1973-74; member Am. Medical Mission to People's Republic of China, 1973. Author: Management of Pain, 1953, Il Dolore, 1959, Tratamiento del Dolor, 1959, Clinical Applications of Diagnostic and Therapeutic Blocks, 1955, Manual of Anesthesiology for Medical Students, Interns and Residents, 1947, Anesthesia for Obstetrical Complications, 1965, Principles and Practice of Obstetric Analgesia and Anesthesia, Volume 1, 1967, Volume 2, 1969, Regional Anesthesia, 1969, Obstetric Analgesia and Anesthesia, 1972, 2d edition, 1980, Blocks of the Sympathetic Nervous System, 1981; also articles professional journals;

Editor: (with P. Procacci, C. Pagni) Recent Advances on Pain, Pathophysiology and Clinical Aspects, 1974, Proceedings International Symposium on Pain, 1974, Obstetric Analgesia-Anesthesia, Recent Advances and Current Status, 1975, (with D. Albe-Fessard) Proceedings First World Congress on Pain, 1976, Advances in Pain Research and Therapy, 1976, (with D. Albe-Fessard, J. Liebeskind) Proceedings 2d World Congress on Pain, Volume 3, 1979, (with V. Ventafridda) Proceedings International Symposium on Pain of Advanced Cancer, 1979, Proceedings ARNMD-Ann. Meeting, 1979; (with L. Ng) Proceedings NIH Conf. of 1979 Pain, Discomfort and Humanitarian Care, 1980; associate editor: Survey of Anesthesiology, 1957-72, Current Contents, 1972-78, Am. Journal Chinese Medicine, 1973-76, Survey of Anesthesiology, 1957-72; editor: Pain, 1975-85; foreign editor: Revista Mexicana de Anestesiologia, 1958-66.

Board of directors Tacoma Symphony, 1951-59, Seattle Opera, 1977-86 . Served from lieutenant to major United States Army, 1944-46. Decorated commander Order of Merit Italy, 1967; recipient Silver medal Swedish Medical Society, 1969; Gold medal for neuroscis. German Neurophysiologic Society, 1972; Gold medal University Palermo, 1954; Distinguished Service award Am. Society Anesthesiologists, 1973; Distinguished Achievement award Modern Medicine, 1975. Fellow Am. College Anesthesiologists, International College Anesthetists, Am. Acad. Anesthesiology, Faculty of Anaesthetists of Royal College Surgeons (hon.); member American Medical Association, King County, Washington State med. socs., Am. Society Anesthesiologists (2d vice president 1961, 1st vice president 1964, president 1966), Association University Anesthestists (president 1969), International Association for Study Pain (chairman organization committee 1973-75, president 1978-81), American Association for the Advancement of Science, World Medical Association, Washington State Society Anesthesiologists (president 1952), International Anesthesia Research Society, New York Acad. Sciences, Seattle, Tacoma surgical socs., Association des Anesthesiologistes Européens (hon.), Society Academic Anesthesia Chairmen, Association Am. Medical Colls., Am. Society Pharmaceutical and Experimental Therapy, Royal College Medicine, World Federation Socs. Anaesthesiologists (chairman sci. adv. committee 1968-72, sec.-gen. 1972-80, president 1980-84); hon. member Cuban Anesthesiology Society, Mexican Anesthesiology Society, Italian Anesthesiology Society (hon. president 1954), Argentinian Anesthesiology Society (hon. president 1955), Venezuelan Anesthesiology Society, Colombian Anesthesiology Society, Brazilian Anesthesiology Society, Chilean Anesthesiology Society, Swedish Anesthesiology Society, Association Anaesthetists of Great Brit. and Ireland, Association Research on Nervous and Mental Diseases (president 1978); member Alpha Omega Alpha. Home: 4732 E Mercer Way Mercer Island Washington 98040 Office: U Washington Department Anesthesiology RN-10 Seattle Washington 98195

BONNER, JOHN TYLER, biology educator; born New York City, May 12, 1920; son of Paul Hyde and Lilly Marguerite (Stehli) B.; married Ruth

Anna Graham, July 11, 1942; children: Rebecca, Jonathan Graham, Jeremy Tyndall, Andrew Duncan. Graduate, Phillips Exeter Academy, 1937; Bachelor of Science, Harvard University, 1941, Master of Arts, 1942, Doctor of Philosophy (Junior fellow 1942, 46-47), 1947; Doctor of Science (honorary), Middlebury College, 1970. Assistant to associate professor Princeton University, 1947-58, professor; 1958—, chairman department biology; 1965-77, 83-84, 87-88; lecturer embryology Marine Biological Laboratory, Woods Hole, Massachusetts, 1951-52; special lecturer University London, 1957; Brooklyn College, 1966; trustee Biological Abstracts, 1958-63; Member board editors Princeton University Press, 1965-68, 71, trustee, 1976-82. Author: Morphogenesis, 1952, Cells and Societies, 1955, The Evolution of Development, 1958, The Cellular Slime Molds, 1959, rev. edition 1967, The Ideas of Biology, 1962, Size and Cycle, 1965, The Scale of Nature, 1969, On Development, 1974, The Evolution of Culture in Animals, 1980, (with T.A. McMahon) On Life and Size, 1983, The Evolution of Complexity, 1988; also scientific papers.; Editor: Growth and Form, 1961, Evolution and Development, 1981; Asso. editor: Am. Scientist, 1961-69; editorial board: Am. Naturalist, 1958-60, 66-68, Journal General Physiology, 1962-69, Growth, 1955—, Differentiation, 1976—. Served from private to 1st lieutenant USAC, 1942-46; staff aeronautical medical lab. Wright Field, Dayton, Ohio. Sheldon traveling fellow Panama, 1941; Rockefeller traveling fellow France, 1953; Guggenheim fellow Scotland, 1958, 71-72; recipient Selman A. Waksman award for contributions to microbiology Theobold Smith Society; National Science Foundation sr. postdoctoral fellow, 1963. Fellow Am. Acad. Arts and Sciences; member Am. Society Naturalists, Society Growth and Devel., Mycological Society Am., Am. Philosophical Society, National Acad. Sciences, Phi Beta Kappa, Sigma Xi.

BONO, PHILIP, aerospace consultant; born Brooklyn, January 14, 1921; son of Julius and Marianna (Culcasi) B.; married Gertrude Camille King, December 15, 1950; children: Richard Philip, Patricia Marianna, Kathryn Camille. Bachelor of Education, University Southern California, 1947; postgraduate, 1948-49. Research and systems analyst North America Aviation, Inglewood, California, 1947; engineering design specialist Douglas Aircraft Company, Long Beach, California, 1948-49; preliminary design engineer Boeing Airplane Company, Seattle, 1950-59; deputy program manager Douglas Aircraft Company, Santa Monica, California, 1960-62; tech. assistant to director advanced launch vehicles and space stations Douglas Aircraft Company, Huntington Beach, California, 1963-65; branch manager advanced studies, senior staff engineer advanced tech. McDonnell Douglas Astronautics Company, Huntington Beach, 1966-73; senior engr.-scientist Douglas Aircraft Company, Long Beach, 1973-83; engineering specialist Northrop Advanced Systems Div., Pico Rivera, California, 1984-86; manager Cal-Pro Engineering Cons., Costa Mesa, 1986—; lecturer seminars, universities and institutes including Soviet Acad. Sciences, 1965. Author: Destination Mars, 1961, (with K. Gatland) Frontiers of Space, 1969; contributor articles to professional journals, chapters in books. Served with United States Naval Reserve, 1943-46. Recipient Golden Eagle award Council International Events, 1964, A.T. Colwell merit award Society Automotive Engrs., 1968, M.N. Golovine award Brit. Interplanetary Society, 1969, cert. of recognition National Aeronautics and Space Administration, 1983, Heritage medallion Project Italia, 1988; named engineer of distinction Engrs. Joint Council, 1971, Knight of Mark Twain, 1979. Fellow American Association for the Advancement of Science, Royal Aeronautical Society, Brit. Interplanetary Society (editorial adv. board), American Institute of Aeronautics and Astronautics (associate); member Am. Astronautical Society (senior), New York Acad. Sciences, International Acad. Astronautics, (academician), American Society of Mechanical Engineers, Society Automotive Engineers (chairman space vehicle committee, Project Italia Gold medallion 1988). Inventor recoverable single-stage space shuttle for NASA. Home: 1951 Sanderling Circle Costa Mesa California 92626

BORDOGNA, JOSEPH, educator, engineer; born Scranton, Pennsylvania, March 22, 1933; son of Raymond and Rose (Yesu) B. Bachelor of Science in Electrical Engineering, University Pennsylvania, 1955, Doctor of Philosophy, 1964; Master of Science, Massachusetts Institute of Technology, 1960. With Radio Corporation of America Corp., 1958-64; assistant professor University Pennsylvania, Philadelphia, 1964-68; associate professor University Pennsylvania, 1968-72, professor; 1972—, associate dean engineering and applied sci.; 1973-80, acting dean; 1980-81, dean; 1981—; director Moore School Electrical Engineering, 1976—, Alfred Fitler Moore chair, 1979—, also board of directors, Weston Incorporated, University City Sci. Center; master Stouffer College House, 1972-76; consultant industry, government, foundations; member National Medal of Sci. Committee, 1989—. Author: (with H. Ruston) Electric Networks, 1966; (with others) The Man-Made World, 1971; chairman editorial board Engring. Education, 1987—. Served with United States Navy, 1955-58. Recipient commendation for first spacecraft recovery, 1957, Lindback award for distinguished teaching University Pennsylvania, 1967, George Westinghouse award Am. Society Engineering Education, 1974, Engineer of Year award Philadelphia, 1984, Centennial medal Philadelphia College Textiles and Sci., 1988. Fellow Institute of Electrical and Electronics Engineers, (chairman Philadelphia section 1987-88, Centennial medal 1984), fellow American Association for the Advancement of Science; member Franklin Institute, Sigma Xi, Eta Kappa Nu, Tau Beta Pi. Home: 1237 Medford Road Wynnewood Pennsylvania 19096

BORLAUG, NORMAN ERNEST, agricultural scientist; born Cresco, Iowa, March 25, 1914; son of Henry O. and Clara (Vaala) B.; married Margaret G. Gibson, September 24, 1937; children: Norma Jean (Mrs. Richard H. Rhoda), William Gibson. Bachelor of Science in Forestry, University Minnesota, 1937, Master of Science in Plant Pathology, 1940, Doctor of Philosophy in Plant Pathology, 1941; Doctor of Science (honoris causa), Punjab (India) Agricultural University,

1969, Kanpur University, India, Royal Norwegian Agricultural College, Luther College, 1970, Michigan State University, University de la Plata, Argentina, Uttar Pradesh Agricultural University, India, 1971; Doctor of Science (honoris causa), University Arizona, 1972, University Florida, 1973, University Católica de Chile, 1974, University Hohenheim, Federal Republic Germany, 1976, University Agriculture, Lyallpur, Faisalabad, Pakistan, 1978, Columbia University, New York City, 1980, Ohio State University, 1981, University Minnesota, 1982, University Notre Dame, 1987; Doctor of Humane Letters, Gustavus Adolphus College, 1971; Doctor of Laws (honorary), New Mexico State University, 1973; Doctor of Agriculture (honorary), Tufts University, 1982; Doctor of Agricultural Scis. (honorary)., University Agricultural Scis., Hungary, 1980, Tokyo University Agriculture, 1981; Doctor Agrl. Scis. (honorary)., University Nacional Pedro Henriques Turena, Dominican Republic, University Central del Estes, Dominican Republic, 1983; Doctor Honoris Causa, University Mayor de San Simón, Bolivia, University de Buenos Aires, 1983, University de Cordoba, Spain, University Politécnica de Catalunya, Barcelon, Spain, 1986. With United States Forest Service, 1935-38; instructor University Minnesota, 1941; microbiologist E.I. DuPont de Nemours, 1942-44; research scientist in charge wheat improvement Cooperative Mexican Agricultural Program, Mexican Ministry Agriculture Rockefeller Foundation, Mexico, 1944-60; associate director assigned to Inter-Am. Food Crop Program Rockefeller Foundation, 1960-63; director wheat research and production program International Maize and Wheat Improvement Center, Mexico City, 1964—; consultant International Maize and Wheat Improvement Center, 1982—; consultant, collaborator Institute Nacional de Investigationes Agricolas, Mexican Ministry Agriculture, 1960-64; consultant Food and Agriculture Organization (of the United Nations), North Africa and Asia, 1960; ex-officio consultant wheat research and production problems to governments in, Latin Am., Africa, Asia.; Member Citizen's Commission on Sci., Law and Food Supply, 1973—, Commission Critical Choices for Am., 1973—, Council Agriculture Sci. and Tech., 1973—, Presdl. Commission on World Hunger United States of America, 1978-79; director Population Crisis Committee, 1971; asesor especial Fundacion para Estudios de la Poblacion A.C., Mexico, 1971—; member adv. council Renewable Natural Resources Foundation, 1973—; A.D. White Distinguished prof.-at-large Cornell University, 1983—; Distinguished professor International Agriculture, Department Soil & Crop Sciences, Texas Agricultural and Mechanical University, Jan.-May, 1984—; advisor The Population Institute, United States of America, 1978; board trustees Winrock International United States of America; life fellow Rockefeller Foundation, 1983—. Recipient Distinguished Service awards Wheat Producers Associations, and state govts. Mexican States of Guanajuato, Queretaro, Sonora, Tlaxcala and Zacatecas, 1954-60; Recognition award Agrl. Institute Can., 1966; Recognition award Instituto Nacional de Tecnologia Agropecuaria de Marcos Juarez, Argentina, 1968; Sci. Service award El Colegio de

Ingenieros Agronomos de Mexico, 1970; Outstanding Achievement award University Minnesota, 1959; E.C. Stakman award, 1961; named Uncle of Paul Bunyan, 1969; recipient Distinguished Citizen award Cresco Centennial Committee, 1966; National Distinguished Service award Am. Agrl. Editors Association,1967; Genetics and Plant Breeding award National Council Commercial Plant Breeders, 1968; Star of Distinction Government of Pakistan, 1968; citation and street named in honor Citizens of Sonora and Rotary Club, 1968; International Agronomy award Am. Society Agronomy, 1968; Distinguished Service award Wheat Farmers of Punjab, Haryana and Himachal Pradesh, 1969; Nobel Peace prize, 1970; Diploma de Merito El Instituto Tecnologico y de Estudios Superiores de Monterrey, Mexico, 1971; medalla y Diploma de Merito Antonio Narro Escuela Superior de Agricultura de la University de Coahuila, Mexico, 1971; Diploma de Merito Escuela Superior de Agricultura Hermanos Escobar, Mexico, 1973; award for service to agr. Am. Farm Bureau Federation, 1971; Outstanding Agrl. Achievement award World Farm Foundation, 1971; Medal of Merit Italian Wheat Scientists, 1971; Service award for outstanding contribution to alleviation of world hunger 8th Latin Am. Food Prodn. Conference, 1972; National award for Agrl. Excellence in Sci. National Agri-Mktg. Association, 1982, Distinguished Achievement award Council for Agrl. Sciences and Tech., 1982; inaugural lecturer, medal recipient Dr. S.B. Hendrick's Memorial Lectureship., 1981, other honored lecturships; named to Halls of Fame Oregon State University Agrl., 1981, Agrl. National Center, Bonner Springs, Kansas, 1984, Scandinavian-Am., U.S.A.,

1986; dedicated in his name Norman E. Borlaug Centro de Capitación y Formación de Agrs., Santa Cruz, Bolivia, 1983, Borlaug Hall University Minnesota, 1985, Borlaug Bldg. International Maize and Wheat Improvement Center, 1986; numerous other honors and awards from govts., educational instns., citizens groups. Hon. fellow Indian Society Genetics and Plant Breeding; member National Acad. Sci., Am. Society Agronomy (1st International Service award 1960, 1st hon. life member), Am. Association Cereal Chemists (hon. life member, Meritorious Service award 1969), Crop Sci. Society Am. (hon. life member), Soil Sci. Society Am. (hon. life member), Sociedad de Agronomia do Rio Grande do Sul Brazil (hon.), India National Sci. Acad. (foreign), Royal Agricultural Society England (hon.), Royal Society Edinburgh (hon.), Hungarian Acad. Sci. (hon.), Royal Swedish Acad. Agriculture and Forestry (foreign), Academia Nacional de Agronomia y Veterinaria (Argentina); hon. academician N.I. Vavilov Acad. Agricultural Sciences Lenin Order (Union of the Soviet Socialist Republics.), Am. Council on Sci. and Health (trustee 1978—), International Food Policy Research Institute (trustee 1976-82), Royal Society. Home: Agustin Ahumada 310-F, Lomas de Chapultepec, Mexico City 10, Mexico Office: Tex A&M U Department Soil & Crop Sci College Station Texas 77843

BORMAN, FRANK, airlines company executive, former astronaut; born Gary, Indiana, March 14, 1928; son of Edwin Borman; married Susan Bugbee; children: Fredrick, Edwin. Bachelor of Science, United States Military Academy, 1950; Master Aeronautical Engineering,

California Institute Tech., 1957; graduate, United States Air Force Aerospace Research Pilots School, 1960, Advanced Management Program, Harvard Business School, 1970. Commissioned 2d lieutenant United States Air Force, advanced through grades to colonel; 1965, retired; 1970; assigned various fighter squadrons United States and Philippines, 1951-56; instructor thermodynamics and fluid mechanics United States Military Acad., 1957-60; instructor United States Air Force Aerospace Research Pilots School, 1960-62; astronaut With Manned Spacecraft Center, National Aeronautics and Space Administration, until 1970; command pilot on 14 day orbital Gemini 7 flight December 1965, including rendezvous with Gemini 6; command pilot Apollo 8, 1st lunar orbital mission; December 1968; senior vice president for operations Eastern Air Lines, Incorporated, Miami, Florida, 1970-74, executive vice president, general operations manager; 1974-75, president, chief executive officer; 1975-85, chief executive officer; 1975-86, chairman board; 1976-86; vice chairman, director Texas Air Corp., Houston, from 1986. Recipient Distinguished Service award National Aeronautics and Space Administration, 1965; Collier Trophy. National Aeros. Association, 1968. Office: Patlex Corp 205 W Boutz Road Building 4 Suite 4 Las Cruces New Mexico 88005 also: Patlex Corp 20415 Nordhoff St Chatsworth California 91324

BOSE, AMAR GOPAL, electrical engineering educator; born Philadelphia, November 2, 1929; son of Noni Gopal and Charlotte (Mechlin) B.; married Prema Sarathy, August 17, 1960; children: Vanu Gopal, Maya. Bachelor of Science, Master of Science, Massachusetts Institute of Technology, 1952, Doctor of Science, 1956. Member faculty Massachusetts Institute of Technology, Cambridge, 1956—, professor electrical engineering; 1966—; chairman, chief executive officer Bose Corp., Framingham, Massachusetts. Author: (with Kenneth N. Stevens) Introductory Network Theory, 1965; patentee in acoustics, nonlinear systems and communications. Fulbright fellow India, 1956-57; recipient Baker Teaching award Massachusetts Institute of Technology, 1964, Teaching award Am. Society Engineering Education, 1965; named Inventor of Year, Intellectual Property Owners, 1987. Fellow Institute of Electrical and Electronics Engineers; member National Acad. Engineering, Sigma Xi, Tau Beta Pi, Eta Kappa Nu. Office: Bose Corp The Mountain Framingham Massachusetts 01701

BOTT, RAOUL, mathematician, educator; born Budapest, Hungary, September 24, 1923; son of Rudolf and Margit (Kovach) B.; married Phyllis Aikman, August 30, 1947; children: Anthony, Jocelyn, Renee, Candace. Bachelor Engineering, McGill University, Montreal, 1945, Master Engineering, 1946, Doctor of Science (honorary), 1987; Doctor of Science, Carnegie Institute Tech., 1949; Doctor of Science (honorary), Notre Dame University, 1979. Fellow Institute Advanced Studies, Princeton University, 1949-51, 55-57; instructor math. University Michigan, Ann Arbor, 1951-52, assistant professor; 1952-55, associate professor; 1957-59; professor Harvard University, Cambridge, Massachusetts, 1959—, W. Casper Graustein professor;

1969—. Author books and papers in various branches of math. and its relation to physics. Sloan fellow, 1956-60; hon. fellow St. Catharines College, 1985; recipient National Sci. Medal, President of U.S., 1987. Fellow Am. Acad. Arts & Sciences, Am. Math. Society (Veblen prize 1964); hon. member London Math. Society. Democrat. Roman Catholic. Avocations: music, nature. Home: 1 Richdale Avenue #9 Cambridge Massachusetts 02140 Office: Harvard University Department of Math 1 Oxford St Cambridge Massachusetts 02138

BOVEE, KENNETH C., veterinary medicine educator; born Chicago, September 1, 1936; married, 1958; 3 children. Bachelor of Science, Ohio State University, 1958, Doctor of Veterinary Medicine, 1961; Master in Medical Science, University Pennsylvania, 1969. Diplomate Am. Coll. Vet. Internal Medicine. Intern, resident Animal Medical Center, New York, 1961-64; from assistant professor to associate professor University Pennsylvania School Vet. Medicine, Philadelphia, 1967-78, professor medicine; 1978—, chairman department clinical studies; 1979-84, Corinne and Henry Bower Chair medicine; 1980—; chairman grad. group Comparative Medical Sci. National Institutes of Health fellow University Pennsylvania Graduate School Medicine, 1964-67. Member Am. Society Nephrology, International Society Nephrology, Am. Federation Clinical Research. Office: U Pennsylvania School Veteran Medicine Philadelphia Pennsylvania 19104

BOVET, DANIEL, physiologist; born Neuchatel, Switzerland, 1907; son of Pierre and Amy (Babut) B.; married Filomena Nitti, 1938; 1 son. Doctor of Science, University Geneva; honorary doctorates, University Palermo, University Rio de Janeiro, others. Assistant in physiology University Geneva, 1928-29; assistant Institute Pasteur, Paris, 1929-39, director laboratory; 1939-47; director laboratories therapeutic chemistry Istituto Superiore di Sanità, Rome, 1947-64; professor pharmacology University Sassari, 1964-71; professor psychobiology University Rome, 1971-82, hon. professor; 1982—; director laboratory psychobiology and psychopharmacology Consiglio Nazionale della Richerche, 1969-75. Author: (with others) Structure chimique et activité pharmacodynamique des medicaments du système nerveux vegetatif, 1948; (with others) Curare and Curare-like Agents, 1959; (with others) Controlling Drugs, 1974. Recipient Nobel prize for physiology and medicine, 1957; decorated grand officer Order Italian Republic. Member Accademia Nazionale dei Lincei, Royal Society (England) (foreign).

BOYER, HERBERT WAYNE, biochemist; born Pittsburgh, July 10, 1936; married Grace B., 1959; 2 children. Bachelor of Arts, St. Vincent College, Latrobe, Pennsylvania, 1958, Doctor of Science (honorary), 1981; Master of Science, University Pittsburgh, 1960, Doctor of Philosophy, 1963. Member faculty University California, San Francisco, 1966—; professor biochemistry University California, 1976—; investigator Howard Hughes Medical Institute, 1976—; co-founder, director Genentech, Incorporated, South San Francisco, California, now consultant. Member editorial board: Biochemistry.

Recipient V.D. Mattai award Roche Institute, 1977; Albert and Mary Lasker award for basic med. research, 1980; U.S. Pub. Health Service postdoctoral fellow, 1963-66. Fellow American Association for the Advancement of Science; member Am. Society Microbiology, Am. Acad. Arts and Sciences, National Acad. Sciences. Office: U California Department Biochemistry HSE 1506 San Francisco California 94143

BOYER, ROBERT ERNST, geologist, educator; born Palmerton, Pennsylvania, August 3, 1929; son of Merritt Ernst and Lizzie Venetta (Reinard) B.; married Elizabeth Estella Bakos, September 1, 1951; children—Robert M., Janice E., Gary K. Bachelor of Arts, Colgate University, 1951; Master of Arts, Ind. University, 1954; Doctor of Philosophy, University Michigan, 1959. Instructor geology University Texas, Austin, 1957-59; assistant professor University Texas, 1959-62, associate professor; 1962-67, professor; 1967—, chairman department geological sciences; 1971-80; dean University Texas (College Natural Sciences), 1980—; executive director Natural Sciences Foundation, 1980—; chairman executive committee Geology Foundation, 1971-80. Author: Activities and Demonstrations for Earth Science, 1970, Geology Fact Book, 1972, Oceanography Fact Book, 1974, The Story of Oceanography, 1975, Solo-Learn in the Earth Sciences, 1975, GEO-Logic, 1976, GEO-VUE, 1978; editor: Texas Journal of Sci, 1962-65, Journal of Geological Edn, 1965-68. Fellow Geological Society Am., American Association for the Advancement of Science; member Texas Acad. Sci.

(hon. life, president 1968), National Association Geology Teachers (president 1974-75), Am. Geological Institute (president 1983), Am. Association Petroleum Geologists, Austin Geological Society (president 1975), Gulf Coast Associate Geological Society (president 1977). Home: 7644 Parkview Circle Austin Texas 78731

BOYLAN, DAVID RAY, chemical engineer, educator; born Belleville, Kansas, July 22, 1922; son of David Ray and Mabel (Jones) B.; married Juanita R. Sheridan, March 24, 1944; children: Sharon Rae, Gerald Ray, Elizabeth Anne, Lisa Dianne. Bachelor of Science in Chemical Engineering, University Kansas, 1943; Doctor of Philosophy, Iowa State University, 1952. Instructor University Kansas, 1942-43; project engineer General Chemical Company, Camden, New Jersey, 1943-47; senior engineer Am. Cyanamid Company, Elizabeth, New Jersey, 1947; plant manager Arlin Chemical Company, Elizabeth, 1947-48; faculty Iowa State University, Ames, 1948—; professor chemical engineering Iowa State University, 1956—; associate director Iowa State University (Engineering Experiment Station), 1959—; director Iowa State University (Engineering Research Institute), 1966—; dean Iowa State University (College Engineering), 1970-88, professor chemical engineering; 1988—. Fellow Am. Institute Chemical Engineers, Am. Chemical Society (Merit award 1987), American Association for the Advancement of Science; member National Society Professional Engineers (vice president), Professional Engineers in Education (chairman), Am. Society Engineering Education, Sigma Xi, Phi Lambda

Upsilon, Sigma Tau, Phi Kappa Phi, Tau Beta Pi. Research in transient behavior and flow of fluids through porous media, unsteady state and fertilizer tech., devel. fused-phosphate fertilizer processes, theoretical and exptl. correlation of filtration Research in transient behavior and flow of fluids through porous media, unsteady state and fertilizer tech., devel. fused-phosphate fertilizer processes, theoretical and exptl. correlation of filtration. Home: 1516 Stafford St Ames Iowa 50010

BRAMBLE, JAMES HENRY, mathematician, educator; born Annapolis, Maryland, December 1, 1930; son of Charles Clinton and Edith (Rinker) B.; married Margaret Hospital Hays, June 25, 1977; children: Margot, Tamara, Mary, James; 1 stepchild, Myron A. Hays. Bachelor of Arts, Brown University, 1953; Master of Arts, University Maryland, 1955, Doctor of Philosophy, 1958; Doctor of Science (honorary), Chalmers University Tech., Góteborg, Sweden, 1985. Mathematician General Electric Company, Cincinnati, 1957-59, Naval Ordnance Laboratory, White Oak, Maryland, 1959-60; assistant professor, associate professor, professor University Maryland, 1960-68; professor Cornell University, Ithaca, New York, 1968—; director Center Applied Math., 1974-80; consultant Brookhaven National Laboratory, 1976—; visiting professor Chalmers University Tech., Göteborg, Sweden, 1970, 72, 73, 76, University Rome, 1966-67, Ecole Polytechnic, Paris, 1978, Lausanne, Switzerland, 1979; visiting professor University Paris, 1981; lecturer in field. Chmn. editorial board Mathematics of Computation, 1975-84; contributor articles professional journals.

Member Am. Math. Society. Offices: Cornell U Department of Math Ithaca New York 14853

BRAND, VANCE DEVOE, astronaut; born Longmont, Colorado, May 9, 1931; son of Rudolph William and Donna (DeVoe) B.; married Joan Virginia Weninger, July 25, 1953; children: Susan Nancy, Stephanie, Patrick Richard, Kevin Stephen; married Beverly Ann Whitnel, November 3, 1979; children—Erik Ryan, Dane Vance. Bachelor of Science in Business, University Colorado, 1953, Bachelor of Science in Aeronautical Engineering, 1960; Master of Business Administration, University of California at Los Angeles, 1964; graduate, United States Naval Test Pilot School, Patuxent River, Maryland, 1963. With Lockheed-Calif. Company, Burbank, 1960-66; flight test engineer Lockheed-Calif. Company, 1961-62, traveling engineer representative; 1962-63, engineering test pilot; 1963-66; astronaut National Aeronautics and Space Administration Johnson Space Center, Houston, 1966—; command module pilot Apollo-Soyuz mission National Aeronautics and Space Administration Johnson Space Center, 1975, commander STS-5 Mission; 1982, commander STS 41-B Mission; 1984. Served with United States Marine Corps Reserve, 1953-57. Recipient Distinguished Service medal National Aeronautics and Space Administration; Exceptional Service medal National Aeronautics and Space Administration.; 2 Space medals National Aeronautics and Space Administration. Fellow Am. Astronomical Society, Society Experimental Test Pilots, American Institute of Aeronautics and Astronautics. Office: Code CB Lyndon

B Johnson Space Center Houston Texas 77058

BRANDENSTEIN, DANIEL CHARLES, astronaut, naval officer; born Watertown, Wisconsin, January 17, 1943; son of Walter C. and Agnes (Holzworth) B.; married Jane A. Wade, January 2, 1966; 1 daughter, Adelle. Bachelor of Science, University Wisconsin, River Falls, 1965; postgraduate, United States Naval Text Pilot School, Patuxent River, Maryland, 1971. Commissioned officer United States Navy, 1965, advanced through grades to captain; student aviator United States Navy, Pensacola, Florida, 1965-67; aviator United States Navy, Whidbey Island, Washington, 1967-71; test pilot United States Navy, Patuxent River, Maryland, 1971-74; aviator United States Navy, Whidbey Island, Washington, 1974-78; astronaut National Aeronautics and Space Administration Johnson Space Center, Houston, 1978—; chief astronaut office National Aeronautics and Space Administration Johnson Space Center, 1987—. Decorated Legion of Honor (France); recipient 26 medals and award USN, 1968-71; recipient Distinguished Alumnus award University Wisconsin, 1982, Space Flight medal National Aeronautics and Space Administration, 1982. Member Society Experimental Text Pilots, American Institute of Aeronautics and Astronautics, United States Naval Institute. Office: NASA Lyndon B Johnson Space Center Houston Texas 77058

BRANSCOMB, LEWIS MCADORY, physicist; born Asheville, North Carolina, August 17, 1926; son of Bennett Harvie and Margaret (Vaughan) B.; married Margaret Anne Wells, October 13, 1951; children—Harvie Hammond, Katharine Capers. Bachelor of Arts summa cum laude, Duke University, 1945, Doctor of Science (honorary); Master of Science, Harvard University, 1947, Doctor of Philosophy, 1949; Doctor of Science (honorary), Polytechnic Institute New York, Clarkson College, Rochester University, University Colorado, Western Michigan University, Lycoming College, University Alabama, Pratt Institute; Rutgers University, Lehigh University, University Notre Dame; Doctor of Humane Letters (honorary), Pace University. Instructor physics Harvard University, 1950-51; lecturer physics University Maryland, 1952-54; visiting staff member University College, London, 1957-58; chief atomic physics section National Bureau Standards, Washington, 1954-60; chief atomic physics div. National Bureau Standards, 1960-62; chairman Joint Institute Laboratory Astrophysics, University Colorado, 1962-65, 68-69; chief laboratory astrophysics div. National Bureau Standards, Boulder, Colorado, 1962-69; professor physics University Colorado, 1962-69; director National Bureau Standards, 1969-72; chief scientist, vice president International Business Machines Corporation, Armonk, New York, 1972-86; member corporate management board International Business Machines Corporation, Armonk, 1983-86; director pub. policy program Kennedy School Government, Harvard University, Cambridge, Massachusetts, 1986—, Albert Pratt pub. service professor; 1988—; mem.-at-large Def. Sci. Board, 1969-72; member high level policy group sci. and tech. information Organization

Economic Cooperative and Devel., 1968-70; member President's Sci. Adv. Committee, 1965-68, chairman panel space sci. and tech., 1967-68; member National Sci. Board, 1978-84, chairman, 1980-84; member President's National Productivity Adv. Committee, 1981-82; member standing committee controlled thermonuclear research Atomic Energy Commission, 1966-68; member adv. committee on sci. and foreign affairs Department State, 1973-74; member U.S.-USSR Joint Commission on Sci. and Tech., 1977-80; chairman Committee on Scholarly Communications with the People's Republic of China, 1977-80; chairman Carnegie Forum Task Force on Teaching as a Profession, 1985-86; director Mobil Corp., Lord Corp., Mitre Corp., Draper Laboratories, Incorporated; member pres.'s board visitors University Oklahoma, 1968-70; member astronomy and applied physics visiting committees Harvard University 1969-83, board overseers, 1984-86 ; member physics visiting committee M.I.T., 1974-79; member President's Committee National Medal Sciences, 1970-72; board of directors Am. National Standards Institute, 1969-72; trustee Carnegie Institution, 1973—, Polytechnic Institute New York, 1974-78, Vanderbilt University, 1980—, National Geog. Society, 1984—, Woods Hole Oceanographic Institution, 1985—. Editor: Rev. Modern Physics, 1968-73. Served to lieutenant (junior grade) United States Naval Reserve, 1945-46. U.S. Pub. Health Service fellow, 1948-49; Junior fellow Harvard Society Fellows, 1949-51; recipient Rockefeller Pub. Service award, 1957-58, Gold medal exceptional service Department Commerce, 1961, Arthur Flemming award District of Columbia Junior Chamber of Commerce, 1962, Samuel Wesley Stratton award Department Commerce, 1966, Career Service award National Civil Service League, 1968, Proctor prize Research Society Am., 1972. Fellow Am. Physical Society (chairman division electron physics 1961-68, president 1979), American Association for the Advancement of Science (director 1969-73), Am. Acad. Arts and Sciences; member National Acad. Sciences (council 1972-75), National Acad. Engineering (Arthur Bueche award), Washington Acad. Sciences (Outstanding Sci. Achievement award 1959), National Acad. Public Administration, Am. Philosophical Society, Phi Beta Kappa, Sigma Xi (president 1985-86). Club: Am. Yacht (Rye, New York). Office: Harvard U Kennedy School Govt 79 J F Kennedy St Cambridge Massachusetts 02138

BREEN, JOHN EDWARD, civil engineer, educator; born Buffalo, May 1, 1932; son of Timothy J. and Alice C. (Keenan) B.; married Marian T. Killian, June 20, 1953; children: Mary L., Michael T., Dennis P., Sheila A., Sean E., Kerry T., Christopher D. Bachelor of Civil Engineering, Marquette University, Milwaukee, 1953; Master of Science in Civil Engineering, University Missouri, 1957; Doctor of Philosophy, University Texas, Austin, 1962. Registered professional engineer, Texas, Missouri. Structural designer Harnischfeger Corp., Milwaukee, 1952-53; assistant professor University Missouri, Columbia, 1957-59; member faculty University Texas, Austin, 1959—, professor civil engineering; 1969—, J.J. McKetta professor engineering; 1977-81, Carol Cockrell Curran chair engineering; 1981-84, Nasser I. Al-

Rashid chair civil engineering; 1984—; director P.M. Ferguson Structural Engineering Laboratory, Balcones Research Center, 1967-85; consultant in field. Contributor articles to professional journals. Served to lieutenant United States Naval Reserve, 1953-56. Recipient Teaching Excellence award General Dynamics Corp., 1971, Teaching Excellence award University Texas Student Association, 1963, Teaching Excellence award Standard Oil Foundation Ind., 1968, Arthur R. Anderson award Am. Concrete Institute, 1987, Arthur J. Boase award Reinforced Concrete Research Council, 1987. Fellow Am. Concrete Institute (board direction 1974-77, Wason medal 1972, 83, Raymond C. Reese Research medal 1972, 79, Kelly medal 1981, Anderson medal 1987, Raymond Davis lecturer 1978), American Society of Civil Engineers (T.Y. Lin medal 1985, A.J. Boase Reinforced Concrete Research Council award 1987); member National Acad. Engineering, Sigma Xi, Chi Epsilon, Tau Beta Pi. Democrat. Roman Catholic. Club: Austin Yacht (commodore 1977). Home: 8603 Azalea Trail Austin Texas 78759 Office: Ferguson Lab University Texas 10100 Burnet Road Austin Texas 78758

BREESE, CHARLES REAGAN, civil engineering educator; born Lewiston, Utah, October 7, 1917; son of Charles L. and Alta L. (Whitt) B.; married Dorothy L. Edholm, November 26, 1958; children by previous marriage: Charles Reagan, Cheryl Breese Wells. Bachelor of Science in Mechanical Engineering, University Nevada, 1948, Master of Science in Civil Engineering, 1956. Member faculty University Nevada, Reno,

1948-51, 55—; professor civil engineering University Nevada, 1967—, dean College Engineering; 1971-82; principal civil engineer, City of Reno, 1951-55, consultant in field. Author articles on mineral aggregate degredation, freeze-thaw behavior of mineral aggregates in Portland cement concretes. Served to lieutenant commander, aviator United States Naval Reserve, 1940-45. Member American Society of Civil Engineers, Tau Beta Pi, Phi Kappa Phi. Lodge: Masons. Office: College Engring University Nevada Reno Nevada 89557

BRENNER, BARRY MORTON, physician; born Brooklyn, October 4, 1937; son of Louis and Sally (Lamm) B.; married Jane P. Deutsch, June 12, 1960; children: Robert, Jennifer. Bachelor of Science, Long Island University; Doctor of Medicine, University Pittsburgh; Master of Arts (honorary), Harvard University; Doctor of Science. (honorary), Long Island University. Assistant professor medicine University Calif.-San Francisco, 1969-72, associate professor medicine and physiology; 1972-75; professor medicine and physiology University California, San Francisco, 1975-76; Samuel A. Levine professor medicine Harvard Medical School, Boston; with Peter Bent Brigham Hospital, Boston, 1976—; director renal div. Brigham and Women's Hospital, Boston, 1979—; director physician-scientist program, Harvard Medical School, 1984—, Harvard Center for Study of Kidney Diseases, 1987—; consultant National Institutes of Health. Co-editor: The Kidney, 2 volumes, 1976, 3d edition, 1986, Contemporary Issues in Nephrology, 1978—, Acute Renal Failure, 1983—, 2d edition, 1988;

contributor numerous articles to various publications. Recipient research award National Institutes of Health, Homer W. Smith award New York Heart Association, George E. Brown award Am. Heart Association; Merit award National Institutes of Health; SKF Distinguished Scientist award. Member Am. Physiological Society, Association Am. Physicians, Western Association Physicians, Am. Society Nephrology (councillor, president), Am. Society Clinical Investigation (councillor, vice president), Salt and Water Club, Interurban Clinical Club, Alpha Omega Alpha, Phi Sigma. Office: 75 Francis St Boston Massachusetts 02115

BRIGGS, RODNEY ARTHUR, agronomist, consultant; born Madison, Wisconsin, March 18, 1923; son of George McSpadden and Mary Etta (McNelly) B.; married Helen Kathleen Ryall, June 1, 1944; children: Carolyn, Kathleen, David, Andrew, Amy. Student, Oshkosh (Wisconsin) State College, 1941-42; Bachelor of Science in Agronomy, University Wisconsin, 1948; Doctor of Philosophy in Field Crops, Rutgers University, 1953. Extension associate farm crops Rutgers University, New Brunswick, New Jersey, 1949-50, 52-53; member faculty University Minnesota, 1953-73; superintendent West Central School and Experiment Station, Morris, Minnesota, 1959-60; professor agronomy, dean University Minnesota; administrv. head, provost University Minnesota (Morris Campus), 1960-69, secretary board regents; 1971-72, executive assistant to president; 1971-73; on leave of absence Ford Foundation as associate director, director research International Institute Tropical Agriculture, Ibadan, Nigeria, 1969-71;

president Eastern Oregon State College, La Grande, 1973-83; executive vice president Am. Society Agronomy/Crop Sci. Society Am./Soil Sci. Society Am., Madison, Wisconsin, 1982-85; independent consultant 1985—; chairman National Silage Evaluation Committee, 1957; secretary Minnesota Corp Improvement Association, 1954-57; columnist crops and soils Minnesota Farmer magazine, 1954-59; judge grain and forage Minnesota State Fair, 1954-61; member educational mission to Taiwan, Am. Association State Colleges and Universities, 1978, chairman educational mission to Colombia, 1982, state representative, 1974-76, member special task force of pres.'s on intercollegiate athletics, 1976-77, member national committee on agriculture, renewable resources and rural devel., 1978-82, national secretary-treasurer, 1980-82; member committee on government relations Am. Council Education Committee, 1981; member Gov.'s Commission on Foreign Language and International Studies, State Oregon, 1980-83; Member Gov.'s Commission Law Enforcement, 1967-69; adv. committee State Planning Agency, 1968-69, Minnesota Interinstnl. TV, 1967-69; invited participant The Role of Sci. & Emergency Societies in Devel., African Regional Seminar American Association for the Advancement of Science, 1984. Com. member African sci. journal AAAS, 1986-88. Board of directors Rural Banking School, 1967-69; board of directors Channel 10 ETV, Appleton, Minnesota, Grande Ronde Hospital, 1980-83; chairman policy adv. committee Oregon Department Environmental Quality, 1979-81. Served with infantry Army of the United States, 1942-46, 50-52.

Recipient Staff award University Minnesota, 1959, special award University Minnesota at Morris, 1961; commendation Soil Conservation Society Am., 1965; Rodney A. Briggs Library named in his honor University Minnesota, Morris, 1974. Fellow American Association for the Advancement of Science, Am. Association Staff Colls. & Univs., Soil Conservation Society Am. (president emeritus 1988); member Am. Society Agronomy, Crop Sci. Society Am., American Association for the Advancement of Science, Wisconsin Acad. Sci. and Arts, Am. Forage and Grassland Council, Am. Institute Biological Sciences (director 1982-83), American Civil Liberties Union, Sigma Xi, Alpha Gamma Rho. Congregationalist. Home: 1109 Gilbert Road Madison Wisconsin 53711

BRIGGS, WILLIAM EGBERT, mathematics educator; born Sioux City, Iowa, March 26, 1925; son of Egbert Estabrook and Berenice (Reynolds) B.; married Muriel Mae Lambert, August 29, 1947; children: William L., Roger P., Barbara E., Lindsey A. Bachelor of Arts, Morningside College, 1948, Doctor of Science, 1968; Master of Arts, University Colorado, 1949, Doctor of Philosophy, 1953. Assistant instructor Morningside College, 1947; math. teacher Elwood (Iowa) High School, 1948, Baseline Junior High School, Boulder, Colo, 1954-55; research associate University Colorado, 1953-54, faculty; 1955—, professor math.; 1964-88, professor emeritus, 1988—; acting dean University Colorado (College Arts and Sciences), 1963-64, dean; 1964-80, acad. dean semester at sea; fall 1980; National Science Foundation faculty fellow, hon.

research associate University College, London, England, 1961-62; member Region XIII Selection committee Woodrow Wilson Foundation Fellowship Program; board of directors Education Projects Incorporated, 1966—; chairman math. adv. committee Colorado Department Education, 1964-66; member commission on arts and sciences National Association State Universities and Land Grant Colleges, 1970-73, 75-78; director Council Colleges Arts and Sciences, 1969-73, 74-77, pres.-elect, 1975, president, 1976. Author: (with others) Analytic Geometry, 1963; also articles. Board of directors Colorado Congregational Conference, 1953-56, Colorado Conference United Church Christ, 1963-68; Board of directors Boulder Council Chs. and Synagogues, 1981-84, Pres.-elect, 1981, president, 1982, 85. Served to 1st lieutenant Army of the United States, 1943-46. Recipient Stearns award Associated Alumni University Colorado; University Colorado medal. Member Math. Association Am. (governor 1963-66), Am. Math. Society, American Association of University Profs., London Math. Society, Rocky Mountain Math. Consortium (chairman 1984), Phi Beta Kappa, Sigma Xi. Home: 1440 Sierra Dr Boulder Colorado 80302

BRIGGS, WINSLOW RUSSELL, plant biologist, educator; born St. Paul, April 29, 1928; son of John DeQuedville and Marjorie (Winslow) B.; married Ann Morrill, June 30, 1955; children: Caroline, Lucia, Marion. Bachelor of Arts, Harvard University, 1951, Master of Arts, 1952, Doctor of Philosophy, 1956. Instructor biological sciences Stanford (California) University, 1955-57, assistant professor; 1957-62, associate professor; 1962-66, professor; 1966-67; professor biology Harvard University, 1967-73; director department plant biology Carnegie Institution of Washington, Stanford, 1973—. Author: (with others) Life on Earth, 1973; Asso. editor: (with others) Annual Review of Plant Physiology, 1961-72; editor (with others), 1972—; Contributor (with others) articles on plant growth and devel. and photobiology to professional journals. Recipient Alexander von Humboldt U.S. sr. scientist award, 1984-85; John Simon Guggenheim fellow, 1973-74, Deutsche Akademie der Naturforscher Leopoldina, 1986. Fellow American Association for the Advancement of Science; member Am. Society Plant Physiologists (president 1975-76), California Botanical Society (president 1976-77), National Acad. Sciences, Am. Acad. Arts and Sciences, Am. Institute Biological Sciences (president 1980-81), Am. Society Photbiology, Botanical Society Am., Nature Conservancy, Deutsche Akademie der Naturforscher Leopoldina, Sigma Xi. Home: 480 Hale St Palo Alto California 94301 Office: Carnegie Institute Wash Department Plant Biology 290 Panama St Stanford California 94305

BRILL, WINSTON JONAS, microbiologist, educator, research director; born London, June 16, 1939; came to United States, 1949; son of Walter and Irmgard (Levy) B.; married Nancy Carol Weisburd, June 11, 1964; 1 child, Eric David. Bachelor of Arts, Rutgers University, 1961; Doctor of Philosophy in Microbiology, University Illinois, 1965. Postdoctoral fellow Massachusetts Institute of Technology, Cambridge, 1965-67; assistant professor department bacteriology University Wisconsin, Madison, 1967-70, associate professor; 1970-74, professor; 1974-79, Vilas research professor; 1979-83; vice president, director research Agracetus, 1981—; panel member National Science Foundation, United States Department Agriculture; member recombinant DNA adv. committee National Institutes of Health, 1979-83; member policy adv. committee United States Department Agriculture, 1985—; member genetic engineering adv. panel to United States secretary state, 1981. Member editorial board Journal Biotech., Trends in Biotech., Critical Revs. in Biotech.; contributor articles to professional journals. Henry Rutgers fellow Rutgers University, 1961; recipient Eli Lilly award in microbiology and immunology, 1979, Alexander von Humboldt Foundation award, 1979. Member Am. Society Microbiology, American Association for the Advancement of Science, Am. Society Plant Physiology. Office: 8520 University Green Middleton Wisconsin 53562

BRINSTER, RALPH LAWRENCE, physiologist, educator; born Montclair, New Jersey, March 10, 1932. Bachelor of Science, Rutgers University, 1953; Doctor of Veterinary Medicine, University Pennsylvania, 1960, Doctor of Philosophy in Physiology, 1964. Teaching fellow University Pennsylvania, Philadelphia, 1961-64, instructor; 1964-65, assistant professor, then associate professor School Vet. Medicine; 1965-70, professor physiology School Vet. Medicine; 1970—, Rich King Mellon professor reproductive physiology; 1975—; lecturer Harvey Society, 1984. Fellow Am. Acad. Arts and Sciences; member Institute Medicine,

National Acad. Sciences, American Veterinary Medical Association, Am. Society Cell Biology, Society Study Reproduction, Brit. Society Study Fertility, Brit. Biochemistry Society. Office: University Pennsylvania School Veteran Medicine Philadelphia Pennsylvania 19104

BROMERY, RANDOLPH WILSON, geologist, educator; born Cumberland, Maryland, January 18, 1926; son of Lawrence Randolph and Edith (Edmondson) B.; married Cecile Trescott, June 8, 1947; children: Keith, Carol, Dennis, David, Christopher. Student, University Michigan, 1945-46; Bachelor of Science, Howard University, 1956; Master of Science, Am. University, 1962; Doctor of Philosophy, Johns Hopkins University, 1968; Doctor of Science (honorary), Frostburg State College; Doctor of Education (honorary), Western New England College; Doctor of Laws, University Hokkaido, 1976; Doctor of Humane Letters (honorary), University Massachusetts, 1979. Geophysicist United States Geological Survey, 1948-68, consultant; 1968-72; professor, lecturer Howard University, Washington, 1961-65; associate professor geology, deputy chairman department University Massachusetts, 1967-68, professor geology, chairman department; 1969-70, professor geology, vice-chancellor; 1970-71, professor geology, chancellor; 1972-77, executive vice president; 1977-79, Commonwealth professor; 1979-88; president Geosci. Engineering Corp., 1983—; acting president Westfield (Massachusetts) State College, 1988—; president Resources Cons. Associates; board of directors Chemical Bank, NYNEX Corp., Exxon Corp., John Hancock Mutual Life Insurance Company; geophysical consultant Kennecott Copper Corp., New England Telephone Company, 1977-81, Northwestern Mutual Life Insurance Company, 1977-79; corp. member Woods Hole Oceanographic Institution. Contributor numerous articles to sci. and professional journals. Trustee Babson College, 1976-81, Johns Hopkins University, Mount Holyoke; trustee Talladega College, 1981-88, Hampshire College, 1971-79, Boston Mus. Sci.; member Committee Collegiate Education Black Students, 1967-72, president, 1968-72; member human devel. committee Catholic Archdiocese, Springfield, 1971-76; vice-chmn. New Coalition for Economic and Social Change; member adv. council National Aeronautics and Space Administration; member National Acad. Engrs. Committee Minorities in Engring; member advisory committee John F. Kennedy Library; member board overseers visiting committee department geological scis. Harvard University, 1975-79. Served with United States Army Air Force, 1943-44. Named hon. president Soodo Women's University, Seoul, Korea; Gillman fellow Johns Hopkins, 1964-65. Fellow American Association for the Advancement of Science, Geological Society Am. (vice president 1987-88, president 1988-89); member Am. Geophysical Union, Society Exploration Geophysicists, New York Acad. Sciences, Explorers Club, Council Foreign Relations, Sigma Xi, Phi Kappa Phi, Phi Eta Sigma. Club: Cosmos. Office: Westfield State College Western Avenue Westfield Massachusetts 01086

BROMLEY, DAVID ALLAN, physicist, educator; born Westmeath, Ontario, Canada, May 4, 1926; son of Milton Escort and Susan Anne (Anderson) B.; married Patricia Jane Brassor, August 30, 1949; children—David John, Karen Lynn. Bachelor of Science in Engineering Physics, Queen's University, Kingston, Ontario, 1948, Master of Science in Physics, 1950; Doctor of Philosophy in Nuclear Physics, University Rochester, 1952; Master of Arts (honorary), Yale University, 1961; Doctor Natural Philosophy (honorary), University Frankfurt, 1978; Docteur (Physique) (honorary), University Strasbourg, 1980; Doctor of Science (honorary), Queen's University, 1981, University Notre Dame, 1982, University Witwatersrand, 1982, Trinity College, 1988; Doctor of Letters (honorary), University Bridgeport, 1981; Dott. (honorary), University Padua, 1983; Doctor of Humane Letters (honorary), University New Haven, 1987. Operating engineer Hydro Electric Power Commission Ontario, 1947-48; research officer National Research Council Can., 1948; instructor, then assistant professor physics University Rochester, 1952-55; senior research officer, section head Atomic Energy Can. Limited, 1955-60; associate professor physics, associate director heavy ion accelerator laboratory Yale, 1960-61, professor physics, director A W Wright Nuclear Structure Laboratory; 1961—, chairman physics department; 1970-77, Henry Ford II professor; 1972—; board of directors UNC Resources Incorporated, Barnes Engineering Company, NE Bancorp Incorporated, Union Trust Company, United Illuminating Corp., Chronar, Incorporated; consultant Brookhaven, Argonne, Berkley and Oak Ridge National Laboratories, Bell Telephone Laboratories, International Business Machines Corporation, General Telephone and Telegraph; member panel nuclear physics National Acad. Sciences, 1964, chairman committee on nuclear sci., 1966-74, chairman physics survey, 1969-74; mem.-at-large, member executive committee div. physical sciences National Research Council, 1970-74, member executive committee, assembly physical and math. sciences, 1974-78, member naval sci. board, 1974-78; member high energy physics adv. panel Energy Research and Development Administration, 1974-78; member nuclear sci. adv. panel National Science Foundation and Department Energy, 1980—; member White House Sci. Council, 1981—, U.S./USSR Joint Coordinating Committee for Research on Fundamental Properties Matter, 1972—, National Sci. Board, 1988—; chairman Office Physical Sciences, 1975-78, Department of Energy INSF Panel on Electron Accelerator Facilities, 1983, Gandhi-Reagan Presdl. Committee on Indo—United States Cooperation in Sci. and Tech., 1983—, Sarney-Reagan Presdl. Committee on Brazil—United States Cooperation in Sci. and Tech., 1987—, Junior Faculty Fellowship Committee David and Lucile Packard Foundation, 1988; vice chairman White House Panel on Health of United States Universities, 1985-86; adv. board Institute Nuclear Power Operations, 1983-85, Electric Power Research Institute, 1984—. Editor: Physics in Perspective, 5 vols, 1972, Large Electrostatic Accelerators, 1974, Nuclear Detectors, 1978, Heavy Ion Science, 8 vols, 1981-84; co-editor: Procs. Kingston International Conf. on Nuclear Structure, 1960, Facets of Physics, 1970, Nuclear

Science in China, 1979; associate editor: Annals of Physics, 1968—, Am. Scientist, 1969-81, Il Nuovo Cimento, 1970—, Nuclear Instruments and Methods, 1974—, Science, Technology and the Humanities, 1978—, Journal Physics, 1978—, Nuclear Science Applications, 1978—, Technology in Soc, 1981—; cons. editor: McGraw Hill Series in Fundamentals of Physics, 1967—, McGraw Hill Encyclopedia Science and Tech. Board of directors Oak Ridge Associate Univs., 1977-80, University Bridgeport, 1981—. Recipient medal Gov. General Can., 1948, U.S. National medal of sci., 1988, Distinguished Alumnus award University Rochester, 1986; National Research Council fellow, 1952; fellow Branford College, 1961—; Guggenheim fellow, 1977-78; Humboldt fellow, 1978, 85; Benjamin Franklin fellow Royal Society Arts, London, 1979—. Fellow Am. Physical Society (member council 1967-71), Am. Acad. Arts and Sciences, American Association for the Advancement of Science (chairman physics section 1977-78, pres.-elect 1980, president 1981—, chairman board 1982—); member Can. Association Physicists, European Physical Society, Connecticut Acad. Arts and Sciences, Connecticut Acad. Sci. and Engineering (council 1976-78), International Union Pure and Applied Physics (United States national committee 1969—, chairman 1975-76, vice president 1975-81, president 1984-87), Southeastern University Research Association (board directors 1984—), Council on Foreign Relations, Sigma Xi (president Yale 1962-63). Home: 35 Tokeneke Dr North Haven Connecticut 06473 Office: Yale Univ/Wright Nuclear Structure Lab 272 Whitney Avenue New Haven Connecticut 06511

BROOKS, FRANK PICKERING, physician, physiologist; born Portsmouth, New Hampshire, January 2, 1920; son of Frank Edwin and Florence Isabel (Towle) B.; married Emily Elizabeth Marden, July 5, 1942; children: William Bradley, Sally Elizabeth, Robert Pickering. Bachelor of Arts, Dartmouth College, 1941; Doctor of Medicine, University Pennsylvania, 1943, Doctor of Science in Medicine, 1951; Doctor Honoris Causa, University Aix-Marseille, 1987. Intern Hospital University Pennsylvania, Philadelphia, 1944; resident Hospital University Pennsylvania, 1944-46; United States Public Health Service research fellow Jefferson Medical College, 1951-52; instructor University Pennsylvania, 1952-53, assistant professor; 1954-60, associate professor; 1960-70, professor medicine and physiology; 1970—, chief gastrointestinal sect; 1972-75, acting chief hospital; 1986-88; senior lecturer in physiology University Edinburgh, Scotland, 1955-56; research associate Veteran's Administration Center, Los Angeles, 1966-67; member National Commission on Digestive Diseases, 1977-79; member council NIADDK, 1983-86; member career awards committee Veteran's Administration, 1983-87. Author: The Control of Gastrointestinal Function, 1970, Gastrointestinal Pathophysiology, 2d edit, 1979, Peptic Ulcer Disease, 1985; editor: Digestive Diseases and Scis., 1982-87. Served to lieutenant (junior grade) United States Naval Reserve, 1946-48. Recipient Research Career Devel. award National Institute Arthritis, Metabolism and Digestive Diseases, 1964-70.

Member Am. Gastroentorological Association (pres.-elect 1979-80, president 1980-81, Friedenwald medal 1988), Am. Physiological Society (chairman gastrointestinal section 1966), Brit. Society Gastroenterology (hon.), Am. Pancreatic Association (president 1980-81), Am. Clinical Climatological Association (vice president 1984), Alpha Omega Alpha (hon.), Belgian Society Gastroentorological Association (Broheé medal 1985). Republican. Episcopalian. Club: Union League Philadelphia. Home: 206 Almur Lane Wynnewood Pennsylvania 19096

BROOKS, FREDERICK PHILLIPS, JR., computer scientist; born Durham, North Carolina, April 19, 1931; son of Frederick Phillips and Octavia Hooker (Broome) B.; married Nancy Lee Greenwood, June 16, 1956; children: Kenneth Phillips, Roger Greenwood, Barbara Suzanne. Bachelor of Arts, Duke University, 1953; Master of Science, Harvard University, 1955, Doctor of Philosophy, 1956. Engineer International Business Machines Corporation, Poughkeepsie, New York, 1956-59, Yorktown Heights, New York, 1959-60; manager devel. computer System/360 International Business Machines Corporation, Poughkeepsie, 1960-64, manager devel. Operating System/360; 1964-65; professor University North Carolina, Chapel Hill, 1964-75, Kenan professor; 1975—, chairman department computer sci.; 1964-84; board of directors Triangle University Computation Center, 1966-84, chairman, 1975-77; board of directors North Carolina Educational Computing Service, 1965—; member Def. Sci. Board, 1982-86, National Sci. Board, 1987—. Author: The Mythical Man-Month-Essays on Software Engineering, 1975; (with K.E. Iverson) Automatic Data Processing, 1963, Automatic Data Processing System/360 Edition, 1969; contributor articles to professional journals; inventor (with D. W. Sweeney) program interruption system, alphabetical read-out device. Chairman executive committee Central Carolina Billy Graham Crusade, 1972-73; trustee Durham Acad., president, 1977-80; member corp. Inter-Varsity Christian Fellowship, 1968-77. Recipient McDowell award Institute of Electrical and Electronic Engineers Computer Society, 1970, Man of Year award Data Processing Mgmt. Association, 1970, National Medal of Tech., 1985; grantee National Science Foundation, Atomic Energy Commission, National Institutes of Health; Guggenheim fellow, 1975. Fellow Institute of Electrical and Electronics Engineers, Am. Acad. Arts and Sciences; member Association Computing Machinery (council mem.-at-large 1966-70, Distinguished Service award 1987), National Acad. Engineering. Methodist. Home: 413 Granville Road Chapel Hill North Carolina 27514 Office: University North Carolina Department Computer Sci Chapel Hill North Carolina 27599-3175

BROWDER, FELIX EARL, mathematician, educator; born Moscow, July 31, 1927; son of Earl and Raissa (Berkmann) B.; married Eva Tislowitz, October 5, 1949; children: Thomas, William. Bachelor of Science, Massachusetts Institute of Technology, 1946; Doctor of Philosophy, Princeton University, 1948. C.L.E Moore instructor math. Massachusetts Institute of Technology, 1948-51, visiting associate professor; 1961-62, visiting professor; 1977-78; instructor math. Boston University, 1951-53; assistant professor Brandeis University, 1955-56; from assistant professor to professor math. Yale University, 1956-63; professor math. University Chicago, 1963-72, Louis Block professor math.; 1972-82, Max Mason Distinguished Service professor math.; 1982-87, chairman department; 1972-77, 80-85; vice president for research Rutgers, State University New Jersey, 1986—; university professor math. Rutgers University, New Brunswick, 1986—; visiting member Institute Advanced Study, Princeton, 1953-54, 63-64; visiting professor Instituto de Matematica Pura e Aplicada, Rio de Janeiro, 1960, Princeton University, 1968; Fairchild distinguished visitor California Institute Tech., 1975-76; senior research fellow University Sussex, England, 1970, 76; visiting professor University Paris, 1973, 75, 78, 81, 83, 85. Served with Army of the United States, 1953-55. Guggenheim fellow, 1953-54, 66-67, Sloan Foundation fellow, 1959-63, National Science Foundation sr. postdoctoral fellow, 1957-58. Fellow Am. Acad. Arts and Sciences; member National Acad. Sciences, Am. Math. Society (editor bull. 1959-68, 78-83, council member 1959-72, 78-83, managing editor 1964-68, 80, executive committee council 1979-80), Math. Association Am., American Association for the Advancement of Science (chairman section A 1982-83), Sigma Xi (president chapter 1985-86).

BROWN, DONALD DAVID, biology educator; born Cincinnati, December 30, 1931; son of Albert Louis and Louise (Rauh) B.; married Linda Jane Weil, July 2, 1957; children: Deborah Lin, Christopher Charles, Sharon Elizabeth. Master of Science, University Chicago, 1956, Doctor of Medicine, 1956, Doctor of Science (honorary), 1976; Doctor of Science (honorary), University Maryland, 1983. Staff member department embryology Carnegie Institution of Washington, Baltimore, 1963-76; director Carnegie Institution of Washington, 1976—; professor department biology Johns Hopkins University, 1968—. President Life Scis. Research Foundation Served with United States Public Health Service, 1957-59. Recipient U.S. Steel Foundation award for molecular biology, 1973; V.D. Mattia award Roche Institute, 1975; Boris Pregel award for biology New York Acad. Sciences, 1976; Ross G. Harrison award International Society Developmental Biology, 1981; Bertner Foundation award, 1982; Rosenstiel award for biomed. sci., 1985, Louisa Gross Horwitz award, 1985; Feodor Lynen award University Miami Winter Symposium, 1987. Fellow Am. Acad. Arts and Sciences, American Association for the Advancement of Science; member National Acad. Sciences, Society Devel. Biology (president 1975), Am. Society Biological Chemists, Am. Society Cell Biology, Am. Philosophical Society. Home: 5721 Oakshire Road Baltimore Maryland 21209 Office: Carnegie Instn of Washington 115 W University Parkway Baltimore Maryland 21210

BROWN, ERIC REEDER, I, immunologist, educator; born Cortland, New York, March 16, 1925; son of Harold McDaniel and Helen (Seitz) B.; married Chloe Cassandra Ledbetter, May 11, 1961; children: Carl F., Christopher H.A., Amy Elizabeth French; children by previous marriage: Eric Reeder II, Christine

Virginia, Dianne Mary, Daniel K. Bachelor of Arts, Syracuse University, 1949, Master of Science, 1951; Doctor of Philosophy, University Kansas, 1957; Doctor of Science, Quincy College, 1966; Doctor of Medicine, University Rochester, 1955. Instructor University Illinois Medical School, 1957-58; assistant professor University Alabama, 1958-60, University Minnesota School Medicine, 1960-61; senior research associate Hektoen Institute, Chicago, 1961-67; associate professor Northwestern University Medical School, Evanston, Illinois, 1964-68; chairman department microbiology Chicago Medical School, North Chicago, Illinois, 1967-82, instructor immunology; consultant Newport Pharms., Incorporated, Strategic Medical Research Corp., University Illinois; medical adviser to Illinois director Selective Service System; reviewer grants National Science Foundation, 1978—; member medical adv. board Leukemia Research Foundation; board of directors Lake Bluff Laboratories, Incorporated, Chesterton, Ind. Co-author: Cancer Disemination and Therapy, 1961; author: Textbook of Micromolecular Biology, 1974, Immunobiological Characteristics of Leukemia, 1975, Sailing Made Easy, 1978; contributor articles to professional journals. Served with United States Coast Guard Reserve, 1942-46, served to colonel United States Air Force Reserve, 1951-55. Am. Cancer Society fellow, 1960-63; Leukemia Society scholar, 1965—. Fellow Am. Institute Chemists, Am. Acad. Microbiology, Chicago Institute Medicine; member Royal Society Medicine, Histochem. Society, International Society Lymphology, American Association of University Women, Am. Mus. Natural History, Medical Mycological Society of Ams., Society Experimental Biology and Medicine, Reserve Officers Association, Phi Beta Kappa, Sigma Xi, Psi Chi, Phi Sigma. Research on virus etiology of cancer and leukemia. Office: Chicago Med School 3333 Greenbay Road North Chicago Illinois 60064

BROWN, HERBERT CHARLES, chemistry educator; born London, May 22, 1912; came to United States, 1914; son of Charles and Pearl (Gorinstein) B.; married Sarah Baylen, February 6, 1937; 1 son, Charles Allan. Associate of Science, Wright Junior College, Chicago, 1935; Bachelor of Science, University Chicago, 1936, Doctor of Philosophy, 1938, Doctor of Science (honorary), 1968; honorary doctorates, Wayne State University, 1980, Lebanon Valley College, 1980, Long Island University, 1980, Hebrew University Jerusalem, 1980, Pontificia Universidad de Chile, 1980, Purdue University, 1980, University Wales, 1981, University Paris, 1982, Butler University, 1982, Ball State University, 1985. Assistant chemistry University Chicago, 1936-38; Eli Lilly post-doctorate research fellow 1938-39, instructor; 1939-43; assistant professor chemistry Wayne University, 1943- 46, associate professor; 1946-47; professor inorganic chemistry Purdue University, 1947-59, Richard B. Wetherill professor chemistry; 1959, Richard B. Wetherill research professor; 1960-78, emeritus; 1978—; visiting professor University California at Los Angeles, 1951, Ohio State University, 1952, University Mexico, 1954, University California at Berkeley, 1957, University Colorado, 1958,

University Heidelberg, 1963, State University New York at Stonybrook, 1966, University California at Santa Barbara, 1967, Hebrew University, Jerusalem, 1969, University Wales, Swansea, 1973, University Cape Town, South Africa, 1974, University California, San Diego, 1979; Harrison Howe lecturer, 1953, Friend East Clark lecturer, 1953, Freud-McCormack lecturer, 1954, Centenary lecturer, England, 1955, Thomas W. Talley lecturer, 1956, Falk-Plaut lecturer, 1957, Julius Stieglitz lecturer, 1958, Max Tishler lecturer, 1958, Kekule-Couper Centenary lecturer, 1958, E C Franklin lecturer, 1960, Ira Remsen lecturer, 1961, Edgar Fahs Smith lecturer, 1962, Seydel-Wooley lecturer, 1966, Baker lecturer, 1969, Benjamin Rush lecturer, 1971, Chemical Society lecturer, Australia, 1972, Armes lecturer, 1973, Henry Gilman lecturer, 1975, others; chemical consultant to industrial corporations. Author: Hydroboration, 1962, Boranes in Organic Chemistry, 1972, Organic Synthesis via Boranes, 1975, The Nonclassical Ion Problem, 1977; Contributor articles to chemical journals. Board governors Hebrew University, 1969—. Served as co-dir. war research projects University Chicago for United States Army, National Def. Research Committee, Manhattan Project, 1940-43. Recipient Purdue Sigma Xi research award, 1951; Nichols medal, 1959; award Am. Chemical Society, 1960; S.O.C.M.A. medal, 1960; H.N. McCoy award, 1965; Linus Pauling medal, 1968; National Medal of Sci., 1969; Roger Adams medal, 1971; Charles Frederick Chandler medal, 1973; Chemical Pioneer award, 1975; CUNY medal for sci. achievement, 1976; Elliott Cresson medal, 1978; C.K. Ingold medal, 1978; Nobel prize in chemistry, 1979; Priestley medal, 1981; Perkin medal, 1982; Gold medal award Am. Institute Chemists, 1985; G.M. Kosolapoff medal, 1987; National Acad. Sciences Award in Chemical Sciences, 1987. Fellow Royal Society Chemistry (hon.), American Association for the Advancement of Science, Indian National Sci. Acad. (foreign); member Am. Acad. Arts and Sciences, National Acad. Sciences, Chemical Society Japan (hon.), Pharmaceutical Society Japan (hon.), Am. Chemical Society (chairman Purdue section 1955-56), Ind. Acad. Sci., Phi Beta Kappa, Sigma Xi, Alpha Chi Sigma, Phi Lambda Upsilon (hon.). Rsch. in phys., organic, inorganic chemistry relating chem. behavior to molecular structure; selective reductions; hydroboration; chemistry of organoboranes. Office: Purdue U Department Chemistry West Lafayette Indiana 47907

BROWN, JACK HAROLD UPTON, university official, educator, biomedical engineer; born Nixon, Texas, November 16, 1918; son of Gilmer W. and Thelma (Patton) B.; married Jessie Carolyn Schulz, April 14, 1943. Bachelor of Science, Southwest Texas State University, 1939; postgraduate, University Texas, 1939-41; Doctor of Philosophy, Rutgers University, 1948. Lecturer physics Southwest Texas State University, San Marcos, 1943-44; instructor physical chemistry Rutgers University, New Brunswick, New Jersey, 1944-45, research associate; 1944-48; lecturer University Pittsburgh, 1948-50; head biological sciences Mellon Institute, Pittsburgh, 1948-50; assistant professor physiology University North Carolina, Chapel Hill, 1950-52; scientist Oak

Ridge Institute Nuclear Studies, 1952, professor biology; associate professor physiology Emory University Medical School, Atlanta, 1952-58, professor; 1959-60, acting chairman department physiology; 1958-60; lecturer physiology George Washington University and Georgetown University medical schools, Washington, 1960-65; executive secretary biomed. engineering and physiology training committees National Institute General Medical Sciences, National Institutes of Health, Bethesda, Maryland, 1960-62; chief special research branch div. Research Facilities and Resources National Institutes of Health, 1962-63, acting chief general clinical research centers branch; 1963-64, assistant director operations Div. Research Facilities and Resources; 1964-65; acting program director pharmacology/toxicology program National Institute General Medical Sciences, National Institutes of Health, 1966-70, assistant director operations; 1965-66, associate director sci. programs; 1967-70, acting director; 1970; special assistant to administrator Health Services and Mental Health Administration, United States Public Health Service, Rockville, Maryland, 1971-72; associate deputy administrator for devel. Health Services and Mental Health Administration, United States Public Health Service, 1972-73; special assistant to administrator Health Resources Administration, 1973-78; coordinator Southwest Research Consortium, San Antonio, 1974-78; professor physiology University Texas Medical School, San Antonio, 1974-78; professor environmental sciences University Texas at San Antonio, 1974-78; adj. professor health services administration Trinity University, 1975-78;

associate provost research and advanced education University Houston, 1978-80, professor biology; 1980—; adj. professor University Texas School Public Health, 1978—; adj. professor public administration Texas Women's University, 1978—; adj. professor community medicine Baylor College Medicine, Houston, 1986-89; Fulbright lecturer University Rangoon, 1950; consultant health systems World Health Organization, Oak Ridge Institute Nuclear Studies, Veteran's Administration, Lockheed Aircraft Company, Drexel Institute Tech., National Aeronautics and Space Administration, Vassar College; member adv. board Center for Cancer Therapy, San Antonio, 1974—; board of directors South Texas Health Education Center; member health adv. board University Texas Health Sci. Center, 1986—. Author: Physiology of Man in Space, 1963, (with A.B. Barker) Basic Endocrinology, 1966, 2d edition, 1970, (with J.F. Dickson) Future Goals of Engineering in Biology and Medicine, 1968, Advances in Biomedical Engineering, volume II, 1972, volumes III, IV, 1973, volume V, 1974, volume VI, 1976, Volume VII, 1978, (with J.E. Jacobs and L.E. Stark) Biomedical Engineering, 1972, (with D.E. Gann) Engineering Principles in Physiology, volumes I, II, 1973, The Health Care Dilemma, 1977, Integration and Control of Biol. Processes, 1978, Politics and Health Care, 1978, Telecommunications in Health Care, 1981, Management in Health Care Systems, 1983, A Laboratory Manual in Animal Physiology, 1984, 3rd edition, 1988, High Cost of Healing, 1985, (with Comolo) Productivity in Health Care, 1986, Guide to Collecting Fine Prints, 1987, (with Comolo) Improving Executive Productivity,

1989; editor: (with Ferguson) Blood and Body Functions, 1966, Life Into Space, (Wunder), 1968; contributor numerous articles on biomed. engring. to sci. journals. Member adv. board San Antonio Mus. Association; member special effects committee Texas Sesquicentennial. Served with United States Naval Reserve, 1941. Recipient special team award National Aeronautics and Space Administration, 1978; Gerard Swope fellow General Electric Company, 1946-48; Fulbright grantee, 1950; National Institutes of Health grantee, 1950-60; Cancer Society grantee, 1958; Damon Runyon Cancer award grantee, 1959; Department Energy grantee, 1980-81; Cert. of Appreciation, National Institutes of Health, 1969; Most Distinguished Alumni award S.W. Texas State University, 1986. Fellow American Association for the Advancement of Science, National Acad. Engineering, Institute of Electrical and Electronics Engineers (joint committee engineering in medicine and biology 1966—); member Am. Chemical Society (senior), Biomed. Engineering Society (president 1969-70, director 1968-69), Institute Radio Engineers (national secretary professional group biomed. engineering 1962-64), New York Acad. Sciences, Endocrine Society, Am. Physiological Society (committee member 1959-63, national committee on animals in research 1985—), Society for Experimental Biology and Medicine, Sigma Xi (research award 1961, president Alamo chapter 1977-78), Council Biology Editors, Society Research Administration, Pi Kappa Delta, Phi Lambda Upsilon, Alpha Chi. Club: Cosmos. Inventor capsule manometer, respirator for small animals and basal metabolic apparatus for small animals, dust sampler, apparatus for partitioning human lung volumes, laser credit card patient record system. Home: 2908 Whisper View San Antonio Texas 78230 Office: U Houston 4800 Calhoun St Houston Texas 77004

BROWN, MICHAEL STUART, geneticist; born New York City, April 13, 1941; son of Harvey and Evelyn (Katz) B.; married Alice Lapin, June 21, 1964; children: Elizabeth Jane, Sara Ellen. Bachelor of Arts, University Pennsylvania, 1962, Doctor of Medicine, 1966. Intern, then resident in medicine Massachusetts General Hospital, Boston, 1966-68; served with United States Public Health Service, 1968-70; clinical associate National Institutes of Health, 1968-71; assistant professor University Texas Southwestern Medical School, Dallas, 1971-74; Paul J. Thomas professor genetics, director Center Genetic Diseases, 1977—. Recipient Pfizer award Am. Chemical Society, 1976, Passano award Passano Foundation, 1978, Lounsbery award U.S. National Acad. Sciences, 1979; Lita Annenberg Hazen award, 1982, Albert Lasker Medical Research award, 1985, Nobel Prize in Medicine or Physiology, 1985. Member National Acad. Sciences, Am. Society Clinical Investigation, Association Am. Physicians, Harvey Society. Office: U Tex Health Sci Center Internal Medicine-Biophysics 5323 Harry Hines Boulevard Dallas Texas 75235

BROWN, RICHARD MALCOLM, JR., botany educator; born Pampa, Texas, January 2, 1939; married; 1 child. Bachelor of Science, University Texas, 1961, Doctor of Philosophy in Botany, 1964. Fellow University Hawaii and University Texas, 1964-65; assistant professor botany University

Texas, Austin, 1965-68; associate professor botany University North Carolina, Chapel Hill, 1968-73, professor; from 1973, director electron microscopy laboratory; from 1970, now Johnson & Johnson Centennial chair in plant cell biology, professor botany; National Science Foundation fellow University Freiburg, 1968-69, research grantee, 1970-72. Research in airborne algae, algal ecology, ultrastructure of algal viruses, algal ultrastructure, immunochemistry of algae, cytology, Golgi apparatus and cell wall formation, sexual reproduction among algae, cellulose biogenesis. Office: University of Tex at Austin Department of Botany Austin Texas 78712

BROWN, ROBERT ARTHUR, chemical engineering educator; born San Antonio, July 22, 1951; son of Ralph and Lillian (Rilling) B.; married Beverly Ann Lamb, June 22, 1972; children: Ryan Arthur, Keith Andrew. Bachelor of Science, University Texas, 1973, Master of Science, 1975; Doctor of Philosophy, University Minnesota, 1979. Instructor University Minnesota, Minneapolis, 1978; assistant professor Massachusetts Institute of Technology, Cambridge, 1979-82, associate professor; 1982-84, professor; 1984—, executive officer department chemical engineering; 1987-88, head department chemical engineering; 1988—; trustee Consortium Sci. Computing, Princeton, New Jersey, 1984—; consultant Lincoln Laboratories, Lexington, Massachusetts, 1985-87, Mobil Solar Energy, Waltham, Massachusetts, 1982—, Lawrence Livermore Laboratory, Livermore, California, 1987—. Contributor over 100 articles to professional journals. Recipient Outstanding Junior Faculty award Amoco Oil Company, 1981, Camille and Henry Dreyfus Tchr.-Scholar award, 1983. Member Am. Institute Chemical Engineers (Allen P. Colburn award 1986), Society Industrial and Applied Math., Am. Association Crystal Growth (young author award 1984), Am. Physical Society. Office: Massachusetts Institute of Technology Department of Chem Engring 66-352 Cambridge Massachusetts 02139

BROWN, ROBERT GROVER, engineering educator; born Shenandoah, Iowa, April 25, 1926; son of Grover Whitney and Irene (Frink) B. Bachelor of Science, Iowa State College, 1948, Master of Science, 1951, Doctor of Philosophy, 1956. Instructor Iowa State College, Ames, 1948-51, 53-55, assistant professor; 1955-56, associate professor; 1956-59, professor; 1959-76, Distinguished professor; 1976—; research engineer North Am. Aviation, Downey, California, 1951-53; consultant various aerospace engineering firms., 1956—. Author: (with R.A. Sharpe, W.L. Hughes) Lines, Waves and Antennas, 1961, (with J.W. Nilsson) Linear Systems Analysis, 1962, Random Signal Analysis and Kalman Filtering, 1983. Member Institute of Electrical and Electronics Engineers, Institute Navigation (Burka award 1978, 84), Am. Society Engineering Education. Office: Iowa State U Ames Iowa 50011

BROWNE, JAMES CLAYTON, computer science educator; born Conway, Arkansas, January 16, 1935; son of Walter E. and Louise (James) B.; married Gayle Moseley; children: Clayton Carleton, Duncan James, Valerie Siobhan. Bachelor of Arts, Hendrix College, 1956; Doctor of

Philosophy, University Texas, 1960. Assistant professor physics University Texas, Austin, 1960-64; professor Computer Sci. Department University Texas, Austin, 1968—, acting chairman; 1968-69, chairman; 1971-75, 85-87, Anonymous professor computer sci. #1; 1987—; postdoctoral fellow Queen's University, Belfast, Ireland, 1964-65, professor computer sci., director computer laboratory; 1965-68; chairman board Information Research Associates, Austin. Associate editor Computer Physics Communications, 1987—; author over 150 papers in computer sci. and physics. Fellow Am. Physical Society, Brit. Computer Society, Association Computing Machinery (chairman special interest group on operating systems 1975-77); member Society Industrial and Applied Math. Avocations: skiing, jogging. Office: University of Tex Department of Computer Scis & Physics/Taylor Hall 5 126 Austin Texas 78712

BROWNSTEIN, BARBARA LAVIN, geneticist, educator, university official; born Philadelphia, Sept. 8, 1931; daughter of Edward A. and Rose (Silverstein) Lavin; married Melvin Brownstein, June 1949 (divorced 1955); children: Judith Brownstein Kaufmann, Dena. Assistant editor Biological Abstracts, Philadelphia, 1957-58; research fellow department microbial genetics Karolinska Institute, Stockholm, 1962-64; associate Wistar Institute, Philadelphia, 1964-68; associate professor molecular biology, department biology Temple University, Philadelphia, 1968-74; professor Temple University, 1974—, chairman department; 1978-81, provost; 1983—; visiting scientist department tumor cell biology Imperial Cancer Research Fund Laboratories, London, 1973-74; member Cancer Scientist Training Program, Temple University, committee institutional grants, Am. Cancer Society; consultant Cancer Information Dissemination Analysis Center, Franklin Institute, Saunders Pubs., Holt, Rinehart, Wadsworth pubs. Recipient Liberal Arts Alumni award for excellence in teaching Temple University, 1980; recipient Outstanding Faculty Woman award Temple University, 1980. Member American Association for the Advancement of Science, Am. Society Cell Biology, New York Acad. Sci., Association Women in Sci. Home: 2201 Pennsylvania Avenue Philadelphia Pennsylvania 19130 Office: Temple U Office of Provost Philadelphia Pennsylvania 19122

BUCHSBAUM, SOLOMON JAN, physicist; born Stryj, Poland, December 4, 1929; came to United States, 1953, naturalized, 1957; son of Jacob and Berta (Rutherfoer) B.; married Phyllis N. Isenman, July 3, 1955; children: Rachel Joy, David Joel, Adam Louis. Bachelor of Science, McGill University, 1952, Master of Science, 1953; Doctor of Philosophy, Massachusetts Institute Tech., 1957. Member tech. staff Bell Laboratories, Murray Hill, New Jersey, 1958-61; department head Bell Laboratories, 1961-65, director; 1965-68; vice president Sandia Laboratories, Albuquerque, 1968-71; executive director Bell Laboratories, 1971-76, vice president; 1976-79, executive vice president; 1979—; research in gaseous and solid state plasmas, communications; senior consultant Def. Sci. Board, chairman, 1972-77, 81—; member Atomic

Energy Commission Controlled Thermonuclear Fusion Committee, 1965-72, President's Sci. Adv. Committee, 1970-73, President's Committee on Sci. and Tech., 1975-76; member fusion power coordinating committee Energy Research and Development Administration, 1972-76, adv. group sci. and tech. National Science Foundation, 1976-77; chairman Energy Research Adv. Board, 1978-81; member Naval Research Adv. Committee, 1978-81; member visiting committee Massachusetts Institute of Technology, 1977—, member corp. devel. committee, 1980—; consultant Office Sci. and Tech., 1976-82; chairman White House Sci. Council, 1982—; trustee Rand Corp., 1982—; member Draper Laboratory Corp., 1983—, board of directors; board Governors Argonne National Laboratory, 1985—. Associate editor: Revs. Modern Physics, 1968-72, Journal Applied Physics, 1968-70, Physics of Fluids, 1963-64; co-author: Waves in Plasmas, 1963; contributor numerous articles to professional journals. Trustee Argonne Univs. Association, 1979-82. Moyse traveling fellow, 1953-54; International Business Machines Corporation fellow, 1954-56; recipient Anne Molson Gold medal, Sec. of Defense medal for Outstanding Pub. Service, 1977; Sec. of Energy award for Exceptional Pub. Service, 1981; National Medal of Sci., 1986. Fellow Am. Physical Society (chairman division plasma physics 1968, member council 1973-76), Institute of Electrical and Electronics Engineers (Frederk Philips award 1987), Am. Acad. Arts and Sciences, American Association for the Advancement of Science; member National Acad. Engineering (executive committee 1975-76), National Acad. Sciences, Cosmos Club. Office: AT&T Bell Labs Crawfords Corner Road Holmdel New Jersey 07733

BULLOCK, THEODORE HOLMES, biologist, educator; born Nanking, China, May 16, 1915; son of Amasa Archibald and Ruth (Beckwith) B.; married Martha Runquist, May 30, 1937; children—Elsie Christine, Stephen Holmes. Student, Pasadena Junior College, 1932-34; Bachelor of Arts, University California at Berkeley, 1936, Doctor of Philosophy, 1940; Sterling fellow zoology, Yale University, 1940-41, Rockefeller fellow experimental neurology, 1941-42. Research associate Yale University School Medicine, 1942-43, instructor neuroanatomy; 1943-44; instructor Marine Biological Laboratory, Woods Hole, Massachusetts, 1944-46; head invertebrate zoology Marine Biological Laboratory, 1955-57, trustee; 1955-57; assistant professor anatomy University Missouri, 1944-46; assistant professor zoology University California at Los Angeles, 1946, associate professor; 1948, professor; 1955-66; Brain Research Institute, University California at Los Angeles, 1960-66; professor neuroscis. Medical School, University California at San Diego, 1966-82, professor emeritus; 1982—; Member Atomic Energy Commission 2d Resurvey of Bikini Expedition, 1948. Author: (with G.A. Horridge) Structure and Function in the Nervous Systems of Invertebrates, 2 vols, 1965; (with others) Introduction to Nervous Systems, 1977; (with W. Heiligenberg) Electroreception, 1986. Fulbright scholar Stazione Zooologica, Naples, 1950-51; fellow Center Advanced Study in Behavioral Sciences, Palo Alto, 1959-60. Fellow

American Association for the Advancement of Science; member Am. Society Zoologists (chairman comparative physiology division 1961, president 1965), Society Neuroscis. (president 1973-74), International Society Neuroethology (president 1984-86), Am. Physiological Society, Society General Physiologists, Am. Acad. Arts and Sciences, National Acad. Sciences, Am. Philosophical Society, International Brain Research Organization, Phi Beta Kappa, Sigma Xi.

BUNCE, DONALD FAIRBAIRN MACDOUGAL, II, physician, anatomist; born Harrisburg, Pennsylvania, July 15, 1920; son of Wesley Hibbard and Jean (Fairbairn) B.; married Lorraine Pelch, May 1, 1954 (deceased November 1975); children: Chip Gregory Alan, Dale Graham Alison; married Suzanne Brockman, July 13, 1973. Bachelor of Science, University Miami, 1951; Master of Science, University Illinois, 1959, Doctor of Philosophy, 1960; Doctor of Osteopathy, College Osteopathic Medicine and Surgery, 1973. President, Bunce School Laboratory Technique, Coral Gables, Florida, 1945-48; clinical physiologist Armour Laboratories, Chicago, 1953-56; director research Chicago Pharmacal Company, 1956-57; instructor anatomy Tulane School Medicine, 1960-62; research professor physiology College Osteopathic Medicine and Surgery, Des Moines, 1962-67; director grad. school College Osteopathic Medicine and Surgery, 1962-73, professor pathology, acting chairman department; 1966-68, professor physiology, chairman department; 1967-73; intern, house physician Des Moines General Hospital, 1973-74;

general practice medicine Forest City, Iowa, 1974-78, Dubuque, Iowa, 1978-80; clinical associate professor department medicine University Alabama School Medicine, Tuscaloosa, 1982—; chief of staff Forest City Hospital, 1977-78; chief physician Acute Medical Care Unit, Bryce Hospital, Tuscaloosa, Alabama, 1980—; vice-chief of staff Bryce Hospital, 1984-85, chief staff; 1985—; president medical staff Hale Memorial Hospital, 1986—; former member staff Mercy, Finley and Xavier hospitals, Dubuque; now member staff departments internal medicine Hale and Druid City hospitals, Tuscaloosa; visiting fellow Institute Experimental Surgery, Copenhagen, 1962; visiting professor Karolinska Institute, Stockholm, 1965, Edinburgh, Scotland, 1966, Kennedy Institute Rheumatology, London, 1969-70; travelling fellow NSF-Internat. Union Physiology; program director grad. training program in medical sciences National Institutes of Health; ofcl. del. 4th International Congress Angiology. Editorial board: Angéiologie, Paris, 1960—, Journal Psychiatric Medicine, 1984—; author: Laboratory Guide to Microscopic Anatomy, 1964, The Nervous System in Canine Medicine, 3d edition, 1968, Atlas of Arterial Histology, 1973; also articles. Board of directors Mus. Sci. and Industry, Des Moines, 1971-75. Recipient Billups Memorial Research award Louisiana Heart Association, 1960. Fellow Am. College Angiology, American Association for the Advancement of Science, New York, Iowa acads sci., Royal Society Medicine; member American Medical Association, Iowa Medical Society, Dubuque County Medical Society, Alabama Medical Association, Tuscaloosa County Medical Society,

Am. Osteopathic Association, Southern Medical Assn, Am. Association Anatomists, Anatomical Society Great Britain, Southern Society Anatomists (executive secretary 1960-62), Pathological Society Great Britain, Society Experimental Biology and Medicine, Am. Association University Profs., Institution Nuclear Engineers, L'Union Internationale d'Angéiologie, Société Français d'Angéiologie et d'Histopathologie, Mensa, Sigma Xi, Sigma Alpha Epsilon. Club: Mason. Research in anatomy and diseases of blood vessels, fetal pathophysiology, medical disease in psychiat. patients. Home: 3203 Arbor Lane Tuscaloosa Alabama 35405

BUNNETT, JOSEPH FREDERICK, chemist, educator; born Portland, Oregon, November 26, 1921; son of Joseph and Louise Helen (Boulan) B.; married Sara Anne Telfer, August 22, 1942; children—Alfred Boulan, David Telfer, Peter Sylvester (deceased September 1972). Bachelor of Arts, Reed College, 1942; Doctor of Philosophy, University Rochester, 1945. Member faculty Reed College, 1946-52, University North Carolina, 1952-58; member faculty Brown University, 1958-66, professor chemistry; 1959-66, chairman department; 1961-64; professor chemistry University California at Santa Cruz, 1966—; Erskine visiting fellow University Canterbury, New Zealand, 1967; visiting professor University Washington, 1956, University Würzburg, Germany, 1974, University Bologna, Italy, 1988; research fellow Japan Society for Promotion of Sci., 1979; Lady Davis visiting professor Hebrew University, Jerusalem, Israel, 1981; member adv. council chemistry department Princeton University. Contributor articles to professional journals. Trustee Reed College, Societá Chimica Italiana (hon.). Fulbright scholar University College, London, England, 1949-50; Guggenheim fellow, Fulbright scholar University Munich, Germany, 1960-61. Fellow American Association for the Advancement of Science; member Am. Acad. Arts and Sciences, Am. Chemical Society (editor journal Accounts of Chemical Research 1966-86), Chemical Society (London), International Union Pure and Applied Chemistry (chairman commission on phys. organic chemistry 1978-83, secretary organic chemistry division 1981-83, vice president 1983-85, president 1985-87), Pharmaceutical Society Japan (hon.), Acad. Gioenia (University Catania, Italy) (hon.). Home: 608 Arroyo Seco Santa Cruz California 95060 Office: U California Santa Cruz California 95064

BURBIDGE, ELEANOR MARGARET PEACHEY, astronomer, educator; born Davenport, England; daughter of Stanley John and Marjorie (Stott) Peachey; married Geoffrey Burbidge, April 2, 1948; 1 child, Sarah. Bachelor of Science, Doctor of Philosophy, University London; Doctor of Science honorary, Smith College, 1963, University Sussex, 1970, University Bristol, 1972, University Leicester, 1972, City University, 1973, University Michigan, 1978, University Massachusetts, 1978, Williams College, 1979, State University of New York, Stony Brook, 1985, Rensselaer Polytechnic Institute, 1986, University Notre Dame, 1986. Member staff University London Observatory, 1948-51; research fellow Yerkes Observatory, University Chicago, 1951-53,

California Institute Tech., Pasadena, 1955-57; Shirley Farr fellow Yerkes Observatory, 1957-59, associate professor; 1959-62; member Enrico Fermi Institute for Nuclear Studies, 1957-62; professor astronomy department physics University Calif.-San Diego, 1964—, university professor; 1984—; director Royal Greenwich Observatory (Herstmonceaux Castle), Hailsham, Sussex, England, 1972-73; Lindsay Memorial lecturer Goddard Space Flight Center, National Aeronautics and Space Administration, 1985; Abby Rockefeller Mauze professor Massachusetts Institute of Technology, 1968; David Elder lecturer University Strathclyde, 1972; V. Gildersleeve lecturer Barnard College, 1974; Jansky lecturer National Radio Astronomy Observatory, 1977; Brode lecturer Whitman College, 1986. Author: (with G. Burbidge) Quasi-Stellar Objects, 1967; editor: Observatory magazine, 1948-51; member editorial board: Astronomy and Astrophysics, 1969—, SUNY-Stonybrook 1985. Recipient (with husband) Warner prize in Astronomy, 1959, Bruce Gold medal Astronomy Society Pacific, 1982; hon. fellow University College, London, Girton College, Lucy Cavendish College, Cambridge; U.S. National medal of sci., 1984; Sesquicentennial medal Mount Holyoke College, 1987. Fellow Royal Society, National Acad. Sciences (chairman section 12 astronomy 1986), Am. Acad. Arts and Sciences, Royal Astronomical Society; member Am. Astronomical Society (vice president 1972-74, president 1976-78; Henry Norris Russell lecturer 1984), International Astronomical Union (president commission 28 1970-73), Grad. Women Sci. (national hon. member).

BURBIDGE, GEOFFREY, astrophysicist, educator; born Chipping Norton, Oxon, England, September 24, 1925; son of Leslie and Eveline Burbidge; married Margaret Peachey, 1948; 1 daughter. Bachelor of Science with special honors in Physics, Bristol University, 1946; Doctor of Philosophy, University College, London, 1951. Assistant lecturer University College, London, 1950-51; Agassiz fellow Harvard, 1951-52; research fellow University Chicago, 1952-53, Cavendish Laboratory, Cambridge, England, 1953-55; Carnegie fellow Mount Wilson and Palomar Observatory, California Institute Tech., 1955-57; assistant professor department astronomy University Chicago,. 1957-58, associate professor; 1958-62; associate professor University California San Diego, La Jolla, 1962-63; professor physics University California San Diego, 1963-83, 88—; director Kitt Peak National Observatory, Tucson, 1978-84; Phillips visiting professor Harvard University, 1968; board of directors Associated Universities Research in Astronomy, 1971-74; trustee Associated Universities, Incorporated, 1973-82. Author: (with Margaret Burbidge) Quasi-Stellar Objects, 1967; editor Annual Rev. Astronomy and Astrophysics, 1973—; contributor articles to sci. journals. Fellow Royal Society London, Am. Acad. Arts and Sciences, Royal Astronomical Society; member Am. Physical Society, Am. Astronomical Society, International Astronomical Union, Astronomical Society of Pacific (president 1974-76).

BURCHENAL, JOSEPH HOLLAND, physician; born Milford, Delaware, December 21, 1912; son of Caleb E.

and Mary E. (Holl) B.; married Margaret Pembroke Thom, October 15, 1938; married Joan Barclay Riley, March 20, 1948; children—Mary Holland, Elizabeth Payne, Joan Littlefield, Barbara Fahys, Caleb Wells, David Holland, Joseph Emory Barclay. Student, Princeton University, 1930-33; Doctor of Medicine, University Pennsylvania, 1937. Diplomate Am. Board Internal Medicine. Rotating intern Union Memorial Hospital, Baltimore, 1937-38; intern pediatrics New York Hospital; also research pathology Cornell University, 1938-39; assistant resident medicine Boston City Hospital, 1940-42; special fellow medicine Memorial Hospital, New York City, 1946-49; assistant attending physician Memorial Hospital, 1949-52, attending physician; 1952-83, attending physician emeritus; 1983—, chief chemotherapy service; 1952-64, associate medical director for clinical investigation; 1964-66, director clinical investigation; 1966-83; research fellow medicine Harvard, 1940-42; research fellow Sloan-Kettering Institute, 1946-48, associate, 1948-52, member, 1952-83, member emeritus, 1983—, vice president, 1964-72, field coordinator human cancer, 1973-80, head Applied Therapy Laboratory, 1973—; asst professor clinical medicine Cornell University, 1949-50, assistant professor medicine, 1950-51, associate professor, 1951-52; professor Cornell University (Sloan-Kettering div.), 1952-55; professor medicine Cornell University Medical College, 1955-80, emeritus, 1980—; special consultant clinical panel Cancer Chemotherapy National Service Center, 1955-64; special consultant pub. health service, hematology study section National Institutes of Health, 1955-58; consultant Am. Cancer Society, 1958-64; chairman United States national committee International Union Against Cancer, 1960-63, chairman chemotherapy panel of research commission, 1962-66; chairman expert committee on cancer chemotherapy World Health Organization, 1961, member expert adv. panel on cancer, 1961-79 ; chairman chemotherapy adv. committee National Cancer Institute, 1970-71; member national panel consultants conquest of cancer United States Senate Committee Labor and Pub. Welfare, 1970; consultant in oncology Stamford (Connecticut), St. Albans (New York) Naval hospitals. Associate editor: Cancer Research, 1969-74; member editorial adv. board Cancer. Member Republican Town Meeting, Darien, Connecticut, 1957-65 . Served with Medical Corps, Army of the United States, 1942-45. Recipient Alfred P. Sloan Cancer Research award, 1963, Albert Lasker award in clinical cancer chemotherapy, 1972, prix Lepold Griffuel, 1970, John Phillips award Phillips Exeter Acad., 1974, David A. Karnofsky memorial award Am. Society Clinical Oncology, 1974, Jeffrey A. Gottlieb Memorial award, 1980, national annual clinical award Am. Cancer Society, 1982, others. Member Am. Society Clinical Investigation, Society Experimental Biology and Medicine, Am. Association for Cancer Research (president 1965-66), European, International, Am. socs. hematology, Am. Society Tropical Medicine, Society Study Blood, Am. Federation Clinical Research, New York Acad. Sciences, Harvey Society, Am. Society Pediatric Research (representative to division med. scis.

National Research Council 1955-58), Society for Pediatric Research, Am. Society Clinical Oncology, American Medical Association, American College of Physicians, New York County Medical Society, New York State Medical Society, Am. Institute Nutrition, Leukemia Society Am. (vice president med. and sci. affairs 1970-75, chairman med. and sci. adv. committee 1970-74), James Ewing Society, Academia Nacional de Medicina de Buenos Aires (corr.), Czechoslovak Medical Society (hon.), Brazilian National Acad. Medicine (corr.). Office: Sloan Kettering Institute Walker Lab 145 Boston Post Road Rye New York 10580

BURNS, NED HAMILTON, civil engineering educator; born Magnolia, Arkansas, November 25, 1932; son of Andrew Louis and Ila Mae (Martin) B.; married Martha Ann Fontaine, June 11, 1955; children: Kathryn Jane, Stephanie Ann, Michael Everett. Bachelor of Science, University Texas, 1954, Master of Science, 1958; Doctor of Philosophy, University Illinois, 1962. Registered professional engineer, Texas. Instructor University Texas, Austin, 1957-59, assistant professor; 1962-65, associate professor; 1965-70, professor civil engineering; 1970-83, Zarrow Centennial professor engineering; 1983—; research assistant University Illinois, Urbana, 1959-62. Author: (with T. Y. Lin) Design of Prestressed Concrete Structures, 1981 (McGraw Hill Book of Month 1982), Staten Island Version—Design of Prestressed Concrete Structures, 1982; contributor tech. papers, reports on structural engring. to professional publications. Served with United States Army, 1955-57. Recipient General Dynamics Teaching award University Texas College Engineering, 1965; recipient AMOCO Teaching award, 1983. Member Am. Concrete Institute (board directors 1983—), Post-Tensioning Institute (director 1975—), American Society of Civil Engineers (committee chairman 1975—), Prestressed Concrete Institute (committee member 1968—), National Society Professional Engineers (chapter president 1970), Texas Society Professional Engineering (Young Engineer of Year award 1970, Travis chapter Engineer of Year award 1987). Democrat. Baptist. Home: 3917 Rockledge Dr Austin Texas 78731 Office: Department Civil Engring U Tex Austin Texas 78712

BURRIS, ROBERT HARZA, biochemist, educator; born Brookings, South Dakota, April 13, 1914; son of Edward T. and Mable C. (Harza) B.; married Katherine Irene Brusse, September 12, 1945; children: Jean Carol, John Edward, Ellen Louise. Bachelor of Science, South Dakota State College, 1936, Doctor of Science, 1966; Master of Science, University Wisconsin, 1938, Doctor of Philosophy, 1940. National Research Council fellow Columbia University, 1940-41; faculty University Wisconsin, Madison, 1941—; professor University Wisconsin, 1951-84; chairman biochemistry College Agriculture, 1958-70, W.H. Peterson professor biochemistry; 1976-84, professor emeritus; 1984—. Recipient Charles Thom award Society Indsl. Microbiology, 1977; National Medal of Sci., 1980; Carty award National Acad. Sciences, 1984; Wolf award in Agr., 1985; Guggenheim fellow Cambridge University, 1954. Member Am. Chemical Society, Am. Society Biochemistry and Molecular Biology,

Am. Society Plant Physiologists (Stephen Hales award 1968, Charles Reid Barnes award 1977, president 1960), Biochem. Society, American Association for the Advancement of Science, Am. Society Microbiology, National Acad. Sciences, Am. Acad. Arts and Sciences, Am. Philosophical Society; foreign associate Indian National Sci. Acad. Home: 1015 University Bay Dr Madison Wisconsin 53705

BURTON, GLENN WILLARD, geneticist; born Clatonia, Nebraska, May 5, 1910; son of Joseph Fearn and Nellie (Rittenburg) B.; married Helen Maurine Jeffryes, December 16, 1934; children: Elizabeth Ann (Mrs. John Edward Fowler), Robert Glenn, Thomas Jeffryes, Joseph William, Richard Bennett. Bachelor of Science, University Nebraska, 1932, Doctor of Science (honorary), 1962; Master of Science, Rutgers University, 1933, Doctor of Philosophy, 1936, Doctor of Science (honorary), 1955. With United States Department Agriculture and University Georgia at Tifton Experimental Station, 1936—; principal geneticist USDA and University Georgia at Tifton Experimental Station, 1952—, chairman div. agronomy; 1950-64; University Foundation professor University Georgia, 1957. Member Tift County Board Education, 1953-58. Recipient 1st Annual Agrl. award Southern Seedsman Association, 1950, Sears-Roebuck Research award, 1953, 60, Superior Service award USDA, 1955, Distinguished Service award, 1980, 1st Ford Almanac Crops and Soils Research award, 1962, President's award for Distinguished Federal Civilian Service, 1981, National Medal of Sci., 1983; named Man of Year in Southern Agriculture Progressive Farmer, 1954, numerous other awards and citations; named to Hall of Fame USDA ARS, 1987. Fellow Am. Society Agronomy (Stevenson award 1949, John Scott award 1957, vice president 1961, president 1962); member Am. Genetic Association, Am. Society Range Management, National Acad. Sci., Sigma Xi, Alpha Zeta, Gamma Sigma Delta. Home: 421 W 10th St Tifton Georgia 31794 Office: University of Georgia Department of Agronomy Tifton Georgia 31794

BUSH, SPENCER HARRISON, metallurgist; born Flint, Michigan, April 4, 1920; son of Edward Charles and Rachel Beatrice (Roser) B.; married Roberta Lee Warren, August 28, 1948; children: David Spencer, Carl Edward. Student, Flint Junior College, 1938-40, Ohio State University, 1943-44, University Michigan, 1946-53. Registered professional engineer, California. Assistant chemist Dow Chemical Company, 1940-42, 46; associate Engineering Research Institute, University Michigan, 1947-53; research assistant Office Naval Research, 1950-53, instructor dental materials; 1951-53; metallurgist Hanford Atomic Products Operation, General Electric Company, 1953-54, supervisor physical metallurgy; 1954-57, supervisor fuels fabrication devel.; 1957-60, metallurgical specialist; 1960-63, consultant metallurgist; 1963-65; consultant to director Battelle Northwest Laboratories, Richland, Washington, 1965-70; senior staff consultant Battelle Northwest Laboratories, 1970-83; president Rev. & Synthesis Associates, consultant, 1983—; lecturer metallurgical engineering Center for Grad. Study, University

Washington, 1953-67, affiliate professor, 1967-78; chairman, committee study group on pressure vessel materials Electric Power Research Institute, 1974-78; consultant University California Lawrence Berkeley Laboratories, 1975-79; chairman committee on reactor safeguards United States Atomic Energy Commission, 1971; member Washington Board Boiler Rules, 1972-85; Gillett lecturer American Society for Testing and Materials, 1975; Mehl lecturer, 1981, member Board Nuclear Codes and Standards, 1983—. Contributor tech. articles to professional journals. Served with United States Army, 1942-46. Recipient Silver Beaver award Boy Scouts Am.; Am. Foundrymens Society fellow, 1948-50; Regents professor University California, Berkeley, 1973-74. Fellow Am. Nuclear Society (adv. editorial board nuclear applications 1965-77, board directors 1984-87, Thompson award 1987), American Society of Mechanical Engineers (chairman section XI 1985—, executive board NDE division 1984—, chairman 1987-88, member national nominating committee, 1988-90, Langer award 1983); member American Institute of Mining, Metallurgy and Petroleum Engineers (chairman ann. seminar committee 1967-68), American Society for Testing and Materials, Am. Society Metals (life, chairman program council 1966-67, trustee 1967-69, chairman fellow committee 1968), National Acad. Engineering, Sigma Xi, Tau Beta Pi, Phi Kappa Phi. Home: 630 Cedar Avenue Richland Washington 99352 Office: Battelle Pacific Northwest Labs Post Office Box 999 Richland Washington 99352

BUSSGANG, JULIAN JAKOB, electronic engineer; born Lwow, Poland, March 26, 1925; came to United States, 1949, naturalized, 1954; son of Joseph and Stephanie (Philipp) B.; married Fay Rita Vogel, August 14, 1960; children: Jessica Edith, Julia Claire, Jeffrey Joseph. Bachelor of Science, University London, 1949; Master of Science in Electrical Engineering, Massachusetts Institute of Technology, 1951; Doctor of Philosophy in Applied Physics, Harvard University, 1955. Member tech. staff Lincoln Laboratory, Massachusetts Institute of Technology, Lexington, 1951-55; manager applied research Radio Corporation of America, Burlington, Massachusetts, 1955-62; president Signatron, Incorporated, Lexington, 1962-87, consultant; 1988—; visiting lecturer Harvard University, 1964; lecturer Northeastern University, Boston, 1962-65; member Massachusetts del. White House Conference on Small Business, 1980. Associate editor: Radio Science, 1976-78; contributor chapters to books, also articles. Member Town Meeting, Lexington, 1975—; member alumni council Massachusetts Institute of Technology, 1965-72. Served with Free Polish Forces, 1942-46. Fellow Institute of Electrical and Electronics Engineers; member Research Management Association, Smaller Business Association New England. Patentee in field. Office: Signatron Incorporated 110 Hartwell Avenue Lexington Massachusetts 02173

BUTENANDT, ADOLF FRIEDRICH JOHANN, physiological chemist; born Bremerhaven, Germany, March 24, 1903; son of Otto and Wilhelmine

(Thomfohrde) B.; married Erika von Ziegner, 1931; 2 sons, 5 daughters. Doctor of Philosophy; educated, Oberrealschule Bremerhaven, University Marburg, University Göttingen. Sci. assistant Chemical Institute Göttingen University, 1927-30, docent in organic and biological chemistry; 1931; professor chemistry, director Organic Chemistry Institute Danzig (Germany) Institute Tech., 1933-36; director Kaiser Wilhelm Institute Biochemistry, Berlin; director Max Planck Institute Biochemistry, Berlin, Munich, 1936-72; professor physiological chemistry Munich University, 1956-71, professor emeritus; 1971—. Author: Biochemie der Wirkstoffe; also articles. Recipient Nobel prize for chemistry, 1939; Adolf von Harnack medal Max Planck Society, 1973; decorated Orden pour le Mérite, 1962, commander Légion d'Honneur, Ordr Palmes Académiques; Österreichisches Ehrenzeichen für Wissenschaft und Kunst. Member Max Planck Society (president 1960-72, hon. president 1972), Acad. Sciences Paris (foreign).

BUTLER, JAMES ROBERT, geology educator; born Macon, Georgia, April 17, 1930; son of Walter Clark and Edna Ruth (Hardwick) B.; married Gail Ann Sargeant, July 30, 1960 (divorced 1980); children—James Robert, Sarah Pace, Erin Gail. Bachelor of Science, University Georgia, 1952; Master of Science, University Colorado, 1955; Doctor of Philosophy, Columbia University, 1962. Lecturer Columbia University, New York City, 1959-60; successively assistant professor, associate professor, professor University North Carolina, Chapel Hill, 1960—; consultant in field. Contributor articles to professional journals. Served to 1st lieutenant United States Army, 1954-56. Fellow Geological Society Am. (chairman Southeast section 1980); member Mineralogical Society Am., National Association Geology Teachers. Democrat. Avocations: travel; hiking. Home: 12 Oakwood Dr Chapel Hill North Carolina 27514 Office: U North Carolina Department Geology Box 3315 Chapel Hill North Carolina 27599-3315

CAFFARELLI, LUIS ANGEL, mathematician, educator; born Buenos Aires, Argentina, December 8, 1948; came to United States, 1973; son of Luis and Hilda Delia (Cespi) C.; married Irene Andrea Martinez-Gamba; children: Alejandro, Nicolas, Mauro. Masters degree, University Buenos Aires, 1969, Doctor of Philosophy, 1972. Postdoctoral assistant, assistant professor University Buenos Aires, 1972-73; assistant professor to professor University Minnesota, 1973-83; professor math. University Chicago, 1983-86; faculty Institute for Advanced Study, Princeton, New Jersey, 1986—; professor New York University, 1980-82. Contributor articles to professional journals. Recipient Stampacchia prize Scuola Normale de Pisa, 1983, Bocher prize Am. Math. Society, 1984; Pius XI medal, 1988; Guggenheim grantee. Member American Association for the Advancement of Science, Accademia dei XL. Office: Institute Advanced Study Olden Lane Princeton New Jersey 08540

CALDWELL, ELWOOD FLEMING, food science educator, researcher, editor; born Gladstone, Manitoba, Canada, April 3, 1923; son of Charles Fleming and Frances Marion (Ridd) C.; married Irene Margaret Sebille, June 13, 1949; children: John

Fleming, Keith Allan; married Florence Annette Zar, June 23, 1979. Bachelor of Science, University Manitoba, 1943; Master of Arts in food chemistry, University Toronto, 1949, Doctor of Philosophy in nutrition, 1953; Master of Business Administration, University Chicago, 1956. Chemist Lake of the Woods Milling Company, Can., 1943-47; research chemist Can. Breweries Limited, Toronto, Ontario, 1948-49; chief chemist Christie, Brown & Company div. Nabisco, Toronto, 1949-51; research associate in nutrition University Toronto, 1951-53; with Quaker Oats Company, Barrington, Illinois, 1953-72, director research and devel.; until 1972; professor, head department food sci. and nutrition University Minnesota, St. Paul, 1972-86, executive associate to dean college agricultural; 1986-88; director sci. services, executive editor Cereal Foods World for Am. Association Cereal Chemists, 1988—; chairman board Dairy Quality Control Institute, Incorporated, St. Paul, 1972-88, R. & D. Associates for Military Food & Packaging, Incorporated, San Antonio, 1970-71; chairman evening program in food sci. Illinois Institute Tech., Chicago, 1965-69. Contributor articles to sci. journals. Chairman North Barrington (Illinois) Board Appeals, 1966-69, mayor, 1969-72; vice-chmn. Barrington Area Council Govts., 1972; board of directors Family Guidance Barrington, 1971-72. Recipient cert. of appreciation for civilian service U.S. Army Materiel Command, 1970. Fellow Institute Food Technologists (Chmn.'s Service award Chicago section 1975, Chmn.'s award Minnesota section 1988); member Am. Home Economics Association, Phi Tau Sigma, Gamma Sigma Delta (award of merit 1988), Phi Upsilon Omicron. Republican. Lutheran. Club: Minnesota Alumni (Minneapolis). Office: Am Association Cereal Chemists 3340 Pilot Knob Road Saint Paul Minnesota 55121

CALLAHAN, HARRY LESLIE, civil engineer; born Kansas City, Missouri, January 11, 1923; son of B. Frank and Myrtle Lou (Anderson) C.; married V. June Yohn, December 16, 1944; children: Michael Thomas, Maureen Lynn, Kevin Leslie. Bachelor of Science in Civil Engineering, University Kansas, 1944; postgraduate, University of California at Los Angeles. Executive partner Black & Veatch Company, Kansas City, Missouri, 1946-89; retired Black & Veatch Company; director B & V Waste Sci. & Tech. Corp.; chairman CCL Construction Cons., Overland Park, Kansas. Contributor articles to professional journals. 1st lieutenant, infantry Army of the United States, 1944-46, Japan. Recipient Missouri Design Excellence award 1st place, 1972. Fellow American Society of Civil Engineers, Am. Cons. Engineers Council; member Am. Nuclear Society, National Society Professional Engineers, Society Military Engineers, Am. Concrete Institute, Water Pollution Control Federation, Combustion Institute, Kappa Sigma. Congregationalist. Clubs: Kansas City, Leawood South Country, Homestead, Chancellor, University Kansas, Sadelle & Sirloin, Rancho Viejo. Office: CCL Constrn Cons 4400 College Boulevard Suite 150 Overland Park Kansas 66211

CALVIN, MELVIN, chemist, educator; born St. Paul, April 8, 1911; son of Elias and Rose I. (Hervitz) C.; married Genevieve Jemtegaard, 1942; children: Elin, Karole, Noel. Bachelor of Science, Michigan College Mining and Tech., 1931, Doctor of Science, 1955; Doctor of Philosophy, University Minnesota, 1935, Doctor of Science, 1969; hon research fellow, University Manchester, England, 1935-37; Guggenheim fellow, 1967; Doctor of Science, Nottingham University, 1958, Oxford (England) University, 1959, Northwestern University, 1961, Wayne State University, 1962, Gustavus Adolphus College, 1963, Polytechnic Institute Brooklyn, 1962, University Notre Dame, 1965, University Gent, Belgium, 1970, Whittier College, 1971, Clarkson College, 1976, University Paris Val-de-Marne, 1977, Columbia University, 1979, Grand Valley University, 1986. With University California, Berkeley, 1937—; successively instructor chemistry, assistant professor, professor, University professor, director Laboratory Chemical Biodynamics University California, 1963-80, associate director Lawrence Berkeley Laboratory; 1967-80; Peter Reilly lecturer University Notre Dame, 1949; Harvey lecturer New York Acad. Medicine, 1951; Harrison Howe lecturer Rochester section Am. Chemical Society, 1954; Falk-Plaut lecturer Columbia University, 1954; Edgar Fahs Smith Memorial lecturer University Pennsylvania and Philadelphia section Am. Chemical Society, 1955; Donegani Foundation lecturer Italian National Acad. Sci., 1955; Max Tishler lecturer Harvard University, 1956; Karl Folkers lecturer University Wisconsin, 1956; Baker lecturer Cornell University, 1958; London lecturer, 1961, Willard lecturer, 1982; Vanuxem lecturer Princeton University, 1969; Distinguished lecturer Michigan State University, 1977; Prather lecturer Harvard University, 1980; Dreyfus lecturer Grinnell College, 1981, Berea College, 1982; Barnes lecturer Colorado College, 1982; Nobel lecturer University Maryland, 1982; Abbott lecturer University North Dakota, 1983; Gunning lecturer University Alberta, 1983; O'Leary distinguished lecturer Gonzaga University, 1984; Danforth lecturer Dartmouth College, 1984, Grinnell College, 1984; R.P. Scherer lecturer University South Florida, 1984; Imperial Oil lecturer University Western Ontario, Can., 1985; distinguished lecturer department chemistry University Calgary, Can., 1986; Melvin Calvin lecturer Michigan Tech. University, 1986; Eastman professor Oxford (England) University, 1967-68. Author: (with G. E. K. Branch) The Theory of Organic Chemistry, 1940, Isotopic Carbon, (with others), 1949, Chemistry of Metal Chelate Compounds, (with Martell), 1952, Path of Carbon in Photosynthesis, (with Bassham), 1957, (with Bassham) Photosynthesis of Carbon Compounds, 1962, Chemical Evolution, 1969; contributor articles to chemical and sci. journals. Recipient prize Sugar Research Foundation, 1950, Flintoff medal prize Brit. Chemical Society, 1953, Stephen Hales award Am. Society Plant Physiologists, 1956, Nobel prize in chemistry, 1961; Davy medal Royal Society, 1964; Virtanen medal, 1975; Priestley medal, 1978; Am. Institute Chemists medal, 1979; Feodor Lynen medal, 1983; Sterling B. Hendricks medal, 1983, Melvin Calvin Medal of Distinction Michigan Tech. University, 1985. Member Britain's Royal Society London (foreign member), Am. Chemical Society (Richards medal N.E. section 1956, Chemical Society Nichols medal New York section 1958, award for nuclear applications in chemistry, president 1971, Gibbs medal Chicago section 1977, Priestley medal 1978, Oesper award Cincinnati section, 1981), Am. Acad. Arts and Sciences, National Acad. Sciences, Royal Dutch Acad. Sciences, Japan Acad., Am. Philosophical Society, Sigma Xi, Tau Beta Pi, Phi Lambda Upsilon. Office: U California Department Chemistry Berkeley California 94720

CAMPBELL, JOHN ROY, animal scientist, educator; born Goodman, Missouri, June 14, 1933; son of Carl J. and Helen (Nicoletti) C.; married Eunice Vieten, August 7, 1954; children: Karen L., Kathy L., Keith L. Bachelor of Science, University Missouri, Columbia, 1955, Master of Science, 1956, Doctor of Philosophy, 1960. Instructor animal sci. University Missouri, Columbia, 1960-61, assistant professor; 1961-65, associate professor; 1965-68, professor; from 1968; associate dean, director resident instruction College Agriculture, University Illinois, Urbana, 1978-83, dean College Agriculture; 1983-88; president Oklahoma State University, Stillwater, 1988—. Author: (with J.F. Lasley) The Science of Animals That Serve Humanity 1969, 2d edition, 1975, 3d edition, 1985, In Touch with Students, 1972, (with R.T. Marshall) The Science of Providing Milk for Man, 1975. Recipient Outstanding Teacher award University Missouri, 1967; Superior Teaching award Gamma Sigma Delta, international award for distinguished service to agr., 1985. Member Am. Dairy Sci. Association (director, president 1980-81, Ralston Purina Distinguished Teaching award 1973), National Association College Teachers Agriculture (Ensminger Interstate Distinguished Teacher award 1973). Office: Oklahoma State Office of President Stillwater Oklahoma 74078

CANNON, PAUL JUDE, physician, educator; born New York City, February 20, 1933; son of John W. and Rita K. Cannon; married Chantal de Cannart d'Hammale, August 5, 1959; children: Christopher P., Peter J., Anne B., Karen C. Bachelor of Arts, Holy Cross College, 1954, Doctor of Science (honorary), 1977; Doctor of Medicine, Harvard University, 1958. Assistant professor medicine Columbia University College Physicians and Surgeons, New York City, 1965-70, associate professor; 1970-75, professor medicine; 1975—; associate attending physician Presbyn. Hospital, New York City, 1970-75, attending physician; 1975—; member cardiovascular and renal study section National Heart, Lung and Blood Institute, 1974-77, member diagnostic radiology study section, 1983—. Contributor articles to professional journals; member editorial board Circulation Journal, 1976—, Am. Journal Medicine, 1980—, Nephron, 1976—. Recipient Career Devel. award National Institutes of Health, 1965-75; grantee National Heart, Lung and Blood Institute, 1965—. Fellow Am. College Cardiology, American College of Physicians; member Am. Association Physicians, Am. Society Clinical Investigation, Am. Physiological Society, Am. Heart Association, Practicioners' Society New York (secretary 1983-85). Democrat. Roman Catholic. Avocations: hiking; tennis; skiing; violin. Home: 96 Avondale Road Ridgewood New Jersey 07450 Office: Columbia College of Physicians and Surgeons 630 W 168th St New York New York 10032

CANTILLI, EDMUND JOSEPH, engineer, planner, educator, author, safety expert; born Yonkers, New York, February 12, 1927; son of Ettore and Maria (deRubeis) C.; married Nella Franco, May 15, 1948; children—Robert, John, Teresa. Bachelor of Arts, Columbia University, 1954, Bachelor of Science, 1955; certificate, Yale Bur. Hwy. Traffic, 1957; Doctor of Philosophy in Transportation Planning, Polytechnic Institute Brooklyn, 1972; postgraduate in urban planning and public safety, New York University. Registered professional engineer, New York, New Jersey, California; certified safety professional. Transportation engineer Port of New York Authority, New York City, 1955-59; project planner Port of New York Authority, 1958-60, terminals analyst; 1960-62, engineer safety research and studies; 1962-67, supervising engineer; 1967-69; research associate div. transportation planning Polytechnic Institute Brooklyn, 1969-72; associate professor transportation engineering Poly University, 1972-77, professor; 1977—; teacher Italian, algebra, traffic engineering, urban planning, transportation planning, urban and transportation geography, land use planning, aesthetics, environment, industrial, traffic and transportation safety engineering, human factors engineering, 1965—; principal Impetus Services Incorporated, 1985—; president Urbitran Associates, 1973-81; consultant community planning, traffic engineering, transportation planning, transportation safety, accident reconstrn., environmental impacts, 1969—; president, chairman board Institute for Safety in Transportation, Incorporated, 1977—. Author: Programming Environmental Improvements in Public Transportation, 1974, Transportation and the Disadvantaged, 1974, Transportation System Safety, 1979; editor: Transportation and Aging, 1971, Pedestrian Planning and Design, 1971, Traffic Engineering Theory and Control, 1973; editor and calligrapher There is No Death That is Not Ennobled by So Great A Cause, 1976; contributor over 200 articles to professional journals and trade journals; developer methods of severity evaluation of accidents, identification and priority-setting of roadside hazards, transp. system safety; introduced diagrammatic traffic signs, collision energy-absorption devices. Served with United States Army, 1945-49, 50-51. Fellow American Society of Civil Engineers, Institute Transportation Engineers; member Am. Planning Association, Am. Institute Cert. Planners (cert.), Am. Society Safety Engineers, System Safety Society, Human Factors Society, Mensa, Sigma Xi. Home: 134 Euston Road S West Hempstead New York 11552 Office: Polytechnic U 333 Jay St Brooklyn New York 11201

CAREY, GRAHAM FRANCIS, engineering educator; born Cairns, Queensland, Australia, November 14, 1944; came to United States, 1968; son of Lionel Dudley and Alma Lilian Carey; married Kira Iljins, January 13, 1968; children: Varis, Tija. Bachelor of Science, University Queensland, 1965, Bachelor of Science with honors, 1966; Master of Science, University Washington, 1970, Doctor of Philosophy, 1974. Registered professional engineer. Research engineer Boeing Company, Seattle, 1968-70; research professor University Washington, Seattle, 1974-76; professor University Texas, Austin,

1977—; United States representative Fenomech Conference, Federal Republic Germany, 1978, U.S.-Germany, Federal Republic Germany, 1981; lecturer Summer Research Institute, Australia, 1984; adj. fellow Minnesota Supercomputer Institute, Mpla., 1986; director computational fluid dynamics laboratory University Texas, 1986—. Author: Introduction to Finite Element Methods, 1974, Finite Element Series, volumes I-VI, 1980-86; editor: (book) Finite Elements in Fluids, 1984; (international journal) Communications in Applied Numerical Methods, 1984—; contributor numerous articles to professional journals. Member National Committee on Undergrad. Math. and Applications, Society for Industrial and Applied Math., International Association for Math. and Computers in Simulation, Am. Acad. Mechanics, Society for Engineering Sci. Office: U Tex Austin Department Aerospace Engring Austin Texas 78712

CARLIN, HERBERT J., electrical engineering educator, researcher; born New York City, May 1, 1917; son of Louis Aaron and Shirley (Salzman) C.; children—Seth Andrew, Elliot Michael; married Mariann J. Hartmann, June 29, 1975. Bachelor of Electrical Engineering, Columbia College, 1938, Master of Electrical Engineering, 1950; Doctor of Philosophy in Electrical Engineering, Polytechnic Institute New York, 1947. Engineer Westinghouse Corp., Newark, 1940-45; from assistant to associate professor Polytechnic Institute Brooklyn, 1945-60, professor, head electrophysics; 1960-66; J. Preston Levis professor engineering Cornell University, Ithaca, New York, 1966—, director electrical engineer-ing; 1966-75; member adv. panel National Bureau Standards, Boulder, Colorado, 1967-70; member rev. committee Lehigh University, Bethlehem, Pennsylvania, 1966-74, University Pennsylvania, Philadelphia, 1979-82; visiting professor Ecole Normale Superieure, Paris, 1964-67, Massachusetts Institute of Technology, Boston, 1973-74; visiting scientist National Center for Telecommunications, Issy Les Moulineaux, France, 1979-80; visiting lecturer University Genoa, Italy, summer 1973, University London, December 1979, The Technion, Haifa, Israel, March 1980, Tianjin University, China, summer 1982, University College, Dublin, Ireland, summer 1983, Polytech. of Turin, Italy, summer 1985. Fellow National Science Foundation, 1964; recipient Outstanding Achievement award U.S. Air Force, 1965. Fellow Institute of Electrical and Electronics Engineers (chairman professional group on circuit theory 1955-56, Centennial medal 1985). Avocations: flute; photography. Home: 8 Highland Park Lane Ithaca New York 14850 Office: Cornell University 201 Phillips Hall Ithaca New York 14853

CARPENTER, MALCOLM SCOTT, astronaut, oceanographer; born Boulder, Colorado, May 1, 1925; son of Marion Scott and Florence Kelso (Noxon) C.; married Rene Louise Price, September 9, 1948 (divorced); children—Marc Scott, Robyn Jay, Kristen Elaine, Candace Noxon; married Maria Roach, 1972; children—Matthew Scott, Nicholas André. Bachelor of Science in Aeronautical Engineering, University Colorado, 1962. Commissioned ensign United States Navy, 1949, advanced through grades to commander; 1959; assigned various flight training schools 1949-51, (Patrol Squadron 6), Barbers Point, Hawaii, 1951; also in (Patrol Squadron 6), Korea, 1951-52; grad. (Navy Test Pilot School), 1954; assigned electronics test div. (Naval Air Test Center), 1954-57, (Naval General Line School), 1957, (Naval Air Intelligence School), 1957-58; air intelligence officer (United States Ship Hornet), 1958-59; joined Project Mercury, man-in-space project National Aeronautics and Space Administration, 1959; completed 3 orbit space flight mission in spacecraft (Aurora 7), May 1962; member (United States Navy Aquanaut Project), 1965-67; retired from United States Navy, 1969; now engaged in private oceanographic and energy research business. Fellow Institute Environmental Sciences (hon.); member Delta Tau Delta. Address: Post Office Box 3161 Vail Colorado 81658

CARR, GERALD PAUL, astronaut; born Denver, August 22, 1932; son of Thomas Ernest and Freda (Wright) C.; divorced; children: Jennifer, Jamee, Jeffrey, John, Jessica, Joshua; married Patricia Musick, September 14, 1979. Bachelor of Science in Mechanical Engineering, University Southern California, 1954; Bachelor of Science in Aeronautical Engineering, United States Naval Postgrad. School, 1961; Master of Science in Aeronautical Engineering, Princeton University, 1962; Doctor of Science, St. Louis University, 1976. Registered professional engineer, Texas. Commissioned 2d lieutenant United States Marine Corps, 1954, advanced through grades to colonel; 1973, retired; 1975; jet fighter pilot United States, Mediterranean, Far East, 1956-65; astronaut National Aeronautics and Space Administration, Houston, 1966-77; commander 3d Skylab Manned Mission, 1973-74; president CAMUS, Incorporated, Huntsville, Arkansas. Board of directors Houston Pops Orchestra, Sunsat Energy Council, Space Foundation. Recipient Group Achievement award National Aeronautics and Space Administration, 1971, Distinguished Service medal, 1974; Gold medal City of Chicago, 1974; Gold medal City of New York, 1974; Alumni Merit award University Southern California, 1974; Distinguished Eagle Scout award Boy Scouts Am., 1974; Robert J. Collier Trophy, 1974; Robert H. Goddard Memorial trophy, 1975; FAI Gold Space medal; others. Fellow Am. Astronautical Society (Flight Achievement award 1975); member Marine Corps Association, Marine Corps Aviation Association, National Society Professional Engineers, Society Experimental Test Pilots, Texas Society Professional Engineers, National Space Institute, University Southern California Alumni Association, Tau Kappa Epsilon. Presbyterian. Office: Post Office Box 919 Huntsville AR 72740-2966

CARRIER, GEORGE FRANCIS, applied mathematics educator; born Millinocket, Maine, May 4, 1918; son of Charles Mosher and Mary (Marcaux) C.; married Mary Casey, June 30, 1946; children: Kenneth, Robert, Mark. Mechanical Engineer, Cornell University, 1939, Doctor of Philosophy, 1944. From assistant professor to professor Brown University, 1946-52; Gordon McKay professor mechanical engineering Harvard University, 1952-72, T. Jefferson Coolidge professor applied math.; 1972-88, emeritus; 1988—;

member council Engineering College, Cornell University. Co-author: Functions of a Complex Variable, 1966, Ordinary Differential Equations, 1968, Partial Differential Equations, 1976; associate editor: Quar. Applied Math. Former trustee Rensselaer Polytechnical Institute, Troy, New York. Recipient Von Karman prize American Society of Civil Engineers, 1977. Fellow Am. Acad. Arts and Sciences; hon. fellow Brit. Institute Math. and Its Applications; hon. member American Society of Mechanical Engineers (Timoshenko medal 1978, Centennial medal 1980); member National Acad. Sciences (award applied math. and mumerical analysis 1980), Society Industrial and Applied Math. (Von Karman prize 1979), National Acad. Engineering, Am. Philosophical Society, Am. Physical Society (Fluid Dynamics prize 1984), National Research Council, Commission on Physical Sciences Math and Resources. Office: Pierce Hall 311 Harvard University Cambridge Massachusetts 02138

CASTRO, JOSEPH RONALD, physician, oncology researcher, educator; born Chicago, April 9, 1934; married Barbara Ann Kauth, October 12, 1957. Bachelor of Science in Natural Science, Loyola University, Chicago, 1956, Doctor of Medicine, 1958. Diplomate: Am. Board Radiology, 1964. Intern Rockford (Illinois) Memorial Hospital; resident United States Naval Hospital, San Diego; associate radiotherapist and associate professor University Tex.-M.D. Anderson Hospital and Tumor Institute, 1967-71; professor radiology/radiation oncology University California School Medicine, San Francisco, 1971—; vice-chairman department radiation oncology University California School Medicine, 1980—; director particle radiotherapy Lawrence Berkeley Laboratory, California, 1975—; member program project rev. committee National Institute Health/Nat. Cancer Institute Cancer Program, 1982-85. Author sci. articles. Past president, chairman board trustees Northern California Cancer Program, 1980-83. Served to lieutenant commander, Medical Corps United States Navy, 1956-66. Recipient Teaching award Mount Zion Hospital and Medical Center, San Francisco, 1972. Fellow Am. College Radiology; member Rocky Mountain Radiological Society (hon.), Am. Society Therapeutic Radiology. Office: Building 55 Lawrence Lawrence Berkeley Lab Berkeley California 94720

CAVINESS, VERNE STRUDWICK, JR., neurologist, educator; born Raleigh, North Carolina, July 25, 1934. Bachelor of Arts, Duke University, 1956; Doctor of Philosophy, Oxford University, England, 1960; Doctor of Medicine, Harvard University, 1962. Assistant professor Harvard University Medical School, Boston, 1971-76, associate professor neurology; 1976-83, Joseph P. and Rose F. Kennedy professor child neurology; 1983—; director research neuropathology devel. Eunice Kennedy Shriver Center, 1976—; assistant neurologist Massachusetts General Hospital, Boston, 1971—; senior investigator East K. Shriver Institute, Waltham, Massachusetts, 1971—. National Institutes of Health specia! research fellow Harvard University Medical School, 1969-71. Member American Association for the Advancement of Science, Am. Neurological Association, Am. Acad. Neurology.

CERNAN, EUGENE A., management company executive, former astronaut; born Chicago, March 14, 1934; son of Andrew G. C.; married Jan Nanna; 1 child, Teresa Dawn. Bachelor of Science in Electrical Engineering, Purdue University, 1956; postgraduate, United States Naval Postgrad. School. Joined United States Navy, 1956; advanced through grades to captain; former member attack squadrons 126, 113 United States Navy, Miramar (California) Naval Air Station; astronaut with Lyndon B. Johnson Space Center, National Aeronautics and Space Administration; pilot Gemini 9; lunar module pilot Apollo 10, 1969; space craft commander (last man to leave footprints on moon) Apollo 17, 1972; Special assistant to program manager Apollo-Soyuz project 1973-76, retired; 1976; executive vice president international Coral Petroleum, Incorporated, Houston, 1976-81; president Cernan Corp., Houston, 1981—. Recipient National Aeronautics and Space Administration Distinguished Service Medal (2), Exceptional Service Medal, Navy Distinguished Service Medal, Distinguished Flying Cross, Gold Space Medal Federation Aeronautique Internationale, Veterans of Foreign Wars Space Medal, New York City Gold medal. Fellow Am. Astronautical Society; member Society Experimental Test Pilots, Sigma Xi, Phi Gamma Delta., Tau Beta Pi. Address: Cernan Corp 900 Town and Country Lane Suite 300 Houston Texas 77024

CHAFFEE, FREDERIC H., JR., astronomer; born West Point, New York, April 4, 1941; son of Frederic H. and Winnifred (Waddell) C.; married Holly Lowry, November 19, 1969 (divorced 1977). Bachelor of Arts, Dartmouth College, 1963; Doctor of Philosophy, University Arizona, 1968. Astronomer Smithsonian Astrophysical Observatory, Cambridge, Massachusetts, 1968-70; resident astronomer Mount Hopkins Observatory, Amado, Arizona, 1970-81, resident director; 1981-84; director Multiple Mirror Telescope Observatory, Tucson, 1984—. Contributor articles to sci. journals. Vice president Arizona Friends of Chamber Music, Tucson, 1984—. With United States Army, 1968-1970. Member Am. Astronomical Society, International Astronomical Union, Astronomical Society of the Pacific. Democrat. Avocations: golf, classical piano. Home: 2256 E Prince Road Tucson Arizona 85719 Office: Multiple Mirror Telescope Obs U Ariz Tempe Arizona 85721

CHAGNON, MRS. ROGER G. See SCHMIDT-NIELSEN, BODIL MIMI

CHAKRABARTY, ANANDA MOHAN, microbiologist; born Sainthia, India, April 4, 1938; son of Satya Dos and Sasthi Bala (Mukherjee) C.; married Krishna Chakraverty, May 26, 1965; children—Kaberi, Asit. Bachelor of Science, St. Xavier's College, 1958; Master of Science, University Calcutta, 1960, Doctor of Philosophy, 1965. Senior research officer University Calcutta, 1964-65; research associate in biochemistry University Illinois, Urbana, 1965-71; member staff General Electric Research and Devel. Center, Schenectady, 1971-79; professor department microbiology University Illinois Medical Center, 1979—. Editor: Genetic Engineering, 1977, Biodegradation and Detoxification of Environmental Pollutants, 1982. Named Scientist of Year Indsl. Research Magazine, 1975; recipient

Inventor of the Year award Patent Lawyers' Association, 1982, Pub. Affairs award Am. Chemical Society, 1984, Distinguished Scientist award U.S. Environmental Protection Agency, 1985, Merit award National Institute Health, 1986. Member Am. Society Microbiology, Society Industrial Microbiology, Am. Society Biological Chemists. Home: 206 Julia Dr Villa Park Illinois 60181 Office: U Illinois Med Center 835 S Wolcott St Chicago Illinois 60612

CHALLINOR, DAVID, scientific institute administrator; born New York City, July 11, 1920; son of David and Mercedes (Crimmins) C.; married Joan Ridder, November 22, 1952; children: Julia M., Mary E., Sarah L., D. Thompson. Bachelor of Arts, Harvard University, 1943; Master of Forestry, Yale University, 1959, Doctor of Philosophy, 1966. With Offerman-Anderson, Clayton & Company, Houston, 1947-51; cotton farmer Culberson County, Texas, 1951-53; assistant secretary First Mortgage Company, Houston, 1953-57; research assistant Connecticut Agriculture Experiment Station, New Haven, 1959-60; deputy director Yale Peabody Mus., New Haven, 1960-65; acting director Yale Peabody Mus., 1965-66; special assistant in tropical biology Smithsonian Institution, Washington, 1966-67, deputy director office international activities; 1967-68, director office international activities; 1968-70, assistant secretary sci.; 1971-87, sci. advisor to secretary; 1988—; Am. administrative secretary Charles Darwin Foundation, 1971—. Contributor articles to sci. journals. Trustee Manhattanville College, 1964-70, Environmental Law Institute, 1975-84, 86—; board of directors Environ Def. Fund, 1982—, African Wildlife Foundation, 1980—. Served with United States Naval Reserve, 1943-46. Fellow American Association for the Advancement of Science; member Sigma Xi. Home: 3117 Hawthorne St Northwest Washington District of Columbia 20008 Office: Smithsonian Institute National Zoo 3000 Connecticut Avenue Northwest Washington District of Columbia 20008

CHALMERS, THOMAS CLARK, physician, educational and research adminstrator; born Forest Hills, New York, December 8, 1917; son of Thomas Clark and Elizabeth (Ducat) C.; married Frances Crawford Talcott, August 31, 1942; children: Elizabeth Ducat Chalmers Wright, Frances Talcott Chalmers Smith, Thomas Clark, Richard Matthew. Student, Yale University, 1936-39; Doctor of Medicine, Columbia University, 1943. Diplomate: Am. Board Internal Medicine. Intern Presbyn. Hospital, New York City, 1943-44; research fellow New York University Malaria Research Unit, Goldwater Memorial Hospital, New York City, 1944-45; resident Harvard Medical Services of Boston City Hospital, 1945-47; private practice internal medicine Cambridge, Massachusetts, 1947-53; assistant physician Thorndike Memorial Laboratory, 1947-53; chief medical services Lemuel Shattuck Hospital, Boston, 1955-68; assistant chief medical director for research and education Veteran's Administration, Washington, 1968-70; associate director clinical care National Institutes of Health, also director clinical center National Institutes of Health, Bethesda, Maryland, 1970-73; president Mount Sinai Medical Center, 1973-83; professor medicine, dean Mount Sinai School Medicine, New

York City, 1973-83, Distinguished Service professor, director clinical trials unit; 1983-86, president emeritus, dean emeritus; 1983—; visiting professor Harvard School Pub. Health, 1983-86, lecturer department health policy and management, Tech. Assessment Group; 1986—; professor medicine Tufts University, 1961-68, George Washington University, 1970-73; member ethics adv. board, special consultant National Institutes of Health, Department of Health and Human Services, 1980; distinguished physician Boston Veteran's Administration Hospital, 1987—. Contributor numerous articles professional journals. Board of directors New England Home for Little Wanderers, 1960-65; board regents National Library Medicine, 1978-79; trustee Dartmouth Hitchcock Medical Center, 1987—, chairman board, 1983-87. Served as captain, Medical Corps Army of the United States, 1953-55. Member Am. Association Study Liver Diseases (president 1959), Am. Clinical and Climatological Association, American College of Physicians, Am. Federation Clinical Research, Am. Gastroentorological Association (president 1969), Am. Society Clinical Investigation, Association Am. Physicians, New York Acad. Medicine, Institute Medicine of National Acad. Sciences, International Physicians for the Prevention of Nuclear War, Eastern Gut Club, Physicians for Social Responsibility, Am. Acad. Arts and Sciences. Office: Harvard School Pub Health Department Health Policy & Management 677 Huntington Avenue Boston Massachusetts 02115

CHAMBERLAIN, JOSEPH MILES, astronomer, educator; born Peoria, Illinois, July 26, 1923; son of Maurice Silloway and Roberta (Miles) C.; married Paula Bruninga, December 12, 1945; children—Janet Ann, Susan Louise, Barbara Jean. Bachelor of Science, United States Merchant Marine Academy, 1944; Bachelor of Arts, Bradley University, 1947; Master of Arts, Teachers College Columbia, 1950, Doctor of Education, 1962. Instructor Columbia Junior High School, Peoria, 1943; instructor navigation War Shipping Administration, 1944-45; boys secretary Young Men's Christian Association, Peoria, 1946-47; instructor United States Merchant Marine Acad., Kings Point, New York, 1947-50; assistant professor United States Merchant Marine Acad., 1950-52; assistant curator Am. Museum-Hayden Planetarium, New York City, 1952-53; general manager, chief astronomer Am. Museum-Hayden Planetarium, 1953-56, chairman; 1956-64; assistant director Am. Mus. Natural History, 1964-68; director Adler Planetarium, Chicago, 1968—; president Adler Planetarium, 1977—; professor astronomy Northwestern University, 1968-78; professorial lecturer University Chicago, 1968-71; led eclipse expeditions to, Can., 1954, 79, Ceylon, 1955, Pacific Ocean, 1977, astro-geodetic expeditions to, Can., 1956, 57, Greenland, 1958; dean council of sci. staff Am. Mus. National History, 1960-62. Co-author: Planets, Stars and Space, 1957; author: Time and the Stars, 1964; also articles on popular astronomy. Active Boy Scouts Am., Metropolitan Chicago Young Men's Christian Association. Served to lieutenant United States Naval Reserve, 1945-46; staff Naval Reserves Officers School 1953-54, New York City. Member Am. Astronomical Society,

International Astronomical Union, International Planetarium Directors Conference (vice chairman 1968-77, chairman 1977-87), Great Lakes Planetarium Association, International Planetarium Society, Midwest Museums Conference, Am. Polar Society, Am. Association Museums (member council 1965-77, vice president 1971-74, president 1974-75), Phi Delta Kappa, Phi Kappa Phi, Kappa Delta Pi. Republican. Presbyterian (elder). Clubs: University (Chicago), Tavern (Chicago), Econ. (Chicago), Metropolitan (Chicago); Dutch Treat. Home: 22428 N Newberry Court Kildeer Illinois 60047 Office: Adler Planetarium 1300 S Lake Shore Dr Chicago Illinois 60605

CHAMBERLAIN, JOSEPH WYAN, astronomer, educator; born Boonville, Missouri, August 24, 1928; son of Gilbert Lee and Jessie (Wyan) C.; married Marilyn Jean Roesler, September 10, 1949; children: Joy Anne, David Wyan, Jeffrey Scott. Bachelor of Arts, University Missouri, 1948, Master of Arts, 1949; Master of Science, University Michigan, 1951, Doctor of Philosophy, 1952. Project sci. aurora and airglow United States Air Force Cambridge Research Center, 1951-53; research associate Yerkes Observatory, Chicago, 1953-55; assistant professor Yerkes Observatory, 1955-59, associate professor; 1959-60, professor; 1961-62, associate director; 1960-62; associate director planetary sciences div. of Kitt Peak National Observatory, 1962-70, astronomer, planetary sciences div.; 1970-71; director Lunar Sci. Institute, Houston, 1971-73; professor department space physics and astronomy Rice University, Houston, 1971—. Author: Physics of the Aurora

and Airglow, 1961, Theory of Planetary Atmospheres, 1978, 2d edition, 1987. Editor: Revs. of Geophysics and Space Physics, 1974-80; member editorial board: Planetary Space Science. Recipient Warner prize Am. Astronomical Society, 1961; Alfred P. Sloan research fellow, 1961-63. Fellow Royal Astronomical Society (foreign), American Association for the Advancement of Science, Am. Geophysical Union (councilor 1968-70); member Am. Astronomical Society (councilor 1961-64, chairman division planetary scis. 1969-71), Am. Physical Society, International Astronomical Union, International Union Geodesy Geophysics, International Sci. Radio Union, National Research Council Assembly Math. and Physical Sciences (executive committee 1973-78), National Acad. Sci. (chairman geophysics section 1972-75), Society Sci. Exploration. Office: Rice U/Dept Space Physics and Astronomy Post Office Box 1892 Houston Texas 77251

CHAMBERLAIN, OWEN, nuclear physicist; born San Francisco, July 10, 1920; divorced 1978; 4 children; married June Steingart, 1980. Bachelor of Arts (Cramer fellow), Dartmouth College, 1941; Doctor of Philosophy, University Chicago, 1949. Instructor physics University California, Berkeley, 1948-50, assistant professor; 1950-54, associate professor; 1954-58, professor; 1958-89, professor emeritus; 1989—; civilian physicist Manhattan District, Berkeley, Los Alamos, 1942-46. Guggenheim fellow, 1957-58; Loeb lecturer at Harvard University, 1959; Recipient Nobel prize (with Emilio Segré) for physics, for discovery anti-proton,

1959. Fellow Am. Physical Society, Am. Acad. Arts and Sciences; member National Acad. Sciences. Office: U California Physics Department Berkeley California 94720

CHANDRA, ASHOK KUMAR, computer scientist; born Allahabad, India, July 30, 1948; son of Harish and Sushila C.; married Mala, September 17, 1974; children: Ankur, Anuj. Bachelor in Tech., Indian Institute Tech., 1969; Master of Science, University Calif.-Berkeley, 1970; Doctor of Philosophy, Stanford University, 1973. Member research staff International Business Machines Corporation Thomas J. Watson Research Center, Yorktown Heights, New York, 1973—; manager theoretical computer sci. International Business Machines Corporation Thomas J. Watson Research Center, 1981-83; tech. adv. office of vice president and chief scientist International Business Machines Corporation, Armonk, New York, 1983-84; manager exploratory computer sci. International Business Machines Corporation, 1984—; conference chairman various symposia, 1985-86. Contributor articles to professional journals. Recipient President's Gold medal Indian Institute Tech., 1969; recipient International Business Machines Corporation Outstanding Innovation award, 1980, Invention Achievement award, 1977, 81. Recipient Outstanding Tech. Achievement award 1985. Member Association Computer Machinery, Computer Society of IEEE (chairman tech. committee on math. founds. of computing 1985-86), Institute of Electrical and Electronics Engineers, Society Industrial and Applied Math. Patentee magnetic bubble tech. (2).

Home: 19 Sassi Dr Croton-on-Hudson New York 10520 Office: Post Office Box 218 Yorktown Heights New York 10598

CHANDRASEKHAR, SUBRAHMANYAN, theoretical astrophysicist, educator; born Lahore, India, October 19, 1910; came to United States, 1936, naturalized, 1953; married Lalitha Doraiswamy, September 1936. Master of Arts, Presidency College, Madras, 1930; Doctor of Philosophy, Trinity College, Cambridge, 1933, Doctor of Science, 1942; Doctor of Science, University Mysore, India, 1961, Northwestern University, 1962, University Newcastle Upon Tyne, England, 1965, Ind. Institute Tech., 1966, University Michigan, 1967, University Liege, Belgium, 1967, Oxford (England) University, 1972, University Delhi, 1973, Carleton University, Can., 1978, Harvard University, 1979. Government India scholar in theoretical physics Cambridge, 1930-34; fellow Trinity College, Cambridge, 1933-37; research associate Yerkes Observatory, Williams Bay and University Chicago, 1937, assistant professor; 1938-41, associate professor; 1942-43, professor; 1944-47, Distinguished Service professor; 1947-52, Morton D. Hull Distinguished Service professor; 1952-86, professor emeritus; 1986—; Nehru Memorial lecturer, Padma Vibhushan, India, 1968. Author: An Introduction to the Study of Stellar Structure, 1939, Principles of Stellar Dynamics, 1942, Radiative Transfer, 1950, Hydrodynamic and Hydromagnetic Stability, 1961, Ellipsoidal Figures of Equilibrium, 1969, The Mathematical Theory of Black Holes, 1983, Eddington: The Most Distinguished Astrophysicist of His Time, 1983,

Truth and Beauty: Aesthetics and Motivations in Science, 1987; managing editor: The Astrophysical Journal, 1952-71; contributor various sci. periodicals. Recipient Bruce medal Astronomical Society Pacific, 1952, gold medal Royal Astronomical Society, London, 1953; Rumford medal Am. Acad. Arts and Sciences, 1957; National Medal of Sci., 1966; Nobel prize in physics, 1983; Dr. Tomalla prize Eidgenössiches Technische Hochschule, Zurich, 1984. Fellow Royal Society (London) (Royal medal 1962, Copley medal 1984); member National Acad. Sciences (Henry Draper medal 1971), Am. Physical Society (Dannie Heineman prize 1974), Am. Philosophical Society, Cambridge Philosophical Society, Am. Astronomical Society, Royal Astronomical Society. Club: Quadrangle (University Chicago). Office: Lab for Astrophysics & Space Research 933 E 56th St Chicago Illinois 60637

CHANG, Y(UAN)-F(ENG), mathematics and computer science educator; born Tientsin, Republic of China, October 7, 1928; came to United States, 1944, naturalized, 1962; son of Peng-Chung and Sieu-Tsu C.; married Hanping Chu, November 21, 1955; children: Claire, Leon. Master of Science in Electrical Engineering, Purdue University, 1950; Doctor of Philosophy in Applied Physics, Harvard University, 1959. Assistant and associate professor Purdue University, Lafayette, Ind., 1958-66; research fellow Battelle Memorial Institute, Columbus, Ohio, 1966-71; visiting associate professor Ind. University, Bloomington, 1972-74; professor computer sci. University Nebraska, Lincoln, 1974-84; W.M.

Keck professor applied math. and computer sci. Claremont (California) McKenna College, 1984—; visiting associate professor University of California at Los Angeles, 1964-65; visiting professor San Diego State University, 1981-82; associate La Jolla (California) Institute. Contributor articles to professional journals. Research grantee National Science Foundation, Naval Air System Command, Office Naval Research, National Aeronautics and Space Administration. Member Am. Math. Society, Association Computing Machinery. 24 years research in numerical analysis and application of Taylor series to sci. problems; indsl. research in solid state physics. Home: 976 W Foothill Boulevard #298 Claremont California 91711

CHAPPELL, CHARLES RICHARD, space scientist; born Greenville, South Carolina, June 2, 1943; son of Gordon Thomas and Mabel Winn (Ownbey) Chappell; married Barbara Lynne Harris, May 15, 1968; 1 child, Christopher Richard. Bachelor of Arts, Vanderbilt University, 1965; Doctor of Philosophy in Space Science, Rice University, 1968. Associate research scientist Lockheed Palo Alto (California) Research Laboratory, 1968-70, research scientist; 1970-72, staff scientist; 1972-74; chief magneto-spheric physics branch NASA-Marshall Space Flight Center, Huntsville, Alabama, 1974-80, chief solar terrestrial physics div.; 1980-87, associate director for sci.; 1987—; selected as Alternate Payload Specialist for the ATLAS-1 mission of the Space Shuttle, 1985. Author: (encyclopedia) Plasmasphere, 1970, Spacelab Mission, 1985; contributor numerous articles to professional journals. Recipient medal for Exceptional Sci. Achievement National Aeronautics and Space Administration, 1981, 84; National Aeronautics and Space Administration trainee, 1966-68. Member Am. Geophysical Union, Congress of Space Research, Phi Beta Kappa, Phi Eta Sigma. Methodist. Avocations: distance running; windsurfing. Home: 2803 Downing Court Huntsville Alabama 35801 Office: NASA-Marshall Space Flight Center Huntsville Alabama 35812

CHARYK, JOSEPH VINCENT, satellite telecommunications company executive; born Canmore, Alberta, Canada, September 9, 1920; came to United States, 1942, naturalized, 1948; son of John and Anna (Dorosh) C.; married Edwina Elizabeth Rhodes, August 18, 1945; children: William R., J. John, Christopher E., Diane E. Bachelor of Science, University Alberta, 1942, Doctor of Laws, 1964; Master of Science, California Institute Tech., 1943, Doctor of Philosophy, 1946; Doctor Engineering (honorary), University Bologna, 1974. Section chief Jet Propulsion Laboratory, California Institute Tech., 1945-46, instructor aeronautics; 1945-46; assistant professor aeronautics Princeton (New Jersey) University, 1946-49, associate professor; 1949-55; director aerophysics and chemistry laboratory, missile systems div. Lockheed Aircraft Corp., 1955-56; director aeronautical laboratory Aeronutronic Systems, Incorporated subsidiary Ford Motor Company, 1956-58, general manager space tech. div.; 1958-59; assistant secretary for research and devel. United States Air Force, 1959, under secretary; 1960-63; president

Communications Satellite Corp., 1963-79, chief executive officer; 1979-85, chairman; 1983-85; chairman Draper Laboratories, 1987—; board of directors Am. Security Corp., Abbott Laboratories, C S Draper Laboratories, MNC, Fin., Incorporated. Recipient National Medal of Tech., 1987. Fellow American Institute of Aeronautics and Astronautics, Institute of Electrical and Electronics Engineers; member National Acad. Engineering, International Acad. Astronautics, National Space Club, Sigma Xi. Clubs: Chevy Chase, Burning Tree, Gulfstream, Met. Home: 5126 Tilden St Northwest Washington District of Columbia 20016

CHAUDHARI, PRAVEEN, scientist; born Ludhiana, Punjab, India, November 30, 1937; came to United States, 1961; son of Hans Raj and Ved (Kumari) C.; married Karin Romhild, June 13, 1964; children: Ashok, Pia. Bachelor of Science, Indian Institute Tech., Kharagpur, 1961; Master of Science, Massachusetts Institute of Technology, 1963, Doctor of Science, 1966. Research associate Massachusetts Institute of Technology, Cambridge, Massachusetts, 1964-66; research staff member International Business Machines Corporation T.J. Watson Research Center, Yorktown Heights, New York, 1966-70, manager; 1970-81, director physical sciences; 1981-82, vice president sci., director physical sciences; 1982-88, vice president sci., corp. tech. committee; 1989—; executive secretary Presidential Adv. Group on Super Conductivity, 1988; member Presidential Commission on Super Conductivity, 1989; member sci. adv. board Hoechst-Celanese, Short Hills,

New Jersey; co-chairman Materials Sci. and Engineering Study by National Research Council; member ad hoc committees University California at Berkeley, University Pennsylvania, Ohio State University; member visiting committee to Department of Materials Sci. and Engineering, Massachusetts Institute of Technology, Div. Physical Sciences, University Chicago, School Engineering, University Illinois, National Sciences Association, University Pennsylvania; member sci. policy board to Stanford Synchrotron Radiation Laboratory, Stanford, Calif; member Brookhaven National Laboratory Physics, ADD, AGS, NSLS, and Instrumentation Visiting Committee; chairman International Union of Pure and Applied Physics Commission on Structure and Dynamics of Condensed Matter; member committee on Physics for the Next Decade, sponsored by National Research Council of National Academy of Sciences. Author of important papers on mechanical properties and defects in crystalline solids, amorphous solids, quantum transport, superconductivity and magnetic monopoles and neutrino mass experiments. Fellow Am. Physical Society (George Pake prize 1987); member American Institute of Mining, Metallurgy and Petroleum Engineers (leadership award 1986), American Association for the Advancement of Science, National Acad. Engineering, Am. Institute Physics (mem.-at-large of governor board), New York State Institute of Superconductivity (mem.-at-large), National Academy of Sciences (Solid State Sciences Committee). Office: International Business Machines Corporation T J Watson Research Center Post Office Box 218 Route 134 Yorktown Heights New York 10598

CHEH, HUK YUK, electrochemist, engineering educator; born Shanghai, China, October 27, 1939; son of Tze Sang and Sue Lan (Che) C.; married An-li, July 26, 1969; children: Emily, Evelyn. Bachelor of Arts in Science in Chemical Engineering, University Ottawa, Can., 1962; Doctor of Philosophy, University Calif.-Berkeley, 1967. Member tech. staff American Telephone and Telegraph Company Bell Laboratories, New Jersey, 1967-70; assistant professor chemical engineering Columbia University, New York City, 1970-73; associate professor Columbia University, 1973-79, professor; 1979—, Ruben-Viele professor; 1982—, chairman department; 1980-86; program director National Science Foundation, 1978-79; visiting research professor National Tsinghua University, Taiwan, 1977. Member editorial adv. board Encyclopedia of Physical Science Tech.; member executive adv. board Dictionary Science Tech.; contributor articles to sci. journals. Recipient Harold C. Urey award, 1980, Electrodeposition Research award The Electrochemical Society, 1988. Member Am. Institute Chemical Engineers, New York Acad. Sciences, Electrochemical Society, Am. Electroplaters Society, Sigma Xi. Office: Columbia U New York New York 10027

CHEN, WAYNE H., electrical engineer, university dean; born Soochow, China, December 13, 1922; came to United States, 1947, naturalized, 1957; son of Ting Li and Yung-Chin (Hu) C.; married Dorothy Teh Hou, June 7, 1957; children: Avis Shirley and Benjamin Timothy (twins). Bachelor of Science in

Electrical Engineering, National Chiao Tung University, China, 1944; Master of Science, University Washington, 1949; Doctor of Philosophy, 1952. Registered professional engineer, Florida. Electronic engineer cyclotron project Applied Physics Laboratory University Washington, 1949-50, associate in math.; 1950-52; member faculty University Florida, Gainesville, 1952—, professor electrical engineering; 1957—, chairman department; 1965-73, dean College Engineering, director Engineering and Industrial Experiment Station; 1973-88; visiting professor National Chiao Tung University, National Taiwan University, spring 1964; visiting scientist National Acad. Sciences to Union of the Soviet Socialist Republics, 1967; member tech. staff Bell Tel. Laboratories, summers 1953, 54, consultant, 1955-60; member tech. staff Hughes Aircraft Company, summer 1962; visiting professor University Carabobo, Venezuela, summer 1972; president College CAD/CAM Consortium Incorporated (not-for-profit corp.), 1985-87. Author: The Analayis of Linear Systems, 1963, Linear Network Design and Synthesis, 1964, The Robotosyncrasies (pseudonym Wayne Hawaii), 1976, The Year of the Robot, 1981. Recipient Florida Blue Key Outstanding Faculty award, 1960, Outstanding Publications award Chia Hsin Cement Company Cultural Fund, Taiwan, 1964, Tchr.-Scholar award University Florida, 1971. Fellow Institute of Electrical and Electronics Engineers; member American Association of University Profs., Am. Society Engineering Education, Florida Engring Society, National Society Professional Engineers, Blue Key, Sigma Xi, Sigma Tau, Eta Kappa Nu, Tau Beta Pi, Epsilon Lambda Chi, Omicron Delta Kappa, Phi Tau Phi., Phi Kappa Phi. Lodge: Rotary. Patentee in field. Office: College Engring U Fla Gainesville Florida 32611

CHERENKOV, PAVEL ALEX-EYEVICH, physicist; born Novaya Chigla, Voronezh, November 28, 1904. Educated, Voronezh University. Professor Moscow Engineering Physical Institute; member Institute Physics Union of the Soviet Socialist Republics Acad. Sciences; member Communist Party of Soviet Union, 1946; corr. member Acad. Sciences, 1964-70, academician, 1970—. Recipient Nobel prize for physics (with Tamm and Frank), 1958, State Prize (3), Order of Lenin (2), Order of Red Banner of Labor (2), Badge of Honor, other decorations. Discoverer of Cherenkov Effect. Member National Academy of Sciences (foreign associate). Office: Union of Soviet Socialist Republics Acad Scis, Lebedev Physics Institute, Leninsky Prospekt 53, Moscow Union of Soviet Socialist Republics

CHERN, SHIING-SHEN, emeritus mathematics educator; born Kashing, Chekiang, China, October 26, 1911; son of Lien Ching and Mei (Han) C.; married Shih-ning Chern, July 28, 1939; children—Paul, May. Bachelor of Science, Nankai University, Tientsin, China, 1930; Master of Science, Tsing Hua University, Peiping, 1934; Doctor of Science, University Hamburg, Germany, 1936, Doctor of Science (honorary), 1972; Doctor of Science (honorary), University Chicago, 1969, SUNY-Stony Brook, 1985; Doctor of Laws honoris causa, Chinese University, Hong Kong, 1969; Doctor Math (honorary), Eidgenossische Technische Hochschule, Zurich,

Switzerland, 1982. Professor math. National Tsing Hua University, China, 1937-43; member Institute Advanced Study, Princeton, New Jersey, 1943-45; acting director Institute Mathematics, Academia Sinica, China, 1946-48; professor math. University Chicago, 1949-60, University California, Berkeley, 1960-79; professor emeritus University California, 1979—; director Math. Sciences Research Institute, 1981-84, director emeritus; 1984—. hon. professor various foreign universities; Recipient Chauvenet prize Math. Association Am., 1970, National Medal of Sci., 1975, Wolf prize Israel, 1983-84. Member Am. Math. Society (Steele prize 1983), National Acad. Sciences, Am. Acad. Arts and Sciences, New York Acad. Sciences (hon. life), Indian Math. Society (hon.), Brazilian Acad. Sciences (corr.), Academia Sinica, Royal Society London (foreign), Academia Peloritana (corr. member 1986), London Math. Society (hon.). Home: 8336 Kent Court El Cerrito California 94530

CHEVALIER, ROGER ALAN, astronomy educator, consultant; born Rome, September 26, 1949; came to United States, 1962; son of Frank Charles and Marion Helen (Janhke) C.; married Margaret Mary With, July 27, 1974.; children: Chase Arthur, Max Toussaint. Bachelor of Science in Astronomy, California Institute Tech., 1970; Doctor of Philosophy in Astronomy (Woodrow Wilson and NSF fellow), Princeton University, 1973. Assistant astronomer Kitt Peak National Observatory, Tucson, 1973-76, associate astronomer; 1976-79; associate professor astronomy University Virginia, Charlottesville, 1979-85, professor astronomy,

chairman department; 1985—; director Leander McCormick Observatory, 1985—; consultant Lawrence Livermore National Laboratory, Livermore, California, 1981—. Contributor numerous research articles to Astrophys. Journal, other astronomy and physics journals. Fellow Woodrow Wilson Foundation, Princeton University, 1970-71, National Science Foundation, Princeton University, 1970-73. Member Am. Astronomical Society, International Astronomical Union, Illinois Sci. Lecturer Association (vice president 1975-85), Sigma Xi. Home: 1891 Westview Road Charlottesville Virginia 22903 Office: U Va Leander McCormick Obs Box 3818 Charlottesville Virginia 22903

CHO, ALFRED YI, electrical engineer; born Beijing, China, July 10, 1937; came to United States, 1955, naturalized, 1962; son of Edward I-Lai and Mildred (Chen) C.; married Mona Lee Willoughby, June 16, 1968; children: Derek Ming, Deidre Lin, Brynna Ying, Wendy Li. Bachelor of Science in Electrical Engineering, University Illinois, 1960, Master of Science, 1961, Doctor of Philosophy, 1968. Research physicist Ion Physics Corp., Burlington, Massachusetts, 1961-62; member tech. staff TRW-Space Tech. Laboratories, Redondo Beach, California, 1962-65; member tech. staff Bell Laboratories, Murray Hill, New Jersey, 1968-84, department head; 1984-87; director Materials Processing Research Laboratory American Telephone and Telegraph Company Bell Laboratories, Murray Hill, 1987—; research assistant University Illinois, Urbana, 1965-68, visiting professor department electrical engineering, visiting research professor coordinated sci. laboratory; 1977-78, adj. professor department electrical engineering adj. research professor coordinated sci. laboratory; 1978—; board of directors Instruments S.A., Metuchen, New Jersey. Contributor articles to professional journals; developer molecular beam epitaxy. Recipient Distinguished Tech. Staff award American Telephone & Telegraph Company Bell Labs., 1982, Electrical and Computer Engineering Distinguished Alumnus award University Illinois, 1985, Distinguished Achievement award Chinese Institute Engrs. U.S.A., 1985, International Gallium Arsenide Symposium award, 1986, Heinrich Welker Gold medal, 1986, The College Engineering Alumni Honor award University Illinois, 1988, World Materials Congress award ASM International, 1988, Achievement award Indsl. Rsch. Institute, Incorporated, 1988. Fellow Institute of Electrical and Electronics Engineers (Morris N. Liebmann award 1982), Am. Physical Society (International prize for new materials 1982); member Am. Vacuum Society (Gaede-Langmuir award 1988), Electrochemical Society (electronic division award 1977, Solid State Sci. and Tech. medal 1987), Materials Research Society, New York Acad. Sciences, National Acad. Engineering, National Acad. Sciences, Sigma Xi, Tau Beta Pi, Eta Kappa Nu, Sigma Tau. Office: AT & T Bell Labs 600 Mountain Avenue Murray Hill New Jersey 07974

CHOPPIN, PURNELL WHIT-TINGTON, research administrator, virology researcher, educator; born Baton Rouge, July 4, 1929; son of Authur Richard and Eunice Dolores (Bolin) C.; married Joan Harriet Macdonald, October 17, 1959; 1 daughter, Kathleen Marie. Doctor of Medicine, Louisiana State University, 1953; Doctor of Science (honorary), Emory University, 1988, Louisiana State University, 1988; Doctor Medicine (honorary), University Cologne, 1988. Diplomate: Am. Board Internal Medicine. Intern Barnes Hospital, St. Louis, 1953-54, assistant resident; 1956-57; postdoctoral fellow, research associate Rockefeller University, New York City, 1957-60, assistant professor; 1960-64, associate professor; 1957-60, professor, senior physician; 1970-85, Leon Hess professor virology; 1980-85, vice president acad. programs; 1983-85; dean grad. studies Rockefeller University, 1985; vice president, chief sci. officer Howard Hughes Medical Institute, 1985-87, president; 1987—; council Institute Medicine, 1987—, executive committee, 1988—; member virology study sect National Institutes of Health, 1968-72, chairman virology study section, 1975-78; board of directors Royal Society Medicine Foundation Incorporated, New York City, 1978—; member adv. committee fundamental research National Multiple Sclerosis Society, 1979-84; chairman adv. committee fundamental research, 1983-84; member adv. council National Institute Allergy and Infectious Diseases, 1980-83; member board sciences consultant Memorial Solan-Ketting Cancer Center, New York City, 1981-86; chairman board sics. cons Member Sloan-Kettering Cancer Center, New York City, 1983-84; member commission on life sciences National Research Council, Wahington, 1982—; member sci. rev. committee Scripps Clinic and Research Foundation, La Jolla, California, 1983-85, chairman sci. rev. committee, La

Jolla, California, 1984; member council for research and clinical investigation Am. Cancer Society, New York City, 1983-85; member committee priotities for vaccine devel. Institute Medicine, Washington. Contributor numerous articles to professional pubs., chapters on virology, cell biology, infectious diseases to professional publications, 1958—; editor: Procs. Society Experimental Biology and Medicine, 1966-69; associate editor Virology, 1969-72, editor, 1973-86; associate editor: Journal Immunology, 1968-72, Journal Supramolecular Structure, 1972-75; member editorial board Journal Virology, 1972, Comprehensive Virology, 1972; member overseas adv. panel Biochem. Journal, 1973-77.

Served as captain United States Air Force, 1954-56, Japan. Recipient Howard Taylor Ricketts award University Chicago, 1978; Waksman award for excellence in microbiology National Acad. Sciences, 1984; named to alumni Hall of Distinction Louisiana State University, Baton Rouge, 1983. Fellow New York Acad. Sciences (committee on reorg. of structure 1985—), American Association for the Advancement of Science; member National Acad. Sciences (chairman Class IV 1983-86), Am. Acad. Arts and Sciences, Am. Philosophical Society, Association Am. Physicians, Am. Society Clinical Investigation, Am. society Microbiology (chairman virology division 1977-79), Am. Society Microbiology (divisional group councilor 1983-85), Harvey Society, Am. Institute Biological Sciences, Am. Association Immunologists, Society Experimental Biology and Medicine, Am. Society Cell Biology, Infectious Diseases Society Am., Practitioners Society New York, Am. Clinical and Climatological Association, Am. Society Virology (president 1985-86), Sigma Xi (president chapter 1980-81), Alpha Omega Alpha. Home: 2700 Calvert St Northwest Washington District of Columbia 20008

CHOW, YUAN SHIH, mathematician, educator; born Nanchang, China, September 1, 1924; came to United States, 1954; son of Ting Chen and Shih (Chang) C.; married Chao Chen Su, December 3, 1949 (divorced 1960); children: Lettia, Eunice; married Yi Chang, June 7, 1963; children: Patrick, Grace, Nelson. Bachelor of Science, Chekian University, Hangchow, China, 1949; Master of Arts, University Illinois, 1954, Doctor of Philosophy, 1958. Assistant Taiwan University, Taipei, Republic of China, 1949-54; research associate University Illinois, Urbana, 1958-59; staff mathematician International Business Machines Corporation Research, New York City, 1959-62; associate professor math. Purdue University, West Lafayette, Ind., 1962-65, professor math.; 1965-68; professor math. Columbia University, New York City, 1968—; director Institute Math., Taipei, Taiwan, Republic of China, 1970-77. Author: Great Expectations, 1972, Probability Theory, 1978; contributor articles to professional journals. Recipient Chung Sam sci. award Republic China, 1973. Fellow Institute Math. Statistics; member Academia Sinica (editor Jour. Math. 1974-78), International Statistical Institute, Am. Math. Society, Chinese Association Statisticians. Office: Columbia U W 116 St New York New York 10027

CLARK, DAVID LEIGH, marine geologist educator; born Albuquerque, New Mexico, June 15, 1931; son of Leigh William and Sadie (Ollerton) C.;

married Louise Boley, August 31, 1951; children: Steven, Douglas, Julee, Linda. Bachelor of Science, Brigham Young University, 1953, Master of Science, 1954; Doctor of Philosophy, University Iowa, 1957. Geologist Standard Oil California, Albuquerque, 1954; assistant professor Southern Methodist University, Dallas, 1957-59; associate professor Brigham Young University, Provo, Utah, 1959-63; professor geology and geophysics University Wis.-Madison, 1963—, chairman department geology and geophysics; 1971-74, associate dean natural sciences; 1986. Author Fossils, Paleontology, Evolution, 1968,72; author and coordinator: Treatise on Invertebrate Paleontology-Conodonts, 1981. Recipient Fulbright award Bonn, Federal Republic of Germany, 1965-66; Distinguished Professorship University Wisconsin, 1974. Fellow Geological Society Am.; member Paleontological Society, Am. Association Petroleum Geologists, Society Econ. Paleontologists and Mineralogists, Am. Geophysical Union, Pander Society, Paleontologisches Gesselschaft, Paleontological Association, North America Micropaleontology Society, American Association for the Advancement of Science. Mormon. Home: 2812 Oxford Road Madison Wisconsin 53705 Office: U Wisconsin Department Geology and Geophysics Madison Wisconsin 53706

CLIFFORD, MAURICE CECIL, physician, former college president, city official; born Washington, August 9, 1920; son of Maurice C. and Rosa P. (Linberry) C.; married Patricia Marie Johnson, June 15, 1945; children: Maurice Cecil III, Jay P.L., Rosemary Clifford McDaniel. Bachelor of Arts, Hamilton College, 1941, Doctor of Science, 1982; Master of Arts, University Chicago, 1942; Doctor of Medicine, Meharry Medical College, 1947; Doctor of Humane Letters, LaSalle College, 1981, Hahnemann University, 1985; Doctor of Laws (honorary), Medical College Pennsylvania, 1986. Diplomate Am. Board Ob-Gyn. Intern Philadelphia General Hospital, 1947-48, resident in ob-gyn; 1948-51, assistant chief service ob-gyn; 1951-60; member faculty Medical College Pennsylvania, Philadelphia, 1955—, professor obgyn.; 1975—, vice president for medical affairs; 1978-80, president; 1980-86; commissioner pub. health City of Philadelphia, 1986—; board of directors Germantown Savings Bank. Contributor articles to professional journals. Trustee Philadelphia Award, Philadelphia Art Mus., Philadelphia College Textiles and Sci.; trustee emeritus Philadelphia Acad. Natural Scis.; life trustee Meharry Medical College; former alumnus trustee Hamilton College; member national medical committee Planned Parenthood, 1975-78; member adv. committee on arts John F. Kennedy Center for Performing Arts, 1978-80. Captain Medical Corps, United States Army, 1952-54. Recipient Dr. Martin Luther King, Junior award PUSH, 1981, Dr. William H. Gray, Junior award Educators Roundtable Association, 1981, Annual award Philadelphia Tribune Charities, 1981, Distinguished Am. award Education and Rsch. Fund Am. Foundation for Negro Affairs, 1980; Outstanding Service award Philadelphia br. National Association for the Advancement of Colored People, 1965, others. Fellow Am. College Obstetricians and Gynecologists (life); member National Medical Association, Pennsylvania Medical Society, Medical Society Eastern Pennsylvania, Philadelphia County Medical Society, Phi Beta Kappa, Alpha Omega Alpha. Office: Mcpl Services Building Philadelphia Pennsylvania 19102

CLOUD, PRESTON, geologist, author, consultant; born West Upton, Massachusetts, September 26, 1912; son of Preston E. and Pauline L. (Wiedemann) C.; married Janice Gibson, 1972; children by previous marriage: Karen, Lisa, Kevin. Bachelor of Science, George Washington University, 1938; Doctor of Philosophy, Yale University, 1940. Instructor Missouri School Mines and Metallurgy, 1940-41; research fellow Yale University, 1941-42; geologist United States Geological Survey, 1942-46, 48-61, 74-79, chief paleontology and stratigraphy branch; 1949-59; research geologist 1959-61, 74-79; assistant professor, curator invertebrate paleontology Harvard University, 1946-48; professor department geology and geophysics University Minnesota, 1961-65, chairman; 1961-63; professor geology University of California at Los Angeles, 1965-68; professor biogeology and environmental studies department geological sciences University California, Santa Barbara, 1968-74, professor emeritus; 1974—; visiting professor University Texas, 1962, 78; H.R. Luce professor cosmology Mount Holyoke College, 1979-80; Senior Queens fellow Baas-Becking Geobiology Laboratory, Canberra, Australia, 1981; internat exchange scholar National Sci. and Engineering Research Council Can., 1982; hon. visiting professor University Ottawa (Ontario Can.), 1982; National Sigma Xi lecturer, 1967; Emmons lecturer

Colorado Sci. Society; Bownocker lecturer Ohio State University; French lecturer Pomona College; Dumaresq-Smith lecturer Acadia College, New Brunswick, Can.; A.L. DuToit Memorial lecturer Royal Society and Geological Society of South Africa; member governing board National Research Council, 1972-75; member Pacific Sci. Board, 1952-56, 62-65; del. international sci. congresses; consultant to government, industry, foundations and agys. Author: Terebratuloid Brachiopoda of the Silurian and Devonian, 1942; (with Virgil E. Barnes) The Ellenburger Group of Central Texas, 1948; (with others) Geology of Saipan, Mariana Islands, 1957; Environment of Calcium Carbonate Deposition West of Andros Island, Bahamas, 1962, Cosmos, Earth and Man, 1978, Oasis in Space, 1988; editor and co-author: (with others) Resources and Man, 1969, Adventures in Earth History, 1970; Author articles. Recipient A. Cressey Morrison prize natural history, 1941, Rockefeller Pub. Service award, 1956, U.S. Department Interior Distinguished Service award and gold medal, 1959, Medal, Paleontol Society Am., 1971, Lucius W. Cross medal Yale University, 1973, Penrose medal Geol. Society Am., 1976, C.D. Walcott medal National Acad. Sciences, 1977, R.C. Moore medal Society Econ. Paleontologists and Mineralogists, 1986; J.S. Guggenheim fellow, 1982-83. Fellow Am. Acad. Arts and Sciences (committee on membership 1978-80, council 1980-83); member Am. Philosophical Society, National Acad. Sciences (committee on sci. and pub. policy 1965-69, member council 1972-75, executive committee 1973-75, chairman committee on resources and man 1965-69, chairman ad hoc committee national materials policy 1972, chairman study group on uses of underground space 1972, chairman committee mineral resources and environment 1972-73, chairman committee geology and climate 1977, chairman section geology 1976-79, member assembly math. and phys. scis. 1976-79), Polish Acad. Sciences (foreign associate), Geological Society Am. (council 1972-75), Paleontological Society Am., Paleontological Society India (hon.), American Association for the Advancement of Science, Geological Society Belgium (hon. foreign corr.), Paläont. Society Deutschland (hon., corresponding member), Phi Beta Kappa, Sigma Xi, Sigma Gamma Epsilon. Field work 6 continents and 2 oceans. Home: 400 Mountain Dr Santa Barbara California 93103 Office: U California Department Geol Scis Santa Barbara California 93106

CLUFF, LEIGHTON EGGERTSEN, physician, foundation executive; born Salt Lake City, June 10, 1923; son of Lehi Eggertsen and Lottie (Brain) C.; married Beth Allen, August 19, 1944; children: Claudia Beth, Patricia Leigh. Bachelor of Science, University Utah, 1944; Doctor of Medicine with distinction, George Washington University, 1949; Doctor of Science (honorary), Hahnemann Medical School, 1979, Long Island University, 1988. Intern Johns Hopkins Hospital, Baltimore, 1949-50, assistant resident; 1951-52; assistant resident physician Duke Hospital, Durham, North Carolina, 1950-51; visiting investigator, assistant physician Rockefeller Institute Medical Research, 1952-54; fellow National Foundation Infantile Paralysis, 1952-54; member faculty Johns Hopkins School Medicine, Baltimore; staff Johns Hopkins Hospital, Baltimore, 1954-66, professor medicine; 1964-66, physician, head div. clinical immunology, allergy and infectious diseases; 1958-66; professor, chairman department medicine University Florida, Gainesville, 1966-76; executive vice president Robert Wood Johnson Foundation, Princeton, New Jersey, 1976-86, president; 1986—; United States del. U.S.-Japan Cooperative Medical Sci. Program, 1972-81; member council drugs American Medical Association, 1965-67; member NRC-Nat. Acad. Sci. Drug Research Board, 1965-71; member expert adv. panel bacterial diseases (coccal infection) World Health Organization; member council National Institute Allergy and Infectious Diseases, 1968-72; consultant Food and Drug Administration; member training grant committee National Institutes of Health, 1964-68. Author, editor books on internal medicine, infectious diseases, clin. pharmacology; contributor articles to professional journals. Markle scholar med. scis., 1955-62; recipient Career Research award National Institutes of Health, 1962. Member Institute Medicine-Nat. Acad. Sciences, Am. Society Clinical Investigation, Association Life Scis.-Nat. Acad. Sciences, Association Am. Physicians, Society Experimental Biology and Medicine, Am. Association Immunologists, Am. Federation Clinical Research, Harvey Society, New York Acad. Sci., Infectious Disease Society Am. (president 1973), Southern Society Clinical Investigation, American College of Physicians (Florida governor 1975-76, Mead-Johnson postgrad. scholar 1954-55, Ordronaux award med. scholarship 1949), Am. Clinical and Climatological Association, Alpha Omega Alpha. Office: Robert Wood Johnson Found Post Office Box 2316 Princeton New Jersey 08543-2316

COAR, RICHARD JOHN, aerospace consultant, mechanical engineer; born Hanover, New Hampshire, May 2, 1921; son of Herbert Greenleaf and Anne (Langill) C.; married Cecilie Berle, 1942 (deceased 1971); children—Gregory, Candace, Andrea, Kenneth; married Lucille Hicks, 1972. Bachelor of Science in Mechanical Engineering, Tufts University, 1942. Engineer Pratt & Whitney Aircraft, East Hartford, Connecticut, 1942-56; chief engineer Florida Research and Devel Ctr Pratt & Whitney Aircraft, 1956-70, assistant general manager; 1970-71; vice president engineering Pratt & Whitney Aircraft, East Hartford, 1971-76, executive vice president; 1976-83, president; 1983-84; senior vice president United Techs., Hartford, 1983-84, executive vice president; 1984-86. Patentee aircraft engines and controls. Corporator Hartford Hospital, 1983; board of directors Hartford Symphony, 1985-87. Member American Society of Mechanical Engineers (George Westinghouse Gold medal 1986), National Acad. Engineering, Society Automotive Engineers, Tau Beta Pi. Clubs: Mayacoo Lakes Country (West Palm Beach, Florida); Sailfish Point Yacht and Country (Stuart, Florida). Avocations: sailing; golf. Home and Office: 2802 Southeast Dunes Dr Stuart Florida 34996 also: 17 Norumbega Dr Camden Maine 04843

COBB, WILLIAM MONTAGUE, anatomist, physical anthropologist, medical editor, emeritus educator; born Washington, October 12, 1904; son of William Elmer and Alexzine E. (Montague) C.; married Hilda B. Smith, June 26, 1929 (deceased June 1976); children: Carolyn Cobb Wilkinson, Hilda Amelia Cobb Gray. Bachelor of Arts (Blodgett scholar), Amherst College, 1925, Doctor of Science (honorary), 1955; Doctor of Medicine, Howard University, 1929, Doctor of Humane Letters (honorary), 1980; Doctor of Philosophy, Western Reserve University, 1932; Doctor of Science (honorary), Colby College, 1984; Doctor of Humane Letters (honorary), Medical College Pennsylvania, 1986; certificate in embryology, Marine Biol. Laboratory, Woods Hole, Massachusetts; student, United States National Museum, Washington University; Doctor of Laws, Morgan State College, 1964, University Witwatersrand, South Africa, 1977; Doctor of Science, Georgetown University, 1978, Medical College Wisconsin, 1979, University Arkansas, 1983; Doctor.Medical Science, Brown University, 1983. Intern Freedmen's Hospital, Washington, 1929-30; instructor embryology Howard University, 1928-29, assistant professor anatomy; 1932-34, associate professor; 1934-42, professor anatomy; 1942-69, head department; 1947-69, distinguished professor anatomy; 1969-73, professor emeritus; 1973—; visiting professor anatomy Stanford University, 1972, University Maryland, 1974, West Virginia University, 1980; Distinguished University professor University Arkansas Medical Sciences Center, 1979; visiting professor, Danz lecturer University Washington, 1978; visiting professor orthopaedic surgery Harvard University, 1981; visiting professor anatomy Medical College Wisconsin, 1982; director Distinguished Senior Scholars Lecture Series University District of Columbia,

1983; junior medical officer United States Department Agriculture, 1935; member Pub. Health Advisory Council of District of Columbia, 1953-61, chairman, 1956-58; chief medical examiner Freedmen's Hospital Board, District of Columbia Selective Service System, 1941; civilian consultant to surgeon general United States Army, 1945; member executive committee White House Conference on Health, 1965; Fellow in anatomy Western Reserve University, 1933-39, associate anatomy, 1942-44.

Founder: Bulletin of Medico-Chirurg. Society D.C, 1941; editor, 1945-54, Journal National Medical Assn, 1949-77; author monographs, articles.

Rosenwald fellow, 1941-42; recipient citations from Opportunity magazine, 1947, citations from Chicago Defender, 1948, citations from Washington Afro-Am., 1948; Distinguished Service award Medico-Chirurg. Society District of Columbia, 1952; Distinguished Service Medal National Medical Association, 1955; Meritorious Service award Medical Society of District of Columbia, 1968; Meritorious Pub. Service award Government of District of Columbia, 1972; Distinguished Public Service award U.S. Navy, 1978, 82; recognized with inaguration of W. Montague Cobb Collection Moorland-Springarn Research Center, Los Angeles, 1979, dedication of W. Montague Cobb Medical Education Bldg., King-Drew Medical Center, Los Angeles, 1984, dedication of A Century of Black Surgeons-The U.S.A. Experience (book) to W. Montague Cobb, Howard University Hospital, 1987. Fellow Am. Anthropological Association, Gerontological Society, American Association for the Advancement of Science (member 1957-59), Association Anatomists (Henry Gray award 1980), Am. Association Physical Anthropologists (vice president 1948-50, president 1957-59), Am. Eugenics Society (director 1957-68), Anatomical Society Great Brit. and Ireland, National Medical Association (state vice president 1943, editor 1949-77, chairman council on med. education and hosps. 1949-63, national president 1964-65), National Urban League (health specialist 1945-47), National Association for the Advancement of Colored People (chairman national med. committee 1950, director 1949—, president 1976-82), Am. Society Mammalogists, Am. Association History of Medicine, Washington Society History of Medicine (president 1972), Association Study of Negro Life and History, Anthropological Society Washington (president 1949-51), Medica-Chirurgical Society District of Columbia (rec. secretary 1935-41, president 1945-47, 54-56), Omega Psi Phi (chairman scholarship committee 1939-48), Sigma Xi, Alpha Omega Alpha. Presbyterian. Club: Cosmos (Washington). Home: 1219 Girard St Northwest Washington District of Columbia 20009 Office: Howard U Washington District of Columbia 20059

COCKERHAM, COLUMBUS CLARK, geneticist, educator; born Mountain Park, North Carolina, December 12, 1921; son of Corbett C. and Nellie Bruce (McCann) C.; married Joyce Evelyn Allen, February 26, 1944; children: Columbus Clark Jr., Jean Allen, Bruce Allen. Bachelor of Science, North Carolina State College, 1943, Master of Science, 1949; Doctor of Philosophy, Iowa State College, 1952. Assistant professor biostats. University North

Carolina, Chapel Hill, 1952-53; member faculty North Carolina State University, Raleigh, 1953—; professor statistics North Carolina State University, 1959-72, William Neal Reynolds professor statistics and genetics; 1972—, Distinguished University professor; 1988—; member genetics study section National Institutes of Health, 1965-69; consultant adv. committee protocols for safety evaluation Food and Drug Administration, 1967-69. Author papers population and quantitative genetics, plant and animal breeding; editor, associate editor: Theoretical Population Biology, 1975—; editorial board: Genetics, 1969-72, Genetic Epidemiology, 1984—; associate editor: Am. Journal Human Genetics, 1978-80. Served with United States Marine Corps Reserve, 1943-46. Recipient North Carolina award in sci., 1976; Oliver Max Gardner award, 1980; D.D. Mason faculty award, 1983, North Carolina State University Alumni Association award, 1986; grantee National Institute General Medical Sciences, 1960—. Fellow American Association for the Advancement of Science, Am. Society Agronomy, Crop Sci. Society Am.; member National Acad. Sciences, Am. Society Animal Sci., Am. Society Naturalists, Biometric Society, Genetics Society Am., Genetics Society Japan (foreign hon. member), Sigma Xi, Gamma Sigma Delta (award merit 1964), Phi Kappa Phi. Office: Department Statistics Box 8203 North Carolina State University Raleigh North Carolina 27695

COFFEY, TIMOTHY, physicist; born Washington, June 27, 1941; son of Timothy and Helen (Stevens) C.; married Paula Marie Smith, August 24, 1963; children: Timothy, Donna, Marie. Bachelor of Science in Electrical Engineering (Cambridge scholar 1958), Massachusetts Institute of Technology, 1962; Master of Science in Physics, University Michigan, 1963, Evening News Assn. fellow, 1964, Doctor of Philosophy, 1967. Research physicist Air Force Cambridge Research Laboratory, 1964; theoretical physicist EGG, Incorporated, Boston, 1966-71; head plasma dynamics branch, then superintendent plasma physics div. Naval Research Laboratory, Washington, 1971-80; associate director research for general sci. and tech. Naval Research Laboratory, 1980-83, director research; 1983—. Recipient award Naval Research Laboratory, 1974, 75. Fellow Am. Physical Society, Washington Acad. Sciences; member Am. Institute Physics, American Association for the Advancement of Science, New York Acad. Sciences, International Union Radio Sci. Office: Naval Research Lab 4555 Overlook Avenue Southwest Washington District of Columbia 20375

COHEN, DONALD JAY, pediatrics, psychiatry and psychology educator, administrator; born Chicago, September 5, 1940; married Phyllis Cohen, 1964; children—Matthew, Rebecca, Rachel, Joseph. Bachelor of Arts in Philosophy and Psychology summa cum laude, Brandeis University, 1961; Student in philosophy and psychology, University Cambridge, 1961-62; Doctor of Medicine, Yale University, 1966. Diplomate Am. Board Psychiatry and Neurology, Am. Board Child Psychiatry. Intern in pediatric medicine Children's Hospital Medical Center, Boston, 1966-67; resident in child psychiatry Judge Baker

Guidance Center, Children's Hospital Medical Center, Boston, 1969-70; resident in psychiatry Massachusetts Mental Health Center, Boston, 1967-69; fellow in child psychiatry Hillcrest Children's Center and Children's Hospital, Washington, 1970-72; assistant in medicine Children's Hospital, Boston, 1967-69; assistant to director child devel. Department Health, Washington, 1970-72; associate professor pediatrics, psychiatry, and psychology Yale University, New Haven, Connecticut, 1972-79; professor pediatrics, psychiatry, psychology Yale University, New Haven, 1979—; Irving B. Harris professor child psychiatry, pediatrics and psychology Yale University, New Haven, Connecticut, 1987—, director Child Study Center; 1983—; clinical associate adult psychiatry board National Institute of Mental Health Section on Twin and Sibling Studies, 1970-72; visiting professor Hebrew University, Hadassah Medical Center, summer 1982. Contributor numerous articles to professional journals, chapters to books; author monographs: Serving School Age Children, 1972, Serving Presch. Children, 1974; editor monographs: Schizophrenia Bulletin, Volume 8, No. 2, 1982, Journal Autism and Devel. Disorders, 1982; co-editor monographs: (with A. Donnellan) Handbook of Autism and Disorders of Atypical Development, 1985; (with A.J. Solnit, J.E. Schowalter) Psychiatry, 1985; author of book revs.; member editorial board Journal Am. Acad. of Child Psychiatry, 1972-76, 80—, Israel Journal Psychiatry, 1983—; member adv. board Journal Child Psychology and Psychiatry, 1977. Chairman professional adv. board National Society for Autistic Children, 1981—;

member medical adv. board Tourette Syndrome Association, 1980—, member professional adv. board Benhaven, New Haven, Connecticut, 1972—; board of directors National Institute of Mental Health Treatment Devel. and Assessment Study Sect., 1979-82, Psychoanalytic Research and Devel. Fund, 1982—, Found.'s Fund for Research in Psychiatry, 1977-81, Special Citizens, Futures Unlimited, Incorporated, 1983—, Ounce of Prevention Fund National Adv. Committee, 1983—, B'nai B'rith Hillel Foundation, Yale University, 1984—; trustee Brandeis University, 1982—, Western New England Institute for Psychoanalysis, 1984—. Served with United States Public Health Service, 1970-72. Woodrow Wilson fellow, 1961, Falk fellow Am. Psychiat. Association, 1970-71; Fulbright scholar Trinity College, University Cambridge, 1961-62; recipient Annual Pub. Service award National Society for Autistic Children, 1972, Special Recognition, Hofheimer Prize Am. Psychiatric Association, 1977, Ittleson award Am. Psychiat. Association, 1981. Fellow Am. Acad. Child Psychiatry (chairman committee on research 1975-81), Am. Pediatric Society, Am. Acad. Pediatrics; member Society for Research in Child Devel., Western New England Psychoanalytic Society, Am. Psychoanalytic Association, International Psychoanalytic Association, Israel Psychoanalytic Society (corr. member), Phi Beta Kappa, Sigma Xi, Alpha Omega Alpha. Office: Yale Child Study Center Post Office Box 3333 New Haven Connecticut 06510

COHEN, KARL PALEY, nuclear energy consultant; born New York City, February 5, 1913; son of Joseph M. and Ray (Paley) C.; married Marthe

H. Malartre, September 20, 1938; children: Martine-Claude Lebouc, Elisabeth M. Brown, Beatrix Josephine Cashmore. Bachelor of Arts, Columbia University, 1933, Master of Arts, 1934, Doctor of Philosophy in Physical Chemistry, 1937; postgraduate, University Paris, 1936-37. Research assistant to Professor H. C. Urey Columbia University, 1937-40; director theoretical div. SAM Manhattan project, 1940-44; physicist Standard Oil Devel. Company, 1944-48; tech. director H.K. Ferguson Company, 1948-52; vice president Walter Kidde Nuclear Laboratory, 1952-55; consultant Atomic Energy Commission, senior sci. Columbia University, 1955; manager advance engineering atomic power equipment department General Electric Company, 1955-65, general manager breeder reactor devel. department; 1965-71, manager strategic planning, nuclear energy div.; 1971-73, chief scientist, nuclear energy group; 1973-78; consultant professor Stanford University, 1978-81. Author: The Theory of Isotope Separation as Applied to Large Scale Production of U-235, 1951; contributor articles to professional journals. Recipient Energy Research prize Alfried Krupp Foundation, 1977; Chemical Pioneer award Am. Institute Chemists, 1979. Fellow Am. Nuclear Society (president 1968-69, director), American Association for the Advancement of Science; member National Acad. Engineering, Am. Physical Society, Cactus and Succulent Society, Phi Beta Kappa, Sigma Xi, Phi Lambda Upsilon. Office: 928 N California Avenue Palo Alto California 94303

COHEN, MELVIN R., physician, educator; born Chicago, May 24, 1911; son of Louis M. and Anna S. (Friedman) C.; married Miriam, May 19, 1946; children—Nancy, Alan. Bachelor of Science, University Illinois, 1931, Master of Science in Pathology, 1933, Doctor of Medicine, 1934, A.O.A.(honorary). Diplomate: Am. Board Ob-Gyn. Practice medicine specializing in infertility Chicago; senior attending physician Michael Reese Medical Center, Chicago, Northwestern Memorial Hospital, Chicago; founder, director Fertility Institute Limited, Chicago; professor Northwestern University Medical School, Chicago, professor emeritus; guest visiting professor first Martin Clyman postgrad. course in infertility Mount Sinai Hospital, New York City, 1982. Author: Laparoscopy, Culdoscopy and Gynecography: Technique and Atlas, 1970; contributor numerous chapters in medical books and articles to medical journals on infertility, endometriosis and Spinnbarkeit. Director, producer: 8 teaching films on infertility; video films during surgery; ektochrome slides established world-wide technique. Pioneer use of Pergonal for stimulating ovulation. Served with MC, Army of the United States, 1942-45. Co-recipient Gold Medal for Infertility exhibit, American Medical Association, 1951; recipient award for film on endometriosis 10th World Congress of Fertility and Sterility, Madrid, Spain, 1980; named Father of Modern Am. Laparoscopy, 1974. Life Fellow Chicago Gynecological Society; member American Medical Association, Am. Fertility Society, Am. College Ob-Gyn., Am. Association Gynecological Laparoscopists, International Fertility Association, International Family Planning Research Association, Illinois State Medical Society, Chicago Gynecological Society, Kansas City Gynecological Society (hon.), Los Angeles Gynecological Society, Institute Medicine Chicago, Medical Research Institute Michael Reese Hospital, Midwest Bio-Laser Institute, Indian Association Gynecological Endoscopists (hon.), Society Reproductive Surgeons, Chicago Association Reproductive Endocrinologists (president 1984-85), Sigma Xi, Alpha Omega Alpha. Named Father of Modern Am. Laparoscopy, 1974. Address: 990 N Lake Shore Dr Chicago Illinois 60611

COHEN, STANLEY, biochemistry educator; born Brooklyn, November 17, 1922; son of Louis and Fannie (Feitel) C.; married Olivia Larson, 1951 (divorced); children: Burt Bishop, Kenneth Larson, Cary; married Jan Elizabeth Jordan, 1981. Bachelor of Arts, Brooklyn College, 1943; Master of Science, Oberlin College, 1945; Doctor of Philosophy in Biochemistry, University Michigan, 1948; Doctor of Philosophy, University Chicago, 1985. Instructor department biochemistry and pediatrics University Colorado, Denver, 1948-52; Am. Cancer Society fellow in radiology Washington University, St. Louis, 1952-53, associate professor department zoology; 1953-59; assistant professor biochemistry, school medicine Vanderbilt University, Nashville, 1959-62, associate professor; 1962-67, professor biochemistry; 1967-86, distinguished professor; 1986—; research professor biochemistry Am. Cancer Society, Nashville, 1976—; Charles B. Smith visiting research professor Sloan Kettering, 1984; Feodor Lynen lecturer University Miami, 1986, Steenbock lecturer University Wisconsin, 1986. Member editorial board Abstracts of Human Developmental Biology, Journal of Cellular Physiology. Cons. Minority Research Center for Excellence. Recipient Research Career Devel. award National Institutes of Health, 1959-69, William Thomson Wakeman award National Paraplegia Foundation, Earl Sutherland Research Prize Vanderbilt University, 1977, Albion O. Bernstein MD award Medical Society State New York, 1978, H.P. Robertson Memorial award National Acad. Sci., 1981, Lewis S. Rosentiel award Brandeis University, 1982, Alfred P. Sloan award General Motors Cancer Research Foundation, 1982, Louisa Gross Horwitz prize Columbia University, 1983, Distinguished Achievement award UCLA Laboratory Biomed. and Environmental Sciences, 1983, Lila Gruber Memorial Cancer Research award Am. Acad. Dermatology, 1983, Bertner award MD Anderson Hospital University Texas, 1983, Gairdner Foundation International award, 1985, Fred Conrad Koch award Endocrine Society, 1986, National Medal Sci., 1986, Albert and Mary Lasker Foundation Basic Medical Research award, 1986, Nobel Prize in physiology medicine, 1986, Tennessean of Year award Tennessee Sports Hall of Fame, 1987, Franklin Medal, 1987, Albert A. Michaelson award Mus. Sci. and Industry, 1987. Fellow Jewish Acad. Arts and Sci.; member National Acad. Sci., Am. Society Biological Chemists, Am. Chemical Society, American Association for the Advancement of Science, International Institute Embryology, International Acad. Sci. (hon. international council for sci. devel.). Office: Vanderbilt U School Medicine Department Biochemistry Nashville Tennessee 37203

COHEN, STANLEY NORMAN, geneticist, educator; born Perth Amboy, New Jersey, February 17, 1935; son of Bernard and Ida (Stolz) C.; married Joanna Lucy Wolter, June 27, 1961; children: Anne, Geoffrey. Bachelor of Arts, Rutgers University, 1956; Doctor of Medicine, University Pennsylvania, 1960. Intern, Mount Sinai Hospital, New York City, 1960-61; resident University Hospital, Ann Arbor, Michigan, 1961-62; clinical associate arthritis and rheumatism branch National Institute Arthritis and Metabolic Diseases, Bethesda, Maryland, 1962-64; senior resident in medicine Duke University Hospital, Durham, North Carolina, 1964-65; Am. Cancer Society postdoctoral research fellow Albert Einstein College Medicine, Bronx, 1965-67, assistant professor devel. biology and cancer; 1967-68; member faculty Stanford (California) University, 1968—, professor medicine; 1975—, professor genetics; 1977, chairman department genetics; 1978-86; member committee recombinant DNA molecules National Acad. Sci.-NRC, 1974; member committee on genetic experimentation International Council Sci. Unions, 1977—. Member editorial board: Journal Bacteriology, 1973-79; asso. editor: Plasmid, 1977-86. Served with United States Public Health Service, 1962-64. Guggenheim fellow, 1975; Josiah Macy Junior Foundation faculty scholar, 1975-76; recipient Burroughs Wellcome Scholar award, 1970, V.D. Mattia award Roche Institute Molecular Biology, 1977, Albert Lasker basic med. research award, 1980, Wolf prize, 1981, Marvin J. Johnson award, 1981, Distinguished Graduate award University Pennsylvania School Medicine, 1986, Distinguished Service award Miami Winter Symposium, 1986, LVMH Institut de la Vie prize, 1988, National Medal of Sci., 1988, City of Medicine award, 1988. Member National Acad. Sci., Institute Medicine, Am. Acad. Arts and Sci., Am. Society Biological Chemists, Genetics Society Am., Am. Society Microbiology (Cetus award 1988), Am. Society Pharmacology and Experimental Therapeutics, Am. Society Clinical Investigation, Phi Beta Kappa, Sigma Xi, Alpha Omega Alpha. Office: Stanford U School Med Department Genetics S-337 Stanford California 94305

COHN, MILDRED, biochemist, educator; born New York City, July 12, 1913; daughter of Isidore M. and Bertha (Klein) Cohn; married Henry Primakoff, May 31, 1938; children: Nina, Paul, Laura. Bachelor of Arts, Hunter College, 1931, Doctor of Science (honorary), 1984; Master of Arts, Columbia University, 1932, Doctor of Philosophy, 1938; Doctor of Science (honorary), Women's Medical College, 1966, Radcliffe College, 1978, Washington University, St. Louis, 1981, Brandeis University, St. Louis, 1984, University Pennsylvania, St. Louis, 1984, University North Carolina, St. Louis, 1985; Doctor of Philosophy (honorary), Weizmann Institute Science, St. Louis, 1988. Research assistant biochemistry George Washington University School Medicine, 1937-38; research associate Cornell University, 1938-46; research associate Washington University, 1946-50, 51-58, associate professor biological chemistry; 1958-60; associate professor biophysics and physical biochemistry University Pennsylvania Medical School, 1960-61, professor; 1961-78, emeritus; 1982—, Benjamin Rush professor physiological chemistry; 1978-82;

senior member Institute Cancer Research, Philadelphia, 1982-85; Chancellor's distinguished professor biophysics University California, Berkeley, spring 1981; visiting professor biological chemistry Johns Hopkins University Medical School, Berkeley, 1985—; research associate Harvard University, 1950-51; established investigator Am. Heart Association, 1953-59, career investigator, 1964-78. Editorial board journal Biol. Chemistry, 1958-63, 67-72. Recipient Cresson medal Franklin Institute, 1976, award International Association Women Biochemists, 1979, National Medal Sci., 1982, Chandler medal Columbia University, 1986, Distinguished Service award College Physicians, Philadelphia, 1987. Member Am. Philosophical Society, National Academy of Sciences, Am. Chemical Society (Garvan medal 1963, Remsen award Maryland section 1988), Harvey Society, Am. Society Biological Chemists, Am. Biophys. Society, Am. Acad. Arts and Sciences, Phi Beta Kappa, Sigma Xi, Iota Sigma Pi (hon. national member 1988). Office: U Pennsylvania Med School Department Biochemistry & Biophysics Philadelphia Pennsylvania 19104-6089

COLEMAN, ANNETTE WILBOIS, biology educator; born Des Moines, February 28, 1934; daughter of Fred J. and Agnes D. Wilbois; married John R. Coleman, July 26, 1958; children: Alan, Benjamin, Suzanne. Bachelor of Arts, Columbia University, 1955; Doctor of Philosophy, University Ind., 1958. Postdoctoral fellow Johns Hopkins University, Baltimore, 1958-61; research associate University Connecticut, 1961-63; research associate Brown University, Providence, 1964-72, assistant professor biology research; 1972-76, assistant professor; 1976-80, associate professor; 1980-84, professor; 1984—, Stephen T. Olney professor natural history; 1984—. National Science Foundation postdoctoral fellow, 1955-58, 58-60; Guggenheim fellow, 1983-84, recipient Provasoli award, 1985, Darbaker award, 1986. Fellow New York Acad. Sciences; member Botanical Society Am., Society Protozoologists, Phcol. Society Am. (president 1981-82). Office: Brown U Department History Providence Rhode Island 02912

COLES, ROBERT, child psychiatrist, educator, author; born Boston, October 12, 1929; son of Philip and Sandra (Young) C.; married Jane Hallowell; children—Robert, Daniel, Michael. Bachelor of Arts, Harvard University, 1950; Doctor of Medicine, Columbia University, 1954; Doctor of Medicine (honorary), Temple University, Notre Dame University, Bates College, 1972, Wayne State University, 1973, Western Michigan University, Holy Cross College, 1974, Hofstra University, 1975, College William and Mary, Bard College, University Lowell, University Cincinnati, 1976, Stonehill College, Lesley College, Rutgers University, 1977, Wesleyan University, Columbia College, Knox College, Cleveland State University, Wooster College, 1978, University North Carolina, Manhattan College, St. Peter's College, College New Rochelle, Pratt Institute and School Design, 1979, Berea College, Brooklyn College, Emmanuel College, 1980, Colby College, 1981, Sienna Heights College, Salem State College, Williams College, 1983, Beloit

College, 1984, Emory University, Fairfield University, Macalaster College, Colgate University, 1986. Intern University Chicago Clinics, 1954-55; resident in psychiatry Massachusetts General Hospital, Boston, 1955-56, McLean Hospital, Belmont, Massachusetts, 1956-57, Judge Baker Guidance Center-Children's Hospital, 1957-58; member staff children's Unit Metropolitan State Hospital, Waltham, Massachusetts, 1957-58; member staff alcoholic clinic Massachusetts General Hospital; teaching fellow in psychiatry, member psychiatric staff and clinical assistant in psychiatry Harvard Medical School, 1955-58; research psychiatrist Harvard University Health Services, 1963—; lecturer general education Harvard University, 1966—, professor psychiatry and medical humanities; 1977—; child psychiatric fellow Judge Baker Guidance Center, Children's Hospital, Boston, 1960-61; member National Adv. Committee on Farm Labor, 1965—; consultant Appalachian Vols., 1965—, Rockefeller Foundation, 1969—, Ford Foundation, 1969—; member Institute of Medicine, National Acad. Sciences, 1973-78; visiting professor public policy Duke University, 1973—; consultant supervisor department psychiatry Cambridge (Massachusetts) Hospital, 1976—; consultant Center for Study of Southern Culture, University Mississippi, 1979—. Author: Children of Crisis: A Study of Courage and Fear, 1967, Dead End School, 1968, Still Hungry in America, 1969, The Grass Pipe, 1969, The Image is Yours, 1969; Wages of Neglect, 1969, Uprooted Children: The Early Lives of Migrant Farmers, 1970, Teachers and the Children of Poverty, 1970, Erik H. Erikson: The Growth of His Work, 1970, The Middle Americans, 1970, Migrants, Sharecroppers and Mountaineers, 1972, The South Goes North, 1972, Saving Face, 1972, Farewell to the South, 1972, A Spectacle Unto the World, 1973, Riding Free, 1973, The Darkness and the Light, 1974, The Buses Roll, 1974, Irony in the Mind's Life: Essays on Novels by James Agee, Elizabeth Bowen and George Eliot, 1974, Headsparks, 1975, The Mind's Fate, 1975, Eskimos, Chicanos and Indians, 1978, Priviledged Ones: The Well-Off and The Rich in America, 1978, Women of Crisis Lives of Struggle and Hope, (with Jane Hallowell Coles), 1978, Walker Percy: An American Search, 1978, Flannery O'Connor's South, 1980, Women of Crisis; Lives of Work and Dreams, 1980,Dorothea Lange: Photographs of a Lifetime, 1982, (with Ross Spears) Agee, 1985, The Political Life of Children, 1986, Dorothy Day: A Radical Devotion, 1987, Simone Weil: A Modern Pilgrimage, 1987; contributing editor: The New Republic, 1966—, Am. Poetry Rev, 1972—, Aperture, 1974—, Literature and Medicine, 1981—, New Oxford Rev, 1981—; member editorial board: Integrated Edn, 1967—, Child Psychiatry and Human Devel, 1969—, Rev. of Books and Religion, 1976—, International Journal Family Therapy, 1977—, Grants mag, 1977—, Learning mag, 1978—, Journal Am. Culture, 1977—, Journal Edn, 1979—; board editors: Parents' Choice, 1978—; editor: Children and Youth Services Rev, 1978—. Board of directors Field Foundation, 1968—; trustee Robert F. Kennedy Memorial, 1968—, Robert F. Kennedy Action Corps, State of Massachusetts, 1968—, Mississippi Institute Early Childhood Education, 1968—, Twentieth Century Fund, 1971—; board of directors Reading is

Fundamental, Smithsonian Institute, 1968—, Am. Freedom from Hunger Foundation, 1968—, Am. Parents Committee, 1971—; member corp. Boston Children's Service, 1970; member adv. council Institute for Nonviolent Social Change of Martin Luther King, Junior Memorial Center, 1971—, Ams. for Children's Relief, 1972—; member national committee for Education of Young Children, 1972—; member national adv. council Rural Am., 1976—; trustee Austen Riggs Foundation, Stockbridge, Massachusetts, 1976—; member national adv. committee Alabama Citizens for Responsive Public Television, 1976—; member adv. committee National Indian Education Association, 1976—; visotor's committee member Boston Mus. Fine Arts, 1977; board of directors Boys Club Boston, 1977; visiting committee Boston College Law School, 1977; adv. Center for Southern Folklore, 1978—; member children's committee Edna McConnell Clark Foundation, 1978—; board of directors Lyndhurst Foundation, 1978—; member national adv. board Foxfire Fund, Incorporated, 1979—. Recipient Ralph Waldo Emerson prize Phi Beta Kappa, 1967; Anisfield-Wolf award in race relations Saturday Rev., 1968; Hofheimer award Am. Psychiat. Association, 1968; Sidney Hillman prize, 1971; Weatherford prize Berea College and Council Southern Mountains, 1973; Lilliam Smith Award Southern Regional Council, 1973; McAlpin medal National Association Mental Health, 1972; Pulitzer prize, 1973 (all received for Children of Crisis, Vols. II, III); distinguished scholar medal Hofstra University, 1974; William A. Shonfeld award Am. Society Adolescent Psychiatry, 1977; MacArthur Foundation award, 1981;

Josepha Hale award, 1986; fellow Davenport College, Yale University, 1976—. Fellow Am. Acad. Arts and Sciences, Institute Society, Ethics and the Life Sciences; member Am. Psychiat. Association, Am. Orthopsychiat. Association (past director), Acad. Psychoanalysis, National Organization Migrant Children. Home: 81 Carr Road Concord Massachusetts 01742 Office: Harvard U Department Psychiatry 75 Mount Auburn St Cambridge Massachusetts 02138

COLLINS, MICHAEL, aerospace consultant, former astronaut; born Rome, October 31, 1930; son of James L. and Virginia (Stewart) C. (parents Am. citizens); married Patricia M. Finnegan, April 28, 1957; children: Kathleen, Ann Stewart, Michael Lawton. Bachelor of Science, United States Military Academy, 1952; graduate, Advanced Management Program, Harvard University, 1974; Doctor of Science, Northeastern University, 1970, Stonehill College, 1970; Doctor of Laws, St. Michael's College, 1970, Southeastern University, 1975. Commissioned officer United States Air Force, advanced through grades to colonel, 1970; fighter pilot, flight commander United States, Europe; experimental flight test officer Edwards Air Force Base, California; astronaut National Aeronautics and Space Administration, 1963-69, Gemini 10, 1966; astronaut, space walker, commander, Command Module pilot Apollo 11, 1969; appointed assistant secretary state for pub. affairs Washington, 1970-71; director National Air and Space Mus., Smithsonian Institution, Washington, 1971-78; undersec. Smithsonian Institution, 1978-80; vice president LTV Aerospace & Defense Company,

1980-85; president Michael Collins Associates, 1985—; board of directors Rand Corp., Avemco Corp. Author: Carrying the Fire, 1974, Flying to the Moon and Other Strange Places, 1976, Liftoff, 1988. Trustee National Geog. Society. Decorated Distinguished Service Medal, Distinguished Flying Cross; recipient Presidential Medal of Freedom, National Aeronautics and Space Administration Distinguished Service and Exceptional Service medals, Hubbard medal, Collier trophy, Goddard Memorial trophy, Harmon trophy, General Thomas D. White USAF Space trophy, gold space medal Federation Aeronautique International. Fellow Am. Institute Aeros. and Astronautics, Am. Astronautical Society; member Washington Institute Foreign Affairs, Society Experimental Test Pilots, Order of Daedalians, Washington National Monument Society. Clubs: Metropolitan, Alfalfa, Alibi. Office: 4206 48th Place Northwest Washington District of Columbia 20016

COLONEY, WAYNE HERNDON, civil engineer; born Bradenton, Florida, March 15, 1925; son of Herndon Percival and Mary Adore (Cramer) C.; married Anne Elizabeth Benedict, June 21, 1950; 1 child, Mary Adore. Bachelor of Civil Engineering summa cum laude, Georgia Institute Tech., 1950. Registered professional engineer and surveyor, Florida, Georgia, Alabama, North Carolina, also Nat. Council Engring. Examiners. Project engineer S.A. Constructora General, Venezuela, 1948-49; project engineer Florida Road Department, 1950-55; highway engineer Gibbs & Hill, Incorporated, Guatemala, 1955-57; project manager Gibbs & Hill, Incorporated, Tampa, Florida, 1957-59; project engineer, then associate J. E. Greiner Company, Tampa, 1959-63; partner Barrett, Daffin & Coloney, Tallahassee, 1963-70; president Wayne H. Coloney Company, Incorporated, Tallahassee, 1970-78, chairman, board chief executive officer; 1978-85; president, secretary Tesseract Corp., 1975-85; chairman board, chief executive officer Coloney Company Cons. Engineers, Incorporated, 1978—; deputy chairman Howden Airdynamics Am., Tallahassee, 1985—; vice president, director Howden Coloney Incorporated, Tallahassee, 1985—; chairman adv. committee Area Vocational Tech. School, 1965-78; president Retro Tech. Corp., 1983—, Professional Management Con. Group, 1983-87, president, board of directors International Enterprises Inc, 1967-73. Patentee roof framing system, dense packing external aircraft fuel tank, tile mounting structure, curler rotating device, bracket system for roof framing; contributor articles to professional journals. President United Fund Leon County, 1971-72; board of directors Springtime Tallahassee, 1970-72, president, 1981-82; board of directors Heritage Foundation, 1965-71, president, 1967; member President's Adv. Council on Industrial Innovation, 1978-79; board of directors LeMoyne Art Foundation, 1973, vice president, 1974-75; board of directors Goodwill Industries, 1972-73, Tallahassee-Popoyan Friendship Commission, 1968-73; member Adv. Committee for Historical and Cultural Preservation, 1969-71, Better Business Bureau Served with Army of the United States, 1943-46. Fellow American Society of Civil Engineers; member Am. Defense Preparedness

Association, NSPE, Florida Engineering Society (senior), National Acad. Forensic Engineers (diplomate), Florida Institute Cons. Engineers, Florida Society Professional Land Surveyors, Tallahassee Chamber of Commerce, Anak, Koseme Society, Am. Arbitration Association, Florida Small business Association (president 1981), Sales & Marketing Executives (1983—), Phi Kappa Phi, Omicron Delta Kappa, Sigma Alpha Epsilon, Tau Beta Pi. Episcopalian. Clubs: Governor's, Killearn Golf and Country, Metropolitan Dinner (past president). Home: 3219 Thomasville Road Apartment 1-D Tallahassee Florida 32312 Office: Coloney Company Cons Engrs Incorporated Post Office Box 668 Tallahassee Florida 32302

COMMONER, BARRY, biologist, educator; born Brooklyn, May 28, 1917; son of Isidore and Goldie (Yarmolinsky) C.; married Lisa Feiner, 1980; children by previous marriage: Lucy Alison, Frederic Gordon. Bachelor of Arts with honors, Columbia University, 1937; Master of Arts, Harvard University, 1938, Doctor of Philosophy, 1941; Doctor of Science, Hahnemann Medical College, 1963, Clark University, 1967, Grinnell College, 1968, Lehigh University, 1969, Williams College, 1970, Ripon College, 1971, Colgate University, 1972, Cleveland State University, 1980; Doctor of Laws, University California, 1974, Grinnell College, 1981; Doctor of Science, St. Lawrence University, 1988. Assistant biology Harvard, 1938-40; instructor biology Queens College, 1940-42; associate editor Sci. Illustrated, 1946-47; associate professor plant physiology Washington University, St. Louis, 1947-53; professor Washington University, 1953-76, chairman department botany; 1965-69; director Washington University (Center for the Biology of Natural Systems), 1965-81, University professor environmental sci.; 1976-81; professor department geology Queens College, Flushing, New York, 1981-87, professor emeritus; 1987—, director Center for the Biology of Natural Systems; 1981—; visiting professor community health Albert Einstein College of Medicine, New York City, 1981-87; President St. Louis Committee for Nuclear Information, 1965-66, board of directors 1966; member National Tuberculosis Commission on Air Conservation, 1966-68; board of directors Scientists Institute Pub. Information, from 1963, co-chairman, 1967-69, chairman, 1969-78, chairman executive committee, from 1978; chairman special consultant group sonic boom Department Interior, 1967-68; adv. council on environmental education Office Education Department of Health, Education and Welfare, 1971; international sponsoring committee Chaim Weizmann Centenary Celebration, 1974-75; adv. committee Coalition Health Communities, 1975; member sec.'s adv. council United States Department Commerce, 1976; sci. adv. council on dioxin Vietnam Vets. Am. Foundation, 1985—; sci. adv. New York State Committee on Sci. and Tech., 1981—; adv. board Committee for Responsible Genetics, 1983—. Author: Science and Survival, 1966, The Closing Circle, 1971 (Phi Beta Kappa award), (International prize City of Cervia, Italy), La Technologia del Profitto, 1973, The Poverty of Power, 1976 (Premio Iglesias award, Sardinia, Italy 1978), Ecologia e Lotte Sociali, 1976, l'energia alternativa, 1978, The

Politics of Energy, 1979 (Premio Iglesias award 1982), Se Scoppia La Bomba, 1984, Il Cerchio Da Chiudere, 1986; Editorial board: World Book Ency, 1968-73, Environment mag, 1977; member adv. board: Science Year, 1967-72; editorial adv. board: Hon. Chemosphere, from 1972; board sponsors: In These Times, 1976—. Board cons. experts Rachel Carson Trust for Living Environment, 1967—; adv. committee Center for Devel. Policy, 1978; member board Univs. National Anti-War Fund; adv. board Fund for Peace, 1978, Citizens Party candidate for president of United States, 1980. Served to lieutenant United States Naval Reserve, 1942-46. Recipient Newcomb Cleveland prize American Association for the Advancement of Science, 1953; 1st Humanist award International Humanist and Ethical Union, 1970; medal American Institute of Architects, 1979; decorated commander Order of Merit Italy, 1977. Fellow American Association for the Advancement of Science (chairman committee sci. in promotion of human welfare 1958-65, director 1967-74, chairman committee on environmental alterations 1969-72), Am. School Health Association (hon.); member Society Biological Chemists, Society General Physiologists, Am. Society Plant Physiologists, Sierra Club, National Parks Association (trustee 1968-70), Soil Association England (hon. life vice president), Am. Chemical Society, Am. Society Biological Chemists, Federation Am. Scientists, Ecological Society Am., Institute Environmental Education (truste), Phi Beta Kappa, Sigma Xi. Office: Queens College Center for Biology Natural Systems Flushing New York 11367

COMPARIN, ROBERT ANTON, mechanical engineering educator; born Hurley, Wisconsin, July 25, 1928; son of Anton Joseph and Evelyn S. (Ebli) C.; married Ida Masone, August 4, 1956; children—Robert J., Evelyn, Thomas, James, Nancy. Bachelor of Science in Mechanical Engineering, Purdue University, 1954, Master of Science, 1958, Doctor of Philosophy, 1960. Instructor Purdue University, 1954-60; staff engineer International Business Machines Corporation Corp., Endicott, New York, Zurich, 1960-62; assistant professor mechanical engineering University Maine, 1962-64; professor mechanical engineering Virginia Polytechnic Institute, Blacksburg, 1964-74; chairman mechanical engineering department New Jersey Institute Tech., Newark, 1974-77; dean engineering Fenn College Engineering, Cleveland State University, 1977-83; chairman department mechanical engineering Virginia Polytechnic Institute, 1983—. Served with United States Air Force, 1946-49, 50-51. Member American Society of Mechanical Engineers, Am., Society Engineering Education, Sigma Xi. Roman Catholic. Home: 1502 Carlson Dr Blacksburg Virginia 24060 Office: Va Polytechnic Institute Blacksburg Virginia 24061

COMPTON, W. DALE, physicist; born Chrisman, Illinois, January 7, 1929; son of Roy L. and Marcia (Wood) D.; married Jeanne C. Parker, October 14, 1951; children: Gayle Corinne, Donald Leonard, Duane Arthur. Bachelor of Arts, Wabash College, 1949; Master of Science, University Oklahoma, 1951; Doctor of Philosophy, University Illinois, 1955; Doctor of Engineering (honorary), Michigan Technological University, 1976. Physicist United

States Naval Ordnance Test Station, China Lake, California, 1951-52, United States Naval Research Laboratory, Washington, 1955-61; professor physics University Illinois at Urbana, 1961-70, director coordinated sci. laboratory; 1965-70; director chemical and physical sciences, executive director sci. research staff, vice president research Ford Motor Company, Dearborn, Michigan, 1971-86; senior fellow National Acad. Engineering, 1986-88; distinguished professor industrial engineering Purdue University, West Lafayette, Ind., 1988—; member Presdl. Commission for Award of Medal of Sci., 1978-80; member visiting committee National Bureau Standards, 1975-79, chairman visiting committee, 1979. Author: (with J.H. Schulman) Color Centers in Solids, 1962; Editor: Interaction of Science and Technology, 1969, Design and Analysis of Integrated Manufacturing Systems, 1988. Board of directors Michigan Cancer Foundation, 1975-84, Coordinating Research Council, 1983-85; adv. committee Combustion Research Facility, Sandia National Lab., 1983-86; member energy research adv. board Department Energy, 1979-80; board governors Argonne National Lab., 1983-86. Fellow Am. Physical Society, American Association for the Advancement of Science, Washington Acad. Sciences, National Acad. Engineering, Society Automotive Engineers, Engineering Society Detroit; member Research Society Am.

CONCORDIA, CHARLES, consulting engineer; born Schenectady, June 20, 1908; son of Francis G. and Susie Elizabeth (Decker) C.; married Frances Butler, December 18, 1948. Doctor of Science (honorary), Union College, 1971. With General Electric Company, Schenectady, 1926-73; in electric utility systems engineering General Electric Company, 1936-73, applications engineer; 1936-49, in aircraft devel.; 1941-45, consultant engineer; 1949-73; consultant electric power systems engineering Venice, Florida, 1973—; lecturer various universities. Author: Synchronous Machines, 1951; contributor 120 articles to professional journals. Recipient Lamme medal Am. Institute Electrical Engrs., 1961; Coffin award General Electric Company, 1942; Steinmetz award, 1973; named Engineer of Year Professional Engrs. Society, 1963. Fellow Institute of Electrical and Electronics Engineers, American Society of Mechanical Engineers, American Association for the Advancement of Science; member Association Computing Machinery (founding member), Conference Internationale des Grands Reseaux Electriques a Haute Tension, National Acad. Engineering, National Society Professional Engineers, Sigma Xi, Tau Beta Pi. Republican. Presbyterian. Clubs: Venice Yacht, Mohawk Golf. Patentee in field (6). Home and Office: 702 Bird Bay Dr W Venice Florida 34292-4030

CONKLIN, HAROLD COLYER, anthropologist, educator; born Easton, Pennsylvania, April 27, 1926; son of Howard S. and May W. (Colyer) C.; married Jean M. Morisuye, June 11, 1954; children: Bruce Robert, Mark William. Bachelor of Arts, University Calif.-Berkeley, 1950; Doctor of Philosophy, Yale University, 1955. From instructor to associate professor anthropology Columbia University, 1954-62; lecturer anthropology Rockefeller Institute,

1961-62; professor anthropology Yale University, 1962—, chairman department; 1964-68; curator of anthropology Yale Peabody Museum Natural History, 1974—; member Institute for Advanced Study, Princeton University, 1972; fellow Center for Advanced Study in Behavioral Sciences, Stanford, California, 1978-79; field research in Philippines, 1945-47, 52-54, 55, 57-58, 61, 62-63, 64, 65, 68-69, 70, 73, 80-81, 82, 83, 84, 85, Malaya and Indonesia, 1948, 57, 83, Melanesia, 1987, California and New York, 1951, 52, Guatemala, 1959, Peru, 1987; director, committee problems and policy Social Sci. Research Council, 1963-70; board of directors Survival International USA; special consultant International Rice Research Institute, Los Baños, Philippines, 1962—; book rev. editor Am. Anthropologist, 1960-62; member Pacific sci. board National Acad. Scis.-NRC, 1962-66. Author: Hanunóo Agriculture, 1957, Folk Classification, 1972, Ethnographic Atlas of Ifugao, 1980; other publications on ethnological, linguistic and ecological. topics. Served with Army of the United States, 1944-46. Guggenheim fellow, 1973; recipient International Sci. prize Fyssen Foundation, 1983. Fellow Am. Acad. Arts and Sciences, Am. Anthropological Association (executive board 1965-68), Royal Anthropological Institute, New York Acad. Sciences (secretary section anthropology 1956), National Academy of Sciences; member Am. Ethnological Society (councilor 1960-62, president 1978-79), Koninklijk Institute voor Taal- Land- en Volkenkunde, Connecticut Acad. Arts and Sciences, Linguistic Society Am., Society Am. Archaeology, Kroeber Anthropological Society, Philadelphia Anthropological Association, Am. Geog. Society, Am. Oriental Society, Association Asian Studies, Classification Society, Linguistic Society Philippines, La Société de Linguistique de Paris, Indo-Pacific Prehistory Association, Society Econ. Botany, International Association Plant Taxonomy, American Association for the Advancement of Science, Phi Beta Kappa, Sigma Xi. Home: 106 York Square New Haven Connecticut 06511 Office: Yale University Department Anthropology New Haven Connecticut 06520

CONN, ROBERT WILLIAM, nuclear engineering educator; born Brooklyn, December 1, 1942; son of William Conrad and Rose Marie (Albanese) C.; married Gloria Trovato, September 21, 1963; children: Carole, William. Bachelor of Science in Chemical Engineering, Pratt Institute, 1964; Master of Science, California Institute Tech., 1965; Doctor of Philosophy in Engineering Science, 1968. National Science Foundation postdoctoral fellow Euratom Community Research Center, Ispra, Italy, 1968-69; research associate Brookhaven National Laboratory, Upton, New York, 1969-70; visiting associate professor University Wisconsin, Madison, 1970-72; member faculty University Wisconsin, 1972-80, professor nuclear engineering; 1975-80, director fusion tech. program; 1974-79; professor engineering and applied sci. University of California at Los Angeles, 1980—, co-director Center for Plasma Physics and Fusion Engineering; 1981-86, director Institute Plasma and Fusion Research; 1987—; consultant to government and industry. Author papers, chapter in book. Recipient Curtis McGraw Research award Am.

Association Engineering Education, 1982; Outstanding Service cert. U.S. Department Energy, also E.O. Lawrence Memorial award, 1984; Romnes Faculty fellow, 1977. Fellow Am. Nuclear Society (Outstanding Achievement award for excellence in research fusion division 1979), Am. Physical Society; member National Acad. Engineering. Office: 6291 Boelter Hall University of California at Los Angeles Los Angeles California 90025

CONNELL, ALASTAIR MCCRAE, physician; born Glasgow, Scotland, December 21, 1929; came to United States, 1970; son of Alex McCrae and Maud (Crawford) C.; married Joyce Dethlefs, 1983; children: Stewart, Fiona, Alison, Iain, Andrew. Bachelor of Science, University Glasgow, 1951, Bachelor of Medicine, ChB, 1954, Doctor of Medicine, 1969. Intern Western Infirmary, Glasgow, 1954-55; resident in gastroenterology Central Middlesex and St. Mark's Hospital, London, 1957-60; practice medicine specializing in gastroenterology 1960—; member medical staff Medical Research Council, 1960-64; senior lecturer clinical sci. Queen's University, Belfast, Northern Ireland, 1964-70; Mark Brown professor medicine Medical Center, University Cincinnati, 1970-79, director div. digestive diseases; 1970-79, professor physiology; 1972-79, associate dean; 1975-77; director Office Clinical Affairs, 1975-77; dean College Medicine, University Nebraska Medical Center, 1979-84, professor internal medicine; 1979-84; vice president health sciences Virginia Commonwealth University, Richmond, 1984—; member sci. adv. board National Foundation for Ileitis and Colitis, 1974—, chairman research

devel. committee, 1974-78; member Personal Health Committee Ohio, 1974-76; trustee Medco Peer Rev., 1974-79. Author: Clinical Tests of Gastric Function, 1973; Associate editor: Am. Journal Digestive Diseases; Contributor articles to professional journals. Served with Medical Corps Royal Army, 1955-57. Fellow Royal College Physicians (Edinburgh), American College of Physicians; member Am. Gas- troentorological Association, Brit. Society Gastroenterology, Medical Research Society, International Group for Study Intestinal Motility (past president), Southwest Ohio Digestive Diseases Society (president 1973-76), Cincinnati Lit. Club. Office: Va Commonwealth U Office of V P Health Scis Box 549 MCV Station Richmond Virginia 23298

CONRAD, CHARLES, JR., former astronaut, business executive; born Philadelphia, June 2, 1930; son of Charles and Frances V. (Sargent) C.; married Jane DuBose, June 17, 1953; children: Peter, Thomas, Andrew, Christopher. Bachelor of Science in Aerospace Engineering, Princeton, 1953. Commissioned ensign United States Navy, 1953, advanced through grades to lieutenant commander; 1964; project test pilot, armaments test div. Navy Department, 1959-60; flight instructor, performance engineer United States Naval Test Pilot School, 1960-61; flight instructor for F4H Naval Air Station, Miramar, California, 1961-62; safety flight officer Fighter Squadron 96 1963; astronaut Manned Spacecraft Center, National Aeronautics and Space Administra- tion, Houston, 1964-74; pilot Manned Spacecraft Center, National Aeronautics and Space Administration (Gemini V), 1965; commanding pilot

Manned Spacecraft Center, National Aeronautics and Space Administration (Gemini XI), 1966; commander Manned Spacecraft Center, National Aeronautics and Space Administration (Apollo 12), 1969, Manned Spacecraft Center, National Aeronautics and Space Administration (Skylab), 1973; vice president operations Am. TV & Communications Corp., Denver, 1974-78; vice president marketing Douglas Aircraft Company, Long Beach, California, 1978-80; senior vice president Douglas Aircraft Company, 1980-86; staff vice president international McDonnell Douglas Corp., 1986—. Recipient Congressional medal of Honor, 1978. Fellow Society Experimental Test Pilots; associate fellow Am. Institute Aeronautical and Astronautics. Office: 3855 Lakewood Boulevard Long Beach California 90846

CONRAD, PAUL, mathematics educator; born New York, October 7, 1921; married; 1 child. Doctor of Philosophy in Math., University Illinois, 1951. From assistant professor to professor math. Newcomb College, Tulane University, 1951-70; professor math. University Kansas, 1970—, now Henry J. Bischoff distinguished professor math.; National Science Foundation senior fellow Australian National University, 1964-65; visiting professor University Paris, 1967. Fulbright lecturer University Ceylon, 1956-57. Member Am. Math. Society. Research in ordered algebraic systems, group theory. Office: U Kansas Department Math Lawrence Kansas 66045

CONWAY, LYNN ANN, computer scientist, educator; born Mount Vernon, New York, January 2, 1938. Bachelor of Science, Columbia University, 1962, Master of Science in Electrical Engineering, 1963. Member research staff International Business Machines Corporation Corp., Yorktown Heights, New York, 1964-68; senior staff engineer Memorex Corp., Santa Clara, California, 1969-73; member research staff Xerox Corp., Palo Alto, California, 1973-78, research fellow, manager VLSI systems area; 1978-82, research fellow, manager knowledge systems area; 1982-83; assistant director for strategic computing Defense Advanced Research Projects Agency, Arlington, Virginia, 1983-85; professor electrical engineering and computer sci., associate dean College Engineering University Michigan, Ann Arbor, Michigan, 1985—; visiting associate professor elec. engineering and computer sci. Massachusetts Institute of Technology, Cambridge, Massachusetts, 1978-79; member sci. adv. board United States Air Force, 1987—. Co-author: textbook Introduction to VLSI Systems, 1980. Recipient Annual Achievement award Electronics magazine, 1981, Harold Pender award University Pennsylvania, 1984, Wetherill Medal Franklin Institute, 1985, Sec. of Defense Meritorious Civilian Service award, 1985; sr. fellow University Michigan Society Fellows, 1987—. Fellow Institute of Electrical and Electronics Engineers; member National Academy of Engineering, Am. Association for Artificial Intelligence, American Association for the Advancement of Science. Office: U Michigan 2307 EECS Building Ann Arbor Michigan 48109

COOKSON, ALBERT ERNEST, telephone and telegraph company executive; born Needham, Massachusetts, October 30, 1921; son of Willard B. and Sarah Jane (Jack) C.;

married Constance J. Buckley, September 10, 1949; children—Constance J., William B. Bachelor of Electrical Engineering, Northeastern University, 1943; Master of Electrical Engineering, Massachusetts Institute Tech., 1951; Doctor of Science, Gordon College, 1974. Group leader Research Laboratory Electronics, Massachusetts Institute Tech., 1947-51; laboratory director International Telephone & Telegraph Corporation Federal Laboratories, Nutley, New Jersey, 1951-59; vice president, director operations International Telephone & Telegraph Corporation Federal Laboratories (International Electrical Corp. div.), Paramus, New Jersey, 1959-62; president International Telephone & Telegraph Corporation Intelcom, Falls Church, Virginia, 1962-65; deputy general tech. director International Telephone & Telegraph Corporation, New York City, 1965-66; vice president, tech. director International Telephone & Telegraph Corporation, 1966-68, senior vice president, general tech. director; 1968—; chairman board International Telephone & Telegraph Corporation Interplan; director International Standard Electric, International Telephone & Telegraph Corporation Industries.; Member Def. Communications Satellite Panel; adviser research and engineering on defense communications satellite systems Department Def.; member industrial panel sci. and tech. National Science Foundation.; Member Fairfax County Economic and Industrial Devel. Committee, 1962-65; member national council Northeastern University; member pride committee University Hartford, 1973-76; electrical engineering/computer adv. board Massachusetts Institute Tech., 1977—. Served with United States Naval Reserve, 1943-46. Fellow Institute of Electrical and Electronics Engineers; member Armed Forces Communications and Electronics Association, Am. Management Association, Am. Institute Aeros. and Astronautics, Electronic Industries Association, Sigma Xi, Tau Beta Pi. Patentee frequency search and track system. Home: 4301 Pond Apple Dr Naples Florida 33999 Office: 320 Park Avenue New York New York 10022

COOLEY, DENTON ARTHUR, surgeon, educator; born Houston, August 22, 1920; son of Ralph C. and Mary (Fraley) C.; married Louise Goldsborough Thomas, January 15, 1949; children: Mary, Susan, Louise, Florence, Helen. Bachelor of Arts, University Texas, 1941; Doctor of Medicine, Johns Hopkins University, 1944; Doctorem Medicinae (honorary), University Turin, Italy, 1969; Doctor of Humanities (honorary), Hellenic College, 1984, Holy Cross Greek Orthodox School of Theology, 1984; DSC honoris causa, College of William and Mary, 1987. Diplomate: Am. Board Surgery, Am. Board Thoracic Surgery. Intern Johns Hopkins School Medicine, Baltimore, 1944-45; resident surgery Johns Hopkins School Medicine, 1945-50; senior surgical registrar thoracic surgery Brompton Hospital for Chest Diseases, London, England, 1950-51; associate professor surgery Baylor University College Medicine, Houston, 1954-62; professor surgery Baylor University College Medicine, 1962-69; clinical professor surgery University Texas Medical School, Houston, 1975—; founder, surgeon-in-chief Texas Heart Institute, 1962—. Served as captain, Medical Corps, 1946-48. Named one of ten Outstanding Young Men in U.S., U.S. Chamber of

Commerce, 1955; Man of the Year award Kappa Sigam, 1964; Rene Leriche prize International Surg. Society, 1965-67; Billings Gold medal Am. Surg. Society, 1967; Vishnevsky medal Vishnevsky Institute, Union of Soviet Socialist Republics, 1971; Theodore Roosevelt Award, 1980; Presidential Medal of Freedom, presented by President Reagan, 1984; Gifted Teacher award Am. College Cardiology, 1987. Hon. fellow Royal College Physicians and Surgeons of Glasgow, Royal College Surgeons of Ireland, Royal Australasian College Surgeons, Royal College Surgeons of England; member American College of Surgeons, Am. Surgical Association, International Cardiovascular Society, Am. Association Thoracic Surgery, Society Thoracic Surgery, Society University Surgeons, Am. College Cardiology, Am. College Chest Physicians, Society Clinical Surgery, Society Vascular Surgery, Western Surgical Association, Texas Surgical, Society Hasted Society. Performed numerous heart transplants; implanted 1st artificial heart, 1969. Office: Tex Heart Institute Post Office Box 20345 Houston Texas 77225

COON, MINOR JESSER, biological chemistry educator; born Englewood, Colorado, July 29, 1921; son of Minor Dillon and Mary (Jesser) C.; married Mary Louise Newburn, June 27, 1948; children: Lawrence R., Susan L. Bachelor of Arts, University Colorado, 1943; Doctor of Philosophy, University Illinois, 1946; Doctor of Science (honorary), Northwestern University, 1983, Northeastern Ohio University College Medicine, 1987. Postdoctoral research assistant in biochemistry University Illinois, 1946-47; instructor department physio-logical chemistry University Pennsylvania, 1947-49, assistant professor; 1949-53; associate professor 1953-55; professor department biological chemistry University Michigan Medical School, 1955—, Victor C. Vaughan Distinguished University professor biological chemistry; 1983—, chairman department; 1970—; research fellow department pharmacology New York University, 1952-53; research fellow Federal Polytechnic Institute, Zürich, Switzerland, 1961-62; consultant Oak Ridge Institute Nuclear Studies, 1956-58; member adv. council Life Insurance Medical Research Fund, 1960-65; member biochem. study section National Institutes of Health, 1963-66, research career award committee, 1966-70; member University Chicago rev. committee for Argonne National Laboratory, 1985—.

Editor-in-chief: Biochemical Preparations, 1962, Microsomes, Drug Oxidations and Chemical Carcinogenesis, 1980; member editorial bds.: Biochemistry, 1971-74, 85—, Molecular Pharmacology, 1972-78, Journal Biol. Chemistry, 1976-81, Proc. Science Conf. on Cytochrome P-450: Structural and Functional Aspects, 1980; contributor articles to professional journals. Recipient Distinguished Faculty achievement award University Michigan, 1976, William C. Rose award in biochemistry, 1978, Bernard B. Brodie award in drug metabolism, 1980, Distinguished Faculty lectureship award in biomed. research University Michigan, 1982, Scientist of Year award State of Michigan, 1988. Fellow New York Acad. Sciences; member Am. Chemical Society (award in enzyme chemistry 1959), Am. Society for Microbiology, Am. Society

Biological Chemists (secretary 1981-84), Am. Society Pharmacology and Experimental Therapeutics, Biophys. Society, American Association for the Advancement of Science, International Society for Biomed. Research on Alcoholism, International Society for Study of Xenobiotics, Research Society for Alcoholism, Association Medical School Departments Biochemistry (president 1974-75), International Union Biochemistry (chairman committee on interest groups, executive committee 1985—), Am. Institute Biological Sciences, Am. Oil Chemists Society, National Acad. Sciences, Am. Acad. Arts and Sciences, Institute of Medicine, National Acad. Sciences, Phi Beta Kappa, Sigma Xi, Phi Kappa Phi, Alpha Chi Sigma, Phi Lambda Upsilon. Home: 1901 Austin Avenue Ann Arbor Michigan 48104 Office: Department Biol Chemistry U Michigan Ann Arbor Michigan 48109

COOPER, EDWIN LOWELL, anatomy educator; born Oakland, Texas, December 23, 1936; son of Edwin Ellis and Ruthesther (Porché) C.; married Helene Marie Antoinette Tournaire, September 13, 1969; children—Astrid Madeleine, Amaury Tournaire. Bachelor of Science, Texas Southern University, 1957; Master of Science, Atlanta, 1959; Doctor of Philosophy, Brown University, 1963. UHPHS postdoctoral fellow University of California at Los Angeles, 1962-64, assistant professor anatomy; 1964-69; associate professor 1969-73, professor; 1973—; visiting professor Instituto Politecnico Nacional, Mexico City, 1966; Member adv. committee Office Sci. Personnel, National Research Council, 1972-73; member board sci. counselors National Institute Dental Research, 1973—. Author: Comparative Immunology; Editor: Phylogeny of Transplantation Reactions, 1970, Invertebrate Immunology, 1974; founding editor: International Journal Developmental and Comparative Immunology, 1977—. Guggenheim fellow, 1970; Fulbright scholar, 1970; Eleanor Roosevelt fellow International Union Against Cancer, 1977-78. Fellow American Association for the Advancement of Science (council 1971, chairman section 1976); member Society Invertebrate Pathology (founding), Pan Am. Congress Anatomy (founding), Am. Association Anatomy, Transplantation Society, Am. Association Immunologists, Am. Society Zoologists (program officer 1974—, founder division comparative immunology 1975), Brit. Society Immunology, Societe d'Immunologie Francaise, Sigma Xi. Office: Department Anatomy School Medicine University California Los Angeles California 90024

COOPER, LEON N., physicist, educator; born New York City, February 28, 1930; son of Irving and Anna (Zola) C.; married Kay Anne Allard, May 18, 1969; children: Kathleen Ann, Coralie Lauren. Bachelor of Arts, Columbia University, 1951, Master of Arts, 1953, Doctor of Philosophy, 1954, Doctor of Science, 1973; Doctor of Science honorary degrees; Doctor of Science, University Sussex, England, 1973, University Illinois, 1974, Brown University, 1974, Gustavus Adolphus College, 1975, Ohio State University, 1976, University Pierre et Marie Curie, Paris, 1977. National Science Foundation postdoctoral fellow, member Institute for Advanced Study,

1954-55; research associate University Illinois, 1955-57; assistant professor Ohio State University, 1957-58; associate professor Brown University, Providence, 1958-62, professor; 1962-66, Henry Ledyard Goddard University professor; 1966-74, Thomas J. Watson Senior professor sci.; 1974—; co-director Center for Neural Sci.; lecturer pub. lectures, international conference and symposia; visiting professor various universities and summer schools; consultant industrial, educational organizations; sponsor Federation Am. Scientists; member counseil superieur de la recherche University Rene Descartes. Author: Introduction to The Meaning and Structure of Phsyics, 1968; Contributor articles to professional journals. Alfred P. Sloan Foundation research fellow, 1959-66; John Simon Guggenheim Memorial Foundation fellow, 1965-66; recipient Nobel prize (with J. Bardeen and J.R. Schrieffer), 1972; award of Excellence, Graduate Facilities Alumni of Columbia, University, 1974; Descartes medal Acad. de Paris, University Rene Descartes, 1977; John Jay award Columbia College, 1985. Fellow Am. Physical Society, Am. Acad. Arts and Sciences; member Am. Philosophical Society, National Acad. Sciences (Comstock prize with J.R. Schrieffer 1968), Society Neurosci, American Association for the Advancement of Science, Phi Beta Kappa, Sigma Xi. Office: Brown U Department Physics Providence Rhode Island 02912

COOPER, LEROY GORDON, JR., former astronaut, business consultant; born Shawnee, Oklahoma, March 6, 1927; son of Leroy Gordon and Hattie Lee (Herd) C.; married Trudy B. Olson, August 29, 1947 (divorced); children—Camala Keoki, Janita Lee; married Susan Taylor, May 6, 1972; children—Elizabeth Jo, Colleen Taylor. Student, University Hawaii, 1946-49, European extension University Maryland, 1951-53; Bachelor of Science in Aeronautical Engineering, Air Force Institute Tech., 1956; graduate, Experimental Test Pilot School, United States Air Force, 1957. Commissioned lieutenant United States Air Force, 1949, advanced through grades to colonel; 1965; jet fighter pilot 1950-54, pilot experimental flight test engineering; 1957-59; astronaut with Project Mercury, National Aeronautics and Space Administration, 1959-70; made 22 orbit flight in Faith 7 1963; worked with Gemini program of Astronaut Office, made 122 Orbit flight in Gemini V; 1965; worked with Apollo lunar program; vice president research and devel. W.E.D. Enterprises, 1974-80; president XL, Incorporated, 1980—. Recipient Harmon trophy; Colliers trophy. Member Am. Institute Aeronautical and Astronautics, Society Experimental Test Pilots, Am. Astronautical Society. Lodge: Masons (Shriner, Jester). Office: XL Incorporated 400 N Rodeo Dr Beverly Hills California 90210

COREY, ELIAS JAMES, chemistry educator; born Methuen, Massachusetts, July 12, 1928; son of Elias and Tina (Hashem) C.; married Claire highham, September 14, 1961; children: David, John, Susan. Bachelor of Science, Massachusetts Institute of Technology, 1948, Doctor of Philosophy, 1951; Master of Arts (honorary), Harvard University, 1959; Doctor of Science (honorary), University Chicago, 1968, Hofstra University, 1974, Oxford University,

1982, University Liege, 1985, University Illinois, 1985. From instructor to assistant professor University Illinois, Champaign-Urbana, 1951-55, professor; 1955-59; professor chemistry Harvard University, Cambridge, Massachusetts, 1959—, Sheldon Emory professor; 1968—. Contributor articles to professional journals. Board of directors physical sci. Alfred P. Sloan Foundation, 1967-72; member sci. adv. board of directors Robert A. Welch Foundation. Recipient Intrasci. Foundation award, 1968, Ernest Guenther award in chemistry of essentials oils and related products, 1968, Harrison Howe award, 1971, Ciba Foundation medal, 1972, Evans award Ohio State University, 1972, Linus Pauling award, 1973, Dickson prize in sci. Carnegie Mellon University, 1973, George Ledlie prize in sci. Harvard University, 1973, Nichols medal, 1977, Buchman award California Institute Tech., 1978, Franklin medal in sci. Franklin Institute, 1978, Sci. Achievement award City College of New York, 1979, J.G. Kirkwood award, Yale University, 1980, Chemical Pioneer award, Am. Institute Chemists, 1981, Wolf prize (chemical), Wolf Foundation, 1986, Japan prize, 1989, numerous others; fellow Swiss-Am. exchange, 1957, Guggenheim Foundation, 1957-58, 68-69, Alfred P. Sloan Foundation, 1956-59. Member Am. Acad. Arts and Sciences, American Association for the Advancement of Science, Am. Chemical Society (award in synthetic chemistry 1971, Pure Chemistry award 1960, Fritzche award 1968, Maryland section Remsen award 1974, Arthur C. Cope award 1976), National Acad. Sci., Sigma Xi. Office: Harvard U Department Chemistry Cambridge Massachusetts 02138

CORMACK, ALLAN MACLEOD, physicist, educator; born Johannesburg, South Africa, February 23, 1924; came to United States, 1957, naturalized, 1966; son of George and Amelia (MacLeod) C.; married Barbara Jeanne Seavey, January 6, 1950; children: Margaret, Jean, Robert. Bachelor of Science, University Cape Town, South Africa, 1944, Master of Science, 1945; research student, Cambridge (England) University, 1947-50. Lecturer University Cape Town, 1946-47, 1950-56; research fellow Harvard University, 1956-57; assistant professor physics Tufts University, Medford, Massachusetts, 1957-60; associate professor Tufts University, 1960-64, professor; 1964-80, University professor; 1980—. Recipient Ballou medal Tufts University, 1978; Nobel prize in medicine and physiology, 1979; Medal of Merit University Cape Town, 1980. Fellow American Association for the Advancement of Science, Am. Physical Society, Am. Acad. Arts and Sci., Royal Society South Africa (foreign); member South African Physical Society, National Acad. Sciences, Am. Association Physicists in Medicine (hon.), Sigma Xi. Research on nuclear and particle physics, computed tomography and related math. topics. Office: Tufts U Physics Department Medford Massachusetts 02155

CORNFORTH, SIR JOHN WARCUP, chemist; born Sydney, Australia, September 7, 1917; son of John William and Hilda (Eipper) C.; married Rita H. Harradence, September 27, 1941; children: Brenda (Mrs. David Osborne), John, Philippa. Bachelor of Science, University Sydney, 1937, Master of Science, 1938; Doctor of

Philosophy, Oxford University, 1941, Doctor of Science (honorary), 1976; Doctor of Science (honorary), E.T.H. Zurich, 1975, Trinity College, Dublin, 1975, Universities Liverpool, Warwick, Aberdeen, Hull, Sussex and Sydney, 1975. Member sci. staff Medical Research Council, London, 1946-62; director Milstead Laboratory Chemical Enzymology, Shell Research Limited, Sittingbourne, Kent, England, 1962-75; Royal Society research professor School Molecular Sciences University Sussex, Brighton, England, 1975-82. Contributor articles on chemistry of penicillin, total synthesis of steroids and other biologically active natural products, chemistry of heterocyclic compounds, biosynthesis of steroids, enzyme chemistry to professional journals. Decorated commander Brit. Empire; knighted, 1977; recipient Stouffer prize, 1967; Prix Roussel, 1972; Nobel prize in chemistry, 1975. Fellow Royal Society, 1953 (Davy medal 1968, Royal medal 1976, Copley medal 1982), Royal Society Chemistry (Corday-Morgan medal 1953, Flintoff medal 1966), Am. Chemical Society (Ernest Guenther award 1969); member Biochem. Society (CIBA medal 1966), Am. Society Biological Chemists (hon.), Am. Acad. (hon. foreign member), Australian Acad. Sci. (corr.), Netherlands Acad. Sci. (foreign), National Academy of Sciences (foreign associate). Home: Saxon Down, Cuilfail, Lewes BN7 2BE, England Office: U Sussex, School Molecular Scis, Falmer, Brighton BN1 9QJ, England

COROTIS, ROSS BARRY, engineering educator; born Woodbury, New Jersey, January 15, 1945; son of A. Charles and Hazel Laura (McCloskey) C.; married Stephanie Michal Fuchs, March 19, 1972; children—Benjamin Randall, Lindsay Sarah. Bachelor of Science, Massachusetts Institute of Technology, Cambridge, 1967, Master of Science, 1968, Doctor of Philosophy, 1971. Licensed professional engineer, Illinois, Maryland, structural engineer, Illinois. Assistant professor department civil engineering Northwestern University, Evanston, Illinois, 1971-74, associate professor department civil engineering; 1975-79, professor department civil engineering; 1979-81; professor department civil engineering Johns Hopkins University, Baltimore, 1981-82, Hackerman professor; 1982-83, Hackerman professor, chairman department civil engineering; 1983—; member building research board National Research Council, Washington, 1985—. Contributor articles to professional journals; lecturer to professional confs. Member Mayor's task force City of Baltimore Construction Management, 1985. Research grantee National Science Foundation, National Bureau Standards, U.S. Department Energy, 1973-87; recipient Engineering Teaching award Northwestern University, 1977. Fellow Am. Society Civil Engineers (chairman safety bldgs. committee 1985—, Walter L. Huber research prize 1984, Civil Engineer of Year award Maryland chapter 1987, vice president Maryland chapter 1987—); member Am. Concrete Institute (chairman structural safety committee 1986—), Am. National Standards Institute (chairman live loads committee 1978-84). Office: Johns Hopkins U Department Civil Engring Baltimore Maryland 21218

COTTON, FRANK ALBERT, chemist, educator; born Philadelphia, April 9, 1930; son of Albert and Helen (Taylor) C.; married Diane Dornacher, June 13, 1959; children: Jennifer Helen, Jane Myrna. Student, Drexel Institute Tech., 1947-49; Bachelor of Arts, Temple University, 1951, Doctor of Science (honorary), 1963; Doctor of Philosophy, Harvard University, 1955; Doctor Natural Science (honorary), Bielefeld University, 1979; Doctor of Science (honorary), Columbia University, 1980, Northwestern University, 1981, University Bordeaux, 1981, St. Joseph's University, 1982, University Louis Pasteur, 1982, University Valencia, 1983, Kenyon College, 1983, Technion-Israel Institute Tech., 1983. Instructor chemistry M.I.T., 1955-57, assistant professor; 1957-60, associate professor; 1960-61, professor; 1961-71; Robert A. Welch Distinguished professor chemistry Texas A&M University, 1971—, director Laboratory for Molecular Stucture and Bonding; 1983—; Cons. Am. Cyanamid, Stamford, Connecticut, 1958-67, Union Carbide, New York City, 1964—. Author: (with G. Wilkinson) Advanced Inorganic Chemistry, 4th edit, 1980, Basic Inorganic Chemistry, 1976, Chemical Applications of Group Theory, 2d edit, 1970, (with L. Lynch and C. Darlington) Chemistry, An Investigative Approach; Editor: (with L. Lynch and C. Darlington) Progress in Inorganic Chemistry, Volumes 1-10, 1959-68, Inorganic Syntheses, Volume 13, 1971, (with L.M. Jackman) Dynamic Nuclear Magnetic Resonance Spectroscopy, (with R.A. Walton) Multiple Bonds between Metal Atoms. Recipient Michelson-Morley award Case Western Res. University, 1980, National Medal of Sci., 1982. Member National Academy of Sciences (chairman phys. scis. 1985—), Am. Society Biological Chemists, Am. Chemical Society (awards 1962, 74, Baekeland medal New Jersey section 1963, Nichols medal New York section 1975, Pauling medal Oregon and Puget Sound section 1976, Kirkwood medal New York section 1978, Gibbs medal Chicago section 1980), Am. Acad. Arts and Sciences, New York Acad. Sciences (hon. life), Göttingen Acad. Sciences (corr.); hon. member Royal Society Chemistry, Royal Danish Acad. Sciences and Letters, Societa Chimica Italiana, Indian Acad. Sciences, Indian National Acad. Sci. Home: Route 2 Box 285 Bryan Texas 77801 Office: Tex A&M University Department of Chemistry College Station Texas 77843

COUSTEAU, JACQUES-YVES, marine explorer, film producer, writer; born St. Andre-de-Cubzac, France, June 11, 1910; son of Daniel P. and Elizabeth (Duranthon) C.; married Simone Melchior, July 11, 1937; children: Jean-Michel, Philippe (deceased). Bachelier, Stanislas Academy, Paris, 1927; midshipman, Brest Naval Academy, 1930; Doctor of Science, University California, Berkeley, 1970, Brandeis University, 1970. Founder Groupe d'etudes et de recherches sous-marines, Toulon, France, 1946; founder, president Campagnes oceanographiques fran-caises, Marseille, 1950, Centre d'etudes marines avancees (formerly Office Francais de recherche sous marine), Marseille, 1952; leader Calypso Oceanographic Expeditions; director Oceanographic Mus., Monaco, 1957—; promoted Conshelf saturation dive program 1962; general secretary I.C.S.E.M., 1966. Recipient numerous awards, including: Motion Picture Acad. Arts and Scis. award (Oscar) for best documentary feature, The Silent World, also for The World Without Sun, 1965, for best short film The Golden Fish 1960, Grand Prix, Gold Palm, Festival Cannes for The Silent World 1956; author and producer documentary films which received awards at Paris, Cannes and Venice film festivals; producer over 70 films for TV; TV series include The World of Jacques-Yves Cousteau, 1966-68, The Undersea World of Jacques-Yves Cousteau, 1968-76, Oasis in Space, 1977, The Cousteau Odyssey Series, 1977-81, The Cousteau/Amazon Series, 1984—; TV specials include The Tragedy of the Red Salmon, The Desert Whales, Lagoon of Lost Ships, The Dragons of Galapagos, Secrets of the Southern Caves, The Unsinkable Sea Otter, A Sound of Sea Dolphins, South to Fire and Ice, The Flight of Penguins, Beneath the Frozen World, Blizzard of Hope Bay, Life at the End of the World; author: Par 18 metres de fonds, 1946, La Plongee en scaphandre, 1950, The Silent World, 1952, (editor with James Dugan) Captain Cousteau's Underwater Treasury, 1959, (with James Dugan) The Living Sea, 1963, World Without Sun, 1965, (with Philippe Cousteau) The Shark: Splendid Savage of the Sea, 1970, (with Philippe Cousteau) Life and Death in a Coral Sea, 1971, Diving for Sunken Treasure, 1971, The Whale: Mighty Monarch of the Sea, 1972, Octopus and Squid, 1973, Three Adventures: Galapagos- Titicaca- the Blue Holes, 1973, The Ocean World of Jacques Cousteau, 1973, Diving Companions, 1974, Dolphins, 1975, Jacques Cousteau: The Ocean World, 1979, A Bill of Rights for Future Generations, 1980, The Cousteau Almanac of the Environment, 1981, Jacques Cousteau's Calypso, 1983, Jacques Cousteau's Amazon Journey, 1984; contributor articles to National Geographic Magazine. Served as lieutenant de vaisseau French Navy, World War II. Decorated commander Legion of Honor, Croix de Guerre with palm, Merite Agricole, Merite Maritime, officier des Arts et des Lettres; Potts medal Franklin Institute, 1970; Gold medal Grand Prix d'oceanographie Albert I, 1971; Presidential medal of Freedom, 1985; Founders award International Council National Acad. Arts and Sciences, 1987; inducte into TV Hall of Fame, 1987. Foreign associate National Acad. Sciences United States of America; member Academie Francaise. Co-inventor of aqualung (with Emile Gagnon); developer of turbosail system (with Malavard and Charrier), 1985; leader sci. cruise around world, 1967, basis for television series The Undersea World of Jacques-Yves Cousteau; leader expedition to Antaratic and Chilian coast, 1972, expedition to Amazon, 1982, Mississippi, 1983, Rediscovery of World (Haiti, Cuba, Marquesas Islands, New Zealand, Australia), 1985—. Office: Found Cousteau, 25 Avenue Wagram, F 75017 Paris France also: care Cousteau Society Incorporated 425 E 52d St New York New York 10022 also: 930 W 21st St Norfolk Virginia 23517 also: 8440 Santa Monica Boulevard Los Angeles California 90069-4221

COVINO, BENJAMIN GENE, anesthesiologist, educator; born Lawrence, Massachusetts, September 12, 1930; son of Nicholas and Mary (Zannini) C.; married Lorraine Gallagher, August 22, 1953; children: Paul, Brian. Bachelor of

Arts, Holy Cross College, 1951; Master of Science, Boston College Graduate School, 1953; Doctor of Philosophy (Life Insurance fellow), Boston University Graduate School, 1955; Doctor of Medicine, University Buffalo, 1962. Teaching fellow Boston University, 1954-55; assistant professor pharmaceutical Tufts University School Medical, Boston, 1957-59; assistant professor physiology University Buffalo School Medical, 1959-62; medical director Astra Pharmaceutical Products, Worcester, 1962-66; vice president sci. affairs Astra Pharmaceutical Products, 1967-78; professor anesthesiology University Massachusetts Medical School, 1976-79; consultant physiologist St. Vincent's Hospital, Worcester, 1963-79; chairman anesthesiology Brigham and Women's Hospital and professor anesthesia Harvard University Medical School, Boston, 1979—. Contributor articles to professional journals. Board of directors St. Vincent's Research Foundation; trustee Assumption College, Worcester, Massachusetts Served to 1st lieutenant United States Air Force, 1955-57. Member Am. Physiological Society, Am. Heart Association, Am. Federation Clinical Research, Am. Society Pharmacology and Experimental Therapeutics, Am. Society Anesthesiology, Alpha Omega Alpha. Office: Harvard U Med School Department Anesthesiology 75 Francis St Boston Massachusetts 02115

COWAN, WILLIAM MAXWELL, neurobiologist; born Johannesburg, South Africa, September 27, 1931; son of Adam and Jessie Sloan (Maxwell) C.; married Margaret Sherlock, March 31, 1956; children: Ruth Cowan Eadon, Stephen Maxwell, David Maxwell. Bachelor of Science, Witwatersrand University, Johannesburg, 1951, Bachelor of Science (honorary), 1952; Doctor of Philosophy, Oxford University, 1956, Bachelor of Medicine, Bachelor.Ch., 1958, Master of Arts, 1959. From demonstrator to lecturer anatomy Oxford University, 1953-66; fellow Pembroke College, 1958-66; visiting professor anatomy Washington University Medical School, St. Louis, 1964-65; associate professor University Wisconsin Medical School, Madison, 1966-68; professor, chairman department anatomy and neurobiology Washington University Medical School, 1968-80; research professor, director Weingart Laboratory Devel. Neurobiology, Salk Institute Biological Studies, La Jolla, California, 1980-86; vice president Salk Institute Biological Studies, 1982-86; provost and executive vice chancellor Washington University, St. Louis, 1986-87; vice president, chief sci. officer Howard Hughes Medical Institute, Bethesda, Maryland, 1988—; member Institute Medicine, National Acad. Sciences, 1978; foreign associate National Acad. Sciences, 1981. Editor-in-chief Journal Neurosci., 1980-87; editor: Annual Revs. Neurosci. Fellow Am. Acad. Arts and Sciences, Royal Society (London), Royal Society S. Africa; member International Brain Research Organization (executive council), American Association for the Advancement of Science, Anatomical Society Great Britain and Ireland, Royal Microscopic Society, Am. Philosophical Society, Am. Association Anatomists, Society Neurosci. (president 1977-78), Norwegian Acad. Sci. (foreign), Sigma Xi, Alpha Omega Alpha, Phi Beta

Kappa. Home: 6337 Windmere Circle Rockville Maryland 20852 Office: Howard Hughes Med Institute 6701 Rockledge Dr Bethesda Maryland 20817

COWIN, STEPHEN CORTEEN, biomedical engineering educator, consultant; born Elmira, New York, October 26, 1934; son of William Corteen and Bernice (Reidy) C.; married Martha Agnes Eisel, August 10, 1956; children—Jennifer Marie, Thomas Burrows. Bachelor of Civil Engineering (Maryland State scholar, Ambrose Howard Carner scholar), Johns Hopkins University, 1956, Master of Civil Engineering (University fellow), 1958; Doctor of Philosophy in Engineering Mechanics, Pennsylvania State University, 1962. Registered professional engineer, Louisiana. Professor mechanical engineering Tulane University, 1969-77, professor mechanics department biomed. engineering; 1977-85, adj. professor orthopedics; 1978-88, prof.-in-charge Tulane-Newcomb Junior Year Abroad program; 1974-75, chairman applied math. program; 1975-79, professor applied statistics; 1979-88, Alden J. Laborde professor engineering; 1985-88; Distinguished professor City University of New York, 1988—; Sci. Research Council Great Brit. senior visiting fellow University Strathclyde, 1974, 80; visiting research professor Instituto de Matematica, Estatistica e Ciencia de Computanao, Universidade Estadual de Campinas, Brazil, 1978; participant United States National Acad. Sciences interacad. exchange program with Bulgaria, 1983; fellow Japan Society for the Promotion Sci., 1987. Editor: (with M. Satake) Continuum Mechanical and Statistical Approaches in the Mechanics of Granular Materials, 1978, Mechanics Applied to the Transport of Granular Materials, 1979, (with M.M. Carroll) The Effects of Voids on Material Deformation, 1976, Bone Mechanics, 1988; associate editor: Journal Applied Mechanics, 1974-82, Journal Biomech. Engring., 1982-88; editorial adv. board Handbook of Materials, Structures and Mechanics, 1981—, Handbook of Bioengineering, 1981, Acta Biomechanica, 1986—; editorial board Annals Biomed. Engring., 1985—; editorial cons. Journal Biomechanics, 1988—. Served to captain United States Army, 1957-64. Research grantee, National Science Foundation, National Institutes of Health, U.S. Army Research Office, Edward G. Schlieder Foundation. Fellow American Association for the Advancement of Science, American Society of Mechanical Engineers, Am. Acad. Mechanics; member Orthopedic Research Society, Society Rheology, Society Natural Philosophy (treasurer 1977-79), Society Engineering Sci., Math. Association Am., New York Acad. Sciences, Sigma Xi. Home: 107 W 86th St Apartment 4F New York New York 10024

CRAIN, CULLEN MALONE, electrical engineer; born Goodnight, Texas, September 10, 1920; son of John Malone and Margaret Elizabeth (Gunn) C.; married Virginia Raftery, January 16, 1943; children—Michael Malone, Karen Elizabeth. Bachelor of Science in Electrical Engineering, University Texas, Austin, 1942, Master of Science, 1947, Doctor of Philosophy, 1952. From instructor to associate professor electrical engineering University Texas, 1943-57; group leader communications and electronics Rand Corp., Santa Monica, California, 1957-69; associate head and head engineering and applied sciences Rand Corp., 1969—; consultant to government, 1958—. Author numerous papers in field. President Austin chapter National Exchange Club, 1954, Santa Monica chapter, 1975. Served with United States Naval Reserve, 1944-46. Fellow Institute of Electrical and Electronics Engineers; member National Acad. Engineering. Inventor microwave atmospheric refractometer. Home: 463 17th St Santa Monica California 90402 Office: 1700 Main St Santa Monica California 90406

CRAM, DONALD JAMES, chemistry educator; born Chester, Vermont, April 22, 1919; son of William Moffet and Joanna (Shelley) C.; married Jane Maxwell, November 25, 1969. Bachelor of Science, Rollins College, 1941; Master of Science, University Nebraska, 1942; Doctor of Philosophy, Harvard University, 1947; Doctor of Philosophy (honorary), University Uppsala, 1977; DSci. (honorary), University Southern California, 1983. Research chemist Merck and Company, 1942-45; assistant professor chemistry University of California at Los Angeles, 1947-50, associate professor; 1950-56, professor; 1956—, named South Winstein professor; 1985—; chemical consultant Upjohn Company, 1952-88, Union Carbide Company, 1960-81, Eastman Kodak Company, 1981—, Technicon Company, 1984—, Institute Guido Donegani, Milan, 1988—; State Department exchange fellow to Institute de Quimica, National University Mexico, 1956; guest professor University Heidelberg, Germany, 1958; guest lecturer, South Africa, 1967; Centenary lecturer Chemical Society London, 1976. Author: (with Pine, Hendrickson and Hammond) Organic Chemistry, 1960, 4th edition, 1980, Fundamentals of Carbanion Chemistry, 1965, (with Richards and Hammond) Elements of Organic Chemistry, 1967, (with Cram) Essence of Organic Chemistry, 1977; contributor chapters to textbooks, articles in field of host-guest complexation chemistry, carbanions, stereochemistry, mold metabolites, large ring chemistry. Named Young Man of Year California Junior Chamber of Commerce, 1954, California Scientist of Year, 1974, Nobel Laureate in Chemistry, 1987; recipient award for creative work in synthetic organic chemistry Am. Chemical Society, 1965, Arthur C. Cope award, 1974, Richard Tolman medal, 1985, Willard Gibbs award, 1985, Roger Adams award, 1985; Herbert Newby McCoy award, 1965, 75; award for creative rsch. organic chemistry Synthetic Organic Chemical Mfrs. Association, 1965; National Rsch. fellow Havard University, 1947, Am. Chemical Society fellow, 1947-48, Guggenheim fellow, 1954-55. Member Am. Chemical Society, National Acad. Sciences, Am. Acad. Arts and Sciences, Royal Society Chemistry, Sigma Xi, Lambda Chi Alpha. Club: San Onofre Surfing. Home: 1250 Roscomare Road Los Angeles California 90077 Office: University of California at Los Angeles Department Chemistry Los Angeles California 90024

CRANE, HORACE RICHARD, educator, physicist; born Turlock, California, November 4, 1907; son of Horace Stephen and Mary Alice (Roselle) C.; married Florence Rohmer LeBaron, December 30, 1934; children—Carol Ann, Janet (deceased), George Richard. Bachelor of Science,

California Institute Tech., 1930, Doctor of Philosophy, 1934. Research fellow California Institute Tech., 1934-35; member faculty University Michigan, Ann Arbor, 1935—; professor physics University Michigan, 1946—, chairman department physics; 1965-72, George P. Williams University professor; 1972-78, emeritus; 1978—; Research associate (radar) Massachusetts Institute Tech., 1940-41; physicist Carnegie Institute Washington, 1941; project director, proximity fuze project University Michigan, 1941-43, atomic energy project, 1943-45; consultant NDRC, 1941-45; member standing committee on controlled thermonuclear research Atomic Energy Commission, 1969-72; Vice president Midwestern Universities Research Association, 1956-57, president, 1957-60; member policy board Argonne National Laboratory, 1957-67; Board governors Am. Institute Physics, 1964-71, chairman, 1971-75; member Commission on Human Resources, 1977-80, Council for International Exchange of Scholars, 1977-80. Contributor sci. articles to professional magazines. Recipient Davisson-Germer prize, 1967; Henry Russel lecturer, 1967; Distinguished Alumni medal Cal. Institute Tech., 1968; Distinguished Service award University Michigan, 1957; National medal of Sci., 1986. Fellow Am. Physical Society, American Association for the Advancement of Science, Am. Acad. Arts and Sciences; member National Acad. Sciences, Am. Association Physics Teachers (president 1965, Oersted medal 1977, Melba Newell Phillips award 1988), Sigma Xi. Clubs: Research University of Michigan (president 1956-57); Science Research (University Michigan) (vice president 1946-47, president 1947-48). Inventor of Race Track, a modified form of synchrotron for nuclear studies, 1946; made early discoveries in field of artificially produced radioactive atoms, 1934-39; measurements of magnetic moment of free electron, 1950. Home: 830 Avon Road Ann Arbor Michigan 48104

CRAVEN, JOHN PINNA, civil engineering educator, lawyer; born Brooklyn, October 30, 1924; son of James McDougal and Mabel (Pinna) C.; married Dorothy Drakesmith, February 4, 1951; children: David John, Sarah Johannah. Bachelor of Science in Civil Engineering, Cornell University, 1946; Master of Science in Civil Engineering, California Institute Tech., 1947; Doctor of Philosophy, University Iowa, 1951; Juris Doctor, George Washington University, 1959. Bar: Hawaii, 1985. Hydrodynamicist David Taylor Model Basin, 1951-59; chief scientist United States Navy Special Projects Office, 1959-71, project manager deep submergence systems project; 1965-67, chief scientist project; 1967-70; visiting professor political sci. and naval architecture Massachusetts Institute Tech., 1969-70; dean marine programs University Hawaii, Honolulu, 1970-81; marine affairs coordinator State Hawaii, 1970-76, 77—; director Law of Sea Institute, 1977—; adj. professor Herbert M. Humphrey Institute, 1983—, emeritus professor ocean engineering; 1985—, professor law; 1983—; president Natural Energy Laboratory of Hawaii, 1974—. Served with United States Naval Reserve, 1943-46. Recipient Meritorious Civilian Service award Navy Department, 1953, Distinguished Civilian Service award, 1960; Fleming award U.S. Chamber of Commerce,

1960; William S. Parsons award Navy League, 1966; Distinguished Civilian Service award Department Defense, 1969; Lockheed award Menne Tech. Society, 1982. Member National Acad. Engineers. Presbyterian. Home: 4921 Waa St Honolulu Hawaii 96821 Office: University of Hawaii Law of Sea Institute Honolulu Hawaii 96822

CRAY, SEYMOUR R., computer designer; born Chippewa Falls, Wisconsin, 1925. Bachelor of Science in Electrical Engineering, University Minnesota, 1950, Bachelor of Science in Math., 1950. Computer scientist Engineering Research Associates (later Remington Rand, Sperry Rand Univac div.), St. Paul, until 1957; co-founder Control Data Corp., 1957, computer scientist; 1957-72; founder Cray Research Incorporated, Mendota Heights, Minnesota, 1972, now consultant, director. Designer first computer made with transistors, Cray-1, Cray-2, other computer systems. Address: care Cray Research Incorporated Post Office Box 154 Minneapolis Minnesota 55440 Office: Cray Research Post Office Box 17500 Colorado Springs Colorado 80935

CRICK, FRANCIS HARRY COMPTON, biologist, educator; born June 8, 1916; son of Harry and Annie Elizabeth (Wilkins) C.; married Ruth Doreen Dodd, 1940 (divorced 1947); 1 son; married Odile Speed, 1949; 2 daughters. Bachelor of Science, University College, London; Doctor of Philosophy, Cambridge University, England. Scientist Brit. Admiralty, 1940-47, Strangeways Laboratory, Cambridge, England, 1947-49; biologist Medical Research Council Laboratory of Molecular Biology, Cambridge, 1949-77; Kieckhefer

Distinguished professor Salk Institute for Biological Studies, San Diego, 1977—, non-resident fellow; 1962-73; adj. professor psychology and chemistry, University Calif.-San Diego; visiting lecturer Rockefeller Institute, New York City, 1959; visiting professor chemistry department Harvard University, 1959, visiting professor biophysics, 1962; fellow Churchill College, Cambridge, 1960-61; Korkes Memorial lecturer Duke University, 1960; Henry Sedgewick Memorial lecturer Cambridge University, 1963; Graham Young lecturer, Glasgow, 1963; Robert Boyle lecturer Oxford University, 1963; Vanuxem lecturer Princeton University, 1964; William T. Sedgwick Memorial lecturer Massachusetts Institute of Technology, 1965; Cherwell-Simon Memorial lecturer Oxford University, 1966; Shell lecturer Stanford University, 1969; Paul Lund lecturer Northwestern University, 1977; Dupont lecturer Harvard University, 1979, numerous other invited, memorial lecturers. Author: Of Molecules and Men, 1966, Life Itself, 1981, What Mad Pursuit, 1988; contributor papers and articles on molecular, cell biology and neurobiology to sci. journals. Recipient Prix Charles Leopold Mayer French Academies des Sciences, 1961; recipient (with J.D. Watson) Research Corp. award, 1961, (with J.D. Watson & Maurice Wilkins) Nobel Prize for medicine, 1962, Gairdner Foundation award, 1962, Royal Medal Royal Society, 1972, Copley Medal, 1976, Michelson-Morley award, 1981, Benjamin P. Cheney medal, Spokane, Washington, 1986, Golden Plate award, Phoenix, 1987, Albert medal Royal Society of Arts, London, 1987, Wright Prize VIII Harvey Mudd College, Claremont, California, 1988,

Joseph Priestly award Dickinson College, 1988. Fellow American Association for the Advancement of Science, Royal Society; member Am. Acad. Arts and Sciences (foreign hon.), Am. Society Biological Chemistry (hon.), United States National Acad. Sciences (foreign associate), German Acad. Sci., Am. Philosophical Society (foreign member), French Acad. Sciences (associate foreign member). Office: Salk Institute Biol Studies Post Office Box 85800 San Diego California 92138

CRIPPEN, ROBERT LAUREL, naval officer, astronaut; born Beaumont, Texas, September 11, 1937; son of Herbert W. and Ruth C. (Andress) C.; married Virginia E. Hill, September 8, 1959; children: Ellen Marie, Susan Lynn, Linda Ruth. Bachelor of Science in Aerospace Engineering, University Texas, 1960; graduate, United States Air Force Aerospace Research Pilot School, 1965. Commissioned ensign United States Navy, 1960, advanced through grades to captain; 1980; assigned to flight training Whiting Field, Florida, 1961, Chase Field, Beeville, Texas, 1961; attack pilot (Fleet Squadron VA-72 aboard United States Ship Independence), 1962-64; instructor United States Air Force Aerospace Research Pilot School, Edwards Air Force Base, California, 1965-66; research pilot United States Air Force Manned Orbiting Laboratory Program, Los Angeles, 1966-69; National Aeronautics and Space Administration astronaut Johnson Space Center, Houston, 1969—; crew member Skylab Medical Experiments Altitude Test, 1972; member astronaut support crew Skylab 2, 3 and 4 missions, 1973-74; pilot Space Shuttle Columbia

STSI, 1981; head Astronaut Office ascent/entry group Lyndon B. Johnson Space Center, Houston, 1981-87; commander Space Shuttle Columbia, 1984; deputy director National Space Transportation System Operations, National Aeronautics and Space Administration, Kennedy Space Center, Florida, 1987—. Recipient Exceptional Service medal National Aeronautics and Space Administration, 1972, Distinguished Service medal, 1981; Distinguished Service medal Department Defense, 1981. Member Society Experimental Test Pilots. Office: Kennedy Space Center Florida 32899

CROFFORD, OSCAR BLEDSOE, JR., internist, medical educator; born Chickahsa, Oklahoma, March 29, 1930; married, 1957; 3 children. Bachelor of Arts, Vanderbilt University, 1952, Doctor of Medicine, 1955. Intern medicine Vanderbilt University Hospital, 1955-56, assistant resident; 1956-57; United States Public Health Service research fellow clinical physiology 1959-62, resident in medicine; 1962-63; United States Public Health Service fellow clinical biochemistry University Geneva, 1963-65; from assistant professor to associate professor 1965-74; professor medicine Vanderbilt University School Medicine, 1974—, associate professor physiology and biophysics; 1970—; investor Howard Hughes Medical Institute, 1965-71; member metabolism study section National Institutes of Health, 1970-74, chairman 1972-74; Addison B. Scoville junior Chair Diabetes & Metabolism, Vanderbilt University, 1973—, div. head diabetes & metab., department medicine, 1973—, director Diabetes-Endocrin. Center,

1973-78; chairman National Commission Diabetes, 1975-76; director Diabetes Research & Training Center, 1978—. Recipient award Am. Diabetes Association, 1970, Charles H. Best award, 1976, Humanitarian award Juvenile Diabetes Association, 1976. Member Am. Diabetes Association (president 1981), Am. Physiological Society, Endocrine Society, Am. Society Clinical Investigation, Association Am. Physicians. Research in hormone control of metabolism in adipocytes; mechanism of action of insulin; sugar transport; pathophysiology and treatment of Diabetes Mellitus; pathophysiology and treatment of obesity. Office: Vanderbilt U School of Medicine Nashville Tennessee 37232

CRONIN, JAMES WATSON, educator, physicist; born Chicago, September 29, 1931; son of James Farley and Dorothy (Watson) C.; married Annette Martin, September 11, 1954; children: Cathryn, Emily, Daniel Watson. Bachelor of Arts, Southern Methodist University (1951); Doctor of Philosophy, University Chicago. Associate Brookhaven National Laboratory, 1955-58; member faculty Princeton, 1958-71, professor physics; 1965-71; professor physics University Chicago, 1971—; Loeb lecturer physics Harvard University, 1967. Trustee Wayland Acad., Beaver Dam, Wisconsin. Recipient Research Corp. Am. award, 1967; John Price Wetherill medal Franklin Institute, 1976; E.O. Lawrence award Energy Research and Development Administration, 1977; Nobel prize for physics, 1980; Sloan fellow, 1964-66; Guggenheim fellow, 1970-71, 82-83. Member Am. Acad. Arts and Sciences, National Acad. Sci. (council member).

Participant early devel. spark chambers; co-discover CP-violation, 1964. Home: 5825 S Dorchester St Chicago Illinois 60637 Office: U Chicago Enrico Fermi Institute 5630 S Ellis Avenue Chicago Illinois 60637

CROSS, RALPH EMERSON, mechanical engineer; born Detroit, June 3, 1910; son of Milton Osgood and Helen (Heim) C.; married Eloise Florence Fountain, June 18, 1932; children: Ralph Emerson, Carol (Mrs. Peter G. Wodtke), Dennis W. Student, Massachusetts Institute of Technology, 1933; Doctor of Engineering (honorary), Lawrence Institute Tech., 1977. Vice president Cross Company, Fraser, Michigan, 1932-67, president, general manager; 1967-79, chairman; 1979-82; chairman board Cross & Trecker, Bloomfield Hills, Michigan, 1979-82, chairman emeritus, director; 1982-86; chairman board, chief executive officer Intelitec Corp., Grosse Pointe Farms, Michigan, 1982—; chairman board, president Cross International A.G., Fribourg, Switzerland, 1965-68; president Cross Export Corp., 1972-80; director Axiomatic Incorporated, Peter G. Wodtke Incorporated; special consultant to assistant secretary Air Force for Material, 1955-59; member corp. Economic Devel. Corp. Greater Detroit, 1968-73, Michigan Blue Shield, 1969-74; member corp. devel. committee Massachusetts Institute Tech., 1970—; member Am. Iranian Joint Business Council, 1975-76; trustee Lawrence Institute Tech., 1979—; president SME Education Foundation, 1979-84, chairman emeritus, director, 1984—. Recipient Engineering citation Am. Society Tool Engrs., 1956; Corp. Leadership award Massachusetts Institute Tech., 1976. Member National Acad. Engineering,

National Machine Tool Builders Association (president 1975), Society Automotive Engineers, Society Manufacturing Engineers (hon.), Engineering Society Detroit. Clubs: Detroit Athletic, Lochmoor, Quail Ridge Country. Home: 4120 Shelldrake Lane Boynton Beach Florida 33436 Office: Intelitec Corp 22 Windemere Dr Grosse Pointe Farms Michigan 48236

CROSSFIELD, ALBERT SCOTT, aeronautical science consultant, pilot; born Berkeley, California, October 2, 1921; son of Albert Scott and Lucia (Dwyer) C.; married Alice Virginia Knoph, April 21, 1943; children: Becky Lee, Thomas Scott, Paul Stanley, Anthony Scott, Sally Virginia, Robert Scott. Bachelor of Science in Aeronautical Engineering, University Washington, 1949, Master of Science in Aeronautical Science, 1950; Doctor of Science (honorary), Florida Institute Tech., 1982. Member University Washington staff charge wind tunnel operation, 1946-50; aerodynamicist, project engineer, also pilot research airplanes X-1, X-4, X-5, D-558-I and II, X-F-92, F-102, F-100, F-86, National Advisory Committee for Aeronautics, 1950-55; participation proposal, design, 1st pilot X-15 research aircraft, design specialist, also chief engineering test pilot Los Angeles div. North America Aviation, Incorporated, 1955-61, director test and quality assurance, space and information systems div.; 1961-66, tech. director research and engineering, space and information systems div.; 1966-67; vice president flight research and devel. div. Eastern Air Lines, Miami, Florida, 1967-71; staff vice president transportation systems devel. Eastern Air Lines, Washington, 1971-74; senior vice president Hawker Siddeley Aviation Incorporated, Washington, 1974; tech. consultant House Committee on Sci. and Tech., Washington, 1977—; special work on the WS-131b Apollo, Saturn S-II, Paraglider programs. Author: Always Another Dawn, 1960; also articles. Served to lieutenant, fighter pilot United States Naval Reserve, 1942-46. Recipient Lawrence Sperry award Institute Aeronautical Sciences, 1954, Octave Chanute award Institute Aeronautical Sciences, 1958; Achievement award Am. Astronomical Society, 1959; California wing Air Force Association, 1959; David C. Shilling award, 1961; Astronautics award Am. Rocket Society, 1960; Ivan C. Kincheloe award Society Experimental Test Pilots, 1960; Achievement award National Aviation Club, 1961; Godfrey Cabot award Aero Club New England, 1961; International Harmon trophy, 1961; Collier trophy, 1962; John J. Montgomery award National Society Aerospace Professionals, 1962; Kitty Hawk Memorial award Los Angeles Chamber of Commerce, 1969; Al J. Engel award Western Res. Historical Society Aviation Hall of Fame, 1983; Ira C. Eaker Historical fellow AFA, 1982; subject of portrait First Flight Society, Kitty Hawk, North Carolina, 1982; named to National Aviation Hall of Fame, 1983. Fellow Society Experimental Pilots (co-founder; chairman East Coast section 1976-77, Ray E. Tenhoff award 1978), Institute Aerospace Sciences, American Institute of Aeronautics and Astronautics (chairman flight test tech. committee 1963-64), Aerospace Medical Association (hon); member Am. Society Quality Control (section chairman Los Angeles 1964-66, Outstanding Contbn. to Quality Control award 1967), Flying Physician

Association (Man of Year 1961), Experimental Aircraft Association (Service to Sport Aviation 1979), National Aviation Club (president 1983), Sigma Xi, Tau Beta Pi. Republican. Episcopalian. Home: 12100 Thoroughbred Road Herndon Virginia 22071 Office: 2321 Rayburn House Office Building Washington District of Columbia 20515

CSANADY, GABRIEL TIBOR, oceanographer, meteorologist, environmental engineer; born Budapest, Hungary, December 10, 1925; son of Arpad Kalman and Elizabeth (Marosi) C.; married Ada Luige, September 3, 1954 (divorced 1968); 1 son, Andrew John; married Joyce Eva Stever, January 19, 1969. Diploma Ing., Technische Hochschule, Munich, Federal Republic of Germany, 1948; Doctor of Philosophy, University New South Wales, Sydney, Australia, 1958. Engineer State Electric Company, Victoria, Melbourne, 1952-54; senior lecturer University New South Wales, Sydney, 1954-61; associate professor mechanical engineering University Windsor, Ontario, Can., 1961-63; professor mechanical engineering University Waterloo, Ontario, Can., 1963-73; senior scientist Woods Hole Oceanographic Institution, Massachusetts, 1972-87; Slover professor of Oceanography Old Dominion University, Norfolk, Virginia, 1987—. Author: Theory of Turbomachines, 1964, Turbulent Diffusion in the Environment, 1973, Circulation in the Coastal Ocean, 1982. Recipient President's prize Can. Meteorological Society, 1970; recipient Chandler-Misener award International Association Great Lakes Research, 1977; Sherman Fairchild distinguished scholar California Institute Tech., 1982. Fellow Royal Meteorological Society London; member Am. Meteorological Society (Editor's award 1975), Am. Geophysical Union, American Society of Mechanical Engineers. Office: Old Dominion U Norfolk Virginia 23529

CUATRECASAS, PEDRO MARTIN, research pharmacologist; born Madrid, September 27, 1936; came to United States, 1947; son of Jose and Martha C.; married Carol Zies, August 15, 1959; children: Paul, Lisa, Diane, Julia. Bachelor of Arts, Washington University, St. Louis, 1958, Doctor of Medicine, 1962; Doctor of Science honoris causa, University Barcelona, 1984, Mount Sinai School Medicine, 1985. Intern, then resident in internal medicine Osler Service, Johns Hopkins Hospital, 1962-64, assistant physician; 1972-75; clinical associate, clinical endocrinology branch National Institute Arthritis and Metabolic Diseases, National Institutes of Health, 1964-66; special United States Public Health Service postdoctoral fellow Laboratory Chemical Biology, 1966-67, medical officer; 1967-70; professorial lecturer biochemistry George Washington University Medical School, 1967-70; associate professor pharmacology and experimental therapeutics, associate professor medicine, director div. clinical pharmacology, Burroughs Wellcome professor clinical pharmacology Johns Hopkins University Medical School, 1970-72, professor pharmacology and experimental therapeutics, associate professor medicine; 1972-75; vice president research, devel. and medical Wellcome Research Laboratories; director Burroughs Wellcome Company, Research Triangle Park, North Carolina, 1975-86; senior vice president research and devel. Glaxo Research Laboratories, Glaxo Incorporated, 1986—; also board of directors Glaxo Research Laboratories, Glaxo Incorporated, Glaxo International Research, Limited, London; adj. professor Duke University Medical School, 1975—; adj. professor, member adv. committee cancer research program University North Carolina Medical School, 1975—; board of directors Burroughs Wellcome Fund, 1975-86, Glaxo International Research. Limited, London. Editor: Receptors and Recognition Series, 1975, Journal Solid-Phase Biochemistry, 1975-80; editorial board: Journal Membrane Biology, 1973, International Journal Biochemistry, 1973, Molecular and Cellular Endocrinology, 1973-77, Biochimica Biophysica Acta, 1973-79, Life Scis., 1978—, Neuropeptides, 1979—, Journal Applied Biochemistry, 1978—, Cancer Research, 1980-81, Journal Applied Biochemistry and Biotech., 1980—, Toxin Revs., 1981—, Biochem. Biophys. Research Communications, 1981—; contributor articles to professional journals. Active Am. Diabetes Association, 1972—, PMA Commission on Drugs and Rare Diseases, 1982—, North Carolina Supercomputer Task Force, 1988—. Recipient John Jacob Abel prize in pharmacology, 1972, Laude prize Pharm. World, 1975, Beerman award Society Investigative Dermatology, 1981, Isco award University Nebraska, 1985, Dupont Splty. Diagnostics award Clinical Ligand Assay Society 1986, Alumni Achievement award Washington University School Medical, 1987. Fellow Am. Acad. Arts. and Sciences; member Am. Society Biological Chemists, National Acad. Sciences, Institute Medicine of National Acad. Sciences (governing council 1988—),

Am. Society Pharmacology and Experimental Therapeutics (Goodman and Gilman award 1982), Am. Society Clinical Investigation, Am. Society Clinical Research, Spanish Biochem. Society, Maryland Acad. Sciences (Outstanding Young Scientist of Year 1970), Am. Cancer Society, Endocrine Society, Am. Chemical Society, Am. Diabetes Association (Eli Lilly award 1975), Am. Diabetes Association, Sigma Xi. Home: 3803 Bluestone Court Chapel Hill North Carolina 27514-9648 Office: Glaxo Incorporated Glaxo Research Labs 5 Moore Dr Research Triangle Park North Carolina 27709 also: Wolf Found, Post Office Box 398, 46103 Herzlia Bet Israel

CULBERSON, WILLIAM LOUIS, botany educator; born Indianapolis, April 5, 1929; son of Louis Henry and Lucy Helene (Hellman) C.; married Chicita Forman, August 24, 1953. Bachelor of Science, University Cincinnati, 1951; Diploma d'Etudes Supérieures, University de Paris, 1952; Doctor of Philosophy, University Wisconsin, 1954. National Science Foundation postdoctoral fellow Harvard University, Cambridge, Massachusetts, 1954-55; instructor Duke University, Durham, North Carolina, 1955-58, assistant professor; 1958-64, associate professor; 1964-70, professor; 1970-84, Hugo L. Blomquist professor; 1984—; visiting research professor Mus. National d'Histoire Naturelle, Paris, 1980. Author 100 research papers. Director Sarah P. Duke Gardens at Duke University, Durham, 1978—. Grantee National Science Foundation, 1957—. Member Am. Bryological and Lichenological Society (president 1987—), Botanical Society Am., Am. Society Plant

Taxonomists, Mycological Society Am. Avocations: greenhouse gardening. Home: Box 297 King Road Rt 7 Durham North Carolina 27707 Office: Duke U Department Botany Durham North Carolina 27706

CULLER, FLOYD LEROY, JR., chemical engineer; born Washington, January 5, 1923; son of Floyd Leroy Culler; married Della Hopper, 1946; 1 son, Floyd Leroy III. Bachelor Chemical Engineering cum laude, Johns Hopkins, 1943. With Eastman Kodak and Tennessee Eastman at Y-12, Oak Ridge, 1943-47; design engineer Oak Ridge National Laboratory, 1947-53, director chemical tech. div.; 1953-64, assistant laboratory director; 1965-70, deputy director; 1970-77; president Electric Power Research Institute, Palo Alto, California, 1978—; research design chemical engineering applied to atomic energy program, chemical processing nuclear reactor plants, energy research. Member sci. adv. committee International Atomic Energy Agency, 1974—; member energy research adv. board Department Energy, 1981-86. Recipient Ernest Orlando Lawrence award, 1964; Atoms for Peace award, 1969; Robert E. Wilson award in nuclear chemical engineering, 1972; Engineering Achievement award East Tennessee Engineers Joint Council, 1974. Fellow Am. Nuclear Society (director 1973-80, special award 1977), Am. Institute Chemists, American Association for the Advancement of Science, Institute Chemical Engineers; member Am. Chemical Society, National Acad. Engineering. Office: Electric Power Research Institute Incorporated 3412 Hillview Avenue Box 10412 Palo Alto California 94303

CUMMINGS, MARTIN MARC, physician, scientific administrator; born Camden, New Jersey, September 7, 1920; son of Samuel and Cecelia (Silverman) C.; married Arlene Sally Avrutine, September 27, 1942; children: Marc Steven, Lee Bernard, Stuart Lewis. Bachelor of Science, Bucknell University, 1941, Doctor of Science, 1969; Doctor of Medicine, Duke University, 1944, Doctor of Science (honorary), 1985; Doctor of Science, University Nebraska, Emory University; Doctor of Humane Letters, Georgetown University, 1971; Doctor of Medicine (honorary), Karolinska Institute, 1972. Diplomate Am. Board Microbiology. Intern, resident Boston Marine Hospital, 1944-46; resident Tb Grasslands Hospital, Valhalla, New York, 1946-47; director Tb evaluation laboratory Communicable Disease Center, United States Public Health Service, Atlanta, 1947-49; instructor medicine Emory University School Medicine, 1948-50, associate medicine; 1950-52, assistant professor; 1953; chief Tb section, also director Tb research laboratory Veteran's Administration Hospital, Atlanta, 1949-53; director research services Veteran's Administration Central Office, Washington, 1953-59; special lecturer microbiology George Washington University School Medicine, 1953-59; professor microbiology, chairman department Oklahoma University School Medicine, 1959-61; chief Office International Research, National Institutes of Health, United States Public Health Service, 1961-63; director National Library of Medicine, 1964-84, director emeritus; 1984—; consultant Council on Library Resources, 1984—; associate director for research grants National Institutes of Health, 1963-64; chairman committee medical research National Tb Association, 1958-59; chairman panel Sarcoidosis NRC-Nat. Acad. Sciences, 1958-60; district professor community medicine Georgetown University School Medicine, 1986—. Author: (with Dr. H.S. Willis) Diagnostic and Experimental Methods in Tuberculosis, 1952, The Economics of Research Libraries, 1986; contributor chapter on Tubercle Bacilli, Diagnostic Procedures and Reagents, 1950. Served with Army of the United States, 1943-44. Recipient Exceptional Service award Veteran's Administration, 1959; Distinguished Service award Department of Health, Education and Welfare, 1968; Rockefeller Pub. Service award, 1973; Distinguished Achievement award Modern Medicine, 1976; Distinguished Service award Am. College Cardiology, 1978; John C. Leonard award Association Hospital Medical Education, 1979. Fellow American Association for the Advancement of Science (director), Royal Society Medicine, Medical Library Association, New York Acad. Medicine (hon.); senior member Am. Society Clinical Investigation, Am. Federation Clinical Research. Home: 11317 Rolling House Road Rockville Maryland 20852 Office: National Library Medicine Bethesda Maryland 20894

CUNNINGHAM, R. WALTER, venture capitalist; born Creston, Iowa, March 16, 1932; son of Walter Wilfred and Gladys (Backen) C.; married Lo Ella Irby, July 8, 1956; children: Brian Keith, Kimberly Ann. Bachelor of Science in Physics, University of California at Los Angeles, 1960, Master of Arts, 1961; AMP, Harvard Graduate School Business, 1974. Research assistant Planning Research Corp., Westwood, California, 1959-60; physicist RAND Corp., Santa Monica, California, 1960-64; astronaut National Aeronautics and Space Administration, 1964-71; crew member of first manned Apollo spacecraft Apollo 7; senior vice president Century Devel., 1971-74; president Hydrotech Devel. Company, Houston, 1974-76; senior vice president 3D/Internat., Houston, 1976-79; founder The Capital Group, Houston, 1979-86; managing partner Genesis Fund, 1986—; director Texas Guaranty Bank, others. Author: The All American Boys, 1977. Judge Rolex awards for enterprise, 1984. Served with United States Naval Reserve, 1951-52; as fighter pilot United States Marine Corps Reserve, 1952-56; colonel Reserves. Recipient National Aeronautics and Space Administration Exceptional Service medal, also; Haley Astronautics award; Professional Achievement award University California at Los Angeles Alumni, 1969; Special Trustee award National Acad. Television Arts and Sciences, 1969; medal of valor Am. Legion, 1975; Outstanding Am. award Am. Conservative Union, 1975; named to International Space Hall of Fame, Houston Hall of Fame. Fellow Am. Astronautical Society; member Society Experimental Test Pilots, Am. Institute Aeros. and Astronautics, Am. Geophysical Union, Sigma Pi Sigma. Office: Acorn Ventures Incorporated 505 Stuart St Houston Texas 77006

CURL, SAMUEL EVERETT, university dean, agricultural scientist; born Fort Worth, December 26, 1937; son of Henry Clay and Mary Elva (Watson) C.; married Betty Doris Savage, June 6, 1957; children: Jane Ellen, Julia Kathleen, Karen

Elizabeth. Student, Tarleton State College, 1955-57; Bachelor of Science, Sam Houston State University, 1959; Master of Science, University Missouri, 1961; Doctor of Philosophy, Texas Agricultural and Mechanical University, 1963. Member faculty Texas Tech University, Lubbock, 1961, 63-76, 79—, teacher, researcher animal physiology and genetics; 1963-68, assistant, associate and interim dean College Agricultural Sci.; 1968-73, associate vice president acad. affairs; 1973-76, dean College Agricultural Sciences, professor; 1979—; president Phillips University, Enid, Oklahoma, 1976-79; agricultural consultant; director Agricultural Workers Mutual Auto Insurance Company; member Gov.'s Task Force on Agricultural Devel. in Texas, 1982-83, 88; member Texas Crop and Livestock Adv. Committee, 1985—; trustee Water, Incorporated; del. Eisenhower Consortium for Western Environmental Forestry Research, 1979-84; management com Southwest Consortium on Plant Genetics and Water Resources, 1984—, chairman 1989—; member USDA National Planning Committee on Hispanic Minority Recruitment, 1988—. Author: (with others) Progress and Change in the Agricultural Industry, 1974, Food and Fiber for a Changing World, 1976, 2d edition, 1982; contributor 90 articles to professional journals. Trustee Consortium for International Devel., member executive committee, 1981-84, 86-87, 89—; farmer member High Plains Research Coordinating Board, Southern Regional Council, United States Joint Council Food and Agricultural Scis.; chairman agricultural and natural resources program rev. task force Sam Houston State University, 1982-83; president Lubbock Economic Council, 1982; board overseers Ranching Heritage Association Served as 2d lieutenant United States Army, 1959; captain United States Army Reserve. Recipient Faculty-Alumni Gold medal University Missouri, 1975, Distinguished Service to Texas Agriculture award Professional Agricultural Workers Texas, 1985, Outstanding Alumnus award Sam Houston State University, 1986, Texas Citation for Outstanding Service award Texas 4-H Foundation, 1987, Distinguished Service award Vocational Agricultural Teachers Association Texas, 1987, Blue and Gold Meritorious Service award Texas Future Farmers of Am., 1988, Texas State University degree Future Farmers Am., 1988; Am. Council Education fellow, 1972-73. Member Am. Society Animal Sci., Am. Association University Agricultural Administrators, Association United States University Directors International Agricultural Programs, Southern Association Agricultural Scientists, National Association of State Univs. and Land-Grant Colls., Texas Agricultural Leadership Council, Council Adminstrv. Heads of Agriculture, Professional Agricultural Workers Texas, West Texas Chamber of Commerce (board directors, chairman agricultural and ranching committee), Lubbock Chamber of Commerce (chairman agriculture task force, chairman research committee 1981-86, member water committee, legis. affairs committee, agriculture committee, gubernatorial appointments task force), Sigma Xi, Phi Kappa Phi, Gamma Sigma Delta. Club: Rotary. Home: 1810 Bangor Avenue Lubbock Texas 79416 Office: Tex Tech U Office Dean Agrl Scis 108 Goddard Building Lubbock Texas 79409

DANSEREAU, PIERRE, ecologist; born Montreal, Canada, October 5, 1911; son of J.-Lucien and Marie (Archambault) D.; married Françoise Masson, August 29, 1935. Bachelor of Arts, University Montréal, 1932, Bachelor of Science Agriculture, 1936; Doctor of Science, University Geneva, Switzerland, 1939; Doctor of Science honorary degrees, University Saskatchewan, 1959, University New Brunswick, 1959, University Strasbourg, France, 1970, University Sherbrooke, 1971, Sir George Williams University, 1971, University Waterloo, 1972, University Guelph, 1973, University Western Ontario, 1973, Memorial University Newfoundland, 1974, McGill University, 1976, University Ottawa, 1978. Member faculty University Montréal, 1940-42, 45, 55-61, 68-71; with Service de Biogéographie, 1943-50; professor botany University Michigan, 1950-55; assistant director, professor ecology New York Botanical Garden, 1961-68; adj. professor Columbia University, 1962-68; member staff University Qué. and Centre de Recherches Écologiques de Montréal, 1971-72; professor ecology University Qué., Montréal, 1972-76, professor emeritus; 1976—; Vice chairman Canadian Environmental Advisory Council, 1972-76, Can. Federal Task Force Housing and Urban Devel., 1968, Natural Sciences and Engineering Research Council, 1978-80; member Sci. Council Can., 1968-72, Canadian Radio-TV Council, 1968; vice president Canadian Commission International Biological Programme, 1968; chairman program urban devel. Sci. Council Can., 1970; president 1st International Film Festival on Human Environment, 1973; secretary general Michigan Acad. Sci., Arts and Letters, 1953; 1st vice president 9th International Botanical Congress, 1959; chairman board Gamma Institute, 1983-86; hon. chairman Fondation de l'ACFAS, 1984. Author: Biogeography: An Ecological Perspective, 1957, Phytogeographia laurentiana II, 1959, Contradictions & Biculture, 1964, (with co-author) Studies on the Vegetation of Puerto Rico I and II, 1966, (with others) A Universal System for Recording Vegetation II, 1966, Dimensions of Environmental Quality, 1971, Inscape and Landscape, 1973, La terre des hommes et le paysage intérieur, 1973, Harmony and Disorder in the Canadian Environment, 1975, Ezaim: Écologie de la Zone de l'Aéroport International de Montréal. Le cadre d'une recherche écologique interdisciplinaire, 1976; co-author: Ecological Grading and Classification of Land-occupation and Land-use Mosaics, 1977; author: An Ecological Grading of Human Settlements, 1978, Harmonie et désordre dans l'environnement canadien, 1980, Essai de classification et de cartographie écologique des espaces, 1985; editor: Challenge for Survival, 1970. Guggenheim fellow, 1949; recipient Pierre Fermat medal, 1960; Commonwealth Prestige fellowship, 1961; Léo Pariseau medal, 1965; Pfizer prize, 1965; Prix David, Qué., 1959; Distinguished Service award New York Botanical Garden, 1969; companion Order Can., 1969; Massey medal, 1973; Molson prize, 1974; Esdras-Minville prize, 1983; Marie-Victorin prize, 1983; Izaak Walton Killam prize, 1985; Knight of Ordre National du Qué., 1985; Can. Botanical Association Lawson medal, 1986; named Great Montrealer in Sci., 1978. Fellow royal socs. Can., New Zealand (hon.); member Canadian Mental Health Association (president

Quebec 1972-74), Am. Teilhard de Chardin Association (president 1967), Ecological Society Am. (vice president 1968), Association Canadienne-Française pour l'Avancement des Sciences (secretary general 1945-46), Geog. Society Montreal (president 1957), Argentina Acad. Environmental Sciences (foreign corresponding member 1984), Acad. Sciences Lisbon (foreign corresponding member 1985), Ordre national du Quebec(president 1987). Office: University du Quebec a Montreal, Case Postale 8888 Station A, Montreal, Province of Quebec Canada H3C 3P8

DANTZIG, GEORGE BERNARD, operations researcher, educator; born Portland, Oregon, November 8, 1914; son of Tobias and Anja (Ourisson) D.; married Anne Shmuner, August 23, 1936; children—David Franklin, Jessica Rose, Paul Michael. Bachelor of Arts in Math., University Maryland, 1936; Master of Arts in Math., University Michigan, 1937; Doctor of Philosophy in Math., University Calif.-Berkeley, 1946; honorary degree, Technion, Israel, Linkoping University, Sweden, University Maryland, Yale University, Louvain University, Belgium, Columbia University, University Zurich, Switzerland, Carnegie-Mellon University. Chief combat analysis, branch statistical control Headquarters United States Army Air Force, 1941-46, math. adv.; 1946-52; research mathematician Rand Corp., Santa Monica, California, 1952-60; professor, chairman Operations Research Center, University Calif.-Berkeley, 1960-66; C.A. Criley professor operations research and computer sci. Stanford University, California, 1966—; chief methodology

International Institute Applied System Analysis, 1973-74; consultant to industry; adv. environmental hazards California Department Health, 1967-70. Author: Linear Programming and Extensions, 1963; co-author: Compact City, 1973; contributor articles to professional journals; associate editor Math. Programming, Math. of Operations Research, others. Recipient Exceptional Civilian Service medal War Department, 1944, National medal of Sci., 1975, Von Neumann theory prize in ops. research, 1975, award National Acad. Sciences, 1977, Harvey prize, 1985, Silver Medal Operational Research Society Great Britain, 1986. Fellow Am. Acad. Arts and Sciences, Econometric Society, Institute Math. Statistics; member National Acad. Sciences, National Acad. Engineering, Ops. Research Society Am., Am. Math. Society, Math. Programming Society (chairman 1973-74), Institute Management Sci. (president 1966), Phi Beta Kappa, Sigma Xi, Phi Kappa Phi, Pi Mu Epsilon. Home: 821 Tolman Dr Stanford California 94305 Office: Stanford University Ops Research Department Stanford California 94305

DAUSSET, JEAN, immunologist; born Toulouse, France, October 19, 1916; son of Henri and Elizabeth D.; married Rose Mayoral, March 17, 1962. Bachelor of Arts, Lycee Michelet, 1939; Doctor of Medicine, University Paris, 1945. Director laboratory National Transfusion Center, 1950-63; professor immunohematology University Paris VII, 1963-77; professor experimental medicine College de France, Paris, 1977-87; director research unit on immunogenetics Hopital Saint-Louis, Paris, 1969-84; director Human Polymorphism Study Center, 1984—.

Served to captain, World War II. Recipient Nobel prize in physiology and medicine, 1980, Honda prize Honda Foundation Japan, 1987. Member Academie des Sciences de l'Institut de France, Am. Acad. Arts and Sci., National Academy of Sciences (Washington). Research in field of man's histocompatibility system, 1952—. Office: 27 rue Juliette Dodu, 75010 Paris France

DAVIES, PETER JOHN, plant physiology educator, researcher; born Sudbury, Middlesex, England, March 7, 1940; came to United States, 1966; son of William Bertram and Ivy Doreen (Parmentier) D.; married Linda Kay DeNoyer, August 2, 1976; children—Kenneth DeNoyer, Caryn Parmentier. Bachelor of Science with honors, University Reading, England, 1962; Master of Science, University Calif.-Davis, 1964; Doctor of Philosophy, University Reading, 1966. Instructor Yale University, New Haven, 1966-69; assistant professor Cornell University, Ithaca, New York, 1969-75; associate professor Cornell University, 1975-83, professor; 1983—. Author: (with others) The Life of the Green Plant, 1980, Control Mechanisms in Plant Development, 1970; editor: Plant Hormones and their Role in Plant Growth and Development, 1987. Member Am. Society Plant Physiology, International Plant Growth Substance Association. Office: Plant Biology Cornell U Plant Sci Building Ithaca New York 14853

DAWID, IGOR BERT, biologist; born Czernowitz, Romania, February 26, 1935; came to United States, 1960, naturalized, 1977; son of Josef and Pepi (Druckmann) D.; married Keiko Naito Ozato, April 5, 1976. Doctor of Philosophy, University Vienna, 1960. Fellow department biology Massachusetts Institute of Technology, 1960-62; fellow department embryology Carnegie Institution of Washington, Baltimore, 1962-66; member staff Carnegie Institution of Washington, 1966-78; chief devel. biochemistry section Laboratory Biochemistry, National Cancer Institute, Bethesda, Maryland, 1978-82; chief laboratory molecular genetics National Institute Child Health and Human Devel. (National Institutes of Health), Bethesda, 1982—; visiting scientist Max Planck Institute for Biology, 1964-67; assistant professor to professor department biology Johns Hopkins University, 1967-78. Editor: Devel. Biology, 1971-75, Cell, 1977-80; editor-in-chief: Devel. Biology, 1975-80, adv. editor, 1980-85. Member Am. Society Biological Chemists, Am. Society Cell Biology, Society Devel. Biology, International Society Devel. Biologists, American Association for the Advancement of Science, National Acad. Sci. (chairman editorial board). Office: 9000 Rockville Pike Bethesda Maryland 20205

DAWSON, WILLIAM RYAN, zoology educator; born Los Angeles, August 24, 1927; son of William Eldon and Mary (Ryan) D.; married Virginia Louise Berwick, September 9, 1950; children: Deborah, Denise, William. Student, Stanford, 1945-46; Bachelor of Arts, University of California at Los Angeles, 1949, Master of Arts, 1950, Doctor of Philosophy, 1953; Doctor of Science, University Western Australia, 1971. Faculty zoology University Michigan, Ann Arbor, 1953—; professor University Michigan, 1962—, D.E.S. Brown professor biological sciences; 1981—, chairman div. biological sciences; 1974-82, director mus. zoology; 1982—; Lecturer Summer Institute Desert Biology, Arizona State University, 1960-71, Maytag professor, 1982; researcher Australian-Am. Education Foundation, University Western Australia, 1969-70; member Speakers Bureau, Am. Institute Biological Sci., 1960-62; Member adv. panel National Science Foundation environmental biology program, 1967-69; member adv. committee for research National Science Foundation, 1973-77; adv. panel National Science Foundation regulatory biology program, 1979-82; member R/V Alpha Helix New Guinea Expedition, 1969; chief scientist R/V Dolphin Gulf of California Expedition, 1976; member R/V Alpha Helix Galapagos Expedition, 1978. Editorial board: Condor, 1960-63, Auk, 1964-68, Ecology, 1968-70, Annual Rev. Physiology, 1973-79, Physiological Zoology, 1976-86; co-editor: Springer-Verlag Zoophysiology and Ecology series, 1968-72; associate editor: Biology of the Reptilia, 1972. Served with United States Naval Reserve, 1945-46. USPHS Postdoctoral Research fellow, 1953; Guggenheim fellow, 1962-63; Recipient Russell award University Michigan, 1959, Distinguished Faculty Achievement award, 1976; Maytag Professor Ariz, State University, 1982; Wheeler Lecturer University North Dakota, 1986. Fellow American Association for the Advancement of Science (council del. 1984-86), Am. Ornithological Union (Brewster medal 1979); member Am. Society Zoologists (president 1986), Am. Physiological Society, Ecological Society Am., Cooper Ornithological Society (hon., Painton award 1963), International Society Biometeorologists, Phi Beta Kappa, Sigma Xi, Kappa Sigma. Home: 1376 Bird Road Ann Arbor Michigan 48103

DAY, EMERSON, physician; born Hanover, New Hampshire, May 2, 1913; son of Edmund Ezra and Emily Sophia (Emerson) D.; married Ruth Fairfield, August 7, 1937; children: Edmund Perry, Robert Fairfield, Nancy, Bonnie, Sheryl. Bachelor of Arts, Dartmouth College, 1934; Doctor of Medicine, Harvard University, 1938. Intern Presbyn. Hospital, New York City, 1938- 40; fellow in cardiology Johns Hopkins University, 1940-42; assistant resident medicine New York Hospital, 1942; medical director international div. Trans World Airline, New York City, 1945-47; assistant professor preventive medicine and pub. health Cornell University Medical College, 1947-50, associate professor clinical preventive medicine and pub. health; 1950-54, professor preventive medicine Sloan Kettering div.; 1954-64; chairman department preventive medicine Memorial Hospital, New York City, 1954-63; director Strang Cancer Prevention Clinic, 1950-63; member, chief div. preventive medicine Sloan-Kettering Institute, New York City, 1954-64; consultant in geriatrics Cold Spring Institute, Cold Spring-on-Hudson, New York, 1952-57; director New York City Department Health Cancer Detection Center, 1947-50, Strang Clinic, Incorporated, 1963-66, PMI-Strang Clinic, 1966-69; president Preventive Medicine Institute, 1963-69, hon. president; 1969—; vice president, medical director Medequip Corp., 1969-76, senior medical consultant; 1976-82; medical vice president Health Management International, Incorporated, 1982-84; medical director Physicians for Medical Cost Containment, Incorporated, 1984—;

professor medicine Northwestern University Medical School, 1976-81, professor emeritus; 1981—; associate director Northwestern University Cancer Center, 1976-81; medical director Portes Cancer Prevention Center, 1978-79; attending physician Northwestern Memorial Hospital, 1976-81, visiting physician; 1981—; lecturer Cook County Grad. School Medical, 1977—; member Northwestern University Medical Associates, 1980-81; medical director, chairman department internal medicine Chicago Specialty Hospital and Medical Center, 1981-84; affiliate staff physician Evanston, Glenbrook hospitals, 1976—; attending physician, member medical board James Ewing Hospital, Memorial Hospital, New York City, 1950-64; senior member PMX Medical Group, New York City, 1956—70; adj. professor biology New York University, 1965-70; member cancer detection committee International Union Against Cancer, 1954-70; president New York City div. Am. Cancer Society, 1963-64; medical consultant Medidata Health Services, Incorporated, 1985—. Contributor numerous articles to professional journals. Served as flight surgeon ATC United States Army Air Force, 1942-45. Recipient Bronze medal Am. Cancer Society, 1956, professorship in early detection Illinois div., 1976-79. Fellow American College of Physicians, New York Acad. Medicine, New York Acad. Sciences (president 1965), Am. Pub. Health Association, Am. Occupational Medical Association, Am. Geriatrics Society, International Acad. Cytology (hon.); member Am. Society Cytology (founding member, president 1958, now hon. member, Papanicolaou award 1978), Am. Society Preventive Oncology, International Health Evaluation Association, Society for Advanced Medical Systems (founding director 1969-81), Am. Association Medical Systems and Informatics (founding director 1981-84), Harvey Society, Illinois, Chicago med. socs., American Medical Association, Phi Beta Kappa, Alpha Omega Alpha, Zeta Psi. Club: Century Association (New York City). Home and Office: 320 Pebblebrook Dr Northbrook Illinois 60062

DEBAKEY, MICHAEL ELLIS, cardiovascular surgeon; born Lake Charles, Louisiana, September 7, 1908; son of Shaker Morris and Raheeja (Zorba) DeB.; married Diana Cooper, October 15, 1936; children: Michael Maurice, Ernest Ochsner, Barry Edward, Denis Alton, Olga Katerina; married Katrin Fehlhaber, July 1975. Bachelor of Science, Tulane University, 1930, Doctor of Medicine, 1932, Master of Science, 1935, Doctor of Laws, 1965; Docteur Honoris Causa, University Lyon, France, 1961, University Brussels, 1962, University Ghent, Belgium, 1964, University Athens, 1964; Doctor.H.C., University Turin, Italy, 1965, University Belgrade, Yugoslavia, 1967; Doctor of Laws, Lafayette College, 1965; Doctor of Medicine (honorary), Aristotelean University of Thessaloniki, Greece, 1972; Doctor of Science, Hahnemann Medical College, 1973, numerous others. Diplomate Nat. Board Medical Examiners, Am. Board Surgery, Am. Board Thoracic Surgery. Intern Charity Hospital, New Orleans, 1932-33, assistant surgery; 1933-35; assistant surgery University Strasbourg, France, 1935-36, University Heidelberg, Federal Republic of Germany, 1936; instructor surgery Tulane University, New Orleans, 1937-40, assistant professor; 1940-46, associate professor; 1946-48; professor, chairman department surgery Baylor (Texas) College Medicine, 1948—, vice president medical affairs; 1968-69, chief executive officer; 1968-69, president; 1969-79, chancellor; 1979—, director National Heart and Blood Vessel Research and Demonstration Center; 1975-85, director DeBakey Heart Center; 1985—; surgeon-in-chief Ben Taub General Hospital, 1963—; senior attending surgeon Methodist Hospital; clinical professor surgery University Texas Dental Branch, Houston; consultant surgery Veteran's Administration Hospital, St. Elizabeth's Hospital, M.D. Anderson Hospital, St. Luke's Hospital, Texas Children's Hospital, Texas Institute Rehabilitation and Research Brooke General Hospital, Brooke Army Medical Center, Fort Sam Houston, Texas, Walter Reed Army Hospital, Washington.; member medical adv. committee Office Secretary Def., 1948-50, Ams. for Substance Abuse Prevention, 1984; Medical Adv. Board, International Brotherhood Teamsters, 1985—; chairman committee surgery National Research Council, 1953, member executive committee, 1953; member committee medical services Hoover Commission; Friends of National Library of Medicine (founding board of directors), 1985—; chairman board regents National Library Medicine, 1959; past member national adv. heart council National Institutes of Health; member National Adv. Health Council, 1961-65, National Adv. Council Regional Medical Programs, 1965—, National Adv. General Medical Sciences Council, 1965, Program Planning Committee, Committee Training, National Heart Institute, 1961—; member civilian health and medical adv. council Office Assistant Secretary Def.; chairman President's Commission Heart Disease, Cancer and Stroke, 1964; member adv. council National Heart Lung and Blood Institute, 1982-87; member Texas Sci. and Tech. Council, 1984-86. Author: (with Robert A. Kilduffe) Blood Transfusion, 1942, (with Gilbert W. Beebe) Battle Casualties, 1952, (with Alton Ochsner) Textbook of Minor Surgery, 1955, (with T. Whayne) Cold Injury, Ground Type, 1958, A Surgeon's Visit to China, 1974, The Living Heart, 1977, The Living Heart Diet, 1985; editor: Yearbook of Surgery, 1958-70; chairman adv. editorial board: Medical History of World War II; editor Journal Vascular Surgery, 1984-88; contributor over 1200 articles to medical journals. Member Texas Constitutional Revision Commission, 1973. Served as colonel Office Surgeon General Army of the United States, 1942-46; now Colonel Reserves; cons. to Surgeon General 1946—. Decorated Legion of Merit, 1946, Independence of Jordan medal 1st class, Merit Order of Republic 1st Class Egypt, , commander Cross of Merit Pro Utiliate Hominum Sovereign Order Knights of Hospital of St. John of Jerusalem in Denmark; recipient Rudolph Matas award, 1nternational Society Surgery Distinguished Service award, 1957, Modern Medicine award, 1957, Roswell Park medal, 1959, Leriche award International Society Surgery, 1959, Great medallion University Ghent, 1961, Grand Cross, Order Leopold Belgium, 1962, Albert Lasker award for clinical research, 1963, Order of Merit Chile, 1964, St. Vincent prize med. scis. University Turin, 1965, Orden del Libertador General San Martin Argentina, 1965,

Centennial medal Albert Einstein Medical Center, 1966, Gold Scalpel award International Cardiology Foundation, 1966, Distinguished Faculty award, 1973; Eleanor Roosevelt Humanities award, 1969; Civilian Service medal Office Sec. Defense, 1970, Union of Soviet Socialist Republics Acad. Sci. 50th Anniversary Jubilee medal, 1973, Phi Delta Epsilon Distinguished Service award, 1974, La Madonnina award, 1974, 30 Year Service award Harris County Hospital District, 1978, Knights Humanity award honoris causa International Register Chivalry, Milan, 1978, diploma de Merito Caja Costarricense de Seguro Social, San Jose, Costa Rica, 1979, Distinguished Service plaque Texas Board Education, 1979, Britannica Achievement in Life award, 1979, Medal of Freedom with Distinction Presidential award, 1969, Distinguished Service award International Society Atherosclerosis, 1979, Centennial award American Society of Mechanical Engineers, 1980, Marian Health Care award St. Mary's University, 1981, Clemson University award, 1983, Humana Heart Institute award, 1985, Theodore E. Cummings award, 1987, National Medical of Sci. award 1987, Markowitz award Acad. Surg. Rsch., 1988, Association Am. Medical Colleges award 1988, Crille award International Platform Association, 1988, Thomas Alva Edison Foundation award, 1988, first issue Michael DeBakey medal American Society of Mechanical Engineers, 1989, Inaugural award Scripps Clinic and Rsch. Foundation, 1989, others; named Dr. of Year, Medical World News, 1965, Medical Man of Year, 1966, Distinguished Service Professor, Baylor University, 1968, Humanitarian Father of Year,

1974, Tulane University Alumnus of Year, 1974, Texas Scientist of Year, Texas Acad. Sci., 1979. Fellow American College of Surgeons (Ann. award Southwestern Pennsylvania chapter 1973), Institute of Medicine Chicago (hon.); member Am. College Cardiology (hon. fellow), Royal Society Medicine, Halsted Society, Am. Heart Association, Southern Society Clinical Research, American Association for the Advancement of Science, Southwestern Surgical Congress (president 1952), Society Vascular Surgery (president 1953), Society Vascular Surgical Education & Research Foundation (president 1988), American Medical Association (Distinguished Service award 1959, Hektoen Gold medal), Am. Surgical Association (Distinguished Service award 1981), Southern Surgical Association, Western Surgical Association, Am. Association Thoracic Surgery (president 1959), International Cardiovascular Society (president 1958, president N.Am chapter 1964), Association International Vascular Surgeons (president 1983), Mexican Acad. Surgery (hon.), Society Clinical Surgical, National Acads. Practice Medicine, Society University Surgeons, International Society Surgery, Society Experimental Biology and Medicine, Hellenic Surgical Society (hon.), Bio-med. Engineering Society (board directors 1968), Houston Heart Association (member adv. council 1968-69), Society Nacional de Cirugia (Cuba), Chamber of Commerce, Sigma Xi, Alpha Omega Alpha. Democrat. Episcopalian. Club: University (Washington). Office: Baylor College Medicine One Baylor Plaza Houston Texas 77030

DE BOLD, ADOLFO J., educator, research scientist; born Paraná, Argentina, February 14, 1942; arrived in Canada, 1968; son of Adolfo E.G. and Ana (Patriarca) deB.; married Mercedes L. Kuroski; children: Adolfo A., Alejandro J., Cecilia I., Gustavo A., Pablo G. Bachelor of Science (honorary), Faculty Chemical Science, Cordoba, Argentina, 1968; Master of Science in Pathology, Queen's University, Kingston, Ontario, 1971, Doctor of Philosophy in Pathology, 1973. Certified clinical chemist. Demonstrator in physics National University Cordoba, 1961-62, demonstrator normal and pathological histology; 1964-67; resident, chief resident National Hospital, Clinicas, Cordoba, 1966-68; assistant professor, laboratory scientist Queen's University and Hotel-Dieu Hospital, Kingston, 1974-82, associate professor; 1982-85, professor; 1985-86; professor pathology and physiology University Ottawa, Ontario, Can., 1986—; board of directors research University Ottawa Heart Institute at Ottawa Civic Hospital, 1986—. Discovered Atrial Natriuretic Hormone, 1981, patented, 1986; contributor over 100 sci. articles and chapters to books in field. Board of directors Heart Institute, Ottawa, 1986—. Recipient Gairdner International award Gairdner Foundation, Toronto, Ontario, 1986, Manning Prin. award Manning Foundation, Alberta, Can., 1986, Sci. Achievement award Am. Society Hypertension, New York, 1986, Research Achievement award Can. Cardiovascular Society, Ottawa, 1986. Fellow Royal Society Can.(McLaughin Medal of Excellence in Research, 1988), Roy. College Physicians and Surgeons (Can.), member Can. Hypertension Society, Am. Society for Hypertension, International Society Heart Rsch, Am. Sect. Can. Federation Biological Socs., Histochem. Society, United States Acad. Pathology, Can. Acad. Pathology, American Association for the Advancement of Science, Am. Society Cell Biology, Can. Society Cell Biology, International Acad. Pathology, Am. Association Pathology, Federation Am. Society Experimental Biology, Microscopial Society Can., Society Experimental Biology and Medicine, Can. Society Anatomy, New York Acad. Sci. Roman Catholic. Avocation: classical guitar. Office: U Ottawa Heart Institute, 1053 Carling Avenue, Ottawa, Ontario Canada K1Y 4E9

DECIUTIIS, ALFRED CHARLES MARIA, medical oncologist, television producer; born New York City, October 16, 1945; son of Alfred Ralph and Theresa Elizabeth (Manko) de C.; married Catherine L. Gohn. Bachelor of Science summa cum laude, Fordham University, 1967; Doctor of Medicine, Columbia University, 1971. Diplomate Am. Board Internal Medicine, Am. Board Medical Oncology. Intern New York Hosp.-Cornell Medical Center, New York City, 1971-72, resident; 1972-74; fellow in clinical immunology Memorial Hosp.-Sloan Kettering Cancer Center, New York City, 1974-75, fellow in clinical oncology; 1975-76, special fellow in immunology; 1974-76; guest investigator, assistant physician experimental hematology Rockefeller University, New York City, 1975-76; practice medicine, specializing in medical oncology Los Angeles, 1977—; host cable TV shows, 1981—; medical editor Cable Health Network, 1983—, Lifetime Network, 1984—; member medical adv. committee 1984

Olympics; active staff South Bay Hospital, Little Company of Mary Hospital, Torrance Memorial Hospital, Bay Harbor Hospital; co-founder Meditrina Medical Center, free out-patient surgical center, Torrance, California. Syndicated columnist Coast Media News "The Subject is Cancer", 1980's; producer numerous medical TV shows; contributor articles to professional journals. Founder Italian-Am. Medical Association, 1982; co-founder Italian-Am. Med.-Legal Alliance, Los Angeles, 1982—; member Italian-Am. Civic Committee, Los Angeles, 1983; member governor board medical council Italian-Am. Foundation; chancellor's associate University of California at Los Angeles. Served to captain Medical Corps, United States Army, 1972-74. Leukemia Society Am. fellow, 1974-76; New York State Regents scholar, 1963-67, 67-71; recipient Physicians Recognition award American Medical Association, 1978-80, 82-85; proclamation Senate Rules Committee, State of California, 1982. Fellow American College of Physicians, International College Physicians and Surgeons; member American Medical Association, Am. Union Physicians and Dentists, Am. Society Clinical Oncology, New York Acad. Sci. (life), California Medical Association, Los Angeles County Medical Association, International Health Society, Am. Pub. Health Association, American Association for the Advancement of Science, Am. Geriatrics Society, Chinese Medical Association, Drug Information Association, Am. Society Hematology (member emeritus), National Geog. Society, International Platform Association, California chapter Catholic League for Civil and Religious Liberty, Nature Conservancy, National Wildlife Federation, World Affiars Council Los Angeles, Am. College Heraldry, Confederation Chivalry, Mensa, Phi Beta Kappa, Alpha Omega Alpha, Sigma Xi. Republican. Roman Catholic. Avocations: collecting; reading; hunting; fishing; astronomy. The deCiutiis family was first ranked among the nobles of Italy in 893, designated a princely family and given the title of "Princes of the Holy Roman Empire" in 1629. Office: care Dr Gene Leone 4305 Torrence Boulevard Suite 101 Torrance California 90503

DE DUVE, CHRISTIAN RENÉ, chemist, biologist, educator; born Thames-Ditton, England, October 2, 1917; son of Alphonse and Madeleine (Pungs) de D.; married Janine Herman, September 30, 1943; children: Thierry, Anne, Françoise, Alain. Doctor of Medicine, University Louvain, Belgium, 1941, Doctor of Philosophy, 1945, Master of Science, 1946; Doctor honoris causa, univs. of Turin, Leiden, Sherbrooke, Lille, Belgium, 1946, Catholic University Santiago, Chile, 1946, University René Descartes, Paris, 1946, State University Ghent, State University Liege, 1946, Gustavus Adolphus College, St. Peter, Minnesota, 1946, University Rosario, Argentina, 1946, University Aix-Marseille II, University Keele, Katholieke Universitet Leuven, 1946, Karolinska Institute, Stockholm, 1946. Lecturer physiological chemistry faculty medicine Catholic University Louvain, 1947-51, professor, head department physiological chemistry; 1951-85, emeritus professor; 1985—; professor biochem. cytology Rockefeller University, New York City, 1962-74, Andrew W. Mellon professor, 1974-88, professor emeritus, 1988—; visiting professor Albert Einstein College

Medicine, Bronx, New York, 1961-62, Chaire Francqui State University Ghent, 1962-63, Free University Brussels, 1963-64, State University Liège, 1972-73; Mayne guest professor University Queensland, Brisbane, Australia, 1972; president International Institute Cellular and Molecular Pathology, Brussels, 1974—. Member editorial board Subcellular Biochemistry, 1971-87, Preparative Biochemistry, 1971-80, Molecular and Cellular Biochemistry, 1973-80. Member Conseil d'Adminstrn. du Fonds National de la Recherche Scientifique, 1958-61; member Conseil de Gestion du Fonds de la Recherche Scientifique Medicale, 1959, 61; member Commission Scientifique du Fonds de la Recherche Scientifique Medicale, 1958, 61; member Comite des Experts du Conseil National de la Politique Scientifique, 1958-61; member adv. board Ciba Foundation; member adult devel. and aging research and training rev. committee National Institute Child Health and Devel., National Institute of Health, 1970-72; member adv. committee for medical research World Health Organization, 1974-79; member sci. adv. committee Max Planck-Inst. für Immunbiologie, 1975-78, Ludwig Institute Cancer Research, 1985—, Mary Imogene Bassett Research Institute, 1986—, Clin. Research Institute Montreal, 1986—; member biology adv. committee New York Hall of Sci., 1986—. Recipient Prix des Alumni, 1949, Prix Pfizer, 1957, Prix Francqui, 1960, Prix Quinquennal Belge des Sciences Médicales, 1967 (Belgium); Gairdner Foundation International award merit (Can.), 1967; Dr. H.P. Heineken prize (Netherlands), 1973; Nobel prize for physiology or medicine, 1974; Harden award Biochem. Society (Great Britain), 1978; Theobald Smith award Albany Medical College, 1981; Jimenez Diaz award, 1985. Fellow American Association for the Advancement of Science; member Royal Acad. Medicine, Royal Acad. Belgium, Am. Chemical Society, Biochem. Society, Am. Society Biological Chemists, Pontifical Acad. Sci., Am. Society Cell Biology (council 1966-69), Society Chimie Biologique, Society Belge Biochim. (president 1962-64), Deutsche Akademie der Naturforscher Leopoldina, Koninklyke Akademie voor Geneeskunde (Belgium), European Association Study Diabetes, European Molecular Biology Organization, European Cell Biology Organization, International Society Cell Biology, New York Acad. Sciences, Society Belge de Physiologie, Sigma Xi; foreign associate Am. Acad. Arts and Sciences, National Acad. Sciences (United States), Royal Society London, Académie des Sciences de Paris, Académie des Sciences d'Athen; numerous hon. memberships. Office: Rockefeller U 1230 York Avenue New York New York 10021 also: ICP, 75 Avenue Hippocrate, B-1200 Brussels Belgium

DE HOFFMANN, FREDERIC, nuclear physicist, research institute executive; born Vienna, Austria, July 8, 1924; came to United States, 1941, naturalized, 1946; son of Otto and Marianne (Halphen) de H.; married Patricia Lynn Stewart, June 10, 1953. Bachelor of Science, Harvard University, 1945, Master of Arts, 1947, Doctor of Philosophy (fellow NRC, 1946-48), 1948. Staff member Los Alamos Sci. Laboratory, 1944-46, 48-55, alternate assistant director; 1950-51; consultant Atomic Energy Commission, 1947-48, committee senior responsible reviewers; 1947-51; consultant Joint Congressional Committee Atomic Energy, 1954; assistant vice president nuclear planning Convair div. Gen Dynamics Corp., San Diego, 1955; vice president General Dynamics Corp., 1955-67, also general manager General Atomic div.; 1955-59, president; 1959-67; president General Atomic Europe, Zurich, Switzerland, 1960-67; vice president Gulf Oil Corp.; also president Gulf General Atomic and Gulf General Atomic Europe, 1967-69; chancellor Salk Institute Biological Studies, 1970-71, president; 1972—; chairman, president Salk Institute Biotech./Indsl. Associates (SIBIA), 1981—; hon. professor theoretical physics University Vienna, 1968—; sci. secretary United Nations International Conference Peaceful Uses Atomic Energy, 1955; president Conference Future Sci. and Tech., Austria, 1972; governing board Courant Institute Math., New York University, 1968-85; director Atomic Industrial Forum, 1962-70; board of directors Salzburg Seminary in Am. Studies, 1978-81; member National Acad. Sci. subcom. management and tech. International Institute Applied Systems Analysis Vienna, 1978-82; chairman international panel of advs. on biological sciences for Sci. Council Singapore; chairman Industrie 2000 Conference, Vienna, 1985; speaker First International Symposium on New Chemistry, Tokyo, 1987. Author: (with K. M. Case and G. Placzek), Volume 1) Introduction to the Theory of Neutron Diffusion, 1954, (with H. A. Bethe and S. S. Schweber) Volumes 1 and 2) Mesons and Fields, 1955. Trustee Salk Institute, 1970—, Scripps Clinic and Research Foundation, 1956-66. Decorated Cross of Honour for Sci. and Arts, Decoration of Honour for Merit in Silver, Decoration of Honour in Gold Republic Austria, Decoration of Honour in Gold Province of Vienna, Austria. Fellow Am. Physical Society, Am. Nuclear Society (board directors 1964-67); member Harvard Alumni Association (director 1961-64), Sigma Xi. Clubs: Bohemian (San Francisco); Duquesne (Pittsburgh); Cosmos (Washington); University (New York City); Atheneum (London). Office: Salk Institute Biol Studies Post Office Box 85800 San Diego California 92138-9216

DEISENHOFER, JOHANN, biochemistry educator, researcher; born Zusamaltheim, Bavaria, Federal Republic of Germany, September 30, 1943; came to United States, 1988; son of Johann and Thekla (Magg) D. Diploma in Physics, Technische Universität, Munich, 1971; Doctor of Philosophy, Technische Universität, 1974, Doctor habil., 1987. Postdoctoral fellow Max-Planck Institut fur Biochemie, Martinsried, Federal Republic of Germany, 1974-76, staff scientist; 1976-88; investigator Howard Hughes Medical Institute, Dallas, 1988—; professor biochemistry University Texas Southwest, Dallas, 1988—. Contributor over 50 sci. papers to professional publications. Recipient Nobel prize for chemistry, 1988; co-recipient Biological Physics prize Am. Physical Society, 1986, Otto Bayer prize, 1988. Member American Association for the Advancement of Science, Am. Crystallographic Association, German Biophys. Society, The Protein Society.

DE JESÚS, NYDIA ROSA, physician, anesthesiologist; born Humacao, Puerto Rico, September 8, 1930; daughter of Manuel Aurelio De Jesus and Luz María González. Bachelor of

Science, University Puerto Rico, 1949, Doctor of Medicine, 1955; certificate medical tech., School Tropical Medicine, San Juan, Puerto Rico, 1950; certificate anesthesiology, Columbia Presbyterian Medical Center, 1958. Diplomate Am. Board Anesthesiology. Director department anesthesiology University Hospital & School Medicine, San Juan, 1960-65; director div. anesthesiology Puerto Rico Medical Center, San Juan, 1965-76; visiting professor anesthesiology Harvard Medical School, Boston, Massachusetts, 1973-74; dean acad. affairs Medical Sciences Campus, University Puerto Rico, San Juan, 1976-78; director cardiovascular surgical center Puerto Rico Medical Center, San Juan, 1980-85; professor anesthesiology University Puerto Rico School Medicine, San Juan, 1965—, dean; 1986—; director intensive care unit University Hospital, San Juan, 1974-75; chief section anesthesiology Veteran's Administration Hospital, San Juan, 1963-76; member cardiovascular commission Secretary of Health, Commonwealth of Puerto Rico, 1985; consultant div. medicine, health resources administration Bur Health Manpower, United States Public Health Service, 1977-79; president consultant board Pediatric University Hospital, San Juan, member board of directors, 1986. Fellow Am. College Anesthesiology; member American College of Physicians, New York Acad. Sciences, American Association for the Advancement of Science, Am. Society Anesthesiology. Avocations: music, gardening, reading. Home: No 8 Jardines De Vedruna Rio Piedras Puerto Rico 00927 Office: University of Puerto Rico School of Medicine GPO Box 5067 San Juan Puerto Rico 00936

DE LAUER, RICHARD D., aerospace consultant, former government official, former aerospace company executive; born Oakland, California, September 23, 1918; son of Michael and Matilda (Giambruno) DeL.; married Ann Carmichael, December 6, 1940; 1 child, Richard Daniel. Bachelor of Arts, Stanford University, 1940; Bachelor of Science, United States Naval Postgrad. School, 1949; Aeronautical Engineer, California Institute Tech., 1950, Doctor of Philosophy, 1953. Structrual designer Glenn L. Martin Company, Baltimore, 1940-42; design engineer Northrop Company, Hawthorne, California, 1942; commissioned ensign United States Navy, 1942, advanced through grades to commander; 1958; assignments in United States, 1943-58; retired 1966; laboratory director Space Tech. Laboratories, El Segundo, California, 1958-60; Titan Program director Space Tech. Laboratories, 1960-62, vice president, director ballistic missile program management; 1962-66; vice president, general manager systems engineering and integration div. TRW Systems Group, Redondo Beach, California, 1966-68; vice president, general manager TRW Systems Group, 1968-70; executive vice president TRW, Incorporated, Redondo Beach, 1970-81; also director; undersec. for research and engineering Department Defense, Washington, 1981-84; chairman The Orion Group Limited, Arlington, Virginia, 1985—; board of directors GenCorp., ERC Incorporated, Daisy Systems; visiting lecturer University California, Los Angeles.; Chairman National Alliance Businessman, 1968-69; chairman Region IX, 1970; member Defense Sci. Board, Department Defense. Author: (with

R.W. Bussard) Nuclear Rocket Propulsion, 1958, Fundamentals of Nuclear Flight, 1965. Former trustee University Redlands. Decorated Department Defense medal for distinguished pub. service; recipient Distinguished Civilian Service award U.S. Army, Exceptional Civilian Service award U.S. Air Force, Distinguished Service medal National Aeronautics and Space Administration. Fellow American Institute of Aeronautics and Astronautics, Am. Astronomical Society; member National Acad. Engineering, American Association for the Advancement of Science, Aerospace Industries Association (former governor), Sigma Xi. Home: 2222 Avenue of the Stars Los Angeles California 90067 Office: Orion Group Limited 1213 Jefferson Davis Highway Suite 1101 Arlington Virginia 22202

DEL REGATO, JUAN ANGEL, radiotherapeutist and oncologist, educator; born Camaguey, Cuba, March 1, 1909; came to United States, 1937, naturalized, 1941; son of Juan and Damiana (Manzano) del R.; married Inez Johnson, May 1, 1939; children: Ann Cynthia del Regato Jaeger, Juanita Inez del Regato Peters, John Carl. Student, University Havana, Cuba, 1930; Doctor of Medicine, University Paris, France, 1937, Laureat, 1937; Doctor of Science (honoris causa), Colorado College, 1969; Doctor of Science (honoris causa, ad gradum), Hahnemann Medical College, 1977; Doctor of Science (honoris causa), Medical College Wisconsin, 1981. Diplomate Am. Board Radiology (trustee 1975-85, historian 1976-85). Assistant Radium Institute, University Paris, 1934-37; assistant Chicago Tumor Institute, 1938; radiotherapeutist Warwick Cancer Clinic, Washington, 1939-40; researcher National Cancer Institute, Baltimore, 1941-43; chief department radiotherapy Ellis Fischel State Cancer Hospital, Columbia, Missouri, 1943-48; director Penrose Cancer Hospital, Colorado Springs, Colorado, 1949-73; professor clinical radiology University Colorado Medical School, 1950-74; professor radiology University South Florida, Tampa, 1974-83, professor emeritus; 1983—; David Gould lecturer Johns Hopkins University, 1983. Author: (with L.V. Ackerman, M.D.) Cancer; Diagnosis Treatment and Prognosis, 1947, 54, 62, 70, (with H.J. Spjut and J.D. Cox), 1985, Radiological Physicists, 1985; editor: Cancer Seminar, 1950-82; contributor articles to professional journals. Decorated Order of Carlos Finlay of Cuba; Order Francisco de Miranda Republic of Venezuela; Béclère medal àtitre exceptionnel, 1980; recipient Gold medal Radiol. Society North Am., 1967; Gold medal Inter-Am. College Radiology, 1967; Gold medal Am. College Radiology, 1968; Gold plaque, 1975; Grubbe gold medal Illinois Radiol. Society, 1973; Prix Bruninghaus French Acad. Medicine, 1979; Distinguished Scientist award University South Florida College Medicine, 1980; Distinguished Service award Am. Cancer Society, 1983; named Distinguished Physician Veteran's Administration, 1974. Member National Adv. Cancer Council, Bethesda, Maryland (1967-71); member med. adv. committee Milheim Foundation, Denver; Fellow Am. College Radiology (board chancellors; chairman commission radiation therapy, committee awards and honors); member American Medical Association, National Acad. Medicine of France (Laureat 1948), Radiological

Society North America (vice president 1959-60, Arthur Erskine lecturer 1978), Am. Roentgen Ray Society, Am. Radium Society (vice president 1963-64, treasurer 1966-68, president 1968-69, chairman executive committee 1971-72, historian 1969—, Janeway gold medal 1973), Association Am. Medical Colls., International Club Radiotherapists (president 1962-65), Inter-Am. College Radiology (president 1967-71, United States counselor 1971-79), Am. Society Therapeutic Radiologists (secretary 1958-68, historian 1968—, president 1974-75, chairman board directors 1975-76, gold medal 1977), Federation Clinical Oncologic Socs. (president board directors 1976-77); hon. member Rocky Mountain, Pacific Northwest, Texas, Oregon, Minnesota radiol. socs., radiol. socs. Cuba, Mexican, Panama, Ecuador, Peru, Paraguay, Can., Argentina, Buenos Aires (Argentina), Am. Institute Radiology (historian 1978—), Arthur Purdy Stout Society Pathologists (hon. member). Home: 3101 Cocos Road Carrollwood Tampa Florida 33618 Office: U South Fla College Medicine Department Radiology Tampa Florida 33618 also: Virginia Med Center 13000 N 30th St Tampa Florida 33612

DE MARIA, ANTHONY J., electrical engineer; born Santa Croce, Italy, October 30, 1931; came to United States, 1935; son of Joseph and Nicolina (Daddona) De M.; married Katherine M. Waybright, August 29, 1953; 1 daughter, Karla Kay. Bachelor of Science in Electrical Engineering, University Connecticut, 1956, Doctor of Philosophy in Electrical Engineering, 1965; Master of Science, Rensselaer Polytechnic Institute, 1960. Acoustic research engineer Anderson Laboratory, West Hartford, Connecticut, 1956-57; magnetic research engineer Hamilton Standard Div. United Techs. Corp., Windsor Locks, Connecticut, 1957-58; scientist United Techs. Research Center, East Hartford, Connecticut, 1958—; instructor in electronics University Hartford, 1957-60; adj. professor physics Rensselaer Polytechnic Institute Grad. Center, Hartford, 1970-77; lecturer in lasers University of California at Los Angeles, 1974-82 ; member Department Defense Adv. Group on Electronic Devices, 1977-86, chairman, 1980-85; member evaluation committee on electromagnetic tech. National Bureau Standards, 1977-79; member Center Electrical and Electronic Engineering, 1979-83. Author: Lasers, Volume III, 1972, Volume IV, 1976; Contributor articles to professional journals. Member Air Force Sci. Adv. Board, 1981-86. Recipient Distinguished Alumnus award University Connecticut, 1978, Distinguished Engineering award University Connecticut, 1983, Davies medal and award Rensselaer Polytechnic Institute, 1980. Fellow Institute of Electrical and Electronics Engineers (editor Jour. Quantum Electronics, Morris N. Liebman memorial award 1980), Optical Society Am. (vice president 1979, president 1981, chairman board editors 1986-88); member Am. Physical Society, National Acad. Engineering (Fairchild Distinguished Scholars 1982-83, California Institute Tech.), Connecticut Acad. Sciences and Engineering. Office: United Techs Research Center 400 Main St East Hartford Connecticut 06108

DEMING, W(ILLIAM) EDWARDS, statistics educator, consultant. Bachelor of Science,

University Wyoming, 1921, Doctor of Laws (honorary), 1958; Master of Science, University Colorado, 1924, Doctor of Laws (honorary), 1987; Doctor of Philosophy, Yale University, 1928; Doctor of Science (honorary), Rivier College, 1981, Ohio State University, 1982, Maryland University, 1983, Clarkson Institute Tech., 1983; Doctor in Engineering (honorary), University Miami, 1985; Doctor of Laws (honorary), George Washington University, 1986, Doctor in Engineering (honorary), 1987; Doctor of Science (hon), University Colorado, 1987. Instructor engineering University Wyoming, 1921-22; assistant professor physics Colorado School Mines, 1922-24, University Colorado, 1924-25; instructor physics Yale University, 1925-27; math. physicist United States Department of Agriculture, 1927-39; adviser in sampling Bureau of Census, 1939-45; professor statistics New York University Grad. School Business Administration, New York City, from 1946; consultant research, industry, 1946—; statistician Allied Mission to Observe Greek Elections, 1946; consultant sampling Government India, 1947, 51, 71; adviser in sampling techniques Supreme Command Allied Powers, Tokyo, 1947-50, High Commission for Germany, 1952, 53; member United Nations Sub-Commn. on Statistical Sampling, 1947-52; lecturer various universities, Germany, Austria, 1953, London School Economics, 1964, Institut de Statistique de University Paris, 1964; consultant Census Mexico, Bank of Mexico, Ministry Economy Mexico, 1954, 55; consultant Statistisches Bundesamt, Wiesbaden, Federal Republic Germany, 1953, Central Statistical Office Turkey, 1959—, China

Productivity Center, Taiwan, 1970, 71; Inter Am. Statistical Institute lecturer, Brazil, Argentina. Author: Quality, Productivity, and Competitive Position, 1982, Out of the Crisis, 1986; contributor numerous articles to professional publications. Decorated 2d Order medal of the Sacred Treasure (Japan); elected Most Distinguished Graduate, University Wyoming, 1972; recipient Taylor Key award Am. Mgmt. Association, 1983; enshrinedin the Engineering and Sci. Hall of Fame, 1986. Fellow Am. Statistical Association, Royal Statistical Society (hon.), Institute Math. Statistics; member Am. Society Quality Control (hon. life, Shewhart medal 1955), International Statistical Institute, Philosophical Society Washington, World Association Pub. Opinion Research, Market Research Council, Biometric Society (hon. life), American Society for Testing and Materials (hon.), Union Japanese Scientists and Engineers (hon. life) (teacher and cons. to Japanese industry 1950-52, 55, 60, 65—, honored in establishment of Deming prizes), Japanese Statistical Association (hon. life), Deutsche Statistische Gesellschaft (hon. life), Operations Research Society Am., National Acad. Engineering, Dayton Hall of Fame. Home and Office: 4924 Butterworth Place Washington District of Columbia 20016

DENNARD, ROBERT HEATH, engineering scientist; born Terrell, Texas, September 5, 1932; son of Buford Leon and Loma (Heath) D.; children—Robert, Amy, Holly. Bachelor of Science in Electrical Engineering, Southern Methodist University, 1954, Master of Science in Electrical Engineering, 1956; Doctor of Philosophy, Carnegie Institute

Tech., 1958. Staff engineer International Business Machines Corporation, Yorktown Heights, New York, 1958-63; research staff member International Business Machines Corporation Research Center, Yorktown Heights, New York, 1963-71, group manager; 1971-79, fellow; 1979—. Contributor articles to professional journals; patentee in field including basic dynamic RAM memory cell. Recipient National Medal of Tech. President of U.S., 1988. Fellow Institute of Electrical and Electronics Engineers; member National Academy of Engineering. Avocation: Scottish country dancing. Office: International Business Machines Corporation Research Center Post Office Box 218 Yorktown Heights New York 10598

DENNIS, JOHN EMORY, JR., mathematics educator; born Coral Gables, Florida, September 24, 1939; son of John Emory and Hazel Violet (Penny) D.; married Ann Watson, March 1, 1960; 1 child, John Emory III. Bachelor of Science in Engineering, University Miami, 1962, Master of Science in Math., 1964; Doctor of Philosophy in Math., University Utah, 1966. Assistant professor math. University Utah, Salt Lake City, 1966-68; lecturer computer sci. University Essex, Colchester, England, 1968-69; visiting assistant professor computer sci. Cornell University, Ithaca, New York, 1969-70, associate professor computer sci.; 1970-76, professor computer sci.; 1976-79, director center for applied math.; 1978-79; professor math. sciences Rice University, Houston, 1979-84, Noah Harding professor math. sciences; 1984—; instructor math. Stillman College, Tuscalusa, Alabama, 1967; Fulbright lecturer,

professor University Buenos Aires, 1986; consultant center for computational research in economics and management sci. Massachusetts Institute of Technology, 1972—, Lawrence Laboratories, 1978—, Argonne National Laboratory, 1978—, Mobil Research and Devel., 1978—, Exxon Production Research, 1978—, Shell Devel., 1978—; research associate National Bureau Economic Research and United Kingdom Atomic Energy Research Establishment, Harwell, Oxfordshire, England, 1975-76; member provosts committee on computer sci. Rice University, 1981-84, member self-study panel on computing, 1983-84, associate Jones College, 1982-86, member undergrad. curriculum committee, 1984-86, member grad. council, 1986—, member engineering dean search committee, 1986—, member faculty council, 1987—, member Computer Information Tech. Institute steering. committee, 1987—; member selection committee grad. fellowships in applications math. National Science Foundation, 1971-72, chairman, 1972-75, member selection committee for postdoctoral fellowships in math. sciences, 1980-82, member panel to evaluate proposals for scientific computing research equipment in the math. sciences, 1982-84; external member search committee for M.D. Anderson chair math. University Houston, 1984-85, Clements chair math. Southern Methodist University, 1985; member national research council committee on recommendations for United States Army Basic Scientific Research, 1986—. Editorial board Math. Programming, 1974—, co-editor, 1986—; contributor articles to scientific journals. National Science Foundation grantee, 1970—, U.S. Army Research Office grantee,

1976—, USAF Office Sponsored Research grantee, 1985—. Member Special Interest Group for Numerical Math. (board directors 1975-77, vice chairman, 1979-81), Am. Math. Society (joint applied math. committee with Society for Industrial and Applies Math., 1980-82), Society for Industrial and Applied Math. (editorial board Jour. for Numericl Analysis 1976-84, board directors 2d summer research conference in numerical analysis 1980-82, member council 1985—, executive committee 1985—, co-organizer international optimization conference 1986—), Math. Programming Society (member international program committee 1987—), Association for Computing Machinery, Operations Research Society Am., Special Interests Group for Math. Programming. Avocations: reading, baseball. Home: 3107 Jarrard West University Place Texas 77005 Office: Rice U Department Math Sci 6100 Main St Houston Texas 77251-1892

DERR, VERNON ELLSWORTH, government research administrator; born Baltimore, November 22, 1921; son of William Edward and Edith May D.; married Mary Louise Van Atta, March 6, 1943; children—Michael Edward, Katherine Mary, Louise Edith, Carol Jean. Bachelor of Arts in Liberal Arts, St. John's College, Annapolis, Maryland, 1948; Doctor of Philosophy, Johns Hopkins University, 1959. Student assistant Applied Physics Laboratory, Baltimore, 1950; research associate Johns Hopkins University, Baltimore, 1951-59; principal scientist Martin Marietta, Orlando, Florida, 1959-67; physicist Environmental Research Laboratories, Wave Propagation Laboratory, National Oceanographic and Atmospheric Administration, Boulder, Colorado, 1967-81; deputy director Environmental Research Laboratories, National Oceanographic and Atmospheric Administration, Boulder, Colorado, 1981-83, director; 1983—; member International Sci. Radio Union Commission II; member International Radiation Commission. Served to captain United States Army 1942-46. Member Am. Geophysical Union, Optical Society Am., Am. Meteorological Society, Institute of Electrical and Electronics Engineers (senior), International Association Meteorology and Atmospheric Physics (United States del. to International Union Geodesy and Geophysics). Office: Department Commerce NOAA Environ Research Labs 325 Broadway R-E Boulder Colorado 80303

DERTOUZOS, MICHAEL LE-ONIDAS, computer scientist, electrical engineer, educator; born Athens, Greece, November 5, 1936; came to United States, 1954, naturalized, 1965; son of Leonidas Michael and Rosana G. (Maris) D.; married Hadwig Gofferje, November 21, 1961; children—Alexandra, Leonidas. Bachelor.S.E.E, University Arkansas, 1957, Master.S.E.E, 1959; Doctor of Philosophy, Massachusetts Institute of Technology, 1964. Head research and devel. Baldwin Electronics, Incorporated, 1958-60; research assistant Massachusetts Institute of Technology, Cambridge, 1960-64, assistant professor; 1964-68, associate professor; 1968-73, professor; 1973—, director Laboratory for Computer Sci.; 1968-74; founder, chairman board Computek, Incorporated, 1964—; consultant in computers to industry; member sci. board Data General Incorporated,

1984—. Author: Threshold Logic: A Synthesis Approach, 1966, (with Athans, Spann and Mason) Systems, Networks and Computation: Multivariable Methods, 1974, Systems, Networks and Computation: Basic Concepts, 1972, (with Clark, Halle, Pool and Wiesner) The Telephone's First Century—and Beyond, 1977, The Computer Age; A Twenty Year View, 1979; Contributor articles professional journals. Trustee Athens College, Greece, 1973—; chairman board Boston Camerata, 1976-80; director Cambridge Society Early Music, 1974-75. Recipient Terman International Education award Am. Society Engineering Education, 1975; Ford postdoctoral fellow, 1964-66; Fulbright scholar, 1954. Fellow Institute of Electrical and Electronics Engineers (Thompson best paper prize 1968); member Acad. Athens, Sigma Xi, Tau Beta Pi, Pi Mu Epsilon. Greek Orthodox. Patentee in field. Home: 15 Bernard Lane Waban Massachusetts 02168 Office: 545 Technology Square Cambridge Massachusetts 02139

DETELS, ROGER, epidemiologist, physician, former university dean; born Brooklyn, October 14, 1936; son of Martin P. and Mary J. (Crooker) D.; married Mary M. Doud, September 14, 1963; children: Martin, Edward. Bachelor of Arts, Harvard University, 1958; Doctor of Medicine, New York University, 1962; Master of Science in Preventive Medicine, University Washington, 1966. Diplomate Am. Board Preventive Medicine. Intern University California General Hospital, San Francisco, 1962-63; resident University Washington, Seattle, 1963-66, practice medicine specializing in preventive medicine; 1966—; medical officer, epidemiologist National Institute Neurological Diseases, Bethesda, Maryland, 1969-71; associate professor epidemiology School Pub. Health, University of California at Los Angeles, 1971-73, professor; 1973—; dean 1980-85; head div. epidemiology School Pub. Health, University of California at Los Angeles, 1972-80; guest lecturer various universities, professional conferences and medical organizations, 1969—; research physician Wadsworth Hospital Center, Los Angeles, 1972; member sci. adv. committee Am. Foundation Acquired Immune Deficiency Syndrome Research. Editor: Oxford Textbook of Public Health, 1985; contributor articles to professional journals. Served as lieutenant commander Medical Corps United States Navy, 1966-69. Grantee in field. Fellow Am. College Preventive Medicine, Am. College Epidemiology (council 1987—); member Am. Epidemiological Society, Society Epidemiologic Research (president 1977-78), Association Teachers Preventive Medicine, California Acad. Preventive Medicine (chairman essay committee 1971), Am. Public Health Association, Am. Association Cancer Education (membership committee 1979-80), Am. Thoracic Society, International Epidemiological Association (treasurer 1984—), American Association for the Advancement of Science, Association Schs. Pub. Health (sec.-treas. 1984-85), Sigma Xi, Delta Omega. Office: University of California at Los Angeles School Public Health Los Angeles California 90024

DEVITA, VINCENT THEODORE, JR., oncologist; born Bronx, New York, March 7, 1935; son of Vincent

Theodore and Isabel DeV.; married Mary Kay Bush, August 3, 1957; children: Teddy (deceased), Elizabeth. Bachelor of Science, College William and Mary, 1957; Doctor of Medicine, George Washington University, 1961. Diplomate: Nat. Board Medical Examiners, Am. Board Internal Medicine (subspecialty hematology, medical oncology). Intern University Michigan Medical Center, Ann Arbor, 1961-62; resident in medicine George Washington University Medical Service District of Columbia General Hospital, 1962-63; clinical associate Laboratory Chemical Pharmacology, National Cancer Institute National Institutes of Health, Bethesda, Maryland, 1963-65; senior resident in medicine Yale New Haven Medical Center, 1965-66; senior investigator solid tumor service, medicine branch National Cancer Institute National Institutes of Health, 1966-68, head solid tumor service, medicine branch; 1968-71, chief medical branch; 1971-74, director div. cancer treatment; 1974-80, clinical director institute; 1975-80; director National Cancer Institute, National Cancer Program, National Institutes of Health, 1980-88; physician-in-chief Memorial Sloan-Kettering Cancer Center, New York City, 1988—, Benno C. Schmidt chair clinical psychology; 1988—; associate professor medicine George Washington University Medical School, 1971-75, professor medicine, 1975—; member expert advisory panel World Health Organization, 1976; member Lasker Award Jury, 1976; chairman Committee French-Am. Agreement on Cancer Treatment Research, 1976—; visiting professor Stanford University Medical School, 1972; 1st annual Clowes lecturer Roswell Park Memorial Institute

Buffalo, 1973. Member editorial board Cancer Research, 1981—, Gynecologic Oncology, 1981—, Hematological Oncology, 1981—, Physicians' Drug Alert, 1982—, Cancer Investigation, 1982—, Journal Clin. Oncology, 1983—; associate editor Cancer Investigation, 1983-87, Am. Journal Medicine, 1983—; member editorial board or adv. editor numerous other medical journals; contributor numerous articles to medical journals. Member awards assembly General Motors Cancer Research Foundation, 1981-85, adv. council, 1984—; member Armand Hammer Cancer Award Committee, 1983—. Served with United States Marine Corps Reserve, 1955-61. Tobacco Research Industry fellow, 1959; decorated Oren del Sol en el Grando de Official, Government of Peru, 1970; recipient Albert and Mary Lasker Medical Research award, 1972; Superior Service award Department of Health, Education and Welfare, 1975; Esther Langer Foundation award, 1976; Alumni medallion College William and Mary, 1976; Jeffrey Gottlieb award, 1976; Bronze medal Am. Society Therapeutic Radiology, 1978, Karnofsky prize and lecture, 1979, Griffuel prize Association for Devel. Research on Cancer, 1980, James Ewing award Society Surgical Oncology, 1982; Memorial Sloan-Kettering Cancer Center award, 1983; Distinguished Service medal U.S. Public Health Service, 1983; Meyer and Anna Prentiss award, 1984; Second Emmanuel Cancer Foundation award, 1984; Pierluigi Nervi award, Rome, 1985; Medal of Honor, Am. Cancer Society, 1985; Barbara Bohen Pfeifer award Am.-Italian Foundation Cancer Research, 1985; Stratton lecturer Am. Society

Hematology, 1985, Leukemia Research Fund lecture, London, 1985; Tenth Richard and Hinda Rosenthal Foundation award, Am. Association Cancer Research Incorporated, 1986; Stanley G. Kay Memorial award, District of Columbia Am. Cancer Society, 1986. Fellow Am. College Physicians; member Am. Society Clinical Oncology (chairman program committee 1972, director 1973-76, president 1977-78), Am. Cancer Society, Am. Society Hematology, Am. Association Cancer Research (director 1976-79), American Medical Association, Am. Federation Clinical Research, Am. Society Clinical Investigation, Society Surgical Oncology, Smith-Reed-Russel Medical Society, Coordinating Council Cancer Research (pres Am. board 1989—), Alpha Omega. Office: Memorial Sloan-Kettering 1275 York Avenue New York New York 10021

DEVRIES, WILLIAM CASTLE, surgeon, educator; born Brooklyn, December 19, 1943; son of Hendrik and Cathryn Lucille (Castle) DeV.; married Ane Karen Olsen, June 12, 1965; children: Jon, Adrie, Kathryn, Andrew, Janna, William, Diana. Bachelor of Science, University Utah, 1966, Doctor of Medicine, 1970. Intern Duke University Medical Center, 1970-71, resident in cardiovascular and thoracic surgery; 1971-79; assistant professor surgery University Utah, until 1984; chairman div. cardiovascular and thoracic surgery; chief thoracic surgery Salt Lake Veteran's Administration Hospital, until 1984; now director artificial heart project, cardiothoracic surgical associates Humana Hospital Audubon, Louisville. Recipient Wintrobe award, 1970. Member Humana Heart Institute International,

American College of Surgeons, Utah Medical Association, American Medical Association, Kentucky Heart Association, Kentucky State Medical Society, Utah Heart Association, Alpha Omega Alpha. Mormon. Office: Audubon Hosp 1 Audubon Dr Louisville Kentucky 40217

DIAMOND, FRED I., electronic engineer; born Brooklyn, December 13, 1925; son of Joseph and Celia (Just) D.; married Edna R. Hutt, September 2, 1956; children: Celia, Joel, Shari. Bachelor of Science in Electrical Engineering, Massachusetts Institute of Technology, 1950; Master of Electrical Engineering, Syracuse University, 1953, Doctor of Philosophy, 1966. Electronic engineer Rome Air Devel. Center, Griffiss Air Force Base, New York, 1950-51; senior scientist Rome Air Devel. Center, 1961-70, chief plans; 1970-73, tech. director communications and control div.; 1973-81, chief scientist; 1981—; chairman avionics panel North Atlantic Treaty Organization Adv. Group for Aerospace Research and Devel.; executive chairman communications subgroup Australian, Canadian, New Zealand, United Kingdom, United States Tech. Coordination Program; instructor department math. Utica College, 1957-59; lecturer department elec. engineering Syracuse University, 1959-61; member educational council Massachusetts Institute of Technology, 1968—. Contributor articles to professional journals. Board of directors Rome Community Concert Association, 1968-80; trustee Jervis Public Library, 1977—, president, 1980-83; member industrial adv. committee University Massachusetts School Engring., Syracuse University School Engring.; ad hoc.

visitor Accreditation Board for Engring. and Tech. Served with United States Army, 1944-46. Recipient Meritorious Civilian Service medal U.S. Air Force, 1968, decoration for exceptional civilian service, 1978, 84, Outstanding Performance award Senior Executive Service, 1982, 83, 84, 85, 86, 87, Presidential Rank award Meritorious Executive. Fellow Institute of Electrical and Electronics Engineers, American Association for the Advancement of Science, American Institute of Aeronautics and Astronautics (associate). Club: Lake Delta Yacht. Office: Rome Air Devel Center Griffiss Air Force Base New York 13441

DIAMOND, SEYMOUR, physician; born Chicago, April 15, 1925; son of Nathan Avruum and Rose (Roth) D.; married Elaine June Flamm, June 20, 1948; children: Judi, Merle, Amy. Student, Loyola University, 1943-45; Bachelor of Medicine, Chicago Medical School, 1948, Doctor of Medicine, 1949. Intern White Cross Hospital, Columbus, Ohio, 1949-50; general practice medicine Chicago, 1950—; director Diamond Headache Clinic, Limited, Chicago, 1970—; member staff St. Joseph Hospital, Chicago; director inpatient headache unit Weiss Memorial Hospital, Chicago; professor neurology Chicago Medical School, 1970-82, adj. professor pharmacology; 1985—; lecturer department community and family medicine Loyola University Stritch School Medicine, 1972-78; consultant member Food and Drug Administration Orphan Products Devel. Initial Rev. Group; lecturer Falconbridge lecture series Laurentian University, Sudbury, Ontario, Can., 1987. Co-author: The Practicing Physician's Approach to Headache, 4th edit, 1986, More Than Two Aspirin: Help for Your Headache Problem, 1976, Advice from the Diamond Headache Clinic, 1982, Coping with Your Headaches, 1982, 2d edition (with Mary Franklin Epstein), 1987, Headache in Contemporary Patient Management series, 1983, Hope for Your Headache Problem, rev. edition, 1988 ; editor: Keeping Current in the Treatment of Headache; member editorial board Headache, Clinical Journal Pain, editorial cons. BIOSIS, 1986; contributor numerous articles on headache and related fields to books and professional journals. President Skokie (Illinois) Board Health, 1965-68. Recipient Distinguished Alumni award Chicago Medical School, 1977; National Migraine Foundation lectureship award, 1982; 1st recipient Migraine Trust lectureship, 1988; British Migraine Trust 7th International Migraine Syposium, London. Member American Medical Association (Physicians Recognition awards 1970-73, 74, 77, 79, 82, del. section clinical pharmacology and therapeutics, member health policy agenda for Am. People, member Cost Effectiveness Conference, del. reference committee "C" on education, reference committee C, 1988), Southern Medical Association, Am. Association Study of Headache (executive director 1971-85, president 1972-74, regent 1984), National Migraine Foundation (president 1971-77, executive director 1977—), World Federation Neurology (executive officer 1980—, research group on migraine and headache), Illinois Acad. General Practice (chairman mental health committee 1966-70), Illinois, Chicago med. socs., Biofeedback Society Am., International Association Study of Pain, Am. Society Clinical Pharmacology and

Therapeutics (chairman headache section 1982—, member committee coordination sci. sects. 1983—), Postgrad. Medical Association (president 1981), Southern Medical Association. Office: Diamond Headache Clinic 5252 N Western Avenue Chicago Illinois 60625

DIDIO, LIBERATO JOHN AL-PHONSE, anatomist, educator; born Sao Paulo, Brazil, May 7, 1920; son of Pascoal and Lydia (Cacace) DiD.; married Lydia S. Silva, March 12, 1960; children: Vera, Rubens, Lydia N.S., Arthur S. Bachelor of Science, Dante Alighieri College, 1939; Doctor of Medicine summa cum laude, University São Paulo, 1945, Doctor of Science summa cum laude, 1949, Doctor of Philosophy summa cum laude, 1951; postgraduate, National College War, Rio de Janeiro, 1957. Instructor physiology Faculty Medicine, University Sao Paulo, Brazil, 1942-43; instructor anatomy Faculty Medicine, University Sao Paulo, 1943-45, assistant professor anatomy; 1945-51, associate professor; 1952-53; teacher chemistry Roosevelt State College, Sao Paulo, 1943-44; professor, chairman department topographical anatomy Faculty Ciencias Medicas, Catholic University Minas Gerais, 1954-55; chairman department anatomy medical school Belo Horizonte, University Minas Gerais, 1954-63, director Institute Morphology; 1962-63; professor anatomy Medical School, Dental School, Grad. School, Northwestern University, Chicago, 1963-67; professor anatomy, chairman department Medical College Ohio, Toledo, 1967-88; dean grad. school Medical College Ohio, 1972-86, assistant to president; 1988—; visiting professor University Messina, Italy,

1955, University Brazil, 1957, University Parma, Italy, 1958, University Rome, 1974, 80, 82, 84, 86-87, University Brescia, University Padua, University Turin, 1988; visiting professor anatomy, Rockefeller Foundation fellow School Medicine, University Washington, 1960-61; guest investigator Rockefeller Institute Medical Research, New York City, 1961, Medical School, Harvard University, 1961; co-chairman 41st session 7th International Congress Anatomy, New York City, 1960; chairman session on heart and arteries International Congress Anatomy, Leningrad, 1970; del. International Congress for Electron Microscopy, Philadelphia, 1962, 8th International Congress Anatomy, Wiesbaden, Federal Republic Germany, 1965; del., co-chairman Session on Embryology I, Pan Am. Congress Anatomy, Mexico City, 1966; president III Congress, New Orleans, 1972; hon. president IV Pan Am. Congress Anatomy, Montreal, Can., 1975, V Congress, São Paulo, 1978, VI Congress, Buenos Aires, 1981, VII Congress, Punta del Este, 1984, VIII Congress Santiago, Chile, 1987; president 4th Symposium on Morphological Sciences, Toledo, Ohio, 1979, hon. president 5th Symposium, Rio, 6th Symposium, Lisbon, 7th Symposium, Brussels, 8th Symposium, Rome; chairman section meeting Chicago Heart Association University Chicago, 1967; adj. professor biology University Toledo, 1967—, adj. professor forensic medicine College Law, 1973—; adj. professor biology Bowling Green University, 1967; seminars at numerous universities, United States, Germany, Italy, Latin Am.; consultant Deputy Assuntos U.-Ministry Education and Culture Brazil, Pan Am.

Health Organization, World Health Organization, Heart Institute, São Paulo; member adv. committee on grad. education Ohio Board Regents; president International Committee of Symposia on Morphological Sciences. Contributor articles to professional journals. Trustee Siena Heights College, Adrian, Michigan, 1979-87. Decorated gt. of cl. Ipiranga Order Government State of Sao Paulo; recipient William H. Rorer award Am. College Gastroenterology, 1970; Andreas Vesalius award Mexican Association Anatomy, 1971; Honor Magistro award Brazilian Society Anatomy, University Rome, 1976; Gold medal Alumni Association Faculty Medicine, University Sao Paulo, 1977; Anatomist of Year award 4th International Symposium on Morphological Sciences, 1979, 5th edit., 1982, 6th, 1984, 7th, 1986; medal Arnaldo V. Carvalho Faculty Medicine, University São Paulo, 1979, University Florence, Italy, 1986, University Siena, Italy, 1987; named hon. citizen Belo Horizonte, Brazil, 1963, hon. citizen New Orleans, 1972, hon. professor Catholic University Chile, 1980, New University, Lisbon, 1986, University Brasilia, 1988; hon. member Acad. Sci. Purkinje, Prague, Czechslovakia, Acad. Medicine Turin, Italy. Fellow American Association for the Advancement of Science, New York Acad. Sciences; member Am. Association Cell Biology, Am. Association Anatomists, American Association of University Profs., Anatomical Society Great Britain and Ireland, Association Am. Medical Colls., Electron Microscopy Society Am., Pan Am. Medical Association, International College Surgeons, International Federation Assns. of Anatomists (secretary general 1980-86, president 1986—), Ohio Acad. Sci.

(president 1979-80), Pan Am. Association Anatomy (hon. president), Association Anatomy (former chairman), Midwest Society Anatomists (former president), Sigma Xi (former secretary and pres). Home: 3563 Edgevale Road Toledo Ohio 43606

DIENER, THEODOR OTTO, plant pathologist; born Zurich, Switzerland, February 28, 1921; came to United States, 1949, naturalized, 1955; son of Theodor Emanuel and Hedwig Rosa (Baumann) D.; married Sybil Mary Fox, May 11, 1968; children by previous marriage: Theodor W., Robert A., Michael S. Diploma, Swiss Federal Institute Tech., 1946; Doctor of Science, National Swiss Federal Institute Tech., 1948. Assistant Swiss Federal Institute Tech., Zurich, 1946-48; plant pathologist Swiss Federal Experimental Station, Waedenswil, 1949-50; assistant professor plant pathology Rhode Island State University, Kingston, 1950; assistant plant pathologist Washington State University, Prosser, 1950-55; associate plant pathologist Washington State University, 1955-59; research plant pathologist Agricultural Research Service, United States Department of Agriculture, Beltsville, Maryland, 1959-88; professor botany, senior staff sci. Agriculture Biotechnology Center, University Maryland, College Park, 1988—; lecturer universities and research institutes; Regents' lecturer University California, Riverside, 1970; A W Dimock lecturer Cornell University, 1975; Andrew D. White prof.-at-large Cornell University, 1979-81; James Law Distinguished lecturer New York State College Vet. Medicine, Cornell University, 1981; Distinguished lecturer Boyce

Thompson Institute for Plant Research, Cornell University, 1987. Author: Viroids and Viroid Diseases, 1979; editor: The Viroids, 1987; associate editor journal Virology, 1964-66, 74-76, editor journal, 1967-71; member editorial com. journal Annual Rev. Phytopathology, 1970-74, Annales de Virologie, 1980—; contributor articles to sci. publications.

Recipient Campbell award Am. Institute Biological Sciences, 1968, Governor's Citation State of Maryland, 1988, E.C. Stakman award University Minnesota, 1988, Alexander von Humboldt award, 1975, Superior Service award U.S. Department of Agriculture, 1969, Distinguished Service award, 1977, Wolf Prize in Agriculture, 1987, U.S. National Medal of Sci., 1987, E.C. Stakman award University Minnesota, 1988. Fellow Am. Phytopath. Society (Ruth Allen award 1976, Distinguished Service award, 1988), New York Acad. Sciences, Am. Acad. Arts and Sciences; member American Association for the Advancement of Science, National Acad. Sciences, Leopoldina, German Acad. Natural Scientists. Discoverer novel class of pathogens (viroids), 1971. Home: 4530 Powder Mill Road Post Office Box 272 Beltsville Maryland 20705 Office: Plant Virology Lab Agrl Research Center USDA Beltsville Maryland 20705

DIERKS, RICHARD ERNEST, veterinarian, educational administrator; born Flandreau, South Dakota, March 11, 1934; son of Martin and Lillian Ester (Benedict) D.; married Eveline Carol Amundson, July 20, 1956; children—Jeffrey Scott, Steven Eric, Joel Richard. Student, South Dakota State University, 1952-55; Bachelor of Science, University Minnesota, 1957, Doctor of Veterinary Medicine, 1959, Master of Public Health, 1964, Doctor of Philosophy, 1964; Master of Business Administration, University Illinois, 1985. Supervisory microbiologist Communicable Disease Center, Atlanta, 1964-68; professor college veterinary medicine Iowa State University, Ames, 1968-74; head department veterinary sci. Montana State University, Bozeman, 1974-76; deanColl. Veterinary Medicine University Illinois, Urbana, 1976-89; dean College Veterinary Medicine University Florida, Gainesville, 1989—; member training grant rev. committee National Institute Allergy and Infectious Diseases, 1973-74. Contributor articles on virology, immunology and epidemiology to professional journals. Served with United States Public Health Service, 1964-67. Career Devel. awardee National Institute Allergy and Infectious Diseases, 1969-74. Member Am., Illinois veterinary medicine associations, Am. Society Microbiologists, Am. College Veterinary Microbiologists, Am. College Veteran Preventive Medicine, Am. Association Immunologists, Society Experimental Biology and Medicine, Gamma Sigma Delta, Phi Kappa Phi, Phi Zeta. Republican. Lutheran. Club: Rotary. Office: U Fla College Veterinary Medicine Health Sci Center Post Office Box J-125 Gainesville Florida 32610-0125

DILCHER, DAVID L., paleobotany educator; born Cedar Falls, Iowa, July 10, 1936; married Katherine Swanson, 1961; children—Peter, Ann. Bachelor of Science in Natural History, University Minnesota, 1958, Master of Science in Botany, Geology and Zoology, 1960; postgraduate,

University Illinois, 1960-62; Doctor of Philosophy in Biology, Geology, Yale University, 1964; participant field course in field dendrology, Costa Rica, 1968. Teaching assistant University Minnesota, Minneapolis, 1958-60, University Illinois, Urbana, 1960-62, Yale University, New Haven, Connecticut, 1962-63; Cullman-Univ. fellow Yale University, 1963-64, instructor biology; 1965-66; National Science Foundation postdoctoral fellow Senckenberg Mus., Frankfurt am Main, Federal Republic of Germany, 1964-65; assistant professor botany Ind. University, Bloomington, 1966-70, associate professor; 1970-76; Guggenheim fellow Imperial College, University London, 1972-73; associate professor geology Ind. University, Bloomington, 1975-77, professor paleobotany; 1977—; panel member for systematic biology program, National Science Foundation, 1977, 78, 79, panel member for selecting North Atlantic Treaty Organization postdoctoral fellow, 1982; visiting lecturer to People's Republic of China National Acad. Sci. committee on scholarly communications with China, 1986. Author: (with D. Redmon, M. Tansey and D. Whitehead) Plant Biology Laboratory Manual, 1973, 2d edition, 1975; editor: (with Tom Taylor and Theodore Delevoryas) Plant Reproduction in the Fossil Record, symposium volume, 1979, (with T. Taylor) Biostratigraphy of Fossil Plants: Successional and Paleoecological Analysis, 1980, (with William L. Crepet) Origin and Evolution of Flowering Plants, Symposium Volume, 1984, (with Michael S. Zavada) Phylogeny of the Hamamedidae, symposium volume, 1986; contributor numerous articles and abstracts to professional journals and books.

Member utilities board City of Bloomington, 1974-76; ruling elder First Presbyterian Church Bloomington, 1975-77; board of directors United Campus Ministries, 1971-72; member council Monroe County United Ministries, 1975-77. District visiting research scholar University Adelaide, Australia, 1981, 88; grantee Sigma Xi, 1961, 62, 66, Ind. University, 1967-68, Organization Tropical Studies, 1971, travel grantee Ind. University, 1968, 71, 77, 80, research grantee National Science Foundation, 1966-69, 69-71, 71-74, 75-77, 77-79, 79, 79-80, 79-84, 82-83, 83-84, 85—, Amax Coal Foundation, 1980-81; Eaton-Hooker fellow, 1963, Cullman-Univ. fellow, 1963-64, Guggenheim fellow, Giessen, Federal Republic Germany, 1972-73, Ind. University, 1972-73, Brit. Mus. Natural History, London, 1973-74; recipient Tracey M. Sonneborn award for distinguished research and excellence in teaching, Ind. University, 1978-88. Fellow Ind. Acad. Sci., Linnean Society; member Botanical Society Am. (chairman paleobotanical section 1974, sec.-treas. 1975-77, representative to journal editorial board 1978-79, member journal editorial board 1981-82, member conservation committee 1978-81, chairman conservation committee 1981, 82, program director 1982-84, member executive board 1982—, secretary 1985-88, pres.-elect 1988-89), Paleontological Society, Paleontological Association, American Association for the Advancement of Science, International Organization Paleobotanists (North America representative 1975-81, vice president 1987—), Association Tropical Biology, Am. Institute Biological Sciences, Am. Association Stratigraphic Palynologists, International Association

Angiosperm Paleobotany (president 1977-80), Society Vertebrate Paleontology, Geological Society Am. (committee on collection and collecting 1978—), Kentucky Acad. Sciences, Sigma Xi (pres.-elect Ind. chapter 1985-86, president 1986-87). Office: Indiana University Department Biology Bloomington Indiana 47405

DIRECTOR, STEPHEN WILLIAM, electrical engineering educator, researcher; born Brooklyn, June 28, 1943; son of Murray and Lillian (Brody) D.; married Lorraine Schwartz, June 20, 1965; children: Joshua, Kimberly, Cynthia, Deborah. Bachelor of Science, State University of New York, Stony Brook, 1965; Master of Science, University Calif.-Berkeley, 1967, Doctor of Philosophy, 1968. Professor electrical engineering University Florida, Gainesville, 1968-77; visiting scientist International Business Machines Corporation Research Laboratories, Yorktown Heights, New York, 1974-75; professor electrical and computer engineering Carnegie-Mellon University, Pittsburgh, 1977—, U.A. and Helen Whitaker professor electronics and electrical engineering; 1980—, professor computer sci.; 1981—, head department electrical and computer engineering; 1982—; consultant Intel Corp., Santa Clara, California, 1977—, Digital Equipment Corp., Hudson, Massachusetts, 1982—, Calma Corp., 1985—; consultant editor McGraw-Hill Book Company, New York City, 1976—; director Research Center Computer-Aided Design, Pittsburgh, 1982—. Author: Introduction to System Theory, 1972, Circuit Theory, 1975; editor: Computer-Aided Design, 1974. Recipient Frederick Emmons Terman award Am. Society Engineering Education, 1976; named Outstanding Alumnus, State University of New York, Stony Brook, 1984. Fellow Institute of Electrical and Electronics Engineers (W.R.G. Prize 1979, Centennial medal 1984); member Institute of Electrical and Electronics Engineers Circuits and Systems Society (president 1981, Best Paper awards 1970, 85), Institute of Electrical and Electronics Engineers (associate editor jour 1973-75), Institute of Electrical and Electronics Engineers Computer Society. Office: Department Elec and Computer Engring Carnegie-Mellon U Schenley Park Pittsburgh Pennsylvania 15213

DJERASSI, CARL, chemist, educator, writer; born Vienna, Austria, October 29, 1923; son of Samuel and Alice (Friedmann) D.; married Norma Lundholm (divorced 1976); children: Dale, Pamela (deceased); married Diane W. Middlebrook, 1985. Bachelor of Arts summa cum laude, Kenyon College, 1942, Doctor of Science (honorary), 1958; Doctor of Philosophy, University Wisconsin, 1945; Doctor of Science (honorary), National University Mexico, 1953, Federal University, Rio de Janeiro, 1969, Worcester Polytechnic Institute, 1972, Wayne State University, 1974, Columbia, 1975, Uppsala University, 1977, Coe College, 1978, University Geneva, 1978, University Ghent, 1985, University Manitoba, 1985. Research chemist Ciba Pharmaceutical Products, Incorporated, Summit, New Jersey, 1942-43, 45-49; associate director research Syntex, Mexico City, 1949-52; research vice president Syntex, 1957-60; vice president Syntex Laboratories, Palo Alto, California, 1960-62; vice president Syntex Research, 1962-68, president; 1968-72; president of Zoecon Corp., 1968-

83, chairman board; 1968-86; professor chemistry Wayne State University, 1952-59, Stanford, 1959—; board of directors Cetus Corp., Monoclonal Antibodies, Incorporated, Affymax, Vitaphore Incorporated; president Djerassi Foundation Resident Artists Program. Member editorial board Journal Organic Chemistry, 1955-59, Tetrahedron, 1958—, Steroids, 1963—, Proceedings of National Acad. Scis, 1964-70, Journal Am. Chemical Soc, 1966-75, Organic Mass Spectrometry, 1968—, Chemica Scripta, 1985—; author 9 books; Contributor numerous articles to professional journals, poems and short stories to lit. publications. Recipient Intrascience Research Foundation award, 1969; Freedman Patent award Am. Institute Chemists, 1970; Chemical Pioneer award, 1973; National Medal Sci., 1973; Perkin medal, 1975; Wolf prize in chemistry, 1978; John and Samuel Bard award in Sci. and Medicine, 1983, Roussel prize, 1988, Discoverers award Pharm. Manual Association, 1988, Esselen award American College of Surgeons, 1988; named to National Inventors Hall of Fame, 1978. Member National Acad. Sciences (Institute Medicine), Am. Chemical Society (award pure chemistry 1958, Baekeland medal 1959, Fritzsche award 1960, award for creative invention 1973, award in chemistry of contemporary tech. problems 1983), Royal Society Chemistry (hon. fellow, Centenary lecturer 1964), Am. Acad. Arts and Sciences, German Acad. (Leopoldina), Royal Swedish Acad. Sciences (foreign), Royal Swedish Acad. Engineering Sciences (foreign), Am. Acad. Pharmaceutical Sciences (hon.), Brazilian Acad. Sciences (foreign), Mexican Acad. Sci. Investigation, Bulgarian Acad. Sciences (foreign), Phi Beta Kappa, Sigma Xi, Phi Lambda Upsilon (hon.). Office: Stanford U Department Chemistry Stanford California 94305

DOLBY, RAY MILTON, engineering company executive, electrical engineer; born Portland, Oregon, January 18, 1933; son of Earl Milton and Esther Eufemia (Strand) D.; married Dagmar Baumert, August 19, 1966; children—Thomas Eric, David Earl. Student, San Jose State College, 1951-52, 55, Washington University, St. Louis, 1953-54; Bachelor of Science in Electrical Engineering, Stanford University, 1957; Doctor of Philosophy in Physics (Marshall scholar 1957-60, Draper's studentship 1959-61, National Science Foundation fellow 1960-61), Cambridge University, England, 1961. Electronic technician/jr. engineer Ampex Corp., Redwood City, California, 1949-53; engineer Ampex Corp., 1955-57, senior engineer; 1957; predoctoral research student in physics Cavendish Laboratory, Cambridge University, 1957-61, research in long wavelength x-rays; 1961-63; fellow Pembroke College, 1961-63; consultant United Kingdom Atomic Energy Authority, 1962-63; United Nations Educational, Scientific and Cultural Organization adviser Central Sci. Instruments Organization, Chandigarh, Punjab, India, 1963-65; owner, chairman Dolby Laboratories Incorporated, San Francisco and London, 1965—. Trustee University High School, San Francisco, 1978-84; board of directors San Francisco Opera; board governors San Francisco Symphony; member Marshall Scholarship selection committee, 1979-85. Served with United States Army, 1953-54. Recipient Beech-Thompson award

Stanford University, 1956; Emmy award for contribution to 1st video recorder, 1957; Trendsetter award Billboard, 1971; Top 200 Executives Bi-Centennial award, 1976; Lyre award Institute High Fidelity, 1972; Emile Berliner Maker of the Microphone award Emile Berliner Association, 1972; Sci. and Engineering award Acad. Motion Picture Arts and Sciences, 1979; Pioneer award International Teleprodn. Society, 1988; named Officer of the Most Excellent Order of the British Empire (O.B.E.), 1986, Man of Year International Tape Association, 1987; hon. fellow Pembroke College, Cambridge University, 1983. Fellow Audio Engineering Society (board govs. 1972-74, 79-84 Silver Medal award 1971, president 1980-81), Brit. Kinematograph, Sound, TV Society, Society Motion Picture and TV Engineers (Samuel L. Warner award 1979, Alexander M. Poniatoff Gold Medal 1982, Progress award 1983), Institute Broadcast Sound; member Institute of Electrical and Electronics Engineers, Tau Beta Pi. Club: St. Francis Yacht. Inventions, research, publications in video tape recording, x-ray microanalysis, noise reduction and quality improvements in audio and video systems; patentee. Office: Dolby Labs 100 Potrero Avenue San Francisco California 94103

DONALDSON, COLEMAN DUPONT, consulting engineer; born Philadelphia, September 22, 1922; son of John W. and Renee (duPont) D.; married Barbara Goldsmith, January 17, 1945; children: B. Beirne, Coleman duPont, Evan F., Alexander M., William M. Bachelor of Science in Aeronautical Engineering, Rensselaer Polytechnic Institute, 1943; Master of Arts, Princeton University, 1954, Doctor of Philosophy, 1957. Staff, National Advisory Committee for Aeronautics, Langley Field, Virginia, 1943-44; head aerophysics section National Advisory Committee for Aeronautics, 1946-52; general aerodynamics USAC, Wright Field, Ohio, 1945-46; aerodynamic evaluation Bell Aircraft, Niagara Falls, New York, 1946; senior consultant, president Aero Research Associates of Princeton, New Jersey, 1954-79, chairman board; 1979-86; group general manager Aero Research Associates Princeton Incorporated, 1986-87; vice president Titan Systems, Incorporated, 1986-87; retired 1987; consultant missile guidance and control General Precision Equipment Corp., 1957-68; consultant magnetohydro-dynamics Thompson Ramo Wooldridge, Incorporated, 1958-61; consultant aerodynamic heating, general aerodynamics Martin Marietta Corp., 1955-72; general editor Princeton series on high speed aerodynamics and jet propulsion, 1955-64; consultant boundary layer stability, aerodynamic heating, missile and ordnance systems department General Electric Company, 1956-72; consultant Grumman Aerospace Corp., 1959-72; Robert H. Goddard visiting lecturer with rank of professor Princeton University, 1970-71; member research and tech. adv. council panel on research National Aeronautics and Space Administration, 1969-76, hypersonic tech. committee, 1986—; member industrial professional adv. committee Pennsylvania State University, 1970-77; member President's Air Quality Adv. Board, 1973-74; chairman laboratory adv. board for air warfare Naval Research Adv. Committee,

1972-77; member Marine Corps panel Naval Reserve Adv. Committee, 1972-77, Naval Research Adv. Committee, 1986—; chairman adv. council department aerospace and mechanical sciences Princeton University, 1973-78. Author articles on aerodynamics. Fellow American Institute of Aeronautics and Astronautics (Dryden Research lecture award 1971, general chairman 13th aerospace scis. meeting 1975), National Acad. Engineering, Am. Physical Society, Sigma Xi, Delta Phi. Home: Glencoe Farm Post Office Box 279 Gloucester Virginia 23061

DONCHIN, EMANUEL, psychologist, educator; born Tel Aviv, April 3, 1935; came to United States, 1961; son of Michael and Guta D.; married Rina Greenfarb, June 3, 1955; children: Gill, Opher, Ayala. Bachelor of Arts, Hebrew University, 1961, Master of Arts, 1963; Doctor of Philosophy, University of California at Los Angeles, 1965. Teaching and research assistant department psychology Hebrew University, 1958-61; research assistant department psychology University of California at Los Angeles, 1961-63, research psychologist; 1964-65; research associate div. neurology Stanford University Medical School, 1965-66, assistant professor in residence; 1966-68; research associate neurobiology branch National Aeronautics and Space Administration, Ames Research Center, Moffett Field, California, 1966-68; associate professor department psychology University Illinois, Urbana-Champaign, 1968-72; professor psychology and physiology University Illinois, 1972—, head department psychology; 1980—. Author: (with Donald P. Lindsley) Averaged Evoked Potentials, 1969; editor: Cognitive

Psychophysiology, 1984, (with M.G.H. Coles and Southwest Porges) Handbook of Psychophysiology, 1986; contributor articles to professional journals. Served with Israeli Army, 1952-55. Fellow American Association for the Advancement of Science, Am. Psychological Association; member Society Psychophysiological Research (president 1980), Federation Behavioral, Cognitive and Psychological Societies (vice president 1981-85), Am. EEG Society, Psychonomic Society, Society Neuroscis. Office: Department Psychology U Illinois 603 E Daniel St Champaign Illinois 61820

DONOVAN, ALLEN FRANCIS, aerospace company executive; born Onondaga, New York, April 22, 1914; son of Paul Andrew and May (Hudson) D.; married Beverly Fay, August 14, 1940 (divorced); 1 son, Allen Michael; married Doris Mildred Efram, April 17, 1953 (divorced); children: Kathryn Ellen, Marshall Stephen; married June Wallace Healy, August 30, 1974. Bachelor of Science in Aeronautical Engineering, University Michigan, 1936, Master of Science, 1936, Doctor Engineering (honorary), 1964. With Curtiss-Wright Corp., Glenn L. Martin, Stinson Aircraft, Vultee Aircraft, 1936-46; head aeronautical mechanics department Cornell University Aeronautical Laboratory, 1946-55; director aeronautical research and devel. staff Ramo-Woolridge Corp. (name changed to Space Tech. Laboratories, Incorporated), 1955-58, vice president; 1958-60; senior vice president tech. Aerospace Corp., 1960-78; executive consultant 1978—; consultant President's Sci. Adv. Committee, 1957-72; member Air Force Sci. Adv. Board, 1948-57, 59-

68; United States del. Geneva Conference, 1959; member space systems committee National Aeronautics and Space Administration, 1972-77; consultant Sci. and Tech. Policy Office, National Science Foundation, 1973-76. Editor volumes on high speed aerodynamics, jet propulsion.; Author tech. papers on space vehicles, aeronautics. Recipient Medal for exceptional civilian services U.S. Air Force, 1968; recipient Sci. award Air Force Association. Fellow American Institute of Aeronautics and Astronautics; member National Acad. Engineering, Sigma Xi. Club: California Yacht. Home: 35 Beachcomber Dr Corona Del Mar California 92625

DOOB, JOSEPH LEO, mathematician, educator; born Cincinnati, February 27, 1910; son of Leo and Mollie (Doerfler) D.; married Elsie Haviland Field, June 26, 1931; children—Stephen, Peter, Deborah. Bachelor of Arts, Harvard University, 1930, Master of Arts, 1931, Doctor of Philosophy, 1932; Doctor of Science (honorary), University Illinois, 1981. Faculty University Illinois, Urbana, 1935—; successively associate, assistant professor, associate professor University Illinois, 1935-45, professor math.; 1945—, now emeritus professor. Recipient National Medal of Sci., 1979. Member National Acad. Sciences, Am. Acad. Arts and Sciences, Acad. Sciences (Paris) (foreign associate). Home: 208 W High St Urbana Illinois 61801

DOUGHERTY, ELMER LLOYD, JR., petroleum engineering educator, consultant; born Dorrance, Kansas, February 7, 1930; son of Elmer Lloyd and Nettie Linda (Anspaugh) D.; married Joan Victoria Benton, November 25, 1952 (divorced June 1963); children—Sharon, Victoria, Timothy, Michael (deceased); married Ann Marie Da Silva. Student, Fort Hays State College, 1946-48; Bachelor of Science in Chemical Engineering, University Kansas, 1950; Master of Science in Chemical Engineering, University Illinois, 1952, Doctor of Philosophy in Chemical Engineering, 1955. Chemical engineer Esso Standard Oil Company, Baton Rouge, 1951-52; chemical engineer Dow Chemical Company, Freeport, Texas, 1955-58; research engineer Standard Oil of California, San Francisco, 1958-65; manager management sci. Union Carbide Corp., New York City, 1965-68; consultant chemical engineering Stamford, Connecticut and Denver, 1968-71; professor petroleum engineering University Southern California, Los Angeles, 1971—; consultant OPEC, Vienna Austria, 1978-82, SANTOS, Limited, Adelaide, Australia, 1980—. Contributor numerous articles to professional journals. Member Society Petroleum Engineers (chairman Los Angeles Basin section 1984-85, Ferguson medal 1964, Distinguished Member award 1983), Am. Institute Chemical Engineers, International Association Energy Economists, Institute Management Sci. Republican. Clubs: El Niguel Country (board dirs. 1976-78) (Laguna Niguel, California). Avocations: golf; poetry recitals. Home: 33531 Marlinspike Dr Laguna Niguel California 92677 Office: U Southern California University Park HED-306 Los Angeles California 90089

DRAKE, FRANK DONALD, astronomy educator; born Chicago, May 28, 1930; son of Richard Carvel and Winifred (Thompson) D.; married Elizabeth Bell, March 7, 1953 (divorced 1979); children: Stephen, Richard, Paul; married Amahl Zekin Shakhashiri, March 4, 1978; children: Nadia, Leila. Bachelor in Engineering Physics, Cornell University, 1952; Master of Arts in Astronomy, Harvard University, 1956, Doctor of Philosophy in Astronomy, 1958. Astronomer National Radio Astronomical Observatory, Green Bank, West Virginia, 1958-63; section chief Jet Propulsion Laboratory, Pasadena, California, 1963-64; professor Cornell University, Ithaca, New York, 1964-84; director National Astronomical and Ionospace Center, Ithaca, 1971-81; dean natural sci. department University California, Santa Cruz, 1984-88, professor; 1984—. Author: Intelligent Life in Space, 1962, Murmurs of Earth, 1978. Lieutenant United States Navy, 1947-55. Fellow American Association for the Advancement of Science, Am. Acad. Arts and Sciences; member National Acad. Sciences, International Astronomical Union (chair United States national committee), Astronomical Society Pacific (president 1988—), Seti Institute (president chapter 1984—). Avocation: jewelry making. Office: U California Santa Cruz California 95064

DRELL, SIDNEY DAVID, physicist; born Atlantic City, September 13, 1926; son of Tulla and Rose (White) D.; married Harriet Stainback, March 22, 1952; children: Daniel White, Persis Sydney, Joanna Harriet. Bachelor of Arts, Princeton University, 1946; Master of Arts, University Illinois, 1947, Doctor of Philosophy, 1949; Doctor of Science (honorary), University Illinois, Chicago, 1981. Research associate University Illinois, 1949-50; instructor physics Stanford, 1950-52, associate professor; 1956-60, professor; 1960-63; professor Stanford Linear Accelerator Center, 1963—, Lewis M. Terman professor and fellow; 1979-84, deputy director; 1969—, executive head theoretical physics; 1969-86; co-director Stanford Center for International Security and Arms Control, 1985—; research associate Massachusetts Institute of Technology, 1952-53, assistant professor, 1953-56; visiting scientist Guggenheim fellow European Organization of Nuclear Research Laboratory, Switzerland, 1961, University Rome, 1972; visiting professor, Loeb lecturer Harvard University, 1962, 70; visiting Schrodinger professor theoretical physics University Vienna, 1975; consultant Office Sci. and Tech., 1960-73, Office Sci. and Tech. Policy, 1977-82, Arms Control and Disarmament Agency, 1969-81, Office Tech. Assessment United States Congress, 1975—, National Security Council, 1973-81; member high energy physics adv. panel Department Energy, 1973-86, chairman, 1974-82, member energy research adv. board, 1978-80; member Jason, 1960—; Richtmyer lecturer to Am. Association Physics Teachers, San Francisco, 1978; visiting fellow All Souls College, Oxford, 1979; Danz lecturer University Washington, 1983; I.I. Rabi visiting professor Columbia University, 1984. Author 3 books; contributor articles to professional journals. Trustee Institute Advanced Study, Princeton, 1974-83; board governors Weizmann Institute Sci., Rehovoth, Israel, 1970—; board of directors Annual Revs., Incorporated, 1976—; member President Sci. Adv. Committee, 1966-70. Recipient Ernest Orlando

Lawrence Memorial award and medal for research in theoretical physics Atomic Energy Commission, 1972; Alumni award for distinguished service in engineering University Illinois, 1973; MacArthur fellow, 1984—. Fellow Am. Physical Society (president 1986, Leo Szilard award for physics in the public interest 1980); member National Acad. Sciences, Am. Acad. Arts and Sciences, Am. Philo. Society, Arms Control Association (board directors 1978—), Council on Foreign Relations. Home: 570 Alvarado Row Stanford California 94305 Office: Stanford Linear Accelerator Center Post Office Box 4349 Stanford California 94305

DRESSELHAUS, MILDRED SPIEWAK, engineering educator; born Brooklyn, November 11, 1930; daughter of Meyer and Ethel (Teichteil) Spiewak; married Gene F. Dresselhaus, May 25, 1958; children: Marianne, Carl Eric, Paul David, Eliot Michael. Bachelor of Arts, Hunter College, 1951, Doctor of Science (honorary), 1982; Fulbright fellow, Cambridge (England) University, 1951-52; Master of Arts, Radcliffe College, 1953; Doctor of Philosophy in Physics, University Chicago, 1958; Doctor Engineering (honorary), Worcester Polytechnic Institute, 1976; Doctor of Science (honorary), Smith College, 1980, Hunter College, 1982, New Jersey Institute Tech., 1984; Doctorat Honoris Causa, University Catholique de Louvain, 1988. National Science Foundation postdoctoral fellow Cornell University, 1958-60; member staff Lincoln Laboratory, Massachusetts Institute of Technology, 1960-67, professor electrical engineering; 1968—, associate department head electrical engineering; 1972-74, professor physics; 1983—; Abby Rockefeller Mauzé visiting professor Massachusetts Institute of Technology, 1967-68, Abby Rockefeller Mauzé professor; 1973-85, Institute professor; 1985—, director Center for Materials Sci. and Engineering; 1977-83; visiting professor department physics University Campinas (Brazil), summer 1971, Technion, Israel Institute Tech., Haifa, Israel, summer 1972, Nihon and Aoyama Gakuin Universities, Tokyo, summer 1973, IVIC, Caracas, Venezuela, summer 1977; Graffin lecturer Am. Carbon Society, 1982; chairman steering committee of evaluation panels National Bureau Standards, 1978-83; member Energy Research Adv. Board, 1984—; board of directors The Alliance Fund, Rogers Corp., Quantum Chemical Corp. Contributor articles to professional journals. Board governors Argonne National Lab.; member governing board National Research Council, 1984-87. Named to Hunter College Hall of Fame, 1972; recipient Alumnae medal Radcliffe College, 1973, Killian Faculty Achievement award, 1986-87. Fellow Am. Physical Society (president 1984), Am. Acad. Arts and Sciences, Institute of Electrical and Electronics Engineers, American Association for the Advancement of Science (board directors 1985—); member National Acad. Engineering (council 1981-87), Society Women Engineers (Achievement award 1977), National Acad. Sciences (council 1987—, chairman engineering section 1987—); corr. member Brazilian Acad. Sci. Home: 147 Jason St Arlington Massachusetts 02174 Office: Massachusetts Institute of Technology Cambridge Massachusetts 02139

DRUCKER, DANIEL CHARLES, engineer, educator; born New York City, June 3, 1918; son of Moses Abraham and Henrietta (Weinstein) D.; married Ann Bodin, August 19, 1939; children: R. David, Mady. Bachelor of Science, Columbia University, 1937, Master of Civil Engineering, 1938, Doctor of Philosophy, 1940; Doctor Engineering (honorary), Lehigh University, 1976; Doctor of Science in Tech. (honorary), Technion, Israel Institute Tech., 1983; Doctor of Science (honorary), Brown University, 1984, Northwestern University, 1985. Instructor Cornell University, 1940-43; supervisor Armour Research Foundation, Chicago, 1943-45; assistant professor Illinois Institute Tech., 1946-47; associate professor Brown University, Providence, 1947-50, professor; 1950-64, L. Herbert Ballou University professor; 1964-68, chairman div. engineering; 1953-59, chairman physical sciences council; 1960-63; dean College Engineering University Illinois, Urbana, 1968-84; grad. research professor engineering sciences University Florida, Gainesville, 1984—; Marburg lecturer American Society for Testing and Materials, 1966; member, past chairman United States National Committee on Theoretical and Applied Mechanics; past chairman adv. committee for engineering National Science Foundation; member National Sci. Board, 1988—; hon. chairman 3d SESA International Congress on Experimental Mechanics. Author: Introduction to Mechanics of Deformable Solids, 1967; contributor chapters to tech. books, papers to mechanical and sci. journals. Recipient Gustave Trasenster medal University Liège, Belgium, 1979, Thomas Egleston medal Columbia University School Engring and Applied Sci., 1978, John Fritz medal Founder Engineering Socs., 1985, National Medal of Sci., 1988; Guggenheim fellow, 1960-61; NATO Senior Sci. fellow, 1968; Fulbright Travel grantee, 1968. Fellow American Institute of Aeronautics and Astronautics (associate), American Society of Mechanical Engineers (hon. member, chairman applied mechanics division 1963-64, vice president policy board communications 1969-71, president 1973-74, Timoshenko medal 1983, Thurston lecturer 1986, Distinguished lecturer 1987-89), Am. Acad. Mechanics (past president), Am. Acad. Arts and Sciences, American Association for the Advancement of Science (past chairman section engineering, member council), American Society of Civil Engineers (von Karman medal 1966, past president New England council, past president Providence section, past chairman executive committee engineering mechanics division); member NSPE, Rhode Island Society Professional Engineers, Illinois Society Professional Engineers (hon.), Society Experimental Stress Analysis (hon.; past president, W.M. Murray lecturer 1967, M.M. Frocht award 1971), Am. Technion Society (past president Southern N.E. chapter), Society Rheology, Am. Society Engineering Education (charter fellow member, past 1st vice president, past chairman engineering coll. council, director, president 1981-82, Lamme award 1967, Distinguished Educator, Mechanics division 1985), National Academy of Engineering (member committee on pub. engineering policy 1972-75, chairman membership policy committee 1982-85), Society Engineering Sci. (William Prager medal 1982), Polish Acad. Sciences (foreign member), International Union Theoretical and Applied Mechanics (treasurer 1972-80, president 1980-84, vice president 1984—), International Council Sci. Unions (past member general committee), Sigma Xi (past president Brown University chapter), Phi Kappa Phi, Tau Beta Pi, Pi Tau Sigma, Chi Epsilon, Sigma Tau. Research in stress-strain relations, finite plasticity, stability, fracture and flow on macroscale and microscale. Office: U Fla 231 Aerospace Engring Building Gainesville Florida 32611

DU BRIDGE, LEE ALVIN, physicist; born Terre Haute, Indiana, September 21, 1901; son of Frederick Alvin and Elizebeth Rebecca (Browne) DuB.; married Doris May Koht, September 1, 1925 (deceased November 1973); children—Barbara (Mrs. David MacLeod), Richard Alvin; married Arrola Bush Cole, November 30, 1974. Bachelor of Arts, Cornell College, Iowa, 1922, Doctor of Science, 1940; Master of Arts, University Wisconsin, 1924, Doctor of Philosophy, 1926; Doctor of Science, Wesleyan University, 1946, Polytechnic Institute Brooklyn, 1946, Washington University, 1948, University British Columbia, 1947, Occidental College, 1952, University Maryland, 1955, Columbia, 1957, Ind. University, 1957, University Wisconsin, 1957, Pennsylvania Military College, De Pauw University, 1962, Pomona College, Rockefeller Institute, Carnegie Institute Tech., 1965, Syracuse University, 1969, Rensselaer Polytechnic Institute, 1970; Doctor of Laws, University California, 1948, University Rochester, 1953, University Southern California, 1957, Northwestern University, 1958, Loyola University of Los Angeles, 1963, University Notre Dame, 1967, Illinois Institute Tech., 1967; Doctor of Humane Letters, Redlands University, 1958, University Judaism, 1958; Doctor of Civil Law, Union College, 1961. Assistant in physics University Wisconsin, 1922-25, instructor; 1925-26; National Research Council fellow California Institute Tech., 1926-28; assistant professor physics Washington University, St. Louis, 1928-33; associate professor Washington University, 1933-34; professor physics, chairman department physics University Rochester, 1934-46, dean faculty arts sciences; 1938-41; investigator National Defense Research Committee; director radiation laboratory Massachusetts Institute of Technology, 1940-45; president California Institute Tech., 1946-69; president emeritus 1970—; sci. adviser to President United States, 1969-70; Trustee Rand Corp., Santa Monica, California, 1948-61; member sci. adv. committee General Motors, 1971-75; Member general adv. committee A.E.C., 1946-52; Naval Research Adv. Committee, 1945-51, Air Force Sci. Adv. Board, 1945-49; sci. advisor Weingart Foundation, 1979—; member President's Communications Policy Board, 1950-51, National Sci. Board, 1950- 54, 58-64; chairman sci. adv. committee Office Defense Mobilization, 1952-56. Author: (with A.L. Hughes) Photoelectric Phenomena, 1932, New Theories of Photoelectric Effect, 1935, Introduction to Space, 1960; Contributor numerous sci. and educational articles to magazines. Member National Manpower Council, 1951-64; member National Adv. Health Council, 1960-61; member distinguished civilan service awards board United States Civil Service

Commission, 1963-65; chairman Greater Los Angeles Urban Coalition, 1968-69; member President's Air Quality Adv. Board, 1968-69, President's Sci. Adv. Committee, 1970-72; board of directors National Merit Scholarship Corp., 1963-69, National Educational TV, New York, 1962-69; Trustee Mellon Institute, 1958-67, Rockefeller Foundation, 1956-67, Nutrition Foundation, 1952-63, Carnegie Endowment International Peace, 1951-57, Community TV Southern California, Los Angeles, 1962-69, Henry E. Huntington Library and Art Gallery, 1962-69, Thomas Alva Edison Foundation, 1960-69, Pasadena Hall Sci., 1977-78.
Recipient Research Corp. award, 1947; Medal for Merit U.S., 1948; King's Medal for Service Great Britain, 1946; Recipient Vannevar Bush award National Science Foundation, 1982; Benjamin Franklin fellow Royal Society Arts. Fellow Am. Physical Society (president 1947); member National Acad. Sci., Am. Philosophical Society, American Association for the Advancement of Science, Phi Beta Kappa, Sigma Pi Sigma, Eta Kappa Nu, Sigma Xi, Tau Kappa Alpha, Tau Beta Pi. Presbyterian. Home: 1730 Homet Road Pasadena California 91106

DUFFY, ROBERT ALOYSIUS, aeronautical engineer; born Buck Run, Pennsylvania, September 9, 1921; son of Joseph Albert and Jane Veronica (Archer) D.; married Elizabeth Reed Orr, August 19, 1945; children: Michael Gordon, Barclay Robert, Marian Orr, Judith Elizabeth, Patricia Archer. Bachelor of Science in Aeronautical Engineering, Georgia Institute Tech., 1951. Commissioned 2d lieutenant United States Army, 1942; commissioned United States Air Force, advanced through grades to brigadier general; 1967; service in Canal Zone, Morocco, Algeria, Tunisia, Sicily, Italy, Vietnam; vice commander United States Air Force Space and Missile Systems Organization, Los Angeles, 1970-71; retired 1971; vice president, director Draper Laboratory div. Massachusetts Institute of Technology, Cambridge, Massachusetts, 1971-73; president, chief executive officer Charles Stark Draper Laboratory, Incorporated, 1973-87, director; 1973—; director Harvard Trust. Contributor articles to professional journals. Decorated Distinguished Service medal, Legion of Merit; recipient Thomas D. White award National Geog. Society, 1970. Fellow American Institute of Aeronautics and Astronautics; member International Acad. Astronautics, National Acad. Engineering, Institute Navigation (Thurlow award 1964, president 1976-77), Air Force Association, Defense Sci. Board, United States Naval Institute. Clubs: Algonquin (Boston); Concord Country. Home: 115 Indian Pipe Lane Concord Massachusetts 01742 Office: Charles Stark Draper Lab 555 Technology Square Cambridge Massachusetts 02139

DUGAN, PATRICK RAYMOND, microbiologist, university dean; born Syracuse, New York, December 14, 1931; son of Francis Patrick and Joan Irma (Clause) D.; married Patricia Ann Murray, September 22, 1956; children: Susan Eileen, Craig Patrick, Wendy Shawn, Carolyn Paige. Bachelor of Science, Syracuse University, 1956, Master of Science, 1959, Doctor of Philosophy, 1964. Associate research scientist Syracuse University Research Corp., 1956-63; member faculty Ohio State University,

Columbus, 1964—, associate professor; 1968-70, professor, chairman department microbiology; 1970-73; acting dean Ohio State University (College Biological Sciences), 1978-79, dean; 1979-85; principal scientist, director Center for Bioprocessing Tech. EG&G Idaho National Engineering Laboratory, Idaho Falls, 1987—. Author: Biochemical Ecology of Water Pollution, 1972. Trustee, Columbus Zool. Association and Zoo, 1982-87. Fellow Am. Acad. Microbiology; member Am. Society Microbiology (Ohio president 1968-70), American Association for the Advancement of Science, Society Industrial Microbiology, Water Pollution Control Federation, Ohio Acad. Sci., Sigma Xi. Club: Creichton.

DUKLER, ABRAHAM EMANUEL, chemical engineer; born Newark, January 5, 1925; son of Louis and Netty (Charles) D.; children—Martin Alan, Ellen Leah, Malcolm Stephen. Bachelor of Science, Yale University, 1945; Master of Science, University Delaware, 1950, Doctor of Philosophy, 1951. Devel. engineer Rohm & Haas Company, Philadelphia, 1945-48; research engineer Shell Oil Company, Houston, 1950-52; member faculty department chemical engineering University Houston, 1952—, professor; 1963—, chairman department; 1967-73, dean engineering; 1976-83; director State of Texas Energy Council, 1973-75; consultant Schlumberger-Doll Research Company, Brookhaven National Laboratory, Shell Devel. Company, Exxon, others. Contributor chapters to books, articles to professional journals. Recipient Research award Alpha Chi Sigma, 1974. Fellow Am. Institute Chemical Engineers (research award), National Acad. Engineering, Am. Society Engineering Education (research lectureship award 1976); member Am. Institute Chemical Engineers, American Society of Mechanical Engineers, American Association for the Advancement of Science, Am. Chemical Society, American Association of University Women, Sigma Xi, Tau Beta Pi. Office: College of Engring University of Houston Houston Texas 77004

DULBECCO, RENATO, biologist, educator; born Catanzaro, Italy, February 22, 1914; came to United States, 1947, naturalized, 1953; son of Leonardo and Maria (Virdia) D.; married Gulseppina Salvo, June 1, 1940 (divorced 1963); children: Peter Leonard (deceased), Maria Vittoria; married Maureen Muir; 1 daughter, Fiona Linsey. Doctor of Medicine, University Torino, Italy, 1936; Doctor of Science (honorary), Yale University, 1968, Vrije Universiteit, Brussels, 1978; Doctor of Laws, University Glasgow, Scotland, 1970. Assistant University Torino, 1940-47; research associate Ind. University, 1947-49; senior research fellow California Institute Tech., 1949-52, associate professor, then professor biology; 1952-63; senior fellow Salk Institute Biological Studies, San Diego, 1963-71; assistant director research Imperial Cancer Research Fund, London, 1971-74; deputy director research Imperial Cancer Research Fund, 1974-77; distinguished research professor Salk Institute, La Jolla, California, 1977—; professor pathology and medicine University California at San Diego Medical School, La Jolla, 1977-81, member Cancer Center; visiting professor Royal Society Great Britain, 1963-64,

Leeuwenhoek lecturer, 1974; Clowes Memorial lecturer, Atlantic City, 1961; Harvey lecturer Harvey Society, 1967; Dunham lecturer Harvard University, 1972; 11th Marjory Stephenson Memorial lecturer, London, 1973, Harden lecturer, Wye, England, 1973, Am. Society for Microbiology lecturer, Los Angeles, 1979; Member California Cancer Adv. Council, 1963-67; adv. board Roche Institute, New Jersey, 1968-71, Institute Immunology, Basel, Switzerland, 1969-84; chairman senior council International Association Breast Cancer Research, 1980-84; president, trustee Am.-Italian Foundation for Cancer Research. Trustee LaJolla Country Day School. Recipient John Scott award City Philadelphia, 1958; Kimball award Conference Pub. Health Laboratory Directors, 1959; Albert and Mary Lasker Basic Medical Research award, 1964; Howard Taylor Ricketts award, 1965; Paul Ehrlich-Ludwig Darmstaedter prize, 1967; Horwitz prize Columbia University, 1973; (with David Baltimore and Howard Martin Temin) Nobel prize in medicine, 1975; Targa d'oro Villa San Giovanni, 1978; Mandel Gold medal Czechoslovak Acad. Sciences, 1982; named Man of Year London, 1975; Italian Am. of Year San Diego County, California, 1978; hon. citizen City of Imperia (Italy), 1983; Guggenheim and Fulbright fellow, 1957-58; decorated grand ufficiale Italian Republic, 1981; hon. founder Hebrew University, 1981. Member National Acad. Sciences (Selman A. Waksman award 1974), Am. Acad. Arts and Sciences, Am. Association Cancer Research, International Physicians for Prevention Nuclear War, Accademia Nazionale dei Lincei (foreign), Accademia Ligure di Scienze e Lettre (hon.), Royal Society (foreign member). Club: Athenaeum. (London).

DUNBAR, MAXWELL JOHN, educator, oceanographer; born Edinburgh, Scotland, September 19, 1914; son of William and Elizabeth (Robertson) D.; married Joan Jackson, August 1, 1945; children: Douglas, William; married Nancy Wosstroff, December 14, 1960; children: Elisabeth, Andrew, Christine, Robyn. Bachelor of Arts, Oxford (England) University, 1937, Master of Arts, 1939; Doctor of Philosophy, McGill University, 1941; Doctor of Science (honorary), Memorial University, Newfoundland, 1979. Member faculty McGill University, Montreal, 1946—, professor; 1959—; also chairman department marine sci., director Marine Sci. Center; director climate research group department Meteorology McGill U, 1987—; director Eastern Arctic Investigations, Can., 1947-55. Author: Eastern Arctic Waters, 1951, Ecological Development in Polar Regions, 1968, Environment and Good Sense, 1971; contributor articles professional journals. Guggenheim fellow Denmark, 1952-53; recipient Bruce medal Royal Society Edinburgh, 1950, Fry medal Can. Society Zoologists, 1979, Arctic Sci. prize North Slope Borough, 1986, Northern Sci. award (Can.), 1987, J.P. Tully medal Can. Meteorol. and Oceanography Society, 1988. Fellow Royal Society Can., Linnaean Society London, Arctic Institute North America (governor, past chairman, recipient Fellows award 1973); member Can. Meteorological and Oceanography Society (medal in oceanography 1988). Home: 488 Strathcona Avenue, Westmount, Province of Quebec Canada H3Y 2X1

DURANT, JOHN RIDGEWAY, physician; born Ann Arbor, Michigan, July 29, 1930; son of Thomas Morton and Jean Margaret (deVries) D.; married Marlene Hamlin, June 28, 1974; children: Christine Joy, Thomas Arthur, Michele Grace, Jennifer Margaret. Bachelor of Arts, Swarthmore (Pennsylvania) College, 1952; Doctor of Medicine, Temple University, Philadelphia, 1956. Diplomate: Am. Board Internal Medicine. Intern, then junior assistant resident in medicine Hartford (Connecticut) Hospital, 1956-58; resident in medicine Temple University Medical Center, 1960-62; special fellow medical neoplasia Memorial Hospital for Cancer and Allied Diseases, New York City, 1962-63; Am. Cancer Society advanced clinical fellow Temple University Health Sciences Center, 1964-67, instructor, then assistant professor medicine; 1963-67; clinical associate chemotherapy Moss Rehabilitation Hospital, Philadelphia, 1964-67; research associate Fels Research Institute, Philadelphia, 1965-67; member faculty University Alabama Medical Center, Birmingham, 1968-82; professor medicine, director comprehensive cancer center University Alabama Medical Center, 1970-82, professor radiation oncology; 1978-82, chairman Southeastern cooperative cancer study group at university; 1975-82, Distinguished faculty lecturer; 1980; president Fox Chase Cancer Center, Philadelphia, 1982-88; senior vice president health affairs and director medical center University Alabama, Birmingham, 1988—; chairman cooperative group executive committee National Cancer Institute, National Institutes of Health, 1977-82, chairman cooperative group chairmen, 1979-82; consultant Veteran's Administration Hospital, Tuskegee, Alabama, 1970-82; executive committee Birmingham chapter American Red Cross, 1972-77; member National Cancer Adv. Board, 1986. Editorial board: Cancer Clinical Trials, 1979-82, associate editor, 1982—; Editorial board: Medical and Pediatric Oncology, 1979-82; editorial adv. board: Oncology News, 1975—; associate editor Cancer, 1984—; contributor numerous articles to medical journals. Served as officer Medical Corps United States Naval Reserve, 1958-60. Named Temple University Medical School Alumnus Year, 1982. Fellow American College of Physicians, College Physicians Philadelphia; member Am. Cancer Society (vice chairman advanced clinical fellowship committee 1974-76, 1985—, member institutional research grant committee 1979-82, president Alabama division 1973-75, 77-79), Am. Association Cancer Research, Am. Radium Society (president 1984), Am. Board Medical Oncology (subcom. 1979-85, chairman 1983-85), Association Am. Cancer Insts. (director 1978—, president 1982-83), Association Community Cancer Centers (director 1979-81), Am. Society Clinical Oncology (chairman public relations committee 1976-79, board directors 1979-82, 1984-87, president 1985-86), American College of Surgeons, Southeastern Cancer Research Association (president 1976—), American Medical Association, Am. Federation Clinical Research, Am. Association Cancer Education, Medical Association Alabama, American Association for the Advancement of Science, Am. Society Hematology, Alpha Omega Alpha. Presbyterian. Office: University

Alabama University Station Birmingham Alabama 35294

DURKEE, JACKSON LELAND, civil engineer; born Tatanagar, India, September 20, 1922; son of E. Leland and Bernice A. (Jackson) D.; married Marian H. Carty, February 20, 1943; children—Janice Durkee Parry, Judith Durkee Burton, Christine Durkee Simpson. Bachelor.S.in Civil Engineering, Worcester Polytechnic Institute, 1943, Civil Engineer, 1951; Master of Civil Engineering, Cornell University, 1947. Registered professional engineer, California, Connecticut, New York, Pennsylvania; chartered engineer, United Kingdom. Various engineering positions Fabricated Steel Construction div. Bethlehem Steel Corp., 1947-65, chief bridge engineer; 1965-76; partner Modjeski and Masters, consultant engineers, Harrisburg, Pennsylvania, 1977-78; consultant structural engineer Bethlehem, Pennsylvania, 1978—; visiting professor structural engineering Cornell University, 1976; member numerous tech. and professional committees. Contributor articles on bridge design, constrn. and research to professional journals; designer, inventor suspension bridge cable and anchorage constrn. techniques. Served to lieutenant United States Naval Reserve, 1944-46, PTO. Recipient constrn. industry citation Engineering News-Record, 1968. Fellow American Society of Civil Engineers (Ernest E. Howard award 1982), Institution Civil Engineers (United Kingdom), Institution Structural Engineers (United Kingdom); member National Society Professional Engineers, Am. Railway Engineering Association, Am. Welding Society, Structural Stability Research Council, Am. Institute Steel Constrn., International Association for Bridge and Structural Engineering. Republican. Member Moravian Church Clubs: Silver Creek Country (Hellertown, Pennsylvania); Cosmos (Washington); St. Andrews Golf, New Golf (St. Andrews, Scotland). Home and Office: 217 Pine Top Trail Bethlehem Pennsylvania 18017

DYNKIN, EUGENE B., mathematics educator; born Leningrad, Union of Soviet Socialist Republics, May 11, 1924; came to United States, 1977, naturalized, 1983; son of Boris and Rebecca (Sheindlin) D.; married Irene Pakshver, June 2, 1959; 1 child, Olga. Bachelor of Arts, Moscow University, 1945, Doctor of Philosophy, 1948, Doctor of Science, 1951. Assistant professor Moscow University, 1948-49, associate professor; 1949-54, professor; 1954-68; senior research scholar Central Institute Math. Economic Acad. of Sci., Moscow, 1968-76; professor math. Cornell University, Ithaca, New York, 1977—. Author: Theory of Markov Processes, 1960, Mathematical Conversations, 1963, Markov Processes, 1965, Mathematical Problems, 1969, Markov Processes-Theorems and Problems, 1969, Controlled Markov Processes, 1979, Markov Processes and Related Problems of Analysis, 1982; contributor articles to professional journals. Fellow American Association for the Advancement of Science, Institute Math. Statistics; member National Acad. Sciences, Am. Math. Society, Bernoulli Society Math. Statistics and Probability. Home: 107 Lake St Ithaca New York 14850 Office: Cornell U Department Math White Hall Ithaca New York 14853

DYSART, BENJAMIN CLAY, III, environmental engineer, educator, consultant; born Columbia, Tennessee, February 12, 1940; son of Benjamin Clay and Kathryne Virginia (Thompson) D.; married Virginia Carole Livesay, September 3, 1960. Bachelor of Civil Engineering, Vanderbilt University, 1961, Master of Science in Sanitary Engineering, 1964; Doctor of Philosophy in Civil Engineering, Georgia Institute Tech., 1969. Staff engineer Union Carbide Corp., 1961-62, 64-65; from assistant professor, associate professor to professor Clemson University, 1968—, McQueen Quattlebaum professor engineering; 1982-83, director South Carolina Waters Resources Research Institute; 1968-75, director water resources engineering grad. program; 1972-75; sci. advisor Office Secretary of Army, Washington, 1975-76; member Environmental Protection Agency Sci. Adv. Board, from 1983; senior fellow The Conservation Foundation, 1985—; member adv. council Electric Power Research Institute, 1989—; member, chief of engineers environmental adv. board United States Army Corps Engineers, 1988—; member Glacier National Park Sci. Council, National Park Service, 1988—; member South Carolina Gov.'s Wetlands Forum, 1989—; secretary appointee Outer Continental Shelf Adv. Board and OCS Sci. Committee Department Interior, 1979-82; member South Carolina Environmental Quality Control Adv. Committee, from 1980, chairman, 1980-81; member Sci. Panel to Rev. Interagy. Research on Impact of Oil Pollution National Oceanographic and Atmospheric Administration, Department Commerce, 1980; member Nuclear Energy Center Environmental Task Force Department Energy-So. States Energy Board, 1978-81; member Nonpoint Source Pollutant Task Force Environmental Protection Agency, 1979-80; member civil works adv. committee Office Secretary Army-Young President's Organization, 1975-76; member South Carolina Heritage Adv. Board South Carolina Wildlife and Marine Resources Department, 1974-76; consultant on environmental protection, water resources, siting, energy production matters to industry and government agys., 1969—. Contributor articles on math. modeling in water quality and environ. mgmt. to professional journals; author numerous professional papers, reports. Trustee Rene Dubos Center for Human Environs., 1985—, secretary, member executive committee, 1988—; board visitors Kanuga Episcopal Conference Center, 1988—. Recipient Tribute of Appreciation for Distinguished Service Environmental Protection Agency, 1981, 86, McQueen Quattlebaum Engineering Faculty Achievement award Clemson University, 1982, Order of Palmetto Gov. South Carolina, 1984, Hon. Member award Water Pollution Control Federation, 1987. Member National Wildlife Federation (board directors 1974—, vice president 1978-83, president, chairman board 1983-85), Am. Geophysical Union, American Society of Civil Engineers, Association Environmental Engineering Profs. (board directors 1978-83, president, chairman board 1981-82), South Carolina Wildlife Federation (board directors from 1969, president, chairman board 1973-74, South Carolina Wildlife Conservationist of Yr), Phi Kappa Phi, Tau Beta Pi, Sigma Xi, Chi Epsilon, Omega Rho, Sigma

Nu. Episcopalian. Club: Cosmos (Washington). Home: 216 Holiday Avenue E Clemson South Carolina 29631 Office: Clemson U 401 Rhodes Research Center Clemson South Carolina 29634-0919

DYSON, FREEMAN JOHN, physicist; born Crowthorne, England, December 15, 1923; son of George and Mildred Lucy (Atkey) D.; married Verena Haefeli-Huber, August 11, 1950 (divorced 1958); children—Esther, George; married Imme Jung, November 21, 1958; children—Dorothy, Emily, Mia, Rebecca. Bachelor of Arts, Cambridge University, 1945. Operations research Royal Air Force Bomber Command, 1943-45; fellow Trinity College, Cambridge University, England, 1946-49; Commonwealth fellow Cornell University, Princeton, 1947-49; professor physics Cornell University, 1951-53; professor Institute Advanced Study, Princeton, 1953—. Author: Disturbing the Universe, 1979, Weapons and Hope, 1984, Origins of Life, 1986, Infinite in all Directions, 1988. Fellow Royal Society London; member Am. Physical Society, National Acad. Sciences. Home: 105 Battle Road Circle Princeton New Jersey 08540

EARLE, SYLVIA ALICE, research biologist, oceanographer; born Gibbstown, New Jersey, August 30, 1935; daughter of Lewis Reade and Alice Freas (Richie) E. Bachelor of Science, Florida State University, 1955; Master of Arts, Duke University, 1956, Doctor of Philosophy, 1966. Resident director Cape Haze Marine Laboratory, Sarasota, Florida, 1966-67; research scholar Radcliffe Institute, 1967-69; research fellow Farlow Herbarium, Harvard University, 1967-75, researcher; 1975—;

research associate in botany Natural History Mus. Los Angeles County, 1970-75; research biologist, curator California Acad. Sciences, San Francisco, from 1976; research associate University California, Berkeley, 1969-75; founder, vice president, secretary-treasurer, board of directors Deep Ocean Tech., Incorporated, Oakland, California; founder, vice president, secretary-treasurer Deep Ocean Engineering, Oakland, 1981-88, chief executive officer, 1988—, also board of directors. Author: Exploring the Deep Frontier, 1980. Editor: Scientific Results of the Tektite II Project, 1972-75. Contributor 60 articles to professional journals. Trustee World Wildlife Fund United States, 1976-82, council member, 1984—; trustee World Wildlife Fund International, 1979-81, council member, 1981—; trustee Charles A. Lindbergh Fund., Ocean Trust Foundation; council member International Union Conservation Nature, 1979-81; corp. member Woods Hole Oceanographic Institute; member National Adv. Committee Oceans and Atmosphere, 1980-84. Recipient Conservation Service award U.S. Department Interior, 1970, Boston Sea Rovers award, 1972, 79, Nogi award Underwater Society Am., 1976, Conservation service award California Acad. Sci., 1979, Lowell Thomas award Explorer's Club, 1980, Order of Golden Ark Prince Netherlands, 1980; named Woman of Year Los Angeles Times, 1970, Scientist of Year, California Mus. Sci. and Industry, 1981. Fellow American Association for the Advancement of Science, Marine Tech. Society, California Acad. Sciences, Explorers Club, California Acad. Sci.; member International Phycological Society (secretary 1974-

80), Phycological Society Am., Am. Society Ichthyologists and Herpetologists, Am. Institute Biological Sciences, Brit. Phycological Society, Ecological Society Am., International Society Plant Taxonomists. Club: Explorers (fellow). Home: 12612 Skyline Boulevard Oakland California 94619 Office: California Acad Scis Golden Gate Park San Francisco California 94118

EASTERDAY, BERNARD CARLYLE, veterinary medicine educator; born Hillsdale, Michigan, September 16, 1929; son of Harley B. and Alberta M. Easterday. Doctor of Veterinary Medicine, Michigan State University, 1952; Master of Science, University Wisconsin, 1958, Doctor of Philosophy, 1961. Diplomate Am. Coll. Veterinary Microbiologists. Private practice veterinary medicine Hillsdale, Michigan, 1952; veterinarian United States Department Defense, Frederick, Maryland, 1955-61; associate professor to professor veterinary medicine University Wis.-Madison, 1961—, dean School Vet. Medicine; 1979—; member, chairman committee animal health National Acad. Sci.-NRC, Washington, 1980-83, member committee on sci. basis meat and poultry inspection program, 1984-85; member tech. adv. committee Binat. Agricultural Research and Devel., Bet-Degan, Israel, 1982-84; member expert adv. panel on zoonoses World Health Organization, Geneva, 1978-84; member tech. adv. committee on avian influenza USDA, 1983-85. Served to 1st lieutenant V.C. United States Army, 1952-54. Recipient Distinguished Alumnus award College Vet. Medicine, Michigan State University, 1975; named Wisconsin Veterinarian of Year, Wisconsin Vet. Medical Association, 1979. Member American Veterinary Medical Association, Am. Association Veteran Medical Colls., Am. Association Avian Pathologists. Office: School Veteran Medicine 2015 Linden Dr W Madison Wisconsin 53706

EBERT, JAMES DAVID, research biologist; born Bentleyville, Pennsylvania, December 11, 1921; son of Alva Charles and Anna Frances (Brundege) E.; married Alma Christine Goodwin, April 19, 1946; children—Frances Diane, David Brian, Rebecca Susan. Bachelor of Arts, Washington and Jefferson College, 1942, Doctor of Science, 1969; Doctor of Philosophy, Johns Hopkins, 1950; Doctor of Science, Yale, 1973, Ind. University, 1975; Doctor of Laws, Moravian College, 1979. Junior instructor biology Johns Hopkins, 1946-49, Adam T. Bruce fellow biology; 1949-50, hon. professor biology; 1956-86; hon. professor embryology Johns Hopkins (School Medicine), 1956-86; instructor biology Massachusetts Institute Tech., 1950-51; assistant professor zoology Ind. University, 1951-54, associate professor; 1954-56, Patten visiting professor; 1963; director department embryology Carnegie Institution of Washington, 1956-76, president; 1978-87, trustee; 1987; director Chesapake Bay Institute Johns Hopkins University, 1987—; visiting scientist medical department Brookhaven National Laboratory, 1953-54; Philips visiting professor Haverford College, 1961; instructor in charge embryology training program Marine Biological Laboratory, summers 1962-66, trustee, 1964—, president, 1970-78, director, 1970-75, 77-78; member Commission on Undergrad. Education in Biological

Sciences, 1963-66; member visiting committee for biological and physical sciences Western Reserve University, 1964-68; Member panels on morphogenesis and biology of neoplasia of committee on growth National Research Council, 1954-56; member adv. panel on genetic and developmental biology National Science Foundation, 1955-56, member divisional committee for biology and medicine, 1962-66, member university sci. devel. panel, 1965-70, adv. committee for institutional devel., 1970-72; member panel basic biological research in aging Am. Institute Biological Sci., 1957-60; member panel on cell biology National Institutes of Health, United States Public Health Service, 1958-62, member child health and human devel. training committee, 1963-66; member board sci. counselors National Cancer Institute, 1967-71, National Institute Child Health, 1973-77; member Committee on Scholarly Communication with People's Republic of China, 1978-81; member visiting committee to department biology Massachusetts Institute Tech., 1959-68; member visiting committee biology Harvard, 1969-75, Princeton, 1970-76; chairman board sci. overseers Jackson Laboratory, 1976-80; member Institute Medicine. Author: (with others) The Chick Embryo in Biological Research, 1952, Molecular Events in Differentiation Related to Specificity of Cell Type, 1955, Aspects of Synthesis and Order in Growth, 1955, Interacting Systems in Development, 2d edit, 1970, Biology, 1973, Mechanisms of Cell Change, 1979; Member editorial board: (with others) Abstracts of Human Developmental Biology; editor: (with others) Oceanus; Contributor (with others) articles to professional journals. Trustee Jackson Lab., Worcester Foundation, Associated Univs. Served as lieutenant United States Naval Reserve, 1942-46. Decorated Purple Heart. Fellow American Association for the Advancement of Science (vice president med. scis. 1964), Am. Acad. Arts and Sciences, International Society Developmental Biology; member National Acad. Sciences (chairman assembly life scis. 1973-77, vice president 1981—, chairman Government, University, INdustry Research Roundtable, 1987—), Am. Philosophical Society, Am. Institute Biological Sciences (president 1963, Pres.'s medal 1972), Am. Society Naturalists, Am. Society Zoologists (president 1970), Society Study Growth and Devel. (president 1957-58), Phi Beta Kappa, Sigma Xi, Phi Sigma. Home: 4100 N Charles St Baltimore Maryland 21218 Office: Johns Hopkins U Chesapeake Bay Institute 711 W 40th St Suite 340 Baltimore Maryland 21211

ECCLES, SIR JOHN CAREW, physiologist; born Melbourne, Australia, January 27, 1903; son of William James and Mary (Carew) E.; married Irene Miller, 1928; 9 children; married Helena Táboríková, 1968. Bachelor of Medicine, Bachelor of Science, Melbourne University, 1925; Master of Arts, Oxford University, 1929, Doctor of Philosophy, 1929; Doctor of Laws, Melbourne University, 1965; Doctor of Science (honorary), University British Columbia, 1966, Cambridge University, 1960, University Tasmania, 1964, Gustavus Adolphus, 1967, Marquette University, 1967, Loyola University, 1969, Yeshiva University, 1969, Charles University, Prague,

1969, Oxford University, 1974, University Fribourg, 1981, University Torino, 1983, Georgetown University, 1984, University Tsukuba, Japan, 1986. Research fellow Exeter College, Oxford University, 1927-34; tutorial fellow Magdalen College, 1934-37; director Kanematsu Memorial Institute Pathology, Sydney (Australia) Hospital, 1937-43; professor physiology Otago University, Dunedin, New Zealand, 1944-51, Australian National University, Canberra, 1951-66; member AMA/E.R.F. Institute Biomed. Research, Chicago, 1966-68; distinguished professor State University of New York, Buffalo, 1968-75. Author: (with others) Reflex Activity of the Spinal Cord, 1932; The Neurophysiological Basis of Mind: The Principles of Neurophysiology, 1953; The Physiology of Nerve Cells, 1957; The Physiology of Synapses, 1964; (with Ito, Szentagothai) The Cerebellum as a Neuronal Machine, 1967; The Inhibitory Pathways of the Central Nervous System, 1968; Facing Reality, 1970; The Understanding of the Brain, 1973; (with Karl Popper) The Self and Its Brain, 1977; (with others) Molecular Neurobiology of the Mammalian Brain, 1978, 2d edition, 1987; (with W. Gibson) Sherrington, His Life and Thought, 1979; The Human Mystery, 1979; The Human Psyche, 1980; (with D.N. Robinson) The Wonder of Being Human: Our Brain, Our Mind, 1984; Evolution of the Brain: Creation of the Conscious Self, 1989. Decorated knight bachelor, 1958; Royal medal Royal Society, 1962; Order of the Rising Sun; Gold and Silver Stars, 1986; Cothenius medal Deutche Akademie der Naturforscher Leopoldina; Nobel prize in physiology and medicine (with A. L. Hodgkin and A. F. Huxley), 1963. Fellow Royal Society, 1941, Australia Acad. Sci. (president 1957-61); member Pontifical Acad. Sciences, Am. Philosophical Society (hon.), Accademia Nazionale del Lincei (foreign hon.), National Academy of Sciences (foreign associate), Am. Physiological Society (foreign hon.), American College of Physicians (hon.), Am. Acad. Arts and Sciences (foreign hon.), Max Planck Society (hon.). Research, numerous publications on the physiology of synapses of the nervous system and chemical transmitters. Home: Ticino, CH-6646 Contra Switzerland

ECKENHOFF, JAMES EDWARD, physician, educator; born Easton, Maryland, April 2, 1915; son of George L. and Ada (Ferguson) E.; married Bonnie Lee Youngerman, June 4, 1938 (divorced January 1973); children: Edward Alvin, James Benjamin, Walter Leroy, Roderic George; married Jane M. Mackey, September 22, 1973. Bachelor of Science, University Kentucky, 1937; Doctor of Medicine, University Pennsylvania, 1941; Doctor of Science, Transylvania University, 1970. Diplomate: Am. Board Anesthesiology (bd. dirs. 1965-73, pres. 1972-73). Intern Good Samaritan Hospital, Lexington, Kentucky, 1941-42; Harrison fellow anesthesia University Pennsylvania, 1945-48; member faculty University Pennsylvania (Medical School and Grad. School), 1948-65, professor anesthesiology; 1955-65; physician anesthetist Hospital University Pennsylvania, 1948-65; professor anesthesia Northwestern University Medical School, Chicago, 1966-85; chairman department Northwestern University Medical School, 1966-70;

dean Northwestern University Medical School (Medical School), 1970-83; president McGaw Medical Center, 1980-85; fellow faculty anesthesia, also Hunterian professor Royal College Surgeons; chief anesthesia Passavant Memorial Hospital, Chicago, 1966-70; chairman anesthesia Chicago Wesley Hospital, 1966-70; consultant Veteran's Administration Research Hospital, Childrens Hospital, Chicago, 1966—, surgeon general United States Navy, 1964—; member surgery study section National Institutes of Health, 1962-66, anesthesia training committee, 1966-70; visiting professor Australian and New Zealand Society Anesthetists, 1968, South African Society Anesthetists, 1970; director National Board Medical Examiners, 1975-87, treasurer, 1979-83. Author: (with others) Introduction to Anesthesia, 7th edit, 1987, Anesthesia from Colonial Times, 1966, also numerous articles.; Editor: (with others) Science and Practice in Anesthesia, 1965, (with J. Beal) Intensive and Recovery Room Care, 1969, Journal Anesthesiology, 1958-62, Yearbook of Anesthesia, 1970-81, Controversy in Anesthesiology, 1979. Trustee Evanston Hospital, 1972-83, Rehabilitation Institute Chicago, 1972-83, Northwestern Memorial Hospital, 1973—, Children's Memorial Hospital, 1977-83, Illinois Hospital Association, 1983-85, La Porte (Indiana) Hospital, 1986—, vice chairman, 1988-89, chairman 1989—. Served to captain Medical Corps Army of the United States, 1942-45, European Theatre of Operations. Commonwealth Fund fellow Queen Victoria Hospital, East Grinstead, England, 1961-62; named Veteran's Administration Distinguished Physician, 1984, 89. Fellow Institute Medicine Chicago (George

Coleman award 1985), American College of Physicians; member Australian, New Zealand, South African socs. anesthesiologists, Philadelphia College Physicians, Society Acad. Anesthesia Chairmen (president 1967-68), Society Medical Consultants to Armed Forces, Am. Society Anesthesiologists (Distinguished Service award 1981), Illinois Society Anesthesiologists (Ralph Waters award 1984), American Medical Association, Association University Anesthetists (president 1962), Am. Association University Profs., Illinois Council Medical Deans (president 1973-74), Chicago, Illinois med. socs., Am. Physicians Art Association, Am. Physiological Society.

ECKSTEIN, JOHN WILLIAM, physician, educator; born Central City, Iowa, November 23, 1923; son of John William and Alice (Ellsworth) E.; married Imogene O'Brien, June 16, 1947; children—John Alan, Charles William, Margaret Ann, Thomas Cody, Steven Gregory. Bachelor of Science, Loras College, 1946; Doctor of Medicine, University Iowa, 1950. Assistant professor internal medicine University Iowa, Iowa City, 1956-60; associate professor University Iowa, 1960-65, professor; 1965—; associate dean Veteran's Administration Hospital affairs, 1969-70, dean college medicine; 1970—; chairman cardiovascular study section National Institutes of Health, 1970-72, National Heart, Lung and Blood Adv. Council, 1974-78; general research support rev. committee National Institutes of Health, 1980-84. Author papers and abstracts. Served with United States Army Air Force, 1943-45. Rockefeller Foundation postdoctoral fellow, 1953-54; Am. Heart Association Research fellow, 1954-55; National Heart Institute special research fellow, 1955-56; Am. Heart Association established investigator, 1958-63; recipient U.S. Pub. Health Service Research Career award, 1963-70. Member Am. Heart Association (member publs. committee subcom. on heart 1986—, vice president 1969, chairman council on circulation 1969-71, president 1978-79), American Medical Association (member health policy agenda panel 1982-86, governing council section on med. schs. 1985—), Am. Federation Clinical Research (chairman Midwestern section 1965), Central Society Clinical Research (sec.-treas. 1965-70, president 1973-74), Am. Society Clinical Investigation, Am. Clinical and Climatological Association, Association Am. Physicians, Association Am. Medical Colls. (executive council 1981-82, adminstrv. board 1980-82, 85-86), Institute of Medicine of National Acad. Sciences. Home: 1415 William White Boulevard Iowa City Iowa 52240 Office: U Iowa 200 HBRF College Medicine Iowa City Iowa 52242

EDELMAN, GERALD MAURICE, biochemist, educator; born New York City, July 1, 1929; son of Edward and Anna (Freedman) E.; married Maxine Morrison, June 11, 1950; children: Eric, David, Judith. Bachelor of Science, Ursinus College, 1950, Doctor of Science, 1974; Doctor of Medicine, University Pennsylvania, 1954, Doctor of Science, 1973; Doctor of Philosophy, Rockefeller University, 1960; Doctor of Medicine (honorary), University Siena, Italy, 1974; Doctor of Science, Gustavus Adolphus College, 1975; Doctor of Science, Williams College, 1976. Medical house officer Massachusetts General Hospital, 1954-55; assistant physician hospital of Rockefeller University, 1957-60, member faculty; 1960—, associate dean grad. studies; 1963-66, professor; 1966-74, Vincent Astor distinguished professor; 1974—; member biophysics and biophys. chemistry study section National Institutes of Health, 1964-67; member Sci. Council, Center for Theoretical Studies, 1970-72; associate, sci. chairman Neurosciences Research Program, 1980—, director Neuroscis. Institute, 1981—; member adv. board Basel Institute Immunology, 1970-77, chairman, 1975-77; non-resident fellow, trustee Salk Institute, 1973-85; board overseers Faculty Arts and Sciences, University Pennsylvania, 1976-83; trustee, member adv. committee Carnegie Institute, Washington, 1980-87; board governors Weizman Institute Sci., 1971-87, member emeritus. Trustee Rockefeller Brothers Fund., 1972-82. Served to captain Medical Corps Army of the United States, 1955-57. Recipient Spencer Morris award University Pennsylvania, 1954; Annual Alumni award Ursinus College, 1969; Nobel prize for physiology or medicine, 1972; Albert Einstein Commemorative award Yeshiva University, 1974; Buchman Memorial award California Institute Tech., 1975; Rabbi Shai Shacknai memorial prize Hebrew U.-Hadassah Medical School, Jerusalem, 1977; Regents medal Excellence, New York State, 1984; Hans Neurath Prize, University Washington, 1986; Sesquicentennial Commemorative award National Library Medicine, 1986. Fellow American Association for the Advancement of Science, New York Acad. Sciences, New York Acad. Medicine; member Am. Philosophical Society, Am. Society Biological

Chemists, Am. Association Immunologists, Genetics Society Am., Harvey Society (president 1975-76, Am. Chemical Society, Eli Lilly award biological chemistry 1965), Am. Acad. Arts and Sciences, National Acad. Sci., Am. Society Cell Biology, Acad. Sciences of Institute France (foreign), Japanese Biochem. Society (hon.), Pharmaceutical Society Japan (hon.), Society Developmental Biology, Council Foreign Relations, Sigma Xi, Alpha Omega Alpha. Research structure of antibodies, molecular and devel. biology. Office: Neuroscis Institute Neuroscis Research Program Smith Hall Annex 1230 York Avenue New York New York 10021

EDGAR, THOMAS FLYNN, chemical engineering educator; born Bartlesville, Oklahoma, April 17, 1945; son of Maurice Russell and Natalie (Flynn) E.; married Donna Jean Proffitt, July 15, 1967; children: Rebecca, Jeffrey. Bachelor of Science in Chemical Engineering, University Kansas, 1967; Doctor of Philosophy in Chemical Engineering, Princeton University, 1971. Registered professional engineer, Texas. Process engineer Conoco, Baltimore, 1968-69; professor chemical engineering University Texas, Austin, 1971—, chairman department; 1985—; professor chemical engineering University California, Berkeley, 1978; president CACHE Corp., Austin, Texas, 1981-84; vice president Am. Automatic Control Council, Chicago, 1988-89. Author: Coal Processing and Pollution Control, 1983; co-author: Real Time Computing, 1982, Optimization of Chemical Processes, 1988, Process Dynamics and Control, 1989; editor: Chemical Process Control, 1981, In Situ (Marcel Dekker), 1977-89; also journals. Member Am. Institute Chemical Engineers (Outstanding Counselor award 1974 Colburn award 1980, editorial board journal 1983-85, chairman cast division 1986, director 1989—), Am. Society Engineering Education (Westinghouse award 1988), Instrument Society Am., Tau Beta Pi, Phi Lambda Upsilon, Omicron Delta Kappa, Phi Kappa Phi (Joe King award University Texas chapter 1989). Democrat. Methodist.

EDGERTON, HAROLD EUGENE, educator, electrical engineer; born Fremont, Nebraska, April 6, 1903; son of Frank Eugene and Mary Nettie (Coe) C.; married Esther May Garrett, February 25, 1928; children—Mary Louise, William Eugene, Robert Frank. Bachelor of Science, University Nebraska, 1925, Doctor of Engineering (honorary), 1948; Master of Science, Massachusetts Institute Tech., 1927, Doctor of Science, 1931; Doctor of Laws (honorary), Doane College, 1969, University South Carolina, 1969. Electrical engineer Nebraska Light & Power Company, 1920-25, General Electric Company, 1925-26; assistant professor Massachusetts Institute of Technology, 1932-38, associate professor; 1938-48, professor; 1948; partner Edgerton and Germeshausen, 1931, Edgerton and Grier, 1934, EG&G Incorporated, 1947. Author: (with James R. Killian, Junior) Moments of Vision, 1979, Electronic Flash, Strobe, 1979, Sonar Timesd, 1986, Stopping the Times: The Photographs of Harold Edgerton, 1987; also numerous tech. articles. Trustee New England Aquarium, Boston, 1965, Mus. Sci., Boston, 1967. Recipient medal Royal Photog. Society, Gold medal National Geog. Society, Modern Pioneer award, Potts medal Franklin Institute, Albert A. Michelson medal, 1969, National Medal Honor, 1973, National Medal Tech., 1988. Fellow Institute of Electrical and Electronics Engineers, Am. Institute Electrical Engineers, Society Motion Pictures and TV Engineers, Royal Society Great Britain; member National Acad. Sciences, National Acad. Engineers, Marine Tech. Society, Sigma Xi, Eta Kappa Nu, Sigma Tau. Republican. Congregationalist Club: Mason. Inventor of stroboscopic high-speed motion and still photography apparatus; designer underwater camera and high-resolution sonar equipment. Home: 100 Memorial Dr Cambridge Massachusetts 02142 Office: Massachusetts Institute of Technology Room 4-405 Cambridge Massachusetts 02139

EDMONDSON, W(ALLACE) THOMAS, limnologist, educator; born Milwaukee, April 24, 1916; son of Clarence Edward and Marie (Kelley) E.; married Yvette Hardman, September 26, 1941. Bachelor of Science, Yale University, 1938, Doctor of Philosophy, 1942; postgraduate, University Wisconsin, 1938-39; Doctor of Science (honorary), University Wisconsin, Milwaukee, 1987. Research associate Am. Mus. Natural History, 1942-43, Woods Hole Oceanographic Institution, 1943-46; lecturer biology Harvard University, Cambridge, Massachusetts, 1946-49; member faculty University Washington, Seattle, 1949—, professor; 1957-86, professor emeritus; 1986—, Jessie and John Danz lecturer; 1987; Brode lecturer Whitman College, 1988. Editor: Freshwater Biology (Ward and Whipple), 2d edit, 1959; contributor articles to professional journals. National Science Foundation sr. postdoctoral fellow Italy, England and Sweden, 1959-60; recipient Einar Naumann-August Thienemann Medal International Association Theoretical and Applied Limnology, 1980, Outstanding Pub. Service award University Washington, Seattle, 1987. Member National Acad. Sciences, Am. Microscopic Society, National Acad. Sciences (Cottrell award 1973), American Association for the Advancement of Science, Am. Society Limnology and Oceanography, International Association Limnology, Am. Society Naturalists, Phycol. Society Am., Ecological Society Am. (Distinguished Ecologist award 1983). Office: U Wash Department Zoology NJ-15 Seattle Washington 98195

EDWARDS, CHARLES, neuroscientist, educator; born Washington, September 22, 1925; son of James Moses and Lola (Rosenthal) Edlavitch; married Lois Bender, August 12, 1951; children: Jan, James, Sally, David. Bachelor of Arts, Johns Hopkins University, 1945, Master of Arts, 1948, Doctor of Philosophy, 1953. Foundation Infantile Paralysis postdoctoral fellow, assistant lecturer University College, London, 1953-55; instructor, assistant professor physiological optics Johns Hopkins University, Baltimore, 1955-58; assistant professor physiology University Utah, Salt Lake City, 1958-60; associate professor physiology University Minnesota, Minneapolis, 1960-65, professor; 1965-67; professor biological sciences, director neurobiology research center State University of New York, Albany, 1967-84; member physiology study section National Institutes of Health, 1971-75; special assistant to sci. director National Institute Diabetes and

Digestive and Kidney Diseases, National Institutes of Health, 1984—. Member editorial board Am. Journal Physiology, 1967-73, General Physiology Biophysics, 1983—, Neurosci., 1979—, Neurosci. Research, 1984—. Lalor fellow, 1957; Lederle fellow, 1959-60; National Acad. Scis.-Czechoslovak Acad. Sci. Exchange fellow, 1980, 82, 84, 87; Japan Society Promotion of Sci. fellow, 1981; Naito Foundation fellow, 1985. Fellow American Association for the Advancement of Science; member Am. Physiological Society, Am. Society Experimental Pharmacology and Therapeutics, Biophys. Society, Society General Physiology (secretary 1971-73), Society Neurosci. Office: National Insts Health Building 8 Room 403 9000 Rockville Pike Bethesda Maryland 20892

EDWARDS, DONALD KENNETH, mechanical engineer, educator; born Richmond, California, October 11, 1932; son of Samuel Harrison and Georgette Marie (Bas) E.; married Nathalie Beatrice Snow, October 11, 1955; children: Victoria Ann, Richard Earl. Bachelor of Science with highest honors in Mechanical Engineering, University Calif.-, Berkeley, 1954, Master of Science in Mechanical Engineering, 1956, Doctor of Philosophy in Mechanical Engineering, 1959. Thermodynamics engineer missile systems div. Lockheed Aircraft Company, Palo Alto, California, 1958-59; assistant professor engineering University of California at Los Angeles, 1959-63, associate professor; 1963-68, professor; 1968-81, chairman department chemical, nuclear and thermal engineering; 1975-78; professor University California, Irvine,

1981—, chairman department mechanical engineering; 1982-86, associate dean; 1986—; director, chairman board Gier Dunkle Instruments, Incorporated, 1963-66. Author: (with others) Transfer Processes, 1973, 2d edition, 1979; associate editor: ASME Journal Heat Transfer, 1975-80, Solar Energy, 1982-85; contributor articles to professional journals. Fellow American Institute of Aeronautics and Astronautics (first Thermophysics award 1976), American Society of Mechanical Engineers (Heat Transfer Memorial award 1973); member Optical Society Am., International Solar Energy Society, Phi Beta Kappa, Sigma Xi, Pi Tau Sigma, Tau Beta Pi. Office: U Calif/Irvine Mech Engring Department Irvine California 92717

EHRLICH, PAUL RALPH, biology educator; born Philadelphia, May 29, 1932; son of William and Ruth (Rosenberg) E.; married Anne Fitzhugh Howland, December 18, 1954; 1 daughter, Lisa Marie. Bachelor of Arts, University Pennsylvania, 1953; Master of Arts, University Kansas, 1955, Doctor of Philosophy, 1957. Research associate University Kansas, Lawrence, 1958-59; assistant professor biological sciences Stanford University, 1959-62, associate professor; 1962-66, professor; 1966—, Bing professor population studies; 1976—, director grad. study department biological sciences; 1966-69, 1974-76, director Center for Conservation Biology; 1988—; consultant Behavioral Research Laboratories, 1963-67. Author: How to Know the Butterflies, 1961, Process of Evolution, 1963, Principles of Modern Biology, 1968, Population Bomb, 1968, 2d edition, 1971,

Population, Resources, Environment: Issues In Human Ecology, 1970, 2d edition, 1972, How to Be a Survivor, 1971, Global Ecology: Readings Toward a Rational Strategy for Man, 1971, Man and the Ecosphere, 1971, Introductory Biology, 1973, Human Ecology: Problems and Solutions, 1973, Ark II: Social Response to Environmental Imperatives, 1974, The End of Affluence: A Blueprint for the Future, 1974, Biology and Society, 1976, Race Bomb, 1977, Ecoscience: Population, Resources, Environment, 1977, Insect Biology, 1978, The Golden Door: International Migration, Mexico, and the United States, 1979, Extinction: The Causes and Consequences of the Disappearance of Species, 1981, The Machinery of Nature, 1986, Earth, 1987, The Science of Ecology, 1987, The Birder's Handbook, 1988, New World/ New Mind, 1989; contributor articles to professional journals. Recipient World Wildlife Federation medal, 1987. Fellow California Acad. Sciences, Am. Acad. Arts and Sciences, Am. Association Advertising Sci.; member National Acad. Sciences, Society for Study Evolution, Society Systematic Zoology, Am. Society Naturalists, Lepidopterists Society, Am. Mus. Natural History (hon. life member). Office: Stanford U Department Biol Scis Stanford California 94305

EIGEN, MANFRED, physicist; born Bochum, Germany, May 9, 1927; son of Ernst E. and Hedwig (Feld) E.; married Elfriede Muller; 2 children. Educated physics and chemistry, University Gottingen, Germany; honorary degrees, Harvard University, University Chicago, Washington University, St. Louis, Nottingham University, St. Louis. Sci.

assistant Institute Physical Chemistry University Gottingen, 1951-53; member staff, then chairman Max Planck Institute Physical Chemistry, Gottingen, 1953—; visiting lecturer Cornell University. Author tech. papers. Co-recipient Nobel prize in chemistry, 1967. Member Bunsen Society Physical Chemistry (Bodenstein Preis), Faraday Society, National Academy of Sciences. Studies on evolution of biol. macromolecules; research on control of enzymes. Office: Max Planck Institute, 3400 Gottingen-Nikolausberg Federal Republic of Germany

EINSPRUCH, NORMAN GERALD, university dean; born New York City, June 27, 1932; son of Adolph and Mala (Goldblatt) E.; married Edith Melnick, December 20, 1953; children—Eric, Andrew, Franklin. Bachelor of Arts in Physics, Rice University, 1953; Master of Science in Physics, University Colorado, 1955; Doctor of Philosophy in Applied Math, Brown University, 1959. Member tech. staff, central research laboratories Texas Instruments, Incorporated, Dallas, 1959-62; manager electron transport physics branch, central research laboratories Texas Instruments, Incorporated, 1962-68, director advanced tech. laboratory, central research laboratories; 1968-69, director tech., chemical materials div.; 1969-72, director central research laboratories; 1972-75, assistant vice president; 1975-77, manager corp. devel.; 1975-76, manager tech. and planning consumer products; 1976-77; professor department electrical and computer engineering College Engineering University Miami, Coral Gables, Florida, 1977—; dean College Engineering University Miami, 1977—;

chairman panel on thin film microstructure sci. and tech. National Research Council, 1978-79; member panel on impact of DoD very high speed integrated circuits program National Research Council, 1980-81, panel on education and utilization of the engineer National Research Council, 1981-82; adv. board Venture Management Associates, Southeast Venture Capital Funds; board of directors Ogden Corp., Biogenix Corp., Image Data Corp. Editor: series VLSI Electronics: Microstructure Science, 18 volumes, VLSI Handbook, 1985; contributor articles to professional journals. Recipient George Washington Honor medal Freedoms Foundation Valley Forge. Fellow Am. Physical Society, Acoustical Society Am., Institute of Electrical and Electronics Engineers, American Association for the Advancement of Science; member Am. Institute Industrial Engineers, Am. Society Engineering Education, Golden Key, Iron Arrow, Sigma Xi, Omicron Delta Kappa, Tau Beta Pi, Eta Kappa Nu, Phi Kappa Phi, Alpha Pi Mu, Tau Sigma Delta. Home: 1415 Trillo Avenue Coral Gables Florida 33146 Office: U Miami College Engring Post Office Box 248294 Coral Gables Florida 33124

EISNER, THOMAS, biologist, educator; born Berlin, June 25, 1929; son of Hans Edouard and Margarete (Heil) E.; married Maria Lobell, June 10, 1952; children: Yvonne, Vivian, Christina. Bachelor of Arts, Harvard University, 1951, Doctor of Philosophy, 1955; Doctor of Science honorary, University Wurzburg, Federal Republic Germany, 1982, University Zurich, Switzerland, 1983. Postdoctoral fellow Harvard University, 1955-57; assistant professor biology Cornell University, Ithaca, New York, 1957-62; associate professor Cornell University, 1962-66, professor; 1966-76, Jacob Gould Schurman professor biology; 1976—; visiting scientist department entomology School Agriculture, Wageningen, Netherlands, 1964-65; visiting scientist Smithsonian Tropical Research Laboratory, Barro Colorado Island, Canal Zone, 1968; senior visiting scientist Max Planck Institute für Verhaltensphysiologie, Seewiesen, Fed/ Republic Germany, 1971, Div. Entomology, CSIRO, Canberra, Australia, 1972-73; Rand fellow Marine Biological Laboratories, Woods Hole, Massachusetts, 1974; visiting research professor University Florida, Gainesville, 1977-78; research associate Archbold Biological Station, 1973—; visiting professor Stanford University, 1979-80, University Zurich, 1980-81. Co-author: Animal Adaptation, 1964, Life on Earth, 1973, and 3 other books.; member editorial board: Sci, 1970-71, Am. Naturalist, 1970-71, Journal Comparative Physiology, 1974-80, Chemical Ecology, 1974—, Behavioral Ecology and Sociobiology, 1976—, Science Year World Books, 1979-83, Human Ecology Forum, 1981-85, Living Bird Quar., 1982-88, Experientia, 1982—, Quar. Review Biology, 1983-87; co-editor: Explorations in Chemical Ecology Series, 1987—; contributor articles to professional journals. Guggenheim fellow, 1964-65, 72-73; recipient Newcomb Cleveland prize American Association for the Advancement of Science, 1967, Founder's Memorial award Entomol. Society Am., 1969, Archie F. Carr medal, 1983, Procter prize Sigma Xi, 1986, Karl Ritter von Frisch medal, 1988. Fellow Am. Acad. Arts and Sciences, Royal Society Arts,

Animal Behavioral Society, Entomological Society Am.; member National Acad. Sci., Am. Philosophical Society, Explorers Club, Deutsche Akad. Naturforsch, Leopoldina, Club of Earth, Zero Population Growth (board directors 1969-70), Nature Conservancy (national council 1969-74), National Audubon Society (board directors 1970-75), Federation Am. Scientists (member council 1977-81), American Association for the Advancement of Science (chairman biology section 1980-81, member Committee on Sci. Freedom and Responsibility 1980-87, chairman subcom. sci. and human rights 1981-87), Center on Consequences Nuclear War (steering committee 1983—), World Wildlife Fund (member sci. adv. council 1983—), Am. Society Naturalists (executive committee 1989-91), National Academy of Sciences (film committee 1986—, committee on human rights 1987—), Monell Chemical Senses Institute (member adv. council 1988—), World Resources Institute (member adv. council 1988—), Committee Concerned Scientists (national sponsor 1988—). Office: Cornell U Department Neurology and Behavior W347 Mudd Hall Ithaca New York 14853

ELDER, REX ALFRED, civil engineer; born Pennsylvania, October 4, 1917; son of George Alfred and Harriet Jane (White) E.; married Janet Stevens Alger, August 10, 1940; children: John A., Carol S., Susan A., William P. Bachelor of Science in Civil Engineering, Carnegie Institute Tech., 1940; Master of Science, Oregon State College, 1942. Hydraulic engineer Tennessee Valley Authority, Norris, Tennessee, 1942-48; director hydraulic laboratory Tennessee Valley

Authority, 1948-61, director engineering laboratory; 1961-73; engineering manager Bechtel Civil & Minerals Incorporated, San Francisco, 1973-85; consultant hydraulic engineer 1986—. Contributor numerous articles on hydraulic structures, hydraulic model studies, reservoir stratification and water quality, hydraulic research and hydraulic machinery to professional journals. Served with United States Navy, 1945-46. Fellow American Society of Civil Engineers (James Laurie prize 1949, Hunter Rouse lecturer 1984); member National Acad. Engineering, American Society of Mechanical Engineers, International Association Hydraulic Research, Permanent International Association Navigation Congresses. Home and Office: 2180 Vistazo E Tiburon California 94920

ELDRED, KENNETH MCKECHNIE, acoustical consultant; born Springfield, Massachusetts, November 25, 1929; son of Robert Moseley and Jean McKechnie (Ashton) E.; married Helene Barbara Koerting Fischer, May 31, 1957; 1 daughter, Heidi Jean. Bachelor of Science, Massachusetts Institute of Technology, 1950, postgraduate, 1951-53; postgraduate, University of California at Los Angeles, 1960-63. Engineer in charge vibration and sound laboratory Boston Naval Shipyard, 1951-54; supervisory physicist, chief physical acoustics section United States Air Force, Wright Field, Ohio, 1956-57; vice president, consultant acoustics Western Electro-Acoustics Laboratories, Los Angeles, 1957-63; vice president, tech. director sci. services and systems group Wyle Laboratories, El Segundo, California, 1963-73; vice president, director div. environmental and noise control tech. Bolt Beranek and Newman Incorporated, Cambridge, Massachusetts, 1973-77; principal consultant Bolt Beranek and Newman Incorporated, 1977-81; director Ken Eldred Engineering; member executive standards council Am. National Standards Institute, 1979—, vice-chairman, 1981-83, chairman, 1985-87, board of directors, 1983-87; member, past chairman Acoustical Standards Board; member committee hearing, bioacoustics and biomechanics National Research Council, 1963—. Served with United States Air Force, 1954-56. Fellow Acoustical Society Am. (standards director 1987—, past chairman coordinating committee environmental acoustics); member National Acad. Engineering, Institute Noise Control Engineering (president 1976, board directors 1987—), Society Automotive Engineers, Society Naval Architects and Marine Engineers, United States Yacht Racing Union. Club: Down East Yacht. Home: 722 Annursnac Hill Road Concord Massachusetts 01742 Office: Post Office Box 1037 Concord Massachusetts 01742

ELION, GERTRUDE BELLE, research scientist, pharmacology educator; born New York City, January 23, 1918; daughter of Robert and Bertha (Cohen) E. Bachelor of Arts, Hunter College, 1937; Master of Science, New York University, 1941; Doctor of Science (honorary), George Washington University, 1969, University Michigan, 1983; Doctor of Medical Science (honorary), Brown University, 1969. Laboratory assistant biochemistry New York Hospital School Nursing, 1937; research assistant in organic chemistry Denver

Chemical Manufacturing Company, New York City, 1938-39; teacher chemistry and physics New York City secondary schools, 1940-42; food analyst Quaker Maid Company, Brooklyn, 1942-43; research assistant in organic synthesis Johnson & Johnson, New Brunswick, New Jersey, 1943-44; biochemist Wellcome Research Laboratories, Tuckahoe, New York, 1944-50; senior research chemist Wellcome Research Laboratories, 1950—; assistant to associate research director 1955-62, assistant to the research director; 1963-66, head experimental therapy; 1966-83, sci. emeritus; 1983—; adj. professor pharmacology and experimental medicine Duke University, 1970, research professor pharmacology; 1983—; adj. professor pharmacology University North Carolina, Chapel Hill, 1973; consultant United States Public Health Service, 1960-64; Chairman Gordon Conference on Coenzymes and Metabolic Pathways, 1966; member board sci. counselors National Cancer Institute, 1980-84; member council Am. Cancer Society, 1983-86; member National Cancer Adv. Board, 1984—. Contributor articles to professional journals. Recipient Garvan medal, 1968; President's medal Hunter College, 1970; Distinguished Chemist award North Carolina Institute Chemists, 1981; Judd award Memorial Sloan-Kettering Cancer Center, 1983; named to Hunter College Hall Fame, 1973. Fellow New York Acad. Sciences; member Am. Chemical Society, American Association for the Advancement of Science, Chemical Society (London), Am. Society Biological Chemists, Am. Association Cancer Research (board directors 1981, 83, president 1983-84, Cain award 1984), Am. Society Hematology, Transplantation Society, Am. Society Pharmacology and Experimental Therapeutics. Patentee in field. Home: 1 Banbury Lane Chapel Hill North Carolina 27514 Office: 3030 Cornwallis Road Research Triangle Park North Carolina 27709

ELKINS, LLOYD EDWIN, petroleum engineer, energy consultant; born Golden, Colorado, April 1, 1912; son of Edwin and Beulah M. (Feltch) E.; married Virginia L. Crosby, May 27, 1934; children: Marylou, Barbara Lee, Lloyd Edwin Jr. Degree in Petroleum Engineering, Colorado School Mines, 1934; Doctor of Philosophy in Science, University Ozarks. With Amoco Production Company, 1934-77; successively field engineer, petroleum engineer Tulsa general office, senior petroleum engineer, petroleum engineering supervisor, assistant chief production engineer, chief production engineer Amoco Production Company, 1949-77; energy consultant 1977—. Contributor articles to professional journals. Named to Engineering Hall of Fame Oklahoma State University, 1961; recipient Distinguished Service medal Colorado School Mines, 1961; named to Engineering Hall of Fame University Tulsa. Member Am. Association Petroleum Geologists, Am. Petroleum Institute (chairman mid-continent district division prodn. 1948-49, chairman adv. com fundamental research on occurrence and recovery petroleum 1941), Am. Institute Mining, Metall, and Petroleum Engineers (hon., vice president 1953-59, president 1962, Anthony F. Lucas gold medal 1966), National Acad. Engineering, Tulsa Geological Society, Australian Institute Mining

and Metallurgy (hon.). Methodist. Clubs: Engineers (Tulsa) (president 1950-51), Petroleum (Tulsa), Tulsa Country (Tulsa). Home and Office: 2806 E 27th St Post Office Box 4745 Tulsa Oklahoma 74114

ELLINGWOOD, BRUCE RUSSELL, structural engineering researcher; born Evanston, Illinois, October 11, 1944; son of Robert W. and Carolyn L. (Ehmen) E.; married Lois J. Drager, June 7, 1969; 1 son, Geoffrey D. Bachelor.S.in Civil Engineering, University Illinois, Urbana, 1968, Master of Science in Civil Engineering, 1969, Doctor of Philosophy, 1972. Structural engineer Naval Ship Research and Devel. Center, Bethesda, Maryland, 1972-75; research structural engineer, leader structural engineering group Center Building Tech., National Bureau Standards, Washington, 1975-86; professor civil engineering Johns Hopkins University, Baltimore, 1986—; lecturer, consultant. Contributor articles to professional journals. Recipient Dural Research prize University Illinois, 1968; recipient National Capital award for Engineering Achievement District of Columbia Joint Council Engineering and Architectural Socs., 1980, Walter L. Huber prize American Society of Civil Engineers, 1980, Silver medal U.S. Department Commerce, 1980; named Engineer of Year of U.S. Department Commerce, National Society Professional Engrs., 1986. Member American Society of Civil Engineers (State of Art in Civil Engring 1983, Norman medal 1983), American Society for Testing and Materials, Am. National Standards Institute, Am. Institute Steel Constrn., Sigma Xi, Chi Epsilon, Tau Beta Pi. Presbyterian. Office: John Hopkins U Department

Civil Engring Baltimore Maryland 21218

ELLNER, PAUL D., clinical microbiologist; born New York City, May 2, 1925; son of George and Cele (Weis) E.; married Estelle Ziswasser, 1948 (divorced 1960); 1 child, Diane; married Cornelia Johns, January 15, 1965; children—David, Jonathan. Bachelor of Science, Long Island University, 1948; Master of Science, University Southern California, 1952; Doctor of Philosophy, University Maryland College Medicine, 1956. Diplomate Am. Board Medical Microbiology; certified clin. laboratory dir. New York City Dept. Health. Clinical bacteriologist Los Angeles hospitals, 1948-52; research assistant Mount Sinai Hospital, New York City, 1952-53; instructor microbiology University Florida College Medicine, 1956-60; assistant professor University Vermont College Medicine, 1960-63; assistant professor Columbia University College Physicians and Surgeons, New York City, 1963-66, associate professor; 1966-70, professor microbiology; 1971-78, professor microbiology and pathology; 1978—, director clinical microbiology service; 1971—; associate microbiologist Presbyn. Hospital, New York City, 1966-70, attending staff; 1971—; consultant in field; visiting professor New York Medical College, Valhalla, 1979; ASM Latin Am. visiting professor, Medellín, Colombia, 1982; Am. Bureau Medical Advancement in China visiting professor, Taiwan, 1982; regional coordinator National Disaster Medical System. Member editorial board Sexually Transmitted Diseases, 1982-84, European Journal Clin. Microbiology, 1985—; author: Current Procedures in Clinical Bacteriology, 1978; editor: Infectious Diarrheal Diseases: Current Concepts and Laboratory Procedures, 1984; contributor chapters to books, numerous articles to sci. journals. Served with Air Corps, United States Navy, 1943-44; to captain United States Public Health Service Reserves, 1956—; health project officer United States Coast Guard, 1982—. U.S. Navy research fellow, 1954-56. Fellow Am. Acad. Microbiology, Association Clinical Scientists, New York Acad. Medicine (associate), Infectious Diseases Society Am.; member Am. Society Microbiology (chairman clinical division 1980-81), American Medical Association (special affiliate), Acad. Clinical Lab. Physicians and Scientists, Am. Veneral Disease Association, Sigma Xi. Republican. Jewish. Avocations: flying; fishing; gardening; photography. Office: Columbia U Department Microbiology 622 W 168th St New York New York 10032

ELSASSER, WALTER MAURICE, physicist, educator; born Mannheim, Germany, March 20, 1904; came to United States, 1936, naturalized, 1940; son of Moritz and Johanna (Masius) E.; married Margaret Trahey, July 17, 1937; children—Barbara, William; married Suzanne Rosenfeld, June 24, 1964. Doctor of Philosophy, University Goettingen, Germany, 1927. Instructor University Frankfurt, Germany, 1930-33; research fellow Sorbonne, Paris, 1933-36, California Institute Tech., 1936-41; war research on radar United States Signal Corps and Radio Corporation of America Laboratories, 1941-47; professor physics University Pennsylvania, 1947-50, University Utah, 1950-56, University California at La Jolla, 1956-

62; chairman department physics University New Mexico, Alburquerque, 1960-61; professor geophysics, department geology Princeton, 1962-68; research professor University Maryland, College Park, 1968-74; adj. professor department earth and planetary sci. Johns Hopkins, 1975—. Author: The Physical Foundation of Biology, 1958, Atom and Organism, 1966, The Chief Abstractions of Biology, 1975, Memoirs of a Physicist in the Atomic Age, 1978; theory of earth's magnetic field. Recipient U.S. National Medal of Sci., 1987, Gauss medal W. Ger., 1977. Fellow Am. Physical Society, Am. Geophysical Union (Bowie medal 1959, Fleming medal 1971); member National Acad. Sci. Home: 500 W University Parkway Apartment 6P Baltimore Maryland 21210

ENGLAND, ANTHONY W., electrical engineering and computer science educator, astronaut, geophysicist; born Indianapolis, May 15, 1942; son of Herman U. and Betty (Steel) E.; married Kathleen Ann Kreutz, August 31, 1962. Bachelor of Science Master of Science, Massachusetts Institute of Technology, 1965, Doctor of Philosophy, 1970. With Texaco Company, 1962; field geologist Ind. University, 1963; scientist-astronaut National Aeronautics and Space Administration, 1967-72, 79—; with United States Geological Survey, 1972-79; crewmember on Spacelab 2 July, 1985; adj. professor Rice University, 1987-88; professor electrical engineering and computer sci. University Michigan, Ann Arbor, 1988—; adj. professor Rice University, 1987—. Asso. editor: Journal Geophysical Research. Recipient Sci. Achievement medal, Antarctic medal, Spaceflight medal National Aeronautics and Space Administration, Spaceflight award Am. Astronomical Society; National Science Foundation grantee, 1965-67. Member Am. Geophysical Union, Society Exploration Geophysicists, Institute of Electrical and Electronics Engineers (adminstrv. committee for geosci. and remote seusing 1988—). Home: 806 S 7th St Ann Arbor Michigan 48103 Office: U Michigan Department EECS Ann Arbor Michigan 48109

ENNS, MARK KYNASTON, electrical engineer; born Hutchinson, Kansas, October 13, 1931; son of Harry and Bernice (Griffith) E.; married Patricia Shupe, December 23, 1956; children: Neil, Paul, Carol. Bachelor of Science in Electrical Engineering, Kansas State University, 1953; Master of Science in Electrical Engineering, University Pittsburgh, 1960, Doctor of Philosophy, 1967. Electrical utility engineer Westinghouse Electrical Corp., East Pittsburgh, Pennsylvania, 1956-64; research laboratories Westinghouse Electrical Corp., Pittsburgh, 1964-67; assistant professor electrical engineering Carnegie-Mellon University, Pittsburgh, 1967-69; associate professor University Michigan, Ann Arbor, 1969-72; professor University Michigan, 1972-78; director Power Systems Laboratory, 1969-78, Harris SAI, Incorporated, Ann Arbor, 1978-81; president, chairman board Electrocon International, Incorporated, Ann Arbor, 1981—. Editor: special issue Procs. of IEEE, 1974. Served with United States Air Force, 1953-55. Fellow Institute of Electrical and Electronics Engineers; member Sigma Xi, Eta Kappa Nu. Patentee in field. Home: 1010 Lincoln Avenue Ann Arbor Michigan 48104 Office:

Electrocon International Incorporated 611 Church St Ann Arbor Michigan 48104

ENOS, PAUL, geologist, educator; born Topeka, July 25, 1934; son of Allen Mason and Marjorie V. (Newell) E.; married Carol Rae Curt, July 5, 1958; children—Curt Alan, Mischa Lisette, Kevin Christopher, Heather Lynne. Bachelor of Science, University Kansas, 1956; postgraduate, University Tubingen, Federal Republic of Germany, 1956-57; Master of Science, Stanford University, 1961; Doctor of Philosophy, Yale University, 1965. Geologist Shell Devel. Company, Coral Gables, Florida, 1964-68, research geologist; 1968-70; from associate professor to professor geology State University of New York, Binghamton, 1970-82; Haas Distinguished professor geology University Kansas, Lawrence, 1982—; consultant to industry; sedimentologist Deep Sea Drilling Project, 1975. Co-author: Quaternary Sedimentation of South Florida, 1977, Mid-Cretaceous, Mexico, 1983; editor: Field Trips: South-Central New York, 1981, Deep-Water Carbonates, 1977; contributor articles to sci. journals. Served to 1st lieutenant Corps of Engineers, United States Army, 1957-59. University Liverpool fellow, 1976-77; National Science Foundation fellow, 1959-62; Fulbright fellow, 1956-57; Summerfield scholar, 1954-56. Member Society Econ. Paleontologists and Mineralogists (associate editor 1976-80, 83-87), International Association Sedimentologists (associate editor 1983-87), Am. Association Petroleum Geologists, American Association for the Advancement of Science, Sigma Xi, Omicron Delta Kappa. Avocations: photography; diving; running; history. Home: 2032 Quail Creek Dr Lawrence Kansas 66046 Office: U Kansas Department Geology 120 Lindley Hall Lawrence Kansas 66045

EPSTEIN, EMANUEL, plant physiologist; born Duisburg, Germany, November 5, 1916; came to United States, 1938, naturalized, 1946; son of Harry and Bertha (Lowe) E.; married Hazel M. Leask, November 26, 1943; children: Jared H. (deceased), Jonathan H. Bachelor of Science, University California, Davis, 1940, Master of Science, 1941; Doctor of Philosophy, University California, Berkeley, 1950. Plant physiologist Department Agriculture, Beltsville, Maryland, 1950-58; lecturer, associate plant physiologist University Calif.-Davis, 1958-65, professor plant nutrition, plant physiologist; 1965-87, professor botany; 1974-87, professor and plant physiologist emeritus; 1987—; consultant to government and private agys. Author: Mineral Nutrition of Plants: Principles and Perspectives, 1972; editorial board: Plant Physiology, 1962-71, 76—, CRC Handbook Series in Nutrition and Food, 1975—, The Biosaline Concept: An Approach to the Utilization of Underexploited Resources, 1978, Plant Science, 1981—, Advances in Plant Nutrition, 1981—. Served with United States Army, 1943-46. Recipient Gold medal Pisa (Italy) University, 1962; Guggenheim fellow, 1958; Fulbright sr. research scholar, 1965-66, 74-75. Fellow American Association for the Advancement of Science; member National Acad. Sciences, Am. Society Plant Physiologists (Charles Reid Barnes Hon. Life Membership award, 1986), Scandinavian Society Plant Physiology, Australian Society Plant

Physiologists, Am. Institute Biological Sciences, Common Cause, Save-the-Redwoods League, University Calif.-Davis Club, Sierra Club, Nature Conservancy, Sigma Xi. Research, publs. on ion transport in plants, mineral nutrition and salt relations of plants, salt tolerant crops. Office: U California Land Air and Water Resources Davis California 95616

EPSTEIN, SAMUEL, geologist, educator; born Poland, December 9, 1919. Bachelor of Science, University Manitoba, Can., 1941, Master of Science, 1942; Doctor of Philosophy in Physical Chemistry, McGill University, Can., 1944; Doctor of Science (honorary), University Manitoba, 1980. Research chemist Natural Resources Council Can., 1944-47; research associate Institute Nuclear Studies, University Chicago, 1948-52, research fellow; 1952-53, senior research fellow; 1953-54, associate professor; 1954-59; professor geochemistry California Institute Tech., Pasadena, 1959-84, William East Leonard professor geology; 1984—. Fellow American Association for the Advancement of Science; member National Acad. Sci., Geological Society Am. (Arthur L. Day medal 1978), Geochem. Society, Am. Geophysical Union. Office: Div Geol and Planetary Sci California Institute Tech Pasadena California 91109

ERICKSON, RALPH O., botany educator; born Duluth, Minnesota, October 27, 1914; son of Charles W. and Stella (Sjostrom) E.; married Elinor M. Borgstedt, June 17, 1945; children—Diane Erickson Field, Elizabeth Jane. Bachelor of Arts, Gustavus Adolphus College, 1935; Master of Science, Washington University, St. Louis, 1941; Doctor of Philosophy, Washington University,

1944. Instructor Gustavus Adolphus College, 1935-39; assistant chemist Western Cartridge Company, East Alton, Illinois, 1942-44; instructor, then assistant professor botany University Rochester, New York, 1944-47; member faculty University Pennsylvania, Philadelphia, 1947—, professor botany; 1954-85; professor emeritus University Pennsylvania, 1985—, chairman grad. group botany; 1957-58, acting director div. biology; 1961-63, chairman grad. group biology; 1968-76, acting chairman department biology; 1977-78. Contributor articles to professional journals. Guggenheim fellow California Institute Tech., 1954-55. Member Botanical Society Am., Society Devel. Biology (president 1959), Am. Society Naturalists, Sigma Xi. Home: 1920 Dog Kennel Road Media Pennsylvania 19063 Office: U Pennsylvania 105B Leidy Labs Philadelphia Pennsylvania 19104

ERIKSON, RAYMOND LEO, biology educator; born Eagle, Wisconsin, January 24, 1936; married, 1958. Bachelor of Science, University Wisconsin, 1958, Master of Science, 1961, Doctor of Philosophy in Molecular Bilogy, 1963. From assistant professor to associate professor University Colorado, Denver, 1965-72, professor pathology; 1972-82; Am. Cancer Society professor cellular and devel. biology Harvard University, Cambridge, Massachusetts, 1982—. U.S. Pub. Health Service fellow, 1963-65; recipient Papaicolau award, 1980, Albert Lasker award, 1982, Robert Koch prize, 1982, Alfred P. Sloan Junior prize General Motors Cancer Research Foundation, 1983. Member Am. Society Biological Chemists, Am. Society Microbiology. Office: Harvard

U Department Biology Cambridge Massachusetts 02138

ERLENMEYER-KIMLING, L., psychiatric and behavior genetics researcher, educator; born Princeton, New Jersey; daughter of Floyd M. and Dorothy F. (Dirst) Erlenmeyer; married Carl F. E. Kimling. Bachelor of Science magna cum laude, Columbia University, 1957, Doctor of Philosophy, 1961. Senior research scientist New York State Psychiat. Institute, New York City, 1960-69; associate research scientist New York State Psychiat. Institute, 1969-75, principal research scientist; 1975-78, director div. devel. behavior studies; 1978—; assistant in psychiatry Columbia University, 1962-66, research associate; 1966-70, assistant professor; 1970-74, associate professor, psychiatry and human genetics; 1974-78, professor; 1978—; visiting professor psychology New School Social Research, 1971—; member peer rev. group National Institutes of Health, 1976-80; member work group on guidance and counseling Congressional Commission on Huntington's Disease, 1976-77; member task force on intervention President's Commission on Mental Health, 1977-78; member initial rev. group National Institute of Mental Health, 1981-85. Editor: Life-span Research in Psychopathology, 1986; issue editor: Differential Reprodn., Social Biology, 1971, Genetics and Mental Disorders, International Journal Mental Health, 1972; member editorial board: Social Biology, 1970-79, Schizophrenia Bulletin, 1978—, Journal Preventive Psychiatry, 1980—. Recipient Merit award National Institute of Mental Health, 1989; National Institute of Mental Health grantee, 1966-69, 71—, Scottish Rite Committee on Schizophrenia grantee, 1970-74, 84-87, W.T. Grant Foundation grantee, 1978-86, MacArthur Foundation grantee 1981. Fellow Am. Psychological Association; member Am. Society Human Genetics, Am. Psychopath. Association, American Association for the Advancement of Science, World Psychiat. Association (committee epidemiology and community psychiatry), Behavior Genetics Association (mem.-at-large 1972-74, Theodosius Dobzhansky award 1985), Society Study Social Biology (director 1969-84, secretary 1972-75, president 1975-78), Scientists Center for Animal Welfare, Scientists Group for Reform of Animal Experimentation, Phi Beta Kappa, Sigma Xi. Office: New York State Psychiat Institute 722 W 168th St New York New York 10032

ERNST, WALLACE GARY, geology educator; born St. Louis, December 14, 1931; son of Fredrick A. and Helen Grace (Mahaffey) E.; married Charlotte Elsa Pfau, September 7, 1956; children: Susan, Warren, Alan, Kevin. Bachelor of Arts, Carleton College, 1953; Master of Science, University Minnesota, 1955; Doctor of Philosophy, Johns Hopkins University, 1959. Geologist United States Geological Survey, Washington, 1955-56; fellow (Geophysical Laboratory), Washington, 1956-59; member faculty University of California at Los Angeles, 1960—, professor geology and geophysics; 1968—, chairman geology department (now earth and space sciences department); 1970-74, 78-82, director Institute Geophysics and Planetary Physics; 1987—. Author: Amphiboles, 1968, Earth Materials, 1969, Metamorphism and Plate Tectonic Regimes, 1975,

Subduction Zone Metamorphism, 1975, Petrologic Phase Equilibria, 1976, The Geotectonic Development of California, 1981, The Environment of the Deep Sea, 1982, Energy for Ourselves and Our Posterity, 1985, Cenozoic Basin Development of Coastal California, 1987, Metamorphic and Crustal Evolution of the Western Cordillera, 1988. Member National Acad. Sci. (chairman geology section 1979-82), American Association for the Advancement of Science, Am. Geophysical Union, Am. Geological Institute, Geological Society Am. (president 1985-86), Am. Acad. Arts and Sci., Geochem. Society, Mineralogical Society Am. (recipient award 1969, president 1979-80), Mineralogical Society London. Office: U California Department Earth and Space Scis Los Angeles California 90024-1567

ESAKI, LEO, physicist; born Osaka, Japan, March 12, 1925; came to United States, 1960; son of Soichiro and Niyoko (Ito) E.; married Masako Kondo, May, 31, 1986; children from previous marriage: Nina Yvonne, Anna Eileen, Eugene Leo. Bachelor of Science, University Tokyo, 1947, Doctor of Philosophy, 1959. With Sony Corp., Japan, 1956-60; with Thomas J. Watson Research Center, International Business Machines Corporation, Yorktown Heights, New York, 1960—; International Business Machines Corporation fellow Thomas J. Watson Research Center, International Business Machines Corporation, 1967—, manager device research; 1965—; director IBM-Japan.

Recipient Morris N. Liebmann Memorial prize I.E.E.E., 1961; Stuart Ballantine medal Franklin Institute, 1961; Japan Acad. award, 1965; Nobel Prize in physics, 1973; decorated Order of Culture Government of Japan, 1974. Fellow Am. Physical Society (councillor-at-large 1971-74); Institute of Electrical and Electronics Engineers; Fellow Japan Physical Society, Am. Vacuum Society (director 1973-74); member Am. Acad. Arts and Sciences, National Academy of Sciences (foreign associate), National Academy of Engineering (foreign associate), Academia Nacional de Ingenieria Mexican (corr.), Japan Acad. Inventor tunnel diode, 1957. Home: Route 4 Box 105 Young Road Katonah New York 10536 Office: Thomas Watson Research Center International Business Machines Corporation Corp Post Office Box 218 Yorktown Heights New York 10598

ESSEX, MYRON ELMER, microbiology educator; born Coventry, Rhode Island, August 17, 1939; son of Myron Elmer and Ruth Hazel (Knight) E.; married Elizabeth Katherine Jordan, June 19, 1966; children—Holly Anne, Carrie Lisa. Bachelor of Science, University Rhode Island, Kingston, 1962; Doctor of Veterinary Medicine, Michigan State University, East Lansing, 1967; Master of Science, Michigan State University, 1967; Doctor of Philosophy, University Calif.-Davis, 1970; Master of Arts (honorary), Harvard University, 1979; Doctor of Science (honorary), University Rhode Island, 1987, Michigan State University, 1988. Research fellow Karolinska Institute, Stockholm, 1970-72; assistant professor Harvard University, Cambridge, Massachusetts, 1972-76, associate professor; 1976-78, professor, chairman department microbiology; 1978-81; chairman department cancer biology Harvard University, 1981—, associate director

Center Infectious Diseases; 1981-88, chairman Acquired Immune Deficiency Syndrome Institute; 1988—; member sci. adv. board Cambridge Biosci. Corp., 1981—, American Red Cross, 1985—; chairman Acquired Immune Deficiency Syndrome Institute Harvard University, 1988—. Editor: Viruses in Cancer, 1980. Co-editor: Human T-cell Leukemia Viruses, 1984. Contributor articles to professional journals Patentee test for human T leukemia virus infection and AIDS blood tests and vaccines. Board sci. counselors National Cancer Institute, 1982—; member Lasker award jury Albert & Mary Lasker Foundation, 1982-84; sci. adv. board American Red Cross, 1985—. Leukemia Society Am. scholar, 1972; Am. Cancer Society National Cancer Institute grantee, 1973—; recipient Bronze medal Am. Cancer Society, 1978, Ralston-Purina research award, 1985, Outstanding Investigator award National Cancer Institute, 1985, Distinguished Alumnus award Michigan State University, 1986, Lasker award, 1986, Carnation Research award, 1987, Distinguished Alumnus award University California Davis, 1987. Member American Association for the Advancement of Science, Am. Association Cancer Research, Am. Society Microbiology, Am. Association Immunologists, American Veterinary Medical Association, International Association Research in Leukemia, Infectious Disease Society Am., Am. Society Virology, National Acad. Practitioners, Reticuloendothelial Society, Society General Microbiology, Am. Cancer Society (research committee Massachusetts branch 1975—), Leukemia Society Am. (adv. board 1978-83, 85—, med./sci. adv. committee 1978—). Office: Harvard School Pub Health Department Cancer Biology 665 Huntington Avenue Boston Massachusetts 02115

EVERHART, THOMAS EUGENE, physicist, educator; born Kansas City, Missouri, February 15, 1932; son of William Elliott and Elizabeth Ann (West) E.; married Doris Arleen Wentz, June 21, 1953; children—Janet Sue, Nancy Jean, David William, John Thomas. Bachelor of Arts in Physics magna cum laude, Harvard, 1953; Master of Science, University of California at Los Angeles, 1955; Doctor of Philosophy in Engineering, Cambridge University, England, 1958. Member tech. staff Hughes Research Laboratories, Culver City, California, 1953-55; member faculty University California, Berkeley, 1958-78, professor electrical engineering and computer sciences; 1967-78, Miller research professor; 1969-70, chairman department; 1972-77; professor electrical engineering, Joseph Silbert dean engineering Cornell University, Ithaca, New York, 1979-84; professor electrical and computer engineering, chancellor University Illinois, Champaign-Urbana, 1984-87; president, professor electrical engineering California Institute Tech., Pasadena, 1987—; fellow scientist Westinghouse Research Laboratories, Pittsburgh, 1962-63; guest professor Institute für Angewandte Physik, University Tuebingen, Federal Republic Germany, 1966-67, Waseda University, Tokyo, Osaka University, Japan, fall 1974; visiting fellow Clare Hall, Cambridge University, 1975; chairman Electron, Ion and Photon Beam Symposium, 1977; consultant to industry; member sci. and educational adv. committee Lawrence

Berkeley Laboratory, 1978-85, chairman, 1980-85; member sci. adv. committee General Motors Corp., 1980—, chairman 1984—; member tech. adv. committee Railroad Donnelley & Sons, 1981—. National Science Foundation sr. postdoctoral fellow, 1966-67; Guggenheim fellow, 1974-75. Fellow Institute of Electrical and Electronics Engineers; member American Association for the Advancement of Science, National Acad. Engineering (educational adv. board 1984—, membership committee 1984—, chairman membership committee 1988—), Electron Microscopy Society Am. (council 1970-72, president 1977), Microbeam Analysis Society Am., Deutsche Gesellschaft für Elektronenmikroskopie, Association Marshall Scholars and Alumni (president 1965-68), National Association State Univs. and Land Grant Colls. (chairman higher education and tech. committee 1986-87), Sigma Xi, Eta Kappa Nu. Clubs: Athenaeum, Chicago. Home: 415 S Hill Avenue Pasadena California 91106 Office: California Institute Tech Office of President 1201 E California Boulevard Pasadena California 91125

FABER, SANDRA MOORE, astronomer, educator; born Boston, December 28, 1944; daughter of Donald Edwin and Elizabeth Mackenzie (Borwick) Moore; married Andrew L. Faber, June 9, 1967; children: Robin, Holly. Bachelor of Arts, Swarthmore College, 1966, Doctor of Science (honorary), 1986; Doctor of Philosophy, Harvard University, 1972. Assistant professor, astronomer Lick Observatory, University California, Santa Crux, 1972-77, associate professor, astronomer; 1977-79, professor, astronomer; 1979—; member National Science Foundation astronomy adv. panel; visiting professor Princeton University, 1978, University Hawaii, 1983, Arizona State University, 1985; Phillips visitor Haverford College, 1982; member National Acad. Astronomy Survey Panel, 1979-81; chairman visiting committee Space Telescope Sci. Institute, 1983-84; co-chairman sci. steering committee Keck Observatory, 1987—. Associate editor: Astrophys. Journal Letters, 1982-87; editorial board: Annual Revs. Astronomy and Astrophysics, 1982-87; contributor articles to professional journals. Trustee Carnegie Instn., Washington, 1985—. Recipient Bart J. Bok prize Harvard University, 1978, Director's Distinguished Lecturer award Liverman National Laboratory, 1986, Carnegie Lecturer Carnegie Institute Washington, 1988; National Science Foundation fellow, 1966-71; Woodrow Wilson fellow, 1966-71; Alfred P. Sloan fellow, 1977-81; listed among 100 best Am. scientists under 40, Sci. Digest, 1984; Tetelman fellow, Yale University, 1987. Member Am. Astronomical Society (councilor 1982-84, Dannie Heineman prize 1986), International Astronomical Union, National Acad. Arts and Sciences, Phi Beta Kappa, Sigma Xi. Office: Lick Obs U California Santa Cruz California 95060

FABIAN, JOHN M., former astronaut, air force officer; born Goosecreek, Texas; married Donna Kay Buboltz; 2 children. Bachelor of Science, Washington State University, 1962; Master of Science, Air Force Institute Tech., 1964; Doctor of Philosophy, University Washington, 1974. Commissioned officer United States Air Force, advanced through grades to colonel; astronaut National Aeronautics and Space Administration, Houston, 1978-86, mission specialist Challenger flight 2; 1983; mission specialist Discovery flight 1985; retired United States Air Force, 1987; vice president ANSER Corp. (Analytical Services Corp.), 1987—; served as pilot United States Air Force, Vietnam. Decorated Vietnam Cross of Gallantry, Defense Superior Service medal; French Legion of Honor; Saudia Arabian King Abdul-Aziz medal. Home: 3303 Circle Hill Road Alexandria Virginia 22305

FALTINGS, GERD, mathematician; born Gelsenkirchen-Buer, Federal Republic of Germany, July 28, 1954. Doctor of Philosophy, University Münster, 1978, Dr.Hab., 1981. Assistant in math. University Münster, 1979-82; professor University Wuppertal, 1982-84; professor math. Princeton University, Princeton, New Jersey, 1984—; co-ed., Math. J., from 1984. Recipient Dannie Heineman Prize Gottingen Acad. of Sciences, 1983, Field's Medal International Congress of Mathematicians, 1986. Member German Math. Union. Office: Princeton U Math Department Princeton New Jersey 08544

FEDOROFF, NINA VSEVOLOD, research scientist, consultant; born Cleveland, April 9, 1942; daughter of Vsevolod N. and Olga S. (Snegireff) Stacy; married T. Patrick Gaganidze, June 18, 1966 (divorced 1978); children: Natasha, Kyr. Bachelor of Science, Syracuse University, 1966; Doctor of Philosophy, Rockefeller University, 1972. Assistant manager transl. bureau Biological Abstracts, Philadelphia, 1962-63; flutist Syracuse (New York) Symphony Orchestra, 1964-66; acting assistant professor University of California at Los Angeles, 1972-74; postdoctoral fellow University of California at Los Angeles and Carnegie Institution Washington, Los Angeles and Baltimore, 1974-78; staff scientist Carnegie Institution Washington, Baltimore, 1978—; professor department biology Johns Hopkins University; member devel. biology panel National Science Foundation, Washington, 1979-80, sci. adv. panel Office of Tech. Assessment, Congress, Washington, 1979-80, recombinant DNA adv. committee National Institutes of Health, Bethesda, Maryland, 1980-84; member commission on life sciences, basic biology board National Research Council, National Academy of Sciences, Washington, 1984—. Contributor articles to professional journals, chapters to books; editor Gene, 1981-84; editor, board of rev. editors Science, 1985—. Grantee National Science Foundation and USDA, 1979-84, National Institutes of Health, 1984—. Member American Association for the Advancement of Science, Phi Beta Kappa (vis. scholar 1984-85), Sigma Xi. Avocations: chamber music, hiking, skiing. Office: Carnegie Institute of Washington Department Embryology 115 W University Parkway Baltimore Maryland 21210

FEFFERMAN, CHARLES LOUIS, mathematics educator; born Washington, April 18, 1949; son of Arthur Stanley and Liselott Ruth (Stern) F.; married Julie Anne Albert, February 1975; children: Nina Heidi, Elaine Marie. Bachelor of Science, University Maryland, 1966, honorary doctorate, 1979; Doctor of Philosophy, Princeton University, 1969; honorary doctorate, Knox College, 1981, Bar-Ilan University,

Israel, 1985. Instructor math. Princeton (New Jersey) University, 1969-70, professor math.; 1974—; member faculty University Chicago, 1970-74, professor math.; 1971-74. Author research papers. Recipient Salem prize for oustanding work in fourier analysis by young mathematician, 1978, Alan T. Waterman award, 1978, Fields medal International Cong. Mathematicians, 1978, 84. Member National Acad. Sciences, Am. Math. Society, Am. Acad. Arts and Sciences. Home: 234 Clover Lane Princeton New Jersey 08540 Office: Fine Hall Princeton U Princeton New Jersey 08540

FEIGENBAUM, EDWARD ALBERT, computer science educator; born Weehawken, New Jersey, January 20, 1936; son of Fred J. and Sara Rachman; married H. Penny Nii, 1975; children: Janet Denise, Carol Leonora, Sheri Bryant, Karin Bryant. Bachelor of Electrical Engineering, Carnegie Institute Tech., 1956, Doctor of Philosophy in Industrial Administration, 1960. Assistant, then associate professor business administration University California at Berkeley, 1960-64; associate professor computer sci., then professor Stanford University, 1965—; principal investigator heuristic programming project 1965—; director Computation Center Stanford University, 1965-68, chairman department computer sci.; 1976-81; president Intelli Genetics Incorporated, 1980-81; chairman, director Teknowledge, Incorporated, 1981-82; member tech. adv. board Intelli Genetics Incorporated, 1983-86; director IntelliCorp, 1984—; consultant to industry, 1957—; director Sperry Corp.; member computer and biomath. sciences study section National Institutes of Health, 1968-72, member adv. committee on artificial intelligence in medicine, 1974—; member adv. committee Health Care Tech. Center, University Missouri, Columbia; member Math. Social Sci. Board, 1975-78; computer sci. adv. committee National Science Foundation, 1977-80; member International Joint Council on Artificial Intelligence, 1973-83. Author: (with others) Information Processing Language V Manual, 1961, (with P. McCorduck) The Fifth Generation; author: (with R. Lindsay, B. Buchanan, J. Lederberg) Applications of Artificial Intelligence to Organic Chemistry: the Dendral Program; Editor: (with J. Feldman) Computers and Thought, 1963, (with A. Barr and P. Cohen) Handbook of Artificial Intelligence, 1981, 82, (with Pamela McCorduck and H. Penny Nii) The Rise of the Expert Company: How Visionary Compaines are using Artificial Intelligence to Achieve Higher Productivity and Profits; member editorial board: Journal Artificial Intelligence, 1970—. Fulbright scholar Great Britain, 1959-60. Fellow American Association for the Advancement of Science; member National Acad. Engineering, Association Computing Machinery (national council 1966-68, chairman special interest group on biological applications 1973-76), Am. Association Artificial Intelligence (president 1980-81), Cognitive Sci. Society (council 1979-82), American Association for the Advancement of Science, Sigma Xi, Tau Beta Pi, Eta Kappa Nu, Pi Delta Epsilon. Home: 1017 Cathcart Way Stanford California 94305 Office: Stanford U Department Computer Sci Stanford California 94305

FEIGENBAUM, MITCHELL JAY, physics educator; born Philadelphia, December 19, 1944; son of Abraham Joseph and Mildred (Sugar) F. Bachelor of Electrical Engineering, City College of New York, 1964; Doctor of Philosophy, Massachusetts Institute of Technology, 1970. Research associate, instructor physics department Cornell University, Ithaca, New York, 1970-72, professor physics; 1982-87; research associate physics department Virginia Polytechnic Institute, Blacksburg, 1972-74; staff member theory div. Los Alamos National Laboratory, 1974-81, laboratory fellow; 1981-82; Toyota professor physics Rockefeller University, New York City, 1987—; visiting member Institute Advanced Study, Princeton, New Jersey, 1978, Institute des Hautes Recherches Scientifiques, Bueres-sur-Yvette, France, 1980—. Editorial board: Journal Statis. Physics, 1982—, Advances in Applied Math. Recipient Distinguished Performance award Los Alamos National Laboratory, 1980, Ernest O. Lawrence award U.S. Department Energy, 1983, MacArthur Foundation award, 1984, Wolf Prize for Physics, 1986. Fellow Am. Physical Society; member Am. Acad. Arts and Sciences, New York Acad. Sciences, Sigma Xi. Discovered theory period doubling route to turbulence, 1976-79. Home: 450 E 63d St 10L New York New York 10021 Office: Physics Department Rockefeller U York Avenue and 66th St New York New York 10021

FERNIE, JOHN DONALD, astronomer, educator; born Pretoria, South Africa, November 13, 1933; emigrated to Canada, 1961, naturalized, 1967; son of John Fernie and Nell (Beattie) F.; married Yvonne Anne Chaney, December 23, 1955; children—Kimberly Jan, Robyn Andrea. Bachelor of Science, University Cape Town, 1953, Bachelor of Science with Honors, 1954, Master of Science, 1955; Doctor of Philosophy, Ind. University, 1958. Lecturer physics, astronomy University Cape Town, 1958-61; assistant professor astronomy University Toronto, 1961-64; associate professor; 1964-67; professor; 1967—, chairman department; 1978-88; director David Dunlap Observatory, 1978-88. Author: Variable Stars in Globular Clusters and Related Systems, 1973, The Whisper and the Vision, 1976; Contributor articles to professional journals. Fellow Royal Society Can.; member Royal Astronomical Society Can. (past president), International Astronomical Union, Am. Astronomical Society, Astronomical Society Pacific, Can. Astronomical Society. Office: U Toronto, David Dunlap Obs, Box 360, Richmond Hill, Ontario Canada L4C 4Y6

FERTIS, DEMETER GEORGE, civil engineering educator; born Athens, Greece, July 25, 1926; son of George P. and Athanasia (Papazschari) F.; married Vaslike J. Beltsos, July 26, 1953; children—Athanasia, Evaggelia. Bachelor of Science, Michigan State University, 1952, Master of Science, 1955, Doctor of Engineering, 1964; diploma in engineering, National Tech. University, Athens, 1962. Planner-in-charge Ohio, Army Corps of Engineers, Greece, 1948-50; research engineer Michigan Highway Department, Lansing, 1952-57; assistant professor mechanics department Wayne State University, Detroit, 1957-63; visiting professor National Tech. University, 1963-64;

associate professor University Iowa, 1964-66; professor civil engineering University Akron, Ohio, 1966—; consultant in field. Author: Tranverse Vibration Theory, 1961, Deflection and Vibration of Engineering Structures, 1964, Notes on Structural Dynamics, 1966, Dynamics of Structural Systems, Volume 1, 1971, Volume 2, 1972, Dynamics and Vibration of Structures, 1973; contributor articles professional publications. Member American Society of Civil Engineers, Am. Society Engineering Education, Ohio Planners-in-Charge, Am. Concrete Institute, Industrial Math. Society, New York Acad. Sciences, Contemporary Authors. Greek Orthodox. Office: U Akron Department Civil Engring 302 E Buchtel Avenue Akron Ohio 44325

FESHBACH, HERMAN, physicist, educator; born New York City, February 2, 1917; son of David and Ida (Lapiner) F.; married Sylvia Harris, January 28, 1940; children: Carolyn Barbara, Theodore Philip, Mark Frederick. Bachelor of Science, City College of New York, 1937; Doctor of Philosophy, Massachusetts Institute of Technology, 1942; Doctor of Science, Lowell Tech. Institute, 1975. Tutor City College of New York, 1937-38; instructor Massachusetts Institute of Technology, Cambridge, 1941-45, assistant professor; 1945-47, associate professor; 1947-55, professor; 1955-87, Cecil and Ida Green professor physics; 1976-83, institute professor; 1983-87, institute professor emeritus; 1987—, director Center for Theoretical Physics; 1967-73, head department physics; 1973-83; consultant Atomic Energy Commission; chairman nuclear sci. adv. committee of Department Energy and National Science Foundation,

1979-82. Author: (with P.M. Morse) Methods of Theoretical Physics, 1953, (with A. deShalit) Theoretical Nuclear Physics, 1974; editor: Annals of Physics, Contemporary Concepts in Physics; contributor articles to sci. journals. John Simon Guggenheim Memorial Foundation fellow, 1954-55; Ford fellow European Organization of Nuclear Research, Geneva, Switzerland, 1962-63; recipient Harris medal City College of New York, 1977; National Medal of Sci., 1986. Member Am. Physical Society (chairman division nuclear physics 1970-71, divisional councillor 1974-78, executive committee 1974-78, chairman panel on pub. affairs 1976-78, vice president 1979-80, president 1980-81, Bonner prize 1973), National Acad. Sciences, National Research Council, Am. Acad. Arts and Sciences (vice president Class I 1973-76, president 1982-86), American Association for the Advancement of Science (chairman physics section 1987-88), International Union Pure and Applied Physics (chairman nuclear physics section 1984—). Home: 5 Sedgwick Road Cambridge Massachusetts 02138

FIELD, GEORGE BROOKS, theoretical astrophysicist; born Providence, October 25, 1929; son of Winthrop Brooks and Pauline (Woodworth) F.; married Sylvia Farrior Smith, June 23, 1956 (divorced October 1979); children: Christopher Lyman, Natasha Suzanne; married Susan Alice Gebhart, February 26, 1981. Bachelor of Science in Physics, Massachusetts Institute of Technology, 1951; Doctor of Philosophy in Astronomy, Princeton University, 1955. Assistant professor, then associate professor astronomy Princeton University, 1957-65; visiting professor California Institute Tech., 1964; professor astronomy University California, Berkeley, 1965-72; chairman department University California, 1970-71; Phillips visitor Haverford (Pennsylvania) College, 1965, 71; visiting professor Cambridge (England) University, 1969; professor astronomy Harvard University, 1972—, now Willson professor applied astronomy; former director Smithsonian Astrophysical Observatory, now senior scientist; lecturer Ecole d'Ete de Physique Theorique, Les Houches, France, 1974; member National Commission on Space, 1985—; member study group NRC-Space Sci. Board. Recipient Public Service medal National Aeronautics and Space Administration, 1977, cert. exceptional service Smithsonian Institute, 1977; Guggenheim fellow, 1960-61. Fellow Am. Physical Society; member Am. Astronomical Society, American Association for the Advancement of Science, Astronomical Society Pacific, International Astronomical Union, Sigma Xi. Office: 60 Garden St Cambridge Massachusetts 02138

FISCHER, ERNST OTTO, chemist, educator; born Munich, Germany, November 10, 1918; son of Karl T. and Valentine (Danzer) F. Diplom, Munich Tech. University, 1949, Doctor rer. national, 1952, Habilitation, 1954, Doctor rer. national h.c., 1972, Doctor.Sc.h.c., 1975, Doctor rer. national h.c., 1977, Dr.h.c., 1983. Associate professor inorganic chemistry University Munich, 1957, professor; 1959; professor inorganic chemistry institute Munich Institute Tech., 1964—. Author: (with H. Werner) Metall-pi-Komplexe mit di- und oligoolefischen Liganden, 1963; transl. Complexes with di- and oligo-

olefinic Ligands, 1966; Contributor (with H. Werner) numerous articles in field to professional journals. Recipient annual prize Göttingen Acad. Sciences, 1957, Alfred Stock Memorial prize Society German Chemists, 1959, Nobel Prize in Chemistry, 1973; Am. Chemical Society Centennial fellow, 1976. Member Bavarian Acad. Sciences, Society German Chemists, German Acad. Sciences Leopoldina, Austrian Acad. Sciences (corr.), Accademia Nazionale dei Lincei, Italy (foreign), Acad. Sciences Göttingen (corr.), Am. Acad. Arts and Sciences (foreign, hon.), Chemical Society (hon.). Spl. research in organometallic chemistry: metal pi complexes of arenes, olefins, carbene and carbyne complexes with metals, ferrocene type sandwich compounds, metal carbonyls. Home: 16 Sohnckestrasse, 8000 Munich 71, Federal Republic of Germany

FISHER, ANNA LEE, physician, astronaut; born St. Albans, New York, August 24, 1949; married William Frederick Fisher; 1 child, Kristin Anne. Bachelor of Science in Chemistry, University of California at Los Angeles, 1971, Doctor of Medicine, 1976, Master of Science in Chemistry, 1987. Physician 1976-78; astronaut National Aeronautics and Space Administration, Johnson Space Center, 1978—, mission specialist STS, 51-A; 1984. Office: NASA Johnson Space Center Astronaut Office Houston Texas 77058

FISHER, LESTER EMIL, zoo administrator; born Chicago, February 24, 1921; son of Louis and Elizabeth (Vodicka) F.; married Wendy Fisher, January 23, 1981; children: Jane Serrita, Katherine Clark. Doctor of Veterinary Medicine, Iowa State University, 1943. Supervisor animal care program Northwestern University Medical School, 1946-47; attending veterinarian Lincoln Park Zoo, Chicago, 1947-62; director zoo Lincoln Park Zoo, 1962—; owner, director Berwyn (Illinois) Animal Hospital, 1947-68; producer, moderator educational closed circuit TV for national vet. meetings, 1949-66; associate professor department biology DePaul University, 1968—; adj. professor zoology University Illinois, from 1972. Editor: Brit. Small Animal Journal and Small Animal Clinician, 1958-72. Member citizens committee University Illinois; chairman zoo and wildlife div. Morris Animal Foundation Served to major, Vet. Corps Army of the United States, 1943-46. Recipient Alumni Merit Award Iowa State University, 1968, Stange award Iowa State University, 1988. Member Am. Animal Hospital Association (regional director, outstanding Service award 1969), Am. Veteran Medical Association, National Recreation and Park Association, International Union Directors Zool. Gardens (vice president 1980-83, president 1983-86), Am. Association Zoo Veterinarians (president 1966-69), Am. Association Zool. Parks and Aquariums (president 1972-73, chairman gorilla species survival plan 1982), Chicago Geographic Society (vice president), Econ. Club Chicago, Theta Xi. Clubs: Adventures (president 1971-72), Execs. of Chicago (board dirs. 1968-71), Arts. Assoc., Chicago Econs. (membership com.) (Chicago). Home: 3180 N Lake Shore Dr Chicago Illinois 60657 Office: Lincoln Park Zoo 2200 N Cannon Dr Chicago Illinois 60614

FISHMAN, ALFRED PAUL, physician; born New York City, September 24, 1918; son of Isaac and Anne (Tinter) F.; married Linda Fishman, August 23, 1948 (deceased); children: Mark, Jay, Hannah Rae. Bachelor of Arts, University Michigan, 1938, Master of Science, 1939; Doctor of Medicine, University Louisville, 1943; Master of Arts (honorary), University Pennsylvania, 1971. Diplomate: Nat. Board Examiners, Am. Board Internal Medicine. Intern Jewish Hospital, Brooklyn, 1943-44; Dazian Foundation fellow pathology Mount Sinai Hospital, New York City, 1946-47; assistant resident, resident medicine Mount Sinai Hospital, 1947-48; Dazian Foundation fellow cardiovascular physiology Michael Reese Hospital, Chicago, 1948-49; Am. Heart Association research fellow Bellevue Hospital, New York City, 1949-50; established investigator Am. Heart Association cardiopulmonary laboratory Bellevue Hospital, 1951-55; Am. Heart Association research fellow physiology Harvard University, Boston, 1950-51; instructor physiology New York University, 1951-53; associate in medicine Columbia College Physicians and Surgeons, New York City, 1953-55; assistant professor Columbia College Physicians and Surgeons, 1955-58, associate professor; 1958-66; professor medicine University Chicago, 1966-69; director Cardiovascular Institute, Chicago, 1966-69; director div. cardiovascular disease Michael Reese Hospital, Chicago, 1966-69; professor medicine University Pennsylvania, 1969—, William Maul Measey professor; 1972—, associate dean School Medicine; 1969-75, director cardiovascular-pulmonary div.; 1969—; director Robinette Foundation, Clinical Cardiovascular Research Center, University Pennsylvania Medical Center, 1969-

82; director Specialized Center of Research (Lung), 1973-81; attending physician Hospital University Pennsylvania, 1969—; senior attending physician Philadelphia General Hospital, 1970-78; physician Massachusetts General Hospital, 1979; consultant to chancellor University Missouri, Kansas City, 1973-78; visiting professor Harvard University, 1970, Oxford (England) University, 1972, Washington University, St. Louis, 1973, Johns Hopkins University, 1974, Ben Gurion University, 1975, Emory University, Atlanta, 1976, University Porto Alegra, Brazilia, Brazil, 1976, University Zurich, Switzerland, 1978, Duke University, 1986, University North Carolina, 1986; visiting scientist for National Institutes of Health to Peking, China, 1980, to Union of the Soviet Socialist Republics, 1985; consultant Executive Office President, 1961-69, University Athens, Greece, 1980; member World Health Organization Expert Panel, Geneva, 1973-76, National Adv. Heart and Lung Council, National Institutes of Health, 1968-71, 79-83; chairman Gov.'s Committee for Research on Respiratory Diseases in Coal Miners, 1974—, International Conference on Lung, Titisee, Germany, Florence, Italy, 1976, 84, Prague, Czeckoslovakia, 1986, 89; member Institute of Medicine, National Acad. Sci., 1980—; chairman Health Sciences Policy Board, Institute Medicine, 1985—; United States chief del. International Union of Physiol. Sciences, Helsinki, Finland, 1989; consultant New York State Board Health, 1987—, Cleveland Foundation, 1984—; visiting committee Case Western Reserve School Medicine, Cleveland, 1987—, Lankenau General Hospital, Philadelphia, 1985. Editor: (with D.W. Richards) Circulation of The Blood-Men and Ideas, 1964, (with H.H. Hecht) The Pulmonary Circulation and Interstitial Space, 1969, Handbooks of Respiratory Physiology, Am. Physiological Society, 1967-72, 79-87—, Physiology in Medicine, New England Journal Medicine, 1969-79, Journal Applied Physiology, 1981-89, cons. editor, 1989—; editor: (with D.W. Richards) Circulation of the Blood Men and Ideas, 1982, Merck Manual, 1972-80, Annual Rev. Physiology, 1977-81, Heart Failure, 1979, (with E. M. Renkin) Pulmonary Edema, 1979, Pulmonary Diseases and Disorders, 1979, 2d edition, 1988, Classics in Biology and Medicine, 1989—; contributor articles to professional journals. Board of directors Polachek Foundation, Philadelphia Zool. Society Served to captain Medical Corps United States Army, 1944-46. Recipient Distinguished Alumni award University Louisville, 1984. Fellow Am. College Chest Physicians (hon.), Royal College Physicians, American College of Physicians; member Am. Physiological Society (chairman publs. board 1974-81, president 1983, editor handbook 1986, chairman centennial celebration committee 1985-87), Am. Society Clinical Investigation, American Association for the Advancement of Science, Royal Society Medicine (London), Association Am. Physicians, Am. Heart Association (board directors 1988—, founder, chairman council on cardiopulmonary disease 1972-74, research council 1974-79, Distinguished Achievement award 1980, sci. pub. committee 1986-88, chairman 1988—, Merit award 1989), New York Heart Association (president 1965-67), Internat Union Physiological Sciences (United States national committee 1982-89, chairman 1986-89), National Acad. Sciences (committee on sci., education and pub. policy 1987—), Institute Medicine of National Acad. Sciences (chairman health scis. board 1984—), Federation Am. Socs. for Experimental Biology (executive board 1983-85), Am. College Cardiology (hon.), Interurban Clinical Club, New York County Medical Society, Philadelphia College Physicians, Heart Association Southeastern Pennsylvania (board directors), Alpha Omega Alpha. Home: 2401 Pennsylvania Avenue Apartment 20-A7 Philadelphia Pennsylvania 19130 Office: Hosp U Pennsylvania 3400 Spruce St Philadelphia Pennsylvania 19104

FISHMAN, ROBERT ALLEN, educator, neurologist; born New York City, May 30, 1924; son of Samuel Benjamin and Miriam (Brinkin) F.; married Margery Ann Satz, January 29, 1956 (deceased May 29, 1980); children: Mary Beth, Alice Ellen, Elizabeth Ann.; married Mary Craig Wilson, January 7, 1983. Bachelor of Arts, Columbia University, 1944; Doctor of Medicine, University Pennsylvania, 1947. Member faculty Columbia College Physicians and Surgeons, 1954-66, associate professor neurology; 1962-66; assistant attending neurologist New York State Psychiatric Institute, 1955-66; assistant attending neurologist Neurological Institute Presbyterian Hospital, New York City, 1955-61, associate; 1961-66; co-director Neurological Clinical Research Center, Neurological Institute, Columbia-Presbyterian Medical Center, 1961-66; professor neurology, chairman department University California Medical Center, San Francisco, 1966—; consultant neurologist San Francisco General Hospital, San Francisco Veteran's Administration Hospital, Letterman General Hospital; director Am. Board Psychiatry and Neurology, 1981-88, vice president, 1986, president, 1987. Author: Cerebrospinal Fluid in Diseases of the Nervous System, 1980; Contributor articles to professional journals. National Multiple Sclerosis Society fellow, 1956-57; John and Mary R. Markle scholar in med. sci., 1960-65. Member Am. Neurological Association (president 1983-84), Am. Federation for Clinical Research, Association for Research in Nervous and Mental Diseases, Am. Acad. Neurology (vice president 1971-73, president 1975-77), Am. Association Physicians, Am. Society for Neurochemistry, Society for Neurosci., New York Neurological Society, Am. Association University Profs. Neurology (president 1972-73), American Association for the Advancement of Science, Am. Epilepsy Society, New York Acad. Sciences, American Medical Association (secretary section on nervous and mental diseases 1964-67, vice president 1967-68, president 1968-69), Alpha Omega Alpha (hon. faculty member). Home: 61 Cloudview Road Sausalito California 94965 Office: U California Med Center 794 Herbert C Moffitt Hosp San Francisco California 94143

FISKE, RICHARD SEWELL, geologist; born Baltimore, September 5, 1932; son of Franklin Shaw and Evelyn Louise (Sewell) F.; married Patricia Powell Leach, November 28, 1959; children: Anne Powell, Peter Sewell. Bachelor of Science in Geological Engineering, Princeton University, 1954, Master of Science, 1955; Doctor of Philosophy in

Geology, Johns Hopkins University, 1960. With United States Geological Survey, 1964-76; chief Office Geochemistry and Geophysics, Reston, Virginia, 1972-76; geologist, curator department mineral sciences Smithsonian Institution, Washington, 1976-80; director National Mus. Natural History, 1980-85, geologist department mineral sciences; 1985—. Am. Chemical Society postdoctoral fellow University Tokyo, 1960-61; recipient Meritorious Service award Department Interior, 1976. Fellow American Association for the Advancement of Science, Geological Society Am.; member Am. Geophysical Union, Geological Society Washington. Club: Cosmos (Washington). Home: 5901 Wynnwood Road Bethesda Maryland 20816 Office: Department Mineral Scis NHB-119 Smithsonian Instn Washington District of Columbia 20560

FITCH, VAL LOGSDON, physics educator; born Merriman, Nebraska, March 10, 1923; son of Fred B. and Frances Marion (Logsdon) F.; married Elise Cunningham, June 11, 1949 (deceased 1972); children: John Craig, Alan Peter; married Daisy Harper Sharp, August 14, 1976. Bachelor of Engineering, McGill University, 1948; Doctor of Philosophy, Columbia University, 1954. Instructor Columbia, 1953; instructor physics Princeton, 1954-56, assistant professor; 1956-59, 1959-60, professor; 1960—, Class 1909 professor physics; 1968-76, Cyrus Fogg Bracket professor physics; 1976-84, James South McDonnel Distinguished University professor physics; 1984—; Member President's Sci. Adv. Committee, 1970-73. Trustee Asso. University, In-corporated, 1961-67. Served with Army of the United States, 1943-46. Recipient Research Corp. award, 1967; E.O. Lawrence award, 1968; Wetherill medal Franklin Institute, 1976; Nobel prize in physics, 1980; Sloan fellow, 1960. Fellow Am. Physical Society, Am. Acad. Arts and Sci., American Association for the Advancement of Science; member National Acad. Sci. Office: Princeton U Department Physics Post Office Box 708 Princeton New Jersey 08544

FITCH, WALTER MONROE, molecular biologist, educator; born San Diego, May 21, 1929; son of Chloral Harrison Monroe and Evelyn Charlotte (Halliday) F.; married Eleanor E. McLean, September 1, 1952; children—Karen Allyn, Kathleen Leslie, Kenton Monroe. Bachelor of Arts, University California, Berkeley, 1953, Doctor of Philosophy, 1958. United States Public Health Service postdoctoral fellow University California Berkeley, 1958-59, Stanford University, Palo Alto, Calif, 1959-61; lecturer University College, London, 1961-62; assistant professor University Wis.-Madison, 1962-67, associate professor; 1967-72, professor; 1972-86; professor University Southern California, Los Angeles, 1986—; visiting Fulbright lecturer, London, 1961-62; National Institutes of Health visiting professor, Hawaii, 1973-74; Macy Foundation visiting professor, Los Angeles, 1981-82. Editor-in-chief Molecular Biology and Evolution; editor Classification Literature, 1975-80; associate editor Journal Molecular Evolution, 1976-80; contributor articles to professional journals. Member Cupertino Planning Commission, California, 1960-61, Madison Planning Commission, 1965-68; member Dane County Regional

Planning Commission, 1968-73; chairman Madison Reapportionment, 1979-81. Grantee National Institutes of Health and National Science Foundation, 1962—. Member Am. Society Biological Chemists, American Association for the Advancement of Science, Am. Chemical Society, Am. Society Naturalists, Biochem. Society (England), Genetics Society Am., Society Study Evolution, Society Systematic Zoology. Office: U Southern California Department Biol Scis University Park Los Angeles California 90089

FLANAGAN, JAMES LOTON, electrical engineer. Bachelor of Science in Electrical Engineering, Mississippi State University, 1948; Master of Science in Electrical Engineering, Massachusetts Institute of Technology, 1950; Doctor of Science in Electrical Engineering, Massachusetts Institute of Technology, 1955. Member electrical engineering faculty Mississippi State University, 1950-52; member tech. staff Bell Laboratories, Murray Hill, New Jersey, 1957-61; head department speech and auditory research Bell Laboratories, 1961-67, head department acoustics research; 1967-85, director information prins. research laboratory; 1985—. Author: Speech Analysis, Synthesis and Perception, 1972; contributor numerous articles to professional journals. Member evaluation panel National Bureau Standards/NRC, 1972-77; member adv. panel on White House tapes United States District Court for D.C., 1973-74; board governors Am. Institute Physics, 1974-77; member sci. adv. board Callier Center, University Texas, Dallas, 1974-76; member sci. adv. panel on

voice communications National Security Agency, 1975-77; member sci. adv. board div. communications research Institute Def. Analyses, 1975-77. Recipient Distinguished Service award in sci. Am. Speech and Hearing Association, 1977. Fellow Institute of Electrical and Electronics Engineers (member fellow selection committee 1979-81, Edison medal 1986), Acoustical Society Am. (associate editor Speech Communication 1959-62, executive council 1970-73, vice president 1976-77, president 1978-79, Gold Medal award 1986); member Acoustics, Speech and Signal Processing Society (vice president 1967-68, president 1969-70, Achievement award 1970, Society award 1976, L.M. Ericsson International prize in telecommunications 1985), National Acad. Engineering, National Acad. Sciences. United States and fgn. patentee in field. Office: AT&T Bell Labs 600 Mountain Avenue Murray Hill New Jersey 07974

FOLKERS, KARL AUGUST, chemistry educator; born Decatur, Illinois, September 1, 1906; married, 1932; 2 children. Bachelor of Science, University Illinois, 1928; Doctor of Philosophy in Organic Chemistry, University Wisconsin, 1931; Doctor of Science (honorary), Philadelphia College Pharmacy and Science, 1962, University Wisconsin, 1969; Doctor of Pharmacy, University Uppsala, 1969; Doctor of Science, University Illinois, 1973. Squibb & Lilly research fellow Yale University, 1931-34; researcher Merck & Company Incorporated, 1934-38, assistant director research; 1938-45, director organic and biological chemistry research div.; 1953-56, executive director fundamental research; 1956-

62, vice president exploration research; 1962-63; president, chief executive officer Stanford Research Institute, 1963-68; Ashbel Smith professor chemistry and director Institute Biomed. Research, University Texas, Austin, 1968—; member div. 9, National Def. Research Committee, 1943-46; Harrison-Howe lecturer, 1949; Baker nonresident lecturer Cornell University, 1953; lecturer medical faculty Lund, Stockholm Uppsala, Gothenburg universities, Sweden, 1954; Strumer lecturer, 1957; chairman adv. council department chemistry Princeton University, 1958-64; Regent's lecturer University of California at Los Angeles, 1960; guest lecturer Am.-Swiss Foundation Sci. Exchange, 1961; Robert A. Welch Foundation lecturer, 1963; courtesy professor Stanford University, 1963—, University Calif.-Berkeley, 1963—; Marchon visiting lecturer University Newcastle, 1964; F.F. Nord lecturer Fordham University, 1971; member rev. committee US Pharmacopoeia; chairman National Acad. Sci., 1975. Recipient Alexander von Humboldt-Stiftung award Federal Republic Germany, 1977; co-recipient Mead Johnson & Company award, 1940, 49; Presidential Cert. of Merit, 1948; Merck & Company Incorporated award, 1951; Spencer award, 1959; Perkin Medal, 1960; co-recipient Van Meter prize Am. Thyroid Association, 1969; Robert A. Welch International award, 1972; Am. Pharm. Association Achievement award, 1974; Priestley medal Am. Chemical Society, 1986. Fellow Am. Institute Nutrition; member American Association for the Advancement of Science, National Acad. Sci., Am. Society Biological Chemistry, Am. Isnt. Chemists. Office: University of Tex Institute Biomed

Research Welch Hall 4.304 Austin Texas 78712

FONDILLER, ROBERT, engineering company executive, management consultant; born New York City, November 29, 1916; son of William and Naomi (Bernfeld) F.; married Vivien Le Vine, September 24, 1940 (divorced September 1944); 1 child, Roger; married Fay Campbell, August 28, 1950 (divorced October 1959); 1 child, Ronald Charles; married Anne Horan, February 16, 1979 (divorced October 1984). Bachelor of Arts in Arts, Columbia College, 1939; Master of Science in Industrial Engineering, Stevens Institute Tech., 1943; Master of Business Administration in Economics, New York University, 1952; Doctor of Philosophy in Psychology, Fremont College, 1956. Registered professional engineer, New Jersey. Engineer General Motors Corp., New York City, 1939; safety supervisor, engineer Western Electric Company, Kearny, New Jersey, 1940-43; president R. Fondiller Management Cons., New York City, 1943—; chairman board Futura Corp., New York City, 1978—, Fondiller Institute, New York City, 1966—, Am. Venture Corp., New York City, 1983—; professor, chairman mechanical tech. div. New York Institute Tech.; associate professor engineering Columbia University, New York City; faculty Columbia Teachers College, New York University, City College of New York, Chaffey College; consultant United States and foreign governments, numerous corporations. Author: Behavioral Science, 1967, Better Product and Package Design, 1968, Purchasing, 1969, Office Management, 1969, Time Management, 1970, Communications, 1971. Inventor fitted sheets, surgical stapler, wristwatch-calculator, swing-up sunglasses, silver-zinc battery, numerous other devices and techniques. Recipient numerous awards including Humanitarian award National Society of Handicapped, 1972, medal of merit Republican Presidential Task Force, 1984. Member Institute of Electrical and Electronics Engineers, American Association of University Profs., New York Acad. Sciences, National Association Professional Engineers, World Future Society, Acad. Management, Am. Designers Institute, Am. Society Metals, Society Advancement of Management, International Society for General Semantics, Plastic Engineers Association, Am. Sociological Association, Am. Psychotherapy Association (diplomate), Acad. Political Sci., Am. Society Cybernetics, Mensa, Seamasters Club, New York Health and Racquet Club, Magellan Club, Explorers Club, Knights of Malta (knight commander). Avocation: solving social problems. Office: Am Venture Corp 200 W 58th St Suite 11B New York New York 10019

FOOTE, ROBERT HUTCHINSON, animal physiology educator; born Gilead, Connecticut, August 20, 1922; son of Robert E. and Annie (Hutchinson) F.; married Ruth E. Parcells, January 12, 1946; children: Robert W., Dale H. Bachelor of Science, University Connecticut, 1943; Master of Science, Cornell University, 1947, Doctor of Philosophy in Animal Physiology and Biochem. Genetics, 1950. Grad. assistant Cornell University, Ithaca, New York, 1946-50, assistant professor animal physiology; 1950-56, associate professor; 1956-63, professor; 1963—, Jacob Gould Schurman chair; 1980—; member study section National Institutes of Health, 1974-78; consultant Shell Oil, 1985—, Environmental Protection Agency, 1988—; program manager United States Department Agriculture competitive grants, 1986-87. Author: Animal Reproduction, 1954; member editorial bds. various journals, 1958—; contributor articles to professional journals, chapters to books. Chairman trustees Congregation Church, Ithaca, 1955-60. Served to captain infantry United States Army 1943-46, European Theatre of Operations. Named Professor of Merit Cornell University, 1967; recipient Sci. medal New York Farmers, 1969; State University of New York Chancellor award, 1980; Superior Service award U.S. Department Agr., 1988. Fellow American Association for the Advancement of Science; member Society Study Reprodn. (board directors 1976-78, president 1985), Am. Society Andrology (member editorial board 1982—, Outstanding Andrologist 1985, Upjohn physiology award 1985), Am. Society Animal Sci. (editorial board 1958-60 National Physiology and Endocrinology award), Am. Society Theriogenology (editorial board 1976—), Sigma Xi, Phi Kappa Phi. Republican. Home: 70 Woodcrest Avenue Ithaca New York 14850 Office: Department Animal Sci Cornell U 201 Morrison Hall Ithaca New York 14853

FORD, WILLIAM KENT, JR., astronomer, researcher; born Clifton Forge, Virginia, April 8, 1931; son of W. Kent and Bernice (Green) F.; married Emily Kathryn Russell, April 4, 1956 (deceased September 10, 1958); 1 child, William Kent III; married Elizabeth Ellen Flack, December 20, 1961; children—Russell Flack, Jeannette Shaw. Bachelor of

Science, Washington and Lee University, 1953; Master of Science, University Virginia, 1955, Doctor of Philosophy in Physics, 1957. Staff member Department Terrestrial Magnetism Carnegie Institution Washington, 1957—; visiting resident scientist Kitt Peak National Observatory, Tucson, 1973-74; adj. staff member Mount Wilson and Las Campanas Observatory, 1981—. Developer electronic imaging devices for astronomical telescopes; designer astronomical instrumentation using electronic image intensifiers; contributor articles to professional journals. Recipient award in physical scis. Washington Acad. Sciences, 1971, Watson medal National Acad. Sciences, 1985. Member Am. Astronomical Society, Astronomical Society of Pacific. Home: Indian Draft Farm Millboro Springs Virginia 24460 Office: Carnegie Instn Washington Department Terrestrial Magnetism 5241 Broad Branch Road Northwest Washington District of Columbia 20015

FORMAN, DONALD T., biochemist; born New York City, February 27, 1932; son of Jack and Fannie (Jaffee) F.; married Florence Sporn, August 22, 1953; children: Joan Diane, Steven Lawrence, Debra Helene. Bachelor of Science, Brooklyn College, 1953; Master of Science, Wayne State University, 1957, Doctor of Philosophy, 1959. Clinical biochemist Mercy Hospital Medical Center, Chicago, 1959-63; director clinical biochemistry, associate professor biochemistry and pathology Evanston Hosp./ Northwestern University Medical School, Chicago, 1963-78; research professor University Stockholm and Royal Postgrad. Medical School,

London, 1975; professor pathology and biochemistry University North Carolina, Chapel Hill, 1978—; director clinical chemistry University North Carolina, 1978—; consultant clinical chemist, industry and government, 1965—. Editor: Clinical Chemistry, 1976. Served with Army of the United States, 1953-55. Recipient Chicago Clinical Chemists Creativity award, 1974; Michigan Heart Association fellow, 1957-59. Member Association Clinical Scientists (president 1973-74), Am. Association Clinical Chemistry (director), Am. Board Clinical Chemistry, National Acad. Clinical Biochemistry, American Association for the Advancement of Science, American Association of University Women, Sigma Xi, Phi Lambda Upsilon, B'nai B'rith. Jewish. Research on enzymology, tumor associated antigens, atherosclerosis. Home: 2559 Owens Court Chapel Hill North Carolina 27514 Office: Department Pathology U North Carolina Med School Chapel Hill North Carolina 27514

FOSTER, HENRY LOUIS, veterinarian, laboratory executive; born Boston, April 6, 1925; son of Joseph and Clara Friedman; married Lois Ann Foster, June 1948; children: James C., John S., Neal R. Doctor of Veterinary Medicine, Middlesex College, 1946; Doctor of Veterinary Medicine Extra Ordinem, Tufts University, 1981; Doctor of Humane Letters (honorary), Brandeis University, 1985. Diplomate: Am. Coll. Lab. Animal Medicine, 1961. Cons. veterinarian United Nations Relief and Rehabilitation Administration, 1946-47; founder, president Charles River Laboratories, Incorporated, Wilmington, Massachusetts, 1947—; vice president, director Century Bancorp; chairman visiting committee Tufts Vet. School, 1980—; chairman board trustees Brandeis University Vet. School, 1979-84, trustee university. Contributor numerous articles to sci. journals; senior editor: The Mouse in Biomedical Research, 4 volumes. Trustee Boston Mus. Fine Arts, Tufts University, Massachusetts General Hospital, Brandeis University. Paul Harris fellow, 1972; recipient human relations award National Conference Christians and Jews, 1983. Member Institute Lab. Animal Resources, National Acad. Sciences, American Veterinary Medical Association, New York Acad. Sci., Am. Association Lab. Animal Sci. (Charles A. Griffin award 1976), Am. College Lab. Animal Medicine (president 1976-77). Home: 11 Drumlin Road Newton Massachusetts 02159 Office: Charles River Labs Incorporated 251 Ballardvale St Wilmington Massachusetts 01887

FOWLER, WILLIAM ALFRED, physicist, educator; born Pittsburgh, August 9, 1911; son of John McLeod and Jennie Summers (Watson) F.; married Ardiane Olmsted, August 24, 1940; children: Mary Emily, Martha Summers Fowler Schoenemann. Bachelor of Engineering Physics, Ohio State University, 1933, Doctor of Science (honorary), 1978; Doctor of Philosophy, California Institute Tech., 1936; Doctor of Science (honorary), University Chicago, 1976, Denison University, 1982, Arizona State University, 1985, Georgetown University, 1986, University Massachusetts, 1987, Williams College, 1988; Doctorat honoris causa, University Liège (Belgium), 1981, Observatoire de Paris, 1981. Research fellow California Institute Tech., Pasadena, 1936-39; assistant professor physics California Institute Tech., 1939-42, associate professor; 1942-46, professor physics; 1946-70, Institute professor physics; 1970—; Recipient Sullivant medal Ohio State University, 1985; Fulbright lecturer Cavendish laboratory University Cambridge, 1954-55; Guggenheim fellow, 1954-55; Guggenheim fellow St. John's College and department applied math. and theoretical physics University Cambridge, 1961-62; visiting fellow Institute Theoretical Astronomy, summers 1967-72; visiting scholar program Phi Beta Kappa, 1980-81; assistant director research, section L National Defense Research Committee, 1941-45; tech. observer, office of field service Office of Scientific Research and Development, South Pacific Theatre, 1944; sci. director, project Volunteers in Service to America, Department Def., 1951-52; member national sci. board National Science Foundation, 1968-74; member space sci. board National Acad. Sciences, 1970-73, 77-80; chairman Office of Physical Sciences, 1981-84; member space program adv. council National Aeronautics and Space Administration, 1971-73; member nuclear sci. adv. committee Department Energy/Nat. Sci. Foundation, 1977-80; Phi Beta Kappa Visiting scholar, 1980-81; E.A. Milne Lecturer Milne Society, 1986; named lecturer universities, colleges. Contributor numerous articles to professional journals. Board of directors Am. Friends of Cambridge University, 1970-78. Recipient Naval Ordnance Devel. award U.S. Navy, 1945, Medal of Merit, 1948; Lammé medal Ohio State University, 1952; Liège medal University Liège, 1955; California Co-Scientist of Year award, 1958; Barnard medal for contribution to sci. Columbia, 1965; Apollo Achievement award National Aeronautics and Space Administration, 1969; Vetlesen prize, 1973; National medal of Sci., 1974; Bruce gold medal Astronomical Society Pacific, 1979; Nobel prize for physics, 1983; Benjamin Franklin fellow Royal Society Arts. Fellow Am. Physical Society (Tom W. Bonner prize 1970, president 1976, 1st recipient William A. Fowler award for excellence in physics Southern Ohio section 1986), Am. Acad. Arts and Sciences, Royal Astronomical Society (associate, Eddington medal 1978); member National Acad. Sciences (council 1974-77), American Association for the Advancement of Science, Am. Astronomical Society, Am. Institute Physics (governing board 1974-80), American Association of University Women, Am. Philosophical Society, Society Royal Sci. Liège (corr. member), Brit. Association Advancement Sci., Society Am. Baseball Research, Mark Twain Society (hon.), Naturvetenskapliga Foreiningen (hon.), Sigma Xi, Tau Beta Pi, Tau Kappa Epsilon. Democrat. Clubs: Athenaeum (Pasadena); Cosmos (Washington). Research on nuclear forces and reaction rates, nuclear spectroscopy, structure of light nuclei, thermonuclear sources of stellar energy and element synthesis in stars and supernovae and the early universe; study of gen. relativistic effects in quasar and pulsar models, nuclear cosmochronology. Office: California Institute Tech Kellogg 106-38 Pasadena California 91125

FOX, MAURICE SANFORD, molecular biologist, educator; born New York City, October 11, 1924; son of Albert and Ray F.; married Sally Cherniavsky, April 1, 1955; children: Jonathan, Gregory, Michael. Bachelor of Science in Meteorology, University Chicago, 1944, Master of Science in Chemistry, 1951, Doctor of Philosophy, 1951. Instructor University Chicago, 1951-53; assistant Rockefeller Institute, 1953-55, assistant professor; 1955-58, associate professor; 1958-62; associate professor Massachusetts Institute of Technology, 1962-66, professor; 1966-79, Lester Wolfe professor molecular biology; 1979—, head department biology; 1985—. Served with United States Army Air Force, 1943-46. U.S. Pub. Health Service fellow, 1952-53; Nuffield Research fellow, 1957. Fellow American Association for the Advancement of Science; member Institute Medicine of National Acad. Sciences (panel on basic biomed. scis.). Office: Massachusetts Institute of Technology Department Biology Cambridge Massachusetts 02139

FOX, MICHAEL WILSON, veterinarian, animal behaviorist; born Bolton, England, August 13, 1937; came to United States, 1962; son of Geoffrey and Elizabeth (Wilson) F.; married Deborah Johnson, August 1974; 1 child, Mara; children by previous marriage: Michael Wilson, Camilla. Bachelor in Vet. Medicine, Royal Vet. College, London, 1962; Doctor of Philosophy, University London, 1967, Doctor of Science, 1975. Postdoctoral fellow Jackson Laboratory, Bar Harbor, Maine, 1962-64; medical research associate State Research Hospital, Galesburg, Illinois, 1964-67; associate professor psychology Washington University, St. Louis, 1967-76; vice president Humane Society United States, Washington; director Center for Respect of Life & Environment;

associate professorial lecturer George Washington University. Contributing editor: McCall's mag; author: syndicated newspaper column Ask Your Animal Doctor; author: Canine Behavior, 1965, Canine Pediatrics, 1966, Integrative Development of Brain and Behavior in the Dog, 1971, Behavior of Wolves, Dogs and Related Canids, 1971, Understanding Your Dog, 1972, Understanding Your Cat, 1974, Concepts in Ethology: Animal and Human Behavior, 1974, Between Animal and Man: The Key to The Kingdom, 1976, The Dog, Domestication and Behavior, 1977, Wild Dogs Three, 1977, What is Your Cat Saying?, 1978; (juveniles), The Wolf, 1973 (Christopher award), Vixie, The Story of a Fox, 1973, Sundance Coyote, 1974, Ramu and Chennai, 1975 (Science Tchrs.' award); co-author: What Is Your Dog Saying?, 1977, Dr. Fox's Fables, 1980, The Touchlings, 1981, Understanding Your Pet, 1978, The Soul of the Wolf, 1980, One Earth One Mind, 1980, Returning to Eden: Animal Rights and Human Responsibility, 1980, How to be Your Pet's Best Friend, 1981, The Healing Touch, 1982, Love is a Happy Cat, 1982, Farm Animal Husbandry, Behavior and Veterinary Practice, 1983, The Whistling Hunters: Field Studies of the Asiatic Wild Dog (Cuon alpinus), 1984; The Animal Doctor's Answer Book, 1984; Laboratory Animal Care, Welfare and Experimental Variables, 1986, Agricide-The Hidden Crisis That Affects Us All, 1986, The New Animal Doctor's Answer Book, 1989, The New Eden, 1989. Editor: Abnormal Behavior in Animals, 1968, Readings in Ethology and Comparative Psychology, 1973, The Wild Canids, 1975, On the Fifth Day: Animal Rights and Human Ethics, 1978, International Journal for Study of Animal Problems, Advances in Animal Welfare Science. Member Brit. Veteran Association, American Veterinary Medical Association, Animal Behavior Society, American Association for the Advancement of Science, Am. Association Lab. Animal Care, Am. Association Animal Sci., Am. Psychological Association, Writers Guild, American Federation of TV and Radio Artists, Am. Massage and Therapy Association. Office: 2100 L St Northwest Washington District of Columbia 20037

FRANK, ILYA MIKHAILOVICH, physicist; born Leningrad, October 23, 1908. Educated, Moscow University. Assistant to professor S I Vavilov 1928; with Leningrad Optical Institute, 1930-34, Lebedev Institute Physics, Union of the Soviet Socialist Republics Acad. Sciences, 1934-70; professor physics Moscow University, 1944—; head laboratory of neutron physics, Joint Institute for Nuclear Research, 1957—; corr. member Union of the Soviet Socialist Republics Acad. Sciences, 1946-48, academician, 1968—. Author: Function of Excitement and Curve of Absorption in Optic Dissociation of Tallium Ioclate, 1933; Coherent Radiation of Fast Electron in a Medium, 1937; Pare Formation in Krypton under Gamma Rays, 1938; Doppler Effect in Refracting Medium, 1942; Radiation of a Uniformly Moving Electron Due to Its Transition from One Medium into Another, 1945; Neutron Multiplication in Uranium-Graphite System, 1955; On Group Velocity of Light in Radiation in Refracting Medium, 1958; Optics of Light Sources Moving in Refracting Media, 1960; On Some Peculiarities of Vavilov-Cherenkov Radiation, 1986.

Recipient Nobel prize for physics (with Tamm and Cherenkov), 1958; State Prize, 1946, 54, 71; Order of Lenin (3); Order of Red Banner of Labor; Order of October Revolution 1978; Varilov Gold medal, 1979. Office: Joint Institute Nuclear Research, Lab Neutron Physics, 141980 Dubna Union of Soviet Socialist Republics

FRANZ, JOHN E., bio-organic chemist, researcher; born Springfield, Illinois, December 21, 1929; married Elinor Thielken, August 7, 1951; children—Judith, Mary, John, Gary. Bachelor of Science, University Illinois, 1951; Doctor of Philosophy, University Minnesota, 1955. Senior research chemist Monsanto Agricultural Company, St. Louis, 1955-60, research group leader; 1960-63, fellow; 1963-75, senior fellow; 1975-80, distinguished fellow; 1980—. Inventor roundup herbicide. Patentee in field. Contributor articles to sci. publications. Recipient Indsl. Research Magazine, 1977; Indsl. Research Institute Achievement award, Washington, 1985; J.F. Queeny award Monsanto Company, 1981; Inventor of Year award St. Louis Bar Association, 1986; The National Medal of Tech., Washington, 1987; Outstanding Achievement award, University Minnesota, 1988; The Missouri award, Gov. of Missouri, 1988. Member Am. Chemical Society (Carothers award Del. section 1989), American Association for the Advancement of Science. Office: Monsanto Agrl Company 800 N Lindbergh Boulevard Saint Louis Missouri 63167

FREEDMAN, DANIEL X., psychiatrist, educator; born Lafayette, Indiana, August 17, 1921; son of Harry and Sophia (Feinstein) F.; married Mary C. Neidigh, March 20, 1945. Bachelor of Arts, Harvard University, 1947; Doctor of Medicine, Yale University, 1951; graduate, Western New England Institute Psychoanalysis, 1966; Doctor of Science (honorary), Wabash College, 1974, Indiana University, 1982. Intern pediatrics Yale Hospital, 1951-52, resident psychiatry; 1952-55; from instructor to professor psychiatry Yale University, 1955-66; chairman department University Chicago, 1966-83, Louis Block professor biological sciences; 1969-83; Judson Braun professor psychiatry and pharmacology University of California at Los Angeles, 1983—; career investigator United States Public Health Service, 1957-66; director psychiatry and biological sci. training program Yale University, 1960-66; consultant National Institute of Mental Health, 1960—, United States Army Chemical Center, Edgewood, Maryland, 1965-66; chairman panel psychiatric drug efficacy study National Acad. Sci.-Nat. Research Council, 1966; member adv. committee Food and Drug Administration, 1967-78; representative to div. medical sciences National Research Council, 1971-82, member committee on brain sciences, 1971-73, member committee on problems of drug dependence, 1971-83; member committee problems drug dependence National Institute Medicine, 1971-76, committee substance abuse, and habitual behavior, 1976-84; advisor President's Biomed. Research Panel, 1975-76; member selection committee, coordinator research task panel President's Commission Mental Health, 1977-78; member Joint Commission Prescription Drug Use, Incorporated, 1977-80. Author: (with New Jersey Giarman) Biochemical Pharmacology of Psychotomimetic

Drugs, 1965, What Is Drug Abuse?, 1970, (with F.C. Redlich) The Theory and Practice of Psychiatry, 1966, (with D. Offer) Modern Psychiatry and Clinical Research, 1972; editor: (with J. Dyrud) American Handbook of Psychiatry, Volume V, 1975, The Biology of the Major Psychoses: A Comparative Analysis, 1975; chief editor: Archives General Psychiatry, 1970—. Board of directors Founds. Fund for Research in Psychiatry, 1969-72, Drug Abuse Council, 1972-80; vice chairman Drug Abuse Council Illinois, 1972-82. Served with Army of the United States, 1942-46. Recipient Distinguished Achievement award Modern Medicine, 1973; William C. Menninger award American College of Physicians, 1975; McAlpin medal for research achievment, 1979; Vestermark award for education, 1981. Fellow Am. Acad. Arts and Sciences, Am. Psychiat. Association (chairman commission on drug abuse 1971-78), Am. College Neuropsychopharmacology (president 1970-71); member Institute Medicine National Acad. Sciences, American College of Physicians (William C. Menninger award 1975), Illinois Psychiat. Society (president 1971-72), Social Sci. Research Council (director 1968-74), Chicago Psychoanalytic Society, Western New England Psychoanalytic Institute, Am. Society Pharmacology and Experimental Therapeutics, American Association for the Advancement of Science, Am. Association Chairmen Departments Psychiatry (president 1972-73), Am. Psychiat. Association (vice president 1975-77, pres.-elect 1980-81, president 1981-82), Group Advancement Psychiatry, Psychiat. Research Society, Am. Psychosomatic Society (councillor 1970-73), Association Research in Nervous and Mental Disease (president 1974), Society Biological Psychiatry (president 1985-86), Sigma Xi, Alpha Omega Alpha. Home: 806 Leonard Road Los Angeles California 90049 Office: University of California at Los Angeles School Medicine 760 Westwood Plaza Los Angeles California 90024

FREEDMAN, MICHAEL HARTLEY, mathematician, educator; born Los Angeles, April 21, 1951; son of Benedict and Nancy (Mars) F.; 1 child by previous marriage, Benedict C.; married Leslie Blair Howland, September 18, 1983; children: Hartley, Whitney. Doctor of Philosophy, Princeton University, 1973. Lecturer University California, 1973-75; member Institute Advanced Study, Princeton, New Jersey, 1975-76; professor University California, San Diego, 1976—; Charles Lee Powell chair math. University California, 1985—. Author: Classification of Four Dimensional Spaces, 1982; associate editor Journal Differential Geometry, 1982—, Annals of Math., 1984—, Journal Am. Math. Society, 1987—. MacArthur Foundation fellow, 1984-89; named California Scientist of Year, California Mus. Association, 1984; recipient Veblen prize Am. Math. Society, 1986, Fields medal International Congress of Mathematicians, 1986, National Medal of Sci., 1987, Humboldt award, 1988. Member National Acad. Sciences, Am. Association Arts and Sciences. Avocation: technical rock climber (soloed Northeast ridge Mount Williamson 1970, Great Western boulder climbing champion 1979).

FREEMAN, ALBERT E., agricultural science educator; born Lewisburg, West Virginia, March 16, 1931; son of

James A. and Grace Vivian (Neal) F.; married Christine Ellen Lewis, December 23, 1950; children—Patricia Ellen, Lynn Elizabeth, Ann Marie. Bachelor of Science, West Virginia University, Morgantown, 1952, Master of Science, 1954; Doctor of Philosophy, Cornell University, 1957. Grad. assistant West Virginia University, Morgantown, 1952-54; grad. assistant Cornell University, Ithaca, New York, 1955-57; assistant prof animal sci Iowa State University, Ames, 1957-61, associate professor animal sci.; 1961-65, professor animal sci.; 1965-78, Charles F. Curtiss Distinguished professor agriculture; 1978—. Contributor numerous articles to professional journals. Active Collegiate Presbyterian Church, Ames. Recipient 1975, Senior Fulbright-Hays award, 1975, First Mississippi Corp. award, 1979, award of appreciation for contributions to Dairy Cattle Breeding 21st Century Genetics, 1984, Distinguished Alumni award West Virginia University, 1985, faculty citation Iowa State University, 1987; named Charles F. Curtiss Distinguished Professor Agr., 1978. Fellow Am. Society Animal Sci. (Rockefeller Prentice Memorial award 1979, award of Honor 1987); member Am. Diary Sci. Association (board directors 1981-83, National Association Animal Breeders Research award 1975, Borden award, 1982, J.L. Lush award 1984), Biometrics Society, Am. Dairy Sci. Association, First Acad. Distinguished Alumni West Virginia University, Gamma Sigma Delta (award of Merit). Office: Iowa State University 239 Kildee Hall Ames Iowa 50011

FREIBERGER, WALTER FREDERICK, mathematics educator, actuarial science consultant, educator; born Vienna, Austria, February 20, 1924; came to United States, 1955, naturalized, 1962; son of Felix and Irene (Tagany) F.; married Christine Mildred Holmberg, October 6, 1956; children: Christopher Allan, Andrew James, Nils H. Bachelor of Arts, University Melbourne, 1947, Master of Arts, 1949; Doctor of Philosophy, University Cambridge, England, 1953. Research officer Aeronautical Research Laboratory Australian Department Supply, 1947-49, senior sci. research officer; 1953-55; tutor University Melbourne, 1947-49, 53-55; assistant professor div. applied math. Brown University, 1956-58, associate professor; 1958-64, professor; 1964—, director Computing Center; 1963-69, director Center for Computer and Information Sciences; 1969-76, chairman div. applied math.; 1976-82, chairman grad. committee; 1985-88, associate chairman div. applied math.; 1988—, chairman university committee on statistical sci.; 1989—; lecturer, consultant program in applied actuarial sci., Bryant College, 1986—; member fellowship selection panel National Science Foundation, Fulbright fellowship selection panel. Author: (with University Grenander) A Short Course in Computational Probability and Statistics, 1971; Editor: The International Dictionary of Applied Mathematics, 1960, (with others) Applications of Digital Computers, 1963, Advances in Computers, Volume 10, 1970, Statistical Computer Performance Evaluation, 1972; Managing editor: Quarterly of Applied Mathematics, 1965—; Contributor numerous articles to professional journals. Served with Australian Army, 1943-45. Fulbright fellow, 1955-56; Guggenheim fellow, 1962-63; National Science Foundation Office Naval

Research grantee in field. Member Am. Math. Society (associate editor Math. Reviews 1957-62), Society for Industrial and Applied Math., Am. Statistical Association, Institute Math. Statistics, Association Computing Machinery. Republican. Episcopalian. Club: University (Providence). Home: 24 Alumni Avenue Providence Rhode Island 02906 Office: 182 George St Providence Rhode Island 02912

FREUND, LAMBERT BEN, engineering educator, researcher, consultant; born McHenry, Illinois, November 23, 1942; son of Bernard and Anita (Schaeffer) F.; married Colleen Jean Hehl, August 21, 1965; children: Jonathan Ben, Jeffrey Alan, Stephen Neil. Bachelor of Science, University Illinois, 1964, Master of Science, 1965; Doctor of Philosophy, Northwestern University, 1967. Postdoctoral fellow Brown University, Providence, 1967-69; assistant professor Brown University, 1969-73, associate professor; 1973-75, professor engineering; 1975—, Henry Ledyard Goddard professor; 1988—, chairman div.; 1979-83; visiting professor Stanford (California) University, 1974-75; consultant Aberdeen Proving Ground, United States Steel Corp., visiting scholar Harvard University, 1983-84; mem.-at-large United States National Committee for Theoretical and Applied Mechanics, National Research Council, 1985—; member IUTAM General Assembly, 1987—. Editor-in-chief: ASME Journal Applied Mechanics, 1983-88 ; contributor articles to tech. journals. National Science Foundation trainee, 1964-67; grantee National Science Foundation, Office Naval Research, Army Research Office, National Bureau Standards. Fellow American Society

of Mechanical Engineers (Henry Hess award 1974), Am. Acad. Mechanics; member Am. Geophysical Union, American Society for Testing and Materials (George R. Irwin medal 1987). Home: 3 Palisade Lane Barrington Rhode Island 02806 Office: Brown U Providence Rhode Island 02912

FREY, DONALD NELSON, engineer, educator, manufacturing company executive; born St. Louis, March 13, 1923; son of Muir Luken and Margaret Bryden (Nelson) F.; married Mary Elizabeth Glynn, June 30, 1971; children by previous marriage: Donald Nelson, Judith Kingsley, Margaret Bente, Catherine, Christopher, Elizabeth. Student, Michigan State College, 1940-42; Bachelor of Science, University Michigan, 1947, Master of Science, 1949, Doctor of Philosophy, 1950, Doctor of Science (honorary), 1965; Doctor of Science, University Missouri, Rolla, 1966. Instructor metallurgical engineering University Michigan, 1949-50, assistant professor chemical and metallurgical engineering; 1950-51; research engineer Babcock & Wilcox Tube Company, Beaver Falls, Pennsylvania, 1951; various research positions Ford Motor Company (Ford div.), 1951-57, various engineering positions; 1958-61, product planning manager; 1961-62, assistant general manager; 1962-65, general manager; 1965-68, company vice president; 1965-67, vice president for product devel.; 1967-68; president General Cable Corp., New York City, 1968-71; president Bell & Howell Company, Chicago, 1973-81, chairman, chief executive officer; 1971-88, also board of directors; professor of industrial engineering and management sci. Northwestern University, Evanston,

Illinois, 1988—; board of directors Clark Equipment Company, Cincinnati Milicron, Spring Industries, Andrew Corp., Spring Industries, Andrew Corp. Co-chairman Gov.'s Commission of Sci. and Industry, Illinois, 1988—. Served with Army of the United States, 1943-46. Named Young Engineer of Year, Engineering Society Detroit, 1953, Outstanding Alumni, University Michigan College Engineering, 1957, Outstanding Young Man of Year, Detroit Junior Board Commerce, 1958. Member Am. Institute Mining Metallurgical and Petroleum Engineers (chairman Detroit chapter 1954, chairman, editor Nat Symposium on Sheet Steels 1956), Am. Society Metals, National Acad. Engineering (member council 1972), American Society of Mechanical Engineers, Society Automotive Engineers (vice chairman Detroit 1958, Russell Springer award 1956), Detroit Engineering Society (board directors 1962-65), National Acad. Engineers, Electrical Manufacturers Club, Council on Foreign Relations, Chicago Club, Saddle and Cycle Club, Tavern Club, Sigma Xi, Phi Kappa Phi, Tau Beta Pi, Phi Delta Theta. Home: 3470 Lake Shore Dr Chicago Illinois 60657 Office: Northwestern U Tech Institute 2145 Sheridan Road Evanston Illinois 60208

FRIED, JOHN H., chemist; born Leipzig, Federal Republic Germany, October 7, 1929; son of Abraham and Frieda F.; married Heléne Gellen, June 29, 1955; children: David, Linda, Deborah. Bachelor of Arts, Cornell University, 1951, Doctor of Philosophy, 1955. Steroid chemist, research associate Merck and Company, Rahway, New Jersey, 1956-64; with Syntex Research, Palo Alto, California, 1964—, director

institute organic chemistry; 1967-74, executive vice president; 1974-76, president; 1976—; senior vice president Syntex Corp., 1981-86, vice chairman; 1986—. Member Am. Chemical Society. Office: Syntex Research 3401 Hillview Avenue Palo Alto California 94304

FRIED, JOSEF, chemist, educator; born Przemysl, Poland, July 21, 1914; came to United States, 1938, naturalized, 1944; son of Abraham and Frieda (Fried) F.; married Erna Werner, September 18, 1939 (deceased November 1986); I daughter, Carol Frances. Student, University Leipzig, 1934-37, University Zurich, 1937-38; Doctor of Philosophy, Columbia University, 1941. Eli Lilly fellow Columbia University, 1941-43; research chemist Givaudan, New York, 1943; head department antibiotics and steroids Squibb Institute Medical Research, New Brunswick, New Jersey, 1944-59; director section organic chemistry Squibb Institute Medical Research, 1959-63; professor chemistry, biochemistry and Ben May Laboratory Cancer Research, University Chicago, 1963—, Louis Block professor; 1973—, chairman department chemistry; 1977-79; member medical chemical study section National Institutes of Health, 1963-67, 68-72, chairman, 1971; member committee arrangements Laurentian Hormone Conference, 1964-71; Knapp Memorial lecturer University Wisconsin, 1958. Member board editors: Journal Organic Chemistry, 1964-69, Steroids, 1966-86, Journal Biol. Chemistry, 1975-81, 83-88; contributor articles to professional journals. Recipient New Jersey Patent award, 1968. Fellow American Association for the Advancement of

Science, New York Acad. Sciences; member Am. Chemical Society (award in medicinal chemistry 1974), National Acad. Sciences, Am. Acad. Arts and Sciences, Am. Society Biological Chemists, Swiss Chemical Socs., Brit. Chemical Socs., Sigma Xi. Patentee in field. Home: 5715 S Kenwood Avenue Chicago Illinois 60637

FRIEDLAENDER, GARY ELLIOTT, orthopedist, educator; born Detroit, May 15, 1945; son of Alex Seymour and Eileen Adrianne (Berman) F.; married Linda Beth Krohner, March 16, 1969; children: Eron Yael, Ari Seth. Bachelor of Science, University Michigan, 1967, Doctor of Medicine, 1969; Master of Arts (honorary), Yale University, 1984. Diplomate Am. Board Orthopaedic Surgery. Intern, resident in surgery University Michigan, Ann Arbor, 1969-71; resident orthopaedics Yale New Haven Hospital, 1971-74; director tissue bank Naval Medical Research Institute, Bethesda, Maryland, 1974-76; instructor surgery Yale University, New Haven, 1974, assistant professor; 1976-79, associate professor; 1979-84, professor, chief orthopaedics; 1984-86, professor chairman department orthopaedics and rehabilitation; 1986—. Board cons. editors Journal Bone and Joint Surgery, Boston, 1981—; board adv. editors, Clin. Orthopaedics and Related Research, 1986—; editor Orthopaedic Rheumatology Digest, 1986—; contributor articles to professional journals, chapters to books. Served to lieutenant commander United States Navy, 1974-76. Recipient Kappa Delta Outstanding Research award, 1982. Fellow American College of Surgeons, Am. Acad. Orthopaedic Surgeons (chairman committee tissue allografts 1986—); member Am. Tissue Banks (president 1983-85), Orthopaedic Research Society, Transplantation Society, Musculoskeletal Tumor Society, Am. Council on Transplantation (president 1983-85), Society for Surgical Oncology, Am. Society Transplant Surgeons, Am. Orthopaedic Association. Jewish. Home: 15 Old Still Road Woodbridge Connecticut 06525 Office: Yale U Department Orthopedics & Rehabilitation 333 Cedar St New Haven Connecticut 06510

FRIEDMAN, AVNER, mathematician; born Petah-Tikva, Israel, November 19, 1932; came to United States, 1956; son of Moshe and Hanna (Rosenthal) F.; married Lillia Lynn, June 7, 1959; children—Alissa, Joel, Naomi, Tamara. Master of Science, Hebrew University, Jerusalem, 1954, Doctor of Philosophy, 1956. Professor math. Northwestern University, Evanston, Illinois, 1962-86; professor math. Purdue University, West Lafayette, Ind., 1984-87, director Center Applied Math.; 1984-87; professor math., director Institute Math. and Its Applications University Minnesota, 1987—. Author: Generalized Functions and Partial Differential Equations, 1963; Partial Differential Equations of Parabolic Type, 1964; Partial Differential Equations, 1969; Foundations of Modern Analysis, 1970; Advanced Calculus, 1971; Differential Games, 1971; Stochastic Differential Equations and Applications, volume 1, 1975, volume 2, 1976; Variational Principles and Free Boundary Problems, 1983. Contributor articles to professional publications. Fellow Sloan Foundation, 1962-65, Guggenheim, 1966-67; recipient Creativity award National Science

Foundation, 1983-85. Member Am. Math. Society.

FRIEDMAN, RONALD MARVIN, cellular biologist; born Brooklyn, April 26, 1930; son of Joseph and Helen (Plotkin) F.; children: Philip, Joelle. Bachelor of Science, Columbia University, 1960; Master of Science, New York University, 1967, Doctor of Philosophy, 1976. Predoctoral fellow Institute Microbiology, 1968-72, New York University, 1972-76; postdoctoral fellow Columbia University, 1976, Yale University, 1977-78; visiting fellow Princeton University, 1978-79; visiting scientist New York State Institute Basic Research, 1979-81; research fellow Albert Einstein College Medicine, 1981-82; sci. advisor Royal Arch Medical Research Foundation, Riverdale, New York, 1982—; research fellow memorial Sloan-Kettering Cancer Center, New York City,. New York, 1984-85; senior research associate department pathology Catholic Medical Center, 1983-84; research associate department biochemistry University Medicine and Dentistry New Jersey, Newark, 1984-85; senior research associate in hematology City University of New York, 1985—; research associate department immunology and biochemistry Roswell Park Memorial Institute, Buffalo, 1986-87; research associate, infectious disease, Channing Laboratory, Harvard Medical School, Boston, 1987—. Volunteer Office of Secretary of Agriculture, 1970-71; conducted survey of emergency medical home call service, Bronx County, NY., 1971-72. Knights Templar fellow, 1973—; National Institutes of Health fellow, 1981-82. Member Harvey Society, Am. Society for Experimental Biology, Am. Society Zoology, Animal Behavior Society, Am. Society Cell Biologists, New York Acad. Sciences, American Association for the Advancement of Science, International Platform Association, Sigma Xi. Clubs: Columbia University Faculty, Nippon. Lodges: Masons, Shriners, Knight Templar. Office: Channing Lab 180 Longwood Avenue Boston Massachusetts 02115

FROSCH, ROBERT ALAN, physicist, automobile manufacturing executive; born New York City, May 22, 1928; son of Herman Louis and Rose (Bernfeld) F.; married Jessica Rachael Denerstein, December 22, 1957; children: Elizabeth Ann, Margery Ellen. Bachelor of Arts, Columbia University, 1947, Master of Arts, 1949, Doctor of Philosophy, 1952; Doctor of Engineering (honorary), University Miami, 1982, Michigan Technological University, 1983. Scientist Hudson Laboratories Columbia University, 1951-53, assistant director theoretical div.; 1953-54, associate director; 1954-56, director; 1956-63; director nuclear test detection Advanced Research Projects Agency, Office Secretary Defense, 1963-65; deputy director Advanced Research Projects Agency, 1965-66; assistant secretary navy for research and devel. Washington, 1966-73; assistant executive director United Nations Environment Programme, 1973-75; associate director for applied oceanography Woods Hole (Massachusetts) Oceanographic Institution, 1975-77; administrator National Aeronautics and Space Administration, Washington, 1977-81; president Am. Association Engineering Societies, New York City, 1981-82; vice president in charge Research Laboratories General

Motors Corp., Warren, Michigan, 1982—; chairman United States del. to Intergovtl. Oceanographic Commission meetings United Nations Educational, Scientific and Cultural Organization, Paris, 1967, 70. Research and publications numerous sci. and tech. articles. Recipient Arthur S. Flemming award, 1966, National Aeronautics and Space Administration Distinguished Service award, 1981. Fellow American Association for the Advancement of Science, American Institute of Aeronautics and Astronautics, Acoustical Society Am., Am. Astronautical Society (John F. Kennedy astronautics award 1981), Institute of Electrical and Electronics Engineers; member Am. Geophysical Union, Seismological Society Am., Society Exploration Geophysicists (Special Commendation award 1981), Marine Tech. Society, National Acad. Engineering, Am. Physical Society, Society Naval Architects and Marine Engineers, Society Automotive Engineers, Engineering Society Detroit. Office: Gen Motors Research Labs Warren Michigan 48090-9055 also: General Motors Gen Motors Building Detroit Michigan 48202

FUJITA, TETSUYA THEODORE, educator, meteorologist; born Kitakyushu City, Japan, October 23, 1920; came to United States, 1953, naturalized, 1968; son of Tomojiro and Yoshie (Kanesue) F.; married Sumiko Yamamoto, June 13, 1969; 1 son, Kazuya. Bachelor.S.Eq. in Mechanical Engineering, Meiji College Tech., Kitakyushu City, 1943; Dr.Science, Tokyo University, 1953. Assistant professor Meiji College Tech., Kitakyushu, 1943-49; assistant professor Kyushu Institute Tech., Kitakyushu, 1949-53; senior

meteorologist University Chicago, 1953-62, associate professor; 1962-65, professor; 1965—. Recipient Okada award Japan Meteorol. Society, 1959, Kamura award Kyushu Institute Tech., 1965, Meisinger award Am. Meteorol. Society, 1967, Aviation Week and Space Tech. Distinguished Service award Flight Safety Foundation, 1977, Adm. Luis de Florez Flight Safety award, 1977, Annual award National Weather Association, 1978, Distinguished Public Service award National Aeronautics and Space Administration, 1979, Losey Atmospheric Sci. award American Institute of Aeronautics and Astronautics, 1982, 25th year Weather Satellite medal Department Commerce, 1985. Member Am. Meteorological Society (applied meteorology award 1988), Japan Meteorological Society, Sigma Xi. Specialized research on tornadoes, microburst-related aircraft accidents and satellite meteorology. Home: 5727 Maryland Avenue Chicago Illinois 60637 Office: Department Geophys Sciences U Chicago 5734 Ellis Avenue Chicago Illinois 60637

FUKUI, KENICHI, chemist; born Nara, Japan, October 4, 1918; son of Ryokichi and Chie Fukui; married Tomoe Horie, 1947; 2 children. Student, Kyoto Imperial University. Researcher synthetic fuel chemistry Army Fuel Laboratory, 1941-45; lecturer in fuel chemistry Kyoto Imperial University, 1943, assistant professor; 1945-51, professor; 1951-82; president Kyoto Institute Tech., 1988; director Institute for Fundamental Chemistry, 1988—; councillor Kyoto University, 1970-73, dean faculty engineering, 1971-73, president industrial arts and textile fibres, 1982—; chemist U.S.-Japan Eminent Scientist Exchange Programme, 1973; counselor Institute Molecular Sci., 1976—. Contributor articles to professional journals. Chairman executive committee 3d International Congress Quantum Chemistry, Kyoto, 1979; foreign associate National Acad. Sci., 1981. Senior Foreign Scientist fellow National Science Foundation, 1970; recipient Japan Acad. medal, 1962, Nobel Prize for chemistry, 1981, Order of Culture award, 1981; named Person of Cultural Merits, 1981. Member Am. Acad. Arts and Sciences (hon. member), European Acad. Arts Sciences and Humanities, Japan Acad., Pontifical Acad. Sciences, Chemical Society (vice president 1978-79, president 1983-84). Home: 23 Kitashirakawa-Hiraicho, Sakyo-ku, Kyoto 606, Japan Office: Institute Fundamental Chemistry, 34-4 Takano-Nishihiraki-cho, Sakyo-ku, Kyoto 606, Japan

FULLERTON, CHARLES GORDON, astronaut; born Rochester, New York, October 11, 1936; son of Charles Renwick and Grace (Sherman) F.; married Marie Jeanette Buettner, July 6, 1968. Bachelor of Science, California Institute Tech., 1957, Master of Science in Mechanical Engineering, 1958. Commissioned 2d lieutenant United States Air Force, 1958, advanced through grades to colonel; 1979; completed pilot training 1959; bomber pilot (Strategic Air Command), Davis-Monthan Air Force Base, Tucson, 1960-64; completed aerospace research pilot school Edwards Air Force Base, 1965; bomber flight test pilot 1966; astronaut (United States Air Force Manned Orbiting Laboratory), 1966-69, (National Aeronautics and Space Administration Johnson Space Center), Houston, 1969—. Decorated Distinguished Flying Cross, National Aeronautics and Space Administration Exceptional Service medal, U.S. Air Force Commendation medal, Meritorious Service medal, Outstanding Unit award, National Defense Service medal, Distinguished Service medal. Fellow Society Experimental Test Pilots (associate); Member Tau Beta Pi. Office: NASA/DFRF/ODF Box 273 Edwards Air Force Base California 93523

FUNG, YUAN-CHENG BERTRAM, bioengineering educator, author; born Yuhong, Changchow, Kiangsu, China, September 15, 1919; came to United States, 1945, naturalized, 1957; son of Chung-Kwang and Lien (Hu) F.; married Luna Hsien-Shih Yu, December 22, 1949; children: Conrad Antung, Brenda Pingsi. Bachelor of Science, National Central University, Chungking, China, 1941, Master of Science, 1943; Doctor of Philosophy, California Institute Tech., 1948. Research fellow Bureau Aeronautical Research China, 1943-45; research assistant, then research fellow California Institute Tech., 1946-51, member faculty; 1951-66, professor aeros.; 1959-66; professor bioengineering and applied mechanics University California, San Diego, 1966—; consultant aerospace industrial firms, 1949—. Author: The Theory of Aeroelasticity, 1956, Foundations of Solid Mechanics, 1965, A First Course in Continuum Mechanics, 1969, 77, Biomechanics, 1972, Biomechanics: Mechanical Properties of Living Tissues, 1980, Biodynamics: Circulation, 1984; also papers.; Editor: Journal Biorheology, Journal Biomechanical Enginerring. Recipient Achievement award

Chinese Institute Engrs., 1965, 68; Landis award Microcirculatory Society, 1975, Poiseville medal International Society Biorheology, 1986, Engineer of Year award San Diego Engineering Society, 1986; von Karman medal American Society of Civil Engineers, 1976; Guggenheim fellow, 1958-59. Fellow American Institute of Aeronautics and Astronautics, American Society of Mechanical Engineers (Lissner award 1978, Centennial medal 1978, Worcester Reed Warner medal 1984); member National Acad. Engring, Society Engineering Sci., Microcirculatory Society, Am. Physiological Society, National Heart Association, Basic Sci. Council, Sigma Xi.

FURTH, HAROLD PAUL, physicist, educator; born Vienna, Austria, January 13, 1930; came to United States, 1941, naturalized, 1947; son of Otto and Gertrude (Harteck) F.; married Alice May Lander, June 19, 1959 (divorced December 1977); 1 son, John Frederick. Graduate, Hill School, 1947; Bachelor of Arts, Harvard University, 1951; Doctor of Philosophy, Harvard, 1960; postgraduate, Cornell University, 1951-52. Physicist University, California Lawrence Radiation Laboratory, Livermore, 1956-65; group leader University, California Lawrence Radiation Laboratory, 1965-67; professor astrophysical sciences Princeton University, 1967—; director Plasma Physics Laboratory, 1981—. Board editors: Physics of Fluids, 1965-67, Nuclear Fusion, 1964—, Revs. Modern Physics, 1975-80, Plasma Physics and Controlled Fusion, 1984—, Journal Fusion Energy, 1984—; contributor articles to professional journals. Recipient E.O. Lawrence award

Atomic Energy Commission, 1974, Joseph Priestley award Dickinson College, 1985. Fellow Am. Physical Society (J. C. Maxwell prize 1983); member National Acad. Sciences. Patentee in field. Home: 36 Lake Lane Princeton New Jersey 08540

GAJDUSEK, DANIEL CARLETON, pediatrician, research virologist; born Yonkers, New York, September 9, 1923; son of Karl A. and Ottilia D. (Dobroczki) G.; children: Ivan Mbagintao, Josede Figirliyong, Jesus Raglmar, Jesus Mororui, Mathias Maradol, Jesus Tamel, Jesus Salalu, John Paul Runman, Yavine Borima, Arthur Yolwa, Joe Yongorimah Kintoki, Thomas Youmog, Toni Wanevi, Toname Ikabala, Magame Prima, Senavayo Anua, Igitava Yoviga, Luwi Ikavara, Iram'bin'ai Undae'mai, Susanna Undapmaina, Steven Malrui, John Fasug Raglmar, Launako Wate, Louise Buwana, Regina Etangthaw Raglmar, Vincent Ayin, Daniel Sumal. Bachelor of Science, University Rochester, 1943; Doctor of Medicine, Harvard University, 1946; NRC fellow, California Institute Tech., 1948-49; Doctor of Science (honorary), University Rochester, 1977, Medical College Ohio, 1977, Washington & Jefferson College, 1980, Harvard University Medical School, 1987, Dental College of New Jersey, 1987; Doctor of Hebrew Literature (honorary), Hamilton College, 1977, University Aix-Marseille, France, 1977, University Hawaii, 1986; Doctor of Laws (honorary), University Aberdeen, Scotland, 1980. Diplomate: Am. Board Pediatrics. Intern, resident Babies Hospital, Columbia Presbyn. Medical Center, New York City, 1946-47; resident pediatrics Children's Hospital, Cincinnati, 1947-

48; pediatric medical mission Germany, 1948; resident, clinical and research fellow Childrens Hospital, Boston, 1949-51; research fellow pediatrics and infectious diseases Harvard University, 1949-52; with Walter Reed Army Institute Research, Washington, 1952-53, Institut Pasteur, Teheran, Iran and department medical University Maryland, 1954-55; visiting investigator National Foundation Infantile Paralysis, Walter and Eliza Hall Institute Medical Research, Melbourne, Australia, 1955-57; director program for study child growth and devel. and disease patterns in primitive cultures and laboratory slow, latent and temperate virus infections National Institute Neurological and Communicative Disorders and Stroke, National Institutes of Health, Bethesda, Maryland, 1958—; chief Central Nervous System Studies Laboratory, 1970—; chief scientist research vessel Alpha Helix expedition to Banks and Torres Islands, New Hebrides, South Solomon Islands, 1972; hon. professor Hupei Medical College, Wuhan, Peoples Republican of China, 1986; hon. professor neurology Beijing Medical University, Republic of China, 1987; hon. faculty Medical School University of Papua New Guinea, Port Moresby, 1980; visiting professor Royal Society of Medicine, 1987. Author: Hemorrhagic Fevers and Mycotoxicoses in the Union of Soviet Socialist Republics, 1951, Journals, 40 volumes, 1954-85, Hemorrhagic Fevers and Mycotoxicoses, 1959, Slow Latent and Temperate Virus Infections, 1965, Correspondence on the Discovery of Kuru, 1976, (with Judith Farquhar) Kuru, 1980. Recipient E. Meade Johnson award Am. Acad. Pediatrics, 1963, Superior Service award National Institutes of Health, Department of Health, Education and Welfare, 1970, Distinguished Service award Department of Health, Education and Welfare, 1975, Professor Lucian Dautrebande prize in pathophysiology Belgium, 1976, Nobel prize in physiology and medicine, 1976; Dyer lecturer National Institutes of Health, 1974; Heath Clark lecturer University London, 1974; B.K. Rachford lecturer Children's Hospital Research Foundation, Cincinnati, 1975; Langmuir lecturer Center for Disease Control, Atlanta, 1975; Withering lecturer University Birmingham, England, 1976; Cannon Elie lecturer Boston Children's Medical Center, 1976; Zale lecturer University Texas, Dallas, 1976; Bayne-Jones lecturer Johns Hopkins Medical School, Baltimore, 1976; Harvey lecturer New York Acad. Medicine, 1977; J.E. Smadel lecturer Infectious Disease Society Am., 1977; Burnet lecturer Australasian Society Infectious Disease, 1978; Mapother lecturer University London, 1978; Distinguished lecturer in medicine Mayo Clinic, 1978; Kaiser Memorial lecturer University Hawaii, 1979; Eli Lilly lecturer University Toronto, 1979; Payne lecturer Children's Hospital District of Columbia, 1981; Ray C. Moon lecturer Angelo State University, Texas, 1981; Silliman lecturer Yale University, 1981; Blackfan lecturer Children's Hospital Medical Center, Boston, 1981; Hitchcock Memorial lecturer University Calif.-Berkeley, 1982; Nelson lecturer University Calif.-Davis, 1982; Derick-MacKerres lecturer Queensland Institute Medical Research, 1982; Bicentennial lecturer Harvard University School Medicine, 1982; Cartwright lecturer Columbia University, 1982; lecturer Chinese

Acad. Medical Sci., 1983; Michelson lecturer, professor, University Tennessee, Memphis, 1986; plenary lecturer, Chinese Association Medical Virology, Yentai, 1986; returned Nobel Laureate, Karolinska Institute, Stockholm and University Tromsö, Norway, 1986. Member National Acad. Sciences, Am. Acad. Arts and Sciences, Am. Philosophical Society, Deutsche Akademie Naturförschen Leopoldina, Royal Acads. Medicine Belgium, Royal Anthropological Institute Great Britain and Ireland, Society Pediatric Research, Am. Pediatric Society, Am. Society Human Genetics, Am. Acad. Neurology (Cotzias prize 1979), Society Neurosci., Am. Epidemiological Society, Infectious Diseases Society Am., Société des Oceanistes, Paris, Papua and New Guinea Sci. Society, Slovak Acad. Sciences, Academia Nacional de Medicina, Mexico and Colombia, Phi Beta Kappa, Sigma Xi. Home: Prospect Hill 6552 Jefferson Pike Frederick Maryland 21701 Office: NIH 36-5B21 Bethesda Maryland 20892

GALASK, RUDOLPH PETER, obstetrician-gynecologist; born Fort Dodge, Iowa, December 23, 1935; son of Peter Otto and Adeline Amelia (Maranesi) G.; married Gloria Jean Vasti, June 19, 1965. Bachelor of Science, Drake University, 1959; Doctor of Medicine, University Iowa, 1964, Master of Science, 1967. Diplomate Am. Board Obstetrics and Gynecology. Research fellow in microbiology University Iowa, Iowa City, 1965-67, resident in obstetrics and gynecology; 1967-70, assistant professor; 1970-74, assistant professor microbiology; 1973-74, associate professor obstetrics and gynecology microbiology; 1974-78,

professor; 1978—; consultant various pharmaceutical and diagnostic companies. Editor: Infectious Diseases in the Female Patient, 1986; contributor numerous articles to professional journals. Served to staff sergeant United States National Guard, 1954-64. Recipient numerous grants to study the efficacy of various antibiotics and chemotherapeutics. Fellow Am. Gynecologal and Obstetrical Society, Am. College Obstetrics and Gynecology, Infectious Disease Am.; member Central Association for Obstetricians and Gynecologists, Infectious Disease Society for Obstetrics and Gynecology (president 1982-84, founding member), Society Gynecological Investigation (council 1987—), Am. Society Microbiology, American Association for the Advancement of Science, Izaac Walton League Sigma Xi. Roman Catholic. Club: Ducks Unltd. (sponsor). Office: University Iowa Hosps Department Ob-Gyn Iowa City Iowa 52242

GALE, ROBERT PETER, physician, medical educator, scientist, researcher; born New York City, October 11, 1945; son of Harvey Thomas and Evelyn (Klein) G.; married Tamar Tishler, June 2, 1976; children—Tal, Shir, Elan. Bachelor of Arts, Hobart College, 1966; Doctor of Medicine, State University of New York, Buffalo, 1970; Doctor of Philosophy, University of California at Los Angeles, 1976. Diplomate Am. Board Internal Medicine, Am. Board Medical Oncology. Intern, then resident department medicine University of California at Los Angeles, 1970-72, resident I and II in hematology and oncology; 1972-74; Postdoctral studies University of California at Los Angeles Med Center;

associate professor medicine University of California at Los Angeles, 1974—; chairman International Bone Marrow Transplant Registry, Milwaukee, 1982—; Meyerhoff visiting professor Weizmann Institute Sci., Israel, 1983; visiting professor Excerpta Medica Foundation, Amsterdam, 1979; president Armand Hammer Center for Advanced Studies in Nuclear Energy and Health. Author 13 books, numerous articles on hematology, oncology and transplantation. Recipient Presidential award New York Acad. Sci., 1986, Olender Peace Prize, 1986; Leukemia Society Am. scholar, 1976-81. Fellow American College of Physicians; member Transplantation Society, Am. Society Hematology, Am. Association Immunologists, International Society Hematology, International Society Experimental Hematology, Am. Society Clinical Oncology, Am. Association Cancer Research. Home: 2316 Donella Circle Bel Air California 90077 Office: University of California at Los Angeles School Medicine Los Angeles California 90024

GALLETTI, PIERRE MARIE, university executive, medical science educator; born Monthey, Switzerland, June 11, 1927; son of Henri and Yvonne (Chamorel) G.; married Sonia Aidan, December 31, 1959; 1 son, Marc-Henri. Bachelor of Arts in Classics, St. Maurice College, Switzerland, 1945; Doctor of Medicine, University Lausanne, Switzerland, 1951; Doctor of Philosophy in Physiology and Biophysics, University Lausanne, 1954; Doctor of Science (honorary), Roger Williams College, University Nancy, France, University Ghent, Belgium. Assistant professor physiology Emory University, 1958-62,

associate professor; 1962-66, professor; 1966-67, visiting professor; 1967-68; professor medical sci. Brown University, 1967—, chairman div. biological sci.; 1968-72, vice president biology and medicine; 1972—; member sci. adv. committee I-Stat, Princeton, New Jersey, 1984—, Cardiopulmonics, Salt Lake City, 1988—, Cell Transplants Incorporated, Menlo Park, California, 1989; chairman board Sorin Biomedica s.p.a., Torino, Italy; chairman Consensus Devel. Conference National Institutes of Health, chairman devices and tech. branch task force; Hastings lecturer National Institutes of Health, 1979; plenary lecturer World Biomaterials Conference, 1980, 88; McNeil Pharmaceutical Spring Sci. lecturer, 1982; lecturer German Surgical Society, 1987, Japan Society Artificial Organs, 1987. Author: Heart-Lung Bypass: Principles and Techniques of Extracorporeal Circulation, 1962; contributor chapters to books, articles, abstracts to professional journals. Recipient John H. Gibbon award Am. Society Extracorporeal Technology, 1980, Rhode Island Governor's Sci. and Tech. award, 1987, Runzi prize, Switzerland, 1988; grantee National Institutes of Health, 1962—. Fellow Am. College Cardiology; member American Association for the Advancement of Science, Am. Physiological Society, Swiss Physiological Society. Office: Box G 97 Waterman St Providence Rhode Island 02912

GALLO, ROBERT CHARLES, research scientist; born Waterbury, Connecticut, March 23, 1937; son of Francis Anton and Louise Mary (Ciancuilli) G.; married Mary Jane Hayes, July 1, 1961; children: Robert

Charles, Marcus. Bachelor of Arts, Providence College, 1959, Doctor of Science (honorary), 1974; Doctor of Medicine, Jefferson Medical College, 1963; postgraduate, Jefferson University, 1987—. Clinical associate medical branch National Cancer Institute National Institutes of Health, Bethesda, Maryland, 1965-68, senior investigator human tumor cell biology branch; 1968-69, head section cellular control mechanisms; 1969-72, chief laboratory tumor cell biology; 1972—; adj. professor genetics George Washington University; adj. professor microbiology Cornell University; consultant Georgetown University Cancer Center; United States representative to world committee International Comparative Leukemia and Lymphoma Association, 1981—; hon. professor biology Johns Hopkins University, 1985—; board governors Franco Am. Acquired Immune Deficiency Syndrome Foundation 1987, World Acquired Immune Deficiency Syndrome Foundation, 1987. Served with United States Public Health Service, 1965-68. Recipient Dameshek award Am. Hematol. Society, 1974, CIBA-GEIGY award in biomed. sci., 1977, 88, Superior Service award USPHS, 1979, Meritorious Service medal, 1983, Stitt award, 1983, Distinguished Service medal, 1984, F. Stohlman lecture award, 1979, Lasker award for basic biomed. research, 1982, 86, Abraham white award in biochemistry George Washington University, 1983, 1st Otto Herz award for cancer research Tel Aviv University, 1982, Griffuel prize Association for Cancer Research, France, 1983, General Motors award in cancer research, 1984, Gruber prize Am. Society Investigative Dermatology, 1984, Lucy Wortham prize in cancer research Society for Surg. Oncology, 1984, Gold medal Am. Chemical Society, 1984, Hammer prize, 1985, Gairdner prize for Biomed. Research from Can., 1987, special award Am. Society Infectious Disease, 1986, Gold Plate award Am. Acad. Achievement, Lions Humanitarian award, 1987, Japan prize in Preventative Medicine, 1988, others. Member International Society Hematology, Am. Society Clinical Investigation, Am. Society Biological Chemists, Am. Microbiology Society, Biochem Society, Am. Association Cancer Research (Rosenthal award 1983), Am. Federation Clinical Research, Federation for Advanced Education in Sciences, Alpha Omega Alpha. Research on viruses, biochemistry and leukemia. Office: National Cancer Institute Tumor Cell Biol Lab 9000 Rockville Pike Bethesda Maryland 20014

GARDNER, CHARLES OLDA, plant geneticist and breeder, design consultant, analysis and interpretation of experiments; born Tecumseh, Neb., March 15, 1919; son of Olda Cecil and Frances E. (Stover) G.; married Wanda Marie Steinkamp, June 9, 1947; children—Charles Olda, Jr., Lynda Frances, Thomas Edward, Richard Alan. Bachelor of Science, University Nebraska, 1941, Master of Science, 1948; Master of Business Administration, Harvard University, 1943; Doctor of Philosophy, North Carolina State University, 1951. Assistant ext. agronomist University Nebraska, Lincoln, 1946-48, associate professor; 1952-57, chairman statistical laboratory; 1957-68, professor; 1957-70, regents professor; 1970—, interim head Biometrics Center; 1988-89; assistant statistician North Carolina State University, Raleigh, 1951-52;

consultant CIMMYT and Rockefeller Foundation, Mexico, Latin Am., 1964—, consultant CIBA-GEIGY, Eastern half of United States, 1983; consultant, lecturer Department Agriculture, Queensland, Australia, 1977. Contributor articles to professional journals. Elder, Eastridge Presbyterian Church; president Eastridge Parent-Teacher Association. Served to captain, United States Army, 1943-46. Recipient International Distinguished Service to Agr. award Gamma Sigma Delta, 1977, Outstanding Research and Creativity award University Nebraska, 1981, USDA Distinguished Service award, 1988. Fellow Am. Society of Agronomy (president 1982, agronomic service award, 1988), Crop Sci. Society of Am. (president 1975, recipient Crop Sci. award, 1978, DeKalb-Pfizer Crop Sci. Distinguished Career award 1984), American Association for the Advancement of Science (chairman section O committee 1987); member Am. Genetic Association, Genetic Society of Am., Biometric Society (member regional committee), Sigma Xi, Gamma Sigma Delta. Republican. Presbyterian. Avocations: photography; golf; fishing; gardening. Home: 5835 Meadowbrook Lane Lincoln NE 68510 Office: Department Agronomy U Neb Lincoln NE 68583

GARFIELD, EUGENE, information scientist, author, publisher; born New York City, September 16, 1925; son of Ernest and Edith (Wolf) Garofano; married Faye Byron, 1945 (divorced); 1 child, Stefan; married Winifred Koziolek, 1955 (divorced); children: Laura, Joshua, Thea.; married Catheryne Stout, 1983; 1 child, Alexander Merton. Bachelor of Science, Columbia University, 1949, Master of Science, 1954; Doctor of Philosophy, University Pennsylvania, 1961; Doctor (honorary), Vrije Universiteit, Brussels, 1988. Research chemist Evans Research & Devel. Corp., 1949-50, Columbia University, 1950-51; member staff machine index project Johns Hopkins University, 1951-53; president Eugene Garfield Associates, Philadelphia, 1954-60; president, founder Institute Sci. Information, Philadelphia, 1960—; pub. The Scientist, 1986—; adj. professor information sci. University Pennsylvania, 1974—; Member council Rockefeller University, 1978—. Inventor: sci. information service Current Contents, 1956; weekly columnist: Current Comments in Current Contents, 1956—, Up Front with Eugene Garfield in The Scientist, 1986—; author: Essays of an Information Scientist, 10 volumes, 1977-89 (Book of Year Am. Society Information Science 1977); Citation Indexing: Its Theory and Application in Science, Technology and Humanities, 1979, Transliterated Dictionary of the Russian Language, 1979; editor-in-chief: Scientometrics; member editorial board Journal Information Science; contributor articles to professional journals; board dirs. Annual Revs.; developer Science Citation Index, 1961—, Index Chemicus, 1960—. Served with Army of the United States, 1943-45. Recipient John Price Wetherill medal Franklin Institute, 1984, Derek de Solla Price Memorial medal, 1984, John Scott award City of Philadelphia, 1986; first Grolier Society fellow, 1953-54. Fellow American Association for the Advancement of Science (chairman section T), Institute Information Scientists London (hon.); corp. member Information Industry Association (past chairman board, past president, Hall of Fame award); member National Association Sci. Writers, Chemical Notation Association (award 1980), Society Scholarly Pub., Special Libraries Association, Association Computing Machinery, Authors League Am., Medical Library Association, Am. Society Information Sci. (award of merit 1975, past president Delaware Valley chapter), Am. Chemical Society (Skolnick award division chemical info. 1977, Patterson-Crane award 1983), Drug Information Association, Federation Am. Scientists. Patentee in field. Office: ISI 3501 Market St University City Sci Center Philadelphia Pennsylvania 19104

GARMEZY, NORMAN, psychologist; born New York City, June 18, 1918; son of Isadore and Laura (Weiss) G.; married Edith Linick, August 8, 1945; children: Kathy, Andrew, Lawrence. Bachelor of Business Administration, City College of New York, 1939; Master of Arts, Columbia University, 1940; Doctor of Philosophy in Clinical Psychology, State University Iowa, 1950. From assistant professor to professor psychology Duke University, Durham, North Carolina, 1950-60; professor University Minnesota, Minneapolis, 1961-88; clinical professor psychiatry department University Rochester (New York) School Medicine, 1969-79; visiting professor University Copenhagen, 1965-66, Cornell University, 1969-70; visiting colleague Institute Psychiatry, Maudsley Hospital, London, 1975-76; visiting professor psychiatry Stanford University Medical School, 1979—; member committee on schizophrenia research Scottish Rite, Boston, 1968-82; consultant National Institute of Mental Health, also past member

grants committee; member task force on research Presdl. Commission on Mental Health, 1977-78; board of directors Foundations Fund for Research in Psychiatry, 1976-82; member overall sci. adv. committee to health program McArthur Foundation, chairman research network on risk and protective factors in major mental disorders. Author: (with G. Kimble and E. Zigler) Principles of General Psychology, 6th edit, 1984; editor: (with Rutter) Stress, Coping and Development in Children, 1983; member international adv. editorial board: Schizophrenia Bull, 1974—, Psychological Medicine, 1976—; corr. editor: Journal Child Psychology and Psychiatry, 1975-85, editorial board, 1986— ; adv. editor, MCGraw-Hill Book Company, 1969-85; Annual Rev. Psychology, 1982-86. Served with United States Army, 1943-45. Recipient Gold medal Am. Psychological Foundation, Lifetime Research Career award National Institute of Mental Health, 1962-88, Distinguished Graduate award in Psychology, University Iowa, 1986, Lifetime Contbns. award Society for Research in Psychopathology, 1987, President's medal Baruch School, CUNY, 1988; co-recipient Stanley Dean award for basic research in schizophrenia, 1967; fellow Center for Advanced Studies in Behavioral Sciences, Palo Alto, California, 1979-80. Fellow American Association for the Advancement of Science, Am. Psychological Association (president division clinical psychology, 1977-78, Distinguished Contbns. award division clinical psychology, 1988), Am. Psychopath. Association; member American Association of University Women, Psychonomic Society, Society Research in Child Devel., Association Advancement

Psychology (chairman board trustees 1977-78), Institute of Medicine, Am. Orthopsy Association (Ittelson Rsch award 1986). Club: Cosmos (Washington). Home: 5115 Lake Ridge Road Edina Minnesota 55436 Office: N419 Elliott Hall University Minnesota Minneapolis Minnesota 55455

GARRIOTT, OWEN K., astronaut, scientist; born Enid, Oklahoma, November 22, 1930; married Helen Mary Walker; children: Randall O., Robert K., Richard A., Linda S. Bachelor of Science in Electrical Engineering, University Oklahoma, 1953; Master of Science, Stanford University, 1957, Doctor of Philosophy, 1960; Doctor of Science (honorary), Phillips University, Enid, 1973. National Science Foundation fellow Cambridge (England) University, Radio Research Station, Slough, England, 1960-61; assistant and associate professor electronics, electro-magnetic theory, ionospheric physics Stanford University, 1961-65, now consultant professor; astronaut, scientist Johnson Space Center National Aeronautics and Space Administration, Houston, 1965—; sci. pilot Skylab-3 National Aeronautics and Space Administration, 1973, deputy director Sci. and Applications Directorate; 1974-76, director Sci. and Applications Directorate; 1976, assistant director for space and life sciences; 77-78, mission specialist on first Spacelab flight; 1983, now program scientist Space Station Program. Former regional editor: Planetary and Space Science. Served with United States Navy, 1953-56. Recipient Distinguished Service medal National Aeronautics and Space Administration, 1973; Gold medal City of Chicago, 1974; Robert J.

Collier trophy, 1974; V.M. Komarov diploma Federation Aeronautique Internationale, 1974; Robert H. Goddard Memorial trophy, 1975. Fellow Am. Astronautical Society; member Am. Geophysical Union, Institute of Electrical and Electronics Engineers, American Association for the Advancement of Science, International Sci. Radio Union, International Acad. Astronautics, Sigma Xi, Tau Beta Pi. Office: Teledyne Brown Engring Mail Stop 52 300 Sparkman Dr Huntsville Alabama 35807

GARTLAND, WILLIAM JOSEPH, JR., research institute administrator; born New York City, April 15, 1941; son of William Joseph and Mary (Klik) G.; married Margaret Louise Wenstadt, June 20, 1981. Bachelor of Science, Holy Cross College, 1962; Master of Arts, Princeton University, 1964, Doctor of Philosophy, 1967. Assistant research scientist New York University Medical Center, New York City, 1967-69; postgrad. research biologist University California, San Diego, 1969-70; grants associate div. research grants National Institutes of Health, Bethesda, Maryland, 1970-71; program administrator genetics program National Institute General Medical Sciences, 1971-76; executive secretary Recombinant DNA Adv. Committee, 1975-88; director Office Recombinant DNA Activities, 1976-88; United States representative European Sci. Foundation Liaison Committee on Recombinant DNA Research, 1976-81; National Institutes of Health representative Recombinant DNA Committee of United States Department Agriculture, 1978-88; assistant director for preclinical sciences Acquired Immune Deficiency Syndrome program

National Institute Allergy and Infectious Diseases, National Institutes of Health; member National Institutes of Health Executive Recombinant DNA Committee, 1976—; United States head U.S.-Japan Cooperative Program for Recombinant DNA Research, 1982—; member faculty CSC executive seminar program, advanced study program Brookings Institution. Co-author articles in field. Member American Association for the Advancement of Science, Am. Society Human Genetics, Am. Society Microbiology. Clubs: Sierra, Washington Ski. Home: 12300 Morning Light Terrace Gaithersburg Maryland 20878 Office: AIDS Program 6003 Executive Boulevard Bethesda Maryland 20892

GATES, LESLIE CLIFFORD, civil engineer; born Dorothy, West Virginia, November 17, 1918; son of Lauren Adolphus and Lillian (Sandburg) G.; married Martha Rose Shrewsbury, December 21, 1940; children—Ellen (Mrs. James G. Anderson III), Leslie Allen. Bachelor of Science, Virginia Polytechnic Institute and State University, 1940. Registered professional engineer, West Virginia, Kentucky, Ohio, Pennsylvania, Illinois, Tennessee, Wyoming, Utah, Virginia, Montana, Ind., Arizona, Colorado, Washington (state), New Mexico, North Dakota, Oklahoma. Member field party Solvey Process Company, Hopewell, Virginia, 1940-41; associate, partner Ferguson-Gates Engineering Company (name changed to Gates Engineering Company 1961), Beckley, West Virginia, also Charleston, West Virginia, Pittsburgh, Chicago, Denver, Sydney, Australia, 1946-54; owner Ferguson-Gates Engineering Com-pany (name changed to Gates Engineering Company 1961), 1958-61; president 1962-78, chairman board, chief executive officer; 1978-82; president Leslie C. Gates Limited, Beckley, 1982—; chairman Los Angeles Gates Company, Beckley, 1986—; director Cardinal State Bank; trustee Engineering Index, In-corporated; Member West Virginia Board Registration for Professional Engineers, 1965-80. President Beckley Business Devel. Corp., 1965; campaign chairman Raleigh County United Fund, 1962-63, president, 1965; president Raleigh County Citizens Scholarship Association, 1966, Flat Top Lake Association, 1965; adv. board West Virginia University, 1970—. Served from 2d lieutenant to major Corps of Engineers Army of the United States, 1951-45, European Theatre of Operations. Fellow American Society of Civil Engineers; member National Society Professional Engineers (president 1974-75), West Virginia Society Professional Engineers (president 1951) socs. professional engrs.), Am. Road Builders Association, Am. Institute Mining, Metallurgical and Petroleum Engineers (chairman Central Appalachian section 1965-66), Am. Mining Congress (resolutions committee 1981), Am. Water Works Association, West Virginia Coal Mining Institute, Hwy. Research Board, West Virginia Chamber of Commerce (pres.-elect), Beckley-Ralegh County Chamber of Commerce (president 1953), Colorado Mining Association, Illinois Mining Institute, Am. Concrete Institute, Am. Arbitration Association, National Coal Association, Am. Society Engineering Education. Presbyterian (elder). Office: Leslie C Gates Limited Beckley West Virginia 25801

GEERTZ, CLIFFORD JAMES, anthropology educator; born San Francisco, August 23, 1926; son of Clifford James and Lois (Brieger) G.; married Hildred Storey, October 30, 1948 (divorced 1981); children: Erika, Benjamin; married Karen Blu, 1987. Bachelor of Arts, Antioch College, 1950; Doctor of Philosophy, Harvard University, 1956, Doctor of Laws (honorary), 1974; Doctor of Humane Letters (honorary), Northern Michigan University, 1975, University Chicago, 1979, Bates College, 1980, Knox College, 1982, Brandeis University, 1984, Swarthmore College, 1984, New School for Social Research, Yale University, 1987. Assistant professor to professor department anthropology University Chicago, 1960-70; professor department social sci. Institute for Advanced Study, Princeton, New Jersey, 1970—; Harold F. Linder professor social sci. Institute for Advanced Study, 1982—; Eastman professor Oxford University, 1978-79. Author: The Religion of Java, 1960, Peddlers and Princes, 1963, Agricultural Involution, 1963, The Social History of an Indonesian Town, 1965, Islam Observed, 1968, The Interpretation of Cultures, 1973, (with H. Geertz) Kinship in Bali, 1975, (with L. Rosen and H. Geertz) Meaning and Order in Moroccan Society, 1979, Negara: The Theatre State in Nineteenth-Century Bali, 1980, Local Knowledge, 1983, Works and Lives, 1988. Served with United States Naval Reserve, 1943-45. National Acad. Sciences fellow, 1973—. Fellow Am. Philosophical Society, Am. Acad. Arts and Sciences, American Association for the Advancement of Science; member Am. Anthropological Association, Association for Asian Studies, Middle East Studies Association. Office: Institute for Advanced Study Princeton New Jersey 08540

GELLHORN, ALFRED, physician, educator; born St. Louis, June 4, 1913; son of George and Edna (Fischel) G.; married Olga Frederick, August 4, 1939; children—Martha, Anne, Christina, Maria, Edna. Student, Amherst College, 1930-32, Doctor of Science (honorary), 1969; Doctor of Medicine, Washington University, St. Louis, 1937; Doctor of Science (honorary), City College of New York, 1979, State University of New York, 1984, Albany Medical College, 1986. Diplomate Am. Board Internal Medicine. General surgical training Barnes Hospital, St. Louis, 1937-39; gynecology trainee Passavant Memorial Hospital, Chicago, 1939-40; fellow Carnegie Institution of Washington, Baltimore, 1940-43; instructor, later assistant professor physiology College Physicians and Surgeons, Columbia University, New York City, 1943-45, assistant, then associate professor pharmacology; 1945-48, associate professor clinical cancer research department medicine; 1948-52, associate professor medicine; 1952-58, professor medicine; 1958-68; professor medicine and pharmacology, dean School Medicine, also director Medical Center University Pennsylvania, Philadelphia, 1968-73; director Center Biomed. Education, City College, vice president for health affairs City University of New York, 1974-79, emeritus; 1979—; director medical affairs New York State Department Health, Albany, 1983—; senior consultant Commonwealth Fund, New York, 1979-80; visiting professor Harvard School Pub. Health, 1980-83; physician Francis

Delafield Hospital, New York City, 1949-52, chief medical service, 1952-68; visiting professor medicine Albert Einstein Medical School; director Institute Cancer Research, Columbia; board regents National Library Medicine. Member American College of Physicians, College Physicians Philadelphia, Society for Clinical Investigation, Association Am. Physicians, New York County Medical Society, Am. Association Cancer Research (president 1962-63), Am. Society Pharmaceutical and Experimental Therapeutics, Institute Medicine, Am. Society Biological Chemistry. Office: State New York Department Health Empire State Plaza Albany New York 12237

GELL-MANN, MURRAY, theoretical physicist; born New York City, September 15, 1929; son of Arthur and Pauline (Reichstein) Gell-M.; married J. Margaret Dow, April 19, 1955 (deceased 1981); children: Elizabeth, Nicholas. Bachelor of Science, Yale University, 1948; Doctor of Philosophy, Massachusetts Institute Tech., 1951; Doctor of Science (honorary), Yale University, 1959, University Chicago, 1967, University Illinois, 1968, Wesleyan University, 1968, University Turin, Italy, 1969, University Utah, 1970, Columbia University, 1977, Cambridge University, 1980. Member Institute for Advanced Study, 1951, 55, 67-68; instructor University Chicago, 1952-53, assistant professor; 1953-54, associate professor; 1954; associate professor California Institute Tech., Pasadena, 1955-56; professor California Institute Tech., 1956—, now R.A. Millikan professor physics.; visiting professor Massachusetts Institute of Technology, spring 1963, European Organization of Nuclear

Research, Geneva, 1971-72, 79-80; Member President's Sci. Adv. Committee, 1969-72; member sci. and grants committee Leakey Foundation, 1977—; chairman board trustees Aspen Center for Physics, 1973-79. Author: (with Y. Ne'eman) Eightfold Way. Regent Smithsonian Instn., 1974-88; board of directors J.D. and C.T. MacArthur Foundation, 1979—. National Science Foundation post doctoral fellow, vis. professor College de France and University Paris, 1959-60; recipient Dannie Heineman prize Am. Physical Society, 1959; E.O. Lawrence Memorial award Atomic Energy Commission, 1966; Overseas fellow Churchill College, Cambridge, England, 1966; Franklin medal, 1967; Carty medal National Acad. Sciences, 1968; Research Corp. award, 1969; Nobel prize in physics, 1969. Fellow Am. Physical Society; member National Academy of Sciences, Royal Society (foreign), Am. Acad. Arts and Sciences (vice president, chairman Western center 1970-76), Council on Foreign Relations, French Physical Society (hon.). Clubs: Cosmos (Washington); Century Association, Explorers (New York City); Athenaeum (Pasadena). Office: California Institute Tech Department Physics Pasadena California 91125

GERWICK, BEN CLIFFORD, JR., construction engineer, educator; born Berkeley, California, February 22, 1919; son of Ben Clifford and Bernice (Coultrap) G.; married Martelle Louise Beverly, July 28, 1941; children: Beverly (Mrs. Robert A. Brian), Virginia (Mrs. Roy Wallace), Ben Clifford III, William. Bachelor of Science, University California, 1940. With Ben C. Gerwick, Incorporated, San Francisco, 1939-70; president Ben C. Gerwick, Incorporated, 1952-70;

executive vice president Santa Fe-Pomeroy, Incorporated, 1968-71; professor civil engineering University California, Berkeley, 1971—; sponsoring manager Richmond-San Rafael Bridge substructure, 1953-56, San Mateo-Hayward bridge, 1964-66; lecturer construction engineering Stanford University, 1962-68; consultant major bridge and marine construction projects; consultant construction engineer for ocean structures and bridges, also offshore structures in North Sea, Arctic Sea, Japan, Australia, Indonesia, Arabian Gulf, Southeast Asia, South Am.; member United States Arctic Research Committee. Author: Russian-English Dictionary of Prestressed Concrete and Concrete Construction, 1966, Construction of Prestressed Concrete Structures, 1971; Construction and Engineering Marketing for Major Project Services, 1981, Construction of Offshore Structures, 1986; contributor articles to professional journals. Served with United States Navy, 1940-46; commander Reserves retired. Recipient Lockheed award Marine Tech. Society, 1977, Frank P. Brown medal Franklin Institute, 1988. Fellow American Society of Civil Engineers (hon. member; Karp award 1976), Am. Concrete Institute (director 1960, hon. member, Turner award 1974, Corbetta award 1981); member Federation Internationale de la Precontrainte (president 1974-78, now hon. president, Freyssinet medal 1982), Prestressed Concrete Institute (president 1957-58, hon.), Deutscher Beton Verein (hon., Emil Mörsch medal 1979), Concrete Society United Kingdom (hon.), Association Francaise pour Constrn. (hon.), Verein Deutscher Ingenieure (hon.), Norwegian Acad. of Tech. Sci., Royal Acad. Tech. Sci. (Sweden), National Acad. Engineering, Moles, Society Naval Architects and Marine Engineers (Blakely Smith award 1981), Beavers (Engineering award 1975), Phi Beta Kappa, Tau Beta Pi, Sigma Xi, Chi Epsilon, Kappa Sigma. Congregationalist. Clubs: Bohemian (San Francisco); Claremont Country (Oakland). Home: 5727 Country Club Dr Oakland California 94618 Office: U California 217 McLaughlin Hall Berkeley California 94720 also: 500 Sansome St San Francisco California 94111

GHAUSI, MOHAMMED SHUAIB, engineering educator, university dean; born Kabul, Afghanistan, February 16, 1930; came to United States, 1951, naturalized, 1963; son of Mohammed Omar and Homaira G.; married Marilyn Buchwold, June 12, 1961; children: Nadjya, Simine. Bachelor of Science summa cum laude, University California, Berkeley, 1956, Master of Science, 1957, Doctor of Philosophy, 1960. Professor electrical engineering New York University, 1960-72; head electrical sciences section National Science Foundation, Washington, 1972-74; professor, chairman electrical engineering department Wayne State University, Detroit, 1974-77; John F. Dodge professor Oakland University, Rochester, Michigan, 1978-83; dean School Engineering and Computer Sci., Oakland University, 1978-83; dean College Engineering, University California, Davis, 1983—; member adv. panel National Science Foundation, 1989. Author: Principles and Design of Linear Active Circuits, 1965, Introduction to Distributed-Parameter Networks, 1968, Electronic Circuits, 1971, Modern Filter Design: Active RC and Switched Capacitor,

1981, Electronic Devices and Circuits: Discrete and Integrated, 1985, also numerous articles. Cons. editor, Van Nostrand Rinehold Pub. Company, 1968-71. Member disting. alumni rev. panel Elec. Engring. and Computer Sci. programs University California, Berkeley, 1973; member external board visitors University Pennsylvania, 1974. Fellow Institute of Electrical and Electronics Engineers (Centennial medal, Alexander von Humboldt prize); member Circuits and System Society (vice president 1970-72, president 1976), New York Acad. Sciences, Engineering Society Detroit, Sigma Xi, Phi Beta Kappa, Tau Beta Pi, Eta Kappa Nu. Office: Dean's Office College Engring U California Davis California 95616

GIACCONI, RICCARDO, astrophysicist; born Genoa, Italy, October 6, 1931; came to United States, 1956, naturalized, 1967; son of Antonio and Elsa (Canni) G.; married Mirella Manaira, February 15, 1957; children: Guia Giacconi Chmiel, Anna Lee, Marc A. Doctor of Philosophy, University Milan, Italy, 1954; Doctor of Science (honorary), University Chicago, 1983; laurea ad honorem in astronomy, University Padua, 1984. Assistant professor physics University Milan, 1954-56; research associate Ind. University, 1956-58, Princeton University, 1958-59; executive vice president, director Am. Sci. & Engineering Company, Cambridge, Massachusetts, 1959-73; professor astronomy Harvard University; also associate director high energy astrophysics div. Center Astrophysics, Smithsonian Astrophysical Obs./ Harvard College Observatory, Cambridge, 1973-81; director Space Telescope Sci. Institute, Baltimore, 1981—; professor astrophysics Johns Hopkins University; member space sci. adv. committee National Aeronautics and Space Administration, 1978-79, member adv. committee innovation study, 1979—; member National Aeronautics and Space Administration Astrophysics Council; member adv. committee innovation study astronomy adv. committee, 1979—; member high energy astronomy survey panel National Acad. Sciences, 1979-80, member Space Sci. Board, 1980-84; member adv. committee Max-Planck Institute für Physik und Astrophysik; chairman board of directors Instituto Guido Donegani, Gruppo Montedison; member visiting committee to div. of physical sciences University Chicago, University Padova. Co-editor: X-ray Astronomy, 1974, The X-Ray Universe, 1985; author numerous articles, papers in field. Fulbright fellow, 1956-58; recipient Röntgen prize astrophysics Physikalish-Medizinische Gesellschaft, Wurzburg, Germany, 1971; Exceptional Sci. Achievement medal National Aeronautics and Space Administration, 1971, 80; Distinguished Public Service award, 1972; Space Sci. award American Institute of Aeronautics and Astronautics, 1976; Elliott Cresson medal Franklin Institute, 1980; Gold medal Royal Astronomical Society, 1982; A. Cressy Morrison award New York Acad. Sci., 1982; Bruce medal; Heinneman award, Wolf Prize in Physics, 1987; Russell lecturer. Member Am. Astronomical Society (Helen B. Warner award 1966, chairman high energy astrophysics division 1976-77, councilor 1979-82, task group on directions in space sci. 1995-2015), Italian Physical Society (Como prize 1967), American Association for the Advancement of Science, International Astronomical Union (National Acad. Sciences astronomical representative 1979-82), National Acad. Sciences, Am. Acad. Arts and Sciences, Maryland Acad. Sci. (sci. council 1982—), Accademia Nazionale dei Lincei (foreign), Italian Physical Society, Am. Physical Society. Club: Cosmos (Washington). Inventor x-ray telescope, discovered x-ray stars. Home: 203 Lambeth Road Baltimore Maryland 21218 Office: Space Telescope Sci Institute 3700 San Martin Dr Baltimore Maryland 21218 also: Wolf Found /Mr Yaron Gruder, Post Office Box 398, 46103 Herzlia Bet Israel

GIAEVER, IVAR, physicist; born Bergen, Norway, April 5, 1929; came to United States, 1957, naturalized, 1963; son of John A. and Gudrun (Skaarud) G.; married Inger Skramstad, November 8, 1952; children: John, Anne Kari, Guri, Trine. Siv. Ing., Norwegian Institute Tech., Trondheim, 1952; Doctor of Philosophy, Rensselaer Polytechnic Institute, 1964. Patent examiner Norwegian Patent Office, Oslo, 1953-54; mechanical engineer Can. General Electric Company, Peterborough, Ontario, 1954-56; applied mathematician General Electric Company, Schenectady, 1956-58, physicist Research and Devel. Center; 1958—. Served with Norwegian Army, 1952-53. Recipient Nobel Prize for Physics, 1973; Guggenheim fellow, 1970. Fellow Am. Physical Society (Oliver E. Buckley prize 1965); member Institute of Electrical and Electronics Engineers, Norwegian Professional Engineers, National Acad. Sci., National Acad. Engineering (V.K. Zworykin award 1974), Am. Acad. Arts and Sciences, Norwegian Acad. Sci., Norwegian

Acad. Tech. Office: General Electric Company R & D Center Post Office Box 8 K1 Room 3C Schenectady New York 12301

GIBBS, MARTIN, educator, biologist; born Philadelphia, November 11, 1922; son of Samuel and Rose (Sugarman) G.; married Svanhild Karen Kvale, October 11, 1950; children—Janet Helene, Laura Jean, Steven Joseph, Michael Seland, Robert Kvale. Bachelor of Science, Philadelphia College Pharmacy, 1943; Doctor of Philosophy, University Illinois, 1947. Scientist Brookhaven National Laboratory, 1947-56; professor biochemistry Cornell University, 1957-64; professor biology, chairman department Brandeis University, Waltham, Massachusetts, 1965—; Cons. National Science Foundation, 1961-64, 69-72, National Institutes of Health, 1966-69; member corp. Marine Biological Laboratory, Woods Hole, Massachusetts, 1970—; RESA lecturer, 1969; North Atlantic Treaty Organization consultant fellowship board, 1968-70; member Council International Exchange of Scholars, 1976—; chairman adv. committee selection Fulbright scholars for Eastern Europe; adj. professor Botanical Institute, University Münster, Federal Republic of Germany. Author: Structure and Function of Chloroplasts, Crop Productivity-Research Imperative, Revisited, Hungarian-USA Binational Symposium on Photosynthesis; editor-in-chief Plant Physiology, 1963—; associate editor: Physiologie Vegetale, 1966-76, Annual Rev. Plant Physiology, 1966-71. Member American Association of University Profs., Am., Japanese socs. plant physiologists; Am. Acad. Arts and

Sciences, Am. Society Biological Chemists, Council Biology Editors, National Acad. Sciences, Sigma Xi. Office: Brandeis University Institute for Photobiology Waltham Massachusetts 02254

GIBSON, ELEANOR JACK (MRS. JAMES J. GIBSON), psychology educator; born Peoria, Illinois, December 7, 1910; daughter of William A. and Isabel (Grier) Jack; married James J. Gibson, September 17, 1932; children: James J., Jean Grier. Bachelor of Arts, Smith College, 1931, Master of Arts, 1933, Doctor of Science, 1972; Doctor of Philosophy, Yale University, 1938; Doctor of Science, Rutgers University, 1973, Trinity College, 1982, Bates College, 1985; Doctor of Humane Letters (honorary), State University of New York, Albany, 1984; Doctor of Science, University South Carolina, 1987. Assistant, instructor, assistant professor Smith College, 1931-49; research associate psychology Cornell University, Ithaca, New York, 1949-66; professor Cornell University, 1972—, Susan Linn Sage professor psychology; 1972—; fellow Institute for Advanced Study, Princeton, 1959-60, Institute for Advanced Study in Behavioral Sciences, Stanford, California, 1963-64; visiting professor Massachusetts Institute Tech., 1973, Institute Child Devel., University Minnesota, 1980; visiting distinguished professor University California, Davis, 1978; visiting scientist Salk Institute, La Jolla, California, 1979; visiting professor University Pennsylvania, 1984; Montgomery fellow Dartmouth College, 1986; Woodruff visiting professor psychology, Emory University, 1988. Author: Principles of Perceptual Learning and Development, 1967 (Century award), (with H. Levin) The Psychology of Reading, 1975. Recipient Wilbur Cross medal Yale University, 1973; Howard Crosby Warren medal, 1977; medal for distinguished service Teachers College, Columbia University, 1983; Guggenheim fellow, 1972-73. Fellow American Association for the Advancement of Science (division chairperson 1983), Am. Psychological Association (Distinguished Scientist award 1968, G. Stanley Hall award 1970, president division 3 1977, Gold medal award 1986); member Eastern Psychological Association (president 1968), Society Experimental Psychologists, National Acad. Education, Psychonomic Society, Society Research in Child Devel. (Distinguished Sci. Contbn. award 1981), National Acad. Sci., Am. Acad. Arts and Sciences, Brit. Psychological Society (hon.), New York Acad. Sciences (hon.), Italian Society Research in Child Devel. (hon.), Phi Beta Kappa, Sigma Xi. Home: RD1 Box 265A Middlebury Vermont 05753

GIBSON, JOHN EGAN, engineering educator; born Providence, June 11, 1926; married; 4 children. Bachelor of Science, University Rhode Island, 1950; Master of Science in Engineering, Yale University, 1952, Doctor of Philosophy in Electrical Engineering, 1956. From instructor to assistant professor electrical engineering Yale University, New Haven, 1952-57; from associate professor to professor Purdue University, West Lafayette, Ind., 1957-65; director Control and Information Systems Laboratories, 1961-65; dean School Engineering Oakland University, Rochester, Michigan, 1965-73, John Dodge professor engineering; 1970-73; Commonwealth professor School Engineering and Applied Sci., University Virginia, Charlottesville, 1973—, former dean. Office: University Va Department Syst Engring Charlottesville Virginia 22903

GIBSON, ROBERT LEE, astronaut; born Cooperstown, New York, October 30, 1946; son of Paul A. Gibson; married Margaret Rhea Seddon; 2 children. Bachelor of Science, California Polytechnic State University. Commissioned 2d lieutenant United States Navy, 1969, advanced through grades to commander, served in Vietnam; astronaut National Aeronautics and Space Administration, Houston, 1978—. Office: Johnson Space Center Houston Texas 77098

GIDDENS, DON PEYTON, engineering educator, researcher; born Augusta, Georgia, October 24, 1940. Bachelor of Arts in Engineering, Georgia Institute Tech., 1963, Master of Science in Aerospace Engineering, 1965, Doctor of Philosophy, 1967. Registered professional engineer, Georgia. Associate aircraft engineer Lockheed-Ga. Company, Atlanta, 1963; member tech. staff Aerospace Corp., San Bernardino, California, 1966-67; assistant professor Georgia Institute Tech., Atlanta, 1968-70, associate professor; 1970-77, professor; 1977-82, Regents professor; 1982—; co-director Emory/Ga. Tech. Biomed. Tech. Research Center, Atlanta, Georgia Tech. Bioengring. Center, Atlanta. Contributor numerous articles to professional journals. Member American Society of Mechanical Engineers (chairman bioengring. division 1986-87), Society of Sigma Xi (national lecturer 1983-87). Avocation: whitewater canoeing. Office: Ga Institute of Tech George W Woodruff School Mech Engring Atlanta Georgia 30332-0405

GIFFORD, ERNEST MILTON, JR., educator, biologist; born Riverside, California, January 17, 1920; son of Ernest Milton and Mildred Wade (Campbell) G.; married Jean Duncan, July 15, 1942; 1 child, Jeanette. Bachelor of Arts, University California, Berkeley, 1942, Doctor of Philosophy, 1950. Assistant professor botany, assistant botanist experiment station University Calif.-Davis, 1950-56, associate professor botany, associate botanist; 1957-61, professor botany, botanist; 1962—, chairman department botany and agricultural botany; 1963-67, 74-78. Author: (with A. S. Foster) Morphology and Evolution of Vascular Plants, 3d edition, 1989, (with T. L. Rost) Mechanisms and control of Cell Division, 1977; editor-in-chief Am. Journal Botany, 1975-79; contributor articles on anatomy, ultrastructure and morphogenesis of higher plants to professional journals. Served to major United States Army, 1942-46; European Theatre of Operations; to colonel United States Army Reserve, 1946-73. Decorated Bronze Star medal; named distinguished contbr. Encyclopaedia Brit., 1964; National Research Council fellow Harvard University, 1956; Fulbright research scholar, France, 1966; John Simon Guggenheim Foundation fellow, France, 1966; NATO sr. postdoctoral fellow, France, 1974; recipient Acad. Senate Distinguished Teaching award University Calif.-Davis, 1986. Fellow Linnean Society (London); member Botanical Society Am. (vice president 1981, president 1982, merit award 1981), International Society Plant Morphologists (vice president 1980-84), Am. Institute Biological Sciences,

California Botanical Society, Sigma Xi. Office: U California Department Botany Robbins Hall Davis California 95616

GILBERT, WALTER, molecular biologist; born Boston, March 21, 1932; son of Richard V. and Emma (Cohen) G.; married Celia Stone, December 29, 1953; children: John Richard, Kate. Bachelor of Arts, Harvard University, 1953, Master of Arts, 1954; Doctor of Philosophy, Cambridge University, 1957; Doctor of Science (honorary), University Chicago, 1978, Columbia University, 1978, University Rochester, 1979, Yeshiva University, 1981. National Science Foundation postdoctoral fellow Harvard University, Cambridge, Massachusetts, 1957-58, lecturer physics; 1958-59, assistant professor physics; 1959-64, associate professor biophysics; 1964-68, professor biochemistry; 1968-72, Am. Cancer Society professor molecular biology; 1972-81, professor biology; 1985-86, H.H. Timken professor sci.; 1986-87, Carl M. Loeb University professor, chair department cellular and devel. biology; 1987—; chairman board, scientist Biogen N.V., Dutch Antilles, 1978-83, co-chairman, supervisory board; 1979-81, chairman supervisory board, chief executive officer; 1981-84; V.D. Mattia lecturer Roche Institute Molecular Biology, 1976. Guggenheim fellow, 1968-69; recipient U.S. Steel Foundation National Acad. Sci., 1968, Ledlie prize Harvard University, 1969, Warren trienneal prize Massachusetts General Hospital, 1977, Louis and Bert Freedman Foundation New York Acad. Sciences, 1977, Prix Charles-Leopold Mayer Academie des Sciences, Institute de France, 1977, Nobel prize in chemistry, 1980; co-winner Louisa Gross Horwitz prize Columbia University, 1979, Gairdner prize, 1979, Albert Lasker Basic Sci., 1979. Member Am. Physical Society, National Acad. Sciences, Am. Society Biological Chemists, Am. Acad. Arts and Sciences; foreign member Royal Society. Office: Harvard U Department Biology Cambridge Massachusetts 02138

GILL, WILLIAM NELSON, chemical engineering educator; born New York City, September 13, 1928; son of William Nelson and Frances (Murphy) G.; married Chandlee Stevens, August 13, 1982; children: Alison Louise, Christine Marie, Douglas Max, Max William. Bachelor of Science in Chemical Engineering, Syracuse University, 1951, Master of Arts, 1955, Doctor of Philosophy, 1960. Field engineer Am. Blower Corp., 1951-55; member faculty Syracuse University, 1957-65, associate professor; 1963-65; professor chemical engineering, chairman department Clarkson College Tech., 1965-71; provost engineering and applied sci. State University of New York, Buffalo, 1971-78, professor chemical engineering; 1982-87; Glenn Murphy Distinguished professor engineering Iowa State University, Ames, 1980-82; professor, chairman chemical engineering Rensselaer Polytech. Institute, Troy, New York, 1987—; consultant in field. Editor: Chemical Engring. Communications, 1979—; member editorial adv. board Fuel, Processing Tech.; member board cons. editors Elsevier Texts in Engring.; editor Chemical Engring. series Elsevier Science Pub. Company; author numerous articles in field. Fulbright-Hays sr. research scholar University College, London, 1977-78, Fulbright sr. research scholar University Old, Australia,

1986-87. Member Am. Institute Chemical Engineers, American Association for the Advancement of Science, Am. Chemical Society, Am. Society Engineering Education, American Association of University Profs., New York Acad. Sci., Sigma Xi. Office: Rensselaer Polytech Institute Chem Engring-Ricketts Troy New York 12180

GILRUTH, ROBERT ROWE, aerospace consultant; born Nashwauk, Minnesota, October 8, 1913; son of Henry Augustus and Frances Marion (Rowe) G.; married E. Jean Barnhill, April 24, 1937 (deceased 1972); 1 daughter, Barbara Jean (Mrs. John Wyatt); married Georgene Hubbard Evans, July 14, 1973. Bachelor of Science in Aeronautical Engineering, University Minnesota, 1935, Master of Science, 1936, Doctor of Science, 1962; Doctor of Science, George Washington University, 1962, Ind. Institute Tech., 1962; Doctor of Engineering, Michigan Tech. University, 1963; Doctor of Laws, New Mexico State University, 1970. Flight research engineer Langley Aeronautical Laboratory, National Advisory Committee for Aeronautics, Langley Field, Virginia, 1937-45; chief pilotless aircraft research div. Langley Aeronautical Laboratory, National Advisory Committee for Aeronautics, 1945-50, assistant director; 1950-58; director National Aeronautics and Space Administration Project Mercury, 1958-61, National Aeronautics and Space Administration Manned Spacecraft Center, Houston, 1961-72; director key personnel devel. National Aeronautics and Space Administration Manned Spacecraft Center, 1972-73, retired; 1973; consultant to administrator National Aeronautics and Space Administration, 1974—; director Bunker Ramo Corp. Ind. experimenter and consultant hydrofoil craft, 1938-58; advisor on guided missiles, aeros. and structures, high temperature facilities United States Department Def., 1947-58; member committee space systems National Aeronautics and Space Administration Space Adv. Council, 1972—; chairman management devel. education panel National Aeronautics and Space Administration, 1972-73; member ad hoc committee fire safety aspects of polymeric materials National Materials Adv. Board, 1973-74. Recipient Outstanding Achievement award University Minnesota, 1954, Great Living Am. award U.S. Chamber of Commerce, 1962, Distinguished Federal Civilian Service award President U.S., 1962, Americanism award CBI Vets. Association, 1965, Spirit of St. Louis medal, 1965, International Astronautics award Daniel and Florence Guggenheim, 1966, Distinguished Service medal National Aeronautics and Space Administration, spring 1969, fall 1969, Pub. Service at Large award Rockefeller Foundation, 1969, American Society of Mechanical Engineers medal, 1970, James Watt International medal, 1971, Achievement award National Aviation Club, 1971, Robert J. Collier trophy with Nat Aeronautical Association, 1972, Space Transp. award Louis W. Hill, Distinguished Service medal National Aeronautics and Space Administration, medal of honor New York City, Robert H. Goddard Memorial trophy National Rocket Club, National Air and Space Mus. trophy, 1985; named to National Space Hall of Fame, 1969, International Space Hall of Fame, 1976. Member National Acad. Engineering (aeros. and space board

1974—), National Acad. Sciences. Home: Route 1 Box 1486 Kilmarnock Virginia 22482

GINGERICH, OWEN JAY, astronomer, educator; born Washington, Iowa, March 24, 1930; 3 children. Bachelor of Arts, Goshen College, 1951; Master of Arts, Harvard University, 1953, Doctor of Philosophy in Astronomy, 1962. Director obs. Am. University, Beirut, 1955-58; instructor Am. University, 1955-57, assistant professor; 1957-58; lecturer astronomy Wellesley College, 1958-59; astrophysicist Smithsonian Astrophysical Observatory, 1961—; lecturer Harvard, 1960-68, associate professor astronomy and history of sci.; 1968-69, professor; 1969—; Sigma Xi national lecturer 1971; George Darwin lecturer Royal Astronomical Society, 1971; councilor Am. Astronomical Society, 1973-76; Member Harvard Observatory eclipse expedition to Ceylon, 1955; member Harvard expedition to observe occultation of Regulus by Venus, Beirut, 1959; astronomy consultant Harvard Project Physics, 1964-69; director, central telegram bureau International Astronomical Union, 1965-67, associate director, 1967-79, president commission history astronomy, 1970-76, chairman United States national committee, 1982-84; council of scholars Library of Congress, 1986-88; adv. committee Center Theological Inquiry, Princeton, 1988—. Asso. editor: Journal History Astronomy, 1975—; member editorial board: Am. Scholar, 1975-80; director: Harvard mag, 1978-85, incorporator, 1986—. Corp. member Boston Mus. Sci., 1979—. Decorated Order of Merit commander class People's Republic of Poland, 1981. Member American Association for the Advancement of Science (chairman section D 1981), Academie Internationale d'Histoire des Sciences Am. Philosophical Society (vice president 1982-85, John F. Lewis prize 1976), Am. Acad. Arts and Sciences, Am. Astronomical Society (councilor 1973-76, chairman historical astronomy division 1983-85), Phi Beta Kappa. Clubs: Examiner. Research and publs. on model stellar atmospheres and in history of astronomy. Office: Center for Astrophysics Cambridge Massachusetts 02138

GINSBERG, HAROLD SAMUEL, virologist, educator; born Daytona Beach, Florida, May 27, 1917; son of Jacob and Anne (Kalb) G.; married Marion Reibstein, August 4, 1949; children: Benjamin Langer, Peter Robert, Ann Meredith, Jane Elizabeth. Bachelor of Arts, Duke University, 1937; Doctor of Medicine, Tulane University, 1941. Resident Mallory Institute Pathology, Boston, 1941-42; intern, assistant resident Boston City Hospital, 4th Medical Service, 1942-43; resident physician, associate Rockefeller Institute, 1946-51; associate professor preventive medicine Western Reserve University School Medicine, 1951-60; professor microbiology, chairman department University Pennsylvania School Medicine, 1960-73; professor microbiology, chairman department College Physical and Surgical Columbia, 1973-85, professor microbiology and medicine, director section molecular pathogenesis of infection; 1986—; member commission acute respiratory diseases Armed Forces Epidemiological Board, 1959-73; consultant National Institutes of Health, 1959-72, 75—, Army Chemical Corps, 1962-64,

National Aeronautics and Space Administration, 1969-73, Am. Cancer Society, 1969-73, member council on research and personnel, 1976-80; vice president International Committee on Nomenclature of Viruses, 1966-75; member space sci. board, chairman panel microbiology National Acad. Sci., 1973-74; chairman microbiology exam. committee National Board Medical Examiners, 1974-79; member microbiology and infectious disease committee National Institute Allergy and Infectious Disease, National Institutes of Health, 1976-81, chairman, 1979-81; co-chairman Institute Noetic Sci. Roundtable: Acquired Immune Deficiency Syndrome: Modern Approaches Vaccines and Anti-Viral Drugs. 1989. Contributor textbooks.; co-author: Microbiology, 1967, 4th edition, 1980, Virology, 2d edition; member editorial board: Journal Infectious Diseases, Journal Immunology, Journal Experimental Medicine, Journal Virology and Bacteriological Revs., Journal Acquired Immune Deficiency Syndromes; editor: Journal Virology, 1979-84, Cancer Research, 1978-82. Served to lieutenant colonel Medical Corps Army of the United States, 1943-46. Decorated Legion of Merit. Member National Acad. Sciences, Institute Medicine of National Acad. Sciences, Association Am. Physicians, Am. Acad. Microbiologists (chairman board govs. 1971-72), Am. Society Clinical Investigation (councillor 1958-60), Am. Association Immunologists, Am. Society Microbiology (chairman virology division 1961-62, councillor division 1977-81), Society Experimental Biology and Medicine, Association Medical School Microbiology Chairmen (president 1972-73), Harvey Society (president 1984coun. 1985-88), Central Society Clinical Research, Am. Society Biological Chemists, Am. Society Virology (president 1983), Alpha Omega Alpha. Office: Columbia U College Physicians and Surgeons Department Medicine 650 W 168th St New York New York 10032

GINZTON, EDWARD LEONARD, engineering corporation executive; born Dnepropetrovsk, Ukraine, December 27, 1915; came to United States, 1929; son of Leonard Louis and Natalie P. (Philipova) G.; married Artemas A. McCann; children: Anne, Leonard, Nancy, David. Bachelor of Science, University California, 1936, Master of Science, 1937; Electrical Engineer, Stanford University, 1938, Doctor of Philosophy, 1940. Research engineer Sperry Gyroscope Company, New York City, 1940-46; assistant professor applied physics and electrical engineering Stanford University, 1946-47, associate professor; 1947-50, professor; 1951-68; director Microwave Laboratory, 1949-59; with Varian Associates, Palo Alto, California, 1948—, chairman board of directors; 1959-84, chief executive officer; 1959-72, president; 1964-68, chairman executive committee; 1984—, also board of directors; director project M Stanford Linear Accelerator Center, 1957-60; member commission 1 United States national committee International Sci. Radio Union, 1958-68; member Lawrence Berkeley Laboratory Sci. and Adv. Committee, 1972-79; chairman adv. board School Engineering, Stanford, 1968-70; board of directors, member executive committee co-chairman Stanford Mid-Peninsula Urban Coalition, 1968-72; board of directors National Bureau Economic Research, 1981-87; member sci. policy board Stanford

Synchrotron Radiation Laboratory, 1985—. Author: Microwave Measurements, 1957; contributor articles to tech. journals. Board of directors Mid-Peninsula Housing Devel. Corp., 1970—, Stanford Hospital, 1975-80; trustee Stanford University, 1977-86. Recipient Morris Liebmann Memorial prize I.R.E., 1958, California Manufacturer of Year award, 1974. Fellow Institute of Electrical and Electronics Engineers (board directors 1971-72, chairman awards board 1971-72, medal of Honor 1969); member National Acad. Sciences (chairman committee on motor vehicle emissions 1971-74, co-chmn. committee nuclear energy study 1975-80, committee on sci. and national security 1982-84, committee on use of lab. animals in biomed. and behavioral research 1985-88), Am. Acad. Arts and Sciences (member executive committee Western Center 1985—), National Acad. Engineering (member council 1974-80), Sigma Xi, Eta Kappa Nu, Tau Beta Pi. Patentee in field. Home: 28014 Natoma Road Los Altos Hills California 94022 Office: Varian Associates 611 Hansen Way Palo Alto California 94303

GLASER, DONALD A(RTHUR), physicist; born Cleveland, September 21, 1926; son of William Joseph Glaser. Bachelor of Science, Case Institute Tech., 1946, Doctor of Science, 1959; Doctor of Philosophy, California Institute Tech., 1949. Professor physics University Michigan, 1949-59; professor physics University California at Berkeley, 1959—, professor physics and molecular biology; 1964—. Recipient Henry Russel award University Michigan, 1955; Charles V. Boys prize Physical Society, London, 1958; Nobel prize in physics, 1960; National Science Foundation fellow, 1961; Guggenheim fellow, 1961-62. Fellow Am. Physics Society (prize 1959); member National Acad. Sciences, Sigma Xi, Tau Kappa Alpha, Theta Tau. Office: U California Department Molecular Physics Berkeley California 94720

GLASER, EDWARD LEWIS, electrical engineer; born Evanston, Illinois, 1929; son of James and Margaret (Barnes) G.; married Anne Sims MacIntyre, November, 1950; children: Eliot, Cheryl Anne. Bachelor of Arts in Physics, Dartmouth College, 1951; Doctor of Science (honorary), Heriot-Watt University, 1980. Member planning group on large size computers International Business Machines Corporation, 1951-55; extension instructor computer architecture University of California at Los Angeles, 1958-59; consultant to director engineering ElectroData Corp. div. Burroughs Corp., 1958-60; manager systems research department Burroughs Corp., 1960-63; associate professor electrical engineering Massachusetts Institute of Technology, Cambridge, 1963-67; director Andrew R. Jennings Computer Center, Case Western Reserve University, Cleveland, 1967-75; manager department product engineering and devel. System Devel. Corp., Santa Monica, California, 1975-78, chief tech. officer, vice president products group; 1978-79; director advanced computer systems tech. Memory Products div. Ampex Corp., El Segundo, California, 1979-82; chairman board IRI, Incorporated, 1982-84; chairman board, chief tech. officer Nucleus International Corp. (formerly Marcus Information Systems), Santa Monica, 1984-85, co-chairman, chief tech. officer; 1985—;

visiting professor University of California at Los Angeles, 1982-85, adj. professor, 1985—. Contributor articles to professional journals. Trustee Seeing Eye, Morristown, New Jersey, 1964. Named Computer Man of Year, Data Processing Association, 1976. Fellow Institute of Electrical and Electronics Engineers; member National Acad. Engineering. Christian Scientist. Office: Nucleus International Corp 1639 11th St Santa Monica California 90404

GLASHOW, SHELDON LEE, physicist, educator; born New York City, December 5, 1932; son of Lewis and Bella (Rubin) G.; married Joan Glashow; children: Jason David, Jordan, Brian Lewis, Rebecca Lee. Bachelor of Arts, Cornell University, 1954; Master of Arts, Harvard University, 1955, Doctor of Philosophy, 1958; Doctor of Science (honorary), Yeshiva University, 1978, University Marseille, 1982. National Science Foundation fellow University Copenhagen, Denmark, 1958-60; research fellow California Institute Tech., 1960-61; assistant professor Stanford University, 1961-62; assistant professor, associate professor University California at Berkeley, 1962-66; faculty Harvard University, 1966—, professor physics; 1967—, Higgins professor physics; 1979—; distinguished visiting scientist Boston University, 1984—; consultant Brookhaven National Laboratory, 1966-73, 75—; member sci. policy committee European Organization of Nuclear Research, 1979-84; visiting professor University Marseille, 1971, Massachusetts Institute of Technology, 1974, 80, Boston University, 1983; affiliated senior scientist University Houston, 1983—; university scholar Texas Agricultural

and Mechanical University, 1983—. Contributor articles to professional journals and popular magazines. President Andrei Sakharov Institute, 1980-85, National Committee for Excellence in Education, 1985—. Recipient J.R. Oppenheimer Memorial prize, 1977; George Ledlie prize, 1978; Nobel prize in physics, 1979; Castiglione di Sicilia prize, 1983; National Science Foundation fellow, 1955-60; Sloan fellow, 1962-66; European Organization of Nuclear Research vis. fellow, 1968. Fellow Am. Physical Society, American Association for the Advancement of Science; member Am. Acad. Arts and Sciences, National Acad. Sciences, Sigma Xi.

GLASSMAN, IRVIN, engineering educator, consultant; born Baltimore, September 19, 1923; son of Abraham and Bessie (Snyder) G.; married Beverly Wolfe, June 17, 1951; children: Shari Powell, Diane Geinger, Barbara Ann. Bachelor of Education, Johns Hopkins University, 1943, Doctor of Engineering, 1950. Research assistant Manhattan Project, Columbia University, New York City, 1943-46; member faculty Princeton University, New Jersey, 1950—, professor mechanical and aeronautical engineering; 1964—, Robert H. Goddard professor mechanical and aeronautical engineering; 1988—, director Center for Energy and Environmental Studies; 1972-79; consultant to industry; visiting professor University Naples, Italy, 1966-67, 78-79, Stanford University, 1975; member adv. committees United Tech. Research Center, Chrysler Corp., CNR Istituto Motori, Italy, National Science Foundation, Center for Fire Research, National Bureau Standards. Author:

(with R.F. Sawyer) Performance of Chemical Propellants, 1971, Combustion, 1977, 2d edition, 1987; editor 3 books; contributor articles to tech. journals. Served with United States Army, 1944-46. National Science Foundation fellow, 1966-67. Member Combustion Institute (Sir Alfred Edgerton Gold medal 1982), Am. Society Engineering Education (Roe award 1984), Am. Chemical Society, American Association of University Profs., Tau Beta Pi. Patentee rocket propellants (2). Home: Post Office Box 14 Princeton New Jersey 08542 Office: Princeton U Princeton New Jersey 08544

GLENN, JOHN HERSCHEL, JR., senator; born Cambridge, Ohio, July 18, 1921; son of John Herschel and Clara (Sproat) G.; married Anna Margaret Castor, April 1943; children: Carolyn Ann, John David. Student, Muskingum College, 1939-42, Bachelor of Science, 1962; naval aviation cadet, University Iowa, 1942; graduate flight school, Naval Air Training Center, Corpus Christi, Texas, 1943, Navy Test Pilot Training School, Patuxent River, Maryland, 1954. Commissioned 2d lieutenant United States Marine Corps, 1943, assigned 4th Marine Aircraft Wing, Marshall Islands campaign; 1944, assigned 9th Marine Aircraft Wing; 1945-46; with 1st Marine Aircraft Wing, North China Patrol, also Guam, 1947-48; flight instructor advanced flight training Corpus Christi, 1949-51; assistant G-2/G-3 Amphibious Warfare School, Quantico, Virginia, 1951; with Marine Fighter Squadron 311, exchange pilot 25th Fighter Interceptor Squadron United States Air Force, Korea, 1953; project officer fighter design branch Navy Bureau Aeronautical Washington, 1956-58;

astronaut Project Mercury, Manned Spacecraft Center National Aeronautics and Space Administration, 1959-65; pilot Mercury-Atlas 6, 1st orbital space flight launched from Cape Canaveral, Florida, February 1962; retired as colonel 1965; vice president corp. devel. and director Royal Crown Cola Company, 1966-74; president Royal Crown International; United States senator from Ohio 1975—. Co-author: We Seven, 1962; author: P.S., I Listened to Your Heart Beat. Trustee Muskingum College. Decorated Distinguished Flying Cross (six), Air medal (18); recipient Astronaut medal USMC, Navy unit commendation, Korean Presidential unit citation, Distinguished Merit award Muskingum College, Medal of Honor New York City, Congl. Space Medal of Honor, 1978, other decorations, awards and hon. degrees. Member Society Experimental Test Pilots, International Acad. of Astronautics (hon.). Democrat. Presbyterian. First supersonic transcontinental Flight, July 16, 1957. Office: United States Senate 503 Hart Senate Building Washington District of Columbia 20510

GLICK, J. LESLIE, biotechnology company executive; born New York City, March 2, 1940; son of Arthur Harvey and Hilda Lillian (Lichtenfeld) G.; married Judith Sumiye Mihara; children: Geoffrey Michael, Jessica Michele. Bachelor of Arts, Columbia University, 1961, Doctor of Philosophy, 1964. National Cancer Institute postdoctoral fellow Princeton University, 1964-65; senior, then associate cancer research scientist Roswell Park Memorial Institute, Buffalo, 1965-69; associate research professor physiology, physiology chairman Roswell Park div. State University of New York, Buffalo, 1968-70; from executive vice president to chairman board Associate Biomedic Systems, Incorporated, Buffalo, 1969-77; president Institute Sci. and Social Accountability, Washington, 1975-79; president, chief executive officer Genex Corp., Gaithersburg, Maryland, 1977-87; chairman, chief executive officer Bionix Corp., Potomac, Maryland, 1987—; chairman HTI Corp., Buffalo, 1972-75; director National Association Life Sci. Industries, 1975-77; research professor biology Niagara University, New York, Canisius College, Buffalo, 1968-70; executive committee State University of New York Grad. School, Buffalo, 1968-70; visiting lecturer North Atlantic Treaty Organization Advanced Study Institute, Brussels, 1970; member biotech. tech. adv. committee United States Department Commerce, 1985-87; adj. professor University Maryland Grad. School, University College, 1988—, member adv. panel, 1988—. Author: Fundamentals of Human Lymphoid Cell Culture, 1980; also articles; member editorial advisors board Strategic Direction, 1984-87; member adv. council High Tech. Marketing Rev., 1986-87; member industrial adv. board Biotech. Process Engring. Center MIT, 1986-87. Board overseers Simon's Rock of Bard College, 1984-85; trustee National Faculty Humanities, Arts and Scis., 1985-87. Member Am. Association Cancer Research, Am. Physiological Society, Tissue Culture Association, Industrial Biotech. Association (board directors 1981-84), New York Acad. Sciences, Sigma Xi.

GLICKSMAN, MAURICE, engineering educator, university dean and provost; born Toronto, Ontario, Canada, October 16, 1928; came to United States, 1949, naturalized, 1961; son of Robert Maxwell and Fanny Bella (Lachowitz) G.; married Yetta Leich, December 18, 1949; children: Howard David, Roslynn Sue, Marcie Ann. Student, Queen's University, 1946-49; Master of Science, University Chicago, 1952, Doctor of Philosophy, 1954. Research associate Institute Nuclear Studies, University Chicago, 1954; member tech. staff Radio Corporation of America Laboratories, Princeton, New Jersey, 1954-61; head Plasma Physics Group Radio Corporation of America Laboratories, 1961-63; director research Radio Corporation of America Research Laboratories, Tokyo, 1963-67; head General Research Group, Princeton, 1967-69; University professor, professor engineering Brown University, 1969—, dean Grad. School; 1974-76, dean faculty and acad. affairs; 1976-78, provost, dean faculty; 1978-86, provost; 1986—; consultant Radio Corporation of America Corp., 1969-77; visiting scientist Massachusetts Institute of Technology, 1983-84; chairman committee materials for radiation detection devices National Acad. Sciences, 1971-74; chairman visiting committee University Pennsylvania, 1977-83, Vanderbilt University, 1977-81; member visiting committee Emory University, 1981—; board of directors center Research Libraries, 1981-87, chairman, 1983-84; board of directors University Research Association, 1983-89. Contributor research articles to professional journals. President, Jewish Center, Princeton, 1962-63; vice president cultural and educational Jewish Community Center, Tokyo, 1965-67; member Bureau Jewish

Education, Rhode Island, 1974—, vice president, 1975-80; vice president Jewish Federation, Rhode Island, 1980-83; trustee Miriam Hospital, 1979-85. Recipient Outstanding Achievement award Radio Corporation of America, 1956, 62. Fellow Am. Physical Society, Institute of Electrical and Electronics Engineers; member New York Acad. Sciences, Am. Society Engineering Education, American Association for the Advancement of Science, Phi Beta Kappa, Sigma Xi. Jewish (trustee 1972—). Patentee frequency multipliers, hall-effect devices, semiconductor devices and circuits. Home: 10 Westwood Lane Barrington Rhode Island 02806 Office: University Hall Brown U Providence Rhode Island 02912

GLIMM, JAMES GILBERT, mathematician; born Peoria, Illinois, March 24, 1934; son of William Frederick and Barbara Gilbert (Hooper) G.; married Adele Strauss, June 30, 1957; 1 daughter, Alison. Bachelor of Arts, Columbia University, 1956, Master of Arts, 1957, Doctor of Philosophy, 1959. From assistant professor to professor math. Massachusetts Institute of Technology, 1960-69; professor Courant Institute, New York University, 1969-74; professor math. Rockefeller University, New York City, 1974-82; professor Courant Institute, New York University, New York City, 1982-89; visiting professor, chair department applied math. and statistics State University of New York, Stony Brook, 1988—. Co-author: Quantum Physics, 1981; Collected Papers, Volumes I and II, 1985; member editorial bds. professional journals; contributor articles to sci. publications. Recipient

Dannie Heineman prize in math. physics, 1980; Guggenheim fellow, 1963, 65. Member International Association Math. Physicists, Am. Physical Society, Am. Math. Society, National Acad. Sciences, Society Industrial and Applied Math., Math. Association Am., Am. Acad. Arts and Sciences, Society Petroleum Engineers, New York Acad. Sciences (award in phys. and math. scis. 1979). Office: Courant Institute 251 Mercer St New York New York 10012

GLOYNA, EARNEST FREDERICK, environmental engineer, educator; born Vernon, Texas, June 30, 1921; son of Herman Ernst and Johanna Bertha (Reithmayer) G.; married Agnes Mary Lehman, February 17, 1946; children: David Frederick, Lisa Anna (Mrs. Jack Grosskopf). Bachelor of Science in Civil Engineering, Texas Technological University, 1946; Master of Science in Civil Engineering, University Texas, 1949; Doctor Engineering, Johns Hopkins University, 1952. Registered professional engineer. Junior engineer Texas Highway Department, 1945-46; office engineer Magnolia Petroleum Company, 1946-47; instructor civil engineering University Texas, Austin, 1947-49, assistant professor; 1949-53, associate professor; 1953-59, professor; 1959-70, Joe J. King professor engineering; 1970-82, Bettie Margaret Smith chair environmental engineering; 1982—, director Environmental Health Engineering Laboratories; 1954-70, director Center for Research in Water Resources; 1963-73, dean College Engineering; 1970-87, director Bureau Engineering Research; 1970-87, Bettie Margaret Smith chair in environmental engineering; 1987—; consultant on water and wastewater treatment and water resources, 1947—; director Parker Drilling Company; consultant numerous industries, World Health Organization, World Bank, United States Air Force, United States Army, United States Senate, foreign cities and governments, United Nations, 1952—; member, past chairman sci. adv. board Environmental Protection Agency; chairman various committees National Research Council, National Acad. Sci., National Acad. Engineering. Author: Waste Stabilization Ponds, 1971 (also French and Spanish edits), (with Joe O. Ledbetter) Principles of Radiological Health, 1969; Editor: (with W. Wesley Eckenfelder, Junior) Advances in Water Quality Improvement, 1968, Water Quality Improvement by Physical and Chemical Processes, 1970, (with William S. Butcher) Conflicts in Water Resources Planning, 1972, (with Woodson and Drew) Water Management by Electric Power Industry, 1975, (with Malina and Davis) Ponds as a Wastewater Treatment Alternative, 1976; Contributor numerous articles to professional journals. Served with Corps Engrs. Army of the United States, 1942-46, European Theatre of Operations, lieutenant colonel Ret. Recipient Harrison Prescott Eddy medal Water Pollution Control Federation, 1959, Gordon Maskew Fair medal, 1979, Hon. Member award, 1980 ; Water Resources Div. award Am. Water Works Association, 1959; named Distinguished Engineer Graduate Texas Tech. University, 1971, Distinguished Alumnus, 1973, Distinguished Engineering Graduate University Texas, Austin, 1982; recipient Joe J. King award University Texas, Austin, 1982; Environmental Protection Agency regional environmental educator award, 1977; National Environmental Devel. award, 1983, Sci. award National Wildlife Federation, 1986; Order of Henri Pittier, National Conservation medal Venezuela, 1983. Fellow American Society of Civil Engineers (hon. member, Meritorious Paper award Texas section 1968, award of honor Texas section 1985, pub. health engrs., Pakistan, 1984, Simon W. Freese environmental engr. award 1986); member National Acad. Engineering, National Society Professional Engineers (director), Am. Institute Chemical Engineers, Association Environmental Engineering Profs. (past president), Am. Society for Engineering Education, Am. Water Works Association, Am. Acad. Environmental Engineers (diplomate, past president, Gordon Maskew Fair award 1982), Water Pollution Control Federation (past president, hon. member), Texas Society Professional Engineers (Engineer of Year award Travis chapter 1972, president 1986), Southwestern Society Nuclear Medicine (hon.), National Acad. Engineering Mexican (foreign corr. member), National Acad. Sciences Venezuela (foreign corr.), Sociedad Mexicana de Aguas (Jack Huppert award), Sigma Xi, Tau Beta Pi, Chi Epsilon, Phi Kappa Phi, Pi Epsilon Tau (hon.), Omicron Delta Kappa. Clubs: Cosmos (Washington); Headliners, Faculty Center, Rotary (Austin). Office: U Tex College of Engring Austin Texas 78712

GODSON, WARREN LEHMAN, meteorologist; born Victoria, British Columbia, Canada, May 4, 1920; son of Walter Ernest Henry and Mary Edna (Lehman) G.; married Harriet Burke,

December 28, 1977; children: Elliott, Marilyn, Murray, Ralph, Ellen; stepchildren—Alan, Alison, Stephen Bloom. Bachelor of Arts, University British Columbia, Vancouver, 1939, Master of Arts, 1941; Master of Arts, University Toronto, Ontario, 1944, Doctor of Philosophy, 1948. Laboratory demonstrator University British Columbia, 1939-41; laboratory demonstrator University Toronto, 1941-42, special lecturer physics department; 1948-61, hon. professor; 1975; meteorologist Can. Meteorol. Service (name changed to Atmospheric Environmental Service 1971), Toronto, 1942-51; super-intendent atmospheric research section Can. Meteorol. Service (name changed to Atmospheric Environ-mental Service 1971), 1951-72, director atmospheric processes research branch; 1972-73; director general Atmospheric Research Directorate, 1973-84, senior sci. advisor; 1984—. Author: (with J.V. Iribarne) Atmospheric Thermodynamics, 1974, 81; Contributor (over 100) articles to professional journals. Recipient Gov.-Gen.'s medal, 1935, Lefevre Gold medal, 1939, Patterson medal, 1968, IMO prize, 1975. Fellow Am. Meteorological Society (councillor 1967-70, associate editor Jour. Atmospheric Sciences 1962-70), Royal Society Can.; member World Meteorological Organization (vice president Commission for Atmospheric Sciences 1957-61, president 1973-77, alternate permanent representative of Can. 1977—, chairman six working groups), International Association Meteorology and Atmospheric Physics (secretary, bureau director 1960-75, vice president 1975-79, president 1979-83, convenor committee on meteorol.

data for research 1960-64), Can. Meteorological Society (executive committee 1955-61, president 1957-59, Pres.'s prize), Can. Association Physicists (councillor 1955-57, chairman earth physics division 1967-68), Royal Meteorological Society (vice president Can. 1959-61, Can. Darton prize, Buchan prize 1964). Pioneer Arctic stratospheric jet stream and final warming process in polar winter stratosphere, Curtis-Godson approximation technique, Ozonagram diagram used for ozone representation. Office: 4905 Dufferin St, North York, Downsview, Ontario Canada M3H 5T4

GOLD, PHIL, physician, educator; born Montreal, Quebec, Canada, September 17, 1936; married Evelyn Katz; 3 children. BSc in Physiology with honors, McGill University, Montreal, 1957, Master of Science, Doctor of Medicine, 1961, Doctor of Philosophy in Physiology, 1965. Licentiate Medical Council Can. Junior rotating intern Montreal General Hospital, 1961-62, junior assistant resident in medicine; 1962-63, senior resident in medicine; 1965-66, junior assistant physician, assistant and associate physician; 1967-73, senior physician; 1973—, physician-in-chief; 1980—, director div. clinical immunology and allergy; 1977-80, director McGill University Medical Clinic; 1980—, also senior investigator Research Ins.; faculty department physiology McGill University, 1964—, member faculty of medicine; 1965—, professor medicine and clinical medicine; 1973—, chairman department medicine and clinical medicine; 1985—, professor physiology; 1974—, member faculty of medicine executive committee representing clinical departments;

1985—, D. G. Cameron professor medicine (inauguaral); 1987—; visiting scientist Pub. Health Research Institute New York City, 1967-68; Chester M. Jones Memorial lecturer Massachusetts General Hospital, 1974; visiting professor University Caracas, Venezuela, 1974; Squires Club visiting professor Wellesley Hospital, Toronto, 1983; Cecil H. and Ida Green visiting professor, 1984 autumn lectures University Brit. Columbia; consultant in allergy and immunology Mount Sinai Hospital, St. Agathe des Monts, Quebec, 1975—; hon. consultant department medicine Royal Victoria Hospital, Montreal; consultant department internal medicine Douglas Hospital Center, Montreal; vice chairman medical adv. committee Council of Physicians, Dentists and Pharmacists, 1985—; member Conseil d'Adminstrn., Foundation Quebecoise du Cancer, 1986—; speaker at convocations and invited lecturer numerous universities. Member editorial board Clin. Immunology and Immunopathology, 1972—, Immunopharmacology, 1978—, Diagnostic Gynecology and Obstetrics, 1978-83, Oncodevelopmental Biology and Medicine, 1979—, Modern Medicine of Can., 1984—; editorial cons. Journal Chronic Diseases, 1981-84; member editorial adv. board Cancer Research, 1971-73, associate editor 1973-80; contributor over 120 articles to medical journals. Recipient Hiram Mills Gold medal, Mosby Scholarship Book award, Wood Gold medal, E.W.R. Steacie prize National Research Council Can., 1973, Can. Silver Jubilee medal, 1977, Johann-Georg-Zemmerman prize for cancer research Medizinische Hochschule, Hannover, Federal Republic Germany, 1978, Gold medal award of merit Graduate Society McGill University, International award Gardner Foundation, Ernest C. Manning prize, F.National Guard Starr award Izzak Walton Killam Prize Can. Council, 1985, numerous others; decorated companion Order of Can., 1986; Great Montrealer, 1986; Knight Commander, Sovereign Order St. John Jerusalem, Knights of Malta, 1986; MacDonald scholar, J. Francis Williams scholar, University scholar. Fellow Royal College Physicians and Surgeons Can. (cert. internal medicine, medal 1965, chairman examing board, 1975-77, member research committee 1986—), Royal Society Can., American College of Physicians ; member American Association for the Advancement of Science, Am. Acad. Allergy and Immunology, Am. Association Cancer Research, Am. Association Immunologists, Am. Federation Clinical Research, Am. Society Clinical Investigation, Association Am. Physicians, Am. Board Medical Lab. Immunology (member adv. panel 1978—), Association Medicale du Quebec, Can. Association Radiologists (hon.), Can. federation Biological Sciences, Can. Oncology Society (founding member, member sci. committee 1979—), Can. Society Alergy and Clinical Immunology, Can. Society Clinical Investigation, Corp. Professional des Medecins Quebec, Federation des Medecins Specialists Quebec, Montreal Physiological Society, New York Acad. Sciences, Reticuloendothelial Society, Alzheimer Society Montreal (patron), Can. Society for Immunology (president 1975-77), Cancer Research Society Montreal (past president med. adv. board), International Society for Oncodevel. Biology and Medicine (editorial board journal 1979—, member constn. committee 1976—, president 9th ann. meeting 1981, Inaugural Outstanding Scientist award 1976), Can. Medical Association (F.N.G.), Medical Research Council Can. (chairman panel 1972-77, chairman grants committee 1981-83, council member 1986—), National Cancer Institute Can. (member cancer grants panel B 1977-79, member research adv. committee 1984—), Med-Chi Society (president 1986—), Sigma Xi, Alpha Omega Alpha, others. Office: Montreal Gen Hosp, 1650 Cedar Avenue, Room 648, Montreal, Province of Quebec Canada H3G 1A4

GOLDHABER, GERTRUDE SCHARFF, physicist; born Mannheim, Federal Republic of Germany, July 14, 1911; came to United States, 1939, naturalized, 1944; daughter of Otto and Nelly (Steinharter) Scharff; married Maurice Goldhaber, May 24, 1939; children: Alfred Scharff, Michael Henry. Student, univs. Freiburg, Zurich, Berlin; Doctor of Philosophy, University Munich, 1935. Research associate Imperial College, London, England, 1935-39; research physicist University Illinois, 1939-48, assistant professor; 1948-50; associate physicist Brookhaven National Laboratory, Upton, New York, 1950-58; physicist Brookhaven National Laboratory, 1958-62, senior physicist; 1962—; consultant nuclear data group National Research Council, National Acad. Sciences, Atomic Energy Commission Laboratories Arms Control and Disarmament Agency, 1974-77; adj. professor Cornell University, 1980-82, Johns Hopkins University, 1983-86; Phi Beta Kappa visiting scholar, 1984-85. Member editorial com. Annual Rev. Nuclear Sci, 1973-77; N. Am. rep. board editors Journal Physics G (Europhysics Journal), 1978-80. Trustee-at-large University Research Association governing Fermi National Accelerator Lab., 1972-77; educational adv. committee New York Acad. Scis., 1982—; National Adv. Committee on Pre-Coll. Material Devel., 1984-88. Fellow Am. Physical Society (council 1979-82, chairman panel on improvement pre-coll. physics literacy 1979-82, chairman audit committee 1980, member committee on professional opportunities 1979-81, committee on history of physics, executive committee 1983-84), American Association for the Advancement of Science (mem.-at-large section B physics committee 1986—); member National Acad. Sciences (member report rev. committee 1973-81, member acad. forum adv. committee 1974-81, member committee on education and employment of women in sci. and engineering 1978-83, commission on human rights 1984-87), Sigma Xi. Home: 91 S Gillette Avenue Bayport New York 11705 Office: Brookhaven National Lab #510A Upton New York 11973

GOLDHABER, MAURICE, physicist; born Lemberg, Austria, April 18, 1911; came to United States, 1938, naturalized, 1944; son of Charles and Ethel (Frisch) G.; married Gertrude Scharff, May 24, 1939; children: Alfred S., Michael H. Doctor of Philosophy, Cambridge University, England, 1936; Doctor of Philosophy (honorary), Tel-Aviv University, Israel, 1974; Doctor (honorary), University Louvain-La-Neuve, Belgium, 1982; Doctor of Science (honorary), State University of New York, Stony Brook, 1983. Bye fellow Magdalene College, Cambridge, 1936-38; assistant professor physics University Illinois, 1938-43, associate professor; 1943-45, professor; 1945-50; senior sci. Brookhaven National Laboratory, 1950-60, chairman department physics; 1960-61, director; 1961-73, AUI distinguished scientist; 1973—; consultant laboratories Atomic Energy Commission; Morris Loeb lectr Harvard University, 1955; adj. professor physics State University of New York, Stony Brook, 1965—; Member nuclear sci. committee National Research Council. Associate editor: Physical Rev, 1951-53; Contributor articles on nuclear physics to sci. journals. Member board governors Weizmann Institute Sci., Rehovoth, Israel, Tel Aviv University; trustee Univs. Research Association. Recipient citation for meritorious contributions U.S. Atomic Energy Commission, 1973, J. Robert Oppenheimer memorial prize, 1982. Fellow Am. Physical Society (president 1982), Am. Acad. Arts and Sciences, American Association for the Advancement of Science; member National Acad. Sci., Am. Philosophical Society (Tom W. Bonner prize in nuclear physics 1971). Office: Brookhaven National Lab Building 510 Upton New York 11973

GOLDMAN, CHARLES REM-INGTON, scientist, educator; born Urbana, Illinois, November 9, 1930; son of Marcus Selden and Olive (Remington) G.; married Shirley Ann Aldous, April 4, 1953 (divorced June 1975); children: Christopher Selden (deceased), Margaret Blanche, Olivia Remington, Ann Aldous; married Evelyne de Amezaga, May 12, 1977. Bachelor of Arts, University Illinois, 1952, Master of Science, 1955; Doctor of Philosophy, University Michigan, 1958. Assistant aquatic

biologist Illinois Natural History Survey, 1954-55; teaching fellow fisheries University Michigan, 1955-58; fishery research biologist United States Fish and Wildlife Service, Alaska, 1957-58; member faculty University California at Davis, 1958—, professor zoology; 1966-71, director Institute Ecology; 1966-69, professor limnology, div. environmental studies; 1971—, chairperson div. environmental studies; 1988—; director Tahoe Research Group, 1973—; chairperson Man and Biosphere Freshwater program (MAB-5), 1988—; consultant hydroelectric and water pollution to government and industry, United States, Africa, South Am., Central Am., Australia and New Zealand, 1959—; consultant United Nations Purari River Dam project, Pupua New Guinea, 1974, Niger River Dam Project, Nigeria, Africa, 1977-78, Parana River Flood Control, Argentina, 1979, El Cajon dam project, Honduras, 1979-84; member California Assembly Sci. and Tech. Adv. Council, 1970-73, California Solid Waste Management Board, 1973-77; University California representative Organization Tropical Studies, 1977—, mem.-at-large, 1985-86; National Science Foundation and National Acad. Sciences on coastal pollutions problems, Taiwan, 1974; member Sci. Committee on Problems of Environmental, National Research Council committees, 1979-87; chairman fresh water resources directorate United States National Committee for Man and the Biosphere. Co-author: Limnology, 1983; editor: Primary Productivity in Aquatic Environments, 1966, Freshwater Crayfish V, 1983; Co-editor: Environmental Quality and Water Development, 1973. Served to captain United States Air Force, 1952-

54. Guggenheim fellow, 1965; National Science Foundation sr. fellow, 1964; Goldman Glacier named in Antarctica, 1967; recipient Antartic Service medal, 1968; Fulbright Distinguished professor, 1985. Fellow American Association for the Advancement of Science, California Acad. Sciences (federal del. to Union of the Soviet Socialist Republics on water pollution 1973); member Am. Society Limnology and Oceanography (editorial board 1964-67, national president 1967-68, president Western section 1966-67), Ecological Society Am. (editorial board 1966-68, mem.-at-large 1972-73, vice president 1973-74), International Society Theoretical and Applied Limnology (national representative); hon. member Culver chapter Cum Laude Society. Club: Explorers. Discoverer trace element limiting factors in N.Am. and New Zealand lakes.

GOLDSTEIN, JOSEPH LEONARD, physician, genetics educator; born Sumter, South Carolina, April 18, 1940; son of Isadore E. and Fannie A. Goldstein. Bachelor of Science, Washington and Lee University, Lexington, Virginia, 1962; Doctor of Medicine, University Texas, Dallas, 1966; Doctor of Science (honorary), University Chicago, 1982, Rensselaer Polytechnic Institute, 1982, Washington and Lee University, 1986. Intern, then resident in medicine Massachusetts General Hospital, Boston, 1966-68; clinical associate National Institutes of Health, 1968-70; postdoctoral fellow University Washington, Seattle, 1970-72; member faculty University Texas Health Sciences Center, Dallas, 1972—, Paul J. Thomas professor medicine, chairman department molecular genetics; 1977—, regental professor; 1985—; Harvey Society lecturer, 1977; member sci. rev. board Howard Hughes Medical Institute, 1978-84, medical adv. board, 1985—; non-resident fellow The Salk Institute, 1983—. Co-author: The Metabolic Basis of Inherited Disease, 5th edition, 1983; editorial board Journal Biol. Chemistry, 1981-85, Cell, 1983—, Journal Clin. Investigation, 1977-82, Annual Rev. Genetics, 1980-85, Arteriosclerosis, 1981-87, Science 1985-87. Sci. adv. board Welch Foundation, 1986—; board of directors Passano Foundation, 1985—. Recipient Heinrich-Wieland prize, 1974, Pfizer award in enzyme chemistry Am. Chemical Society, 1976; Passano award Johns Hopkins University, 1978; Gairdner Foundation award, 1981; award in biological and med. scis. New York Acad. Sciences, 1981; Lita Annenberg Hazen award, 1982; Research Achievement reward Am. Heart Association, 1984; Louisa Gross Horwitz award, 1984; 3M Life Sciences award, 1984, Albert Lasker award in Basic Medical Research, 1985; Nobel Prize in Physiology or Medicine, 1985, Trustees' medal Massachusetts General Hospital, 1986. Member National Acad. Sciences (Lounsbery award 1979), Association Am. Physicians, Am. Society Clinical Investigation (president 1985-86), Am. Society Human Genetics, Amer. Acad. Arts and Sciences, Am. Society Biological Chemists, American College of Physicians (award 1986), Am. Federation Clinical Research, Am. Philosophical Society, Phi Beta Kappa, Alpha Omega Alpha. Home: 3831 Turtle Creek Boulevard Apartment #22-B Dallas Texas 75219 Office: U Tex Health Sci Center 5323 Harry Hines Boulevard Dallas Texas 75235

GOLDSTEIN, MURRAY, osteopathic physician, government official; born New York City, October 13, 1925; son of Israel and Yetta (Zeigen) G.; married Mary Susan Michael, June 13, 1957; children—Patricia Sue, Barbara Jean. Bachelor of Arts in Biology, New York University, 1947; Doctor of Osteopathy, Des Moines Still College Osteo Medicine, 1950; Master of Public Health in Epidemiology, University California, 1959; Doctor of Science (honorary), Kirksville College Osteopathic Medicine, 1966, University New England, 1984, Ohio University, 1987; D.D.L. (honorary), New York Institute Tech., 1982; Doctor honoris causa, Medical University of Pecs, Hungary, 1985. Diplomate Am. Osteopathic Board Preventive Medicine (sec.-treas. 1987—). Intern Des Moines Still College Osteo Medicine Hospital, 1950-51, resident in internal medicine; 1951-53; commissioned senior assistant surgeon United States Public Health Service, 1953, advanced through ranks to assistant surgeon general; 1980; assistant chief grants and training branch National Heart Institute, National Institutes of Health, Bethesda, Maryland, 1953-58; assistant chief research grants rev. branch, director epidemiology and biometry training grant program div. research grants National Institutes of Health, Bethesda, 1956-60; acting section chief Bureau Acute Communicable Disease, California Department Public Health, Berkeley, 1958; chief special projects branch National Institute Neurological Diseases and Blindness National Institutes of Health, Bethesda, 1960-61; director extramural programs National Institute Neurological and Communicative Disorders and Stroke, National Institutes of Health, Bethesda, 1961-76; director stroke and trauma program National Institute Neurological and Communicative Disorders and Stroke, National Institutes of Health, 1976-78; deputy director National Institute Neurological and Communicative Disorders and Stroke—NIH, 1978-82, director; 1982—; director World Health Organization Collaborative Center in Neurosci., Bethesda, 1982—; visiting scientist Mayo Clinic and Grad. School, Rochester, Minnesota, 1967-68; vice president Eisenhower Institute for Stroke Research; consultant World Health Organization, chairman task force on stroke, 1986—; clinical professor medicine New York College Osteo Medicine, New York Institute Tech.; senior lecturer (neurology) Uniformed Services University of Health Sciences, 1986—; board of directors United Cerebral Palsy Research and Education Foundation. Editorial board Osteopathic Annals, 1973—, International Journal Neurology, 1980—, Journal Neuroepidemiology. Served with United States Army, 1943-45. Decorated Silver Star, Purple Heart.; Recipient Meritorious Service medal USPHS, 1971, Distinguished Service medal USPHS, 1983. Fellow Am. Pub. Health Association, Am. Heart Association (liaison member executive committee Council on Stroke, associate editor Stroke, Jour. Cerebral Circulation 1976—), Am. College Osteopathic Internists (hon.), Am. Acad. Neurology, Am. Osteopathic College Preventive Medicine (trustee); member Am. Neurological Association (2d vice president, cert. merit), Am. Osteopathic Association, American Association for the Advancement of Science, Association Research in Nervous and Mental Disease, Society

Neurosci., Am. College Neuropsychiatrists (distinguished service award), World Federation Neurology. Office: 9000 Rockville Pike Bethesda Maryland 20892

GOLDSTINE, HERMAN HEINE, mathematician, association executive; born Chicago, September 13, 1913; son of Isaac Oscar and Bessie (Lipsey) G.; married Adele Katz, September 15, 1941 (deceased 1964); children—Madlen, Jonathan; married Ellen Watson, January 8, 1966. Bachelor of Science, University Chicago, 1933, Master of Science, 1934, Doctor of Philosophy, 1936; Doctor of Philosophy honoris causa, University Lund, Sweden, 1974; Doctor of Science (honorary), Amherst College, 1978, Adelphi University, 1978. Research assistant University Chicago, 1936-37, instructor; 1937-39; instructor University Michigan, Ann Arbor, 1939-42, assistant professor; 1942-50; assistant project director electronic computer project Institute Advanced Study, Princeton, New Jersey, 1946-55, acting project director; 1954-57, permanent member; 1952—; director math. sciences department International Business Machines Corporation Research, 1960-65; director sci. devel. International Business Machines Corporation Data Processing Headquarters, White Plains, New York, 1965-67; consultant to director research International Business Machines Corporation, 1967-69, fellow; 1969—; executive officer Am. Philos Society, Philadelphia, 1984—; consultant various government, military agys., 1984—; trustee University Pennsylvania Press, 1985—. Author: The Computer from Pascal to vonNeumann, 1972, New and Full

Moons 1001 British Columbia to A.D. 1651, 1973, A History of Numerical Analysis from the 16th through the 19th Century, 1977; A History of the Calculus of variations from the 17th Through the 19th Century, 1980. Member adv. council history of sci. program. Princeton University, 1982—; member visiting committee physical sci. div. University Chicago, 1976-86; member acad. committee Annenberg Research Institute, 1987—; board of directors National Constitution Center, 1987—. Served to lieutenant colonel Army of the United States, World War II. Recipient University Chicago Alumni Achievement award, 1975; Harry Goode award AFIPS, 1979; Charter Pioneer award Institute of Electrical and Electronic Engineers, 1982; National Medal of Sci., 1983; Outstanding Civilian Service award U.S. Army, 1984. Member Am. Math. Society, Am. Philosophical Society, Am. Acad. Arts and Sciences, National Acad. Sci., Math. Association Am., Phi Beta Kappa (book award in sci. 1973), Sigma Xi. Home: 1900 Rittenhouse Square Philadelphia Pennsylvania 19103 Office: Am Philos Society 104 S 5th St Philadelphia Pennsylvania 19106

GOLDTEIN, MOISE H., JR., electrical engineering educator; born New Orleans, December 26, 1926; married; 4 children. Bachelor of Science in Electrical Engineering, Tulane University, New Orleans, 1949; Master of Science, Massachusetts Institute of Technology, 1951, Doctor of Science, 1957. Teaching, research assistant Massachusetts Institute of Technology, Cambridge, 1949-51, member staff; 1952-55, biophysicist; 1955-63, instructor electrical engineering; 1955-56, assistant professor electrical engineering; 1956-61, associate professor electrical engineering; 1961-63; research engineer Texas Company, Houston, 1951-52; associate professor electrical engineering Johns Hopkins University, Baltimore, 1963-67, associate professor biomedical engineering; 1963-75, professor electrical engineering; 1967—, professor biomedical engineering; 1975—, Edward J. Schaefer professor electrical engineering; 1975—; consultant and lecturer in field. Contributor chapters to books, articles to professional journals. Guggenheim fellow, 1970-71; National Science Foundation fellow, 1959-60; University College London hon. research fellow, 1982; National Institutes of Health fellow, 1981-82. Fellow Acoustical Society Am.; member Institute of Electrical and Electronics Engineers, Society Neurosci., International Brain Research Organization, Am. Auditory Society, American Association for the Advancement of Science, Am. Speech Language Hearing Association.

GOLOMB, SOLOMON WOLF, mathematician, electrical engineer, educator, university official; born Baltimore, May 31, 1932; son of Elhanan Hirsh and Minna (Nadel) G. Bachelor of Arts, Johns Hopkins University, 1951; Master of Arts, Harvard University, 1953, Doctor of Philosophy, 1957; postgraduate, University Oslo, 1955-56. Member faculty Boston University, 1954-55, Harvard University, 1954-55, University of California at Los Angeles, 1957-61, California Institute Tech., 1960-62; senior research engineer Jet Propulsion Laboratory, Pasadena, California, 1956-58, research group supervisor; 1958-60, assistant chief

telecommunications research section; 1960-63; associate professor University Southern California, Los Angeles, 1963-64, professor electrical engineering and math.; 1964—; vice provost for research University Southern California, 1986—; director Cyclotomics Incorporated; consultant to government and industry. Author: Digital Communications with Space Applications, 1964, Polyominoes, 1965, Shift Register Sequences, 1967, 82; contributor articles to professional journals. Recipient Rogers prize in math. Harvard University, 1953-54; recipient University Assocs. Research award University Southern California, 1968-69, Archimedes Circle award, 1978; Presidential medal, 1985. Fellow Institute of Electrical and Electronics Engineers; member National Acad. Engineering, International Sci. Radio Union, Am. Math. Society, Math. Association Am., Society Industrial and Applied Math., American Association for the Advancement of Science, American Association of University Women, Golden Key, Phi Beta Kappa, Sigma Xi, Pi Delta Epsilon, Eta Kappa Nu, Phi Kappa Phi. Office: PHE 506 U Southern California Los Angeles California 90089

GOMORY, RALPH EDWARD, mathematician, business machines manufacturing company and foundation executive; born Brooklyn Heights, New York, May 7, 1929; son of Andrew L. and Marian (Schellenberg) G.; married Laura Dumper, 1954 (divorced 1968); children: Andrew C., Susan S., Stephen H. Bachelor of Arts, Williams College, 1950, Doctor of Science (honorary), 1973; postgraduate, Kings College, Cambridge University, England, 1950-51; Doctor of Philosophy, Princeton University, 1954; Doctor of Humane Letters (honorary), Pace University, 1986; Doctor of Science (honorary), Polytechnic University, 1987, Syracuse University, 1989, Worcester Polytechnic University, 1989, Carnegie-Mellon University, 1989. Research associate Princeton University, 1951-54, assistant professor math., Higgins lecturer; 1957-59; with International Business Machines Corporation, Yorktown Heights, New York, 1959-86; director math. sciences, research div. International Business Machines Corporation, Armonk, 1968-70, director research; 1970-86, vice president; 1973-84, senior vice president; 1985-89, senior vice president for sci. and tech.; 1986-89, also member corp. management board; 1983-89, director Asia Pacific Group; 1982-88; president Alfred P. Sloan Foundation, New York City, 1989—; Andrew D. White prof.-at-large Cornell University, 1970-76; board director Bank of New York, Nova Pharmaceutical Corp., Washington Post Company; member adv. council department math. Princeton, 1982-85, chairman, 1984-85; member adv. council School Engineering Stanford University, 1978-85; chairman visiting committee div. applied sciences Harvard University, 1987—; member White House sci. council, Council on Foreign Relations; chairman adv. committee to President on High Temperature Superconductivity, 1987-88; member council on grad. school Yale University, 1988—; member visiting committee elec. engineering and comuter sci. Massachusetts Institute of Technology, 1988—; researcher in integer and linear programming, non-linear differential equations. Trustee Hampshire College, 1977-86, Princeton University, 1985-89, Alfred P. Sloan Foundation, 1988-89; member governing board National Research Council, 1980-83. With United States Navy, 1954-57. Recipient Lanchester prize Ops. Rsch. Society Am., 1964, Harry Goode Memorial award Am. Federation Info. Processing Socs., 1984, John Von Neumann Theory prize Ops. Rsch. Society Am. and Institute Mgmt. Sciences, 1984, IRI medal Indsl. Rsch. Institute, 1985, Engineering Leadership Recognition award Institute of Electrical and Electronic Engineers, 1988, National Medal of Sci., 1988; International Business Machines Corporation fellow, 1964. Fellow Econometric Society, Am. Acad. Arts and Sciences; member National Acad. Sciences (council 1977-78, 80-83), National Acad. Engineering (council 1986—), Am. Philosophical Society (council 1986—). Home: 260 Douglas Road Chappaqua New York 10514 Office: Alfred P Sloan Found 630 Fifth Avenue New York New York 10111

GOOD, MARY LOWE (MRS. BILLY JEWEL GOOD), business executive, chemist; born Grapevine, Texas, June 20, 1931; daughter of John W. and Winnie (Mercer) Lowe; married Billy Jewel Good, May 17, 1952; children: Billy, James. Bachelor of Science, Arkansas State Teachers College, 1950; Master of Science, University Arkansas, 1953, Doctor of Philosophy, 1955, Doctor of Laws (honorary), 1979; Doctor of Science (honorary), University Illinois, Chicago, 1983, Clarkson University, 1984, Eastern Michigan University, 1986, Duke University, 1987; honorary degree, St. Mary's College, 1988, Kenyon College, 1988. Instructor Arkansas

State Teachers College, Conway, summer 1949; instructor Louisiana State University, Baton Rouge, 1954-56; assistant professor Louisiana State University, 1956-58; associate professor Louisiana State University, New Orleans, 1958-63; professor Louisiana State University, 1963-80; Boyd professor materials sci., div. engineering research Louisiana State University, Baton Rouge, 1979-80; vice president, director research UOP, Incorporated, Des Plaines, Illinois, 1980-84; president Signal Research Center Incorporated, 1985—; president engineered materials research div. Allied-Signal Incorporated, Des Plaines, Illinois, 1986-88; senior v.p.-tech., Morristown, New Jersey, 1988—; chairman President's Committee for National Medal Sci., 1979-82; member National Sci. Board, 1980—; adv. board National Science Foundation chemistry section, 1972-76, committee medicinal chemistry National Institutes of Health, 1972-76, Office of United States Air Force Research, 1974-78, chemist div. Brookhaven and Oak Ridge National Laboratories, 1973-83, chemical tech. div. Oak Ridge National Laboratory, catalysis program Lawrence-Berkeley Laboratory, college engineering Louisiana State University; vice chairman National Sci. Board, 1984, chairman, 1988—. Contributor articles to professional journals. Board of directors Oak Ridge Associate Univs., Industrial Research Institute; trustee Renssalaer Polytech. Institute; adv. board Mayor Byrne's Chicago Task Force High Tech. Devel. Recipient Agnes Faye Morgan research award, 1969, Distinguished Alumni citation University Arkansas, 1973, Scientist of Year award Indsl. R & D Magazine, 1982, Delmer S. Fahrney medal Franklin Institute,

1988; Atomic Energy Commission tng. grantee, 1967, National Science Foundation international travel grantee, 1968, National Science Foundation research grantee, 1969-80. Fellow American Association for the Advancement of Science, Am. Institute Chemistry (Gold medal 1983), Chemical Society London; member Am. Chemical Society (1st woman director 1971-74, regional director 1972-80, chairman board 1978, 80, president 1987, Garvan medal 1973, Herty medal 1975, award Florida section 1979), International Union Pure and Applied Chmistry (president inorganic division 1980-85), National Acad. Engineering, Phi Beta Kappa, Sigma Xi, Iota Sigma Pi (regional director 1967—, hon. member 1983). Club: Zonta (past president New Orleans club, chmn. dist. status of women com. and nominating com., chmn. internat. Amelia Earhart scholarship com. 1978-88, president Found. 1988—). Home: 21 Oak Park Dr Convent Station New Jersey 07961 Office: Allied-Signal Incorporated Post Office Box 1021R Morristown New Jersey 07960-1021

GOOD, ROBERT ALAN, physician, educator; born Crosby, Minnesota, May 21, 1922; son of Roy Homer and Ethel Gay (Whitcomb) G.; married Noorbibi K. Day, 1986; children from previous marriage: Robert Michael, Mark Thomas, Alan Maclyn, Margaret Eugenia, Mary Elizabeth. Bachelor of Arts, University Minnesota, 1944, Bachelor of Medicine, 1946, Doctor of Philosophy, 1947, Doctor of Medicine, 1947, Doctor of Science (honorary), 1989; Doctor of Medicine (honorary), University Uppsala, Sweden, 1966; Doctor of Science (honorary), New York Medical College, 1973, Medical College Ohio, 1973, College Medicine and Dentistry New Jersey, 1974, Hahnemann Medical College, 1974, University Chicago, 1974, St. John's University, 1977, University Health Scis., Chicago Medical School, 1978. Teaching assistant department anatomy University Minnesota, Minneapolis, 1944-45; instructor pediatrics University Minnesota (Medical School), 1950-51, assistant professor; 1951-53, associate professor; 1953-54, Am. Legion Memorial research professor pediatrics; 1954-73, professor microbiology; 1962-72, Regents professor pediatrics and microbiology; 1969-73, professor, head department pathology; 1970-72; intern University Minnesota Hospitals, 1947, assistant resident pediatrics; 1948-49; president, director Sloan-Kettering Institute for Cancer Research, 1973-80, member; 1973-81; professor pathology Sloan-Kettering div. Grad. School Medical Sciences Cornell University, 1973-81, director; 1973-80; adj. professor, visiting physician Rockefeller University, 1973-81; professor medicine and pediatrics Cornell University Medical College, 1973-81; director research Memorial Sloan-Kettering Cancer Center, vice president; 1980-81; director research Memorial Hospital for Cancer and Allied Diseases, 1973-80, also attending physician departments medicine and pediatrics; attending pediatrician New York Hospital, 1973-81; member, head cancer research program Oklahoma Medical Research Foundation, 1982-85; professor pediatrics, research professor medicine, Oklahoma Medical Research Foundation professor microbiology and immunology University Oklahoma Health Sciences Center, 1982-85; attending physician, head div. immunology Oklahoma

Children's Memorial Hospital, 1982-85; attending physician in internal medicine Oklahoma Memorial Hospital, 1983-85; physician-in-chief All Children's Hospital, St. Petersburg, Florida, 1985—; professor, chairman department pediatrics University South Florida, St. Petersburg, 1985—; visiting investigator Rockefeller Institute for Medical Research, New York City, 1949-50, assistant physician to Hospital, 1949-50; attending pediatrician Hennepin County General Hospital, 1950-73, consultant, 1960-73; Member Unitarian Service Commission Medical Exchange Team to, France, Germany, Switzerland and Czechoslovakia, 1958; consultant Veteran's Administration Hospital, Minneapolis, 1959-60; consultant, sci. adviser National Jewish Hospital, Denver and Childrens Asthma Research Institute and Hospital, Denver, 1964-69; member study sections United States Public Health Service, 1952-69; member expert adv. panel on immunology World Health Organization, 1967—; consultant Merck & Company, New Jersey, 1968—, National Cancer Institute, 1973-74; member ad hoc committee President's Sci. Adv. Council on Biological and Medical Sci., 1970, President's Cancer Panel, 1972; member Lyndon B. Johnson Foundation awards committee, 1972; member adv. committee Bone Marrow Transplant Registry, 1973—; foreign adv. Acad. Medical Sciences, People's Republic of China, 1980—. Author, editor numerous books; contributor articles to professional journals. Member adv. council Childrens Hospital Research Foundation, Cincinnati, 1954-58; board of directors Allergy Foundation Am., 1973; board sci. advisers Jane

Coffin Childs Memorial Fund Medical Research, 1972-74, Merck Institute Therapeutic Research, 1972-76; chairman International Bone Marrow Registry, 1977-79. Recipient Borden Undergrad. Researchaward University Minnesota Medical School, 1946; E. Mead Johnson First award, 1955; Theobald Smith award, 1955; Parke-Davis 6th Annual award, 1962; Rectors medal University Helsinki, 1963-64; Pemberton Lectureship award, 1966; Gordon Wilson Gold medal, 1967; R.E. Dyer Lectureship award, 1967; Clemens Von Pirquet Gold medal 9th Annual Forum on Allergy, 1968; Presidents medal University Padua, Italy, 1968; Robert A. Cooke Gold medal Am. Acad. Allergy, 1968; John Stewart Memorial award Dalhousie University, 1969; Borden award Association Am. Medical Colleges, 1970; Howard Taylor Ricketts award University Chicago, 1970; Gairdner Foundation award, 1970; City of Hope award, 1970; Am. Acad. Achievement golden plate award, 1970; Albert Lasker award for clinical and med. research, 1970; Am. College of Physicians award, 1972; Am. College Chest Physicians award, 1974; Lila Gruber award Am. Acad. Dermatology, 1974; award in cancer immunology Cancer Research Institute New York, 1975; Outstanding Achievement award University Minnesota, 1978; award Am. Dermatological Society Allergy and Immunology, 1978; 1st Sarasota Medical award, 1979; sect. on mil. pediatrics award Am. Acad. Pediatrics, 1980; recipient University medal Hacettepe University, Ankara, Turkey, 1982, President's medal University Lyon, France, 1986, Merieux Foundation award International Society Preventive Oncology, 1987; numerous others.; Fellow National Foundation for Infantile Paralysis, 1947; Helen Hay Whitney Foundation fellow, 1948-50; Markle Foundation scholar, 1950-55. Fellow Acad. Multidisciplinary Research, American Association for the Advancement of Science, New York Acad. Sci., Am. Acad. Arts and Sciences; member Am. Association History of Medicine, Am. Federation Clinical Research, Am. Association Anatomists, Am. Association Immunologists (past president), American Association of University Women, Am. Pediatric Society (John Howland award 1987), Minneapolis Pediatric Society, Northwestern Pediatric Society, Am. Rheumatism Association, Am. Society Clinical Investigation (past president), Am. Society Experimental Pathology (past president), Am. Society Microbiology, Association Am. Physicians, Central Society Clinical Research (past president), Harvey Society, Infectious Disease Society Am. (Squibb award 1968), International Society Nephrology, International Acad. Pathology, International Society for Transplantation Biology, Minnesota State Medical Association, National Acad. Sci., National Acad. Sci. Institute Medicine (charter), Reticuloendothelial Society (past president), Society for Experimental Biology and Medicine (president), Society for Pediatric Research, Am. Clinical and Climatological Association (Gordon Wilson Gold medal 1967), Detroit Surgical Association (McGraw medal 1969), International Society Blood, Transfusion, Practitioners' Society, Am. Association Pathologists, International Society Experimental Hematology, Transplant Society, Western Association Immunologists, International Society Immunopharmacology (founding member),

Phi Beta Kappa, Sigma Xi, Alpha Omega Alpha. Office: All Children's Hosp 801 6th St S Saint Petersburg Florida 33701

GOODENOUGH, WARD HUNT, anthropologist, educator; born Cambridge, Massachusetts, May 30, 1919; son of Erwin Ramsdell and Helen Miriam (Lewis) G.; married Ruth Gallagher, February 8, 1941; children: Hester G. Goodenough Gelber, Deborah L. Goodenough Gordon, Oliver R., Garrick G. Graduate, Groton (Massachusetts) School, 1937; Bachelor of Arts, Cornell University, 1940; Doctor of Philosophy, Yale University, 1949. Instructor anthropology University Wisconsin, 1948-49; member faculty University Pennsylvania, Philadelphia, 1949—, professor anthropology; 1962-89, university professor; 1980-89, emeritus university professor; 1989—, chairman department anthropology; 1976-82; visiting professor Cornell University, Ithaca, New York, 1961-62, visiting lecturer, summer 1950; visiting lecturer Swarthmore College, spring 1955, Bryn Mawr College, fall 1955, University Hawaii, summer 1959, 75-77; visiting professor University Wisconsin, Milwaukee, summer 1967, Yale University, New Haven, spring 1969, Colorado College, spring 1979, University Hawaii, 1982-83; anthropological studies in Truk, 1947, 64-65, Gilbert Islands, 1951, New Guinea, 1951, 54; Pacific Sci. board National Acad. Scis.-NRC, 1962-66; standing committee anthropology and social sciences Pacific Sci. Association, 1962-66; consultant Office Sci. and Tech., 1961-62. Author: Property, Kin and Community on Truk, 1951, Cooperation in Change, 1963, Explorations in Cultural Anthropology, 1964, Description and Comparison in Cultural Anthropology, 1970, Culture, Language and Society, 1971, Trukese-English Dictionary, 1980. Member health committee Philadelphia District Health and Welfare Council, 1963-64; Board of directors Human Relations Area Files, Incorporated, 1964-86, chairman, 1971-81. Served with Army of the United States, 1941-45. Fellow Center Advanced Study Behavioral Sciences, 1957-58; Guggenheim fellow, 1979-80; Fulbright lecturer St. Patrick's College, Ireland, 1987. Member National Acad. Sciences; fellow Am. Philosophical Society, Am. Acad. Arts and Sciences; member Royal Anthropological Institute, Am. Anthropological Association (editor 1966-70, Distinguished Service award 1986), American Association for the Advancement of Science (vice president, chairman section H 1971, director 1972-75), Am. Ethnological Society (president 1962), Society Applied Anthropology (president 1963), Linguistics Society Am., Institute on Religion in an Age of Sci. (president 1987-89), Polynesian Society, Association Social Anthropology in Oceania, Phi Beta Kappa, Sigma Xi, Phi Kappa Phi. Office: University Museum Philadelphia Pennsylvania 19104

GORDON, JOHN CHARLES, forestry educator; born Nampa, Idaho, June 10, 1939; son of John Nicholas and Ada Elizabeth (Scheuermann) G.; married Helka Lehtinen, August 6, 1964; 1 child, Sean Nicholas. Bachelor of Science, Iowa State University, Ames, 1961, Doctor of Philosophy, 1966; postgraduate, University Helsinki, Finland, 1961-62; MAP (honorary), Yale University, New Haven, 1984. Instructor forestry Iowa

State University, Ames, 1965-66; plant physiologist United States Forest Service, Rhinelander, Wisconsin, 1966-70; professor forestry Iowa State University, Ames, 1970-77; professor, head department forestry Oregon State University, Corvallis, 1977-83; professor, dean School Forestry Yale University, New Haven, 1983—. Editor: Symbiotic Nitrogen Fixation, 1983. Contributor articles to professional journals. Board of directors Friends of Gray Towers, Milford, Pennsylvania, 1983-87, Yale University Alumni Fund, 1985—; visiting committee Harvard University, 1985—; president C.V. Riley Foundation, New York City, 1985-86, Connecticut Fund for Environment, 1986—. Fulbright scholar, 1961, 84; hon. sr. fellow University Glasgow, Scotland, 1975-76; Green vis. professor University British Columbia, Vancouver, 1985. Member American Association for the Advancement of Science, Society Am. Foresters, Am. Forestry Association, Sigma Xi (hon.), Phi Kappa Phi (hon.). Presbyterian. Club: Yale (New York City), Morys (New Haven). Avocations: hiking; fishing; writing short stories. Home: 125 Lawrence St New Haven Connecticut 06511 Office: Yale U School Forestry 205 Prospect St New Haven Connecticut 06511

GOULD, DAVID SCOTT, equipment manufacturing company executive; born Decatur, Illinois, August 28, 1926; son of Favre and Helen (States) G.; married Grace Sitter, June 26, 1955; children: David, Frances. Bachelor of Science, Missouri School Mines, 1951, Master of Science, 1954; Doctor of Philosophy, University Missouri, 1957; Master of Science, Massachusetts Institute of Technology, 1964; Doctor of Engineering, University Missouri, Rolla, 1986. Registered professional engineer. Metallurgical engineer Laclede Steel Company, 1950-52; metallurgist Air Craft Engine div. Houdaille-Hershey Corp., 1952-53; with Caterpillar Tractor Company, Peoria, Illinois, 1957—, executive vice president; from 1983; now executive vice president Caterpillar Incorporated, Peoria. Served to sergeant United States Army, 1945-47. Fellow Am. Society Metals; mem Am. Foundryman's Association, Society Automotive Engineers. Office: Caterpillar Incorporated 100 NE Adams St Peoria Illinois 61629

GOULD, GORDON, physicist, retired optical communications executive; born New York City, July 17, 1920; son of Kenneth Miller and Helen Vaughn (Rue) G. Bachelor of Science in Physics, Union College, 1941, Doctor of Science, 1978; Master of Science in Physics, Yale University, 1943, Columbia University, 1952. Physicist Western Electric Company, Kearny, New Jersey, 1941; instructor Yale University, 1941-43; physicist Manhattan Project, 1943-45; engineer Semon Bache Company, New York City, 1945-50; instructor City College of New York, 1947-54; research assistant Columbia University, 1954-57; research director TRG, Inc./ Control Data Corp., Melville, New York, 1958-67; professor electrophysics Brooklyn Polytechnic Institute, 1967-74; vice president engineering/marketing, director Optelecom, Incorporated, Gaithersburg, Maryland, 1974-85; director Optelecom, Incorporated, 1979—; director Patlex Corp., Chatsworth, California, Polygon Incorporated, Dillon, Colorado. Contributor sci. articles to professional journals.

Recipient 63 research grants and contracts, 1958—; named Inventor of Year for laser amplifier Patent Office Society, 1978; John Scott award for laser Philadelphia City Trust, 1983. Member Am. Institute Physics, Optical Society Am., Institute of Electrical and Electronics Engineers, American Association for the Advancement of Science, Fiber Optic Communications Society, Laser Institute Am. (president 1971-73, director 1971—). Patentee in field. Home and Office: Route 1 Box 112 Kinsale Virginia 22488

GOULD, PHILLIP L., civil engineering educator, consultant; born Chicago, May 24, 1937; son of David J. and Belle (Blair) G.; married Deborah Paula Rothholtz, February 5, 1961; children—Elizabeth, Nathan, Rebecca, Joshua. Bachelor of Science, University Illinois, 1959, Master of Science, 1960; Doctor of Philosophy, Northwestern University, 1966. Structural designer Skidmore, Owings & Merrill, Chicago, 1960-63; principal structural engineer Westenhoff & Novick, Chicago, 1963-64; National Aeronautics and Space Administration trainee Northwestern University, Evanston, Illinois, 1964-66; assistant professor civil engineering Washington University, St. Louis, 1966-68, associate professor; 1968-74, professor; 1974—, chairman department civil engineering; 1978—, Harold D. Jolly professor civil engineering; 1981—; visiting professor Ruhr University, Federal Republic Germany, 1974-75, University Sydney, Australia, 1981, Shanghai Institute Tech., Peoples Republic of China, 1986; director Great Lakes chapter Earthquake Engineering Research Institute. Author: Static Analysis of Shells: A Unified Development of Surface Structures, 1977, Introduction to Linear Elasticity, 1984, Finite Element Analysis of Shells of Revolution, 1985, Analysis of Shells and Plates, 1987; co-author: Dynamic Response of Structures to Wind and Earthquake Loading, 1980; co-editor: Environmental Forces on Engineering Structures, 1979, Natural Draught Cooling Towers, 1985. Served to 1st lieutenant United States Army, 1959-61. Recipient Senior Scientist award Alexander von Humboldt Foundation, Federal Republic Germany, 1974-75. Fellow American Society of Civil Engineers (board directors St. Louis section 1985-87); member Am. Society Engineering Education, International Association Shell Structures, Am. Acad. Mechanics, Structural Engineers Association Illinois, Sigma Xi. Home: 102 Lake Forest Richmond Heights Missouri 63117 Office: Washington U Department Civil Engring Campus Box 1130 Saint Louis Missouri 63130

GOULD, STEPHEN JAY, paleontologist, educator; born New York City, September 10, 1941; son of Leonard and Eleanor (Rosenberg) G.; married Deborah Ann Lee, October 3, 1965; children: Jesse, Ethan. Bachelor of Arts in Geology, Antioch College, Yellow Springs, Ohio, 1963; Doctor of Philosophy, Columbia University, 1967; Doctor of Laws (honorary), Antioch College, 1983; Doctor of Humane Letters (honorary), Marlboro College, 1982, MacAlester College, 1983, Colgate University, 1984, Pace University, 1984, Suffolk University, 1984; DSci (honorary), Bucknell University, 1982, Denison University, 1984, University Maryland, 1984, Williams College, 1985, Rutgers University, 1987; and numerous others. Assistant professor, then associate professor geology, assistant curator, then associate curator invertebrate paleontology Harvard University, Cambridge, Massachusetts, 1967-73, professor geology; 1973—, curator invertebrate paleontology Mus. Comparative Zoology; 1973—, Alexander Agassiz professor zoology; 1982—, member committee profs. Department Biology, adj. member Department History of Sci.; 1973—; member Smithsonian Council, 1976—; board of directors biological sciences curriculum study, 1976-79; adv. board Children's TV Workshop, 1978-81; adv. board TV program NOVA, 1980—. Author: Ontogeny and Phylogeny, 1977, Ever Since Darwin, 1977, The Panda's Thumb, 1980 (Am. Book award Science 1981), The Mismeasure of Man (1981 National Book Critics Circle award for general non-fiction 1982, Outstanding Book award Am. Educational Research Association 1983), Hen's Teeth and Horse's Toes, 1983 (Phi Beta Kappa Book award in Science 1983), The Flamingo's Smile, 1985, Time's Arrow, Time's Cyce, 1987, An Urchin in the Storm, 1987; also numerous articles, monthly column This View of Life in Natural History magazine (National Magazine award for essays and criticism 1980); associate editor Evolution, 1970-72; edition board Systematic Zoology, 1970-72, Paleobiology, 1974-76, Am. Naturalist, 1977-80. Recipient Scientist of Year award Discover Magazine, 1981, Medal of Excellence Columbia University, 1982, F.V. Haydn medal Philadelphia Acad. Sciences, 1982, J. Priestley award and medal Dickinson College, 1983, Neil Miner award for excellence in teaching National Association Geology Teachers, 1983, Distinguished Service award Am. Humanists' Association, 1984, Silver medal Zool. Society London, 1984, Meritorious Service award Am. Association Systematics Collections, 1984, Bradford Washburn award and Gold medal Mus. Sci. Boston, 1984, John and Samuel Bard award in Medicine and Sci. Bard College, 1984; named Humanist Laureate Acad. of Humanism, 1983; Tanner lecturer Cambridge University, 1984, Buwalda lecturer California Institute Tech., 1985; McArthur Foundation prize fellow 1981-86; subject of film profile for TV program NOVA, 1985 (Westinghouse Sci. Film award to producers 1985); prin. investigator numerous grants National Science Foundation, 1969—; National Science Foundation fellow, Woodrow Wilson hon. fellow, Columbia University hon. fellow, 1963-67. Fellow Am. Acad. Arts and Sciences, European Union Geosciences (hon.), American Association for the Advancement of Science (member council 1974-76, committee council affairs 1976-77); member Paleontological Society (president 1985—, Schuchert award for excellence in paleontol. research (under age 40) 1975), Society Study Evolution (vice president 1975), Society Systematic Zoology, Am. Society Naturalists (president 1977-80), Paleontological Society United Kingdom, Society Vertebrate Paleontology, Linnean Society, History of Sci. Society, Sigma Xi (secretary treasurer Harvard-Radcliffe chapter 1968-70). Office: Mus Comparative Zoology Harvard U Cambridge Massachusetts 02138

GOWEN, RICHARD JOSEPH, electrical engineering educator, college president; born New Brunswick, New Jersey, July 6, 1935; son of Charles David and Esther Ann

(Hughes) G.; married Nancy A. Applegate, December 28, 1955; children: Jeff, Cindy, Betsy, Susan, Kerry. Bachelor of Science in Electrical Engineering, Rutgers University, 1957; Master of Science, Iowa State University, 1961, Doctor of Philosophy, 1962. Registered professional engineer, Colorado. Research engineer Radio Corporation of America Laboratories, Princeton, New Jersey, 1957; commissioned United States Air Force; ground electronics officer Yaak Air Force Base, Montana, 1957-59; instructor United States Air Force Acad., 1962-63, research associate; 1963-64, assistant professor; 1964-65, associate professor; 1965-66, tenured associate professor electrical engineering; 1966-70, tenured professor; 1971-77, director, principal investigator National Aeronautics and Space Administration instrumentation group for cardiovascular studies; 1968-77; member launch and recovery medical team Johnson Space Center, National Aeronautics and Space Administration, 1971-77; vice president, dean engineering, professor South Dakota School Mines and Tech., Rapid City, 1977-84, president; 1987—; president Dakota State University, Madison, 1984-87; principal investigator program in support space cardiovascular studies National Aeronautics and Space Administration, 1977-81; co-chairman Joint Industry, Nuclear Regulatory Institute of Electrical and Electronics Engineers, Am. Nuclear Society Probabilistic Risk Assessment Guidelines for Nuclear Power Plants Project, 1980-83; member Department Def. Software Engineering Institute Panel, 1983; board of directors ETA Systems, Incorporated, St. Paul, Minnesota, 1983-89.

Contributor articles to professional journals; patentee in field. Board of directors St. Martins Acad., Rapid City, South Dakota. Named Outstanding Young Man of Colorado Springs Jaycees, 1967; reicpient Marrs Arnold Air Society, 1967; recipient Outstanding Achievement in Field of Engineering Rutgers University, 1977, Professional Achievement Citation in Engineering Iowa State University, 1983. Fellow Institute of Electrical and Electronics Engineers (Centennial International president 1984, USAB/ IEEE Distinguished Contbns. to Engineering Professionalism award 1986); member Am. Association Engineering Socs. (chairman 1988—), Sigma Xi, Phi Kappa Phi, Tau Beta Phi, Eta Kappa Nu, Pi Mu Epsilon. Roman Catholic. Lodge: Rotary. Home: 1609 Palo Verde Rapid City South Dakota 57701 Office: South Dakota School Mines and Tech Office of President Rapid City South Dakota 57701

GRAHAM, RONALD LEWIS, mathematician; born Taft, California, October 31, 1935; son of Leo Lewis and Margaret Jane (Anderson) G.; children: Cheryl, Marc. Student, University Chicago, 1951-54; Bachelor of Science, University Alaska, 1958; Master of Arts, University California, Berkeley, 1961, Doctor of Philosophy, 1962; Doctor of Laws (honorary), Western Michigan University, 1984; Doctor of Science, St. Olaf College, 1985, University Alaska, 1988. Member tech. staff Bell Laboratories, Murray Hill, New Jersey, 1962—, head department discrete math.; 1968—, director Math. Sciences Research Center; 1983—, adj. director research, information sciences div.; 1987—; professor Rutgers University, 1987—; Regents' professor University of California at Los Angeles, 1975;

visiting professor computer sci. Stanford University, 1979, 81, Princeton (New Jersey) University, 1987. Author: Ramsey Theory, 1980. Served with United States Air Force, 1955-59. Recipient Polya prize, 1975; named Scientist of Year, World Book Encyclopedia, 1981; scholar Ford Foundation, 1958, Fairchild Foundation Distinguished scholar California Institute Tech., 1983; fellow National Science Foundation, 1961, Woodrow Wilson Foundation, 1962. Fellow Am. Acad. Arts and Sics., New York Acad. Sciences; member National Acad. Sciences, Am. Math. Society, Math. Association Am., Society Industrial and Applied Math., Ops. Research Society Am., Association Computing Machinery, Math. Program Society. Club: International Jugglers Association (past president). Office: AT&T Bell Labs Murray Hill New Jersey 07974

GRAHAM, WILLIAM ROBERT, government official; born San Antonio, June 15, 1937; son of William Robert Sr. and Dorothy Pearl (Sargent) G.; married Nina Harrison Winter, July 20, 1963; children: Ian Robert, Elizabeth Holley. Bachelor of Science in Physics with honors, California Institute Tech., 1959; Master in Engineering Science, Stanford University, 1960, Doctor of Philosophy in Electrical Engineering, 1963. Member tech. staff Hughes Aircraft Company, Malibu and Culver City, California, 1959-62, RAND Corp., Santa Monica, California, 1965-71; senior associate, co-founder Research & Development Associates, Marina del Rey, California, 1971-85; acting administrator National Aeronautics and Space Administration, Washington, 1985-86, deputy administrator; 1985-86; sci. advisor to president, director office of sci. and tech. policy Executive Office of President, Washington, 1986—; chairman Pres.' General Adv. Committee on Arms Control and Disarmament, Washington, 1982-85; member Pres.' Commission on Compensation of Career Federal Executives, 1987—; consultant U.S.-U.K. Joint Working Group on Atomic Weapons, Washington, 1964-71, Def. Sci. Board Task Force, Washington, 1970-81, Office of Secretary of Def., Washington, 1970-81, Def. Nuclear Agency, Washington, 1975-85. Contributing author: Strategic Options for the Early Eighties, 1979, NATO's Strategic Options, 1981, Arms Control: Myth Versus Reality, 1984, Soviet Strategic Deception, 1987; contributor articles on electromagnetics and statistics to professional journals. Member Def. Policy Adv. Group Reagan presidential campaign, 1980; campaigner, member Republican National Committee, Washington, 1983—; executive committee, board of directors Committee on the Present Danger, Washington, 1979-85. Served to 1st lieutenant United States Air Force, 1962-65. Dupont Travel fellow California Institute Tech., 1958, Hughes Masters fellow Stanford University, 1959-60, Hughes Staff Doctoral fellow Stanford University, 1960-62. Member Council Foreign Relations, Ethics and Pub. Policy Center, American Association for the Advancement of Science, New York Acad. Sciences, Am. Institute Aeros. and Astronautics, Tau Beta Pi, Sigma Xi. Clubs: Met., Cosmos (Washington). Avocations: skiing, photography. Office: Office of Sci and Tech Policy 360 Old Exec Office Building Washington District of Columbia 20506

GRANIT, RAGNAR ARTHUR, neurophysiologist; born Finland, October 30, 1900; married Baroness Marguerite (Daisy) Bruun; 1 child, Michael. Graduate, Swedish Normallyceum, Helsinki, Finland, 1919; Mag. phil., Helsinki University, Doctor of Medicine, 1927, Doctor of Science (honorary); Doctor of Science (honorary), University Oslo, University Oxford, Loyola University, University Pisa, University Göttingen, others. Docent Helsinki University, 1932-37, professor physiology; 1937-40; fellow medical physics Eldridge Reeves Johnson Research Foundation, University Pennsylvania, 1929-31; member staff Royal Caroline Institute, Stockholm, 1940-67; emeritus member Royal Caroline Institute, 1967—, professor neurophysiology; 1946-67; Thomas Young orator Physical Society London, England, 1945; Silliman lecturer Yale University, 1954; Sherrington lecturer London, 1967, Liverpool, 1970; Murlin lecturer Rochester, New York, 1973; Jackson lecturer McGill University, 1975; visiting professor Rockefeller University, New York City, 1956-66, St. Catherine's College, Oxford, 1967, Smith-Kettlewell Institute Medical Sci., San Francisco, 1969, Fogarty International Center, National Institutes of Health, Bethesda, Maryland, 1971-72, 75, Düsseldorf University, 1974, Max-Planck Institute, Bad Nauheim, Federal Republic of Germany, 1976. Author: Ung Mans Vägtill Minerva, 1941, Sensory Mechanisms of the Retina, 1947, Receptors and Sensory Perception, 1955, Charles Scott Sherrington, An Appraisal, 1966, Basis of Motor Control, 1970, Regulation of the Discharge of Motoneurons, 1971, The Purposive Brain, 1977, Hur Det Kom Sig (autobiography), 1983. Co-recipient Nobel prize in medicine, 1967; recipient Donders, Retzius, Sherrington, Purkinje, Tigerstedt medals; 3d International St. Vincent prize, 1961; Jahre prize Oslo University, 1961. Member Royal Swedish Acad. Sci. (president 1963-65, vice president 1965-69), Royal Society London (foreign member), National Acad. Sci. (United States), Am. Philosophical Society, Indian Acad. Sci. (hon.), Acad. di Medical (hon.) (Turin), Acad. National d. Lincei (Rome), Physiological Society England (hon.), Physiological Society United States (hon.), Am. Acad. Arts and Sciences (hon.), Societas Scientiarum Fennicae (hon.), Royal Danish Acad., Acad. Finland (foreign member). Address: 14 Eriksbergsgatan, 11430 Stockholm Sweden

GRAY, HARRY BARKUS, chemistry educator; born Woodburn, Kentucky, November 14, 1935; son of Barkus and Ruby (Hopper) G.; married Shirley Barnes, June 2, 1957; children: Victoria Lynn, Andrew Thomas, Noah Harry Barkus. Bachelor of Science, Western Kentucky University, 1957; Doctor of Philosophy, Northwestern University, 1960, Doctor of Science (honorary), 1984; Doctor of Science (honorary), University Chicago, 1987, University Rochester, 1987. Postdoctoral fellow University Copenhagen, 1960-61; faculty Columbia University, 1961-66, professor; 1965-66; professor chemistry California Institute Tech., Pasadena, 1966—; now Arnold O. Beckman professor chemistry and director Beckman Institute California Institute Tech.; visiting professor Rockefeller University, Harvard University, University Iowa, Pennsylvania State University,

Yeshiva University, University Copenhagen, University Witwatersrand, Johannesburg, South Africa, University Canterbury, Christchurch, New Zealand; consultant government, industry. Author: Electrons and Chemical Bonding, 1965, Molecular Orbital Theory, 1965, Ligand Substitution Processes, 1966, Basic Principles of Chemistry, 1967, Chemical Dynamics, 1968, Chemical Principles, 1970, Models in Chemical Science, 1971, Chemical Bonds, 1973, Chemical Structure and Bonding, 1980, Molecular Electronic Structures, 1980. Recipient Franklin Memorial award, 1967; Fresenius award, 1970; Shoemaker award, 1970; Harrison Howe award, 1972; award for excellence in teaching Mfg. Chemists Association, 1972; Remsen Memorial award, 1979; Tolman medal, 1979; Centenary Medal of Royal Society Chemistry, 1985, Pauling Medal, 1986, National medal of Sci., 1986; Guggenheim fellow, 1972-73; Phi Beta Kappa scholar, 1973-74; named California Scientist of Year, 1988. Member National Acad. Sciences, Am. Chemical Society (award pure chemistry 1970, award inorganic chemistry 1978, award for distinguished service in advancement of inorganic chemistry 1984), Royal Danish Acad. Sciences and Letters, Alpha Chi Sigma, Phi Lambda Upsilon. Home: 1415 E California Boulevard Pasadena California 91106 Office: California Institute Tech Chemistry 127-72 Pasadena California 91125

GRAY, KENNETH EUGENE, petroleum engineering educator; born Herrin, Illinois, January 11, 1930; married, 1955; 3 children. Bachelor of Science, University Tulsa, 1956, Master of Science, 1957; Doctor of Philosophy, University Texas, 1963.

Drilling engineer California Company, 1957-59; reservoir engineer Sohio Petroleum Company, 1959-60; faculty member University Texas, Austin, 1962—, chairman department; 1966-74, Halliburton professor petroleum engineering, director Center Earth Sci.; 1968—; Zarrow Centennial professor petroleum engineering; consultant research department Continental Oil Company, 1963—; member United States National Committee on Rock Mechanics. Research grantee Petroleum Research Fund, Am. Chemical Society, Texas Petroleum Research Committee, 1963—; research grantee Am. Petroleum Institute, Gulf Research & Devel. Company, 1964—. Fellow Am. Institute Chemists, New York Acad. Sciences, Am. Acad. Mechanics; member Society Petroleum Engineers (Distinguished Lecturer). Office: Department Petroleum Engring U Tex Austin Texas 78712

GRAY, MARY W., statistician, lawyer; born Hastings, Nebraska, 1939; daughter of Neil C. and Lillie W. (Alves) Wheat; married Alfred Gray, August 20, 1964. Bachelor of Arts summa cum laude, Hastings College, 1959; postgraduate, J.W. Goethe University, Frankfurt, Federal Republic Germany, 1959-60; Master of Arts, University Kansas, 1962, Doctor of Philosophy, 1964; Juris Doctor summa cum laude, Am. University, 1979. Bar: District of Columbia 1979, United States Supreme Court 1983, United States District Court, District of Columbia 1980. Physicist National Bureau Standards, Washington, summers 1959-63; assistant instructor University Kansas, Lawrence, 1963-64; instructor department math.

University California, Berkeley, 1965; assistant professor California State University, Hayward, 1965-67; associate professor California State University, 1967-68; associate professor department math., statistics and computer sci. Am. University, 1968-71, professor; 1971—, chairman department; 1977-79, 80-81, 83—; statistical consultant for government agys., universities and private firms, 1976—. Author: A Radical Approach to Algebra, 1970; Calculus with Finite Mathematics for Social Sciences, 1972; contributor numerous articles to professional journals. National treasurer, director Women's Equity Action League, from 1981, president, from 1982; board of directors treasurer American Civil Liberties Union, Montgomery County, Maryland; member adv. committee D.C. Department Employment Services, 1983—; director Amnesty International United States of America, 1985—; member Commission on College Retirement, 1984-86; director Am.-Middle East Education Foundation, 1983—. Fulbright grantee, 1959-60; National Science Foundation fellow, 1963-64, NDEA fellow, 1960-63. Fellow American Association for the Advancement of Science (chairman committee on women); member American Association of University Profs., (regional counsel 1984—, committee on acad. freedom 1978—, director Legal Defense Fund 1974-78, board directors Exxon Project on Salary Discrimination 1974-76, committee on status of women 1972-78, Georgina Smith award), Am. Math. Society (vice president 1976-78, council 1973-78), Conference Board Math. Sciences (chairman committee on affirmative action 1977-78), Math. Association Am. (chairman committee on school lectrs. 1973-75, vis. lecturer 1974—), Association for Women in Math (founding president 1971-74, executive committee 1974-80, general counsel 1980—), District of Columbia Bar Association, American Bar Association, Am. Society International Law, London Math. Society, Societe de Mathematique de France, Brit. Society History of Math., Can. Society History of Math., Association Computing Machinery, New York Acad. Sciences, Am. Statistical Association, Phi Beta Kappa, Sigma Xi, Phi Kappa Phi, Alpha Chi, Pi Mu Epsilon. Home: 6807 Connecticut Chevy Chase Maryland 20815 Office: Math Stats and Computer Sci Department American U Washington District of Columbia 20016

GREATBATCH, WILSON, biomedical engineer; born Buffalo, September 6, 1919; married; 5 children. Bachelor of Electrical Engineering, Cornell University, 1950; Master of Science in Electrical Engineering, University Buffalo, 1957; Doctor of Science (honorary), Houghton College, 1971, State University of New York, Buffalo, 1984, Clarkson University, 1987, Roberts Wesleyan College, 1988. Project engineer Cornell Aeronaut Laboratory Incorporated, 1950-52; assistant professor electrical engineering University Buffalo, 1952-57; manager electronics div. Taber Instrument Corp., 1957-60; vice president Mennen Greatbatch Electronics Incorporated, 1962-78; adj. professor elec. engineering State University of New York, Buffalo, 1981—; adj. professor engineering Cornell University, Ithaca, New York, 1989—. Contributor over 100 articles to sci. jours; holder over 150 United States and foreign patents. Recipient Holley medal American Society of

Mechanical Engineers, 1986; inducted Am. Inventors Hall of Fame, 1986. Fellow Institute of Electrical and Electronics Engineers, Am. College Cardiology, Royal Society Health; member National Academy of Engineering, Am. Society Angiology, Association Advancement Medical Instrumentation, New York Acad. Sci., Sigma Xi. Inventor implantable cardiac pacemaker; research in implantable power supplies for medical uses, biomass energy, genetic engineering. Office: Greatbatch Gen Aid Limited 10871 Main St Clarence New York 14031

GREEN, DON WESLEY, chemical and petroleum engineering educator; born Tulsa, July 8, 1932; son of Earl Leslie and Erma Pansy (Brackins) G.; married Patricia Louise Polston, November 26, 1954; children—Guy Leslie, Don Michael, Charles Patrick. Bachelor of Science in Petroleum Engineering, University Tulsa, 1955; Master of Science in Chemical Engineering, University Oklahoma, 1959, Doctor of Philosophy in Chemical Engineering, 1963. Research scientist Continental Oil Company, Ponca City, Oklahoma, 1962-64; assistant to associate professor University Kansas, Lawrence, 1964-71, professor chemical and petroleum engineering; 1971-82, chairman department chemical and petroleum engineering; 1970-74, co-director Tertiary Oil Recovery project; 1974—, Conger-Gabel Distinguished professor; 1982—. Editor: Perry's Chemical Engineers' Handbook, 1984; contributor articles to professional journals. Served to 1st lieutenant United States Air Force, 1955-57. Fellow Am. Institute Chemical Engineers; member Society

Petroleum Engineers (Distinguished Achievement award 1983, chairman education and accreditation committee 1980-81, Distinguished member 1986). Democrat. Avocations: handball; baseball; mountain hiking. Home: 1020 Sunset Dr Lawrence Kansas 66044 Office: U Kans/Dept Chem and Petroleum Engring 4008 Learned Hall Lawrence Kansas 66045

GREEN, HOWARD, cellular physiologist, educator, administrator; born Toronto, Ontario, Canada, 1925. Doctor of Medicine, University Toronto, 1947; Master of Science in Physiology, Northwestern University, 1950. Research assistant department physiology Northwestern University, Evanston, Illinois, 1948-50; research associate, instructor biochemistry University Chicago, 1951-53; instructor pharmacology New York University School Medicine, 1954-55, assistant professor chemical pathology; 1956-59, associate professor pathology; 1959-65, professor; 1965-68, professor, chairman cell biology department; 1968-70; professor cell biology Massachusetts Institute of Technology, Cambridge, 1970-80; Higgins professor cellular physiology Harvard University Medical School, Boston, 1980-86; George Higginson professor physiology Harvard University Medical School, 1986—, chairman department physiology and biophysics; 1986-88, chairman department cellular and molecular physiology; 1988—; lecturer in field. Served to captain Medical Corps United States Army Reserve, 1955-56. Recipient Mr. And Mrs. J. N. Taub International Memorial award, 1977; recipient Selman A. Waksman award, 1978, Lewis S. Rosenstiel award,

1980, Lila Gruber Research award Am. Acad. Dermatology, 1980. Member Am. Acad. Arts and Sciences, National Acad. Sciences. Home: 82 Williston Road Brookline Massachusetts 02146 Office: Harvard Med School Department Cellular & Molecular Physiology 25 Shattuck St Boston Massachusetts 02115

GREEN, LEON, JR., mechanical engineer; born Austin, Texas, August 13, 1922; son of Leon and Notra (Anderson) G.; married Eleanor Broome Samuels, April 14, 1951; children: John Anderson, Emily Broome, Charles Leon. Bachelor of Science in Physics, California Institute Tech., 1944, Master of Science in Mechanical Engineering, 1947, Doctor of Philosophy, 1950. With North America Aviation, Incorporated, 1949-51, Aerojet-Gen. Corp., 1951-59, Aeronutronic div. Ford Motor Company, 1959-62; chief scientist Lockheed Propulsion Company, 1962-64; sci. director research and tech. div. Air Force Systems Command, Washington, 1964-67; director planning Washington area Lockheed Aircraft Corp., 1967-70; executive secretary Defense Sci. Board, Department Defense, 1970-73; senior staff engineer applied physics laboratory Johns Hopkins University; also consultant Atomic Energy Commission, 1973-74; member tech. staff Mitre Corp., McLean, Virginia, 1974-77; consultant General Atomic Company, 1977-80; president Energy Conversion Alternatives, Limited, Washington, 1980-88, consultant; 1988—; vice president Clean Coal Coalition, Incorporated, 1983-86. Contributor articles to professional journals. Member American Society of Mechanical Engineers, Combustion Institute, American Association for the Advancement of Science. Club: Cosmos (Washington). Home and Office: 2101 Connecticut Avenue Northwest Suite 67 Washington District of Columbia 20008

GREEN, PAUL ELIOT, JR., electrical engineer, communications scientist; born Durham, North Carolina, January 14, 1924; son of Paul Eliot and Elizabeth Atkinson (Lay) G.; married Dorrit L. Gegan, October 30, 1948; children: Dorrit Green Rodemeyer, Nancy E., Judith Green Godin, Paul M., Gordon M. Bachelor of Arts, University North Carolina, Chapel Hill, 1943; Master of Science, North Carolina State University, 1948; Doctor of Science, Massachusetts Institute of Technology, 1953. Group leader Massachusetts Institute of Technology Lincoln Laboratory, Lexington, 1951-69; senior manager International Business Machines Corporation Research Div., Yorktown Heights, New York, 1969-81; member corp. tech. committee International Business Machines Corporation Research Div., Armonk, New York, 1981-83; staff International Business Machines Corporation Research Div., Yorktown Heights, New York, 1983—; member radio engineering adv. committee Voice of Am., United States Information Agency, 1983—; member committee on survivable communications National Research Council, 1982—. Co-editor: Computer Communication, 1974; editor: Computer Network Architectures and Protocols, 1982. Served to lieutenant commander United States Naval Reserve, 1943-60; retired. Named Distinguished Engineering Alumnus North Carolina State University, 1983. Fellow Institute of Electrical and Electronics Engineers (Aerospace Pioneer award 1981, chairman info.

theory group 1960); member Communications Society Institute of Electrical and Electronics Engineers (vice president for tech. affairs 1988—), National Acad. Engineering. Home: Roseholm Place Mount Kisco New York 10549 Office: International Business Machines Corporation Post Office Box 218 Yorktown Heights New York 10598

GREENBERG, JOSEPH H., anthropologist; born Brooklyn, May 28, 1915; son of Jacob and Florence (Pilzer) G.; married Selma Berkowitz, November 23, 1940. Bachelor of Arts, Columbia, 1936; Doctor of Philosophy in Anthropology, Northwestern University, 1940, Doctor of Science (honorary), 1982. Faculty University Minnesota, 1946-48; assistant professor Columbia, 1948-53, associate professor; 1953-57, professor anthropology; 1957-62; professor Stanford, 1962-85, Ray Lyman Wilbur professor social sciences in anthropology; 1971; director National Defense Education Act. African Language and Area Center, 1967-78; Visiting professor Summer Linguistic Institute, Michigan University, 1957, University Minnesota, 1960; member panel anthropology and philosophy and history of sci. National Science Foundation, 1959-61; visiting professor summer institute University Colorado, 1961; director West African Languages Survey, 1959-66; Linguistic Society Am. professor Summer Linguistic Institute, Oswego, New York, 1976; Collitz professor Summer Linguistic Institute, Stanford, 1987, coordinator Stanford Project on Language Universals. Author: Languages of Africa, 1963, Essays in Linguistics, 1957, Universals of Language, 1963, Influence of Islam on a Sudanese Religion, 1946, Anthropological Linguistics: An Introduction, 1968, Language, Culture and Communication: Essays by Joseph H. Greenberg, 1971, Language Typology, 1974, A New Invitation to Linguistics, 1977, Universals of Human Language, 4 vols, 1978, Language in the Americas, 1987; co-editor: Word, 1950-54. Served with Signal Intelligence Corp. Army of the United States, 1940-45. Social Sci. Research Council fellow Northwestern University, 1940; Stanford humanities fellow, 1958-59, 82-83; Ford Foundation grantee, 1952, 57-62; recipient Demobilization award Social Sci. Research Council, 1945-46; Guggenheim award, 1954-55, 58-59; Haile Selassie award for African research, 1967; award in behavioral scis. New York Acad. Sciences, 1980. Member Am. Anthropological Association (representative to governor board International Institute 1955—, 1st distinguished lecturer 1970), Linguistic Society Am. (executive committee 1953-55, vice president 1976, president 1977), West African Linguistics Society (chairman 1965-66), African Studies Association (executive committee, also committee on langs. and linguistics 1959—, president 1964-65), National Acad. Sciences, Am. Acad. Arts and Sciences, Am. Philosophical Society, Phi Beta Kappa. Home: 860 Mayfield Avenue Stanford California 94305

GREENWALD, PETER, physician, government medical research director; born Newburgh, New York, November 7, 1936; son of Louis and Pearl (Reingold) G.; married Harriet Reif, September 6, 1968; children—Rebecca, Laura, Daniel. Bachelor of Arts, Colgate

University, 1957; Doctor of Medicine, State University of New York College Medicine, 1961; Master of Public Health, Harvard University, 1967, Doctor of Public Health, 1974. Intern Los Angeles County Hospital, 1961-62; resident in internal medicine Boston City Hospital, 1964-66; assistant in medicine Peter Bent Brigham Hospital, 1967-68; member epidemiology and disease control study section National Institutes of Health, 1974-78; member New York State Gov.'s Breast Task Force, 1976-78; with New York State Department Health, Albany, 1968-81; director New York State Department Health, 1968-76, director epidemiology; 1976-81; professor medicine Albany Medical College, 1976-81; attending physician Albany Medical Center Hospital, 1968-81; adj. professor biomed. engineering Rensselaer Polytechnic Institute, Troy, New York, 1976-81; associate scientist Sloan-Kettering Institute for Cancer Research, New York City, 1977-81; director Div. Cancer Prevention and Control, National Cancer Institute, National Institutes of Health, 1981—; member Veteran's Administration Merit Rev. Board Medical Oncology, Washington, 1972-74. Editor-in-chief Journal National Cancer Institute, National Institute Health, 1981-87; contributor articles to professional journals. Served with United States Public Health Service, 1962-64, 81—. Recipient Distinguished Service award New York State Department Health, 1975; Redway medal and award for med. writing New York State Journal Medicine, 1977; New York State Governor's Citation for pub. health achievement, 1981. Fellow American College of Physicians, Am. College Preventive Medicine, Am. Pub. Health Association (epidemiology section chairman 1981); member Am. Association Cancer Research, Am. College Epidemiology (board directors 1981-82), Am. Cancer Society, National Committee Cancer Prevention and Detection, Am. Society Preventive Oncology, International Cancer Registry Association, International Epidemiology Society, National Acad. Sciences (food and nutrition board). Office: NIH Building 31 Room 10A52 9000 Rockville Pike Bethesda Maryland 20892-3100

GREVE, JOHN HENRY, veterinary parasitologist, educator; born Pittsburgh, August 11, 1934; son of John Welch and Edna Viola (Thuenen) G.; married Sally Jeanette Doane, June 21, 1956; children—John Haven, Suzanne Carol, Pamela Jean. Bachelor of Science, Michigan State University, East Lansing, 1956, Doctor of Veterinary Medicine, 1958, Master of Science, 1959; Doctor of Philosophy, Purdue University, West Lafayette, Ind., 1963. Associate instructor Michigan State University, East Lansing, 1958-59; instructor Purdue University, West Lafayette, 1959-63; assistant professor Iowa State University, Ames, 1963-64, associate professor; 1964-68, professor department vet. pathology; 1968—; consultant parasitologist various zoos. Contributor chapters to books, articles to professional jours; member editorial board Vet. Research Communications, the Netherlands, 1977-84, Vet. Parasitology, 1984—. District chairman Broken Arrow District, Boy Scouts Am., Ames, Iowa, 1975-77. Named Distinguished Teacher Norden Labs., 1965; Outstanding Teacher Amoco Oil, Iowa State University, 1972; recipient Faculty Citation Iowa State University

Alumni Association, 1978. Member American Veterinary Medical Association (member editorial board journal 1975—), Iowa Veteran Medical Association, Am. Society Parasitologists, Midwestern Conference Parasitologists (sec.-treas. 1967-75, presiding officer 1975-76), Am. Association Vetcran Parasitologists (president 1968-70), Helminthological Society Washington, World Association for Advancement Veteran Parasitology, Am. Association Veteran Medical Colls., Izaak Walton League (board directors Iowa 1968-70), Honor Society Cardinal Key, Gamma Sigma Delta, Phi Eta Sigma, Phi Kappa Phi, Phi Zeta. Republican. Lodges: Kiwanis (Town and Country-Ames president 1967, Nebr.-Iowa lt. gov. 1972-73). Avocations: philately; camping. Office: Iowa State U Department Veteran Pathology Ames Iowa 50011

GREY, ROBERT DEAN, biology educator; born Liberal, Kansas, September 5, 1939; son of McHenry Wesley and Kathryn (Brown) G.; married Alice Kathleen Archer, June 11, 1961; children: Erin Kathleen, Joel Michael. Bachelor of Arts, Phillips University, 1961; Doctor of Philosophy, Washington University, 1966. Assistant professor Washington University, St. Louis, 1966-67; from assistant professor to full professor zoology University California, Davis, 1967—, chairman department; 1979-83, dean biological sciences; 1985—. Author: (with others) A Laboratory Text for Developmental Biology, 1980; contributor articles to professional journals. Recipient Distinguished Teaching award Acad. Senate University California, Davis, 1977, Magnar Ronning award for teaching Associated Students University California, Davis, 1978. Member Am. Society Cell Biology, Society Developmental Biology, Phi Sigma. Lodge: Rotary. Avocations: music, hiking, gardening. Office: U California Davis Div of Biol Scis Davis California 95616

GRIFFITHS, PHILLIP A., mathematician, university provost. Bachelor of Science, Wake Forest University, 1959; Doctor of Philosophy, Princeton University, 1963; Doctor Honoris Causa, Angers University, France, 1979; Honorary degree, Wake Forest University, 1973, University Peking, Peoples Republic China, 1983. Miller fellow University Calif.-Berkeley, 1963-64, assistant professor; 1964-66, associate professor; 1966-68; professor math. Princeton University, New Jersey, 1968-72, Harvard University, 1972-83; Dwight Parker Robinson professor math. Princeton University; provost, James B. Duke professor math. Duke University, Durham, North Carolina, 1984—. Recipient LeRoy P. Steel prize Am. Math. Society, 1971, Dinnie-Heineman-Preis prize Acad. Sciences, 1979. Office: Office of Provost Duke U Durham North Carolina 27706

GROSS, PAUL RANDOLPH, biologist, academic administrator; born Philadelphia, November 27, 1928; son of Nathan and Kate (Segal) G.; married Joan M. Edstrom, May 23, 1987; 1 child, Wendy Loren. Bachelor of Arts, University Pennsylvania, 1950, Doctor of Philosophy (Harrison and NSF fellow), 1954; Master of Arts, Brown University, 1963; Doctor of Science, Medical College Ohio, 1979. Assistant professor biology New York University, 1954-58, associate professor; 1958-61; associate professor biology Brown University, 1962-65; professor biology Massachusetts Institute of Technology, 1965-71; professor, chairman department biology University Rochester, 1972-78, dean grad. studies; 1975-78, chairman sci. adv. committee Cancer Center; 1974-78; president, director Marine Biological Laboratory, Woods Hole, Massachusetts, 1978-86; Taylor professor biology, professor physology, vice president, provost University Virginia, Charlottesville, 1986—; principal investigator research and training grants from National Science Foundation and National Institutes of Health, 1955—; member, advisor to doctoral council New York State Education Department; member adv. committee cell and devel. biology Am. Cancer Society; member oversight committee Association Am. Colleges; member national adv. council National Institute Child Health and Human Devel.; member sci. adv. committee Tufts University School Vet. Medicine, Stazione Zoologica, Naples, Italy; member council National Sci. Association, University Pennsylvania; member committee on oceans and international environmental and sci. affairs United States Department State. Contributor sci. articles to professional journals. Trustee University Rochester, 1980-86. Lalor fellow, 1954-55; National Science Foundation fellow University Edinburgh, 1961-62. Fellow Am. Acad. Arts and Sciences; member International Society for Developmental Biology, Am. Physiological Society, Am. Society Zoologists (chairman section on developmental biology), American Association for the Advancement of Science, Am. Society

Cell Biology. Clubs: Woods Hole Yacht, Cosmos.

GUILLEMIN, ROGER, physiologist; born Dijon, France, January 11, 1924; came to United States, 1953, naturalized, 1963; son of Raymond and Blanche (Rigollot) G.; married Lucienne Jeanne Billard, March 22, 1951; children—Chantal, Francois, Claire, Helene, Elizabeth, Cecile. Bachelor of Arts, University Dijon, 1941, Bachelor of Science, 1942; Doctor of Medicine, Faculty of Medicine, Lyons, France, 1949; Doctor of Philosophy, University Montreal, 1953; Doctor of Philosophy (honorary), University Rochester, 1976, University Chicago, 1977, Baylor College Medicine, 1978, University Ulm, Germany, 1978, University Dijon, France, 1978, Free University Brussels, 1979, University Montreal, 1979, University Manitoba, Can, 1984, University Turin, Italy, 1985. Intern, resident universities hospitals Dijon, 1949-51; associate director, assistant professor Institute Experimental Medicine and Surgery, University Montreal, 1951-53; associate director department experimental endocrinology College de France, Paris, 1960-63; assistant professor physiology Baylor College Medicine, 1953-57, associate professor; 1957-63, professor, director laboratories neuroendocrinology; 1963-70, adj. professor; 1970—; adj. professor medicine University California at San Diego, 1970—; research fellow, chairman laboratories neuroendocrinology Salk Institute, 1970—. Decorated chevalier Legion of Honor (France), 1974, officier, 1984; recipient Gairdner International award, 1974; U.S. National Medal of Sci., 1977; co-recipient Nobel prize for medicine,

1977; recipient Lasker Foundation award, 1975; Dickson prize in medicine, 1976; Passano award med. sci., 1976; Schmitt medal neurosci., 1977; Barren gold medal, 1979; Dale medal Society for Endocrinology United Kingdom, 1980. Fellow American Association for the Advancement of Science; Member Am. Physiological Society, Endocrine Society (president) 1986), Society Experimental Biology and Medicine, International Brain Research Organization, International Society Research Biology Reprodn., Society Neuro-scis., National Acad. Sciences, Am. Acad. Arts and Sciences, Académie nationale de Médecine (foreign associate), Swedish Society Medical Sciences (hon.), Académie des Sciences (foreign associate), Académie Royale de Médecine de Belgique (corr. foreign), Club of Rome. Office: Salk Institute Box 85800 San Diego California 92138

GURALNICK, SIDNEY AARON, civil engineering educator; born Philadelphia, April 25, 1929; son of Philip and Kenia (Dudnik) G.; married Eleanor Alban, March 10, 1951; children—Sara Dian, Jeremy. Bachelor of Science, Drexel Institute Tech., Philadelphia, 1952; Master of Science, Cornell University, 1955, Doctor of Philosophy, 1958. Registered professional engineer, Pennsylvania; registered structural engineer, Illinois. Instructor, then assistant professor Cornell University, 1952-58, manager structural research laboratory; 1956-58; member faculty Illinois Institute Tech., Chicago, 1958—; professor civil engineering Illinois Institute Tech., 1967—, distinguished professor engineering; 1982—, director structural engineering laboratories; 1968-71, dean Grad. School; 1971-75, executive vice president, provost; 1975-82, trustee; 1976-82; devel. engineer Portland Cement Association, Skokie, Illinois, 1959-61; participant international conferences; consultant to government and industry. Author numerous papers in field. Trustee Institute Gas Tech., 1976-81; commr.-at-large North Central Association Schools and Colls., 1985—. Served with Army of the United States, 1950-51. McGraw fellow, 1952-53; Faculty Research fellow Illinois Institute Tech., 1960; European travel grantee, 1961. Fellow Am. Concrete Institute, American Society of Civil Engineers (Collingwood prize 1961); member Am. Society for Engineering Education, Society Experimental Stress Analysis, Sigma Xi, Phi Kappa Phi, Tau Beta Pi, Chi Epsilon. Office: Illinois Institute Tech 3300 S Federal St Chicago Illinois 60616

GUTH, ALAN HARVEY, physicist, educator; born New Brunswick, New Jersey, February 27, 1947; son of Hyman and Elaine (Cheiten) G.; married Susan Tisch, March 28, 1971; children—Lawrence David, Jennifer Lynn. Bachelor of Science and Master of Science, Massachusetts Institute of Technology, 1969, Doctor of Philosophy in Physics, 1972. Instructor Princeton University, 1971-74; research associate Columbia University, New York City, 1974-77, Cornell University, Ithaca, New York, 1977-79, Stanford Linear Accelerator Center, California, 1979-80; associate professor Physics Massachusetts Institute of Technology, Cambridge, 1980-86, professor; 1986—; physicist Harvard-Smithsonian Center for Astrophysics, 1984—. Alfred P. Sloan fellow, 1981; on Sci. Digest's list of America's 100 Brightest Scientists

Under 40, 1984; on Esquire Mag.'s list of Men and Women Under 40 Who Are Changing the Nation, 1985. Fellow Am. Physical Society (member executive committee astrophysics division 1986-88, vice chairman astrophysics division 1988-89, chairman division 1989-90), Am. Acad. Arts and Sciences, National Academy of Sciences; member Am. Astronomical Society, American Association for the Advancement of Science. Originator of inflationary model of early universe. Office: Center Theoretical Physics Massachusetts Institute of Technology Cambridge Massachusetts 02139

HAHN, ERWIN LOUIS, physicist, educator; born Sharon, Pennsylvania, June 9, 1921; son of Israel and Mary (Weiss) H.; married Marian Ethel Failing, April 8, 1944 (deceased September 1978); children: David L., Deborah A., Katherine L.; married Natalie Woodford Hodgson, April 12, 1980. Bachelor of Science, Juniata College, 1943, Doctor of Science, 1966; Master of Science, University Illinois, 1947, Doctor of Philosophy, 1949; Doctor of Science, Purdue University, 1975. Assistant Purdue University, 1943-44; research associate University Illinois, 1950; National Research Council fellow Stanford, 1950-51, instructor; 1951-52; research physicist Watson International Business Machines Corporation Laboratory, New York City, 1952-55; associate Columbia University, 1952-55; faculty University California at Berkeley, 1955—, professor physics; 1961—, associate professor, then professor Miller Institute for Basic Research; 1958-59, 66-67, 85-86; visiting fellow Brasenose College, Oxford (England)

University, 1981-82; Eastman visiting professor Oxford University, 1988-89; consultant Office Naval Research, Stanford, 1950-52, Atomic Energy Commission, 1955—; special consultant United States Navy, 1959; adv. panel member National Bureau Standards, Radio Standards div., 1961-64; member National Acad. Sci./Nat. Research Council committee on basic research; adv. to United States Army Research Office, 1967-69. Author: (with T.P. Das) Nuclear Quadrupole Resonance Spectroscopy, 1958. Served with United States Naval Reserve, 1944-46. Recipient Oliver E. Buckley prize Am. Physical Society, 1971; prize International Society Magnetic Resonance, 1971; award Humboldt Foundation, Germany, 1976-77; co-winner Wolf Foundation prize in physics, 1983-84; named to California Inventor Hall of Fame, 1984; Guggenheim fellow, 1961-62, 69-70; National Science Foundation fellow, 1961-62; vis. fellow Brasenose College, Oxford, 1969-70; lifetime hon. fellow Brasenose College, Oxford, 1984, Alumni Achievement award, Juniata College, 1986. Fellow Am. Physical Society (past member executive committee division solid state physics); member Am. Acad. Arts and Sciences, National Acad. Sciences, Slovenian Acad. Sciences and Arts (foreign). Home: 69 Stevenson Avenue Berkeley California 94708 Office: Department Physics U California Berkeley California 94720

HAILMAN, JACK PARKER, zoology educator; born St. Louis, May 6, 1936; son of David E. and Katharine Lillard (Butts) H.; married Elizabeth Bailey Davis, August 26, 1958; children—Karl Andrew, Peter

Eric. Bachelor of Arts, Harvard University, 1958; Doctor of Philosophy, Duke University, 1964. National Institutes of Health postdoctoral fellow University Tubingen, Germany, 1964, Rutgers University, 1964-66; assistant professor zoology University Maryland, 1966-69; associate professor University Wisconsin, Madison, 1969-72; professor University Wisconsin, 1972—; hon. research associate Smithsonian Institution, Washington, 1966-69. Author: Ontogeny of an Instinct, 1967, Optical Signals, 1977; co-author: Introduction to Animal Behavior, 1967; co-editor: Fascinating World of Animals, 1971. Board of directors County chapter American Civil Liberties Union, 1968. Served with United States Navy, 1958-61. James P. Duke fellow, 1961; National Institutes of Health fellow, 1962, 64; National Institutes of Health research grantee, 1966-69; National Science Foundation research grantee, 1970-85; Fulbright research scholar University Trondheim, Norway, 1987. Fellow American Association for the Advancement of Science, Am. Ornithologists Union, Animal Behavior Society (president 1981-82). Office: Department Zoology Birge Hall U Wisconsin Madison Wisconsin 53706

HAISE, FRED WALLACE, JR., aerospace company executive, former astronaut; born Biloxi, Mississippi, November 14, 1933; son of Fred Wallace and Lucille (Blacksher) H.; married Mary Griffin Grant, June 4, 1954; children: Mary Margaret, Frederick Thomas, Stephen William, Thomas Jesse. Associate of Arts, Perkinston Junior College, 1952; Bachelor of Science in Aeronautical Engineering, University Oklahoma,

1959; Doctor of Science (honorary), Western Michigan University. Naval aviation cadet United States Navy, 1952-54; fighter pilot United States Marine Corps, 1954-56, Air National Guard, Oklahoma, Ohio, 1957-63; captain United States Air Force, 1961-62; research pilot National Aeronautics and Space Administration Lewis Research Center, Cleveland, 1959-63, National Aeronautics and Space Administration Flight Research Center, Edwards Air Force Base, California, 1963-66; astronaut National Aeronautics and Space Administration Manned Spacecraft Center, Houston, 1966-77; commander Space Shuttle Orbiter Crew, 1977-79; vice president for space programs Grumman Aerospace Corp. (now Grumman Corp.), Bethpage, New York, from 1979; now president Grumman Tech. Services Incorporated div. Grumman Corp., Titusville, Florida; member crew Apollo 13, 1970; backup commander Apollo 16, 1972. Recipient AB Honts trophy U.S. Air Force Aerospace Research Pilot School, Edwards Air Force Base, 1964; Presidential Medal Freedom; Mississippi Distinguished Civilian Service Medal; Jeff Davis award; Pine Burr award; City Houston Medal Valour. Member Society Experimental Test Pilots, Phi Theta Kappa, Tau Beta Pi, Sigma Gamma Tau. Address: Grumman Tech Services Incorporated 5195 S Washington Avenue Titusville Florida 32780

HALL, CARL WILLIAM, mechanical and agricultural engineer, scientific research foundation executive; born Tiffin, Ohio, November 16, 1924; son of Lester and Irene (Routzahn) H.; married Mildred Evelyn Wagner, September 5, 1949; 1 daughter,

Claudia Elizabeth. Bachelor of Science, Bachelor in Agricultural Engineering summa cum laude, Ohio State University, 1948; Master of Mechanical Engineering, University Delaware, 1950; Doctor of Philosophy, Michigan State University, 1952. Registered professional engineer, Michigan, Ohio, Washington (state). Instructor University Del., 1948-50, assistant professor; 1950-51; assistant professor Michigan State University, 1951-53, associate professor; 1953-55, professor; 1955-70, research adviser; 1957-64, chairman department agricultural engineering; 1964-70; dean, director research (College Engineering); professor mechanical engineering Washington State University, Pullman, 1970-82; president Research Foundation Washington State University, 1973-82; deputy assistant director Directorate for Engineering National Science Foundation, 1982—; acting assistant director ESCOE, Incorporated, Washington, 1979; research consultant University Puerto Rico, 1957, 63; consultant University Nacional de Colombia, 1960; consultant dairy engineering, India, 1961, consultant food engineering, China, 1961; Mission to Ecuador, 1966; University Nigeria, 1967; consultant UNDP/SF Project 80 (higher education Latin Am.), 1964-70, Council Grad. Schools, Washington, 1970, Brazil project, world food and nutrition study National Acad. Sci., 1976-77, member engineering education del. to, People's Republic of China, 1978; co-chairman National Acad. Sci.-India National Sci. Acad. Workshop, New Delhi, 1979; with ACA, Incorporated (consultant engineering), 1956-70, president, 1962-70; chairman National Dairy Engineering Conference, 1953-66; member United States sci. exchange del. to Union of the Soviet Socialist Republics, 1958, 87; member postgrad. education select committee United States Navy, Monterey, California, 1975. Author: Drying Farm Crops, 1957, Agricultural Engineering Index 1907-1960, 1961-70, 71-80, (with others) Drying of Milk and Milk Products, 1966, 71, Agricultural Mechanization for Developing Countries, 1973; co-editor: Agricultural Engineers Handbook, 1960, Processing Equipment for Agricultural Products, 1963, 2d edition, 1979, Spanish edition, 1968, Milk Pasteurization, 1968, Encyclopedia of Food Engineering, 1971, 86, Drying Cereal Grains, 1974, 2d. edition, 1989, Dairy Technology and Engineering, 1976, Errors in Experimentation, 1977, Dictionary of Drying, 1979, Drying and Storage of Agricultural Products, 1980, Biomass as an Alternative Fuel, 1981, Dictionary of Energy, 1983, Food and Energy, 1984, Food and Natural Resources, 1988, Biomass Handbook, 1989; editor: Drying Technology:Marcel Dekker, Inc; Contributor yearbooks, encys., handbooks. Secretary Tefft Foundation for Bible Study, 1960-70. Served with Army of the United States, 1943-46, European Theatre of Operations. Decorated Bronze Star; recipient outstanding teacher award Alpha Zeta, 1957, 58; Distinguished Faculty award Michigan State University, 1963; Centennial Achievement award Ohio State University, 1970; Massey-Ferguson Education medal, 1976; Max Eyth medal Germany, 1979; medal du Merite France, 1979; La Medaille d'Argent Paris, 1980, Cyrus Hall McCormick medal, 1984, National Science Foundation Distinguished

Service award and medal, 1988. Fellow American Association for the Advancement of Science (life), American Society of Mechanical Engineers (life, chairman central Michigan 1959-60), Accreditation Board Engineering and Tech.; member Am. Society Agricultural Engineers (chairman electric power and processing division 1960, division director 1962-64, 67-69, president 1974-75, Engineer of Year award Michigan chapter 1964, Pacific Northeast region 1973), Am. Society Engineering Education, Am. Institute Biological Sciences, NSPE (National Science Foundaton engr. of year 1986), Washington Society Professional Engineers (national director 1975-79), Virginia Society Professional Engineers (president Northern Virginia chapter 1987-88), National Acad. Engineering, International Commission Agricultural Engineers (vice president 1965-74), Engineers Council for Professional Devel. (executive committee, director, secretary 1973-74, chairman engineering accreditation commission 1979-80), 99th Inf. Div. Association, Institute Food Tech., Sigma Xi, Alpha Zeta, Tau Beta Pi, Phi Kappa Phi, Gamma Sigma Delta, Phi Lambda Tau. Office: NSF Dir Engring Washington District of Columbia 20550 also: 2454 N Rockingham St Arlington Virginia 22207-1033

HALL, CHARLES ALLAN, numerical analyst; born Pittsburgh, March 19, 1941; son of George Orbin and Minnie (Carter) H.; married Mary Katherine Harris, August 11, 1962; children—Charles, Eric, Katherine. Bachelor of Science, University Pittsburgh, 1962, Master of Science, 1963, Doctor of Philosophy, 1964. Senior mathematician Bettis Atomic Power Laboratory, West Mifflin, Pennsylvania, 1966-70; associate professor math. statistics University Pittsburgh, 1970-78, professor; 1978—; executive director Institute Computational Maths. and Applications, 1978—; consultant General Motors Research, 1971—, Westinghouse Electric Corp., Pittsburgh, 1974-81, Pittsburgh Corning Company, 1980-86, Contraves, 1986—. Contributor articles to professional journals. Served to 1st lieutenant United States Army, 1964-66. Member Math. Association Am., Society Industrial and Applied Math. Home: Box 83 Murrysville Pennsylvania 15668 Office: ICMA U Pittsburgh Pittsburgh Pennsylvania 15260

HALL, DONALD NORMAN BLAKE, astronomer; born Sydney, New South Wales, Australia, June 26, 1944; came to United States, 1967; son of Norman F.B. and Joan B. Hall. Bachelor of Science with honors, University Sydney, 1966; Doctor of Philosophy in Astronomy, Harvard University, 1970. Research associate Kitt Peak National Observatory, Tucson, 1970-72, associate astronomer; 1972-76, astronomer; 1976-81; deputy director Space Telescope Sci. Institute, Baltimore, 1982-84; director Institute Astronomy University Hawaii, Honolulu, 1984—; member space sci. board National Acad. Sci., 1984-88, member astronomy adv. committee National Science Foundation, 1984-87; member astrophysics council National Aeronautics and Space Administration, 1984-88. Member Am. Astronomical Society (Newton Lacey Pierce prize 1978), International Astronomical Union. Office: U Hawaii Institute Astronomy 2680 Woodlawn Dr Honolulu Hawaii 96822

HALL, MARION TRUFANT, botany educator, arboretum director; born Gorman, Texas, September 6, 1920; son of Frank Marion and Nora Gertrude (Wharton) H.; married Virginia Riddle, November 9, 1944; children: Susan, Alan Lee, John Lane. Bachelor of Science, University Oklahoma, 1943, Master of Science, 1947; Doctor of Philosophy (Henrietta Heerman scholar 1951), Washington University, St. Louis, 1951; Doctor of Science (honorary), North Central College, Illinois, 1977. Ranger National Park Service, Department Interior, 1942; instructor botany University Oklahoma, 1946-47; curator Bebb Herbarium, 1949; field botanist, instructor Texas Nature Camp, National Audubon Society, Kerrville, Texas, 1948; grad. assistant zoology, teaching fellow Washington University, 1948-50; special lecturer genetics and evolution Henry Shaw School Botany, 1952; botanist Cranbrook Institute Sci., Bloomfield Hills, Michigan, 1950-56; acting director Cranbrook Institute Sci., 1955-56; professor, head department botany Butler University, 1956-62; visiting professor botany University Oklahoma, 1962; director Stovall Mus. Sci. and History, 1962-66, Morton Arboretum, Lisle, Illinois, 1966—; professor botany, acting director University Michigan Botanical Gardens, 1963-64; professor horticulture University Illinois, Urbana; adj. professor biology Northern Illinois University; Cons. Michigan Department Conservation, Handbook Biological Materials for Museums. Contributor numerous research articles to professional journals. Board of directors Joyce Foundation, Chicago; governing member Forest Foundation DuPage County. Served to lieutenant (junior grade) United States Naval Reserve, 1943-45. National Science Foundation grantee; recipient Alumni award for achievement University Oklahoma, 1953. Fellow Ind. Acad. Sci., Cranbrook Institute Sci.; member Am. Society Plant Taxonomists, International Association Plant Taxonomists, Ecological Society Am., Asa Gray Memorial Association, Society Study Evolution, Michigan Natural Areas Council, Oklahoma Acad. Sci., Botanical Society Am., Michigan Botanical Club (past president Detroit), Phi Beta Kappa, Sigma Xi, Phi Sigma. Home: Morton Arboretum Lisle Illinois 60532 Office: Morton Arboretum Route 53 Lisle Illinois 60532

HALLETT, MARK, physician, neurologist, health research institute administrator; born Philadelphia, October 22, 1943; son of Joseph Woodrow and Estelle (Barg) H.; married Judith E. Peller, June 26, 1966; children—Nicholas L., Victoria C. Bachelor of Arts magna cum laude, Harvard University, 1965, Doctor of Medicine cum laude, 1969. Diplomate Am. Board Neurology and Psychiatry. Resident in neurology Massachusetts General Hospital, Boston, 1972-75; Moseley fellow Harvard University, London, 1975-76; lecturer, associate professor neurology Harvard University, Boston, 1976-84; head clinical neurophysiology laboratory Brigham and Women's Hospital, Boston, 1976-84; clinical director National Institute Neurological and Communicative Disorders and Stroke, National Institutes of Health, Bethesda, Maryland, 1984—. Author: (with others) Entrapment Neuropathies, 1983; contributor numerous articles to professional journals. Board of directors Easter Seal Research

Foundation, Chicago, 1985-87. Member Am. Association Electromyography and Electrodiagnosis, Am. Acad. Neurology, Am. Neurological Association, Am. EEG Society, Society for Neurosci., Phi Beta Kappa, Alpha Omega Alpha. Democrat. Jewish. Home: 5147 Westbard Avenue Bethesda Maryland 20816 Office: National Institute Neurol & Communicative Disorders & Stroke NIH Building 10 Room 5N226 Bethesda Maryland 20892

HALLGREN, RICHARD EDWIN, meteorologist; born Kersey, Pennsylvania, March 15, 1932; son of Edwin Leonard and Edith Marie H.; married Maxine Hope Anderson, April 17, 1954; children—Scott, Douglas, Lynette. Bachelor of Science, Pennsylvania State University, 1953, Doctor of Philosophy, 1960; Doctor of Science (honorary), State University of New York, 1989. Systems engineer International Business Machines Corporation Corp., 1960-64; sci. adv. to assistant secretary of commerce 1964-66; director world weather systems Environmental Science Services Administration, Rockville, Maryland, 1966-69; assistant administration Environmental Science Services Administration, 1969-70; assistant administrator National Oceanographic and Atmospheric Administration, Rockville, 1970-71; associate administrator environmental monitoring and prediction National Oceanographic and Atmospheric Administration, 1971-73, assistant administrator for ocean and atmospheric sciences; 1977-79; deputy director National Weather Service, Silver Spring, Maryland, 1973-77; director National Weather Service, 1979-88; executive director Am. Meteorol. Society, 1988—;

permanent United States representative World Meteorol. Organization. Contributor articles to sci. journals. Served with United States Air Force, 1954-56. Recipient Arthur S. Flemming award U.S. Chamber of Commerce, 1968; Gold medal Department Commerce, 1969; named Meritorious Senior Executive, 1980, Distinguished Senior Executive, 1986; alumni fellow Pennsylvania State University, 1987. Fellow Am. Meteorological Society (president, C.F. Brooks award); member Oceanographic Society, Am. Geogphys. Union, Sigma Xi. Lutheran. Home: 6121 Wayside Dr Rockville Maryland 20852 Office: National Weather Service 8060 13th St Silver Spring Maryland 20910

HALPERN, BRUCE PETER, psychology and biology educator; born Newark, August 18, 1933; son of Leo and Thelma (Rubin) H.; married Pauline Touber Anklowitz, June 9, 1956; children—Michael Touber, Stacey Rachael. Bachelor of Arts, Rutgers University, 1955; Master of Science, Brown University, 1957, Doctor of Philosophy, 1959. Assistant professor physiology Upstate Medical Center, Syracuse, New York, 1961-66; associate professor psychology, neurobiology and behavior Cornell University, Ithaca, New York, 1966-73; professor Cornell University, 1973—, chairman department psychology; 1974-80; member Advisory Panel Sensory Physiology and Perception National Science Foundation, 1976-79; member adv. committee National Institute Neurological and Communicative Disorders and Stroke, National Institutes of Health, 1978-79, 85-87, International Commission on Olfaction and Taste, Union of Physiological Sciences, 1986-89; Fogarty senior international fellow, visiting professor in oral physiology Osaka University, 1982-83; chairman Gordon Conference on Chemical Senses: Taste and Smell, 1987—. Executive editor Chemical Senses, 1984-88; contributor articles to professional journals. National Institute of Mental Health grantee, 1958-62; National Institutes of Health grantee, 1963-72; National Science Foundation grantee, 1972—. Member Am. Physiological Society, Association Chemoreception Sciences (executive chair 1982-83). Home: 113 Winston Dr Ithaca New York 14850-1935

HALPIN, DANIEL WILLIAM, civil engineering educator, consultant; born Covington, Kentucky, September 29, 1938; son of Jordan W. and Gladys E. (Moore) H.; married Maria Kirchner, February 8, 1963; 1 son, Rainer. Bachelor of Science, United States Military Academy, 1961; Master of Science in Civil Engineering, University Illinois, 1969, Doctor of Philosophy, 1973. Research analyst Construction Engineering Research Laboratory, Champaign, Illinois, 1970-72; faculty University Illinois, Urbana, 1972-73; member faculty Georgia Institute Tech., Atlanta, 1973-85, professor; 1981-85; A.J. Clark professor, director Construction Engineering and Management University Maryland, 1985-87; director div. Construction Engineering and Management Purdue University, 1987—; consultant construction management; visiting associate professor University Sydney, Australia, 1981; visiting professor Swiss Federal Institute Tech., 1985; visiting scholar Tech. University, Munich, 1979; visiting lecturer Center Cybernetics in Construction, Bucharest, Romania, 1973. Author:

Design of Construction and Process Operations, 1976, Construction Management, 1980, Planung und Kontrolle von Bauproduktion-sprozessen, 1979, Constructo - A Heuristic Game for Construction Management, 1973, Financial and Cost Control Concepts for Construction Management, 1985. Served with Corps of Engineers, United States Army, 1961-67. Decorated Bronze Star; recipient Walter L.Huber prize American Society of Civil Engineers, 1979; grantee National Science Foundation, Department Energy. Member American Society of Civil Engineers (past section president 1981-82, chairman constrn. research council 1985-86), Am. Society Engineering Education, Sigma Xi. Methodist.

HAM, JAMES MILTON, engineering educator; born Coboconk, Ontario, Canada, September 21, 1920; son of James Arthur and Harriet Boomer (Gandier) H.; married Mary Caroline Augustine, June 4, 1955; chidren: Peter Stace, Mary Martha, Jane Elizabeth. Bachelor of Arts Sc., University Toronto, 1943; Master of Science, Massachusetts Institute of Technology, 1947, Doctor of Science, 1952; Doctor ès Sc.A., University Montreal, 1973; Doctor of Science, Queen's University, 1974, University New Brunswick, 1979, McGill University, 1979, McMaster University, 1980; Doctor of Laws, University Manitoba, 1980, Hanyang University, Seoul, Korea, 1981, Concordia College, 1983; Doctor of Engineering, Nova Scotia Tech. University, 1980, Memorial University, 1981; Doctor.S.L., Wycliffe College, University Toronto, 1983. Lecturer, housemaster Ajax div. University Toronto, 1945-46; research associate

Massachusetts Institute of Technology, 1949-51, assistant professor electrical engineering; 1951-52; member faculty University Toronto, 1952-88, head electrical engineering; 1964-66, dean faculty applied sci. and engineering; 1966-73, chairman research board; 1974-76, dean grad. studies; 1976-78, president; 1978-83, professor sci., tech. and pub. policy; 1983-88; adv. to president Can. Institute for Advanced Research, Toronto, 1988—; vice president Can. Acad. Engineering, Toronto, 1988—; fellow New College, 1962; visiting scientist University Cambridge (England) and Union of the Soviet Socialist Republics, 1960-61; director Shell Can. Limited; fellow Brookings Institution, 1983-84; chairman Industrial Disease Standards Panel, 1985-87. Author: (with G.R. Slemon) Scientific Basis of Electrical Engrineering, 1961, Royal Commission on Health and Safety of Workers in Mines, 1976. Board governors Ontario Reserves Federation Served with Royal Canadian Navy, 1944-45. Decorated officer Order of Can.; recipient Sci. medal Brit. Association Advancement Sci., 1943; Centennial medal Can., 1967; Engineering Alumni medal, 1973; Engineering medal Assoc. Professional Engrs. Ontario, 1974, Gold medal, 1984; Queen's Jubilee medal, 1977; Order of Ontario, 1989; rsch. fellow electronics Massachusetts Institute of Technology, 1950. Fellow Engineering Institute Can. (Sir John Kennedy medal 1983), Institute of Electrical and Electronics Engineers (McNaughton medal 1977), Can. Acad. Engineering; member Sigma Xi. Home: 135 Glencairn Avenue, Toronto, Ontario Canada M4R 1N1

HAMMOND, DONALD L., computer company executive; born Kansas City, Missouri, August 7, 1927; son of Clark E. and Laila G. (Morris) H.; married Phyllis E. Whitmore, August 21, 1949; children—Deborah Ruth, Katherine Ilene, Carol Linda, Nancy Linda, Paul David. Bachelor of Science in Physics, Colorado State University, 1950, Master of Science, 1952, Doctor of Science (honorary), 1974; Doctor of Science (honorary), Bristol University, 1987. Chief crystal research United States Army Electronics, Fort Monmouth, New Jersey, 1952-56; director research Sci. Electronic Products, Loveland, Colorado, 1956-59; manager precision time and frequency Hewlett-Packard Laboratories, Palo Alto, California, 1959-64, manager physical research and devel.; 1964-66, director physical electrical laboratory; 1966-79, director physics research center; 1979-84, director Europe research center; 1984-86, associate, acting director; 1986—; lecturer CB Sawyer Frequency Control Symposium, 1970. Member board education Palo Unified School District, 1971-81, also president Served as ensign United States Navy, 1945-52. Fellow Institute of Electrical and Electronics Engineers; member National Acad. Engineering, Am. Institute Physics. Home: 12660 Corte Madera Lane Los Altos Hills California 94022 Office: Hewlett-Packard Labs 1501 Page Mill Road Palo Alto California 94304

HANNAY, N(ORMAN) BRUCE, chemist, industrial research and business consultant; born Mount Vernon, Washington, February 9, 1921; son of Norman Bond and Winnie (Evans) H.; married Joan Anderson, May 27, 1943; children: Robin, Brooke. Bachelor of Arts,

Swarthmore College, 1942, Doctor of Science (honorary), 1979; Master of Science, Princeton University, 1943, Doctor of Philosophy, 1944; Doctor of Philosophy (honorary), Tel Aviv University, 1978; Doctor of Science (honorary), Polytechnic Institute New York, 1981. With Bell Telephone Laboratories, Murray Hill, New Jersey, 1944-82; executive director materials research div. Bell Telephone Laboratories, 1967-73, vice president research and patents; 1973-82, retired, 1982; researcher on dipole moments and molecular structure, thermionic emission, mass spectroscopy, analysis of solids, solid state chemistry, semiconductors, superconductors; member sci. adv. committee SRI International, tech. adv. council Chrysler Corp.; research adv. committee United Techs., Regents' professor University of California at Los Angeles, 1976, University California, San Diego, 1979; consultant Alexander von Humboldt Foundation; board of directors Plenum Pub. Company, General Signal Corp., Rohm and Haas Company, Alex Brown Cash Reserve Fund, Tax-Free Investments Trust, and Flag Investors Telephone Income Trust, International Trust, Corp. Cash Trust and Emerging Growth Fund. Author: Solid State Chemistry, 1967, also articles.; Member numerous editorial bds.; editor: Semiconductors, 1959, Treatise on Solid State Chemistry, 1974. Recipient Acheson medal, 1976; Perkin medal, 1983; Gold medal Am. Institute Chemists, 1986. member National Acad. Engineering (past foreign secretary), National Acad. Sciences, Am. Acad. Arts and Sciences, Mexican National Acad. Engineering, Electrochemical Society (past president), Industrial Research Institute (past president, medal 1982), Directors of Industrial Research (past chairman).

HANSON, JOHN M., research and consulting engineering company executive; born Brookings, South Dakota, November 16, 1932; married Mary Josephson, January 16, 1980. Bachelor of Science in Civil Engineering, South Dakota State University, 1949; Master of Science in Structural Engineering, Iowa State University, 1957; Doctor of Philosophy in Civil Engineering, Lehigh University, 1964. Structural engineer J.T. Banner & Associate, Laramie, Wyoming, 1957-58, Phillips, Carter, Osborn, Denver, 1958-60; research professor Lehigh University, Bethlehem, Pennsylvania, 1960-65; engineer, assistant manager structural devel. Portland Cement Association, Skokie, Illinois, 1965-72; research director, vice president, president Wiss, Janney, Elstner, Northbrook, Illinois, 1972—. Contributor articles to professional journals. Served to lieutenant United States Air Force, 1953-55, Korea. Recipient Distinguished Engineering award South Dakota State University, 1979; Professional Achievement citation Iowa State University, 1980. Fellow American Society of Civil Engineers, Am. Concrete Institute (board directors 1981-84, Bloem award 1976); member Prestressed Concrete Institute (board directors, Korn award 1978), Transportation Research Board, International Association Bridge and Structural Engineers. Lutheran. Office: Wiss Janney Elstner Associate Incorporated 330 Pfingsten Road Northbrook Illinois 60062

HARLAN, JACK RODNEY, geneticist, emeritus educator; born Washington, June 7, 1917; son of Harry Vaughn and Augusta (Griffing)

H.; married Jean Yocum, August 4, 1939; children: Sue (Mrs. Robert Hughes), Harry, Sherry (Mrs. Mark Wilson), Richard Edwin. Bachelor of Science in Botany with distinction, George Washington University, 1938; Doctor of Philosophy in Genetics, University California at Berkeley, 1942. Research assistant Tela Railroad Company, Honduras, 1942; geneticist Department Agriculture, Woodward, Oklahoma, 1942-51, Stillwater, Oklahoma, 1951-61; professor agronomy Oklahoma State University, 1951-66; professor genetics University Illinois at Urbana, 1966-84, professor emeritus; 1984—; botanist Department of Agriculture (plant exploration and introduction), Turkey, Syria and Iraq, 1948, Department of Agriculture, Iran, Afghanistan, Pakistan, India and Ethiopia, 1960; senior staff member Iranian prehistoric project Oriental Institute University Chicago, 1960, senior staff member Turkish prehistoric project, 1964; member Dead Sea Archaeol. Project, 1977, 79, 83; plant exploration, Africa, Asia, Latin Am.; Cons. Food and Agriculture Organization (of the United Nations), 1970-71. Member international board: Plant Genetic Resources, 1974-79; contributor professional journals. Fellow American Association for the Advancement of Science, Am. Society Agronomy, Am. Acad. Arts and Sci.; member National Acad. Sciences, Crop Sci. Society Am. (president 1966), Am. Institute Biological Scientists, Botanical Society Am., Am. Society Agronomy, Society for Econ. Botany, Phi Beta Kappa, Sigma Xi, Phi Kappa Phi. Presbyterian (elder). Office: U Illinois Department Agronomy AE-120 Turner Hall Urbana Illinois 61801

HARPER, DOYAL ALEXANDER, JR., astronomer, educator; born Atlanta, October 9, 1944; son of Doyal Alexander and Emliy (Brown) H.; married Carolyn James, March 11, 1967; children: Scott Alexander, Nathan Todd, Amy Claire, Evan James. Bachelor of Arts in Electrical Engineering, Rice University, 1966, Doctor of Philosophy in Space Science, 1971. Assistant professor astronomy and astrophysics University Chicago, 1971-76, associate professor; 1976-80, professor; 1980—; director Yerkes Observatory 1982—. Member Am. Astronomical Society (Newton Lacy Pierce prize 1979), Astronomical Society Pacific. Current work: infared observations of galaxies, stars, planets, star formation regions, far infared detectors, cryogenics, optical systems. Subspecialty: infared astronomy. Office: U Chicago Yerkes Obs Post Office Box 258 Williams Bay Wisconsin 53191

HARRIS, CYRIL MANTON, physicist, engineering and architecture educator, consulting acoustical engineer; born Detroit; son of Bernard O. and Ida (Moss) H.; married Ann Schakne, July 12, 1949; children: Nicholas Bennett, Katherine Anne. Bachelor of Arts, University of California at Los Angeles, 1938, Master of Arts, 1940; Doctor of Philosophy, Massachusetts Institute of Technology, 1945; Doctor of Science (honorary), New Jersey Institute Tech., 1981, Northwestern University, 1989. Teaching assistant University of California at Los Angeles, 1939-40; research fellow Massachusetts Institute of Technology, 1940; war research Office of Scientific Research and Development, 1941-44, teaching fellow; 1943-45; war research Carnegie Institution Washington, 1941; member staff Bell Telephone Laboratories, 1945-51; consultant Office Naval Research, London, England, 1951; Fulbright lecturer Tech. University, Delft, Holland, 1951-52; Charles Batchelor professor electrical engineering, professor architecture and past chairman div. architectural tech. Columbia University; now professor emeritus; visiting Fulbright professor University Tokyo, 1960; acoustical consultant Metropolitan Opera House, New York City, John F. Kennedy Center for Performing Arts, Washington, Krannert Center for Performing Arts, University Illinois, Powell Symphony Hall, St. Louis, National Acad. Sciences Auditorium, Washington, Minnesota Orchestra Hall, Minneapolis, National Centre for Performing Arts, Bombay, India, new Avery Fisher Hall, New York State Theater reconstructions, Lincoln Center, New York City, Symphony Hall, Salt Lake City; past director United States Institute Theatre Tech.; member noise control group, committee undersea warfare National Research Council, 1955-57; member council hearing and bio-acoustics Armed Forces-NRC, 1953-55; member National Research Council adv. panel 213 to National Bureau Standards, 1966-69, chairman, 1969-71; member building research adv. board National Research Council, 1977-79. Author: (with V.O. Knudsen) Acoustical Designing in Architecture, 1950, rev., 1980, Handbook of Noise Control, 1957, 2d edition, 1979; Shock and Vibration Handbook, 3d edition, 1987, Dictionary of Architecture and Construction, 1975; author: Historic Architecture Sourcebook, 1977, Illustrated Dictionary of Historic Architecture, 1983; Contributor articles to professional journals; Editorial adv. board: Physics Today, 1955-66. Board of directors Armstrong Memorial Research Foundation, 1976—; hon. vice president St. Louis Symphony Society, 1977—; member national adv. board Utah Symphony Orchestra, 1976-85; vice president New York Acad. of Scis., 1988. Recipient Franklin medal, 1977; Emile Berliner award, 1977; Hon. award U.S. International Telephone and Telegraph Corporation, 1977; Wallace Clement Sabine medal, 1979; American Institute of Architects medal, 1980; Gold Medal Audio Engineering Society, 1984; award of honor for sci. and tech. City of New York, 1985; Alumni award UCLA, 1989. Fellow Acoustical Society Am. (president 1964-65, associate editor journal 1959-70, Gold medal 1987), Institute of Electrical and Electronics Engineers (chairman professional group ultrasonic engineering 1957-58, professional group audio 1961-62), Audio Engineering Society (hon. member); member Am. Institute Physics (governing board 1965-66), National Acad. Sciences, National Acad. Engineering, Am. Philosophical Society, Sigma Xi, Tau Beta Pi. Office: Mudd Building Columbia U New York New York 10027

HARRISON, ANNA JANE, chemist, educator; born Benton City, Missouri, December 23, 1912; daughter of Albert S.J. and Mary (Jones) H. Student, Lindenwood College, 1929-31, Doctor of Humane Letters (honorary), 1977; Bachelor of Arts, University Missouri, 1933, Bachelor of Science, 1935, Master of Arts, 1937, Doctor of Philosophy, 1940, Doctor of Science (honorary), 1983; Doctor of Science (honorary), Tulane University,

1975, Smith College, 1975, Williams College, 1978, Am. International College, 1978, Vincennes University, 1978, Lehigh University, 1979, Hood College, 1979, Hartford University, 1979, Worcester Polytechnic Institute, 1979, Suffolk University, 1979, Eastern Michigan University, 1983, Russell Sage College, 1984, Mount Holyoke College, 1984, Mills College, 1985; Doctor of Humane Letters (honorary), Emmanuel College, 1983; Doctor of Hebrew Literature, St. Joseph College, 1985, Elms College, 1985. Instructor chemistry Newcomb College, 1940-42, assistant professor; 1942-45; assistant professor chemistry Mount Holyoke College, 1945-47, associate professor; 1947-50, professor; 1950-76, professor emeritus; 1976—, chairman department; 1960-66, William R. Kenan, Junior professor; 1976-79; Member National Sci. Board, 1972-78; Distinguished Visiting professor United States Naval Acad., 1980. Author: (textbook with Edwin S. Weaver) Chemistry: A Search to Understand, 1989; contributor articles to professional journals. Recipient Frank Forrest award Am. Ceramic Society, 1949; James Flack Norris award in chemical education Northeastern sect. Am. Chemical Society, 1977; American Association of University Women Sarah Berliner fellow Cambridge University, England, 1952-53; Am. Chemical Society Petroleum Research Fund International fellow National Research Council Can., 1959-60; recipient College Chemistry Teacher award Mfg. Chemists Association, 1969. Member American Association for the Advancement of Science (director 1979-85, president 1983, chairman board 1984-85), Am. Chemical Society (chairman division chemical education 1971, president 1978, director 1976-79, award in chemical education 1982), International Union Pure and Applied Chemistry (United States national committee 1978-81), Sigma Xi (board directors 1988—). Address: Mt Holyoke College Department Chemistry South Hadley Massachusetts 01075

HART, TERRY JONATHAN, communications executive; born Pittsburgh, October 27, 1946; son of Jonathan Smith Hart and Lillian Dorothy (Zugates) Hart Pierson; married Wendy Marie Eberhardt, December 20, 1975; children: Amy, Lori. Bachelor of Mechanical Engineering, Lehigh University, 1968, Doctor of Engineering (honorary), 1988; Master of Science, Massachusetts Institute of Technology, 1969; Master of Electrical Engineering, Rutgers University, 1978. Member tech. staff American Telephone and Telegraph Company Bell Laboratories, Whippany, New Jersey, 1968-69, 73-78, supervisor; 1984—; astronaut National Aeronautics and Space Administration Johnson Space Center, Houston, 1978-84; captured solar maximum satellite National Aeronautics and Space Administration Johnson Space Center, 1984; head government data systems American Telephone and Telegraph Company Nordics AB, Stockholm, Sweden, 1989—. Patentee in field. Served to lieutenant colonel United States Air Force Air National Guard, 1969—. Recipient New Jersey Distinguished Service medal, National Aeronautics and Space Administration Space Flight medal, Pride of Pennsylvania medal. Member Institute of Electrical and Electronics Engineers, Sigma Xi, Tau Beta Pi. Avocations: skiing; golf.

Office: AT&T Nordics Alberta, Klarabergsviadukten 70, Box 703 63, 10723 Stockholm Sweden

HARTL, DANIEL LEE, genetics educator; born Marshfield, Wisconsin, January 1, 1943; son of James W. and Catherine E. (Stieber) H.; married Carolyn Teske, September 5, 1964 (divorced April 1978); children: Dana Margaret, Theodore James; married Christine Blazynski, July 23, 1980; 1 child, Christopher Lee. Bachelor of Science, University Wisconsin, 1965, Doctor of Philosophy, 1968. Postdoctoral fellow in genetics University California, Berkeley, 1968-69; assistant professor genetics and cell biology University Minnesota, St. Paul, 1969-73, associate professor; 1973-74; associate professor biological sciences Purdue University, West Lafayette, Ind., 1974-78, professor; 1978-81; professor genetics Washington University School Medicine, St. Louis, 1981-84, James South McDonnell professor genetics, head genetics department; 1984—, director div. biology and biomed. sciences; 1986—; member genetics study section National Institutes of Health, Washington, 1976-80, genetic basis of disease rev. committee National Institutes of Health, 1983-87. Author: Principles of Population Genetics, 1980, Human Genetics, 1983, General Genetics, 1985, Primer of Population Genetics, 1988, Basic Genetics, 1988; associate editor Annual Revs. Incorporated, 1984—, Molecular Biology and Evolution, 1983—, Genetics, 1977-85, BioSci., 1974-80, Theoretical Population Biology, 1975-81. Recipient Career Devel. award National Institutes of Health, 1974-79. Member Genetics Society Am. (pres.-elect 1988, board directors 1984-87),

Phi Beta Kappa. Office: Washington U School Medicine Department of Genetics Box 8031 Saint Louis Missouri 63110-1095

HARTMANIS, JURIS, computer scientist, educator; born Riga, Latvia, July 5, 1928; came to United States, 1950, naturalized, 1956; son of Martins and Irma (Liepins) H.; married Ellymaria Rehwald, May 16, 1959; children—Reneta, Martin, Audrey. Student, University Marburg, 1947-49; Master of Arts, University Kansas City, 1951; Doctor of Philosophy, California Institute Tech., 1955. Instructor Cornell University, Ithaca, New York, 1955-57; professor Cornell University, 1965—, Walter R. Read professor engineering; 1980—, chairman department computer sci.; 1965-71, 77-82; assistant professor Ohio State University, 1957-58; research mathematician General Electric Research & Devel. Center, Schenectady, 1957-65. Author: (with R.E. Stearns) Algebraic Structure Theory For Sequential Machines, 1966; Feasible Computations and Provable Complexity Properties, 1978; editor: SIAM Journal Computing; associate editor: Journal Computer and Systems Scis, 1966—, Journal Math. Systems Theory, 1966—; co-editor: Springer-Verlag Lecture Notes in Computer Sci, 1973—. Fellow American Association for the Advancement of Science; member National Academy of Engineering, Am. Math. Society, Math. Association Am., Association Computing Machinery, New York Acad. Sciences, Sigma Xi. Home: 324 Brookfield Road Ithaca New York 14850 Office: Computer Sci Department Upson Hall Cornell University Ithaca New York 14853

HARTSFIELD, HENRY WARREN, JR., astronaut; born Birmingham, Alabama, November 21, 1933; son of Henry Warren and Alice Norma (Sorrell) H.; married Judy Frances Massey, June 30, 1957; children: Judy Lynn, Keely Warren. Bachelor of Science, Auburn University, 1954; postgraduate, Duke University, 1954-55, Air Force Institute Tech., 1960-61; Master of Science, University Tennessee, 1970; Doctor of Science (honorary), Auburn University, 1986. Commissioned 2d lieutenant United States Air Force, 1955, advanced through grades to colonel; 1974; assigned to tour with 53d Tactical Fighter Squadron United States Air Force, Bitburg, Federal Republic Germany, 1961-64; instructor United States Air Force Test Pilot School, Edwards Air Force Base, California, 1965-66; assigned to Manned Orbiting Laboratory United States Air Force, 1966-69; astronaut, National Aeronautics and Space Administration Lyndon B. Johnson Space Center, 1969—, member support crew Apollo 16, Skylabs 2, 3, 4 missions, pilot STS-4; commander STS-41D, STS-61A, retired; 1977; civilian astronaut National Aeronautics and Space Administration; deputy director Flight Crew Operations Directorate, 1987—. In space: 483 hours. Decorated Meritorious Service medal, Distinguished Service Medal National Aeronautics and Space Administration, 1982, 88, Space Flight medal National Aeronautics and Space Administration, 1982, 84, 85; recipient National Geog. White Space Trophy, 1973. Member Society Experimental Test Pilots, Air Force Association, Sigma Pi Sigma. Office: NASA Flight Crew Ops Code California Lyndon B Johnson Space Center Houston Texas 77058

HARZA, RICHARD DAVIDSON, civil engineer; born Chicago, October 7, 1923; son of Leroy F. and Zelma D. H.; married Dorothy Goettsch, April 23, 1956; children: Laura A., John D. Bachelor of Science in Mechanical Engineering, Northwestern University, 1944, Master of Science in Civil Engineering, 1947; Doctor of Science, University Wisconsin, 1987. Registered professional engineer, Illinois. Instructor civil engineering department Northwestern University, 1946-47; with Harza Engineering Company, Chicago, 1947—; vice president, director, director United States Water and Land Resources Management Group, 1962-76, vice president, director, director administrative, financial and corporate operations; 1976-77, president, board of directors; 1977—, chairman; 1987—; director Harza Engineering Company International. Contributor tech. articles to professional journals. Served to ensign United States Naval Reserve, 1943-46. Member Am. Institute Cons. Engineers, American Society of Civil Engineers, Am. Water Resources Association (past president), Cons. Engineers Association Illinois, Cons. Engineers Council, National, Illinois socs. professional engrs., United States Commission on Large Dams (past chairman). Clubs: Metropolitan; Union League, Chicago; Tower. Lodge: Moles. Office: Harza Engineering Company 150 S Wacker Dr Chicago Illinois 60606

HAUCK, FREDERICK HAMILTON, naval officer, astronaut; born Long Beach, California, April 11, 1941; son of Philip and Virginia (Hustvedt) H.; married Dolly Bowman, August 27, 1962; children: Whitney Irene, Stephen Christopher. Bachelor of

Science, Tufts University, 1962; Master of Science, Massachusetts Institute of Technology, 1966. Commissioned ensign United States Navy, 1962, advanced through grades to captain; 1983; pilot Attack Squadron 35, United States Ship Coral Sea, 1968-70; instructor pilot Attack Squadron 42, Oceana, Virginia, 1970-71; test pilot Naval Air Test Center, Patuxent River, Maryland, 1971-74; operations officer Carrier Air Wing 14, Miramar, California, United States Ship Enterprise, 1974-76; executive officer Attack Squadron 145, Washington, 1976-78; astronaut National Aeronautics and Space Administration, Houston, 1978-89; space shuttle pilot shuttle transportation system mission 7, 1983; space shuttle commander STS-51A, 1984; associate administrator for external relations National Aeronautics and Space Administration, 1986; space shuttle commander STS-26, 1988; director Navy Space Systems (OP-943), Washington, 1989. Decorated Navy Commendation medal (2), Distinguished Flying Cross, Air medal (9), National Aeronautics and Space Administration Space Flight medal (2), D.Distinguished Service Medal, silver medal for Meritorious Service Lloyd's of London; recipient Yuri Gagarin gold medal Federation Aeronautique International, 1985, Flight Achievement award Am. Aeronautical Society, 1985, President medal Tufts University, Distinguished Alumni medal Delta Upsilon; recipient National Aeronautics and Space Administration Outstanding Leadership Medal., Distinguished Sci. medal National Aeronautics and Space Administration, Haley Space Flight award AAA. Associate fellow American Institute of Aeronautics and Astronautics, Society Experimental Test Pilots. Office: Navy Space Systems OP-943 Washington District of Columbia

HAUPTMAN, HERBERT AARON, mathematician, educator, researcher; born New York City, February 14, 1917; son of Israel and Leah (Rosenfeld) H.; married Edith Citrynell; children—Barbara, Carol Fullerton. Bachelor of Science in Math., City College of New York, New York City, 1937; Master of Arts, Columbia University, New York City, 1939; Doctor of Philosophy, University Maryland, College Park, 1955. Statistician United States Census Bureau, 1940-42; civilian instructor electronics and radar United States Army Air Force, 1942-43, 46-47; physicist, mathematician Naval Research Laboratory, 1947-70, head math. physics branch; 1965-67, acting superintendent math. and information sciences div.; 1967-68, head applied math. branch; 1968-69, head math. staff; 1969-70; research professor biophys. sciences State University of New York, Buffalo, 1970—; professor math. University Maryland, 1956-70; head math. biophysics laboratory Medical Foundation of Buffalo Incorporated, 1970-72, deputy research director, 1972, executive vice president, research director, 1972-85, president, research director, 1986-88, president, 1988—; consultant and lecturer in field. Contributor chapters to books, articles to professional journals. Board of directors Medical Foundation, Buffalo. Served with United States Naval Reserve, 1943-46. Recipient numerous prizes for excellence in math. including co-recipient Nobel Prize in Chemistry, 1985. Fellow Washington Acad. Sciences; member

National Acad. Sciences, Endocrine Society, Am. Math. Society, Am. Physical Society, Am. Crystallographic Association, Math. Association Am., American Association for the Advancement of Science, Sigma Xi. Clubs: Cosmos (Washington); Saturn (Buffalo). Avocations: stained glass art; swimming; hiking. Office: Med Found 73 High St Buffalo New York 14203

HAWKING, STEPHEN W., astrophysicist, mathematician; born Oxford, England, January 8, 1942; son of F. and E.I. Hawking; married Jane Wilde, 1965; two sons, one daughter. Bachelor of Arts, Oxford University, Doctor of Science (honorary), 1978; Doctor of Philosophy, Cambridge University; Doctor of Science (honorary), University Chicago, 1981, Notre Dame University, 1982, New York University, 1982, Leicester University, 1982. Research assistant Institute Astronomy, Cambridge, England, 1972-73; research assistant department applied maths. and theoretical physics Institute Astronomy, Cambridge, 1973-75, reader in gravitational physics; 1975-77, professor; 1977-79, Lucasian professor math.; 1979—. Author: (with G.F.R. Ellis) The Large Scale Structure of Space-Time, 1973; A Brief History of Time: From the Big Bang to Black Holes, 1988; co-editor: 300 Years of Gravitation, 1987. Decorated commander Brit. Empire, 1981; recipient Eddington medal Royal Acad. Sci., 1975, Pius XI Gold medal Pontifical Acad. Sci., 1975, Danne Heinemann prize for math. and physics Am. Physical Soc.-Am. Institute Physics, 1976, William Hopkins prize Cambridge Philos. Society, 1976, Maxwell medal Institute Physics, 1976, Einstein award Strauss Foundation, 1978, Albert Einstein medal Albert Einstein Society of Berne, 1979, Wolf Prize in physics, 1988. Foreign member Am. Philosophical Society, American Association for the Advancement of Science; fellow Royal Society (Hughes medal 1976). Address: 5 West Road, Cambridge England 351905

HAXO, FRANCIS THEODORE, marine biologist; born Grand Forks, North Dakota, March 9, 1921; son of Henry Emile and Florence (Shull) H.; married Judith Morgan McLaughlin, April 15, 1961; children: John Frederick, Barbara, Philip, Francis Theodore, Aileen. Bachelor of Arts, University North Dakota, 1941; Doctor of Philosophy, Stanford University, 1947. Teaching, research assistant Stanford University, 1941-44, acting instructor; 1943; research assistant California Institute Tech., 1946; research associate Hopkins Marine Station, Pacific Grove, California, 1946-47; from instructor to assistant professor plant physiology Johns Hopkins University, 1947-52; member faculty University California Scripps Institute Oceanography, La Jolla, 1952—; professor biology University California Scripps Institute Oceanography, 1963—, chairman marine biology department; 1960-65, chairman marine biology research div.; 1971-77; instructor marine botany Marine Biological Laboratory, Woods Hole, Massachusetts, 1949-52, 70; visiting faculty botany University California at Berkeley, 1957, University Washington Marine Laboratory, Friday Harbor, 1963. Abraham Rosenberg fellow Stanford, 1945. Fellow American Association for the Advancement of Science, San

Diego Zool. Society; member Am. Society Photobiology, Phycological Society Am., Western Society Naturalists, International Phycological Society, Phi Beta Kappa, Sigma Xi. Spl. research photosynthesis, plant pigments, physiology of algae.

HECKER, SIEGFRIED STEPHEN, metallurgist; born Tomasow, Poland, October 2, 1943; came to United States, 1956; son of Robert and Maria (Schaller) Mayerhofer; married Janina Kabacinski, June 19, 1965; children—Lisa, Linda, Lori, Leslie. Bachelor of Science, Case Institute Tech., 1965, Master of Science, 1967; Doctor of Philosophy, Case Western Reserve University, 1968. Postdoctoral associate Los Alamos Sci. Laboratory, 1968-70, member staff; 1973-80, associate div. leader; 1980-81, deputy div. leader; 1981-83, div. leader; 1983-85, chairman Center for Materials Sci.; 1985-86, director; 1986—; senior research metallurgist General Motors Research Laboratories, Warren, Michigan, 1970-73. Author, editor: Formability, 1977. Board regents University New Mexico; board of directors Carrie Tingley Hospital; board of directors Council on Superconductivity for Am. Competitiveness. Recipient E. O. Lawrence award Department Energy, 1984; named One of 100 Top Innovators, Sci. Digest, 1985. Fellow Am. Society Metals (member national commission superconductivity 1989—); member Metallurgical Society (board directors 1983-84), National Acad. Engineering. Republican. Roman Catholic. Clubs: Los Alamos Ski (president 1980-81). Avocation: skiing. Home: 117 Rim Road Los Alamos New Mexico 87544 Office: Los Alamos National Lab Mail Stop A100 Los Alamos New Mexico 87545

HEEGER, ALAN JAY, physicist; born Sioux City, Iowa, January 22, 1936; son of Peter J. and Alice (Minkin) H.; married Ruthann Chudacoff, August 11, 1957; children: Peter S., David J. Bachelor of Arts, University Nebraska, 1957; Doctor of Philosophy, University California, Berkeley, 1961. Assistant professor University Pennsylvania, Philadelphia, 1962-64; associate professor University Pennsylvania, 1964-66, professor physics; 1966-82; professor physics University California at Santa Barbara, 1982—, director Institute for Polymers and Organic Solids; 1983—; director Laboratory for Research on Structure of Matter, 1974-81, acting vice provost for research, 1981-82; Morris Loeb lecturer Harvard University, 1973; consultant various sci. laboratories. Contributor sci. articles to professional journals. Recipient Oliver E. Buckley prize in solid state physics, 1983; Alfred P. Sloan fellow; Guggenheim fellow; Government grantee; International Exchange scholar Union of Soviet Socialist Republics, 1976; International Exchange scholar Japan, 1978. Member Am. Physical Society. Patentee in field. Office: U California Department Physics Santa Barbara California 93103

HEESCHEN, DAVID SUTPHIN, astronomer, educator; born Davenport, Iowa, March 12, 1926; son of Richard George and Emily (Sutphin) H.; married Eloise St. Clair, June 11, 1950; children: Lisa Clair, David William, Richard Mark. Bachelor of Science, University Illinois, 1949, Master of Science, 1951; Doctor of Philosophy, Harvard University, 1954; Doctor of Science (honorary), West

Virginia Institute Tech., 1974. Instructor Wesleyan University, Middletown, Connecticut, 1954-55; lecturer, research associate Harvard University, 1955-56; scientist National Radio Astronomy Observatory, 1956-77, senior scientist; 1977—, director; 1962-78; research professor astronomy University Virginia, 1980—; Cons. National Aeronautics and Space Administration, 1960-61, 68-72. Contributor sci. journals. G.R. Agassiz fellow Harvard Obs., 1953-54; Recipient Distinguished Public Service award National Science Foundation, 1980, Alexander von Humboldt Senior Scientist award 1985. Fellow American Association for the Advancement of Science; member Am. Astronomical Society (vice president 1969-71, president 1980-82), International Astronomical Union (vice president 1976-82), Internat Sci. Radio Union, National Acad. Sci., Am. Acad. Arts and Sci., Am. Philosophical Society.

HEIDER, KARL GUSTAV, anthropology educator; born Northampton, Massachusetts, January 21, 1935; son of Fritz and Grace (Moore) H.; married Eleanor Rosch, January 1967 (divorced 1973); married 2d Mary Elizabeth Bruton, November 27, 1976; children: Mary Winn, John Bruton, Paul Moore. Student, Williams College, 1952-54; Bachelor of Arts, Harvard University, 1956; postgraduate, University Vienna, Austria, 1957-58; Master of Arts, Harvard University, 1959, Doctor of Philosophy, 1966. Instructor Harvard University, Cambridge, Massachusetts, 1965-66; assistant professor, then associate professor Brown University, Providence, 1966-71; visiting associate professor University Calif.-

Berkeley, 1971-73; lecturer Stanford University, California, 1972-74, University of California at Los Angeles, 1973-74; professor anthropology, chairman department University South Carolina, Columbia, 1975—. Co-author: Gardens of War, 1969; author: Ethnographic Film, 1976, Grand Valley Dani, 1979; producer: film Dani Sweet Potatoes, 1974. Sheldon Traveling fellow in Asia Harvard University, 1956-57; Center for Advanced Study fellow Stanford University, 1974-75. Fellow Am. Anthropological Association (chairman ethics committee 1978-79), Royal Anthropological Institute; member Am. Ethnological Society, Association Social Anthropology in Oceania, Polynesian Society (life), Society Visual Anthropology (president 1987—). Presbyterian. Club: Kosmos (Columbia). Home: 211 Southwood Dr Columbia South Carolina 29205 Office: Department Anthropology U South Carolina Columbia South Carolina 29208

HEILMEIER, GEORGE HARRY, research electrical engineer; born Philadelphia, May 22, 1936; son of George C. and Anna I. (Heineman) H.; married Janet S. Faunce, June 24, 1961; 1 daughter, Elizabeth. Bachelor of Science in Electrical Engineering, University Pennsylvania, 1958; Master of Science in Engineering, Princeton University, 1960, Master of Arts, 1961, Doctor of Philosophy, 1962. With Radio Corporation of America Laboratories, Princeton, New Jersey, 1958-70; director solid state device research Radio Corporation of America Laboratories, 1965-68, director device concepts; 1968-70; White House fellow, special assistant to secretary defense Washington,

1970-71; assistant director defense research and engineering Office Secretary Defense, 1971-75; director Defense Advanced Projects Agency, 1975-77; vice president research, devel. and engineering Texas Instruments Incorporated, 1978-83, senior vice president, chief tech. officer; 1983—; member Def. Sci. Board; member adv. group on electron devices Department Def.; member adv. board Stanford Center for Integrated Systems. Pantentee in field. Recipient Institute of Electrical and Electronic Engineers David Sarnoff award, 1976; IR-100 New Product award Indsl. Rsch. Association, 1968, 69; Sec. Defense Distinguished Civilian Service award, 1975, 77; Arthur Flemming award U.S. Jaycees, 1974. Fellow Institute of Electrical and Electronics Engineers (Outstanding Achievement award Dallas chapter 1984, Philips award 1985, Founder's award 1986); member University Pennsylvania, Princeton University Grad. alumni associations, National Acad. Engineering, Sigma Xi, Tau Beta Pi, Eta Kappa Nu (Outstanding Young Engineer in United States award 1969). Methodist. Office: Tex Instruments Incorporated 13500 N Central Expressway Box 655474 Mississippi 400 Dallas Texas 75265

HEIMLICH, HENRY JAY, physician, surgeon; born Wilmington, Delaware, February 3, 1920; son of Philip and Mary (Epstein) H.; married Jane Murray, June 3, 1951; children: Philip, Peter, Janet and Elizabeth (twins). Bachelor of Arts, Cornell University, 1941, Doctor of Medicine, 1943; Doctor of Science (honorary), Wilmington College, 1981, Adelphi University, 1982, Rider College, 1983. Diplomate: Am. Board Surgery, Am. Board Thoracic Surgery. Intern Boston City Hospital, 1944; resident Veteran's Administration Hospital, Bronx, 1946-47, Mount Sinai Hospital, New York City, 1947-48, Bellevue Hospital, New York City, 1948-49, Triboro Hospital, Jamaica, New York, 1949-50; attending surgeon div. surgery Montefiore Hospital, New York City, 1950-69; director surgery Jewish Hospital, Cincinnati, 1969-77; professor advanced clinical sciences Xavier University, Cincinnati, 1977—; associate clinical professor surgery University Cincinnati College Medicine, 1969—; member President Commission on Heart Disease, Cancer and Stroke, 1965; President National Cancer Foundation, 1963-68, board of directors, 1960-70; founder, president Dysphagia Foundation. Author: Postoperative Care in Thoracic Surgery, 1962, (with M.O. Cantor, C.H. Lupton) Surgery of the Stomach, Duodenum and Diaphragm, Questions and Answers, 1965; also; contributor chapters to books; numerous articles to medical journals; Producer: films Esophageal Replacement with a Reversed Gastric Tube (awarded Medaglione Di Bronzo Minerva 1961), Reversed Gastric Tube Esophagoplasty Using Stapling Technique, How to Save a Choking Victim: The Heimlich Maneuver, 1976, 2d edition, 1982, How To Save a Drowning Victim: The Heimlich Maneuver, 1981, Stress Relief: The Heimlich Method, 1983; member editorial board: films Reporte's Medicos. Board of directors Community Devel. Foundation, 1967-70; board of directors Save the Children Federation, 1967-68, United Cancer Council, 1967-70. Served to lieutenant (senior grade) United States Naval Reserve, 1944-46. Recipient Lasker Award for Pub.

Service, Lasker Foundation, 1984, China-Burma-India Vets. Association Americanism award, 1988. Fellow American College of Surgeons (chapter president 1964), Am. College Chest Physicians, Am. College Gastroenterology; member Society Thoracic Surgeons (founding member), American Medical Association (cons. to journal), Cincinnati Society Thoracic Surgery, New York Society Thoracic Surgery, Society Surgery Alimentary Tract, Am. Gastroentorological Association, Pan Am. Medical Association, Collegium International Chirurgiae Digestive, Central Surgical Association. Developer Heimlich Operation reversed gastric tube esophagoplasty) for replacement of esophagus; inventor Heimlich chest drain valve; developer Heimlich Maneuver to save lives of victims of food choking (listed in Random House, Oxford Am. and Webster dictionaries); developer Computers for Peace, a program to maintain peace throughout world. Office: Xavier U Cincinnati Ohio 45207

HEISER, ARNOLD MELVIN, astronomer; born Brooklyn, February 9, 1933; son of Hyman Samuel and Sadie (Kretchmer) H.; married Vivian Carol Jacobs, June 6, 1964; children—Naomi Elizabeth, David Alan. Bachelor of Arts, Ind. University, 1954, Master of Arts, 1956; Doctor of Philosophy, University Chicago, 1961. Research assistant Ind. University, 1954-56; research fellow University Chicago, 1956-61; assistant professor physics and astronomy Vanderbilt University, Nashville, 1961-66; associate professor Vanderbilt University, 1966—; director A.J. Dyer Observatory, 1972-86; H. Shapley visiting professor Am. Astronomical Society, 1969—. Contributor articles to astron. journals. Member Am. Astronomical Society, International Astronomical Union, Royal Astronomical Society, Tennessee Acad. Sci., Sigma Xi. Home: 6132 Gardendale Dr Nashville Tennessee 37215 Office: A J Dyer Observatory Vanderbilt University Nashville Tennessee 37235

HENDRIE, JOSEPH MALLAM, physicist, nuclear engineer, government official; born Janesville, Wisconsin, March 18, 1925; son of Joseph Munier and Margaret Prudence (Hocking) H.; married Elaine Kostell, July 9, 1949; children: Susan Debra, Barbara Ellen. Bachelor of Science, Case Institute Tech., 1950; Doctor of Philosophy, Columbia University, 1957. Registered professional engineer, New York, California. Assistant physicist Brookhaven National Laboratory, Upton, New York, 1955-57; associate physicist Brookhaven National Laboratory, 1957-60, physicist; 1960-71, senior physicist; 1971—, chairman steering committee, project chief engineer high flux beam reactor design and construction; 1958-65, acting head experimental reactor physics div.; 1965-66, project manager pulsed fast reactor project; 1967-70, associate head engineering div., department applied sci.; 1967-71, head; 1971-72, chairman department applied sci.; 1975-77, special assistant to director; 1981—; director Tenera Corp., 1984-85, Houston Industries, Incorporated, Houston Lighting and Power Company, System Energy Resources, Incorporated; deputy director licensing for tech. rev. United States Atomic Energy Commission, 1972-74; chairman United States Nuclear Regulatory

Commission, Washington, 1977-79, 81, commissioner, 1980, member adv. committee on enforcement policy, 1984-85; lecturer nuclear power plant safety Massachusetts Institute of Technology, Georgia Institute Tech., Northwestern University, summers 1970-77; consultant radiation safety committee Columbia University, 1964-72; member adv. committee reactor safeguards Atomic Energy Commission, 1966-72, chairman, 1970; United States member senior adv. group on reactor safety standards International Atomic Energy Agency, 1974-78; member national research council committee International Cooperation in Magnetic Fusion, 1983-85; consultant Atomic Energy Commission, Nuclear Regulatory Commission, 1974-75, General Accounting Office, 1975-77, Electric Power Research Institute, 1982, various nuclear utilities, 1981—. Member editorial adv. board Nuclear Tech, 1967-77. Served with Army of the United States, 1943-45. Recipient E.O. Lawrence award, 1970; decorated commander Order of Leopold II (Belgium), 1982. Fellow Am. Nuclear Society (director 1976-77, vice president 1983-84, president 1984-85), American Society of Mechanical Engineers; member National Acad. Engineering, Am. Physical Society, American Society for Testing and Materials (committee on research and tech. planning 1985—), Am. Concrete Institute, Institute Nuclear Power Operation (adv. council 1984—), Institute of Electrical and Electronics Engineers, National Society Professional Engineers, Sigma Xi, Tau Beta Pi. Research, publs. on physics nuclear reactors, nuclear power plant safety, engring. design reactors, elec. power transmission, chem. physics nitrogen dissociation process, structure oxygen molecule. Office: Brookhaven National Lab Upton New York 11973

HENIZE, KARL GORDON, astronomer, astronaut; born Cincinnati, October 17, 1926; son of Fred R. and Mabel (Redmon) H.; married Caroline Rose Weber, June 27, 1953; children: Kurt Gordon, Marcia Lynn, Skye Karen, Vance Karl. Student, Denison University, 1944-45; Bachelor of Arts, University Virginia, 1947, Master of Arts, 1948; Doctor of Philosophy, University Michigan, 1954. Observer University Michigan Lamont-Hussey Observatory, Bloemfontein, Union South Africa, 1948-51; Carnegie postdoctoral fellow Mount Wilson Observatory, Pasadena, California, 1954-56; senior astronomer in charge photographic satellite tracking stations Smithsonian Astrophysical Observatory, Cambridge, Massachusetts, 1956-59; associate professor department astronomy Northwestern University, Evanston, Illinois, 1959-64, professor; 1964-72; scientist-astronaut National Aeronautics and Space Administration Johnson Space Center, Houston, 1967-86, senior scientist; 1986—; guest observer Mount Stromlo Observatory, Canberra, Australia, 1961-62; principal investigator astronomy experiments for Gemini 10, 11, 12 and Skylab 1, 2, 3 1964-78; member astronomy subcom. National Aeronautics and Space Administration Space Sci. Steering Committee, 1965-68; adj. professor department astronomy University Texas, Austin, 1972—; team leader National Aeronautics and Space Administration Facility Definition Team for Starlab Telescope, 1974-78; chairman National Aeronautics and Space Administration working group for

Spacelab Wide-Angle Telescope, 1978-79; jet pilot training Vance Air Force Base, Enid, Oklahoma, 1968-69; member support crew Apollo 15 and Skylab 1, 2, 3 1970-73, mission specialist ASSESS 2 Spacelab simulation; 1976-77, mission specialist Shuttle flight 51F (Spacelab 2); 1985. Served with United States Naval Reserve, 1944-46; lieutenant commander Reserves, retired. Recipient Robert Gordon Memorial award, 1968; National Aeronautics and Space Administration medal for exceptional sci. achievement, 1974, Space Flight medal, 1985, Flight Achievement award Am. Astronautical Society, 1985. Member Am., Royal, Pacific astronomical socs., International Astronomical Union, Phi Beta Kappa. Research on planetary nebulae, emission-line stars, ultraviolet stellar spectra, space debris. Home: 18630 Point Lookout Dr Houston Texas 77058 Office: NASA Space Physics Br Johnson Space Center Houston Texas 77058

HENLE, ROBERT ATHANASIUS, engineer; born Virginia, Minnesota, April 27, 1924; son of Robert Alois and Ethel (O'Donnel) H.; married Eleanor Bonnel, September 9, 1950 (deceased 1972); children—Robert, David, Barbara, John. Bachelor of Science in Electrical Engineering, University Minnesota, 1949, Master of Science in Electrical Engineering, 1951. Fellow components div. International Business Machines Corporation, Fishkill, New York, 1964-70; with corp. tech. committee International Business Machines Corporation, Armonk, New York, 1970-73; fellow International Business Machines Corporation, Fishkill, New York, 1973-75, manager advanced tech. components div.; 1975-80;

director silicon tech. laboratory International Business Machines Corporation, Yorktown Heights, New York, 1980—; member adv. board National Security Agency, 1968-73. Patentee in field. Contributor articles to professional journals. Served to lieutenant (junior grade) United States Navy, 1944-46. Fellow International Business Machines Corporation, 1964, Institute of Electrical and Electronic Engineers, 1966. Fellow Institute of Electrical and Electronics Engineers (Edison medal 1987); member National Academy of Engineering, New York Acad. Sci., American Association for the Advancement of Science, Sigma Xi. Republican. Roman Catholic. Avocations: sailing; skiing; tennis. Home: RR2-255 Sunset Trail Clinton Corners New York 12514-9629 Office: International Business Machines Corporation Research Div 89 NO8 Post Office Box 218 Yorktown Heights New York 10598

HERBERT, GEORGE RICHARD, research executive; born Grand Rapids, Michigan, October 3, 1922; son of George Richard and Violet (Wilton) H.; married Lois Anne Watkins, August 11, 1945; children: Gordon, Patricia, Alison, Douglas, Margaret. Student, Michigan State University, 1940-42; Bachelor of Science, United States Naval Academy, 1945; Doctor of Science (honorary), North Carolina State University, 1967; Doctor of Laws (honorary), Duke University, 1978, University N.C.-Chapel Hill, 1984. Line officer United States Navy, 1945-47; instructor electrical engineering Michigan State University, 1947-48; assistant to director Stanford Research Institute, 1948-51, manager business operations; 1951-55, executive associate director; 1955-56, assistant secretary; 1950-56; treasurer Am. & Foreign Power Company, Incorporated, New York City, 1956-58; president Research Triangle Institute, 1958—; board of directors Microelectronics Center North Carolina; board of directors North Carolina Biotech. Center, Central Carolina Bank & Trust Company, Duke Power Company, Triangle Universities Center for Advanced Studies, Incorporated; member North Carolina Board Sci. and Tech., 1963-79; member tech. adv. board United States Department Commerce, 1964-69, North Carolina Atomic Energy Adv. Committee, 1964-71; member Korea-United States joint committee for sci. cooperation National Acad. Sciences, 1973-78; member board sci. and tech. for international devel. National Acad. Sci., 1978-81. Board of directors Oak Ridge Associate Universities, 1971-73, 78-85; trustee Duke University, 1985—. Member Sigma Alpha Epsilon. Club: Hope Valley Country. Office: Research Triangle Institute 3040 Cornwallis Road Box 12194 Research Triangle Park North Carolina 27709

HERSCHBACH, DUDLEY ROBERT, chemistry educator; born San Jose, California, June 18, 1932; son of Robert Dudley and Dorothy Edith (Beer) H.; married Georgene Lee Botyos, December 26, 1964; children: Lisa Marie, Brenda Michele. Bachelor of Science in Math., Stanford University, 1954, Master of Science in Chemistry, 1955; Master of Arts in Physics, Harvard University, 1956, Doctor of Philosophy in Chemical Physics, 1958; Doctor of Science (honorary), University Toronto, 1977. Junior fellow Harvard University, Cambridge, Massachusetts, 1957-59, professor chemistry; 1963-76, Frank B. Baird professor sci.; 1976—, member faculty council; 1980-83, master Currier House; 1981-86; assistant professor University California, Berkeley, 1959-61, associate professor; 1961-63; consultant editor W.H. Freeman lecturer Haverford College, 1962; Falk-Plaut lecturer Columbia, 1963; visiting professor Göttingen (Germany) University, summer 1963, University California at Santa Cruz, 1972; Harvard lecturer Yale University, 1964; Debye lecturer Cornell University, 1966; Rollefson lecturer University California at Berkeley, 1969; Reilly lecturer University Notre Dame, 1969; Phillips lecturer University Pittsburgh, 1971; Distinguished visiting professor University Arizona, 1971, University Texas, 1977, University Utah, 1978, Gordon Lecturer University Toronto, 1971, Clark lecturer San Jose State University, 1979, Hill lecturer Duke University, 1988, Flory lecturer Stanford University, 1988, Flugare lecturer University Illinois, 1988. Associate editor: Jour Physical Chemistry. Guggenheim fellow University Freiburg, Germany, 1968; visiting fellow Joint Institute for Laboratory Astrophysics University Colorado, 1969; Fairchild Distinguished scholar California Institute Tech., 1976; Sloan fellow, 1959-63, Exxon Faculty fellow, 1980—; recipient pure chemistry award Am. Chemical Society, 1965, Centenary medal, 1977, Pauling medal, 1978; Spiers medal Faraday Society, 1976, Polanyi medal, 1981, Langmuir prize, 1983, Nobel Prize in Chemistry, 1986; named to California Pub. Education Hall of Fame, 1987. Fellow Am. Physical Society (chairman chemical physics division 1971-72), Am. Acad. Arts and Sciences; member Am. Chem Society, American Association for the Advancement of Science, National Acad. Sciences, Royal Society Chemistry (foreign hon. member), Phi Beta Kappa, Sigma Xi. Office: Harvard U Department Chemistry 12 Oxford St Cambridge Massachusetts 02138

HERSHEY, ALFRED DAY, geneticist; born Owosso, Michigan, December 4, 1908; son of Robert Day and Alma (Wilbur) H.; married Harriet Davidson, November 15, 1945; 1 son, Peter. Bachelor of Science, Michigan State University, 1930, Doctor of Philosophy in Chemistry, 1934, Doctor of Medical Science, 1970; Doctor of Science (honorary), University Chicago, 1967. Assistant bacteriologist Washington University School Medicine, St. Louis, 1934-36; instructor Washington University School Medicine, 1936-38, assistant professor; 1938-42, associate professor; 1942-50; member staff, genetics research unit Carnegie Institute of Washington, Cold Spring Harbor, New York, 1950-62; director Carnegie Institute of Washington, 1962-74; retired 1974. Contributor articles to professional journals. Recipient Nobel prize in Medicine (joint), 1969; Albert Lasker award Am. Pub. Health Association, 1958; Kimber Genetics award National Acad. Sciences, 1965. Member National Acad. Sciences. Address: Rural Delivery 1640 Moores Hill Road Syosset New York 11791

HERTZBERG, ABRAHAM, university research scientist, educator; born New York City, July 8, 1922; son of Rubin and Paulien (Kalif) H.; married Ruth Cohen, September 3, 1950; children: Eleanor Ruth, Paul Elliot, Jean R. Bachelor of Science in Aeronautical Engineering, Virginia Polytechnic Institute, 1943; Master of Science in Aeronautical Engineering, Cornell University, 1949; postgraduate, University Buffalo, 1949-53. Engineer Cornell Aeronautical Laboratory, 1949-57, assistant head aerodynamics research; 1957-59, head aerodynamics research; 1959-65; professor astronautics, director aerospace & energetics research program University Washington, 1966—; consultant Aerospace Corp., Spectra Tech., Incorporated; past member sci. adv. board United States Air Force; past member electro-optics panel SAB, member various ad hoc committees; member space systems & tech. adv. committee, research and tech. subcom., past member research and tech. adv. council National Aeronautics and Space Administration; member plasma dynamics rev. panel National Science Foundation, United States Army.; honored speaker Laser Institute Am., 1975; member theory adv. committee Los Alamos National Laboratory; visiting lecturer Chinese Acad. Sciences, Beijing, 1983. Editor: Physics of Fluids, 1968-70; Contributor numerous articles on modern high energy engring., high powered lasers, controlled thermonuclear fusions processes, space laser solar energy concepts, space energy concepts and new ultra velocity propulsion concepts to professional journals. Served with Army of the United States, 1944-46. Honored speaker Laser Institute Am.; prin. investigator on numerous federal research grants. Fellow American Institute of Aeronautics and Astronautics (Dryden lecturer 1977, Agard lecturer 1978); member Am. Physical Society, National Acad. Engineers, Sigma Xi. Patentee in field.

Office: U Washington Aerospace & Engring Research Building F1-10 Seattle Washington 98195

HERZBERG, GERHARD, physicist; born Hamburg, Germany, December 25, 1904; emigrated to Canada, 1935, naturalized, 1945; son of Albin and Ella (Biber) H.; married Luise H. Oettinger, December 29, 1929 (deceased); children: Paul Albin, Agnes Margaret; married Monika Tenthoff, March 21, 1972. Doctor Ing., Darmstadt Institute Tech., 1928; postgraduate, University Goettingen, University Bristol, 1928-30; Doctor of Science hon causa, Oxford University, 1960; Doctor of Science, University Chicago, 1967, Drexel University, 1972, University Montreal, 1972, University Sherbrooke, 1972, McGill University, 1972, Cambridge University, 1972, University Manitoba, 1973, Andhra University, 1975, Osmania University, 1976, University Delhi, 1976, University Bristol, 1975, University Western Ontario, 1976; Fil. Hed. Doctor, University Stockholm, 1966; Doctor of Philosophy (honorary), Weizmann Institute Science, 1976, University Toledo, 1984; Doctor of Laws, St. Francis Xavier University, 1972, Simon Fraser University, 1972; Doctor phil. national, University Frankfurt, 1983, others. Lecturer, chief assistant physics Darmstadt Institute Tech., 1930-35; research professor physics University Saskatchewan, Saskatoon, 1935-45; professor spectroscopy Yerkes Observatory, University Chicago, 1945-48; principal research officer National Research Council Can., Ottawa, 1948; director div. pure physics National Research Council Can., 1949-69, distinguished research scientist; 1969—; Bakerian lecturer Royal Society London, 1960; holder

Francqui chair University Liege, 1960. Author books including: Spectra of Diatomic Molecules, 1950; Electronic Spectra and Electronic Structure of Polyatomic Molecules, 1966, The Spectra and Structures of Simple Free Radicals, 1971, (with K.P. Huber) Constants of Diatomic Molecules, 1979. Recipient Faraday medal Chemical Society London, 1970, Nobel prize in Chemistry, 1971; named companion Order of Can., 1968, academician Pontifical Acad. Sciences, 1964. Fellow Royal Society London (Royal medal 1971), Royal Society Can. (president 1966, Henry Marshall Tory medal 1953), Hungarian Acad. Sci. (hon.), Indian Acad. Sciences (hon.), Am. Physical Society (Earle K. Plyler prize 1985), Chemical Institute Can.; member International Union Pure and Applied Physics (past vice president), Am. Acad. Arts and Sciences (hon. foreign member), Am. Chemical Society (Willard Gibbs medal 1969, Centennial foreign fellow 1976), National Acad. Sci. India, Indian Physical Society (hon.), Japan Acad. (hon.), Chemical Society Japan (hon.), Royal Swedish Acad. Sciences (foreign, physics section), National Acad. Sci. (foreign associate), Faraday Society, Am. Astronomical Society, Can. Association Physicists (past president, Achievement award 1957), Optical Society Am. (hon., Frederic Ives medal 1964). Home: 190 Lakeway Dr, Rockcliffe Park, Ottawa, Ontario Canada K1L 5B3 Office: National Research Coun, Ottawa, Ontario Canada K1A 0R6

HESS, WILMOT NORTON, science administrator; born Oberlin, Ohio, October 16, 1926; son of Walter Norton and Rachel Victoria (Metcalf) H.; married Winifred Esther Lowdermilk, June 16, 1950;

children—Walter Craig, Alison Lee, Carl Ernest. Bachelor of Science in Electrical Engineering, Columbia, 1946; Master of Arts in Physics, Oberlin Coll, 1949, Doctor of Science, 1970; Doctor of Philosophy, University California, Berkeley, 1954. Staff Lawrence Radiation Laboratory, University California, Berkeley and Livermore, 1954-59; head plowshare div. Lawrence Radiation Laboratory, University California, Livermore, 1959-61; director theoretical div. Goddard Spaceflight Center (National Aeronautics and Space Administration), Greenbelt, Maryland, 1961-67; director sci. and applications Manned Spacecraft Center, Houston, 1967-69; director National Oceanographic and Atmospheric Administration Research Laboratories (Commerce Department), Boulder, Colorado, 1969-80, National Center for Atmospheric Research, Boulder, 1980-86; director high energy and nuclear physics United States Department Energy Office of Energy Research, Germantown, Maryland, 1986—; adj. professor University Colorado, 1970-78. Contributor articles to professional journals; editor: Introduction to Space Science, 1965; author: Radiation Belt and Magnetosphere, 1968, (with others) Weather and Climate Modification, 1974; associate editor: (with others) Journal Geophysical Research, 1961-67, Journal Atmospheric Sci, 1961-67, Journal Am. Institute Aeros. and Astronautics, 1967-69. Served with United States Navy, 1944-46. Fellow Am. Geophysical Union, Am. Physical Society; member National Acad. Engineering. Club: Cosmos (Washington). Home: 14508 Pebble Hill Lane Gaithersburg Maryland 20878 Office: United States Department Energy Office of Energy Research Germantown Maryland 20874

HEWISH, ANTONY, radioastronomer; born May 11, 1924; son of Ernest William and Frances Grace Lanyon (Pinch) H.; married Marjorie Elizabeth Catherine Richards, 1950; 1 son, 1 daughter. Bachelor of Arts, Cambridge University, 1948, Master of Arts, 1950, Doctor of Philosophy, 1952; Doctor of Science (honorary), University Leicester, 1976, University Exeter, 1977. Research fellow Gonville and Caius College, 1952-54, assistant director research; 1954-62, fellow; 1955-62, hon. fellow; 1976—; lecturer physics University Cambridge, 1962-69, professor radioastronomy; 1971—, reader; 1969-71, fellow Churchill College; 1962—; visiting professor astronomy Yale University, 1963; professor astronomy Royal Institution Great Britain, 1977—; director Mullard Radio Astronomy Observatory, Cambridge, 1982—. Recipient Eddington medal Royal Astronomical Society, 1969; Charles Vernon Boys prize Institute Physics and Physical Society, 1970; Dellinger Gold medal International Union Radio Sci., 1972; Michelson medal Franklin Institute, 1973; Hopkins prize Cambridge Philos. Society, 1973; Holweck medal and prize Society Française de Physique, 1974; Nobel prize for Physics (with other), 1974; Hughes medal Royal Society London, 1977. Fellow Royal Society London, Indian Acad. Sciences (foreign); member Am. Acad. Arts and Sciences. Home: Pryor's Cottage, Kingston, Cambridge England Office: U Cambridge, Cavendish Lab, Cambridge CB3 OHE, England

HEWLETT, WILLIAM (REDINGTON), manufacturing company executive, electrical engineer; born Ann Arbor,

Michigan, May 20, 1913; son of Albion Walter and Louise (Redington) H.; married Flora Lamson, August 10, 1939 (deceased 1977); children: Eleanor Hewlett Gimon, Walter B., James S., William A., Mary Hewlett Jaffe; married Rosemary Bradford, May 24, 1978. Bachelor of Arts, Stanford University, 1934, Electrical Engineer, 1939; Master of Science, Massachusetts Institute of Technology, 1936; Doctor of Laws, University California, Berkeley, 1966, Yale University, 1976, Mills College, 1983; Doctor of Science (honorary), Kenyon College, 1978, Poly Institute New York, 1978; Doctor of Humane Letters, Johns Hopkins University, 1985; Doctor Engineering, University Notre Dame, 1980, Utah State University, 1980, Dartmouth College, 1983; Doctor of Philosophy, Rand Graduate Institute. Electromedical. researcher 1936-39; co-founder Hewlett-Packard Company, Palo Alto, California, 1939, partner; 1939-46, executive vice president, director; 1947-64, president; 1964-77, chief executive officer; 1969-78, chairman executive committee; 1977-83, vice chairman board of directors; 1983-87, emeritus director; 1987—; member international adv. council Wells Fargo Bank, 1986—; trustee Rand Corp., 1962-72, Carnegie Institute, Washington, 1971—, chairman board trustees, 1980-86; director Overseas Devel. Council, 1969-77; board of directors Institute Radio Engineers (now Institute of Electrical and Electronics Engineers), 1950-57, president 1954. Contributor articles to professional journals; patentee in field. Trustee Stanford University, 1963-74, Mills College, Oakland, California, 1958-68; member President's General Adv. Committee on Foreign Assistance Programs,

Washington, 1965-68, President's Sci. Adv. Committee, 1966-69; member San Francisco regional panel Commission on White House Fellows, 1969-70, chairman, 1970; president board of directors Palo Alto Stanford Hospital Center, 1956-58, board of directors, 1958-62; director Drug Abuse Council, Washington, 1972-74, Kaiser Foundation Hospital & Health Plan Board, 1972-78; chairman The William and Flora Hewlett Foundation, 1966—; board of directors San Francisco Bay Area Council, 1969-81, Institute Medicine, Washington, 1971-72, The National Acads. Corp., 1986—, Monterey Bay Aquarium Research Institute, 1987—, University Corp. for Atmospheric Research Foundation, 1986—. Lieutenant colonel Army of the United States, 1942-45. Recipient California Manufacturer of Year California Manufacturers Association, 1969, Business Statesman of Year Harvard Business School Northern California, 1970, Medal of Achievement Western Electronic Mfrs. Association, 1971, Industrialist of Year (with David Packard) California Mus. Sci. and Industry and California Mus. Foundation, 1973, Award with David Packard presented by Scientific Apparatus Makers Association, 1975, Corp. Leadership award Massachusetts Institute of Technology, 1976, Medal of Honor City of Boeblingen, Germany, 1977, Herbert Hoover medal for distinguished service Stanford University Alumni Association, 1977, Henry Heald award Illinois Institute Tech., 1984, National Medal of Sci. U.S. National Sci. Committee, 1985. Fellow Institute of Electrical and Electronics Engineers (president 1954, Founders medal with David Packard 1973), Franklin Institute (life, Vermilye medal with

David Packard 1976), Am. Acad. Arts and Sciences; member National Acad. Sciences (panel on advanced tech. competition 1982-83), National Acad. Engineering, Instrument Society Am. (hon. life), Am. Philosophical Society, California Acad. Sci. (trustee 1963-68), Association Quadrato della Radio, Century Association New York City. Clubs: Bohemian, Pacific-Union (San Francisco); Menlo Country (Woodside, California). Office: Hewlett-Packard Company 1501 Page Mill Road Palo Alto California 94304

HEYERDAHL, THOR, anthropologist, explorer, author; born Larvik, Norway, October 6, 1914; son of Thor and Alison (Lyng) H.; married Liv Coucheron Torp, December 24, 1936; children—Thor, Bjorn; married Yvonne Dedekam-Simonsen, March 7, 1949; children—Anette, Marian, Bettina. Realartium, Larvik College, 1933; postgraduate, field study, University Oslo, Polynesia, British Columbia, 1937; Doctor of Philosophy (honorary), Oslo University, 1961. Ethnological collection and research primitive man, his habits Polynesia and British Columbia, 1937-40; produced documentary film Kon-Tiki, 1951; leader, organizer Norwegian archeological expedition, Galapagos, 1953; research Andes region, 1954; produced film Galapagos, 1955; leader, organizer Norwegian archaeol. expedition, Easter Island and the East Pacific, 1955-56, Ra expeditions, 1969-70, Tigris Expeditions, 1977-78; leader, organizer archaeol. expeditions, Republic of Maladives, 1982-84, Easter Island, 1986-87; Member, lecturer International Congress Americanists, Cambridge, 1952, São Paulo, 1954, San Jose, 1958, Vienna, 1960, Barcelona, Madrid, Sevilla, 1964; Member, lecturer International Congress Anthropology and Ethnology, Paris, 1960, Moscow, 1964; Member, lecturer International Pacific Sci. Congress, Honolulu, 1961, Tokyo, 1965, Vancouver, 1976. Author: Paa Jakt Efter Paradiset, Oslo, 1938, Kon-Tiki (Am. edition), 1950, American Indians in the Pacific: The Theory Behind the Kon-Tiki Expedition, 1952, Archaeological Evidence of pre-Spanish visits to the Galapagos Island, 1956, Aku-Aku, The Secret of Easter Island (Am. edition), 1958, Reports of the Norwegian Archaeological Expedition to Easter Island and the East Pacific: Volume 1, Archaeology of Easter Island, 1961, Volume 2, Miscellaneous Papers, 1965, Sea Routes to Polynesia, 1968, The Ra Expeditions, 1972, Fatu-Hiva, Back to Nature (Am. edition), 1975, Zwischen den Kontinenten, 1975, The Art of Easter Island, 1975, Early Man and The Ocean (Am. edition), 1979, Tigris, 1979; The Maldive Mystery, 1985; contributor articles to sci. and popular magazines. Founder, board member Kon-Tiki Mus., Oslo; international patron United World Colls.; trustee World Wildlife Fund International. Decorated grand officer Order Al Merito della Repubblica Italiana; Order of Merit First Class Egypt; grand officer Royal Alaouites Order, Morocco; Kirll i Metodi Order of 1st Class Bulgaria; commander with star Order St. Olav, Norway; Order Golden Ark Netherlands; recipient Retzius medal Royal Swedish Anthropological and Geog. Society, 1950, Vega gold medal, 1962; Mungo Park medal Royal Scottish Geog. Society, 1951; Oscar for camera achievement National Acad. Motion Picture Arts and Sciences, 1951; Prix Bonaparte-Wyse Société de Geographie Paris, 1951; Elish Kane gold medal, Geog. Society Philadelphia, 1952; Lomonosov medal Moscow University, 1962; Patron's Gold medal Royal Geog. Society, 1964; co-recipient International Pahlavi environmental prize United Nations, 1978; named hon. professor El Instituto Politécnico Nacional Mexico, others. Fellow New York Acad. Sciences; member Belgian, Brazilian, Peruvian, Russian, Swedish (hon.) anthropological geog. societies, Norwegian Acad. Sci., Norwegian Geog. Society (hon.), World Association World Federalists (vice president), Worldview International (vice president), Explorers Club (hon. director). Office: care Mng Editor Simon & Shuster 1230 Avenue of the Americas New York New York 10020 other: Colla Micheri, Laigueglia Italy

HICKEY, LEO J(OSEPH), museum curator, educator; born Philadelphia, April 26, 1940; son of James J(oseph) and Helen Marie (Schwartz) H.; married Judith McKendry, June 29, 1968; children: Geoffrey Alan, Damian Michael, Jason Alexander. Bachelor of Science, Villanova University, 1962; Master of Arts, Princeton University, 1964; postgraduate, Rutgers University, 1963-65; Doctor of Philosophy, Princeton University, 1967; Master of Arts (privatim), Yale University, 1983. Postdoctoral fellow NRC-Smithsonian Institute, Washington, 1966-69, associate curator; 1969-80; chairman exhibits committee Natural History Museum, Smithsonian, 1973-75, curator; 1980-82; professor biology and geology Yale University, New Haven, Connecticut, 1982—; director Peabody Museum, Yale University, 1982-87; adj. professor botany University Maryland, College Park, 1981-85; adj. professor geology University Pennsylvania, Philadelphia,

1982-86; past president, president, vice president Yellowston-Bighorn Research Association, Red Lodge, Montana, 1979—; director Mus. of Am. Theatre, New Haven, Connecticut, 1983-87. Author: Stratigraphy and Paleobotany of Golden Valley Formation, 1977; co-author: Early Evolution of Flowering Plants, 1976-77 (H.A. Gleason award 1977); author: classification system Leaf Architecture, 1972. Recipient best paper award Geol. Society Washington, 1981; recipient Distinguished Alumnus award Villanova University, 1982; grantee Smithsonian Research Foundation, 1972-76, National Geog. Society, 1979. 84, 85. Member Geological Society Am., Botanical Society Am., American Association for the Advancement of Science, Paleontological Society. Democrat. Roman Catholic. Club: Morys (New Haven). Office: Peabody Mus of Natural History Post Office Box 6666 New Haven Connecticut 06511

HICKMAN, JAMES CHARLES, business and statistics educator, business school dean; born Indianola, Iowa, August 27, 1927; son of James C. and Mabel L. (Fisher) H.; married Margaret W. McKee, June 12, 1950; children—Charles Wallace, Donald Robert, Barbara Jean. Bachelor of Arts, Simpson College, 1950; Master of Science, University Iowa, 1952, Doctor of Philosophy, 1961. Actuarial assistant Bankers Life Company, Des Moines, 1952-57; assistant professor department statistics University Iowa, 1961-64, associate professor; 1964-67, professor; 1967-72; professor business and statistics University Wisconsin, Madison, 1972—; dean School Business University Wisconsin, 1985—; member panel of consultant on social security fin. Senate Fin. and House Ways and Means Committee, 1975-76; member adv. committee to Joint Board for Enrollment of Actuaries, 1976-78; member Actuarial Standards Board, 1985—. Served with United States Army Air Force, 1945-47. Recipient Alumni Achievement award Simpson College, 1979; David Halmstad award for actuarial research Actuarial Educational Research Fund, 1979, 81.

Fellow Society Actuaries (vice president 1975-77); member Casualty Actuarial Society, Am. Acad. Actuaries, Am. Statistical Association. Presbyterian. Home: 4917 Woodburn Dr Madison Wisconsin 53711 Office: U Wisconsin School Business Madison Wisconsin 53706

HILL, HENRY ALLEN, physicist, educator; born Port Arthur, Texas, November 25, 1933; son of Douglas and Florence (Kilgore) H.; married Ethel Louise Eplin, August 23, 1954; children—Henry Allen, Pamela Lynne, Kimberly Renee. Bachelor of Science, University Houston, 1953; Master of Science, University Minnesota, 1956, Doctor of Philosophy, 1957; Master of Arts (honorary), Wesleyan University, 1966. Research assistant University Houston, 1952-53; teaching assistant University Minnesota, 1953-54, research assistant; 1954-57; research associate Princeton University, 1957-58, instructor, then assistant professor; 1958-64; associate professor Wesleyan University, Middletown, Connecticut, 1964-66; professor physics Wesleyan University, 1966-74, chairman department; 1969-71; professor physics University Arizona, 1966—. Contributor articles to professional journals. Sloan fellow, 1966-68.

Fellow Am. Physical Society; member American Association for the Advancement of Science, Am. Astronomical Society, Royal Astronomical Society, Optical Society Am., Am. Association Advancement Sci. Research on nuclear physics, relativity and astrophysics. Office: U Ariz Department Physics Tucson Arizona 85721

HILLEMAN, MAURICE RALPH, virus research scientist; born Miles City, Montana, August 30, 1919; son of Robert A. and Edith (Matson) H.; married Lorraine Witmer, August 3, 1963; children—Jeryl Lynn, Kirsten Jeanne. Bachelor of Science, Montana State University, 1941, Doctor of Science, 1966; Doctor of Philosophy, University Chicago, 1944; Doctor of Science, University Maryland, 1968. Assistant bacteriologist University Chicago, 1942-44; research associate virus laboratories E.R. Squibb & Sons, 1944-47, chief virus department; 1947-48; chief research and diagnostic sections virus and rickettsial diseases Army Medical Service Grad. School, Walter Reed Army Medical Center, 1948-56, assistant chief laboratory affairs; 1953-56; chief respiratory diseases Walter Reed Army Institute Research, Washington, 1956-57; director virus and cell biological research Merck Institute Therapeutic Research, Merck & Company Incorporated, 1957-66, executive director; 1966-71, vice president; 1971-78, senior vice president; 1978—; director virus and cell biology research, vice president Merck, Sharp & Dohme Research Laboratories, 1970-78, senior vice president; 1978—; visiting investigator Hospital of Rockefeller Institute for Medical Research, 1951; visiting professor bacteriology University Maryland, 1953-57; adj. professor virology pediatrics School Medicine University Pennsylvania, 1968—; consultant Children's Hospital of Philadelphia, 1968—; member council div. biological sciences Pritzker School Medicine, 1977—; John Herr Musser lecturer Musser-Burch Society, Tulane University School Medicine, 1969, 19th Graugnard lecturer, 1978; Member, special consultant panel respiratory and related viruses United States Public Health Service, 1960-64; member National Cancer Institute primate study group, 1964-70; member council analysis and projection Am. Cancer Society, 1971-76; member expert adv. panel on virus diseases World Health Organization, 1952—; board of directors W. Alton Jones Cell Sci. Center, Lake Placid, New York, 1980-82; member overseas medical research laboratories committee Department Def., 1980; member virology department rev. committee Am. Type Culture Collection, 1980. Editorial board: International Journal Cancer, 1964-71, Institute Science Information, 1968-70, Am. Journal Epidemiology, 1969-75, Infection and Immunity, 1970-76, Excerpta Medica, 1971—, Proc. Society Experimental Biology and Medicine, 1976—, Journal Antiviral Research, 1980—; Contributor 400 articles to sci., professional, medical journals. Phi Kappa Phi fellow, 1941-42; Koessler fellow, 1943-44; Recipient Howard Taylor Ricketts prize, 1945; Distinguished Civilian Service award sec. def., 1957; Walter Reed Army Medical Incentive award, 1960; Dean M. McCann award, 1970; Procter award, 1971; Achievement award Indsl. Research Institute, 1975. Fellow Am. Acad. Microbiology, Am. Acad. Arts and Sciences; member National Acad. Sci., Am. Society Microbiology, Society Experimental Biology and Medicine (member editorial and publs. committee 1977—), Tissue Culture Association (member council 1977—), Am. Association Immunologists, Am. Association Cancer Research, Infectious Diseases Society, Permanent section Microbiological Standardization International Association Microbiological Socs. Office: Merck Sharp & Dohme Research Labs West Point Pennsylvania 19486

HILTON, JAMES L., plant physiologist, agricultural research administrator; born Bristol, Virginia, April 14, 1930; son of William Rhea and Hattie Lee (Moore) H.; married Mary Katherine Reasor, December 27, 1958; children—Julie Elizabeth, Ann Katherine, Mary Martha. Bachelor of Arts, Duke University, 1952; Master of Science, Iowa State University, 1954, Doctor of Philosophy, 1955. Research scientist United States Department Agriculture Agricultural Research Service, Raleigh, North Carolina, 1956; research scientist United States Department Agriculture Agricultural Research Service, Beltsville, Maryland, 1956-72, laboratory chief; 1972-76, institute director; 1976-88; associate area director United States Department Agriculture Agricultural Research Service, South Atlantic Area, Athens, Georgia, 1988—. Author: Hiltons of Scott County, Virginia, 1965; editor: Herbicide Handbook, 1974, Agricultural Chemicals of the Future, 1985; contributor numerous articles to professional journals. Recipient Contributions to Agriculture award CIBA-GEIGY Corp., 1976; Superior Service award U.S. Department

Agriculture, 1982. Fellow Weed Sci. Society Am. (associate editor 1973-77, editor in chief 1978-87, Best paper award 1972, Research award 1976, Special award 1987), Washington Acad. Sci. (Contributions to Biology award 1966); member Am. Society Plant Physiologists (representative to Am. National Standards Institute 1969-82), Pesticide Sci. Society Washington (member adv. board 1981-86), American Association for the Advancement of Science, Organization Professional Employees Department Agriculture (chapter president 1984-85, national councilman 1985-88, board directors 1986-88). Methodist. Avocation: wood carving. Home: 635 River Bottom Road Athens Georgia 30606 Office: United States Department Agr ARS/Russel Research Ctr/College Station Road Post Office Box 5677 Athens Georgia 30613

HIRSCHOWITZ, BASIL ISAAC, physician; born Bethal, S. Africa, May 29, 1925; came to United States, 1953, naturalized, 1961; son of Morris and Dorothy (Drieband) H.; married Barbara L. Burns, July 6, 1958; children: David E., Karen, Edward A., Vanessa. Bachelor of Science, Witwatersrand University, Johannesburg, 1943, Bachelor of Medicine, Bachelor.Ch., 1947, Doctor of Medicine, 1954. Intern, resident Johannesburg General Hospital, 1948-50; house physician Postgraduate Medical School, London, England, 1950; registrar Central Middlesex Hospital, London, 1951-53; instructor, assistant professor University Michigan, 1953-56; assistant professor Temple University, 1957-59; associate professor medicine, director div. gastroenterology University Alabama Medical Center, Birmingham, 1959-64; professor medicine, associate professor physiology University Alabama Medical Center, 1964-70, professor physiology; 1970—; director gastroenterology department medicine University Alabama Hospital and Clinics, 1959-87; chairman executive committee University Alabama Hospital, 1986—. Recipient Charles F. Kettering Prize, General Motors Cancer Foundation, 1987. Fellow American Association for the Advancement of Science, American College of Physicians, Royal College Physicians (Edinburgh), Royal College Physicians (London); member American Medical Association, South African, Brit., Alabama Medical Assns., Medical Research Society Great Britain, Am. Federation Clinical Research, Southern Society Clinical Investigation, Am. Physiological Society, Biophys. Society, Am. Gastroentorological Association, Alabama Acad. Sci., Am. Society Gastro-Intestinal Endoscopy (Schindler medal 1974), British Society Gastro-Intestinal Endoscopy (hon.), William Beaumont Society (Eddy Palmer award for contributions to endoscopy 1976), Society Experimental Biology and Medicine, Sigma Xi, Alpha Omega Alpha. Office: U Alabama Med Center Birmingham Alabama 35294

HITCHINGS, GEORGE HERBERT, retired chemical company executive, educator; born Hoquiam, Washington, April 18, 1905; son of George Herbert and Lillian (Matthews) H.; married Beverly Reimer, June 24, 1933 (deceased 1985); children—Laramie (Mrs. Robert C. Brown), Thomas E.; married Joyce Shaver, 1989. Bachelor of Science, University Washington, 1927, Master of Science, 1928; Doctor of Philosophy, Harvard University, 1933; Doctor of Science, University Michigan, 1971, University Strathcylde, 1977; Doctor of Science (honorary), New York Medical College, Valhalla, 1981, Emory University, Atlanta, 1981, Duke University, Durham, North Carolina, 1982, University North Carolina, Chapel Hill, 1982, Mount Sinai School Medicine, City University of New York, New York City, 1983, Harvard University, 1987, Medical University of South Carolina, 1988. Instructor University Washington, 1926-28; from teaching fellow to associate Harvard University, 1928-39; senior instructor Western Reserve University, 1939-42; with Burroughs Wellcome Company, Research Triangle Park, North Carolina, 1942—, research director; 1955-67, vice president; 1967-75, director; 1968-84, scientist emeritus; 1975—; professor pharmacology Brown University, 1968-80; adj. professor pharmacology and experimental medicine Duke University, 1970—; adj. professor University North Carolina, 1972—; Hartung lecturer, 1972; Dohme lecturer, Johns Hopkins University, 1969; Michael Cross lecturer Cambridge University, England, 1974; consultant National Research Council, 1952-53, United States Public Health Service, 1955-60, 74-78, Am. Cancer Society, 1963-66, Leukemia Society Am., 1969-73. Author, patentee in field. Member Am. Cancer Society; board of directors Durham United Fund; president Greater Durham Community Foundation, 1983-85; board of directors Burroughs Wellcome Fund, 1968—, president, 1972—. Recipient Gairdner award, 1968; Passano award, 1969; de Villier award, 1969; Cameron prize practical

therapeutics, 1972, Bertner Federation award, 1974, Royal Society Mullard award, 1976, Papanicolaou Cancer Society award, 1979, C. Chester Stock medal, 1981, Distinguished Service award University North Carolina, 1982, Oscar B. Hunter award, 1984, Alfred Burger award, 1984; Distinguished Achievement award modern medicine, 1973; Gregor Mendel medal Czechoslovakia Acad., 1968; Purkinje medal, 1971; Medicinal Chemistry award, 1972; Ministry of Health medal, Warsaw, Poland, 1988; Institute Lekow medal, Warsaw, 1988; Nobel prize in Medicine & Physiology, 1988; Albert Schweitzer International prize for Medicine, 1989. Fellow Royal Society Chemistry (hon.); member National Acad. Sci., Am. Association for Cancer Research (hon.), American Association for the Advancement of Science, Society Experimental Biological Medicine, Royal Society Medicine (foreign member), Hope Valley Country Club. Fields of interest: chemotherapy, antimetabolites, organic chemistry of hetercycles, antimalarial and antibacterial drugs. Home: Carolina Meadows Apartment 1-102 Chapel Hill North Carolina 27514 Office: Burroughs Wellcome Company 3030 Cornwallis Road Research Triangle Park North Carolina 27709

HOCHSTADT, JOY, biomedical research scientist, scientific and research director; born New York City, May 6, 1939; daughter of Julius Louis and Edith (Tabatchnick) H.; married Harvey Leon Ozer, February 3, 1960; 1 child, Juliane Natasha Hochstadt-Ozer. Bachelor of Arts in Zoology, Barnard College, 1960; Master of Arts in Biologic Scis. (graduate fellow 1961-62), Stanford University, 1963;

visiting fellow in tumor biology, Karolinska Institute, Stockholm, 1964-65; research fellow in biological chemistry, Harvard University, 1965-66; Doctor of Philosophy in Microbiology, Georgetown University, 1968; postdoctoral fellow National Institutes of Health, 1968-70. Diplomate Am. Board Clinical Chemistry. Instructor biology College San Mateo, California, 1962-63; teaching assistant microbiology Georgetown Medical School, 1967-68; established investigator Am. Heart Association; laboratory biochemistry National Heart and Lung Institute, Bethesda, Maryland, 1970-72; senior scientist Worcester Foundation Experimental Biology, Shrewsbury, Massachusetts, 1972-76; adj. professor biochemistry Central New England College, Worcester, Massachusetts, 1974-75; visiting professor membrane research Weizmann Institute Sci., Rehovot, Israel, 1976; visiting professor biochemistry and biophysics University Rhode Island, Kingston, 1976-77; research professor microbiology New York Medical College, Valhalla, 1977-81; director Div. Clinical Biochemistry and Basic Research in Pathology, Catholic Medical Center, Queens, 1981-88; professor clinical microbiology Cornell University Medical School, 1986—; vice president, scientific director Hercon Laboratories Corp. subsidiary Health Chem Corp., New York City, 1988—; member National Science Foundation postdoctoral fellowship evaluation panel in biology National Research Council, 1975—, North Atlantic Treaty Organization postdoctoral fellowship evaluation panel, 1978—; member cell biology study section National Institutes of Health, 1979—, Biomedical sciences fellowship committee, 1979—. Editorial board Journal Bacteriology, 1975-80; contributor research papers, methods articles and monographs to professional lit. Member national policy committee Professional Women's Caucus, 1970-73; member alumnae council Barnard College, 1975—. Recipient Stanford Graduate award, 1963; Cancer International Research Coop. Snell scholar, 1965; predoctoral trainee United States Public Health Service, 1966-67, predoctoral fellow, 1967-68, postdoctoral fellow, 1968-70, special trainee, 1973; Am. Heart Association investigatorship, 1970-75; National Institutes of Health grantee, 1973—; National Science Foundation grantee, 1978—; Travel award to Stockholm, Am. Society Biological Chemists, 1973, to Hamburg, 1976; Travel award to Jerusalem, Am. Society Microbiology, 1973. Fellow Am. Acad. Microbiology, Am. Institute Chemists (professional opportunities committee, legis. committee), National Acad. Clinical Biochemistry; member Am. Heart Association (basic sci. council), Am. Society Microbiology (status of women committee 1970-73, secretary physiology division 1972-74, member divisional nominating committee 1973), Am. Society Biological Chemists, Am. Association Clinical Chemists, American Association for the Advancement of Science, Am. Society Clinical Research, Am. Chemical Society, Genetics Society Am., Harvey Society, Am. Association Cancer Research, New York Acad. Sciences, Federation Am. Scientists, Association Women in Sci. (affirmative goals and actions committee 1973-75), Tissue Culture Association (Northeast planning committee 1986—), Am. Society for Cell Biology. Discoverer that penicillinase is involved in bacterial cell wall metabolism (differentiation to spore wall in bacillus); elucidator of mechanisms of utilization of several purines and pyrimidines in bacterial and animal cells; developer of first cell-free vesicle system permitting study of nutrient transport across membranes isolated from mammalian cells in culture; identifier transport changes with growth, quiescence and reactivation involve membrane alterations; viral transformation, differentiation, recombinant DNA gene cloning; developer and implementer of new diagnostics procedures and tests for genetic analysis. Home: 300 Central Park W New York New York 10024 also: 1347 Cambridge Court Saw Creek Bushkill Pennsylvania 18324 also: 21 Spur Road Roaring Brook Lake Putnam Valley New York 10579 Office: Health Chem Corp 1212 Avenue of the Americas New York New York 10036

HOCHSTER, MELVIN, mathematician, educator; born Brooklyn, August 2, 1943; son of Lothar and Rose (Gruber) H.; married Anita Klitzner, August 29, 1965 (divorced February 1983); 1 child, Michael Adam. Bachelor of Arts, Harvard University, 1964; Master of Arts, Princeton University, 1966, Doctor of Philosophy, 1967. Assistant professor math. University Minnesota, Minneapolis, 1967-70, associate professor; 1970-73; professor math. Purdue University, West Lafayette, Ind., 1973-77; professor math. University Michigan, Ann Arbor, 1977-84, Raymond L. Wilder professor math.; 1984—; guest professor Math. Institute Aarhus, Denmark, 1973-74; trustee Math. Sci. Research Institute, Berkeley, California; board governors Institute for Math. and its Application,

Minneapolis. Chairman editorial com. Math. Revs., 1984—. Guggenheim fellow, 1982. Member Am. Math. Society (Frank Nelson Cole prize 1980), Math. Association Am. Office: U Michigan Math Department Angell Hall Ann Arbor Michigan 48109

HODGE, PHILIP GIBSON, JR., mechanical and aerospace engineering educator; born New Haven, November 9, 1920; son of Philip Gibson and Muriel (Miller) H.; married Thea Drell, January 3, 1943; children: Susan E., Philip T., Elizabeth M. Bachelor of Arts, Antioch College, 1943; Doctor of Philosophy, Brown University, 1949. Research assistant Brown University, 1947-49, associate; 1949; assistant professor math. University of California at Los Angeles, 1949-53; associate professor applied mechanics Polytechnic Institute Brooklyn, 1953-56, professor; 1956-57; professor mechanics Illinois Institute Tech., 1953-71, University Minnesota, Minneapolis, 1971—; Russell Severance Springer visiting professor University California, 1976; secretary United States National Com./Theoretical and Applied Mechanics, 1982—. Author: 5 books, the most recent being Limit Analysis of Rotationally Symmetric Plates and Shells, 1963, Continuum Mechanics, 1971; research numerous publications in field, 1949—; tech. editor: Journal Applied Mechanics, 1971-76. Recipient Distinguished Service award Am. Acad. Mechanics, 1984; Karman medal American Society of Civil Engineers, 1985. National Science Foundation senior postdoctoral fellow, 1963. Member American Society of Mechanical Engineers (hon., Worcester Reed Warner medal 1975, medal 1987), NSPE, National Acad. Engineering.

Member Democratic Farm Labor Party. Home: 2962 W River Parkway Minneapolis Minnesota 55406 Office: U Minnesota 107 Akerman Hall Minneapolis Minnesota 55455

HODGES, ROBERT EDGAR, physician, educator; born Marshalltown, Iowa, July 30, 1922; son of Wayne Harold and Blanche Emma (McDowell) H.; married Norma Lee Stempel, June 8, 1946; children: Jeannette Louise, Robert William, Karl Wayne, James Wolter. Bachelor of Arts, State University Iowa, 1944, Doctor of Medicine, 1947, Master of Science in Physiology, 1949. Diplomate: National Board Medical Examiners, Am. Board Internal Medicine. Intern Memorial Hospital, Johnstown, Pennsylvania, 1947-48; fellow physiology, also obstetrics and gynecology, then resident in internal medicine State University Iowa Hospital, 1948-52, director metabolic ward; 1952-71; member faculty State University Iowa Medical School, 1952-71, professor internal medicine; 1964-71, chairman committee nutritional education, administration grad. educational program nutrition; 1968-71; member liaison committee Maximum Security Hospital, Iowa City, 1966-71; professor internal medicine, chief section nutrition University California Medical School, Davis, 1971-80, University Nebraska College Medicine, Omaha, 1980-82; professor and director nutrition program, department family medicine, professor department internal medicine University California Irvine School Medicine, 1982—; member nutrition study section National Institutes of Health, 1964-68; chairman subcom. ascorbic acid and pantothenic acid American Red Cross, 1966-68; member committee nutrition overview

and adjustment of food on demand National Acad. Scis.-NRC, 1976; consultant to hospitals, other government agencies. Author: Nutrition in Medical Practice, 1980, also articles.; Editor: Human Nutrition, A Comprehensive Treatise, 1980; Member editorial bds. medical journals. Served to captain Medical Corps Army of the United States, 1943-46, 54-56. Fellow American College of Physicians; member American Medical Association, Am. Heart Association (fellow councils atherosclerosis, epidemiology; chairman committee nutrition 1966-68), Am. Board Nutrition (president 1973-74), International Society Parenteral Nutrition, Am. Society Parenteral and Enteral Nutrition, Society Experimental Biology and Medicine, Am. Federation Clinical Research, Am. Institute Nutrition, Am. Society Clinical Nutrition (president 1966-67), Nutrition Society (London). Office: U California Irvine School Medicine Department Internal Medicine 101 City Dr South Orange California 92668

HODGKIN, ALAN LLOYD, biophysicist; born February 5, 1914; son of G.L. and M.F. (Wilson) H.; married Marion de Kay Rous, 1944; 1 son, 3 daughters. Student, Trinity College; (fellow), Cambridge University, 1936, Master of Arts, Doctor of Science; Doctor of Medicine (honorary), universities of Berne, Louvain; Doctor of Science (honorary), univs. of Sheffield, Newcastle-upon-Tyne, East Anglia, Manchester, Leicester, London, Newfoundland, Wales, Rockefeller University, Bristol, Oxford; Doctor of Laws, University Aberdeen. Sci. officer radar Air Ministry, also Ministry Aircraft Production, 1939-45; lecturer, then assistant director research Cambridge University, 1945-52; Foulerton research professor Royal Society, 1952-69; John Humphrey Plummer professor biophysics University Cambridge, 1970-81; master Trinity College, Cambridge, 1978-84; member Medical Research Council, 1959-63; chancellor University Leicester, 1971—. Author: Conduction of the Nervous Impulse, 1963; also sci. papers on nature of nervous conduction, muscle, and vision. Devised (with Andrew Huxley) system of math. equations describing nerve impulse; worked with giant nerve fibers of squid, proving that electricity was direct causal agent of impulse propagation. Decorated knight Order Brit. Empire, 1972, Order of Merit, 1973; recipient Baly medal, 1955, Nobel prize for medicine or physiology (with A.F. Huxley, J.C. Eccles), 1963, Lord Crook Medal, 1983. Fellow Royal Society (Royal medal 1958, Copley medal 1965, president 1970-75), Imperial College Sci., Indian National Sci. Acad. (hon.) Girton College, Cambridge (hon.); member Physiological Society (foreign secretary 1960-67), National Acad. Sciences, Am. Acad. Arts and Sciences (foreign hon.), Royal Danish Acad. Sciences (foreign), Leopoldina Acad., Royal Swedish Acad. Sciences (foreign), Pontifical Acad. Sciences, Am. Philosophical Society (foreign), Royal Irish Acad. (hon.), Union of the Soviet Socialist Republics Acad. Sciences (foreign), Marine Biological Association United Kingdom (president 1966-76). Office: Cambridge U Physiol Lab, Downing St, Cambridge CB2 3EG, England

HODGKIN, DOROTHY CROWFOOT, chemist; born Cairo, 1910; married Thomas L. Hodgkin, 1937 (deceased 1982). Student, Somerville College, Oxford, England, 1928-32, Cambridge University, 1932-34; Doctor of Science (honorary), University Leeds, University Manchester, Cambridge University, others, 1932-34. Member faculty Oxford University, 1934—, professor emeritus; 1934—; chancellor Bristol University, 1970—. Decorated Order of Merit; First Freedom of Beccles; recipient Nobel Prize in chemistry, 1964; Mikhail Lomonosov gold medal, 1982. Fellow Royal Society (Royal medal 1956, Copley medal 1976), Australian Acad. Sci., Akad. Leopoldina; member National Acad. Sciences, Brit. Association Advancement of Sci. (president 1977-78); foreign member Royal Netherlands Acad. of Sci. and Letters, Am. Acad. Arts and Sciences; hon. foreign member Union of the Soviet Socialist Republics Acad. Sciences. Determined structure of vitamin B12, cholesterol iodide, and penicillin using X-ray crystallographic analysis. Home: Crab Mill, Ilmington, Shipston-on-Stour Warwickshire, England Office: U Oxford, Chem Crystallography Lab, 9 Parks Road, Oxford OX1 3PS, England

HODGSON, ERNEST, toxicology educator; born Durham, England, July 26, 1932; came to United States, 1955; son of Ernest Victor and Emily (Moses) H.; married Mary Kathleen Devlin, December 21, 1957; children—Mary Elizabeth, Audrey Catherine, Patricia Emily Devlin, Ernest Victor Felix. Bachelor of Science with honors, Kings College University Durham, England, 1955; Doctor of Philosophy, Oregon State University, 1959. Research fellow Oregon State University, Corvallis, 1955-59, University Wisconsin, Madison, 1959-61; assistant professor, professor North Carolina State University, Raleigh, 1961-65, professor toxicology, William Neal Reynolds professor; 1977—, chairman toxicology department; 1982—, distinguished alumni research professor; 1987—; member adv. panel United States Environmental Protection Agency, Washington, 1982-85; member toxicology study section National Institutes of Health, Washington, 1985—; president Toxicology Communications, Raleigh, 1982—; visiting scientist University Washington, Seattle, 1975. Author, editor: Introduction to Biochemical Toxicology, 1980, Modern Toxicology, 1987, Dictionary of Toxicology; editor: Reviews in Biochemical Toxicology, 1979—, Reviews in Environmental Toxicology, 1984—, Journal Biochemical Toxicology; contributor articles to professional journals; member editorial board Chemico-Biological Interactions, Journal Toxicology and Applied Pharmacology. Chairman policy rev. committee Gov.'s Waste Management Board, Raleigh, 1984. National Institutes of Health grantee, 1964—. Member Society Toxicology (education committee 1984—, Education award 1984, North Carolina chapter president 1984-85), Am. Society Pharmacology (drug metabolism committee 1981-84), Am. Chemical Society, American Association for the Advancement of Science, International Society Study Xenobiotics (council member 1986-89), Sigma Xi (chapter president 1974). Democrat. Avocations: history, writing, travel. Office: North Carolina State U Toxicology Program Box 7633 Raleigh North Carolina 27695

HOFFMAN, ALAN JEROME, mathematician, educator; born New York City, May 30, 1924; son of Jesse and Muriel (Schrager) H.; married Esther Atkins Walker, May 30, 1947; children—Eleanor, Elizabeth Hoffman Perry. Bachelor of Arts, Columbia University, 1947, Doctor of Philosophy, 1950; Doctor of Science (honorary), Technion University, 1986. Member Institute Advanced Study, Princeton, New Jersey, 1950-51; mathematician National Bureau Standards, Washington, 1951-56; sci. liaison officer Office Naval Research, London, 1956-57; consultant General Electric Company, New York City, 1957-61; research staff member International Business Machines Corporation Research Center, Yorktown Heights, New York, 1961—; fellow International Business Machines Corporation Research Center, 1978—; visiting professor Technion, Haifa, Israel, 1965, Stanford University, 1980—; adj. professor City University of New York, 1965-76, Yale University, 1976-85. Served with United States Army, 1943-46, European Theatre of Operations, PTO. Fellow New York Acad. Sci., Am. Acad. Arts and Sciences; member Am. Math. Society (council 1982-84), National Acad. Sciences. Office: International Business Machines Corporation TJ Watson Research Center Post Office Box 218 Yorktown Heights New York 10598

HOFFMANN, ROALD, chemist, educator; born Zloczow, Poland, July 18, 1937; came to United States, 1949, naturalized, 1955; son of Hillel and Clara (Rosen) Safran (stepson Paul Hoffmann); married Eva Börjesson, April 30, 1960; children: Hillel Jan, Ingrid Helena. Bachelor of

Arts, Columbia University, 1958; Master of Arts, Harvard University, 1960, Doctor of Philosophy, 1962; Doctor Tech. (honorary), Royal Institute Tech., Stockholm, 1977; Doctor of Science (honorary), Yale University, 1980, Columbia University, 1982, Hartford University, 1982, City University of New York, 1983, University Puerto Rico, 1983, University Uruguay, 1984, University La Plata, State University of New York, Binghampton, 1985, Colgate University, Rennes University, 1987. Junior fellow Society Fellows Harvard, 1962-65; associate professor Cornell University, Ithaca, New York, 1965-68; professor Cornell University, 1968-74, John A. Newman professor physical sci.; 1974—. Author: (with R.B. Woodward) Conservation of Orbital Symmetry, 1970, (poetry) The Metamict State, 1987. Recipient award in pure chemistry Am. Chemical Society, 1969, Arthur C. Cope award, 1973; Fresenius award Phi Lambda Upsilon, 1969; Harrison Howe award Rochester sect. Am. Chemical Society, 1970; annual award International Acad. Quantum Molecular Sciences, 1970; Pauling award, 1974; Nobel prize in chemistry, 1981; inorganic chemistry award; Am. Chemical Society, 1982; National Medal of Sci., 1983; Award in Chemical Sciences, National Acad. Sci., 1986. Member National Acad. Sciences, Am. Acad. Arts and Sciences, International Acad. Quantum Molecular Sciences; foreign member Royal Society, Indian National Sci. Acad., Royal Swedish Acad. Sciences.

HOFSTADTER, DOUGLAS RICHARD, cognitive scientist, educator; born New York City, February 15, 1945; son of Robert and Nancy (Givan) H.; married Carol Ann Brush, 1985; 1 child, Daniel Frederic. Bachelor of Science in Math. with distinction, Stanford University, 1965; Master of Science, University Oregon, 1972, Doctor of Philosophy in Physics, 1975. Assistant professor computer sci. Ind. University, Bloomington, 1977-80; associate professor Ind. University, 1980-84; Walgreen professor Cognitive Sci. University Michigan, Ann Arbor, 1984-88; professor cognitive sci. Ind. University, Bloomington, 1988—. Author: Gödel, Escher, Bach: an Eternal Golden Braid, 1979, Metamagical Themas, 1985, Ambigrammi, 1987; editor: (with Daniel C. Dennett) The Mind's I, 1981; columnist: Metamagical Themas in Science Am., 1981-83. Recipient Pulitzer prize for general nonfiction, 1980; Am. Book award, 1980; Guggenheim fellow, 1980-81. Member Cognitive Sci. Society, Am. Association Artificial Intelligence. Office: Center for Research on Concepts & Cognition 510 N Fess St Bloomington Indiana 47408

HOFSTADTER, ROBERT, physicist, educator; born New York City, February 5, 1915; son of Louis and Henrietta (Koenigsberg) H.; married Nancy Givan, May 9, 1942; children: Douglas Richard, Laura James, Mary Hinda. Bachelor of Science magna cum laude (Kenyon prize), College City New York, 1935; Master of Arts (Procter fellow), Princeton University, 1938, Doctor of Philosophy, 1938; Doctor of Laws, City University New York, 1961; Doctor of Science, Gustavus Adolphus College, 1963; Laureate Honoris Causa, University Padua, 1965; Doctor of Science (honorary), Carleton University, Ottawa, Can., 1967, Seoul National

University, 1967; Honoris Causa, University Clermont-Ferrand, 1967; Doctor Rerum Naturalium honoris causa, Julius Maximilians University, Würzburg, Federal Republic Germany, 1982, Johannes Gutenberg University Mainz, Federal Republic Germany, 1983; Doctor of Science (honorary), Israel Institute Tech., 1985. Coffin fellow General Electric Company, 1935-36; Harrison fellow University Pennsylvania, 1939; instructor physics Princeton University, 1940-41, City College of New York, 1941-42; physicist Norden Laboratory Corp., 1943-46; assistant professor physics Princeton University, 1946-50; associate professor physics Stanford University, 1950-54, professor; 1954-85, Max H. Stein professor physics; 1971-85, professor emeritus; 1985—, director high energy physics laboratory; 1967-74; director John Fluke Manufacturing Company, 1979-88. Author: (with Robert Herman) High-Energy Electron Scattering Tables, 1960; editor: Investigations in Physics, 1958-65, Electron Scattering and Nucleon Structure, 1963; co-editor: Nucleon Structure, 1964; associate editor: Physical Review, 1951-53; member editorial board: Review Science Instruments, 1953-55, Reviews of Modern Physics, 1958-61. Board governors Technion, Israel Institute Tech., Weizmann Institute Sci. California Scientist of Year, 1959; co-recipient of Nobel prize in physics, 1961; Townsend Harris medal College City New York, 1961; Guggenheim fellow Geneva, Switzerland, 1958-59; Ford Foundation fellow; recipient Röntgen medal, Wurzburg, Germany, 1985, U.S. National Medal Sci., 1986, Prize of Cultural Foundation of Fiuggi, Italy, 1986. Fellow Am. Physical Society, Physical Society London; member National Acad. Sciences, Am. Acad. Arts and Sciences, American Association of University Profs., Phi Beta Kappa, Sigma Xi. Home: 639 Mirada Avenue Stanford California 94305 Office: Stanford U Department Physics Stanford California 94305

HOGNESTAD, EIVIND, civil engineer; born Time, Norway, July 17, 1921; came to United States, 1947, naturalized, 1954; son of Hans E. and Dorthea (Norheim) H.; married Andree S. Hognestad, April 4, 1964; children: Hans E., Marta Marie, Kirsten Andree. Master of Science, Norwegian Tech. University, 1947, Doctor of Science, 1952; Master of Science, University Illinois, 1949. Research assistant to associate professor University Illinois, 1947-53; manager structural devel. section Portland Cement Association, Skokie, Illinois, 1953-66; director engineering devel. department Portland Cement Association, 1966-74, director tech. and sci. devel.; 1974-86; principal consultant Construction Tech. Laboratories, Incorporated, 1987—; consultant offshore devel. petroleum fields various oil companies and contractors; field and laboratory investigations of concrete structures. Contributor to: Encyclopedia Britannica, 1966, also over 100 articles on structural engring. and concrete tech. to tech. journals. Served with Royal Norwegian Navy, 1944-46. Fellow Am. Concrete Institute (past chairman committee 357 offshore concrete structures, Wason medal 1956, Henry L. Kennedy award 1971, hon. member 1976, Alfred E. Lindau award 1977, Delmar L. Bloem award 1980), American Society of Civil Engineers (past chairman adminstrv. committee on masonry and reinforced concrete,

Research prize 1956, Chicago Civil Engineer of Year award 1977, Arthur J. Boase award 1981); member National Acad. Engineering, Prestressed Concrete Institute (past chairman tech. activities committee), European Concrete Committee, International Prestressing Federation, Structural Engineering Society Puerto Rico (hon.), Norwegian Acad. Engineering, Royal Norwegian Acad. Sci. Home: 2222 Prairie St Glenview Illinois 60025 Office: 5420 Old Orchard Road Skokie Illinois 60077

HOLLEY, ROBERT WILLIAM, biologist; born Urbana, Illinois, January 28, 1922; son of Charles E. and Viola (Wolfe) H.; married Ann Dworkin, March 3, 1945; 1 son, Frederick. Bachelor of Arts, University Illinois, 1942; Doctor of Philosophy, Cornell University, 1947. Fellow Am. Chemical Society State College Washington, 1947-48; assistant professor, then associate professor organic chemistry New York State Agriculture Experiment Station Cornell University, Ithaca, 1948-57, research chemist plant, soil and nutrition laboratory United States Department of Agriculture; 1957-64, professor biochemistry; 1964-69, chairman department biochemistry; 1965-66; resident fellow Salk Institute Biological Studies, La Jolla, California, 1968—; member biochemistry study section National Institutes of Health, 1962-66; visiting fellow Salk Institute Biological Studies; visiting professor Scripps Clinic and Research Foundation, La Jolla, 1966-67. Recipient Distinguished Service award U.S. Department Agr., 1965, Albert Lasker award basic medcal research, 1965; U.S. Steel Foundation award in molecular biology National Acad. Sciences, 1967; Nobel prize for

medicine and physiology, 1968; Guggenheim fellow California Institute Tech., 1955-56. Fellow American Association for the Advancement of Science; member Am. Acad. Arts and Sciences, Am. Society Biological Chemists, Am. Chemical Society, National Acad. Sciences, Phi Beta Kappa, Sigma Xi. Office: Salk Institute Biolog Studies Post Office Box 85800 San Diego California 92138

HOLMQUEST, DONALD LEE, physician, astronaut, lawyer; born Dallas, April 7, 1939; son of Sidney Browder and Lillie Mae (Waite) H.; married Ann Nixon James, October 24, 1972. Bachelor of Science in Electrical Engineering, Southern Methodist University, 1962; Doctor of Medicine, Baylor University, 1967, Doctor of Philosophy in Physiology, 1968; Juris Doctor, University Houston, 1980. Student engineer Ling-Temco-Vought, Dallas, 1958-61; electronics engineer Texas Instruments, Incorporated, Dallas, 1962; intern Methodist Hospital, Houston, 1967-68; pilot training United States Air Force, Williams Air Force Base, Arizona, 1968-69; scientist-astronaut National Aeronautics and Space Administration, Houston, 1967-73; research associate Massachusetts Institute of Technology, 1968-70; assistant professor radiology and physiology Baylor College Medicine, 1970-73; director nuclear medicine Eisenhower Medical Center, Palm Desert, California, 1973-74; associate dean medicine, associate professor Texas A&M University, College Station, 1974-76; director nuclear medicine Navasota (Texas) Medical Center, 1976-84, Medical Arts Hospital, Houston, 1977-85; partner Wood Lucksinger & Epstein, Houston, 1980—. Contributor articles to medical journals. Member Society Nuclear Medicine, Am. College Nuclear Physicians, Texas Bar Association, Am. Fighter Pilots Association, Sigma Xi, Alpha Omega Alpha, Sigma Tau. Home: 3721 Tangley Road Houston Texas 77005

HOLT, STEPHEN S., astrophysicist; born New York City, May 17, 1940; son of Aaron J. and Faye E. (Schwartz) Holtz; married Carol Ann Weissman, June 3, 1961; children: Peter David, Eric Lawrence, Laura Kimberly. Bachelor of Science, New York University, 1961, Doctor of Philosophy in Physics, 1966. Instructor physics New York University, 1964-66; astrophysicist Goddard Space Flight Center, Greenbelt, Maryland, 1966—; chief high energy astrophysics National Aeronautics and Space Administration Headquarters, 1980-81; director Laboratory for High Energy Astrophysics Goddard Space Flight Center, Greenbelt, Maryland, 1983—; lecturer physics University Maryland, 1967-87, adj. professor astronomy, 1988—. Contributor articles to professional journals. Recipient medal for exceptional sci. achievement National Aeronautics and Space Administration, 1977, 80. Fellow Am. Physical Society; member Am. Astronomical Society (chair division), Sigma Xi, Tau Beta Pi, Sigma Pi Sigma. Home: 1207 Mimosa Lane Silver Spring Maryland 20904 Office: Code 660 Goddard Space Flight Center Greenbelt Maryland 20771

HONDEGHEM, LUC M., cardiovascular and pharmacology educator; born Jabbeke, Belgium, September 22, 1944; married; 3 children. Doctor of Medicine, University Louvain, Belgium, 1970, Master of Science in Physiology, 1971; Doctor of Philosophy in Pharmacology, University California, San Francisco, 1973. From assistant professor to associate professor pharmacology University California, San Francisco, 1973-85; professor medicine and pharmacology, Stahlman chairman cardiovascular research program Vanderbilt University, 1985—. Member Am. Heart Association, Medical Electronics and Data Society, Am. Society Pharmacology and Experimental Therapeutics, Sigma Xi. Fields of research include ultrastructural and electrophysiological aspects of impulse transmission in cardiac tissue; mechanisms of cardiac arrhythmias; effects of antiarrhythmic drugs on normal and abnormal impulse transmission in the heart. Office: Vanderbilt U School of Medicine Nashville Tennessee 37132

HOOD, LEROY EDWARD, biologist; born Missoula, Montana, October 10, 1938; son of Thomas Edward and Myrtle Evylan (Wadsworth) H.; married Valerie Anne Logan, December 14, 1963; children: Eran William, Marqui Leigh Jennifer. Bachelor of Science, California Institute Tech., 1960, Doctor of Philosophy in Biochemistry, 1968; Doctor of Medicine, Johns Hopkins University, 1964. Medical officer United States Public Health Service, 1967-70; senior investigator National Cancer Institute, 1967-70; assistant professor biology California Institute Tech., Pasadena, 1970-73; associate professor California Institute Tech., 1973-75, professor; 1975—, Bowles professor biology; 1977—, chairman div. biology; 1980—. Author: (with others) Biochemistry, a Problems Approach, 1974, Molecular Biology of Eukaryotic Cells, 1975, Immunology, 1978,

Essential Concepts of Immunology, 1978. Co-recipient, Albert Lasker Basic Medical Research Award, 1987.

Member Am. Association Immunologists, Am. Association Sci., National Acad. Sciences, Am. Acad. Arts and Sciences, Sigma Xi. Home: 1453 E California Boulevard Pasadena California 91106 Office: California Institute Tech Div Biology Pasadena California 91125

HOPPENSTEADT, FRANK CHARLES, mathematics educator, university dean; born Oak Park, Illinois, April 29, 1938; son of Frank Carl and Margaret (Goltermann) H.; married Leslie Thomas, December 27, 1986; children: Charles, Matthew, Sarah. Bachelor of Arts, Butler University, 1960; Master of Science, University Wisconsin, 1962, Doctor of Philosophy, 1965. Instructor maths. University Wisconsin, Madison, 1965; assistant professor maths. Michigan State University, East Lansing, 1965-68, dean College Natural Sci.; 1986—; associate professor New York University, New York City, 1968-76, professor; 1976-79; professor University Utah, Salt Lake City, 1977-86, chairman department maths.; 1982-85. Author: Mathematical Methods in Population Biology, 1982, An Introduction to Mathematics of Neurons, 1986. Member Am. Math. Society (chairman applied math. committee 1976-80), Society Industrial and Applied Maths., Sigma Xi. Office: Michigan State University Dean College Natural Sci 103 Natural Sci East Lansing Michigan 48824

HOPPER, GRACE M., mathematician; born New York City, December 9, 1906; daughter of Walter Fletcher and Mary Campbell (Van Horne) Murray; married Vincent Foster Hopper, June 15, 1930 (divorced 1945). Bachelor of Arts, Vassar College, 1928; Master of Arts (Vassar fellow, Sterling scholar), Yale University, 1930, Doctor of Philosophy, 1934; postgraduate (Vassar faculty fellow), New York University, 1941-42; Doctor of Engineering (honorary), Newark College Engineering, 1972; Doctor of Science (honorary), C.W. Post College Long Island University, 1973, Pratt Institute, 1976, Linkoping (Sweden) University, 1980, Bucknell University, 1980, Acadia (Can.) University, 1980, Southern Illinois University, 1981, Loyola University, Chicago, 1981; Doctor of Laws (honorary), University Pennsylvania, 1974; Doctor Pub. Service (honorary), George Washington University, 1981. From instructor to associate professor math. Vassar College, Poughkeepsie, New York, 1931-44; assistant professor math Barnard College, New York City, summer 1943; research fellow engineering sciences, applied physics computation lab Harvard University, Cambridge, Massachusetts, 1946-49; senior mathematician Eckert-Mauchly Computer Corp., Philadelphia, 1949-50; senior programmer Eckert-Mauchly div. Remington Rand, 1950-59; systems engineer, director automatic programming devel. UNIVAC div. Sperry Rand Corp., Philadelphia, 1959-64, staff scientist systems programming; 1964-71; visiting lecturer Moore School Electrical Engineering, University Pennsylvania, 1959-63, visiting associate professor electrical engineering, 1963-74, adj. professor, 1974; professorial lecturer George Washington University from 1971. Contributor articles to professional journals. Served to comdr United States Navy Women's Reserve, 1944-46, from 1967, captain United States

Naval Reserve, 1973; later served active duty NAVDAC. Decorated Legion of Merit, Meritorious Service award; recipient Naval Ordnance Devel. award, 1946, Connelly Memorial award, 1968, Wilbur L. Cross medal Yale University, 1972, Sci. Achievement award Am. Mother's Committee, 1970, others. Fellow Brit. Computer Society (distinguished), Association Computer Programmers and Analysts, Institute of Electrical and Electronics Engineers (McDowell award 1979), American Association for the Advancement of Science; member National Acad. Engineering, Association Computing Machinery, Data Processing Management Association (Man of Year award 1969), Am. Federation Information Processing Socs. (Harry Goode Memorial award 1970), Society Women Engrs (Achievement award 1964, Franklin Institute, United States Naval Institute, International Oceanographic Foundation, Daughters of the American Revolution, Dames Loyal Legion, Historical Society Pennsylvania, Genealogical Society Pennsylvania, New Hampshire Historical Society, New England Historical Genealogical Society, Valley Forge Historical Association, Retired Officers Association, Huguenot Society Pennsylvania, National, New York genealogical socs., Pechin Society, Phi Beta Kappa, Sigma Xi. Home: 1400 S Joyce St Arlington Virginia 22202

HORNE, GREGORY STUART, geologist, educator; born Minneapolis, June 11, 1935; married; 2 children. Bachelor of Arts, Dartmouth College, 1957; Doctor of Philosophy in Geology, Columbia University, 1968. Geologist Tidewater Oil Company, 1957-64; geologist Pan Am. Petrol Corp., 1965; associate professor earth sci. Wesleyan University, Middletown, Connecticut, 1967-80, professor earth and environmental sci.; 1980—, George I. Seney professor geology and professor earth and environmental sciences; president Essex Marine Laboratory, 1975—. Member Geological Society Am., Am. Association Petroleum Geologists, Society Econ. Paleontology and Minerals. Office: Wesleyan U Department Earth and Environ Sci Middletown Connecticut 06457

HOUNSFIELD, GODFREY NEWBOLD, scientist; born August 28, 1919; son of Thomas H. Educated, City and Guilds College, London; diploma, Faraday House Electrical Engineering College, London; Doctor of Medicine (honorary), University Basel, 1975; Doctor of Science (honorary), City University, 1976, University London, 1976; Doctor.Tech. (honorary), University Loughborough, 1976. Joined EMI Limited, Hayes, Middlesex, England, 1951, head medical systems section, central research laboratories; 1972-76, senior staff scientist; 1977—; professorial fellow in imaging sciences Manchester University, 1978—. Contributor articles to sci. journals. Recipient Nobel prize in Physiology or Medicine, 1979; MacRobert award, 1972; Wilhelm-Exner medal Austrian Indsl. Association, 1974; Ziedses des Plantes medal Physikalishe Medizinische Gesellschaft, Würzburg, 1974; Prince Philip Medal award CGLI, 1975; ANS Radiation Industry award Georgia Institute Tech., 1975; Lasker award Lasker Foundation, 1975; Duddell Bronze medal Institute Physics, 1976; Golden Plate award Am. Acad. Achievement, 1976;

Reginald Mitchell Gold medal Stoke-on-Trent Association Engrs., 1976; Churchill Gold medal, 1976; Gairdner Foundation award, 1976; decorated commander Order Brit. Empire, 1976, knight, 1981. Fellow Royal Society. Led design team for 1st large all-transistor computer to be built in Great Britain; invented EMI-scanner computerized transverse axial tomography system for X-ray exam.; developed new X-ray technique (EMI-scanner system). Office: Thorn EMI Research Labs, Dawley Road, Hayes, Middlesex UB3 1HH, England

HOUSNER, GEORGE WILLIAM, civil engineering educator, consultant; born Saginaw, Michigan, December 9, 1910; son of Charles and Sophie Ida (Schust) H. Bachelor of Science in Civil Engineering, University Michigan, 1933; Doctor of Philosophy, California Institute Tech., 1941. Registered professional engineer, California. Engineer United States Corps Engineers, Los Angeles, 1941-42; operations analyst 15th Air Force, Libya and Italy, 1943-45; professor engineering California Institute Tech., Pasadena, 1945—; earthquake engineering consultant Pasadena, 1945—; member Gov.'s Earthquake Council, 1971-76, Los Angeles County Earthquake Commission, 1971-72, adv. panel on Earthquake Hazard National Acad. Sciences, 1981-83; chairman Committee on Earthquake Engineering, National Research Council, 1983—, Committee on International Decade Natural Hazard Reduction, National Research Council, 1986-88. Author 3 textbooks, numerous tech. papers. Recipient Distinguished Civilian Service award U.S. War Department, 1945, Bendix Research award Am. Society Engineering Education, 1967,

National Medal Sci., 1988. Member National Acad. Engineering, National Acad. Sciences, Seismological Society Am. (president 1977-78, medal 1981), American Society of Civil Engineers (von Karman medal 1972, Newmark medal 1981), International Association Earthquake Engineering (president 1969-73), Earthquake Engineering Research Institute (president 1954-65). Home: 4084 Chevy Chase Dr Louisiana Canada California 91011 Office: California Institute Tech 1201 E California Boulevard Pasadena California 91125

HOWARD, ROBERT FRANKLIN, observatory administrator, astronomer; born Delaware, Ohio, December 30, 1932; son of David Dale and Clarine Edna (Morehouse) H.; married Margaret Teresa Farnon, October 4, 1958; children—Thomas Colin, Moira Catharine. Bachelor of Arts, Ohio Wesleyan University, 1954; Doctor of Philosophy, Princeton University, 1957. Carnegie fellow Mount Wilson and Palomar Observatory, Pasadena, California, 1957-59; staff member Mount Wilson and Palomar Observatory, 1961-81; assistant professor University Massachusetts, Amherst, 1959-61; assistant director for Mount Wilson Mount Wilson & Las Campanas Observatory, Pasadena, 1981-84; director National Solar Observatory, Tucson, 1984-88, astronomer; 1988—. Editor: Solar Magnetic Fields, 1971; editor: (journal) Solar Physics, 1987—; contributor articles to professional journals. Member Am. Astronomical Society, International Astronomical Union. Office: National Solar Obs 950 N Cherry Avenue Tucson Arizona 85726

HOWELL, JOHN REID, mechanical engineering educator; born Columbus,

Ohio, June 13, 1936; son of Frederick Edward and Hilma Lavilla (Kief) H.; married Arlene Elizabeth Pollitt, June 20, 1959 (divorced 1974); married Susan Gooch Conway, May 20, 1979; children: John Reid Jr., Keli Dianne, David Lee. Bachelor of Science in Chemical Engineering, Case Institute Tech., 1958, Master of Science in Chemical Engineering, 1960, Doctor of Philosophy, 1962. Registered professional engineer. Aerospace engineer National Aeronautics and Space Administration Lewis Research Center, Cleveland, 1961-68; associate professor University Houston, 1969-73, professor; 1973-78; director Energy Institute University Houston, 1975-78; visiting professor mechanical engineering University Texas, Austin, 1978-79, professor; 1979-82, E.C.H. Bantel professor; 1982—, chairman mechanical engineering department; 1986—; director Center for Energy Studies, 1988—. Co-author: Thermal Radiation Heat Transfer, 1981, Design of Solar Thermal Systems, 1984, Fundamentals of Engineering Thermodynamics, 1987; contributor over 60 articles to professional journals. Commissioner Renewable Energy Resources Commission, Austin, 1980-81. Served to 1st lieutenant United States Air Force, 1962-65. Recipient Special Service award National Aeronautics and Space Administration, 1965; named to Hon. Order Kentucky Colonels, 1980. Fellow American Society of Mechanical Engineers; associate fellow American Institute of Aeronautics and Astronautics; member Am. Society Engineering Education (Ralph Coats Roe award 1987), International Solar Energy Society. Office: U Tex/Austin Department Mech Engring Austin Texas 78712

HUBEL, DAVID HUNTER, physiologist, educator; born Windsor, Ontario, Canada, February 27, 1926; son of Jesse Hervey and Elsie (Hunter) H.; married Shirley Ruth Izzard, June 20, 1953; children: Carl Andrew, Eric David, Paul Matthew. Bachelor of Science, McGill University, 1947, Doctor of Medicine, 1951, Doctor of Science (honorary), 1978; Master of Arts (honorary), Harvard University, 1962; Doctor of Science (honorary), University Manitoba, 1983. Intern Montreal General Hospital, 1951-52; assistant resident neurology Montreal Neurological Institute, 1952-53, fellow clinical neurophysiology; 1953-54; assistant resident neurology Johns Hopkins Hospital, 1954-55; senior fellow neurological sciences group Johns Hopkins University, 1958-59; faculty Harvard University Medical School, 1959—, George Packer Berry professor physiology, chairman department; 1967-68, George Packer Berry professor neurobiology; 1968-82, John Franklin Enders university professor; 1982—; George H. Bishop lecturer experimental neurology Washington University, St. Louis, 1964; Jessup lecturer biological sciences Columbia, 1970; James Arthur lecturer Am. Mus. Natural History, 1972; Ferrier lecturer Royal Society London, 1972; Harvey lecturer Rockefeller University, 1976; Weizmann memorial lecturer Weizmann Institute Sci., Rehovot, Israel, 1979; Fenn lecturer 30th international congress International Union Psychological Sci., Vancouver, British Columbia, Can., 1986. Served with Army of the United States, 1955-58. Recipient Trustees Research to

Prevent Blindness award, 1971; Lewis S. Rosenstiel award for distinguished work in basic med. research, 1972; Karl Spencer Lashley prize Am. Philos. Society, 1977; Louisa Gross Horwitz prize Columbia University, 1978; Dickson prize in Medicine University Pitts., 1979; Ledlie prize Harvard University, 1980; Nobel prize, 1981; Senior fellow Harvard Society Fellows, 1971—. Fellow Am. Acad. Arts and Sciences; member National Acad. Sci., Am. Physiological Society (Bowditch lecturer 1966), Deutsche Akademie der Naturforscher Leopoldina, Society for Neurosci. (Grass lecture 1976), Association for Research in Vision and Ophthalmology (Friedenwald award 1975), Johns Hopkins University Society Scholars, Am. Philosophical Society (Karl Spencer Lashley prize 1977), Royal Society London (foreign). Research brain mechanisms in vision; bd. syndics Harvard University Press, 1979-83. Home: 98 Collins Road Waban Massachusetts 02168 Office: Harvard Med School Department Neurobiology 220 Longwood Avenue Boston Massachusetts 02115

HUBER, ROBERT, biochemist; born Munich, February 20, 1937; son of Sebastian and Helene (Kebinger) H.; married Christa Huber, 1960; children: Ulrike, Martin, Robert, Julia. Diploma, Tech. Universität Munich, 1960, Doctor of Philosophy, 1963, habil., 1968. Professor, director Max-Planck-Institute für Biochemie, Martinsreid, Federal Republic of Germany, 1971—. Editor Journal Molecular Biology and Biophysics of Structure and Mechanism. Recipient E. K. Frey prize deutschen Gesellschaft für Chirurgie, 1972, Otto Warburg medal deutschen Gesellschaft für Biologische Chemie, 1977; co-recipient Nobel prize for chemistry, 1988. Member European Molecular Biology Organization (member committees). Office: Max Planck Institute, Biochemistry, Am Klopferspitz 18A, 8033 Martinsried bei Munchen Federal Republic of Germany *

HUDSON, WILLIAM RONALD, transportation engineering educator; born Temple, Texas, May 17, 1933; son of Clarence W. and Nan S. Hudson; married Martha Ann Collins, May 6, 1936; children: Stuart William, Alan David, Paul Collin. Bachelor of Science, Texas Agricultural and Mechanical University, 1954, Master of Science, 1955; Doctor of Philosophy, University Texas, Austin, 1965. Registered professional engineer, Texas, Arizona, Kansas, Ind., Illinois; registered pub. surveyor, Texas. Civil engineer S. J. Buchanan and Associates Cons. Engineers, Bryan, Texas, 1957-58; assistant chief rigid pavement research branch AASHO Road Test, National Acad. Sciences, Ottawa, Illinois, 1985-61; assistant project engineer National Cooperative Hwy Research Program Project I-1 National Acad. Sciences, 1964-65; supervising designing research engineer Highway Design Div. Texas Highway Department, Austin, 1961-63; instructor civil engineering, research engineer University Texas, Austin, 1963-65; assistant professor, research engineer Center for Hwy Research, University Texas, Austin, 1965-68, acting director; 1969; assistant dean engineering University Texas, 1969-70, associate dean engineering; 1970-72, associate professor civil engineering, director Pavement Systems Research

Laboratory; 1968-73, professor civil engineering; 1973—, director Council for Advanced Transportation Studies; 1972-75, international tech. director Brazilian Hwy Project; 1975-80, coordinator of chair of free enterprise; 1977-78, area coordinator for transportation, director Pavement Systems Research Laboratory; 1977-81, Dewitt C. Greer Centennial professor engineering, area coordinator transportation; 1981—; member student affairs dean's council, 1969-70, University Texas, Austin, chairman university committee on fin. aid to students, 1970-71. Author: Pavement Management Systems, 1978; over 250 tech. reports and papers; over 300 oral presentations at national and international meetings. Served to major United States Air Force, 1955-57. Recipient Engineering Foundation Adv. Council award, 1977-78; also various awards for research papers; named keynote speaker several confs. on pavement and transp. topics. Member American Society of Civil Engineers (chairman executive committee hwy. division 1983-84, chairman econ. affairs Texas section 1983-85; numerous other committee activities; J. James R. Croes medal 1968), Am. Society Testing and Materials, Am. Society Engineering Education, Association Asphalt Paving Technologists, Am. Concrete Institute, Transportation Research Board, National Acad. Sciences (numerous committee activities on pavement management and design), International Society Soil Mechanics and Foundation Engineering, National Society Professional Engineers, Texas Society Professional Engineers, Texas Association College Teachers, Sigma Xi, Chi Epsilon, Tau Beta Pi. Republican. Office: The University of Tex at Austin Department of Civil Engring ECJ 6.10 Austin Texas 78712-1076

HUEBNER, JOHN STEPHEN, geologist; born Bryn Mawr, Pennsylvania, September 9, 1940; son of John Mudie and Elizabeth (Converse) H.; married Emily Mayer Zug, June 16, 1962; children: Christopher Converse, Jeffrey Worrell. Bachelor of Arts magna cum laude, Princeton University, 1962; Doctor of Philosophy, Johns Hopkins University, 1967. Research geologist United States Geological Survey, 1967—; consultant National Aeronautics and Space Administration, 1976-78; lecturer George Washington University, 1971; secretary-treasurer Am. Geological Institute, 1974-75. Associate editor: Journal Geophysical Research, 1977-79; Contributor articles professional journals. President Wood Acres Citizens Association, 1977-78. Fellow Mineralogical Society Am. (board directors 1985—, recipient award 1978); member Geochem. Society (treasurer 1972-75), Am. Geophysical Union, American Association for the Advancement of Science, Geological Society Washington, Sigma Xi. Club: Cosmos (Washington). Home: 6102 Cromwell Dr Bethesda Maryland 20816 Office: 959 National Center Reston Virginia 22092

HUEBNER, ROBERT JOSEPH, medical research scientist; born Cincinnati, February 23, 1914; son of Joseph Frederick and Philomena (Brickner) H.; married Harriet Lee, February 5, 1975; children by previous marriage—Elizabeth, Frances, Geraldine, James, Virginia, Roberta, Edward, Louise, Daniel. Student, Xavier University, 1932-35, University Cincinnati, 1937-38; Doctor of

Medicine, St. Louis University, 1942; Doctor of Laws, University Cincinnati, 1965; Doctor of Science (honorary), Edgecliff College, 1970, University Parma, Italy, 1970; Doctor of Science honorary degree, University Leuven, 1973. Commissioned junior assistant surgeon United States Public Health Service, 1942, advanced through grades to medical director; 1953; military duty Alaskan area United States Coast Guard, 1943- 44; virus and rickettsial disease research National Institutes of Health, 1944-56, chief virus section; 1949-56; chief laboratory infectious disease National Institute Allergy and Infectious Diseases, 1956-68; chief viral carcinogenesis branch National Cancer Institute, Bethesda, Maryland, 1968—; Gehrman lecturer University Illinois, 1955, Eli Lilly lecturer, 1957; Gudakunst lecturer University Michigan, 1958, Harvey lecturer, 1960, Puckett lecturer, 1960. Contributor numerous articles to professional journals. Recipient Bailey K. Ashford award, 1949; certificate merit St. Louis University, 1949; James D. Bruce Memorial award, 1964; Pasteur medal, 1965; Distinguished Service medal USPHS, 1966; Howard Taylor Ricketts award, 1968; National medal Sci., 1969; Kimble award, 1970; Rockefeller award, 1970; Guido Lenghi award, 1971. Fellow Am. Pub. Health Association, New York Acad. Sciences; member National Acad. Sciences, American Association for the Advancement of Science, Am. Association Immunologists, Am. Epidemiological Society, Federation Am. Socs. Experimental Biology and Medicine, Washington Acad. Sci. (award biological scis. 1949), International Union Against Cancer, Am. Acad. Microbiology, Am. Association Cancer Research, American Medical Association, Maryland Angus Association (president 1959-60), Sigma Xi, Alpha Omega Alpha. Home: 12100 Whippoorwill Lane Rockville Maryland 20852 Office: National Cancer Institute Lab Cellular/Molecular Biology Bethesda Maryland 20205

HUELKE, DONALD FRED, anatomy and cell biology educator, research scientist; born Illinois, August 20, 1930; son of Arthur August and Laura Sophia (Malon) H.; married Jean Louise Kilbert, May 17, 1932 (deceased); children—Donna, David. Bachelor of Science in Zoology, University Illinois, 1952, Master of Science in Physiology, 1954; Doctor of Philosophy in Anatomy, University Michigan, 1957. Teaching fellow University Illinois, Urbana, 1952-54; Teaching fellow University Michigan, Ann Arbor, 1954-57, instructor in anatomy; 1957-60, assistant professor anatomy; 1960-63, associate professor anatomy; 1963-68, professor; 1968—; consultant, General Motors, Warren, Michigan, 1965—, Ford Motor Company, Dearborn, Michigan, 1966—, Chrysler, Highland Park, Illinois, 1980—. Member Am. Association Automotive Medicine (award of merit 1982), Association Advancement Automotive Medicine, Society Automotive Engineers (Ralph Isbrandt award 1980, award for excellence in oral presentation 1980, 1982), International Association Auto and Traffic Medicine, Am. Trauma Society. Republican. Lutheran. Home: 861 Greenhills Dr Ann Arbor Michigan 48105 Office: U Michigan Department Anatomy Ann Arbor Michigan 48109 also: 2901 Baxter Road Ann Arbor Michigan 48109

HUGGINS, CHARLES BRENTON,

surgical educator; born Halifax, Nova Scotia, Canada, September 22, 1901; son of Charles Edward and Bessie (Spencer) H.; married Margaret Wellman, July 29, 1927; children: Charles Edward, Emily Wellman Huggins Fine. Bachelor of Arts, Acadia University, 1920, Doctor of Science (honorary), 1946; Doctor of Medicine, Harvard University, 1924; Master of Science, Yale, 1947; Doctor of Science (honorary), Washington University, St. Louis, 1950, Leeds University, 1953, Turin University, 1957, Trinity College, 1965, University Wales, 1967, University Michigan, 1968, Medical College Ohio, 1973, Gustavus Adolphus College, 1975, Wilmington (Ohio) College, 1980, University Louisville, 1980; Doctor of Laws (honorary), University Aberdeen, 1966, York University, Toronto, 1968, University California, Berkeley, 1968; Doctor of Pub. Service (honorary), George Washington University, 1967; Doctor of Pub. Service (honorary) sigillum magnum, Bologna University, 1964. Intern in surgery University Michigan, 1924-26, instructor surgery; 1926-27; with University Chicago, 1927—, instructor surgery; 1927-29, assistant professor; 1929-33, associate professor; 1933-36, professor surgery; 1936—, director Ben May Laboratory for Cancer Research; 1951-69, William B. Ogden Distinguished Service professor; 1962—; chancellor Acadia University, Wolfville, Nova Scotia, 1972-79; Macewen lecturer University Glasgow, 1958, Ravdin lecturer, 1974, Powell lecturer, Lucy Wortham James lecturer, 1975, Robert V. Day lecturer, 1975, Cartwright lecturer, 1975. Trustee Worcester Foundation Exptl. Biology; board governors Weizmann Institute Sci., Rehovot, Israel, 1973—.

Decorated Order Pour le Mérite Germany; Order of The Sun Peru; recipient Nobel prize for medicine, 1966, Am. Urological Association award, 1948, Francis Amory award, 1948, American Medical Association Gold medals, 1936, 40, Société Internationale d'Urologie award, 1948, Am. Cancer Society award, 1953, Bertner award M.D. Anderson Hospital, 1953, Am. Pharmaceutical Manufacturers Association award, 1953, Gold medal Am. Association Genito-Urinary Surgeons, 1955, Borden award Association Am. Medical Colleges, 1955, Comfort Crookshank award Middlesex Hospital, London, 1957, Cameron prize Edinburg University, 1958, Valentine prize New York Acad. Medicine, 1962, Hunter award Am. Therapeutic Society, 1962, Lasker award for med. research, 1963, Gold medal Virchow Society, 1964, Laurea award Am. Urological Association, 1966, Gold medal Worshipful Society Apothecaries of London, 1966, Gairdner award Toronto, 1966, Chicago Medical Society award, 1967, Centennial medal Acadia University, 1967, Hamilton award Illinois Medical Society, 1967, Bigelow medal Boston Surgical Society, 1967, Distinguished Service award Am. Society Abdominal Surgeons, 1972, Sheen award American Medical Association, 1970, Sesquicentennial Commemorative award National Library of Medicine, 1986; Charles Mickle fellow, 1958. Fellow American College of Surgeons (hon.), Royal College Surgeons Can. (hon.), Royal College Surgeons Scotland (hon.), Royal College Surgeons England (hon.), Royal Society Edinburgh (hon.), La Academia Nacional de Medicina (Mexico, hon.); member National Academy of Sciences (Charles L.

Meyer award for cancer research 1943), Am. Philos Society (Franklin medal 1985), Am. Association Cancer Research, Can. Medical Association (hon.), Alpha Omega Alpha. Home: 5807 Dorchester Avenue Chicago Illinois 60637 Office: U Chicago Ben May Lab Cancer Research 5841 S Maryland Avenue Chicago Illinois 60637

HULL, DAVID GEORGE, aerospace engineering educator, research; born Oak Park, Illinois, March 27, 1937; son of John Lawrence Hull and Elizabeth Christine (Carstensen) Meyer; married Meredith Lynn Kiesel, June 2, 1962 (divorced July 1980); children: David, Andrew, Matthew; married Vicki Jan Poole, June 30, 1983; 1 child, Katherine. Bachelor of Science, Purdue University, 1959; Master of Science, University Washington, 1962; Doctor of Philosophy, Rice University, 1967. Staff associate Boeing Sci. Research Laboratories, Seattle, 1959-64; research associate Rice University, Houston, 1964-66; assistant professor University Texas, Austin, 1966-71, associate professor; 1971-77, professor; 1977-85, M.J. Thompson Regents professor; 1985—; consultant several aerospace companies. Reviewer several engring. journals; contributor over 50 articles to professional journals. Recipient, co-recipient over 30 grants and contracts. Associate fellow American Institute of Aeronautics and Astronautics (atmospheric flight mechanics tech. committee 1974-77, guidance and control tech. committee 1984-87); member Delta Tau Delta (treasurer Purdue University 1958-59). Avocations: handball, softball, weekend farming. Office: U Tex Austin ASE/EM WRW 217 Austin Texas 78712

HUTCHINSON, JOHN WOODSIDE, applied mechanics educator, consultant; born Hartford, Connecticut, April 10, 1939; son of John Woodside and Evelyn (Eastburn) H.; married Helle Vilsen, August 28, 1964; children: Leif, David, Robert. Bachelor of Science, Lehigh University, 1960; Master of Science, Harvard University, 1961, Doctor of Philosophy, 1963; Doctor of Science (honorary), Royal Institute Tech., Stockholm, 1985. Assistant professor Harvard University, Cambridge, Massachusetts, 1964-69, Gordon McKay professor applied mechanics; 1969—; consultant to various industries; consultant Mobil Solar, Arthur D. Little, General Electric, Westinghouse, Alcoa. Contributor articles to professional journals. Guggenheim Foundation fellow, 1974.
Fellow American Society of Mechanical Engineers; member American Association for the Advancement of Science, National Acad. Engineering, American Society for Testing and Materials (Irwin medal 1982).

HUTCHINSON, THOMAS EUGENE, biomedical engineering educator; born York, South Carolina, August 1, 1936; married Colleen Ray, 1959; 2 children. Bachelor of Science, Clemson University, 1958, Master of Science, 1959; Doctor of Philosophy in Physics, University Virginia, 1963. Teaching assistant University Virginia, 1960-61; research fellow Atomic Energy Commission, 1962; senior scientist 3M Company, 1963-66, research specialist; 1966-67; associate professor chemical engineering and material sci. University Minnesota, 1967-74, professor; 1974-76; professor bioengring. and chemical engineering

University Washington, from 1976, associate dean engineering research; from 1982; William Stanfield Calcott professor biomed. engineering University Virginia, 1982—; consultant various organizations including 3M Company, Radio Corporation of America, North Star Research, 1967-73, on polography, federal agys., 1988; chairman Gordon Research Conference, 1970; visiting professor Cavendish Laboratory Cambridge, England, 1971; senior research fellow University Glasgow, Scotland, 1974—; chairman Bettelle Conference Microprobe Analysis, 1980, Acad. Conference on the Future of Sci. in the Southeast, 1987, Southeastern Universities Reasearch Association Materials Sci. committee, 1984—, SURA Conference on Synchrotron Radiation, 1986, 87, SURA select committee on the Future of Materials Service; member National Sci. Foundation select committee for Materials Service Centers, 1985-88; director SURA-COM Satellite Video Network, 1988. Patentee Eyegaze Response Computer Aid (ERICA), 1987. 2nd lieutenant Civil Air Patrol, 1987. Recipient Distinguished Service award Virginia Track Association, 1988. Elected senior fellow Biomedical Engineering Society; member Electron Microscopy Society Am., Am. Vaccuum Society, Virginia Advanced Tech. Association (board directors 1985—), Cosmos Club. Fields of research include microprobe analysis of biol. tissue-an application of physics tools to solution of questions of ion transport in excitable cells, eye gaze computer interface for the handicapped, psychological and drug impairment testing using eye gaze response analysis. Home: Hardendale Ivy Virginia 22945 Office: University Va School of Engring & Applied Sci Charlottesville Virginia 22903

HUTCHINSON, WILLIAM BURKE, surgeon, research center director; born Seattle, September 6, 1909; son of Joseph Lambert and Nona Bernice (Burke) H.; married Charlotte Rigdon, March 25, 1939; children: Charlotte J. Hutchinson Reed, William B., John L., Stuart R., Mary Hutchinson Wiese. Bachelor of Science, University Washington, Seattle, 1931; Doctor of Medicine, McGill University, 1936; Doctor of Humanities (honorary), University Seattle, 1982. Diplomate: Am. Board Surgery. Intern Baltimore City Hospital, 1936-37; resident Union Memorial Hospital, Baltimore, 1937-39, James Walker Memorial Hospital, Wilmington, North Carolina, 1939-40; surgeon Swedish Hospital and Medical Center, Seattle, 1941—, Providence Hospital, Seattle, 1941—; president, founding director Pacific Northwest Research Foundation, Seattle, 1955—; founding director Fred Hutchinson Cancer Research Center, Seattle, 1972-85; director Surgical Cancer Cons. Service, 1982—; clinical professor surgery emeritus University Washington; president 13th International Cancer Congress, 1978-82; member Yarborough committee for writing National Cancer Act, 1970. Contributing editor, 13th International Cancer Congress. Recipient 1st Citizen of Seattle award, 1976, Alumnus Summa Laude Dignatus award University Washington, 1983, Washington State award of Merit, 1988. Fellow American College of Surgeons; member American Medical Association, King County Medical Society, Seattle Surgical Association, North Pacific Surgical Association, Pacific Coast Surgical Association,

Western Surgical Association, Society Surgical Oncologists, National Research Council, Alpha Sigma Phi. Clubs: Men's University (Seattle); Seattle Golf and Country. Home: 7126-55th Avenue Southern Seattle Washington 98118 Office: Pacific Northwest Research Found 720 Broadway Seattle Washington 98122

HUTCHISON, CLYDE ALLEN, III, microbiology educator; born New York City, November 26, 1938; married; 3 children. Bachelor of Science, Yale University, 1960; Doctor of Philosophy in Biophysics, California Institute Tech., 1969. From assistant professor to associate professor University North Carolina, Chapel Hill, 1968-78, professor bacteriology School Medicine; 1978—, now Kenan professor microbiology and immunology. National Institutes of Health grantee, 1969-82; recipient Research Career Devel. award National Institutes of Health, 1973-78. Fields of research include physiol. genetics of bacterial viruses; phys. genetic analysis of eukaryotic DNA; restriction enzymes; gene putrification; DNA sequencing. Office: U of North Carolina Department Biology Chapel Hill North Carolina 27514

HUXLEY, SIR ANDREW (FIELDING), physiologist, educator emeritus; born London, November 22, 1917; son of Leonard and Rosalind (Bruce) H.; married Jocelyn Richenda Gammell Pease, July 5, 1947; children: Janet Rachel, Stewart Leonard, Camilla Rosalind, Eleanor Bruce, Henrietta Catherine, Clare Marjory Pease. Bachelor of Arts, Cambridge (England) University, 1938, Master of Arts, 1941, Doctor of Science (honorary), 1978; Doctor of Medicine (honorary), University Saar, 1964; Doctor of Science (honorary), University Sheffield, England, 1964, University Leicester, England, 1967, London University, 1973, University St. Andrews, Scotland, 1974, University Aston, Birmingham, England, 1977; Doctor of Laws (honorary), University Birmingham, 1979, Marseille University, 1979, York University, 1981, University Western Australia, 1982, New York University, 1982, Oxford University, 1983, University Pennsylvania, 1984, Dundee University, 1984, Harvard University, 1984, University Keele, 1985, East Anglia University, 1985, Humboldt University, East Berlin, 1985, Maryland University, 1987, Brunel University, 1988. Member research staff Anti-Aircraft Command, 1940-42, Admiralty, 1942-45; fellow Trinity College, Cambridge, 1941-60, hon. fellow; 1967—, master; 1984—, director studies; 1952-60; demonstrator Cambridge University, 1946-50, assistant director research, 1951-59, reader experimental biophysics, 1959-60; Jodrell professor physiology University College London, 1960-69, Royal Society research professor, 1969-83, hon. fellow, 1980; emeritus professor physiology University London, 1983—; Herter lecturer Johns Hopkins University, 1959; Jesup lecturer Columbia University, 1964; Forbes lecturer, 1966; Croonian lecturer Royal Society, 1967, Florey lecturer, 1982, Blackett Memorial lecturer, 1984; Fullerian professor Royal Institute, London, 1967-73; Hans Hecht lecturer, Chicago, 1975; Sherrington lecturer Liverpool University, 1976-77; Centenary Colloquium lecturer Berlin Institute Physiology, 1977; Cecil H. and Ida Green visiting professor University British Columbia, 1980; 6th annual Darwin Lecture, 1982; Tarner lecturers Trinity College, Cambridge,

1988; chairman Brit. National Committee for Physiol. Sciences, 1979. Author: Reflections on Muscle, 1980; editor: Journal Physiology, 1950-57, chairman board Publications on analysis of nerve conduction (with Hodgkin), physiology of striated muscle, devel. of interference microscope and ultramicrotome. Trustee Brit. Mus. (Natural History), 1981—, Sci. Mus., 1984-88. Created knight bachelor, 1974; decorated Order of Merit, 1983; recipient (with A.L. Hodgkin and J.C. Eccles) Nobel prize for physiology or medicine, 1963; Imperial College Sci. and Tech. fellow, 1980; fellowship of engineering (hon.) 1986. Fellow Royal Society (Copley medal 1973, council 1960-62, 77-79, 80-85, president 1980-85), Institute Biology (hon.), Royal Society Can. (hon.), Royal Society Edinburgh (hon.), Indian National Sci. Acad. (foreign); member Physiological Society (hon., rev. lecturer on muscular contraction 1973), International Union Physiological Sciences (president 1986—), Brit. Biophys. Society, Royal Acad. Sciences, Letters and Fine Arts Belgium (associate), Muscular Dystrophy Group Great Britain and Northern Ireland (chairman med. research committee 1974-81, vice president, 1981—), Royal Institution Great Britain (hon.), Anatomical Society Great Britain and Ireland (hon.), Am. Philosophical Society, Brit. Association Advancement Sci. (president 1976-77), National Academy of Sciences (United States) (foreign associate), Agricultural Research Council, Royal Acad. Medicine Belgium (associate), Dutch Society Sciences (foreign), Am. Society Zoologists (hon.), Royal Irish Acad. (hon.), Japan Acad. (hon.), Nature Conservancy (council 1985-87). Office: Trinity College, Master's Lodge, Cambridge CB2 1TQ, England also: care Royal Society, 6 Carlton House Terrace, London SW1Y 5AG, England

HYMES, DELL HATHAWAY, anthropologist; born Portland, Oregon, June 7, 1927; son of Howard Hathaway and Dorothy (Bowman) H.; married Virginia Margaret Dosch, April 10, 1954; 1 adopted child, Robert Paul; children: Alison Bowman, Kenneth Dell; 1 stepchild, Vicki (Mrs. David Unruh). Bachelor of Arts, Reed College, 1950; Master of Arts, Ind. University, 1953, Doctor of Philosophy, 1955; postgraduate, University of California at Los Angeles, 1954-55. Instructor, then assistant professor Harvard University, 1955-60; associate professor, then professor University California, Berkeley, 1960-65; professor anthropology University Pennsylvania, 1965-72, professor folklore and linguistics; 1972-88, professor sociology; 1974-88, professor education; 1975-88, dean University Grad. School Education; 1975-87; professor anthropology and English University Virginia, 1987—; board of directors Social Sci. Research Council, 1965-67, 69-70, 71-72; trustee Center for Applied Linguistics, 1973-78. Author: Language in Culture and Society, 1964, The Use of Computers in Anthropology, 1965, Studies in Southwestern Ethnolinguistics, 1967, Pidginization and Creolization of Languages, 1971, Reinventing Anthropology, 1972, Foundations in Sociolinguistics, 1974, Studies in the History of Linguistics, 1974, Soziolinguistik, 1980, Language in Education, 1980, In Vain I Tried to Tell You, 1981, (with John Fought) American Structuralism, 1981, Essays in the History of Linguistic Anthropology, 1983, Vers la Competence Communicative, 1984; associate editor: Journal History Behavioral Scis, 1966—, Am. Journal Sociology, 1977-80, Journal Pragmatics, 1977—; contributing editor: Alcheringa, 1973-80, Theory and Society, 1976—; editor: Language in Society, 1972—. Served with Army of the United States, 1945-47. Fellow Center Advanced Study Behavioral Sciences, 1957-58; fellow Clare Hall, Cambridge, England; Guggenheim fellow, 1969—; National Endowment for Humanities sr. fellow, 1972-73. Fellow Am. Folklore Society (president 1973-74); member Am. Anthropological Association (executive board 1968-70, president 1983), Am. Association Applied Linguistics (president 1986), Linguistic Society Am. (executive board 1967-69, president 1982), Am. Acad. Arts and Sciences (council 1979-80), Council on Anthropology and Education (president 1978), Consortium Social Sci. Assns. (president 1984-85). Home: 205 Montvue Dr Charlottesville Virginia 22901

INGLE, JAMES CHESNEY, JR., geology educator; born Los Angeles, November 6, 1935; son of James Chesney and Florence Adelaide (Geldart) I.; married Fredricka Ann Bornholdt, June 14, 1958; 1 child, Douglas James. Bachelor of Science in Geology, University Southern California, 1959, Master of Science in Geology, 1962, Doctor of Philosophy in Geology, 1966. Registered geologist, California. Research associate University Southern California, 1961-65; visiting scholar Tohoku University, Sendai, Japan, 1966-67; assistant, associate to full professor Stanford University,

California, 1968—; W.M. Keck professor earth sciences Stanford University, 1984—, chairman department geology; 1982—; co-chief scientist Leg 31 Deep Sea Drilling Project, 1973; geologist United States Geological Survey W.A.E, 1978-81. Author: Movement of Beach Sand, 1966; contributor articles to professional journals. Recipient W.A. Tarr award Sigma Gamma Epsilon, 1958; named Distinguished lecturer Am. Association Petroleum Geologists, 1986-87; A.I. Leverson award Am. Association Petroleum Geologists, 1988. Fellow Geological Society Am., California Acad. of Sciences; member Cushman Foundation (board directors 1984—), Society Professional Paleontological and Mineralogists (Pacific section 1958—), American Association for the Advancement of Science.

IRWIN, JAMES BENSON, former astronaut, foundation executive, aeronautical engineer; born Pittsburgh, March 17, 1930; son of James and Elsie (Strebel) I.; married Mary Ellen Monroe, September 4, 1959; children: Joy Carmel, Jill Cherie, James Benson, Jan Caron, Joe Chau. Bachelor of Science, United States Naval Academy, 1951; Master of Science in Aeronautical Engineering, University Michigan, 1957, Doctor Astronautical Science, 1971; Doctor of Science, William Jewell College, 1971, Samford University, 1972. Commissioned 2d lieutenant United States Air Force, 1951, advanced through grades to colonel; 1971; project officer Wright Patterson Air Force Base, 1957-60; test director (ASG-18/AIM-47 armament system), Edwards Air Force Base, California, 1961-63; test pilot (F-12 Test Force), Edwards Air Force

Base, 1963-65; branch chief (Advanced Systems Headquarters Air Defense Command), Colorado Springs, Colorado, 1965-66; astronaut National Aeronautics and Space Administration, 1966-72. Author: To Rule the Night, 1973, rev. edition, 1982, More Than Earthlings, 1983, More Than an Ark on Ararat, 1985. Founder, president evang. foundation High Flight, Colorado Springs, Colorado, 1972. Decorated National Aeronautics and Space Administration Distinguished Service Medal, Distinguished Service Medal USAF, City New York Gold Medal, United Nations Peace medal, City Chicago Gold medal; order Leopold Belgium; recipient David C. Schilling trophy, 1971, Kitty Hawk memorial award, 1971, Haley Astronautics award American Institute of Aeronautics and Astronautics, 1972, John F. Kennedy trophy Arnold Air Society, 1972, Freedoms Foundation Washington medal, 1976, National Citizenship award Mil. Chaplains Association, 1978, others. Member Air Force Association, Society Experimental Test Pilots. Baptist. Member support crew Apollo 10; backup lunar module pilot Apollo 12; lunar module pilot Apollo 15 moon landing crew, July 30, 1971. Office: High Flight Post Office Box 1387 Colorado Springs Colorado 80901

ITOH, TATSUO, engineering educator; born Tokyo, May 5, 1940; son of Yohnosuke and Kimi (Okamoto) I.; married Seiko Fukumori, June 16, 1969; children: Akihiro, Eiko. Bachelor of Science, Yokohama National University, Japan, 1964, Master of Science, 1966; Doctor of Philosophy, University Illinois, 1969. Registered prof. engineer, Texas. Research associate University Illinois, Urbana, 1969-71, research assistant professor; 1971-76; senior research engineer Stanford Research Institute, Menlo Park, California, 1976-77; associate professor University Kentucky, Lexington, 1977-78; associate professor University Texas, Austin, 1978-81, professor; 1981—, Hayden Head professor; 1983—; guest researcher AEG-Telefunken, Ulm, W. Ger., 1979; consultant Texas Instruments, Dallas, 1979, Hughes Aircraft. Guest editor: Transactions, 1981; inventor millimeter-wave line, 1975, quasi-optical mixer, 1982. Recipient Engineering Foundation faculty awards, 1980-81, Billy and Claude Hocott Distinguished Rsch. award, 1988. Fellow Institute of Electrical and Electronics Engineers; member Microwave Theory and Techniques Society (editor 1983-85), International Sci. Radio Union (chairman USNC commission D), Institute Electronics and Communication Engineers. Home: 3801 Green Trails N Austin Texas 78731 Office: U Texas Department Elec Engring Austin Texas 78712

IVERSEN, JAMES DELANO, aerospace engineering educator, consultant; born Omaha, April 1, 1933; son of Alfred and Asta Marie (Jorgensen) I.; married Margery Lynn Peters, August 20, 1960; children—David S., Philip W. Bachelor of Science, Iowa State University, Ames, 1956, Master of Science, 1958, Doctor of Philosophy, 1964. Professor aerospace engineering Iowa State University, Ames, 1958—; aerodynamicist Sandia Corp., Albuquerque, 1966, National Aeronautics and Space Administration Ames Research Center, Mountain View, California, 1973-74, Boeing Commercial Airplane Company,

Seattle, 1978, Skibsteknisk Laboratory, Lyngby, Denmark, 1981; consultant to governmental agys., industry. Co-author: Wind As A Geological Process, 1985; also articles to professional journals. Board of directors Black Elk-Neihardt Park, Blair, Nebraska, 1984—, Danish Immigrant Mus., Elk Horn, Iowa, 1985—. Recipient Faculty citation Iowa State University, 1982, Distinguished Alumnus award Dana College, 1987. Associate fellow American Institute of Aeronautics and Astronautics (senior scholar 1956, section president 1975-77); member Am. Geophysical Union, The Planetary Society, Am. Society Engineering Education, (affiliate) American Society of Civil Engineers, Sigma Xi, Phi Kappa Phi, Tau Beta Pi, Sigma Gamma Tau. Republican. Lutheran. Lodge: Rotary (Ames). Avocations: photography; genealogy. Office: Iowa State U 304 Town Engr Building Ames Iowa 50011

JACOB, FRANÇOIS, biologist; born Nancy, France, June 17, 1920; son of Simon and Therese (Franck) J.; married Lysiane Bloch, November 27, 1947 (deceased 1984); children: Pierre, Laurent, Odile, Henri. Doctor of Medicine, Faculty of Medicine, Paris, 1947; Doctor of Science, Faculty of Scis., Paris, 1954; Doctor of Science (honorary), University Chicago, 1965. Assistant Pasteur Institute, 1950-56, head department cellular genetics; 1960—, president, director; 1982—; professor cellular genetics College of France, 1964—. Author: The Logic of Life, 1970; The Possible and the Actual, 1981, The Statue Within, 1987. Recipient Charles Leopold Mayer prize, 1962; Nobel prize in physiology and medicine (with A. Lwoff and J.

Monod), 1965. Member Académie des Sciences (Paris); foreign member Am. Acad. Arts and Sciences, National Acad. Sciences (United States), Am. Philosophical Society, Royal Society (London), Académie Royale de Médecine de Belgique, Acad. Sciences Hungary, Royal Acad. Sciences Madrid. Research on genetics bacterial cells and viruses; contbr. to mechanisms of info. transfer (messenger RNA) and genetic basis of regulatory circuits, early stages of the mouse embryo. Office: Pasteur Institute, 25 Rue de D'Roux, 75015 Paris France

JACOBS, JOSEPH DONOVAN, engineering firm executive; born Motley, Minnesota, December 24, 1908; son of Sherman William and Edith Mary (Donovan) J.; married Virginia Mary O'Meara, February 8, 1937; 1 son, John Michael. Bachelor of Science in Civil Engineering, University Minnesota, 1934. Civil engineer, construction supervisor Walsh Construction Company, New York City and San Francisco, 1934-54; chief engineer Kaiser-Walsh-Perini-Raymond, Australia, 1954-55; founder, senior officer Jacobs Associates, San Francisco, 1955—; Chairman, United States national committee on tunnelling tech. National Acad. Sciences, 1977. Recipient Golden Beaver award for engineering, 1980; Non-Mem. award Moles, 1981. Fellow American Society of Civil Engineers, Institution Engineers Australia; member National Acad. Engineering, Am. Institute Mining and Metallurgical Engineers, National Society Professional Engineers, Delta Chi. Clubs: Corinthian Yacht, World Trade, Engineers (San Francisco). Inventor in field of mining and tunnel excavation. Office: Jacobs Engring Group Incorporated 500 Sansome St San Francisco California 94111

JAMES, THOMAS NAUM, cardiologist, educator; born Amory, Mississippi, October 24, 1925; son of Naum and Kata J.; married Gleaves Elizabeth Tynes, June 22, 1948; children—Thomas Mark, Terrence Fenner, Peter Naum. Bachelor of Science, Tulane University, 1946, Doctor of Medicine, 1949. Diplomate Am. Board Internal Medicine (bd. govs. 1982-88), Board Cardiovascular Diseases (bd. dirs. 1972-78). Intern Henry Ford Hospital, Detroit, 1949-50, resident in internal medicine and cardiology; 1950-53, member staff; 1959-68; practice medicine specializing in cardiology Birmingham, Alabama, 1968-87; member staff University Alabama Hospitals, 1968-87; instructor medicine Tulane University, New Orleans, 1955-58, assistant professor; 1959; professor medicine University Alabama Medical Center, Birmingham, 1968-87, professor pathology; 1968-73, associate professor physiology and biophysics; 1969-73, director Cardiovascular Research and Training Center; 1970-77, chairman department medicine, director div. cardiovascular disease; 1973-81, Mary Gertrude Waters professor cardiology; 1976-87, Distinguished professor of university; 1981-87; professor medicine and pathology, president University Texas Medical Branch, Galveston, 1987—; member adv. council National Heart Lung and Blood Institute, 1975-79; president 10th World Congress Cardiology, 1986; member cardiology del. invited by Chinese Medical Association to People's Republic of China, 1978. Author: Anatomy of the Coronary Arteries, 1961, The Etiology of Myocardial Infarction, 1963; Member editorial board: Circulation, 1966-83; member editorial board: Am. Journal Cardiology, 1968-76; associate editor, 1976-82; member editorial board: Am. Heart Jour, 1976-79; Contributor articles on cardiovascular diseases to medical journals. Served as captain Medical Corps United States Army, 1953-55. Fellow American College of Physicians (governor Alabama 1975-79, master 1983); member American Medical Association, Am. Clinical and Climatological Association, Association Am. Physicians, Am. Society Clinical Investigation, Association University Cardiologists (president 1978-79), Am. Heart Association (president 1979-80), Am. College Cardiology (vice president 1970-71, trustee 1970-71, 76-81, First Distinguished Scientist award 1982), Am. Society Pharmacology and Experimental Therapeutics, Society Experimental Biology of Medicine, Am. College Chest Physicians, Central Society Clinical Research, International Society and Federation Cardiology (president 1983-84), Southern Society Clinical Investigation, Am. Federation Clinical Research, Phi Beta Kappa, Sigma Xi, Omicron Delta Kappa, Alabama Acad. Honor, Alpha Omega Alpha, Alpha Tau Omega, Phi Chi. Presbyterian. Clubs: Cosmos, Mountain Brook, Galveston Artillery. Office: U Tex Med Br 301 University Boulevard Galveston Texas 77550

JANZEN, DANIEL HUNT, biology educator; born Milwaukee, January 18, 1939; son of Daniel Hugo and Floyd (Foster) J. Bachelor of Science, University Minnesota, 1961; Doctor of Philosophy, University California, Berkeley, 1965. Assistant professor University Kansas, Lawrence, 1965-68; associate professor University Chicago, 1969-72; associate professor, professor biology University Michigan, Ann Arbor, 1972-76; professor biology University Pennsylvania, Philadelphia, 1976—; member faculty Organization for Tropical Studies, City University, Costa Rica, 1965—; friend National Park Service Costa Rica, San Jose, 1972—. Co-editor: Herbivores, 1979; editor Costa Rican Natural History, 1983; contributor over 250 articles on ecology, evolution, systematics, and tropical biology to sci. journals. Served with Member of Parliament, United States Army, 1957. Recipient Crafoord prize for coevolutionary ecology Swedish Royal Acad. Sciences, 1984. Member Brit. Ecological Society, Ecological Society Am., Am. Society Naturalists, Association for Tropical Biology, American Association for the Advancement of Science. Avocation: tropical biology. Office: U Pennsylvania Department Biology Philadelphia Pennsylvania 19104

JARVIK, ROBERT K., biomedical research scientist; born Midland, Michigan, May 11, 1946; son of Norman Eugene and Edythe (Koffler) J. Bachelor of Arts, Syracuse University, 1968, Doctor of Science (honorary), 1983; Master of Arts, New York University, 1971; Doctor of Medicine, University Utah, 1976; Doctor Science (honorary), Hahnemann University, 1985. Research assistant Div. Artificial Organs-U. Utah, Salt Lake City, 1971-76, assistant director experimental laboratories; 1976-82; president Symbion, Incorporated, Salt Lake City, 1981-87; assistant research professor University Utah, 1979-87;

member national selection panel National Aeronautics and Space Administration Teacher in Space Project, Washington, 1985; president Jarvik Research Incorporated, New York City, 1987—. Sect. editor: International Journal Artificial Organs, 1979—; inventor repeating hemostatic clip instruments and cartridges, total artificial hearts powered by electrohydraulic energy; patentee in field. Named Inventor of Year Intellectual Property Owners, 1983; named John W. Hyatt award Society Plastics Engrs., 1983, Golden Plate Am. Acad. Achievement, 1983, Gold Heart award Utah Heart Association, 1983. Member Am. Society Artificial Internal Organs. Office: Jarvik Research Incorporated 124 W 60th St New York New York 10023

JASTROW, ROBERT, physicist; born New York City, September 7, 1925; son of Abraham and Marie (Greenfield) J. Bachelor of Arts, Columbia, 1944, Master of Arts, 1945, Doctor of Philosophy, 1948; post-doctoral fellow, Leiden University, 1948-49, Princeton Institute Advanced Study, 1949-50, 53, University California at Berkeley, 1950-53; Doctor of Science (honorary), Manhattan College, 1980, New Jersey Institute Tech., 1987. Assistant professor Yale, 1953-54; consultant nuclear physics United States Naval Research Laboratory, Washington, 1958-62; head theoretical div. Goddard Space Flight Center National Aeronautics and Space Administration, 1958-61, chairman lunar exploration committee; 1959-60, member committee; 1960-62; director Goddard Institute Space Studies, New York City, 1961-81; adj. professor geology Columbia, 1961-81, director Summer Institute Space Physics;

1962-70; adj. professor astronomy Columbia (Summer Institute Space Physics), 1977-82; adj. professor earth sci. Dartmouth, 1973—; president G.C. Marshall Institute, 1985—. Author: The Evolution of Stars, Planets and Life, 1967, Astronomy: Fundamentals and Frontiers, 1972, Until the Sun Dies, 1977, God and the Astronomers, 1978, Red Giants-White Dwarfs, 1979, The Enchanted Loom, 1981, How To Make Nuclear Weapons Obsolete, 1985; editor: Exploration of Space, 1960; co-editor: Journal Atmospheric Scis, 1962-74, The Origin of the Solar System, 1963, The Venus Atmosphere, 1969. Recipient Medal of Excellence Columbia, 1962, Graduate Faculties Alumni award, 1967; Arthur S. Flemming award, 1965; medal for exceptional sci. achievement National Aeronautics and Space Administration, 1968. Fellow Am. Geophysical Union, A.A.A.S., Am. Physical Society; member International Acad. Astronautics, Council Foreign Relations, Leakey Foundation. Clubs: Cosmos, Explorers, Century. Home: Box 191 Hanover New Hampshire 03755

JEFFERIES, JOHN TREVOR, astronomer, astrophysicist, observatory administrator; born Kellerberrin, Australia, April 2, 1925; came to United States, 1956, naturalized, 1967; son of John and Vera (Healy) J.; married Charmian Candy, September 10, 1949; children: Stephen R., Helen C., Trevor R. Master of Arts, Cambridge (England) University, 1949; Doctor of Science, University Western Australia, Nedlands, 1962. Senior research staff High Altitude Observatory, Boulder, Colorado, 1957-59, Sacramento Peak Observatory, Sunspot, New Mexico, 1957-59; professor adjoint University Colorado, Boulder, 1961-64; professor physics and astronomy University Hawaii, Honolulu, 1964-83; director, Institute Astronomy; 1967-83; director National Optical Astronomy Observatory, Tucson, 1983-87; consultant National Bureau Standards, Boulder, 1960-62. Author: (monograph) Spectral Line Formation, 1968; contributor articles to professional journals. Guggenheim fellow, 1970-71. Fellow American Association for the Advancement of Science, Royal Astronomical Society; member International Astronomical Union, Am. Astronomical Society, Australian Astronomical Society. Home: 6760 N Placita Manzanita Tucson Arizona 85718 Office: National Optical Astronomy Obs Post Office Box 26732 Tucson Arizona 85726

JENNINGS, JESSE DAVID, anthropology educator; born Oklahoma City, July 7, 1909; son of Daniel Wellman and Grace (Cruce) J.; married Jane Noyes Chase, September 7, 1935; children: Jesse David, Herbert Lee. Bachelor of Arts, Montezuma College, 1929; Doctor of Philosophy, University Chicago, 1943; Doctor of Science, University Utah, 1980. Anthropologist National Park Service, 1937-42, 45-48; member faculty University Utah, 1948—, professor anthropology; 1949-86, professor emeritus; 1986—, distinguished research professor; 1970—, distinguished professor anthropology; 1975—; Member anthropology-psychology div. National Acad. Sci.-NRC, 1954-56; visiting professor anthropology Northwestern University, 1960, University Minnesota, 1961, University Hawaii,

1965, 67-68; adj. professor University Oregon, 1980—; lecturer summer institute anthropology University Colorado, 1961, Fairmont College, 1962; lecturer semi-centennial symposium Am. archeology Rice University, 1962; Reynolds lecturer University Utah, 1962, Leigh lecturer, 1975; director Glen Canyon Archeological Salvage Project, 1957-66, Utah Mus. Natural History, 1965-73; consultant institutional studies National Science Foundation, 1964-66. Author: (with A.V. Kidder and E.M. Shook) Excavations at Kaminal Juyu, Guatemala, 1946, (with E.A. Hoebel) Readings in Anthropology, 3d edit, 1972, The Archeology of the Plains: An Assessment, 1956, Danger Cave, 1957, also numerous articles, reports, papers.; Editor: (with Edward Norbeck) Prehistoric Man in the New World, 1964, (with Robert F. Spencer) Native Americans, 1965, 2d edition, 1977, Prehistory of North America, 1968, 3d edition, 1989, Warner Modular Publications in Anthropology, 1972-74, (with others) Pacific Anthrop. Records Northern 25, 1976, Ancient Native Americans, 1978, (with others) Prehistory of Utah and the Eastern Great Basin, 1978, Prehistory of Polynesia, 1979, Cowboy Cave, 1980, Bull Creek, 1981, Ancient North Americans, Ancient South Americans; editor for: (with others) North America, Atlas of Archaeology, Rainbird Reference Books, 1972. Served to commander United States Naval Reserve, 1942-45. Recipient Viking medal in archaeology Wenner Gren Foundation Anthrop. Research, 1958. Member National Acad. Sci., Society Am. Archaeology (editor bull. 1950-54, president 1958-59, Distinguished Service award 1982), Am. Anthropological Association (executive board 1953-56), American Association for the Advancement of Science (national vice president, chairman section H 1961, 69), Sigma Xi, Phi Kappa Phi. Home: 21801 Siletz Highway Siletz Oregon 97380

JENNINGS, PAUL CHRISTIAN, engineering educator; born Brigham City, Utah, May 21, 1936; son of Robert Webb and Elva S. (Simonsen) J.; married Millicent Marie Backman, August 28, 1981; married Barbara Elaine Morgan, September 3, 1960 (divorced 1981); children—Kathryn Diane, Margaret Ann. Bachelor of Science in Civil Engineering, Colorado State University, 1958; Master of Science in Civil Engineering, California Institute Tech., 1960, Doctor of Philosophy, 1963. Professor civil engineering, applied mechanics California Tech. Institute, Pasadena, 1966—, chairman div. engring, applied sci.; 1985—; member faculty board California Tech. Institute, 1974-76, steering committee, 1974-76, chairman nominating committee, 1975, engineering applied sci. div. undergrad. council, 1973-75, grad. studies committee, 1978-80; consultant in field. Author: (with others) Earthquake Design Criteria. Contributor numerous articles to professional journals. Served to 1st lieutenant United States Air Force, 1965-66. Recipient Walter Huber award American Society of Civil Engineers, 1973; Erskine fellow University Canterbury, New Zealand, 1970, 85. Fellow American Association for the Advancement of Science, New Zealand Society Earthquake Engineering; member American Society of Civil Engineers, Seismological Society Am. (president 1980), Earthquake Engineering Research Institute (president 1981-83). Club: Athenaeum (Pasadena).

Avocations: fly fishing; running. Home: 1414 Edgecliff Lane Pasadena California 91107 Office: California Institute Tech Div Engring Applied Sci Pasadena California 91125

JERNE, NIELS KAJ, scientist; born London, December 23, 1911; son of Hans Jessen and Else Marie (Lindberg) J.; married Ursula Alexandra Kohl, 1964; 2 children. Graduate, University Leiden, University Copenhagen; honorary degrees, University Chicago, University Copenhagen, University Basel, University Rotterdam, Columbia University. Research worker Danish State Serum Institute, Copenhagen, 1943-55; chief medical officer World Health Organization, Geneva, 1956-62; professor biophysics University Geneva, 1960-62; chairman department microbiology University Pittsburgh, 1962-66; professor experimental therapy J.W. Goethe University, Frankfurt, 1966-69; director Basel Institute for Immunology, 1969-80; professor Institute Pasteur, Paris, 1981-82. Contributor articles to professional journals. Recipient Marcel Benoist prize, Berne, 1979, Paul Ehrlich prize, Frankfurt, 1982; shared Nobel prize for medicine, 1984. Member Am. Philosophical Society, Acad. des Sciences de l'Inst. de France, member Am. Acad. Arts and Sciences, United States of America National Acad. Sciences, others. Office: Basel Institute Immunology, CH-4058 Basel Switzerland also: Chateau de Bellevue, Castillon-du-Nord, 30210 Gard France

JIRSA, JAMES OTIS, civil engineering educator; born Lincoln, Nebraska, July 30, 1938; son of Otis Frank and Anna Marie (Skutchan) J.; married Marion Ansley Coad, August 7, 1941; children: David, Stephen. Bachelor of Science, University Nebraska, 1960; Master of Science, University Illinois, 1962, Doctor of Philosophy, 1963. Registered professional engineer, Texas. Assistant professor civil engineering University Nebraska, Lincoln, 1964-65; assistant professor then associate professor Rice University, Houston, 1965-72; associate professor then professor University Texas, Austin, 1972-82, Finch professor engineering; 1982-84, Ferguson professor civil engineering; 1984-88, director Ferguson Structural Engineering Laboratory; 1985-88, Janet South Cockrell Centennial chair in engineering; 1988—; research engineer Portland Cement Associates, 1965; engineer J.J. Degenkolb Associates, San Francisco, 1980. Contributor articles to professional journals. Fulbright scholar, Paris, 1963-64. Fellow Am. Concrete Institute (TAC chairman 1985-88, board directors 1987—, Alfred Lindau award 1986, Wason medal 1977, Reese award 1977, 79); member American Society of Civil Engineers (committee chairman 1972-81, Reese award 1970, Huber Research prize 1978), Earthquake Engineering Research Institute, Structural Engring Association Texas, International Association for Bridge and Structural Engineers, National Acad. Engineering. Office: U Tex/Austin - Ferguson Structural Engring Lab 10100 Burnet Road Austin Texas 78758

JOBS, STEVEN PAUL, computer corporation executive; born 1955; adopted son of Paul J. and Clara J. (Jobs). Student, Reed College. With Hewlett-Packard, Palo Alto, California; designer video games Atari Incorporated, 1974; co-founder Apple

Computer Incorporated, Cupertino, California, chairman board; 1975-85, former director; president NeXT, Incorporated, Palo Alto, California, 1985—. Co-designer: (with Stephan Wozniak) Apple I Computer, 1976. Office: NeXT Incorporated 3475 Deer Creek Road Palo Alto California 94304

JOHANSON, DONALD CARL, physical anthropologist; born Chicago, June 28, 1943; son of Carl Torsten and Sally Eugenia (Johnson) J. ; married Lenora Carey, 1988. Bachelor of Arts, University Illinois, 1966; Master of Arts, University Chicago, 1970, Doctor of Philosophy, 1974; Doctor of Science (honorary), John Carroll University, 1979; Doctor of Science (honorary), College of Wooster, 1985. Member department physical anthropology Cleveland Mus. Natural History, 1972-81, curator; 1974-81; director Institute Human Origins, Berkeley, California, 1981—; professor anthropology Stanford University, 1983—; adj. professor Case Western Reserve University, 1978-81, Kent State University, 1978-81. Co-author: (with M.A. Edey) Of Lucy: The Beginning of Humankind, 1982 (Am. Book award 1982), Blue Prints: Solving the Mystery of Evolution, 1989; film producer: The First Family, 1981, Lucy in Disguise, 1982; contributor numerous sci. articles, papers, reviews; host, narrator Pub. Broadcasting Service NATURE series, 1982. Recipient Jared Potter Kirtland award for outstanding sci. achievement Cleveland Mus. Natural History, 1979, Professional Achievement award, University Chicago, 1980, Gold Mercury International ad personem award Ethiopia, 1982, Humanist Laureate award Acad. of Humanism, 1983, Distinguished Service award Am. Humanist Association, 1983, San Francisco Exploratorium award, 1986, International Premio Fregene award, 1987; grantee Wenner-Gren Foundation, National Science Foundation, National Geog. Society, L.S.B. Leakey Foundation, Cleveland Foundation, George Gund Foundation, Roush Foundation, National Geog. Society. Fellow American Association for the Advancement of Science, California Acad. Sciences, Rochester (New York) Mus., Royal Geog. Society; member Am. Association Physical Anthropologists, International Association Dental Research, International Association Human Biologists, Am. Association Africanist Archaeologists, Society Vertebrate Paleontology, Society Study of Human Biology, Explorers Club, Societe de l'Anthropologie de Paris, Centro Studi Ricerche Ligabue (Venice), Founders' Council, Chicago Field Mus. Natural History (hon.), Association Internationale pour l'etude de Paleontologie Humaine, Mus. National d'Histoire Naturelle de Paris (corr.), National Center Sci. Education (supporting scientist). Office: Institute Human Origins 2453 Ridge Road Berkeley California 94709

JOHN, FRITZ, mathematician, educator; born Berlin, Germany, June 14, 1910; came to United States, 1935, naturalized, 1941; son of Hermann and Hedwig (Buergel) Jacobsohn-John; married Charlotte Woellmer; children—Thomas Franklin, Charles Frederic. Doctor of Philosophy, Goettingen (Germany) University, 1933; student, Cambridge (England) University, 1934-35; honorary degrees, University Rome, University Bath, University Heidelberg. Assistant, the associate professor University Kentucky, 1935-42;

mathematician Aberdeen Proving Grounds, 1942-45; professor math. New York University, 1946—; Courant professor Courant Institute, 1976-79; director Research Institute Numerical Analysis, National Bureau Standards, 1950-51; special research applied math., math. analysis; Sherman Fairchild distinguished scholar California Institute Tech., 1979-80; Josiah Willard Gibbs lecturer Am. Math. Society, 1975. Author: Plane Waves and Spherical Means, 1955, (with L. Bers and M.S. Schechter) Partial Differential Equations, 1964, (with R. Courant) Introduction to Calculus and Analysis, 1965, Partial Differential Equations, 1978. Recipient G.D. Birkhoff prize in Applied Math., 1973; Rockefeller fellow, 1935, 42; Fulbright lecturer Goettingen University, 1955; Guggenheim travel grantee, 1963, 70; Senior U.S. Scientist Humboldt award, W. Ger., 1980-81; Benjamin Franklin fellow Royal Society Arts; MacArthur fellow, 1984. Member National Acad. Sciences, Am. Math. Society (Steele prize 1982), American Association for the Advancement of Science, Math. Association Am., Deutsche Akademie der Naturforscher Leopoldina, Sigma Xi. Office: NYU Courant Institute 251 Mercer St New York New York 10012

JOHNSON, BARRY LEE, public health research administrator; born Sanders, Kentucky, October 24, 1938; son of Otto Lee and Sarah Josephine (Deatherage) J.; married Billie Reed, August 19, 1960; children—Lee, Clay, Scott, Reed, Sarah. Bachelor of Science, University Kentucky, 1960; Master of Science, Iowa State University, 1962, Doctor of Philosophy, 1967. Electrical engineer United States Public Health Service, Cincinnati, 1960-70; bioengr.

Environmental Protection Agency, Cincinnati, 1970-71; bioengr. National Institute for Occupational Safety and Health, Department of Health and Human Services, Cincinnati, 1971-77, research administrator; 1978-86; associate administrator Agency for Toxic Substances and Disease Registry, 1986—. Editor: Behavioral Toxicology, 1974, Neurotoxicology, 1986; editor Neurotoxicology, 1979, Archives Environ. Health journal, 1980, Toxicology and Industrial Health, 1985, Prevention of Neurotoxic Illness, 1987, Risk Analysis, 1987. President Southeast Cincinnati Soccer Association, 1978-80. Recipient commendation medal USPHS, 1980, 84, Superior Performance medal USPHS, 1986, Meritorious Service award USPHS, 1988; USPHS fellow, 1962-65. Member Am. Pub. Health Association, Am. Conference Government Hygienists, Am. Association Clinical Toxicology, International Conference Occupational Health, Am. College Toxicology. Avocation: amateur sports. Home: 2618 Riverglenn Circle Atlanta Georgia 30338 Office: Agency for Toxic Substances and Disease Registry Atlanta Georgia 30333

JOHNSON, IRVING STANLEY, pharmaceutical company executive, scientist; born Grand Junction, Colorado, June 30, 1925; son of Walter Glen and Frances Lucetta (Tuttle) J.; married Alwyn Neville Ginther, January 29, 1949; children: Rebecca Lyn, Bryan Glenn, Kirsten Shawn, Kevin Bruce. Bachelor of Arts, Washburn University, Topeka, 1948; Doctor of Philosophy, University Kansas, 1953. With Lilly Research Laboratories, Indianapolis, 1953—; vice president research Lilly Research Laboratories, 1973—; member professional education committee Am. Cancer Society, 1972—; active in several areas of biological research including cancer, virus, genetic engineering; member Recombinant Adv. Committee, National Institutes of Health, 1985—; member University of California at Los Angeles Symposia Board, 1986—; consultant in field. Author articles in field; associate editor: Cancer Research, 1974—; editorial board: Chemico-Biol. Interactions, 1968-73. Member education committee Indianapolis Urban League, 1968-70; president Indianapolis chapter Am. Field Service Exchange Program, 1969-70; board of directors Walther Cancer Research Foundation; board of directors Indianapolis Center Advanced Research, vice president executive committees, 1985—. Served with United States Naval Reserve, 1943-46. Recipient 1st annual Congl. award for sci. and tech., 1984. Member American Association for the Advancement of Science, Am. Association Cancer Research (Cain Memorial award for outstanding preclin. research in cancer chemotherapy 1986), Am. Society Cell Biology (pub. policy committee), Environmental Mutagen Society, International Society Chemotherapy, Kansas Acad. Sci., New York Acad. Sciences, Society Experimental Biology and Medicine, Sigma Xi, Phi Sigma. Episcopalian. Patentee in field. Office: 307 E McCarty St Indianapolis Indiana 46285

JOHNSON, PATRICIA R., cell biologist, academic administrator; born Waco, Texas, February 28, 1931. Bachelor of Arts, Baylor University, 1952, Master of Arts, 1958; Doctor of Philosophy in Biochemistry, Rutgers University, 1967. Health

physicist Rocky Flats Plant div. Dow Chemical Company, 1952-53; analytical chemist Virginia Carolina Chemical Corp., Texas, 1953-54; teacher high school Texas, 1956-60; instructor biology, chemistry Malone College, 1960-61; research assistant Bureau Biological Research Rutgers University, 1961-64, from instructor to associate professor biology; 1964-75; professor biology, chairman biology department Vassar College, 1975—, William R. Keenan chairman; 1981—; adj. associate professor Rockefeller University, 1971-75, adj. professor, 1975-80. Member American Association for the Advancement of Science, New York Acad. Sci., Am. Institute Nutrition, Sigma Xi. Office: Vassar College Department of Biology Poughkeepsie New York 12601

JONES, GEOFFREY MELVILL, physiology research educator; born Cambridge, England, January 14, 1923; son of Benett and Dorothy Laxton (Jotham) J.; married Jenny Marigold Burnaby, June 21, 1953; children—Katharine, Francis, Andrew, Dorothy. Bachelor of Arts, Cambridge University, 1944, Master of Arts, 1947, Doctor of Medicine, 1949. House surgeon Middlesex Hospital, London, England, 1949-50; senior house surgeon Addenbrookes Hospital, Cambridge, England, 1950-51; sci. medical officer Royal Air Force Institute Aviation Medicine, Farnborough, England, 1951-55; sci. officer Medical Research Council, England, 1955-61; associate professor physiology, director aviation medical research unit McGill University, Montreal, Quebec, Can., 1961-68, professor, director; 1968-88, Hosmer research professor; 1978—. Author: (with another) Mammalian Vestibular Physiology, 1979. Editor (with another) Adaptive Mechanisms in Gaze Control, 1985. Served to squadron leader Royal Air Force, 1951-55. Senior rsch. assoc. National Acad. Sci., 1971-72; recipient Skylab Achievement award National Aeronautics and Space Administration, 1974, 1st recipient Dohlman medal Dohlman Socicty Toronto University, 1987, Quinquennial Gold medal Barany Society International, 1988, Wilbur Franks Annual award Can. Society Aerospace Medicine. Fellow Canadian Aeronautics and Space Institute, Aerospace Medical Association (Harry Armstrong award 1968, Arnold D. Tuttle award 1971), Royal Society Can., Royal Society London, Royal Aeronautical Society London. Avocations: outdoor activities; reading; choral singing. Office: Aerospace Med Research Unit, 3655 Drummond St, Montreal, Province of Quebec Canada H3G 1Y6

JOSEPH, RICHARD ISAAC, electrical engineering and computer science educator; born Brooklyn, May 25, 1936. Bachelor of Science, City College of New York, 1957; Doctor of Philosophy in Physics, Harvard University, 1962. Senior research scientist solid state physics Raytheon Company, 1961-66; from assistant professor to associate professor Johns Hopkins University, Baltimore, 1966-70, professor electrical engineering; from 1970, now Jacob Suter Jammer professor electrical engineering and computer sci. Office: Johns Hopkins University GWC Whiting School Engring Baltimore Maryland 21218

JOSEPHSON, BRIAN DAVID, physicist; born January 4, 1940; son of Abraham and Mimi Josephson; married Carol Anne Olivier, 1976; 1 daughter. Bachelor of Arts, Cambridge University, 1960, Master of Arts, Doctor of Philosophy, 1964; Doctor of Science (honorary), University Wales, 1974. Assistant director research in physics Cambridge University, 1967-72, reader; 1972-74, professor physics; 1974—; visiting faculty Maharishi European Reserve University, 1975. Author papers on physics and theory of intelligence; co-editor: Consciousness and the Physical World, 1980. Recipient Nobel prize in Physics, 1973; fellow Trinity College, Cambridge, 1962—; New Scientist award, 1969; Guthrie medal, 1972; van der Pol medal, 1972; Elliott Cresson medal, 1972; Hughes medal, 1972; Holweck medal, 1973; Faraday medal, 1982. Fellow Royal Society; member Institute of Electrical and Electronics Engineers (hon.), Am. Acad. Arts and Sciences (foreign, hon.). Office: U Cambridge, Cavendish Lab, Madingley Road, Cambridge CB3 OHE, England

JUDD, O'DEAN P., government scientist; born Austin, Minnesota, May 26, 1937. Master of Science in Physics, University of California at Los Angeles, 1961, Doctor of Philosophy in Physics, 1968. Staff physicist and project director Hughes Research Laboratory, Malibu, California, 1959-67; postdoctoral fellow University of California at Los Angeles Department Physics, 1968-69; researcher Hughes Research Laboratory, Malibu, California, 1969-72; researcher, associate group leader Los Alamos National Laboratory, 1972-82, chief scientist for defense research and applications; 1981; chief scientist Strategic Defense Initiative Organization, Washington; laser consultant to National Oceanographic and Atmospheric Administration;

member government committees related to strategic defense; tech. advisor to SDIO; adj. professor of physics University New Mexico, Albuquerque. Patentee in laser field; contributor articles to sci. and def. related journals. Member Institute of Electrical and Electronics Engineers, Am. Physical Society, American Association for the Advancement of Science. Office: United States Department Def Strategic Def Initiative Orgn The Pentagon Washington District of Columbia 20301

JUKES, THOMAS HUGHES, biological chemist, educator; born Hastings, England, August 25, 1906; came to United States, 1925, naturalized, 1939; son of Edward Hughes and Ann Mary (Barton) J.; married Marguerite Esposito, July 2, 1942; children—Kenneth Hughes, Caroline Elizabeth (Mrs. Nicholas Knueppel), Dorothy Mavis (Mrs. Robert Hudson). Bachelor of Agricultural Science, University Toronto, 1930, Doctor of Philosophy, 1933; NRC fellow medical scis., University California at Berkeley, 1933-34; Doctor of Science (honoris causa), University Guelph, 1972. Instructor, assistant professor University California at Davis, 1934-42; with pharmaceutical div. Lederle Laboratories, 1942-45; director nutrition and physiology research section research div. Am. Cyanamid Company, Pearl River, New York, 1945-58; director research agricultural div. Am. Cyanamid Company, 1958-59, director biochemistry; 1960-62; visiting senior research fellow in biochemistry Princeton, 1962-63; professor in residence department biophysics and medical physics, department nutritional sciences, research biochemist Space Sciences Laboratory, University California at Berkeley, 1963—, associate director; 1968-70; consultant Chemical Warfare Service, Army of the United States, 1944-45, National Aeronautics and Space Administration, 1969-70; guest lecturer various universities; Storer lecturer University California at Davis, 1973; Fred W. Tanner lecturer Institute Food Technologists, 1979; visiting professor University Wisconsin, River Falls, 1985; plenary lecturer Japanese Molecular Biology and Genetics Societies, Nagoya, 1986; consultant California Cancer Adv. Council, 1981—. Author: B Vitamins for Blood Formation, 1952, Antibiotics in Nutrition, 1955, Molecules and Evolution, 1965; member editorial bds., Biochem. Genetics, BioSystems; biographical editor: Journal Nutrition; associate editor: Journal Molecular Evolution; Contributor articles to professional journals. Member National Adv. Board Accuracy in Media, Washington, 1976—; adv. board Consumer Alert, 1978—. Recipient Borden award Poultry Sci. Association, 1947; Spencer award Am. Chemical Society, 1976; Agrl. and Food Chemistry award, 1979; Distinguished Service award Am. Agrl. Editors Association, 1978; Cain Memorial award Am. Association Cancer Research, 1987; Klaus Schwarz commemorative medal International Association Bioinorganic Scientists, 1988. Fellow Am. Society Animal Sci., Poultry Sci. Association, Am. Institute Nutrition (council 1941-45, pub. affairs officer 1978-81, chairman committee on history 1979-83); member International Council Sci. Unions (chairman biology working group COSPAR 1978-80, chairman interdisciplinary sci. commission F

1980-84), Am. Society Biological Chemists, Biophys. Society, Society for Experimental Biology and Medicine, Am. Chemical Society, Trustees for Conservation (San Francisco) (president 1970-71), Sigma Xi, Delta Tau Delta. Clubs: Am. Alpine (New York City), Explorers (New York City); Chit Chat (San Francisco), Sierra (San Francisco); Faculty (Berkeley). Home: 170 Arlington Avenue Berkeley California 94707 Office: Space Scis Lab U California 6701 San Pablo Avenue Oakland California 94608

JULESZ, BELA, experimental psychologist, communications company executive, educator, electrical engineer; born Budapest, Hungary, February 19, 1928; came to United States, 1956; son of Jeno and Klementin (Fleiner) J.; married Margit Fasy, August 7, 1953. Dipl. Electrical Engineering, Tech. University, Budapest, 1950; Doctor Ing., Hungarian Academy Science, Budapest, 1956. Assistant professor department communication Tech University Budapest, Hungary, 1950-51; member tech. staff Telecommunication Research Institute, Budapest, 1951-56; member tech. staff Bell Laboratories, Murray Hill, New Jersey, 1956-64, head sensory and perceptual processes; 1964-83; research head visual perception research American Telephone and Telegraph Company Bell Laboratories, Murray Hill, New Jersey, 1984—; continuing visiting professor biology department California Tech. Institute, Pasadena, 1985—. Author: Foundations of Cyclopean Perception, 1971; author over 140 sci. papers on visual perception; discover computer generated random-dot stereogram technique. Fairchild distinguished scholar California Institute Tech., 1977-79, 87, assoc. Neurosci. Research Progam, 1982; MacArthur Foundation fellow, 1983—; Dr. H.P. Heineken prize Royal Netherlands Acad. Arts and Sciences, 1985. Fellow Am. Acad. Arts and Sciences, American Association for the Advancement of Science; member National Acad. Sciences, Goettingen Acad. Sciences (corr.), Hungarian Acad. Sciences (hon.). Home: 30 Valley View Road Warren New Jersey 07060 Office: AT&T Bell Labs Murray Hill New Jersey 07974

KABAT, ELVIN ABRAHAM, immunochemist, biochemist, educator; born New York City, September 1, 1914; son of Harris and Doreen (Otis) K.; married Sally Lennick, November 28, 1942; children: Jonathan, Geoffrey, David. Bachelor of Science, City College of New York, 1932; Master of Arts, Columbia University, 1934, Doctor of Philosophy, 1937; Doctor of Laws (honorary), University Glasgow, 1976; Doctoral degree (honorary), University Orleans (France); Doctor of Philosophy (honorary), Weizmann Institute Science, Rehovot, Israel; Doctor of Science honoris causa, Columbia University, 1987. Laboratory assistant immunochemistry Presbyn. Hospital, 1933-37; Rockefeller Foundation fellow Institute Physical Chemical, Upsala, Sweden, 1937-38; instructor pathology Cornell University, 1938-41; member faculty Columbia University, New York City, 1941—; assistant professor bacteriology Columbia University, 1946-48, associate professor; 1948-52, professor microbiology; 1952-85, professor human genetics and devel.; 1969-85, Higgins professor microbiology; 1984-

85, Higgins professor emeritus microbiology; 1985—; member adv. panel on immunology World Health Organization, 1965—; lecturer 25th Michael Heidelberger Lecture, College Physicians and Surgeons, Columbia University, 1986; expert consultant National Cancer Institute, 1975-82, National Institute Allergy and Infectious Disease, 1983-88, National Institutes of Health, Office of Director, 1989—; Alexander South Wiener lecturer New York Blood Center, 1979. Author: (with M.M. Mayer) Experimental Immunochemistry, 1948, 2d edition, 1961, Blood Group Substances, Their Chemistry and Immunochemistry, 1956, Structural Concepts in Immunology and Immunochemistry, 1968, 2d edition, 1976, (with T.T. Wu and H. Bilofsky) Variable Regions of Immunoglobulin Chains, 1976, Sequences of Immunoglobulin Chains, (with others) Sequences of Proteins of Immunological Interest, 1983, 4th edition 1987 (with T.T. Wu, M. Reid-Miller, H.M. Perry and K.S. Gottesman)., member editorial board: Journal Immunology, 1961-76, Transplantation Bull, 1957-60. Recipient numerous awards including: Annual Research award City of Hope, 1974, award Center for Immunology, State University New York, Buffalo, 1976, Louisa Gross Horwitz award Columbia University, 1977, R.E. Dyer lecturer award National Institutes of Health, 1979, Townsend Harris medal City College of New York, 1980, Philip Levine award Am. Society Clinical Pathology, 1982, award for excellence Graduate Faculties Alumni Columbia University, 1982, Distinguished Service award Columbia University College Physicians and Surgeons, 1988, Dickson Prize for Medicine University Pitts, 1986, Academy medal, New York Acad. Medicine, 1989; named Pierre Grabar Lecturer Societe Francaise d'Immunologie and German Society of Immunology; Fogarty scholar National Institutes of Health, 1974-75. Fellow American Association for the Advancement of Science, Am. Acad. Allergy (hon.); member National Acad. Sciences, Am. Acad. Arts and Sciences, Am. Association Immunologists (past president), Am. Society Biological Chemists, Am. Chemical Society, Harvey Society (president 1976-77), Am. Society Microbiology, International Association Allergists, Societe Franciaise d'Allergie (hon.), Biochem. Society (England), Association for Research in Nervous and Mental Diseases, American Association of University Women, Association de Microbiologists de Langue Francaise, Société de Biologie, Société de Immunologie (hon.), Phi Beta Kappa, Sigma Xi. Home: 70 Haven Avenue New York New York 10032 Office: Columbia U Department Microbiology/Coll Physicians and Surgeons 701 W 168th St New York New York 10032

KAHN, ROBERT E., electrical engineer; born December 23, 1938. Bachelor of Electrical Engineering, City College of New York; Master of Electrical Engineering, Princeton University, Doctor of Philosophy in Electrical Engineering. Assistant professor electrical engineering Massachusetts Institute of Technology, Cambridge; engineer Bolt, Beranek & Newman; director information processing techniques DARPA; founder, president Corp. National Research Initiatives, Reston, Virginia, 1986—. Fellow Institute of Electrical and Electronics Engineers. Office: Corp for National Reserve

Initiatives 1899 Preston White Dr Reston Virginia 22091

KALINER, MICHAEL ARON, immunologist, allergist, medical association administrator; born Baltimore, 1941. Doctor of Medicine, 1967. Intern Hospital Maryland, 1967-68; resident in medicine University California, San Francisco; assistant in medicine Peter Bent Brigham Hospital, Boston, 1972-73; chief allergy and immunology Keesler Air Force Base (Mississippi) Medical Center, 1973-75; senior investigator National Institute Allergy and Infectious Disease, National Institutes of Health, Bethesda, Maryland, 1975—; now also chairman Am. Board Allergy and Immunology Incorporated.

Served to major Medical Corps, United States Air Force. Fellow in allergy and immunology Harvard University, 1970-73. Member Am. Thoracic Society, Am. Acad. Allergy and Immunology, Am. Association Immunologists. Office: NIH Room 10 11C 205 Bethesda Maryland 20205

KALMAN, RUDOLF EMIL, research mathematician, system scientist; born Budapest, Hungary, May 19, 1930; son of Otto and Ursula (Grundmann) K.; married Constantina Stavrou, September 12, 1959; children: Andrew E.F.C., Elisabeth K. Bachelor of Science, Massachusetts Institute of Technology, 1953, Master of Science, 1954; Doctor of Science, Columbia University, 1957. Staff engineer International Business Machines Corporation Research Laboratory, Poughkeepsie, New York, 1957-58; research mathematician Research Institute Advanced Studies, Baltimore, 1958-64; professor engineering mechanical and electrical engineering Stanford University, 1964-67, professor math. system theory; 1967-71; grad. research professor, director Center for Math. System Theory, University Florida, 1971—; professor math. system theory Swiss Federal Institute Tech., Zurich, 1973—; sci. adviser Ecole Nationale Superieure des Mines de Paris, 1968—; member sci. adv. board Laboratorio di Cibernetica, Naples, 1970-73. Author: Topics in Mathematical System Theory, 1969; over 120 sci. and tech. papers.; editorial board: Journal Math. Modelling, Math. Systems Theory, Journal Computer and Systems Scis., Journal Nonlinear Analysis, Advances in Applied Math., Journal Optimization Theory and Applications, Systems and Control Letters. Named outstanding young scientist Maryland Acad. Sci., 1962; recipient Institute of Electrical and Electronic Engineers medal of honor, 1974, Rufus Oldenburger medal American Society of Mechanical Engineers, 1976, Centennial medal Institute of Electrical and Electronic Engineers, 1984, 1st Kyoto Prize Inamori Foundation, 1985, Steele prize Am. Math. Society, 1987; Guggenheim fellow IHES Bures-sur-Yvette, 1971. Foreign hon. member Hungarian Acad. Sciences. Office: U Fla Department Math Gainesville Florida 32611 also: ETH-Hauptgebaude, 8092 Zurich Switzerland

KAN, YUET WAI, physician, investigator; born Hong Kong, June 11, 1936; came to United States, 1960; son of Tong-Po and Lai-Wai (Li) K.; married Alvera Lorraine Limauro, May 10, 1964; children—Susan Jennifer, Deborah Ann. Bachelor of Science, Bachelor of Medicine, University of Hong Kong, 1958, Doctor of Science, 1980, Doctor of Science (Honorary), 1987; Doctor of Science (Honorary), Chinese University, Hong

Kong, 1981; Doctor of Medicine (Honorary), University of Cagliari, Sardinia, Italy, 1981. Investigator Howard Hughes Medical Institute, San Francisco, 1976—; professor medicine and laboratory medicine University California, San Francisco, 1977—, Louis K. Diamond professor hematology; 1983—, chief div. genetics and molecular hematology; 1983—; member basic research adv. committee March of Dimes, White Plains, New York, 1985-88; member blood diseases and resources adv. committee National Institutes of Health, 1985-88; hon. member board of directors Institute Molecular Biology University Hong Kong, 1988—. Contributor more than 170 articles to medical books, journals. Recipient Damashek award Am. Society Hematology, 1979, Stratton Lecture award International Society Hematology, 1980, George Thorn award Howard Hughes Medical Institute, 1980, Gairdner Foundation International award, 1984, Allan award Am. Society Human Genetics, 1984, Lita Annenberg Hazen award for Excellence in Clinical Research, 1984, Waterford award, 1987, ACP's award, 1988. Fellow Royal College of Physicians (London), Royal Society (London), Third World Acad. Sciences; member National Acad. Sciences, Acad. Sinica (Chinese Acad. Sciences), Association Am. Physicians. Avocations: tennis; skiing. Home: 20 Yerba Buena Avenue San Francisco California 94127 Office: U California Room U-426 San Francisco California 94143

KANTOR, FRED STUART, medical educator, physician, researcher; born New York City, July 2, 1931; son of Nathan G. and Sylvia R. (Rosenthal) K.; married Linda Ruth Silverman, December 20, 1958; children—Michael A., Karen S., Theodore R. Bachelor of Science, Union College, Schenectady, 1952; Doctor of Medicine, New York University, 1956; Master of Arts (honorary), Yale University, 1971. Diplomate Am. Board Internal Medicine, Am. Board Allergy and Clinical Immunology. Intern ward medical service Barnes Hospital, St. Louis, 1956-57; research associate National Institute Allergy and Infectious Disease, National Institutes of Health, Bethesda, Maryland, 1957-59; assistant resident in internal medicine Yale-New Haven Hospital, 1959-60; fellow in immunology New York University, 1961-62; assistant professor medicine Yale University, New Haven, 1962-66, associate professor; 1966-71, professor; 1971-83, Paul B. Beeson professor medicine; 1983—; consultant West Haven Veteran's Administration Hospital, Connecticut, 1966—, Middlesex Memorial Hospital, Middletown, Connecticut, 1980—; member and chairman rev. boards National Institutes of Health, 1969-84; visiting scientist Walter & Eliza Hall Institute, Australia, 1968-69, Weizmann Institute, 1969, University College, London, 1975; visiting professor Hunan Medical College, China, 1983, Harvard Medical School, 1984. Contributor numerous articles to professional publications. Served to senior assistant surgeon United States Public Health Service, 1957-59. Union College exchange scholar, St. Andrews, Scotland, 1950. Fellow American College of Physicians, Am. Acad. Allergy; member Am. Society Clinical Investigation, Am. Association Am. Physicians, Interurban Clinical Club (sec.-treas. 1970-74, president 1986-87), Sigma Xi, Alpha Omega Alpha. Avocation: flying. Office: Yale

U Med School 333 Cedar St New Haven Connecticut 06510

KANTROWITZ, ADRIAN, surgeon, educator; born New York City, October 4, 1918; son of Bernard Abraham and Rose (Esserman) K.; married Jean Rosensaft, November 25, 1948; children—Niki, Lisa, Allen. Bachelor of Arts, New York University, 1940; Doctor of Medicine, Long Island College Medicine, 1943; postgraduate physiology, Western Reserve University, 1950. Diplomate: Am. Board Surgery, Am. Board Thoracic Surgery. General rotating intern Jewish Hospital Brooklyn, 1944; assistant resident, then resident surgery Mount Sinai Hospital, New York City, 1947; assistant resident Montefiore Hospital, New York City, 1948; assistant resident pathology Montefiore Hospital, 1949, fellow cardiovascular research group; 1949, chief resident surgery; 1950, adj. surgical service; 1951-55; United States Public Health Service fellow cardiovascular research, department physiology Western Reserve University, 1951-52, teaching fellow physiology; 1951-52; instructor surgery New York Medical College, 1952-55; consultant surgeon Good Samaritan Hospital, Suffern, New York, 1954-55; assistant professor surgery State University New York College Medicine, 1955-56, associate professor surgery; 1957-64, professor; 1964-70; director cardiovascular surgery Maimonides Medical Center, Brooklyn, 1955-64; director surgery Maimonides Medical Center, 1964-70; chairman department surgery Sinai Hospital Detroit, 1970—; professor surgery Wayne State University School Medicine, 1970—. Contributor articles professional journals. Served from 1st lieutenant to captain, Medical Corps Army of the United States, 1944-46. Recipient H.L. Moses prize to Montefiore Alumnus for outstanding research accomplishment, 1949; 1st prize sci. exhibit Convention New York State Medical Society, 1952; Gold Plate award Am. Acad. Achievement, 1966; Max Berg award for outstanding achievement in prolonging human life, 1966; Theodore and Susan B. Cummings humanitarian award Am. College Cardiology, 1967. Fellow New York Acad. Sci., A.C.S.; member International Society Angiology, Am. Society Artificial Internal Organs (president 1968-69), New York County Medical Society, Harvey Society, New York Society Thoracic Surgery, New York Society Cardiovascular Surgery, Am. Heart Association, Am. Physiological Society, Am. College Cardiology, Am. College Chest Physicians, Brooklyn Thoracic Surgery Society (president 1967-68), Pan Am. Medical Association, Soaring Society Am., Am. Ski Association. Pub. pioneer motion pictures taken inside living heart, 1950; contbr. to devel. pump- oxygenators for human heart surgey; pioneer devel. mech., artificial hearts; performed 1st permanent partial mech. heart surgery in humans, 1966; 1st use phase-shift intra-aortic balloon pump in patient in cardiogenic shock; 1st human heart transplant in United States, Dec. 1967. Home: 70 Gallogly Road Pontiac Michigan 48053 Office: 6767 W Outer Dr Detroit Michigan 48253

KANTROWITZ, ARTHUR, physicist, educator; born New York City, October 20, 1913; son of Bernard A. and Rose (Esserman) K.; married Rosalind Joseph, September 12, 1943 (divorced); children: Barbara, Lore, Andrea; married Lee Stuart, December 25, 1980. Bachelor of

Science, Columbia University, 1934, Master of Arts, 1936, Doctor of Philosophy, 1947; Doctor of Engineering (honorary), Montana College Mineral Science and Tech., 1975; Doctor of Science (honorary), New Jersey Institute Tech., 1981. Physicist National Advisory Committee for Aeronautics, 1935-46; professor aeronautical engineering and engineering physics Cornell University, 1946-56; director Avco-Everett Research Laboratory, Everett, Massachusetts, 1955-72; chairman, chief executive officer Avco-Everett Research Laboratory, 1972-78; senior vice president, director Avco Corp., 1956-79; professor Thayer School Engineering, Dartmouth College, 1978—; visiting lecturer Harvard University, 1952; Fulbright and Guggenheim fellow Cambridge and Manchester universities, 1954; fellow School Advanced Study, Massachusetts Institute of Technology, 1957, visiting institute professor, 1957—; Messenger lecturer Cornell University, 1978; hon. professor Huazhong Institute Tech., Wuhan, China, 1980; member Presdl. Adv. Group on Anticipated Advances in Sci. and Tech., head task force on sci. court, 1975-76; member tech. adv. board United States Department Commerce, 1974-77; member adv. panel NOVA, Station WGBH-TV; board overseers Center for Naval Analyses, 1973-83; member adv. council Israel-United States Binational Industrial Research and Devel. Foundation; board governors The Technion (hon. life); member adv. council National Aeronautics and Space Administration, 1979, 80; life trustee, past member mechanical engineering adv. committee University Rochester; member adv. council department aeronautical and mechanical sciences Princeton University, 1959-77; member engineering adv. council Stanford University, 1966-82; member adv. board engineering Rensselaer Polytechnic Institute, 1981—; visiting professor University California, Berkeley, 1983. Contributor articles to professional journals. Board of directors Hertz Found, 1972—. Recipient Kayan medal Columbia University, 1973, MHD Faraday Memorial medal, 1983, Theodore Roosevelt medal of honor for Distinguished Service in Sci., 1967. Fellow Am. Acad. Arts and Sciences, Am. Physical Society, American Association for the Advancement of Science, American Institute of Aeronautics and Astronautics (Fluid and Plasmadynamics award and medal 1981), Am. Astronautical Society; member International Acad. Astronautics, National Acad. Sciences, National Acad. Engineering, Am. Institute Physics, Sigma Xi. Home: 4 Downing Road Hanover New Hampshire 03755

KAO, CHARLES KUEN, electrical engineer; born Shanghai, China, November 4, 1933; son of Chun-Hsien and Tising Fong K.; married May Wan Wong, September 19, 1959; children—Simon M.T., Amanda M.C. Bachelor of Science in Electrical Engineering, University London, 1957, Doctor of Philosophy in Electrical Engineering, 1965. Devel. engineer Standard Telephones & Cables Limited, London, 1957-60; principal research engineer Standard Telecommunications Laboratory Limited, Harlow, England, 1960-70; professor electronics, chairman department Chinese University Hong Kong, 1970-74; chief scientist Electro Optical Products div./ITT, Roanoke,

Virginia, 1974-81; vice president, director engineering; 1981-83, now executive scientist, director research International Telephone & Telegraph Corporation Advanced Tech. Center, Shelton, Connecticut. Author: Optical Fiber Technology II, Optical Fibers Systems; contributor articles to professional journals; patentee in field. Recipient Morey award Am. Ceramic Society, 1976; Stewart Ballentine medal Franklin Institute, 1977; Rank prize Rank Trust Funds, 1978; LM Ericsson International prize, 1979; gold medal Armed Forces Communications and Electronics Association, 1980; Marconi International fellow, 1985. Fellow Institute of Electrical and Electronics Engineers (Morris Liebmann Memorial award 1978, Alexander Graham Bell medal 1985), Institute Electrical Engineers (United Kingdom); member Optical Society Am. Office: ITT/Alcatel Advanced Tech Center 1 Research Dr Shelton Connecticut 06484

KARLE, JEROME, research physicist; born New York City, June 18, 1918; married, 1942; 3 children. Bachelor of Science, City College of New York, 1937; Master of Arts, Harvard University, 1938; Master of Science, University Michigan, 1942, Doctor of Philosophy in Physical Chemistry, 1943. Research associate Manhattan project, Chicago, 1943-44, United States Navy Project, Michigan, 1944-46; head electron diffraction section Naval Research Laboratory, Washington, 1946-58; head diffraction branch Naval Research Laboratory, 1958, now head laboratory for structure matter; member National Research Council, 1954-56, 67-75, 78-87; chairman United States National Committee for Crystal-

lography, 1973-75. Recipient Nobel prize in chemistry, 1985. Fellow Am. Physical Society; member Am. Chemical Society, Crystallograph. Association (treasurer 1950-52, president 1972), International Union Crystallography (executive committee 1978-87, president 1981-84), Am. Math. Society, American Association for the Advancement of Science, National Acad. Sciences. Research in structure atoms, molecules, crystals, solid surfaces. Office: United States Naval Research Lab Structure Matter Code 6030 Washington District of Columbia 20375

KARNOVSKY, MORRIS JOHN, pathologist, biologist; born Johannesburg, South Africa, June 28, 1926; came to United States, 1955; son of Herman Louis and Florence (Rosenberg) K.; married Shirley Esther Katz, August 26, 1952; children; David Mark, Nina Jane. Bachelor of Science, University Witwatersrand, Johannesburg, 1946, Bachelor of Medicine, BCh, 1950, Doctor of Science, 1984; diploma clin. pathology, University London, 1954; Master of Arts (honorary), Harvard University, 1965. Professor pathology Harvard University Medical School, Boston, 1968-72, Shattuck professor; 1972—, chairman program in cell and devel. biology; 1975—. Fellow Royal Microbiology Society; member Am. Society Cell Biology (president 1983-84), Am. Association Pathologists (co-pres. 1978-79 Rous-Whipple award). Club: Harvard (Boston). Office: Harvard Med School 25 Shattuck St Boston Massachusetts 02115

KASTEN, PAUL RUDOLPH, nuclear engineer, educator; born Jackson, Missouri, December 10, 1923; son of Arthur John and Hattie L. (Krueger) K.;

married Eileen Alma Kiehne, December 28, 1947; children: Susan (Mrs. Robert M. Goebbert), Kim Patrick, Jennifer. Bachelor of Science in Chemical Engineering, University Missouri, Rolla, 1944, Master of Science, 1947; Doctor of Philosophy in Chemical Engineering, University Minnesota, 1950. Staff member Oak Ridge National Laboratory, 1950-88, director gas-cooled reactor and thorium utilization programs; 1970-78, director HTGR and GCFR programs; 1978-86, tech. director gas cooled reactor programs; 1986-88; consultant engineer 1988—; guest director Institute Reactor Devel., Nuclear Research Center, Jülich, Federal Republic Germany, 1963-64; member faculty University Tennessee, Knoxville, 1953—, part-time professor nuclear engineering, 1965—. Fellow American Association for the Advancement of Science, Am. Nuclear Society; member National Society Professional Engineers, Sigma Xi, Tau Beta Pi, Phi Lambda Upsilon. Lutheran. Research and publ. in role of thorium in power reactor devel. and high temperature gas-cooled reactors. Office: 341 Louisiana Avenue Oak Ridge Tennessee 37830 also: U Tennessee Department Nuclear Engring Knoxville Tennessee 37996-2300

KATZ, BERNARD, physiologist; born Leipzig, Germany, March 26, 1911; son of Max and Eugenie (Rabinowitz) K.; married Marguerite Penly, October 27, 1945; children: David, Jonathan. Doctor of Medicine, University Leipzig, 1934; Doctor of Philosophy, University London, 1938, Doctor of Science, 1943; Doctor of Science (honorary), Southampton, 1971, Melbourne, 1971, Cambridge, 1980; Doctor of Philosophy (honorary), Weizmann Institute Science, 1979. Beit Memorial Research fellow 1938-39; Carnegie Research fellow Sydney, Australia, 1939-42; assistant director biophys. research University College, London, 1946-50, reader; 1950, professor, head biophysics department; 1952-78; lecturer universities, societies. Author: Electric Excitation of Nerve, 1939; Nerve, Muscle and Synapse, 1966; The Release of Neural Transmitter Substances, 1969; also articles. Member Agricultural Research Council, 1967-77. Recipient Garten prize University Leipzig, 1934; Feldberg award, 1965; Baly medal Royal College Physicians, 1967; Copley medal Royal Society, 1967; Nobel prize in medicine-physiology, 1970; created knight, 1969. Fellow Royal Society (council 1964-65, vice president 1965, biological secretary 1968-76), Royal College Physicians; foreign member Royal Danish Acad. Sciences and Letters, Acad. National Lincei, Am. Acad. Arts and Sci., National Acad. Sciences United States (foreign associate), Order Pour le Mérite für Wissenschaften und Künste (foreign). Research on nerve and muscle function especially transmission of impulses from nerve to muscle fibers. Office: U College Department Biophysics, Gower St, London WC1E 6BT, England

KAUFMAN, SEYMOUR, biochemist; born Brooklyn, March 13, 1924; son of Charles and Anna Kaufman; married Elaine Elkins, February 6, 1948; children: Allan, Emily, Leslie. Bachelor of Science, University Illinois, 1945, Master of Science, 1946; Doctor of Philosophy, Duke University, 1949. Fellow Department Pharmacology, New York University

Medical School, 1949-50, instructor; 1950-53, assistant professor; 1953-54; biochemist Laboratory Cellular Pharmacology National Institute of Mental Health, Bethesda, Maryland, 1954-56, chief section on cellular regulatory mechanisms Laboratory of General and Comparative Biochemistry; 1956-68, acting chief Laboratory Neurochemistry; 1968-71, chief Laboratory Neurochemistry; 1971—. Contributor articles to professional journals. U.S. Pub. Health fellow Duke University, 1949. Member Am. Society Biological Chemists, Am. Chemical Society, Am. Acad. Arts and Sciences, International Society for Neurochemistry, Am. Society for Neurochemistry, National Acad. Sci. Home: 10300 Rossmore Court Bethesda Maryland 20814 Office: Mental Health Intramural Reserve Div Lab Neurochem 3D30 NIH Building 36 Bethesda Maryland 20205

KEAR, BERNARD HENRY, materials scientist; born Port Talbot, South Wales, July 5, 1931; came to United States, 1959, naturalized, 1965; son of Herbert and Catherine Ann (Rees) K.; married Jacqueline Margaret Smith, August 22, 1959; children: Andrew, Gareth, Edward, Gwyneth. Bachelor of Science, University Birmingham, 1954, Doctor of Philosophy, 1957, Doctor of Science, 1970. With Tube Investments Limited, England, 1957-59; staff scientist Franklin Institute, Philadelphia, 1959-63; with United Technologies Corp., East Hartford, Connecticut, 1963-81; senior consultant scientist United Technologies Corp., 1977-81; sci. adv. Exxon Research and Engineering Company, 1981-86; professor, chairman dept mechs. and materials sci., director center for materials synthesis Rutgers University, New

Jersey, 1986—; John Dorn Memorial lecturer, 1980, Henry Krumb lecturer, 1983. Editor 7 books in field; contributor 130 articles to professional journals; holder 23 patents. Board of directors, president Interfaith Housing for Elderly Project, Madison, Connecticut, 1974-79. Recipient Mathewson gold medal Am. Institute Metall. Engrs., 1971. Fellow Am. Society Metals (Howe medal 1970); member National Acad. Engineering, National Materials Adv. Board (chairman 1986), Metallurgical Society, Am. Society Metals. Office: Rutgers U/Dept Mechanics and Materials Sci Post Office Box 909 Piscataway New Jersey 08854

KEIL, KLAUS, geology educator, consultant; born Hamburg, Germany, November 15, 1934; son of Walter and Elsbeth K.; married Rosemarie, March 30, 1961; children: Kathrin R., Mark K.; married Linde, January 28, 1984. Master of Science, Schiller University, Jena, Germany, 1958; Doctor of Philosophy, Gutenberg University, Mainz, Federal Republic Germany, 1961. Research associate Mineralogical Institute, Jena, 1958-60, Max Planck-Inst. Chemistry, Mainz, 1961, University California, San Diego, 1961-63; research scientist Ames Research Center National Aeronautics and Space Administration, Moffett Field, California, 1964-68; professor geology, director Institute Meteoritics, University New Mexico, Albuquerque, 1968—; president professor University New Mexico, 1985—; chairman department of geology University New Mexico, Albuquerque, 1986—; consultant Sandia Laboratories, others. Contributor over 400 articles to sci. journals. Recipient Apollo Achievement award National

Aeronautics and Space Administration, 1970; recipient George P. Merrill medal National Acad. Sciences, 1970, Exceptional Sci. Achievement medal National Aeronautics and Space Administration, 1977, Regents Meritorious Service medal University New Mexico, 1983, Leonard medal Meteoritical Society, 1988, Zimmerman award University New Mexico, 1988, numerous others. Fellow Meteoritical Society, American Association for the Advancement of Science, Mineralogical Society Am.; member Am. Geophysical Union, German Mineralogical Society, others. Office: U N Mexican Department Geology Albuquerque New Mexico 87131

KELLER, JOSEPH BISHOP, mathematician, educator; born Paterson, New Jersey, July 31, 1923; son of Isaac and Sally (Bishop) K.; married Evelyn Fox, August 29, 1963 (divorced November 17, 1976); children—Jeffrey M., Sarah N. Bachelor of Arts, New York University, 1943, Master of Science, 1946, Doctor of Philosophy, 1948. Professor math. Courant Institute Math. Sciences, New York University, 1948-79; chairman department math. University College Arts and Sciences and Grad. School Engineering and Sci., 1967-73; professor math. and mechanical engineering Stanford University, 1979—. Contributor articles to professional journals. Recipient U.S. National Medal of Sci., 1988. Member National Acad. Sciences, Am. Acad. Arts and Sciences, Am. Math. Society, Am. Physical Society, Society Industrial and Applied Math., Foreign Member Royal Society. Home: 820 Sonoma Terrace Stanford California 94305

Office: Stanford U Department Math Stanford California 94305

KELLEY, JAY HILARY, engineer; born Greensburg, Pennsylvania, March 9, 1920; son of Augustine Bernard and Ellen Marie (Bates) K.; married Catherine Jane Holway, May 10, 1949; children: Leonard, Christine, Catherine, Mary, Gerard, Patrick, Joyce, Michele, Sheila. Bachelor of Science, Pennsylvania State University, 1942, Master of Science, 1947, Doctor of Philosophy, 1952; postdoctoral, University Pittsburgh, 1952-60. Vice president Calora Coal Company, Mammoth, Pennsylvania, 1946-50; station manager and senior engineer Joy Machinery Company, Saltsburg, Pennsylvania, 1952-57; senior engineer Westinghouse Electric Company, Pittsburgh, 1957-62; member White House Sci. Staff, Washington, 1962-65; professor, director Rutgers University, New Brunswick, New Jersey, 1965-66; manager advanced tech. Ford Motor Corp., Philadelphia, 1966-69; president Elders Ridge Mining Company, Greensburg, Pennsylvania, 1964—; dean, distinguished professor minerals college West Virginia University, Morgantown, 1970-87, emeritus; 1987—; engineering consultant Kelastic/Urbdata Engineers, Greensburg, 1967—; adj. professor Drexel University, Philadelphia, 1968-69. Patentee; contributor articles to professional journals. Chairman Buffalo Creek Disaster Commission, Charleston, West Virginia, 1973, West Virginia Coal Mine Inspection Board, Charleston, 1970-78; general chairman National Safety Council, Chicago, 1978-79; president, vice president, board of directors trustee Engring. Index, 1965-79; board of directors Engring. Foundation, 1980—, chairman project committee, 1987—. Served as 1st lieutenant United States Army, 1943-46, European Theatre of Operations. Member Institute of Electrical and Electronics Engineers, Society Mining Engineers of American Institute of Mining, Metallurgy and Petroleum Engineers, Ops. Research Society Am., Am. Mining Congress, Cosmos Club (Washington). Roman Catholic. Avocations: tennis, golf. Home: 300 Maple Dr Greensburg Pennsylvania 15601 Office: West Virginia University College of Mineral and Energy Resources Morgantown West Virginia 26506 also: Urbdata Limited 307 S Pennsylvania Avenue Greensburg Pennsylvania 15601

KELLOGG, WILLIAM WELCH, meteorologist; born New York Mills, New York, February 14, 1917; son of Frederick S. and Elizabeth (Walcott) K.; married Elizabeth Thorson, February 14, 1942; children: Karl S., Judith K. Liebert, Joseph W., Jane K. Holien, Thomas W. Bachelor of Arts, Yale University, 1939; Master of Arts, University of California at Los Angeles, 1942, Doctor of Philosophy, 1949. With Institute Geophysics University of California at Los Angeles, Los Angeles, 1946-52, assistant professor; 1950-52; scientist Rand Corp., Santa Monica, California, 1947-59, head planetary sciences department; 1959-64; associate director National Center Atmospheric Research, Boulder, Colorado, also director laboratory atmospheric sciences; 1964-73, senior scientist; 1973-87; Member earth satellite panel International Geophysical Year, 1956-59; member space sci. board National Acad. Sciences, 1959-68, member committee meteorol. aspects of effects of atomic radiation, 1956-58, member committee atmospheric sciences, 1966-72, member polar research board, 1972-77; member Rocket and Satellite Research Panel, 1957-62; member adv. group supporting tech. for operational meteorol. satellites NASA-NOAA, 1964-72; rapporteur meteorology of high atmosphere, commission aerology World Meteorol. Organization, 1965-71; chairman international commission meteorology upper atmosphere International Union Geodesy and Geophysics, 1960-67, member, 1967-75; member international committee climate International Association Meteorology and Atmospheric Physics, 1978-87; member sci. adv. board United States Air Force, 1956-65; chairman meteorol. satellite committee Advanced Research Projects Agency, 1958-59; member panel on environment President's Sci. Adv. Committee, 1968-72; member space program adv. council National Aeronautics and Space Administration, 1976-77; chairman meteorol. adv. committee Environmental Protection Agency, 1970-74, member national air quality criteria adv. committee, 1975-76, air pollution transport and transformation adv. committee, 1976-78; member council on carbon dioxide environmental assessment Department Energy, 1976-78; adv. to secretary general on World Climate Program, World Meteorol. Organization, 1978-79; director research Naval Environmental Prediction Research Facility, Monterey, California, 1983-84; chairman adv. committee Div. Polar Programs National Science Foundation, 1983-86. Served as pilot-weather officer United States Army Air Force, 1941-46. Co-recipient special award pioneering work in planning meteorol. satellite Am. Meteorol. Society, 1961; recipient Risseca award contribution human relations in scis. Jewish War Vets. U.S.A., 1962-63, Exceptional Civilian Service award Department Air Force, 1966, Special award for pioneering meteorol. satellites Department Commerce, 1985, Special Citation award for atmospheric conservation Garden Club of Am., 1988. Fellow Am. Geophysical Union (president meteorol. section 1972-74), Am. Meteorological Society (council 1960-63, president 1973-74), American Association for the Advancement of Science (chairman atmospheric and hydrospheric section 1984); member International Acad. Astronautics, Sigma Xi. Club: Cosmos (Washington). Research on meteorology, dynamics and turbulence of upper atmosphere, use rockets and satellites for atmospheric research; prediction radioactive fallout and dispersal; applications of infrared techniques; atmospheres of Mars and Venus; theory of climate and causes of climate change. Home: 445 College Avenue Boulder Colorado 80302 Office: Adjunct/Nat Center Atmospheric Research Boulder Colorado 80307

KELLY, WILLIAM CROWLEY, geological sciences educator; born Philadelphia, May 10, 1929; married Anna Zauner; children—Geroge, Ted. Bachelor of Arts in Geology, Columbia University, 1951, Master of Arts in Geology, 1953, Doctor of Philosophy in Geology, 1954. Map clerk Royal Liverpool Ins. Company, New York City, 1946-47; geologist Naica mine Eagle Picher Company, Chihuahua, 1950; assistant in economic geology Columbia University, New York City, 1951-53; instructor geology Hunter College, New York City, 1954; instructor Department Geological Sciences University Michigan, Ann Arbor, 1956-58, assistant professor; 1958-62, associate professor; 1962-67, professor; 1967-83, C. Scott Turner professor; 1984—, chairman department; 1978-81; interim director Institute Sci. and Tech., University Michigan, 1986-87, assistant vice president for research, 1989—; acting director Michigan Sea Grant College Program University Michigan; visiting professor geology University Toronto, 1973, University Texas, Arlington, 1978; Distinguished visiting professor University Alberta, 1982; member adv. panel in earth sciences National Science Foundation, 1977-80, member adv. panel on problem focused research, 1980, member oversight committee earth sciences div., 1983; member task force on submarine polymetallic sulfide deposits National Oceanographic and Atmospheric Administration, 1982; director Economic Geology Publishing Company; lecturer and consultant in field. Member board associate editors: Journal Econ. Geology, 1966-73, The Canadian Mineralogist, 76-80; contributor chapters to books and articles, and revs. to professional journals. Trustee, Cranbrook Institute Sci., 1964-71, chairman personnel compensation, 1971. New Mexico Bureau Mines fellow, 1953; grantee in field. Fellow Geological Society Am., Mineralogical Society Am. (chairman publications committee 1976); member International Society Econ. Geologists (councilor 1973-76, vice president 1978, president 1984), Geochem. Society Am. (co-editor journal 1962, editor, 1963-64), Econ. Geology Foundation (trustee 1983-

85), Geological Association Can., Michigan Acad. Sci., Phi Kappa Phi. Home: 2970 Burlington St Ann Arbor Michigan 48105 Office: Department Geol Scis U Michigan Ann Arbor Michigan 48109

KEMENY, JOHN GEORGE, mathematics educator; born Budapest, Hungary, May 31, 1926; came to United States, 1940, naturalized, 1945; son of Tibor and Lucy (Fried) K.; married Jean Alexander, November 5, 1950; children: Jennifer M., Robert A. Bachelor of Arts, Princeton University, 1947, Doctor of Philosophy, 1949, Doctor of Laws, 1971; Doctor of Science, Middlebury College, 1965, Boston College, 1973, University Pennsylvania, 1975, Bard College, 1978, Dickinson College, 1981; Doctor of Laws, Columbia University, 1971, University New Hampshire, 1972, Colby College, 1976, Lafayette College, 1976, Brown University, 1980, Dartmouth College, 1981; Doctor of Science, Claremont Graduate School, 1982; Doctor of Laws, Tufts University, 1982; Doctor of Science, Rockford College, 1983; Doctor of Laws, Western Michigan University, 1983, York University, Can., 1984; Doctor of Humane Letters, Skidmore College, 1984. Assistant theoretical div. Los Alamos Project, 1945-46; assistant teaching and research Princeton, 1946-48; Fine instructor Office Naval Research fellow math., 1949-51, assistant professor philosophy; 1951-53; research assistant to Dr. Albert Einstein, Institute Advanced Study, 1948-49; professor math. Dartmouth College, 1953-70, 81—, adj. professor math; 1972-81, chairman math. department; 1955- 67, Albert Bradley 3d Century professor; 1969-72,

president; 1970-81, professor math. and computer sci.; 1981—; coordinator ednl. plans and devel. 1967-69; lecturer in Austria, Israel, India, Japan, 1964-65; Vanuxem lecturer Princeton University, 1974; chairman True BASIC, Incorporated, Hanover, New Hampshire, 1983— (implemented on a variety of microcomputers); consultant Rand Corp., Santa Monica, California, 1953-69; member National Commission Libraries and Information Sci., 1971-73; member regional dir.'s adv. committee Department of Health, Education and Welfare, 1971-73. Author: Man and the Computer, Back to BASIC, 1985, 12 other books; co-author: Finite Mathematics with Business Applications: Denumerable Markov Chains; Basic Programming, 1967; contributor to Encyclopedia Brit., articles to professional journals; cons. editor: Journal Symbolic Logic, 1950-59; associate editor: Journal Math. Analysis and Applications, 1959-70; member editorial board ABACUS, 1983-88; co-inventor of computer language BASIC, Dartmouth Time-Sharing System. Chairman United States Commission on Math. Instrn., 1958-60; member NRC, 1963-66; chairman President's Commission on Accident at Three Mile Island, 1979; member Hanover School Board (New Hampshire), 1961-64; Trustee Foundation Center, 1970-76, Carnegie Foundation Advancement Teaching, 1972-78; board of directors Council for Fin. Aid to Education, 1976-79; chairman Consortium on Financing Higher Education, 1979-80. Served with Army of the United States, 1945-46. Recipient Priestley award, 1976, Education award, Am. Federation Info. Processing Socs., 1983, New York Acad. Sci. award, 1984, Institute of Electrical and

Electronic Engineers Computer Pioneer medal, 1986. Member Association Symbolic Logic, Math. Association Am. (chairman New England section 1959-60, board govs. 1960-63, chairman panel biological and social scis. 1963-64), Am. Math. Society, Am. Philosophical Association, Am. Acad. Arts and Sciences, Phi Beta Kappa, Sigma Xi (national lecturer 1967). Club: Century Association. Office: Dartmouth College 231 Baker Libr Hanover New Hampshire 03755

KENDREW, JOHN COWDERY, former college president, molecular biologist; born Oxford, England, March 24, 1917; son of Wilfrid George and Evelyn May Graham (Sandberg) K. Bachelor of Arts, Trinity College, Cambridge University, 1939, Master of Arts, 1943, Doctor of Philosophy, 1949; Doctor of Science, 1962, 1949. With Ministry Aircraft Production, 1940-45; sci. adv. allied air commander in chief Southeast Asia, 1944; deputy chairman Medical Research Council Laboratory for Molecular Biology, Cambridge University, Southeast Asia, 1947-75; fellow of Peterhouse, Cambridge University, 1947-75 (hon. fellow 1975); reader Davy-Faraday Laboratory, Royal Institution, London, 1954-68; dir.-gen. European Molecular Biology Laboratory, Heidelberg, Germany, 1975-82; president St. John's College, Oxford University, 1981-87 (hon. fellw 1987). Editor in chief Journal Molecular Biology, 1959-87. Member council United Nations University, 1980-86, chairman, 1983-85. Decorated knight bachelor and commander Order Brit. Empire; recipient (with Max Perutz) Nobel prize in chemistry, 1962; Cambridge University hon. fellow, 1972. Fellow Royal Society, 1960; foreign associate National Acad. Sciences (United States); foreign hon. member Am. Acad. Arts and Sciences; hon. member Am. Society Biological Chemists; member Brit., Am. biophys. socs., International Organization Pure and Applied Biophysics (president 1969), International Council Sci. Unions (secretary general 1974-80, president 1983-88). In work with myoglobin, determined structure of a protein in general outline (1957) and atomic detail (1959); observed alpha-helix arrangement of the polypeptide chain, thereby confirming Pauling's earlier description. Home: Guildhall, 4 Church Lane, Linton, Cambridge CB1 6JX, England

KERR, DONALD MACLEAN, JR., physicist; born Philadelphia, April 8, 1939; son of Donald MacLean and Harriet (Fell) K.; married Alison Richards Kyle, June 10, 1961; 1 daughter, Margot Kyle. Bachelor of Electrical Engineering (National Merit scholar), Cornell University, 1963, Master of Science, 1964, Doctor of Philosophy (Ford Foundation fellow, 1964-65, James Clerk Maxwell fellow 1965-66), 1966. Staff Los Alamos National Laboratory, 1966-76, group leader; 1971-72, assistant div. leader; 1972-73, assistant to director; 1973-75, alternate div. leader; 1975-76; deputy manager Nevada operations office Department Energy, Las Vegas, 1976-77; acting assistant secretary defense programs Department Energy, Washington, 1978; deputy assistant secretary defense programs Department Energy, 1977-79, deputy assistant secretary energy tech.; 1979; dir Los Alamos National Laboratory, 1979-85; senior vice president EG&G, Incorporated, Wellesley, Massachusetts, 1985-88, executive vice president; 1988-89, president; 1989—; member Navajo Sci. Committee, 1974-77; member sci. adv. panel United States Army, 1975-78; member engineering advs. board University Nev.-Las Vegas, 1976-78; chairman committee research and devel. International Energy Agency, 1979-85; member national security adv. council SRI International, 1980—; member adv. board University Alaska Geophysical Institute, 1980-85; member sci. adv. group Joint Strategic Planning Staff, 1981—; member Naval Research Adv. Committee, 1982-85; adv. board Georgetown University Center Strategic and International Studies, 1981-87; member corp. Charles Stark Draper Laboratory, 1982—; board of directors Mirase Systems, Sunnyvale, California, 1988—. Published research on plasma physics, microwave electronics, ionospheric physics, energy and national security. Trustee New England Aquarium, 1989—. Fellow American Association for the Advancement of Science; member Am. Physical Society, Am. Geophysical Union, National Association Manufacturers (board directors 1986—), Southwestern Association Indian Affairs, World Affairs Council Boston (board directors 1988—), Sigma Xi, Tau Beta Pi, Eta Kappa Nu. Club: Cosmos (Washington). Office: EG&G Incorporated 45 William St Wellesley Massachusetts 02181

KERWIN, JOSEPH PETER, physician, former astronaut; born Oak Park, Illinois, February 19, 1932; married Shirley Ann Good; children: Sharon, Joanna, Kristina. Bachelor of Arts, College Holy Cross, 1953; Doctor of Medicine, Northwestern University, 1957. Flight surgeon United States Navy, 1959, aviator; 1962; astronaut 1965; member Skylab 2 Crew, 1973; representative Australia National Aeronautics and Space Administration, 1982-83; director Space-Life Sci., 1984-87; manager EVA systems Lockheed Missiles & Space Company, 1987—. Address: 1150 Gemini A23 Houston Texas 77058

KESTIN, JOSEPH, mechanical engineer, educator; born Warsaw, Poland, September 18, 1913; came to United States, 1952, naturalized, 1960; son of Paul and Leah K.; married Alicja Wanda Drabienko, March 12, 1949; 1 daughter, Anita Susan. Dipl. Ing., Engineering, University Warsaw, 1937; Doctor of Philosophy, Imperial College, London, 1945; Master of Arts ad eundem, Brown University, 1955; Doctor of Science, University London, 1966; Doctor h.c., Universite Claude Bernard (Lyon I). Senior lecturer department mechanical engineering Polish University College, London, 1944-46; department head Polish University College, 1947-52; professor engineering, director Center for Energy Studies, Brown University, Providence, 1952-84; visiting professor Imperial College, London, 1958, 83-86, Summer School in Jablonna, Warsaw Polish Acad. Sciences, 1973, University Maryland, 1983—; Distinguished visiting professor University Del., 1989; professeur associe University Paris, 1966, Université Claude Bernard (Lyon I) and Ecole Centrale de Lyon, 1974; Fulbright lecturer Instituto Superior Tecnico, Lisbon, 1972; special lecturer Norges Tekniske, Hogskole, Trondheim, Norway, 1963, 71; lecturer Nobel Committee Berzelius Symposium, 1979; fellow Institute Advanced Studies, West

Berlin; special adv. on engineering education to Chancellor of University Tehran, Iran, 1968; chairman National Research Council Eval. Panel for Office of Standard Reformed Data of National Bureau Standards, 1976-80, summer school on internal variables in thermodynamics and continuum mechanics International Center for Mechanical Sciences, Udine, Italy, 1988; member Eval. Panel for National Measurement Laboratory of National Bureau Standards, 1978-80, Numerical Data Adv. Board, National Acad. Sciences, 1976-80; consultant National Bureau Standards, North Atlantic Treaty Organization, Rand Corp.; member visiting committee University Virginia, Charlottesville, 1964; member executive committee National Bureau Standards Evaluation Panels, 1974-78. Author 4 books on thermodynamics; also 250 research papers in field; translator 5 books on thermodynamics and fluid mechanics; editor-in-chief Department Energy Sourcebook on Production of Electricity from Geothermal Energy; tech. editor Journal Applied Mechanics, 1956-71; member editorial board International Journal Heat and Mass Transfer, 1961-71, Heat Transfer-Soviet Research, 1968—, Heat Transfer-Japanese Research, 1972—, Mechanics Research Communications, 1973—, Journal Non-Equilibrium Thermodynamics, 1976—, Revue Generale de Thermique, 1975—, Physica A, 1978—, International Journal Thermophysics, 1979—, Journal Chemical and Engring. Data, 1980—; contributor articles to professional journals. Recipient Alexander von Humboldt Senior U.S. Scientist award, 1986, Japan Society for Advancement of Sci. fellowship, 1986, Humboldt prize Government

Federal Republic Germany, 1987. Fellow Institute Mechanical Engineers (London) (Water Arbitration prize 1949), American Society of Mechanical Engineers (task group on energy 1974-76, applied mechanics division 1967-78, chairman 1978, national nominating committee 1976-78, Centennial medals for research achievements and distinguished service, James Harry Potter Gold medal 1981, special fellowship), Japan Society Promotion of Sci., International Union Pure and Applied Chemical (hon.) (chairman subcom. transport properties, 1981—, hon. fellow 1987), Imperial College Sci., Tech. and Medicine (London); member Am. Society Engineering Education (chairman Curtis W. McGraw Research award committee 1976-78), International Association Properties of Steam (United States del. executive committee 1954—, chief of del., 1972-88, president 1974-76), Council Energy Engineering Research, National Acad. Engineering (peer committee mech. engineering 1987—), Polish Acad. Sciences (elected foreign member),Sigma Xi (president Brown University chapter 1979-84), Tau Beta Pi. Clubs: University (Providence), Faculty Brown University (Providence). Home: 140 Woodbury St Providence Rhode Island 02906 Office: Brown U Providence Rhode Island 02912

KETCHUM, MILO SMITH, civil engineer; born Denver, March 8, 1910; son of Milo Smith and Esther (Beatty) K.; married Gretchen Allenbach, February 28, 1944; children: David Milo, Marcia Anne, Matthew Phillip, Mark Allen. Bachelor of Science, University Illinois, 1931, Master of Science, 1932; Doctor of Science (honorary), University Colorado, 1976.

Assistant professor Case School Applied Sci., Cleveland, 1937-44; engineer F.G. Browne, Marion, Ohio, 1944-45; owner, operator Milo S Ketchum, Cons. Engineers, Denver, 1945-52; partner, principal Ketchum, Konkel, Barrett, Nickel & Austin, Cons. Engineers and predecessor firm, Denver, 1952—; professor civil engineering University Connecticut, Storrs, 1967-78; emeritus University Connecticut, 1978—; member Progressive Architecture Design Awards Jury, 1958, Am. Institute Steel Construction Design Awards Jury, 1975, James F. Lincoln Arc Welding Foundation Design Awards Jury, 1977; Stanton Walker lecturer University Maryland, 1966. Author: Handbook of Standard Structural Details for Buildings, 1956; editor-in-chief Structural Engineering Practice, 1981-84; contributor engring. articles to tech. magazines and journals. Recipient Distinguished Alumnus award University Illinois, 1979. Member Am. Concrete Institute (hon.; director, Turner medal 1966), American Society of Civil Engineers (president Colorado section, hon.), Am. Cons. Engineers Council, National Acad. Engineering, Am. Society Engineering Education, International Association Shell and Space Structures, Structural Engineers Association Colorado (president), Cons. Engineers Council Colorado (president), Sigma Xi, Tau Beta Pi, Chi Epsilon, Phi Kappa Phi, Alpha Delta Phi.

KETY, SEYMOUR S(OLOMON), physiologist, psychobiologist; born Philadelphia, August 25, 1915; son of Louis and Ethel (Snyderman) K.; married Josephine R. Gross, June 18, 1940; children: Lawrence Philip, Roberta Frances. Bachelor of Arts, University Pennsylvania, 1936, Doctor of Medicine, 1940, Doctor of Science (honorary), 1965; Doctor of Science (honorary), Loyola University, 1969, University Illinois, 1981, Mount Sinai University, 1982, Medical College Pennsylvania, 1985, Georgetown University, 1987, Washington University, 1989; Doctor of Medicine (honorary), University Copenhagen, 1979. Intern Philadelphia General Hospital, 1940-42; National Research Council fellow Harvard University, 1943-44; from instructor to assistant professor pharmacology University Pennsylvania School Medicine, 1943-48; professor clinical physiology Grad. School Medicine, 1948-51; scientific director National Institutes Mental Health and Neurological Diseases and Blindness, 1951-56; chief Laboratory Clinical Sci. National Institute of Mental Health, 1956-61, 62-67, senior scientist; 1983—; Henry Phipps professor, director department psychiatry Johns Hopkins School Medicine, 1961-62; professor psychiatry Harvard Medical School, 1967-80, professor neurosci.; 1980-83, professor emeritus neurosci.; 1983—; director psychiatric research laboratories Massachusetts General Hospital, Boston, 1967-77, Mailman Research Center, McLean Hospital, Belmont, Massachusetts, 1977-83; Thomas Dent Mütter lecturer, 1951, Eastman lecturer, 1957, National Institutes of Health lecturer, 1960, Thomas William Salmon lecturer, 1961, Alvarenga Prize lecturer, 1961, Acad. lecturer Am. Psychiat. Association, 1961, Saul Korey lecturer, 1964, James Arthur lecturer, 1966, 3d Mental Health Research Fund lecturer, London, 1965, Heinrich Waelsch lecturer, 1969, Benjamin Musser lecturer, 1970, Edward Mapother lecturer, London, 1974,

George Bishop lecturer, 1975, Harvey lecturer, 1975, Grass Foundation lecturer, 1975, Henry Maudsley lecturer, 1978, Edward Sachar lecturer, 1985. Editor-in-chief Journal Psychiatric Research, 1959-83, founding editor, 1983—; hon. editor Journal Cerebral Circulationand Metabolism, 1980; contributor sci. articles to professional publications. Organizing committee International Neurochem. Symposia, 1952-60; sci. advisory committee Massachusetts General Hospital, 1956-60; director Foundation Fund Research in Pyschiatry, 1962-65; associate Neuroscis. Research Foundation, 1962-83; trustee Rockefeller University, 1976-85. Recipient Theobald Smith award American Association for the Advancement of Science, 1949, Max Weinstein award, 1954, Distinguished Service award Department of Health, Education and Welfare, 1958, Stanley Dean award, 1962, McAlpin award National Association for Mental Health, 1972, Intra-Sci. award, 1975, William C. Menninger award American College of Physicians, 1976, Fromm-Reichman award, 1978, Foundations Fund award, 1979, Passano award, 1980, Thomas W. Salmon medal, 1982, Emil Kraepelin medal, 1984, Mihara Fund award, 1984, de Hevesy award Society Nuclear Medical, 1988, Schizophrenia rsch. award National Congress Rsch. in Schizophrenia, 1989. Distinguished fellow Am. Psychiat. Association (Distinguished Service award 1980); fellow Royal College Psychiatrists London (hon.); member National Acad. Sciences (Kovalenko award 1973, Neuroscience award 1988), Am. Acad. Arts and Sciences, Am. Philosophical Society, Association Research Nervous and Mental Disease (trustee, president 1965, 80, Research Achievement award 1980), Am. Psychopath. Association (president 1965, Paul Hoch award 1973), Society for Psychiat. Research, Am. Society Clinical Investigation, Am. Society Pharmacology and Experimental Therapeutics, Society for Neurosci. (Grass Foundation award 1975, Ralph Gerard award 1986), Phi Beta Kappa, Sigma Xi, Alpha Omega Alpha. Office: NIH Clin Center 4C-110 Bethesda Maryland 20892

KEYWORTH, GEORGE ALBERT, II, physicist, consulting company executive; born Boston, November 30, 1939; son of Robert Allen and Leontine (Briggs) K.; married Polly Lauterbach, July 28, 1962; children: Deirdre Anne, George Albert III. Bachelor of Science in Physics, Yale University, 1963; Doctor of Philosophy in Nuclear Physics, Duke University, 1968; Doctor of Science (honorary), Rensselaer Polytechnic Institute, Troy, New York, 1982; Doctor Engineering (honorary), Michigan Tech. University, 1984; Doctor of Science (honorary), University Alabama, 1985. Staff physicist Los Alamos (New Mexico) National Laboratory, 1968-74, group leader neutron physics; 1974-78, div. leader; 1978-81; sci. advisor to President, director Office Sci. and Tech. Policy The White House, Washington, 1981-85; chairman The Keyworth Company, Washington, 1986—; director research Hudson Institute, Indianapolis, 1988—; hon. professor Fudan University, Shanghai People's Republican of China, 1984; member V.P.'s Task Force on Regulatory Relief, Pres.' Commission on Industrial Competitiveness. Recipient Chmn.'s award Am. Association Engineering Sci., 1982,

Hertz Foundation award, 1987. Fellow Am. Physical Society; member American Association for the Advancement of Science, Sigma Xi. Republican. Club: Cosmos (Washington). Office: Hudson Institute 5395 Emerson Way Post Office Box 26-919 Indianapolis Indiana 46226

KHORANA, HAR GOBIND, chemist, educator; born Raipur, India, January 9, 1922; son of Shri Ganpat Rai and Shrimati Krishna (Devi) K.; married Esther Elizabeth Sibler, 1952; children: Julia, Emilie, Dave Roy. Bachelor of Science, Punjab University, 1943, Master of Science, 1945; Doctor of Philosophy, Liverpool (England) University, 1948; Doctor of Science, University Chicago, 1967. Head organic chemistry group British Columbia Research Council, 1952-60; visiting professor Rockefeller Institute, New York City, 1958—; professor co-director Institute Enzyme Research, University Wisconsin, Madison, 1960-70, professor department biochemistry; 1962-70, Conrad A. Elvehjem professor life sciences; 1964-70; Alfred P. Sloan professor biology and chemistry Massachusetts Institute of Technology, Cambridge, 1970—; visiting professor Stanford University, 1964; member adv. board Biopolymers. Author: Some Recent Developments in the Chemistry of Phosphate Esters of Biological Interests, 1961; Member editorial board: Journal Am. Chemical Soc, 1963—. Recipient Merck award Chemical Institute Can., 1958, Gold medal Professional Institute Pub. Service Can., 1960, Dannie-Heinneman Preiz Göttingen, Germany, 1967, Remsen award Johns Hopkins University, 1968, Am. Chemical Society award for creative work in synthetic organic chemistry, 1968, Louisa Gross Horwitz prize, 1968, Lasker Foundation award for basic med. research, 1968, Nobel prize in medicine, 1968; elected to Deutsche Akademie der Naturforscher Leopoldina HalleSaale, Germany, 1968; Overseas fellow Churchill College, Cambridge, England, 1967. Fellow Chemical Institute Can., Am. Acad. Arts and Sciences; member National Acad. Sci. Research and numerous publs. on chem. methods for synthesis of nuccleotides, coenzymes and nucleic acids; elucidation on the genetic code, lab. synthesis of genes, biol. membrane, light-transducing pigments. Office: Massachusetts Institute of Technology Department Biology & Chemistry Room 180511 Cambridge Massachusetts 02139

KIEFFER, STEPHEN AARON, radiologist, educator; born Minneapolis, December 20, 1935; son of Julius Hyman and Anita Elaine (Brudnick) K.; married Cyrile Frada Kaplan, December 21, 1958; children—Alisa, Mitchell, Stuart, Paula. Bachelor of Arts summa cum laude, University Minnesota, 1956, Bachelor of Science, 1957, Doctor of Medicine, 1959. Diplomate: Am. Board Radiology. Intern Wadsworth Veteran's Administration Hospital, Los Angeles, 1959-60; resident in radiology University Minnesota Hospitals, Minneapolis, 1960-62, 64-65; National Institutes of Health fellow in neuroradiology 1966-68; instructor University Minnesota Medical School, Minneapolis, 1966-67; assistant professor University Minnesota Medical School, 1967-68, associate professor; 1968-72, professor; 1972-74; chief radiology service Minneapolis Veteran's Administration

Hospital, 1968-74; professor, chairman department radiology SUNY-Health Sci. Center, Syracuse, 1974—, chairman governing board clinical practice management plan; 1985-88; vice president University Hospital member medical board 1988—; consultant Syracuse Veteran's Administration Medical Center, Crouse-Irving-Meml. Hospital. Co-author: Introduction to Neuroradiology, 1972; co-editor: An Atlas of Cross-sectional Anatomy, 1979; contributor numerous articles to professional journals, also chapters to books; editorial adv. board: Radiology, 1980-85, associate editor, 1986, cons. to editor, 1987—; cons. to editorial board Am. Journal Neuroradiology, 1980—; associate editor: Yearbook of Radiology, 1981-86; editorial board RadioGraphics, 1987—. Chairman tech. adv. subcom. on computed tomography Central New York Health Systems Agency, 1979-80; member tech. adv. committee on computed tomography New York State Office Health Systems Mgmt., 1981; Board Directors Syracuse Jewish Federation, 1975-81. Served to captain, Medical Corps United States Army, 1962-64. National Heart Institute trainee, 1961-62; National Institute Neurol. Diseases and Blindness fellow, 1966; James Picker Foundation scholar, 1966-68. Fellow Am. College Radiology (councilor 1986—); member Am. Roentgen Ray Society (publs. committee 1979-84), Am. Society Neuroradiology (president 1978-79), American Medical Association, Association University Radiologists (program committee 1985-86), Central New York Radiological Society (chairman program committee 1979-82), Medical Society State of New York, Minnesota Radiological Society (secretary 1974),

Neurosurg. Society Am., Onondaga County Medical Society, Radiological Society North America (refresher course committee 1977-82, program committee 1984—), Society Chairmen Acad. Radiology Departments, New York State Radiological Society (vice president 1985-86, president 1987-88), Phi Beta Kappa, Alpha Omega Alpha. Jewish. Home: 503 Standish Dr Syracuse New York 13224 Office: 750 E Adams St Syracuse New York 13210

KILBY, JACK ST. CLAIR, inventor; born Jefferson City, Missouri, November 8, 1923; son of Hubert St. Clair and Vina (Freitag) K.; married Barbara Annegers, June 27, 1948; children: Ann, Janet Lee. Bachelor of Electrical Engineering, University Illinois, 1947; Master of Science, University Wisconsin, 1950; Doctor of Engineering (honorary), University Miami, 1982, Rochester Institute Tech., 1986; Doctor of Science (honorary), University Illinois, 1988. Program manager Globe-Union, Incorporated, Milwaukee, 1948-58; assistant vice president Texas Instruments, Incorporated, Dallas, 1958-70; self-employed inventor Dallas, 1970—; distinguished professor electrical engineering Texas A & M University, 1978-85; inventor monolithic integrated circuit, others; consultant to government and industry. Served with Army of the United States, 1943-45. Recipient National Medal Sci., 1969; Ballentine medal Franklin Institute, 1967; Alumni Achievement award University Illinois, 1974; named to Holley medal American Society of Mechanical Engineers, 1982, National Inventors Hall of Fame U.S. Patent Office, 1981. Fellow Institute of Electrical and Electronics Engineers (Sarnoff medal

1966, Brunetti award 1978, Medal of honor 1986); member National Acad. Engineering (Zworykin medal 1975). Home: 7723 Midbury St Dallas Texas 75230 Office: 6600 LBJ Freeway Suite 4155 Dallas Texas 75240

KING, JONATHAN ALAN, molecular biology educator; born Brooklyn, August 20, 1941; married Jacqueline Dee. Bachelor of Science in Zoology, magna cum laude with high honors, Yale University, 1962; Doctor of Philosophy, California Institute Tech., 1968. With National Science Foundation Antarctic Service, 1969; Brit. Medical Research Council postdoctoral fellow Cambridge (England) University, 1970; assistant professor Massachusetts Institute of Technology, Cambridge, 1971-73; associate professor Massachusetts Institute of Technology, 1974-78, professor molecular biology; 1979—, director biology electron microscope facility; 1971—; chairman microbial physiology study section National Institutes of Health, 1982-83. Contributor numerous articles to sci. journals. Chairman National Jobs with Peace Campaign. General Motors National scholar, 1958-62; Jane Coffin Shields Fund fellow, 1968-70; recipient U.S. Antarctic Service medal, 1968; Woodrow Wilson fellow, 1962-63; National Institutes of Health fellow, 1963-67. Fellow American Association for the Advancement of Science; member Genetics Society Am., Am. Society Microbiology, Biophysics Society, Teratology Society, Am. Society Biological Chemists, Am. Pub. Health Association. Home: 1023 Washington St Boston Massachusetts 02124 Office: Massachusetts Institute of Technology Department Biology Cambridge Massachusetts 02139

KING, MARY-CLAIRE, epidemiologist, educator, geneticist; born Evanston, Illinois, February 27, 1946; 1 child, Emily King Colwell. Bachelor of Arts in Math., Carleton College, 1966; Doctor of Philosophy in Genetics, University California, Berkeley, 1973. Assistant professor University California, Berkeley, 1976-80, associate professor; 1980-84, professor; 1984—; member board sci. counselors National Cancer Institute; consultant Committee for Investigation of Disappearance of Persons, Government Argentina, Buenos Aires, 1984—. Contributor more than 80 articles to professional journals. Recipient Alumni Achievement award Carleton College. Member American Association for the Advancement of Science, Am. Society Human Genetics, Society Epidemiologic Research, Phi Beta Kappa, Sigma Xi. Office: U California School Pub Health Berkeley California 94720

KINSELLA, JOHN EDWARD, food science and chemistry researcher, educator, administrator; born Wexford, Ireland, February 22, 1938; married Ruth Ann De Angelis, July 10, 1965; children: Sean, Helen, Kathryn, Kevin. Bachelor of Science in Biology, University Dublin, 1961; Master of Science in Biology and Biochemistry, Pennsylvania State University, 1965, Doctor of Philosophy in Food Biochemistry, 1967. Assistant professor food biochemistry Cornell University, Ithaca, New York, 1967-73, associate professor food chemistry; 1973-77, professor food chemistry, chairman food sci. department; 1977—, Liberty Hyde Bailey professor food chemistry; 1981—, General Foods Distinguished professor food sci.; 1984-87; State University of New York Leading professor 1987; director

Institute Food Sci. Cornell University, Ithaca, New York, 1980-87; consultant United States Food industry, World Bank; cons National Science Foundation, Brazil, Government Indonesia; member food and nutrition board National Research Council. Author: Fish Oil/Seafood Health and Disease; editor: Advanced Food Research; contributor numerous articles to professional jours; patentee protein tech. and plant cell culture. Recipient Borden Award Borden Foundation, 1976, Fulbright award, 1984, Philadelphia Lectureship award, 1986; research grantee National Science Foundation, National Institutes of Health, USDA, various industry assns. Member Am. Chemical Society, Institute Food Technologists (executive committee 1982-85, Am. Institute Nutrition, Babcock Hart award 1987), American Association for the Advancement of Science, Am. Dairy Sci. Association, Am. Oil Chemical Society, International Dairy Federation. Office: Cornell University Food Sci Department Ithaca New York 14853

KIRK, JAMES ROBERT, research and development executive; born DuBois, Pennsylvania, October 30, 1941; son of Joseph James and Vinetta Helen (Fromm) K.; married Elaine Gralton, January 5, 1963 (divorced July 1985); children—Leanne, James Joseph, John Daniel; married Paulette DeJong, September 15, 1985. Bachelor of Science in Biology, Holy Cross College, 1964; Master of Science in Food Science, Michigan State University, 1966, Doctor of Philosophy, 1971. Assistant professor Michigan State University, East Lansing, 1971-74; associate professor Michigan State University, 1974-78, professor; 1978; professor,

chairman department food sci. and human nutrition University Florida, Gainesville, 1978-83; corp. vice president research and devel. Campbell Soup Company, Camden, New Jersey, 1983—; executive vice president Campbell Institute Research and Tech., Camden, 1983-88, president; 1988—; director National Nutrition Consortium, 1979-83; chairman food and nutrition conference Gordon Research Conference, 1982; member food nutrition board National Acad. Sciences, 1982-87; member food and nutrition board National Research Council, 1982—; director DNA Plant Tech. Corp., 1987—. Contributor over 100 articles to professional journals. Recipient Future Leader award Nutrition Foundation, 1977. Fellow Institute Food Technologists (Babcock Hart award 1983; executive committee 1983-86); member Am. Society Agricultural Engineers, Research and Devel. Association, Am. Chemical Society. Avocations: tennis; photography; golf. Office: Campbell Soup Company Campbell Place Camden New Jersey 08101

KLINGMAN, DARWIN DEE, business and computer science educator, consultant; born Dickinson, North Dakota, February 5, 1944; son of Virgil Wayne and Ethel Lara (Foster) K.; married Brenda Mabel Sargent, August 29, 1964 (divorced March 1974). Bachelor of Arts in Math., Washington State University, 1966, Master of Arts, 1967; Doctor of Philosophy interdisciplinary, University Texas, 1969. Assistant professor business and computer sci. University Texas, Austin, 1969-71, associate professor; 1972-75, professor; 1976—; director Center Business Decision Analysis University Tex,

Austin, 1982—; Bruton Centennial chair University Texas, Austin, 1983-85, Cullen Centennial chair; 1985—; visiting professor computer sci. Free University, Berlin, 1975; visiting professor math. Washington State University, Pullman, 1977. Editor Network Models and Associated Applications, 1982; contributor numerous articles to professional journals, 1969-82. Recipient Outstanding Graduate Teacher award University Texas, 1983, Outstanding Research award Golden Key National Honor Society, 1983, Franz Edelman award for Mgmt. Sci. Achievement, 1986, Jack G. Taylor award for Excellence in Teaching University Texas, 1987; Alexander von Humboldt fellow Bonn, Federal Republic of Germany, 1974. Member Institute Management Sci. (vice president at large 1981-82), Math. Association Am. (1977-81), Association Computing Machinery, Math. Programming Society (charter), Ops. Research Society Am., Naval Research Logistics Quar. Society. Office: U Tex CBA S.202 Austin Texas 78712

KLITZING, KLAUS VON, institute administrator, physicist; born Schroda, June 28, 1943; son of Bogislav and Anny (Ulbrich) von K.; married Renate Falkenberg, May 27, 1971; children: Andreas, Christine, Thomas. Diploma, Tech. University Braunschweig, 1969; Doctor of Philosophy, University Wuerzburg, 1972; Habilitation, 1978. Faculty member Tech. University, Munich, 1980-84; director Max Planck Institute for Festkörperforschung, Stuttgart, Federal Republic Germany, 1985—. Recipient Schottky prize Deutsche Physical Gesellschaft, 1981, Hewlett Packard prize European Physical Society, 1982, Nobel prize in physics Royal Swedish Acad. Sci., 1985. Office: Max Planck Institute, fur Festkörperforschung, Heisenbergstr 1, D-7000 Stuttgart 80 Federal Republic of Germany

KLUG, AARON, molecular biologist; born August 11, 1926; son of Lazar and Bella (Silin) K.; married Liebe Bobrow, 1948; 2 children. Bachelor of Science, University Witwatersrand; Master of Science, University Cape Town; Doctor of Philosophy, Cambridge University; Doctor of Science (honorary), University Chicago, 1978, Columbia University, 1978; Doctor (honorary), University Strasbourg, 1978; Doctor Fil. (honorary), University Stockholm, 1980; Doctor of Philosophy (honorary), University St. Andrews, 1987. Junior lecturer 1947-48; research student Cavendish Laboratory Cambridge (England) University, 1949-52; Rouse-Ball research student Trinity College, 1949-52; colloid sci. department 1953; Nuffield research fellow Birkbeck College, London, 1954-57, director virus structure research group; 1958-61; member staff Medical Research Council Laboratory Molecular Biology, Cambridge University, 1962—, joint head div. structural studies; 1978-86, director; 1987—; Leeuwenhoek lecturer Royal Society, 1973; Dunham lecturer Harvard University Medical School, 1975; Harvey lecturer, New York City, 1979; Lane lecturer Stanford University, 1983; Cetus lecturer Berkeley University, 1986; Pauli lecturer, Zürich, 1986; Nishina Memorial lecturer, Tokyo, 1986. Contributor articles to sci. journals. Recipient Heineken prize Royal Netherlands Acad. Sci., 1979, Louisa Gross Horwitz prize Columbia University, 1981, Nobel prize in chemistry, 1982; Gold medal of Merit, University Cape Town, 1983; Copley medal Royal Society, 1985; Knight, 1988. Fellow Royal Society; member Am. Acad. Arts and Sciences (foreign hon.), French Acad. Sciences (foreign associate), Max-Planck-Gesellschaft, Federal Republic of Germany (foreign associate), National Academy of Sciences (foreign associate). Office: Med Research Coun, Lab Molecular Biology, Cambridge CB2 2QH, England

KNAPP, EDWARD ALAN, government administrator; born Salem, Oregon, March 7, 1932; son of Gardner and Lucille (Moore) K.; married Jean Elaine Hartwell, June 27, 1954; children: Sandra, David, Robert, Mary. Bachelor of Arts, Pomona College, 1954; Doctor of Philosophy, University California, Berkeley, 1958; Doctor of Science (honorary), Pomona College, 1984, Bucknell University, 1984. With Los Alamos Sci. Laboratory, University California, 1958-82, director accelerator tech. div.; 1977-82; assistant director, then director National Science Foundation, Washington, 1982-84; senior fellow Los Alamos National Laboratory, 1984; president Universities Research Association, Washington, 1985—; consultant in field. Contributor articles to professional journals. Fellow American Association for the Advancement of Science, Am. Physical Society; member Institute of Electrical and Electronics Engineers, Sigma Xi. Methodist. Office: Univs Research Association 1111 19th St Northwest Washington District of Columbia 20036

KNUTH, DONALD ERVIN, computer sciences educator; born Milwaukee, January 10, 1938; son of Ervin Henry and Louise Marie (Bohning) K.; married Jill Carter, June 24, 1961; children: John Martin, Jennifer Sierra. Bachelor of Science, Master of Science, Case Institute Tech., 1960; Doctor of Philosophy, California Institute Tech., 1963; Doctor of Science (honorary), Case Western Reserve University, 1980, Luther College, Decorah, Iowa, 1985, Lawrence University, 1985, Muhlenberg College, 1986, University Pennsylvania, 1986, State University of New York, Stony Brook, 1987; Docteur, University Paris-Sud, Orsay, 1986. Assistant professor California Institute Tech., Pasadena, 1963-66, associate professor; 1966-68; professor Stanford (California) University, 1968—; consultant Burroughs Corp., Pasadena, 1960-68. Author: The Art of Computer Programming, 1968 (Steele prize 1987), Computers and Typesetting, 1986. Guggenheim Foundation fellow, 1972-73; recipient National Medal of Sci., President James Carter, 1979, Distinguished Alumni award, California Institute Tech., 1978, Priestly award, Dickinson College, 1981. Fellow Am. Acad. Arts and Sciences; member National Acad. Sciences, National Acad. Engineering, Association for Computing Machinery (Grace Murray Hopper award 1971, Alan M. Turing award 1974, Computer Sci. Edn award 1986, Software Systems award 1986), Institute of Electrical and Electronics Engineers (hon.; McDowell award 1980, Computer Pioneer award 1982). Lutheran. Avocation: playing pipe organ. Office: Computer Sci Department Stanford U Stanford California 94305

KOEN, BILLY VAUGHN, mechanical engineering educator; born Graham, Texas, May 2, 1938; son of Ottis

Vaughn and Margaret (Branch) K.; married Deanne Rollins, June 3, 1967; children: Kent, Douglas. Bachelor of Arts in Chemistry, University Texas, 1961, Bachelor of Science in Chemical Engineering, 1961; Master of Science in Nuclear Engineering, Massachusetts Institute of Technology, 1962, Doctor of Science in Nuclear Engineering, 1968; Diplome d'ingenieur en Genie Atomique, L'institut National des Scis. et Techniques Nucleaires, France, 1963. Assistant professor mechanical engineering University Texas, Austin, 1968-71, associate professor; 1971-80, Minnie S. Piper professor; 1980, professor; 1981—; director Bureau Engineering Teaching University Tex.-Austin, 1973-76; professor Ecole Centrale, Paris, 1983; consultant, lecturer in field. Contributor articles to professional journals. Board of directors Oak Ridge Associated Univs., 1975-76. Recipient Standard Oil Ind. award, 1970. Fellow Am. Society Engineering Education (Chester Carlson award 1980, Ben Dasher best paper award 1985, 86, Helen Plants award 1986, William Elgin Wickenden best paper award 1986, Olmsted award, director 1982-84, vice president 1987—); member Am. Nuclear Society, Texas Society Professional Engineers, New York Acad. Sci., Association des Ingenieurs en Genie Atomique, Phi Beta Kappa, Sigma Xi (distinguished lecturer 1981-83), Tau Beta Pi. Quaker. Club: Rotary (Austin) (International fellow 1962). Office: U Tex Department Mech Engring ETC 5 160 Austin Texas 78712

KÖHLER, GEORGES J. F., scientist, immunologist; born April 17, 1946. Scientist, immunologist Max-Planck Institut fur Immunologie, Stubeweg, Federal Republic Germany. Recipient Nobel prize in Medicine and Physiology, 1984, Albert Lasker Medical Research award, 1984.

KOHN, WALTER, educator, physicist; born Vienna, Austria, March 9, 1923. Bachelor of Arts, University Toronto, Ontario, Can., 1945, Master of Arts, 1946, Doctor of Laws (honorary), 1967; Doctor of Philosophy in Physics, Harvard University, 1948; Docteur es Sciences honoris causa, University Paris, 1980; Doctor of Science (honorary), Brandeis University, 1981; Doctor of Philosophy (honorary), Hebrew University Jerusalem, 1981. Industrial physicist Sutton Horsley Company, Can., 1941-43; geophysicist Koulomzine, Quebec, 1944-46; instructor physics Harvard University, 1948-50; assistant professor Carnegie Institute Tech., 1950-53, associate professor; 1953-57, professor; 1957-60; professor physics University California, San Diego, 1960-79, chairman department; 1961-63; director Institute for Theoretical Physics, University California, Santa Barbara, 1979-84, professor department physics; 1984—. Recipient Oliver Buckley prize, 1960, Davisson-Germer prize, 1977; National Research Council fellow, 1951; National Science Foundation fellow, 1958; Guggenheim fellow, 1963; National Science Foundation sr. postdoctoral fellow, 1967. Fellow American Association for the Advancement of Science, Am. Physical Society (counselor-at-large 1968-72), Am. Acad. Arts and Sciences; member National Acad. Sciences Research on electron theory of solids and solid surfaces. Office:

Department Physics U California Santa Barbara California 93106

KOLFF, WILLEM JOHAN, surgeon, educator; born Leiden, Holland, February 14, 1911; came to United States, 1950, naturalized, 1956; son of Jacob and Adriana (de Jonge) K.; married Janke C. Huidekoper, Sept 4, 1937; children: Jacob, Adriana P., Albert C., Cornelis A., Gualtherus C.M. Student, University Leiden Medical School, 1930-38; Doctor of Medicine summa cum laude, University Groningen, 1946; Doctor of Medicine (honorary), University Turin, Italy, 1969, Rostock (Germany) University, 1975, University Bologna, Italy, 1983; Doctor of Science (honorary), Allegheny College, Meadville, Pennsylvania, 1960, Tulane University, 1975, City University of New York, 1982, Temple University, 1983, University Utah, 1983; Doctor of Tech. Scis. (honorary), Tech. University Twente, Enscheded, the Netherlands, 1986. Internist, head medical department Municipal Hospital, Kampen, Holland; staff research div. Cleveland Clinic Foundation, 1950-67; privaat docent, department medicine University Leiden, Nether-Bunts Educational Institute, Cleveland, 1950-67; head department artificial organs University Leiden, Nether-Bunts Educational Institute, 1958-67; professor surgery University Utah College Medicine, Salt Lake City, 1967-86, Distinguished professor medicine and surgery; 1979—; professor internal medicine University Utah College Medicine, 1981—; research professor engineering Institute Biomed. Engineering, 1967—. Decorated commandeur Orde Van Oranje Netherlands, 1970; Orden de Mayo al Merito en el Grado de Gran Official

Argentina, 1974; recipient Landsteiner medal for establishment blood banks during war in Holland Netherlands Red Cross, 1942; Cameron prize University Edinburgh (Scotland), 1964; 5,000 award Gairdner Foundation, 1966; Valentine award New York Acad. Medicine, 1969; 1st Gold medal Netherlands Surg. Society, 1970; Leo Harvey prize Technion, Israel, 1972; Senior U.S. Scientist award Alexander Von Humboldt Foundation, 1978; Austrian Gewerbeverein's Wilhelm-Exner award, 1980; John Scott medal City of Philadelphia, 1984; named to National Inventors Hall of Fame, 1984; recipient Japan prize Japan Foundation Sci. and Tech., 1986, Research prize Netherlands Royal Institute Engrs., 1986; recipient 1st Jean Hamburger award International Society Nephrology, 1987. Member American Medical Association (Sci. Achievement award 1982), American Association of University Profs., Am. Physiological Society, Society Experimental Biology and Medicine, American Association for the Advancement of Science, New York Acad. Sciences, Am. Society Artificial Internal Organs, National Kidney Foundation, European Dialysis and Transplant Association, American College of Physicians, Austrian Society Nephrology (hon.), Academia Nacional de Medicine (Colombia) (hon.). Lodge: Rotary. Devel. artificial kidney for clin. use, 1943; oxygenator, 1956. Office: U Utah Med Center Div Artificial Organs Building 535 Salt Lake City Utah 84112

KOOP, CHARLES EVERETT, surgeon, government official; born Brooklyn, October 14, 1916; son of John Everett and Helen (Apel) K.; married Elizabeth Flanagan,

September 19, 1938; children: Allen van Benschoten, Norman Apel, David Charles Everett, Elizabeth. Bachelor of Arts, Dartmouth College, 1937; Doctor of Medicine, Cornell University, 1941; Doctor of Science in Medicine, University Pennsylvania, 1947; Doctor of Laws, Eastern Baptist College, 1960, La Salle College, Philadelphia, 1983; Doctor of Medicine (honorary), University Liverpool, England, 1968; Doctor of Humane Letters, Wheaton College, 1973; Doctor of Science, Gwynedd Mercy College, 1978. Intern Pennsylvania Hospital, Philadelphia, 1941-42; fellow in surgery Boston Children's Hospital, 1946; surgeon-in-chief Children's Hospital of Philadelphia, 1948—; with University Pennsylvania School Medicine, 1942—, professor; 1959—; deputy assistant secretary for health Department of Health and Human Services; surgical general United States Public Health Service, 1981—, director international health; 1982—; surgeon general of United States 1985-89; consultant United States Navy, 1964—. Editor in chief: Journal Pediatric Surgery, 1965-77; contributor publications in surgical physiology, biomed. ethics, physiology of surgical neonate, tech. advances in pediatric surgery. Board of directors Medical Assistance Programs, Incorporated, Wheaton, Illinois, Evangelical Ministries, Incorporated, Philadelphia, Daystar Communications, Incorporated, Eugene, Ore., Ea. Baptist Sem. and College, Philadelphia. Decorated chevalier Legion of Honor (France); recipient medal City of Marseille, Kopernicus medal Polish Surg. Society. Fellow American College of Surgeons, Am. Acad. Pediatrics (William E. Ladd Gold medal), Royal College Surgeons England (hon.); member Am. Surgical Association, Society University Surgeons, Brit. Association Pediatric Surgeons (Dennis Browne Gold medal), International Society Surgery, Association Military Surgeons United States (president 1982, 87, Founders medal), Societe Francaise de Chirugie Infantile, American Medical Association, Deutschen Gesselschaft für Kinderchirugi, Societé Suisse De Chirurgie Infantile, Order Duarte, Sanchez y Mella Dominican Republic, Sigma Xi. Office: Department of Health & Human Services Surgeon Gen Office 200 Independence Avenue Southwest Washington District of Columbia 20201

KOPP, RICHARD EDGAR, electrical engineer; born Brooklyn, July 12, 1931; son of Edgar A. and Anna M. (Barto) K.; married Elaine Hecker, June 14, 1953; children: Debra, Richard (deceased), Lisa, Barbara. Bachelor of Electrical Engineering, Polytechnic Institute Brooklyn, 1953; Master of Science, Brooklyn Institute, 1957, Doctor.Electrical Engineer, 1960. With Grumman Aerospace, Bethpage, New York, 1953—, director system sciences research; 1976—; adj. professor Polytechnic Institute Brooklyn, 1961-70; member adv. committee Polytechnic Institute Imaging Sciences. Contributor articles to professional journals. Fellow American Institute of Aeronautics and Astronautics (associate); member Institute of Electrical and Electronics Engineers (senior), United States Power Squadron. Club: Smithtown Bay Yacht. Home: 12 Cygnet Dr Smithtown New York 11787 Office: Grumman Aerospace Corp. A-08-35 Bethpage New York 11714

KOPROWSKI, HILARY, medical scientist; born Warsaw, Poland; son of

Paul and Sarah (Berland) K.; married Dr. Irena Grasberg; children: Claude Eugene, Christopher Dorian. Bachelor of Arts, Nikolaj Rej Gymnasium of Lutheran Congregation, Warsaw; Doctor of Medicine, University Warsaw; graduate, Warsaw Conservatory Music and Santa Cecilia Academy, Rome; Doctor honoris causa, Widener College, Philadelphia, Ludwig-Maximilian University, Ger., University Helsinki, Finland, University Uppsala (Sweden), Thomas Jefferson University, Philadelphia. Research assistant department experimental and general pathology University Warsaw, 1936-39; staff Yellow Fever Research Service, Rio de Janeiro, 1940-44; staff research div. Am. Cyanamid Company, 1944-46; assistant director viral and rickettsial research Lederle Laboratory, Pearl River, New York, 1946-57; director Wistar Institute, Philadelphia, 1957—; professor microbiology Faculty Arts and Sciences, University Pennsylvania, 1957—; Wistar professor research medicine University Pennsylvania, 1957—; consultant World Health Organization, National Cancer Institute, National Institutes of Health, United States Public Health Service, 1962-70. Co-editor: Methods in Virology, Viruses and Immunity, Current Topics in Microbiology and Immunology, 1965—, Cancer Research, Viral Immunology, Hybridoma. Decorated Commandeur Ordre du Mérite pour la Recherche et l'Invention; Chevalier Order Royal De Lion Belgium; recipient Alvarenga prize. College Physicians Philadelphia, 1959; Alfred Jurzykowski Found Polish Millenium prize, 1966; Felix Wankel Tierschutz prize, 1979; Alexander Von Humboldt Senior U.S. Scientist award; Fulbright Scholar Max Planck Institute für Verhaltensphysio-logie, Seewiesen, Germany, 1971. Fellow New York Acad. Medicine, Philadelphia College Physicians; member Am. Acad. Arts and Sciences, National Acad. Sciences, New York Acad. Sciences (president 1959, trustee 1960-72). Research cell biology, virology and immunology; vaccine against poliomyelitis, hog cholera, rabies. Home: 334 Fairhill Road Wynnewood Pennsylvania 19096 Office: Wistar Institute Anatomy & Biology 36th & Spruce Sts Philadelphia Pennsylvania 19104

KORCHYNSKY, MICHAEL, metallurgical engineer; born Kiev, Ukraine, April 11, 1918; came to United States, 1950, naturalized, 1956; son of Michael and Jadwiga (Zdanowicz) K.; married Taisija Lapin, November 22, 1951; children—Michael, Marina, Roksana. Dipl. Ing. in Metals Tech., Tech. University Lviv, 1942. Lecturer Tech. University Lviv, 1942-44; chief engineer Corps of Engineers, United States Army, Federal Republic Germany, 1945-50; research metallurgist Union Carbide Company, Niagara Falls, New York, 1951-61; research supervisor Jones & Laughlin Steel Corp., Pittsburgh, 1962-68; director product research Jones & Laughlin Steel Corp., 1969-72; director alloy devel. metals div. Union Carbide Company, New York City, 1973-77, Pittsburgh, 1978-86; consultant, principal Korchynsky and Associates, Pittsburgh, 1986—; lecturer Niagara University, 1957-58. Author, patentee in field. Union Carbide sr. fellow, 1979. Fellow Am. Society Metals (Andrew Carnegie lecturer 1973; W.H. Eisenman medal 1984, F.C. Bain award 1986); member Am. Iron and Steel Institute (medalist), Institute Metals, Am. Society Metals International, American Institute of

Mining, Metallurgy and Petroleum Engineers (Howe Memorial lecturer 1983), Iron and Steel Institute Japan, Institute Metals (United Kingdom). Home: 2770 Milford Dr Bethel Park Pennsylvania 15102

KORNBERG, ARTHUR, biochemist; born New York City, March 3, 1918; son of Joseph and Lena (Katz) K.; married Sylvy R. Levy, November 21, 1943; children: Roger, Thomas Bill, Kenneth Andrew. Bachelor of Science (New York State scholar), City College of New York, 1937, Doctor of Laws (honorary), 1960; Doctor of Medicine (Buswell scholar), University Rochester, 1941, Doctor of Science (honorary), 1962; Doctor of Science (honorary), University Pennsylvania, University Notre Dame, 1965, Washington University, 1968, Princeton University, 1970, Colby College, 1970; Doctor of Humane Letters (honorary), Yeshiva University, 1963; Doctor of Medicine honoris causa, University Barcelona, Italy, 1970. Intern in medicine Strong Memorial Hospital, Rochester, New York, 1941-42; commissioned officer United States Public Health Service, 1942, advanced through grades to medical director; 1951; member staff National Institutes of Health, Bethesda, Maryland, 1942-52, nutrition section, div. physiology; 1942-45; chief section enzymes and metabolism National Institute Arthritis and Metabolic Diseases, 1947-52; guest research worker departments chemistry and pharmacology college medicine New York University, 1946; department biological chemistry medical school Washington University, 1947; department plant biochemistry University California, 1951; professor, head department microbiology, medical school

Washington University, St. Louis, 1953-59; professor biochemistry Stanford University School Medicine, 1959—, chairman department; 1959-69; Member sci. adv. board Massachusetts General Hospital, 1964-67; board governors Weizmann Institute, Israel. Contributor sci. articles to professional journals. Served lieutenant (junior grade), medical officer United States Coast Guard Reserve, 1942. Recipient Paul-Lewis award in enzyme chemistry, 1951; co-recipient of Nobel prize in medicine, 1959; Max Berg award prolonging human life, 1968; Sci. Achievement award American Medical Association, 1968; Lucy Wortham James award James Ewing Society, 1968; Borden award Am. Association Medical Colleges, 1968. Member Am. Society Biological Chemists (president 1965), Am. Chemical Society, Harvey Society, Am. Acad. Arts and Sciences, Royal Society, National Acad. Sciences (member council 1963-66), Am. Philosophical Society, Phi Beta Kappa, Sigma Xi, Alpha Omega Alpha. Office: Stanford U Med Center Department Biochemistry Stanford California 94305

KOROS, WILLIAM JOHN, chemical engineering educator; born Omaha, August 31, 1947; son of William Alexander and Mary Ellen (Roth) K.; married Ann Marie Teahan, December 19, 1970. Bachelor of Science in Chemical Engineering, University Texas, 1969, Master of Science in Chemical Engineering, 1975, Doctor of Science in Chemical Engineering, 1977. Registered professional engineer, Texas. Chemical engineer E.I. DuPont, Wilmington, Del., 1969-71, consultant; 1982—; engineer E.I. DuPont, Camden, South Carolina,

1971-73; research assistant University Texas, Austin, 1973-77, professor; 1983—, Meek Petrofina professor in Chemical Engineering; 1985—; assistant professor chemical engineering North Carolina State University, Raleigh, 1977-80, associate professor chemical engineering; 1980-83. Recipient Sigma Xi Research award, 1980, Young Investigators award National Science Foundation, 1983, Alcoa Found Research award North Carolina State University, 1983. Member American College of Surgeons, Am. Institute Chemical Engineers. Office: U Tex CPE Building Department Chem Engring Austin Texas 78712

KOSHLAND, DANIEL EDWARD, JR., biochemist, educator; born New York City, March 30, 1920; son of Daniel Edward and Eleanor (Haas) K.; married Marian Elliott, May 25, 1945; children: Ellen, Phyllis, James, Gail, Douglas. Bachelor of Science, University California, Berkeley, 1941; Doctor of Philosophy, University Chicago, 1949; Doctor of Philosophy (honorary), Weizmann Institute Science, 1984; Doctor of Science (honorary), Carnegie Mellon University, 1985; Doctor of Laws (honorary), Simon Fraser University, 1986. Chemist Shell Chemical Company, Martinez, 1941-42; research associate Manhattan District University Chicago, 1942-44; group leader Oak Ridge National Laboratories, 1944-46; postdoctoral fellow Harvard, 1949-51; staff Brookhaven National Laboratory, Upton, New York, 1951-65; affiliate Rockefeller Institute, New York City, 1958-65; professor biochemistry University California at Berkeley, 1965—, chairman department; 1973-78; Harvey lecturer, 1969; fellow All Souls, Oxford University, 1972; Phi Beta Kappa lecturer, 1976; John Edsall lecturer Harvard University, 1980; William H. Stein lecturer, Rockefeller University, 1985; Robert Woodward visiting professor Harvard University, 1986. Author: Bacterial Chemotaxis as A Model Behavioral System, 1980; member editorial bds.: journal Accounts Chemical Research; editor: journal Procs. National Acad. Scis, 1980-85; editor Science magazine, 1985—. Recipient T. Duckett Jones award Helen Hay Whitney Foundation, 1977; Guggenheim fellow, 1972; delivered Rudin Lectures, Columbia University, 1985. Member National Acad. Sciences, Am. Chemical Society (Edgar Fahs Smith award 1979, Pauling award 1979, Rosenstiel award 1984, Waterford prize 1984), Am. Philosophical Society, Am. Society Biological Chemists (president), Am. Acad. Arts and Sciences (council), Academy Forum (chairman), Japanese Biochem. Society (hon.), Royal Swedish Acad. Sciences (hon.), Alpha Omega Aplha. Home: 3991 Happy Valley Road Lafayette California 94549 Office: Biochemistry Department U California Berkeley California 94720

KOSHLAND, MARIAN ELLIOTT, immunologist, educator; born New Haven, October 25, 1921; daughter of Waller Watkins and Margaret Ann (Smith) Elliott; married Daniel Edward Koshland, Jr., May 25, 1945; children—Ellen R., Phyllis A., James M., Gail F., Douglas E. Bachelor of Arts, Vassar College, 1942, Master of Science, 1943; Doctor of Philosophy, University Chicago, 1949. Research assistant Manhattan District Atomic Bomb Project, 1945-46; fellow department bacteriology Harvard Medical School, 1949-51; associate bacteriologist biology department Brookhaven National Laboratory, 1952-62, bacteriologist; 1963-65; associate research immunologist virus laboratory University California, Berkeley, 1965-69; lecturer department molecular biology University California, 1966-70, professor department microbiology and immunology; 1970—, chairman department; 1982—; member National Sci. Board, 1976-82; member adv. committee to director National Institutes of Health, 1972-75. Contributor articles to professional journals. Member National Acad. Sciences, Am. Acad. Microbiology, Am. Association Immunologists (president 1982-1983), Am. Society Biological Chemists, Phi Beta Kappa, Sigma Xi. Office: U California Department Microbiology & Immunology Berkeley California 94720

KOWAL, CHARLES THOMAS, astronomer; born Buffalo, November 8, 1940; son of Charles Joseph and Rose (Myszkowiak) K.; married Maria Antonietta Ruffino, October 17, 1968; 1 daughter, Loretta. Bachelor of Arts, University Southern California, 1963. Research assistant Mount Wilson and Palomar observatories, 1961-63, California Institute Tech., Pasadena, 1963-65, 66-75, University Hawaii, 1965-66; associate scientist California Institute Tech., 1976-78, scientist; 1978-81, member professional staff; 1981-85; staff scientist Computer Sci Corp., 1986—; staff associate Hale Observatory, 1979-80; lecturer in field. Recipient James Craig Watson award National Acad. Sciences, 1979. Member Am. Astronomical Society, International Astronomical Union.

Discovered bright supernova, 1972, 13th satellite of Jupiter, 1974, large planetoid between orbits of Saturn and Uranus, 1977, also asteroids and comets; recovered lost comets and asteroids. Office: Space Telescope Sci Institute CSC Homewood Campus Baltimore Maryland 21218

KRAFT, DAVID CHRISTIAN, civil engineering educator; born Marion, Ohio, September 10, 1937; son of Walter Christian and Marie Francis K.; married Suzanne Bintz, August 24, 1959; children—Susan, Michael, Jeannine. Bachelor of Civil Engineering, University Dayton, 1959; Master of Science in Civil Engineering, University Notre Dame, 1961; Doctor of Philosophy in Civil Engineering, Ohio State University, 1964. Registered professional engineer, Ohio, Kansas. Associate research engineer University New Mexico, 1964; assistant professor civil engineering University Dayton, 1965-68, associate professor; 1969-72, professor; 1972-78, assistant dean; 1970-72, dean School Engineering; 1972-78; dean School Engineering University Kansas, Lawrence, 1978-84; professor civil engineering University Kansas, 1984—; partner Kraft-Shaw-Weiss and Associates (Cons. Engineers), 1968-78. Named Professor of Year University Dayton, 1970, Outstanding Dayton Area Engineering Educator Engineering Affiliate Socs. Council, 1971; recipient Neil Armstrong award Ohio Society Professional Engrs., 1972. Member National Society Professional Engineers, American Society of Civil Engineers, Am. Society Engineering Education. Roman Catholic. Office: U Kansas 2111 Learned Hall Lawrence Kansas 66045

KRAUSE, RICHARD MICHAEL, medical scientist, government official, educator; born Marietta, Ohio, January 4, 1925; son of Ellis L. and Jennie (Waterman) K. Bachelor of Arts, Marietta College, 1947, Doctor of Science (honorary), 1978; Doctor of Medicine, Case Western Reserve University, 1952; Doctor of Science (honorary), University Rochester, 1979, Medical College Ohio, Toledo, 1981, Hahnemann Medical College and Hospital, 1982; Doctor of Laws (honorary), Thomas Jefferson University, 1982. Research fellow department preventive medicine Case Western Reserve University, 1950-51; intern Ward Medical Service, Barnes Hospital, St. Louis, 1952-53; assistant resident Ward Medical Service, Barnes Hospital, 1953-54; assistant physician to hospital Rockefeller Institute, 1954-57, assistant professor, associate physician to hospital; 1957-61; professor epidemiology School Medicine, Washington University, St. Louis, 1962-66; associate professor medicine School Medicine, Washington University, 1962-65, professor medicine; 1965-66; associate professor, physician to hospital Rockefeller University, 1966-68, professor, senior physician; 1968-75; director Rockefeller University (Animal Research Center), 1974-75, National Institute Allergy and Infectious Diseases, National Institutes of Health, Department of Health, Education and Welfare, Bethesda, Maryland, 1975-84; United States Public Health Service surgeon 1975-77, assistant surgeon general; 1977-84; dean Emory University School Medicine, Atlanta, 1984-88; member program committee Institute Medicine 1986-87; senior sci. adv. Fogerty International Center National Institutes of Health, Bethesda,

1989—; Board directors Mo.-St. Louis Heart Association, 1962-66, member research committee, 1963-66; member executive committee council on rheumatic fever and congenital heart disease Am. Heart Association, 1963-66, chairman council research study committee, 1963-66, member association research committee, 1963-66, member policy committee, 1966-70; member commission streptococcal and staphylococcal diseases United States Armed Forces Epidemiological Board, 1963-72, deputy director, 1968-72; board of directors New York Heart Association, 1967-73, chairman adv. council on research, 1969-71, member directors council, 1973-75; consultant, member coccal expert committee World Health Organization, 1967—; member steering committee Biomed. Sci. Scientific Working Group, World Health Organization, 1978; member infectious disease adv. committee National Institute Allergy and Infectious Disease, National Institutes of Health, 1970-74; board of directors Royal Society Medicine Foundation, Incorporated, 1971-77, treasurer, 1973-75; board of directors Allergy and Asthma Foundation Am., 1976-77, Lupus Foundation Am., 1977—.
Asso. editor: Journal Immunology, 1963-71; sect. editor: Viral and Microbial Immunology, 1974-75; editor: Journal Experimental Medicine, 1973-75; adv. editor, 1976-84; member editorial board: Bacteriological Revs, 1969-73, Infection and Immunity, 1970-78, Immunochemistry, 1973-80, Clin. Immunology and Immunopathology, 1976-78, 1978—; Contributor numerous articles to professional journals. Served with United States Army, 1944-46. Decorated Gumhuria medal Egypt; recipient Distinguished Service medal

Department of Health, Education and Welfare, 1979; C. William O'Neal Distinguished Am. Service award; Robert Koch Medal in Gold, Berlin, 1985; Senior U.S. Scientist award Alexander Von Humboldt Foundation, Federal Republic Germany, 1986. Member United States National Acad. Sciences, Institute Medicine, Association Am. Physicians, Am. Acad. Allergy, Am. Society Biological Chemists, Am. Society Clinical Investigation, Am. Association Immunologists, Am. Society Microbiology, Harvey Society, Am. College Allergists, American Association for the Advancement of Science, Infectious Diseases Society Am., Royal Society Medicine, Practitioner's Society New York, Am. Epidemiological Society. Clubs: Century Association (New York City); Cosmos (Washington). Research on pathogenesis and epidemiology of streptococcal diseases; immunochemical studies on streptococcal antigens; immunogenetics; recognition of rabbit antibodies with molecular uniformity, genetics of immune response. Home: 4000 Cathedral Avenue Apartment 715B Washington District of Columbia 20016 Office: Fogerty International Center NIH Building 38A Room B2N13 Bethesda Maryland 20892

KRAUSS, ROBERT WALLFAR, botanist, university dean; born Cleveland, December 27, 1921; son of Wallfar Gradifer and Emma Eleanor (Mueller) K.; married Wilberta Tucker Bunker, August 29, 1947 (divorced 1969); children: Robert Geoffrey, Douglas Andrew; married Marilyn J. Marsh, December 19, 1986. Bachelor of Arts, Oberlin College, 1947; Master of Science, University Hawaii, 1949; Doctor of Philosophy, University Maryland, 1951. Research fellow Carnegie Institution, 1951-54; research fellow University Maryland, College Park, 1951-54, member faculty; 1955-72, professor botany; 1959-72, head department; 1964-73; dean College Sci. Oregon State University, Corvallis, 1973-79; executive director Federation Am. Societies Experimental Biology, Bethesda, Maryland, 1979—; staff member Marine Biological Laboratory, Woods Hole, Massachusetts, 1955, 56, 57; consultant United States Air Force School Aviation Medicine, 1961—; special advisor on U.S./Soviet relations to administrator National Aeronautics and Space Administration, 1964—; senior research affiliate Chesapeake Biological Laboratory, 1968—. Contributor numerous articles to tech. journals. Served to 2d lieutenant Army of the United States, 1943-46. Recipient Achievement award in biology Washington Acad. Sciences, 1961. Fellow American Association for the Advancement of Science (council member); member Am. Society Plant Physiologists (trustee 1964-70), Am. Institute Biological Sciences (special award 1974, sec.-treas. 1963-68, president 1973), Botanical Society Am. (Darbaker award 1956), Botanical Society Washington (president 1964), Phycological Society Am. (president 1963—), Phi Beta Kappa, Sigma Xi. Club: Cosmos (Washington). Office: Federation Am Socs Exptl Biology 9650 Rockville Pike Bethesda Maryland 20814

KRUMHANSL, JAMES ARTHUR, physicist, educator, Industrial consultant; born Cleveland, August 2, 1919; son of James and Marcella (Kelly) K.; married Barbara Dean

Schminck, December 26, 1944 (divorced 1983); children: James Lee, Carol Lynne, Peter Allen.; married Marilyn Cupp Dahl, February 19, 1983. Bachelor of Science in Electrical Engineering, University Dayton, 1939; Master of Science, Case Institute Tech., 1940, Doctor of Science (honorary), 1980; Doctor of Philosophy in Physics, Cornell University, 1943. Instructor Cornell University, 1943-44; physicist Stromberg-Carlson Company, 1944-46; member faculty Brown University, 1946-48, associate professor; 1947-48; assistant professor, then associate professor Cornell University, 1948-55; assistant director research National Carbon Company, 1955-57, associate director research; 1957-58; professor physics Cornell University, 1959—, Horace White professor; 1980; director Laboratory Atomic and Solid State Physics, 1960-64; adj. professor University Pennsylvania, 1979; fellow Los Alamos Laboratory, 1980; assistant director for math., physical sci. and engineering National Science Foundation, 1977-79; consultant to industry, 1946—; adv. com. for Atomic Energy Commission, Department Def., National Acad. Sci.; visiting fellow All Souls College, Oxford University, 1977, Gonville and Caius College, Cambridge University, 1983, Royal Society London, 1983; Fulbright lecturer, Yugoslavia, 1975. Editor Journal Applied Physics, 1957-60; associate editor Solid State Communications, 1963—, Rev. Modern Physics, 1968-73; editor Physical Rev. Letters, 1974-78, physics Oxford University Press; Contributor articles to professional journals. Guggenheim fellow, 1959-60; National Science Foundation sr. postdoctoral fellow Oxford University,

1966-67. Fellow Am. Physical Society (chairman division solid state physics 1968, councillor 1970-74, vice president 1987, pres.-elect 1988), American Association for the Advancement of Science, Am. Institute Physics (governing board 1987); member American Association of University Profs., Sigma Xi, Phi Kappa Phi. Republican. Presbyterian Club: Ithaca Yacht. Home: 2 Genung Road Ithaca New York 14850

KRUSKAL, MARTIN DAVID, mathematical physicist, educator; born New York City, September 28, 1925; married 1950; 3 children. Bachelor of Science, University Chicago, 1945; Master of Science, New York University, 1948, Doctor of Philosophy in Math., 1952. Assistant instructor department math. New York University, 1946-51; research scientist Plasma Physics Laboratory, Princeton University, 1951—, senior research associate; 1959—, professor astrophysical sci.; 1961—, professor math.; 1981—; consultant Los Alamos Sci. Laboratory, 1953-59; consultant radiation laboratory University California, 1954-57; consultant Oak Ridge National Laboratory, 1955-58, from 1963, Radio Corporation of America, 1960-62, International Business Machines Corporation, from 1963; lecturer in field. Recipient Dannie Heineman prize in math. physics, 1983; sr. fellow National Science Foundation, 1959-60. Member Am. Math. Society, Math. Association Am., Am. Physical Society, Am. Acad. Arts and Sciences, National Acad. Sciences. Office: Princeton U Department Astrophysics Princeton New Jersey 08540

KUBLER-ROSS, ELISABETH, physician; born Zurich, Switzerland,

July 8, 1926; came to United States, 1958, naturalized, 1961; daughter of Ernst and Emma (Villiger) K.; children: Kenneth Lawrence, Barbara Lee. Doctor of Medicine, University Zurich, 1957; Doctor of Science (honorary), Albany (New York) Medical College, 1974, Smith College, 1975, Molloy College, Rockville Centre, New York, 1976, Regis College, Weston, Massachusetts, 1977, Fairleigh Dickinson University, 1979; Doctor of Laws, University Notre Dame, 1974, Hamline University, 1975; honorary degree, Medical College Pennsylvania, 1975, Anna Maria College, Paxton, Massachusetts, 1978; Doctor of Letters (honorary), St. Mary's College, Notre Dame, Ind., 1975, Hood College, 1976, Rosary College, River Forest, Illinois, 1976; Doctor of Humane Letters (honorary), Amherst College, 1975, Loyola University, Chicago, 1975, Bard College, Annandale-on-Hudson, New York, 1977, Union College, Schenectady, 1978, D'Youville College, Buffalo, 1979, University Miami, Florida, 1976; Doctor.Pedagogy, Keuka College, Keuka Park, New York, 1976.

Rotating intern Community Hospital, Glen Cove, New York, 1958-59; research fellow Manhattan State Hospital, 1959-62; resident Montefiore Hospital, New York City, 1961-62; fellow psychiatry Psychopathic Hospital, University Colorado Medical School, 1962-63; instructor psychiatry Colorado General Hospital, University Colorado Medical School, 1962-65; member staff LaRabida Children's Hospital and Research Center, Chicago, 1965-70; chief consultant and research liaison section LaRabida Children's Hospital and Research Center, 1969-70; assistant professor psychiatry Billings Hospital, University Chicago, 1965-70; medical director Family Service and Mental Health Center South Cook County, Chicago Heights, Illinois, 1970-73; president Ross Medical Associates (South Carolina), Flossmoor, Illinois, 1973-77; president, chairman board Shanti Nilaya Growth and Health Center, Escondido, California, 1977—; member numerous adv., consultant boards in field. Author: On Death and Dying, 1969, Questions and Answers on Death and Dying, 1974, Death-The Final Stages of Growth, 1975, To Live Until We Say Goodbye, 1978, Working It Through, 1981, Living With Death and Dying, 1981, Remember The Secret, 1981, On Children and Death, 1985, AIDS: The Ultimate Challenge, 1988; contributor chapters to books, articles to professional journals.

Recipient Teilhard prize Teilhard Foundation, 1981; Golden Plate award Am. Acad. Achievement, 1980; Modern Samaritan award Elk Grove Village, Illinois, 1976; named Woman of the Decade Ladies Home Journal, 1979; numerous others. Member American Association for the Advancement of Science, Am. Holistic Medical Association (a founder), Am. Medical Women's Association, Am. Psychiat. Association, Am. Psychosomatic Society, Association Cancer Victims and Friends, Illinois Psychiat. Society, Society Swiss Physicians, Society Psychophysiol. Research, Second Attempt at Living. Address: care Celestial Arts Pub Post Office Box 7327 Berkeley California 94707

KUEHLER, JACK DWYER, manufacturing company executive; born Grand Island, Nebraska, August 29, 1932; son of August C. and Theresa (Dwyer) K.; married Carmen

Ann Kubas, July 16, 1955; children—Cynthia Marie, Daniel Scott, Christina L., David D., Michael P. Bachelor of Science in Mechanical Engineering, University Santa Clara. Design engineer jet engines department General Electric Company, Evandale, Ohio, 1954-55; with International Business Machines Corporation, 1958—; director International Business Machines Corporation Raleigh Comunications Laboratory, 1967-70, International Business Machines Corporation San Jose and Menlo Park Laboratories, 1970-72; vice president devel. general products div. International Business Machines Corporation, 1972-77, assistant group executive data processing product group; 1977-78, president system products div.; 1978-80, vice president International Business Machines Corporation Corp.; from 1980; president general tech. div. International Business Machines Corporation, White Plains, New York, 1980-81, information systems and tech. group executive; 1981-82, senior vice president; 1982-88, now vice chairman; 1982-88. Patentee in field. Trustee University Santa Clara (California). Served as 1st lieutenant United States Army, 1955-57. Member Institute of Electrical and Electronics Engineers (senior), National Acad. Engineering, Am. Electronics Association. Office: International Business Machines Corporation Old Orchard Road Armonk New York 10504 also: International Business Machines Corporation Corp Info Systems & Tech Group 1000 Westchester Avenue White Plains New York 10604

KUESEL, THOMAS ROBERT, civil engineer; born Richmond Hill, New York, July 30, 1926; son of Henry N. and Marie D. (Butt) K.; married Lucia Elodia Fisher, January 31, 1959; children—Robert Livingston, William Baldwin. Bachelor.in Engineering with highest honors, Yale University, 1946, Master in Engineering, 1947. With Parsons, Brinckerhoff, Quade & Douglas, 1947—; project manager Parsons, Brinckerhoff, Quade & Douglas, San Francisco, 1967-68; partner, senior vice president Parsons, Brinckerhoff, Quade & Douglas, New York City, 1968-83, chairman board, director; 1983—, director; 1968—; vice chairman Organization of European Cooperation and Development Tunneling Conference, Washington, 1970; mem United States National Committee on Tunneling Tech., 1972-74. Contributor 60 articles to professional journals Designer more than 120 bridges, 135 tunnels, and numerous other structures in 36 states and 20 foreign countries most recent: Great Belt Railway Tunnel, Denmark, 1986-88, Fort McHenry Tunnel, Baltimore, 1978-85; Rogers Pass Railway Tunnel, British Columbia, 1981-85, Glenwood Canyon Tunnel, Colorado, 1981—, Trans Koolan Tunnel, Hawaii, 1985—, Cumberland Gap Tunnel, Kentucky-Tennessee, 1986—; subways Boston, New York, Baltimore, Washington, Atlanta, Pittsburgh, Seattle, Los Angeles, Singapore, Taipei. Fellow American Society of Civil Engineers, Am. Cons. Engineers Council: member National Acad. Engineering, International Association for Bridge and Structural Engineering, Brit. Tunnelling Society, Yale Sci. and Engineering Association, Geotechnical Board of National Research Council (chairman 1988—), Yale Club (New York City); Wee Burn Club (Darien, Connecticut), The Moles, Sigma Xi, Tau Beta Pi. Clubs:

Yale (New York City); Wee Burn (Darien, Connecticut). Office: One Penn Plaza 250 W 34th St New York New York 10119

KUHI, LEONARD VELLO, astronomer, university administrator; born Hamilton, Ontario, Canada, October 22, 1936; came to United States, 1958; son of John and Sinaida (Rose) K.; married Patricia Suzanne Brown, September 3, 1958; children—Alison Diane, Christopher Paul. Bachelor of Science, University Toronto, Can., 1958; Doctor of Philosophy, University California, Berkeley, 1964. Carnegie postdoctoral fellow Hale Observatory, Pasadena, California, 1963-65; assistant professor University California, Berkeley, 1965-69, associate professor; 1969-74, professor; 1974—, chairman department astronomy; 1975-76, dean physical sciences College Letters and Sci.; 1976-81, provost; 1983—; visiting professor University Colorado, 1969, College de France, Paris, 1972-73, University Heidelberg, 1978. Contributor articles to professional journals. National Science Foundation research grantee, 1966—. Fellow American Association for the Advancement of Science; member Am. Astronomical Society (treasurer), Astronomical Society Pacific (president 1978-80), Royal Astronomical Society (Can.), International Astronomical Union, Simga Xi. Office: U California Department Astronomy Berkeley California 94720

KURZWEIL, RAYMOND C., computer scientist, entrepreneur; born New York City, February 12, 1948; son of Fredric and Hannah K.; married Sonya Rosenwald, August 3, 1975. Bachelor of Science, Massachusetts Institute of Technology, 1970; Doctor of Philosophy (honorary), Hofstra University, 1982, Berklee College Music, 1987, Rensselaer Polytech. Institute, 1988. Chairman Kurzweil Computer Products, Incorporated div. Xerox, Cambridge, Massachusetts, 1974—; chairman, chief executive officer Kurzweil Music Systems, Incorporated, Waltham, Massachusetts, 1982—; chairman Kurzweil Applied Intelligence, Incorporated, Waltham, Massachusetts, 1982—; chairman exhibition board Age of Intelligent Machines Exhibition Mus. of Sci., Boston, 1985—. Recipient Grace Murray Hopper Outstanding Young Computer Scientist of Year award Association for Computing Machinery, 1978, Personal Computing to Aid the Handicapped National award Johns Hopkins University, 1981, Francis Joseph Campbell award Am. Library Association, 1983, Entrepreneurial Excellence award White House Conference on Small Business, 1986; named to Computer Design Hall Fame, Computer Design Magazine, 1982, New England Inventor of the Year, 1988. Avocation: music. Office: Kurzweil Applied Intelligence Incorporated 411 Waverley Oaks Road Waltham Massachusetts 02154

KUSCH, POLYKARP, physicist, educator; born Blankenburg, Germany, January 26, 1911; came to United States, 1912, naturalized, 1923; son of John Matthias and Henrietta (van der Haas) K.; married Edith Starr McRoberts, August 12, 1935 (deceased 1959); children—Kathryn, Judith, Sara; married Betty Jane Pezzoni, 1960; children—Diana, Maria. Bachelor of Science, Case Institute Tech., 1931,

Doctor of Science, 1956; Master of Science, University Illinois, 1933, Doctor of Philosophy, 1936, Doctor of Science (honorary), 1961; Doctor of Science (honorary), Ohio State University, 1959, Colby College, 1961, Gustavus Adolphus College, St. Peter, Minnesota, 1962, Yeshiva University, 1976, College of Incarnate Word, 1980, Columbia University, 1983. Engaged as teaching assistant University Illinois, 1931-36; research assistant University Minnesota, 1936-37; instructor Columbia University, 1937-41, associate professor physics; 1946-49, professor; 1949-72, chairman department physics; 1949-52, 60-63, acad. vice president and provost; 1969-72; engineer Westinghouse, 1941-42; research associate Columbia University, 1942-44; member tech. staff Bell Telephone Laboratories, 1944-46; professor physics University Tex.-Dallas, 1972—, Eugene McDermott professor; 1974-80, Regental professor; 1980-82, Regental professor emeritus; 1982—. Recipient Nobel prize in physics, 1955, Illinois Achievement award University Illinois, 1975; Fellow; Center for Advanced Study in Behavioral Sciences, 1964-65. Fellow Am. Physical Society, American Association for the Advancement of Science; member Am. Acad. Arts and Sciences, Am. Philosophical Society, National Acad. Sciences. Democrat. Research in atomic and molecular beams and optical molecular spectroscopy. Office: U Tex-Dallas Post Office Box 830688 Richardson Texas 75083

LACKNER, JAMES ROBERT, aerospace medicine educator; born Virginia, Minnesota, November 11, 1940; son of William and Lillian Mae (Galbraith) L.; married Ann Martin Graybiel, August 26, 1970. BSc, Massachusetts Institute of Technology, 1966, Doctor of Philosophy, 1970. Assistant professor psychology Brandeis University, Waltham, Massachusetts, 1970-74, associate professor psychology; 1974-79, Riklis professor behavioral physiology department psychology; 1977—, chairman department psychology; 1975-83, provost, dean faculty; 1986-89, director Ashton Graybiel Spatial Orientation Laboratory; 1982—; research associate department psychology and clinical research center Massachusetts Institute of Technology, Cambridge, 1970-80; sci. adv. board Space Biomed. Research Institute, Houston, 1982—, Aphasia Research Center Boston University School Medical, 1977-82, Eunice Kennedy Shriver Center Harvard University Medical School, Cambridge, 1980—; sci. adv. panel astronaut longitudinal health program Johnson Space Center, National Aeronautics and Space Administration, 1983, executive secretary space adaptation syndrome steering committee, 1982-84, pre-adaption trainer working group, 1986—, artificial gravity working group, 1987—; fabricant committee life sciences experiments for a space station, 1982; space sciences board sensory motor panel National Acad. Sciences, 1984-86; committee on hearing, bioacoustics and biomechanics National Research Council, 1985—. Contributor over 100 articles to sci. journals. Member Am. Society for Gravitational and Space Biology, Aerospace Medical Association (Arnold B. Tuttle award), Society for Neurosci., Psychonomics Society, International Brain Research Organization, Barany Society (hon.),

International Acad. Astronautics (hon.). Research in human sensory-motor coordination and spatial orientation. Home: Boyce Farm Road Lincoln Center Massachusetts 01773 Office: Brandeis University Ashton Graybiel Spatial Orientation Lab Waltham Massachusetts 02254-9110

LAHR, C. DWIGHT, mathematics educator, college dean; born Philadelphia, February 6, 1945; son of Charles and Helen L.; married Dora (divorced); children—Elena, Maria, Emilio; married Beatriz Pastor. Bachelor of Arts, Temple University, 1966; Master of Arts, Syracuse University, 1968, Doctor of Philosophy, 1971. Associate professor math. Dartmouth College, Hanover, New Hampshire, 1979-84, professor math. and computer sci.; 1984—, associate dean sciences, dean grad. studies; 1981-84, dean of faculty; 1984—; consultant Alfred P. Sloan Foundation, 1983—; reviewer Math. Revs.; project director Fund for the Improvement of Post-Secondary Education, Washington, 1982—. Sloan Foundation grantee, 1983, Fund for Improvement Postsecondary Education grantee, 1982. Member Am. Math. Society, Math. Association Am., American Association for the Advancement of Science. Office: Dartmouth College 301 Wentworth Hanover New Hampshire 03755

LAKE, LARRY WAYNE, petroleum engineer; born Del Norte, Colorado, January 31, 1946; son of Ralph Wayne and Ina Belle (Card) L.; married Carole Sue Holmes, March 22, 1975; children: Leslie Sue, Jeffrey Wayne. Bachelor of Science, Arizona State University, 1967; Doctor of Philosophy, Rice University, 1973. Registered professional engineer, Texas. Production engineer Motorola

Company, Phoenix, 1968-70; senior research engineer Shell Devel. Company, Houston, 1973-78; professor petroleum engineering, Shell distinguished chairman University Texas, Austin, 1978—; consultant enhanced oil recovery AMOCO, Malapai Resources, IFE, Norway. Recipient University Texas Engineering Foundation award, 1979, Distinguished Faculty Adv. award University Texas, 1981, Graduate Engineering Council award, University Texas, 1987. Member Society Mining Engineers, Society Petroleum Engineers (member editorial rev. committee, chairman continuing education committee, author video, Distinguished Achievement award 1981), Am. Institute Chemical Engineers, Sigma Xi, Tau Beta Pi, Pi Epsilon Tau. Baptist. Home: 4003 Edgefield Court Austin Texas 78731 Office: U Tex Department Petroleum Engring Austin Texas 78712

LAM, SIMON SHIN-SING, computer science educator; born Macao, July 31, 1947; came to United States, 1966; son of Chak Han and Kit Ying (Tang) L.; married Amy Leung, March 29, 1971; 1 child, Eric. Bachelor of Science in Electrical Engineering with distinction, Washington State University, 1969; Master of Science in Engineering, University of California at Los Angeles, 1970, Doctor of Philosophy, 1974. Research engineer ARPA Network Measurement Center, University of California at Los Angeles, Los Angeles, 1971-74; research staff member International Business Machines Corporation Watson Research Ctr, Yorktown Heights, New York, 1974-77; assistant professor University Tex.-Austin, 1977-79, associate professor; 1979-83, professor computer sci.; 1983—,

David South Bruton Centennial professor; 1985—. Contributor articles to professional journals, conference procs.; editor: Principles of Communicaton and Networking Protocols. National Science Foundation grantee, 1978—; Chancellor's Teaching fellow UCLA, 1969-73. Fellow Institute of Electrical and Electronics Engineers (Leonard G. Abraham prize 1975); member Association for Computing Machinery (program chairman symposium 1983). Avocations: tennis; swimming; golf; travelling. Office: University Texas Department of Computer Sci Austin Texas 78712

LAMB, WILLIS EUGENE, JR., physicist, educator; born Los Angeles, July 12, 1913; son of Willis Eugene and Marie Helen (Metcalf) L.; married Ursula Schaefer, June 5, 1939. Bachelor of Science, University California, 1934, Doctor of Philosophy, 1938; Doctor of Science, University Pennsylvania, 1953, Gustavus Adolphus College, 1975; Master of Arts, Oxford (England) University, 1956, Yale, 1961; Doctor of Humane Letters, Yeshiva University, 1965. Member faculty Columbia, 1938-52, professor physics; 1948-52; professor physics Stanford, 1951-56; Wykeham professor physics and fellow New College, Oxford University, 1956-62; Henry Ford 2d professor physics Yale, 1962-72, J. Willard Gibbs professor physics; 1972-74; professor physics and optical sciences University Arizona, Tucson, 1974—; Morris Loeb lecturer Harvard, 1953-54; consultant Philips Laboratories, Bell Telephone Laboratories, Perkin-Elmer, National Aeronautics and Space Administration.; Visiting committee Brookhaven National Laboratory. Recipient (with Dr. Polykarp Kusch) Nobel prize in physics, 1955; Rumford premium Am. Acad. Arts and Sciences, 1953; Research Corp. award, 1955; Guggenheim fellow, 1960-61; recipient Yeshiva award, 1962. Fellow Am. Physical Society, New York Acad. Sciences; hon. fellow Institute Physics and Physical Society (Guthrie lecturer 1958), Royal Society Edinburgh (foreign member); member National Acad. Sciences, Phi Beta Kappa, Sigma Xi. Office: U Ariz Department Physics Tucson Arizona 85721

LAMBERT, DAVID L., astronomy educator. Bachelor of Science, University College, Oxford, England; Doctor of Philosophy, Balliol College, Oxford. Research fellow California Institute Tech., Pasadena, Mount Wilson Palomar Observatories; with department astronomy University Texas, Austin, 1969, professor; 1974—, now Isabel McCutcheon Harte Centennial professor astronomy. Recipient Dannie Heineman Prize for Astrophysics award Am. Astronomical Society, 1987; Guggenheim fellow, vis. Erskine fellow University Canterbury, New Zealand, 1985. Fellow Royal Astronomical Society; member Am. Astronomical Society, International Astronomical Union. Office: U Tex Austin Department Astronomy Austin Texas 78712

LAND, EDWIN HERBERT, physicist, inventor; born Bridgeport, Connecticut, May 7, 1909; son of Harry M. and Matha F. L.; married Helen Maislen, 1929; children: Jennifer, Valerie. Educated, Norwich Academy; student, Harvard University, Doctor of Science (honorary), 1957; Doctor of Science (honorary), Tufts College, 1947, Polytechnic Institute Brooklyn, 1952, Colby College, 1955,

Northeastern University, 1959, Carnegie Institute Tech., 1964, Yale University, 1966, Columbia University, 1967, Loyola University, 1970, New York University, 1973; Doctor of Laws (honorary), Bates College, 1953, Washington University, 1966; Doctor of Laws (honorary), University Massachusetts, 1967, Brandeis University, 1980; Doctor of Humane Letters (honorary), Williams College, 1968. Founder Polaroid Corp., Cambridge, Massachusetts, 1937; president, chairman board Polaroid Corp., 1982; founder, director research, scientist Rowland Institute Sci., Cambridge, Massachusetts, from 1981; William James lecturer psychology Harvard, 1966-67, Morris Loeb lecturer physics, 1974; visiting Institute professor Massachusetts Institute Tech., from 1956; member President's Sci. Adv. Committee, 1957-59, cons.-at-large, 1960-73; member President's Committee National Medal of Sci., 1969-72, Carnegie Commission on Educational TV, 1966-67, National Commission on Tech., Automation and Economic Progress, 1964-66; foreign member Royal Society, 1986. Trustee Ford Foundation, 1967-75. Recipient Presidential Medal of Freedom, 1963, National Medal of Sci., 1967, Hood medal Royal Photog. Society, 1935, Cresson medal, 1937, Potts medal, 1956, Vermilye medal Franklin Institute, Philadelphia, 1974, John Scott medal and award, 1938, Rumford medal Am. Acad. Arts and Sciences, 1945, Holley medal American Society of Mechanical Engineers, 1948, Duddell medal Brit. Physical Society, 1949, Progress medal Society Photographic Engineers, 1955, Albert A. Michelson award Case Institute Tech., 1966, Kulturpreis Photographic Society

Germany, 1967, Perkin medal Society Chemical Industry, 1974, Proctor award, 1963, Photographic Sci. and Engineering Journal award, 1971, Progress medal Photographic Society Am., 1960, Kosar Memorial award, 1973, Golden Society medal Photographic Society Vienna, 1961, Interkamera award, 1973, Cosmos Club award, 1970, National Association of Manufacturers award, 1940, 66, Jefferson medal New Jersey Patent Law Association, 1960, Indsl. Research medal, 1965, Diesel medal in gold, 1966; named National Inventors Hall of Fame, 1977. Fellow National Academy of Sciences, Photographic Society Am., Am. Acad. Arts and Sciences (president 1951-53), Royal Photographic Society Great Britain (Progress medal 1957), Royal Microscopic Society (hon.), Society Photographic Scientists and Engineers (hon., Lieven-Gevaert medal 1976); member New York Acad. Sciences, National Acad. Engineering (Founders medal 1972), Optical Society Am. (hon. member 1972, director 1950-51, Frederick Ives medal 1967, Dudley Wright prize 1980), Royal Institution Great Britain (hon.), Am. Philosophical Society, German Photographic Society (hon.), Society Photographic Sci. and Tech. Japan (hon.), Institute of Electrical and Electronics Engineers (hon.), Sigma Xi. During college years invented first light-polarizer in form of an extensive synthetic sheet; developed a sequence of subsequent polarizers, theories and applications of polarized light, including automobile headlight system, 3 dimensional pictures, camera filters; during World War II developed optical, other systems for military use; created cameras, films that give instantaneous dry photographs in black and white and color; proposed Retinex Theory for mechanism of color perception and designed series of supporting experiments. Office: Rowland Institute Sci 100 Cambridge Parkway Cambridge Massachusetts 02142

LANDAU, WILLIAM MILTON, neurologist; born St. Louis, October 10, 1924; son of Milton S. and Amelia (Rich) L.; married Roberta Anne Hornbein, April 3, 1947; children: David, John, Julia, George. Student, University Chicago, 1941-43; Doctor of Medicine cum laude, Washington University, St. Louis, 1947. Diplomate: Am. Board Psychiatry and Neurology (dir. 1967, pres. 1975). Intern University Chicago Clinics, 1947; resident St. Louis City Hospital, 1948; fellow Washington University, St. Louis, 1949-52, National Institutes of Health, Bethesda, Maryland, 1952-54; instructor neurology Washington University, 1952-54, assistant professor; 1954-58, associate professor; 1958-63, professor; 1963—, department head; 1970—, co-head department neurology and neur. surgery; 1975; chairman National Committee for Research in Neurological and Communicative Disorders, 1980. Editorial board: Neurology, 1963, A.M.A. Archives Neurology, 1965, Annals Neurology, 1977. Member American Civil Liberties Union (trustee East Missouri 1956—), Am. Neurological Association (president 1977), Am. Acad. Neurology, Association University Profs. Neurology (president 1978), Society Neurosci., Am. Physiological Society, Am. Electro-encephalography Society. Research neurophysiology. Office: 660 S Euclid Avenue Saint Louis Missouri 63110

LANDEAU, RALPH, chemical engineer; born Philadelphia, May 19, 1916; son of Stanley and Deanna L.; married Claire, July 14, 1940; 1 daughter. Bachelor of Science, University Pennsylvania, 1937; Doctor of Science, Massachusetts Institute of Technology, 1941. Research assistant chemical engineering Massachusetts Institute of Technology, 1939-41; devel. engineer M.W Kellogg Company, 1939, 41-43, 46; head chemicals department Kellex Corp., 1943-45; executive vice president, director Sci. Design Company, Incorporated, New York City, 1946-63; president Halcon International, Incorporated, 1963-75, chairman; 1975-81; chairman Halcon-SD Group, 1981-82, Listowel Incorporated, 1982—; consultant professor economic Stanford University; fellow faculty Harvard Kennedy School; board of directors Alcoa Corp. Author papers, chapters; patentee in field. Life member corp. Massachusetts Institute of Technology; life trustee University Pennsylvania; trustee California Institute Tech., Cold Spring Harbor Lab. Recipient Chemical Industry medal, Perkin medal, National Medal Tech. Member National Acad. Engineering (vice president), Am. Acad. Arts and Sciences, Sigma Xi, Tau Beta Pi. Clubs: Sky, Harvard, Princeton, Yale, Chemists (New York City), French (San Francisco). Office: 2 Park Avenue New York New York 10016

LANDIS, FRED, mechanical engineering educator; born Munich, Germany, March 21, 1923; came to United States, 1947, naturalized, 1954; son of Julius and Elsie (Schulhoff) L.; married Billie H. Schiff, August 26, 1951 (deceased January 10, 1985); children—John David, Deborah Ellen, Mark Edward. Bachelor of Engineering, McGill University, 1945; Master of Science, Massachusetts Institute of Technology, 1949, Doctor of Science, 1950. Design engineer Canadian Vickers, Limited, Montreal, Can., 1945-47; assistant professor mechanical engineering Stanford University, 1950-52; research engineer Northrop Aircraft, Incorporated, Hawthorne, California, 1952-53; assistant professor New York University, 1953-56, associate professor; 1956-61, professor; 1961-73, chairman department mechanical engineering; 1963-73; dean, professor mechanical engineering Polytechnic University, Brooklyn, 1973-74; dean College Engineering and Applied Sci., University Wisconsin, Milwaukee, 1974-83, professor mechanical engineering; 1984—; staff consultant Pratt & Whitney Aircraft Company, 1957—. Cons. editor, Macmillan Company, 1960-68; cons. editorial board: Funk & Wagnalls Ency, 1969—, Compton's Encyclopedia, 1984—; Contributor numerous research articles to professional journals. Member Board Education, Dobbs Ferry, New York, 1965-71, vice president, 1966-67, 70-71, president, 1967-68; board of directors Westchester County, School Boards Association, 1969-70, vice president, 1970, president, 1970-71; board of directors Engring. Foundation, 1986—. Fellow American Society of Mechanical Engineers (division executive committee 1965-73, policy board 1973—, vice president 1985—), Am. Society Engineering Education; associate fellow American Institute of Aeronautics and Astronautics; member Sigma Xi, Tau Beta Pi, Pi Tau Sigma. Home: 2420 W Acacia Road Milwaukee Wisconsin 53209

LANFORD, OSCAR ERASMUS, III, mathematics educator; born New York City, January 6, 1940; son of Oscar E. and Caroline Clapp (Sherman) L.; married Regina Victoria Krigman, December 29, 1961; 1 child, Lizabeth Lanford Miller. Bachelor of Arts, Wesleyan University, Middletown, Connecticut, 1960; Master of Arts, Princeton University, 1962, Doctor of Philosophy, 1966. Assistant, associate to professor math. University California, Berkeley, 1966—; professor physics Institute des Hautes Etudes Scientiques, Bures-sur-Yvette, France, 1982-87. Recipient award in applied math and numerical analysis, U.S. National Acad. Sci., 1986. Member Am. Math. Society. Home: 1841 Berryman St Berkeley California 94703 Office: University of California Department of Math Berkeley California 94720

LANGSTON, WANN, JR., paleontologist educator, researcher; born Oklahoma City, July 10, 1921; married; 2 children. Bachelor of Science, University Oklahoma, 1943, Master of Science, 1947; Doctor of Philosophy in Paleontology, University California, 1951. Instructor geology Texas Tech. College, 1946-48; preparator Mus. Paleontology-U. California, 1949-54; lecturer Mus. Paleontology, University California, 1951-52; paleontologist National Mus. Can., 1954-62; research scientist Texas Memorial Mus., Austin, 1962-86; director vertebrate paleontology laboratory University Texas, Austin, 1969-86, professor department geological sci.; 1975-85; retired 1986; 1st Mr. and Mrs. Charles East Yager professor geological sciences University Texas, Austin, 1986—; research associate Cleveland Mus. Natural History, 1974-79. Member Geological Society Am.,

Society Vertebrate Paleontology (vice president 1973-74, president 1974-75), Am. Society Ichtvol. and Herpetology, Am. Association Petroleum Geologists. Office: U Tex Department Geol Sci Utah Station Austin Texas 78712

LARAGH, JOHN HENRY, physician, scientist, educator; born Yonkers, New York, November 18, 1924; son of Harry Joseph and Grace Catherine (Coyne) L.; married Adonia Kennedy, April 28, 1949; children—John Henry, Peter Christian, Robert Sealey; married Jean E. Sealey, September 22, 1974. Doctor of Medicine, Cornell University, 1948. Diplomate: Am. Board Internal Medicine. Intern medicine Presbyn. Hospital, New York City, 1948-49; assistant resident Presbyn. Hospital, 1949-50; fellow cardiology, trainee National Heart Institute, 1950-51; research fellow New York Heart Association, 1951-52; assistant physician Presbyn. Hospital, 1950-55, assistant attending; 1954-61, associate attending; 1961-69, attending physician; 1969-75, president elect medical board; 1972-74; director cardiology Delafield Hospital, New York City, 1954-55; member faculty Columbia College Physicians and Surgeons, 1950-75, professor clinical medicine; 1967-75, spokesman executive committee faculty council; 1971-73; vice chairman board trustees for professional and sci. affairs Presbyn. Hospital, 1974-75; director Hypertension Center Columbia-Presbyn. Medical Center, 1971-75, chief Nephrology div.; 1968-75; Hilda Altschul Master professor medicine, director Cardiovascular Center and Hypertension Center New York Hosp.-Cornell Medical Center, 1975—, chief Cardiology div.; 1976—; consultant United States Public Health Service, 1964—. Editor-in-chief: Am. Journal Hypertension, Cardiovascular Reviews and Reports; Editor: Hypertension Manual, 1974, Topics in Hypertension, 1980, Frontiers in Hypertension Research, 1981; Editorial board: Am. Journal Medicine, Am. Journal Cardiology, Kidney International, Journal Clin. Endocrinology and Metabolism, Hypertension, Journal Hypertension, Circulation, Am. Heart Journal, Procs. of Society Experimental Biology and Medicine, Heart and Vessels. Member policy adv. board detection and follow-up program National Heart and Lung Institute, 1971, board sci. counselors, 1974-79; chairman U.S.A.-USSR Joint Program in Hypertension, 1977—. Served with Army of the United States, 1943-46. Recipient Stouffer prize med. research, 1969. Fellow A.C.P., Am. College Cardiology; member Am. Heart Association (chairman med. adv. board council high blood pressure research 1968-72), Am. Society Clinical Investigation, Association Am. Physicians., Am. Society Contemporary Medicine and Surgery (adv. board), Am. Society Hypertension (founder, 1st president 1986-88), International Society Hypertension (president 1986-88, vice president sci. council), Harvey Society, Kappa Sigma, Nu Sigma Nu, Alpha Omega Alpha. Clubs: Winged Foot (Mamaroneck, New York); Shinnecock Hills Golf (Southampton). Research on hormones and electrolyte metabolism and renal physiology, on mechanisms of edema formation and on causes and treatment of high blood pressure. Home: 435 E 70th St New York New York 10021 Office: New York Hosp-

Cornell Med Center 525 E 68th St New York New York 10021

LARKIN, PETER ANTHONY, zoology educator, university dean and official; born Auckland, New Zealand, December 11, 1924; son of Frank Wilfred and Caroline Jane (Knapp) L.; married Lois Boughton Rayner, August 21, 1948; children: Barbara, Kathleen, Patricia, Margaret, Gillian. Bachelor of Arts, Master of Arts, University Saskatchewan, 1946; Doctor of Philosophy (Rhodes scholar), Oxford University, 1948. Bubonic plague survey Government of Saskatchewan, 1942-43; fisheries investigator Fisheries Research Board of Can., 1944-46; chief fisheries biologist British Columbia Game Commission, 1948-55; assistant professor University British Columbia, 1948-55, professor department zoology; 1959-63, 66-69; professor Institute Animal Resource Ecology, 1969—, also director fisheries; 1955-63, 66-69, head department zoology; 1972-75, dean grad. studies; 1975-84, associate vice president research; 1980-86, vice president research; 1986-88, university professor; 1988—; Hon. life governor Vancouver Pub. Aquarium; member Canadian national committee Special Committee on Problems Environment, 1971—; member Killam selection committee Can. Council, 1974-77; member Sci. Council Can., 1971-76; governmental research committees; member National Research Council Can., 1981-84; member Can. Committee on Seals and Sealing, 1981—, Can. Institute Advanced Research, 1982-85, International Center for Living Aquatic Resources Management, 1977—; director British Columbia Packers, 1980—; board governors International Devel. Research Center;

member National Sci. England Research Council Can., 1987—; president Rawson Acad., 1988—. Contributor articles to professional journals. Recipient Centennial medal Government of Can., 1967, Master Teacher award University British Columbia, 1970, Silver Jubilee medal, 1977, award Can. Sport Fishing Institute, 1979; Nuffield Foundation fellow, 1961-62. Fellow Royal Society Can.; member International Limnological Association, Am. Fisheries Society (award of excellence 1983), British Columbia Natural Resources Conference (president 1954), British Columbia Wildlife Federation, Canadian Society Zoologists (president 1972, Fry medal 1978), Canadian Association University Research Administration (president 1979), Am. Institute Fisheries Biologists (Outstanding Achievement award 1986). Home: 4166 Crown Crescent, Vancouver, British Columbia Canada V6R 2A9

LASTER, LEONARD, physician, academic administrator; born New York City, August 24, 1928; son of Isaac and Mary (Ehrenreich) L.; married Ruth Ann Leventhal, December 16, 1956; children: Judith Eve, Susan Beth, Stephen Jay. Bachelor of Arts, Harvard University, 1949, Doctor of Medicine, 1950. Diplomate Nat. Board Medical Examiners, Am. Board Internal Medicine (gastroenterology). From intern to resident in medicine Massachusetts General Hospital, Boston, 1950-53; fellow gastroenterology Massachusetts Memorial Hospital, 1958-59; visiting investigator Pub. Health Research Institute, New York City, 1953-54; commissioned lieutenant United States Public Health Service, 1954, advanced through grades to assistant surgeon general (rear admiral); 1971; member staff National Institute Arthritis, Metabolic and Digestive Diseases, National Institutes of Health, Bethesda, Maryland, 1954-73, chief digestive and hereditary diseases branch; 1969-73; special assistant, then assistant director human resources President's Office Sci. and Tech., 1969-73; executive director Assembly Life Sciences; also div. medical sciences National Acad. Scis.-NRC, 1973-74; retired United States Public Health Service, 1973; vice president acad. affairs and clinical affairs Medical Center, also dean College Medicine, professor medicine Downstate Medical Center, State University of New York, Brooklyn, 1974-78; president Oregon Health Sciences University, Portland, 1978-87, professor medicine; 1978-87; chancellor University Massachusetts Medical Center, Worcester, 1987—; director Tektronix Incorporated, Standard Insurance. Author articles on gastrointestinal disease, inborn errors metabolism, devel. biology; member editorial bds. medical journals. Board of directors Foundation Advanced Education Scis., Bethesda, 1965-69, Bedford Stuyvesant Family Health Center, Brooklyn, 1976-78, Medical Research Foundation Oregon, 1978—, Oregon Symphony, 1979-85, Oregon Contemporary Theatre, 1981-83; president Burning Tree Elementary School Parent-Teacher Association, Bethesda, 1972-73. Fellow American College of Physicians; member Am. Association Study Liver Diseases, Am. Federation Clinical Research, Am. Gastroenterol. Association, Am. Society Biological Chemists, Am. Society Clinical Investigation, Association Am. Medical Colls.

(council deans 1974-78), Multnomah County Medical Society (trustee), Marine Biological Lab. Corp., Portland Chamber of Commerce (director 1980-84), Phi Beta Kappa, Sigma Xi, Alpha Omega Alpha. Clubs: Cosmos (Washington); Harvard (New York City); University, City, Arlington (Portland). Lodge: Downtown Rotary (Portland). Home: 47 Pine Arden Dr West Boylston Massachusetts 01583 Office: U Mass Med Center 55 Lake Avenue N Worcester Massachusetts 01655

LATANISION, RONALD MICHAEL, materials science and engineering educator, consultant; born Richmondale, Pennsylvania, July 2, 1942; son of Stephen and Mary (Kopach) L.; married Carolyn Marie Domenig, June 27, 1964; children—Ivan, Sara. Bachelor of Science, Pennsylvania State University, 1964; Doctor of Philosophy in Metallurgical Engineering, Ohio State University, 1968. Postdoctoral fellow National Bureau Standards, Washington, 1968-69; research scientist Martin Marietta, Baltimore, 1969-73, acting head materials sci.; 1973-74; director H.H. Uhlig Corrosion Laboratory Massachusetts Institute of Technology, Cambridge, 1975—, Shell Distinguished professor materials sci. and engineering; 1983-88, director Materials Processing Center; 1984—; tech. adv. board MODAR, Incorporated, Natick, Massachusetts, 1981—; sci. advisor United States House of Representatives Committee on Sci. and Technology, Washington, 1982-83; chairman ad hoc committee Massachusetts Advanced Materials Center, Boston, 1985—; member adv. board Massachusetts Office Sci. and Tech. Editor: Surface Effects in

Crystal Plasticity, 1977, Atomistics of Fracture, 1983, Chemistry and Physics of Fracture, 1987, Advances in Mechanics and Physics of Fracture, 1981, 83, 86; contributor articles to professional journals. Coach Winchester Soccer Club, Massachusetts. Recipient A.B. Campbell award NACE, 1971; Senior Scientist award Humboldt Foundation, 1974-75; Henry Krumb lecturer American Institute of Mining, Metallurgy and Petroleum Engineers, 1984; David Ford McFarland award Pennsylvania State University, 1986. Fellow Am. Society Metals International; member National Acad. Engineering, Am. Society Metals (member government and pub. affairs committee 1984), National Association Corrosion Engineers. Roman Catholic. Office: Massachusetts Institute of Technology Department Materials Sci and Engring 77 Massachusetts Avenue Cambridge Massachusetts 02139

LAUFF, GEORGE HOWARD, biologist; born Milan, Michigan, March 23, 1927; son of George John and Mary Anna (Klein) L. Bachelor of Science, Michigan State University, 1949, Master of Science, 1951; postgraduate, University Montana, 1951, University Washington, 1952; Doctor of Philosophy, Cornell University, 1953. Fisheries research technician Michigan Department Conservation, 1950; teaching assistant Cornell University, 1952-53; instructor University Michigan, 1953-57, assistant professor; 1957-61, associate professor; 1961-62; research associate Great Lakes Research Institute, University Michigan, 1954-59; director University Georgia Marine Institute, 1960-62; associate professor University

Georgia, 1960-62; research coordinator Sapelo Island Research Foundation, 1962-64; director Kellogg Biological Station; department fisheries and wildlife and zoology Michigan State University, East Lansing, 1964—; member consultant and rev. panels for Smithsonian Institute, National Water Commission, National Science Foundation, National Acad. Sci., Am. Institute Biological Sci., United States Atomic Energy Commission, Institute Ecology, others. Editor: Estuaries, 1967, Experimental Ecological Reserves, 1977. Served with infantry United States Army, 1944-46. Office of Naval Research grantee; U.S. Department Interior grantee; National Science Foundation grantee; others. Fellow American Association for the Advancement of Science; member Am. Institute Biological Sci., Am. Society Limnology and Oceanography (president 1972-73), Ecological Society Am., Freshwater Biology Association, INTECOL, Societas Internationalis Limnologiae, Organization Biological Field Stas., Sigma Xi, Phi Kappa Phi. Home: 3818 Heights Dr Hickory Corners Michigan 49060 Office: 3700 E Gull Lake Dr Hickory Corners Michigan 49060

LAUTERBUR, PAUL C(HRISTIAN), professor; born Sidney, Ohio, May 6, 1929. Bachelor of Science, Case Institute Tech., 1951; Doctor of Philosophy, University Pittsburgh, 1962; Doctor of Philosophy (honorary), University Liege, Belgium, 1984; Doctor of Science, Carnegie Mellon University, 1987. Research assistant Carnegie Mellon Institute, Pittsburgh, 1951-53, associate fellow; 1955-63; with State University of New York, Stony Brook, 1963-85, resident professor radiology; 1978-85,

University professor; 1984-85; professor (4) departments University Illinois, Urbana, 1985—. Contributor articles to professional journals; member editorial bds.; member sci. couns. Corporal United States Army, 1953-55. Recipient Clinical Rsch. award Lasker Foundation, 1984, National Medal of Sci., U.S.A., 1987, Fiuggi International prize Fondazione Fiuggi, 1987. Fellow Am. Physical Society, American Association for the Advancement of Science; member National Acad. Sciences, Am. Chemical Society. Office: U Ill-Urbana-Champaign 1307 W Park St Urbana Illinois 61801

LAX, PETER DAVID, mathematician; born Budapest, Hungary, May 1, 1926; came to United States, 1941, naturalized, 1944; son of Henry and Klara (Kornfeld) L.; married Anneli Cahn, 1948; children: John, James D. Bachelor of Arts, New York University, 1947, Doctor of Philosophy, 1949; Doctor of Science (honorary), Kent State University, 1976; Doctor honoris causa, University Paris, 1979. Assistant professor New York University, 1949-57, professor; 1957—; director Courant Institute Math. Sciences, 1972-80. Author: (with Ralph Phillips) Scattering Theory, 1967, Scattering Theory for Automorphic Functions, 1976, (with A. Lax and S.Z. Burstein) Calculus with applications and computing), 1976, Hyperbolic Systems of Conservation Laws and the Mathematical Theory of Shock Waves, 1973. Member President's Committee on National Medal of Sci., 1976, National Sci. Board, 1980-86. Served with Army of the United States, 1944-46. Recipient Semmelweis medal Semmelweis Medical Society, 1975, National Medal Sci., 1986, Wolf Prize, 1987. Member Am. Math. Society (president 1979-80, Norbert Wiener prize), National Acad. Sciences (applied math. and numerical analysis award 1983), Am. Acad. Arts and Sciences, Math. Association Am. (board govs., Chauvenet prize), Society Industrial and Applied Math.; foreign associate Académie des Sciences (France). Office: Courant Institute Math Scis 251 Mercer St New York New York 10012

LEADER, ROBERT WARDELL, pathologist; born Tacoma, January 16, 1919; son of Robert Joseph and Edith May (Wardell) L.; married Isabel Parra, September 20, 1969; children: Cheri, Mary, Robert, Lorraine, Carol. Bachelor of Science, Washington State University, 1952, Doctor of Veterinary Medicine, 1952, Master of Science, 1955; Doctor of Science (honorary), Medical College Ohio, 1976. From instructor to professor pathology Washington State University, 1952-65; associate professor, head comparative pathology laboratory Rockefeller University, 1965-71; professor, head department pathobiology University Connecticut, 1971-75; professor pathology, chairman department Michigan State University, East Lansing, 1975-80; dean research and grad. studies Michigan State University, 1980-85, acting director Center Environmental Tech.; 1983-85, now professor pathology; member pathological training grant committee National Institutes of Health, 1967-71, virology study section, 1971-75; medical adv. committee Leukemia Society, 1965-71; Robert Miller lecturer Dartmouth College, 1968. Author: Dictionary of Comparative Pathology, 1971, also articles.;

Editorial board: Journal Toxicol. Pathology; member edition board Health and Environment Digest. Served with United States Naval Reserve, 1937-46. Borden scholar, 1951; postdoctoral fellow National Institutes of Health, 1954-55; tng. grantee, 1959-65. Member Am. Association Pathologists, Am. College Veteran Pathologists, American Association for the Advancement of Science, American Veterinary Medical Association, International Acad. Pathology, Harvey Society, Reticuloendothelial Society, Michigan Society Pathologists., Am. College Veteran Pathologist (president 1980), International Acad. Pathology (president 1986), Society Toxicol. Pathologists, National Association Environmental Professionals. Office: Department of Pathology E Fee Hall Michigan State University East Lansing Michigan 48824

LEAKEY, MARY DOUGLAS, archaeologist, anthropologist; born February 6, 1913; daughter of Erskine Edward and Cecilia Marion (Frere) Nicol; married Louis Seymour Bazett Leakey, 1936 (deceased 1972); 3 sons. Educated private schools; Doctor of Science (honorary), University Witwatersrand, 1968, University Western Michigan, 1980, University Chicago, 1981, Yale University, 1976, University Cambridge, 1987; Doctor of Literature (honorary), University Oxford, 1981, Emory University, 1988, Massachusetts University, 1988. Former director Olduvai Gorge Excavations. Author: Excavation in Beds I and II, 1971, Africa's Vanishing Art, Disclosing the Past; also articles; editor: (with J.M. Harris) Laetoli, A Pliocene Site in North Tanzania. Joint recipient (with L.S.B. Leakey)

Prestwich medal of Geol. Society London; recipient National Geog. Society Hubbard medal; Gold medal Society Women Geographers; Lineus medal Stockholm, 1978; Stopes medal Geol. Association London, 1980; Bradford Washburn prize Boston Mus. of Sci., 1980; Elizabeth Blackwell award Hobart and Smith College, 1980. Member Royal Swedish Acad. Sciences (hon.), Am. Acad. Arts and Sciences (associate), National Acad. Sci. (foreign). Office: care National Mus, Post Office Box 30239, Nairobi Kenya

LEAKEY, RICHARD ERSKINE, palaeoanthropologist, museum director; born Nairobi, Kenya, December 19, 1944; son of Louis Seymour and Mary Douglas (Nicol) L.; married Meave Epps, 1970; children: Anna, Louise, Samira. Student, Lenana School, Nairobi; Doctor of Science (honorary), Wooster College, 1978, Rockford College, 1983. Director tour company Kenya, 1965-66; assistant director Center for Prehistory and Palaeontology, 1966-67; administrative director National Museums of Kenya, Nairobi, 1968-74; director, chief executive National Museums of Kenya, 1974—; leader expedition to West Lake Baringo, Kenya, 1966, International Omo River Expedition in, Southern Ethiopia, 1967, East Rudolf Expedition, 1968; leader, coordinator Koobi Fora Research Project, Lake Turkana, 1969—; member Kenya del. United Nations Educational, Scientific and Cultural Organization, 1972, 76; chairman Foundation Research into Origins of Man; trustee, vice chairman Foundation Social Habilitation; vice-chairman Environmental Prep. Group, Kenya, 1972-74; member Nakali/Suguta Valley Expedition, 1978, West

Turkana Research Project, 1982, 84, 85, 86, Buluk-Early Miocene Project, 1982, advisor TV series The Making of Mankind; numerous pub. and scholarly lectures, United States, Can., United Kingdom, Scandinavia, New Zealand, Kenya, China, 1968—. Author: (with R. Lewin) Origins, 1977, Koobi Fora Research Project: a Catalogue of Hominid Fossils, Volume I, 1978, People of the Lake, 1978, Making of Mankind, 1981, One Life An Autobiography, 1984; films include The Ape that Stood Up, 1977; lecture films on prehistory; various sci. programs, talk shows and news interviews since 1968; contributor (with R. Lewin) chapters to books, articles to professional journals. Trustee National Fund for the Disabled in Kenya, trustee Rockford College, National Kidney Foundation Kenya, Agricultural Research Foundation, Kenya, Gallmann Memorial Foundation, Kenya. Recipient Franklin Burr prize, 1965, 73. Fellow Royal Anthropological Institute, American Association for the Advancement of Science, Kenya Acad. Sciences (founding fellow), Institute Cultural Research United Kingdom; member Explorers Club, Wildlife Clubs of Kenya (trustee, hon. chairman 1969-85), Kenya Exploration Society (chairman 1969-72), East African Wildlife Society (hon. chairman 1984—), Pan African Association Prehistoric Studies (secretary), Sigma Xi.

LEDER, PHILIP, geneticist, educator; born Washington, November 19, 1934; married; 3 children. Bachelor of Arts, Harvard University, 1956, Doctor of Medicine, 1960. Research associate National Heart Institute, National Cancer Institute; lab chief molecular genetics National Institute

Child Health and Human Devel., National Institutes of Health, 1972-80; professor genetics Harvard University Medical School, Boston, Massachusetts, 1980—, now John Wesley Andrus professor genetics; senior investigator Howard Hughes Medical Institute. Recipient Albert Lasker Medical Research award, 1987. Member National Acad. Sciences, Institute Medicine. Office: Department Genetics Harvard U Med School 25 Shattuck St Boston Massachusetts 02115

LEDERBERG, JOSHUA, university president, geneticist; born Montclair, New Jersey, May 23, 1925; son of Zwi Hirsch and Esther (Goldenbaum) L.; married Marguerite S. Kirsch, April 5, 1968; children: David Kirsch, Anne. Bachelor of Arts, Columbia University, 1944; Doctor of Philosophy, Yale University, 1947. With University Wisconsin, 1947-58; professor genetics School Medicine, Stanford (California) University, 1959-78; president Rockefeller University, New York City, 1978—; member adv. committee medical research World Health Organization, 1971-76; member board sci. advisors Cetus Corp., Emeryville, California, Affymax, N.V., Palo Alto, California, J.D. Wolfensohn, Incorporated, New York City, Hoechst-Celanese Corp., New York City; member study sections National Science Foundation, National Institutes of Health; member United States Def. Sci. Board; consultant National Aeronautics and Space Administration, Arms Control and Disarmament Agency; board of directors Institute Sci. Information Incorporated, Philadelphia, Procter & Gamble Company, Cincinnati, Annual Revs., Incorporated, Palo Alto, California. Trustee Revson

Foundation Incorporated, Carnegie Corp., Camille and Henry Dreyfus Foundation; board of directors Chem. Industry Institute Toxicology, North Carolina, New York City Ptnrship.; member President's Panel on Mental Retardation, 1961-62; member national mental health adv. council National Institute of Mental Health, 1967-71. Served with United States Navy, 1943-45. Recipient Nobel prize in physiology and medicine for research genetics of bacteria, 1958. Fellow American Association for the Advancement of Science, Am. Philosophical Society, Am. Acad. Arts and Sciences, New York Acad. Medicine (hon.); member National Acad. Sciences (past council member Institute of Medicine), Royal Society London (foreign), New York Acad. Sciences (hon. life), Alpha Omega Alpha (hon.). Office: Rockefeller U 1230 York Avenue New York New York 10021

LEDERMAN, LEON MAX, physicist, educator; born New York City, July 15, 1922; son of Morris and Minna (Rosenberg) L.; married Florence Gordon, September 19, 1945; children: Rena S., Jesse A., Heidi R. Bachelor of Science, College City New York, 1943, Doctor of Science (honorary), 1985; Master of Arts, Columbia University, 1948, Doctor of Philosophy, 1951; Doctor of Science (honorary), Northern Illinois University, 1984, University Chicago, 1985, Illinois Institute Tech., 1987. Associate in physics Columbia, New York City, 1951; assistant professor Columbia, 1952-54, associate professor; 1954-58, professor; 1958—, Eugene Higgins professor physics; 1973—; director Fermi National Accelerator Laboratory, Batavia, Illinois, 1979—; director Nevis Laboratories, Irvington, New York, 1960-67, 69—; guest scientist Brookhaven National Laboratories, 1955—; consultant, national accelerator laboratory European Organization for Nuclear Research (European Organization of Nuclear Research), 1970—; member high energy physics adv. panel Atomic Energy Commission, 1966-70; member adv. committee to div. math. and physical sciences National Science Foundation, 1970-72. Contributor articles to professional journals. Served to 2d lieutenant Signal Corps, Army of the United States, 1943-46. Recipient National Medal of Sci., 1965, Wolf Prize, 1983; National Science Foundation fellow, 1967; Guggenheim fellow, 1958-59; Ford Foundation fellow European Center For Nuclear Research, Geneva, 1958-59; recipient Townsend Harris medal City University New York, 1973, Elliot Cresson medal Franklin Institute, 1976, Nobel prize in physics, 1988. Fellow American Association for the Advancement of Science, Am. Physical Society; member Italian Physical Society, National Acad. Sci. Office: Fermi National Accelerator Lab Post Office Box 500 Batavia Illinois 60510

LEE, GEORGE C., civil engineer, university adminstrator; born Peking, China, July 17, 1933; son of Shun C. and J. T. (Chang) L.; married Grace S. Su, July 29, 1961; children—David S., Kelvin H. Bachelor of Science, Taiwan University, 1955; Master of Science in Civil Engineering, Lehigh University, 1958, Doctor of Philosophy, 1960. Research associate Lehigh University, 1960-61; member faculty department civil engineering State University of New York, Buffalo, 1961—; professor State

University of New York, 1967—, chairman department; 1974-77, dean faculty of engineering and applied sciences; 1978—; head engineering mechanics section National Science Foundation, Washington, 1977-78; sci. consultant National Heart Lung and Blood Institute. Author: Structural Analysis and Design, 1979, Design of Single Story Rigid Frames, 1981, Cold Region Structural Engineering, 1986; Contributor articles to professional journals in areas of structural design, nonlinear structural mechanics, biomed. engring. and cold region structural engring. Recipient Adams Memorial award Am. Welding Society, 1974; Superior Accomplishment award National Science Foundation, 1977. Member American Society of Civil Engineers, Am. Welding Society, Welding Research Council, Structural Stability Research, Council, Am. Society Engineering Education, American Association for the Advancement of Science, Sigma Xi, Chi Epsilon, Tau Beta Pi. Office: State University of New York Buffalo 412 Bonner Hall Amherst New York 14260

LEE, THOMAS HENRY, research institute director; born Shanghai, China, May 11, 1923; came to United States, 1948, naturalized, 1953; son of Y. C. and Nan Tien (Ho) L.; married Kin Ping, June 12, 1948; children—William F., Thomas H. Jr., Richard T. Bachelor of Science in Mechanical Engineering, National Chiao Tung University, Shanghai, 1946; Master of Science in Electrical Engineering, Union College, Schenectady, 1950; Doctor of Philosophy, Rensselaer Polytechnic Institute, 1954. Registered professional engineer, Pennsylvania. Manager research and devel. General Electric Company, Philadelphia, 1959-74; manager

strategic planning Fairfield, Connecticut, 1974-78, staff executive; 1978-80; professor electrical engineering Massachusetts Institute of Technology, Cambridge, 1980-84, 87—; director International Institute for Applied Systems Analysis, Laxenburg, Austria, 1984-87; president Tech. Associate Group, Schenectady, 1980-84. Author: Physics and Engineering of High Power Switching Devices, 1973; patentee in field. Recipient Davis medal for outstanding engineering accomplishment Rensselaer Polytechnic Institute, 1987. Fellow Institute of Electrical and Electronics Engineers (Power Life award 1980, Haraden Pratt award 1983), American Association for the Advancement of Science; member National Acad. Engineering, Swiss Acad. Engineering Sci., Power Engineering Society (president 1974-76). Office: Massachusetts Institute of Technology 77 Massachusetts Avenue Cambridge Massachusetts 02139

LEE, TSUNG-DAO, physicist, educator; born Shanghai, People's Republic of China, November 25, 1926; son of Tsing-Kong L. and Ming-Chang (Chang); married Jeannette Chin, June 3, 1950; children: James, Stephen. Student, National Chekiang University, Kweichow, China, 1943-44, National Southwest Associated University, Kunming, China, 1945-46; Doctor of Philosophy, University Chicago, 1950; Doctor of Science (honorary), Princeton University, 1958; Doctor of Laws (honorary), Chinese University, Hong Kong, 1969; Doctor of Science (honorary), City College of New York, 1978. Research associate in astronomy University Chicago, 1950; research associate, lecturer physics University California, Berkeley, 1950-51; member Institute for Advanced Study, Princeton (New Jersey) University, 1951-53, professor physics; 1960-63; assistant professor Columbia University, New York City, 1953-55, associate professor; 1955-56, professor; 1956-60, 63—, Enrico Fermi professor physics; 1964—, adj. professor; 1960-62; Loeb lecturer Harvard University, Cambridge, Massachusetts, 1957, 64. Editor: Weak Interactions and High Energy Nutrino Physics, 1966, Particle Physics and Introduction to Field Theory, 1981. Recipient Albert Einstein Sci. award Yeshiva University, 1957, (with Chen Ning Yang) Nobel prize in physics, 1957. Member National Acad. Sci., Acad. Sinica, Am. Acad. Arts and Sciences, Am. Philosophical Society, Acad. Nazionale dei Lincei. Office: Columbia U Department Physics Morningside Heights New York New York 10027

LEE, YUAN T(SEH), chemistry educator; born Hsinchu, Taiwan, China, November 29, 1936; came to United States, 1962, naturalized, 1974; son of Tsefan and Pei (Tasi) L.; married Bernice Wu, June 28, 1963; children: Ted, Sidney, Charlotte. Bachelor of Science, National Taiwan University, 1959; Master of Science, National Tsinghua University, Taiwan, 1961; Doctor of Philosophy, University California, Berkeley, 1965. From assistant professor to professor chemistry University Chicago, 1968-74; professor University California, Berkeley, 1974—, also principal investigator Lawrence Berkeley Laboratory. Contributor numerous articles on chemical physics to professional journals. Recipient Nobel Prize in Chemistry, 1986, Ernest O. Lawrence award Department Energy, 1981, National Medal of Sci., 1986, Peter Debye award for Physical Chemistry, 1986; fellow Alfred P. Sloan, 1969-71, John Simon Guggenheim, 1976-77; Camille and Henry Dreyfus Foundation Teacher scholar, 1971-74. Fellow Am. Physical Society; member Am. Acad. Arts and Sciences, Am. Chemical Society, American Association for the Advancement of Science, National Acad. Sciences. Office: U California Department Chemistry Berkeley California 94720

LEGGETT, WILLIAM C., biology educator, educational administrator; born Orangeville, Ontario, Canada, June 25, 1939; son of Frank William and Edna Irene (Wheeler) L.; married Claire Holman, May 9, 1964; children: David, John. Bachelor of Arts, Waterloo University College, 1962; Master of Science, University Waterloo, 1965; Doctor of Philosophy, McGill University, 1969. Don of men St. Pauls College University Waterloo, 1963-65; research scientist Essex (Connecticut) Marine Laboratory, 1965-70, research associate; 1970-73; assistant professor McGill University, Montreal, Quebec, Can., 1970-72; associate professor McGill University, 1972-79, professor; 1979—, chairman department biology; 1981-85; dean of sci. 1986—; president, chairman board Huntsman Marine Laboratory, 1980-85; president Groupe Interuniversitatre De Recherche Oceanographique Du Quebec, 1986—; chairman grant selection committee for population biology Natural Sciences and Engineering Research Council Can., 1980-81, chairman grant selection committee for oceans, 1986-87. Member editorial board: Can. Journal

Fisheries and Aquatic Sciences, 1980-85, Le Naturaliste Canadien, 1980—, Can. Journal Zoology, 1982—; contributor in field. Grantee in field. Member Am. Fisheries Society (president North-East division 1977-78), Can. Committee for Fishery Research, Can. Society Zoologists, Am. Society Limnology and Oceanography. Office: 1205 Avenue Docteur Penfield, Montreal, Province of Quebec Canada H3A 1B1

LEHN, JEAN-MARIE PIERRE, chemistry educator; born Rosheim, Bas-Rhin, France, September 30, 1939; son of Pierre and Marie (Salomon) L.; married Sylvie Lederer, 1965; 2 children. Graduate, University Strasbourg, France, 1960, Doctor of Philosophy, 1963; Doctor of Philosophy (honorary), University Jerusalem, 1984, University Autonoma, Madrid, Spain, 1985, University Göttingen, Federal Republic of Germany, 1987, University Bruxelles, 1987. Various posts National Center Sci. Research, 1960-66; postdoctoral research associate Harvard University, Cambridge, Massachusetts, 1963-64; assistant professor chemistry University Strasbourg, 1966-70, associate professor; 1970, professor; 1970-79; professor College de France, Paris, 1979—; with Center National Sci. Research, France, 1960-66; assistant professor University Strasbourg, France, 1966-69; associate professor University Louis Pasteur of Strasbourg, 1970, professor of chemistry; 1970-79; professor College France, Paris, 1979—; visiting professor chemistry Harvard University, 1972, 74, E.T.H., Zurich, Switzerland, 1977, Cambridge (England) University, 1984, Barcelona (Spain) University, 1985, Frankfurt University (Federal Republic Germany), 1985-86. Contributor about 307 articles to sci. publications. Recipient Gold medal Pontifical Acad. Sciences, 1981, Paracelsus prize Swiss Chemical Society, 1982, von Humboldt prize, 1983, Nobel Prize for Chemistry, 1987; named to Officier Légion d'Honneur, Chevalier Ordre National du Mérite. Member Institute de France, Deutsche Acad. der Naturforscher Leopoldina, Acad. Nazionale dei Lincei, National Academy of Sciences (foreign associate), NAs (foreign member), American Association for the Advancement of Science (foreign hon.), Royal Netherlands Acad. Arts and Sciences (foreign member). Home: 21 Rue d'Oslo, 67000 Strasbourg France Office: College France, 11 Place Marcelin Berthelot, 75005 Paris France also: U Louis Pasteur, 4 Rue Blaise Pascal, 67000 Strasbourg France

LEIDEL, FREDERICK OTTO, mechanical engineer, educator; born Milwaukee, December 3, 1916; son of Otto Frederick and Alma (Losse) L.; married Margarette Frona Lerum, June 5, 1963; children: Linda K., James M.; stepchildren: Dennis, Russell, James. Bachelor of Science in Mechanical Engineering, University Wisconsin, 1940. Registered professional engineer, Wisconsin. Design engineer Hamilton Standard Propeller div. United Aircraft Corp., East Hartford, Connecticut, 1940-45; instructor University Illinois, Champaign, 1946; member faculty College Engineering, University Wisconsin, Madison, 1946—, professor; 1966-82, professor emeritus; 1982—; associate dean College Engineering, 1966-82; transfer student adviser University

Wisconsin, 1983—; director University Book Store, 1967-75, chairman, 1973-75. Board of directors University Young Men's Christian Association, 1962-69. Clubs: Masons, Shriners, Order Eastern Star. Office: U Wisconsin College Engring Madison Wisconsin 53706

LEIGHTON, ROBERT B(ENJAMIN), physicist; born Detroit, September 10, 1919; son of George Benjamin and Olga Ottilie (Homrig) L.; married Alice M. Winger, July 31, 1943 (divorced 1973); children: Ralph Edward, Alan Paul; married Margaret Laura Lauritsen, January 7, 1977; stepchildren: Eric, Margaret Ann. Associate of Arts, Los Angeles City College, 1938; Bachelor of Science in Electrical Engineering, California Institute Tech., 1941, Master of Science in Physics, 1944, Doctor of Philosophy in Physics, 1947. Resident fellow California Institute Tech., Pasadena, 1947-49, assistant professor; 1949-53, associate professor; 1953-59, professor; 1953-85, William R. Valentine professor physics; 1984-85, professor emeritus; 1985—, chairman div. physics, math, and astronomy, principal investigator; 1971-75. Author: Principals of Modern Physics, 1960; editor: Feynman Lectures on Physics, Volume I, 1963; designer/inventor in field. Fellow Am. Physics Society; member National Acad. Sci. (James Craig Watson medal 1988), American Association for the Advancement of Science (Rumford prize 1986), Am. Astronomical Society. Democrat. Office: California Institute of Tech Department of Physics Pasadena California 91125

LELAND, JOY HANSON, anthropologist, alcohol specialist, educator; born Glendale, California, July 29, 1927; daughter of David Emmett and Florence (Sockerson) Hanson; married Robert Leland, May 6, 1961 (deceased October 1986); 1 stepson, John. Bachelor of Arts in English Literature, Pomona College, Claremont, California, 1949; Master of Business Administration, Stanford University, 1960; Master of Arts in Anthropology, University Nevada, 1972; Doctor of Philosophy in Anthropology, University California, Irvine, 1975. With Desert Research Institute, University Nevada, 1961—, assistant research professor; 1975-77, associate research professor; 1977-79, research professor; 1979—. Author: monograph Firewater Myths.; contributing author: Smithsonian Handbook of North American Indians; also articles, book chapters. National Institute of Mental Health grantee, 1972-73; National Institute Alcohol Abuse and Alcoholism grantee, 1974-75, 79-81. Member Am. Anthropological Association, Southwestern Anthropological Association, American Association for the Advancement of Science, Society Applied Anthropology, Society Medical Anthropology, Society Psychological Anthropology, Great Basin Anthropological Conference. Office: Desert Research Institute U Nevada Post Office Box 60220 7010 Dandini Boulevard Reno Nevada 89506

LEMESSURIER, WILLIAM JAMES, structural engineer; born Pontiac, Michigan, June 12, 1926; son of William James and Bertha Emma (Sherman) LeM.; married Dorothy Wright Judd, June 20, 1953; children: Claire Elizabeth, Irene Louise, Peter Wright. Bachelor of Arts cum laude, Harvard University, 1947, postgraduate, 1948; Master of Science,

Massachusetts Institute of Technology, 1953. Registered professional engineer, Massachusetts, District of Columbia, New York, Tennessee, Colorado. Partner Goldberg, LeMessurier Associate, Boston, 1952-61; president LeMessurier Associates Incorporated, Boston and Cambridge, 1961-73; chairman Sippican Cons. International Incorporated, Cambridge, 1973-85, LeMessurier Cons. Incorporated, Cambridge, 1985—; instructor department building construction and engineering Massachusetts Institute of Technology, 1951-52, assistant professor, 1952-56, associate professor department architecture, 1964-67, senior lecturer department civil engineering, 1976-77, lecturer, 1983-86; associate professor grad. school design Harvard University, 1956-61, adj. professor, 1973—; visiting lecturer Yale University, University Michigan, University Illinois, Chicago, Rice University, Washington University, St. Louis, Northeastern University, Rhode Island School Design, Cornell University, University Pennsylvania, Roger Williams College, University California, Berkeley, University Texas, Austin; speaker Association Collegiate Schools of Architecture Construction Materials and Tech. Institute, Harvard University; member sci. adv. committee National Center Earthquake Engineering Research. Co-author: Structural Engineering Handbook, 1968, 2d edition, 1979; principal works include New Boston City Hall, Shawmut Bank Boston, 1st National Bank Boston, Federal Res. Bank Boston, Citicorp Center, New York City, Dallas-Ft. Worth Airport Terminal Bldgs., Ralston Purina Headquarters, Saint Louis, National Air and Space Mus., Washington, Am. Institute Architects Headquarters, Washington, One Post Office Square, Boston, Bank Southwest Tower, Houston, InterFirst Plaza Dallas Main Center, Treasury Building, Singapore, King Khalid Military City, Al Batin, Saudi Arabia, TVA Headquarters, Chattanooga, Lafayette Place Hotel, Boston, academic bldgs. at Harvard University, Princeton University, Amherst College, Bowdoin College, Williams College, University Massachusetts, University Wisconsin, University Illinois, Colby College, University New Hampshire, Northeastern University, Kirkland College, Cornell University. Member Cambridge Experimentation Reverend Board, 1977; juror Capitol area archtl. and planning board State Capitol Bldg. Extension, St. Paul, 1977, Am. Institute Architects Regional Awards Program, Northern Vermont, 1980, Progressive Architecutre mag., Portland Cement Association Awards, 1986, Fazlur Rahman Kahn International Fellowship, New York City, 1987; tech. advisor to jury Boston Archtl. Center Competition. Recipient Am. Institute Architects' Allied Professions medal, 1968, Professional Service award Engineering News-Record, 1978, Prestressed Concrete Institute award, 1984. Fellow American Society of Civil Engineers (hon.), Am. Concrete Institute; member National Institute Architects (hon.), Boston Society Architects (hon.), Boston Society Civil Engineers (hon.), Boston Association Structural Engineers (past president), Am. Institute Steel Constrn. (specifications adv. committee 1961—, Award of Excellence 1962, 66, 70, 77, 79, Special award 1972), Veterans' Administration (adv. board division constrn.), National Committee on Housing Tech., Structural Clay

Products Institute (bldg. code committee), National Acad. Engineering, Seismic Safety Council (task committee), Boston Society Architects (hon.), Bldg. Code Committee, International Masonry Institute (research council), Tau Beta Pi. Episcopalian. Club: Met. (New York City). Developed Mah-LeMessurier high-rise housing system; conceived and developed Staggered Truss System for use in high-rise steel sctures; conceived, developed and applied Tuned Mass Damper System to reduce tall bldg. motion. Avocation: music. Office: LeMessurier Cons 1033 Massachusetts Avenue Cambridge Massachusetts 02238

LENFANT, CLAUDE JEAN-MARIE, physician; born Paris, October 12, 1928; came to United States, 1960, naturalized, 1965; son of Robert and Jeanine (Leclerc) L.; children: Philipe, Bernard, Martine Lenfant Wayman, Brigitte Lenfant Martin, Christine Lenfant Duke. Bachelor of Science, University Rennes, France, 1948; Doctor of Medicine, University Paris, 1956; Doctor of Science (honorary), State University of New York, 1988. Assistant professor physiology University Lille, France, 1959-60; from clinical instructor to professor medicine physiology and biophysics University Washington Medical School, 1961-72; associate director lung programs National Heart, Lung and Blood Institute National Institutes of Health, Bethesda, Maryland, 1970-72; director div. lung diseases National Heart, Lung and Blood Institute National Institutes of Health, 1972-80; director Fogarty International Center National Institutes of Health, 1980-82, associate director international research; 1980-82; director National Heart, Lung and Blood Institute, 1982—. Associate editor: Journal Applied Physiology, 1976-82, Am. Journal Medicine, 1979—; member editorial board: Undersea Biomed. Research, 1973-75, Respiration Physiology, 1971-78, Am. Journal Physiology and Journal Applied Physiology, 1970-76, Am. Rev. Respiratory Disease, 1973-79; editor-in-chief: Lung Biology in Health and Disease. Member Association Am. Physicians, Am. Society Clinical Investigation, French Physiological Society, Am. Physiological Society, New York Acad. Sciences, Undersea Medical Society, Institute of Medicine of National Acad. Sci., Union of the Soviet Socialist Republics Acad. Medical Sciences. Home: 13201 Glen Road Gaithersburg Maryland 20878 Office: National Heart Lung and Blood Institute Building 31A Room 5A52 Bethesda Maryland 20014

LENOIR, WILLIAM BENJAMIN, aeronautical scientist-astronaut; born Miami, Florida, March 14, 1939; son of Samuel S. Lenoir; married Elizabeth Lenoir, 1964; children: William Benjamin, Samantha. Bachelor of Science, Massachusetts Institute of Technology, 1961, Master of Science, 1962, Doctor of Philosophy, 1965. Assistant electrical engineer Massachusetts Institute of Technology, Cambridge, 1962-64, instructor; 1964-65, assistant professor; 1965-67, Ford fellow engineering; 1965-66; scientist-astronaut National Aeronautics and Space Administration Johnson Space Center, Houston, 1967-84; mission specialist 5th Mission of Columbia, National Aeronautics and Space Administration, 1982; with Booz Allen & Hamilton, Incorporated, Arlington, Virginia, 1984—. Member American

Association for the Advancement of Science, Am. Geophysical Union.

LEONARD, EDWARD F., chemical engineer, educator; born Paterson, New Jersey, July 6, 1932; son of Edward F. and Adelyn (Minder) L.; children—Mary, Edward F., Gerald, Louise, Joseph. Bachelor of Science in Chemical Engineering, Massachusetts Institute of Technology, 1953; Master of Science in Chemical Engineering, University Pennsylvania, 1955, Doctor of Philosophy, 1960. Member faculty Columbia University, 1958—, professor chemical engineering; 1968—, also founder seminar on biomaterials. Author articles in field. Member Am. Institute Chemical Engineers (William H. Walker award), Am. Society Artificial Internal Organs (president 1972-73), Biomed. Engineering Society (a founder), New York Acad. Medicine. Home: 42 Tanglewylde Avenue Bronxville New York 10708 Office: Columbia University 351 Engring Terrace New York New York 10027

LEVI-MONTALCINI, RITA, neurologist, researcher; born Torino, Italy, April 22, 1909. Doctor of Medicine, University Turin, 1940. Resident, associate zoologist Washington University, 1947-51, associate professor; 1951-58, professor; 1958-81; with Laboratory Cellular Biology, Rome, 1981—. Author: In Praise of Imperfection: My Life and Work, 1988. Recipient Albert Lasker Medical Research award, 1986, Nobel prize Physiology-Medicine, 1986. Member American Association for the Advancement of Science, Society Devel. Biology, Am. Association Anatomists, Tissue Culture Association. Office: Lab di Biologia Cellulare, Via 6 Romagnosa, 00196 Rome Italy

LEVIN, WILLIAM COHN, physician, former university president; born Waco, Texas, March 2, 1917; son of Samuel P. and Jeanette (Cohn) L.; married Edna Seinsheimer, June 23, 1941; children: Gerry Lee Levin Hornstein, Carol Lynn Levin Cantini. Bachelor of Arts, University Texas, 1938, Doctor of Medicine, 1941; Doctor of Medicine (honorary), University Montpellier, 1980. Diplomate: Am. Board Internal Medicine. Intern Michael Reese Hospital, Chicago, 1941-42; resident John Sealy Hospital, Galveston, Texas, 1942-44; member staff University Texas Medical Branch Hospitals, Galveston, 1944—, associate professor internal medicine; 1948-65, professor; 1965—; Warmoth professor hematology University Texas Medical Branch, 1968-86, Ashbel Smith professor; 1986—, president; 1974-87; past chairman, past member cancer clinical investigation rev. committee National Cancer Institute. Executive committee, member national board Union Am. Hebrew Congregations; trustee Houston-Galveston Psychoanalytic Foundation, 1975-78, Menil Foundation, 1976-83. Recipient Nicholas and Katherine Leone award for adminstrv. excellence, 1977; decorated Palmes Académiques France. Fellow American College of Physicians, International Society Hematology; member Am. Federation Clinical Research, Central Society Clinical Research, Am. Society Hematology, Phi Beta Kappa, Sigma Xi, Alpha Omega Alpha. Office: U Tex Med Br Ashbel Smith Building Suite 2.212 301 University Boulevard Galveston Texas 77550

LEVINE, ARNOLD JAY, molecular biology educator, researcher; born

Brooklyn, July 30, 1939; son of Samuel and Marion (Wisot) L.; married Linda Hirst, June 5, 1962; children—Samantha, Alison. Bachelor of Arts, Harper College State University of New York, 1961; Doctor of Philosophy, University Pennsylvania, 1966. Postdoctoral fellow California Institute Tcch., Pasadena, 1968; assistant professor Princeton University, New Jersey, 1968-73, associate professor; 1973-76, professor biochemistry; 1976-79, chairman, Harry C. Wiess professor molecular biology; 1978—; chairman, professor department molecular biology State University of New York, Stony Brook, 1979-83; member human cell biology panel National Science Foundation, 1971-72, member genetics and biology panel, 1972-73. Associate editor Journal Cellular and Molecular Biology, 1984—; editor-in-chief Journal Virology, 1984—; editor Virology Journal, 1974-84; contributor articles to professional journals. Member cell biology panel Am. Heart Association, 1978-80; member adv. committee virology and cell biology Am. Cancer Society, 1974-78, vice chairman, 1976, chairman 1977; member National Board Medical Examiners. Dryfus fellow. Member Am. Society Microbiology, American Association for the Advancement of Science, Association Medical School Microbiology (chairman adv. and educational committees), Sigma Xi. Office: Princeton University Molecular Biology Biochem Scis Lab Princeton New Jersey 08544

LEVY, ROBERT ISAAC, physician, educator, research director; born Bronx, New York, May 3, 1937; son of George Gerson and Sarah (Levinson) L.; married Ellen Marie Feis, 1958; children: Andrew, Joanne, Karen, Patricia. Bachelor of Arts with high honors and distinction, Cornell University, 1957; Doctor of Medicine cum laude, Yale University, 1961. Intern, then assistant resident in medicine Yale-New Haven Medical Center, 1961-63; clinical associate molecular diseases National Heart, Lung and Blood Institute, Bethesda, Maryland, 1963-66, chief resident; 1965-66, attending physician molecular disease branch; 1965-80, head section lipoproteins; 1966-80, deputy clinical director institute; 1968-69, chief clinical services molecular diseases branch; 1969-73, chief lipid metabolism branch; 1970-74, director div. heart and vascular diseases; 1973-75, director institute; 1975-81; vice president health sciences, dean School Medicine Tufts University, Boston, 1981-83, professor medicine; 1981-83; vice president health sciences Columbia University, New York City, 1983-84, professor; 1983—, senior assistant vice president health sciences; 1985-87; president Sandoz Research Institute, East Hanover, New Jersey, 1988—; attending physician Georgetown University medical div. District of Columbia General Hospital, 1966-68; special consultant anti-lipid drugs Food and Drug Administration. Editor: Journal Lipid Research, 1972-80, Circulation, 1974-76, Am. Heart jour, 1980—; contributor articles to professional journals. Served as surgeon United States Public Health Service, 1963-66. Recipient Kees Thesis prize Yale University, 1961; Arthur S. Flemming award, 1975; Superior Service award Department of Health, Education and Welfare, 1975; Research award and Van Slyke award Am. Society Clinical Chemists, 1980. Member Am. Heart Association (mem.-at-large executive committee council basic sci., member executive council on atherosclerosis), Am. Institute Nutrition, Am. Federation Clinical Research, New York Acad. Sciences, Am. Society Clinical Nutrition, Am. Society Clinical Investigation, Am. College Cardiology, Institute Medicine of National Acad. Sciences, Am. Society Clinical Pharmacology and Therapeutics, Association Am. Physicians, Phi Beta Kappa, Sigma Xi, Alpha Omega Alpha, Alpha Epsilon Delta, Phi Kappa Phi. Office: Sandoz Pharms Corp East Hanover New Jersey 07936

LEVY, RONALD, medical educator, researcher; born Carmel, California Bachelor of Science, Harvard University; Doctor of Medicine, Stanford University, 1968. Diplomate Am. Board Internal Medicine. Intern Massachusetts General Hospital, Boston, 1968-69; researcher Massachusetts General Hospital, 1969-70; Helen Hay Whitney Foundation fellow in department chemical immunology Weizmann Institute Sci., Rehovot, Israel, 1973-75; member faculty Stanford University, California, 1975—, now associate professor department medicine-oncology. Co-recipient (with G. Telford) 1st award for cancer research Armand Hammer Foundation. Member American College of Physicians, Am. Society Clinical Oncology. Office: Stanford U Department Medicine-Oncology Stanford California 94305

LEWIS, HARRY ROY, computer science educator; born Boston, April 19, 1947; son of Emil Harold and Anne H. (Kowal) L.; married Marlyn Elizabeth McGrath, June 15, 1968; children—Elizabeth Medb, Anne MacLachlan. Bachelor of Arts in Applied Math., Harvard College, 1968; Master of Arts, Harvard University, 1973, Doctor of Philosophy, 1974. Mathematician National Institutes of Health, Bethesda, Maryland, 1968-70; assistant professor Harvard University, Cambridge, Massachusetts, 1974-78, associate professor; 1978-81, Gordon McKay professor computer sci.; 1981—. Author: (with C.H. Papadimitriou) Elements of the Theory of Computation, 1981. Trustee Roxbury Latin School, West Roxbury, Massachusetts, 1979—, vice president board trustees, 1984—. Served with United States Public Health Service, 1968-70. Member Association Computing Machinery, Association Symbolic Logic, Society Industrial and Applied Math. Home: 310 Kent St Brookline Massachusetts 02146 Office: Aiken Computation Lab Harvard University Cambridge Massachusetts 02138

LEWIS, ROBERT ALAN, biologist, researcher, educator, administrator; born Chillicothe, Ohio, April 23, 1933; son of Clarence Albert and Ethel (Hamm) L.; married Carolyn Jane Weber, December 22, 1960; 1 child, Cynthia Anne. Bachelor of Science, Ohio State University, 1959; Master of Science, Rutgers University, 1963; Doctor of Philosophy, University Washington, 1971. Assistant curator vertebrate collections Ohio Historical Mus., Columbus, 1958-60; field representative for vet. pub. health New Jersey Department Health, Trenton, 1960-61; acting chairman department biology Monroe College, Rochester, New York, 1963; zoologist Avian Physiology Laboratory, University Washington, Seattle, 1966-73, research associate Avian Physiology Laboratory; 1973-74, senior research associate Avian

Physiology Laboratory; 1974-77; senior scientist, environmental physiologist National Ecological Research Laboratory, Corvallis, Oregon, 1973-77; general ecologist, program manager Office Health and Environmental Research United States Department Energy, Washington, 1977-81; professor, director Institute Biogeography University Saarland, Saarbruecken, Federal Republic Germany, 1982, professor School Biogeography; 1982—; adj. professor Grad. School, Hood College, Frederick, Maryland, 1978—; member President's Water Policy Study; member Interagy. Committee on Health and Environmental Effects of Advanced Energy Tech.; member Working Group on Western Range Management of Commission on Food and Renewable Resources, Federal Coordinating Council for Sci., Engineering and Tech.; board examiners Banares University, India; lecturer in field; advisor to governments, facilitator cooperative activities between United States and West German agys.; official liaison between Man and the Biosphere Program of United States Department State and Federal Republic Germany, 1986—; evaluated and recommended system of National Ecological Research Parks to be established by Federal Republic Germany. Author, editor: Guidelines for the Establishment of an Environmental Specimen Bank in the Federal Republic of Germany: Ecological Foundations, 1985; editor: Environmental Specimen Banking and Monitoring as Related to Banking, 1984; contributor numerous articles to professional journals. Served with United States Army, 1955-58. Grantee in field. Member American Association for the Advancement of Science, Am. Ornithologists Union (member foreign research committee 1983—), Am. Physiological Society, Cooper Ornithological Society, Delattinia, Ecological Society Am., International Association Ecology, International Society Chronobiology, International Statistical Program, North America Association Environmental Education, Northeastern Bird-Banding Association, Society Environmental Toxicology and Chemistry, Wilson Ornithological Society, Sigma Xi. Republican. Club: Wheaton of Ohio (Columbus). Avocations: hiking; bicycling; camping; natural history. Home: 7213 James I Harris Dr Frederick Maryland 21701 Office: U Saarland, Department Biogeography, D-6600 Saarbruecken Saarland Federal Republic of Germany

LI, HUI-LIN, botanist, educator; born Soochow, China, July 15, 1911; came to United States, 1940, naturalized, 1962; son of Yung-Wu and Wen-Chen (Wang) L.; married Chih Ying Hsu, September 5, 1946; children: June Sing-ju, Anne Sing-yong. Bachelor of Science, Soochow University, 1930; Master of Science, Yenching University, 1932; Doctor of Philosophy, Harvard University, 1942. Instructor biology Soochow University, (China), 1932-40, professor; 1946-47; professor botany, chairman department National Taiwan University, Taipei, 1947-49; research associate Morris Arboretum, University Pennsylvania, 1952-54, taxonomist; 1954-70, director; 1970-74, associate professor botany; 1958-64, professor; 1964-73, John Bartram professor botany and horticulture; 1973-80, emeritus; 1980—; professor biology, director university studies in biology Chinese University Hong

Kong, 1964-65. Author: Chinese Flower Arrangement, 1956, (rev. edition), 1959, The Garden Flowers of China, 1959, The Origin and Cultivation of Shade and Ornamental Trees, 1964, Woody Flora of Taiwan, 1964, Trees of Pennsylvania, The Atlantic States and the Lake States, 1972, Nan-fang t'sao-mu chang, A Fourth Century Flora of Southeast Asia, 1979; contributor: Botany, 1983; head editor, contributor: Flora of Taiwan, 6 vols, 1975, 76, 77, 78, 79; contributor numerous articles to professional journals. Research grantee Am. Philos. Society, 1947, 52, 73, 76; research grantee National Science Foundation, 1956-59, 63, National Library Medicine, 1968, Am. Council Learned Societies, 1976; Harrison fellow University Pennsylvania, 1943-46; Guggenheim Foundation fellow, 1961-62; Fulbright fellow, 1968; National Research Council Fellow, 1969. Member Academia Sinica (Academician 1964—). Office: Department Biology U Pennsylvania Philadelphia Pennsylvania 19104

LICHSTEIN, HERMAN CARLTON, microbiology educator emeritus; born New York City, January 14, 1918; son of Siegfried W. and Luba (Berson) L.; married Shirley Riback, January 24, 1942; children: Michael, Peter. Bachelor of Arts, New York University, 1939; Master of Science in Pub. Health, University Michigan, 1940, Doctor of Science in Bacteriology, 1943. Diplomate: Am. Board Microbiology. Instructor University Wisconsin, 1943-46; associate professor, then professor University Tennessee, 1947-50, University Minnesota, 1950-61; professor microbiology, director department University Cincinnati College Medicine, 1961-78, director grad. studies microbiology; 1962-78, 81-83, professor microbiology; 1961-84, professor emeritus; 1984—; member Linacre College, Oxford University, 1976; member microbiology training committee National Institutes of Health, 1963-66, microbiology fellowships committee, 1966-70; member sci. faculty fellowship panel National Science Foundation, 1960-63; Herman C. Lichstein distinguished lectureship micobial physiology and genetics endowed, 1987. Author: (with Evelyn Oginsky) Experimental Microbial Physiology, 1965; editor: Bacterial Nutrition, 1983; Author also articles. Member Governor Minnesota Committee Education Exceptional Child, 1956-57; Board of directors Walnut Hills (Ohio) High School Association, 1964-66. National Research Council fellow Cornell University, 1946-47; fellow University Cincinnati Graduate School, 1965. Fellow American Association for the Advancement of Science, Am. Acad. Microbiology (governor 1972-75, chairman 1973); member Am. Society Microbiology (hon. 1986), Am. Society Biological Chemistry, Society General Microbiology, Association Medical School Microbiology Chairmen (council 1970-72, trustee 1974-77), Society Experimental Biology and Medicine, Am. Institute Biological Sciences, Sigma Xi (president Cincinnati chapter 1971-73), Phi Kappa Phi, Pi Kappa Epsilon.

LICHTENBERG, BYRON K., space flight consultant; born Stroudsburg, Pennsylvania, February 19, 1948; son of Glenn John and Georgianna (Bierei) L.; married Lee Lombard, July 25, 1970 (divorced); children—Kristin, Kimberly. Bachelor of Science,

Brown University, 1969; Master of Science, Massachusetts Institute of Technology, 1975, Doctor of Science, 1979. Research scientist Massachusetts Institute of Technology, Cambridge, 1978-84; president Payload Systems, Incorporated, Wellesley, Massachusetts, 1984—. Contributor articles to professional journals. Served to lieutenant colonel United States Air Force, Massachusetts Air National Guard, 1969—. Recipient National Aeronautics and Space Administration Space Flight award, 1983, Spaceflight award Veterans of Foreign Wars, 1983, Haley Spaceflight award American Institute of Aeronautics and Astronautics, 1983. Member Tau Beta Pi, Sigma Xi. Avocations: golf; racquetball; windsurfing; skiing. Office: Payload Systems Incorporated 66 Central St Suite 18 Wellesley Massachusetts 02181

LICHTER, PAUL RICHARD, ophthalmology educator; born Detroit, March 7, 1939; son of Max L. and Buena (Epstein) L.; married Carolyn Goode, 1960; children: Laurie, Susan. Bachelor of Arts, University Michigan, 1960, Doctor of Medicine, 1964, Master of Science, 1968. Diplomate Am. Board Ophthalmology. Assistant to associate professor ophthalmology University Michigan, Ann Arbor, 1971-78, professor, chairman department ophthalmology; 1978—; chairman Am. Board Ophthalmology, 1987—. Editor (journal) Ophthalmology, 1987—. Served to lieutenant commander United States Navy, 1969-71. Fellow Am. Acad. Ophthalmology (board directors 1981—, Senior Honor award 1986); member American Medical Association, Pan Am. Association Ophthalmology, Michigan State Medical Society, Washtenaw County Medical Society, Alpha Omega Alpha. Office: University of Michigan Medical School Kellogg Eye Center 1000 Wall St Ann Arbor Michigan 48105

LIEBERMAN, GERALD J., statistics educator; born New York City, December 31, 1925; son of Joseph and Ida (Margolis) L.; married Helen Herbert, October 27, 1950; children—Janet, Joanne, Michael, Diana. Bachelor of Science in Mechanical Engineering, Cooper Union, 1948; Master of Arts in Math. Statistics, Columbia University, 1949; Doctor of Philosophy, Stanford University, 1953. Math. statistician National Bureau Standards, 1949-50; member faculty Stanford University, 1953—, professor statistics and industrial engineering; 1959-67, professor statistics and operations research; 1967—, chairman department operations research; 1967-75, associate dean School Humanities and Sciences; 1975-77, acting vice president and provost; 1979, vice provost; 1977-85, dean research; 1977-80, dean grad. studies and research; 1980-85; consultant to government and industry, 1953—. Author: (with A. H. Bowker) Engineering Statistics, 1959, 2d edition, 1972, (with F.S. Hillier) Introduction to Operations Research, 1967, 4th edition, 1986. Center Advanced Studies in Behavioral Sciences fellow, 1985-86. Fellow Am. Statistical Association, Institute Math. Statistics, Am. Society Quality Control (Shewhart medal 1972), American Association for the Advancement of Science; member National Acad. Engineering, Institute Management Sci. (president 1980-81), Ops. Research Society Am., National Acad.

Engineering (elected), Sigma Xi, Pi Tau Sigma. Home: 811 San Francisco Terrace Stanford California 94305

LIEBOWITZ, HAROLD, aeronautical engineering educator, university dean; born Brooklyn, June 25, 1924; son of Samuel and Sarah (Kaplan) L.; married Marilyn Iris Lampert, June 24, 1951; children: Alisa Lynn, Jay, Jill Denice. Bachelor in Aeronautical Engineering, Polytechnic Institute Brooklyn, 1944, Master in Aeronautical Engineering, 1946, Doctor in Aeronautical Engineering, 1948. With Office Naval Research, 1948-60; assistant dean Grad. School, executive director engineering experiment station University Colorado, Boulder, 1960-61; also visiting professor aeronautical engineering University Colorado; head structural mechs. branch Office Naval Research, 1961-68, director Navy programs in solid propellant mechanics; 1962-68; dean School Engineering and Applied Sci., George Washington University, Washington, 1968 ; research professor Calholic University, Washington, 1962-68; Cons. Office Naval Research, 1960—, Pratt & Whitney Aircraft Company, 1981-82, Pergamon Press, 1968—, Acad. Press, 1968—; member Israeli-Am. Materials Adv. Group, 1970—; sci. adviser Congressional Ad Hoc Committee on Environmental Quality, 1969—; co-director Joint Institute for Advancement Flight Sciences NASA-Langley Research Center, Hampton, Virginia, 1971—. Editor: Advanced Treatise on Fracture, 7 volumes, 1969-72; founder, editor-in-chief International Journal Computers and Structures, 1971—; founder, editor International Journal Engineering Fracture Mechanics, 1968—; contributor articles to professional

journals. Board governors University Denver, 1987—. Recipient Outstanding award Office Naval Research, 1961, Research Accomplishment Superior award, 1961; Superior Civilian Service award USN, 1965, 67; Commendation Outstanding Contbns. sec. navy, 1966; Washington Society Engrs. award, Educational Service award, Washington Society Engrs., Fundacion Gran Mariscal de Avacucho, Service cert. Tech. Contbns. to Structures and Materials Panel, NATO, Distinguished Alumnus award Polytechnic Institute Nklyn., Tech. Achievement cert. Washington sect. American Society of Mechanical Engineers, Civilian Service award U.S. Navy. Fellow American Association for the Advancement of Science, American Institute of Aeronautics and Astronautics, Am. Society Metals; member Society Engineering Sciences (past president), Sci. Research Society Am., Am. Technion Society (director), Am. Acad. Mechanics (founder, president), International Cooperative Fracture Institute (founder, vice president), Engineers Council for Professional Devel., National Acad. Engineering (home secretary), Sigma Xi, Tau Beta Pi, Sigma Gamma Tau, Omega Rho, Pi Tau Sigma, Sigma Tau. Office: 725 23d St Northwest Washington District of Columbia 20052

LIEPMANN, HANS WOLFGANG, physicist, educator; born Berlin, July 3, 1914; came to United States 1939, naturalized, 1945.; son of Wilhelm and Emma (Leser) L.; married Kate Kaschinsky, June 19, 1939 (divorced); married Dietlind Wegener Goldschmidt, 1954; 2 chil-dren. Student, University Istanbul, 1933-35, University Prague, 1935;

Doctor of Philosophy, University Zurich, 1938; Doctor Engineering (honorary), Tech. University Aachen, 1985. Research fellow University Zurich, 1938-39; member faculty California Institute Tech., Pasadena, 1939, professor aeronautics; 1949—, director Grad. Aeronautical Laboratories; 1972-85, Charles Lee Powell professor fluid mechanics and thermodynamics; 1976-83, Theodore von Kármán professor aeronautics; 1983-85, Theodore von Kármán professor aeronautics emeritus; 1985—; member research and tech. adv. committee on basic research National Aeronautics and Space Administration. Co-author: (with A.E. Puckett) Aerodynamics of a Compressible Fluid, 1947; (with A. Roshko) Elements of Gas-dynamics, 1957. Contributor articles to professional journals. Recipient Physics prize University Zurich, 1939, Prandtl Ring, German Society Aeros. and Astronautics, 1968, Worcester Reed Warner medal American Society of Mechanical Engineers, 1969, National Medal of Sci., 1986, Guggenheim medal, 1986. Fellow Am. Acad. Arts and Sciences, American Institute of Aeronautics and Astronautics, Am. Physical Society (Fluid Dynamics prize 1980, Otto Laporte award 1985); hon. fellow Indian Acad. Sciences, 1985; foreign fellow Max-Planck Institut, 1988; member National Acad. Engineering (award 1965), International Acad. Astronautics, American Association for the Advancement of Science, National Acad. Sciences (award 1971), Sigma Xi (Monie A. Ferst award 1978). Address: California Institute Tech care Department Aeronautics Pasadena California 91125

LIN, TUNG YEN, civil engineer, educator; born Foochow, China, November 14, 1911; came to United States, 1946, naturalized, 1951; son of Ting Chang and Feng Yi (Kuo) L.; married Margaret Kao, July 20, 1941; children: Paul, Verna. Bachelor of Science in Civil Engineering, Chiaotung University, Tangshan, Republic of China, 1931; Master of Science, University California, Berkeley, 1933; Doctor of Laws, Chinese University Hong Kong, 1972, Golden Gate University, San Francisco, 1982, Tongji University, Shanghai, 1987, Chiaotung University, Taiwan, 1987. Chief bridge engineer, chief design engineer Chinese Government Railways, 1933-46; assistant, then associate professor University California, 1946-55, professor; 1955-76, chairman div. structural engineering; 1960-63, director structural laboratory; 1960-63; chairman board T.Y. Lin International, 1953—, hon. chairman board; 1987—; president Inter-Continental Peace Bridge, Incorporated, 1968—; consultant to State of California, Def. Department, also to industry; chairman World Conference Prestressed Concrete, 1957, Western Conference Prestressed Concrete Buildings, 1960. Author: Design of Prestressed Concrete Structures, 1955, rev. edition, 1963, 3d edition (with New Hampshire Burns), 1981, (with B. Bresler, Jack Scalzi) Design of Steel Structures, rev. edit, 1968, (with South Dakota Statesbury) Structural Concepts and Systems, 1981, 2d edition, 1988; contributor articles to professional journals. Recipient Berkeley citation award, 1976, National Research Council Quarter Century award, 1977, American Institute of Architects Honor award, 1984, President's National Medal of

Sci., 1986, Merit award Am. Cons. Engrs. Council, 1987; named Outstanding Alumni of Year, University California Engineering Alumni Association, 1984, Hon. Professor, Chiaotung University, 1982, Hon. Professor, Tongji University, 1984, Hon. Professor, Shanghai Chiaotung University, 1985; University California at Berkeley fellow. Member American Society of Civil Engineers (hon., life, Wellington award, Howard medal), National Acad. Engineering, Academia Sinica, International Federation Prestressing (Freyssinet medal), Am. Concrete Institute (hon.), Prestressed Concrete Institute (medal of honor). Home: 8701 Don Carol Dr El Cerrito California 94530 Office: 315 Bay St San Francisco California 94133

LINDBERG, DONALD ALLAN BROR, library administrator, pathologist, educator; born New York City, September 21, 1933; son of Harry B. and Frances Seeley (Little) L.; married Mary Musick, June 8, 1957; children—Donald Allan Bror, Christopher Charles Seeley, Jonathan Edward Moyer. Bachelor of Arts, Amherst College, 1954, Doctor of Science (honorary), 1979; Doctor of Medicine, College Physicians and Surgeons, Columbia University, 1958. Diplomate Am. Board Pathology. Research assistant Amherst College, 1954-55; intern in pathology Columbia-Presbyterian Medical Center, 1958-59; assistant resident in pathology Columbia-Presbyn. Medical Center, 1959-60; assistant in pathology Columbia University College Physicians and Surgeons, New York City, 1958-60; instructor pathology University Missouri School of Medicine, 1962-63, assistant professor; 1963-66, associate professor; 1966-69, professor; 1969-

84, director Diagnostic Microbiology Laboratory; 1960-63, director Medical Center Computer Program; 1962-70, staff, executive director for health affairs; 1968-70, professor, chairman department information sci.; 1969-71; director National Library of Medicine, Bethesda, Maryland, 1984—; member computer sci. and engineering board National Acad. Sci., 1971-74 chairman National Adv. Committee Artificial Intelligence in Medicine, Stanford University, 1975-84; United States representative to International Medical Informatics Association of International Federation for Information Processing, 1975-84, also trustee; member peer rev. group Department Def., 1979-84; director Symposium on Computer Applications in Medical Care, 1981—; member board sci. counselors Lister Hill National Center for Biomedical Communications, National Library of Medicine, Bethesda, 1983—. Author: The Computer and Medical Care, 1968; The Growth of Medical Information Systems in the United States, 1979; editor: (with W. Siler) Computers in Life Science Research, 1975; (with others) Computer Applications in Medical Care, 1982; editor Methods of Information in Medicine, 1970-83, associate editor, 1983—; editor Journal Medical Systems, 1976—, Medical Informatics Journal, 1976—; chief editor procs. 3d World Conf. on Medical Informatics, 1980; contributor articles to sci. journals, chapters to books. Simpson fellow Amherst College, 1954-55; Markle scholar in acad. medicine, 1964-69; member Institute Medicine, National Acad. Sci., 1985—. Member American Association for the Advancement of Science, Am. Society Clinical Pathologists (intersoc. pathology telecommunications network committee 1984—), College Am. Pathologists (commission on computer policy and coordination 1981—), National Board Medical Examiners (executive board 1987—), Missouri State Medical Association, Association for Computing Machines, Salutis Unitas (Am. vice president 1981—), Am. Association for Medical Systems and Informatics (international committee 1982—, board directors 1982—, editor conference procs. 1983, 84), Gorgas Memorial Institute Tropical and Preventive Medicine (board directors 1987—), Sigma Xi. Democrat. Club: Cosmos (Washington). Avocations: photography; riding. Home: 13601 Esworthy Road Germantown Maryland 20874 Office: National Library of Medicine 8600 Rockville Pike Bethesda Maryland 20894

LINDOW, STEVEN EARL, plant pathologist, researcher; born Portland, May 20, 1951; son of Clarence George and Dorothy (Ficken) L.; married Kathryn Preston, June 12, 1974 (divorced June 1981). Bachelor of Science, Oregon State University, 1973; Doctor of Philosophy, University Wisconsin, Madison, 1977. Assistant professor plant pathology University California at Berkeley, 1978-83, associate professor plant pathology; 1983—; consultant Advanced Genetic Sciences, Berkeley, 1983-85; member sci. adv. panel Shell Devel., Modesto, California, 1984—. Recipient Research Inititives award National Acad. Sciences, 1985. Member Am. Phytopathol. Society (CIBA-GEIGY award 1985), Am. Society Plant Physiology, Am. Society Cryobiology, Am. Society Microbiology. Avocations: hiking; running; skiing; golf.

Office: U California Department Plant Pathology Berkeley California 94720

LINDSEY, CASIMIR CHARLES, zoologist; born Toronto, Ontario, Canada, March 22, 1923; son of Charles Bethune and Wanda Casimira (Gzowski) L.; married Shelagh Pauline Lindsey, May 29, 1948. Bachelor of Arts, University Toronto, 1948; Master of Arts, University British Columbia, Vancouver, 1950; Doctor of Philosophy, Cambridge (England) University, 1952. Div. biologist British Columbia Game Department, 1952-57; with Institute Fisheries, also department zoology University British Columbia, 1953-66; professor zoology University Manitoba, Winnipeg, 1966-79; director Institute Animal Resource Ecology, University British Columbia, 1980-85; member Fisheries and Oceans Adv. Council, 1981-86; board governors Vancouver Public Aquarium, 1956-66, 80—; external assessor universities Singapore and Nanyang, 1979-81; consultant in field. Author papers in field. Served with Can. Army, 1943-45. Recipient Publ. award Wildlife Society, 1972; Saunderson award for excellence in teaching University Manitoba, 1977; Rh Institute award, 1979; Nuffield Foundation grantee, 1973; Killam sr. fellow, 1985-86. Fellow Royal Society Can.; member Can. Society Zoologists (president 1977-78), Can. Society Environmental Biologists (vice president 1974-75), Am. Society Ichthyologists and Herpetologists (governor). Office: U British Columbia Department Zoology, 2204 Main Mall, Vancouver, British Columbia Canada V6T 1W5

LINDZEN, RICHARD SIEGMUND, meteorologist, educator; born Webster, Massachusetts, February 8, 1940; son of Abe and Sara

(Blachman) L.; married Nadine Lucie Kalougine, April 7, 1965; children: Eric, Nathaniel. Bachelor of Arts, Harvard University, 1960, Master of Science, 1961, Doctor of Philosophy, 1964. Research associate University Washington, Seattle, 1964-65; Research associate University Oslo, 1965-66; with National Center Atmospheric Research, Boulder, Colorado, 1966-68; member faculty University Chicago, 1968-72; professor meteorology Harvard University, 1972-83, director Center for Earth and Planetary Physics; 1980-83; Alfred P. Sloan professor meteorology Massachusetts Institute of Technology, 1983—; Lady Davis visiting professor Hebrew University, 1979; Vikram Sarabhai professor Physical Research Laboratory, Ahmedabad, India, 1985; consultant Naval Research Laboratories, National Aeronautics and Space Administration, others. Co-author: Atmospheric Tides; contributor to professional journals. Recipient Macelwane award Am. Geophys. Union, 1968. Fellow Am. Meteorological Society (Meisinger award 1969, councillor 1972-75, Charney award 1985), National Acad. Sciences, Am. Acad. Arts and Sciences. Jewish. Office: 54-1416 Mass Institute Tech Cambridge Massachusetts 02139

LINHART, JOSEPH WAYLAND, cardiologist, educator; born New York City, February 7, 1933; son of Joseph and Myrla Watson (Wayl) L.; married Marilyn Adele Voight, September 1, 1956; children—Joseph Wayland, Mary Ellen, Richard, Jennifer, Donna Lisa, Daria. Bachelor of Science, George Washington University, 1954, Doctor of Medicine, 1958. Diplomate Am. Board Internal Medicine, Am. Board Cardiology. Intern Washington Hospital Center, 1958-59; resident in internal medicine George Washington University, 1959-60, Duke University, Durham, North Carolina, 1961; fellow in cardiology Duke University, 1962-63, National Heart Institute and Johns Hopkins University, 1963-64; assistant professor medicine University Florida, Gainesville, 1965-67; associate professor medicine and physiology University Texas, San Antonio, 1968-71; professor medicine, director cardiology Hahnemann Medical School, Philadelphia, 1971-75; professor, chairman department medicine Chicago Medical School, 1975-79, Oral Roberts University, Tulsa, 1979-83; associate dean clinical affairs Oral Roberts University, 1980-81; professor medicine University South Florida, 1983—; assistant chief medicine Veteran's Administration Medical Center, Bay Pines, Florida, 1983-85, chief cardiology; 1983—; medical director Young Men's Christian Association Cardiac Rehabilitation Program, Niles, Illinois, 1976-79; governor Philadelphia Heart Association, 1972-75. Author: 4 books in field including Diagnostic Echocardiography, 1982; contributor 135 articles on clin., invasive and non-invasive cardiology to professional journals. Fellow Am. College Cardiology, American College of Physicians, Am. College Chest Physicians, Council Clinical Cardiology, Institute Medicine Chicago; member American Association for the Advancement of Science, American Medical Association, American Association of University Women, Association Profs. Medicine, Am. Federation Clinical Research, Alpha Omega Alpha. Republican. Office: Med Service

Virginia Med Center Bay Pines Florida 33504

LIPPARD, STEPHEN JAMES, chemist, educator; born Pittsburgh, October 12, 1940; son of Alvin I. and Ruth (Green) L.; married Judith Ann Drezner, August 16, 1964; children: Andrew (deceased), Joshua, Alexander. Bachelor of Arts, Haverford College, 1962; Doctor of Philosophy, Massachusetts Institute of Technology, 1965. Postdoctoral research associate chemistry Massachusetts Institute of Technology, Cambridge, 1965-66, professor chemistry; 1983-89, Arthur Amos Noyes professor chemistry; 1989—; assistant professor chemistry Columbia University, New York City, 1966-69; associate professor Columbia University, 1969-72, professor; 1972-83; member study section medicinal chemistry National Institutes of Health, 1973-77. Editor: Progress in Inorganic Chemistry, 1967—; member editorial board Inorganic Chemistry, 1981-83, 89—, associate editor, 1983; member editorial board Account Chemical Res., 1986-88; contributor articles to professional journals. Coach Demarest Borough Soccer Team, 1975-82, league administrator, 1979-82. National Science Foundation fellow, 1965-66; Alfred P. Sloan fellow, 1968-70; Guggenheim fellow, 1972; recipient Tchr.-Scholar award Camille and Henry Dreyfus Foundation, 1971-76, Henry J. Albert award International Precious Metals Institute, 1985, Alexander von Humboldt U.S. Senior Scientist award, 1988; sr. international fellow John E. Fogarty International Center, 1979. Fellow American Association for the Advancement of Science, Am. Acad. Arts and Sciences; member National Academy of Sciences, Am. Chemical Society (chairman bioinorganic subdiv. 1987-88, Inorganic Chemistry award 1987, Remson award 1987, associate editor journal 1989—), Am. Crystallographic Association, Am. Society Biological Chemists, Chemical Society (London), Biophys. Society, Phi Beta Kappa. Home: 15 Humboldt St Cambridge Massachusetts 02140 Office: Massachusetts Institute of Technology Department Chemistry Room 18-290 Cambridge Massachusetts 02139

LIPSCOMB, WILLIAM NUNN, JR., physical chemist, educator; born Cleveland, December 9, 1919; son of William Nunn and Edna Patterson (Porter) L.; married Mary Adele Sargent, May 20, 1944; children: Dorothy Jean, James Sargent; married Jean Craig Evans, 1983. Bachelor of Science, University Kentucky, 1941, Doctor of Science (honorary), 1963; Doctor of Philosophy, California Institute Tech., 1946; DrHC, University Munich, 1976; Doctor of Science (honorary), Long Island University, 1977, Rutgers University, 1979, Gustavus Adolphus College, 1980, Marietta College, 1981. Physical chemist Office of Scientific Research and Development, 1942-46; with University Minnesota, 1946-59, successively assistant professor, associate professor and acting chief physical chemistry div., professor and chief physical chemistry div.; 1954-59; professor chemistry Harvard University, Cambridge, Massachusetts, 1959-71, Abbott and James Lawrence professor; 1971—, chairman department chemistry; 1962-65; member United States National Committee for Crystallography, 1954-59, 60-63, 65-67; chairman program committee 4th

International Congress of Crystallography, Montreal, 1957; member sci. adv. board Robert A. Welch Foundation; member research adv. board Michigan Molecular Biological Institute; member adv. committee Institute for Amorphous Studies; board of directors Dow Chemical Company. Author: The Boron Hydrides, 1963, (with G.R. Eaton) NMR Studies of Boron Hydrides and Related Compounds, 1969; associate editor: (with G.R. Eaton) Journal Chemical Physics, 1955-57; contributor articles to professional journals; clarinetist, member: Amateur Chamber Music Players. Guggenheim fellow Oxford University, England, 1954-55; Guggenheim fellow Cambridge University, England, 1972-73; National Science Foundation sr. postdoctoral fellow, 1965-66; Overseas fellow Churchill College, Cambridge, England, 1966, 73; Robert Welch Foundation lecturer, 1966, 71; Howard University distinguished lecture series, 1966; George Fisher Baker lecturer Cornell University, 1969; centenary lecturer Chemical Society, London, 1972; lecturer Weizmann Institute, Rehovoth, Israel, 1974; Evans award lecturer Ohio State University, 1974; Gilbert Newton Lewis Memorial lecturer University California, Berkeley, 1974; also lectureships Michigan State University, 1975, University Iowa, 1975, Illinois Institute Tech., 1976, numerous others; also speaker confs.; Recipient Harrison Howe award in Chemistry, 1958; Distinguished Alumni Centennial award University Kentucky, 1965; Distinguished Service in advancement inorganic chemistry Am. Chemical Society, 1968; George Ledlie prize Harvard, 1971; Nobel prize in chemistry, 1976; Distinguished Alumni award California Institute

Tech., 1977; sr. U.S. scientist award Alexander von Humboldt-Stiftung, 1979; award lecture International Acad. Quantum Molecular Sci., 1980. Fellow Am. Acad. Arts and Sciences, Am. Physical Society; member Am. Chemical Society (Peter Debye award phys. chemistry 1973, chairman Minnesota section 1949-50), Am. Crystallographic Association (president 1955), National Acad. Sci., Netherlands Acad. Arts and Sciences (foreign), Math. Association Bioinorganic Scientists (hon.), Academie Europeenne des Sciences, des Arts et des Lettres, Royal Society Chemistry (hon.), Phi Beta Kappa, Sigma Xi, Alpha Chi Sigma, Phi Lambda Upsilon, Sigma Pi Sigma, Phi Mu Epsilon. Office: Harvard U Department Chemistry Cambridge Massachusetts 02138

LITTLEFIELD, JOHN WALLEY, geneticist, cell biologist, educator, pediatrician; born Providence, December 3, 1925; son of Ivory and Mary Russell (Walley) L.; married Elizabeth Legge, November 11, 1950; children: Peter P., John W., Elizabeth L. Doctor of Medicine, Harvard University, 1947. Diplomate: Am. Board Internal Medicine. Intern Massachusetts General Hospital, Boston, 1947-48; resident in medicine Massachusetts General Hospital, 1948-50, staff; 1956-74, chief genetics unit children's service; 1966-73; associate in medicine Harvard University Medical School, 1956-62, assistant professor medicine; 1962-66, assistant professor pediatrics; 1966-69, professor pediatrics; 1970-73; professor, chairman department pediatrics Johns Hopkins University School Medicine, Baltimore, 1974-85, professor, chairman department physiology; 1985—; pediatrician-in-chief Johns Hopkins University Hospital, 1974-85. Author: Variation, Senescence and Neoplasia in Cultured Somatic Cells, 1976. Served with United States Naval Reserve, 1952-54. Guggenheim fellow, 1965-66; Josiah Macy Junior Foundation fellow Oxford University. Member Am. Acad. Arts and Sciences, National Acad. Sciences, Am. Society Biological Chemists, Am. Society Clinical Investigation, Tissue Culture Association, Society Pediatric Research, Am. Society Human Genetics, Am. Pediatric Society, Association Am. Physicians, Phi Beta Kappa, Alpha Omega Alpha. Home: 304 Golf Course Road Owings Mills Maryland 21117 Office: Johns Hopkins U School Medicine Department Physiology Baltimore Maryland 21205

LIVINGSTON, ROBERT BURR, neuroscientist, educator; born Boston, October 9, 1918; son of William Kenneth and Ruth Forbes (Brown) L.; married Mandana Beckner, December 21, 1954 (divorced 1977); children: Louise, Dana, Justyn. Bachelor of Arts, Stanford University, 1940, Doctor of Medicine, 1944. Intern, assistant resident internal medicine Stanford Hospital, Palo Alto, California, 1943-44; instructor physiology Yale University, New Haven, Connecticut, 1946-48; assistant professor Yale University, New Haven, 1950-52; research assistant psychiatry Harvard University, Cambridge, Massachusetts, 1947-48; National Research Council senior fellow neurology Institute Physiology, Geneva, Switzerland, 1948-49; Wilhelm Gruber fellow neurophysiology Switzerland, France, England, 1949-50; executive assistant to president National Acad. Scis.—Nat. Research Council, 1951-52; associate professor physiology and anatomy University of California at Los Angeles, 1952-56, professor; 1956-57; director basic research National Institute of Mental Health and National Institute Neurological Diseases and Blindness, 1956-61; chief neurobiology laboratory National Institute of Mental Health, 1960-65; professor department neuroscis. University California, San Diego, 1965—, chairman department neuroscis.; 1965-70; Gast professor University Zurich, Switzerland, 1971-72; Ernest Sachs lecturer Dartmouth Medical School, 1981; consultant National Research Council, Veteran's Administration, National Aeronautics and Space Administration, Department of Health, Education and Welfare, National Science Foundation, Department Def.; associate neuroscis. research program Massachusetts Institute of Technology, 1963-76, hon. associate, 1976—; emissary to 6 Arab nations for International Physicians for the Prevention of Nuclear War, September, 1986; del. International Conflict Resolution in Central Am., Rust, Austria, International Conference The Central Am. Challenge, Costa Rica, 1988; neuroscis. tutor to Dalai Lama, Dharamsala, India, October, 1987. Adv. editorial board: Journal Neurophysiology, 1959-65; editorial board: International Journal Psychobiology, 1970-80, Neurol. Rsch., 1979—; cons. editor: Journal Neurosci. Rsch., 1975-85. Board of directors Foundations' Fund for Research in Psychiatry, 1954-57; board incorporators Journal History of Medicine and Allied Scis.; incorporator Institute Policy Studies, 1963, Elmwood Institute, 1984. Lieutenant (junior grade) Medical Corps United States Naval Reserve, 1944-46. Decorated Bronze Star; recipient Award for Excellence Matrix: Midland Festival, 1981. Fellow American Association for the Advancement of Science (chairman commission sci. education 1968-71), Am. Acad. Arts and Sciences; member Am. Physiological Society, Am. Association Anatomists, Am. Neurological Association, Am. Acad. Neurology, Association for Research in Nervous and Mental Diseases, Am. Association Neurological Surgeons, Society for Neurosci.

LIVINGSTONE, DANIEL ARCHIBALD, zoology educator; born Detroit, August 3, 1927; son of Harrison Lincoln and Elizabeth Agnes (Matheson) L.; married Bertha Griffin Ross, June 17, 1952 (divorced); children: Laura Ross, Mary Lisa, John Malcolm, Christina Ann, Elizabeth. Bachelor of Science, Dalhousie University, Halifax, Nova Scotia, Can., 1948, Master of Science, 1950; Doctor of Philosophy, Yale University, 1953. Postdoctoral fellow Cambridge University, England, 1953-54, Dalhousie University, Halifax, 1954-55; assistant professor zoology University Maryland, College Park, 1955-56; assistant professor zoology Duke University, Durham, North Carolina, 1956-59, associate professor; 1959-66, professor; 1966—, James B. Duke professor zoology; 1980—; limnogist United States Geological Survey, Washington, summers 1956-58; member adv. panel Environmental Biology branch National Science Foundation, 1964-67, Tundra Biome Project, 1974-76, member human origins panel, 1978, member river-ocean interaction panel, 1978; member United States

National Committee for International Hydrological Decade, 1964; member adv. council for systematic and environmental biology Foreign Currency program, Smithsonian Institution, 1977-80; member external rev. committee University Minnesota Department Ecology and Behavioral Biology, 1979; collaborator National Park Service United States Department Interior, 1974; consultant on geochemistry to A.D. Little Incorporated, 1972-73, on study on mineral cycling in Volta Lake, Ghana, Smithsonian Institution, 1973, to South-East Consortium for International Devel., Kakamega, Kenya, 1985; convenor various workshop sessions. Member editorial board Limnology and Oceanography, 1969-72, Ecology, 1970-72, Annual Rev. Ecology and Systematics, 1975-80, African Archaeol. Rev., 1985—; associate editor Paleobiology, 1974-79; member editorial/adv. board Tropical Freshwater Biology, 1987—; contributor articles to professional journals. National Research Council fellow, 1953, 54-55; John Simon Guggenheim Memorial Foundation fellow, 1960-61. Fellow American Association for the Advancement of Science; member Nova Scotian Institute Sci., International Union for Quaternary Research (United States national committee 1970-78, sub.-commn. for African stratigraphy 1973-82), Am. Quaternary Association (council 1982, counselor 1971-73, 81—), Am. Society Ichthyologists and Herpetologists, Ecological Society Am. (council 1961-66, ecology study committee 1964, chairman weather working group 1965-66), Am. Society for Limnology and Oceanography, North Carolina Acad. Sciences, Freshwater Biological Association United Kingdom, Southeast Electron

Microscopy Society, Hydrobiol. Society East Africa, Can. Quaternary Association, Am. Association Stratigraphic Palynologists, International Association for Fundamental and Applied Limnology, Limnological Society Southern Africa, Association Pour l'Etude Taxonomique de la Flore d'Afrique Tropicale, Association Sénégalaise Pour l'Etude du Quaternaire de l'Ouest Africain, Association des Palynologues de la Langue Française, Sigma Xi. Avocation: woodworking. Home: 853 Louise Circle Durham North Carolina 27705 Office: Duke U Department Zoology Durham North Carolina 27706

LÖE, HARALD, dentist, educator, researcher; born Steinkjer, Norway, July 19, 1926; son of Haakon and Anna (Bruem) L.; married Inga Johansen, July 3, 1948; children: Haakon, Marianne. Doctor of Dental Surgery, University Oslo, 1952; Dr.Odont., 1961; honorary degrees, University Gothenburg, 1973, Royal Dental College, 1980, University Athens, 1980, Catholic University, Leuven, 1980, University Lund, 1983, Georgetown University, 1983, University Bergen, 1985, University Maryland, 1986, University New Jersey, 1987, Royal Dental College, Copenhagen, 1988, University Toronto, 1989. Instructor School Dentistry, Oslo University, 1952-55; research associate Norwegian Institute Dental Research, 1956-62; Fulbright research fellow, research associate department oral pathology University Illinois, Chicago, 1957-58; University research fellow Oslo University, 1959-62, associate professor department periodontology; 1960-61; professor dentistry, chairman department periodontology

Royal Dental College, Aarhus, Denmark, 1962-72; associate dean, dean-elect Royal Dental College, 1971-72; professor, director Dental Research Institute University Michigan, Ann Arbor, 1972-74; dean, professor periodontology School Dental Medicine University Connecticut, Farmington, 1974-82; director National Institute Dental Research, Bethesda, Maryland, 1983—; visiting professor periodontics Hebrew University, Jerusalem, 1966-67; hon. professor Medical Sciences University Beijing, 1987; consultant World Health Organization, National Institutes of Health. Served with Norwegian Army, 1944-48. Recipient 75th Anniversary award Norwegian Dental Association, 1958, Aalborg Dental Society prize Denmark, 1965, William J. Gies Periodontology award, 1978, numerous others. Member American Association for the Advancement of Science, American Dental Association, Danish Dental Association, Am. Acad. Periodontology, Am. Association Dental Research, Am. Society Preventive Dentistry (international award), Massachusetts Dental Society (international award), International Association Dental Research (award for basic research in periodontology 1969, president 1980), International College Dentists, Scandinavian Association Dental Research, Scandinavian Society Periodontology. Office: National Institute Dental Research 9000 Rockville Pike Bethesda Maryland 20892

LONG, CARL FERDINAND, engineering educator; born New York City, August 6, 1928; son of Carl and Marie Victoria (Wellnitz) L.; married Joanna Margarida Tavares, July 23,

1955; children: Carl Ferdinand, Barbara Anne. Bachelor of Science, Massachusetts Institute of Technology, 1950, Master of Science, 1952; Doctor of Engineering, Yale University, 1964; Master of Arts (honorary), Dartmouth College, 1971. Registered professional engineer, New Hampshire. Instructor Thayer School Engineering, Dartmouth College, Hanover, New Hampshire, 1954-57; assistant professor Thayer School Engineering, Dartmouth College, 1957-64, associate professor; 1964-70, professor; 1970—, associate dean; 1972, dean; 1972-84, dean emeritus; 1984—, director Cook Design Center; 1984—; engineer Western Electric Company, Alaska, 1956-57; vice president operations, director Controlled Environment, 1975-81; president, director Q-S Oxygen Processes, Incorporated, 1979-87; New Hampshire Water Supply and Pollution Control Committee, United States Army Small Arms Systems Agency; member New England Construction Education Adv. Council, 1971-74; member adv. committee United States Patent and Trademark Office, 1975-79; member ad hoc visiting committee Engineers Council for Professional Devel., 1973-81; president, director Roan of Thayer, Incorporated, 1986—; board of directors Micro Tool Company, Incorporated, Micro Weighing Systems, Incorporated, 1986—, Roan Ventures, Incorporated, 1987—. Member Hanover Town Planning Board, 1963-75, chairman, 1966-74; trustee Mount Washington Observatory, 1975—; board of directors Eastman Community Association, 1977-80; member corp. Mary Hitchcock Memorial Hospital, 1974—. National Science Foundation Sci.

Faculty fellow, 1961-62; recipient Robert Fletcher award Thayer School of Engineering, 1985. Fellow American Association for the Advancement of Science, American Society of Civil Engineers; member Am. Society Engineering Education (chairman New England section 1977-78, chairman council of sects. Zone 1, director 1981-83), Sigma Xi, Chi Epsilon, Tau Beta Pi. Republican. Baptist. Home: Reservoir Road Hanover New Hampshire 03755

LORENZ, EDWARD NORTON, meteorologist, educator; born West Hartford, Connecticut, May 23, 1917; 3 children. Bachelor of Arts, Dartmouth College, 1938; Master of Arts, Harvard University, 1940; Master of Science, Massachusetts Institute of Technology, 1943, Doctor of Science, 1948. Assistant meteorologist Massachusetts Institute of Technology, Cambridge, 1946-48, member staff; 1948-54, assistant professor, then associate professor; 1955-62, professor meteorology; 1962—; head department Massachusetts Institute of Technology; visiting associate professor University of California at Los Angeles, 1954-55. Recipient Crafoord prize Swedish Acad. Sciences, 1983. Member National Acad. Sciences. Office: Massachusetts Institute of Technology Department Meteorology Cambridge Massachusetts 02139

LOVELL, JAMES A., JR., business executive, former astronaut; born Cleveland, March 25, 1928; son of James A. and Blanch L.; married Marilyn Gerlach; children: Barbara Lynn, James Arthur, Susan Kay, Jeffrey C. Student, University Wisconsin, 1946-48; Bachelor of Science, United States Naval Academy, 1952; graduate, Aviation

Safety School, University Southern California, 1961. Commissioned in United States Navy, advanced through grades to captain; 1965; test pilot Navy Air Test Center Patuxent River, Maryland, 1958-61; flight instructor, safety officer Fighter Squadron 101, Naval Air Station Oceana, Va; became astronaut with Manned Spacecraft Center, National Aeronautics and Space Administration 1962, deputy director sci. and applications directorate Manned Spacecraft Center, National Aeronautics and Space Administration; 1971-73, retired; 1973; president Fisk Telephone Systems, Incorporated, 1977-81; senior vice president administration Centel Corp., Chicago, 1980—. Recipient Distinguished Service award National Aeronautics and Space Administration, 1965, Medal of Honor, 1970; recipient Robert J. Collier trophy, 1969, Grand Medallion award Aero Club France, 1972. Fellow Am. Astronautical Society. Club: Toastmasters. Made 14 day orbital Gemini 7 flight, Dec. 1965, including rendezvous with Gemini 6, Gemini 12 (last of Gemini series) Nov. 1966, Apollo 8 1st journey to moon, Dec. 21-27, 1968, Apollo 13, aborted and returned to earth, Apr. 11-17, 1970. Office: Centel Corp 8725 Higgins Road Chicago Illinois 60631

LOWN, BERNARD, cardiologist, educator; born Utena, Lithuania, June 7, 1921; came to United States, 1935; son of Nisson and Bella (Grossbard) L.; married Louise Charlotte Lown, December 29, 1946; children—Anne Lown Green, Frederick, Naomi Lown Lewiton. Bachelor of Science summa cum laude, University Maine, 1942, DS (honorary), 1982; Doctor of Medicine, Johns Hopkins University, 1945; Doctor of Science (honorary), Worcester State College, 1983, Charles University, Prague, 1987, Bowdoin College, 1988, State University of New York, Syracuse, 1988; Doctor of Laws (honorary), Bates College, Lewiston, Maine, 1983, Queen's University, Kingston, Ontario, Can., 1985; Doctor of Humane Letters (honorary), Colby College, 1986; Doctor of Philosophy (honorary), University Buenos Aires, 1986; Doctor of Humane Letters, Thomas Jefferson University, 1988. Assistant in pathology Yale U.-New Haven Hospital, 1945-46; intern in medicine Jewish Hospital, New York City, 1947-48; assistant resident in medicine Montefiore Hospital, New York City, 1948-50; research fellow in cardiology Peter Bent Brigham Hospital, Boston, 1950-53, assistant in medicine; 1955-56, director Samuel A. Levine Cardiovascular Research Laboratory; 1956-58, junior associate in medicine; 1956-62, research associate in medicine; 1958-59, associate in medicine; 1962-63, senior associate in medicine; 1963-70, director Samuel A. Levine Coronary Care Unit; 1965-74, physician; 1973-81, senior physician; 1982—; assistant in medicine Harvard University, Boston, 1955-58, assistant professor medicine department nutrition School Pub. Health; 1961-67, associate professor cardiology; 1967-73, professor cardiology; 1974—, director cardiovascular research laboratory School Pub. Health; 1961—; consultant in cardiology Newton-Wellesley Hospital, Massachusetts, 1963-77, Beth Israel Hospital, Boston, 1963—, Children's Hospital Medical Center, Boston, 1964—; special consultant World Health Organization, Copenhagen, 1971; coordinator U.S.-USSR Cooperative Study, 1973-81; member lipid metabolism adv. committee National Institutes of Health, Bethesda, Maryland, 1975-79; visiting professor, lecturer, guest speaker numerous universities, hospitals, organizations. Author: (with Samuel A. Levine) Current Advances in Digitalis Therapy, 1954; (with Harold D. Levine) Atrial Arrhythmias, Digitalis and Potassium, 1958, (with A. Malliani) Nueral Mechanisms and Cardiovascular Disease, 1986; member editorial board Circulation, Coeur et Medecine Interne, Journal Electrocardiology; member editorial adv. board Journal Soviet Research in Cardiovascular Diseases; contributor numerous articles to professional journals; member international adv. board International Medical Tribune, 1987—; inventor cardioverter; introduced Lidocaine as antiarrythmic drug. Recipient Modern Medicine award, 1972, Ray C. Fish award and Silver medal Texas Heart Institute, Houston, 1978, A. Ross McIntyre award and Gold medal University Nebraska Medical Center, Omaha, 1979, Richard and Hinda Rosenthal award Am. Heart Association, 1980, George W. Thorn award Brigham and Women's Hospital, 1982, 1st Cardinal Medeiros Peace medallion, 1982, Nikolay Burdenko medal Acad. Medical Sciences Union of Soviet Socialist Republics, 1983; co-recipient Peace Education award United Nations Education, Sci. and Cultural Organization, 1984, Beyond War award, 1984, Nobel Preace prize, 1985, Ghandi Peace award, 1985, New Priorities award, 1986, Andres Bello medal 1st class Ministry Education and Ministry Sci., Venezuela, 1986, Gold Shiel, University Havana, Cuba, 1986, Dr. Tomas Romay y Cahcon Medallion Acad. Sci., Havana, 1986, George F.

Kennan award, 1986, Fritz Gietzelt Medaille Council of Medico-Sci. Socs. of German Democratic Republic, 1987; named hon. citizen City of New Orleans, 1978; named Distinguished Citizen and recipient Key to City Buenos Aires, 1986. Fellow Am. College Cardiology; member Am. Society for Clinical Investigation, Am. Heart Association, Association Am. Physicians, American Association for the Advancement of Science, Physicians for Social Responsibility (founder, 1st president 1960-70), U.S.-China Physicians Friendship Association (president 1974-78), International Physicians for Prevention Nuclear War (president 1980—); corr. member Brit. Cardiac Society, Cardiac Society Australia and New Zealand, Swiss Society Cardiology, Belgian Royal Acad. Medicine, Acad. Medicine of Columbia (hon.), National Acad. Sciences (senior member institute medicine), Phi Beta Kappa, Alpha Omega Alpha. Club: Harvard (Boston). Avocations: photography; music; philosophy; bicycling. Office: Lown Cardiovascular Group PC 221 Longwood Avenue Boston Massachusetts 02115

LUK, KING SING, engineering company executive, educator; born Canton, China, September 1, 1932; came to United States, 1954, naturalized, 1964; son of Yau Kong and Liang Yu L.; married Kit Ming Wong, July 14, 1957; children—Doris, Stephen, Eric, Marcus. Bachelor of Science, California State University, Los Angeles, 1957; Master of Science in Civil Engineering, University Southern California, 1960; Doctor of Philosophy with distinction, University of California at Los Angeles, 1971. Chief engineer R.E Rule Incorporated,

1958-60; president King S Luk & Associate, Incorporated Cons. Engineers, Los Angeles, 1960—; professor civil engineering California State University, Los Angeles, 1960-82, professor emeritus; 1982—, chairman civil engineering department; 1968-74; commissioner California Seismic Safety Commission, 1979-83; director, corp. director, executive officer Mechanics National Bank, Cathay Pacific Incorporated, Luk & Luk, Incorporated. Author: Civil Engineering Reviews, 1964; contributor articles in field to professional journals; research in reinforced concrete and earthquake engring. National Science Foundation fellow, 1966, 70. Fellow American Society of Civil Engineers. Office: Luk & Luk Incorporated 55 S Raymond Avenue #302 Alhambra California 91801

LUKASIK, STEPHEN JOSEPH, aerospace company executive; born Staten Island, New York, March 19, 1931; son of Stephen Joseph and Mildred Florence (Tynan) L.; married Marilyn Bertha Trappiel, January 31, 1953 (divorced 1982); children: Carol J., Gregory C., Elizabeth A., Jeffrey P.; married Virginia Dogan Armstrong, February 11, 1983; stepchildren: Elizabeth L., Alan D. Bachelor of Science, Rensselaer Polytechnic Institute, 1951; Master of Science, Massachusetts Institute of Technology, 1953, Doctor of Philosophy, 1956. Director Advanced Research Project Agency, Washington, 1966-74; vice president Xerox Corp., Rochester, New York, 1974-76; chief scientist and senior vice president Rand Corp., Santa Monica, California, 1977-79; chief scientist Federal Communications Commission, Washington, 1979-82; vice president and manager Northrop Research and Tech. Center, Palos Verdes, California, 1982—; consultant numerous governor organizations. Associate editor: The Information Society. Trustee Stevens Institute Tech., Hoboken, New Jersey; member computer sci. adv. committee Stanford University Served to captain United States Army Reserve. Recipient Sec. Defense Distinguished Civilian Service medal, 1973, 74. Member Am. Physical Society, American Association for the Advancement of Science. Club: Cosmos. Home: 429 S Bentley Avenue Los Angeles California 90049 Office: Northrop Corp 1840 Century Park E Los Angeles California 90067

LURIA, SALVADOR EDWARD, biologist; born Turin, Italy, August 13, 1912; came to United States, 1940, naturalized, 1947; son of David and Ester (Sacerdote) L.; married Zella Hurwitz, April 18, 1945; 1 son, Daniel. Doctor of Medicine, University Turin, 1935. Research fellow Curie Laboratory, Institute of Radium, Paris, 1938-40; research assistant surgical bacteriology Columbia University, 1940-42; successively instructor, assistant professor, associate professor bacteriology Ind. University, 1943-50; professor bacteriology University Illinois, 1950-59; professor microbiology M.I.T., 1959-64, Sedgwick professor biology; 1964—, Institute professor; 1970—, director center cancer research; 1972—; nonresident fellow Salk Institute Biological Studies, 1965—; lecturer biophysics University Colorado, 1950; Jesup lecturer zoology Columbia University, 1950; Nieuwland lecturer biology University Notre Dame, 1959; Dyer lecturer National Institutes of Health,

1963; with Office of Scientific Research and Development, Carnegie Institution, Washington, 1945-46. Asso. editor: Journal Bacteriology, 1950-55; editor: Virology, 1955—; sect. editor: Biol. Abstracts, 1958-62; editorial board: Experimental Cell Research Jour, 1948—; adv. board: Journal Molecular Biology, 1958-64; hon. editorial adv. board: Journal Photochemistry and Photobiology, 1961—. Guggenheim fellow Vanderbilt University and Princeton University, 1942-43; Guggenheim fellow Pasteur Institute, Paris, 1963-64; Co-recipient Nobel prize for medicine, 1969. Member Am. Philosophical Society, Am. Society Microbiology (president 1967-68), National Acad. Sciences, Am. Acad. Arts and Sciences, American Association for the Advancement of Science, Society General Microbiology, Genetics Society Am., American Association of University Women, Sigma Xi. Office: Massachusetts Institute of Technology Department Biology Room E17-113 Cambridge Massachusetts 02139

LURIE, HAROLD, educator; born Durban, South Africa, March 28, 1919; came to United States, 1946, naturalized, 1952; son of Samuel Isaac and Dora (Mitchell) L.; married Patricia Elkin, March 26, 1959 (divorced 1978); children—Diana Isabel, David Andrew. Bachelor of Science, University Natal, South Africa, 1940, Master of Science, 1946; Doctor of Philosophy, California Institute Tech., 1950. Lecturer aeros. California Institute Tech., 1948-50, assistant professor applied mechanics; 1953-56, associate professor; 1956-64, professor engineering sci.; 1964-70, associate

dean grad. studies; 1964-70; director research and devel. New England Electric System, 1971-79; dean engineering Polytechnic Institute New York, Brooklyn, 1979-81; dean College Engineering, Northeastern University, 1981-86; acting director Advanced Systems department Electric Power Research Institute, 1974-75; consultant Yankee Atomic Electric Company, 1970-71; head weapons effectiveness group RAND Corp., 1950-52; senior devel. engineer Oak Ridge National Laboratory, 1956-57. Home: 193 Saint Botolph St Boston Massachusetts 02115

LWOFF, ANDRE MICHEL, microbiologist, virologist; born Ainy-le-Chateau, France, May 8, 1902; son of Salomon and Marie (Siminovitch) L.; married Marguerite Bourdaleix, December 5, 1925. Licence es Scis. Naturelles, Paris, 1921, Doctor Medical, 1927, Doctor Scis. Naturelles, 1932; honorary doctorates, University Chicago, Oxford University, 1959. Became fellow Pasteur Institute, Paris, 1921, assistant; 1925, head laboratory; 1929, head department microbiol. physiology; 1938; professor microbiology Faculty Sciences, University Sorbonne, Paris, 1959-68; head Cancer Research Institute, Villejeuf, 1968-72; president French Family Planning Movement, 1970—. Author: Problems of Morphogenesis in Ciliates: the Kinetosomes in Development, Reproduction and Evolution, 1950; Biological Order, 1962; also articles. Recipient Nobel prize (with François Jacob and Jacques Monod) in medicine and physiology, 1965. Fellow Royal Society (foreign); member New York Acad. Sciences, National Acad. Sciences, Academie des Sciences,

1976. Research on nature and function of growth factors, physiology of viruses; induction and repression of enzymes; explained phenomenon of lysogenic bacteria; demonstrated existence latent bacterial virus; conductor studies on protozoa nutrition; identified vitamins as microbial growth factors, demonstrated that vitamins function as co-enzymes. Home: 69 ave de Suffren, 75007 Paris France Office: Institute Pasteur, 25 rue du Dr Roux, F-75024 Paris France

LYNCH, NANCY ANN, computer science educator; born Brooklyn, January 19, 1948; daughter of Roland David and Marie Catherine (Adinolfi) Evraets; married Dennis Christopher Lynch, June 14, 1969; children: Patrick, Kathleen (deceased), Mary. Bachelor of Science, Brooklyn College, 1968; Doctor of Philosophy, Massachusetts Institute of Technology, 1972. Assistant professor math. Tufts University, Medford, Massachusetts, 1972-73, University Southern California, Los Angeles, 1973-76, Florida International University, Miami, 1976-77; associate professor computer sci. Georgia Tech. University, Atlanta, 1977-82; associate professor computer sci. Massachusetts Institute of Technology, Cambridge, 1982-86, professor computer sci.; 1986—; Ellen Swallow Richards chair Massachusetts Institute of Technology, 1982-87; consultant Computer Corp. Am., Cambridge, 1984-86, Apollo Computer, Chelmsford, Massachusetts, 1986—, American Telephone and Telegraph Company Bell Labs, Murray Hill, New Jersey, 1986—. Contributor numerous articles to professional journals. Member Association Computing Machinery. Roman Catholic. Office: Massachusetts Institute of Technology NE43-525 Cambridge Massachusetts 02139

MACCHESNEY, JOHN BURNETTE, materials scientist, researcher; born Caldwell, New Jersey, July 8, 1929; son of Samuel Burnette and Helen Frances (Van Houten) MacC.; married Janice Hoyt, March 22, 1952; 1 child, John Burnette. Bachelor of Arts, Bowdoin College, 1951; Doctor of Philosophy, Pennsylvania State University, 1959. Chemist Oakite Products, New York City, 1953-55; materials scientist American Telephone and Telegraph Company Bell Laboratories, Murray Hill, New Jersey, 1959—. Contributor numerous articles to professional journals; patentee in field. Served with United States Army, 1951-53. Bell Labs. fellow, 1982. Fellow Am. Ceramic Society (George M. Murey award 1976); member Institute of Electrical and Electronics Engineers (N. Liebman award 1978), National Acad. Engineering, Sigma Xi. Presbyterian. Home: Rural Delivery 1 Cratetown Road Lebanon New Jersey 08833 Office: AT&T Bell Labs 600 Mountain Avenue Murray Hill New Jersey 07974

MAC CREADY, PAUL BEATTIE, aeronautical engineer; born New Haven, September 29, 1925. Bachelor of Science in Physics, Yale University, 1947; Master of Science, California Institute Tech., 1948, Doctor of Philosophy in Aeronautical Engineering cum laude, 1952. Founder, president Meteorology Research Incorporated, 1951-70, Atmospheric Research Group, 1958-70; founder, 1971, since president, now also chairman AeroVironment Incorporated,

Pasadena, California; consultant in field, 1951—; member numerous government tech. adv. committees. Author research papers in field. Recipient Collier trophy National Aeronautical Association, 1979, Edward Longsreth medal Franklin Institute, 1979, Gold Air medal Federation Aeronautical International, 1981; Inventor of Year award Association Advancement Innovation and Invention, 1981; named Engineer of Century American Society of Mechanical Engineers, 1980. Member National Acad. Engineering, Am. Acad. Arts and Sciences, Am. Meteorological Society (chairman committee atmospheric measurements 1968-69, councillor 1971-74), American Institute of Aeronautics and Astronautics (Reed Aeronautical award 1979). Leader team that developed Gossamer Condor (Kremer prize 1977), 1976-77, Gossamer Albatross (Kremer prize 1979) for human-powered flight across English Channel, 1979, Solar Challenger, ultralight aircraft powered by solar cells, 1981, Gossamer Penguin. Office: Aerovironment Incorporated 825 Myrtle Avenue Monrovia California 91106-3424

MACKEY, GEORGE WHITELAW, educator, mathematician; born St. Louis, February 1, 1916; son of William Sturges and Dorothy Frances (Allison) M.; married Alice Willard, December 9, 1960; 1 child, Ann Sturges Mackey. Bachelor of Arts, Rice Institute, 1938; Master of Arts, Harvard University, 1939, Doctor of Philosophy, 1942; Master of Arts, Oxford, 1966. Instructor math. Illinois Institute Tech., 1942-43; faculty instructor math. Harvard, 1943-46, assistant professor; 1946-48, associate professor; 1948-56,

professor math.; 1956-69, Landon T. Clay professor math. and theoretical sci.; 1969-85, professor emeritus; 1985—; visiting professor University Chicago, summer 1955, University of California at Los Angeles, summer 1959, Tata Institute Fundamental Research, Bombay, India, 1970-71; Walker Ames visiting professor University Washington, summer 1961; Eastman visiting professor Oxford, 1966-67; associate professor University Paris, 1978; visiting researcher Math. Sci. Institute, Berkeley, 6 mos. 1983; visiting professor University California, Berkeley, spring 1984. Author: Mathematical Foundations of Quantum Mechanics, 1963, Lectures on the Theory of Functions of a Complex Variable, 1967, Induced Representations and Quantum Mechanics, 1968, The Theory of Unitary Group Representations, 1976, Unitary Group Representations in Physics, Probability and Number Theory, 1978; Contributor articles math. journals. Served as civilian, operational research section 8th Air Force, 1944; applied math. panel NDRC, 1945. Guggenheim fellow, 1949-50, 61-62, 70-71; recipient Humboldt prize Max Planck Institute, Bonn, Federal Republic of Germany, 1985-86. Member Am. Math. Society (vice president 1964-65, Steele prize 1974), National Acad. Sciences, Am. Philosophical Society, Am. Acad. Arts and Sciences, Phi Beta Kappa, Sigma Xi. Office: Harvard U Department Math Cambridge Massachusetts 02138

MAC QUEEN, ROBERT MOFFAT, solar physicist; born Memphis, March 28, 1938; son of Marion Leigh and Grace (Gilfillan) MacQ.; married Caroline Gibbs, June 25, 1960;

children: Andrew, Marjorie. Bachelor of Science, Rhodes College, 1960; Doctor of Philosophy, Johns Hopkins University, 1968. Assistant professor physics Rhodes College, 1961-63; instructor physics and astronomy Goucher College, Towson, Maryland, 1964-66; senior research scientist National Center for Atmospheric Research, Boulder, Colorado, 1967—, director High Altitude Observatory; 1979-86, assistant director; 1986-87, associate director; 1987—; principal investigator National Aeronautics and Space Administration Apollo program, 1971-75, National Aeronautics and Space Administration Skylab program, 1970-76, National Aeronautics and Space Administration Solar Maximum Mission, 1976-79, NASA/ESA International Solar Polar Mission, 1978-83; lecturer University Colorado, 1968-79, adj. professor, 1979—; member committee on space astronomy National Acad. Sciences, 1973-76, member committee on space physics, 1977-79; member Space Sci. Board, 1983-86. Recipient Exceptional Sci. Achievement medal National Aeronautics and Space Administration, 1974. Fellow Optical Society Am.; member Am. Astronomical Society (chairman solar physics division 1976-78), Association University Research Astronomy (dir.-at-large 1984—), Am. Association Physics Teachers, Sigma Xi. Home: 1366 Northridge Court Boulder Colorado 80302 Office: National Center Atmospheric Research Post Office Box 3000 1850 Table Mesa Dr Boulder Colorado 80307

MAHLMAN, JERRY DAVID, research meteorologist; born Crawford, Nebraska, February 21, 1940; son of Earl Lewis and Ruth Margaret (Callendar) M.; married Janet Kay Hilgenberg, June 10, 1962; children—Gary Martin, Julie Kay. Bachelor of Arts, Chadron State College, Nebraska, 1962; Master of Science, Colorado State University, 1964, Doctor of Philosophy, 1967. Instructor Colorado State University, Fort Collins, 1964-67; from assistant professor to associate professor Naval Postgrad. School, Monterey, California, 1967-70; reseach meteorologist National Oceanographic and Atmospheric Administration Geophysical Fluid Dynamics Laboratory, Princeton, New Jersey, 1970-84, laboratory director; 1984—; lecturer with rank of professor Princeton University, 1980—; member committee on global ecology US-USSR Joint National Acad. Sciences; chairman panel on middle atmosphere program National Acad. Sci., 1982-84. Contributor over 60 articles to professional journals. Elder Monterey Presbyterian Church, 1968-70, Lawrence Road Presbyterian Church, Lawrenceville, New Jersey, 1972-75; board of directors Lawrence Non-Profit Housing Incorporated, 1978-88. Recipient Distinguished Authorship award Department Commerce, 1980, 81, cert. of recognition, 1983, Gold medal, 1986; Distinguished Service award Chadron State College, 1984. Fellow Am. Geographic Union, Am. Meteorological Society (awards committee 1984, chairman upper atmosphere committee 1979, associate editor Jour. Atmospheric Sci. 1979-86, editor's award 1978); member Sigma Xi. Democrat. Home: 9 Camelia Road Lawrenceville New Jersey 08648 Office: Geophys Fluid Dynamics Lab Princeton U Box 308 Princeton New Jersey 08542

MAI, WILLIAM FREDERICK, plant nematologist, educator; born

Greenwood, Delaware, July 23, 1916; son of William Frederick and Laurana (Owens) M.; married Barbara Lee Morrell, June 2, 1941; children: Virginia Mai Abrams, William Howard, Eliabeth Hardy. Bachelor of Science, University Delaware, 1939; Doctor of Philosophy, Cornell University, 1945. Assistant professor Cornell University, Ithaca, New York, 1946-49, associate professor; 1949-52, professor; 1952-81, Liberty Hyde professor plant pathology; 1981-83, professor emeritus; 1983—; consultant National Acad. Sciences, International Potato Center, Brands Company, Agency for International Development. Author (with H.H. Lyon), Pictoral Key to Genera of Plant Parasitic Nemtodes, 1960, Plant Parasitic Nematodes, 1971; editor: Control of Plant Parasitic Nematodes, 1968. Coach Little League Baseball and Football, Ithaca, 1955-60; chairman Community Organization, 1960-65. Recipient award of distinction International Plant Protection Conference, 1979. Fellow Am. Phytopath. Society (president Northeastern division 1968-69 award of merit Northeastern div); member Society Nematologists (president 1969 hon. life); Member Helminthological Society Washington; member Society European Nematologists; American Association for the Advancement of Science; member Potato Association Am. Lodge: Rotary. Home: 613 E Shore Dr Ithaca New York 14850 Office: Cornell U Department Plant Pathology Ithaca New York 14853

MAIER, ROBERT HAWTHORNE, biology educator; born New York City, October 26, 1927; son of Ernest Henry and Clara Louise M.; married Jane Hiob, August 31, 1952; children: Pamela, David, Daniel. Bachelor of Science, University Miami, 1951; Master of Science, University Illinois, 1952, Doctor of Philosophy, 1954. Assistant dean Grad. College, University Arizona, 1966-67; assistant chancellor for instruction and research University Wisconsin, Green Bay, 1967-69, vice chancellor and deputy chancellor, professor; 1969-75, professor sci. and environmental change, public and environmental administration; 1975-79; vice chancellor acad. affairs East Carolina University, Greenville, North Carolina, 1979-83; professor experimental surgery, biology, political sci. East Carolina University, 1983—, director Trace Element Center, School Medicine; 1984—; member council biotech. University North Carolina System, 1981-83; board of directors Agronomic Sci. Foundation, 1987—. Contributor articles to professional journals. Board of directors Lakeland chapter American Red Cross, 1978-79, Children's Services Ea. North Carolina, 1987—; member Education Task Force, City of Green Bay, 1977-78, North Carolina State Panel Advancement of Women in Administration, 1981-84, Gov.'s Commission on Future of North Carolina, 1981-84; treasurer Ronald McDonald House, 1987—. Served with United States Army, 1954-56. Fellow American Association for the Advancement of Science, Am. Institute Chemists, Am. Society Agronomy, Soil Sci. Society Am.; member Am. Chemical Society, Am. Society Plant Physiologists, Am. Institute Biological Sciences, Am. Management Association. Presbyterian. Office: East Carolina U Greenville North Carolina 27858-4354

MAIMAN, THEODORE HAROLD, physicist; born Los Angeles, July 11,

1927. Bachelor of Science in Engineering Physics, University Colorado, 1949; Master of Science in Electrical Engineering, Stanford University, 1951, Doctor of Philosophy in Physics, 1955. Section head Hughes Research Laboratories, 1955-61; president, founder Korad Corp., Santa Monica, California, 1961-68, Maiman Associates, Los Angeles, 1968—; vice president, founder Laser Video Corp., Los Angeles, 1972-75; vice president advanced tech. and new ventures TRW Incorporated Electronics and Defense Sector, Los Angeles, 1975-83; director Plesscor Optronics Incorporated. Author papers in field. Adv. board Industrial Research magazine. Served with United States Naval Reserve, 1945-46. Recipient award Fannie and John Hertz Foundation, 1966; Ballantine award Franklin Institute, 1962; award for development laser Aerospace Electrical Soc.-Am. Astronomical Society, 1965, Light award Braille Institute, 1982, Wolf prize in physics, 1984; named Alumni of Century University Colorado, 1976; inducted into U.S. National Inventors Hall of Fame, 1984; named Laureate Japan Prize (electro-optics), 1987. Fellow Society Motion Picture and TV Engineers, Am. Physical Society (Oliver E. Buckley prize 1966), Optical Society Am. (R.W. Wood prize 1976), Society Photog. and Instrumentation Engineers; member National Acad. Engineers, National Acad. Sciences, Institute of Electrical and Electronics Engineers, Society Information Display, Sigma Xi, Sigma Pi Sigma, Sigma Tau, Pi Mu Epsilon. Responsible devel. 1st laser.

MAKI, DENNIS G., medical educator, researcher; born River Falls, Wisconsin, May 8, 1940; married Gail Dawson, 1962; children: Kimberly, Sarah, Daniel. Bachelor of Science with high honors in Physics, University Wisconsin, 1962, Master of Science in Physics, 1964, Doctor of Medicine, 1967. Diplomate Am. Board Internal Medicine, Am. Board Infectious Diseases. Physicist, computer programmer Lawrence Radiation Laboratory, Atomic Energy Commission, Livermore, California, 1962; intern, assistant resident Harvard Medical unit Boston City Hospital, 1967-69, chief resident; 1972-73; with Hospital Infections section Centers for Disease Control, United States Public Health Service, Atlanta, 1969-71; acting chief national nosocomial infections study Center for Disease Control, United States Public Health Service, Atlanta, 1970-71; senior resident department medicine Massachusetts General Hospital, 1971-72, clinical and research fellow infectious disease unit; 1973-74; assistant professor medicine University Wisconsin, Madison, 1974-78, associate professor; 1978-82, professor; 1982—; chief section infectious diseases, hospital, epidemiologist University Wisconsin Hospital and Clinic, Madison, 1974—; Ovid O. Meyer chair in medicine University Wisconsin, Madison, 1975—, head secretary infectious diseases; 1979—; attending physician Center for Trauma and Life Support University Wisconsin, 1976—; lecturer in field. Contributor research articles to medical journals; associate editor: Infection Control, 1979—; member editorial board: Journal Lab. and Clin. Investigation, 1980-86, Critical Care Monitor, 1982-85, Journal Critical Care, 1985—. Recipient Ingersoll award in Physics, 1960, others; General Motors Scholar, 1960-62; numerous teaching awards; First award for distinguished research in Antibiotic Rev., 1980. Fellow American College of Physicians, Infectious Diseases Society Am., Society for Critical Care Medicine, Surgical Infection Society; member Society Hospital Epidemiologists Am. (vice president 1988—), Central Society for Clinical Research (specialty counsellor for infectious diseases), American Association for the Advancement of Science, Am. Society Microbiology, Am. Federation for Clinical Research, Alpha Omega Alpha. Office: U Wisconsin Department Medicine 600 Highland Avenue H4/574 Madison Wisconsin 53792

MALKUS, WILLEM VAN RENSSE-LAER, mathematics educator; born Brooklyn, November 19, 1923; son of Hubert Paul and Alida Fitzhugh (Wright) M.; married Joanne Starr Simpson, 1948; married Ulla Charlotte, December 28, 1964; children: David S., Steven W., Karen E., Per N. Doctor of Philosophy in Physics, University Chicago, 1950. Assistant professor natural sci. University Chicago, 1950-51; physical oceanographer Woods Hole (Massachusetts) Oceanographic Institution, 1951-60; professor geophysics University of California at Los Angeles, 1960-67, professor geophysics and math.; 1967-69; professor applied math. Massachusetts Institute of Technology, Cambridge, 1969—. Contributor articles to sci. journals. Served to lieutenant (junior grade) United States Naval Reserve, 1942-46. Guggenheim fellow University Cambridge, (England) and Stockholm, 1971-72, University Cambridge, 1979-80; National Science Foundation fellow, 1964-65. Fellow Am. Physical

Society, Am. Acad. Arts and Sciences, Am. Geophysical Union; member National Acad. Sci. Home: 72 Shade St Lexington Massachusetts 02173 Office: Massachusetts Institute of Technology Room 2-369 Cambridge Massachusetts 02139

MALONE, JOSEPH JAMES, mathematics educator, researcher; born St. Louis, September 9, 1932; son of Joseph James and Aurelia Theresa (Shoemaker) M.; married Dorothy Sue Cleary, November 24, 1960; children—Michael, Barbara, Philip, Patrick. Bachelor of Science, St. Louis University, 1954, Master of Science, 1958, Doctor of Philosophy, 1962. Instructor math Rockhurst College, Kansas City, Missouri, 1960-62; assistant professor University Houston, 1962-67; associate professor Texas A&M University, College Station, 1967-70, professor; 1970-71; professor Worcester Polytechnic Institute, Massachusetts, 1971—, chairman department math.; 1971-78. Contributor articles to professional journals. Member Westborough Pub. Schools Board, Massachusetts, 1974-83, 84-87. Served with United States Army, 1954-56. Member Am. Math. Society, Math. Association Am., Consortium for Math. and Its Applications, American Association of University Profs., Society Industrial and Applied Math. Democrat. Roman Catholic. Active reform calculus instrn. movement. Avocations: jogging; softball. Home: 45 Adams St Westborough Massachusetts 01581 Office: Worcester Polytechnic Institute 100 Institute Road Worcester Massachusetts 01609

MANDEL, LEONARD, physicist. married Jeanne Elizabeth Kear, August 20, 1953; children:

Karen Rose, Barry Paul. Bachelor of Science, University London, England, 1947, University London, England, 1948; Doctor of Philosophy, University London, England, 1951. Tech. officer Imperial Chemical Industries, 1951-54; lecturer, senior lecturer Imperial College, University London, 1954-64; professor physics University Rochester, New York, 1964—; professor optics University Rochester, 1977-80; joint secretary Rochester Confs. on Coherence and Quantum Optics, 1966, 72, 77, 83; visiting professor University Texas, Austin, 1984. Editor books; associate editor: Optics Letters, 1977-79; Contributor articles to professional journals.
Recipient Marconi medal Italian National Rsch. Council, 1987, Thomas Young medal Institute Physics Great Britain, 1989. Fellow Am. Physical Society, Optical Society Am. (board directors 1985-87, associate editor journal 1970-76, 82-84, board editors Physical Rev. 1988—, chairman committee for society objectives and policy 1977, chairman Wood prize committee 1988, 1st recipient Max Born prize 1982). Office: U Rochester Department Physics and Astronomy Rochester New York 14627

MANDELBROT, BENOIT B., mathematician, scientist, educator; born Warsaw, Poland, November 20, 1924; came to United States, 1958; son of Charles and Belle (Lurie) M.; married Aliette Kagan, November 5, 1955; children: Laurent, Didier. Diploma, Ecole Polytechnique, Paris, 1947; Master of Science in Aeronautics, California Institute Tech., 1948; Doctor of Philosophy in Math., University Paris, 1952; Doctor of Science (honorary), Syracuse University, 1986, Laurentian University, 1986, Boston University, 1987. Junior member and Rockefeller scholar Institute for Advanced Study, Princeton, New Jersey, 1953-54; junior professor math. University Geneva, Switzerland, 1955-57, University Lille and Ecole Polytechnique, Paris, 1957-58; research staff member International Business Machines Corporation Watson Research Center, Yorktown Heights, New York, 1958-74; International Business Machines Corporation fellow International Business Machines Corporation Watson Research Center, 1974—; visiting professor economics Harvard University, 1962-63, visiting professor applied math., 1963-64, visiting professor math., 1979-80, professor practice math., 1984-87; visiting professor engineering Yale University, 1970, adj. professional math. Sciences, 1987—; visiting professor physiology Einstein College Medicine, 1970; visitor M.I.T., 1953; also Institute lecturer; visitor University Paris, 1966; visitor College de France, Paris, 1973, and various times, Institut des Hautes Etudes Scientifiques, Bures, 1980, Mittag-Leffler Institute, Sweden, 1984; Trumbull lecturer Yale University, 1970; speaker and organizer professional conferences. Author: books including Logique, Langage et Théorie de l'Information, 1957, Les Objets Fractals, 1975, 2d edition, 1984, Fractals: Form, Chance and Dimension, 1977, The Fractal Geometry of Nature, 1982, Fraktal Kikaguku, 1984, Die Fraktale Geametrie du Natur, Gli Oggetti Frattali, 1987, Los Objetos Fractales, 1987; contributor articles to professional journals. Recipient Frederick Barnard medal National Acad. Sciences, 1985, Franklin medal Franklin Institute, 1986, Alexander von Humboldt Preis, 1987; National lecturer Sigma Xi, 1980-82; Guggenheim fellow, 1968. Fellow Am. Acad. Arts and Sciences, Am. Physical Society, European Acad. Arts Sciences and Humanities, Institute of Electrical and Electronics Engineers, Institute Math. Statistics, Econometric Society, Am. Geophys, Union, Am. Statistic Association, American Association for the Advancement of Science; member National Acad. Sci. USA (foreign associate), International Statistical Institute (elected), Am. Math. Society, French Math. Society. Originator of theory of fractals, an interdisciplinary enterprise concerned with shapes and phenomena that are rough, irregular or broken-up at all scales. Office: International Business Machines Corporation Post Office Box 218 Yorktown Heights New York 10598 also: Yale U Math Department New Haven Connecticut 06520

MAR, JAMES WAH, aeronautics engineer, educator; born Oakland, California, March 10, 1920; married, 1942; 4 children. Bachelor of Science, Massachusetts Institute of Technology, 1941, Master of Science, 1947, Doctor of Science, 1949. Head structural test section Curtiss-Wright Corp., 1941-44; engineer structural research group Massachusetts Institute of Technology, Cambridge, 1949-50, member faculty; 1950—, professor aeros. and astronautics; 1964—, head department; 1981-83; member panel thermal protection systems Materials Adv. Board, National Acad. Sci.-NRC, 1957-69, member committee thermal protection aerospace vehicles; 1963-65; consultant committee space vehicle structures National Aeronautics and Space Administration, 1963—; member adv. board materials committee on structural design with

fibrous composites National Acad. Sci-NRC-Nat. Acad. Engineering, 1967—; chief scientist United States Air Force, 1971-72, member sci. adv. board vehicles panel. Member American Institute of Aeronautics and Astronautics. Office: Department Aeros and Astronautics Massachusetts Institute of Technology Room 33-207 77 Massachusetts Avenue Cambridge Massachusetts 02139

MARAN, STEPHEN PAUL, astronomer; born Brooklyn, December 25, 1938; son of Alexander P. and Clara F. (Schoenfeld) M.; married Sally Ann Scott, February 14, 1971; children: Michael Scott, Enid Rebecca, Elissa Jean. Bachelor of Science, Brooklyn College, 1959; Master of Arts, University Michigan, 1961, Doctor of Philosophy, 1964. Astronomer Kitt Peak National Observatory, Tucson, 1964-69; project scientist for orbiting solar observatories NASA-Goddard Space Flight Center, Greenbelt, Maryland, 1969-75; head advanced systems and ground observations branch NASA-Goddard Space Flight Center, 1970-77; manager operation Kohoutek, 1973-74, senior staff scientist; 1977—; Cons. Westinghouse Research Laboratories, 1966; visiting lecturer University Maryland, College Park, 1969-70; senior lecturer University California at Los Angeles, 1976. Author: (with John C. Brandt) New Horizons in Astronomy, 1972, 2d edition, 1979, Arabic edition, 1979; Editor: Physics of Nonthermal Radio Sources, 1964, The Gum Nebula and Related Problems, 1971, Possible Relations Between Solar Activity and Meteorological Phenomena, 1975, New Astronomy and Space Science Reader, 1977, A Meeting with the

Universe, 1981, Astrophysics of Brown Dwarfs, 1986; associate editor: Earth, Extraterrestrial Scis, 1969-79; editor: Astrophys. Letters, 1974-77, associate editor, 1977-85; Contributor articles on astronomy, space to popular magazines. Named Distinguished Visitor Boston University, 1970; recipient Group Achievement awards National Aeronautics and Space Administration, 1969, 74, Hon. Mention AAAS-Westinghouse Sci. Writing Award, 1970. Member International Astronomical Union (editor daily newspaper 1988), American Association for the Advancement of Science, Am. Astronomical Society (Harlow Shapley vis. lecturer 1981—, press officer 1985—), Royal Astronomical Society, Am. Physical Society, Am. Geophysical Union, Am. Institute Aeros. and Astronautics. Office: NASA-Goddard Space Flight Center Code 680 Greenbelt Maryland 20771

MARCUS, HARRIS L., materials science and engineering educator; born Ellenville, New York, July 5, 1931; son of David and Bertha (Messite) M.; married Leona Gorker, August 28, 1962; children: Leland, M'Risa. Bachelor of Science, Purdue University, 1963; Doctor of Philosophy, Northwestern University, 1966. Registered professional engineer, Texas. Tech. staff Texas Instruments, Dallas, 1966-68, Rockwell Sci. Center, 1968-70; group leader Rockwell Sic. Center, 1971-75; professor mechanical engineering University Texas, Austin, 1975-79, H.L. Kent Junior professor; 1979—, director Materials Sci. and Engineering Center, director program. Contributor numerous articles to professional publications. Recipient

University Texas faculty University Texas Engineering Foundation, 1983; Krengel lecturer Technion, Israel, 1983; Alumni Merit medal Northwestern University, 1988. Fellow Am. Society Metals; member American Society of Mechanical Engineers, University Materials Council, American Institute of Mining, Metallurgy and Petroleum Engineers (board directors Metallurgical Society), American Society for Testing and Materials, Am. Physical Society. Home: 4102 Hyridge Austin Texas 78759 Office: U Tex Department Mech Engring Austin Texas 78712

MARCUS, STEVEN IRL, electrical engineering educator; born St. Louis, April 2, 1949; son of Herbert A. and Peggy L. (Polishuk) M.; married Jeanne M. Wilde, June 4, 1978; children: Jeremy A., Tobin L. Bachelor of Arts, Rice University, 1971; Master of Science, Massachusetts Institute of Technology, 1972, Doctor of Philosophy, 1975. Research engineer The Analytic Sciences Corp., Reading, Massachusetts, 1973; assistant professor University Texas, Austin, 1975-80, associate professor; 1980-84, professor; 1984—, associate chairman, department electrical and computer engineering; 1984—, L.B. Meaders professor engineering; 1987—; consultant Tracor Incorporated, Austin, 1977. Associate editor Math. of Control Signals & Systems, 1987—; contributor articles to professional journals. National Science Foundation fellow, 1971-74; Werner W. Dornberger Centennial Teaching fellowship in engineering, University Texas, Austin, 1982-84. Fellow Institute of Electrical and Electronics Engineers (prize paper awards committee 1985-88), Institute of Electrical and Electronics Engineers Control Systems Society (board govs. 1985—, chairman conference on decision and control program commission 1983, chairman working group on stochastic control and estimation 1984-87); member Am. Math. Society, Society Industrial and Applied Math., Eta Kappa Nu, Tau Beta Pi. Home: 1703 W 32d St Austin Texas 78703 Office: University Tex at Austin Department Elec & Computer Engring Austin Texas 78712

MARKESBERY, WILLIAM R., neurology and pathology educator, physician; born Florence, Kentucky, September 30, 1932; son of William M. and Sarah E. (Tanner) M.; married Barbara A. Abram, September 5, 1958; children—Susanne Hartley, Catherine Kendall, Elizabeth Allison. Bachelor of Arts, University Kentucky, 1960, Doctor of Medicine with distinction, 1964. Diplomate Am. Board Neurology and Psychiatry Diplomate Am. Board Pathology. Resident neurology, neuropathology Columbia University, New York City, 1965-69; assistant professor pathology, neurology University Rochester, New York, 1969-72; associate professor pathology, neurology University Kentucky, Lexington, 1972-77, professor neurology, pathology, anatomy; 1977—, director research institute; 1979—, professor neurology, pathology, director; 1977—; member pathology study section National Institutes of Health, Washington, 1982-85; member medical sci. adv. board National Alzheimer's Association, Chicago, 1985-86; member adv. panel on dementia United States Congress of Tech., Washington, 1985-86; director Alzheimer's Disease Research Center. Member editorial board Journal Neuropathology and Experimental Neurology, 1983—, Neurobiology of Aging, 1986—; contributor numerous articles to professional journals. Served to United States Army, 1954-56. Recipient Distinguished Achievement award Kentucky Research Foundation, Lexington, 1978; named University Kentucky Distinguished Alumni professor, 1985, Distinguished Research professor, University Kentucky, 1977; prin. investigator National Institutes of Health, Washington, 1977—. Member Am. Acad. Neurology, Am. Association Neuropathologists (executive committee 1984-86), Am. Neurological Association, Alpha Omega Alpha. Home: 1555 Tates Creek Road Lexington Kentucky 40502 Office: U Ky/Multidisciplinary Center for Gerontology 101 Sanders-Brown Building Lexington Kentucky 40536

MARKS, PAUL ALAN, oncologist, cell biologist; born New York City, August 16, 1926; son of Robert R. and Sarah (Bohorad) M.; married Joan Harriet Rosen, November 28, 1953; children: Andrew Robert, Elizabeth Susan, Matthew Stuart. Bachelor of Arts with general honors, Columbia University, 1945, Doctor of Medicine, 1949; Doctor Biol. Science (honorary), University Urbino, Italy, 1982; Doctor of Philosophy (honorary), Hebrew University, Jerusalem, Israel, 1987. Fellow Columbia College Physicians and Surgeons, 1952-53, associate; 1955-56, member faculty; 1956—, director hematology training; 1961-74, professor medicine; 1967-82, dean faculty of medicine, vice president medical affairs; 1970-73, director Comprehensive Cancer Center; 1972-80, vice president health sciences, 1973-80; professor human genetics and devel., 1969-82; Frode Jensen professor medicine, 1974-80; professor medicine and genetics Cornell University College Medicine, New York City, 1981—; attending physician Presbyterian Hospital, New York City, 1967-82; president, chief executlve officer Memorial Sloan-Kettering Cancer Center, 1980—; attending physician Memorial Hospital for Cancer and Allied Diseases, 1980—; member Sloan-Kettering Institute for Cancer Research, 1980—; adj. professor Rockefeller University, 1980—; visiting professor College de France, Paris, 1988; visiting physician Rockefeller University Hospital, 1980—; instructor School Medicine, George Washington University, 1954-55; consultant Veteran's Administration Hospital, New York City, 1962-66; associate investigator National Institute Arthritis and Metabolic Diseases, National Institutes of Health, Bethesda, Maryland, 1953-55; member adv. panel hematology training grants program National Institutes of Health, 1969-73, chairman hematology training grants program, 1971-73; visiting scientist Laboratory Cellular Biochemistry, Pasteur Institute, 1961-62; visiting professor Chemica Biologica, University Genoa, Italy, 1963; member adv. panel on developmental biology National Science Foundation, 1964-67; member Delos Conference, Athens, Greece, 1971, 72; member founding committee Radiation Effects Research Foundation, Japan, 1975; member President's Biomed. Research Panel, 1975-76, President's Cancer Panel, 1976-79, President's Commission on Accident at Three Mile Island, 1979; chairman executive committee div. medical sciences National Acad. Scis.-NRC, 1973-76; ad hoc adviser White House Conference on Aging, 1981; council div. cancer treatment National Cancer Institute, 1980-83; adviser Leopold Schepp Foundation; director Pfizer, Incorporated, Life Techs., Incorporated, Dreyfus Mutual Funds. Editor: Monographs in Human Biology, 1963; Contributor over 300 articles to professional journals; member editorial board: Blood, 1964-71, associate editor, 1976-77, editor-in-chief, 1978-82; editor-in-chief Journal Clin. Investigation, 1967-72. Trustee St. Luke's Hospital, 1970-80, Roosevelt Hospital, 1970-80, Presbyterian Hospital, 1972-80; member jury Albert Lasker Awards, 1974-82; board of directors Pub. Health Research Institute, New York City, 1971-74; board governors Weizmann Institute, 1976—; board of directors Revson Foundation, 1976—; board sci. counselors, div. cancer treatment National Cancer Institute, 1980-83; member council div. biol. scis. and Pritzker School Medicine, University Chicago; member tech. board Milbank Memorial Fund, 1978-85 ; trustee Metpath Institute Medical Education, 1977-79. Recipient Charles Janeway prize Columbia, 1949, Joseph Mather Smith prize, 1959, Stevens Triennial prize, 1960, Swiss-Am. Foundation award in med. research, 1965, Columbia University College Physicians and Surgeons Distinguished Service medal, 1980, Centenary medal Institute Pasteur, 1987, Medal of College de France, 1988; Foundation for Promotion of Cancer Research, Japan Medal, 1984; Commonwealth Fund fellow, 1961-62, Ayrey fellow postgrad. med. sch. University London, 1985. Fellow Am. Acad. Arts andSciences, American Association for the Advancement of

Science; member Institute Medicine (member council 1973-76), National Acad. Sciences (chairman section med. genetics, hematology and oncology 1980-83, chairman Acad. Forum Adv. Committee 1980-81, member council 1984-87), Red Cell Club (past chairman), Am. Federation Clinical Research (past councillor Eastern district), Am. Society Clinical Investigation (president 1972-73), Am. Society Biological Chemists, Am. Society Human Genetics (past member program committee), Am. Association Cancer Research, American College of Physicians, Am. Society Cell Biology, Am. Society Hematology (pres.-elect 1983, president 1984), Association Am. Physicians, Enzyme Club, Harvey Society (president 1973-74), International Society Developmental Biologists, Interurban Clinical Club, Society for Study Devel. and Growth. Home: Beach Hill Road Bridgewater Connecticut 06752 Office: Memorial Sloan-Kettering Cancer Center 1275 York Avenue New York New York 10021

MARTIN, ARCHER JOHN PORTER, retired chemistry educator; born London, March 1, 1910; son of William Archer Porter and Lilian Kate (Brown) M.; married Judith Bagenal, January 9, 1943; 5 children. Student, Peterhouse, Cambridge, England, 1929-32, Master of Arts, 1936; Doctor of Philosophy, Doctor of Science, Leeds University, 1968; Doctor of Laws (honorary), University Glasgow, Scotland, 1973; laurea honoris causa, University Urbino, Italy, 1985. Chemist Nutritional Laboratory, Cambridge, 1933-38, Wool Industries Research Association, Leeds, 1938-46; research department Boots Pure Drug Company, Nottingham, England,

1946-48; staff Medical Research Council, 1948-52; head physical chemistry div. National Institute Medical Research, Mill Hill, 1952-56; chemical consultant 1956-59; director Abbotsbury (England) Laboratories Limited, 1959-73; professional fellow University Sussex, England, 1973-77; Robert A. Welch professor chemistry University Houston, 1974-78; guest professor Ecole Polytechnique Federal de Lausanne, Switzerland, 1980-85; consultant Wellcome Research Laboratories, Beckenham, England, 1970-73; Extraordinary professor Tech. University, Eindhoven, The Netherlands, 1965-74. Decorated commander Brit. Empire; Order of Rising Sun Japan; recipient Berzelius Gold medal Swedish Medical Society, 1951, Nobel prize chemistry (with R.L.M. Synge) for invention of partition chromatography, 1952, John Scott award, 1958, John Price Wetherill medal, 1959, Franklin Institute medal, 1959, Koltoff medal Acad. Pharm. Sci., 1969, Callendar medal Institute Measurement & Control, 1971, Fritz-Pregl medal Austrian Chemical Society, 1985. Fellow Royal Society; member (Leverhulme medal 1964). Club: Chemist's (New York City) (honorary). Home: 47 Roseford Road, Cambridge CB4 2HA, England Office: U Houston Chemistry Department Houston Texas 77004

MASON, DEAN TOWLE, cardiologist; born Berkeley, California, September 20, 1932; son of Ira Jenckes and Florence Mabel (Towle) M.; married Maureen O'Brien, June 22, 1957; children: Kathleen, Alison. Bachelor of Arts in Chemistry, Duke University, 1954, Doctor of Medicine, 1958. Diplomate: Nat. Board Medical Examiners, Am. Board Internal

Medicine (cardiovascular diseases). Intern, then resident in medicine Johns Hopkins Hospital, 1958-61; clinical associate cardiology branch, senior assistant surgeon United States Public Health Service, National Heart Institute, National Institutes of Health, 1961-63, assistant section director cardiovascular diagnosis, attending physician, senior investigator cardiology branch; 1963-68; professor medicine, professor physiology, chief cardiovascular medicine University California Medical School, Davis-Sacramento Medical Center, 1968-82; director cardiac center Cedars Medical Center, Miami, Florida, 1982-83; physician-in chief Western Heart Institute, San Francisco, 1983—; chairman department cardiovascular medicine St. Mary's Medical Center, San Francisco, 1986—; co-chairman cardiovascular-renal drugs United States Pharmacopeia Committee Revision, 1970-75; member life sciences committee National Aeronautics and Space Administration; medical research rev. board Veteran's Administration, National Institutes of Health; visiting professor numerous universities, consultant in field; member Am. Cardiovascular Specialty Certification Board, 1972-78. Author: Cardiovascular Management, 1974, Congestive Heart Failure, 1976, Advances in Heart Disease, Volume 1, 1977, Volume 2, 1978, Volume 3, 1980, Cardiovascular Emergencies, 1978, Principles of Noninvasive Cardiac Imaging, 1980, Myocardial Revascularization, 1981, Cardiology, 1981, 82, 83, 84, 85, 86, 87, 88, Clinical Nuclear Cardiology, 1981, Love Your Heart, 1982; also numerous articles.; associate editor: Clin. Cardiol. Jour; editor-in-chief: Am. Heart Jour; member editorial bds. sci. journals. Recipient Research award Am. Therapeutic Society, 1965; Theodore and Susan B. Cummings Humanitarian award State Dept.-Am. College Cardiology, 1972, 73, 75, 78; Skylab Achievement award National Aeronautics and Space Administration, 1974; University California Faculty Research award, 1978; named Outstanding Professor University California Medical School, Davis, 1972. Fellow Am. College Cardiology (president 1977-78), A.C.P., Am. Heart Association, Am. College Chest Physicians, Royal Society Medicine; member Am. Society Clinical Investigation, Am. Physiological Society, Am. Society Pharmacology and Experimental Therapeutics (Experimental Therapeutics award 1973), Am. Federation Clinical Research, New York Acad. Sciences, Am. Association University Cardiologists, Am. Society Clinical Pharmacology and Therapeutics, Western Association Physicians, American Association of University Profs., Western Society of Clinical Research (past president), Phi Beta Kappa, Alpha Omega Alpha. Republican. Methodist. Club: El Marcero Country. Home: 3015 Country Club Dr El Macero California 95618 Office: Western Heart Institute St Mary's Med Center 450 Stanyan St San Francisco California 94117

MASON, JAMES OSTERMANN, medical center administrator; born Salt Lake City, June 19, 1930; son of Ambrose Stanton and Neoma (Thorup) M.; married Lydia Maria Smith, December 29, 1952; children—James, Susan, Bruce, Ralph, Samuel, Sara, Benjamin. Bachelor of Arts, University Utah, 1954, Doctor of Medicine, 1958; Master of Public

Health, Harvard University, 1963, Doctor of Public Health, 1967. Diplomate Am. Board Preventive Medicine. Intern Johns Hopkins Hospital, Baltimore, 1958-59; chief epidemic intelligence service Center Disease Control, Atlanta, 1959, chief hepatitis surveillance unit epidemiology branch; 1960, chief surveillance section epidemiology branch; 1961, deputy director bureau laboratories; 1964-68, 69-70; director Center Disease Control, 1983—; resident in internal medicine Peter Bent Brigham Hosp.-Harvard Medical Service, Boston, 1961-62; chief infectious diseases Latter-day Saints Hospital, Salt Lake City, 1968-69; commissioner Health Services Corp., Church of Jesus Christ of Latter-day Saints, 1970-76; deputy director health Utah Div. Health, 1976-78, executive director; 1979-83; acting assistant secretary health Department of Health and Human Services, Washington, 1985; assistant professor department medicine and preventive medicine University Utah, Salt Lake City, 1968-69; associate professor, chairman div. community medicine, department family and community medicine University Utah, 1978-79; physician, consultant to medical services Salt Lake Veteran's Administration Hospital, 1977-83; clinical professor department family and community medicine, University Utah. College Medicine, 1979-83, clinical professor department pathology, 1980-83; clinical professor community health Emory University School Medicine, 1984—; chairman joint residency committee in preventive medicine and pub. health Utah College Medicine, 1975-80; member Utah Cancer Registry Research Adv. Committee, 1976-83; member adv. committee Utah Center

Health Statistics, 1977-79; chairman board Hospital Cooperative Utah, 1977-79; chairman executive committee Utah Health Planning and Resource Devel. Adv. Group, 1977-79; chairman Utah Gov.'s Adv. Committee for Comprehensive Health Planning, 1975-77; member recombinant DNA adv. committee National Institutes of Health, 1979-83; member Gov.'s Nuclear Waste Repository Task Force, 1980-83, chairman, 1980-82; board of directors Utah Health Cost Management Foundation, 1980-83; member adv. committee for programs and policies Centers for Disease Control, 1980; member committee on future of local health departments, Institute Medicine, 1980-82; member executive committee, chairman tech. adv. committee Thrasher Research Foundation, 1980—; member Robert Wood Johnson Foundation Program for Hospital Initiatives in Long-Term Care, 1982—; administrator Agency for Toxic Substances and Disease Registry, 1983—; member sci. and tech. adv. committee UNDP-World Bank-WHO Special Programme for Research and Training in Tropical Diseases, 1984—; member Utah Resource for Genetic and Epidemiologic Research, 1982—, chairman board, 1982-83. Author: (with H.L. Bodily and E.L. Updyke) Diagnostic Procedures for Bacterial, Mycotic and Parasitic Infections, 5th edition, 1970; (with M.H. Maxell, K.H. Bousfield and D.A. Ostler) Funding Water Quality Control in Utah, Procs. for Lincoln Institute, 1982; contributor articles to professional journals. Member national scouting committee Boy Scouts Am., 1974-78. Served to assistant surgeon general United States Public Health Service, 1983—. Recipient Roche award University

Utah, 1957, Wintrobe award University Utah, 1958, distinguished alumni award University Utah, 1973, Adminstr. of Year award Brigham University, 1980, special award for outstanding pub. service Am. Society Pub. Administration 1984). Member Am. Pub. Health Association (task force for credentialing of lab. personnel 1976-78, program devel. board 1979-81), American Medical Association, Utah State Medical Association (trustee 1979-83), Deseret Mutual Benefit Association (board directors 1972-79), Utah Acad. Preventive Medicine (president 1982-83), Utah Cancer Society, Utah Pub. Health Association (president 1980-82, Beatty award 1979), National Acad. Sciences (Institute Medicine), Education for Health (adv. council 1986—), Medical Association Atlanta, Sigma Xi, Alpha Epsilon Delta, Phi Kappa Phi, Alpha Omega Alpha, Delta Omega. Mormon. Lodge: Rotary. Home: 2520 Oak Crossing Dr Atlanta Georgia 30033 Office: Ctrs for Disease Control 1600 Clifton Dr NE Atlanta Georgia 30333

MASSEY, WALTER EUGENE, physicist, university official; born Hattiesburg, Mississippi, April 5, 1938; son of Almar and Essie (Nelson) M.; married Shirley Streeter, October 25, 1969; children: Keith Anthony, Eric Eugene. Bachelor of Science, Morehouse College, 1958; Master of Arts, Washington University, St. Louis, 1966, Doctor of Philosophy, 1966. Physicist Argonne (Illinois) National Laboratory, 1966-68; assistant professor physics University Illinois, Urbana, 1968-70; associate professor Brown University, Providence, 1970-75, professor, dean of College; 1975-79; professor physics University Chicago, 1979—, vice president for research; 1983-84; director Argonne National Laboratory, 1979-84; vice president for research and for Argonne National Laboratory University Chicago, 1984—; member National Science Foundation, 1975-77, 85—, NSB, 1978-84; consultant National Acad. Sciences, 1973-76. Contributor articles on sci. education in secondary schools and in theory of quantum fluids to professional journals. Trustee Brown University, 1980—, Mus. Sci. and Industry, Chicago, 1980—, Illinois Math. and Sci. Acad., 1985-88; board of directors Urban League Rhode Island, 1973-74. National Academy of Sciences fellow, 1961, NDEA fellow, 1959-60, American Association for the Advancement of Science fellow, 1962. Member American Association for the Advancement of Science (board directors 1981-85, pres.-elect 1987, president 1988, chairman 1989), Am. Physical Society (councillor-at-large 1980-83), Sigma Xi. Home: 4950 Chicago Beach Dr Chicago Illinois 60615 Office: University Chicago 5801 S Ellis Chicago Illinois 60637

MASURSKY, HAROLD, geologist; born Fort Wayne, Indiana, December 23, 1923; son of Louis and Celia (Ochstein) M.; 4 children. Bachelor of Science in Geology, Yale University, 1943, Master of Science, 1951; Doctor of Science (honorary), Northern Arizona University, 1981. With United States Geological Survey, 1951—, chief astrogeologic studies branch; 1967-71; chief scientist United States Geological Survey (Center Astrogeology), Flagstaff, Arizona, 1971-75; senior scientist United States Geological Survey (Center Astrogeology), 1975—; lunar orbiter Surveyor Missions, 1965-67; team leader, principal investigator TV experiment

(Mariner Mars), 1971; co-investigator Apollo field geological team Apollo 16 and 17, also member Apollo orbital sci. photographic team, Apollo site selection group; leader Viking Mars Missions Site Selection and cert. team, 1975; member imaging teams Voyager (Jupiter, Saturn, Uranus, Neptune), 1977; chairman mission operations group Venus Pioneer Mission 1978, co-chairman mission operational group Galileo Mission; 1981, mission operations leader, radar team Magellan mission Magellan Mission; 1981—; member camera team Mars observer, 1986; member Space Sci. Adv. Committee, 1978-81, solar system exploration committee, 1980-86; member Space Sci. Board, 1982-85; president intedisc committee B, COSPAR; secretary Coordinating Committee of Moon and Planets. Associate editor: Icarus, Geophysical Rev. Letters, Geodynamics. Served with Army of the United States, 1943-46. Fellow Geological Society Am. (associate editor bull., president planetary geol. division), American Association for the Advancement of Science, Am. Geophysical Union (president nomenclature workgroup), International Astronomical Union (executive committee compar planet interan. Union Geological Sci.), Am. Astronomical Association (director planet studies, member executive committee 1987). Office: United States Geol Survey 2255 N Gemini St Flagstaff Arizona 86001

MATHIAS, MILDRED ESTHER, botany educator; born Sappington, Missouri, September 19, 1906; daughter of John Oliver and Julia Hannah (Fawcett) M.; married Gerald L. Hassler, August 30, 1930; children: Frances, John, Julia, James (deceased). Bachelor of Arts, Washington University, 1926, Master of Science, 1927, Doctor of Philosophy in Systematic Botany, 1929. Assistant Missouri Botanical Garden, 1929-30; research associate New York Botanical Garden, 1932-36, University California, 1937-42; herbarium botanist University of California at Los Angeles, 1947-51, lecturer botany; 1951-55, from assistant professor to professor; 1955-74, vice chairman department; 1955-62; director botanical garden 1956-74, professor emertius; 1974—; assistant specialist University of California at Los Angeles Experimental Station, 1951-55, assistant plant systematist; 1955-57, associate plant systematist; 1957-62; president Organization Tropical Studies, 1968-70; secretary board trustees Institute Ecology, 1975-77; executive director Am. Association Botanical Gardens and Arboreta, 1977-81. Recipient Medal of Honor Garden Club Am., 1982; Mildred E. Mathias Botanical Garden, UCLA, 1979. Fellow California Acad. Sciences; member American Association for the Advancement of Science (president Pacific division 1977) Am. Society Plant Taxonomy (president 1964), Botanical Society Am. (Merit award 1973, president 1984), Society Study of Evolution, Am. Society Naturalist, Am. Horticulture Society (Sci. citation 1974, Liberty Hyde Bailey medal 1980). Office: University of California at Los Angeles Department Biology Los Angeles California 90024

MATTAUCH, ROBERT JOSEPH, electrical engineering educator; born Rochester, Pennsylvania, May 30, 1940; son of Henry Paul and Anna Marie (Mlinarcik) M.; married Frances Sabo, December 29, 1962;

children—Lori Ann, Thomas J. Bachelor of Science, Carnegie Institute Tech., Pittsburgh, 1962; Master of Electrical Engineering, North Carolina State University, Raleigh, 1963, Doctor of Philosophy, 1967. Assistant professor electrical engineering University Virginia, Charlottesville, 1966-70, associate professor electrical engineering; 1970-76, professor electrical engineering; 1976-83, Wilson professor electrical engineering; 1983-86; Standard Oil Company professor sci. and tech. University Virginia, 1986—, chairman department elect. engineering; 1987—; director semiconductor device laboratory University Virginia; consultant Foreign Sci. and Tech. Center, Charlottesville, 1973—, The Rochester Corp., Culpepper, Virginia, 1983—, Milltech Corp., Deerfield, Massachusetts, 1985. Patentee: infrared detector; solid state switching capacitor; thin wire pointing method. Board of directors Children's Home Society, Richmond, Virginia. Recipient Excellence in Instruction of Engineering Students award Western Electric, 1980. Fellow Institute of Electrical and Electronics Engineers (Centennial medal 1984); member Eta Kappa Nu (recipient Oustanding Professor in Electrical Engineering 1975), Sigma Xi, Tau Beta Pi. Office: Department Elec Engring Thornton Hall U Va Charlottesville Virginia 22901

MATTINGLY, THOMAS K., astronaut; born Chicago, March 17, 1936; son of Thomas K. Mattingly. Bachelor Aeronautical Engineering, Auburn University, 1958. Commissioned officer United States Navy, 1958; now commander assigned to space shuttle operations National Aeronautics and Space Administration; astronaut (National Aeronautics and Space Administration Manned Spacecraft Center), Houston; crew member (Apollo 16), 1972, (4th Test Mission, Columbia), 1982, Shuttle Mission 51-C, 1985; rear admiral in charge Department Navy (Space Sensor Systems), Washington, 1986—. Office: Space Sensor Systems/Space & Naval Warfare Systems Command Department Navy PD-40 Washington District of Columbia 20363-5100

MAURER, ROBERT DISTLER, industrial physicist; born St. Louis, July 20, 1924; son of John and Elizabeth J. (Distler) M.; married Barbara A. Mansfield, June 9, 1951; children: Robert M., James B., Janet L. Bachelor of Science, University Arkansas, 1948, Doctor of Laws, 1980; Doctor of Philosophy, Massachusetts Institute of Technology, 1951. Member staff Massachusetts Institute of Technology, 1951-52; with Corning Glass Works, New York, 1952—; manager physics research Corning Glass Works, 1963-78, research fellow; 1978—. Contributor articles to professional journals, chapters to books. Served with United States Army, 1943-46. Recipient Indsl. Physics prize Am. Institute Physics, 1978, L.M. Ericsson International prize in telecommunications, 1979, Indsl. Research Institute Achievement award, 1986, Optical Society Am./IEEE Leos Tyndall award, 1987. Fellow Am. Ceramic Society (George W. Morey award 1976); member Institute of Electrical and Electronics Engineers (Morris N. Liebmann award 1978), Am. Physical Society, National Acad. Engineering. Patentee in field. Home: 6 Roche Dr Painted Post New York 14870 Office: Corning Glass

Works Sullivan Park Corning New York 14830

MAY, ROLLO, psychoanalyst; born Ada, Ohio, April 21, 1909; son of Earl Tittle and Matie (Boughton) M.; married Florence DeFrees, June 5, 1938 (divorced 1968); children: Robert Rollo, Allegra Anne, Carolyn Jane; married Ingrid Schöll, 1971 (divorced 1978). Bachelor of Arts, Oberlin College, 1930, Doctor of Humanities (honorary), 1980; Bachelor of Divinity cum laude, Union Theological Seminary, New York City, 1938; Doctor of Philosophy summa cum laude, Columbia University, 1949; Doctor of Hebrew Literature (honorary), University Oklahoma, 1970; Doctor of Laws (honorary), Regis College, 1971; Doctor of Humane Letters (honorary), St. Vincent College, 1972, Michigan State University, 1976, Rockford College, 1977, Ohio Northern University, 1978, Oberlin College, 1980, Sacred Heart University, 1982, California School Professional Psychology, 1983, Rivera College, 1986, Gonzaga University, 1986, Saybrook Institute, 1987. Teacher Am. College, Saloniki, Greece, 1930-33; student adviser Michigan State College, 1934-36; student counselor City College of New York, 1943-44; member faculty William Alanson White Institute Psychiatry, Psychology and Psychoanalysis, 1958-75; lecturer New School Social Research, New York City, 1955-76; training fellow supervisory analyst Williams Alanson White Institute Psychiatry, 1958—; co-chairman Conference on Psychotherapy and Counseling, New York Acad. Sciences, 1953-54; visiting professor Harvard University, summer 1964, Princeton University, 1967, Yale University, 1972; Dean's scholar New York University, 1971; Regents' professor University California, Santa Cruz, 1973; distinguished visiting professor Brooklyn College, 1974-75. Author: Art of Counseling, 1939, Meaning of Anxiety, 1950, rev. edition, 1977, Man's Search for Himself, 1953, Psychology and the Human Dilemma, 1966, Existence: A New Dimension in Psychiatry and Psychology, 1958, Love and Will, 1969, Power and Innocence, 1972, Paulus-Reminiscences of a Friendship, 1973, The Courage to Create, 1975, Freedom and Destiny, 1981, The Discovery of Being, 1983; Editor: Existence: A New Dimension in Psychiatry and Psychology, 1958, Existential Psychology, 2d edit, 1961, Symbolism in Religion and Literature, 1960, My Quest for Beauty, 1985. Trustee Am. Foundation Mental Health; board of directors Society Arts, Religion and Culture. Recipient award for distinguished contribution to profession and sci. of psychology New York Society Clinical Psychology, 1955; Ralph Waldo Emerson award for Love and Will Phi Beta Kappa, 1970; Distinguished Contbns. award New York University, 1971; Centennial Medallion St. Peter's College, 1972; annual citation Merrill-Palmer Institute, Detroit, 1973; special Dr. Martin Luther King, Junior award New York Society Clinical Psychologists, 1974; Distinguished Graduate award Columbia University Teachers College, 1975; fellow Branford College Yale University, 1960—; Whole Life Humanitarian award Whole Life Exposition, 1986. Fellow Am. Psychological Association (award for distinguished contbn. to sci. and profession of clinical psychology 1971, Gold medal for Distinguished Career 1987), National Council Religion Higher Education, William

Alanson White Psychoanalytic Society (past president); member New York State Psychological Association (past president).

MAYBERRY, WILLIAM EUGENE, physician; born Cookeville, Tennessee, August 22, 1929; son of Henry Eugene and Beatrice Lucille (Maynard) M.; married Jane G. Foster, December 29, 1953; children: Ann Graves, Paul Foster. Student, Tennessee Tech. University, 1947-49; Doctor of Medicine, University Tennessee, 1953; Master of Science in Medicine, University Minnesota, 1959, Doctor of Humane Letters (honorary), Jacksonville University, 1983. Diplomate: Am. Board Internal Medicine. Intern United States Naval Hospital, Philadelphia, 1953-54; resident Mayo Grad. School Medicine, Rochester, Minnesota, 1956-59; member staff New England Medical Center, Boston, 1959-60, National Institute Arthritis and Metabolic Diseases, 1962-64; consultant internal medicine, endocrine research and laboratory medicine, chairman department laboratory medicine Mayo Clinic, Rochester, 1971-75, board governors, 1971-87, vice chairman, 1974-75, chairman, chief executive officer, 1976-87, professor laboratory medicine, 1971—, professor medicine, 1983—; assistant in medicine Tufts University Medical School, 1959-60; member faculty Mayo Grad. School Medicine and Mayo Medical School, 1960—; trustee Mayo Foundation, 1971-87, vice chairman, 1974-85, president 1986-87, chairman board devel. 1988—; trustee Minnesota Mutual Life Insurance, 1983—; director Northwestern Bell Corp., Kahler Corp., George A. Hormel & Company, Minnesota Business Partnership,

Incorporated. Member editorial board (Journal of Clin. Endocrinology and Metabolism), 1971-73; contributor articles to professional journals. Trustee Minneapolis Society Fine Arts, 1983—, Cumberland University, 1984-86; board overseers Minneapolis College Art and Design, 1983-86, University Minnesota School Mgmt., 1985—; board of directors Greater Rochester Area University Center, 1986-87, Minnesota Acad. Excellence Foundation, 1986-87; representative Congl. District I State of Minnesota Compensation Council, 1986; chairman Presidential Commission on Human Immunodeficiency Virus Epidemic, 1987. Recipient Distinguished Alumni award Tennessee Technol. University, 1976, Outstanding Alumni award University Tennessee, 1982, Medical Executive Award Am. College Medical Group Administrators, 1986; research fellow National Institutes of Health, 1959-60, Am. Cancer Society, 1962-64; National Institutes of Health research grantee, 1965-71. Fellow American College of Physicians; member Am. Thyroid Association, Am. Clinical and Climatological Society, Endocrine Society, Society Medical Administrs., Am. Acad. Medical Directors, Am. College Physician Executives (board regents 1983, vice chairman 1985-86), Institute Medicine of National Acad. Sciences, Sigma Xi. Clubs: Minnesota, Rochester Golf and Country, Minneapolis; The Club at Pelican Bay (Naples, Florida). Home: 705 Southwest 8th Avenue Rochester Minnesota 55901 Office: Bd Devel Mayo Found Rochester Minnesota 55905

MAYR, ERNST, emeritus zoology educator; born Kempten, Germany, July 5, 1904; came to United States,

1931; son of Otto and Helene (Pusinelli) M.; married Margarete Simon, May 4, 1935; children: Christa E., Susanne. Cand. medical, University Greifswald, 1925; Doctor of Philosophy, University Berlin, 1926; Doctor of Philosophy (honorary), Uppsala University, Sweden, 1957; Doctor of Science (honorary), Yale University, 1959, University Melbourne, 1959, Oxford University, 1966, University Munich, 1968, University Paris, 1974, Harvard University, 1980, Guelph University, University Cambridge, 1982, University Vermont, 1984. Assistant curator zoological mus. University Berlin, 1926-32; member Rothschild expedition to Dutch New Guinea, 1928, expedition to Mandated Ty. of New Guinea, 1928-29, Whitney Expedition, 1929-30; research associate Am. Mus. Natural History, New York City, 1931-32; associate curator Am. Mus. Natural History, 1932-44, curator; 1944-53; Jesup lecturer Columbia University, 1941; Alexander Agassiz professor zoology Harvard University, 1953-75, emeritus; 1975—; director Harvard (Mus. Comparative Zoology), 1961-70; Messenger lecturer Cornell University, 1985; Hitchcock professor University California, 1987. Author: List of New Guinea Birds, 1941, Systematics and the Origin of Species, 1942, Birds of the Southwest Pacific, 1945, Birds of the Philippines, (with Jean Delacour), 1946, Methods and Principles of Systematic Zoology, (with E. G. Linsley and R. L. Usinger), 1953, Animal Species and Evolution, 1963, Principles of Systematic Zoology, 1969, Populations, Species and Evolution, 1970, Evolution and the Diversity of Life, 1976, (with W. Provine) Evolutionary Synthesis, 1980, Biologie de l'Evolution, 1981,

The Growth of Biological Thought, 1982, Toward a New Philosophy of Biology, 1988; editor: Evolution, 1947-49. President XIII International Ornith. Congress, 1962. Recipient Leidy medal, 1946, Wallace Darwin medal, 1958, Brewster medal Am. Ornithologists Union, 1965, Daniel Giraud Elliot medal, 1967, National Medal of Sci., 1970, Molina prize Accademia delle Scienze, Bologna, Italy, 1972, Linnean medal, 1977, Gregor Mendel medal, 1980, Balzan prize, 1983, Darwin medal Royal Society, 1987. Fellow Linnean Society New York (past secretary editor), Am. Ornithological Union (president 1956-59), New York Zool. Society; member Am. Philosophical Society, National Acad. Sci., Am. Acad. Arts and Sciences, Am. Society Zoologists, Society Systematic Zoology (president 1966), Society Study Evolution (secretary 1946, president 1950); hon. or corr. member Royal Society, Royal Australian, Brit. ornithol. unions, Zool. Society London, Society Ornithological France, Royal Society New Zealand, Botanical Gardens Indonesia, S. Africa Ornithological Society, Linnean Society London, Deutsche Akademie der Naturforsch Leopoldina., Accad. Naz. dei Lincei, Royal Society, Académie des Sci. Office: Mus Comparative Zoology Harvard U Cambridge Massachusetts 02138

MCBRIDE, JON ANDREW, astronaut, aerospace engineer; born Charleston, West Virginia, August 14, 1943; son of William Lester and Catherine (Byus) McB.; married Sharon White; children: Richard, Melissa, Jon II, Michael. Bachelor of Science, Aeronautical Engineering Naval Postgrad. School, Monterey, California, 1971; Doctor of Philosophy (honorary), Salem College, West Virginia, 1984, University Charleston, West Virginia, 1987. Commissioned ensign United States Navy, 1965, advanced through grades to captain; 1985, served as naval officer/aviator; 1965-78; astronaut, assistant administrator National Aeronautics and Space Administration, Houston, 1978—. Avocations: athletics, carpentry, cooking, numismatics. Office: NASA JSC Houston Texas 77058

MC CANDLESS, BRUCE, II, astronaut; born Boston, June 8, 1937; son of Bruce and Sue (Bradley) McC.; married Alfreda Bernice Doyle, August 6, 1960; children: Bruce III, Tracy. Bachelor of Science, United States Naval Academy, 1958; Master of Science in Electrical Engineering, Stanford University, 1965; Master of Business Administration, University Houston, Clear Lake, 1987.

Commissioned ensign United States Navy, 1958, advanced through grades to captain; 1979, naval aviator; 1960, with Fighter Squadron 102; 1960-64; astronaut Johnson Space Center, National Aeronautics and Space Administration, Houston, 1966—; member Skylab 1 backup crew Johnson Space Center, National Aeronautics and Space Administration, member STS-11 shuttle crew, member STS-31 Hubble Space Telescope deployment crew.

Decorated Legion of Merit; recipient Defense Superior Service medal, National Aeronautics and Space Administration Exceptional Service medal, National Aeronautics and Space Administration Spaceflight medal, National Aeronautics and Space Administration Exceptional Engineering Achievement medal, Collier Trophy, 1985. Fellow Am. Astronomical Society; member Institute of Electrical and Electronics Engineers, United States Naval Institute, National Audubon Society, Houston Audubon Society (past president). Episcopalian. Executed 1st untethered free flight in space using Manned Maneuvering Unit. Office: Code CB NASA Johnson Space Center Houston Texas 77058

MCCARTHY, JOHN, computer scientist, educator; born Boston, September 4, 1927; son of Patrick Joseph and Ida McC.; children: Susan Joanne, Sarah Kathleen, Timothy Talcott. Bachelor of Science, California Institute Tech., 1948; Doctor of Philosophy, Princeton University, 1951. Instructor Princeton University, 1951-53; acting assistant professor math. Stanford University, 1953-55; assistant professor Dartmouth College, 1955-58; assistant and associate professor communications sciences M.I.T., Cambridge, 1958-62; professor computer sci. Stanford University, 1962—, Charles M. Pigott professor School Engineering; 1987—; director Information International Incorporated, Inference Corp., MAD Intelligent Systems. Served with Army of the United States, 1945-46. Recipient Kyoto prize, 1988. Member Association Computing Machinery (A.M. Turing award 1971), Am. Math Society, Am. Association Artificial Intelligence (president 1983-84), National Acad. Engineering, National Academy of Sciences. Republican. Home: 885 Allardice Way Stanford California 94305 Office: Department Computer Sci Stanford U Stanford California 94305

MCCARTY, MACLYN, medical scientist; born South Bend, Indiana, June 9, 1911; son of Earl Hauser and

Hazel Dell (Beagle) McC.; married Anita Alleyne Davies, June 20, 1934 (divorced 1966); children: Maclyn, Richard E., Dale, Colin; married Marjorie Steiner, September 3, 1966. Bachelor of Arts, Stanford University, 1933; Doctor of Medicine, Johns Hopkins University, 1937; Doctor of Science, Columbia University, 1976, University Florida, 1977, Rockefeller University, 1982, Medical College Ohio, 1985, Emory University, 1987. House officer, assistant resident physician Johns Hopkins Hospital, 1937-40; associate Rockefeller Institute, 1946-48, associate member; 1948-50, member; 1950—, professor; 1957—, vice president; 1965-78, physician in chief to hospital; 1961-74; research in streptococcal disease and rheumatic fever.; Cons. United States Public Health Service, National Institutes of Health. Author: The Transforming Principle: Discovering That Genes are Made of DNA, 1985. Member distribution committee New York Community Trust, 1966-74; chairman Health Research Council City New York, 1972-75; Member board trustees Helen Hay Whitney Found; chairman board of directors Pub. Health Research Institute of New York, 1985—. Served with Naval Medical Research Unit, Rockefeller Hospital United States Naval Reserve, 1942-46. Fellow medicine New York University College Medicine, 1940-41; National Research Council fellow med. scis. Rockefeller Institute, 1941-42; Recipient Eli Lilly award in bacteriology and immunology, 1946, 1st Waterford Biomed. Research award, 1977. Member Am. Society for Clinical Investigation, Am. Association Immunologists, Society Am. Bacteriologists, Society for Experimental Biology and Medicine (president 1973-75), Harvey Society (secretary 1947-50, president 1971-72), New York Acad. Medicine, Association Am. Physicians, National Acad. Sciences, Am. Acad. Arts and Sciences, New York Heart Association (1st vice president 1967, president 1969-71), Am. Philosophical Society. Home: 500 E 63d St New York New York 10021 Office: Rockefeller U 66th St and York Avenue New York New York 10021

MC CLELLAN, CATHARINE, educator, anthropologist; born York, Pennsylvania, March 1, 1921; daughter of William Smith and Josephine (Niles) McClellan; married John Thayer Hitchcock, June 6, 1974. Bachelor of Arts magna cum laude in Classical Archaeology, Bryn Mawr College, 1942; Doctor of Philosophy (Anthropology fellow), University California at Berkeley, 1950. Visiting assistant professor University Missouri at Columbia, 1952; assistant professor anthropology University Washington, Seattle, 1952-56; anthropological consultant United States Public Health Service, Arctic Health Research Center, Alaska, 1956; assistant professor anthropology, chairman department anthropology Barnard College, Columbia University, 1956-61; associate professor anthropology University Wisconsin at Madison, 1961-65, professor, 1965-83, professor emeritus, 1983—, John Bascom professor, 1973; visiting lecturer Bryn Mawr (Pennsylvania) College, 1954; visiting professor University Alaska, 1973, 87. Associate editor: Arctic Anthropology, 1961; editor, 1975-82; associate editor: The Western Canadian Journal of Anthropology, 1970-73. Served to lieutenant United States Navy

Women's Reserve, 1942-46. Margaret Snell fellow American Association of University Women, 1950-51; Am. Acad. Arts and Sciences grantee, 1963-64; National Mus. Can. grantee, 1948-74. Fellow Am. Anthropological Association, Royal Anthropological Institute Great Britain and Ireland, American Association for the Advancement of Science, Arctic Institute North America; member Am. Ethnological Society (sec.-treas. 1958-59, vice president 1964, president 1965), Kroeber Anthropological Society, Am. Folklore Society, Am. Society Ethnohistory (executive committee 1968-71), Sigma Xi. Various archaeol. and ethnographic field investigations in Alaska and Yukon Territory in Can. Home: 4110 Veith Avenue Madison Wisconsin 53704 Office: Department Anthropology Social Sci Building U Wisconsin Madison Wisconsin 53706

MCCLINTOCK, BARBARA, geneticist, educator; born June 16, 1902. Doctor of Philosophy in Botany, Cornell University, 1927; Doctor of Science (honorary), University Rochester, University Missouri, Smith College, Williams College, Western College for Women. Instructor botany Cornell University, Ithaca, New York, 1927-31, research associate; 1934-36, Andrew D. White professor-at-large; 1965—; assistant professor University Missouri, 1936-41; member staff Carnegie Institution of Washington, Cold Spring Harbor, New York, 1941-47, Distinguished Service member, 1967—; consultant agricultural sci. program Rockefeller Foundation, 1962-69. National Research Council fellow, 1931-33; Guggenheim Foundation fellow, 1933-34; recipient Achievement award American Association of University

Women, 1947; National medal of Sci., 1970; MacArthur Foundation prize; Rosentiel award, 1978; Nobel prize, 1983. Member National Acad. Sciences (Kimber genetics award 1967), Am. Philosophical Society, Am. Acad. Arts and Sciences, Genetics Society Am. (president 1945), Botanical Society Am. (award of merit 1957), American Association for the Advancement of Science, Am. Institute Biological Sci., Am. Society Naturalists. Office: Carnegie Instn Washington Cold Spring Harbor Lab Cold Spring Harbor New York 11724

MCCOLLUM, ROBERT WAYNE, physician, educator; born Waco, Texas, January 29, 1925; son of Robert Wayne and Minnie (Brown) McC.; married Audrey Talmage, October 16, 1954; children: Cynthia, Douglas Scott. Bachelor of Arts, Baylor University, 1945; Doctor of Medicine, Johns Hopkins, 1948; Doctor of Public Health, London School Hygiene and Tropical Medicine, 1958. Intern pathology Columbia-Presbyn. Medical Center, New York City, 1948-49; intern internal medicine Vanderbilt Hospital, Nashville, 1949-50; assistant resident internal medicine New Haven Medical Center, 1950-51; member faculty Yale School Medicine, 1951-81, professor epidemiology; 1965-81, chairman department epidemiology and public health; 1969-81; associate physician Yale-New Haven Hospital, from 1954; dean School Medicine, Dartmouth College, Hanover, New Hampshire, 1982—; vice president Dartmouth-Hitchcock Medical Center; consultant World Health Organization, 1962-79; surgeon general United States Army, from 1960. Contributor articles on epidemiology and control infectious diseases to professional journals.

Board sci. advisers Merck Institute, 1981-85; trustee Mary Hitchcock Memorial Hospital, Hanover, New Hampshire, 1982—. Served to captain Medical Corps Army of the United States, 1952-54. Member Association Teachers Preventive Medicine, Am. Epidemiological Society, International Epidemiological Association, Infectious Diseases Society Am., Connecticut Acad. Sci. and Engineering, Am. College Epidemiology. Office: Dartmouth Med School Office of Dean Hanover New Hampshire 03756

MCCONNELL, HARDEN MARSDEN, biophysical chemistry researcher, chemistry educator; born Richmond, Virginia, July 18, 1927; son of Harry Raymond and Frances (Coffee) McC.; married Sophia Milo Glogovac, October 6, 1956; children: Hunter, Trevor, Jane. Bachelor of Science, George Washington University, 1947; Doctor of Philosophy, California Institute Tech., 1951. National Research Council fellow department physics University Chicago, 1950-52; research chemist Shell Devel. Company, Emeryville, California, 1952-56; assistant professor chemistry California Institute Tech., 1956-58, professor chemistry and physics; 1963-64; professor chemistry Stanford University, California, 1964-79, Robert Eckles professor chemistry; 1979—; founder Molecular Devices Corp., 1983—; consultant in field. Contributor numerous articles to professional publications; patentee (in field). Recipient California sect. award Am. Chemical Society, 1961; recipient award in pure chemistry Am. Chemical Society, 1962, Irving Langmuir award in chemical physics Am. Chemical Society, 1971, Dickinson prize for sci. Carnegie-Mellon University, 1982, Wolf prize in chemistry, 1984, ISCO award, 1984, Pauling medal Puget Sound and Oregon sects. Am. Chemical Society, 1987, Wheland medal University Chicago, 1988. Fellow American Association for the Advancement of Science, Am. Physical Society; member National Acad. Sciences (award in chemical scis. 1988), Am. Acad. Arts and Sciences, Am. Society Biological Chemists. Office: Stanford U Department Chemistry Stanford California 94305

MCCRAW, LESLIE GLADSTONE, construction and design engineering executive; born Sandy Springs, South Carolina, November 3, 1934; son of Leslie Gladstone and Cornelia (Milam) McC.; married Mary Earle Brown; children: Leslie Gladstone III, James C., John. Bachelor of Science in Civil Engineering, Clemson University, 1956. Registerd professional engineer, Delaware. Design engineer Gulf Oil Corp., Philadelphia, 1956-57; various engineering and construction positions E.I. duPont Company, Wilmington, Del., 1960-75; vice president, manager div. Daniel Construction Company, Greenville, South Carolina, 1975-82, president; 1982-84; president, chief executive officer Daniel International, Greenville, 1984-86, Fluor Daniel, Greenville and Irvine, California, 1986-88; president Fluor Daniel, Irvine, 1988—; board of directors Fluor Corp., Irvine, Palmetto Bank, Greenville. Trustee Columbia College, South Carolina, Hampden sydney College; member engring. adv. council Clemson University, chairman president's adv. council; board of directors Greenville Tech. College Foundation Served to captain United States Air Force, 1957-60. Member Business Roundtable (constrn.

committee, adv. committee, contractor), South Carolina State Chamber of Commerce (board directors). Republican. Presbyterian. Club: Greenville Country, Commerce (board governors); Vintage Country (Indian Wells, California); Center (Cosa Mesa, California); Pacific (Newport Beach, California). Home: 57 Hillside Dr Newport Beach California 92660 Office: Fluor Daniel 3333 Michelson Dr Irvine California 92730

MCDEVITT, HUGH O'NEILL, physician, medical educator; born Cincinnati, 1930. Doctor of Medicine, Harvard University, 1955. Diplomate: Am. Board Internal Medicine. Intern Peter Bent Brigham Hospital, Boston, 1955-56, senior assistant resident in medicine; 1961-62; assistant resident Bell Hospital, 1956-57; research fellow department bacteriology and immunology Harvard University, 1959-61; United States Public Health Service special fellow National Institute Medical Research, Mill Hill, London, 1962-64; physician Stanford University Hospital, California, 1966—; associate professor Stanford University School Medicine, California, 1969-72, professor medical immunology; 1972—, professor medical microbiology, medicine; 1980—; consultant physician Veteran's Administration Hospital, Palo Alto, California, 1968—. Served as captain Medical Corps, Army of the United States, 1957-59. Member National Academy of Sciences, American Association for the Advancement of Science, Am. Federation Clinical Research, Am. Society Clinical Investigation, Am. Association Immunologists, Transplantation Society, Institute Medicine. Office: Stanford U Department Med Microbiology D-345 Fairchild Building Stanford California 94305

MCDIVITT, JAMES ALTON, electronics executive, astronaut; born Chicago, June 10, 1929; son of James A. and Margaret M. (Maxwell) McD.; married Patricia A. Haas, June 16, 1956 (divorced 1981); married 2d, Judith Odell; children: Michael A., Ann L., Patrick W., Kathleen M., Josephy Bagby, Jeffrey Bagby. Bachelor of Science in Aeronautical Engineering, University Michigan, 1959, Doctor Astronautical Science (honorary), 1965; Doctor of Science (honorary), Seton Hall University, 1969, Miami University, 1970; Doctor of Laws (honorary), Eastern Michigan University, 1975. Commissioned United States Air Force, 1952, grad. experimental test pilot school; 1960, grad. aerospace research pilot school; 1961, advanced through grades to brigadier general; 1972, assigned as astronaut to National Aeronautics and Space Administration; 1962, program manager Apollo Spacecraft, National Aeronautics and Space Administration; 1969-72, retired; 1972; executive vice president Consumers Power Company, Jackson, Michigan, 1972-75, Pullman Incorporated, Chicago, 1975-81; executive vice president electronics operations Rockwell International, Arlington, Virginia, 1981, executive vice president defense electronics, senior vice president sci. and tech., senior vice president strategic management; 1981—. Member adv. council University Michigan, College Engrinr., 1988—, University Notre Dame, College Engring., 1975—. Fellow Society Experimental Test Pilots (Kinchloe award 1969). Avocations: hunting, fishing, outdoor activities. Office: Rockwell International Corp 1745

Jefferson Davis Highway Arlington Virginia 22202

MC DONALD, FRANK BETHUNE, physicist; born Columbus, Georgia, May 28, 1925; son of Frank B. and Lucy (Kyle) McD.; married Virginia Ballew, June 15, 1951 (deceased 1977); children: Kyle Louise McDonald Jossi, Robert Kyle, Douglas Frank; married Irene Negosh Kelejian, November 7, 1987. Bachelor of Science, Duke University, 1948; Master of Science, University Minnesota, 1951, Doctor of Philosophy (AEC fellow), 1955. Research associate State University Iowa, Iowa City, 1953-56; assistant professor physics State University Iowa, 1956-59; chief laboratory for high energy astrophysics Goddard Space Flight Center National Aeronautics and Space Administration, Greenbelt, Maryland, 1959-82; chief scientist National Aeronautics and Space Administration, 1982-87, associate director, chief scientist Goddard Space Flight Center; 1987—, member physical sciences committee space program adv. council; 1974-76; senior policy analyst Office Sci. and Tech. Policy, Executive Office of President, Washington, 1982; professor University Maryland, College Park, part-time 1963-82; member Geophysics Research Forum, 1985-88; International Union Pure and Applied Physics member International Commission on Cosmic Rays, 1981-84, secretary to commission, 1984-87, chairman, 1987—; National Aeronautics and Space Administration representative to National Aeronautics and Space Administration Adv. Council, 1984—. Editor: High Energy Particles and Quanta in Astrophysics, 1974; associate editor: Journal Geophysical Research, 1964-67; member editorial board: Space Science Revs.; Research in cosmic ray physics. Served with United States Naval Reserve, 1942-45. Recipient Exceptional Sci. Achievement award National Aeronautics and Space Administration, 1964, Outstanding Leadership medal, 1981; Presidential Mgmt. Improvement cert., 1971; Presidential rank of meritorious executive Senior Executive Service, 1980. Fellow Am. Physical Society (chairman division cosmic physics 1973-74, member council 1982—, member executive committee 1983); member Am. Institute Physics (council, governing board 1983-86), Am. Geophysical Union, Washington Philosophical Society, Am. Astronom. Society, National Acad. Sci., Sigma Xi, Phi Beta Kappa. Office: NASA Goddard Space Flight Center Code 100 Greenbelt Maryland 20771

MCFADDEN, PETER WILLIAM, mechanical engineering educator; born Stamford, Connecticut, August 2, 1932; son of Kenneth E. and Marie (Gleason) McF.; children: Peter, Kathleen, Mary. Bachelor of Science in Mechanical Engineering, University Connecticut, 1954, Master of Science, 1956; Doctor of Philosophy, Purdue University, 1959. Registered professional engineer, Ind., Connecticut. Assistant instructor University Connecticut, 1954-56, professor mechanical engineering; 1971—, dean School Engineering; 1971-85, director devel.; 1985—, provost, vice president; 1988; member faculty Purdue University, 1956-71; professor mechanical engineering, head Purdue University (School Mechanical Engineering), 1965-71; postdoctoral research Swiss Federal Institute, Zurich, 1960-61; consultant to industry, 1959—. Member American Society of Mechanical Engineers, Am. Society Engineering Education. Research in cryogenics, heat transfer, mass. transfer.

MC KENNA, MALCOLM CARNEGIE, vertebrate paleontologist, curator, educator; born Pomona, California, July 21, 1930; son of Donald Carnegie and Bernice Caroline (Waller) McK.; married Priscilla Coffey, June 17, 1952; children—Douglas M., Katharine L., Andrew M., Bruce C. Bachelor of Arts, University California, Berkeley, 1954, Doctor of Philosophy, 1958. Instructor department paleontology University California, Berkeley, 1958-59; assistant curator department vertebrate paleontology Am. Mus. Natural History, New York City, 1960-64; associate curator Am. Mus. Natural History, 1964-65; Frick associate curator, chairman Frick Laboratory, 1965-68, Frick curator; 1968—; assistant professor geology Columbia University, New York City, 1960-64, associate professor, 1964-72, professor geological sciences, 1972—; research associate University Colorado Mus., Boulder, 1962—. Contributor articles on fossil mammals and their evolution, the dating of Mesozoic and Tertiary sedimentary rocks, and paleogeography and plate tectonics to professional journals. Board of directors Bergen Community (New Jersey) Mus., 1964-67, president, 1965-66; trustee Flat Rock Brook Nature Association, New Jersey, 1979—, Raymond Alf Mus., Webb School of California, 1980—, Dwight-Englewood School, Englewood, New Jersey, 1968-80; board of directors Flat Rock Brook Nature Association, New Jersey, 1979-84; trustee Claremont McKenna College, California, 1983—; Planned Parenthood Bergen County, New Jersey, 1979—, Mus. Northern Arizona, 1978-85, 87—. National Acad. Sciences exchange fellow Union of Soviet Socialist Republics, 1965. Fellow Explorers Club, Geological Society Am.; member Grand Canyon Natural History Association (director 1972-76), American Association for the Advancement of Science, Society Systematic Zoology (council 1974-77), Society Vertebrate Paleontology (vice president 1975, president 1976), Am. Geophysical Union, Am. Society Mammalogists, Paleontological Society, Society for Study Evolution, Sigma Xi. Office: Am Mus National History Vertebrate Paleontology Central Park W at 79th St New York New York 10024

MCKENNY, JERE WESLEY, geological engineering firm executive; born Okmulgee, Oklahoma, February 14, 1929; son of Jere Claus and Juanita (Hunter) McK.; married Anne Ross Stewart, May 4, 1957; children: Jere James, Robert Stewart. Bachelor of Science in Geological Engineering, University Oklahoma, 1951, Master of Science in Geological Engineering, 1952. With Kerr-McGee Corp., Oklahoma City, 1953—, manager oil and gas exploration; 1968-69, vice president oil and gas; 1969-74, vice president exploration; 1974-77, vice chairman; 1977—, president; 1983—, chief operating officer; 1988—; Member alumni adv. council School Geology and Geophysics University Oklahoma. Served with United States Army, 1953-55. Member Am. Association Petroleum Geologists, Am. Petroleum Institute (director), Ind. Petroleum Association Am. (director), Houston

Geological Society, Oklahoma City Geological Society, Sigma Xi, Sigma Gamma Epsilon. Episcopalian. Clubs: Oklahoma City Golf and Country, Whitehall. Home: 2932 Cornwall Place Oklahoma City Oklahoma 73120 Office: Kerr-McGee Corp Post Office Box 25861 Oklahoma City Oklahoma 73125

MC LAREN, DIGBY JOHNS, geologist, educator; born Carrickfergus, Northern Ireland, December 11, 1919; married Phyllis Mary Matkin, March 25, 1942; children: Ian, Patrick, Alison. Student, Queens' College, Cambridge University, 1938-40; Bachelor of Arts, Cambridge University, 1941, Master of Arts (Harkness scholar), 1948; Doctor of Philosophy, Michigan University, 1951; Doctor of Science (honorary), University Ottawa, 1980. Geologist Geological Survey Can., Ottawa, Ontario, 1948-80; director general Geological Survey Can., 1973-80; senior sci. advisor Can. Department Energy, Mines and Resources, Ottawa, 1981-84; visiting professor University Ottawa, 1981—; 1st director Institute Sedimentary and Petroleum Geology, Calgary, Alberta, Can., 1967-73; president Commission on Stratigraphy, International Union Geological Sciences, 1972-76; appointed 14th director Geological Survey Can., 1973; chairman board International Geological Correlation Program, United Nations Educational, Scientific and Cultural Organization, 1976-80. Contributor memoirs, bulls., papers, geological maps, sci. articles in field to professional lit. Served to captain Royal Artillery Brit. Army, 1940-46. Gold medalist (sci.) Professional Institute Pub. Service of Can., 1979. Fellow Royal Society Can. (president 1987—), Royal

Society London, European Union of Geoscis. (hon.); United States National Acad. Scis (foreign associate), Geological Society France (hon.); member Geological Society London, Geological Society Germany (hon., Leopold von Buch medal 1983), Geological Society Am. (president 1982), Paleontological Society (president 1969), Geological Association Can. (Logan medal 1987), Can. Society Petroleum Geologists (president 1971, hon.). Office: Royal Society Can, 344 Wellington St, Ottawa, Ontario Canada K1N 6N5

MC LAUGHLIN, JOHN FRANCIS, civil engineer, educator; born New York City, September 21, 1927; son of William Francis and Anna (Goodwin) McL.; married Eleanor Thomas Trethewey, November 22, 1950; children: Susan, Donald, Cynthia, Kevin. Bachelor of Civil Engineering, Syracuse University, 1950; Master of Science in Civil Engineering, Purdue University, 1953, Doctor of Philosophy, 1957. Member faculty Purdue University, 1950—, professor civil engineering; 1963—, head School Civil Engineering; 1968-78, assistant dean engineering School Civil Engineering; 1977-80, associate dean engineering; 1980—; consultant in field. Served with United States Army Air Force, 1945-47. Fellow American Society of Civil Engineers, Highway Research Board; member Am. Concrete Institute (hon. member, board directors, vice president 1977-79, president 1979), American Society for Testing and Materials (board directors 1984-86), Sigma Xi, Tau Beta Pi, Chi Epsilon, Theta Tau. Home: 112 Sumac Dr West Lafayette Indiana 47906 Office: Civil Engring Department Purdue University Lafayette Indiana 47907

MCMAHON, THOMAS ARTHUR, applied mechanics and biology educator; born Dayton, Ohio, April 21, 1943; son of Howard Oldford and Lucille (Nelson) McM.; married Carol Ehlers, June 20, 1965; children: James Robert, Elizabeth Kirsten. Bachelor of Science, Cornell University, 1965; Master of Science, Massachusetts Institute of Technology, 1967, Doctor of Philosophy, 1970. Postdoctoral fellow Harvard University, Cambridge, Massachusetts, 1969-70, lecturer bioengineering; 1970-71, assistant professor; 1971-74, associate professor; 1974-77, professor applied mechanics and biology; 1977—; consultant numerous indusries, legal firms. Author: (novels), Principles of American Nuclear Chemistry, 1970, McKay's Bees, 1979, Loving Little Egypt, 1987; (non-Fiction) Muscles, Reflexes and Locomotion, 1984; (with others) On Size and Life, 1983. Grantee National Institutes of Health; System Devel. Foundation, Sloan Foundation. Member Biomed. Engineering Society, Am. Physiological Society, New York Acad. Sciences, Poets, Playwrights, Editors, Essayists and Novelists. Home: 65 Crest Road Wellesley Massachusetts 02181 Office: Harvard U Department Applied Scis Pierce Hall Cambridge Massachusetts 02138

MCMILLAN, EDWIN MATTISON, physicist, educator; born Redondo Beach, California, September 18, 1907; son of Edwin Harbaugh and Anna Marie (Mattison) McM.; married Elsie Walford Blumer, June 7, 1941; children—Ann B., David M., Stephen W. Bachelor of Science, California Institute Tech., 1928, Master of Science, 1929; Doctor of Philosophy, Princeton University, 1932; Doctor of Science, Rensselaer Polytechnic Institute, 1961, Gustavus Adolphus College, 1963. National research fellow University California at Berkeley, 1932-34, research associate; 1934-35, instructor in physics; 1935-36, assistant professor physics; 1936-41, associate professor; 1941-46, professor physics; 1946-73, emeritus; 1973—; member staff Lawrence Radiation Laboratory, 1934—, associate director, 1954-58, director, 1958-73; on leave for defense research at Massachusetts Institute Tech. Radiation Laboratory, United States Navy Radio and Sound Laboratory, San Diego, and Los Alamos Sci. Laboratory, 1940-45; member general adv. committee Atomic Energy Commission, 1954-58; member commission high energy physics International Union Pure and Applied Physics, 1960-67; member sci. policy committee Stanford Linear Accelerator Center, 1962-66; member physics adv. committee National Accelerator Laboratory, 1967-69; chairman 13th International Conference on High Energy Physics, 1966; guest professor European Organization of Nuclear Research, Geneva, 1974. Trustee Rand Corp., 1959-69; Board of directors San Francisco Palace Arts and Scis. Foundation, 1968—; trustee Univs. Research Association, 1969-74. Recipient Research Corp. Sci. award, 1951; (with Glenn T. Seaborg) Nobel prize in chemistry, 1951; (with Vladimir I. Veksler) Atoms for Peace award, 1963; Alumni Distinguished Service award California Institute Tech., 1966; Centennial citation University California at Berkeley, 1968; Faculty Research lecturer University California at Berkeley, 1955. Fellow Am. Acad. Arts and Sciences, Am.

Physical Society; member National Acad. Sciences (chairman class I 1968-71), Am. Philosophical Society, Sigma Xi, Tau Beta Pi. Office: U California Lawrence Berkeley Lab Berkeley California 94720

MCNOWN, JOHN STEPHENSON, hydraulic engineer, educator; born Kansas City, Kansas, January 15, 1916; son of William Coleman and Florence Marie (Klahr) Mc.N.; married Miriam Leigh Ellis, September 6, 1938 (divorced November 1971); children: Stephen Ellis, Robert Neville, Cynthia Leigh, Mark William. Bachelor of Science, University Kansas, 1936; Master of Science, University Iowa, 1937; Doctor of Philosophy, University Minnesota, 1942; Doctor.esSc., University Grenoble, France, 1951. Registered professional engineer, Kansas. Instructor Math. and mechanics University Minnesota, 1937-42; research associate div. war research University California, San Diego, 1942-43; assistant professor mechanics and hydraulics College Engineering University Iowa, Iowa City, 1943-47, associate professor, 1947-52, professor, 1952-54; research engineer Iowa Institute Hydraulic Research, 1943-51, associate director; 1951-54; Fulbright research scholar Grenoble, France, 1950-51; professor engineering mechanics University Michigan, Ann Arbor, 1954-57; professor engineering mechanics University Kansas, 1957-65, Albert P. Learned professor civil engineering, from 1965, dean School Engineering and Architecture, 1957-65; executive director Center Research in Engineering Sci., 1959-62, director engineering div; 1962-65; director overseas liason committee Am. Council Education, 1967-69; tech. education specialist International Bank for Reconstruction and Development, 1972-73; hydraulic engineer Ministry of Agriculture, Government of Swaziland, 1981—; hydraulic engineering consultant throughout world; tech. lecturer Colorado Agricultural and Mechanical College, 1949, University Michigan, 1950, Universities Lille, Grenoble, Toulouse and Poitiers, France, 1951, University Bogota, Colombia, 1952, Ecole Polytechnique, Montreal, 1953, University Nebraska, 1958, Purdue University, 1959, New Mexico State University, 1966, California Institute Tech., 1967, University Karlsruhe, 1976, University Aachen, University Lulea, 1978, Chalmers University, Goteborg, Sweden, 1977-78, Royal Institute Tech., Stockholm, 1978; member numerous international study committees. Author: Technical Education in Africa; contributor articles to professional journals. Trustee, University Kansas Center for Research Incorporated, 1962—. Recipient J.C. Stevens award, 1946, research program prize, 1949. Fellow American Society of Civil Engineers (chairman adv. committee 1960, J. Jas. R. Croes medal 1955), Am. Acad. Mechanics; member National Conference Engineering Education (coordinator 1961), International Association Hydraulic Research (council 1955-59), Am. Society Engineering Education (executive committee, vice chairman international division 1975-77), Committee Engineering Education (Middle Africa), American Association for the Advancement of Science, Permanent International Association for Navigation Congresses, American Association of University Profs., Am. Canal Society, Sigma Xi, Theta Tau, Phi Delta Theta, Tau Beta Pi, Phi Kappa Phi, Chi Epsilon.

Congregationalist. Office: Department Civil Engring U Kansas Lawrence Kansas 66045

MEAD, CARVER ANDRESS, computer science educator; born Bakersfield, California, May 1, 1934. Bachelor of Science, California Institute Tech., 1956, Master of Science, 1957, Doctor of Philosophy, 1960. Professor California Institute Tech., Pasadena, 1957—, Gordon and Betty Moore professor computer sci.; 1980—; director Silicon Compilers, Incorporated, San Jose, California, Intern Microelectronic, San Jose, Computer Mus., Boston. Author: Introduction to VLSI Systems, 1979 (Electronic Achievements award 1981, Harold Pender award 1984, John Price Wetherhill award 1985). Member editorial board Integration, 1983—. Recipient T.D. Callinan award Electrochemical Society, 1971, Centennial medal Institute of Electrical and Electronic Engineers, 1984, Harry Goode Memorial award Am. Federation Info. Processing Socs., Incorporated, 1985. Fellow Am. Physical Society; member National Acad. Engineering, Royal Swedish Acad. Engineering Sci., Sigma Xi. Office: California Institute Tech Department Computer Sci 1201 E California Boulevard Pasadena California 91125

MEIER, PAUL, statistician, mathematics educator; born New York City, July 24, 1924. Bachelor of Science in Physics, Math., Oberlin College, 1945; postgraduate program in applied math., Brown University, 1945; Master of Arts in Math., Princeton University, 1947, Doctor of Philosophy, 1951. Assistant professor math. Lehigh University, 1948-49; research secretary Philadelphia Tb and Health Association, 1949-51;

research associate analytical research group, Forrestal Research Center Princeton University, 1951-52; research associate department biostats. School of Hygiene and Pub. Health, Johns Hopkins University, 1952-57, assistant professor; 1953-55, associate professor; 1955-57; associate professor department statistics div. biological sciences University Chicago, 1957-62, professor statistics; 1962—, chairman department statistics; 1960-66, director Biomed. Computation Facilities; 1962-69, professor theoretical biology; 1968-74, acting chairman department statistics; 1970-71, chairman department statistics; 1973-74, 83—, Ralph and Mary Otis Isham Distinguished Service Professor Statistics and the Pharmaceutical and Physiological Sciences; 1975-84; special fellow National Institutes of Health University London School of Hygiene and Tropical Medicine and Imperial College, 1966-67; visiting professor department statistics, Center for Analysis of Health Practices Harvard School Pub. Health, 1975-76; member committee on lung cancer Am. Cancer Society, 1959-62; member special study section biomath. and statistics National Institute General Medical Sciences National Institutes of Health, 1965-70, member therapeutic evaluation committee, National Heart Institute, 1967-71; member adv. board Environmental Health Resource Center State of Illinois Institute Environmental Quality, 1971—; member Task Force on Health Considerations of National Energy Policy Am. Pub. Health Association, 1972-74; member adv. board Veteran's Administration Cooperative Study of the Pathogenic Effects of Sickle Cell Trait, 1973-78; member adv. council department statistics Princeton University, 1974-76; member Computer and Biomath. Sciences Study Section National Institutes of Health, 1974-77; director Data Quality Control Center for Persantine-Aspirin Reinfarction Study, 1975-81; member Policy Adv. Board Multiple Risk Factor Intervention Trial, 1976—; member Committee on National Statistics, 1978—; member Clinical Trials Rev. Committee, National Heart, Lung and Blood Institute, National Institutes of Health, 1978—; director Data Audit Center for International Mexiletine and Placebo Antiarrhythmic Coronary Trial (IMPACT), 1979—. Am. Acad. Arts and Sciences fellow; John Simon Guggenheim Memorial Foundation fellow; Center for Advanced Study in Behavioral Sciences fellow, Stanford University, 1982-83; Sigma Xi lecturer, 1974-76. Fellow Am. Statistical Association (board directors, vice president 1965-67, chairman committee on computers in stats. 1967, chairman section on training 1974), Royal Statistical Society, Am. Pub. Health Association, Am. Thoracic Society, Institute Math Statistics (chairman committee on fellows 1979), American Association for the Advancement of Science, Am. Heart Association (council on epidemiology, committee on fellows 1978); member Biometric Society (executive committee Eastern North America Region, president Eastern North America Region, 1967), Am. Math. Society, Math Association Am., Association for Symbolic Logic, Society for Industrial and Applied Math. Office: University Chicago Department Stats 5734 University Avenue Chicago Illinois 60637

MEIGHAN, CLEMENT WOODWARD, anthropologist, archaeologist; born San Francisco, January 21, 1925; son of Charles Woodward and Lucille Christine (Mellin) M.; married Joan Seibert, June 1, 1960; 1 daughter, Maeve. Bachelor of Arts, University California, Berkeley, 1949, Doctor of Philosophy, 1953. Faculty anthropology University of California at Los Angeles, 1952—, professor; 1962—. Author: The Maru Cult of the Pomo Indians, 1972; The Archaeology of Amapa, Nayarit, 1977; Prehistoric Trails of Atacama, 1980. Served with United States Army, 1943-47. Fellow Am. Anthropol. Association, American Association for the Advancement of Science, Am. Geog. Society. Field research, publs. on archaeology of California, Western United States, Mexico, Chile. Office: Department Anthropology U California Los Angeles California 90024

MEINDL, JAMES DONALD, electrical engineer; born Pittsburgh, April 20, 1933; son of Louis M. and Elizabeth F. (Steinhauser) M.; married Frederica Ziegler, May 21, 1961; children: Peter James, Candace Ann. Bachelor of Science, Carnegie Mellon University, 1955, Master of Science, 1956, Doctor of Philosophy, 1958. Engineer Autonetics Company, Downey, California, 1957, Westinghouse Company, Pittsburgh, 1958-59; head section microelectronics United States Army Electronics Command, Fort Monmouth, New Jersey, 1959-62; chief branch semicondr. and microelectronics United States Army Electronics Command, 1962-65, director div. integrated electronics; 1965-67; associate professor electrical engineering Stanford University, 1967-70, professor; 1970-84, John M. Fluke professor electrical engineering, 1984-86, associate dean research, 1984-86, director integrated circuits laboratory, 1969-84, director Electronics Laboratories, 1972-86, director Center Integrated Systems, 1981-86; vice president acad. affairs, provost, dean Rensselaer Polytechnic Institute, Troy, New York, 1986—; director Telesensory Systems Incorporated, Palo Alto, California, 1971-84; consultant to government, industry. Author: Micropower Circuits, 1969; contributor numerous articles to professional publications. Served to 1st lieutenant Army of the United States, 1959-61. Recipient Arthur S. Flemming Commn. award Washington Junior Chamber of Commerce, 1967; J.J. Ebers award Institute of Electrical and Electronic Engineers Electron Devices Society, 1980. Fellow Institute of Electrical and Electronics Engineers (editor Jour. Solid State Circuits 1966-71, International Solid-State Circuits Conference Out-standing Paper award 1970, 75, 76, 77, 78), American Association for the Advancement of Science; member National Acad. Engineering, Electrochemical Society, Biomedical Engineering Society (co-editor Annals of Biomedical Engineering 1976-80), American Association of University Profs., Sigma Xi, Tau Beta Pi, Eta Kappa Nu, Phi Kappa Phi. Patentee integrated circuit field.

MELBY, EDWARD CARLOS, JR., veterinarian; born Burlington, Vermont, August 10, 1929; son of Edward C. and Dorothy H. (Folsom) M.; married Jean Day File, August 15, 1953; children: Scott E., Susan J., Jeffrey T., Richard A. Student, University Pennsylvania, 1948-50; Doctor of Veterinary Medicine, Cornell University, 1954. Diplomate: Am. Coll. Lab. Animal Medicine. Practice veterinary medicine Middlebury, Vermont, 1954-62; instructor laboratory animal medicine Johns Hopkins University School Medicine, Baltimore, 1962-64; assistant professor Johns Hopkins University School Medicine, 1964-66, associate professor, 1966-71, professor, director div. comparative medicine, 1971-74; professor medicine, dean College Veterinary Medicine, Cornell University, Ithaca, New York, 1974-84; vice president research and devel. SmithKline AHP div. SmithKline Beckman Corp., 1985—; consultant Veteran's Administration, National Research Council, National Institutes of Health. Author: Handbook of Laboratory Animal Science, Volumes I, II, III, 1974-76. Served with United States Military Corps, 1946-48. Member Am., New York State, Southern Tier, Vermont veterinary med. associations, Am. Association Lab. Animal Sci., Am. College Lab. Animal Medicine, Am. Association Accreditation Lab. Animal Care, American Association for the Advancement of Science, Phi Zeta. Home: 770 Newtown Road Villanova Pennsylvania 19085 Office: Smith Kline Beckman Corp One Franklin Plaza Box 7929 Philadelphia Pennsylvania 19101

MELMON, KENNETH LLOYD, physician, biologist, consultant; born San Francisco, July 20, 1934; son of Abe Irving and Jean (Kahn) M.; married Elyce Edelman, June 9, 1957; children: Bradley S., Debra W. Bachelor of Arts in Biology with honors, Stanford University, 1956; Doctor of Medicine, University California at San Francisco, 1959. Intern, then resident in internal medicine University California Medical Center, San Francisco, 1959-61;

clinical associate, surgeon United States Public Health Service, National Heart, Lung and Kidney Institute, National Institutes of Health, 1961-64; chief resident in medicine University Washington Medical Center, Seattle, 1964-65; chief div. clinical pharmacology University California Medical Center, 1965-78; chief department medicine Stanford University Medical Center, 1978-84, Arthur Bloomfield professor medicine, professor pharmacology; 1978—; director office new clinical program devel. Stanford University Hospital, 1986—; member senior staff Cardiovascular Research Institute; chairman joint commission prescription drug use Senate Subcom. on Health, Institute Medicine and HEW-Pharm. Manufacturers Association; member National Board Medical Examiners, 1987—; president Bio 2000, Woodside, California, 1983—; founder, Immulogic, Boston, Palo Alto, California, 1988; sci. advisor Syntex, Hoffman LaRoche, Recordati, LTI, Cetus, other consultant Food and Drug Administration, 1965-82, Office Tech. Assessment, 1974-75, Senate Subcom. on Health, 1975—; board of directors Pharmatrix, Techno-Gentics, New York City; consultant to government. Author articles, chapters in books, sects. encys.; Editor: Clinical Pharmacology: Basic Principles in Therapeutics, 2d edit, 1978, Cardiovascular Therapeutics, 1974; associate editor: The Pharmacological Basis of Therapeutics (Goodman and Gilman), 1984; member editorial board numerous professional journals. Surgeon United States Public Health Service, 1961-64. Burroughs Wellcome clinical pharmacology scholar, 1966-71; John Simon Guggenheim fellow Weizman Institution, Israel, 1971; National Institutes of Health fellow, Bethesda, 1972. Fellow American Association for the Advancement of Science (national council 1985—); member Am. Federation Clinical Research (president 1973-74), Am. Society Clinical Investigation (past president 1978-79), Association Am. Physicians, Western Association Physicians (past president 1983-84), Am. Society Pharmacology and Experimental Therapeutics, Institute Medicine of National Acad. Sci., Am. Physiological Society, California Acad. Medicine, Medical Friends of Wine, Phi Beta Kappa. Democrat. Jewish. Avocations: woodworking, hiking, cycling, swimming, squash. Home: 51 Cragmont Way Woodside California 94062 Office: Stanford U Med Center Department Medicine S025 Stanford California 94305

MENNINGER, KARL AUGUSTUS, psychiatrist; born Topeka, July 22, 1893; son of Charles Frederick (M.D.) and Flora (Knisely) M.; married Grace Gaines, September 1916 (divorced February 1941); children: Julia Menninger Gottesman, Robert Gaines, Martha Menninger Nichols; married Jeanetta Lyle, September 1941; 1 daughter, Rosemary Jeanetta Karla. Student, Washburn College, 1910-12, Ind. University, summer 1910; Bachelor of Arts, University Wisconsin, 1914, Master of Science, 1915, Doctor of Science (honorary), 1965; Doctor of Medicine cum laude, Harvard University, 1917; Doctor of Humane Letters (honorary), Park College, 1955, St. Benedict's College, 1963, Loyola University, 1972, DePaul University, 1974; Doctor of Laws, Jefferson Medical College, 1956, Parsons College, 1960, Kansas State University, 1962, Baker University, 1965, Pepperdine University, 1973,

John Jay College Criminal Justice, New York, 1978; Doctor of Science, Washburn University, 1949, Oklahoma City University, 1966. Chairman board trustees Menninger Foundation; professor at large University Kansas; distinguished professor psychiatry Chicago Medical School; professor Loyola University, Chicago, University Cincinnati; visiting professor University Chicago; consultant Illinois Department Mental Health, Illinois State Psychiat. Institute, 1967-73; founder Menninger School Psychiatry, 1946, dean; 1946-69; consultant Topeka Veteran's Administration Hospital, Topeka State Hospital, Stormont-Vail Hospital, Kansas Reception and Diagnostic Center, Kansas Neurological Institute, Federal Bureau Prisons, Office Vocational Rehabilitation, Department of Health, Education and Welfare, President's Task Force on Prisoner Rehabilitation, 1969, Mount Sinai Medical Center, Chicago, Am. Bar Association committee on correctional facilities and services, 1970-76, Committee on Penal Reform, Kansas Association Mental Health; member special committee on psychiatry, Office of Scientific Research and Development, European Theatre of Operations, adv. to surgeon general United States Army, 1945; adviser on penology to Governor Kansas, 1966-75; member National Council on Crime and Delinquency, Open Lands Project; member adv. board Adult div. Illinois Department Corrections, Illinois State Psychiat. Institute; medical adv. council Governor Illinois; member adv. committees many other civic, governmental organizations. Author: (with others) Why Men Fail, 1918, The Human Mind, 1930, rev., 1945, The Healthy-Minded Child, 1930, Man Against Himself, 1938, America Now, 1938, (with Mrs. Menninger) Love Against Hate, 1942, (with Devereux) A Guide to Psychiatric Books, 1950, 2d rev. edition, 1958, 3d rev. edition, 1972, Manual for Psychiatric Case Study, 1952, Theory of Psychoanalytic Technique, 1958, rev. edit, (with Holzman), 1973; selected papers A Psychiatrist's World, 1959, The Vital Balance, 1963, The Crime of Punishment, 1968, (with Lucy Freeman) Sparks, 1973, Whatever Became of Sin, 1974; also articles.; Editorial board: (with Lucy Freeman) Bulletin Menninger Clinic. Board overseers Lemberg Center for Study Violence, Brandeis University; board of directors Chicago Boys Club, John Howard Association Chicago, W. Clement and Jessie V. Stone Foundation, Chicago; founder, chairman board of directors the Villages, Incorporated, Topeka. Commd. lieutenant (junior grade) United States Naval Reserves Force, 1918-21. Recipient T.W. Salmon award New York Acad. Medicine, 1967, Good Samaritan award Eagles Lodge, 1968, 69, Annual Service award John Howard Association, 1969, Good Shepherd award The Lambs, Chicago, 1969, award Am. Acad. Psychiatry and Law, 1974, Roscoe Pound award National Council Crime and Delinquency, 1975, Special award Kansas Department Corrections, 1976, Sheen award American Medical Association, 1978, Presidential Medal of Freedom, 1981, numerous others. Life fellow Am. Psychiatric Association (Isaac Ray award 1962, 1st distinguished service award 1965, 1st Founders award 1977), American College of Physicians (life master), Am. College Psychiatrists, Am. Medical Writers Association; hon. fellow Royal College Psychiatrists; life member American

Medical Association, Am. Psychological Association, Chicago Psychoanalytic Society, Am. Orthopsychiat. Association, Am. Psychoanalytic Association (founder; president 1941-43); hon. member Am. Association Suicidology, International Association for Suicide Prevention, Sigmund Freud Archives; joint founder, charter member Central Neuropsychiatric Association, Central Psychiatric Hospital Association, Medical Association for Research Nervous and Mental Diseases; member Am. Association for Child Psychoanalysis, Am. Society Criminology, Illinois Acad. Criminology, Association for Psychiatric Treatment Offenders, Am. Acad. Psychiatry and Law, Am. Justice Institute (adv. committee sponsors), Association Clinical Pastoral Education, Illinois Committee on Family Law, International Psychoanalytic Association, Kansas Medical Society, Sigmund Freud Society Vienna, World Society Ekistics, National Congress Am. Indians, Am. Horticultural Council, American Association for the Advancement of Science, American Civil Liberties Union (national adv. council), National Association for the Advancement of Colored People, Sierra Club, Chicago Orchestral Association (governor), Am. Association Botanical Gardens and Arboreta, Friends of the Earth, Am. Indian Center (Chicago Grand Council), Aspen Institute for Humanistic Studies (former trustee, now hon. trustee), Am. Humanics Foundation, National Commission for Prevention of Child Abuse (co-chmn. hon. board), Save the Tallgrass Prairie Incorporated (chairman national hon. board), others. Presbyterian. Clubs: University (Chicago); Country (Topeka) Lodge: Masons. Office: Menninger Found Box 829 Topeka Kansas 66601 also: Topeka Virginia Hosp Topeka Kansas 66601

MENNINGER, WILLIAM WALTER, psychiatrist; born Topeka, October 23, 1931; son of William Claire and Catharine Louisa (Wright) M.; married Constance Arnold Libbey, June 15, 1953; children: Frederick Prince, John Alexander, Eliza Wright, Marian Stuart, William Libbey, David Henry. Bachelor of Arts, Stanford University, 1953; Doctor of Medicine, Cornell University, 1957; Doctor of Letters (honorary), Middlebury College, 1982; Doctor of Science (honorary), Washburn University, 1982; Doctor of Humane Letters (honorary), Ottawa University, 1986. Diplomate: Am. Board Psychiatry and Neurology, Am. Board Forensic Psychiatry. Intern Harvard Medical Service, Boston City Hospital, 1957-58; resident in psychiatry Menninger School Psychiatry, 1958-61; chief medical officer, psychiatrist Federal Reformatory, El Reno, Oklahoma, 1961-63; associate psychiatrist Peace Corps, 1963-64; staff psychiatrist Menninger Foundation, Topeka, 1965—, coordinator for devel.; 1967-69, director law and psychiatry; 1981-85, director department education, dean Karl Menninger School Psychiatry and Mental Health Sciences; 1984—, executive vice president, chief of staff; 1984—; clinical supervisor Topeka State Hospital, 1969-70, section director; 1970-72, assistant superintendent, clinical, director residency training; 1972-81; clinical professor Kansas University Medical College; adj. professor Washburn University, Wichita State University; instructor Topeka Institute for Psychoanalysis;

member adv. board National Institute Corrections, 1975-88 , chairman, 1980-84; consultant United States Bureau Prisons; member Federal Prison Facilities Planning Council, 1970-73. Syndicated columnist: Insights, 1975-83; author: Happiness Without Sex and Other Things Too Good to Miss, 1976, Caution: Living May Be Hazardous, 1978, Behavioral Science and the Secret Service, 1981, Chronic Mental Patient II, 1987; editor: Psychiatry Digest, 1971-74; member editorial board Bulletin Menninger Clinic, 1985—; contributor chapters to books, articles to professional journals. Member national health and safety committee Boy Scouts Am., 1970—, chairman, 1980-85, member national executive board, 1980—; member Kansas Gov.'s Adv. Commission on Mental Health, Mental Retardation and Community Mental Health Services, 1983—; board of directors National Committee for Prevention Child Abuse, 1975-83; member national adv. health council Department of Health Education and Welfare, 1967-71; member National Commission Causes and Prevention Violence, 1968-69, Kansas Gov.'s Penal Planning Council, 1970. Served with United States Public Health Service, 1959-64. Fellow American College of Physicians, Am. Psychiatric Association (chairman committee on chronically mentally ill 1984-86), Am. College Psychiatrists; member American Medical Association, Group for Advancement of Psychiatry (chairman committee mental health services 1974-77), Institute Medicine National Acad. Sciences, Am. Psychoanalytic Association (chairman committee on psychoanalysis, community, and society 1984—), Am. Acad. Psychiatry and Law, American Association for the Advancement of Science. Office: Menninger Found Box 829 Topeka Kansas 66601

MERMIN, N. DAVID, physicist, educator; born New Haven, March 30, 1935; son of John and Eva (Gordon) M.; married Dorothy E. Milman, June 9, 1957; children—Jonathan George, Elizabeth Ruth. Bachelor of Arts summa cum laude, Harvard University, 1956, Master of Arts, 1957, Doctor of Philosophy, 1961. National Science Foundation postdoctral fellow University Birmingham, England, 1961-63; postdoctoral fellow University California, San Diego, 1963-64; assistant professor physics Cornell University, Ithaca, New York, 1964-67; associate professor physics Cornell University, 1967-72, professor physics; 1972—, director Laboratory Atomic and Solid State Physics; 1984—; Loeb lecturer Harvard University, Cambridge, 1980 Emil Warburg professor University Bayreuth, Ger., 1981 Walker Ames professor University Washington, Seattle, 1984; Japan Society for Promotion of Sci. fellow Nagoya University, 1982. Author: Space and Time in Special Relativity, 1968; Solid State Physics, 1976; contributor articles to professional journals. Sloan Foundation fellow, 1966-68; Guggenheim Foundation fellow, 1970-71. Fellow Am. Acad. Arts and Sciences, Am. Physical Society (Julius Edgar Lillienfeld prize 1989), American Association for the Advancement of Science. Avocation: piano. Home: 75 Hickory Road Ithaca New York 14850 Office: Cornell University Lab of Atomic and Solid State Physics Clark Hall Ithaca New York 14853

MERRIFIELD, ROBERT BRUCE, educator, biochemist; born Fort Worth, July 15, 1921; son of George E.

and Lorene (Lucas) M.; married Elizabeth Furlong, June 20, 1949; children: Nancy, James, Betsy, Cathy, Laurie, Sally. Bachelor of Arts, University of California at Los Angeles, 1943, Doctor of Philosophy, 1949. Chemist Park Research Foundation, 1943-44; research assistant Medical School, University of California at Los Angeles, 1948-49; assistant Rockefeller Institute for Medical Research, 1949-53, associate; 1953-57; assistant professor Rockefeller University, 1957-58, associate professor; 1958-66, professor; 1966—. Associate editor: International Journal Peptide and Protein Research; contributor articles to sci. journals. Recipient Lasker award biomed. research, 1969; Gairdner award, 1970; Intra-Sci. award, 1970; Nichols medal, 1973; Alan E. Pierce award Am. Peptide Symposium, 1979; Nobel prize in chemistry, 1984. Member Am. Chemical Society (award creative work synthetic organic chemistry 1972), National Acad. Sciences, Am. Society Biological Chemists, Sigma Xi, Phi Lambda Upsilon, Alpha Chi Sigma. Developed solid phase peptide synthesis; completed (with B. Gutte) 1st total synthesis of an enzyme, 1969. Office: Rockefeller U New York New York 10021

MERTZ, WALTER, government research executive; born Mainz, Germany, May 4, 1923; son of Oskar and Anne (Gabelmann) M.; married Marianne C. Maret, August 8, 1953. Doctor of Medicine, University Mainz, 1951. Intern County Hospital, Hersfeld, Germany, 1952-53; resident University Hospital, Frankfurt, Germany, 1953; visiting scientist National Institutes of Health, Bethesda, Maryland, 1953-61; chief department biological chemistry Walter Reed Army Institute Research, Washington, 1961-69; member staff Nutrition Institute, Agricultural Research Service, Department Agricultural, Beltsville, Maryland, 1969-72, chairman institute; 1972—; director Human Nutrition Research Center; lecturer George Washington University Medical School, 1963-73. Served with German Army, 1941-46. Recipient Osborne and Mendel award Am. Institute Nutrition, 1971; recipient Superior Performance award Department Agr., 1972. Member Am. Institute Nutrition, Am. Society Biological Chemists, Am. Society Clinical Nutrition. Office: Department Agr Human Nutrition Research Center Beltsville Maryland 20705

MESELSON, MATTHEW STANLEY, educator, biochemist; born Denver, May 24, 1930; son of Hymen Avram and Ann (Swedlow) M.; married Jeanne Guillemin, 1986; children: Zoe, Amy Valor. Bachelor of Philosophy, University Chicago, 1951, Doctor of Science (honorary), 1975; Doctor of Philosophy, California Institute Tech., 1957; Doctor of Science (honorary), Oakland College, 1964, Columbia, 1971, Yale University, 1987, Princeton University, 1988. From research fellow to senior research fellow California Institute Tech., 1957-60; associate professor biology Harvard University, 1960—, professor biology; 1964-76, Thomas Dudley Cabot professor natural sciences; 1976—. Recipient prize for molecular biology National Acad. Sciences, 1963, Eli Lilly award microbiology and immunology, 1964, Alumni medal University Chicago, 1971; Lehman award 1975, Presidential award 1983, New York Acad. Sciences, 1975; Alumni Distinguished Service award

California Institute Tech., 1975; Leo Szilard award Am. Physical Society, 1978; MacArthur fellow, 1984—. Fellow American Association for the Advancement of Science; member Am. Acad. Arts and Sciences, Federation Am. Scientists (chairman 1986-88, Pub., Service award 1972), Council Foreign Relations, Accademia Santa Chiara, National Acad. Sciences, Institute Medicine, Am. Philosophical Society, Royal Society (London), Académie des Sciences (Paris). Office: Harvard U Fairchild Biochem Building 7 Divinity Avenue Cambridge Massachusetts 02138

METCALFE, DARREL SEYMOUR, educator, agronomist; born Arkansaw, Wisconsin, August 28, 1913; son of Howard Lee and Mabel (De Marce) M.; married Ellen Lucille Moore, May 16, 1942; children: Dean Darrel, Alan Moore. Tchr. certificate, University Wisconsin at River Falls, 1931; Bachelor of Science in Agronomy, University Wisconsin, 1941; Master of Science, Kansas State University, 1942; Doctor of Philosophy, Iowa State University, 1950. From instructor to professor agronomy Iowa State University, 1946-56, assistant director student affairs; 1956-58; associate dean, director resident instruction, assistant director agricultural experiment station, agronomist University Arizona, Tucson, 1958—; dean University Arizona, 1978-82, dean emeritus; 1982—; Chairman resident instruction section, div. agriculture National Association State Universities and Land Grant Colleges, 1958-59; member committee education agriculture and natural resources National Acad. Sci., 1966-70, member rev. panel for Egypt, 1980-83, member Institute International Education Committee, Somalia and Kenya, 1980-82; United States representative Organization of European Cooperation and Development Conference Higher Education in Agriculture, Paris, 1963-65; trustee Consortium for International Devel., 1978-82; member Agency for International Development missions to Brazil, 1962, 64, 66, 69, 71, 72, 73, Sultan Zaboos University Committee, Oman, 1982-86. Co-author: Forages, 4th edition, 1985, Crop Production, rev. edits, 1957, 72, 80. Served with Army of the United States, 1942-46, Pacific Theatre of Operations. Named Hon. Alumnus University Virginia, 1985, University Arizona, 1985. Fellow Am. Society Agronomy (Agronomic education award 1958, Agronomic Service award 1980, chairman student activities section 1950-53, education division 1956, editorial board, tech. editor journal 1961-65), National Association Colls. and Teachers Agriculture (E.B. Knight award 1967, president 1970-71, Distinguished Educator award 1980), Sigma Xi, Phi Kappa Phi, Phi Eta Sigma, Gamma Sigma Delta, Alpha Tau Alpha, Delta Theta Sigma, Acacia (medallion of merit 1966). Club: Kiwanian. Home: 5811 E 9th St Tucson Arizona 85711

METZ, CHARLES EDGAR, radiology educator; born Bayshore, New York, September 11, 1942; son of Clinton Edgar and Grace Muriel (Schienke) M.; married Maryanne Theresa Bahr, July 1, 1967 (divorced October 1988); children: Rebecca, Molly. Bachelor of Arts, Bowdoin College, 1964; Master of Science, University Pennsylvania, 1966, Doctor of Philosophy, 1969. Instructor radiology University Chicago, 1969-71, assistant professor; 1971-75, associate professor; 1976-80, director grad.

programs in medical physics; 1979-85, professor; 1980—, professor structural biology; 1984-86; member diagnostic research adv. group National Cancer Institute, 1980-81; member sci. committee National Council on Radiation Protection and Measurements, 1982—, International Commission on Radiation Units and Measurements, 1988—; consultant and lecturer in field. Associate editor Radiology journal, 1985—; member editorial board Medical Decision Making, 1980-84; contributor over 55 articles to sci. journals and over 30 chapters to books. Member Radiological Society North America, Am. Association Physicists in Medicine, Society Medical Decision Making, Phi Beta Kappa, Sigma Xi. Office: U Chicago Department Radiology Box 429 5841 S Maryland Avenue Chicago Illinois 60637

MEYER, PETER, educator, physicist; born Berlin, January 6, 1920; came to United States, 1952, naturalized, 1962; son of Franz and Frida (Lehmann) M.; married Luise Schützmeister, July 20, 1946 (deceased 1981); children: Stephan S., Andreas S.; married Patricia G. Spear, June 14, 1983. Dipl.Ing., Tech. University, Berlin, 1942; Doctor of Philosophy, University Goettingen, Germany, 1948. Faculty University Goettingen, 1946-49; fellow University Cambridge, England, 1949-50; member sci. staff Max-Planck Institute fuer Physik, Goettingen, 1950-52; faculty University Chicago, 1953—, professor physics; 1965—, chairman Department Physics; 1986—; director Enrico Fermi Institute, 1978-83; consultant National Aeronautics and Space Administration, National Science Foundation.; member cosmic ray commission International Union Pure and Applied Physics, 1966-72; member space sci. board National Acad. Sciences, 1975-78. Recipient Alexander von Humboldt Senior U.S. Scientist award, 1984, Llewellyn John and Harriet Manchester Quantrell award, 1971. Fellow Am. Physical Society (chairman division cosmic physics 1972-73), American Association for the Advancement of Science; member Am. Astronomical Society, Am. Geophysical Union, Max Planck Institute fuer Physik und Astrophysik (foreign), Sigma Xi. Office: 933 E 56th St Chicago Illinois 60637

MICHEL,   HARTMUT, biochemist. Postdoctoral student, University Wurzburg. With Max Planck Institute Biophysics, Martinsreid, Federal Republic of Germany, 1979—. Co-recipient Nobel prize for chemistry, 1988. Office: Max Planck Institute Biophysics, Kennedyallee 70, 6000 Frankfurt am 70, Federal Republic of Germany *

MICHL, JOSEF, chemistry educator; born Prague, Czechoslovakia, March 12, 1939; came to United States, 1969; son of Josef and Vera (Polakova) M.; married Sara Margaret Allensworth, March 14, 1969; children: Georgina Frances, John Allensworth. Master of Science, Charles University, Prague, 1961; Doctor of Philosophy, Czechoslovakia Academy Science, Prague, 1965. Postdoctoral University Houston, 1965-66, University Texas, Austin, 1966-67; research scientist Czechoslovak Acad. Sci., 1967-68; amanuensis Aarhus (Denmark) University, 1968-69; postdoctoral research University Utah, Salt Lake City, 1969-70, research associate professor chemistry; 1970-71, associate professor; 1971-75, professor; 1975-

86, chairman department; 1979-84; M.K. Collie-Welch Regents professor chemistry University Texas, Austin, 1986—; chairman commission photochemistry International Union Pure Applied Chemistry, 1985—. Editor: Chemical Revs., 1984—; member editorial adv. board, Accounts of Chemical Research, 1984—, Journal Physics and Chemistry Reference Data, 1985—; associate editor Theoretica Chim. Acta, 1985—; contributor numerous sci. papers. Recipient Alexander von Humboldt Senior U.S. Scientist award, 1980, distinguished research award University Utah, 1978-79; Alfred P. Sloan fellow, 1971-75, Guggenheim fellow. Member National Acad. Sciences, Am. Chemical Society (executive committee division phys. chemistry, 1982-86, Utah section award 1986), Interam. Photochem. Society (executive committee 1977-80), Chemical Society, Am. Society Mass Spectroscopy. Roman Catholic.

Office: University of Texas/Austin Department of Chemistry Austin Texas 78712

MIDDLEBROOKS, EDDIE JOE, environmental engineer; born Crawford County, Georgia, October 16, 1932; son of Robert Harold and Jewell LaVerne (Dixon) M.; married Charlotte Linda Hardy, December 6, 1958; 1 child, Linda Tracey. Bachelor of Civil Engineering, University Florida, 1956, Master of Science, 1960; Doctor of Philosophy, Mississippi State University, 1966. Diplomate: Am. Acad. Environmental Engineers; registered professional engineer, Arizona, Mississippi, Utah; registered land surveyor, Florida. Assistant sanitary engineer United States Public Health Service, Cincinnati, 1956-58; field engineer T.T. Jones Construction

Company, Atlanta, 1958-59; grad. teaching assistant University Florida, 1959-60; research assistant University Arizona, 1960-61; assistant professor, associate professor Mississippi State University, 1962-67; research engineer, assistant director Sanitary Engineering Research Laboratory, University Calif.-Berkeley, 1968-70; professor Utah State University, Logan, 1970-82, dean College Engineering; 1974-82; Newman chair natural resources engineering Clemson University, 1982-83; provost, vice president acad. affairs Tennessee Tech. University, 1983-88; provost, vice president acad. affairs, professor chemical engineering University Tulsa, 1988—; member national drinking water adv. council Environmental Protection Agency, 1981-83; consultant Environmental Protection Agency, United Nations Industrial Devel. Organization, California Water Resources Control Board, also numerous industrial and engineering firms. Author: Modeling the Eutrophication Process, 1974, Statistical Calculations-How To Solve Statistical Problems, 1976, Biostimulation and Nutrient Assessment, 1976, Water Supply Engineering Design, 1977, Lagoon Information Source Book, 1978, Industrial Pollution Control, Volume 1: Agro-Industries, 1979, Wastewater Collection and Treatment: Principles and Practices, 1979, Water Reuse, 1982, Wastewater Stabilization Lagoon Design, Performance and Upgrading, 1982, Reverse Osmosis Treatment of Drinking Water, 1986, Pollution Control in the Petrochemicals Industry, 1987, Natural Systems for Waste Management and Treatment, 1988; member editorial adv. board Lewis Pubs. Incorporated, Envionment

International; contributor tech. articles to professional journals. Fellow American Society of Civil Engineers; member American Association for the Advancement of Science, Water Pollution Control Federation (Eddy medal 1969, director 1979-81), Association Environmental Engineering Profs. (president 1974), Utah Water Pollution Control Association (president 1976), International Association on Water Pollution Research, Am. Society Engineering Education, Am. Society Limnology and Oceanography, Sigma Xi, Omicron Delta Kappa, Phi Kappa Phi, Tau Beta Pi, Sigma Tau. Home: 1115 E 20th St Tulsa Oklahoma 74120 Office: U Tulsa 600 S College Avenue Tulsa Oklahoma 74104-3189

MILEY, GEORGE HUNTER, nuclear engineering educator; born Shreveport, Louisiana, August 6, 1933; son of George Hunter and Norma Angeline (Dowling) M.; married Elizabeth Burroughs, November 22, 1958; children: Susan Elizabeth, Hunter Robert. Bachelor of Science in Chemical Engineering, Carnegie-Mellon University, 1955; Master of Science, University Michigan, 1956, Doctor of Philosophy in Chem.-Nuclear Engineering, 1959. Nuclear engineer Knolls Atomic Power Laboratory, General Electric Company, Schenectady, 1959-61; member faculty University Illinois, Urbana, 1961—; professor University Illinois, 1967—, chairman nuclear engineering program; 1975-86, director Fusion Studies Laboratory; 1976—, fellow Center for Advanced Study; 1985-86; visiting professor University Colorado, 1967, Cornell University, 1969-70, University New South Wales, 1986, Imperial College of London, 1987. Author: Direct Conversion of Nuclear Radiation Energy, 1971, Fusion Energy Conversion, 1976; editor: Journal Fusion Tech., 1980—; United States associate editor Laser and Particle Beams, 1982-86, managing editor, 1987—. Served with Corps of Engineers Army of the United States, 1960. Recipient Western Electric Teaching-Research award, 1977; NATO sr. sci. fellow, 1975-76; Guggenheim fellow, 1985-86. Fellow Am. Nuclear Society (director 1980-83, Distinguished Service award 1980), Am. Physical Society, Institute of Electrical and Electronics Engineers; member Am. Society Engineering Education (chairman energy conversion committee 1967-70, president University Illinois chapter 1973-74, chairman nuclear division 1975-76, Outstanding Teacher award 1973), Sigma Xi, Tau Beta Pi. Presbyterian. Lodge: Kiwanis.
   Research on fusion, energy conversion, reactor kinetics Research on fusion, energy conversion, reactor kinetics. Office: U Illinois 214 Nuclear Engring Lab 103 S Goodwin Avenue Urbana Illinois 61801

MILLER, GEORGE ARMITAGE, psychologist, educator; born Charleston, West Virginia, February 3, 1920; son of George E. and Florence (Armitage) M.; married Katherine James, November 29, 1939; children: Nancy, Donnally James. Bachelor of Arts, University Alabama, 1940, Master of Arts, 1941; Master of Arts, Harvard University, 1944, Doctor of Philosophy, 1946; Doctorat honoris causa, University Louvain, 1976; Doctor Social Science (honorary), Yale University, 1979; Doctor of Science honoris causa, Columbia University, 1980; Doctor of Science (honorary), University Sussex, 1984. Instructor psychology University Alabama, 1941-43; research fellow Harvard Psycho-Acoustic Laboratory, 1944-48; assistant professor psychology Harvard University, 1948-51, associate professor; 1955-58, professor; 1958-68, chairman dept psychology; 1964-67, co-director Center for Cognitive Studies; 1960-67; professor Rockefeller University, New York City, 1968-79; adj. professor Rockefeller University, 1979-82; professor Princeton University, 1979—, James S McDonnell Distinguished University professor psychology; 1982—; associate professor Massachusetts Institute of Technology, 1951-55; visiting Institute for Advanced Study, Princeton, 1972-76, 82-83, member, 1950, 70-72; visiting professor Rockefeller University, 1967-68; visiting professor Massachusetts Institute of Technology, 1976-79, group leader Lincoln Laboratory, 1953-55; fellow Center Advanced Study in Behavioral Sciences, Stanford University, 1958-59; Fulbright research professor Oxford (England) University, 1963-64; Sesquicentennial professor University Alabama, 1981. Author: Language and Communication, 1951, (with Galanter and Pribram) Plans and the Structure of Behavior, 1960, Psychology, 1962, (with Johnson-Laird) Language and Perception, 1976, Spontaneous Apprentices, 1977, Language and Speech, 1981; editor Psychological Bulletin, 1981-82. Recipient Distinguished Service award Am. Speech and Hearing Association, 1976, award in behavioral scis. New York Acad. Sciences, 1982. Member Am. Psychological Association (president 1968-69, Distinguished Scientific Contbn. award 1963), Eastern Psychological Association (president 1961-62), Acoustical Society Am., Linguistic Society Am., Am. Statistical Association, Am. Philosophical Society, Am. Physiological Society, Psychometric Society, Society Experimental Psychologists (Warren medal 1972), Am. Acad. Arts and Sciences, Psychonomic Society, National Acad. Sci., American Association for the Advancement of Science (chairman section J 1981), Royal Netherlands Acad. Arts and Sciences (foreign), Sigma Xi. Home: 478 Lake Dr Princeton New Jersey 08540 Office: Department Psychology Green Hall Princeton U Princeton New Jersey 08544

MILLER, IRVING FRANKLIN, chemical engineering educator, academic administrator; born New York City, September 27, 1934; son of Sol and Gertrude (Rochkind) M.; married Baila Hannah Milner, January 28, 1962; children—Eugenia Lynne, Jonathan Mark. Bachelor of Science in Chemical Engineering, New York University, 1955; Master of Science, Purdue University, 1956; Doctor of Philosophy, University Michigan, 1960. Research scientist United Aircraft Corp., Hartford, 1959-61; from assistant professor to professor, head chemical engineering Polytechnic Institute Brooklyn, 1961-72; professor bioengring., head bioengring. program University Illinois, Chicago, 1973-79, acting head systems engineering department; 1978-79, associate vice chancellor for research, dean Grad. College; 1979-85, professor chemical engineering, head chemical engineering; 1986—; consultant to industry, also National Acad. Sciences, National Institutes of Health. Editor: Electrochemical Bioscience and Bioengineering, 1973;

Contributor articles professional journals. Member Am. Institute Chemical Engineers, Am. Chemical Society, American Association for the Advancement of Science, Biomed. Engineering Society, New York Acad Sciences. Home: 2600 Orrington Avenue Evanston Illinois 60201 Office: Box 4348 Chicago Illinois 60680

MILLER, RAYMOND JARVIS, agronomist, college dean, university official; born Claresholm, Alberta, Canada, March 19, 1934; came to United States, 1957, naturalized, 1975; son of Charles Jarvis and Wilma Macy (Anderson) M.; married Frances Anne Davidson, April 28, 1956; children—Cheryl Rae, Jeffrey John, Jay Robert. Bachelor of Science (Federal Provincial grantee 1954-56, Dan Baker scholar 1954-56), University Alberta, Edmonton, 1957; Master of Science, Washington State University, 1960; Doctor of Philosophy, Purdue University, 1962. Member faculty North Carolina State University, 1962-65, University Illinois, 1965-69; assistant director, then associate director Illinois Agricultural Experiment Station, 1969-73; director Idaho Agricultural Experiment Station, 1973-79; dean University Idaho College Agriculture, 1979-85, vice president for agriculture; dean College Agriculture and College Life Sci. University Maryland, College Park, 1986—. Author numerous papers in field. President Idaho Research Foundation, 1980-85; board governors Agricultural Research Institute, 1979-80; chairman legis. subcom. Expt. Sta. Committee on Policy, 1981-82, chairman board div. agriculture Land Grant Association, 1985-86; board of directors C.V. Riley Foundation, 1985—. Grantee International Congress Soil Sci., 1960, Purdue University Research Foundation, summers 1960, 61. Fellow Am. Society Agronomy, Soil Sci. Society Am.; member International Society Soil Sci., Clay and Clay Minerals Society, Am. Chemical Society, Am. Society Plant Physiologists, Sigma Xi, Phi Kappa Phi, Gamma Sigma Delta, Alpha Zeta. Clubs: Elks, Lions. Home: 3319 Gumwood Dr Adelphi Maryland 20783 Office: U Maryland College Agr and Life Sci College Park Maryland 20742

MILLER, RENE HARCOURT, aerospace engineering educator; born Tenafly, New Jersey, May 19, 1916; son of Arthur C. and Elizabeth M. (Tobin) M.; married Marcelle Hansotte, July 16, 1948 (divorced 1968); children: Christal L., John M.; married Maureen Michael, November 20, 1973. Bachelor of Arts, Cambridge University, 1937, Master of Arts, 1954. Registered professional engineer, Massachusetts. Aeronautical engineer G.L. Martin Company, Baltimore, 1937-39; chief aeronautical and devel. McDonnell Aircraft Corp., St. Louis, 1939-44; member faculty aeronautical engineering Massachusetts Institute of Technology, Cambridge, 1944—, professor; 1957-86, Slater professor flight transportation; 1986—; head department aerospace and astronautics Massachusetts Institute of Technology, 1968-78, professor emeritus; 1986—; vice president engineering Kaman Aircraft Corp., Bloomfield, Connecticut, 1952-53; member tech. adv. board Federal Aviation Administration, 1964-66; member Aircraft panel President's Sci. Adv. Committee, 1960-72, Army Sci. Adv. Panel, 1966-73; chairman Army Aviation Sci. Adv. Group, 1963-73;

member Air Force Sci. Adv. Board, 1959-70; committee on aircraft aerodynamics National Aeronautics and Space Administration, 1960-70. Contributor articles to professional journals. Recipient U.S. Army Decoration for Meritorious Civilian Service, 1967, 70; recipient L.B. Laskowitz award New York Acad. Sciences, 1976. Fellow Am. Helicopter Society (hon. tech. director 1957-59, editor Jour. 1957-59 Klemin award, Hon. Nikolsky lecturer 1983), American Institute of Aeronautics and Astronautics (hon., president 1977-78 Sylvanus Albert Reed award), Royal Aeronautical Society (Great Britain); member National Acad. Engineering, International Acad. Astronautics. Home: San Jose New Road, Penzance Cornwall TR18 4PN, England Office: Massachusetts Institute of Technology Department Aerospace and Astronautics 33-411 Cambridge Massachusetts 02139

MILLER, ROBERT JAMES, anthropologist, educator, editor; born Detroit, September 18, 1923; son of Robert Paul and Desdemona (Jelinek) M.; married Beatrice Diamond, November 6, 1943; children: Karla M., Erik T., Terin T. Student, India studies University Pennsylvania, 1947; Bachelor of Arts in Oriental Civilization, University Michigan, 1948; Doctor of Philosophy in Anthropology, University Washington, 1956. Asia research fellow University Washington, 1948-50, instructor in anthropology; 1950; fellow Inner Asia Project, 1951-52; research anthropologist Inner Mongolia Project, 1955-56; assistant professor sociology-anthropology Washington University, St. Louis, 1956-59; assistant professor anthropology University Wisconsin, Madison, 1959-

61; associate professor University Wisconsin, 1962-64, professor; 1965-88, professor emeritus; 1988—, chairman department anthropology; 1965-69, 76-78, professor South Asian studies; 1959-88; resident director Am. Institute Indian Studies, New Delhi, 1970-72; associate director Qualitative Systems Analysts Company; consultant in field. Author: Monasteries and Culture Change in Inner Mongolia, 1959; contributor numerous articles to professional publications; editor: Religious Ferment in Asia, 1974, Robotics: Future Factories, Future Workers. Founding member board of directors Council on Understanding of Tech. in Human Affairs. Served with United States Coast Guard, 1942-44. Social Sci. Research Council fellow, 1952-53; Ford Foundation fellow, 1953-55; National Science Foundation grantee, 1963-64; Am. Institute Indian Studies sr. fellow, 1963-64; Smithsonian fellow, 1970-72; Sloan Foundation grantee, 1976. Fellow Am. Anthropological Association, American Association for the Advancement of Science, Sigma Xi; member Association Asian Studies, Am. Ethnological Society, Society General Systems Research, Current Anthropology (associate), American Association of University Women, Council Anthropology and Education (director 1980-84, chairman committee on education futures 1981-84), Indian Anthropol. Association (founding), International Association Buddhist Studies (founding, general secretary 1982-86), World Future Society, Bioelectromagnetics Society, Am. Radio Relay League, Society Wireless Pioneers. Office: U Wisconsin 5243 Social Sci Building Observatory Dr Madison Wisconsin 53706

MILLER, WILLIAM FREDERICK, research company executive, computer science educator; born Vincennes, Indiana, November 19, 1925; son of William and Elsie M. (Everts) M.; married Patty J. Smith, June 19, 1949; 1 son, Rodney Wayne. Student, Vincennes University, 1946-47; Bachelor of Science, Purdue University, 1949, Master of Science, 1951, Doctor of Philosophy, 1956; Doctor of Science, 1972. Member staff Argonne National Laboratory, 1955-64, associate physicist; 1956-59, director applied math. div.; 1959-64; professor computer sci. Stanford University, Palo Alto, California, 1965—; Herbert Hoover professor pub. and private management Stanford University, 1979—, associate provost for computing; 1968-70, vice president for research; 1970-71, vice president, provost; 1971-78; member Stanford Associates, 1972—; president, chief executive officer SRI International, Menlo Park, California, 1979—; chairman board, chief executive officer SRI Devel. Company, Menlo Park, David Sarnoff Research Center, Incorporated, Princeton, New Jersey; professional lecturer applied math. University Chicago, 1962-64; visiting professor math. Purdue University, 1962-63; visiting scholar Center for Advanced Study in Behavioral Sciences, 1976; board of directors Fireman's Fund Insurance Company, Annual Revs. Incorporated, Varian Associates Incorporated, 1st Interstate Bancorp, 1st Interstate Bank of California, Pacific Gas and Electric Company; member computer sci. and engineering board National Acad. Sci., 1968-71; member National Sci. Board, 1982-88; member corp. committee on computers in education Brown University, 1972-79; member policy board EDUCOM Planning Council on Computing in Education, 1974-79, chairman, 1974-76; educational adv. board Guggenheim Memorial Foundation, 1976-80; committee postdoctoral and doctoral research staff National Research Council, 1977-80. Associate editor: Pattern Recognition Jour, 1968-72, Journal Computational Physics, 1970-74. Served to 2d lieutenant Field Artillery Army of the United States, 1943-46. Fellow Institute of Electrical and Electronics Engineers, Am. Acad. Arts and Sciences, American Association for the Advancement of Science; member Am. Math. Society, Am. Physical Society, Society Industrial and Applied Math., Association Computing Machinery, National Acad. Engineering, Sigma Xi. Office: SRI International 333 Ravenswood Avenue Menlo Park California 94025

MILLIKEN, FRANK ROSCOE, mining engineer; born Malden, Massachusetts, January 25, 1914; son of Frank R. and Alice (Gould) M.; married Barbara Kingsbury, September 14, 1935; children—Frank R., David C. Bachelor of Science in Mining Engineering, Massachusetts Institute of Technology, 1934. Chief metallurgist General Engineering Company, Salt Lake City, 1936-41; assistant manager Titanium div. National Lead Company, 1941-52; vice president charge mining operations Kennecott Copper Corp., New York City, 1952—; executive vice president Kennecott Copper Corp., 1958-61, director; 1958—, president, chief executive officer; 1961-78, chairman, chief executive officer; 1978-79; chairman Federal Reserve Bank New York, 1976-77. Life member corp. M.I.T. Named Copper

Man of Year Am. Mining Congress, 1973; recipient 1st Distinguished award, Distinguished Service award U.S. Treasury, 1965, 68. Member National Acad. Engineering, Mining and Metallurgical Society Am., Am. Institute Mining Metallurgical and Petroleum Engineers (Robert H. Richards award of minerals beneficiation division 1951), The Business Council. Clubs: River (New York City); Wee Burn Country (Darien, Connecticut).

MILSTEIN, CÉSAR, molecular biologist; born October 8, 1927; son of Lázaro and Maxima Milstein; married Celia Prilleltensky, 1953. Educated, Colegio Nacional De Bahia Blanca, University Nacional de Buenos Aires, Fitzwilliam College, Cambridge. Brit. Council fellow 1958-60; staff Instituto Nacional de Microbiologia, Buenos Aires, 1957-63; head Div. de Biologia Molecular, 1961-63; member staff M.R.C. Laboratory of Molecular Biology, 1963—, member governor board; 1975-79. Contributor articles to professional journals. Recipient Royal medal Royal Society, 1982, Nobel prize for medicine, 1984; Rozenberg prize, 1979, Mattia award, 1979, Gross Howit prize, 1980, Koch prize, 1980, Wolf prize in medicine, 1980, Wellcome Foundation medal, 1980, Gimene Dia medal, 1981, Sloan prize General Motors Cancer Research Foundation, 1981, Gardner award Gardner Foundation, 1981. Fellow Royal College Physicians (hon.); member National Acad. Sciences (foreign associate). Avocation: cooking. Office: Med Research Coun Centre, Hills Road, Cambridge England

MINDLIN, RAYMOND DAVID, educator, civil engineer; born New York City, September 17, 1906; son of Henry and Beatrice (Levy) M.; married Elizabeth Roth, 1940 (deceased 1950); married Patricia Kaveney, 1953 (deceased 1976). Student, Ethical Culture School, New York City, 1918-24; Bachelor of Arts, Columbia University, 1928, Bachelor of Science, 1931, Civil Engineer, 1932, Doctor of Philosophy, 1936; Doctor of Science (honorary), Northwestern University, 1975. Research assistant department civil engineering Columbia University, New York City, 1932-38; Bridgham fellow Columbia University, 1934-35, instructor civil engineering; 1938-40, assistant professor; 1940-45, associate professor; 1945-47, professor civil engineering; 1947-67, James Kip Finch professor applied sci.; 1967-75, professor emeritus; 1975—; consultant Bell Telephone Laboratories Incorporated, New York City, 1943-51; consultant physicist Department Terrestrial Magnetism, Carnegie Institution of Washington, 1940-42; consultant National Defense Research Committee, 1941-42; section T Office Sci. Research and Devel., Applied Physics Laboratory, Johns Hopkins University, Baltimore, 1942-45. Member adv. board: Applied Mechanical Reviews; Contributor articles to tech. and sci. journals. Recipient Illig medal Columbia University, 1932, U.S. Naval Ordnance Devel. award, 1945, Presidential Medal for Merit, 1946, Class of 1889 School Mines medal Columbia University, 1947, research prize American Society of Civil Engineers, 1958, Great Teacher award Columbia University, 1960, von Karman medal American Society of Civil Engineers, 1961, Timoshenko medal American Society of Mechanical Engineers, 1964, American Society of Mechanical Engineers medal, 1976, C.B. Sawyer Piezoelectric Resonator award, 1967,

Egleston medal Columbia University, 1971, Trent-Crede medal Acoustical Society, Am., 1971, Frocht award Society Exptl. Stress Analysis, 1974, National medal of Sci., 1979. Fellow Acoustical Society Am., Am. Acad. Arts and Sciences; member Society Experimental Stress Analysis (founding member; executive committee 1943-50, vice president 1946, president 1947, hon. member 1986), American Society of Civil Engineers (secretary committee applied mechanics 1940-42, chairman 1942-45), Eastern Photoelasticity Conference (executive committee 1938-41), Am. Physical Society, National Acad. Engineering, National Acad. Sci., Connecticut Acad. Sci. and Engineering, United States National Committee Theoretical and Applied Mechanics, International Union Theoretical and Applied Mechanics, American Society of Mechanical Engineers (hon.), Tau Beta Pi, Sigma Xi. Home: South Cove Vista Grantham New Hampshire 03753

MINKOWYCZ, W. J., engineering educator; born Libokhora, Ukraine, Union of Soviet Socialist Republics, October 21, 1937; son of Alexander and Anna (Tokan) M.; married Diana Eva Szandra, May 12, 1973; 1 child, Liliana Christine Anne. Bachelor of Science in Mechanical Engineering, University Minnesota, 1958, Master of Science in Mechanical Engineering, 1961, Doctor of Philosophy in Mechanical Engineering, 1965. Assistant professor University Illinois, Chicago, 1966-68, associate professor; 1968-78, professor; 1978—; consultant Argonne National Lab, Illinois, 1970-82, University Hawaii, Honolulu, 1974—. founding editor-in-chief Journal Numerical Heat Transfer, 1978—; co-editor International Journal Heat and Mass Transfer, 1968—, International Communications In Heat and Mass Transfer Journal, 1974—; editor book series: Computational Methods in Thermal Scis., 1979—; editor: Rheologically Complex Fluids, 1972, Handbook of Numerical Heat Transfer, 1988; contributor articles to professional journals. Recipient Silver Circle for Excellence in Teaching, University Ill.-Chgo., 1975, 76, 81, 86, Harold A. Simon award Excellence in Teaching, 1986, Ralph Coats Roe Outstanding Teacher award Am. Society Engineering Education, 1988. Fellow American Society of Mechanical Engineers; member Sigma Xi, Pi Tau Sigma. Republican. Greek Catholic. Office: U Illinois Department Mech Engring Chicago Illinois 60680

MINSKY, MARVIN LEE, mathematician, educator; born New York City, August 9, 1927; son of Henry and Fannie (Reyser) M.; married Gloria Anna Rudisch, July 30, 1952; children: Margaret, Henry, Juliana. Bachelor of Arts, Harvard University, 1950; Doctor of Philosophy, Princeton University, 1954. Member Harvard Society Fellows, 1954-57; with Lincoln Laboratory, Massachusetts Institute of Technology, 1957-58, professor math.; 1958-61, professor electrical engineering; 1961—, Donner professor sci.; 1973, director artificial intelligence group MAC project; from 1958, director artificial intelligence laboratory MAC project; from 1970. Author: Computation, 1967, Semantic Information Processing, 1968, Perceptrons, (with S. Papert), 1968, Robotics, 1985. Served with United States Naval Reserve, 1945-46. Recipient Turing award Association for Computing Machinery, 1970. Fellow I.E.E.E., Am. Acad. Arts and Sciences, New York Acad. Sciences, National Acad. Sci. Office: Massachusetts Institute of Technology Department Elec Engring - Computer Sci Cambridge Massachusetts 02139

MISRA, JAYADEV, computer science educator; born Cuttack, Orissa, India, October 17, 1947; son of Sashibhusan and Shanty (Kar) M.; married Mamata Das, November 30, 1972; children: Amitav, Anuj. Bachelor Tech, Indian Institute Tech., Kanpur, 1969; Doctor of Philosophy, Johns Hopkins University, 1972. Staff scientist International Business Machines Corporation, Gaithersburg, Maryland, 1973-74; from assistant professor to professor computer science University Texas, Austin, 1974—; visiting professor Stanford (California) University, 1983-84; consultant on software and hardware design. Contributor articles to professional journals. Guggenheim fellow, 1988-89. Member Institute of Electrical and Electronics Engineers, Association Computing Machinery (Samuel N. Alexander Memorial award, 1970). Office: University Tex Department Computer Sci Austin Texas 78712

MITCHELL, PETER DENNIS, biochemist; born Mitcham, Surrey, England, September 29, 1920; son of Christopher Gibbs and Kate Beatrice Dorothy (Taplin) M.; married Patricia Helen Mary French, November 1, 1958; children: Julia, Jeremy, Vanessa, Daniel, Jason, Gideon. Bachelor of Arts, Jesus College, Cambridge University, 1943, Doctor of Philosophy, 1950, Doctor of Science (honorary), 1985; Dr.rer.national (honorary), Tech. University Berlin, 1976; Doctor of Science (honorary),

Exeter University, 1977, University Chicago, 1978, University Liverpool, 1979, University Bristol, 1980, University Edinburgh, 1980, University Hull, 1980, University East Anglia, 1981, University York, 1982. With department biochemistry Cambridge University, 1943-55, demonstrator; 1950-55; director chemical biology unit, department zoology University Edinburgh, Scotland, 1955-63, senior lecturer, then reader; 1961-63, James Rennie Bequest lecturer; 1980; director research Glynn Research Institute, Bodmin, Cornwall, 1964-87; chairman hon. director Glynn Research Foundation, 1987—; Sir Hans Krebs lecturer Federation European Biochem. Societies, 1978; Fritz Lipmann lecturer German Society Biological Chemistry, 1978; Humphry Davy memorial lecturer Royal Institute Chemistry and The Chilterns and Middlesex section of Chemical Society, 1980; Croonian lecturer The Royal Society, 1987. Author: Chemiosmotic Coupling in Oxidative and Photosynthetic Phosphorylation, 1966, Chemiosmotic Coupling and Energy Transduction, 1968; also papers. Hon. adv. editor Biosci. Reports. Recipient Louis and Bert Freedman Foundation award New York Acad. Sciences, 1974; Wilhelm Feldberg prize Feldberg Foundation Anglo/German Sci. Exchange, 1976; Lewis S. Rosenstiel award Brandeis University, 1977; Nobel Prize in chemistry, 1978; Medal of Honor, Athens (Greece) Mcpl. Council; co-recipient Warren Triennial prize Massachusetts General Hospital, Boston, 1974; fellow Jesus College, Cambridge. Fellow Royal Society (Copley medal 1981); hon. fellow Royal Society Edinburgh; member Biochem. Society (CIBA medal 1973), Econ. Research Council,

European Molecular Biology Organization; foreign associate United States National Acad. Sciences, French Acad. Sciences; hon. member Society General Microbiology, Am. Society Biological Chemists, Am. Acad. Arts and Sciences, Japanese Biochem. Society. Office: Glynn Research Found Limited, Glynn House, Bodmin, Cornwall PL30 4AU, England

MOELLERING, ROBERT CHARLES, JR., internist, educator; born Lafayette, Indiana, June 9, 1936; son of Robert Charles and Irene Pauline (Nolde) M.; married Mary Tigg Johnston, June 14, 1964 (divorced 1987); children: Anne Elizabeth, Robert Charles, Catherine Irene; married Mary Jane Ferraro, July 11, 1987. Bachelor of Arts, Valparaiso University, 1958, Doctor of Science, 1980; Doctor of Medicine cum laude, Harvard University, 1962. Diplomate: Am. Board Internal Medicine. Intern Massachusetts General Hospital, Boston, 1962-63, resident; 1963-64, postdoctoral fellow in infectious diseases; 1967-70, resident; 1966-67, member infectious disease unit and assistant physician; 1970-76, associate physician; 1976-83, hon. physician; 1983—, consultant bacteriology; 1972—; instructor medicine Harvard University Medical School, Boston, 1970-72, assistant professor; 1972-76, associate professor; 1976-80, professor; 1980—; chairman department medicine, physician-in-chief New England Deaconess Hospital, 1981—; Shields Warren-Mallinckrodt professor clinical research Harvard University Medical School, Boston, 1981—; member subcom. on susceptibility testing National Committee for Clinical Laboratory Standards, 1976—; member subcom. on antimicrobial agents and chemotheraph, 1978—, subcom. on antimicrobiol disc. diffusion suceptibility testing, 1980—. Member editorial board New England Journal Medicine, 1977-81, Antimicrobial Agts. and Chemical Therapy, 1977-81, European Journal Clin. Microbiology, 1981—, Journal Infectious Deseases, 1981-85, Infectious Disease Alert, 1981—, Pharmacotherapy, 1982—, Antimicrobial Agts. Annual, 1984—, Zentralblatt Fur Bacteriologie, Microbiologie und Hygiene, 1984—, Journal of Infection, 1986—, Innovations, 1986—, Residents Forum in Internal Medicine, 1988—; editor Antimicrobial Agts. and Chemotherapy, 1982-85, Les Infections, 1983; editor-in-chief Amtimicrobial Agts. and Chemical Therapy, 1985—, editor; Antimicrobial Agents Annual, 1984—; cons. editor: Infectious Disease Clinics North America, 1986—; contributor articles to professional journals. Served with United States Public Health Service, 1964-66. Grantee USPHS. Fellow American College of Physicians, Infectious Diseases Society Am.; member Am. Society Microbiology, Am. Clinical and Climatological Association, International Society Chemotherapy, Am. Society Clinical Investigation, European Society Clinical Microbiology, Am. Federation Clinical Research, Roxbury Clinical Records Club, Massachusetts Medical Society, Alpha Omega Alpha, Phi Kappa Psi. Cardiovascular epidemiology, mechanism action of and resistance to antibiotics, pharmacology, susceptibility testing and automated techniques for clin. microbiology. Home: 16 Breakwater Dr Chesla Massachusetts 02150 Office: New England Deaconess Hosp

Department Medicine 110 Francis St Boston Massachusetts 02215

MONTAGNA, WILLIAM, scientist; born Roccacasale, Italy, July 6, 1913; son of Cherubino and Adele (Giannangelo) M.; married Martha Helen Fife, September 1, 1939 (divorced 1975); children: Eleanor, Margaret, James and John (twins); married Leona Rebecca Montagna, April 19, 1980. Bachelor of Arts, Bethany College, 1936, Doctor of Science, 1960; Doctor of Philosophy, Cornell University, 1944; Doctor Bachelor of Science, Universitá di Sassari, 1964. Instructor Cornell University, 1944-45; assistant professor Long Island College Medicine, 1945-48; assistant, associate professor Brown University, 1948-52, professor; 1952-63, L. Herbert Ballou university professor biology; 1960-63; professor, head experimental biology University Oregon Health Sciences Center; director Oregon Regional Primate Research Center, Beaverton, 1963—. Author: The Structure and Function of Skin, 1956, 3d edition, 1974, Comparative Anatomy, 1959, Nonhuman Primates in Biomedical Research, 1976, Science Is Not Enough, 1980; co-author: Man, 1969, 2d edition, 1973; editor: The Biology of Hair Growth, 1958, Advances in Biology of Skin, 20 vols, The Epidermis, 1965, Advances in Primatology, 1970, Reproductive Behavior, 1974. Decorated Order di Cavaliere, 1963, Cavaliere Ufficiale, 1969, Commendator della Repubblica Italiana, 1975; Italy; recipient special award Society Cosmetic Chemists, 1957; Gold award Am. Acad. Dermatology, 1958; gold medal for meritorious achievement Universitá di Sassari, 1964; Aubrey R. Watzek award Lewis and Clark College, 1977; Hans Schwarzkopf Research award German Dermatol. Society, 1980. Fellow American Association for the Advancement of Science, New York Acad. Sciences, Society Gerontology; hon. member Acad. Dermatology and Syphilology, Society Investigative Dermatology (president 1969, recipient Stephen Rothman award 1972, ann. William Montagna lecturer 1975—), Sigma Xi (President 1960-62). Research in biology mammalian skin with emphasis on primates. Office: ORPRC 505 Northwest 185th Avenue Beaverton Oregon 97006

MONTAGU, ASHLEY, anthropologist, social biologist; born London, June 28, 1905; came to United States, 1927, 30; naturalized, 1940; son of Charles Ashley and Mary (Plot) M.; married Helen Marjorie Peakes, September 18, 1931; children—Audrey, Barbara, Geoffrey. Student, University London, 1922-25, University Florence, 1928-29; Doctor of Philosophy, Columbia University, 1937; Doctor of Science (honorary), Grinnell College, 1967, University North Carolina, 1987; Doctor of Literature (honorary), Ursinus College, 1972. Research associate Brit. Mus. Natural History, London, 1926-27; curator physical anthropology Wellcome Historical Medical Mus., 1929-30; assistant professor anatomy New York University, 1931-38; associate professor anatomy Hahnemann Medical College and Hospital, Philadelphia, 1938-49; chairman department anthropology Rutgers University, 1949-55; visiting lecturer department social sci. Harvard, 1945; senior lecturer Veteran's Administration Postgrad. Training Program Psychiatry and Neurology, 1946—;

lecturer New School Social Research, 1931-59; visiting professor University Del., 1955; Regents professor, University California, Santa Barbara, 1962; lecturer Princeton University, 1978-83; director Institute Natural Philosophy, 1979-81; director research New Jersey committee physical devel. and health, 1953-57; family affairs editor, anthropological adv. NBC-TV, 1954; chairman Anisfield-Wolf Award Committee, 1954—; Responsible for drafting statement on race for United Nations Educational, Scientific and Cultural Organization, 1949-50, consultant, 1949; a drafter National Science Foundation Bill, 1946-47; Hon. corr. member anthropological societies Paris and Florence. Produced, financed, wrote and directed: film One World or None for, National Commn. on Atomic Information and Am. Federation Science Workers, 1946; Author: Coming into Being Among the Australian Aborigines, 1937, 2d edition, 1974, Man's Most Dangerous Myth: The Fallacy of Race, 1942, 5th edition, 1974, Edward Tyson, M.D., F.R.S., (1650-1708): and the rise of human and comparative anatomy in England, 1943, Introduction to Physical Anthropology, 1945, 3d edition, 1960, Adolescent Sterility, 1946, On Being Human, 1950, 2d edition, 1966, On Being Intelligent, 1951, Statement on Race, 1952, 3d edition, 1972, Darwin, Competition and Cooperation, 1952, The Natural Superiority of Women, 1953, 2d edition, 1974, The Direction of Human Development, 1955, 2d edition, 1970, Immortality, 1955, Biosocial Nature of Man, 1956, Anthropology And Human Nature, 1957, Man: His First Million Years, 1957, The Reproductive Development of the Female, 1957, 3d edition, 1979, Education and Human Relations, 1958, The Cultured Man, 1958, Human Heredity, 1959, 2d edition, 1963, Handbook of Anthropometry, 1960, Man in Process, 1961, Prenatal Influences, 1962, The Humanization of Man, 1962, Race, Science, and Humanity, 1963, The Dolphin in History, 1963, Life Before Birth, 1964, 2d edition, 1978, The Science of Man, 1964, (with E. Steen) Anatomy and Physiology, 1959, 2d edition, 1983, (with C. L. Brace) Man's Evolution, 1965, The Idea of Race, 1965, The Human Revolution, 1965, Up the Ivy, 1966, The American Way of Life, 1967, The Anatomy of Swearing, 1967, (with E. Darling) The Prevalance of Nonsense, 1967, Man Observed, 1968, Man, His First Two Million Years, 1957, 2d edition, 1969, Sex, Man, and Society, 1969, the Ignorance of Certainty, 1970, Immortality, Religion, and Morals, 1971, Touching, 1971, 3d edition, 1986, (with M. Levitan) Textbook of Human Genetics, 1971, 2d edition, 1977, The Elephant Man, 1971, 2d edition, 1979, (with S.S. Snyder) Man and the Computer, 1972, The Nature of Human Aggression, 1976, (with C.L. Brace) Human Evolution, 1977, (with Floyd Matson) The Human Connection, 1979, (with Floyd Matson) The Dehumanization of Man, 1983, Growing Young, 1981, The Peace of the World, 1986, Living and Loving, 1986, The World of Humanity, 1987; editor National Historical Society Series, Classics of Anthropology; adv. editor Science, Tech. and Humanities; anthrology editor Isis, 1936-56, publications editor, 1937—. Guardsman with Welsh Guards, 1919. Recipient 1st prize Morris Chaim prize Centennary 2d District Dental Society, New York, 1936, Chicago Forum Literary contest, 1943; Distinguished Service awards

Association Childbirth at Home International, 1970, Am. Anthrop. Association, 1984, Phi Beta Kappa, 1985, Institute Human Behavior, 1986, National Association Parents and Professionals Safe Alternatives in Childbirth, 1986. Fellow American Association for the Advancement of Science; member International Society Study of Race Relations, Am. Association Anatomists, Am. Society Study of Child Growth and Devel., Am. Association Maternal and Child Health, International Association Human Biologists, Sigma Xi. Expert witness on legal, sci. problems relating to race and anthrop. matters, 1930. Home: 321 Cherry Hill Road Princeton New Jersey 08540

MOORE, C. BRADLEY, chemistry educator; born Boston, December 7, 1939; son of Charles Walden and Dorothy (Lutz) M.; married Penelope Williamson Percival, August 27, 1960; children—Megan Bradley, Scott Woodward. Bachelor of Arts, Harvard University, 1960; Doctor of Philosophy, University California, Berkeley, 1963. Assistant professor chemistry University California, Berkeley, 1963-68, associate professor; 1968-72, professor; 1972—, vice chairman department; 1971-75, chairman department chemistry; 1982-86, dean College of Chemistry; 1988—; visiting professor Faculté des Sciences, Paris, 1970, 75, Institute for Molecular Sci., Okazaki, Japan, 1979, Fudan University, Shanghai, Peoples Republic China, 1979, Joint Institute for Laboratory Astrophysics, University Colorado, Boulder, 1981-82; adv. professor Fudan University, Shanghai, 1988—. Editor: Chemical and Biochemical Applications of Lasers; contributor articles to professional journals.

Fellow Alfred P. Sloan Foundation, 1968, Guggenheim Foundation, 1969; recipient Coblentz award, 1973, E.O. Lawrence award 1986, Lippincott award, 1987, 1st Inter-Am. Photochem. Society award., 1988. Fellow Am. Physical Society, American Association for the Advancement of Science; member Am. Chemical Society (past chairman division phys. chemistry, California section award 1977), National Acad. Sciences. Avocation: cycling. Home: 936 Oxford St Berkeley California 94707 Office: U California Department Chemistry 211 Lewis Hall Berkeley California 94720

MOORE, SALLY FALK, anthropology educator; born New York City, January 18, 1924; daughter of Henry Charles and Mildred (Hymanson) Falk; married Cresap Moore, July 14, 1951; children: Penelope, Nicola. Bachelor of Arts, Barnard College, 1943; Bachelor of Laws, Columbia University, 1945, Doctor of Philosophy, 1957. Assistant professor University Southern California, Los Angeles, 1963-65, associate professor; 1965-70, professor; 1970-77; professor University of California at Los Angeles, 1977-81; professor anthropology Harvard University, Cambridge, Massachusetts, 1981—; dean Grad. School Arts and Sciences Harvard University, 1985—. Author: Power and Property in Inca Peru, 1958 (Ansley Prize 1957), Law as Process, 1978, Social Facts and Fabrications, 1986. Research grantee Social Sci. Research Council, New York City, 1968-69; research grantee National Science Foundation, Washington, 1972-75, 79-80, Wenner Gren Foundation, 1983. Fellow Am. Anthropological Association, Royal Anthropological Institute; member

Association Political and Legal Anthropology (president 1983), Am. Ethnological Society (president 1987—). Democrat. Office: Harvard U Masters Residence Dunster House 935 Memorial Dr Cambridge Massachusetts 02138

MORAWETZ, CATHLEEN SYNGE, mathematician; born Toronto, Ontario, Canada, May 5, 1923; came to United States, 1945, naturalized, 1950; daughter of John Lighton and Elizabeth Eleanor Mabel (Allen) Synge; married Herbert Morawetz, October 28, 1945; children: Pegeen Ann, John Synge, Lida Joan, Nancy Babette. Bachelor of Arts, University Toronto, 1945; Master of Science, Massachusetts Institute of Technology, 1946; Doctor of Philosophy, New York University, 1951; honorary degrees, Eastern Michigan University, 1980, Smith College, 1982, Brown University, 1982, Princeton University, 1986. Research associate Courant Institute, New York University, 1952-57, assistant professor math.; 1957-60, associate professor; 1960-65, professor; 1965—, associate director; 1978-84, director; 1984—; director NCR Corp., 1978— ; trustee Sloan Foundation, 1980—. Editor: Journal Math Anal Appl., Communications in PDE, Advanced Applicationa Math.; contributor articles on applications of partial differential equations, especially transonic flow and scattering theory, to professional journals. Guggenheim fellow, 1967, 79; Office Naval Research grantee. Fellow American Association for the Advancement of Science; member Am. Math. Society (trustee), Am. Acad. Arts & Sciences, Society Industrial and Applied Math. Office:

251 Mercer St New York New York 10012

MORFORPOULOS, VASSILIS CONSTANTINOS PANTELEIMON, technical and scientific consultant; born Athens, Greece, October 22, 1937; came to United States, 1955, naturalized, 1963; son of Constantinos Vassilis and Dina Michael (Constantinou) M.; married Irini-Nike Sarlis, December 31, 1962; 1 son, Constantine Alexander Michael, III. Bachelor of Science, Purdue University, 1958, Master of Science, 1960; Doctor of Science, Columbia University, 1964. Research associate Purdue University, 1958-60; research and devel. engineer United States Steel Corp., 1961, Atomic Energy Commission, 1963; instructor City University New York, 1961-63; research associate, fellow Columbia University, 1960-65; tech. director Am. Standards Testing Bureau, Incorporated, New York City, 1966—; also head laboratory Am. Standards Testing Bureau, Incorporated; director Atlantic X-Ray, Incorporated, Philadelphia, Architectural Research Corp., Philadelphia, Am. Polymer Concrete Corp., Augusta, Georgia, E.B.T.A., Incorporated, Athens; board of directors Franklin Research International, Incorporated, Philadelphia; member transportation research board National Research Council; consultant in field. Contributor articles to professional journals. Recipient J. Starr award Purdue University, 1959; William Campbell fellow, 1960-62; H. Krumb fellow, 1960-62; Am. Iron and Steel Institute fellow, 1962-64. Fellow Am. Institute Chemists; member Association Cons. Chemists and Chemical Engineers, American Institute of Mining, Metallurgy and

Petroleum Engineers, Am. Ordnance Association, Am. Society Metals, Am. Society Safety Enfrs., Am. Society Non-Destructive Testing, American Society for Testing and Materials, American Association for the Advancement of Science, Am. Society Engineering Education, Brit. Iron and Steel Institute, Electro-Chem. Socicty, International Chemical Union, National Fire Protection Association, New York Acad. Sciences, Society International Devel., Society Automotive Engineers, Society Aerospace Materials and Process Engineers, Society Plastics Engineers, Am. Welding Society. Patentee in field. Office: 40 Water St New York New York 10004

MORRISON, PHILIP, physicist, educator; born Somerville, New Jersey, November 7, 1915; married Phyllis Singer. Bachelor of Science, Carnegie Institute Tech., 1936; Doctor of Philosophy in Theoretical Physics, University California, Berkeley, 1940; Doctor of Science (honorary), Case Western Reserve University, Rutgers University, Denison University, Amherst College, Carleton College. Instructor physics San Francisco State College, 1941, University Illinois, 1941-42; physicist Metallurgical Laboratory University Chicago, 1943-44; physicist, group leader Los Alamos Sci. Laboratory, University California, 1944-46; from associate professor to professor physics Cornell University, Ithaca, New York, 1946-65; professor physics Massachusetts Institute of Technology, Cambridge, 1965—. Author: Cosmic Rays, 1961, My Father's Watch: Aspects of the Physical World, 1969; author: Winding Down: The Price of Defense, 1979, (with others) Powers of Ten: The Relative Size of Things in the Universe, 1982; editor: The Search for Extraterrestrial Intelligence, 1977; author (with Phylis Morrison) public television series, The Ring of Truth, 1987. Recipient Pregel prize, 1955, Babson prize, 1957, Oerstad medal, 1965; first recipient Gemant Award (Am. Institute Physics), 1987. Member National Acad. Sci., Am. Physical Society, Am. Astronomical Society, Federation Am. Scientists (chairman 1972-76). Office: Massachusetts Institute of Technology Department Physics Cambridge Massachusetts 02139

MORROW, WALTER EDWIN, JR., electrical engineer, university laboratory adminstrator; born Springfield, Massachusetts, July 24, 1928; son of Walter Edwin and Mary Elizabeth (Ganley) M.; married Janice Lila Lombard, February 25, 1951; children—Clifford E., Gregory A., Carolyn F. Bachelor of Science, Massachusetts Institute of Technology, 1949, Master of Science, 1951. Member staff Lincoln Laboratory, Massachusetts Institute of Technology, Lexington, Massachusetts, 1951-55, group leader; 1956-65; head div. communications Massachusetts Institute of Technology Lincoln Laboratory, 1966-68, assistant director; 1968-71, associate director; 1972-77, director; 1977—. Contributor articles to professional publications. Recipient award for outstanding achievement President M.I.T., 1963, Edwin Howard Armstrong Achievement award Institute of Electrical and Electronic Engineers Communications Society, 1976. Fellow Institute of Electrical and Electronics Engineers, National Acad. Engineering. Patentee synchronous satellite, electric power plant using electrolytic cell-fuel cell combination.

Office: Post Office Box 73 Lexington Massachusetts 02173

MÖSSBAUER, RUDOLF L., physicist, educator; born Munich, January 31, 1929; son of Ludwig and Erna M.; 3 children. Educated, Technische Hochschule, Munich; Doctor of Science (honorary), Oxford University, 1973, University Leicester, England, 1975; Doctor honoris causa, University Grenoble, France, 1974. Research assistant Max-Planck Institute, Heidelberg, Federal Republic Germany, 1955-57; research fellow Technische Hochschule, Munich, 1958-60; research fellow California Institute Tech., 1960, senior research fellow; 1961, professor physics; 1961; professor experimental physics Tech. University Munich, 1964-72, 77—; director Institute Max von Laue, Grenoble, France and German-French-Brit. High Flux Reactor, 1972-77. Author publications on recoilless nuclear resonance absorption and neutrino physics. Recipient Research Corp. award, 1960; Röntgen prize University Giessen, 1961; Elliott Cresson medal Franklin Institute, Philadelphia, 1961; Nobel prize for physics, 1961; Guthrie medal Institute Physics (London), 1974; Lomonos-sovmedal Acad. Sci. Union of Soviet Socialist Republics, 1984; Einstein medal Albert Einstein Society, Bern, 1986. Member Deutsche Physikalische Gesellschaft, Deutsche Gesellschaft der Naturforscher, Leopoldina, Am. Physical Society, European Physical Society, Indian Acad. Sciences, Am. Acad. Sci. (foreign), Am. Acad. Arts Sciences (fgn), National Acad. Sciences (foreign associate), Bavarian Acad. Sciences, Academia Nazionale dei XL Roma, Pontifical Acad. Sciences, Acad. Sci. Union of the Soviet Socialist Republics (foreign). Office: Tech U Munich, Department Physics, 8046 Garching Federal Republic of Germany

MOSTELLER, FREDERICK, mathematical statistician, educator; born Clarksburg, West Virginia, December 24, 1916; son of William Roy and Helen (Kelley) M.; married Virginia Gilroy, May 17, 1941; children: William, Gale. Bachelor of Science, Carnegie Institute Tech. (now Carnegie-Mellon University), 1938, Master of Science, 1939, Doctor of Science (honorary), 1974; Master of Arts, Princeton University, 1942, Doctor of Philosophy, 1946; Doctor of Science (honorary), University Chicago, 1973, Wesleyan University, 1983; Doctor of Social Scis. (honorary), Yale University, 1981. Instructor math. Princeton University, 1942-44; research associate Office Pub. Opinion Research, 1942-44; special consultant research branch War Department, 1942-43; research mathematician Statistical Research Group, Princeton, applied math. panel National Devel. and Research Council, 1944-46; member faculty Harvard University, 1946—, professor math. statistics; 1951—, chairman department statistics; 1957-69, 75-77, chairman department biostats.; 1977-81, chairman department health policy and management; 1981-87, Roger I. Lee professor; 1978-87; director Tech. Assessment Group, 1987—; vice chairman President's Commission on Federal Statistics, 1970-71; member National Adv. Council Equality of Educational Opportunity, 1973-78, National Sci. Board Commission on Pre-coll. Education in Math., Sci. and Tech., 1982-83; Fund for Advancement of Education fellow, 1954-55; national teacher NBC's

Continental Class-room TV course in probability and statistics, 1960-61; fellow Center Advanced Study Behavioral Sciences, 1962-63, board of directors, 1980-86; Guggenheim fellow, 1969-70; Miller research professor University California at Berkeley, 1974-75; Hitchcock Foundation lecturer University California, 1985. Co-author: Gauging Public Opinion (editor Hadley Cantril), 1944, Sampling Inspection, 1948, The Pre-election Polls, 1948, 1949, Stochastic Models for Learning, 1955, Probability with Statistical Applications, 1961, Inference and Disputed Authorship, The Federalist, 1964, The National Halothane Study, 1969, Statistics: A Guide to the Unknown, 1972, On Equality of Educational Opportunity, 1972, Sturdy Statistics, 1973, 3d edition, 1988, Statistics By Example, 1973, Cost, Risks and Benefits of Surgery, 1977, Data Analysis and Regression, 1977, Statistics and Public Policy, 1977, Data for Decisions, 1982, Understanding Robust and Exploratory Data Analysis, 1983, Biostatistics in Clinical Medicine, 1983, 2d. edition 1986, Beginning Statistics with Data Analysis, 1983, Exploring Data Tables, Trends and Shapes, 1985, Medical Uses of Statistics, 1986, Quality of Life and Technology Assessment, 1989; author articles in field. Trustee Russell Sage Foundation; member board National Opinion Research Center, 1962-66. Recipient Outstanding Statistician award Chicago chapter Am. Statis. Association, 1971, Myrdal prize Evaluation Research Society, 1978, Paul F. Lazarsfeld prize Council Applied Social Research, 1979, R.A. Fisher award Committee of President's of Statis. Socs., 1987,

Medallion of Ctrs. for Disease Control, 1988. Fellow American Association for the Advancement of Science (chairman section U 1973, director 1974-78, president 1980, chairman board 1981), Institute Math. Statistics (president 1974-75), Am. Statistical Association (vice president 1962-64, president 1967, Samuel S. Wilks medal 1986), Social Sci. Research Council (chairman board directors 1966-68), Math. Social Sci. Board (acad. governing board 1962-67), Am. Acad. Arts and Sciences (council 1986-88), Royal Statistical Society (hon.); member Am. Philosophical Society (council 1986-88), International Statistical Institute (vice president 1986-88, pres.-elect 1989), Math. Association Am., Psychometric Society (president 1957-58), Institute Medicine of National Acad. Sciences (council 1978), National Acad. Sciences, Biometric Society. Office: 1 Oxford St Cambridge Massachusetts 02138

MOTT, SIR NEVILL (FRANCIS), physicist, educator, author; born Leeds, England, September 30, 1905; son of C.F. and Lilian Mary (Reynolds) M.; married Ruth Horder, March 21, 1930; children: Elizabeth, Alice. Master of Arts, St. John's College, Cambridge, England, 1929; Doctor of Science (honorary), Universities of Sheffield, London, Louvain, Grenoble, Paris, Poitiers, Bristol, Universities of Ottawa, Liverpool, Reading, Warwick, Lancaster, Heriot Watt, Bordeaux, Universities of St. Andrews, Essex, Stuttgart, Sussex, William and Mary, Marburg, Universities of Bar Ilan, Lille, Rome, Lisbon; Doctor Tech., Linköping. Lecturer math. Cambridge University, 1930-33, Cavendish professor experimental physics; 1954-

71; master Gonville and Caius College, 1959-66; professor physics University Bristol, 1933-54, also director H.H. Wills Physical Laboratory, 1948-54; Page-Barbour lecturer University Virginia, 1956. Author: An Outline of Wave Mechanics, 1930; (with H.Southwest Massey) The Theory of Atomic Collisions, 1933; (with H. Jones) The Theory of the Properties of Metals and Alloys, 1936; (with R. W. Gurney) Electronic Processes in Ionic Crystals, 1940; Wave (with I. N. Snedden) Wave Mechanics and Its Applications, 1948; Elements of Wave Mechanics, 1952; Atomic Structure and the Strength of Metals, 1956; (with E. A. Davis) Electronic Processes in Noncrystalline 1971, 2d edit, 1979; Elements of Quantum Mechanics, 1972; Metal-Insulator Transitions, 1974; (autobiography) A Life in Science, 1986. Member central adv. council Ministry of Education, 1956-59; chairman committee physics education Nuffield Foundation, 1965-75. Sci. adviser to Anti Aircraft Command, also supt. theoretical research in armaments Armament Research Department, World War II. Decorated knight bachelor; recipient Nobel prize for physics, 1977. Fellow Royal Society (Hughes medalist 1941, Royal medal 1953, Copley medal 1972), Physical Society of Great Britain (president 1956-58); member National Acad. Sciences, Am. Acad. Arts and Sciences (corr.), Institute Physics (hon. fellow), International Union Pure and Applied Physics (president 1951-57), Modern Langs. Association (president 1955), Société Française de Physique (hon.).

MOTTELSON, BEN R., physicist; born Chicago, July 9, 1926; naturalized Danish citizen, 1971; son of Goodman and Georgia (Blum) M.; married Nancy Jane Reno, 1948 (deceased 1975); 3 children. Bachelor of Science, Purdue University, 1947; Doctor of Philosophy, Harvard University, 1950; honorary degrees, Purdue University, University Heidelberg, Federal Republic Germany. Fellow Institute Theoretical Physics, Copenhagen, 1950-51, United States Atomic Energy Commission fellow; 1951-53; with theoretical study group European Organization for Nuclear Research, Copenhagen; professor Nordic Institute for Theoretical Atomic Physics, Copenhagen, 1957—; physicist Bohr Institute; board of directors Nordita; visiting professor University California, Berkeley, 1959. Author: Nuclear Structure, vol 1, 1969, volume 2 (with A. Bohr), 1975; numerous other publications in field. Recipient Nobel prize for physics, 1975. Member National Acad. Sciences (foreign associate). Address: Nordita, Blegdamsvej 17, DK-2100 Copenhagen Denmark

MOULDER, JAMES EDWIN, civil engineer; born Roach, Missouri, August 29, 1926; son of Cyrus B. and Lela (Morgan) M.; married Eldora Rhodes, December 19, 1954; children: Robin Edwin, Bradley James. Bachelor of Science in Civil Engineering, University Missouri, 1953, Master of Science, 1955. Registered professional engineer, Missouri. Structural engineer Boeing Airplane Company, Wichita, 1953; research engineer University Missouri, Columbia, 1953-56; consultant engineer Smith & Gillespie (engineers), Jacksonville, Florida, 1956-60; with Booker Associates, Incorporated, St. Louis, 1961—; executive vice president, then president Booker Associates

Incorporated, St. Louis, 1968-80, chairman board, president; 1977-80, chief executive officer; 1980—, also director; past chairman adv. council College Engineering, University Missouri, Columbia, 1984—. Board of directors Downtown St. Louis, 1981—, St. Louis County Library, 1988—, Hawthorn Foundation, 1983—; member Missouri Coordinating Board Higher Education, 1978-82; member committee on access to engring. education in urban areas University Missouri, 1988. Served with United States Military Corps, 1945-46; served with Army of the United States, 1950-52. Recipient Missouri honor award, 1977, Faculty Alumni award University Missouri, 1979, Distinguished Service award, 1982. Fellow Am. Cons. Engineers Council; member National Society Professional Engineers (joint NSPE/Profl. Engineers in Private Practice merit award 1988), American Society of Civil Engineers, National Association Housing and Redevel. Officials, Missouri Society Professional Engineers (treasurer 1981-82, vice president 1983-84 president 1984-85, Engineer of Year award 1983), Missouri Planning Association, Cons. Engineers Council Missouri (president 1975-76), others. Clubs: St. Louis Engrs. (award merit 1981), Rotary. Home: 13433 Conway Road Saint Louis Missouri 63141 Office: 1139 Olive St Saint Louis Missouri 63101

MOW, VAN C., researcher and engineering educator; born Chengdu, China, January 10, 1939. Bachelor Aeronautical Engineering, Rensselaer Polytechnic Institute, 1962, Doctor of Philosophy, 1966. Member tech. staff Bell Telephone Laboratories, Whippany, New Jersey, 1968-69; associate professor mechanics Rensselaer Polytechnic Institute, Troy, New York, 1969-76, professor mechanics and biomed. engineering; 1976-82, John A. Clark and Edward T. Crossan professor engineering; 1982-86; professor mechanical engineering and orthopedic bioengring. Columbia University, New York City, 1986—; director Orthopedic Research Laboratory, Columbia-Presbyn. Medical Center, New York City, 1986—; visiting member Courant Institute Math. Sci., New York University, 1967-68; visiting professor Harvard University, Boston, 1976-77; chairman orthopaedics and musculoskeletal study section National Institutes of Health, Bethesda, Maryland, 1982-84; hon. professor Chengdu University Sci. Tech., 1981, Shanhai Jiao Tong University, 1987; consultant in field. Associate editor: Journal Biomech., 1981—, Journal Biomech. Engr., 1979-86; edition adv. board chairman Journal Orthopedic Research, 1983—; contributor numerous articles to professional journals. Founder Gordon Research Conference on Bioengring. and Orthopedic Sci., 1980. NATO sr. fellow, 1978; recipient William H. Wiley Distinguished Faculty award Rensselaer Polytechnic Institute, 1981; Japan Society for Promotion Sci. Fellow, 1986, Fogarty Senior International fellow, 1987; Alza distinguished lecturer Biomed. Engineering Society, 1987; H.R. Lissner award American Society of Mechanical Engineers, 1987. Fellow American Society of Mechanical Engineers (chairman biomechanics division 1984-85, Melville medal 1982); member Orthopaedic Research Society (president 1982-83), Am. Society Biomechanics (founding), International Society Biorheology, United States National

Committee on Biomechanics (sec.-treas. 1985—). Office: Columbia-Presbyn Med Center 630 W 168th St New York New York 10032

MUELLER, GEORGE E., corporation executive; born St. Louis, July 16, 1918; married Maude Rosenbaum (divorced); children: Karen, Jean; married Darla Hix, 1978. Bachelor of Science in Electrical Engineering, Missouri School Mines, 1939; Master of Science in Electrical Engineering, Purdue University, 1940; Doctor of Philosophy in Physics, Ohio State University, 1951; honorary degrees, Wayne State University, New Mexico State University, University Missouri, 1964, Purdue University, Ohio State University, 1965. Member tech. staff Bell Telephone Laboratories, 1940-46; professor electrical engineering Ohio State University, 1946-57; consultant electronics Ramo-Wooldridge, Incorporated, 1955-57; from director electronic laboratory to vice president research and devel. Space Tech. Laboratories, 1958-62; associate administrator for manned space flight National Aeronautics and Space Administration, 1963-69; corporate officer, senior vice president General Dynamics Corp., New York City, 1969-71; chairman, president System Devel. Corp., Santa Monica, California, 1971-83, chairman, chief executive officer; 1983; senior vice president Burroughs Corp., 1981-83; president Jojoba Propagation Labs, from 1981, George East Mueller Corp., 1984—, International Acad. Astronautics, 1983—. Author: (with E.R. Spangler) Communications Satellites. Recipient 3 Distinguished Service medals National Aeronautics and Space Administration, 1966, 68, 69; Eugen Sanger award, 1970; National Medal Sci., 1970; National Transp. award, 1979. Fellow American Association for the Advancement of Science, Institute of Electrical and Electronics Engineers, American Institute of Aeronautics and Astronautics (Goddard medal 1983, Sperry award 1986), Am. Physical Society, Am. Astronautical Society (Space Flight award), Am. Geophysical Union, Brit. Interplanetary Society; member International Acad. Astronautics (president 1982—), National Acad. Engineering, New York Acad. Sciences. Patentee in field. Home: Santa Barbara California Office: Post Office Box 5856 Santa Barbara California 93150

MUHLENBRUCH, CARL W., civil engineer; born Decatur, Illinois, November 21, 1915; son of Carl William and Clara (Theobald) M.; married Agnes M. Kringel, November 22, 1939; children: Phyllis Elaine (Mrs. Richard B. Wallace), Joan Carol (Mrs. Frederick B. Wenk). Bachelor of Civil Engineering, University Illinois, 1937, Civil Engineer, 1945; Master of Civil Engineering, Carnegie Institute Tech., 1943. Research engineer Aluminum Research Laboratories, Pittsburgh, 1937-39; consultant engineering 1939-50; member faculty Carnegie Institute Tech., 1939-48; associate professor civil engineering Northwestern University, 1948-54; president TEC-SEARCH, Incorporated (formerly Educational and Tech. Consultants Incorporated), 1954-67, chairman board; 1967—; President Professional Centers building Corp., 1961-77. Author: Experimental Mechanics and Properties of Materials; Contributor articles engring. publications. Treasurer, board of directors Concordia College Foundation; director Missouri Lutheran Synod, 1965-77, vice chairman 1977-79.

Recipient Stanford E. Thompson award, 1945. Member Am. Econ. Devel. Council (certified indsl. developer), Am. Society Engineering Education (editor Educational Aids in Engineering), National Society Professional Engineers, American Society of Civil Engineers, Sigma Xi, Tau Beta Phi, Omicron Delta Kappa. Club: University (Evanston). Lodge: Rotary (dist. gov. 1980-81, mem. service projects Ghana and the Bahamas). Office: Tec-Search Incorporated 1000 Skokie Boulevard Wilmette Illinois 60091

MÜLLER, K. ALEX, physicist, researcher; born April 20, 1927. Doctor of Philosophy in Physics, Swiss Federal Institute Tech., 1958; Doctor of Science (honorary), University Geneva, 1987, Tech. University Munich, 1987, University Studi di Pavia, Italy, 1987. Project manager Battelle Institute, Geneva, 1958-63; lecturer University Zurich, Switzerland, 1962—, titular professor physics; 1970—; researcher solid-state physics International Business Machines Corporation Zurich Research Laboratory, Rüschlikon, Switzerland, 1963-73, manager department physics; 1973-82, fellow; 1982-85; researcher Switzerland, 1985—. Contributor over 200 articles to tech. publications. Recipient Marcel-Benoist Foundation prize, 1986, Nobel prize in physics, 1987, (with J. Georg Bednorz) Fritz London Memorial award, 1987, Dannie Heineman prize Acad. Sciences Göttingen, Federal Republic of Germany, 1987, Robert Wichard Pohl prize German Physical Society, 1987, Europhysics prize Hewlett-Packard Company, 1988. Fellow Am. Physical Society (International prize for new materials research 1988); member European Physical Society (member ferroelectricity group), Swiss Physical Society, Zurich Physical Society (president 1968-69), Groupement Ampère. Office: International Business Machines Corporation Zurich Research Lab, Saumerstrasse 4, CH-8803 Ruschlikon Switzerland

MULLINS, WILLIAM WILSON, physical metallurgist; born Boonville, Indiana, March 5, 1927; son of Thomas Clinton and Ruth (Wilson) M.; married June Bonner, June 26, 1948; children—William Wilson, Oliver Clinton, Timothy Bonner, Garrick Russell. Bachelor of Philosophy, University Chicago, 1949, Master of Science in Physics, 1951, Doctor of Philosophy, 1955. Research physicist, then adv. physicist Westinghouse Research Laboratories, 1955-60; associate professor metallurgical engineering Carnegie Mellon University Pittsburgh, 1960-63, professor, head department; 1963-66, dean engineering and sci., professor applied sci.; 1970—; Chairman physical metallurgy Gordon Conference, 1966. Author articles in field. Served with United States Naval Reserve, 1944-46. Fulbright and Guggenheim fellowships University Paris, France, 1961-62. Member Am. Institute Metallurgical Engineers (Mathewson gold medal 1963), Am. Institute Mining, Metallurgical and Petroleum Engineers, National Acad. Sciences, Am. Physical Society, Am. Society Engineering Education, New York Acad. Sciences, American Civil Liberties Union, Sigma Xi, Alpha Sigma Nu. Club: Unitarian. Address: Department Applied Sci Carnegie-Mellon U 5000 Forbes Avenue Pittsburgh Pennsylvania 15213

MUMFORD, DAVID BRYANT, mathematics educator; born Worth,

Sussex, England, June 11, 1937; came to United States, 1940; son of William Bryant and Grace (Schiott) M.; married Erika Jentsch, June 27, 1959; children: Stephen, Peter, Jeremy, Suchitra. Bachelor of Arts, Harvard University, 1957, Doctor of Philosophy, 1961; Doctor of Science (honorary), University Warwick, 1983. Junior fellow Harvard University, 1958-61, associate professor; 1962-66, professor math.; 1966—, chairman department math; 1981-84. Author: Geometric Invariant Theory, 1965, Abelian Varieties, 1970, Introduction to Algebraic Geometry, 1976. Recipient Fields medal International Congress Mathematicians, 1974; MacArthur Foundation fellow, 1987—. Fellow Tata Institute (hon.); member National Acad. Sciences, Am. Acad. Arts and Sciences. Home: 26 Gray St Cambridge Massachusetts 02138 Office: 1 Oxford St Cambridge Massachusetts 02138

MUNK, WALTER HEINRICH, geophysics educator; born Vienna, Austria, October 19, 1917; came to United States, 1933; married Edith Kendall Horton, June 20, 1953; children: Edith, Kendall. Bachelor of Science, California Institute Tech., 1939, Master of Science, 1940; Doctor of Philosophy, University California, 1947; Doctor of Philosophy (honorary), University Bergen, Norway, 1975, Cambridge (England) University, 1986. From assistant professor to professor geophysics Scripps Institute Oceanography University California San Diego, La Jolla, 1947—. Contributor over 180 articles to professional journals. Recipient Gold medal Royal Astronomical Society, 1968, Capt. Robert Dexter Conrad award Department Navy, 1978; named California Scientist of Year, California Mus. Sci. and Industry, 1969; fellow Guggenheim Foundation, 1948, 55, 62, Overseas Foundation, 1962, 81-82, Fulbright Foundation, 1981-82, Senior Queen's Foundation, 1978, National Medal Sci., 1985. Fellow Am. Geophysical Union (Maurice Ewing medal 1976), American Association for the Advancement of Science, Am. Meteorological Society (Sverdrup Gold medal 1966), Accoustical Society Am., Marine Tech. Society; member National Acad. Sciences (chairman Agassiz medal 1976), Am. Philosophical Society, Royal Society London (foreign member), Deutsche Akademie der Naturforscher Leopoldina, Am. Acad. Arts and Sciences (Arthur L. Day medal 1965), Am. Geological Society.

MUROFF, LAWRENCE ROSS, physician; born Philadelphia, December 26, 1942; son of John M. and Carolyn (Kramer) M.; married Carol R. Savoy, July 12, 1969; children: Michael Bruce, Julie Anne. Bachelor of Arts cum laude, Dartmouth College, 1964, Bachelor of Medical Science, 1965; Doctor of Medicine cum laude, Harvard University, 1967. Diplomate Am. Board Radiology, Am. Board Nuclear Medicine. Intern Boston City Hospital, Harvard, 1968; resident in radiology Columbia Presbyn. Medical Center, New York City, 1970-73, chief resident; 1973; instructor, assistant radiologist 1973-74; director department nuclear medicine, computed tomography and magnetic resonance imaging University Community Hospital, Tampa, Florida, 1974—; clinical assistant professor radiology University South Florida, 1974-78, clinical associate professor, 1978-82, clinical professor, 1982—;

clinical professor radiology University Florida, 1988—. Contributor articles to professional journals. Served to lieutenant commander United States Public Health Service, 1968-70. Fellow Am. College Nuclear Medicine (distinguished fellow, Florida del.), Am. College Nuclear Physicians (regents 1976-78, pres.-elect 1978, president 1979, fellow 1980), Am. College Radiology (councilor 1979-80, chancellor 1981-87, chairman commission on nuclear medicine 1981-87, fellow 1981); member Am. Association Acad. Chief Residents Radiology (chairman 1973), American Medical Association, Boylston Society, Florida Association Nuclear Physicians (president 1976), Florida Medical Association, Hillsborough County Medical Association, Radiological Society North America, Society Nuclear Medicine (council 1975—, trustee 1980-84, 86-89, president Southeastern chapter 1983, vice chairman correlative imaging council 1983), Florida Radiological Society (executive committee 1976—, treasurer 1984, secretary 1985, vice president 1986, president elect 1987, president 1988—), West Coast Radiological Society, Society Magazine Resonance Imaging (board directors 1988-89, chairman educational program 1988), Phi Beta Kappa, Alpha Omega Alpha. Office: 13550 N 31st St Tampa Florida 33612

MURPHY, ROBERT EARL, scientist, government agency administrator; born Yakima, Washington, September 24, 1941; son of William Barry and Caroline Norbeth (Boyd) M.; married Nancy Jane Hybner, June 26, 1965; children: Kimberly Elizabeth, Mark Hybner. Bachelor of Science in Math, Worcester (Massachusetts) Polytechnic Institute, 1963; Master of

Arts in Astronomy, Georgetown University, 1966; Doctor of Philosophy, Case Western Reserve University, 1969. Astronomer United States Army Map Service, 1965-66; assistant professor astronomy Institute Astronomy, University Hawaii, 1969-73; executive director Maryland Acad. Sciences, Baltimore, 1973-76; president Scientia Incorporated, Baltimore, 1976—; chief planetary atmospheres programs and program scientist Galileo project National Aeronautics and Space Administration, Washington, 1977-81; head earth resources branch, project scientist heat capacity mapping mission Goddard Space Flight Center, Greenbelt, Maryland, 1981-84; chief land processes branch National Aeronautics and Space Administration Headquarters, Washington, 1984—. Author curriculum materials, articles in field. Member American Association for the Advancement of Science, Am. Astronomical Society, Am. Geophysical Union. Republican. Baptist. Office: NASA Hdqrs Land Processes Br Code EE Washington District of Columbia 20546

MURRAY, JOSEPH JAMES, JR., zoologist, educator; born Lexington, Virginia, March 13, 1930; son of Joseph James and Jane Dickson (Vardell) M.; married Elizabeth Hickson, August 24, 1957; children—Joseph James III, Alison Joan, William Lister. Bachelor of Science, Davidson College, 1951; Bachelor of Arts, Oxford University, England, 1954, Master of Arts, 1957, Doctor of Philosophy, 1962. Instructor biology Washington & Lee University, Lexington, Virginia, 1956-58; assistant professor biology University Virginia, Charlottesville, 1962-67, associate professor; 1967-73, professor; 1973-

77, Samuel Miller professor biology; 1977—, chairman department biology; 1984-87; co-director Mountain Lake Biological Station, Pembroke, Virginia, 1963-84. Author: Genetic Diversity and Natural Selection, 1972. Contributor articles to professional journals. Served with United States Army, 1955-56. Rhodes scholar, 1951-54. Fellow American Association for the Advancement of Science, Virginia Acad. Sci.; member Am. Society Naturalists, Genetics Society Am., Society Study Evolution, Am. Society Ichthyologists and Herpetologists, Virginia Acad. Sci. (president 1986-87), Virginia Society Ornithology (president 1976-79). Avocations: walking; mountaineering; shooting. Office: U Va Department Biology Gilmer Hall Charlottesville Virginia 22901

MURRAY, RUSSELL, II, defense analyst; born Woodmere, New York, December 5, 1925; son of Herman Stump and Susanne Elizabeth (Warren) M.; married Sally Tingue Gardiner, May 22, 1954; children: Ann Tingue, Prudence Warren, Alexandria Gardiner. Bachelor of Science in Aeronautical Engineering, Massachusetts Institute Tech., 1949, Master of Science, 1950. Guided missile flight test engineer Grumman Aircraft Engineering Corp., Bethpage, New York, 1950-53; assistant chief operations analysis Grumman Aircraft Engineering Corp., 1953-62; principal deputy assistant secretary of defense for systems analysis The Pentagon, Washington, 1962-69; director long range planning Pfizer International, New York City, 1969-73; director review Center for Naval Analyses, Arlington, Virginia, 1973-77; assistant secretary of defense for program analysis and evaluation Department of Defense, The Pentagon, Washington, 1977-81; principal Systems Research & Applications Corp., Arlington, Virginia, 1981-85; special counsellor Committee on Armed Services United States House of Representatives, 1985—. Served with United States Army Air Force, 1944-45. Recipient Sec. of Defense Medal for meritorious civilian service, 1968; Distinguished Public Service medal Department Defense, 1981. Office: Room 2120 Rayburn House Office Building Washington District of Columbia 20515

MUSGRAVE, F. STORY, astronaut, surgeon, physiologist, educator; born Boston, August 19, 1935; children: Lorelei Lisa, Bradley Scott, Lane Linwood, Holly Kay, Christopher Todd, Jeffrey Paul. Bachelor of Science in Math. and Statistics, Syracuse University, 1958; Master of Business Administration, University of California at Los Angeles, 1959; Bachelor of Arts in Chemistry, Marietta College, 1960; Doctor of Medicine, Columbia University, 1964; Master of Science in Biophysics, University Kentucky, 1966, Doctor of Philosophy in Physiology and Biophysics, 1987. Surgical intern University Kentucky Medical Center, Lexington, 1964-65; part-time resident general surgery Denver General Hospital, 1967—; part-time professor department physiology and biophysics University Kentucky Medical College, 1967—; scientist-astronaut National Aeronautics and Space Administration, Houston, 1967—; participant in design and devel. of Skylab program, backup sci.-pilot on 1st Skylab mission, capsule communicator on 2d and 3d Skylab missions, National Aeronautics and Space Administration, flew on space shuttle mission STS-6, Apr. 3,

1983, on Spacelab 2 mission, 1985; I S Ravdin lecturer American College of Surgeons, 1973. Contributor articles to professional journals. Served with United States Military Corps, 1953-56. USAF postdoctoral fellow, 1965-66; National Heart Institute postdoctoral fellow, 1966-67; recipient Reese AFB Comdr.'s trophy, 1969, National Aeronautics and Space Administration Exceptional Service medal, 1974. Member Air Force Association, American Association for the Advancement of Science, American Institute of Aeronautics and Astronautics, Flying Physicians Association (Airman of Year award 1974), National Aeronautical Association, National Aerospace Education Council, International Acad. Astronautics, Civil Aviation Medical Association, New York Acad. Sciences, National Geog. Society, Soaring Society Am., United States Parachute Association, Marine Corps Association, Alpha Kappa Psi, Phi Delta Theta. Address: NASA Code CB Houston Texas 77058

NAJARIAN, JOHN SARKIS, surgeon, educator; born Oakland, California, December 22, 1927; son of Garabed L. and Siranoush (Demirjian) N.; married Arlys Viola Mignette Anderson, April 27, 1952; children: Jon, David, Paul, Peter. Bachelor of Arts with honors, University California Berkeley, 1948; Doctor of Medicine, University Calif.-San Francisco, 1952; Doctor of Science (honorary), Gustavus Adolphus College, 1981; Doctor of Humane Letters (honorary), California Lutheran College, 1983. Diplomate: Am. Board Surgery. Surgical intern University Calif.-San Francisco, 1952-53, surgical resident; 1955-60, assistant professor surgery, director surgical research laborato-

ries, chief transplant service department surgery; 1963-66, professor, vice chairman; 1966-67; special research fellow in immunopathology University Pittsburgh Medical School, 1960-61; National Institutes of Health senior fellow and associate in tissue transplantation immunology Scripps Clinic and Research Foundation, La Jolla, California, 1961-63; professor, chairman department surgery University Minnesota Hospital, Minneapolis, 1967—; now Regents professor University Minnesota Hospital, chief hospital staff; 1970; Special consultant United States Public Health Service, National Institutes of Health Clinical Research Training Committee, Institute General Medical Sciences, 1965-69; consultant United States Bureau Budget, 1966-68; member sci. adv. board National Kidney Foundation, 1968—; member surgery study section A div. research grants National Institutes of Health, 1970—; chairman renal transplant adv. group Veteran's Administration Hospitals, 1971; member board sci. consultant Sloan-Kettering Institute Cancer Research, 1971-78; member screening committee Dernham Postdoctoral Fellowships in Oncology, California div. Am. Cancer Society. Editor: (with Richard L. Simmons) Transplantation, 1971; editorial board: Journal Surgical Research, 1968—, Minnesota Medicine, 1968—, Journal Surgical Oncology, 1968—, Am. Journal Surgery, 1967-82, associate editor, 1982—; editorial board: Year Book of Surgery, 1970—, Transplantation, 1970, Transplantation Procs, 1970, Annals of Surgery, 1972—, World Journal Surgery, 1976—; associate editor: Surgery, 1971. Board of directors, vice president Variety Club Heart Hospital, University Minnesota; trustee, vice president Minnesota Medical Foundation Served with United States Air Force, 1953-55. Recipient award California Trudeau Society, 1962; named Alumnus of Year University California Medical School at San Francisco, 1977; recipient Annual Brotherhood award National Conference of Christians and Jews, 1978; Distinguished Achievement award Modern Medicine, 1978; Distinguished Achievement award International Great Am. award B'nai B'rith Foundation, 1982; Uncommon Citizen award, 1985; Markle scholar in acad. medicine, 1964-69. Fellow American College of Surgeons; member Society University Surgeons, Society Experimental Biology and Medicine, American Association for the Advancement of Science, Am. Society Experimental Pathology, Am. Surgical Association, Am. Association Immunologists, American Medical Association, Transplantation Society, Am. Society Nephrology, International Society Nephrology, Am. Association Lab. Animal Sci., Association Acad. Surgery (president 1969), Internat Society Surgery, Society Surgical Chairmen, Society Clinical Surgery, Central Surgical Association, Minnesota, Hennepin County med. socs., Minneapolis, St. Paul, Minnesota, Howard C. Naffziger, Portland, Halsted surgical socs., Am. Heart Association, Am. Society Transplant Surgeons (president 1977-78), Council on Kidney in Cardiovascular Disease, Hagfish Society, Italian Research Society, Minnesota Acad. Medicine, Minnesota Medical Association, Minnesota Medical Foundation, Surgical Biology Club, Sigma Xi, Alpha Omega Alpha, others. Office: U Minnesota Health Sci Center Mayo Memorial Building Box 195 Minneapolis Minnesota 55455

NAKANISHI, KOJI, chemistry educator, research institute administrator; born Hong Kong, May 11, 1925; came to United States, 1969; son of Yuzo and Yoshiko (Sakata) N.; married Yasuko Abe, October 25, 1947; children: Keiko, Jun. Bachelor of Science, Nagoya University, Japan, 1947; Doctor of Science (honorary), Williams College, 1987; Doctor of Philosophy, Nagoya University, 1954; Doctor of Science (honorary), Williams College, 1987. Assistant professor Nagoya University, 1955-58; professor Tokyo Kyoiku University, 1958-63, Tohoku University, Sendai, Japan, 1963-69; professor chemistry Columbia University, New York City, 1969-80; centennial professor chemistry Columbia University, 1980—; director research International Center Insect Physiology and Ecology, Nairobi, Kenya, 1969-77; director Suntory Institute for Bioorganic Research, Osaka, Japan, 1979—. Author: Infrared Spectroscopy—Practical, 1962, rev. edition, 1977, Circular Dichroic Spectroscopy—Exciton Coupling in Organic Stereochemistry, 1983. Recipient Asahi Cultural award Asahi Press, Tokyo, 1968, E.E. Smissmann medal University Kansas, 1979, H.C. Urey award Phi Lambda Upsilon chapter Columbia University, 1980, Alcon award in ophthalmology, 1986, Paul Karrer gold medal University Zurich, 1986, Egbert Havinga medal Havinga Foundation, Leiden, 1989. Member Chemical Society Japan (society award 1954, 79), Am. Chemical Society (E. Guenther award 1978, Remsen award, Maryland section 1981), Brit.

Chemical Society (Centenary medal 1979), Am. Acad. Arts and Sciences, Am. Society Pharmacognosy (research achievement award 1985). Home: 560 Riverside Dr New York New York 10027 Office: Department Chemistry Columbia U 116th St Broadway New York New York 10027

NAMBU, YOICHIRO, physics educator; born Toyko, January 18, 1921; came to United States, 1952; son of Kichiro and Kimiko (Kikuchi) N.; married Chieko Hida, November 3, 1945; children: Jun-ichi, Albert Kenji. Research assistant University Tokyo, 1945-49; professor physics Osada City University, Japan, 1950-56; member Institute Advanced Study, 1952-54; research associate University Chicago, 1954-56, member faculty; 1956—, professor physics; 1958, Distinguished professor; 1971—. Contributor articles to professional journals. Member National Acad. Sciences, Am. Acad. Arts and Sciences, Am. Physical Society. Office: Fermi Institute U Chicago Chicago Illinois 60637

NATHANS, DANIEL, biologist; born Wilmington, Delaware, October 30, 1928; son of Samuel and Sarah (Levitan) N.; married Joanne E. Gomberg, March 4, 1956; children: Eli, Jeremy, Benjamin. Bachelor of Science, University Delaware, 1950; Doctor of Medicine, Washington University, 1954. Intern Presbyn. Hospital, New York City, 1954-55; resident in medicine Presbyn. Hospital, 1957-59; clinical associate National Cancer Institute, 1955-57; guest investigator Rockefeller University, New York City, 1959-62; professor microbiology School Medicine, Johns Hopkins, 1962-72, professor, director department microbiology; 1972-82, University

professor; 1982—; senior investigator Howard Hughes Medical Institute, 1982—. Recipient Nobel prize in physiology or medicine, 1978. Fellow Am. Acad. Arts and Sciences; member National Acad. Sciences. Office: Johns Hopkins U Department Molecular Biology & Genetics 725 N Wolfe St Baltimore Maryland 21205

NAUGHTON, JOHN PATRICK, cardiologist, medical school administrator; born West Nanticoke, Pennsylvania, May 20, 1933; son of John Patrick and Anne Frances (McCormick) N.; married Margaret Louise Fox; children: Bruce, Marcia, Lisa, George, Michael, Thomas. Associate of Arts, Cameron State College, Lawton, Oklahoma, 1952; Bachelor of Science, St. Louis University, 1954; Doctor of Medicine, Oklahoma University, 1958. Intern George Washington University Hospital, Washington, 1958-59; resident University Oklahoma Medical Center, 1959-64; assistant professor medicine University Oklahoma, 1966-68; associate professor medicine University Illinois, 1968-70; professor medicine George Washington University, 1970-75, dean acad. affairs; 1973-75, director div. rehabilitation medicine and Regional Rehabilitation Research and Training Center; 1970-75; dean School Medicine, State University of New York, Buffalo, 1975—; professor medicine and physiology School Medicine, State University of New York, 1975—, lecturer in rehabilitation medicine; 1975; acting vice president for health sciences State University of New York, 1983-84, vice president clinical affairs; 1984—; Director National Exercise and Heart Disease Project, 1972—; chairman policy adv. board Beta-blocker heart attack trial

National Heart, Lung and Blood Institute, 1977-82; president Western New York chapter Am. Heart Association, 1983-85, vice president New York State affiliate, 1985, president New York state affiliate, 1988-90; chairman clinical applications and preventions adv. committee National Heart, Lung and Blood Institute, 1984; member New York Gov.'s Commission on Grad. Medical Education, 1985; member New York State Council on Grad. Medical Education, 1988—; president Associate Medical Schools New York, 1982-84, member administrative committee Council of deans, 1983—; member New York State Department of Health Adv. Committee on Physician Recredentialing. Author: Exercise Testing and Exercise Training in Coronary Heart Disease, 1973, Exercise Testing: Physiological, Biochemical, and Clinical Principles, 1988. Career Devel. awardee National Heart Institute, 1966-71; recipient Brotherhood-Sisterhood award in medicine National Conference of Christians and Jews. Fellow American College of Physicians, Am. College Cardiology, Am. College Sports Medicine, Am. College Chest Physicians; member New York State Heart Association (president).

NAYMARK, SHERMAN, consulting engineer; born Duluth, Minnesota, May 12, 1920; son of David N. and Lena (Naymark); children by previous marriage: Ronald L., Janet Naymark Stone. Bachelor of Science in Engineering, United States Naval Academy, 1941; Master of Science in Engineering and Construction, Massachusetts Institute of Technology, 1946. Registred professional engineer, New York,

Illinois, Iowa, Wisconsin, Minnesota, Pennsylvania registered electrical and nuclear engineer, California. Senior scientist Argonne National Laboratory, (Illinois), 1948-52; director reactor div. project, engineering manager Schenectady office Atomic Energy Commission, 1952-56; with General Electric Company, 1956-70; engineering manager nuclear turnkey plants San Jose, 1967-69; president Quadrex Corp., Campbell, California, 1970-86; chairman Quadrex Corp., 1986; lecturer University Virginia, Massachusetts Institute of Technology, United States Naval Reserve Officer training Schools; adviser to United States del. 3d International Conference on Peaceful Uses of Atomic Energy, Geneva, 1964; senior examiner Professional Engineers State of California, 1960-70 member fusion power coordinating committee Department Energy. Contributor numerous articles on nuclear research, devel., engring. to professional journals. Served to captain United States Navy, 1941-54. Fellow Am. Nuclear Society (general chairman ann. meeting, national treasurer 1978-80), national treasurer (member governing board Nuclear Tech. 1979-81); member American Association for the Advancement of Science, Am. Pub. Power Association (associate), United States Naval Institute (hon. life). Democrat. Jewish. Home: 218 Forrester Road Los Gatos California 95030

NEEL, JAMES VAN GUNDIA, geneticist, educator; born Hamilton, Ohio, March 22, 1915; son of Hiram Alexander and Elizabeth (Van Gundia) N.; married Priscilla Baxter, May 6, 1943; children—Frances, James Van Gundia, Alexander Baxter. Bachelor of Arts, College Wooster, 1935,

Doctor of Science (honorary), 1959; Doctor of Philosophy, University Rochester, 1939, Doctor of Medicine, 1944, Doctor of Science (honorary), 1974; Doctor of Science (honorary), Medical College Ohio, 1981. Instructor zoology Dartmouth, 1939-41; fellow zoology National Research Council, 1941-42; intern, assistant resident medicine Strong Memorial Hospital, 1944-46; associate geneticist laboratory vertebrate biology, assistant professor internal medicine University Michigan Medical School, 1948-51, geneticist Institute Human Biology, associate professor medical genetics; 1951-56, professor human genetics, chairman department; 1956-85, professor internal medicine; 1957-85, Lee R. Dice University professor human genetics; 1966-85, professor emeritus; 1985—; Galton lecturer University London, 1955; Cutter lecturer Harvard, 1956; Russel lecturer University Michigan, 1966; consultant United States Public Health Service, Atomic Energy Commission, National Research Council, World Health Organization., Environmental Protection Agency, Veteran's Administration; president 6th International Congress Human Genetics; chairman 7th International Symposium Smithsonian Institution, Washington, 1981. Author medical articles; member editorial board: Blood, 1950-62, Perspectives in Biology and Medicine, 1956—, Human Genetics Abstracts, 1962—, Mutation Research, 1964-75. Served to 1st lieutenant Medical Corps Army of the United States, 1943-44, 46-47; acting director field studies Atomic Bomb Casualty Commission, 1947-48. Recipient Albert Lasker award, 1960, Allan award Am. Society Human Genetics, 1965; National Medal Sci., 1974, Smithsonian Institution Medal, 1981, Wilhemene E. Key lecturer Am. Genetic Association, 1982; named Michigan Scientist of Year, 1984. Member Am. Philosophical Association, Am. Acad. Arts and Sciences, Institute of Medicine, National Acad. Sciences (member council 1970-72), Genetics Society Am., Am. Society Human Genetics (vice president 1952-53, president 1953-54), Am. Federation Clinical Research, Am. Society Naturalists, Association Am. Physicians, Japanese, Association Am. Physicians, Brazilian socs. human genetics, Phi Beta Kappa, Sigma Xi, Alpha Omega Alpha. Avocation: orchid cultivation.

NEEL, LOUIS EUGENE FELIX, physicist; born Lyons, France, November 22, 1904; son of Louis Antoine and Marie Antoinette (Hartmayer) N.; married Hélène Hourticq, September 14, 1931; children: Marie-Francoise, Marguerite Guély, Pierre. Agrégé de l'Université, Ecole Normale Supérieure, 1928; Docteur es-Sciences, Ecole Normale Supérieure, Strasbourg, France, 1932.

With Faculté des Sciences, Strasbourg, 1928-45, professor; 1937-45; professor Faculté des Sciences Grenoble, France, 1945-76; director Laboratory Electrostatics and Physics of Metal, 1940-71; president Institut National Polytechnique, Grenoble, 1970-76; director Centre d'Etudes Nucléaires, Grenoble, 1957-71; French representative sci. council North Atlantic Treaty Organization, 1960-82; president Conseil Sup. Sûreté nucléaire, 1973-86. Decorated grand croix Legion of Honor, Gold medal National Center Sci. Research; Nobel prize in physics, 1970. Member French Acad. Sci., acads. sci. Moscow, Halle, Royal Society

London, Romanian Acad., Royal Netherlands Acad. Sciences, Am. Acad. Arts and Sciences, French Society Physics (hon. president), International Union Pure and Applied Physics (hon. president). Research and numerous publs. on magnetic properties of solids; introduced sci. ideas of ferrimagnetism and antiferromagnetism; discoveries of certain magnetic properties of fine grains and crystals, directional order of magnetism, magnetic after effect. Home: 15 rue Marcel-Allégot, 92190 Meudon-Bellevue France

NELSON, FREDERICK CARL, mechanical engineering educator, academic administrator; born Braintree, Massachusetts, August 8, 1932; son of Carl Edwin and Marjorie May (Miller) N.; married Delia Ann Dwaresky, July 15, 1931; children: Jeffrey, Karen, Richard, Christine. Bachelor of Science in Mechanical Engineering, Tufts University, 1954; Master of Science, Harvard University, 1955, Doctor of Philosophy, 1961. Registered professional engineer, Massachusetts. Instructor Tufts University, Medford, Massachusetts, 1955-57; associate professor mechanical engineering Tufts University, Medford, 1964-71, professor mechanical engineering; 1971—, dean engineering; 1980—; board of directors Massachusetts Tech. Park Corp., Westboro. Translator: (book) Mechanical Vibrations for Engineers, 1983. Fellow Acoustical Society Am.; member Am. Society Mechanical Engineers (Centennial Medallion 1980), American Association for the Advancement of Science, National Institute Applied Sciences of Lyons (medal 1988). Office: Tufts University College of Engring Office of the Dean Medford Massachusetts 02155

NELSON, GEORGE DRIVER, astronaut, astronomer; born Charles City, Iowa, July 13, 1950; son of George Vernon and Evelyn Elenor (Driver) N.; married Susan Lynn Howard, June 19, 1971; children: Aimee Tess, Marti Ann. Bachelor of Science, Harvey Mudd Coll, 1972; Master of Science, University Washington, 1974, Doctor of Philosophy, 1978. Astronaut National Aeronautics and Space Administration, Houston, 1978—; mission specialist Space Shuttle flight, 1984. Unitarian. Avocations: reading; athletics; guitar. Office: NASA Johnson Space Center Code CB Houston Texas 77058

NELSON, GORDON LEIGH, chemist, educator; born Palo Alto, California, May 27, 1943; son of Nels Folke and Alice Virginia (Fredrickson) N. Bachelor of Science in Chemistry, University Nevada, 1965; Master of Science, Yale University, 1967, Doctor of Philosophy, 1970. Staff research chemist corp. research and devel. General Electric Company, Schenectady, New York, 1970-74; manager combustibility tech. plastics div. General Electric Company, Pittsfield, Massachusetts, 1974-79, manager environmental protection plastics div.; 1979-82; vice president materials sci. and tech. Springborn Laboratories Incorporated, Enfield, Connecticut, 1982-83; professor, chairman department polymer sci. University Southern Mississippi, Hattiesburg, 1983—; consultant in field. Author: Carbon-13 Nuclear Magnetic Resonance For Organic Chemists, 1972; editor books on coatings sci. tech.; contributor articles to professional journals. Member Am.

Institute of Chemists, Society Plastics Engineers, Am. Chemical Society (president 1988, board directors 1977-85, 87-89, Henry Hill award 1986), Computer and Business Equipment Manufacturers Association (chairman Plastics Task Group), American Society for Testing and Materials (E5 cert. of appreciation 1985), Southern Society for Coatings Technology, National Fire Protection Association, IEC (United States tech. adv. group on info. processing equipment), Structural Plastics division Society of the Plastics Industry (member executive committee, chairman combustibility committee, Man of Year 1979), Mississippi Acad. Sciences, Yale Chemists Association (president 1981—), Nevada Historical Society, Sigma Xi. Republican. Presbyterian. Avocations: travel, western United States history. Office: U Southern Miss Department Polymer Sci Southern Station Box 10063 Hattiesburg Mississippi 39406-0063

NELSON, NEAL N., computer science educator; born Albany, Oregon, September 3, 1952; son of Richard G. and Mary Alice (Strickler) N. Bachelor of Arts in Math., Washington State University, 1974, Master of Science in Computer Science, 1976; postgraduate, Oregon Grad Center, 1984—. Software engineer Texas Instruments Incorporated, Austin, Texas, 1976-77; MOS design engineer Texas Instruments Incorporated, Houston, 1977-79; senior design engineer Intel Corp., Aloha, Oregon, 1979-82; senior tech. marketing engineer Intel Corp., Hillsboro, Oregon, 1982-84; MacArthur professor computer sci. Reed College, Portland, Oregon, 1984—, acad. director computing master plan; 1984-86. Vice chairman

adv. council Oregon Institute Tech., Portland Center, 1985—. Avocation: travel in desert wilderness areas.

NELSON, OLIVER EVANS, JR, geneticist, educator; born Seattle, August 16, 1920; son of Oliver Evans and Mary Isabella (Grant) N.; married Gerda Kjer Hansen, March 28, 1963. Bachelor of Arts, Colgate University, 1941; Master of Science, Yale, 1943, Doctor of Philosophy, 1947. Assistant professor genetics Purdue University, 1947-49, associate professor; 1949-54, professor; 1954-69; professor genetics University Wisconsin, Madison, 1969—, Brink professor genetics; 1982—, chairman Laboratory of Genetics; 1986—; visiting investigator Biochem. Institute, University Stockholm and National Forest Research Institute, Stockholm, 1954-55; National Science Foundation, senior postdoctoral fellow California Institute Tech., Pasadena, 1961-62. Contributor articles on controlling elements, genes affecting starch synthesis to professional publications. Recipient John Scott medal City of Philadelphia, 1967; Hoblitzelle award Texas Research Foundation, 1968; Browning award Am. Society Agronomy, 1974; Donald F. Jones medal Connecticut Agrl. Exptl. Station, 1976. Member National Acad. Sciences, Am. Acad. Arts and Sciences, Genetics Society Am., Am. Genetics Association, Am. Society Plant Physiologists (Stephen Hales award, 1988), Crop Sci. Society, American Association for the Advancement of Science, Sigma Xi. Home: 4197 Barlow Road Cross Plains Wisconsin 53528 Office: Lab Genetics University Wisconsin Madison Wisconsin 53706

NELSON, RONALD HARVEY, animal science educator, researcher; born

Union Grove, Wisconsin, August 10, 1918; son of Harvey August and Myra Frances (Sheen) N.; married Elizabeth Jane Lappley, April 13, 1940; children—David Peter, Marjorie Jean, Linda Louise, Ronda Elizabeth. Bachelor of Science, University Wisconsin, 1939; Master of Science, Oklahoma Agricultural and Mechanical University, 1941; Doctor of Philosophy, Iowa State University, 1943. Member faculty Michigan State University, 1946—, professor, head, animal sci. department; 1950-84; chief of party Michigan State University tech. assistance project, Balcarce, Pcia, Buenos Aires, 1966-68. Recipient Graduate Distinction award Okla State University, 1987. Fellow Am. Society Animal Sci. (International Animal Agriculture award 1978, Animal Industry award 1984); member Am. Angus Association (chairman research advisory committee 1956-60), Michigan Angus Association (president 1977-78), Animal Sci. Association, Sigma Xi, Phi Kappa Phi, Alpha Zeta. Home: 1545 N Harrison St East Lansing Michigan 48823

NEUFELD, ELIZABETH FONDAL, biochemist, educator; born Paris, September 27, 1928; United States citizen; married 1951. Doctor of Philosophy, University California, 1956; Doctor.H.C. (honorary), University Rene Descartes, Paris, 1978; Doctor of Science (honorary), Russell Sage College, Troy, New York, 1981, Hahnemann University School Medicine, 1984. Assistant research biochemist University California, Berkeley, 1957-63; with National Institute Arthritis, Metabolism and Digestive Diseases, Bethesda, Maryland, 1963-84, research biochemist; 1963-73, chief section human biochem. genetics; 1973-79, chief genetics and biochem. branch; 1979-84; professor, chairman department biological chemistry University of California at Los Angeles School Medicine, 1984—; United States Public Health Service fellow University California, Berkeley, 1956-57. Recipient Dickson prize University Pitts., 1974, Hillebrand award, 1975, Gairdner Foundation award 1982; Albert Lasker Clinical Medical Research award, 1982; Elliott Cresson Medal, 1984; Wolf Foundation prize, 1988. Member National Acad. Sci., Am. Acad. Arts and Sci., Am. Society Human Genetics, Am. Chemical Society, Am. Society Biological Chemists, Am. Society Cell Biology, Am. Society Clinical Investigation. Office: University of California at Los Angeles School Medicine Department Biol Chemistry Los Angeles California 90024-1737

NEUGEBAUER, GERRY, astrophysicist; born Gottingen, Germany, September 3, 1932; came to United States, 1939; son of Otto E. and Grete (Brück) N.; married Marcia MacDonald, August 26, 1956; children: Carol, Lee. Bachelor of Science, Cornell University, 1954; Doctor of Philosophy, California Institute Tech., 1960. Member faculty California Institute Tech., Pasadena, 1962—, professor physics; 1970—; member staff Hale Observatory, 1970-80; acting director Palomar Observatory, 1980-81, director; 1981—. Served with Army of the United States, 1961-63. Fellow Am. Acad. Arts and Sciences; member National Acad. Sciences. Office: California Institute Tech Palomar Obs 105-24 Pasadena California 91125

NEUMANN, ANDREW CONRAD, geological oceanography educator; born Oak Bluffs, Massachusetts,

December 21, 1933; son of Andrew Conrad Neumann and Faye Watson (Gilmore) Gilmour; married Jane Spaeth, July 7, 1962; children: Jennifer, Christopher, Jonathan. Bachelor of Science in Geology, Brooklyn College, 1955; Master of Science in Oceanography, Texas Agricultural and Mechanical University, 1958; Doctor of Philosophy in Geology, Lehigh University, 1963. Assistant professor marine geology Lehigh University, Bethlehem, Pennsylvania, 1963-65; assistant professor marine sci. University Miami, Florida, 1965-69, associate professor marine sci.; 1969-72; professor marine sci. University North Carolina, Chapel Hill, 1972-85, Bowman and Gray professor geological oceanography; 1985-88; program director National Science Foundation, Washington, 1969-70; Kenan professor University Edinburgh, Scotland, 1978; summer visiting investigator United States Geological Survey, Woods Hole, Massachusetts, 1981—, Woods Hole Oceanographic Institute, 1981—; visiting professor University Naples, Italy, 1984. Contributor articles to professional journals. Trustee Bermuda Biol. Sta. for Research Incorporated, 1972-76. Recipient Distinguished Alumni award Brooklyn College, 1987. Fellow Geological Society Am.; member Society Econ. Paleontologists and Mineralogists, Am. Association Petroleum Geologists, North Carolina Acad. Sci. Avocations: fishing, gardening, sailing. Office: U North Carolina Department Marine Scis 1205 Venable Hall Chapel Hill North Carolina 27514

NICHOLSON, THOMAS DOMINIC, astronomer; born New York City, December 14, 1922; son of Dominic J. and Catherine (Brown) N.; married Branca Costa, December 26, 1946; children—Lester C., Diana C., Glen C., Gail C. Bachelor of Science, United States Mcht. Marine Academy; Bachelor of Arts, St. John's University, 1950; Master of Science, Fordham University, 1953, Doctor of Philosophy, 1962; Doctor of Science (honorary), Lawrence University, 1988. Marine deck officer Moore-McCormack Lines, 1941-46; from instructor to assistant professor nautical sci. and assistant to department head United States Merchant Marine Acad., 1946-53; lecturer, instructor department astronomy Hayden Planetarium, Am. Mus. Natural History, New York City, 1952-53; associate astronomer Hayden Planetarium, Am. Mus. Natural History, 1953-57, astronomer; 1957-67, chairman; 1964-67, mus. assistant director; 1967-68, deputy director; 1968-69, director; 1969—; TV weather forecaster station WNBC, New York City, 1967-72; has lectured in astronomy United States Military Acad., Yale, New York University; geodetic surveying, Arctic, 1956, Greenland Ice Cap, 1958; member adv. council Astrophysical Observatory, Princeton University; member national adv. board Monell Chemical Senses Center. Author: (with J. M. Chamberlain) Planets, Stars and Space, 1957, Adventure with Stars, 1958, also numerous articles; Editor: Curator; Contributing editor: Christian Science Monitor, Natural History Magazine. Served with United States Merchant Marine, 1941-46; lieutenant (junior grade) United States Naval Reserve. Recipient Medal of Honor St. John's University, 1959. Fellow A.A.A.S., Royal Astronomical Society, Am. Astronomical Association; member

Institute Navigation (past president), Astronomical Society Pacific, Am. Meteorological Society, Am. Association Museums (vice president), Association Systematics Collections (president). Office: Am Mus Natural History Central Park W at 79th St New York New York 10024

NIERENBERG, WILLIAM AARON, oceanography educator; born New York City, February 13, 1919; son of Joseph and Minnie (Drucker) N.; married Edith Meyerson, November 21, 1941; children—Victoria Jean (Mrs. Tschinkel), Nicolas Clarke Eugene. Aaron Naumberg scholar, University Paris, 1937-38; Bachelor of Science, City College of New York, 1939; Master of Arts, Columbia University, 1942, Doctor of Philosophy (NRC predoctoral fellow), 1947. Tutor City College of New York, 1939-42; section leader Manhattan Project, 1942-45; instructor physics Columbia University, 1946-48; assistant professor physics University Michigan, 1948-50; associate professor physics University California at Berkeley, 1950-53, professor; 1954-65; director Scripps Institution Oceanography, 1965-86, director emeritus; 1986—; vice chancellor for marine sciences University California at San Diego, 1969-86; director Hudson Laboratories, Columbia, 1953-54; associate professor University Paris, 1960-62; assistant secretary general North Atlantic Treaty Organization for sci. affairs, 1960-62; special consultant Executive Office President, 1958-60; senior consultant White House Office Sci. and Tech. Policy, 1976-78. Contributor papers to professional journals. E.O. Lawrence lectr. National Acad. Sci., 1958, Miller Foundation fellow, 1957-59, Sloan Foundation fellow, 1958, Fulbright fellow, 1960-61; member United States National Commission United Nations Educational, Scientific and Cultural Organization, 1964-68, California Adv. Committee on Marine and Coastal Resources, 1967-71; adviser-at-large United States Department State, 1968—; member National Sci. Board, 1972-78, 82-88, cons., 1988—; chairman USNC/PSA, NRC, 1988—; member National Adv. Committee on Oceans and Atmosphere, 1971-77, chairman, 1971-75; member sci. and tech. adv. Council California Assembly; member adv. council National Aeronautics and Space Administration, 1978-83, chairman adv. council, 1978-82; member council National Acad. Scis., 1979—. NATO Senior Sci. fellow, 1969; Decorated officer National Order of Merit France; recipient Golden Dolphin award Association Artistico Letteraria Internazionale, Distinguished Pub. Service medal National Aeronautics and Space Administration, 1982, Delmer S. Fahrney medal The Franklin Institute, 1987, Compass award Marine Tech. Society, 1975. Fellow Am. Physical Society (council, secretary Pacific Coast section 1955-64); member Am. Acad. Arts and Sciences, National Acad. Engineering, National Acad. Sciences, Am. Philosophical Society, Am. Association Naval Architects, Navy League, Foreign Policy Association (member national council), Sigma Xi (president 1981-82, Proctor prize, 1977). Club: Cosmos.

NIEVERGELT, JURG, computer science educator; born Luzern, Switzerland, June 6, 1938; came to United States, 1962; son of Albert and Hedwig Nievergelt; married Teresa Quiambao; children: Mark, Derek. Diploma in math., Swiss Federal

Institute Tech. (ETH), Zurich, Switzerland, 1962; Doctor of Philosophy in Math., University Illinois, 1965. Research fellow Department Computer Sci. and Math. University Illinois, 1962-65; assistant professor computer sci. and math. University Illinois, Urbana, 1965-68, associate professor computer sci.; 1968-72, professor; 1972-77; professor Swiss Federal Institute Tech. (ETH), Zurich, 1975-85, 89—; Kenan professor, chairman department computer sci. University North Carolina, Chapel Hill, 1985-89; research scientist various research laboratories and universities, summers 1964, 69-74, 81, 84, springs 1978-79, fall 1982; visiting associate professor University of California at Los Angeles, summer 1969. Co-author: (with E.M. Reingold and N. Deo) Combinational Algorithms: Theory and Practice, 1977, (with A. Ventura and H. Hinterberger) Interactive Computer Programs for Education-Philosophy, Techniques and Examples, 1986; member editorial board Science Computer Programming, Journal Symbolic Computation, Future Generations Computer Systems, Decision Support Systems, Computer Compacts, Education and Computing, Informatik Spektrum; contributor articles to professional journals. Grantee National Science Foundation, 1972-76, 86—, Office Naval Research, 1986—. Fellow Institute of Electrical and Electronics Engineers, American Association for the Advancement of Science; member Association Computing Machinery, Computing Research Board. Research interests include algorithms and data structures, geometric computation, interactive systems. Office: ETH Informatik, CH-8092 Zurich Switzerland

NILAN, ROBERT ARTHUR, agronomy educator; born New Westminster, British Columbia, Canada, December 26, 1923; son of Jack Galway and Phyllis May (Houghton) N.; married Winona Patricia Ross, June 11, 1948; children: Judith, Gregory, Patricia. Bachelor of Agricultural Science, University British Columbia, Vancouver, 1946, MSA, 1948; Doctor of Philosophy, University Wisconsin, Madison, 1951. Research associate Washington State University, Pullman, 1951-52; assistant professor Washington State University, 1952-56, associate professor; 1956-61, professor; 1961—, assistant agronomist; 1952-56, associate agronomist; 1956-61, agronomist; 1961-65, chairman genetics program; 1965-79, dean div. sci.; 1979—; lecturer Institute Plant Breeding & Genetics, Castelar, Argentina, 1972-73. Contributor articles in field to professional journals. Guggenheim fellow, 1959-60; USPHS fellow, 1967-68. Member Pullman Chamber of Commerce, Am. Society Agronomy, Genetics Society Am., Environmental Mutagen Society, Danish Acad. Sci. (foreign). Office: Div of Scis Wash State U Pullman Washington 99164

NIRENBERG, LOUIS, mathematician, educator; born Hamilton, Ontario, Canada, February 28, 1925; came to United States, 1945, naturalized, 1954; son of Zuzie and Bina (Katz) N.; married Susan Blank, January 25, 1948; children: Marc, Lisa. BSc, McGill University, Montreal, 1945; Master of Science, New York University, 1947, Doctor of Philosophy, 1949; Doctor of Science (honorary), McGill University, 1986. Member faculty New York University, 1949—, professor math.; 1957—, director Courant Institute; 1970-72; visitor Institute Advanced Study, 1958; hon. professor Nankai University. Author research articles. Recipient Crafoord prize Royal Swedish Acad., 1982; National Research Council fellow, 1951-52; Sloan Foundation fellow, 1958-60; Guggenheim Foundation fellow, 1966-67, 75-76; Fulbright fellow, 1965. Member National Acad. Sciences, Am. Acad. Arts and Sciences, Am. Math. Society (vice president 1976-78, M. Bôcher prize 1959), Am. Philosophical Society, French Acad. Sciences (foreign associate). Home: 221 W 82d St New York New York 10024 Office: Courant Institute 251 Mercer St New York New York 10012

NIRENBERG, MARSHALL WARREN, biochemist; born New York City, April 10, 1927; son of Harry Edward and Minerva (Bykowsky) N.; married Perola Zaltzman, July 14, 1961. Bachelor of Science in Zoology, University Florida, 1948, Master of Science, 1952; Doctor of Philosophy in Biochemistry, University Michigan, 1957. Postdoctoral fellow Am. Cancer Society at National Institutes of Health, 1957-59; postdoctoral fellow United States Public Health Service at National Institutes of Health, 1959-60; member staff National Institutes of Health, 1960—; research biochemist, chief laboratory biochem. genetics National Heart, Lung and Blood Institute, 1962—. Recipient Molecular Biology award National Acad. Sciences, 1962, award in biological scis. Washington Acad. Sciences, 1962, medal Department of Health, Education and Welfare, 1964, Modern Medicine award, 1963, Harrison Howe award Am. Chemical Society, 1964, National Medal Sci. President Johnson, 1965,

Hildebrand award Am. Chemical Society, 1966, Research Corp. award, 1966, A.C.P. award, 1967, Gairdner Foundation award merit Can., 1967, Prix Charles Leopold Meyer French Acad. Sciences, 1967, Franklin medal Franklin Institute, 1968, Albert Lasker Medical Research award, 1968, Priestly award, 1968; co-recipient Louisa Gross Horowitz prize Columbia, 1968, Nobel prize in medicine and physiology, 1968. Fellow American Association for the Advancement of Science, New York Acad. Sciences; member Am. Society Biological Chemists, Am. Chemical Society (Paul Lewis award enzyme chemistry 1964), Am. Acad. Arts and Sciences, Biophys. Society, National Acad. Sciences, Washington Acad. Sciences, Society for Study Devel. and Growth, Harvey Society (hon.), Leopoldina Deutsche Akademie der Naturforscher, Pontifical Acad. Sciences. Spl. research mechanism protein synthesis, genetic code, nucleic acids, regulatory mechanisms in synthesis macromolecules, neurobiology. Office: Lab Biochem Genetics NIH 9000 Rockville Pike Bethesda Maryland 20892

NOLAN, THOMAS BRENNAN, research geologist; born Greenfield, Massachusetts, May 21, 1901; son of Frank Wesley and Anna (Brennan) N.; married Mabelle Orleman, December 3, 1927; 1 son, Thomas Brennan. Bachelor of Philosophy in Metallurgy, Yale University, 1921, Doctor of Philosophy in Geology, 1924; Doctor of Laws (honorary), University St. Andrews, 1962. Geologist United States Geological Survey, 1924-44, assistant director; 1944-56, director; 1956-65, research geologist; 1965—. Contributor numerous articles, reports, bulls. to professional and governmental journals. Recipient Spendiaroff prize International Geol. Congress, 1933; K. C. Li prize and medal Columbia, 1954; Rockefeller Pub. Service award Princeton, 1961; Silver medal Tokyo Geog. Society, 1965; Wilbur Cross medal Yale University, 1987. Fellow Geological Society Am. (president 1961), Society Econ. Geologists (president 1950), Am. Geophysical Union, Mineralogical Society Am., Royal Society Edinburgh (hon.); member National Acad. Sciences, Geological Society Washington, Am. Philosophical Society, Tokyo Geog. Society (hon. member), International Union Geological Sciences, Am. Acad. Arts and Sciences, Geological Society London (foreign member), Am. Ornithologists Union, Sigma Xi. Clubs: Cosmos (Washington); Yale. Office: United States Geological Survey Reston Virginia 22092

NOVALES, RONALD RICHARDS, zoologist, educator; born San Francisco, April 24, 1928; son of William Henry and Dorothy (Richards) N.; married Barbara Jean Martin, December 19, 1953; children: Nancy Ann, Mary Elizabeth. Bachelor of Arts, University California, Berkeley, 1950, Master of Arts, 1953, Doctor of Philosophy, 1958; postgraduate, University California, Los Angeles, 1951-52. Assistant professor biological sciences Northwestern University, Evanston, Illinois, 1958-64; associate professor Northwestern University, 1964-70, professor; 1970-80, professor neurobiology and physiology; 1981—; consultant A.J. Nystrom Company, 1969. Member editorial board: The American Zoologist, 1969-73; Contributor: articles to professional journals Encyclopedia Brit. Book of Year.

Served with United States Army, 1953-55. National Science Foundation research grantee, 1959-73, 75-78. Fellow American Association for the Advancement of Science; member Am. Society Zoologists (secretary 1966-67, chairman division comparative endocrinology 1974-75), International Pigment Cell Society, Phi Beta Kappa, Sigma Xi. Unitarian. Home: 2008 McDaniel Avenue Evanston Illinois 60201 Office: Northwestern University Department Neurobiology and Physiology Evanston Illinois 60201

NOYCE, ROBERT NORTON, electronics company executive; born Burlington, Iowa, December 12, 1927; son of Ralph B. and Harriet (Norton) N.; married Ann S. Bowers; children: William B., Pendred, Priscilla, Margaret. Bachelor of Arts, Grinnell College, 1949; Doctor of Philosophy, Massachusetts Institute of Technology, 1953. Research engineer Philco Corp., Philadelphia, 1953-56, Shockley Semicondr. Laboratory, Mountain View, California, 1956-57; founder, director research Fairchild Semicondr., Mountain View, 1957-59; vice president, general manager Fairchild Semicondr., 1959-65; group vice president Fairchild Camera & Instrument, Mountain View, 1965-68; founder, president Intel Corp., Santa Clara, California, 1968-75; chairman Intel Corp., 1968-75, vice chairman; 1979—; president, chief executive officer Sematech, Austin, Texas, 1988—. Patentee in field. Trustee Grinnell College, 1962—. Recipient Stuart Ballentine award Franklin Institute, 1967, Harry Goode award AFIPS, 1978, National Medal of Sci., 1979, National Medal of Tech. President of U.S., 1987, Harold Pender award University Pennsylvania, 1980, John Fritz medal, 1989; named to National Business Hall of Fame, 1989. Fellow Institute of Electrical and Electronics Engineers (Cledo Brunetti award 1978, medal of honor 1978, Faraday medal 1979); member National Acad. Engineering, American Association for the Advancement of Science, National Acad. Sci. Office: Sematech 2706 Montopolis Dr Austin Texas 78741

NYE, EDWIN PACKARD, mechanical engineering educator; born Atkinson, New Hampshire, January 29, 1920; son of Eben W. and Gertrude Florence (Dunn) N.; married Persephone Fern Drumheller, August 12, 1944; children: David Edwin, Sarah Leone, Benjamin Alfred. Bachelor of Science with high honor, University New Hampshire, 1941; Master of Science, Harvard, 1947. Registered professional engineer, Pennsylvania, Connecticut. Service engineer Bailey Meter Company, Cleveland, 1941-42; instructor mechanical engineering University New Hampshire, 1942-44; project engineer National Advisory Committee for Aeronautics, 1944-46; from instructor to associate professor mechanical engineering Pennsylvania State University, 1947-59; Hallden professor Trinity College, Hartford, Connecticut, 1959-83; chairman department engineering Trinity College, 1960-70, dean of faculty; 1970-79; Secretary University Research Institute Connecticut, 1964-68, president, 1968-71, chairman, 1971-74; director Hallden Machine Company; chairman college work Episcopal Diocese Connecticut, 1960-64. Co-author: Steam Power Plants, 1952, Power Plants, 1956, Thermal Engineering, 1959. Member board education, Bloomfield, Connecticut, 1961-65; member State Board Acad.

Awards, 1974—, dean faculty, 1979-83; corporator Hartford Public Library, 1978-82. Member American Society of Mechanical Engineers, Am. Society Engineering Education, Connecticut Acad. Sci. and Engineering, Phi Kappa Phi, Pi Tau Sigma. Home: Bug Hill Road Ashfield Massachusetts 01330

OCHOA, SEVERO, biochemist; born Luarca, Spain, September 24, 1905; came to United States, 1940, naturalized, 1956; son of Severo and Carmen (Albornoz) O.; married Carmen G. Cobian, July 8, 1931. Bachelor of Arts, Malaga (Spain) College, 1921; Doctor of Medicine, University Madrid, Spain, 1929; Doctor of Science, Washington University, University Brazil, 1957, University Guadalajara, Mexico, 1959, Wesleyan University, University Oxford, England, University Salamanca, Spain, 1961, Gustavus Adolphus College, 1963, University Pennsylvania, 1964, Brandeis University, 1965, University Granada, Spain, University Oviedo, Spain, 1967, University Perugia, Italy, 1968, University Michigan, Weizman Institute, Israel, 1982; Doctor Medical Science (honorary), University Santo Tomas, Manila, Philippines, 1963, University Buenos Aires, 1968, University Tucuman, Argentina, 1968; Doctor of Humane Letters, Yeshiva University, 1966; Doctor of Laws, University Glasgow, Scotland, 1959. Lecturer physiology University Madrid Medical School, 1931-35; head physiological div. Institute for Medical Research, 1935-36; guest research assistant in physiology Kaiser-Wilhelm Institute for Medical Research, Heidelberg, Germany, 1936-37; Ray Lankester investigator Marine Biological Laboratory, Plymouth, England, 1937; demonstrator Nuffield research assistant biochemistry Oxford (England) University Medical School, 1938-41; instructor, research associate pharmacology Washington University School of Medicine, St. Louis, 1941-42; research associate medicine New York University School Medicine, 1942-45, assistant professor biochemistry; 1945-46, professor pharmacology, chairman department; 1946-54, professor, chairman department biochemistry; 1954-76, professor; 1976—; distinguished member Roche Institute Molecular Biology. Author publications on biochem. of muscles, glycolysis in heart and brain, transphosphorylations in yeast fermentation, pyruvic acid oxidation in brain and role of vitamin B1; RNA and Protein biosynthesis; genetic code. Decorated Order Rising Sun Japan; recipient (with Arthur Kornberg) 1959 Nobel prize in medicine, Albert Gallatin medal New York University, 1970, National Medal of Sci., 1980. Fellow New York Acad. Sciences, New York Acad. Medicine, Am. Acad. of Arts and Sci., American Association for the Advancement of Science; member National Academy of Sciences, Am. Philosophical Society, Society for Experimental Biology and Medicine, Society of Biological Chemists (president 1958, editor journal 1950-60), International Union Biochemistry (president 1961-67), Biochem. Society (England), Harvey Society (president 1953-54), Alpha Omega Alpha (hon.); foreign member German Acad. National Sciences, Royal Spanish, Union of the Soviet Socialist Republics, Polish, Pullian, Italian, Argentinian, Barcelona (Spain), Brazilian acads. sci., Royal Society (England), Pontifical Acad. Sci., G D R Acad. Sciences, Argentinian National Acad. Medicine.

Office: Roche Institute Molecular Biol Nutley New Jersey 07110

OGG, JAMES ELVIS, microbiologist, educator; born Centralia, Illinois, December 24, 1924; son of James and Amelia (Glammeyer) O.; married Betty Jane Ackerson, December 27, 1948; children—James George, Susan Kay. Bachelor of Science, University Illinois, 1949; Doctor of Philosophy, Cornell University, 1956. Bacteriologist Biological Laboratories, Fort Detrick, Maryland, 1950-53; consultant Biological Laboratories, 1953-56, medical bacteriologist; 1956-58; professor microbiology Colorado State University, Fort Collins, 1958—; assistant dean Grad. School, 1965-66, head department microbiology; 1967-77; director Advanced Sci. Education Program div. grad. education in sci. National Science Foundation, Washington, 1966-67; Fulbright-Hays senior lecturer in microbiology, Nepal, 1976-77, 81; acad. administration advisor Institute Agriculture and Animal Sci., Tribhuvan University, Nepal, 1988—; consultant National Aeronautics and Space Administration, 1968-69, National Science Foundation, 1968-73, Martin Marietta Corp., 1970-76; cons.-evaluator North Central Association Colleges and Secondary Schools, 1974—. Contributor articles to professional journals. Served with Army of the United States, 1943-46, 50-51. Fellow American Association for the Advancement of Science, Am. Acad. Microbiology; member Am. Society Microbiology (chairman pub. service and adult education committee 1975-80), Fulbright Alumni Association, Sigma Xi, Phi Kappa Phi, Gamma Sigma Delta. Home: 1442 Ivy St Fort Collins Colorado 80525

OKRENT, DAVID, engineering educator; born Passaic, New Jersey, April 19, 1922; son of Abram and Gussie (Pearlman) O.; married Rita Gilda Holtzman, February 1, 1948; children—Neil, Nina, Jocelyne. Mechanical Engineer, Stevens Institute Tech., 1943; Master of Arts, Harvard, 1948, Doctor of Philosophy in Physics, 1951. Mechanical engineer National Advisory Committee for Aeronautics, Cleveland, 1943-46; senior physicist Argonne (Illinois) National Laboratory, 1951-71; regents lecturer University of California at Los Angeles, 1968, professor engineering; 1971—; visiting professor University Washington, Seattle, 1963, University Arizona, Tucson, 1970-71; Isaac Taylor chair Technion, 1977-78. Author: Fast Reactor Cross Sections, 1960, Computing Methods in Reactor Physics, 1968, Reactivity Coefficients in Large Fast Power Reactors, 1970, Nuclear Reactor Safety, 1981; contributor articles to professional journals. Member adv. committee on reactor safeguards Atomic Energy Commission, 1963—, also chairman, 1966; sci. secretary to secretary general of Geneva Conference, 1958; member United States del. to all Geneva Atoms for Peace Confs. Guggenheim fellow, 1961-62, 77-78; recipient Distinguished Appointment award Argonne Universities Association, 1970, Distinguished Service award U.S. Nuclear Regulatory Commn., 1985. Fellow Am. Physical Society, Am. Nuclear Society (Tommy Thompson award 1980, Glenn Seaborg medal 1987), National Acad. Engineering. Home: 439 Veteran Avenue Los Angeles California 90024

OKUN, DANIEL ALEXANDER, environmental engineering educator, consulting engineer; born New York City, June 19, 1917; son of William Howard and Leah (Seligman) O.; married Elizabeth Griffin, January 14, 1946; children—Michael Griffin, Tema Jon. Bachelor of Science, Cooper Union, 1937; Master of Science, California Institute Tech., 1938; Doctor of Science, Harvard, 1948. Registered professional engineer, North Carolina, New York. With United States Public Health Service, 1940-42; teaching fellow Harvard, 1946-48; with Malcolm Pirnie (consultant environmental engineers), New York City, 1948-52; associate professor department environmental sciences and engineering University North Carolina at Chapel Hill, 1952-55, professor; 1955-73, Kenan professor; 1973-87, Kenan professor emeritus; 1987—, head department environmental sciences and engineering; 1955-73; director Water Resources Research Institute, 1965-84, chairman faculty; 1970-73; visiting professor Technological University Delft, 1960-61, University College, London, 1966-67, 73-75, Tianjin University, 1981; editor environmental sciences series Acad. Press, 1968-75; consultant to industry, consultant engineers, governmental agys. World Bank, World Health Organization, with special service in Switzerland, Peru, Egypt, Kenya, People's Republic China; member environmental adv. council Rohm & Haas, Incorporated, 1985—. Author: (with Gordon M. Fair and John C. Geyer) Water and Wastewater Engineering, 2 vols, 1966, 68, Elements of Water Supply and Wastewater Disposal, 1971, (with George Ponghis) Community Wastewater Collection and Disposal, 1975, Regionalization of Water

Management—A Revolution in England and Wales, 1977; Editor: (with M.B. Pescod) Water Supply and Wastewater Disposal in Developing Countries, 1971, (with C.R. Schulz) Surface Water Treatment for Communities in Developing Countries; contributor to publications in field. Adv. board Ackland Memorial Art Mus., 1973-78; board of directors Warren Regional Planning Corp., 1971-77, Inter-Ch. Council Housing Corp., 1975-83, North Carolina Water Quality Council, 1975-77; adv. committee for medical research Pan Am. Health Organization, 1976-79; chairman Washington Metropolitan Area Water Supply Study Committee, 1976-80, National Acad Scis.-Nat. Research Council; board sci. and tech. for international devel. National Research Council, 1978-81, vice chairman environmental studies board, 1980-83; member committee on human rights National Acad. Scis., 1988-91. Served from lieutenant to major Army of the United States, 1942-46. Recipient Harrison Prescott Eddy medal for research Water Pollution Control Federation, 1950, Gordon Maskew Fair award Am. Acad. Environmental Engrs., 1973, Thomas Jefferson award University North Carolina at Chapel Hill, 1973, Gordon Y. Billard award New York Acad. Sciences, 1975; Gordon Maskew Fair medal Water Pollution Control Federation, 1978; Friendship medal Institute Water Engrs. and Scientists (England), 1984; National Science Foundation fellow, 1960-61; Federal Water Pollution Control Administration fellow, 1966-67; Fulbright-Hayes lecturer, 1973-74. Fellow American Society of Civil Engineers (chairman environmental engineering division 1967-68, Simon W. Freese award 1977), American Association for the Advancement of Science, Institute Water Pollution Control (England) (corp. fellow); member Am. Water Works Association (hon.; North Carolina Fuller award 1983, best paper award educational division 1985), National Acad. Engineering, Institute Medicine, American Association of University Women (University North Carolina chapter president 1963-64), Water Pollution Control Federation (hon. member; chairman research committee 1961-66, dir.-at-large 1969-72), Am. Acad. Engineering (hon. diplomate), Order of Golden Fleece, Sigma Xi (University North Carolina president chapter 1968-69). Home: Linden Road Route 7 Chapel Hill North Carolina 27514

OLESEN, DOUGLAS EUGENE, research institute executive; born Tonasket, Washington, January 12, 1939; son of Magnus and Esther Rae (Myers) O.; married Michaele Ann Engdahl, November 18, 1964; children: Douglas Eugene, Stephen Christian. Bachelor of Science, University Washington, 1962, Master of Science, 1963, postgraduate, 1965-67, Doctor of Philosophy, 1972. Research engineer space research div. Boeing Aircraft Company, Seattle, 1963-64; with Battelle Memorial Institute, Pacific NW Laboratories, Richland, Washington, 1967-84, manager water resources systems section, water and land resources department; 1970-71, manager department; 1971-75, deputy director research laboratories; 1975, director research; 1975-79, vice president institute, director NW div.; 1979-84; executive vice president, chief operating officer Battelle Memorial Institute, Columbus, Ohio, 1984-87, president, chief executive officer; 1987—. Patentee process and system for treating waste water. Trustees Capital University, Columbus Mus. of Art, Riverside Hospital, Columbus Zoo, INROADS/Columbus Incorporated, Franklin County United Way, Columbus 1992 Commission, Columbus Symphony Orchestra; member Columbus Capital Corp. for Civic Improvement; board of directors Ohio State University Foundation. Member Ohio Chamber of Commerce (trustee), Columbus Area Chamber of Commerce (executive committee, board directors). Office: Battelle Memorial Institute 505 King Avenue Columbus Ohio 43201

OLIVE, LINDSAY SHEPHERD, emeritus botany educator; born Florence, South Carolina, April 30, 1917; son of Lindsay Shepherd and Sarah Carolyn (Williamson) O.; married Anna Jean Grant, August 28, 1942. Bachelor of Arts, University North Carolina, 1938; Master of Arts, 1940, Doctor of Philosophy, 1942. Instructor botany University North Carolina, 1942-44; mycologist, plant disease diagnostician Department Agriculture, 1944-45; assistant professor botany University Georgia, 1945-46; associate professor botany Louisiana State University, 1946-49; associate professor botany Columbia University, 1949-57, professor; 1957-67; professor department botany University North Carolina, Chapel Hill, 1968-69; distinguished university professor University North Carolina, 1970-82, distinguished university professor emeritus; 1982—. Contributor to: Encyclopedia Americana; contributor chapters to books.; Author: The Mycetozoans, 1975; also numerous articles on classification, life histories, cytology, genetics, evolution of fungi and mycetozoans. Guggenheim fellow,

1956. Fellow American Association for the Advancement of Science; member Nature Conservancy (hon. life member; former project committee chairman), Am. Botanical Society, Mycological Society Am. (president 1966, Distinguished Mycologist award 1981), Society Protozoologists, Torrey Botanical Club (president 1962), Brit. Mycological Society (hon.), National Acad. Sciences, Phi Beta Kappa, Sigma Xi. Home: Bowery Road Highlands North Carolina 28741

OLIVER, BERNARD MORE, electrical engineer, technical consultant; born Soquel, California, May 27, 1916; son of William H. and Margaret E. (More) O.; married Priscilla June Newton, June 22, 1946; children: Karen, Gretchen, Eric. Bachelor of Arts in Electrical Engineering, Stanford University, 1935; Master of Science, California Institute Tech., 1936, Doctor of Philosophy, 1940. Member tech. staff Bell Telephone Laboratories, New York City, 1940-52; director Research & Development, Hewlett-Packard Company, Palo Alto, California, 1952-57, vice president Research & Development; 1957-81, tech. adviser to president; 1981—; lecturer Stanford University, 1957-60; consultant Army Sci. Adv. Committee, from 1966; member sci. and tech. adv. committee California State Assembly, 1970-76. Contributor articles on electronic tech. and instrumentation to professional journals; patentee electronic circuits and devices. Member President's Commission on the Patent System, 1966, State Senate Panel for the Bay Area Rapid Transit System, 1973; trustee Palo Alto Unified School District, 1961-71. Recipient Distinguished Alumni award California Institute Tech., 1972; National Medal of Sci., 1986. Fellow

Institute of Electrical and Electronics Engineers (Lamme medal 1977); member American Association for the Advancement of Science, Astronomical Society, National Acad. Sci., National Acad. Engineering. Republican. Club: Palo Alto. Office: Hewlett-Packard Company 1501 Page Mill Road Palo Alto California 94304

OLSEN, RICHARD GEORGE, microbiology educator; born Independence, Missouri, June 25, 1937; son of Benjamin Barth and Ruth Naomi (Myrtle) O.; married Melinda J. Tarr; children—Cynthia Olsen-Noll, David G., Susan B., John D. Bachelor of Arts, University Missouri, Kansas City, 1959; Master of Science, Atlanta University, 1963; Doctor of Philosophy, State University of New York, Buffalo, 1969. Teacher Rustin High School, Kansas City, Missouri, 1960-61; instructor Metropolitan Junior College, Kansas City, 1963-67; from assistant professor to professor microbiology Ohio State University, Columbus, 1969—. Author: Immunology and Immunopathology, 1979, Feline Leukemia, 1981; also numerous papers. Inventor method of recovering cell antigen and preparation of feline leukemia vaccine. National Institutes of Health fellow SUNY-Buffalo, 1967-68; National Cancer Institute grantee, 1973—. Member Am. Society Microbiology, International Association Research Leukemia, Am. Association Cancer Research, International Society Immunopharmacology, Am. Society Virology. Avocation: farming. Home: 2255 State Route 56 London Ohio 43140 Office: Ohio State U 1925 Coffey Road Columbus Ohio 43210

OLUM, PAUL, mathematician, former university president; born Binghamton, New York, August 16, 1918; son of Jacob and Rose (Citlen) O.; married Vivian Goldstein, June 8, 1942 (deceased March 1986); children—Judith Ann, Joyce Margaret, Kenneth Daniel. Bachelor of Arts summa cum laude, Harvard, 1940, Doctor of Philosophy (NRC predoctoral fellow 1946-47), 1947; Master of Arts, Princeton, 1942. Theoretical physicist Manhattan Project, Princeton, 1941-42, Los Alamos Sci. Laboratory, 1943-45; Frank B. Jewett postdoctoral fellow Harvard, 1947-48, Institute Advanced Study, 1948-49; member faculty Cornell University, Ithaca, New York, 1949-74, professor math.; 1957-74, chairman department; 1963-66, trustee; 1971-75; professor math., dean College Natural Sciences University Texas at Austin, 1974-76; professor math., vice president for acad. affairs, provost University Oregon, Eugene, 1976-80, acting president; 1980-81, president; 1981-89; member Institute Advanced Study, 1955-56; on leave at University Paris (France) and Hebrew University, Jerusalem, 1962-63; visiting professor University Washington, 1970-71. Author monograph, research articles on algebraic topology. Member adv. committee Office Ordnance Research, NRC, 1958-61. National Science Foundation fellow Stanford, 1966-67. Member Am. Math. Society, American Association of University Profs., Math Association Am., Phi Beta Kappa, Sigma Xi. Office: U Oregon Main Campus Office of President Eugene Oregon 97403-1226

O'MEARA, ONORATO TIMOTHY, university administrator, mathematician; born Cape Town, Republic of South Africa, January 29,

1928; came to United States, 1950; son of Daniel and Fiorina (Allorto) O'M.; married Jean T. Fadden, September 12, 1953; children—Maria, Timothy, Jean, Kathleen, Eileen. Bachelor of Science, University Cape Town, 1947, Master of Science, 1948; Doctor of Philosophy, Princeton University, 1953; Doctor of Laws (honorary), University Notre Dame, 1987. Assistant lecturer University Natal, Republic South Africa, 1949; lecturer University Otago, New Zealand, 1954-56; member Institute for Advanced Study, Princeton, New Jersey, 1957-58, 62; assistant professor Princeton, 1958-62; professor math. University Notre Dame, Ind., 1962-75; chairman department University Notre Dame, 1965-66, 68-72, Kenna professor math.; 1976—, provost; 1978—; visiting professor California Institute Tech., 1968; Gauss professor Göttingen Acad. Sci., 1978; member adv. panel math. sciences National Science Foundation, 1974-77, consultant, 1960—. Author: Introduction to Quadratic Forms, 1963, 71, 73, Lectures on Linear Groups, 1974, 2d edition, 1977, Russian transl., 1976, Symplectic Groups, 1978, 82, Russian transl., 1979; contributor articles on arithmetic theory of quadratic forms and isomorphism theory of linear groups to Am. and European professional journals. Member Catholic Commission Intellectual and Cultural Affairs, 1962—. Recipient Marianist award University Dayton, 1988; Alfred P. Sloan fellow, 1960-63. Member Am. Math. Society, Association Catholic Colls. and Univs. (board directors 1986—, executive committee board 1986—). Roman Catholic. Home: 1227 E Irvington Avenue South Bend Indiana 46614

Office: University Notre Dame Office of Provost Notre Dame Indiana 46556

O'NEILL, ROBERT CHARLES, consultant, inventor; born Buffalo, December 3, 1923; son of Albert T. and Helen (Lynch) O'N.; married Agnes Balischak; 1 daughter, Eileen Anne. Bachelor of Science in Chemistry, Rensselaer Polytechnic Institute, 1945; Doctor of Philosophy in Organic Chemistry, Massachusetts Institute Tech., 1950. Senior chemist Merck & Company, Incorporated, Rahway, New Jersey, 1950-56; marketing devel. specialist Merck & Company, Incorporated, 1956-58; vice president Stauffer Pharms. div. Stauffer Chemical Company, New York City, 1958-61; vice president, director research and devel. Cooper Laboratories, Incorporated, 1961-70, executive vice president; 1970-76, general manager; 1975-76, president; 1976-77, also director; consultant, inventor, 1977—. Contributor articles to professional journals. Served with United States Naval Reserve, 1943-46. Member Am. Chemical Society, Chemists Club New York. Patentee in field. Home: 10 Whitlaw Close Chappaqua New York 10514

O'NEILL, RUSSELL RICHARD, engineering educator; born Chicago, June 6, 1916; son of Dennis Alysious and Florence Agnes (Mathurin) O'N.; married Margaret Bock, December 15, 1939; children: Richard A., John R.; married Sallie Boyd, June 30, 1967. Bachelor of Science in Mechanical Engineering, University California at Berkeley, Master of Science in Mechanical Engineering, 1940; Doctor of Philosophy, University of California at Los Angeles, 1956. Registered professional engineer, California. Design engineer Dowell, Incorporated, Midland, Michigan,

1940-41; design engineer Dow Chemical Company, Midland, 1941-44, Airesearch Manufacturing Company, Los Angeles, 1944-46; lecturer engineering University of California at Los Angeles, 1946-56, professor engineering; 1956, assistant dean engineering; 1956-61, associate dean; 1961-73, acting dean; 1965-66, dean; 1974-83, dean emeritus; 1983—; staff engineer National Acad. Sci.-Nat. Research Council, 1954; director Data Design Laboratories, 1977-86, director emeritus; 1986—; Member engineering task force Space Era Education Study Florida Board Control, 1963; member regional Export Expansion Council Department Commerce, 1960-66, Los Angeles Mayor's Space Adv. Committee, 1964-69; member Maritime Transportation Research Board, 1974-81; board advisers Naval Postgrad. School, 1976-84; member National Nuclear Accreditation Board, 1983—. Trustee West Coast University, 1981—; board of directors Western region United Way, 1982—. Member National Acad. Engineering, Am. Society Engineering Education, Society Naval Architects and Marine Engineers, Triangle, Sigma Xi, Tau Beta Pi. Home: 15430 Longbow Dr Sherman Oaks California 91403 Office: 405 Hilgard Avenue Los Angeles California 90024

OPPENHEIMER, JANE MARION, biologist, historian, educator; born Philadelphia, September 19, 1911; daughter of James Harry and Sylvia (Stern) O. Bachelor of Arts, Bryn Mawr College, 1932; Doctor of Philosophy, Yale University, 1935, postgraduate (Sterling fellow), 1935-36, Am. Assn. University Women fellow, 1936-37; Doctor of Science (honorary), Brown University, 1976.

Research fellow embryology University Rochester, 1937-38; faculty Bryn Mawr (Pennsylvania) College, 1938—, professor; 1953-80, professor emeritus; 1980—, acting dean grad. school, 2d semester; 1946-47; Visiting professor biology Johns Hopkins, 1966-67; exchange professor University Paris, 1969. Author: New Aspects of John and William Hunter, 1946, Essays in History of Embryology and Biology, 1967; editor: Autobiography of Dt. Karl Ernst von Baer, 1986; co-editor: Founds. Experimental Embryology, 1964, editor 2d edition, 1974; associate editor: Journal Morphology, 1956-58, Quarterly Rev. Biol, 1963-64; member editorial board: Am. Zoologist, 1965-70, Journal History Biology, 1967-75, Quarterly Rev. Biology, 1968-75; sect. editor developmental biology: Biol. Abstracts, 1970-73. Member history life scis. study section National Institute of Health, 1966-70. Recipient Lucius Wilbur Cross medal Yale Graduate Alumni Association, 1971; Guggenheim Memorial Foundation fellow, 1942-43, 52-53; Rockefeller Foundation fellow, 1950-51; National Science Foundation postdoctoral fellow, 1959-60. Fellow American Association for the Advancement of Science (secretary section L 1955-58, council del. section G 1980-83, committee on council affairs 1981-82), Philadelphia College Physicians (hon.); member Am. Society Zoologists (treasurer 1957-59, chairman division devel. biology 1967, president 1973), Am. Association Anatomists, History of Sci. Society (member council 1975-77), Am. Association History Medicine (member council 1971-74), Am. Society Naturalists, Society for Developmental Biology, International Society for Developmental Biology,

Am. Institute Biological Sciences (member at large governing board 1974-77), International Society History Medicine, International Acad. History of Sci. (Paris) (corr.), International Acad. History Medicine (Paris), Am. Philosophical Society (council 1982—, executive committee 1984—, secretary 1987—). Office: Biology Building Bryn Mawr College Bryn Mawr Pennsylvania 19010

ORDUNG, PHILIP FRANKLIN, electrical engineering educator; born Luverne, Minnesota, August 12, 1919; son of Philip N. and Katherine (Franklin) O.; married Betty Jane Soergel, December 22, 1945; children—Christine Soergel, Katherine Louise. Bachelor of Science, South Dakota State College, 1940; Master Engineering, Yale University, 1942, Doctor Engineering, 1949. Grad. assistant department electrical engineering Yale, 1940- 42, instructor to associate professor; 1942-57, professor electrical engineering; 1957-62; professor electrical engineering University California, Santa Barbara, 1962—; chairman department electrical engineering University California, 1962-68; Visiting professor Tech. University Norway, 1969-70; Director Optoelectronics, 1969-85. Member board education, Branford, Connecticut, 1955-61, chairman, 1959-61; Board of directors Santa Barbara Sci. and Engineering Council, 1969-72; regent California Lutheran College Served as ensign United States Naval Reserve, 1944-45. Fellow Institute of Electrical and Electronics Engineers (regional sec.-treas. 1956-58, Royal W. Sorenson fellow 1962, Centennial award 1984), American Association for the Advancement of Science; member

New York Acad. Sciences, Yale Engineering Association (award for advancement basic and applied scis. 1953), Sigma Xi, Sigma Tau, Eta Kappa Nu. Home: 226 Northridge Road Santa Barbara California 93105

ORR, ROBERT THOMAS, biologist; born San Francisco, August 17, 1908; son of Robert Harris and Agnes (Cockburn) O.; married Dorothy Sutton, June 1934; 1 daughter, Nancy Jane (Mrs. Richard A. Davis); married Dorothy Bowen, August 1942; married Margaret Barry Cunningham, August 1972. Bachelor of Science, University San Francisco, 1929, Doctor of Science, 1976; Master of Arts, University California at Berkeley, 1931, Doctor of Philosophy, 1937. Research assistant Museum Vertebrate Zoology, University California at Berkeley, 1932-35; wildlife technician United States National Park Service, 1935-36; assistant professor biology University San Francisco, 1942-48, associate professor; 1949-54, professor; 1955-64; assistant curator department ornithology and mammalogy California Acad. Sciences, San Francisco, 1936-43; associate curator California Acad. Sciences, 1944, curator; 1945-75, associate director; 1964-75, senior scientist; 1975—; visiting professor zoology University California at Berkeley, summer, 1962, spring, 1965; Trustee Western Foundation for Vertebrate Zoology; member adv. board Point Reyes Bird Observatory. Author numerous books and articles in field. Fellow American Association for the Advancement of Science (past president Pacific division), Am. Ornithologists Union, California Acad. Sciences (Fellows' medal), Explorers Club; hon. member Am. Society Mammalogists (past president), Cooper Ornithological Society (past president), San Francisco Mycological Society; member Australian Mammal Society, Biological Society Washington, National Audubon Society, Nature Conservancy, Society Systematic Zoology, Friends of Sea Otter (vice president). Home: 30 Elm Avenue Larkspur California 94939 Office: California Acad Scis San Francisco California 94118

OSTRIKER, JEREMIAH PAUL, astrophysicist, educator; born New York City, April 13, 1937; son of Martin and Jeanne (Sumpf) O.; married Alicia Suskin, December 1, 1958; children—Rebecca, Eve, Gabriel. Bachelor of Arts, Harvard, 1959; Doctor of Philosophy (NSF fellow), University Chicago, 1964; postgraduate, University Cambridge, England, 1964-65. Research associate, lecturer astrophysics Princeton University (New Jersey), 1965-66, assistant professor; 1966-68, associate professor; 1968-71, professor; 1971—; chairman department astronomy, director obs. Princeton (New Jersey) University, 1979—; Charles A. Young professor astronomy Princeton University (New Jersey), 1982—. Editorial board, trustee Princeton University Press; Contributor articles to professional journals. Alfred P. Sloan Foundation fellow, 1970-72. Member Am. Astronomical Society (councilor 1978-80, Warner prize 1972, Russell prize 1980), International Astronomical Union, National Acad. Sciences, Am. Acad. Arts and Sciences. Home: 33 Philip Dr Princeton New Jersey 08540 Office: Princeton University Obs Peyton Hall Princeton New Jersey 08544

OSTROW, JAY DONALD, gastroenterology educator, researcher; born New York City, January 1, 1930; son of Herman and Anne Sylvia (Epstein) O.; married Judith Fargo, September 9, 1956; children: Geroge Herman, Bruce Donald, Margaret Anne. Bachelor of Science in Chemistry, Yale University, 1950; Doctor of Medicine, Harvard University, 1954; Master of Science in Biochemistry, University College, London, 1970. Diplomate Am. Board Internal Medicine, Am. Board Gastroenterology. Intern Johns Hopkins Hospital, Baltimore, 1954-55; resident Peter Bent Brigham Hospital, Boston, 1957-58; National Institutes of Health trainee in gastroenterology 1958-59; National Institutes of Health trainee in liver disease Thorndike Member Laboratory Boston City Hospital, 1959-62; instructor in medicine Harvard University, Boston, 1959-62; assistant professor medicine Case-Western Reserve University, Cleveland, 1962-70; associate professor University Pennsylvania, Philadelphia, 1970-76, professor; 1977-78; Sprague professor medicine Northwestern University, Chicago, 1978—, chief gastroenterology section; 1978-87; medical investigator Veteran's Administration Hospital, Philadelphia, 1973-78. Editor, contributing author: Bile Pigments and Jaundice, 1986. Assistant scoutmaster Valley Forge council Boy Scouts Am., Merion, Pennsylvania, 1972-78; assistant scoutmaster Northeast Illinois council Boy Scouts Am., 1978-81; vestryman St. Matthew's Episcopal Church, Evanston, Illinois, 1979-82; treasurer Classical Children's Chorale, Evanston, 1982. Served to lieutenant commander Medical Corps United States Navy, 1955-57. Recipient

Gastroenterology Research award Beaumont Society, El Paso, Texas, 1979; National Institutes of Health fellow, 1958-62; National Institutes of Health grantee, 1962—; Veteran's Administration grantee, 1970—. Member Am. Association Study Liver Diseases (councillor 1983-85, vice president 1985-86, president 1987), Am. Gastroentorological Association (chairman exhibit committee 1969-72), Am. Society Clinical Investigation, Am. Physiological Society (assistant editor 1979-84), International Association Study Liver, Am. Society Photobiology. Club: Peripatetic (Bethesda, Maryland). Office: Northwestern U Department Medicine Gastroenterology Section 251 E Chicago Avenue Chicago Illinois 60611

OVERMYER, ROBERT FRANKLYN, astronaut, marine corps officer; born Lorain, Ohio, July 14, 1936; son of Rolandus and Margaret (Fabian) O.; married Katherine Ellen Jones, October 17, 1959; children: Carolyn Marie, Patricia Ann, Robert Rolandus. Bachelor of Science in Physics, Baldwin Wallace College, 1958; Master of Science in Aeros., United States Naval Postgrad. School, 1964. Commissioned 2d lieutenant United States Marine Corps., 1958, advanced through grades to lieutenant colonel; 1972; completed aerospace research pilot school Edward Air Force Base, 1966; astronaut with Manned Orbiting Laboratory National Aeronautics and Space Administration, 1966-69; astronaut with Manned Spacecraft Center National Aeronautics and Space Administration, Houston, from 1969; member support crew Appolo-Soyuz Test Project, 1973-75; co-pilot on 5th mission Columbia National Aeronautics and Space Administration, Houston, 1982; commander Spacelab 3 mission National Aeronautics and Space Administration, 1985. Recipient Alumni Merit award Baldwin Wallace College, 1967. Member Society Experimental Test Pilots (associate), Sigma Xi. Office: 18510 Point Lookout Dr Houston Texas 77058

OVSHINSKY, STANFORD ROBERT, engineering company executive; born Akron, Ohio, November 24, 1922; son of Benjamin and Bertha T. (Munitz) O.; married Iris L. Miroy, November 24, 1959; children—Benjamin, Harvey, Dale, Robin Dibner, Steven Dibner. Student public schools, Akron; Doctor of Science (honorary), Lawrence Institute Tech., 1980; Doctor of Engineering (honorary), Bowling Green State University, 1981; Doctor of Science, Jordan College, Cedar Springs, Michigan, 1989. President Stanford Roberts Manufacturing Company, Akron, 1946-50; manager centre drive department New Britain Machine Company, Connecticut, 1950-52; director research Hupp Corp., Detroit, 1952-55; president General Automation, Incorporated, Detroit, 1955-58, Ovitron Corp., Detroit, 1958-59; president, chairman board Energy Conversion Devices, Incorporated, Troy, Michigan, 1960-78; president, chief executive officer, chief scientist Energy Conversion Devices, Incorporated, 1978—; adj. professor engineering sciences College Engineering, Wayne State University; hon. advisor for sci. and tech. Beijing (China) Institute Aeronautics and Astronautics; chairman Institute for Amorphous Studies. Contributor articles on physics of amorphous materials, neurophysiology and neuropsychiatry to professional journals. Recipient Diesel Gold medal German Inventors Association, 1968, Coors Am. Ingenuity award, 1988; named to Michigan Chemical Engineering Hall of Fame, 1983, Michigan Scientist of Year, Impression 5 Sci. Mus., 1987. Fellow American Association for the Advancement of Science, Am. Physical Society; member Institute of Electrical and Electronics Engineers (senior), Society Automotive Engineers, New York Acad. Sciences, Detroit Physiological Society, Electrochemical Society, Engineering Society Detroit, Cranbrook Institute Sci. (board govs. 1981). Office: Energy Conversion Devices Incorporated 1675 W Maple Road Troy Michigan 48084

OWEN, DUNCAN SHAW, JR., physician, medical educator; born Fayetteville, North Carolina, October 24, 1935; son of Duncan S. and Mary Gwyn (Hickerson) O.; married Irene Lacy Rose, October 22, 1966; children: Duncan Shaw III, Robert Burwell, Frances Gwyn. Bachelor of Science, University North Carolina, 1957, Doctor of Medicine, 1960. Diplomate Am. Board Internal Medicine. Intern Medical College Virginia, Richmond, 1960-61; junior assistant resident in medicine North Carolina Memorial Hospital, Chapel Hill, 1961-62; assistant resident in medicine Medical College Virginia, Richmond, 1964-65, fellow in rheumatic diseases; 1965-66; practice medicine specializing in internal medicine and rheumatology Richmond, Virginia, 1966—; instructor in medicine Medical College Virginia, Richmond, 1966-67, assistant professor; 1967-71, associate professor; 1971-78, professor medicine; 1978—; member staff Medical College Virginia Hospital, McGuire Veteran's Administration; director clinical training div. immunology and connective tissue diseases, chairman clinical activities comm., department internal medicine; chairman medical adv. committee Richmond Branch Arthritis Foundation, 1966-75, board of directors, 1966—, member national patient education committee, 1979-80; medical adv. Social Security Administration, Department of Health and Human Services, 1967—; board of directors Blue Shield Virginia, 1975-77; co-chairman Arthritis Project Virginia Regional Medical Program, 1975-76; board of directors University Internal Medicine Foundation, 1979—; producer Your Health TV Series, Virginia Educational TV, 1978-79; producer Update in Medicine, Good Morning Virginia TV Show, 1980; member various committees in field; proctor Am. Board Internal Medicine, 1977—. Contributor numerous papers, chapters in books, articles to professional journals; associate editor: Virginia Medical, 1978—; editorial reviewer Journal AMA, 1979—, Arthritis Rehumatism, 1981—, Journal Rheumatology, 1984—. Member usher's guild First Presbyterian Church, Richmond, Virginia, 1966-70, deacon, 1974-77, chairman of diaconate, 1976-77, elder, 1978—, chairman witness committee, 1978-80; co-chairman physicians statewide capital funds campaign Virginia Commission University, 1986-87; board of directors Mooreland Farms Association, 1971-73, 77-81, Virginia chapter Arthitis Foundation, 1970-85; member Virginia Mus., Richmond Symphony; board of directors Richmond Area Health Care Coalition, 1980-84. Served to captain

MC, 1962-64. Recipient Army Commendation medal, 1964. National Institute Arthritis and Metabolic Diseases fellow, 1965-66; recipient Gerard B. Lambert award, 1974-75, Distinguished Service award Arthritis Foundation, 1971. Fellow American College of Physicians; member Am. Rheumatism Association (executive committee 1979-80), Richmond Acad. Medicine (president 1982, chairman board 1983), Medical Society Virginia (member committee on aging 1980—, vice president 1973, 75, del. 1972—, scholarship committee 1980—), American Medical Association (7 awards for continuing med. education 1969-87, editorial reviewer journal 1979—), Richmond Society Internal Medicine (board directors 1971-73), Junior Clinical Club, Metropolitan Richmond Chamber of Commerce (board directors 1981-84). Club: Country Virginia. Avocations: hunting, fishing, photography, amateur radio. Home: 8910 Brieryle Road Richmond Virginia 23229 Office: Med College Va Room 742 Nelson Clinic Post Office Box 647 Richmond Virginia 23298-0647

OXNARD, CHARLES ERNEST, anatomist, anthropologist, educator; born Durham, England, September 9, 1933; arrived in Australia, 1987; son of Charles and Frances Ann (Golightly) O.; married Eleanor Mary Arthur, February 2, 1959; children: Hugh Charles Neville, David Charles Guy. Bachelor of Science with 1st class honors, University Birmingham, England, 1955, Bachelor of Medicine, Bachelor of Surgery in Medicine, 1958, Doctor of Philosophy, 1962, Doctor of Science, 1975. Medical intern Queen Elizabeth Hospital, Birmingham, 1958-59; research fellow University Birmingham, 1959-62, lecturer; 1962-65, senior lecturer; 1965-66, court governors; 1958-66; associate professor anatomy, anthropology and evolutionary biology University Chicago, 1966-70, professor; 1970-78, governor biology collegiate div.; 1970-78, dean college; 1973-77; dean grad. school University Southern California, Los Angeles, 1978-83; university research professor biology and anatomy University Southern California, 1978-83, university professor, professor anatomy and cell biology, professor biological sciences; 1983-87; professor anatomy and human biology, head department of anatomy and human biology University Western Australia, 1987—; research associate Field Mus. Natural History, Chicago, 1967—; overseas associate University Birmingham, 1968—; Lo Yuk Tong lecturer University Hong Kong, 1973, hon. professor, 1978—, Chan Shu Tzu lecturer, 1980, Octagan lecturer University Western Australia, 1987, Latta lecturer University Nebraska, Omaha, 1987; research associate Los Angeles County Natural History Mus., 1984—, George C. Page Mus., Los Angeles, 1986—. Author: Form and Pattern in Human Evolution, 1973, Uniqueness and Diversity in Human Evolution, 1975, Human Fossils: The New Revolution, 1977, The Order of Man, 1983, Humans, Apes and Chinese Fossils, 1985, Fossils, Teeth and Sex, 1987, Animal Anatomies and Lifestyles, 1988; member editorial board Annals of Human Biology; cons. editor: Am. Journal Primatology; contributor articles to anat. and anthrop. journals. Recipient Book award Hong Kong Council, 1984, S.T. Chan Silver Medal, University of Hong Kong, 1980; grantee U.S. Pub. Health Service, 1960-71, 74—, National Science Foundation, 1971—. Fellow

New York Acad. Sci., American Association for the Advancement of Science, Southern California Acad. Sci. (board directors 1985); Member Chicago Acad. Society (hon. life), Australasian Society for Human Biology (president), Society for Study Human Biology (treasurer 1962-66), Sigma Xi (president chapter, national lecturer 1987—), Phi Beta Kappa (president chapter), Phi Kappa Phi (president chapter, Book award 1984). Office: U Western Australia, Nedlands Washington 6009, Australia

PACKARD, DAVID, manufacturing company executive, electrical engineer; born Pueblo, Colorado, September 7, 1912; son of Sperry Sidney and Ella Lorna (Graber) P.; married Lucile Salter, April 8, 1938 (deceased, 1987); children: David Woodley, Nancy Ann Packard Burnett, Susan Packard Orr, Julie Elizabeth Stephens. Bachelor of Arts, Stanford University, 1934, Master of Electrical Engineering, 1939; Doctor of Laws (honorary), University California, Santa Cruz, 1966, Catholic University, 1970, Pepperdine University, 1972; Doctor of Science (honorary), Colorado College, 1964; Doctor of Letters (honorary), Southern Colorado State College, 1973; Doctor of Engineering (honorary), University Notre Dame, 1974. With vacuum tube engineering department General Electric Company, Schenectady, 1936-38; co-founder, partner Hewlett-Packard Company, Palo Alto, California, 1939-47, president; 1947-64, chief executive officer; 1964-68, chairman board; 1964-68, 72—; United States deputy secretary defense Washington, 1969-71; director Genetech, Incorporated, 1981—; board of directors Caterpillar Tractor Company, 1972-83, Chevron,

1972-85; chairman Presdl. Commission on Def. Management, 1985-86; member White House Sci. Council. Member President's Commission Personnel Interchange, 1972-74, Trilateral Commission, 1973-81, Directors Council Exploratorium, 1987; president board regents Uniformed Services University of Health Scis., 1975-82; member U.S.-USSR Trade and Economic Council, 1975-82; trustee The Ronald Reagan Presidential Foundation, 1986—; member board overseers Hoover Instn., 1972—; board of directors National Merit Scholarship Corp., 1963-69; director Foundation for Study of Presidential and Congl. Terms, 1978—, Alliance to Save Energy, 1977-87, Atlantic Council, 1972-83, (vice chairman 1972-80), Am. Enterprise Institute for Public Policy Research, 1978—, National Fish and Wildlife Foundation, 1985-87, Hitachi Foundation Adv. Council, 1986—; trustee Herbert Hoover Foundation, 1974—, director Wolf Trap Foundation; vice chairman The California Nature Conservancy, 1983—; trustee Stanford University, 1954-69, (president board trustees 1958-60), Hoover Instn., The Herbert Hoover Foundation; member Dir.'s Council Exploratium, 1987. Decorated Grand Cross of Merit Federal Republic of Germany, 1972, Medal Honor Electronic Industries, 1974; numerous other awards including Silver Helmet Defense award American Veterans of World War II, Korea, Vietnam, 1973, Washington award Western Society Engrs., 1975, Hoover medal American Society of Mechanical Engineers, 1975, Gold Medal award National Football Foundation and Hall of Fame, 1975, Good Scout award Boy Scouts Am., 1975, Vermilye medal Franklin Institute, 1976, International

Achievement award World Trade Club of San Francisco, 1976, Merit award Am. Cons. Engrs. Council Fellows, 1977, Achievement in Life award Encyclopaedia Britannica, 1977, Engineering Award of Distinction San Jose State University, 1980, Thomas D. White National Defense award USAF Acad., 1981, Distinguished Info. Sciences award Data Processing Mgmt. Association, 1981, Sylvanus Thayer award U.S. Mil. Acad., 1982, Environmental Leadership award Natural Resources Defense Council, 1983, Dollar award National Foreign Trade Council, 1985, Presidential MEdal of Freedom, 1988. Fellow Institute of Electrical and Electronics Engineers (Founders medal 1973); member National Acad. Engineering (Founders award 1979), Instrument Society Am. (hon. lifetime member), Wilson Council, The Business Roundtable, Business Council, Am. Ordnance Association (Crozier Gold medal 1970, Henry M. Jackson award 1988, National Medal Tech. 1988, Presidential Medal of Freedom 1988), Sigma Xi, Phi Beta Kappa, Tau Beta Pi, Alpha Delta Phi (Distinguished Alumnus of Year 1970). Clubs: Bohemian, Commonwealth, Pacific Union, World Trade, Engrs. (San Francisco); The Links (New York City); Alfalfa, Capitol Hill (Washington). Office: Hewlett-Packard Company 1501 Page Mill Road Palo Alto California 94304

PAGE, ROBERT HENRY, engineering educator, researcher; born Philadelphia, November 5, 1927; son of Ernest Fraser and Marguerite (MacFarl) P.; married Lola Marie Griffin, November 12, 1948; children: Lola Linda, Patricia Jean, William Ernest, Nancy Lee, Martin Fraser. Bachelor of Science in Mechanical Engineering, Ohio University, 1949; Master of Science, University Illinois, 1951, Doctor of Philosophy, 1955. Instructor, research associate University Illinois, 1949-55; research engineer fluid dynamics Esso Research & Engineering Company, 1955-57; visiting lecturer Stevens Institute Tech., 1956-57, director fluid dynamics laboratory, professor mechanical engineering; 1957-61; professor mechanical engineering, chairman department mechanical, industrial and aerospace engineering Rutgers-The State University, 1961-76, professor, research consultant; 1976-79; dean engineering Texas A&M University, 1979-83, Forsyth professor; 1983—; special research base pressure and heat transfer, wake flow and flow separation. Author papers in field. Served with Army of the United States, 1945-47, Pacific Theatre of Operations. Recipient Western Electric Fund award for excellence in engineering education Am. Society Engring Education, 1968; Lindback Foundation award for distinguished teaching, 1969; Distinguished Alumnus award University Illinois, 1971; Distinguished Service award, 1973; Life Quality Engineering award, 1974, James Harry Potter Gold medal, 1983, Ohio University medal, 1983; named hon. professor Ruhr University, Buchum, W. Ger., 1984. Fellow American Society of Mechanical Engineers, Am. Astronautical Society (chairman National Space Engineering Committee 1969-70, 72-76), American Association for the Advancement of Science, Am. Society Engineering Education; associate fellow Am. Institute Aeros. and Astronautics; member Am. Physical Society. Home:

1905 Comal Circle College Station Texas 77840

PAIS, ABRAHAM, educator, physicist; born Amsterdam, Holland, May 19, 1918; son of Jesaja and Kaatje (van Kleeff) P.; married Lila Atwill, December 15, 1956 (divorced 1962); 1 child, Joshua. Bachelor of Science, University Amsterdam, 1938; Master of Science, University Utrecht, 1940, Doctor of Philosophy, 1941. Research fellow Institute Theoretical Physics, Copenhagen, Denmark, 1946; professor Institute Advanced Study, Princeton, New Jersey, 1950-63; professor physics Rockefeller University, New York City, 1963-81, Detlev Bronk professor; 1981—, professor emeritus; 1988—; Balfour professor Weizmann Institute, Israel, 1977. Author: Subtle is the Lord (Am. Book award 1983, Am. Institute Physics award 1983), Inward Bound. Recipient J.R. Oppenheimer Memorial prize, 1979; Guggenheim fellow, 1960. Fellow Am. Physical Society; member Royal Acad. Sciences Holland (corr.), Royal Acad. Sciences and Letters, Denmark, Am. Acad. Arts and Sciences, Am. Philosophical Society, National Acad. Sciences, Council on Foreign Relations. Home: 450 E 63d St New York New York 10021 Office: Rockefeller University New York New York 10021

PAKE, GEORGE EDWARD, research executive, physicist; born Jeffersonville, Ohio, April 1, 1924; son of Edward Howe and Mary Mabel (Fry) P.; married Marjorie Elizabeth Semon, May 31, 1947; children—Warren E., Catherine E., Stephen G., Bruce E. Bachelor of Science, Master of Science, Carnegie Institute Tech., 1945; Doctor of Philosophy, Harvard University, 1948. Physicist Westinghouse Research Laboratories, 1945-46; member faculty Washington University, St. Louis, 1948-56, 62-70; professor physics, provost Washington University, 1962-69, executive vice chancellor; 1965-69, Edward Mallinckrodt professor physics; 1969-70; vice president Xerox Corp.; manager Xerox Palo Alto (California) Research Center, 1970-78, vice president corp. research; 1978-83, group vice president; 1983-86; director Institute for Research on Learning, Palo Alto, California, 1987—; professor physics Stanford University, 1956-62. Author: (with E. Feenberg) Quantum Theory of Angular Momentum, 1953, Paramagnetic Resonance, 1962, (with T. Estle) The Physical Principles of Electron Paramagnetic Resonance, 1973. Member governor board Am. Institute Physics, 1957-59; board of directors St. Louis Research Council, 1964-70; member physics adv. panel National Science Foundation, 1958-60, 63- 66; chairman physics survey committee National Acad. Sci.-NRC, 1964-66; Member St. Louis County Business and Indl. Devel. Commission, 1963-66; chairman board Regional Industrial Devel. Corp., St. Louis, 1966-67, St. Louis Research Council, 1967-70; member President's Sci. Adv. Committee, 1965-69; Board of directors St. Louis Country Day School, 1964-70, Central Institute for Deaf, 1965-70; trustee Washington University, 1970—, Danforth Foundation, 1971—, University Rochester, 1982—; trustee Center for Advanced Study in Behavioral Scis., Palo Alto, 1986—, The Exploratorium, San Francisco, 1987—; board overseers Superconducting Super Collider, Univs. Research Association, 1984—. Fellow Am. Physical Society (president 1977); member Am.

Association Physics Teachers, American Association of University Profs., American Association for the Advancement of Science, Am. Acad. Arts and Sciences, National Acad. Sci., Sigma Xi, Tau Beta Pi. Club: University (Palo Alto). Home: 2 Yerba Buena Road Los Altos California 94022 Office: Institute for Research on Learning 3333 Coyote Hill Road Palo Alto California 94304

PALADE, GEORGE EMIL, cell biologist, educator; born Jassy, Romania, November 19, 1912; came to United States, 1946, naturalized, 1952; son of Emil and Constanta (Cantemir) P.; married Irina Malaxa, June 12, 1941 (deceased 1969); children—Georgia Teodora, Philip Theodore; married Marilyn G. Farquhar, 1970. Bachelor, Hasdeu Lyceum, Buzau, Romania; Doctor of Medicine, University Bucharest, Romania. Instructor, assistant professor, then associate professor anatomy School Medicine, University Bucharest, 1935-45; visiting investigator, assistant associate, professor cell biology Rockefeller University, 1946-73; professor cell biology Yale University, New Haven, 1973-83; senior research scientist Yale University, 1983—; correlated biochem. and morphological analysis cell structures. Author sci. papers. Recipient Albert Lasker Basic Research award, 1966, Gairdner Special award, 1967, Horwitz prize, 1970, Nobel prize in Physiology or Medicine, 1974, National Medal Sci., 1986. Fellow Am. Acad. Arts and Sciences; member National Acad. Sci., Pontifical Acad. Sci., Royal Society (London), Leopoldina Acad. (Halle), Romanian Acad., Royal Belgian Acad. Medicine. Office: Yale U School Medicine Cell Biology Department 333 Cedar St New Haven Connecticut 06510

PALLADINO, NUNZIO JOSEPH, retired nuclear engineer; born Allentown, Pennsylvania, November 10, 1916; son of Joseph and Angelina (Trentalange) P.; married Virginia Marchetto, June 16, 1945; children: Linda Susan, Lisa Anne, Cynthia Madaline. Bachelor of Science, Lehigh University, 1938, Master of Science, 1939, Doctor of Engineering (honorary), 1964. Registered professional engineer, Pennsylvania. Engineer Westinghouse Electric Company, Philadelphia, 1939-42; nuclear reactor designer Oak Ridge National Laboratory, 1946-48; staff assistant to div. manager Argonne National Laboratory, Lemont, Illinois, 1948-50; manager PWR reactor design subdiv. Westinghouse Electric Corp., Pittsburgh, 1950-59; head nuclear engineering department Pennsylvania State University, University Park, 1959-66, dean College Engineering; 1966-81; chairman Nuclear Regulatory Commission, Washington, 1981-86; past member Pennsylvania Gov.'s Sci. Advisory Committee, Gov.'s Energy Council; past member Pa.'s Commission to Investigate TMI. Contributor tech. articles to professional journals. Served to captain Army of the United States, 1942-45. Recipient Order of Merit Westinghouse Electric Corp. Fellow American Society of Mechanical Engineers (Prime Movers award), Am. Nuclear Society (past president, A.H. Compton award, W. Zinn award), Am. Society Engineering Education; member National Society Professional Engineers, Argonne Univs. Association (past interim president, past director), National Acad.

Engineers. Roman Catholic. Club: Rotary.

PALSER, BARBARA F., botany researcher, retired educator; born Worcester, Massachusetts, June 2, 1916; daughter of G. Norman and Cora A. (Munson) P. Bachelor of Arts, Mount Holyoke College, 1938, Master of Arts, 1940, Doctor of Science (honorary), 1978; Doctor of Philosophy, University Chicago, 1942. From instructor to professor botany University Chicago, 1942-65; from associate professor to professor botany Rutgers University, New Brunswick, New Jersey, 1965-83, director grad. program in botany; 1973-80, emeritus professor; 1983—; Erskine fellow University Canterbury, Christchurch, New Zealand 1969; visiting professor Duke University, Durham, North Carolina, fall 1962; visiting research fellow University Melbourne, Australia, fall 1984-85. Author lab. manual Principles of Botany, 1973, also numerous research papers in bot. journals; bot. adviser Encyclopedia Brit., Chicago, 1958-59; editor Bot. Gazette, Chicago, 1960-65. Named Outstanding Teacher, Rutgers College, 1977. Member Botanical Society Am. (secretary 1970-74, vice president 1975, president 1976, Merit award 1985), Torrey Botanical Club (president 1968), International Society Plant Morphologists, New Jersey Acad. Sciences (president elect 1987-88, president 1988-89, Outstanding Service award 1985), Am. Institute Biological Sciences. Avocations: mountain hiking and climbing; stamp collecting; photography. Home: 18 Charlotte Dr Bridgewater New Jersey 08807 Office: Rutgers U Department Biol Scis Post Office Box 1059 Piscataway New Jersey 08855

PAN, CODA H. T., mechanical engineering educator, consultant, researcher; born Shanghai, China, February 10, 1929; came to United States, 1948; son of Ming H. Pai and Chih S. Ling; married Vivian Y.C. Chang, June 2, 1951; children—Lydia Codetta, Philip Daniel. Student, Tsing Hwa University, Beijing, China, 1946-48; Bachelor of Science in Mechanical Engineering, Illinois Institute Tech., 1950; Master of Science in Aeronautical Engineering, Rensselaer Polytechnic Institute, 1958, Doctor of Philosophy, 1961. Engineer General Electric Company, Schenectady, 1950-61; director research Mechanical Tech. Incorporated, Latham, New York, 1961-73; tech. director Shaker Research Corp., Ballston Lake, New York, 1973-81; professor mechanical engineering Columbia University, New York City, 1981—; adj. professor Rensselaer Polytechnic Institute, 1961-81; visiting professor Tech. University Denmark, Copenhagen, 1971, University Poitiers, France, 1987; member adv. panel Rand Corp., 1974; consultant in field; vice president Industrial Tribology Institute, Troy, New York, 1982—; co-prin. investigator Spacelab I, 1984. Contributing author: Tribology, 1980, Structural Mechanical Software Series 3, 1980; contributor articles to professional journals. Recipient IR-100 award, 1967; National Institutes of Health fellow, 1972. Fellow Am. Society Lubrication Engineers, American Society of Mechanical Engineers; member American Association for the Advancement of Science, Am. Physical Society, Am. Acad. Mechanics. Avocation: classical music. Home: 501 Plantation St Apartment 409 Worcester Massachusetts 01605 Office: Columbia U New York New York 10027

PANOFSKY, WOLFGANG KURT HERMANN, physicist, educator; born Berlin, Germany, April 24, 1919; came to United States, 1934, naturalized, 1942; son of Erwin and Dorothea (Mosse) P.; married Adele Du Mond, July 21, 1942; children: Richard, Margaret, Edward, Carol, Steven. Bachelor of Arts, Princeton University, 1938, honorary doctorate, 1983; Doctor of Philosophy, California Institute Tech., 1942; Doctor of Science (honorary), Case Institute Tech., 1963, University Saskatchewan, 1964, Columbia University, 1977, University Hamburg, Federal Republic Germany, 1984, Yale University, 1985. Member staff member radiation laboratory University California, 1945-51, assistant professor; 1947-48, associate professor; 1948-51; professor Stanford, 1951—; director Stanford (High Energy Physics Laboratory, Stanford Linear Accelerator Center), 1962-84, director emeritus; 1984—; Am. del. Conference Cessation Nuclear Tests, Geneva, 1959; member President's Sci. Adv. Committee, 1960-65; consultant Office Sci. and Tech., Executive Office President, 1965—, United States Arms Control and Disarmament Agency, 1968-81; member general adv. committee to White House, 1977-81; member panel Office of Sci. and Tech. Policy, 1977—; national defense research California Institute Tech. and Los Alamos, 1942-45. Decorated officer Legion of Honor; recipient Lawrence prize Atomic Energy Commission, 1961; National Medal Sci., 1969; Franklin medal, 1970; Annual Pub. Service award Federation Am. Scientists, 1973; Enrico Fermi award Department Energy, 1979; Shoong Foundation award for sci., 1983; named California Scientist Year, 1966.

Member National Acad. Sciences (chairman Committee on International Security and Arms Control 1985—), Am. Physical Society (vice president, president 1974), Am. Acad. Arts and Sciences, Phi Beta Kappa, Sigma Xi. Home: 25671 Chapin Avenue Los Altos California 94022 Office: Stanford Linear Accelerator Center Post Office 4349 Stanford California 94305

PAPERT, SEYMOUR, mathematician, educator, writer; born Pretoria, South Africa, March 1, 1928; came to United States, 1964; son of Jack and Betty P.; married Androula Christofides, April 10, 1963 (divorced); 1 daughter, Artemis; married Sherry Turkle, December 18, 1977. Bachelor of Arts, University Witwatersrand, S. Africa, 1949, Doctor of Philosophy, 1952; Doctor of Philosophy, Cambridge University, England, 1959. Co-dir. artificial intelligence laboratory Massachusetts Institute of Technology, Cambridge, 1967-73, director Logo Group; 1970-81, professor math. and education; 1964—, Cecil and Ida Green professor education; 1974-80; visiting professor math. Rockefeller University, New York City, 1980-81; sci. director Centre Mondial Informatique et Ressource Humaine, Paris, 1982-83. Author: (with Marvin Minsky) Perceptrons, 1969, Artificial Intelligence, 1974, (with McNaughton) Non-Counting Automata, 1971, Mindstorms: Children, Computers..., 1980. Marconi International fellow, 1981; J.S. Guggenheim fellow, 1980. Office: Massachusetts Institute of

Technology Department Media Tech Cambridge Massachusetts 02139

PARDEN, ROBERT JAMES, engineering educator, management consultant; born Mason City, Iowa, April 17, 1922; son of James Ambrose and Mary Ellen (Fahey) P.; married Elizabeth Jane Taylor, June 15, 1955; children—Patricia Gale, James A., John R., Nancy Ann. Bachelor of Science in Mechanical Engineering, State University Iowa, 1947, Master of Science, 1951, Doctor of Philosophy, 1953. Industrial engineer LaCrosse Rubber Mills, 1947-50; associate director Iowa Management Course, 1951-53; associate professor industrial engineering Illinois Institute Tech., 1953-54; professor engineering management University Santa Clara, 1955—, dean School Engineering; 1955-82; principal Saratoga Cons. Group (California), 1982—; Member Secretary Navy's Survey Board Grad. Education, 1964. Member Saratoga Planning Commission, 1959-61. Served to 1st lieutenant, Quartermaster Corps Army of the United States, 1943-46. Member American Society of Mechanical Engineers (chairman Santa Clara Valley section 1958), Am. Society Engineering Education (chairman Pacific Northwest section 1960), Am. Institute Industrial Engineers (education chairman 1958-63, director ASEE-ECPD affairs 1963-68), National Society Professional Engineers, Engineers Council Professional Devel. (director 1964-65, 66-69), Society Advancement Management, American Society of Mechanical Engineers, Sigma Xi, Tau Beta Pi. Roman Catholic. Home: 19832 Bonnie Ridge Way Saratoga California 95070 Office: U Santa Clara School Engring Santa Clara California 95053 also: Saratoga Cons Group Box 3145 Saratoga California 95070

PARIZEK, ELDON JOSEPH, geologist, college dean; born Iowa City, April 30, 1920; son of William Joseph and Libbie S. P.; married Mildred Marie Burger, August 9, 1944; children—Richard, Marianne, Elizabeth, Amy. Bachelor of Science, University Iowa, 1942, Master of Science, 1946, Doctor of Philosophy, 1949. Instructor University Iowa, 1947-49; assistant professor geology University Georgia, 1949-54, associate professor; 1954-56; associate professor University Kansas City, 1956-63; professor University Missouri, Kansas City, 1963—; chairman department geoscis. University Missouri, 1968-78; dean University Missouri (College Arts and Sciences), 1979-86. Served with United States Navy, 1942-45. Fellow Geological Society Am.; member American Association of University Profs., Association Missouri Geologists, American Association for the Advancement of Science, Sigma Xi. Roman Catholic. Research, numerous publs. on mass wasting, slope failure, underground space, geology of West Missouri. Home: 6913 W 100 Overland Park Kansas 66212 Office: 5100 Rockhill Kansas City Missouri 64110

PARKER, DONN BLANCHARD, computer security specialist; born San Jose, California, October 9, 1929; son of Donald William and Miriam Estelle (Blanchard) P.; married Lorna Ruth Schroeder, August 16, 1952; children: Diane Parker Wisdom, David. Bachelor of Arts, University Calif, Berkeley, 1952, Master of Arts, 1954. Senior engineer General Dynamics Company, San Diego, 1954-62; staff consultant Control Data

Corp., Palo Alto, California, 1962-69; senior management systems consultant SRI International, Menlo Park, California, 1969—. Author: Crime by Computer, 1976; Ethical Conflicts in Computer Technology, 1977; Computer Security Management, 1982; Fighting Computer Crime, 1983. Research grantee National Science Foundation, 1971-79, U.S. Department Justice, 19796. Member Association Computing Machinery (secretary 1969-75), Am. Federation Information Processing Socs. (board directors 1974-76), Am. Society Industrial Security. Republican. Lutheran. Lodge: Rotary. Office: SRI International Menlo Park California 94025

PARKER, ROBERT ALLAN RIDLEY, astronaut; born New York City, December 14, 1936; son of Allan Elwood and Alice (Heywood) P.; married Joan Audrey Capers, June 14, 1958 (divorced 1980); children: Kimberly Ellen, Brian David Capers; married Judith S. Woodruff, April 2, 1981. Bachelor of Arts, Amherst College, 1958; Doctor of Philosophy, California Institute Tech., 1962. National Science Foundation postdoctoral fellow University Wisconsin, 1962-63, assistant professor, then associate professor astronomy; 1963-74; astronaut National Aeronautics and Space Administration, Johnson Space Center, 1967—; member support crew Apollo XV and XVII; mission scientist Apollo XVII; program scientist Skylab program; mission specialist for Spacelab I. Member Am. Astronomical Society, Phi Beta Kappa, Sigma Xi. Office: Code CB NASA-JSC Houston Texas 77058

PASACHOFF, JAY MYRON, astronomer, educator; born New York City, July 1, 1943; son of Samuel S. and Anne (Traub) P.; married Naomi Schwartz, March 31, 1974; children: Eloise Hilary, Deborah Donna. Bachelor of Arts, Harvard University, 1963, Master of Arts (NSF fellow), 1965, Doctor of Philosophy (NSF fellow, New York State Regents fellow for advanced graduate study), 1969. Research physicist Air Force Cambridge Research Laboratories, Bedford, Massachusetts, 1968-69; Menzel research fellow Harvard College Observatory, Cambridge, Massachusetts, 1969-70; research fellow Hale Observatory, Carnegie Institution, Washington, and California Institute Tech., Pasadena, 1970-72; director Hopkins Observatory Williams College, Williamstown, Massachusetts, 1972—; chairman astronomy department Williams College, 1972-77, assistant professor astronomy; 1972-77, associate professor; 1977-84, professor; 1984, Field Memorial professor of astronomy; 1984—; adj. assistant professor astronomy University Massachusetts, Amherst, 1975-77, adj. associate professor, 1977-83, adj. professor, 1986—; visiting colleague and visiting associate professor astronomy Institute for Astronomy, University Hawaii, 1980-81, visiting colleague, 1984-85; eclipse expeditions, Massachusetts, 1959, Quebec, Can., 1963, Mexico, 1970, assistant director Harvard-Smithsonian-Nat. Geog. Expedition, Prince Edward Island, Can., 1972, National Science Foundation expedition, Harvard-Smithsonian-Williams Expedition, Kenya, 1973; National Science Foundation expedition, Colombia, 1973 (annular eclipse), Australia, 1974, Pacific Ocean, 1977, Manitoba, Can., 1979, National Science Foundation expedition, India, 1980, Hawaii/ Pacific, 1981, National Science Foundation expedition, Indonesia, 1983, Mississippi, 1983 (annular eclipse), Papua New Guinea, 1984, Sumatra, Indonesia, 1988; research fellow Owens Valley Radio Observatory, summer 1973, U.S.-Australia Cooperative Sci. Program, Australian National Radio Astronomical Observatory, 1974; guest investigator National Aeronautics and Space Administration Orbiting Solar Obs.-8, 1975-79; Lockhart lecturer University Manitoba, 1979. Author: Contemporary Astronomy, 1977, 4th edition, 1989, Astronomy Now, 1978, Astronomy: From Earth to the Universe, 1979, 3d edit, 1987, A Brief View of Astronomy, 1986, First Guide to Astronomy, 1988; co-author: (with Marc L. Kutner, Naomi Pasachoff) Student Study Guide to Contemporary Astronomy, 1977, (with Kutner, Pasachoff and N.P. Kutner) Student Study Guide to Astronomy Now, 1978; (with M.L. Kutner) University Astronomy, 1978, Invitation to Physics, 1981; (with N. Pasachoff, T. Cooney) Physical Science, 1983, Earth Science, 1983; (with D.H. Menzel) A Field Guide to the Stars and Planets, 2d edition, 1983; (with R. Wolfson) Physics, 1987, (with N. Pasachoff, R.W. Clark, M.H. Westermann) Physical Science Today, 1987; associate editor: Journal Irreproducible Results, 1972—; abstractor from Am. journals for Solar Physics, 1968-78; cons. editor McGraw-Hill Encyclopedia Science and Tech., 1983—; cons. Random House Dictionary, 1983-86; contributor articles to professional journals and encys., articles and photographs to non-tech. publications. Recipient Bronze medal Nikon Photo Contest International, 1971;

photograph aboard National Aeronautics and Space Administration Voyagers, 1977; Dudley award Dudley Obs., 1985; National Science Foundation grantee, 1973-75, 79-83; National Geog. Society grantee, 1973-86; Research Corp. grantee, 1973-74, 75-78, 82-88. Fellow Royal Astronomical Society, American Association for the Advancement of Science (chair section D. 1987-88), Am. Physical Society, New York Acad. Sci.; member International Astronomical Union (United States national representative to Commission on Teaching Astronomy 1976—), Am. Astronomical Society, Astronomical Society Pacific, International Union Radio Sci., American Association of University Women (chapter president 1977-80), Am. Association Physics Teachers (astronomy committee 1983-87), Sigma Xi (chapter president 1973-74). Home: 1305 Main St Williamstown Massachusetts 01267 Office: Hopkins Obs Williams College Williamstown Massachusetts 01267

PATEL, CHANDRA KUMAR NARANBHAI, research company executive; born Baramati, India, July 2, 1938; came to United States, 1958, naturalized, 1970; son of Naranbhai Chaturbhai and Maniben P.; married Shela Dixit, August 20, 196l; children: Neela, Meena. Bachelor of Engineering., Poona University, 1958; Master of Science, Stanford University, 1959, Doctor of Philosophy, 1961. Member tech. staff Bell Telephone Laboratories, Murray Hill, New Jersey, 1961—, head infrared physics and electronics research department; 1967-70, director electronics research department; 1970-76, director physical research laboratory; 1976-81, executive director research physics and acad. affairs div.; 1981-87, executive director research, materials sci., engineering and acad. affairs div.; 1987—; trustee Aerospace Corp., Los Angeles, 1979—; director Newport Corp., Fountain Valley, California. Contributor articles to tech. journals. Recipient Adolph Lomb medal Optical Society Am., 1966; Ballantine medal Franklin Institute, 1968; Coblentz award Am. Chemical Society, 1974; Honor award Association Indians in Am., 1975; Zworykin award National Acad. Engineering, 1976; Lamme medal Institute of Electrical and Electronic Engineers, 1976; Founders prize Texas Instruments Foundation, 1978; award New York sect. Society Applied Spectroscopy, 1982; Schawlow medal Laser Institute Am., 1984; Thomas Alva Edison Sci. award New Jersey Gov., 1987; George E. Pake prize Am. Physical Society, 1988. Fellow Am. Acad. Arts and Sciences, Am. Physical Society, Institute of Electrical and Electronics Engineers, American Association for the Advancement of Science, Optical Society Am. (Townes medal 1982), Indian National Sci. Acad. (foreign); member National Acad. Sciences, National Acad. Engineering, Gynecologic Laser Surgery Society (hon.), Am. Society for Laser Medicine and Surgery (hon.), Third World Acad. Sciences (associate). Home: 77 Colt Road Summit New Jersey 07901 Office: AT&T Bell Labs 600 Mountain Avenue Murray Hill New Jersey 07974

PATRICK, RUTH (MRS. CHARLES HODGE), limnologist, diatom taxonomist, educator; born Topeka, Kansas; daughter of Frank and Myrtle (Jetmore) P.; married Charles Hodge, IV, July 10, 1931; 1 son, Charles, V. Bachelor of Science, Coker College, 1929, Doctor of Laws, 1971; Master of Arts, University Virginia, 1931, Doctor of Philosophy, 1934; Doctor of Science, Beaver College, 1970, PMC Colls., 1971, Philadelphia College Pharmacy and Science, 1973, Wilkes College, 1974, Cedar Crest College, 1974, University New Haven, 1975, Hood College, 1975, Medical College Pennsylvania, 1975, Drexel University, 1975, Swarthmore College, 1975, Bucknell University, 1976, Rensselaer Polytechnic Institute, 1976, St. Lawrence University, 1978; Doctor of Humane Letters, Chestnut Hill Coll, 1974. Associate curator microscopy department Acad. Natural Sciences, Philadelphia, 1939-47; curator Leidy Microscopic Society, 1937-47, curator limnology department; 1947—, chairman limnology department; 1947-73; occupant Francis Boyer Research Chair, 1973—, chairman board trustees; 1973-76, hon. chairman board trustees; 1976—; lecturer botany University Pennsylvania, 1950-70, adj. professor; 1970—; guest Fellow of Saybrook Yale, 1975; participant Am. Philosophical Society limnology expedition to, Mexico, 1947; leader Catherwood Foundation expedition to, Peru and Brazil, 1955; del. General Assembly, International Union Biological Sciences, Bergen, Norway, 1973; Director E.I. duPont, Pennsylvania Power and Light Company; Chairman algae committee Smithsonian Oceanographic Sorting Center, 1963-68; member panel on water blooms President's Sci. Adv. Committee, 1966; member panel on water resources and water pollution Gov.'s Sci. Adv. Committee, 1966; member national tech. adv. committee on water quality requirements for fish and other aquatic life and wildlife Department Interior, 1967-68; member citizen's adv. council

Pennsylvania Department Environmental Resources, 1971-73; member hazardous materials adv. committee Environmental Protection Agency, 1971-74, executive adv. committee, 1974-79, chairman com.'s panel on ecology, 1974-76; member Pennsylvania Gov.'s Sci. Adv. Council, 1972-78; member executive adv. committee national power survey Federal Power Commission., 1972-75; member council Smithsonian Institution, 1973—; member Philadelphia Adv. Council, 1973-76; member energy research and devel. adv. council President's, Energy Policy Office, 1973-74; member adv. council Renewable Natural Resources Foundation, 1973-76, Electric Power Research Foundation, 1973-77; member adv. committee for research National Science Foundation., 1973-74; member general adv. committee Energy Research and Development Administration, 1975-77; member committee on human resources National Research Council, 1975-76; member adv. council department biology Princeton, 1975—; member committee on sci. and arts Franklin Institute, 1978—; member university council committee Yale School Forestry and Environmental Studies, 1978—; member sci. adv. council World Wildlife Fund-U.South, 1978—; trustee Aquarium Society Philadelphia, 1951-58, Chesnut Hill Acad., Lacawac Sanctuary Foundation, Henry Foundation; board of directors Wissahickon Valley Watershed Association; member adv. council French and Pickering Creeks Conservation Trust; board governors Nature Conservancy; board managers Wistar Institute Anatomy and Biology. Author: (with Dr. C.W. Reimer) Diatoms of the United States, Volume 1, 1966, Volume II, Part 1, 1975;

member editorial board: (with Dr. C.W. Reimer) Science, 1974-76, American Naturalist; trustee: (with Dr. C.W. Reimer) Biological Abstracts, 1974-76; contributor (with Dr. C.W. Reimer) articles to professional journals.

Recipient Distinguished Dau. of Pennsylvania award, 1952; Richard Hopper Day Memorial medal Acad. Natural Sciences, 1969; Gimbel Philadelphia award, 1969; Gold medal YWCA, 1970; Lewis L. Dollinger Pure Environment award Franklin Institute, 1970; Pennsylvania award for excellence in sci. and tech., 1970; Eminent Ecologist award Ecol. Society Am., 1972; Philadelphia award, 1973; Gold medal Pennsylvania State Fish and Game Protective Association, 1974; International John and Alice Tyler Ecology award, 1975; Gold medal Philadelphia Society for Promoting Agr., 1975; Pub. Service award Department Interior, 1975; Iben award Am. Water Resources Association, 1976; Outstanding Alumni award Coker College, 1977; Francis K. Hutchinson medal Garden Club of Am., 1977; Golden medal Royal Zool. Society Antwerp, 1978.

Fellow American Association for the Advancement of Science (committee environmental alterations 1973-74); member National Acad. Sciences (chairman panel committee on pollution 1966, member committee sci. and pub. policy 1973-77, member environmental measurements panel of committee on remote sensing programs for earth resource surveys 1973-74, member nominating committee 1973-75), National Acad. Engineering (committee environmental engring.'s ad hoc study on explicit criteria for decisions in power plant siting 1973), Am. Philosophical Society, Am. Acad. Arts and Sciences, Botanical Society Am. (member

Darbarker prize committee 1956, merit award 1971), Phycol. Society Am. (president 1954), International Limnological Society, International Society Plant Taxonomists, Am. Society Plant Taxonomy, Am. Society Limnology and Oceanography, Pennsylvania Zool. Society, Water Pollution Control Federation (hon.), Colonial Dames Am., Society Study Evolution, Water Resources Association, Del. River Basin, Am. Society Naturalists (president 1975-76), Ecological Society Am., Am. Institute Biological Sciences, International Phycol. Society, Society Sigma Xi. Presbyterian. Office: Acad Natural Scis 19th at Benjamin Franklin Parkway Philadelphia Pennsylvania 19103

PAULING, LINUS CARL, chemistry educator; born Portland, Oregon, February 28, 1901; son of Herman Henry William and Lucy Isabelle (Darling) P.; married Ava Helen Miller, June 17, 1923 (deceased December 7, 1981); children: Linus Carl, Peter Jeffress, Linda Helen, Edward Crellin. Bachelor of Science, Oregon State College, Corvallis, 1922, Doctor of Science (honorary), 1933; Doctor of Philosophy, California Institute Tech., 1925; Doctor of Science (honorary), University Chicago, 1941, Princeton, 1946, University Cambridge, University London, Yale University, 1947, Oxford University, 1948, Brooklyn Polytechnic Institute, 1955, Humboldt University, 1959, University Melbourne, 1964, University Delhi, Adelphi University, 1967, Marquette University School Medicine, 1969; Doctor of Humane Letters, Tampa University, 1950; Ultriusque Juris Doctor, University New Brunswick, 1950; Doctor of Laws, Reed College, 1959; Doctor h.c., Jagiellonian University, Montpellier (France), 1964; Doctor of Fine Arts, Chouinard Art Institute, 1958; also others. Teaching fellow California Institute Tech., 1922-25, research fellow; 1925-27, assistant professor; 1927-29, associate professor; 1929-31, professor chemistry; 1931-64; chairman div. chemical and chemical engineering, director California Institute Tech. (Gates and Crellin Laboratories of Chemistry), 1936-58, member executive committee, board trustees; 1945-48; research professor (Center for Study Dem. Institutions), 1963-67; professor chemistry University California at San Diego, 1967-69, Stanford, 1969-74; president Linus Pauling Institute Sci. and Medicine, 1973-75, 78—, research professor; 1973—; George Eastman professor Oxford University, 1948; lecturer chemistry several universities.

Author several books, 1930—, including How to Live Longer and Feel Better, 1986. Contributor articles to professional journals. Fellow Balliol College, 1948; Fellow National Research Council, 1925-26; Fellow John S. Guggenheim Memorial Foundation, 1926-27; Recipient numerous awards in field of chemistry, including; U.S. Presidential Medal for Merit, 1948, Nobel prize in chemistry, 1954, Nobel Peace prize, 1962, International Lenin Peace prize, 1972, U.S. National Medal of Sci., 1974, Fermat medal, Paul Sabatier medal, Pasteur medal, medal with laurel wreath of International Grotius Foundation, 1957, Lomonosov medal, 1978, U.S. National Acad. Sci. medal in Chemical Sciences, 1979, Priestley medal Am. Chemical Society, 1984, award for chemistry Arthur M. Sackler Foundation, 1984, Chemical Education award Am. Chemical Society, 1987. Hon., corr., foreign member numerous associations and orgns. Home: Salmon Creek 15 Big Sur California 93920 Office: Institute Sci & Medicine 440 Page Mill Road Palo Alto California 94306

PAYNE, WILLIAM JACKSON, educator, microbiologist; born Chattanooga, August 30, 1925; son of Henry Frederick and Maude (Fonda) P.; married Jane Lindsey Marshall, June 16, 1949; children: William Jackson, Marshall, Lindsey. Bachelor of Science, College William and Mary, 1950; Master of Science, University Tennessee, 1952, Doctor of Philosophy, 1955. Instructor bacteriology University Tennessee, 1953-54; member faculty University Georgia, 1955—, professor microbiology, head department; 1962-77, Alumni Foundation Distinguished professor; 1982—, acting dean Franklin College Arts and Sciences; 1977-78, dean Franklin College Arts and Sciences; 1978-88; visiting professorial fellow University Wales, Cardiff, 1975, hon. professorial fellow, 1977-87; consultant University Alabama, 1959, 68, 70, 85, Philip Morris Company, 1981, Iowa State University, 1988, Howard University, 1989; summer research participant Oak Ridge National Laboratory, 1960; chairman Committee National Registry Microbiologists, 1966-72; consultant United States Environmental Protection Agency, 1971; member biological oceanography panel National Science Foundation, 1976-77; member nitrogen-fixation panel CRGO United States Department Agriculture, 1982; member visiting committee Southern Association Colleges, Mississippi State University, 1983. Author: (with D.R. Brown) Microbiology: A Programmed Presentation, 1968, 2d

edition, 1972, (transl. to Spanish, 1975), Denitrification, 1981, also articles; member editorial board Applied and Environ. Microbiology, 1974-79, University Georgia Press, 1975-78, 88—. Trustee Athens Acad., 1967-72. Served with United States Naval Reserve, 1943-46. Recipient M.G. Michael research award University Georgia, 1960; Creative Research award University Georgia, 1982. Fellow Am. Acad. Microbiology; member Am. Society Microbiology (president Southeastern branch 1963, Puerto Rico Edwards award Southeastern branch 1972, foundation lecturer 1972-73, director foundation 1973-76, chairman foundation committee 1977-82, chairman committee undergrad. and grad. education 1974-77), Am. Society Biochemistry and Molecular Biology, Society General Microbiology (England), Georgia Acad. Sci., Sigma Xi (University Georgia Chapter Research award 1973, president University Georgia chapter 1963), Phi Kappa Phi (president University Georgia chapter 1983), Sigma Alpha Epsilon. Episcopalian. Club: Athens City. Home: 111 Alpine Way Athens Georgia 30606

PEARSON, JAMES BOYD, JR., electrical engineering educator; born McGehee, Arkansas, June 3, 1930; son of James Boyd and Lydia Frances (Lacey) P.; married Marian Scarborough, February 16, 1957; children: Sarah, Jane, Carol, Catherine, Susan, Joanne. Bachelor of Science in Electrical Engineering, University Arkansas, 1958, Master of Electrical Engineering, 1959; Doctor of Philosophy, Purdue University, 1962. Assistant professor electrical engineering Purdue University, Lafayette, Ind., 1962-65; associate professor Rice University, Houston, 1965-70, professor; 1970-79, J. S. Abercrombie professor; 1979—. Served to captain United States Army Reserve, 1952-55. Fellow Institute of Electrical and Electronics Engineers. Office: Rice University Department Elec and Computer Engring Houston Texas 77251

PECK, DALLAS LYNN, geologist; born Cheney, Washington, March 28, 1929; son of Lynn Averill and Mary Hazel (Carlyle) P.; married Tevis Sue Lewis, March 28, 1951; children—Ann, Stephen, Gerritt. Bachelor of Science, California Institute Tech., 1951, Master of Science, 1953; Doctor of Philosophy, Harvard University, 1960. With United States Geological Survey, 1954—; assistant chief geologist, office of geochemistry and geophysics United States Geological Survey, Washington, 1967-72; geologist, geologic div. United States Geological Survey, 1972-77, chief geologist; 1977-81, director; 1981—; member Lunar Sample Rev. Board, 1970-71; chairman earth sciences adv. committee National Science Foundation, 1970-72; visiting committee department geological sciences Harvard University, 1972-78; member Earthscis. Adv. Board, Stanford University, 1982—. Recipient Meritorious Service award Department Interior, 1971, Distinguished Service award, 1979; Presidential Meritorious Executive award, 1980, Distinguished Alumni award California Institute Tech., 1985. Fellow Geological Society Am., American Association for the Advancement of Science; member Am. Geophysical Union (president section volcanology, geochemistry and petrology 1976-78), Mineralogical

Society Am. Home: 2524 Heathcliff Lane Reston Virginia 22091 Office: United States Geol Survey Reston Virginia 22092

PEDERSEN, CHARLES J., chemist; born Fusan, Republic of Korea, October 3, 1904; came to United States, 1922; naturalized, 1953; widowed; 2 children. Master of Science, Massachusetts Institute of Technology, 1927. Research chemist E.I. du Pont de Nemours and Company, Wilmington, Del., 1927-69. Recipient Nobel Prize in Chemistry, 1987. Home: 57 Market St Salem New Jersey 08079

PEEPLES, WILLIAM DEWEY, JR., educator; born Bessemer, Alabama, April 19, 1928; son of William Dewey and Thelma Jeannette (Chastain) P.; married Katie Ray Blackerby, August 30, 1956; children: Mary Jeannette, William Dewey III, Gerald Lewis, Stephen Ray. Bachelor of Science, Samford University, 1948; Master of Science, University Wisconsin, 1949; Doctor of Philosophy, University Georgia, 1951. Research mathematician Ballistics Research Laboratory, Aberdeen, Maryland, summer 1951; member faculty Samford University, 1951-56, Auburn University, 1956-59; professor math. Samford University, 1959—, head department; 1967—; consultant Hayes International Corp. Co-author: Modern Mathematics for Business Students, 1969, Finite Mathematics, 1974, Modern Mathematics with Applications to Business and the Social Sciences, 4th edit, 1986, Finite Mathematics with Applications to Business and the Social Sciences, 1981, 2d edition, 1987; Contributor articles to professional publications. Served to 1st lieutenant Army of the United States, 1954-56. Member Am.

Math. Society, Math. Association Am., National Council Teachers Math., Alabama College Teachers Math. (president 1969), Sigma Xi, Pi Mu Epsilon, Phi Kappa Phi (president 1977), Lambda Chi Alpha. Baptist (deacon, chmn. 1986). Club: Mason (Shriner). Home: 419 Poinciana Dr Birmingham Alabama 35209

PELL, WILLIAM HICKS, mathematician; born Lewisport, Kentucky, October 15, 1914; son of William Clay and Florence Beulah (Hicks) P.; married Dorothy Small, August 23, 1939. Bachelor of Science, University Kentucky, 1936, Master of Science, 1938; Doctor of Philosophy, University Wisconsin, 1943. Grad. assistant math. University Kentucky, 1936-38, University Wisconsin, 1938-42; instructor Math. Brown University, 1943; research aerodynamicist Bell Aircraft Corp., 1943-47; research associate div. applied math. Brown University, 1947-48, assistant professor, then associate professor; 1948-56; professor, head math. department University Kentucky, 1952-53; mathematician National Bureau Standards, Washington, 1956-58; acting chief, then chief math. physics section National Bureau Standards, 1958-65; program director applied math. and statistics National Science Foundation, 1965-67, head math. sciences section; 1967-80, special projects program; 1980—, Cons.; 1981-83; visiting professor University Maryland, 1983—. Associate editor: Journal Research, sect. B, National Bur. Standards, 1961-65, Society Industrial and Applied Math. Journal Applied Math, 1962-68. Postdoctoral fellow School Applied Math., Brown University, 1942-43; postdoctoral fellow Institute Fluid Dynamics and Applied Math., University Maryland, 1955-56. Fellow American Association for the Advancement of Science (section committee math.); member Am. Math. Society, American Society of Mechanical Engineers, Society Industrial and Applied Math., Math. Association Am., Am. Acad. Mechanics, Society Natural Philosophy, Phi Beta Kappa, Sigma Xi, Omicron Delta Kappa. Home and Office: Rural Rt 2 Box 1501 Lewisport Kentucky 42351

PENROSE, ROGER, mathematics educator; born Colchester, Essex, England, August 8, 1931; son of Lionel Sharples; married Joan Isabel Wedge (marriage dissolved 1981); three children. Bachelor of Science in Math., University London; Doctor of Philosophy, St. John's College, Cambridge, London, 1975. Assistant lecturer math. Bedford College, London, 1956-57; research fellow St. John's College, Cambridge, 1957-60; North Atlantic Treaty Organization research fellow Princeton University and Syracuse University, 1959-61; research associate King's College, London, 1961-63; visiting associate professor University Texas, Austin, 1963-64, reader; 1964-66, professor applied math.; 1966-73; Lovett professor Rice University, Houston, 1983-87; Rouse Ball professor math. University Oxford, 1987—; vis professor Yeshiva University, Princeton University, Cornell University, 1966-67, 69. Author: Techniques of Differential Topology in Relativity, 1973; (with W. Rindler) Spinors and Space-time, volume 1, 1984, volume 2, 1986; contributor many articles in sci. journals. Recipient Adams Prize Cambridge University, 1966-67, Dannie Heineman Prize Am. Physical Society and Am. Institute Physics, 1971, Eddington Medal RAS, 1975, Royal Medal Royal Society, 1985, Wolf Prize in physics, 1988. Member London Math. Society, Cambridge Philosophical Society, Institute for Math. and its Applications, International Society for General Relativity and Gravitation. Avocations: reading sci. fiction, 3 dimensional puzzles, miniature stone carving, piano. Office: Oxford U, Math Institute, 24-29 St Giles, Oxford OX1 3LB, England

PENZIAS, ARNO ALLAN, astrophysicist, research scientist; born Munich, Germany, April 26, 1933; came to United States, 1940, naturalized, 1946; son of Karl and Justine (Eisenreich) P.; married Anne Pearl Barras, November 25, 1954; children: David Simon, Mindy Gail, Laurie Ruth. Bachelor of Science in Physics, City College of New York, 1954; Master of Arts in Physics, Columbia University, 1958, Doctor of Philosophy in Physics, 1962; Doctor honoris causa, Observatoire de Paris, 1976; Doctor of Science (honorary), Rutgers University, 1979, Wilkes College, 1979, City College of New York, 1979, Yeshiva University, 1979, Bar Ilan University, 1983, Monmouth College, 1984, Technion-Israel Institute Tech., 1986, University Pittsburgh, 1986, Ball State University, 1986, Kean College, 1986, Ohio State University, 1988, Iona College, 1988. Member tech. staff Bell Laboratories, Holmdel, New Jersey, 1961-72, head radiophysics research department; 1972-76; director radio research laboratory Bell Laboratories, 1976-79, executive director research, communications sciences div.; 1979-81, vice president research; 1981—; adj. professor earth and sciences State University of New York, Stony Brook, 1974-84; lecturer department astrophysical sciences Princeton University, 1967-72, visiting professor, 1972-85; research associate Harvard College Observatory, 1968-80; Edison lecturer United States Naval Research Laboratory, 1979, Kompfner lecturer Stanford University, 1979, Gamow lecturer University Colorado, 1980, Jansky lecturer National Radio Astronomy Observatory, 1983; member astronomy adv. panel National Science Foundation, 1978-79, member industrial panel on sci. and tech., 1982—; affiliate Max-Planck-Inst. für Radioastronomie, 1978-85, chairman Fachbeirat, 1981-83; lecturer Michelson Memorial, 1985, Grace Adams Tanner, 1987; distinguished lecturer National Science Foundation, 1987; Klopsteg lecturer Northwestern University, 1987. Author: Ideas and Information, 1989; member editorial board Annual Rev. Astronomy and Astrophysics, 1974-78; member editorial board AT&T Bell Labs. Tech. Journal, 1978-84, chairman, 1981-84; associate editor Astrophys. Jour, 1978-82; contributor over 80 articles to tech. journals; patentee in field. Trustee Trenton (New Jersey) State College, 1977-79; member board overseers University Pennsylvania School Engring. and Applied Sci., 1983-86; member visiting committee California Institute Tech., 1977-79; member Committee Concerned Scientists, 1975—, vice chairman, 1976—; member adv. board Union of Councils for Soviet Jews, 1983—. Served to lieutenant Signal Corps United States Army, 1954-56. Recipient Nobel prize for physics, 1978, Herschel medal Royal Astronomical Society, 1977, Townsend Harris medal City College of New York, 1979, Newman award

City College of New York, 1983, Joseph Handleman prize, 1983, Graduate Faculties Alumni award Columbia University, 1984, Achievment in Sci. award Big Bros., Incorporated, New York City, 1985. member Am. Acad. Arts and Sciences, Am. Astronomical Society, Am. Physical Society, National Acad. Sciences (Henry Draper medal 1977), International Astronomical Union. Republican. Jewish. Research in astrophysics, info. tech., its potential applications and impacts.

PERKINS, BOB(BY) F(RANK), university official, geologist; born Greenville, Texas, December 9, 1929; son of William Frank and Vela Beatrice (Richey) P.; married Patricia Katharine Woodhull, May 25, 1954; children: Katharine Harriet, Marianna Lea, Orrin Woodhull. Bachelor of Science, Southern Methodist University, 1949, Master of Science, 1950; Doctor of Philosophy, University Michigan, 1956. Instructor geology and biology Southern Methodist University, 1950-51, 53-56; assistant professor geology University Houston, 1956-57; research paleontologist Shell Devel. Corp., Houston, 1957-66; professor geology Louisiana State University, Baton Rouge, 1966-75; chairman, director School Geosci. Louisiana State University, 1973-75; professor geology, dean Grad. School, University Texas, Arlington, 1975—, also associate vice president research; executive director Gulf Coast section Society Economic Paleontologists and Mineralogists Foundation, 1983—. Editor: 15 volume series Geoscience and Man, 1970-75; contributor articles to professional journals. Fellow Geological Society Am., American Association for the Advancement of Science, Texas Acad. Sci.; member Paleontological Society, Am. Association Petroleum Geologists, Paleontological Society Great Britain, Society Econ. Paleontologists and Mineralologists, Malacological Society London. Home: 1416 Creekford Dr Arlington Texas 76012

PERRY, ROBERT MICHAEL, construction engineering company executive; born New York City, December 5, 1931; son of Jerome and Rose P.; married Frances Diane Gross, February 2, 1957; children—Karen, David, Janice. Bachelor of Science in Engineering, University Michigan, 1953; postgraduate, Columbia University, 1955-57. Engineer Dames & Moore (Cons. Engineers), Los Angeles, 1955-60; associate Dames & Moore (Cons. Engineers), 1960-65, partner; 1965-75, managing partner; 1975—, chief fin. officer; 1980—, director; 1981—; president, director RMP Incorporated, 1972—. Served with Corps of Engineers United States Army, 1953-55. Member American Society of Civil Engineers (director, treasurer New York section 1964-68), Professional Services Management Association. Club: University (Los Angeles). Home: 2736 Via Victoria Palos Verdes Estates California 90274 Office: 911 Wilshire Boulevard Los Angeles California 90071

PERRY, SEYMOUR MONROE, physician; born New York City, May 26, 1921; son of Max and Manya (Rosenthal) P.; married Judith Kaplan, March 18, 1951; children: Grant Matthew, Anne Lisa, David Bennett. Bachelor of Arts with honors, University of California at Los Angeles, 1943; Doctor of Medicine with honors, University Southern California, 1947. Diplomate: Am.

Board Internal Medicine. Intern Los Angeles County Hospital, 1946-48, resident; 1948-51, member staff outpatient department; 1951; examining physician Los Angeles Pub. Schools, 1951-52; senior assistant surgeon Phoenix Indian General Hospital, United States Public Health Service, 1952; charge internal medicine United States Public Health Service Outpatient Clinic, Washington, 1952-54; fellow hematology University of California at Los Angeles, 1954-55, assistant research physician atomic energy project; 1955-57; assistant professor medicine, head Hematology Training Program, Medical Center, 1957-60; instructor medicine College Medical Evangelists, 1951-57; attending specialist internal medicine Wadsworth Veteran's Administration Hospital, Los Angeles, 1958-61; senior investigator, medicine branch National Cancer Institute, 1961-65, chief medicine branch; 1965-68, member clinical cancer training committee; 1966-69, chief human tumor cell biology branch; 1968-71, associate sci. director clinical trials; 1966-71, associate sci. director for program planning, div. cancer treatment; 1971-73, deputy director; 1973-74, acting director; 1974; special assistant to director National Institutes of Health, 1974-78, associate director; 1978-80, acting deputy assistant secretary health (tech.); 1978-79; acting director National Center Health Care Tech., OASH, 1978-80, director; 1980-82; deputy director Institute for Health Policy Analysis Georgetown University Medical Center, Washington, 1983—, professor medicine, professor community and family medicine; 1983—; member adv. committee research therapy cancer Am. Cancer Society, 1966-70, adv. committee

chemotherapy and hematology, 1975-77, chairman epidemiology, diagnosis and therapy committee, 1971, grantee, 1959-60; medical director United States Public Health Service, 1961-80; assistant surgical general, 1980-82; member radiation committee National Institutes of Health, 1963-70, co-chairman, 1971-73; president National Blood Club, 1971; chairman Interagy. Committee on New Therapies for Pain and Discomfort, 1978-80; member adv. panel on medical tech. and costs of medicare program Congress of United States, 1982-84; chairman criteria working group (bioseparation) National Aeronautics and Space Administration, 1984; consultant National Center Health Services Research and Health Care Tech., DHHS, 1985—; consultant National Library of Medicine, 1985—; member procedures rev. committee and professional adv. panel Blue Cross/Blue Shield National Capitol Area, 1987—. Associate editor: International Journal Tech. Assessment and Health Care, 1984—; member editorial board Journal Health Care Tech., 1984-87, Health Care Instrumentation, 1984-87; member editorial adv. board Health Tech.: Critical Issues for Decision Makers. Decorated comendador Order of Merit, Peru; comendador Orden Hipólito Unanue, Peru; Pub. Health Service commendation, 1967; Meritorious Service medal USPHS, 1980. Fellow American College of Physicians (adv. committee to governor Maryland on coll. affairs 1969-76, governor for United States Public Health Service and Department of Health and Human Services 1980-82, subcom. on clinical efficacy assessment 1982-85, chairman health and pub. policy committee District of

Columbia met. area 1987—); member Am. Federation Clinical Research, Am. Society Hematology (chairman leukocyte subcom. 1969-71, member sci. affairs committee 1969-70, chairman 1971), Institute Medicine, National Acad. Sci., Institute of Medicine Council Health Care Tech. (member evaluation panel 1987—), Institute of Medicine committee on evaluation med. techs. in clinical use 1981-84),International Society Tech. Assessment in Health Care (president 1985-87). Club: Cosmos. Office: Institute Health Policy Analysis Georgetown U Med Center 2121 Wisconsin Avenue Northwest # 220 Washington District of Columbia 20007

PERUTZ, MAX FERDINAND, molecular biologist; born May 19, 1914; son of Hugo and Adele Perutz; married Gisela Peiser, 1942; 1 son, 1 daughter. Educated, University Vienna; Doctor of Philosophy, University Cambridge, 1940. Director Medical Research Council Unit for Molecular Biology, 1947-62; chairman European Molecular Biology Organization, 1963-69; reader Davy Faraday Research Laboratory, 1954-68, Fullerian professor physiology; 1973-79; chairman Medical Research Council Laboratory Molecular Biology, 1962-79. Author: Proteins and Nucleic Acids, Structure and Function, 1962, Is Science Necessary and Other Essays, 1988. Decorated commander Order Brit. Empire, Companion of Honor, Order of Merit, Orden für Wissenschaft und Kunst, Austria, Order Pour le Mérite, Federal Republic Germany; recipient Nobel prize for chemistry, 1962. Fellow Royal Society (Royal medal 1971, Copley medal, 1979); member Royal Society Edinburgh, Am. Acad. Arts and Sciences (hon.), Austrian Acad. Sciences (corr.), Am. Philosophical Society (foreign), National Acad. Sciences (foreign associate), Royal Netherlands Acad. (foreign), French Acad. Sciences, Bavarian Acad. Sciences, National Acad. Sciences of Rome (foreign), Accademia dei Lincei (Rome) (foreign), Pontifical Acad. Sciences. Office: MRC Lab Molecular Biology, Cambridge CB2 2QH, England

PETERSDORF, ROBERT GEORGE, osteopath, educator, university dean; born Berlin, February 14, 1926; son of Hans H. and Sonja P.; married Patricia Horton Qua, June 2, 1951; children: Stephen Hans, John Eric. Bachelor of Arts, Brown University, 1948, Doctor of Medical Science (honorary), 1983; Doctor of Medicine cum laude, Yale University, 1952; Doctor of Science (honorary), Albany Medical College, 1979; Master of Arts (honorary), Harvard University, 1980; Doctor of Medical Science (honorary), Medical College Pennsylvania, 1982, Brown University, 1983; Doctor of Medical Science, Bowman-Gray School Medicine, 1986; Doctor of Humane Letters (honorary), New York Medical College, 1986; Doctor of Science (honorary), State University of New York, Brooklyn, 1987, Medical College Ohio, 1987, University Health Scis., The Chicago Medical School, 1987, St. Louis University, 1988; Doctor of Humane Letters (honorary), Eastern Virginia Medical School, 1988. Diplomate Am. Board Internal Medicine. Intern, assistant resident Yale University, New Haven, 1952-54; senior assistant resident Peter Bent Brigham Hospital, Boston, 1954-55; fellow Johns Hopkins Hospital, Baltimore, 1955-59; chief resident, instructor medicine Yale University,

1957-58; assistant professor medicine Johns Hopkins University, 1957-60, physician; 1958-60; associate professor medicine University Washington, Seattle, 1960-62, professor; 1962-79, chairman department medicine; 1964-79; physician-in-chief University Washington Hospital, 1964-79; president Brigham and Women's Hospital, Boston, 1979-81; professor medicine Harvard University Medical School, Boston, 1979-81; dean, vice chancellor health sciences University Calif.-San Diego School Medicine, 1981-86; president Association Am. Medical Colleges, Washington, 1986—; consultant to surgeon general United States Public Health Service, 1960-79; consultant United States Public Health Service Hospital, Seattle, 1962-79. Editor: Harrison's Priciples of Internal Medicine, 1968—; contributor numerous articles to professional journals. Served with United States Army Air Force, 1944-46. Recipient Lilly medal Royal College Physicians, London, 1978; recipient Wiggers award Albany Medical College, 1979; Robert H. Williams award Association Profs. Medicine, 1983; Keen award Brown University, 1980; named Distinguished Internist of 1987, Am. Society Internal Medicine. Fellow Am. Acad. Arts and Sciences; member American College of Physicians (president 1975-76 Stengel award), Institute Medicine of National Acad. Sciences (councillor 1977-80), Association Am. Physicians (president 1976-77). Club: Cosmos (Washington). Home: 1827 Phelps Place Northwest Washington District of Columbia 20008

PETERSON, ROGER TORY, ornithologist, artist; born Jamestown, New York, August 28, 1908; son of Charles Gustav and Henrietta (Bader) P.; married Mildred Warner Washington, December 19, 1936; married Barbara Coulter, July 29, 1943; children: Tory, Lee; married Virginia Westervelt, 1976. Student, Art Students League, 1927-28, N.A.D., 1929-31; Doctor of Science, Franklin and Marshall College, 1952, Ohio State University, 1962, Fairfield University, 1967, Allegheny College, 1967, Wesleyan University, 1970, Colby College, 1974, Gustavus Adolphus College, 1978, Connecticut College, 1985; DH, Hamilton College, 1976; Doctor of Hebrew Literature, Amherst College, 1977, Skidmore College, 1981, Yale University, 1986; Doctor of Fine Arts, University Hartford, 1981, State University of New York, 1986, Middlebury College, 1986; Doctor of Fine Arts (honorary), Long Island University, 1987; Doctor of Science (honorary), University Connecticut, 1987, Memorial University Newfoundland, 1987. Decorative artist 1926; instructor sci. and art River School, Brookline, Massachusetts, 1931-34; member administrative staff National Audubon Society; charge ednl. activitles; art editor Audubon magazine, 1934-43; Audubon screen tour lecturer from 1946; editor Houghton-Mifflin Company Field Guide Series, 1946—; art director Nat Wildlife Federation; founder Roger Tory Peterson Institute Study Natural History, 1986—; distinguished scholar-in-residence Fallingwater-Western Pennsylvania Conservancy, 1968; del. 11th International Ornithological Congress, Basel, Switzerland, 1954, 12th, Helsinki, 1958, 13th, Ithaca, New York, 1962, 14th, Oxford, England, 1966, 15th, The Hague, Netherlands, 1970, International Bird Protection

Convention, Tokyo, 1960, Cambridge, England, 1966; member International Galapagos Sci. Project, 1964, USARP-Operation Deepfreeze, Antarctica, 1965; chairman Am. section International Bird Protection Committee; Hon. trustee Uganda (Africa) National Parks; secretary National Audubon Society, 1960-64; member council Cornell Laboratory Ornithology; board of directors World Wildlife Fund, 1962-76; 1st vice president Am. Ornithologists Union, 1962-63. Engaged in bird painting and illustration bird books, 1934—; Author: Field Guide to the Birds, 1934, Junior Book of Birds, 1939, A Field Guide to Western Birds, 1941, Birds Over America, 1948, How to Know the Birds, 1949, Wildlife in Color, 1951, A Bird-Watchers Anthology, 1957, A Field Guide to the Birds of Texas, 1959, Penguins, 1979; Illustrator: Birds of South Carolina, 1949, Birds of Newfoundland, 1951, Arizona and Its Bird Life, 1952, Birds of Nova Scotia, 1961, Birds of Colorado, 1965, limited edition prints of birds, Mill Pond Press, 1974; Co-author: The Audubon Guide to Attracting Birds, 1941, Field Guide to Birds of Europe, 1953, Wild America, 1955, The World of Birds, 1964, The Birds, 1963, Field Guide to Wildflowers, 1968, Field Guide to Birds of Mexico, 1973, Peterson First Guide to Birds, 1986, Peterson First Guide to Wildflowers, 1986; editor: American Naturalist series, 1965—; Contributor articles to natural history and popular publications; lecturer in field. Del. 19th International Ornithological Congress, Quebec, 1986. Served with Corps of Engineers United States Army, 1943-45. Recipient Brewster Memorial medal Am. Ornithologists Union, 1944; John Burroughs medal exemplary nature writing, 1950; Geoffrey St. Hilaire gold medal French Natural History Society, 1958; gold medal New York Zool. Society, 1961; Arthur A. Allen medal Laboratory Ornithology, 1967; White Memorial Foundation Conservation award, 1968; Gold medal Safari Club Philadelphia, 1968; Paul Bartsch award Audubon Naturalist Society, 1969; Frances Hutchinson award Garden Club Am., 1970; Gold medal New Jersey Garden Club, 1970; Gold medal World Wildlife Fund, 1972; Joseph Wood Krutch medal, 1973; Explorers Club medal, 1974; Teacher of Year award, 1974; Distinguished Pub. Service award Connecticut Bar Association, 1974; Cosmos Club award, 1976; Linné Gold medal Royal Swedish Acad. Sciences, 1976; Green World award New York Botanical Garden, 1976; Sarah Joseph Hale award Richards Library, 1977; Master Bird Artist medal Leigh Yankee Mus., 1978; Presidential Medal of Freedom, 1980, Gold medal Philadelphia Acad. Natural Sciences, 1980, Ludlow Griscom award Am. Birding Association, 1980, Smithsonian medal, 1984, Roger Tory Peterson award Thames Sci. Center, 1985—, Eisenmann medal Linnaean Society, 1986, award of Merit Chicago Field Mus. Natural History, 1986, Distinguished Community Citizen award University Connecticut ALumni Association, 1986, New York State Legis. award, 1987; named Swedish-Am. of 1977, Vasa Order of Am.; officer Order of Golden Ark Holland, 1978; Connecticut Citizen of Year, 1986, hon. president International Council Bird Preservation, 1986; Silver Buffalo award Boy Scouts Am., 1986; fellow Davenport College, Yale, 1966—. Fellow American Association for the Advancement of Science, New York Zool. Society, Am. Ornithologists Union, Linnaean Society New York (hon.), London Zool. Society (hon.); member National Audubon Society (life; director 1958-60, 65-67, Audubon medal 1971, special cons. 1972—), Society Wildlife Artists (England) (vice president), Wilson Ornithological Society (life president 1964-65), Brit. Ornithologists Union (hon.), Cooper Ornithological Society, National Association Biology Teachers (hon.). Clubs: Nuttall (Cambridge, Massachusetts); Cosmos, Biologists Field (Washington); Century Association, Explorers (New York City); Intrepids (president). Office: care Houghton-Mifflin Company 2 Park St Boston Massachusetts 02108

PETRIDES, GEORGE ATHAN, ecologist, educator; born New York City, August 1, 1916; son of George Athan and Grace Emeline (Ladd) P.; married Miriam Clarissa Pasma, November 30, 1940; children: George H., Olivia L., Lisa B. Bachelor of Science, George Washington University, 1938; Master of Science, Cornell University, 1940; Doctor of Philosophy, Ohio State University, 1948; postdoctoral fellow, University Georgia, 1963-64. Naturalist National Park Service, Washington and Yosemite, California, 1938-43, Glacier National Park, Montana, 1947, Mount McKinley National Park, Alaska, 1959; game technician West Virginia Conservation Commission, Charleston, 1941; instructor Am. University, 1942-43, Ohio State University, 1946-48; leader Texas Cooperative Wildlife Unit; associate professor wildlife management Texas A. and M. College, 1948-50; associate professor wildlife management, zoological and African studies Michigan State University, 1950-58, professor; 1958—; research professor University Pretoria, South Africa, 1965; visiting professor University Kiel, Germany, 1967; visiting professor wildlife management Kanha National Park, India, 1983; del. sci. conferences Warsaw, 1960, Nairobi and Salisbury, 1963, Sao Paulo, Aberdeen, 1965, Lucerne, 1966, Varanasi, India, Nairobi, 1967, Oxford, England, Paris, 1968, Durban, 1971, Mexico City, 1971, 73, Banff, 1972, Nairobi, Moscow, The Hague, 1974, Johannesburg, 1977, Sydney, 1978, Kuala Lumpur, 1979, Cairns, Australia, Mogadishu, Somalia, Peshawar, Pakistan, 1980; participant National Science Foundation Expedition, Antarctic, 1972, Food and Agriculture Organization (of the United Nations) mission to, Afghanistan, 1972, World Bank mission to, Malaysia, 1975. Author: Field Guide to Trees and Shrubs, 1958, 2d edition, 1972; Editor wildlife mgmt. terrestial sect.: Biol. Abstracts, 1947-72; Contributor articles to biol. publications. Served to lieutenant United States Naval Reserve, 1943-46. Fulbright research awards in E. Africa National Parks Kenya, 1953-54; Fulbright research awards in E. Africa National Parks Kenya, Uganda, 1956-57; New York Zool. Society grantee Ethiopia, Sudan, 1957; New York Zool. Society grantee Thailand, 1977; Michigan State University grantee Nigeria, 1962; Michigan State University grantee Zambia, 1966; Michigan State University grantee Kenya, 1969; Michigan State University grantee Africa, 1970, 71, 73, 81; Michigan State University grantee Greece, 1974, 83; Michigan State University grantee Iran, 1974; Michigan State University grantee Botswana, 1977; Michigan State University grantee Papua New Guinea, Thailand, 1979; Iran Department Environment grantee, 1977; Smithsonian Institution grantee India and Nepal, 1967, 68, 75, 77, 83, 85; World Wildlife Fund grantee W. Africa, 1968. Member Am. Ornithologists Union, Am. Society Mammalogists, Wildlife Society (executive secretary 1953), Wilderness Society, Am. Comm. International Wildlife Protection, Ecological Society, Fauna Preservation Society, E. African Wildlife Society, International Union Conservation Nature, Zool. Society Southern Africa, Sigma Xi. Presbyterian. Home: 4895 Barton Road Williamston Michigan 48895 Office: Department Fisheries and Wildlife Michigan State U East Lansing Michigan 48824

PETRONE, ROCCO A., aerospace manufacturing executive; born Amsterdam, New York, March 31, 1926; son of Anthony and Theresa (DeLuca) P.; married Ruth Holley, October 29, 1955; children—Teresa, Nancy, Kathryn, Michael. Bachelor of Science, United States Military Academy, 1946; degree in mechanical engineering, Massachusetts Institute of Technology, 1952; Doctor of Science (honorary), Rollins College, 1969. Devel. officer Redstone Missile Devel., Huntsville, Alabama, 1952-55; member army general staff Department Army, Washington, 1956-60; manager Apollo program Kennedy Space Center, 1960-66, director launch operations; 1966-69; Apollo program director National Aeronautics and Space Administration, Washington, 1969-73; director Marshall Space Flight Center, Huntsville, Alabama, 1973-74; associate administrator National Aeronautics and Space Administration, Washington, 1974-75; president, chief executive officer National Center for Resource Recovery, Washington, 1975-81; executive vice president Space Transportation and Systems Group, Rockwell International, Downey, California, 1981-82, president; 1982—. Decorated Distinguished Service Medal with 2 clusters National Aeronautics and Space Administration; Commendatore Ordine al Merito, Italy). Fellow Am. Institute Aeros. and Astronautics; member National Acad. Engineering, Sigma Xi. Home: Space Transp System Div 12214 Lakewood Boulevard Downey California 90241

PÉWÉ, TROY LEWIS, geologist, educator; born Rock Island, Illinois, June 28, 1918; son of Richard E. and Olga (Pomrank) P.; married Mary Jean Hill, December 21, 1944; children—David Lee, Richard Hill, Elizabeth Anne. Bachelor of Arts in Geology, Augustana College, 1940; Master of Science, State University Iowa, 1942; Doctor of Philosophy, Stanford University, 1952. Head department geology Augustana College, 1942-46; civilian instructor USAAC, 1943-44; instructor geomorphology Stanford, 1946; geologist Alaskan branch United States Geological Survey, 1946—; chief glacial geologist United States National Committee International Geophysical Year, Antarctica, 1958; professor geology, head department University Alaska, 1958-65; professor geology Arizona State University, 1965—, chairman department; 1965-76; director Mus. Geology, 1976—; lecturer in field, 1942—; Member organizing committee 1st International Permafrost Conference National Acad. Sci., 1962-63, chairman United States planning committee 2d International Permafrost Conference, 1972-74, chairman United States del.

3d International Permafrost Conference, 1978, chairman United States organizing committee 4th International Permafrost Conference, 1979-83; committee to study Good Friday Alaska Earthquake National Acad. Sciences, 1964-70, member glaciological committee polar research board, 1971-73, chairman permafrost committee, member polar research board, 1975-81; organizing chairman International Association Quarternary Research Symposium and International Field Trip Alaska, 1965; member International Commission Periglacial Morophology, 1964-71, 80-88 ; member polar research board National Research Council, 1975-78, late Cenozoic study group, sci. committee Antarctic research, 1977-80. Contributor numerous papers to professional lit. Recipient U.S. Antarctic Service medal, 1966; Outstanding Achieve-ment award Augustana College, 1969; recipient International Geophysics medal Union of Soviet Socialist Republics National Acad. Sci., 1985; named second hon. international fellow Chinese Society Glaciology and Geocryology, 1985. Fellow American Association for the Advancement of Science (president Alaska division 1956, committee on arid lands 1972-79), Geological Society Am. (editorial board 1975-82, chairman cordilleran section 1979-80, chairman geomorphology division 1981-82), Arctic Institute North America (board govs. 1969-74, executive board 1972-73), Iowa Acad. Sci., Arizona Acad. Sci. (president 1982-83); member Association Geology Teachers, Glaciological Society, New Zealand Antarctic Society, Am. Society Engineering Geologists, International Permafrost Association (founding vice president 1983, president 1988—), Am. Quaternary Association (president 1984-86), International Geog. Union. Club: Cosmos. Home: 538 E Fairmont Dr Tempe Arizona 85282

PFENNINGER, KARL H., cell biology and neuroscience educator; born Stafa, Switzerland, December 17, 1944; son of Hans Rudolf and Delie Maria (Zahn) P.; married Marie-France Maylié, July 12, 1974; children—Jan Patrick, Alexandra Christina. Doctor of Medicine, University Zurich, 1971. Research instructor department anatomy Washington University, St. Louis, 1971-73; research associate section cell biology Yale University, New Haven, 1973-76; associate professor department anatomy and cell biology Columbia University, New York City, 1976-81, professor; 1981-86; professor, chairman department cellular and structural biology University Colorado School Medicine, Denver, 1986—; director interdept-mental program in cell and molecular biology Columbia University College Physicians and Surgeons, New York City, 1980-85. Contributor articles to professional journals. Recipient C.J. Herrick award Am. Association Anatomists, 1977; I.T. Hirschl Career Scientist award, 1977; Javits neurosci. investigator award National Institutes of Health, 1984. Member Am. Society for Cell Biology, American Association for the Advancement of Science, Harvey Society, Society for Neurosci., International Brain Research Organization, International Society for Neurochemistry, Am. Society Biological Chemists. Office: U Colorado Health Scis Center Department Cellular and Structural Biology 4200 E 9th Avenue Denver Colorado 80262

PFRANG, EDWARD OSCAR, association executive; born New Haven, August 9, 1929; son of Luitpold and Anna P.; married Jacquelyn Marcia Montefalco, June 7, 1958; children: Lori Ann, Leslie Jean, Philip Edward. Bachelor of Science, University Connecticut, 1951; Mechanical Engineer, Yale University, 1952; Doctor of Philosophy, University Illinois, 1961. Registered professional engineer, Maryland, New York, California. Section chief structures section, building research div. National Bureau Standards, Washington, 1966-83; manager housing tech. program National Bureau Standards, 1970-73, chief structures materials safety div.; 1973-83; executive director American Society of Civil Engineers, New York City, 1983—. Contributor articles to professional journals. Served with United States Naval Reserve, 1953-56. Fellow American Society of Civil Engineers, Am. Concrete Institute (president); member Earthquake Engineering Institute, Sigma Xi, Tau Beta Phi, Chi Epsilon, Sigma Tau. Office: Amer Society Civil Engineer 345 E 47th St New York New York 10017

PHINNEY, WILLIAM CHARLES, geologist; born South Portland, Maine, November 16, 1930; son of Clement Woodbridge and Margaret Florence (Foster) P.; married Colleen Dorothy Murphy, May 31, 1953; children—Glenn, Duane, John, Marla. Bachelor of Science, Massachusetts Institute of Technology, 1953, Master of Science, 1956, Doctor of Philosophy, 1959. Faculty geology University Minnesota, 1959-70; chief geology branch National Aeronautics and Space Administration Lyndon B. Johnson Space Center, Houston, 1970-82; chief planetology branch National Aeronautics and Space Administration Lyndon B. Johnson Space Center, 1982—; National Aeronautics and Space Administration principal investigator lunar samples. Contributor articles to professional journals. Served with Corps of Engineers Army of the United States, 1953-55. Recipient National Aeronautics and Space Administration Exceptional Sci. Achievement medal, 1972; National Aeronautics and Space Administration Cert. of Commendation, 1987; National Aeronautics and Space Administration research grantee, 1972—; National Science Foundation research grantee, 1960-70. Member Am. Geophysical Union, American Association for the Advancement of Science, Mineralogical Society Am., Geological Society Am., Minnesota Acad. Sci. (director), Sigma Xi. Home: 18523 Barbuda Lane Houston Texas 77058 Office: NASA Lyndon B Johnson Space Center SN 2 Houston Texas 77058

PIASECKI, FRANK NICHOLAS, corporation executive, aeronautics engineer; born Philadelphia, October 24, 1919; son of Nikodem and Emilia (Lotocki) P.; married Vivian O'Gara Weyerhaeuser, December 1958; children: Lynn, Nicole, Frederick, Frank, John, Michael, Gregory. Student, University Pennsylvania, 1936-39; Bachelor of Science in Aeronautical Engineering, New York University, 1940, Doctor Aeronautical Engineering (honorary), 1955; Doctor.Aeronautical Science, Pennsylvania Military College, 1953; Doctor.Science, Alliance College, 1970. Registered professional engineer, Pennsylvania. Aircraft designer Platt-LePage Aircraft Corp., Eddystone, Pennsylvania, 1940-41; aerodynamicist Edward G. Budd Manufacturing Company, Philadelphia, 1941-43; founded an engineering research group 1940, (inc. as P-V Engineering Forum), 1943, (became Piasecki Helicopter Corp.), 1946; later chairman board; founded Piasecki Aircraft Corp., 1955; president; director Crown Cork International Corp.; Member industrial consultant committee National Advisory Committee for Aeronautics; member National Science Foundation Commission on Innovation. Member Citizens' Adv. Committee Transportation Quality Department Transportation; member adv. committee industrial innovation presentation, subcom. sci., tech. and space Senate Committee on Commerce, Sci. and Transportation; Trustee Kosciuszko Foundation, New York City. Named hon. Coast Guard pilot, 1945, Elder Statesman of Aviation, 1987; recipient Lawrence Sperry award Institute Aeronautical Sciences, 1951; Mendel award Villanova University, 1954; Philip H. Ward, Junior medal Franklin Institute, 1979; Penjerdel's Aviation award, 1983; Spirit of St. Louis award American Society of Mechanical Engineers, 1983; Explorers award Philadelphia chapter Explorers Club, 1984; Distinguished Citizen award Valley Forge council Boy Scouts Am., 1985; Presidential National Medal of Tech., 1986; Contemporary Pioneer award Colonial Society Pennsylvania, 1987; named to Army Aviation Hall of Fame, 1974; chosen one of nation's ten outstanding young men of year U.S. Junior Chamber of Commerce, 1952. Fellow Institute Aeronautical Sciences, Society Automotive Engineers; hon. fellow Am. Helicopter Society (past president); member Am. Society Professional Engineers, Society Experimental Test Pilots. Clubs: Wings (New York City); Merion Golf, Merion Cricket (Haverford, Pennsylvania); Engineers (Philadelphia), Union League, Corinthian Yacht (Philadelphia); Twirly Birds (founder mem.). Home: Tunbridge Road and Andover Road Haverford Pennsylvania 19041 Office: Piasecki Aircraft Corp W Terminus of 2nd St Essington Pennsylvania 19029

PIEL, GERARD, editor, publisher; born Woodmere, Long Island, New York, March 1, 1915; son of William F.J. and Loretto (Scott) P.; married Mary Tapp Bird, February 4, 1938; children: Jonathan Bird, Samuel Bird (deceased); married Eleanor Virden Jackson, June 24, 1955; child, Eleanor Jackson. Bachelor of Arts magna cum laude, Harvard University, 1937; Doctor of Science, Lawrence College, 1956, Colby College, 1960; University British Columbia, Brandeis University, 1965, Lebanon Valley College, 1977, Long Island University, 1978, Bard College, 1979, City University of New York, 1979, University Missouri, 1985, Blackburn College, 1985; Doctor of Letters, Rutgers University, 1961, Bates College, 1974; Doctor of Humane Letters, Columbia, 1962, Williams College, 1966, Rush University, 1979, Hahnemann Medical College, 1981, Mount Sinai Medical School, 1985; Doctor of Laws, Tuskegee Institute, 1963, University Bridgeport, 1964, Brooklyn Polytechnic Institute, 1965, Carnegie-Mellon University, 1968, Lowell University, 1986; Doctor (honoris causa), Moscow State (Lomonosov) University, 1985. Sci. editor Life magazine, 1938-44; assistant to president Henry J. Kaiser Company (and associate companies), 1945-46;

organizer (with Dennis Flanagan, Donald H. Miller, Junior), president Sci. Am., Incorporated, 1946-84, chairman; 1984-87, chairman emeritus; 1987—; pub. magazine Sci. Am., 1947-84. Translated editions: Le Scienze, 1968, Saiensu, 1971, Investigacion y Ciencia, 1976, Pour la Science, 1977, Spektrum der Wissenschaft, 1978, KeXue, 1979, V Mire Nauki, 1983, Tudomany, 1985, Majallat Al Oloom, 1986; Author: Science in the Cause of Man, 1961, The Acceleration of History, 1972. Chairman Commission Delivery Personal Health Services City New York, 1967-68; trustee Am. Mus. National History, New York Botanical Garden, René Dubos Center; trustee emeritus Radcliffe College, Phillips Acad., Mayo Clinic, Henry J. Kaiser Family Foundation, Foundation for Child Devel.; pub. member Am. Board Medical Specialities; board overseers Harvard University, 1966-68, 73-79. Recipient George Polk award, 1961, Kalinga prize, 1962, Bradford Washburn award, 1966, Arches of Sci. award, 1969; Rosenberger medal University Chicago, 1973, A.I. Djavakhishvili medal University Tbilisi, 1985; named Pub. of Year Magazine Pubs. Association, 1980. Fellow Am. Acad. Arts and Sciences, American Association for the Advancement of Science (president 1985, chairman 1986); member Council Foreign Relations, Am. Philosophical Society, National Acad. Sciences (trustee), National Acad. Sci. Institute Medicine, Phi Beta Kappa, Sigma Xi. Clubs: Harvard, Century, Cosmos (Washington), Somerset (Boston). Office: care Sci Am Incorporated 41 Madison Avenue New York New York 10010

PIERCE, ALLAN DALE, engineering educator, researcher; born Clarinda,

Iowa, December 18, 1936; son of Franklin Dale and Ruth Pauline (Wright) P.; married Penelope Claffey, October 27, 1961; children: Jennifer Irene, Bradford Loren. Bachelor of Science, New Mexico College Agrl. and Mechanic Arts, 1957; Doctor of Philosophy, Massachusetts Institute of Technology, 1962. Registered professional engineer, Massachusetts. Staff researcher RAND Corp., Santa Monica, California, 1961-63; senior staff scientist Avco Corp., Wilmington, Massachusetts, 1963-66; assistant professor Massachusetts Institute of Technology, Cambridge, 1966-68, associate professor; 1968-73; professor mechanical engineering Georgia Institute Tech., Atlanta, 1973-76, Regent's professor; 1976-88; William Leonard professor Pennsylvania State University, University Park, 1988—; visiting professor Max Planck Institute, Goettingen, Federal Republic Germany, 1976-77; consultant in field. Author: Acoustics: An Introduction to it Physical Principles and Applications, 1981; editor physical acoustics monograph series, 1988—; contributor articles on acoustics, wave propagation, vibrations, oil and fluid mechanics to professional journals. National Science Foundation fellow, 1957-60, Shell oil fellow, 1960-61, U.S Department Transp. faculty fellow, 1979-80; recipient Senior U.S. Scientist award Alexander von Humboldt Foundation, 1976, Cert. of Recognition National Aeronautics and Space Administration, 1984. Fellow Acoustical Society Am., American Society of Mechanical Engineers; member Institute of Electrical and Electronics Engineers, Am. National Standards Institute. Home: 4229 Arbor Club Dr Marietta Georgia 30066 Office: Pennsylvania State University

Department of Mech Engring
University Park Pennsylvania 16802

PIERCE, JOHN ROBINSON,
educator, electric engineer; born Des
Moines, March 27, 1910; son of John
Starr and Harriet Anne (Robinson) P.;
married Martha Peacock, November
5, 1938 (divorced March 1964);
children—John Jeremy, Elizabeth
Anne; married Ellen R. McKown, April
1, 1964 (deceased September 1986);
married Brenda K. Woodard, October
17, 1987. Bachelor of Science,
California Institute Tech., 1933,
Master of Science, 1934, Doctor of
Philosophy, 1936; Doctor of
Engineering, Newark College
Engineering, 1961; Doctor of Science,
Northwestern University, 1961,
Polytechnic Institute Bklyn, 1963,
Columbia University, 1965, University
Nevada, 1970, University of California
at Los Angeles, 1977; Doctor of
Engineering, Carnegie Institute Tech.,
1964; Doctor.Electrical Engineer,
University Bologna, Italy, 1974; Doctor
of Laws, University Pennsylvania,
1974; Doctor.Science, University
Southern California, 1978. With Bell
Telephone Laboratories, Incorporated, Murray Hill, New Jersey,
1936-71; member tech. staff, director
electronics research 1952-55, director
research, communication principles;
1958-62, executive director research,
communications principles and
systems div.; 1963-65, executive
director research, communications
sciences div.; 1965-71; professor
engineering California Institute Tech.,
Pasadena, 1971-80; chief technologist Jet Propulsion Laboratory, 1979-
82; visiting professor music emeritus
Stanford University, California,
1983—; past member President's Sci.
Adv. Committee, President's
Committee of National Medal of Sci.

Author: Theory and Design of Electron
Beams, rev. edition, 1954, Traveling
Wave Tubes, 1950, Electrons, Waves
and Messages, 1956, Man's World of
Sound, 1958, Symbols, Signals and
Noise, 1961, (with A.G. Tressler) The
Research State: A History of Science
in New Jersey, 1964, The Beginnings
of Satellite Communications, 1968,
Science, Art and Communication,
1968, Almost All About Waves, 1973;
(with E.C. Posner) Introduction to
Communication Science and
Systems, 1980, Signals: The
Telephone and Beyond, 1981, The
Science of Musical Sound, 1983, (with
Hiroshi Inose) Information Technology
and Civilization, 1984; articles on
popular sci.; short stories. Associate
trustee Batelle Memorial Institute.
Recipient Morris Liebmann memorial
prize Institute Radio Engrs., 1947;
Stuart Ballantine medal 1960, Man of
Year, Air Force Association, 1962;
Golden Plate award Acad.
Achievement, 1962; General Hoyt S.
Vandenberg trophy Arnold Air Society,
1963; National Medal of Sci., 1963;
Edison medal American Institute of
Electrical Engineers, 1963; Valdemar
Poulsen Gold medal, 1963; H.T.
Cedergren medal, 1964; Marconi
award, 1974; John C. Scott award,
1975; Japan Prize, 1985; Marconi
international fellow, 1979. Fellow
Acoustical Society Am., Am. Physical
Society, Institute of Electrical and
Electronics Engineers (medal of honor
1976); member National Acad.
Engineering (Founders award 1977),
Am. Acad. Arts and Sciences,
National Acad. Sciences, Royal Acad.
Sci. (Sweden), Institute Electronic and
Communications Engineers Japan
(hon.), Institute TV Engineers Japan
(hon.), Am. Philosophical Society.
Home: 7 Peter Coutts Circle Stanford
California 94305 Office: Stanford

University Center for Computer Research in Music and Accoustics Stanford California 94305

PILBEAM, DAVID ROGER, paleoanthropology educator; born Brighton, Sussex, England, November 21, 1940; came to United States, 1968; son of Ernest Winton and Edith (Clack) P.; married Maryellen Ruvolo, December 18, 1982. Bachelor of Arts, Cambridge University, 1962, Master of Arts, 1966; Doctor of Philosophy, Yale University, 1967; Master of Arts (honorary), Harvard University, 1982. Demonstrator in anthropology Cambridge University, England, 1965-68; assistant professor anthropology Yale University, 1968-70, associate professor; 1970-74, professor; 1974-81, professor anthropology, geology and geophysics; 1974-81; professor anthropology Harvard University, 1981—, associate dean undergraduate education; 1987—. Author: Evolution of Man, 1970, Ascent of Man, 1972. Fellow Am. Anthropol. Association; member Am. Acad. Arts and Sciences. Office: Harvard U Peabody Mus Cambridge Massachusetts 02138

PIMENTEL, GEORGE CLAUDE, chemist; born Rolinda, California, May 2, 1922; son of Emile J. and Lorraine Alice (Reid) P.; married; children: Anne Christine, Tess Loren, Janice Amy. Bachelor of Arts, University of California at Los Angeles, 1943; Doctor of Philosophy in Chemistry, University California, Berkeley, 1949; Doctor of Philosophy (honorary), University Arizona, 1986, Colorado School Mines, 1987, University Rochester, 1988. From instructor to associate professor chemistry University California, Berkeley, 1949-59, professor; 1959—; deputy director National Science Foundation, Washington, 1977-80; director Laboratory Chemical Biodynamics, University California, Berkeley, 1981—; participant U.S.-Japan Eminent Scientists Exchange Program, 1973-74. Editor: Chemistry-An Experimental Science, 1963; co-author: Understanding Chemistry, 1971, Introductory Quantitative Chemistry, 1956; editor: Chemical Study, 1960; contributor papers to professional journals. Served with United States Naval Reserve, 1944-46. Guggenheim fellow, 1955; recipient Campus Teaching award University California, Berkeley, 1968, College Chemistry Teaching award Mfg. Chemists Association, 1971, Joseph Priestley Memorial award Dickinson College, 1972, Spectroscopy Society Pitts., 1974, Alexander von Humboldt Senior Scientist award, 1974, Pauling medal, 1982, Wolf prize, 1982, Debye award, 1983, Madison Marshall award, 1983, National Medal of Sci. award, 1985, Gesselleschaft Deutscher Chemiker medal, August-Wilhelm-von Hofmann-Denkumnze, 1985, William Proctor prize, 1985, Robert A. Welch award in Chemistry, 1986, Maurice F. Hasler award, 1987, Gold medal Am. Institute Chemistry, 1988. Fellow Am. Acad. Arts and Sci., Royal Society Chemistry (hon.); member National Acad. Sciences, Am. Chemical Society (president 1986—, Precision Sci. award 1959, award California section 1957, Priestley medal 1989), Am. Physical Society (Earle K. Plyer prize 1979, Lippencott medal 1980), Optical Society Am., Phi Beta Kappa, Sigma Xi., Phi Eta Sigma, Phi Lambda Epsilon, Alpha Chi Sigma. Home: 754 Coventry Road Kensington California 94707 Office: University of California

Lab Chem Biodynamics Berkeley California 94720

PITTENDRIGH,   COLIN STEPHENSON, biology educator; born Whitley Bay, England, October 13, 1918; came to United States, 1945, naturalized, 1950; son of Alexander and Florence Hemy (Stephenson) P.; married Margaret Dorothy Eitelbach, May 1, 1943; children: Robin   Ann,   Colin Stephenson. Bachelor of Science with 1st class honors, University Durham, England, 1940; AICTA, Imperial College, Trinidad, British West Indies, 1942; Doctor of Philosophy, Columbia, 1947; Doctor of Science, University Newcastle upon Tyne, 1985.   Biologist international health div. Rockefeller Foundation, 1942-45; adviser Brommellad-malaria Brazilian government, 1945; assistant professor biology Princeton (New Jersey) University, 1947-50, associate professor; 1950-57, professor; 1957-69, Class of 1877 professor zoology; 1963-69, dean Grad. School; 1965-69; professional   biology   Stanford (California) University, 1969—, Bing professor human biology; 1970-76, Miller professor biology, director Hopkins Marine Station; 1976-84; visiting professor Rockefeller Institute, 1962; Phillipps lecturer Haverford College, 1956; Timothy Hopkins lecturer Stanford, 1957; Phi Beta Kappa national lecturer, 1976-77, Sigma Xi national lecturer, 1977-78, 78-79; Adviser Brit. colonial office on Bromeliad-malaria, 1958; member National Acad. Scis.-NRC Committee oceanography. Author: (with George Gaylord Simpson, L. H. Tiffany) Life, 1957;   Contributor   to   books, professional journals.   Past vice president, trustee Rocky Mountain Biol. Lab. Guggenheim fellow, 1959.

Fellow Am. Acad. Arts and Sciences; member Am. Philosophical Society, Am. Society Zoologists, Am. Society Naturalists (president 1968), National Acad. Sci., American Association for the Advancement of Science (vice president for zoology 1968). Home: 8434 Wagon Boss Road Bozeman Montana 59715

PITTMAN, JAMES ALLEN, JR., physician; born Orlando, Florida, April 12, 1927; son of James Allen and Jean C. (Garretson) P.; married Constance   Ming-Chung   Shen, February 19, 1955; children—James Clinton, John Merrill. Bachelor of Science, Davidson College, 1948, Doctor of Science (honorary); Doctor of Medicine, Harvard, 1952; Doctor of Science   (honorary),   University Alabama at Birmingham.   Intern, assistant   resident   medicine Massachusetts General Hospital, Boston, 1952-54; teaching fellow medicine Harvard, 1953-54; clinical associate National Institutes of Health, Bethesda, Maryland, 1954-56; instructor   medicine   George Washington University, 1955-56; chief resident University Alabama Medical Center,   Birmingham,   1956-58, instructor   medicine;   1956-59, assistant   professor;   1959-62, associate   professor;   1962-64, professor medicine; 1964—, director endocrinology and metabolism div.; 1962-71,   co-chairman   department medicine; 1969-71, also professor, physiology and biophysics; 1967—, professor medicine; 1964—; dean University Alabama Medical Center (School Medicine), 1973—; assistant chief medical director research and education in medicine United States Veteran's   Administration,   1971-73; professor   medicine   Georgetown University   Medical   School,   Washington, 1971-73; member endocrinology study section National Institutes of Health, 1963-67; member pharmacology, endcrinology fellowships rev. committees, 1967-68; chairman Liaison Committee Grad. Medical Education, 1976; member Grad. Medical Education National Adv. Committee, 1977-78, United States Department Health and Human Services Council on Grad. Medical Education, 1986. Author: Diagnosis and Treatment of Thyroid Diseases, 1963; Contributor articles in field to professional journals. Fellow American College of Physicians (life); member Association Am. Physicians, Endocrine Society, Am. Thyroid Association, New York Acad. Sciences (life), Society Nuclear Medicine, Am. Diabetes Association, Am. Chemical Society, Wilson Ornithological Club (life), Am. Ornithologists Union, Am. Federation Clinical Research (president Southern section, member national council 1962-66), Southern Society Clinical Investigation, Harvard University Medical Alumni Association (president 1986-88, member committee on grad. med. evaluation 1987—), Phi Beta Kappa, Alpha Omega Alpha, Omicron Delta Kappa. Office: U Alabama School Medicine Office Dean Birmingham Alabama 35294

PODOS, STEVEN MAURICE, ophthalmologist; born New York City, November 7, 1937; son of Mark A. and Sophia L. (Landress) P.; married Salle Garber, June 20, 1959; children: Richard Lance, Lisa Beth. Bachelor of Arts, Princeton University, 1958; Doctor of Medicine, Harvard University, 1962. Diplomate Am. Board Ophthalmology. Intern University Utah Affiliated Hospital, Salt Lake City, 1962-63; resident in ophthalmology Washington University Medical Center, St. Louis, 1963-67, from assistant professor to professor; 1969-75; practice medicine specializing in ophthalmology New York City, 1975—; clinical associate National Institutes of Health, 1967-69; professor ophthalmology, chairman department Mount Sinai Medical School, New York City; also ophthalmologist in chief Mount Sinai Hospital, New York City, 1975—. Member editorial bds. various professional journals; contributor articles to medical journals. Member sci. adv. board Fight for Sight, 1975—; board of directors National Society Prevention Blindness, 1977—. Grantee USPHS, 1975—. Member Am. Acad. Ophthalmology and Otolaryngology (award of merit), American College of Surgeons, Am. Ophthalmol. Society, American Association for the Advancement of Science, New York Acad. Medicine, Association Research Vision and Ophthalmology (trustee 1977-81). Jewish. Club: Princeton. Office: Mt Sinai Med Center 1 Gustave Levy Place New York New York 10029

POGUE, WILLIAM REID, former astronaut, foundation executive, business and aerospace consultant; born Okemah, Oklahoma, January 23, 1930; son of Alex W. and Margaret (McDow) P.; married Jean Ann Pogue; children: William Richard, Layna Sue, Thomas Reid. Bachelor of Science in Secondary Education, Oklahoma Baptist University, 1951, Doctor of Science (honorary), 1974; Master of Science in Math., Oklahoma State University, 1960. Commissioned 2d lieutenant United States Air Force, 1952, advanced through grades to colonel; 1973; combat fighter pilot Korea, 1953; gunnery instructor Luke

Air Force Base, Arizona, 1954; member acrobatic team United States Air Force Thunderbirds, Luke Air Force Base and Nellis Air Force Base, Nevada, 1955-57; assistant professor math. United States Air Force Acad., 1960-63; exchange test pilot Brit. Royal Aircraft Establishment, Ministry Aviation, Farnborough, England, 1964-65; instructor United States Air Force Aerospace Research Pilots School, Edwards Air Force Base, California, 1965-66; astronaut National Aeronautics and Space Administration Manned Spacecraft Center, Houston, 1966-75; vice president High Flight Foundation, Colorado Springs, Colorado, 1975—; pilot 3d manned visit to Skylab space station; now with Vutara Services of Springdale, Arkansas. Decorated Air medal with oak leaf cluster, Air Force Commendation medal, Distinguished Service Medal USAF; named to Five Civilized Tribes Hall of Fame, Choctaw descent; recipient Distinguished Service medal National Aeronautics and Space Administration, Collier trophy National Aeronautical Association; Robert H. Goddard medal National Space Club; General Thomas D. White USAF Space Trophy National Geog. Society; Halley Astronautics award, 1975; de la Vaalx medal Federation Aeronautique International, 1974; V.M. Komarov diploma, 1974. Fellow Acad. Arts and Sciences of Oklahoma State University, Am. Astronomical Society; member Society Experimental Test Pilots, Explorers Club, Sigma Xi, Pi Mu Epsilon. Baptist (deacon). Office: care High Flight Post Office Box 1387 Colorado Springs Colorado 80901 Address: Vutara Services 1101 S Old Missouri Road Suite 30 Springdale AR 72764

POHM, ARTHUR V., electrical engineering educator; born Olmsted Falls, Ohio, January 11, 1927; married; 3 children. Bachelor of Electrical Engineering, Bachelor.E.S., Fenn College, 1950; Master of Science, Iowa State University, 1953, Doctor of Philosophy in Physics, 1954. Laboratory instructor Fenn College, 1949-50; assistant Ames Laboratories, Iowa, 1950-54, Atomic Energy Commission, 1950-54; research physicist Remington Rand Univac div. Sperry Rand Corp., 1954-55, project physicist; 1955-56, research supervisor; 1957-58; associate professor electrical engring Iowa State University, Ames, 1958-62, professor electrical engineering; 1962—, Anson Marston Distinguished professor; lecturer University Michigan, 1956. Fellow Institute of Electrical and Electronics Engineers. Office: Department Elec Engring Iowa State U Ames Iowa 50010

POIROT, JAMES WESLEY, engineering company executive; born Douglas, Wyoming, 1931; married Raeda Poirot. Bachelor of Civil Engineering, Oregon State University, 1953. With various construction firms, Alaska and Oregon; with CH2M Hill Incorporated, 1953—, vice president, Seattle and Atlanta; from 1967, chairman board, Englewood, Colorado; 1983—; former chairman CEO Western Regional Council, Design Profls. Coalition. Named ENR Constrn. Man of Year, 1988. Fellow American Society of Civil Engineers (chairman steering committee quality manual from 1985, board directors); member Am. Cons. Engineers Council (president 1989—). Office: CH2M Hill Incorporated 6060 S Willow Dr Englewood Colorado 80111

POLANYI, JOHN CHARLES, chemist, educator; born January 23, 1929; married Anne Ferrar Davidson, 1958; 2 children. BSc, Manchester (England) University, 1949, Master of Science, 1950, Doctor of Philosophy, 1952, Doctor of Science, 1964; Doctor of Science (honorary), University Waterloo, 1970, Memorial University, 1976, McMaster University, 1977, Carleton University, 1981, Harvard University, 1982, Rensselaer University, Brock University, 1984, Lethbridge University, Sherbrooke University, Laval University, Victoria University, Ottawa University, 1987, University Manchester, York University, 1988, University Montreal, Acadia University, 1989; Doctor of Laws (honorary), Trent University, 1977, Dalhousie University, 1983, St. Francis-Xavier University, 1984. Member faculty department chemistry University Toronto, Ontario, Can., 1956—; professor University Toronto, 1962—, University professor; from 1974; William D. Harkins lecturer University Chicago, 1970; Reilly lecturer University Notre Dame, 1970; Purves lecturer McGill University, 1971; F.J. Toole lecturer University New Brunswick, 1974; Philips lecturer Haverford College, 1974; Kistiakowsky lecturer Harvard University, 1975; Camille and Henry Dreyfus lecturer University Kansas, 1975; J.W.T. Spinks lecturer University Saskatchewan, Can., 1976; Laird lecturer University Western Ontario, 1976; CIL Distinguished lecturer Simon Fraser University, 1977; Gucker lecturer Ind. University, 1977; Jacob Bronowski memorial lecturer University Toronto, 1978; Hutchinson lecturer University Rochester, New York, 1979; Priestley lecturer Pennsylvania State University, 1980; Barré lecturer University Montreal, 1982; Sherman Fairchild distinguished scholar California Institute Tech., 1982; Chute lecturer Dalhousie University, 1983, Redman lecturer McMaster University, 1983, Wiegand lecturer University Toronto, 1984, Edward University Condon lecturer University Colorado, 1984, John A. Allan lecturer University Alberta, 1984, John East Willard lecturer University Wisconsin, 1984, Owen Holmes lecturer University Lethbridge, 1985, Walker-Ames professor University Washington, 1986, John W. Cowper distinguished visiting lecturer University Buffalo, State University of New York, 1986, visiting professor chemistry Texas Agricultural and Mechanical University, 1986, Distinguished Visiting speaker University Calgary, 1987, Morino lecturer University Japan, 1987, J.T. Wilson lecturer Ontario Sci. Center, 1987, Welsh lecturer University Toronto, 1987, Spiers Memorial lecturer Faraday div. Royal Society Chemistry, 1987, Polanyi lecturer International Union Pure & Applied Chemistry, 1988, W.N. Leis lecturer Atomic Energy of Can. Limited, 1988, Consolidated Bathurst visiting lecturer Concordia University, 1988, Priestman lecturer University New Brunswick, 1988, Killam lecturer, University Windsor, 1988, Herzberg lectr, Carleton University, 1988, Falconbridge lecturer, Lauretian University, 1988; member sci. adv. board Max Plank Institute for Quantum Optics, Federal Republic Germany, 1982; member National Adv. Board on Sci. and Tech., 1987; founding member Can. Committee on Sci. and Scholars. Co-editor: (with F.G. Griffiths) The Dangers of Nuclear War, 1979; contributor articles to journals, magazines, newspapers; producer: film Concepts in Reaction Dynamics,

1970. Board of directors Can. Center for Arms Control and Environment; founding member Can. Pugwash Committee, 1960. Decorated officer Order of Can., companion Order of Can.; recipient Marlow medal Faraday Society, 1962; Centenary medal Chemical Society Great Brit., 1965; with N. Bartlett Steacie prize, 1965; Mack award and lectureship Ohio State University, 1969; Noranda award Chemical Institute Can., 1967; award Brit. Chemical Society, 1971; Mack award and lectureship Ohio State University, 1969; medal Chemical Institute Can., 1976; Henry Marshall Tory medal Royal Society Can., 1977; Remsen award and lectureship Am. Chemical Society, 1978, Nobel Prize in chemistry, 1986, Isaac Walton Killam Memorial prize, 1988; Sloan Foundation fellow, 1959-63; Guggenheim fellow, 1979-80. Fellow Royal Society Can. (founding member committee on scholarly freedom), Royal Society London, Royal Society Edinburgh; member National Acad. Sciences United States (foreign), Am. Acad. Arts and Sci. (hon. foreign, member committee on international security studies), Pontifical Acad. Sciences, Rome. Office: U Toronto Department Chemistry, 80 St George St, Toronto, Ontario Canada M5S 1A1

PONNAMPERUMA, CYRIL AN-DREW, chemist; born Galle, Sri Lanka, October 16, 1923; came to United States, 1959, naturalized; son of Andrew and Grace (Siriwardene) P.; married Valli Pal, March 9, 1955; 1 child, Roshini. Bachelor of Arts, University Madras, 1948; BSc, University London, 1959; Doctor of Philosophy, University California, Berkeley, 1962; Doctor of Science, University Sri Lanka, 1978. Research associate Lawrence Radiation Laboratory, University California, 1960-62; research scientist Ames Research Center, National Aeronautics and Space Administration, Mountain View, California, 1962-70; professor chemistry University Maryland, College Park, 1971—; director Arthur C. Clarke Center, Sri Lanka, 1984-86; sci. advisor to president, Sri Lanka, 1984; director Institute Fundamental Studies, Sri Lanka, 1988—. Author: Origins of Life, 1972; Cosmic Evolution, 1978. Contributor articles to professional journals. Fellow Royal Institute Chemistry; member Am. Chemical Society, Astronomical Association, Am. Society Biological Chemists, American Association for the Advancement of Science, Geochem. Society, Radiation Research Society. Office: U Maryland Lab Chem Evolution College Park Maryland 20742

POPE, MICHAEL, electrical engineer; born New York City, May 16, 1924; son of Philip and Anna (Frimet) P.; married Sally Ganong Farrell, May 1, 1977; children: Barbara Lisa, Joseph David, Michele Burton; stepchildren: Jackson Elliott Dube, Ian Hans Farrell. Bachelor of Electrical Engineering, City College of New York, 1944. With Pope Evans and Robbins, Incorporated, and predecessor firms, New York City, 1946-83; chief executive officer, chairman board Pope Evans and Robbins, Incorporated, 1969-83; senior partner Pope Engineers, New York City, 1983-84; president Parsons Brinckerhoff Devel. Corp., 1984-87, Agoil, Incorporated, 1988-89; vice president Robbins, Pope and Griffis, 1989—; board of directors Aegis Incorporated; member New York

State Temporary Study Commission to Rev. Procedures of State University and State University Construction Fund, 1971, New York State Ad Hoc Committee on Energy Conservation in Large Buildings, 1973. Trustee Manhattan Country School, New York City, 1966—, chairman, 1974-78; board of directors City College Fund, 1965—, president, 1976-79; board of directors New Theater of Brooklyn, 1983—. Served with United States Maritime Service, 1944-46. Recipient 125th Anniversary medal to distinguished alumni City College of New York, 1973, also; President's medal, 1979; David B. Steinman medal, 1981; Townsend Harris medal, 1983; Award of Honor, Am. Cons. Engrs. Council, 1979. Fellow Am. Cons. Engineers Council; member American Society of Mechanical Engineers, National Society Professional Engineers, Institute of Electrical and Electronics Engineers. Research in fluidized bed combustion of coal. Home: 115 Central Park West New York New York 10023 also: Basket Neck Lane Remsenburg New York 11960 Office: 2929 Broadway New York New York 10025-7899

PORTER, SIR GEORGE, chemist, educator; born Stainforth, Yorkshire, England, December 6, 1920; son of John Smith and Alice Ann (Roebuck) P.; married Stella Jean Brooke, August 12, 1949; children: John B., Andrew C. G. Bachelor of Science, University Leeds, England, 1941; Master of Arts, Doctor of Philosophy, Cambridge (England) University, 1949, Doctor of Science, 1959; Doctor of Science (honorary), University Utah, 1968, Sheffield University, 1968, University East Anglia, University Surrey, University Durham, 1970, University Leicester, University Leeds, University Heriot-Watt, City University, 1971, University Manchester, University St. Andrews, London University, 1972, Kent University, 1973, Oxford University, 1974, University Hull, 1980, Institute Quimico de Sarria, Barcelona, 1984, University Coimbra, Portugal, 1984, Open University, University Pennsylvania, 1984, University Philippines, 1985, University Notre Dame, University Bristol, University Reading, 1986, University Loughborough, 1987. Assistant research director physical chemistry Cambridge University, 1952-54; assistant director Brit. Rayon Research, 1954-55; professor physical chemistry University Sheffield, England, 1955-63, Firth professor, head department chemistry; 1963-66; director, Fullerian professor chemistry Royal Institution, 1966—; president The Royal Society, 1985—; professor photochemistry Imperial College, London; visiting professor chemistry University College London; hon. fellow Emmanuel College, Cambridge; hon. professor physical chemistry University Kent; Richard Dimbleby lecturer, 1988, John P. McGovern lecturer, 1988. Author: Chemistry for the Modern World, 1962; author BBC TV series Laws of Disorder, 1965; Time Machines, 1969-70; Natural History of a Sunbeam, 1976. Editor: Progress in Reaction Kinetics; contributor to professional journals. Trustee Bristol Exploratory, 1986—; president London International Youth Sci. Fortnight, 1987, 88. Served with Royal Navy, 1941-45. Recipient (with M. Eigen and R. G. W. Norrish) Nobel prize in chemistry, 1967; Kalinga prize, 1977; created knight, 1972. Fellow Royal Society (Davy medal 1971, Rumford medal 1978), Royal Institute Chemistry, Royal Scottish Society of

Arts, Royal Society of Edinburgh; member Chemical Society (president 1970-72, president Faraday division 1973-74, Faraday medal 1979, 80, Longstaff medal 1981), Sci. Research Council (Brit.) (council, sci. board 1976-80), Comite International de. Photobiologie (president 1968-72), New York (hon.), Göttingen (corr.), Pontifical acads. scis., National Acad. Sciences (foreign associate Washington), La Real Academia de Ciencias (Madrid; foreign corr.), Am. Acad. Arts and Sciences (foreign hon.), National Association Gifted Children (president 1975-80). Research on fast chem. reactions, photochemistry, photosynthesis. Office: Royal Society, 6 Carlton House Terrace, London SW14 5AG, England

POSTMA, HERMAN, aerospace company executive; born Wilmington, North Carolina, March 29, 1933; son of Gilbert and Sophie Hadrian (Verzaal) P.; married Patricia Dunigan, November 25, 1960; children: Peter, Pamela. Bachelor of Science summa cum laude, Duke University, 1955; Master of Science, Harvard University, 1957, Doctor of Philosophy, 1959. Registered professional engineer, California. Summer staff Oak Ridge National Laboratory, 1954-57, physicist thermonuclear div.; 1959-62, co-leader DCX-1 group; 1962-66, assistant director thermonuclear div.; 1966, associate director div.; 1967, director div.; 1967-73, director national laboratory; from 1974; vice president Martin Marietta, 1984-88, senior vice president; 1988—; visiting scientist FOM-Instituut voor Plasma-Fysica, The Netherlands, 1963; consultant Laboratory Laser Energetics, University Rochester; member energy research adv. board special panel Department Energy;

board of directors Federal Reserve Bank Atlanta, Nashville branch. Editorial board: Nuclear Fusion, 1968-74; contributor numerous articles to professional journals. Board of directors The Nucleus; chairman board trustees Hospital of Methodist Church; member adv. board College Business Administration, University Tennessee, 1976-84, Energy Institute, State of North Carolina; board of directors, executive committee Tennessee Tech. Foundation, 1982—, Venture Capital Fund; vice chairman Tennessee Higher Education Commission, 1984—; member adv. board Institute Pub. Policy Vanderbilt University, 1986—, conference chairman 1987; board trustees Duke University, 1987—, Federal Reserves Bank of Atlanta. Fellow Am. Physical Society (executive committee division plasma physics), American Association for the Advancement of Science, Am. Nuclear Society (director); member Chamber of Commerce (vice president 1981-83, chairman 1987), Industrial Research Institute, Gas Research Institute (adv. board 1986—), Phi Beta Kappa, Beta Gamma Sigma, Sigma Pi Sigma, Omicron Delta Kappa, Sigma Xi, Pi Mu Epsilon, Phi Eta Sigma. Home: 104 Berea Road Oak Ridge Tennessee 37830 Office: Martin Marietta Energy System Post Office Box 2009 Oak Ridge Tennessee 37831-8002

POTTER, JOHN LEITH, aerospace and mechanical engineer, educator, consultant; born Metz, Missouri, February 5, 1923; son of Jay Francis Lee and Pearl Delores (Leeth) P.; married Dorothy Jean Williams, December 15, 1957; children: Stephen, Anne, Carol. Bachelor of Science in Aerospace Engineering,

University Alabama, Tuscaloosa, 1944, Master of Science in Engineering, 1949; Master of Science in Engineering Management, Vanderbilt University, 1976, Doctor of Philosophy in Mechanical Engineering, 1974. Registered professional engineer, Tennessee. Engineer, educator various industrial, ednl. and government organizations, 1944-52; chief, flight and aerodynamics laboratory Redstone Arsenal, Alabama, 1952-56; manager, div. chief, deputy tech. director, senior staff scientist Sverdrup Tech., Incorporated, Tullahoma, Tennessee, 1956-83; research professor Vanderbilt University, Nashville, 1983—; consultant engineer Nashville, 1983—; part-time professor mechanical and aerospace engineering, University Tennessee, Tullahoma, 1956—; convener NATO-AGARD, United States and England, 1980-82, member working group, 1984-88; member adv. committee International Symposium on Rarefied Gasdynamics, 1970—; invited lecturer Union of the Soviet Socialist Republics Acad. Sciences, 1967; member National Research Council committee on assessment national aeronautical wind tunnel facilities, 1987-88; member National Aeronautics and Space Administration working groups, 1987—. Editor: Rarefied Gas Dynamics, 1977. Contributor articles to professional publications, chapters to books. Chairman board of directors Coffee County Historical Society, Tennessee, 1971-72; board of directors Southeastern Amateur Athletic Union, 1972-73; president Tullahoma Swim Club, 1972-73, Sheffield Homeowners Association, Nashville, 1983-84. Recipient Outstanding Fellow award University Alabama Aerospace Engineering Department, 1987; elected 150th Anniversary Distinguished Engineering Fellow University Alabama College Engineering, 1988. Fellow American Institute of Aeronautics and Astronautics (associate editor American Institute of Aeronautics and Astronautics Jour., 1970-73, member publs. committee 1973-78, associate editor Progress in Astronautics and Aeronautics, 1981-85; recipient General H. H. Arnold award Tennessee section 1964); member Engring Accreditation Commission 1985—, Capstone Engineering Society (regional director 1972-77), Sigma Xi, Tau Beta Pi, Theta Tau. Clubs: University, Cheekwood (Nashville). Office: Vanderbilt University Nashville Tennessee 37235

POTTER, MICHAEL, medical researcher; born East Orange, New Jersey, February 27, 1924. Bachelor of Arts, Princeton University, 1945; Doctor of Medicine, University Virginia, 1949. Research assistant department microbiology University Virginia Medical School, 1952-54, biologist; 1954-70, head immunochemistry section Laboratory Cell Biology; 1970-82; head genetics laboratory, cancer biology and diagnosis div. National Cancer Institute, Bethesda, Maryland, 1982—. Recipient Paul-Ehrlick & Ludwig-Darmstaedter prize, 1983, Lasker award in basic med. research, 1984. Member National Acad. Sci., Am. Association Cancer Research, Am. Association Immunologists. Office: National Cancer Institute Building 31 9000 Rockville Pike Bethesda Maryland 20892

POULSON, DONALD FREDERICK, biologist; born Idaho Falls, Ida., October 5, 1910; son of Christian

Frederick and Esther (Johnson) P.; married Margaret Judd Boardman, June 18, 1934; children: Donald Boardman, Christian Frederick. Bachelor of Science, California Institute Tech., 1933, Doctor of Philosophy, 1936; Master of Arts, Yale University, 1955. Teaching fellow biology California Institute Tech., 1934-36, Gosney research fellow biology; 1949; research assistant department embryology Carnegie Institute Washington, 1936-37; instructor biology Yale University, 1937-40, assistant professor; 1940-46, associate professor; 1946-55, professor; 1955-81, professor emeritus; 1981—, senior research biologist; 1981—, chairman department biology; 1962-65; research collaborator Brookhaven National Laboratory, 1951-55; Fulbright committee National Research Council, 1958-60; Central qualifications board National Institutes Health, 1961-63. Author: The Embryonic Development of Drosophila Melanogaster, 1937; contributor Biology of Drosophila, 1950; Contributor articles sci. journals.

Fellow Calhoun College, Yale, 1954—; Fulbright sr. research scholar Commonwealth Sci. and Indsl. Research Organization, Canberra, Australia, 1957-58, 66-67; Guggenheim fellow, 1957-58; Japan Society Promotion of Sci. fellow, 1979.

Fellow American Association for the Advancement of Science (council 1960-62); member International Society Developmental Biologists, Am. Society Naturalists (treasurer 1951-53), Am. Society Zoologists, Genetics Society Am., Society Developmental Biology, Connecticut Acad. Arts and Sciences, Sigma Xi. Home: 96 Green Hill Road Orange Connecticut 06477 Office: Osborn Memorial Lab Yale U New Haven Connecticut 06511

PRAY, LLOYD CHARLES, geologist, educator; born Chicago, June 25, 1919; son of Allan Theron and Helen (Palmer) P.; married Carrel Myers, September 14, 1946; children: Lawrence Myers, John Allan, Kenneth Palmer, Douglas Carrel. Bachelor of Arts, Carleton College, 1941; Master of Science, California Institute Tech., 1943, Doctor of Philosophy (NRC fellow 1946-49), 1952. Geologist Magnolia Petroleum Company, summer 1942, United States Geological Survey, 1943-44, 1946-56; instructor to associate professor geology California Institute Tech., 1949-56; senior research geologist Denver Research Center, Marathon Oil Company, 1956-62, research associate; 1962-68; professor geology University Wisconsin, Madison, 1968—; short course visiting professor University Texas, 1964, University Colorado, 1967, University Miami, 1971, University Alberta, 1969, Colorado School Mines, 1985; visiting scientist Imperial College Sci. and Tech., London, 1977, University California Santa Cruz, 1987. Author articles sedimentary carbonates, the Permian Reef complex, stratigraphy and structural geology Southern N.M. and W. Texas, porosity of carbonate facies, California rare earth mineral deposits. President Colorado Diabetes Association, 1963-67, vice president, 1968; member adv. panel earth scis. National Science Foundation, 1973-76. Served as hydrographic officer United States Naval Reserve, 1944-46. Named Layman of Year Am. Diabetes Association, 1968; recipient Distinguished Teaching award University Wisconsin Madison, 1988.

Fellow Geological Society Am. (research grants committee 1965-67, committee on nominations 1973, committee Penrose medal 1979-81); member Am. Association Petroleum Geologists (research committee 1958-61, lecturer continuing education program 1966-69, Matson trophy 1967, continuing education committee 1978-80, distinguished lecturer 1986-87, 87-88), Society Econ. Paleontologists and Mineralogists (hon. life member Permian Basin section; hon. member national assn.; sec.-treas. 1961-63, vice president 1966-67, president 1969-70), Am. Geological Institute (education committee 1966-68, house board of dels. 1970-72), Phi Beta Kappa. Office: U Wisconsin Madison Wisconsin 53706

PRELOG, VLADIMIR, chemist; born Sarajevo, Yugoslavia, July 23, 1906; son of Milan and Mara (Cettolo) P.; married Kamila Vítek, October 31, 1933; 1 son, January. Ing.chemical, Institute Tech. School Chemistry, Prague, Czechoslovakia, 1928, Doctor, 1929; Doctor h.c., University Zagreb, Yugoslavia, 1954, University Liverpool, England, University Paris, 1963, Cambridge University, University Brussels, 1969, University Manchester, 1971, Institute Quim. Sarria, Barcelona, 1978, Weizmann Institute, Rehovot, 1985. Chemist Laboratory G.J. Dríza, Prague, 1929-35; docent University Zagreb, 1935-40, associate professor; 1940-41; member faculty Swiss Federal Institute Tech., Zurich, 1942—, professor chemistry; 1950—, head Laboratory Organic Chemistry; 1957-65, retired; 1976; director CIBA Geigy Limited, Basel, Switzerland, 1963-78. Recipient Werner medal, 1945; Stas medal, 1962; medal of honour Rice University, 1962; Marcel Benoist award, 1965; A.W. Hofmann medal, 1968; Davy medal, 1968; Roger Adams prize, 1969; Nobel prize for chemistry, 1975; Paracelsus medal, 1976. Fellow Royal Society, 1962; member Am. Acad. Arts and Sciences (hon.), National Acad. Sciences (foreign associate), Acad. dei Lincei (Rome) (foreign), Leopoldina, Halle/Saale, Acad. Sciences Union of the Soviet Socialist Republics (foreign), Royal Irish Acad. (hon.), Royal Danish Acad. Sciences (hon.), Acad. Pharmaceutical Sciences (hon.), Am. Philosophical Society, Acad. Sciences (Paris) (foreign member), Pontificia Acad. Sci., Rome. Research, numerous publs. on constn. and stereochemistry alkaloids, antibiotics, enzymes, other natural compounds, alicyclic chemistry, chem. topology. Office: Eidgenossische Techn, Hochschule, Universitatsstrasse 16, 8092 Zurich Switzerland

PRESS, FRANK, educator, geophysicist; born Brooklyn, December 4, 1924; son of Solomon and Dora (Steinholz) P.; married Billie Kallick, June 9, 1946; children: William Henry, Paula Evelyn. Bachelor of Science, City College of New York, 1944, Doctor of Laws (honorary), 1972; Master of Arts, Columbia University, 1946, Doctor of Philosophy, 1949; Doctor of Science (honorary), 23 univs. Research associate Columbia, 1946-49, instructor geology; 1949-51, assistant professor geology; 1951-52, associate professor; 1952-55; professor geophysics Cal. Institute Tech., 1955-65, director seismological laboratory; 1957-65; professor geophysics, chairman department earth and planetary sciences Massachusetts Institute Tech., 1965-77; sci. advisor to President, director Office Sci. and Tech. Policy, Washington, 1977-80; Institute professor M.I.T., 1981; president National Acad. Sciences, 1981—; member President's Sci. Adv. Committee, 1961-64; member Baker and Ramo President's Sci. Adv. Committee, 1974-76; member National Sci. Board, 1970—; member lunar and planetary missions board National Aeronautics and Space Administration; participant bilateral sciences agreement with Peoples Republic of China and Union of the Soviet Socialist Republics; member United States delegation to Nuclear Test Ban Negotiations, Geneva and Moscow. Author: (with M. Ewing, W.S. Jardetzky) Propagation of Elastic Waves in Layered Media, 1957, (with R. Siever) Earth, 1986; also over 160 publications; co-editor: (with R. Siever) Physics and Chemistry of the Earth, 1957—. Recipient Columbia medal for excellence, 1960, pub. service award U.S. Department Interior, 1972, gold medal Royal Astronomical Society, 1972, pub. service medal National Aeronautics and Space Administration, 1973; named as most influential scientist in Am., U.S. News and World Report, 1982, 84, 85. Member Am. Acad. Arts and Sciences, Geological Society Am. (councilor), Am. Geophysical Union (president 1973), Society Exploration Geophysicists, Seismological Society Am. (president 1963), American Association of University Women, National Acad. Sciences (councilor), Am. Philosophical Society, French Acad. Sciences, Royal Society (UK), National Acad. Pub. Administration, Phi Beta Kappa. Office: National Acad Scis 2101 Constitution Avenue Washington District of Columbia 20418

PRIGOGINE, ILYA, physics educator; born Moscow, January 25, 1917; son of Roman and Julie (Wichmann) P.; married Marina Prokopowicz, February 25, 1961; children: Yves, Pascal. Doctor of Philosophy, Free University Brussels, 1942; honorary degrees, University Newcastle (England), 1966, University Poitiers (France), 1966, University Chicago, 1969, University Bordeaux (France), 1972, University de Liege, Belgium, 1977, University Uppsala, Sweden, 1977, U de Droit, D'Economie et des Sciences, d'Aix-Marseille, France, 1979, University Georgetown, 1980, University Cracovie, Poland, 1981, University Rio de Janeiro, 1981, Stevens Institute Tech., 1981, Heriot-Watt University, Scotland, 1985, l'Universidad Nacional de Educacion a Distancia, Madrid, 1985, University Francois Rabelais de Tours, 1986, University Nankin, University Peking, People's Republic of China, 1986; honorary prof., Banaras Hindle University, Varasani, India, 1988. Professor University Brussels, 1947—; director International Institutes Physics and Chemistry, Solvay, Belgium, 1959—; director Ilya Prigogine Center for studies in statistical mechanics and thermodynamics University Texas, Austin, 1967—; director social sciences l'Ecole des Hautes Etudes, France, 1987. Author: (with R. Defay) Traite de Thermodynamique, conformement aux methodes de Gibbs et de De Donder, 1944, 50, Etude Thermodynamique des Phenomenes Irreversibles, 1947, Introduction to Thermodynamics of Irreversible Processes, 1962, (with A. Bellemans, V. Mathot) The Molecular Theory of Solutions, 1957, Statistical Mechanics of Irreversible Processes, 1962, (with others) Non Equilibrium

Thermodynamics, Variational Techniques and Stability, 1966, (with R. Herman) Kinetic Theory of Vehicular Traffic, 1971, (with R. Glansdorff) Thermodynamic Theory of Structure, Stability and Fluctuations, 1971, (with G. Nicolis) Self-Organization in Nonequilibrium Systems, 1977, From Being to Becoming-Time and Complexity in Physical Sciences, 1979, French, German, Japanese, Russian, Chinese and Italian editions, (with I. Stengers), Order Out of Chaos, 1983, La Nouvelle Alliance, Les Métamorphoses de la Science, 1979, German, English, Italian, Spanish, Serbo-Croatian, Romanian, Swedish, Dutch, Danish, Russian, Japanese, Chinese and Portugese editions, (with G. Nicolis) Die Erforschung des Komplexen, 1987. Decorated officier de la Légion d'Honneur (France); recipient Prix Francqui, 1955; Prix Solvay, 1965; Nobel prize in chemistry, 1977; Honda prize, 1983; medal Association Advancement of Sci., France, 1975; Rumford gold medal Royal Society London, 1976; Karcher medal Am. Crystallographic Association, 1978; Descartes medal University Paris, 1979; Prix Umberto Biancamano, 1987; award Gravity Rsch. Foundation, 1988, others. Member Royal Acad. Belgium, Am. Acad. Sci., Royal Society Sciences Uppsala (Sweden), National Acad. Sciences United States of America (foreign associate), Society Royale des Sciences Liège Belgium (corr.), Acad. Gottingen Ger., Deutscher Akademie der Naturforscher Leopoldina (medaille Cothenius 1975), Osterreichische Akademie der Wissenschaften (corr.), Chemical Society Poland (hon.), International Society General Systems Research (pres.-elect 1988), Royal Society Chemistry of Belgium (hon.), du Conseil Consultatif de la Section Scientifique de la Fondazione dell'Istituto Bancario San Paolo di Torino per la cultura, la scienzia e l'artre, Torino, Italy, 1988, others. Address: 67 Avenue Fond' Roy, 1180 Brussels Belgium Office: U Tex Ilya Prigogine Center for Studies Stat Mechanics & Thermodynamics Austin Texas 78712

PRITCHARD, DONALD WILLIAM, oceanographer; born Santa Ana, California, October 20, 1922; son of Charles Lorenzo and Madeleine (Sievers) P.; married Thelma Lydia Amling, April 25, 1943; children—Marian Lydia, Jo Anne, Suzanne Louise, Donald William, Albert Charles. Bachelor of Arts, University of California at Los Angeles, 1942; Master of Science Scripps Institution Oceanography, La Jolla, 1948, Doctor of Philosophy, 1951; Doctor of Science (honorary), College William and Mary, 1985. Research assistant Scripps Institution Oceanography, 1946-47; oceanographer United States Navy Electronics Laboratory, 1947-49; associate director Chesapeake Bay Institute, Johns Hopkins, Baltimore, 1949-51; director Chesapeake Bay Institute, Johns Hopkins, 1951-74, chief scientist; 1974-79, professor; 1958-79, chairman department oceanography; 1951-68; associate director for research, professor Marine Sciences Research Center, State University of New York at Stony Brook, 1979-86, acting director, dean; 1986-87, associate dean; 1987-88, professor emeritus; 1988—; consultant Corps of Engineers, United States Army, United States Public Health Service, Atomic Energy Commission, International Atomic

Energy Commission, National Science Foundation, Adv. Panel Earth Sciences; member adv. board to Secretary Natural Resources, State of Maryland. Board editors: Journal Marine Research, 1953-70, Bulletin Bingham oceanographic Collection, 1960-70, Geophysical Monograph Board, Am. Geophysical Union, 1959-70, Johns Hopkins Oceanographic Studies, 1962—; Author articles in field. Served from 2d lieutenant to captain United States Army Air Force, 1943-46. Fellow Am. Geophysical Union (past president oceanography section); member Am. Society Limnology and Oceanography (past vice president), Am. Meteorological Society, American Association for the Advancement of Science, National Acad. Sciences (past member committee oceanography, past chairman panel radioactivity in marine environment), Sigma Xi (past chapter president). Office: MSRC State University of New York Stony Brook New York 11794

PROKHOROV,   ALEKSANDR MIKHAILOVICH, radiophysicist; born Atherton, Australia, June 28, 1916. Graduate, Leningrad State University, 1939; postgraduate, Physics Institute Union of the Soviet Socialist Republics Academy Scis., 1939-41, 44-46. Joined Communist Party Soviet Union, 1950; member staff Lebedev Physics Institute, Union of the Soviet Socialist Republics Acad. Sciences, 1954-72, head of laboratory; 1972-83, vice director; 1983—, also board of directors, academician-sec. gen physics and astronomy department; 1971—; chairman National Commission Soviet Physicists. Author standard works on laser. Served with Soviet Army, 1941-43. Decorated Hero of Socialist Labor; recipient Lenin prize, 1959; Nobel prize, 1964; Lomonosov medal Soviet Acad. Sciences, 1987. Member Am. Acad. Sci. and Art. Office: Union of Soviet Socialist Republics Acad Scis Department Gen, Physics & Astronomy, Leninsky Prospect 14, Moscow Union of Soviet Socialist Republics

PUCK,   THEODORE   THOMAS, geneticist, biophysicist, educator; born Chicago, September 24, 1916; son of Joseph and Bessie (Shapiro) Puckowitz; married Mary Hill, April 17, 1946; children: Stirling, Jennifer, Laurel. Bachelor of Science, University Chicago, 1937, Doctor of Philosophy, 1940. Member commission airborne infections Office Surgeon General, Army Epidemiological Board, 1944-46; assistant professor departments medicine and biochemistry University Chicago, 1945-47; senior fellow Am. Cancer Society, California Institute Tech., Pasadena, 1947-48; professor biophysics University Colorado Medical School, 1948—, chairman department; 1948-67, distinguished professor; 1986—; director Eleanor Roosevelt Institute Cancer Research, 1962—; Distinguished research professor Am. Cancer Society, 1966—; national lecturer Sigma Xi, 1975-76. Author: The Mammalian Cell as a Microorganism: Genetic and Biochemical Studies in Vitro, 1972. Member Commission on Physicians for the Future. Recipient Albert Lasker award, 1958; Borden award med. research, 1959; Louisa Gross Horwitz prize, 1973; Gordon Wilson medal Am. Clinical and Climatol. Association, 1977; award Environmental Mutagen Society, 1981; Heritage Foundation scholar, 1983; E.B. Wilson medal Am. Society Cell

Biology, 1984; Bonfils-Stanton award in sci., 1984; Phi Beta Kappa scholar, 1985. Fellow Am. Acad. Arts and Sciences; member Am. Chemical Society, Society Experimental Biology and Medicine, American Association for the Advancement of Science (Phi Beta Kappa award and lecturer 1983), Am. Association Immunologists, Radiation Research Society, Biophys. Society, Genetics Society Am., National Acad. Sci., Tissue Culture Association (Hon. award 1987), Paideia Group, Santa Fe Institute Sci. Board, Phi Beta Kappa, Sigma Xi. Recipient University Colorado Disting. Prof. award, 1987; ARCS Man of Sci. award, 1987. Office: Eleanor Roosevelt Institute for Cancer Research 1899 Gaylord St Denver Colorado 80206

PUCKETT, ALLEN EMERSON, aeronautical engineer; born Springfield, Ohio, July 25, 1919; son of Roswell C. and Catherine C. (Morrill) P.; married Betty J. Howlett; children—Allen W., Nancy L., Susan E.; married Marilyn I. McFarland; children—Margaret A., James R. Bachelor of Science, Harvard, 1939, Master of Science, 1941; Doctor of Philosophy, California Institute Tech., 1949. Lecturer aeronautics, chief wind tunnel section Jet Propulsion Laboratory, California Institute Tech., 1945-49; tech. consultant United States Army Ordnance, Aberdeen Proving Ground, Maryland, 1945-60; member sci. adv. committee Ballistic Research Laboratories, 1958-65; with Hughes Aircraft Company, Culver City, California, 1949—, executive vice president; 1965-77, president; 1977-78, chairman board, chief executive officer; 1978-87, chairman emeritus Hughes Aircraft Company, Culver City,

1987—; director General Dynamics, Fluor, Logicon Investment Company of Am., Am. Mutual Fund, Lone Star Industries; member steering group OASD adv. panel on aeros.; consultant President's Sci. Adv. Committee; chairman research adv. committee control, guidance and navigation National Aeronautics and Space Administration, 1959-64; vice-chairman Def. Sci. Board, 1962-66; member Army Sci. Adv. Panel, 1965-69, National Aeronautics and Space Administration tech. and research adv. committee, 1968-72, space program adv. council 1974-78; Wilbur and Orville Memorial lecturer Royal Aeronautical Society, London, 1981. Author: (with Hans W. Liepmann) Introduction to Aerodynamics of a Compressible Fluid, 1947; editor: (with Simon Ramo) Guided Missile Engineering, 1959; contributor tech. papers on high-speed aerodynamics. Trustee University Southern California. Recipient Lawrence Sperry award Institute Aeronautical Sciences, 1949, Lloyd V. Berkner award Am. Astronautical Society, 1974; named California Mfr. of Year, 1980. Fellow American Institute of Aeronautics and Astronautics (president 1972); member Aerospace Industries Association (chairman 1979), Los Angeles World Affairs Council (president), National Acad. Sciences, National Acad. Engineering, American Association for the Advancement of Science, Sigma Xi, Phi Beta Kappa. Office: Hughes Aircraft Company Post Office Box 45066 Los Angeles California 90045

PURCELL, EDWARD MILLS, physics educator; born Taylorville, Illinois, August 30, 1912; son of Edward A. and Mary Elizabeth (Mills) P.; married Beth C. Busser, January 22, 1937;

children: Dennis W., Frank B. Bachelor of Science in Electrical Engineering, Purdue University, 1933, Doctor Engineering (honorary), 1953; International Exchange student, Technische Hochschule, Karlsruhe, Germany, 1933-34; Master of Arts, Harvard University, 1935, Doctor of Philosophy, 1938. Instructor physics Harvard University, 1938-40, associate professor; 1946-49, professor physics; 1949-58, Donner professor sci.; 1958-60, Gerhard Gade University professor; 1960-80, emeritus; 1980—; senior fellow Society of Fellows, 1949-71; group leader Radiation Laboratory, Massachusetts Institute of Technology, 1941-45. Contributing author: Radiation Lab. series, 1949, Berkeley Physics Course, 1965; contributor sci. papers on nuclear magnetism, radio astronomy, astrophysics, biophysics. Member President's Sci. Advisory Committee, 1957-60, 62-65. Co-winner Nobel prize in Physics, 1952; recipient Oersted medal Am. Association Physics Teachers, 1968, National Medal of Sci., 1980, Harvard medal, 1986. Member Am. Philosophical Society, National Acad. Sci., Physical Society, Am. Acad. Arts and Sciences. Office: Harvard U Department Physics Cambridge Massachusetts 02138

PURPURA, DOMINICK P., neuroscientist, university dean; born New York City, April 2, 1927; married Florence Williams, 1948; children—Craig, Kent, Keith, Allyson. Bachelor of Arts, Columbia University, 1949; Doctor of Medicine, Harvard University, 1953. Intern Presbyn Hospital, New York City, 1953-54; assistant resident in neurology Neurological Institute, New York City, 1954-55; Professor, chairman department anatomy Albert Einstein College Medicine, Yeshiva University, New York City, 1967-74, sci. director Kennedy Center; 1969-72, director Kennedy Center; 1972-82, professor, chairman department neurosci.; 1974-82, dean; 1984—; dean Stanford University, California, 1982-84; member neurophysiol. panel International Brain Research Organization, president, 1986, vice president medical affairs, 1987, United Nations Educational, Scientific and Cultural Organization, 1961—; chairman international congress committee International Brain Research Orgn./World Foundation Neuroscientists, 1983—. Member editorial board Brain Research, 1965—, editor-in-chief, 1975—; editor-in-chief Brain Research Revs., 1975—; editor-in-chief Developmental Brain Research, 1981—. Served with United States Army Air Force, 1945-47. Fellow New York Acad. Sciences; member Institute Medicine of National Acad. Sciences, National Acad. Sciences, Am. Acad. Neurology, Am. Association Anatomists, Am. Association Neurological Surgeons, Am. Epilepsy Society, Am. Physiological Society, Association Research in Nervous and Mental Disease, Society Neurosci., Sigma Xi. Office: Albert Einstein College Medicine 1300 Morris Park Avenue Bronx New York 10461

PURVIN, ROBERT LEMAN, chemical engineer; born Farmersville, Texas, June 5, 1917; son of Julius L. and Adelaide F. (Mittenthal) P.; married Maria Czartoryski Chajecki, February 1972; children—James Kenneth, Laura Jill Purvin Zinner, Duane Emory, Robert Leman, Jeffrey Leon, Lisa Purvin Oliner. Bachelor of Arts with highest honors, University Texas, 1937, Bachelor of Science with highest honors, 1938; Doctor of Science in Chemical Engineering, Massachusetts Institute Tech., 1941; Doctor of Laws (honorary), Manhattan College, 1981. Engineer refinery tech. service Humble Oil & Refining Company, 1941-46; consultant 1946-50; consultant senior partner Purvin & Gertz, Incorporated, 1946-57; president, director Purmil Corp., from 1953; executive vice president, director Foster Grant Company, Incorporated, 1957-62, consultant; 1962-70; vice president, director TransAtlantic Trading Limited, 1965-66; manager TransAtlantic Gas Associates, 1963-69; sub. director general Fertilizantes Fosfatados Mexicanos (S.A. de C.V.), 1965-67, consultant; 1962-70; executive vice president, director Distrigas Corp., 1969-70; chairman board Purvin & Lee, Incorporated, 1970-75; president, chief executive officer Barber Oil, 1975-78; consultant 1978—; Consultor Manhattan College, 1967-81. Recipient Distinguished Engineering Graduate award University Texas, 1969. Fellow Am. Institute Chemical Engineers; member Am. Chemical Society, National Society Professional Engineers, Society Gas Operators, Ind. Petroleum Association Am., Phi Beta Kappa, Sigma Xi, Phi Lambda Upsilon, Tau Beta Pi. Club: Sky (New York City). Lodges: Masons, Shriners. Office: Robert L Purvin & Associates 770 Taylors Lane Mamaroneck New York 10543

PUTNAM, PAUL ADIN, government agency official; born Springfield, Vermont, July 12, 1930; son of Horace Adin and Beatrice Nellie (Baldwin) P.; married Elsie Mae (Ramseyer) June 12, 1956; children: Pamela Ann, Penelope Jayne, Adin Tyler II, Paula Anna. Bachelor of Science, University Vermont, 1952; Master of Science, Washington State University, 1954; Doctor of Philosophy, Cornell University, 1957. Research animal scientist Agricultural Research Service, United States Department Agriculture, Beltsville, Maryland, 1957-66, investigation leader beef cattle nutrition; 1966-68, chief beef cattle research branch; 1968-72, assistant director Beltsville Agricultural Research Center, 1972-80, director; 1980-84; director Central Plains Area, Ames, Iowa, 1984—. Contributor articles to professional journals. Recipient Kidder medal University Vermont; Outstanding Performance award USDA, also cert. merit; Danforth fellow; Borden fellow; Purina Research fellow. Fellow American Association for the Advancement of Science (representative section O), Am. Society Animal Sci.; member Am. Society Animal Sci. (president North Atlantic section, chairman various committees; N.E. section Distinguished Service award), Am. Dairy Sci. Association, Organization Professional Employees USDA (president Beltsville chapter), Council for Agricultural Sci. and Tech. Home: 3D Schilletter Village Ames Iowa 50010 Office: USDA-ARS Central Plains Area Post Office Box 70 Dayton Avenue Ames Iowa 50010

PYKE, THOMAS NICHOLAS, JR., government science and engineering administrator; born Washington, July 16, 1942; son of Thomas Nicholas and Pauline Marie (Pingitore) P.; married Carol June Renville, June 22, 1968; children—Christopher Renville, Alexander Nicholas. Bachelor of Science,

Carnegie Institute Tech., 1964; Master of Science in Engineering, University Pennsylvania, 1965. Electronic engineer National Bureau Standards, Gaithersburg, Maryland, 1964-69, chief computer networking section; 1969-75, chief computer systems engineering div.; 1975-79, director center for computer systems engineering; 1979-81, director center programming sci. and tech.; 1981-86; assistant administrator for satellite and information services National Oceanographic and Atmospheric Administration, Washington, 1986—; organizer professional computer conferences, 1970—; member Presdl. Adv. Committee on Networking Structure and Function, 1980; program chairman Interagy. committee on Information Resources Management, 1983-84, board of directors, 1984-87, vice chairman 1986-87; speaker in field. Editorial board Computer Networks Journal, 1976-86; contributor articles to professional journals. Board of directors Glebe Commons Association, Arlington, Virginia, 1976-79, vice president, 1977-79; chairman Student Congress, Carnegie Institute Tech., 1963-64; member Task Force on Computers in Schools, Arlington, 1982-85; president Parent-Teacher Association, Arlington, 1983-84. Recipient Silver medal Department Commerce, 1973, award for exemplary achievement in pub. administration William A. Jump Foundation, 1975, 76; Westinghouse scholar Carnegie Institute Tech., Pitts., 1960-64; Ford Foundation fellow University Pennsylvania, Philadelphia, 1964-66. Fellow Washington Acad. Sciences (Engineering Sci. award 1974); member Am. Federation Information Processing Socs. (board directors 1974-76), Institute of Electrical and Electronics Engineers (senior member), Computer Society of Institute of Electrical and Electronics Engineers (board govs. 1971-73, 75-77, vice chairman tech. committee on personal computing 1982-86, chairman 1986-87), American Association for the Advancement of Science, Association Computing Machinery, Sigma Xi, Eta Kappa Nu, Omicron Delta Kappa, Pi Kappa Alpha (chapter vice president 1963-64). Episcopalian. Office: NOAA National Environ Satellite Data and Info Service Washington District of Columbia 20233

QUIMBY, GEORGE IRVING, anthropologist, former museum director; born Grand Rapids, Michigan, May 4, 1913; son of George Irving and Ethelwyn (Sweet) Q.; married Helen M. Ziehm, October 13, 1940; children: Sedna H., G. Edward, John E., Robert W. Bachelor of Arts, University Michigan, 1936, Master of Arts, 1937, graduate fellow, 1937-38; postgraduate, University Chicago, 1938-39. State supervisor Federal Archaeol. Project in Louisiana, 1939-41; director Muskegon (Michigan) Mus., 1941-42; assistant curator North America archaeology and ethnology Field Mus. Natural History, 1942-43, curator exhibits, anthropology; 1943-54, curator North America archeology and ethnology; 1954-65, research associate in North Am. archaeology and ethnology; 1965—; curator anthropology Thomas Burke Memorial Washington State Mus.; professor anthropology University Washington, 1965-83, emeritus professor; 1983—, mus. director; 1968-83, emeritus director; 1983—; lecturer University Chicago, 1947-65, Northwestern University, 1949-53; Fulbright visiting professor, University Oslo, Norway, 1952; archaeol. expeditions and field work, Michigan, 1935, 37, 42, 56-63, Wisconsin, 1936, Hudson's Bay, 1939, Louisiana, 1940-41, New Mexico, 1947, Lake Superior, 1956-61. Author: Aleutian Islanders, 1944, (with J. A. Ford) The Tchefuncte Culture, an Early Occupation of the Lower Mississippi Valley, 1945, (with P. S. Martin, D. Collier) Indians Before Columbus, 1947, Indian Life in the Upper Great Lakes, 1960, Indian Culture and European Grade Goods, 1966; producer documentary film (with Bill Holm) In the Land of the War Canoes, 1973; Edward S. Curtis in the Land of the War Canoes: A Pioneer Cinematographer in the Pacific Northwest, 1980; Contributor articles to professional journals. Honored by festschrift University Michigan Mus. Anthropology, 1983. Fellow American Association for the Advancement of Science, Am. Anthropological Association; member Society Am. Archaeology (president 1958, 50th Anniversary award 1983), Am. Society Ethnohistory, Wisconsin Archeological Society, Society Historical Archeology (council 1971-74, 75-78, J.C. Harrington medal 1986), Association Sci. Mus. Directors (president 1973—), Arctic Institute North America, Am. Association Museums (council 1971-74), Sigma Xi, Phi Sigma, Chi Gamma Phi, Zeta Psi. Home: 6001 52d Avenue NE Seattle Washington 98115 Office: U Washington Thomas Burke Memorial Wash State Mus Seattle Washington 98195

RABB, GEORGE B., zoologist; born Charleston, South Carolina, January 2, 1930; son of Joseph and Teresa C. (Redmond) R.; married Mary Sughrue, June 10, 1953. Bachelor of Science,

College Charleston., 1951; Master of Arts, University Michigan, 1952, Doctor of Philosophy, 1957. Teaching fellow zoology University Michigan, 1954-56; curator. coordinator research Chicago Zool. Park, Brookfield., Illinois, 1956-64; associate director research and education Chicago Zool. Park, 1964-75, deputy director; 1969-75, director; 1976—; research associate Field Mus. Natural History, 1965—; lecturer department biology University Chicago, 1965—; member Committee on Evolution Biology, 1969—; president Chicago Zool. Society, 1976—; member steering committee Species Survival Commission, International Union Conservation of Nature, 1983—, vice chairman for North America, 1986—, board of directors 1987—. Fellow American Association for the Advancement of Science; member Am. Society Ichthyologists and Herpetologists (president 1978), Herpetologists League, Society Systematic Zoology, Society Mammalogists, Society Study Evolution, Ecological Society Am., Society Conservation Biology (council member 1986—), Am. Society Zoologists, Society Study Animal Behavior, Am. Association Museums, Am. Society Naturalists, Am. Association Zool. Parks and Aquariums (director 1979-80), International Union Directors Zool. Gardens, Am. Committee International Conservation, Chicago Council Foreign Relations (Chicago committee), Sigma Xi. Club: Economic (Chicago). Office: Chicago Zool Park 8400 W 31st St Brookfield Illinois 60513

RABIN, MICHAEL O., computer scientist, mathematician; born Breslau, Germany, September 1,

1931; son of Israel A. and Else (Hess) R.; married Ruth Scherzer, May 31, 1954; children: Tal, Sharon. Master of Science in Math., Hebrew University, Jerusalem; Doctor of Philosophy, Princeton University, 1956. Instructor Princeton (New Jersey) University, 1956-57; member Institute Advanced Study, Princeton, 1957-58; professor computer sci. Harvard University, Cambridge, Massachusetts, 1981—, Gordon McKay professor, now Thomas J. Watson senior professor computer sci.; visiting professor University Calif.-Berkeley, 1962, Massachusetts Institute of Technology, 1972-78, University Paris, 1965, Yale University, 1967, New York University, 1970; Albert Einstein professor Hebrew University, Jerusalem, 1965—; consultant computer industry. Inventor (oblivious transfer algorithm). Recipient Rothschild prize in math., 1974, Turing award in computer sci., 1976, Harvey prize in sci. and tech., 1980. Member Israel Acad. Sci., National Academy of Sciences (foreign hon. member), Am. Acad. Arts and Sciences, Am. Philosophical Society. Office: Harvard U Department Applied Scis Cambridge Massachusetts 02138

RABINOW, JACOB, electrical engineer; born Kharkov, Russia, January 8, 1910; came to United States, 1921, naturalized, 1930; son of Aaron and Helen (Fleisher) Rabinovich; married Gladys Lieder, September 26, 1943; children: Jean Ellen, Clare Lynn. Bachelor of Science in Electrical Engineering, College City New York, 1933, Electrical Engineer, 1934; Doctor of Hebrew Literature (honorary), Towson State University, 1983. Radio serviceman New York City, 1934-38; mechanical engineer National Bureau Standards, Washington, 1938-54; president Rabinow Engineering Company, Washington, 1954-64; vice president Control Data Corp., Washington, 1964-72; research engineer National Bureau Standards, 1972—; Regent's lecturer University Calif.-Berkeley, 1972; lecturer, consultant in field. Author. Recipient President's Certificate of Merit, 1948; certificate appreciation War Department, 1949; Exceptional Service award Department Commerce, 1949; Edward Longstreth medal Franklin Institute, 1959; Jeffersom medal New Jersey Patent Law Association, 1973; named Scientist of Year Indsl. R&D magazine, 1980. Fellow Institute of Electrical and Electronics Engineers (Harry Diamond award 1977), American Association for the Advancement of Science; member National Acad. Engineering, Philosophical Society Washington, Audio Engineering Society, Sigma Xi. Club: Cosmos (Washington). Patentee in field. Home: 6920 Selkirk Dr Bethesada Maryland 20817 Office: National Bur Standards Gaithersburg Maryland 20899

RAHN, HERMANN, physiologist; born East Lansing, Michigan, July 5, 1912; son of Otto and Bell S. (Farrand) R.; married Katharine F. Wilson, August 29, 1939; children: Robert F., Katharine B. Bachelor of Arts, Cornell University, 1933; student, University Kiel, 1933-34; Doctor of Philosophy, University Rochester, 1938, Doctor of Science (honorary), 1973; Docteur Honoris Causa, University Paris, 1964; Doctor of Laws (honorary), Yonsei University, Korea, 1965; Titulo de Profesor Honorario University Peruana Cayetano Heredia,

Peru, 1980; Doctor Medicinae h.c., University Bern, Switzerland, 1981. National Research Council fellow Harvard University, 1938-39; instructor physiology University Wyoming, 1939-41; assistant physiology School Medicine, University Rochester, 1941-42, instructor; 1942-46, assistant professor; 1946-50, associate professor, vice chairman department; 1950-56; Lawrence D. Bell professor physiology, chairman department School Medicine, University Buffalo (now SUNY-Buffalo), 1956-73; distinguished professor physiology School Medicine, University Buffalo, 1973—; visiting professor Medical Faculty San Marcos University, Lima, Peru, 1955, Dartmouth Medical School, 1962, Laboratory de Physiologie Respiratoire, CNRS, Strasbourg, France, 1971, Max-Planck-Inst. für experimentelle Medizin, Göttingen, Federal Republic Germany, 1977; member adv. committee biological sci. Air Force Office Sci. Research and Devel., 1958-64; member physiological study section National Institutes of Health, 1958-62; member working committee space sci. board National Acad. Sci.-NRC, 1962-65; member general medical research program project committee National Institutes of Health, 1964-67; member research career award committee National Institute General Medical Sciences, 1968-72; cardiopulmonary adv. committee National Heart Institute, 1968-71; member national adv. board R/V Alpha Helix, 1968-71; chairman committee on underwater physiology and medicine National Research Council, 1972-74. Author: (with W.O. Fenn) A Graphical Analysis of the Respiratory Gas Exchange, 1955, (with others) Blood Gases:

Hemoglobin, Base Excess and Maldistribution, 1973; editorial board: Am. Journal Physiology, Journal Applied Physiology, 1953-62, sect. editor for respiration, 1962, board publication trustees, 1959-62; editor: (with W.O. Fenn) Handbook of Physiology-Respiration, Volumes I, II, 1964-65, Physiology of Breath-Hold Diving and the Ama of Japan, 1965, (with G. C. Whittow) Seabird Energetics, 1984, (with O. Prakash) Acid-Base Balance and Body Temperature, 1985. Recipient Senior U.S. Scientist award Alexander von Humboldt Foundation, 1976. Member Am. Institute Biological Sci. (adv. committee physiol. 1957-64, adv. panel 1967-71), Am. Physiological Society (council 1960-65, president 1963-64), National Acad. Sci., Institute Medicine, National Acad. Sci., Harvey Society (hon.), Society Experimental Biology and Medicine, International Union Physiological Sciences (council 1965-74, United States national committee 1966-74, vice president 1971-74, executive committee 1971-74), Am. Society Zoologists, Am. Acad. Arts and Sci., Sigma Xi. Research in pulmonary, comparative and environmental physiology. Home: 75 Windsor Avenue Buffalo New York 14209

RALL, JOSEPH EDWARD, physician; born Naperville, Illinois, February 3, 1920; son of Edward Everett and Nell (Platt) R.; married Caroline Domm, September 28, 1944 (deceased April 1976); children—Priscilla, Edward Christian; married Nancy Lamontagne, April 15, 1978. Bachelor of Arts, North Central College, 1940, Doctor of Science (honorary), 1966; Master of Science, Northwestern University, 1944, Doctor of Medicine, 1945; Doctor of

Philosophy, University Minnesota, 1952; Doctor honoris causa, Faculty of Medicine, Free University Brussels, Belgium, 1975; Doctor of Medicine (honorary), University Naples, 1985. Associate member Sloan Kettering Institute, New York City, 1950-55; chief clinical endocrinology branch National Institute Arthritis, Metabolism and Digestive Diseases, National Institutes of Health, 1955-62; director intramural research National Institute Arthritis, Diabetes, Digestive and Kidney Diseases, 1962-83; deputy director intramural research National Institutes of Health, 1983—; Member National Research Council, 1960-65. Author numerous articles, chapters in books on thyroid gland and radiation. Served to captain Medical Corps Army of the United States, 1946-48. Recipient Van Meter prize Am. Goiter Association, 1950, Fleming award, 1959, Outstanding Achievement award Mayo Clinic and University Minnesota, 1964; Distinguished Service award Am. Thyroid Association, 1967; Distinguished Service award Department of Health, Education and Welfare, 1968, Distinguished Executive rank, sr. executive service, 1980, R.H. Williams Distinguished Leadership award in endocrinology, 1983. named Outstanding Alumnus N. Central College, 1966. Member American Association for the Advancement of Science, Am. Acad. Arts and Sciences, Am. Society Clinical Investigation, Am. Physical Society, Endocrine Society, Association Am. Physicians, Societe de Biologie (France), Royal Acad. Medicine (Brussels), National Acad. Sciences, National Acad. Arts and Sciences. Home: 3947 Baltimore St Kensington Maryland 20895 Office: National Institutes Health Building 1 Room 122 Bethesda Maryland 20892

RAMEY, HENRY JACKSON, JR., petroleum engineering educator; born Pittsburgh, November 30, 1925; married, 1948; 4 children. Bachelor of Science, Purdue University, 1949, Doctor of Philosophy, 1952. Assistant chemical engineer unit operations laboratory Purdue University, 1949, assistant radiant heat transfer from gases; 1951-52; senior research technologist petroleum production research Magnolia Petroleum Company, Socony Mobil Oil Company, Incorporated, 1952-55; project engineer General Petroleum Corp., 1955-60; staff reservoir engineer Mobil Oil Company Div., 1960-63; member faculty petroleum engineering department Texas A&M University, 1963-66; professor petroleum engineering Stanford University, California, 1966—, also chairman department; consultant Chinese Petroleum Corp., Taiwan, 1962-63, other companies. Contributor papers, articles to professional lit.; patentee in field. Served as officer United States Army Air Force, 1943-46. Recipient Purdue University Distinguished Engineer award, 1975, Mineral Education award American Institute of Mining, Metallurgy and Petroleum Engineers, 1987. Member Am. Institute Chemical Engineers, American Institute of Mining, Metallurgy and Petroleum Engineers (Ferguson medal 1959), National Acad. Engineering. Office: Stanford U Department Petroleum Engring Stanford California 94305

RAMO, SIMON, engineering executive; born Salt Lake City, May 7, 1913; son of Benjamin and Clara (Trestman) R.; married Virginia Smith, July 25, 1937; children: James Brian,

Alan Martin. Bachelor of Science, University Utah, 1933, Doctor of Science (honorary), 1961; Doctor of Philosophy, California Institute Tech., 1936; Doctor of Engineering (honorary), Case Institute Tech., 1960, University Michigan, 1966, Polytechnic Institute New York, 1971; Doctor of Science (honorary), Union College, 1963, Worcester Polytechnic Institute, 1968, University Akron, 1969, Cleveland State University, 1976; Doctor of Laws (honorary), Carnegie-Mellon University, 1970, University Southern California, 1972, Gonzaga University, 1983, Occidental College, 1984, Gonzaga University, 1983, Occidental College, 1984. With General Electric Company, 1936-46; vice president operations Hughes Aircraft Company, 1946-53; with Ramo-Woolridge Corp., 1953-58; sci. director United States intercontinental guided missile program 1954-58; director TRW Incorporated, 1954—, vice chairman board; 1961-78, chairman executive committee; 1969-78; chairman board TRW-Fujitsu Company, 1980-83; president The Bunker-Ramo Corp., 1964-66; visiting professor management sci. California Institute Tech., 1978—; Regents lecturer University of California at Los Angeles, 1981-82, University California at Santa Cruz, 1978-79; chairman Center for Study Am. Experience, University Southern California, 1978-80; Faculty fellow John F. Kennedy School Government, Harvard University, 1980—; director Union Bank, 1965—, Atlantic Richfield Company, 1984-86; past director Times Mirror Company, 1968-83; Member White House Energy Research and Devel. Adv. Council, 1973-75; member adv. committee on sci. and foreign affairs United States State Department, 1973-75; chairman President's Committee on Sci. and Tech., 1976-77; member adv. council to Secretary Commerce, 1976-77; co-chairman Transitition Task Force on Sci. and Tech. for Pres.-elect Reagan; member roster consultants to administrator Energy Research and Development Administration, 1976-77; board advisors for sci. and tech. Republic of China, 1981—. Author: The Business of Science, 1988, other sci., engring. and mgmt. books. Board of directors Los Angeles World Affairs Council; board of directors Music Center Foundation, Los Angeles, Los Angeles Philharmonic Association; trustee California Institute Tech., National Symphony Orchestra Association, 1973-83; trustee emeritus California State Univs.; board visitors University of California at Los Angeles School Medicine, 1980—; board of directors W. M. Keck Foundation, 1983—; board governors Performing Arts Council of Music Center Los Angeles, president, 1976-77. Recipient award IAS, 1956; award Am. Institute Electrical Engrs., 1959; award Arnold Air Society, 1960; Am. Acad. Achievement award, 1964; award Am. Iron and Steel Institute, 1968; Distinguished Service medal Armed Forces Communication and Electronics Association, 1970; medal of achievement WEMA, 1970; awards University Southern California, 1971, 79; Kayan medal Columbia University, 1972; award Am. Cons. Engrs. Council, 1974; medal Franklin Institute, 1978; award Harvard Business School Association, 1979; award National Medal Sci., 1979; Distinguished Alumnus award University Utah, 1981; UCLA medal, 1982; Presidential Medal of Freedom, 1983; Junior Achievement Business Hall of Fame award, 1984; others. Fellow Institute of Electrical and

Electronics Engineers (Electronic Achievement award 1953, Golden Omega award 1975, Founders medal 1980), Am. Acad. Arts and Sciences; member National Acad. Engineering (founder, council member Bueche award), National Acad. Sciences, Am. Physical Society, Am. Philosophical Society, Institute Advancement Engineering, International Acad. Astronautics, Eta Kappa Nu (eminent member award 1966). Office: TRW 1 Space Park Redondo Beach California 90278

RAMSEY, NORMAN, physicist, educator; born Washington, August 27, 1915; son of Norman F. and Minna (Bauer) R.; married Elinor Jameson, June 3, 1940 (deceased December 1983); children: Margaret, Patricia, Janet, Winifred; married Ellie Welch, May 11, 1985. Bachelor of Arts, Columbia University, 1935; Bachelor of Arts, Cambridge (England) University, 1937, Master of Arts, 1941, Doctor of Science, 1954; Doctor of Philosophy, Columbia University, 1940; Master of Arts (honorary), Harvard University, 1947; Doctor of Science (honorary), Case Western Reserve University, 1968, Middlebury College, 1969, Oxford (England) University, 1973, Rockefeller University, 1986. Kellett fellow Columbia University, 1935-37, Tyndall fellow; 1938-39; Carnegie fellow Carnegie Institute Washington, 1939-40; associate University Illinois, 1940-42; assistant professor Columbia University, 1942-46; associate Massachusetts Institute of Technology Radiation Laboratory, 1940-43; consultant National Defense Research Committee, 1940-45; expert consultant secretary of war 1942-45; group leader, associate div. head Los Alamos Laboratory, 1943-45; associate professor Columbia University, 1945-47; head physics department Brookhaven National Laboratory of Atomic Energy Commission, 1946-47; associate professor physics Harvard University, 1947-50, professor physics; 1950-66, Higgins professor physics; 1966—; senior fellow Harvard Society of Fellows, 1970—; Eastman professor Oxford University, 1973-74; Luce professor cosmology Mount Holyoke College, 1982-83; professor University Virginia, 1983-84; director Harvard Nuclear Laboratory, 1948-50, 52-53, Varlan Associates, 1963-66; member Air Forces Sci. Adv. Committee, 1947-54; sci. adviser North Atlantic Treaty Organization, 1958-59; member Department Def. Panel Atomic Energy; executive committee Cambridge Electron Accelerator and general adv. committee Atomic Energy Commission. Author: Nuclear Moments and Statistics, 1953, Nuclear Two Body Problems, 1953, Molecular Beams, 1956, 85, Quick Calculus, 1965; contributor: articles Physical Rev.; other sci. journals on nuclear physics, molecular beam experiments, radar, nuclear magnetic moments, radiofrequency spectroscopy, masers, nucleon scattering. Trustee Asso. Univs., Incorporated, Brookhaven National Lab., Carnegie Endowment International Peace, 1962—, Rockefeller University, 1977—; president Univs. Research Assos., Incorporated, 1966-72, 73-81, president emeritus, 1981—. Recipient Presidential Order of Merit for radar development work, 1947, E.O. Lawrence award Atomic Energy Commission, 1960, Columbia award for excellence in sci., 1980, medal of honor Institute of Electrical and Electronic Engineers, 1983, Rabi prize, 1985, Monie Ferst award, 1985,

Compton medal, 1985, Oersted medal, 1988; Rumford premium, 1985; Guggenheim fellow Oxford University, 1954-55. Fellow Am. Acad. Sci., Am. Physical Society (council 1956-60, president 1978-79, Davisson-Germer prize 1974); member New York, National acads. sci., Am. Philosophical Association, American Association for the Advancement of Science (chairman physics section 1977), Am. Institute Physics (chairman board govs. 1980—), Phi Beta Kappa (senator 1979—, vice president 1982-85, president 1985—), Sigma Xi. Home: 4420 Greenbriar Boulevard Boulder Colorado 80303-7051 Office: Lyman Lab Harvard University Cambridge Massachusetts 02138

RAPP, FRED, virologist; born Fulda, Germany, March 13, 1929; came to United States, 1936, naturalized, 1945; son of Albert and Rita (Hain) R.; children: Stanley I., Richard J., Kenneth A.; married Pamela A. Miles, August 28, 1988. Bachelor of Science, Brooklyn College, 1951; Master of Science, Albany Medical College, Union University, 1956; Doctor of Philosophy, University Southern California, 1958. Diplomate: fellow Am. Acad. Microbiology. Junior Bacteriologist, div. laboratories and research New York State Department Health, 1952-55; from teaching assistant to instructor department medical microbiology School Medicine, University Southern California, 1956-59; consultant supervisory microbiologist Hospital Special Surgery, New York City, 1959-62; also virologist div. pathology Philip D. Wilson Research Foundation, New York City; assistant professor micorbiology and immunology Cornell University Medical College, New York City, 1961-62; associate professor Baylor University School Medicine, Waco, Texas, 1962-66, professor; 1966-69; professor, chairman department microbiology and immunology Pennsylvania State University College Medicine, University Park, 1969—, Evan Pugh professor microbiology; 1978—, associate provost, dean health affairs; 1973-80, senior member grad. faculty, associate dean acad. affairs, research and grad. studies; 1987—; researh career professor of virology Am. Cancer Society, 1966-69, professor virology, 1977—; director College Medical Pennsylvania State University (Specialized Cancer Research Center), 1973-84; member delegation on viral oncology, U.S./USSR Joint Committee Health Cooperation; chairman, Gordon Research Conference in Cancer, 1975; virology Task Force, 1976-79; chairman Atlantic Coast Tumor Virology Group, National Cancer Institutes Health, 1971-77; member council for projection and analysis Am. Cancer Society, 1976-80; chairman standards and exam. committee on virology Am. Board Medical Microbiology, 1977, 80; chairman subsect. on virology program committee Am. Association Cancer Research, 1978-79; member adv. council virology div. International Union Microbiol. Societies, 1978-84; referee Macy Faculty Scholar Award Program, 1979-81; member programme committee Fifth International Congress for Virology, Strasbourg, France, 1981; member basic cancer research group U.S.-France Agreement for Cooperation in Cancer Research, 1980—; member organizing committee International Workshop on Herpes viruses, Bologna, Italy, 1980-81, North Atlantic Treaty Organization International Advanced Study Institute, Corfu

Island, Greece, 1981; member Herpes viruses Study Group, 1981-84; member sci. adv. committee Wilmot Fellowship Program, University Rochester Medical Center, 1981—; member scientific rev. committee Hubert H. Humphrey Cancer Research Center, Boston University, 1981; member fin. committee Am. Society Virology, 1982—; member adv. committee persistent virus-host interactions research program R.J. Reynolds Scientific Bd./Wistar Institute, 1983—; member medical adv. board Herpes Resource Center, Am. Social Health Association, 1983—; board of directors U.S.-Japan Foundation Biomedicine, 1983—; member council Society Experimental Biology and Medicine, 1983-87; member scientific adv. committee International Association Study and Prevention of Virus-Associated Cancers, 1983—; member Basil O'Connor Starter Research Adv. Committee, 1984—; member council for research and clinical investigation awards Am. Cancer Society, 1984—; member recombinant DNA adv. committee National Institutes of Health, 1984-87; member council Am. Society Virology, 1984—; member outstanding investigator grant rev. committee National Cancer Institute, 1984—; member organizing committee Fourth Symposium Sapporo Cancer Seminar, Japan, 1984, Second International Conference Immunobiology and Prophylaxis of Human Herpes virus Infections, Fort Lauderdale, Floor, 1984-85, International Congress of Virology, Sendai, Japan, 1984; member international sci. committee International Meeting on Adv. in Virology, Catania, Italy, 1984-85; member adv. board Cancer Information, Dissemination and

Analysis Center Carcinogenesis and Cancer Biology, 1984—; member international programme committee 7th International Congress of Virology, Edmonton, Can., 1985-87; councilor div. DNA viruses Am. Society Microbiology, 1985-87; member adv. committee research on etiology, diagnosis, natural history, prevention and therapy of multiple sclerosis National Multiple Sclerosis Society, 1985—; member sci. adv. board Showa University Research Institute for Biomedicine in Florida, 1985—; member sci. adv. council Pittsburgh Center Acquired Immune Deficiency Syndrome Research University Pittsburgh, 1988. Sect. editor on oncology: Intervirology, 1972-84, associate editor, 1978-84, editor-in-chief, 1985—; adv. board: Archives Virology, 1976-81; editorial board Journal Immunology, 1966-73, Journal Virology, 1968—; associate editor Cancer Research 1972-79. Recipient 1st CIBA-Geigy Drew award for biomed. research, 1977, National award for teaching excellence in microbiology, University Medicine and Dentistry New Jersey Medical School, 1988. Member Am. Society Microbiology (member committee med. microbiology and immunology, board pub. scientific affairs, 1979—, chairman DNA viruses division 1981-82), Am. Society Virology (chairman fin. committee 1987-88), American Association for the Advancement of Science, Am. Association Immunologists, The Harvey Society, Society Experimental Biology and Medicine, Am. Association Cancer Research, American Association of University Women, Association Medical School Microbiology Chairman (president 1980-81), Alpha Omega Alpha, Sigma Xi. Home: 2 Laurel Ridge Road Hershey Pennsylvania 17033

RAPSON, WILLIAM HOWARD, chemical engineering educator; born Toronto, Ontario, Canada, September 15, 1912; son of Alfred Ernest and Lillian Jane (Cannicott) R.; married Mary Margaret Campbell, January 29, 1937; children—Margaret (Mrs. Brian A. Fox), Linda (Mrs. Morris Manning), Lorna (Mrs. John A. Ferguson), William Howard II. Bachelor of Arts in Science, University Toronto, 1934, Master of Arts in Science, 1935, Doctor of Philosophy, 1941; Doctor of Engineering, University Waterloo, 1976; Doctor of Science, McGill, 1980. Demonstrator chemical engineering University Toronto, 1934-40, instructor; 1940, professor; 1953—, University professor; 1976-81; with research department Canadian International Paper Company, 1940-42, head pioneering research, 1942-53; consultant in field, 1953—; vice president Chemical Engineering Research Cons., Limited, 1962-70, president, 1970-81; president W.H. Rapson Limited, 1964-77, chairman board, 1977—; chairman board Rapson Farms Limited, 1971-78. Author, editor: The Bleaching of Pulp, 1963; patentee in field; pioneer use of chlorine dioxide for pulp bleaching. Trustee Hawkesbury (Ontario) Pub. School Board, 1947-52, chairman, 1949-52; Board governors Ontario Institute Studies in Education, 1971-77. Recipient Weldon medal, 1954; R.S. Jane Memorial award, 1965; McCharles prize, 1966; Canadian Centennial medal, 1967; Brazilian Pulp and Paper Association medal, 1974; Shalimar Gold medal Indian Pulp and Paper Association, 1976; Forest Products Div. award Am. Institute Chemical Engrs., 1976; Anselme Payen award Am. Chemical Society, 1978; Can. medal Society Chemical Industry, 1978; named to Engineering Hall of Distinction University Toronto, 1979; Engineering Alumni medal, 1979; Palladium medal Chemical Institute Can., 1980; Izaak Walton Killam Memorial prize Can. Council, 1986. Fellow Royal Society Can. (Eadie medal 1981), Chemical Institute Can. (hon., Palladium medal 1980, president 1985-86), Technical Association of the Pulp and Paper Industry (hon. life; Manufacturing Div. award 1967, Gold medal 1976, board directors 1972-75), Can. Pulp and Paper Association (tech. section)(senior, hon. life member; chairman 1970-71), Canadian Society Chemical Engineering (director 1966-68), Association Professional Engineers Province Ontario (Gold medal 1975), Royal Swedish Acad. Engineering Sci. (foreign). Club: Faculty (University Toronto). Home: 110 Bloor St W, Suite 1001, Toronto, Ontario Canada M5S 2W7 Office: University Toronto, Department Chem Engring, Toronto, Ontario Canada M5S 1A4

RATNOFF, OSCAR DAVIS, physician, educator; born New York City, August 23, 1916; son of Hyman L. and Ethel (Davis) R.; married Marian Foreman, March 31, 1945; children: William Davis, Martha. Bachelor of Arts, Columbia University, 1936, Doctor of Medicine, 1939; Doctor of Laws (honorary), University Aberdeen, 1981. Intern Johns Hopkins Hospital, Baltimore, 1939-40; Austin fellow in physiology Harvard Medical School, Boston, 1940-41; assistant resident Montefiore Hospital, New York City, 1942; resident Goldwater Memorial Hospital, New York City, 1942-43; assistant in medicine Columbia College Physicians and Surgeons, New York City, 1942-46; fellow in medicine Johns Hopkins, 1946-48, instructor medicine; 1948-50, instructor bacteriology; 1949-50; assistant professor medicine Case Western Reserve University, Cleveland, 1950-56; associate professor Case Western Reserve University, 1956-61, professor; 1961—; assistant physician (University Hospital), Cleveland, 1952-56; associate physician (University Hospital), 1956-67, physician; 1967—. Author: Bleeding Syndromes, 1960; member editorial board: Journal Lab. Clin. Medicine, 1956-62, associate editor, 1986—; editor: Treatment of Hemorrhagic Disorders, 1968, (with C. D. Forbes) Disorders of Hemostasis, 1984; member editorial board Circulation, 1961-65, Blood, 1963-69, 78-81, Am. Journal Physiology, 1966-72, Journal Applied Physiology, 1966-72, Journal Lipid Research, 1967-69, Journal Clin. Investigation, 1969-71, Circulation Research, 1970-75, Annals Internal Medicine, 1973-76, Perspectives in Biology and Medicine, 1974—, Thrombosis Research, 1981-84, Journal Urology, 1981-88; contributor articles to medical journals. Career investigator Am. Heart Association, 1960-86. Served to major Medical Corps, 1943-46, Ind. Recipient Henry Moses award Montefiore Hospital, 1949; Distinguished Achievement award Modern Medicine, 1967; James F. Mitchell award, 1971; Murray Thelin award National Hemophilia Foundation, 1971; H.P. Smith award Am. Society Clinical Pathology, 1975; Joseph Mather Smith prize Columbia College Physicians and Surgeons, 1976; Kober medal, 1988. Member American College of Physicians (John Phillips award 1974, master 1983), American Medical Association, Am. Federation Clinical Research (emeritus), National Acad. Sciences (Kovalenko award 1985), Society Scholars of Johns Hopkins University, Am. Society Clinical Investigation (emeritus), Central Society Clinical Research, Association Am. Physicians (Kober lecturer 1985), Am. Society Hematology (Dameshek award 1972), International Society Hematology, International Society Thrombosis (Grant award 1981), Am. Physiological Society, Am. Society Biological Chemists, Royal College Physicians and Surgeons Glasgow (hon.), Sigma Xi, Alpha Omega Alpha. Home: 2916 Sedgewick Road Shaker Heights Ohio 44120 Office: University Hosps of Cleveland Cleveland Ohio 44106

RAVEN, PETER HAMILTON, botanical garden administrator, botany educator; born Shanghai, China, June 13, 1936; son of Walter Francis and Isabelle Marion (Breen) R.; married Tamra Engelhorn, November 29, 1968; children—Alice Catherine, Elizabeth Marie, Francis Clark, Kathryn Amelia. Bachelor of Arts with honors, University Calif.-Berkeley, 1957; Doctor of Philosophy, University of California at Los Angeles, 1960; Doctor of Science (honorary), St. Louis University, 1982, Knox College, 1983, Southern Illinois University, 1983, Miami University, 1986, University Goteborg, 1987, Rutgers University, 1988, University Massachusetts, 1988. Taxonomist, curator Rancho Santa Ana Botanic Garden, Claremont, California, 1961-62; assistant professor, then associate professor biological sciences Stanford University, California, 1962-71; director Missouri Botanical Garden, St. Louis, 1971—; Engelmann professor botany Washington University, St. Louis, 1971—; adj. professor biology St. Louis University, University Missouri,

St. Louis; senior research fellow New Zealand Department Sci. and Industrial Research, 1969-70; vice president XIII International Botanical Congress, Sydney, 1981; home secretary National Acad. Sciences, 1987—; chairman report rev. committee National Research Council, 1988—. Author: Native Shrubs of Southern California, 1966, (with PR Ehrlich, R.W. Holm) Papers on Evolution, 1969, (with H. Curtis) Biology of Plants, 1971, 4th edition, 1986; Principles of Tzeltal Plant Classification, 1974; (with G. Johnson) Biology, 1986, Understanding Biology, 1988; editor: (with L.E. Gilbert) Coevolution of Animals and Plants, 1981, (with F.J. Radovsky & S.H. Sohmer) Biography of the Tropical Pacific, 1984, (with others) Topics in Plant Population Biology, 1979, Advances in Legume Systematics, 1981; editor in chief Brittonia, 1963-66, Flora Neotropica, 1965-84; member editorial board Evolution, 1963-65, 76-79, Memoirs of New York Botanical Garden, 1966-84, North America Flora, 1966-84, Am. Naturalist, 1967-70, Annual Rev. Ecology and Systematics, 1971-75, Flora of Ecuador, 1974—, Evolutionary Theory, 1975—, Adansonia, 1976—, Journal Biogeography, 1978—, Science, 1979-82, Proceedings of United States National Acad. Scis., 1980-87, World Book, Incorporated, 1982-86, Diversity, 1985—, Bothalia, 1985—, others; member adv. board Applied Botany Abstracts, 1981—, Tropical Plant Science Research, 1982—, Darwinania, 1985—; member international edition com. Acta Botanica Mexicana, 1987—; editorial advisor Plants Today, 1988—; member editorial board Botanical Bulletin Academia Sinica, 1988—,

Botanical Meg., 1988—, Cathaya, 1988—, Ecological Applications, 1989—; co-chmn. editorial com. Flora of China, 1988—; contributor over 390 articles to professional journals. Board curators University Missouri, 1985; commissioner Tower Grove Park, St. Louis, 1971—; member Arnold Arboretum Vis. Committee, 1974-81, chairman 1976-81; board overseers Morris Arboretum; member sci. adv. board Pacific Tropical Botanical Garden, 1975—; member Smithsonian Council, 1985—, Commission for Flora Neotropica, 1985—; member Commission on Mus. for New Century, 1981-84; member sci. and engring. panel Committee on Scholarly Communication with People's Republic China, 1981-85; chairman committee to visit department organismic and evolutionary biology Harvard University, 1982-84, member 84-85; chairman St. Louis Mus. Collaborative, 1985—; educational adv. board John Simon Guggenheim Memorial Foundation, 1986—; research associate botany Bernice P. Bishop Mus., 1985—; associate trustee University Pennsylvania, 1977-81; hon. trustee Acad. Sci. of St. Louis, 1986—; hon. chairman International Union for the Conservation of Nature, World Wildlife Fund, 1987; member council Intenrat. Association for Plant Taxonomy, 1981—; member adv. and tech. board Fundacion de Parques Nacionales and Fundacion Neotropica, Costa Rics, 1988—; member National Council World Wildlife Fund and Conservati, scientific adv. committee Conservation International, 1988—. Recipient Associated Press DeCandolle prize, Geneva, 1970; Distinguished Service award Japan Am. Society Southern California, 1977; award of Merit,

Botanical Society Am., 1977; Achievement medal Garden Club Am., 1978; Willdenow medal Berlin Botanical Garden, 1979; Distinguished Service award Am. Institute Biological Sciences, 1981; Joseph Priestly medal, Dickinson College, 1982; Gold Seal medal National Council of State Garden Clubs, 1982; International Environmental Leadership medal United Nations Environmental Program, 1982; Special citiation Doña Doris Yankelewitz de Monge, 1985, Award Biology Association for Teachers, 1985, International Prize for Biology, Government Japan, 1986, Archie F. Carr medal, 1987, Global 500 Honor Roll United Nations Environmental Program, 1987, Am. Fuschsia Society Achievement Medal, 1987, George Robert White Medal of Honor Massachusetts Horticultural Society, 1987, Robert Allerton Medal Pacific Tropical Botanical Garden, 1988, and numerous other botanical awards and honors; Guggenheim fellow, 1969-70; John D. and Catherine T. MacArthur Federation fellow, 1985-89, National Science Foundation postdoctoral fellow, Brit. Mus. London, 1960-61. Fellow Am. Acad. Arts and Sciences (committee on membership 1980-82), Linnean Society London, California Acad. Sciences, American Association for the Advancement of Science; member National Science Foundation (systematic biology panel 1973-76, adv. committee for biological behavioral and social scis. 1984—), National Acad. Sciences (committee on human rights 1984-87, home secretary 1987—), Royal Danish Acad. Sciences and Letters (foreign), Royal Swedish Acad. Sciences (foreign), Royal Society New Zealand (hon.), National Research Council (board govs. 1983-86, 87—, chairman committee on research priorities in tropical biology 1977-79, assembly life scis. 1979-81, committee on selected research problems in humid tropics 1980-82, commission international relations 1981-82, adv. con. on ICSU 1985—, California Botanical Society (vice president 1968-69), Am. Society Plant Taxonomists (president 1972), Association Systematics Collections (president 1980-82, Federal Council Arts and Humanities, World Wildlife Fund-U.S. (board directors 1983-88), Conservation Foundation (board directors 1985-88), National Mus. Services Board (chairman 1984-88), National Geographic Society (committee on research and exploration 1982—), International Association for Plant Taxonomy (council 1981—), Organization Tropical Studies (treasurer 1981-84, vice president devel. 1984-85, president 1985-88), Am. Society Naturalists (president 1983), Miller Institute Basic Research in Sci. (adv. board 1983—), Smithsonian Institute (council 1985—), Am. Institute Biological Sciences (president 1983-84), Missouri Acad. Sciences, Geological Society Am., Botanical Society Am. (president 1975, chairman committee on sci. exchange with People's Republic China 1978-84), International Union for Conservation of Nature and Natural Resources (chairman plants adv. group 1984-87), Association Tropical Biology (board directors 1981-85), Am. Association Mus. (executive committee 1980-83), Association Sci. Mus. Directors, Association Pacific Systematists, Sociedad Argentina de Botanica (hon.), Fundación Miguel Lillo (hon.), Society Systematic Zool., Sociedad Botánica de México (life), Association pour l"Etude Tazonomique de la Flore d'Afrique

Tropicale, Organization for Phyto-Taxonomic Investigation of Mediterranean Area (council 1975—), All Union Botanical Society Union of the Soviet Socialist Republics (hon. foreign member), Phi Beta Kappa, Sigma Xi. Office: Missouri Bot Garden Post Office Box 299 Saint Louis Missouri 63166

REBHUN, LIONEL ISRAEL, cell biologist, zoologist, educator; born Bronx, New York, April 19, 1926; married; 2 children. Bachelor of Science, City College of New York, 1949; Master of Science, University Chicago, 1951, Doctor of Philosophy in Zoology, 1955. From instructor to assistant professor anatomy College Medicine, University Illinois, 1955-58; from assistant to associate professor biology Princeton University, 1958-69, professor; 1969-77; commonwealth professor biology University Virginia, Charlottesville, 1977—. Lalor fellow, 1956, Guggenheim fellow, 1962. Member Am. Society Cell Biologists, Biophys. Society, Electron Microscopy Society Am., Society Developmental Biology, Society Genetic Physiologists. Research in control of cell division, cellular motility, cell ultrastructure, cryobiology. Office: U of Va Department Biology Charlottesville Virginia 22903

RECHTIN, EBERHARDT, aerospace educator; born East Orange, New Jersey, January 16, 1926; son of Eberhardt Carl and Ida H. (Pfarrer) R.; married Dorothy Diane Denebrink, June 10, 1951; children: Andrea C., Nina, Julie Anne, Erica, Mark. Bachelor of Science, California Institute Tech., 1946, Doctor of Philosophy cum laude, 1950. Director Deep Space Network, California Institute Tech. Jet Propulsion Laboratory, 1949-67; director Advanced Research Projects Agency, Department Defense, 1967-70, principal deputy director defense research and engineering; 1970-71, assistant secretary defense for telecommunications; 1972-73; chief engineer Hewlett-Packard Company, Palo Alto, California, 1973-77; president, chief executive officer Aerospace Corp., El Segundo, California, 1977-87; professor University Southern California, 1988—. Served to lieutenant United States Naval Reserve, 1943-56. Recipient major awards National Aeronautics and Space Administration, Department Defense. Fellow American Institute of Aeronautics and Astronautics (major awards), Institute of Electrical and Electronics Engineers (major awards); member National Acad. Engineering, Tau Beta Pi. Home: 1665 Cataluna Place Palos Verdes Estates California 90274 Office: U Southern California University Park Los Angeles California 90089-1454

REECE, ROBERT WILLIAM, zoological park administrator; born Saginaw, Michigan, January 21, 1942; son of William Andrews and Mary Barbara (Murphy) R.; married Jill Whetstone, August 21, 1965; children: William Clayton, Gregory Scott, Mark Andrews. Bachelor of Science, Michigan State University, 1964; postgraduate, University West Florida, 1969-71, University South Florida, 1974-76. Director Northwest Florida Zool. Gardens, Pensacola, Florida, 1970-72; zoological director Lion Country Georgia, Stockbridge, 1972-73; assistant director Salisbury Zoo, Maryland, 1976-77; director zoology Wild Animal Habitat, Kings Island, Ohio, 1977—. Associate editor: Science Journal Zoo Biology, 1982—.

Served to lieutenant United States Navy, 1964-69, Korea. Professional fellow Am. Association Zool. Parks and Aqariums; member Cincinnati Wildlife Research Federation, Am. Society Mammalogists, Animal Behavior Society. Republican. Episcopalian. Home: 2772 Turnkey Court Cincinnati Ohio 45244 Office: Wild Animal Habitat Kings Island Ohio 45034

REESE, LYMON CLIFTON, civil engineering educator; born Murfreesboro, Arkansas, April 27, 1917; son of Samuel Wesley and Nancy Elizabeth (Daniels) R.; married Eva Lee Jett, May 28, 1948; children: Sally Reese Melant, John, Nancy. Rodman. Bachelor of Science, University Texas at Austin, 1949, Master of Science, 1950; Doctor of Philosophy (General Education Board California fellow, NSF fellow), University California at Berkeley, 1955. Diplomate: Registered professional engineer, Texas. International Boundary Commission San Benito, Texas, 1939-41; layout engineer E.I. DuPont Company de Nemours & Company, Incorporated, Pryor, Oklahoma, Childersburg, Alabama, 1941-42; surveyor United States Naval Construction Battalions, Aleutian Islands, Okinawa, 1942-45; field engineer Associate Contractors & Engineers, Houston, 1945; draftsman Phillips Petroleum Company, Austin, 1946-48; research engineer University Texas, Austin, 1948-50; assistant professor civil engineering Mississippi State College, State College, 1950-51, 53-55; assistant professor University Texas, Austin, 1955-57; associate professor University Texas, 1957-64, professor; 1964—, chairman department; 1965-72, Taylor professor engineering; 1972-81, associate dean engineering for program planning; 1972-79, Nasser I. Al-Rashid Chair; 1981-84; consultant Shell Oil Company, Shell Devel. Company, 1955-65, Dames & Moore, 1970—, McClelland Engineers, Houston, 1970—, Association Drilled Shaft Contractors, 1971—, Florida Department Transportation, 1975—, others. Contributor articles to professional journals. Served with United States Naval Reserve, 1942-45. Recipient Thomas Middlebrooks award American Society of Civil Engineers, 1958; Joe J. King Professional Engineering Achievement award, 1977, Offshore Tech. Conference Distinguished Achievement award for Individuals, 1985, Distinguished grad. College of Engineering, University Texas, Austin., 1985. Fellow American Society of Civil Engineers (Karl Terzaghi lecturer 1976 Terzaghi award, 1983, Texas section award of Hon. 1985, hon. member 1984—); member National Acad. Engineering, Am. Society Engineering Education, National Society Professional Engineers, American Society for Testing and Materials, Sigma Xi, Tau Beta Pi, Chi Epsilon, Phi Kappa Phi. Baptist (deacon). Office: U Tex Department Civil Engring Austin Texas 78712

REEVES, ROBERT GRIER LEFEVRE, scientist, educator; born York, Pennsylvania, May 30, 1920; son of Edward LeGrande and Helen (Baker) R.; married Elizabeth Bodette Simmons, June 11, 1942; children: Dale Ann, Edward Boyd. Student, Yuba College, 1938-40; Bachelor of Science, University Nevada, 1949; Master of Science, Stanford University, 1950, Doctor of Philosophy, 1965. Registered professional engineer, Texas. Geophysicist, geologist United States Geological Survey, 1949-69; with assignments as project chief iron ore deposits of Nevada, tech. adviser Foreign Aid Program; visiting professor economic geology University Rio Grande do Sul, Brazil; staff geologist for research contracts and grants and professional staffing Washington; professor geology Colorado School Mines, Golden, 1969-73; staff scientist Earth Resources Observation Systems Data Center, United States Geological Survey, Sioux Falls, South Dakota, 1973-78; professor geology University Tex.-Permian Basin, Odessa, 1978-85, chairman earth sciences; 1978-82; dean College Sci. and Engineering University Texas Permian Basin, 1979-84; consultant geologist, engineer partner Orion, Limited, Midland, Texas, 1984-87, consultant engineer, geologist; 1987—; leader People to People Economic Geology Trip to Brazil and Peru, 1985; co-leader Am. Geological Institute International Field Institute to Brazil, 1966; visiting geological scientist Boston College, Boston University, 1967; senior Fulbright lecturer University Adelaide, Australia, 1969. Contributor articles professional journals. Served to major Signal Corps Army of the United States, 1941-46, European Theatre of Operations. Recipient Outstanding Service award U.S. Geol. Survey, 1965. Fellow Geological Society Am., Geological Society Brazil; member Am. Institute Mining, Metallurgical and Petroleum Engineers (secretary Washington 1964), Am. Society Photogrammetry (editor-in-chief Manual of Remote Sensing), Society Econ. Geologists, Society Ind. Professional Earth Scientists. Home

and Office: 4040 Lakeside Dr Odessa Texas 79762 also: Post Office Box 796 Battle Mountain Nevada 89820

REICHSTEIN, TADEUS, scientist, educator; born Wloclawek, Poland, July 20, 1897; son of Isidor and Gustava (Brokman) R.; married Luise Henriette Quarles v. Ufford, July 21, 1927; children: Margrit, Ruth. Student, Industrieschule, Zurich, 1914-16; diploma in chemical engineering, Eidg. Tech. Hochschule, Zurich, 1920, Doctor Ing.-Chem., 1922; Doctor of Science (honorary), University Sorbonne, Paris, 1947, University Basel, Paris, 1951, University Geneva, University Abidjan, Paris, 1967, University London, Paris, 1968, University Leeds, Paris, 1970. Professor Eidg. Techn. Hochschule, 1934-38; professor University Basel, Switzerland, 1938-67, professor emeritus; 1967—; director Pharmacol. Institute, 1938-48, Institute Organic Chemistry, 1946-67; research botanist on ferns, 1967—. Contributor articles to professional publications. Recipient Marcel-Benoist prize, 1948; co-recipient Nobel prize in physiology or medicine, 1950, various other prizes. Fellow Royal Society London, National Acad. Sci. (Washington), Royal Irish Acad., Chemical Society London (hon.), Swiss Medical Acad. (hon.), Indian Acad. Sci. (hon.); member Mus. Historical National Paris (corr.), Medical Faculty University Basel (hon.). Home: 22 Weissensteinstrasse, CH-4059 Basel Switzerland Office: Institute fur Organische Chemie, St Johanns-Ring 19, CH-4056 Basel Switzerland

REINES, FREDERICK, physicist, educator; born Paterson, New Jersey, March 16, 1918; son of Israel and Gussie (Cohen) R.; married Sylvia Samuels, August 30, 1940; children:

Robert G., Alisa K. Mechanical Engineer, Stevens Institute Tech., 1939, Master of Science, 1941; Doctor of Philosophy, New York University, 1944; Doctor of Science (honorary), University Witwatersrand, 1966, Doctor Engineering (honorary), 1984. Member staff Los Alamos Sci. Laboratory, 1944-59; group leader Los Alamos Sci. Laboratory (Theoretical div.), 1945-59; director (Atomic Energy Commission experiments on Eniwetok Atoll), 1951; professor physics, head department Case Institute Tech., 1959-66; professor physics University Calif.-Irvine, 1966—, dean physical sciences; 1966-74, distinguished professor physics; 1987—.
Contributor numerous articles to professional journals; Contributing author: Effects of Atomic Weapons, 1950. Member Cleveland Symphony Chorus, 1959-62. Recipient J. Robert Oppenheimer memorial prize, 1981, National medal of Sci., 1983, University California Irvine medal, 1987; Guggenheim fellow, 1958-59; Sloan fellow, 1959-63. Fellow Am. Physical Society, American Association for the Advancement of Science; member Am. Association Physics Teachers, Argonne University Association (trustee 1965-66), Am. Acad. Arts and Sciences, National Acad. Sci., Phi Beta Kappa, Sigma Xi, Tau Beta Pi. Co-discoverer elementary nuclear particle, free antineutrino, 1956. Office: U California at Irvine Irvine California 92717

REINHARDT, CHARLES FRANCIS, toxicologist; born Spring Grove, Indiana, November 25, 1933; son of Charles H. and Frances N. R.; married Linda Helen Ieler, September 1, 1956; children: Amy Linn, Jeff Charles, Meg Susan, Jane Ellen. Bachelor of Arts, Wabash College, 1955; Doctor of Medicine, Ind. University, 1959; Master of Science, Ohio State University, 1964. Diplomate: Am. Board Preventive Medicine, Am. Board Toxicology (pres. 1983-84). Resident in occupational medicine Ohio State University; plant physician Chambers Works, E.I. du Pont de Nemours & Company, 1964-66; physiologist Haskell Laboratory, Newark, Del., 1966-69; chief physiology Haskell Laboratory, 1969-70; research manager Environmental Sciences Group, 1970-71, assistant director; 1971-74, associate director; 1974-76, director; 1976—; member sci. adv. panel Chemical Industry Institute Toxicology, 1980-83.
Contributor in field. Member sci. ad. board Environmental Protection Agency, 1985—. Served to captain, Medical Corps United States Air Force, 1960-62. Member American Medical Association, Am. Acad. Occupational Medicine (president 1985-86), Am. Occupational Medical Association, Society Toxicology, Am. Industrial Hygiene Association. Office: Haskell Laboratory El du Pont De Nemours and Company Elkton Road Newark Delaware 19714

REIS, DONALD JEFFERY, neurologist, neurobiologist, educator; born New York City, September 9, 1931; son of Samuel H. and Alice (Kiesler) R.; married Cornelia Langer Noland, April 13, 1985. Bachelor of Arts, Cornell University, 1953, Doctor of Medicine, 1956. Intern New York Hospital, New York City, 1956; resident in neurology Boston City Hosp.-Harvard Medical School, 1957-59; Fulbright fellow, United Cerebral Palsy Foundation fellow London and Stockholm, 1959-60; research associate National Institute of Mental

Health, Bethesda, Maryland, 1960-62; special fellow National Institutes of Health, Nobel Neurophysiology Institute, Stockholm, 1962-63; assistant professor neurology Cornell University Medical School, New York City, 1963-67; associate professor neurology and psychiatry Cornell University Medical School, 1967-71, professor; 1971—, First George C. Cotzias Distinguished professor neurology; 1982—; Member U.S.-Soviet Exchange Program; adv. councils National Institutes of Health; board sci. advisers Merck, Sharpe and Dohm; consultant biomed. companies. Contributor articles to professional journals; member editorial board various professional journals. Recipient CIBA Prize award Am. Heart Association. Member Am. Physiological Society, Am. Neurological Association, Am. Pharmacol. Society, Am. Association Physicians, Telluride Association, Am. Society Clinical Investigation, Phi Beta Kappa, Sigma Xi, Alpha Omega Alpha. Club: Century Association. Home: 190 E 72d St New York New York 10021 Office: 1300 York Avenue New York New York 10021

RELMAN, ARNOLD SEYMOUR, physician, educator; born New York City, June 17, 1923; son of Simon and Rose (Mallach) R.; married Harriet Morse Vitkin, June 26, 1953; children: David Arnold, John Peter, Margaret Rose. Bachelor of Arts, Cornell University, 1943; Doctor of Medicine, Columbia University, 1946; Master of Arts (honorary), University Pennsylvania; Doctor of Science (honorary), Medical College Wisconsin; Sc. Doctor (honorary), Union University; DMSc (honorary), Brown University; Doctor.L.H. (honorary), State University of New York. Diplomate: Am. Board Internal Medicine. House officer New Haven Hospital, Yale, 1946-49; National Research Council fellow Evans Memorial, Massachusetts Memorial hospitals, 1949-50; practice medicine, specializing in internal medicine Boston, 1950-68, Philadelphia, 1968-77; assistant professor, professor medicine Boston University School Medicine, 1950-68; director Boston University Medical Services, Boston City Hospital, 1967-68; professor medicine, chairman department medicine University Pennsylvania; chief medical services Hospital of University Pennsylvania, 1968-77; editor New England Journal Medicine, Boston, 1977—; senior physician Brigham and Women's Hospital, Boston, 1977—; professor medicine Harvard Medical School, 1977—; Cons. National Institutes of Health, United States Public Health Service. Editor: Journal Clin. Investigation, 1962-67, (with F.J. Ingelfinger and M. Finland) Controversy in Internal Medicine, Volume 1, 1966, Volume 2, 1974; Contributor (with F.J. Ingelfinger and M. Finland) articles professional journals. Recipient Columbia Alumni Gold medal, 1980, Distinguished Service award Am. College Cardiology, 1987. Fellow Am. Acad. Arts and Sciences, American College of Physicians (master, John Phillips medal 1985); member Association Am. Physicians (council, president 1983-84), Am. Physiological Society, American Medical Association, Massachusetts Medical Society, Institute Medicine of National Acad. Sciences (council 1979-82), Am. Society Clinical Investigation (past president), Am. Federation Clinical Research (past president), Phi Beta Kappa, Alpha Omega Alpha. Office: New England Jour of Medicine 10

Shattuck St Boston Massachusetts 02115

REYNOLDS, WILLIAM CRAIG, mechanical engineer, educator; born Berkeley, California, March 16, 1933; son of Merrill and Patricia Pope (Galt) R.; married Janice Erma, September 18, 1953; children—Russell, Peter, Margery. Bachelor of Science in Mechanical Engineering, Stanford University, 1954, Master of Science in Mechanical Engineering, 1955, Doctor of Philosophy in Mechanical Engineering, 1957. Faculty mechanical engineering Stanford University, 1957—, chairman department mechanical engineering; 1972-82, Donald Whittier professor mechanical engineering; 1986—, chmn.Institute for Energy Studies; 1974-81. Author: books, including Energy Thermodynamics, 2d edit, 1976; contributor numerous articles to professional journals. National Science Foundation sr. scientist fellow England, 1964. Fellow American Society of Mechanical Engineers; fellow Am. Physical Society; member American Association of University Profs., American Institute of Aeronautics and Astronautics, National Acad. Engineering, Sigma Xi, Tau Beta Pi. Research in fluid mechanics and applied thermodynamics. Office: Stanford U Department Mech Engring Building 500 Stanford California 94305

RHODES, DONALD ROBERT, electrical engineer, educator; born Detroit, December 31, 1923; son of Donald Eber and Edna Mae (Fulmer) R.; children: Joyce Rhodes Holbert, Jane Rhodes Stranz, Roger Charles, Diane Rhodes Herran. Bachelor of Electrical Engineering, Ohio State University, 1945, Master of Science, 1948, Doctor of Philosophy, 1953. Research associate Ohio State University, Columbus, 1945-54; research engineer Cornell Aeronautical Laboratory, Buffalo, 1954-57; head basic research department Radiation, Incorporated, Orlando, Florida, 1957-61; senior scientist Radiation, Incorporated, Melbourne, Florida, 1961-66; University professor North Carolina State University, Raleigh, 1966—. Author: Introduction to Monopulse, 1959, 2d edition, 1980, Synthesis of Planar Antenna Sources, 1974. Co-founder Central Florida Community Orchestra, Winter Park, 1961, president, 1961-62. Recipient Benjamin G. Lamme medal Ohio State University, 1975; Eminent Engineer award Tau Beta Pi, 1976; named to North Carolina State University Acad. Outstanding Teachers, 1980. Fellow American Association for the Advancement of Science, Institute of Electrical and Electronics Engineers (John T. Bolljahn award 1963, president Antenna and Propagation Society 1969); member Sigma Xi, Theta Tau, Eta Kappa Nu, Sigma Pi Sigma. Home: 625 Cardinal Gibbons Dr Apartment 101 Raleigh North Carolina 27606 Office: Post Office Box 7911 Raleigh North Carolina 27695

RICH, ALEXANDER, molecular biologist, educator; born Hartford, Connecticut, November 15, 1924; son of Max and Bella (Shub) R.; married Jane Erving King, July 5, 1952; children—Benjamin, Josiah, Rebecca, Jessica. Bachelor of Arts magna cum laude in Biochem. Scis, Harvard University, 1947, Doctor of Medicine cum laude, 1949; Doctor (honorary), Federal University Rio de Janeiro, 1981. Research fellow Gates and Crellin Laboratories, California Institute Tech., Pasadena, 1949-54; chief section physical chemistry

National Institute of Mental Health, Bethesda, Maryland, 1954-58; visiting scientist Cavendish Laboratory, Cambridge (England) University, 1955-56; associate professor biophysics Massachusetts Institute of Technology, Cambridge, 1958-61; professor Massachusetts Institute of Technology, 1961—, William Thompson Sedgwick professor biophysics; 1974—; Fairchild distinguished scholar California Institute Tech., Pasadena, 1976; member committee career devel. awards National Institutes of Health, 1964-67, member postdoctoral fellowship board, 1955-58; member committee exobiology space sci. board National Academy of Sciences, 1964-65; member United States national committee International Organization Pure Applied Biophysics, 1965-67; member visiting committee department biology Weizmann Institute Sci., 1965-66; member life sciences committee National Aeronautics and Space Administration, 1970-75, member lunar planetary missions board, 1968-70; member biology team Viking Mars Mission, 1969—; member corp. Marine Biological Laboratory, Woods Hole, Massachusetts, 1965-77; member sci. rev. committee Howard Hughes Medical Institute, Miami, Florida, 1978—; member visiting committee biology div. Oak Ridge National Laboratory, 1972-76; member sci. adv. board Stanford Synchrotron Radiation Project, 1976—, Massachusetts General Hospital, Boston, 1978—; member United States National Sci. Board, 1976—; member board governors Weizmann Institute Sci., 1976—; member research committee Medical Foundation, Boston, 1976-80; member U.S.-USSR Joint Commission on Sci. and Tech.,

Department State, Washington, 1977—; senior consultant Office of Sci. and Tech. Policy, Executive Office of President, Washington, 1977-81; member council Pugwash Confs. on Sci. and World Affairs, Geneva, 1977—; chairman basic research committee National Sci. Board, Washington, 1978—; member United States National Committee for International Union for Pure and Applied Biophysics, National Acad. Sciences, 1979—; member nominating committee National Acad. Sciences, 1980, member executive committee of council, 1985—, member govt.-univ.-industry research round table, 1984—; chairman sci. adv. committee department molecular biology Massachusetts General Hospital, Boston, 1983—; member governing board National Research Council, 1985—; member national adv. committee Pew Scholars program Pew Memorial Trust, 1986—; member committee on Union of the Soviet Socialist Republics and Eastern Europe National Research COuncil, Washington, 1986—, governing board, 1985—. Editor: (with Norman Davidson) Structural Chemistry and Molecular Biology, 1968; editorial board Biophys. Jour, 1961-63, Currents Modern Biology, 1966-72, Science, 1963-69, Analytical Biochemistry, 1969—, Bio-Systems, 1973-78, Molecular Biology Reports, 1974—, Procs. National Acad. Sci, 1973—, Journal Molecular and Applied Genetics, 1980—, Recombinant DNA, 1981—; editorial advisory board: Journal Molecular Biology, 1959-66, Accounts of Chemical Research, 1980—; contributor articles to professional journals. Served with United States Navy, 1943-46. Recipient Skylab Achievement award National Aeronautics and Space

Administration, 1974, Theodore von Karmin award Viking Mars Mission, 1976, Presidential award New York Acad. Sciences, 1977; James R. Killian faculty achievement award M.I.T., 1980; Jabotinsky medal Jabotinsky Foundation, 1980; James R. Killian Faculty Achievement award Massachusetts Institute of Technology, 180; Lewis S. Rosenstiel award in basic biomed. research Brandeis University, 1983; National Research Council fellow, 1949-51; Guggenheim Foundation fellow, 1963; member Pontifical Acad. Sciences The Vatican, 1978. Fellow Am. Acad. Arts and Sciences, American Association for the Advancement of Science; member National Acad. Sciences (chairman biotech, program, committee on scholarly communication with the Peoples Republic China 1986—, executive committee 1985—), Am. Chemical Society, Biophys. Society (council 1960-69), Am. Society Biological Chemists, Am. Crystallographic Society, International Society for Study of Origin of Life, French Acad. Sciences (foreign member), European Molecular Biology Organization (associate), Japanese Biochem. Society (hon. member), Physicians for Social Responsibility (national adv. board 1983—), Phi Beta Kappa. Office: Massachusetts Institute of Technology Department Biology Cambridge Massachusetts 02139

RICHTER, BURTON, physicist, educator; born New York City, March 22, 1931; son of Abraham and Fanny (Pollack) R.; married Laurose Becker, July 1, 1960; children: Elizabeth, Matthew. Bachelor of Science, Massachusetts Institute of Technology, 1952, Doctor of Philosophy, 1956. Research associate Stanford University, 1956-60, assistant professor physics; 1960-63, associate professor; 1963-67, professor; 1967—, Paul Pigott professor physical sci.; 1980—, tech. director Linear Accelerator Center; 1982-84, director Linear Accelerator Center; 1984—; consultant National Science Foundation, Department Energy; director Teknowledge Incorporated, Middlefield Capital Corp. Contributor over 200 articles to professional publications. Recipient E.O. Lawrence medal Department Energy, 1975; Nobel prize in physics, 1976. Fellow Am. Physical Society, American Association for the Advancement of Science; member National Acad. Sci. Research elementary particle physics, Am. Acad. Arts and Sciences. Office: Stanford U Post Office Box 4349 Stanford California 94305

RICK, CHARLES MADEIRA, JR., geneticist, educator; born Reading, Pennsylvania, April 30, 1915; son of Charles Madeira and Miriam Charlotte (Yeager) R.; married Martha Elizabeth Overholts, September 3, 1938 (deceased); children: Susan Charlotte Rick Baldi, John Winfield. Bachelor of Science, Pennsylvania State University, 1937; Master of Arts, Harvard University, 1939, Doctor of Philosophy, 1940. Assistant plant breeder W. Atlee Burpee Company, Lompoc, California, 1936, 37; instructor, junior geneticist University California, Davis, 1940-44; assistant professor, assistant geneticist University California, 1944-49, associate professor, associate geneticist; 1949-55, professor, geneticist; 1955—; chairman coordinating committee Tomato Genetics Cooperative, 1950-82; member genetics study section

National Institutes of Health, 1958-62; member Galapagos International Sci. Project, 1964; member genetic biology panel National Science Foundation, 1971-72; member national plant genetics resources board Department Agriculture, 1975-82; General Education Board visiting lecturer North Carolina State University, 1956; Faculty Research lecturer University California, 1961; Carnegie visiting professor University Hawaii, 1963; visiting professor Universidade São Paulo, Brazil, 1965; visiting scientist University Puerto Rico, 1968; centennial lecturer Ontario Agriculture College University Guelph, Ontario, Can., 1974; adj. professor University de Rosario, Argentina, 1980; university lecturer Cornell University, 1987; member Plant Breeding Research Forum, 1982-84. Contributor numerous articles in field to books and sci. journals. Guggenheim fellow, 1948, 50; grantee National Science Foundation, USPHS/NIH, Rockefeller Foundation, 1953-83. Fellow California Acad. Sci., American Association for the Advancement of Science (Campbell award 1959); member National Acad. Sciences, Botanical Society Am. (Merit award 1976), Am. Society Horticultural Sci. (M.A. Blake award 1974, Vaughan Research award 1946), Massachusetts Horticultural Society (Thomas Roland medal 1983), Society Econ. Botany (named Distinguished Econ. Botanist 1987), National Council Commercial Plant Breeders (Genetic and Plant Breeding award 1987), Am. Genetics Association (Frank N. Meyer medal 1982). Office: U California Davis California 95616

RIDE, SALLY KRISTEN, scientist, former astronaut; born Los Angeles, May 26, 1951; daughter of Dale Burdell and Carol Joyce (Anderson) R.; married Steven Alan Hawley, July 26, 1982 (divorced). Bachelor of Arts in English, Stanford University, 1973, Bachelor of Science in Physics, 1973, Doctor of Philosophy in Physics, 1978.

Teaching assistant Stanford University, Palo Alto, California; researcher department physics Stanford University; astronaut candidate, trainee National Aeronautics and Space Administration, 1978-79, astronaut; 1979-87; on-orbit capsule communicator STS-2 mission Johnson Space Center National Aeronautics and Space Administration, Houston; on-orbit capsule communicator STS-3 mission National Aeronautics and Space Administration, mission specialist STS-7; 1983; sci. fellow Stanford (California) University, 1987—; member Presdl. Commission on Space Shuttle, 1986; director Apple Computer Incorporated. Author: (with Susan Okie) To Space and Back, 1986. Office: Stanford U Center International Security & Arms Control Stanford California 94305-1684

RIEGEL, KURT WETHERHOLD, astronomy centers administrator; born Lexington, Virginia, February 28, 1939; son of Oscar Wetherhold and Jane Cordelia (Butterworth) R.; married Lenore R. Engelmann, November 15, 1974; children: Tatiana Suzanne, Samuel Brent Oscar, Eden Sonja Jane. Bachelor of Arts, Johns Hopkins University, 1961; Doctor of Philosophy, University Maryland, 1966. Assistant professor astronomy University of California at Los Angeles, 1966-74; professor astronomy University California Extension, Los Angeles, 1968-74; manager energy conservation program Federal Energy

Administration, Washington, 1974-75; chief tech. and consumer products energy conservation Department Energy, Washington, 1975—; director consumer products div., conservation and solar energy Department Energy, 1979; associate director environmental engineering and tech. Environmental Protection Agency, 1979-82; head Astronomy Centers National Science Foundation, 1982—; consultant Aerospace Corp., El Segundo, California, 1967-70, Rand Corp., Santa Monica, California, 1973-74; visiting fellow University Leiden, Netherlands, 1972-73; Member Casualty Council Underwriters Laboratories, National Radio Astronomical Observatory Users Committee, 1968-74. Contributor articles to professional journals. Member American Association for the Advancement of Science, Am. Physical Society, Sierra Club, Audubon Society, International Radio Sci. Union, Am. Astronomical Society, International Astronomical Union. Office: National Sci Found 1800 G St Northwest Washington District of Columbia 20550

RILEY, CARROLL LAVERN, anthropology educator; born Summersville, Missouri, April 18, 1923; daughter of Benjamin F. and Minnie B. (Smith) R.; married Brent Robinson Locke, March 25, 1948; children—Benjamin Locke, Victoria Smith Evans, Cynthia Winningham. Bachelor of Arts, University New Mexico, 1948, Doctor of Philosophy, 1952; Master of Arts, University of California at Los Angeles, 1950. Instructor University Colorado, Boulder, 1953-54; assistant professor University North Carolina, Chapel Hill, 1954-55; assistant professor Southern Illinois University, Carbondale, 1955-

60, associate professor; 1960-67, professor; 1967-86, distinguished professor; 1986-87, distinguished professor emeritus; 1987—, chairman department; 1979-82, director Mus.; 1972-74; research associate Mus. New Mexico, 1987—; research collaborator Smithsonian Institution, 1988—. Author: The Origins of Civilization, 1969, The Frontier People, 1982, expanded edition, 1987; editor: Man Across the Sea, 1971, Southwestern Journals of Adolph F. Bandelier, 4 volumes, 1966, 70, 75, 84, Across the Chichimec Sea, 1978; others; contributor numerous articles to professional journals. Served in United States Army Air Force, 1942-45. Decorated 4 battle stars; grantee Social Sci. Research Council, National Institutes of Health, Am. Philos. Society, Am. Council Learned Socs., National Endowment for the Humanities, others. Fellow Explorers Club, Am. Anthropological Association, American Association for the Advancement of Science; member Society Am. Archaeology, Am. Society Ethnohistory, Sigma Xi. Home: 1106 6th St Las Vegas New Mexico 87701

RILEY, WILLIAM FRANKLIN, engineering educator; born Allenport, Pennsylvania, March 1, 1925; son of William Andrew and Margaret (James) R.; married Helen Elizabeth Chilzer, November 5, 1945; children—Carol Ann, William Franklin. Bachelor of Science in Mechanical Engineering, Carnegie Institute Tech., 1951; Master of Science in Mechanics, Illinois Institute Tech., 1958. Mechanical engineer Mesta Machine Company, West Homestead, Pennsylvania, 1951-54; research engineer Armour Research Foundation, Chicago, 1954-61; section manager IIT Research Institute, Chicago, 1961-64, sci.

adviser; 1964-66; professor Iowa State University, Ames, 1966-78, distinguished professor engineering; 1978—; educational consultant Bihar Institute Tech., Sindri, India, 1966, Indian Institute Tech., Kanpur, summer 1970. Author: (with A.J. Durelli) Introduction to Photomechanics, 1965; (with J. W. Dally) Experimental Stress Analysis, 1978; (with D. Young, K. McConnell and T. Rogge) Essentials of Mechanics, 1974; (with A. Higdon, E. Ohlsen, W. Stiles and J. Weese) Mechanics of Materials, 4th edition, 1985; (with J. Dally and K. McConnell) Instrumentation for Engineering Measurements, 1984; also numerous articles and tech. papers. Served to lieutenant colonel United States Army Air Force, 1943-46. Fellow Society for Experimental Mechanics (hon. member); member American Society of Mechanical Engineers, Society for Experimental Stress Analysis (hon., M.M. Frocht award 1977). Home: 1518 Meadowlane Avenue Ames Iowa 50010 Office: Iowa State U Engring Sci and Mechanics Department Ames Iowa 50011

RIPLEY, SIDNEY DILLON, II, zoologist, museum director; born New York City, September 20, 1913; son of Louis Arthur and Constance Baillie (Rose) R.; married Mary Moncrieffe Livingston, August 18, 1949; children: Julie Dillon Ripley Miller, Rosemary Livingston Ripley Lanius, Sylvia McNeill Ripley Addison. Bachelor of Arts, Yale University, 1936, Master of Arts, 1961, Doctor of Laws (honorary), 1975; Doctor of Philosophy, Harvard University (teaching asst.), 1943; Doctor of Humane Letters, Harvard University, 1984; Doctor of Hebrew Literature, Marlboro College, 1965, Williams College, 1972, Johns Hopkins University, 1984; Doctor of Engineering, Stevens Institute Tech., 1977; Doctor of Science, George Washington University, 1966, Catholic University, 1968, University Maryland, 1970, Cambridge University, England, 1974, Brown University, 1975, Trinity College, 1977; Doctor of Laws, Dickinson College, 1967, Hofstra University, 1968, Gallaudet College, 1981. Staff Acad. Natural Sci., Philadelphia, 1936-39; volunteer assistant Am. Mus. Natural History, New York City, 1939-40; assistant curator boards Smithsonian Institution, Washington, 1942; secretary Smithsonian Institution, 1964-84, secretary emeritus; 1984—; lecturer Yale University, 1946-49, associate curator; 1946-52, assistant professor; 1949-55, curator; 1952-64, associate professor zoology; 1955-61, professor biology; 1961-64; director Peabody Mus. Natural History, 1959-64; expeditions to, Nepal, South Pacific, Southeast Asia, India, Bhutan; United States del. Stockholm Conference on Human Environment, 1972; director Research Corp. (hon.), White Memorial Foundation, Hitachi Foundation. Author: Trail of the Money Bird, 1942, Search for the Spiny Babbler, 1953, A Paddling of Ducks, 1959, (with L. Scribner) Ornithological Books in Yale Library, 1961, Synopsis Birds India and Pakistan, 1961, 2d edition, 1982, Land and Wildlife of Tropical Asia, 1964, (with Sálim Ali) A Handbook of Birds of India and Pakistan, 10 vols, 1968-74, 2d editions, 1978, 80, 81, 83, (with Sálim Ali) A Pictoral Guide to Birds of the Indian Subcontinent, 1983, The Sacred Grove, 1969, 2d edition, 1978, Paradox of the Human Condition, 1975, 2d edition, 1985, Rails of the World, 1977, portfolio edition, 1984; contributor articles to Yale University

Bulletin, Journal Bombay Natural History Society, and other professional journals. Trustee emeritus Henry Francis du Pont Winterthur Mus., Forman School, George Washington University; president International Council of Bird Preservation, 1958-82, president emeritus, 1982—; United States board of directors World Wildlife Fund, 1961-80, 81—; chairman English Speaking Union U.S.A., 1984-87. Served as civilian Office of Strategic Services, 1942-45. Decorated Officer Legion d'Honneur (France), Presidential Medal of Freedom. (U.S.), Order White Elephant, Freedom medal (Thailand); grand cross Order al Merito Civil (Spain); commander's cross Order of Dannebrog (Denmark); officier Ordre des Arts et Lettres (France); knight commander Order Brit. Empire; officier Ordre Leopold (Belgium); commander Order Orange Nassau; commander Order Golden Ark (Netherlands); Order Sacred Treasurer (Japan); Padma Bhushan (India); Order James Smithson; recipient Gold medal New York Zool. Society, 1966; Gold medal Royal Zool. Society Antwerp, 1970; Gold medal Holland Society New York, 1977; Thomas Jefferson award Am. Society Interior Designers, 1975; F.K. Hutchinson medal Garden Club Am., 1979; Henry Shaw medal Missouri Botanical Garden, 1982; Ram Deo medal, India 1985; Cosmos Club award, 1988; Barnard College medal, 1986; Addison Emery Verrill medal Peabody Mus. of Yale University, 1984; Fulbright fellow, 1950; Guggenheim fellow, 1954; National Science Foundation fellow, 1954; Ben Franklin Fellow Royal Society Arts, 1968, 87. Fellow American Association for the Advancement of Science, Am. Ornithologists Union,

Zool. Society India; member National Acad. Sciences, Am. Philosophical Society, Am. Acad. Arts and Letters, International Council Mus. Founds., Council Foreign Relations, French Institute, Alliance Française, Am. Naturalists Society, Brit. Ornithological Union, French Ornithological Society (hon.), Argentine Ornithological Society (hon.), S. African Ornithological Society (corr.), New Zealand Ornithological Society, Cooper Ornithological Society, Wilson Ornithological Society, Society Systematic Zoology, Bombay Natural History Society, Society Study Evolution, International Wild Waterfowl Association, Charles Darwin Sci. Foundation (chairman), American Institute of Architects (hon.), Society Cincinnati (hon.), Sigma Xi. Clubs: Century, Knickerbocker, New York, Cosmos, Alibi, Metropolitan, Washington, Yale. Third level of new Smithsonian mus. complex named S. Dillon Ripley Ctr., 1987. Home: 2324 Massachusetts Avenue Northwest Washington District of Columbia 20008 also: Litchfield Connecticut 06759

RIS, HANS, zoologist, educator; born Bern, Switzerland, June 15, 1914; came to United States, 1938, naturalized, 1945; son of August and Martha (Egger) R.; married Hania Wislicka, December 26, 1947 (divorced 1971); children: Christopher Robert, Annette Margo; married Theron Caldwell, July 14, 1980. Diploma high school teaching, University Bern, 1936; Doctor of Philosophy, Columbia, 1942. Lecturer zoology Columbia University, 1942; Seessel fellow in zoology Yale University, 1942; instructor biology Johns Hopkins University, 1942-44; assistant Rockefeller Institute, New

York City, 1944-46; associate Rockefeller Institute, 1946-49; associate professor zoology University Wisconsin, Madison, 1949-53; professor University Wisconsin, 1953-84, professor emeritus; 1984—. Member Am. Acad. Arts Sciences, National Acad. Sciences, American Association for the Advancement of Science. Researcher mechanisms of nuclear div., chromosome structure, cell ultrastructure, electron microscopy. Office: Zoology Research U Wisconsin Madison Wisconsin 53706

ROBBINS, FREDERICK CHAPMAN, physician, emeritus medical school dean; born Auburn, Alabama, August 25, 1916; son of William J. and Christine (Chapman) R.; married Alice Havemeyer Northrop, June 19, 1948; children: Alice, Louise. Bachelor of Arts, University Missouri, 1936, Bachelor of Science, 1938; Doctor of Medicine, Harvard University, 1940; Doctor of Science (honorary), John Carroll University, 1955, University Missouri, 1958; Doctor.Science (honorary), University North Carolina, 1979, Tufts University, 1983, Medical College Ohio, 1983; Doctor of Laws, University New Mexico, 1968. Diplomate Am. Board Pediatrics. Senior fellow virus disease National Research Council, 1948-50; staff research div. infectious diseases Children's Hospital, Boston, 1948-50, associate physician, associate director isolation service, associate research div. infectious diseases; 1950-52; instructor, associate in pediatrics Harvard Medical School, 1950-52; director department pediatrics and contagious diseases Cleveland Metropolitan General Hospital, 1952-66; professor pediatrics Case-Western Reserve

University, 1952-80, dean School Medicine; 1966-80, Univ professor, dean emeritus; 1980—, University professor emeritus; 1987—; president Institute Medicine, National Acad. Sciences, 1980-85; visiting scientist Donner Laboratory, University California, 1963-64. Served as major Army of the United States, 1942-46; chief virus and rickettsial disease section 15th Medical General Lab. investigations infectious hepatitis, typhus fever and Q fever. Decorated Bronze Star, 1945; recipient 1st Mead Johnson prize application tissue culture methods to study of viral infections, 1953; co-recipient Nobel prize in physiology and medicine, 1954; Medical Mut. Honor Award for, 1969; Ohio Governor's award, 1971. Member National Acad. Sciences, Am. Acad. Arts and Sciences, Am. Society Clinical Investigation (emeritus member), Am. Acad. Pediatrics, Society Pediatric Research (president 1961-62, emeritus member), Am. Pediatric Society, Am. Philosophical Society, Phi Beta Kappa, Sigma Xi, Phi Gamma Delta. Office: Case Western Reserve U School Medicine 2119 Abington Road Cleveland Ohio 44106

ROBBINS, PHILLIPS WESLEY, biology educator; born Barre, Massachusetts, August 10, 1930; married, 1953; 2 children. Bachelor of Arts, Depauw University, 1952; Doctor of Philosophy, University Illinois, 1955. Research associate Massachusetts General Hospital, Boston, 1955-57; assistant professor Rockefeller Institute, New York City, 1957-59; member faculty Massachusetts Institute of Technology, Cambridge, 1959—; professor biochemistry Massachusetts Institute of Technology, 1965—, now Am.

Cancer Society professor biology. Recipeint Eli Lilly award in biological chemistry, 1966. Member Am. Society Biological Chemistry, Am. Chemical Society, Am. Acad. Arts and Sciences. Office: Department Biology Mass Institute Tech Cambridge Massachusetts 02139

ROBERTS, LORIN WATSON, botanist, educator; born Clarksdale, Missouri, June 28, 1923; son of Lorin Cornelius and Irene (Watson) R.; married Florence Ruth Greathouse, July 10, 1967; children: Michael Hamlin, Daniel Hamlin, Margaret Susan. Bachelor of Arts, University Mo.-Columbia, 1948, Master of Arts, 1950, Doctor of Philosophy in Botany, 1952. Assistant professor, then associate professor botany Agnes Scott College, Decaur, Georgia, 1952-57; visiting assistant professor Emory University, 1952-55; member faculty University Idaho, 1957—, professor botany; 1967—; Fulbright research professor Kyoto (Japan) University, 1967-68; research fellow University Bari, Italy, 1968; Cabot fellow Harvard, 1974; Fulbright teaching fellow North-Eastern Hill University, Shillong, Meghalaya, India, 1977; Fulbright senior scholar and fellow Australian National University, Canberra, 1980; senior researcher University London, 1984; president botany section 1st International Congress Histochemistry and Cytochemistry, Paris, 1960. Author: Cytodifferentiation in Plants, 1976, (with J.H. Dodds) Experiments in Plant Tissue Culture, 1982, 2d edition, 1985, (with P.B. Gahan and R. Aloni) Vascular Differentiation and Plant Growth Regulators, 1988; contributor articles to professional journals. Served with United States Army Air Force, 1943-46. Decorated chevalier de l'Ordre du Merite Agricole

France, 1961. Fellow American Association for the Advancement of Science; member Northwest Sci. Association (president 1970-71), Botanical Society Am., Am. Society Plant Physiologists, International Association Plant Tissue Culture, International Society Plant Morphologists, Am. Institute Biological Sciences, Idaho Acad. Sciences, Sigma Xi, Phi Kappa Phi, Phi Sigma. Home: 920 Mabelle Avenue Moscow Idaho 83843

ROBERTS, WALTER ORR, solar astronomer; born West Bridgewater, Massachusetts, August 20, 1915; son of Ernest Marion and Alice Elliott (Orr) R.; married Janet Naomi Smock, June 8, 1940; children—David Stuart, Alan Arthur, Jennifer Roberts McCarthy, Jonathan Orr. Bachelor of Arts, Amherst College, 1938, Doctor of Science (honorary), 1959; Master of Arts, Harvard, 1940, Doctor of Philosophy, 1943; Doctor of Science (honorary), Ripon College, 1958, Colorado College, 1962, C.W. Post College of Long Island University, 1964, Carleton College, 1966, Southwestern at Memphis, 1968, University Colorado, 1968, University Denver, 1969, University Alaska, 1975. Operator High Altitude Observatory, Climax, Colorado, 1940-47; director charge solar research program High Altitude Observatory, 1947-50; director High Altitude Observatory, Boulder; also High Altitude Observatory, Climax, Colorado, 1940-60; instructor Harvard, 1947-48, Radcliffe College, 1947-48; research associate Harvard College Observatory, 1948-73; director National Center for Atmospheric Research, 1960-70, research associate; 1975—; professor astro-geophysics University Colorado,

Boulder, 1957—; director program in food, climate and world's future Aspen Institute Humanistic Studies, 1974-81; Trustee University Corp. Atmospheric Research, 1959, president, 1960-73, president emeritus, 1980—; trustee Mitre Corp., 1960-87, Upper Atmosphere Research Corp., 1971-74; Chairman committee on arctic sci. and tech. National Acad. Sciences, 1972-73, member committee on international environmental programs, 1971-77; member committee consultant Report on State of Human Environment, United Nations Stockholm Conference, 1972; member United States National Commission for United Nations Educational, Scientific and Cultural Organization, 1964-67; member defense sci. board Department Def., 1972-75; member adv. panel for National Science Foundation Journalistic History, 1972; member adv. committee World Meteorol. Organization, 1963-68; member bureau committee effects solar terrestrial disturbances in lower atmosphere Special Committee Solar-Terrestrial Physics, 1972-77; member subcom. U.S.-USSR cooperative program man's impact on environment Department State, 1973-80; member visiting committee Smithsonian Astrophysical Observatory, 1975-78; member founding board, chairman task force sci. and tech. Civilian/Mil. Institute, Air Force Acad., 1975-83; member Council on Sci. and Tech. for Devel., 1977-84; president University Corp. for Atmospheric Research Foundation, 1986-87. Asso. editor: Journal Geophysical Research, 1960-64; editorial board: Science, 1970-72, Journal Planetary and Space Science. Trustee Max C. Fleischmann Foundation, 1967-80, Charles F. Kettering Foundation, 1964-70, Amherst College, 1964-70; member Am. council United Nations University; trustee Aspen Institute for Humanistic Studies, 1970—; secretary Marconi International Fellowship Council, 1974-86; trustee International Federation Insts. Advanced Study, 1971-81, chairman program committee; board of directors International Institute Environment and Devel., 1971-76, Worldwatch Institute, 1975-85. Recipient Hodgkins medal Smithsonian Institution, 1973, Mitchell Prize award, 1979, International Environmental Leadership medal, 1982, Man Sci. award Achievement Rewards for College Scientists Foundation, 1986, Sci. award Bonfils-Stanton Foundation, 1986, Pacesetter award Boulder County, 1986; named Man of Sci., American Red Cross Foundation, 1986. Fellow American Association for the Advancement of Science (director 1963-70, president 1967, member committee on arid lands 1973-83), Am. Acad. Arts and Sciences, Royal Astronomical Society; member Acad. Ind. Scholars, Aspen Society Fellows, Am. Rocket Society, Am. Astronomical Society (member council), Am. Meteorological Society, International Astronomical Union, Colo.-Wyo. Acad. Sci., Am. Geophysical Union, Am. Philosophical Society, Federation Am. Scientists, American Institute of Aeronautics and Astronautics, International Acad. Astronautics , Council Foreign Relations, Royal Society Arts, Explorers Club, Sigma Xi, Phi Beta Kappa, Sigma Pi Sigma. Clubs: Rocky Mountain Harvard. Home: 1829 Bluebell Avenue Boulder Colorado 80302

ROBINSON, DENIS MORRELL, engineer; born London, November 19, 1907; came to United States, 1941, naturalized, 1951; son of Ernest Herbert and Marion (Morrell) R.; married Alix Casagrande, May 6, 1932; children—Marius Arthur, Harald Denis. Bachelor of Science, London University, 1927, Doctor of Philosophy, 1929; Master of Science, Massachusetts Institute of Technology, 1931. High voltage research, devel. Callender's Cable Company, London, 1931-35; with Scophony TV, London, 1935-39; Brit. government scientist 1939-45; assigned radiation laboratory Massachusetts Institute of Technology, 1941-45; head electrical engineering department Birmingham (England) University, 1945-46; co-founder, president High Voltage Engineering Corp., 1946-70, chairman board; 1970-80, senior consultant; 1980—. Author: Dielectric Phenomena in High Voltage Cables, 1936; Contributor articles to professional journals. Chairman board trustees Marine Biol. Lab., Woods Hole, Massachusetts, 1971-77; now hon. chairman Marine Biol. Lab, Woods Hole, Massachusetts. Fellow Am. Acad. Arts and Sciences (secretary), Institute Electrical Engineers London; member National Acad. Engineering. Office: High Voltage Engring Corp S Bedford St Burlington Massachusetts 01803

ROBINSON, STEPHEN HOWARD, physician, educator; born New York City, April 3, 1933; son of Nathan and Beatrice Leonia (Koen) R.; married Carole Latter, June 25, 1956; children: Lisa, Susan, Michael. Bachelor of Arts summa cum laude, Harvard University, 1954, Doctor of Medicine, 1958. Diplomate Am. Board Internal Medicine. Intern then resident Boston City Hospital, 1958-61; assistant professor medicine University Chicago, 1963-65; from assistant professor medicine to George C. Reisman professor medicine Harvard University, Boston, 1965—; chief hematology Beth Israel Hospital, Boston, 1971—, clinical director department medicine; 1980—; chairman Veteran's Administration Merit Rev. Board Hematology, Washington, 1979-81; master William B. Castle Acad. Society, Harvard Medical School, 1987—. Contributor over 100 articles to professional journals and chapters to books. Member adv. board Am. Cancer Society, New York City, 1983-87; board of directors American Red Cross, Boston, 1985-88. Served as surgeon United States Public Health Service, 1961-63. Fellow Am. College Physicians; member Am. Society Hematology (executive secretary 1970-73), Association Am. Physicians, Am. Society Clinical Investigation, Phi Beta Kappa. Clubs: Newton Tennis and Squash (Massachusetts), Lakewood Tennis. Avocations: literature, sports, travel. Office: Beth Israel Hosp 330 Brookline Avenue Boston Massachusetts 02215

ROELOFS, WENDELL LEE, biochemistry educator, consultant; born Orange City, Iowa, July 26, 1938; son of Edward and Edith (Beyers) R.; married Marilyn Joyce Kuiken, September 3, 1960; children: Brenda Jo, Caryn Jean, Jeffrey Lee, Kevin Jon. Bachelor of Arts, Central College, Pella, Iowa, 1960; Doctor of Philosophy, Ind. University, 1964; postdoctoral fellow, Massachusetts Institute of Technology, 1965; Doctor of Science (honorary), Central College, 1985—. Assistant professor

New York State Agricultural Experiment Station, Geneva, 1965-69; associate professor New York State Agricultural Experiment Station, 1969-76, professor; 1976—, Liberty Hyde Bailey professor insect biochemistry; 1978—; consultant Albany International Company. Contributor over 200 articles to sci. journals. Recipient Alexander von Humboldt award in Agr., 1977; recipient Outstanding Alumni award Central College, 1978, Wolf prize for Agr., 1982, Distinguished Alumnus award Ind. University, 1983, National Medal of Sci., 1983, Distinguished Service award USDA, 1986. Fellow American Association for the Advancement of Science, Entomological Society Am. (J. Everett Bussart Memorial award 1973, Founder's Memorial award 1980, Distinguished Achievement award Eastern branch 1983); member Am. Chemical Society, National Acad. Sci., Am. Acad. Arts and Sci., Sigma Xi. Republican. Presbyterian. Patentee in field (10). Home: 4 Crescence Dr Geneva New York 14456 Office: New York State Agrl Expt Station Geneva New York 14456

ROEMER, ELIZABETH, astronomer, educator; born Oakland, California, September 4, 1929; daughter of Richard Quirin and Elsie (Barlow) R. Bachelor of Arts with Honors (Bertha Dolbeer scholar), University California at Berkeley, 1950, Doctor of Philosophy (Lick Obs. fellow), 1955. Teacher adult class Oakland pub. schools, 1950-52; lab technician University California at Mount Hamilton, 1954-55; grad. research astronomer University California at Berkeley, 1955-56; research associate Yerkes Observatory University Chicago, 1956; astronomer United States Naval Observatory, Flagstaff, Arizona, 1957-66; associate professor department astronomy, also in lunar and planetary laboratory University Arizona, Tucson, 1966-69; professor University Arizona, 1969—; astronomer Steward Observatory, 1980—; Chairman working group on orbits and ephemerides of comets commission 20 International Astronomical Union, 1964-79, 85-88, vice president comm. 20, 1979-82, president, 1982-85, vice president commission 6, 1973-76, 85-88, president, 1976-79, 88—; Member adv. panels Office Naval Research, National Acad. Scis.-NRC, National Aeronautics and Space Administration. Recipient Dorothea Klumpke Roberts prize University California at Berkeley, 1950, Mademoiselle Merit award, 1959; asteroid (1657) named Roemera, 1965; Benjamin Apthorp Gould prize National Acad. Sciences, 1971; National Aeronautics and Space Administration Special award, 1986. Fellow American Association for the Advancement of Science (council 1966-69, 72-73), Royal Astronomical Society (London); member Am. Astronomical Society (program vis. profs. astronomy 1960-75, council 1967-70, chairman division dynamical astronomy 1974), Astronomical Society Pacific (publs. committee 1962-73, Comet medal committee 1968-74, Donohoe lecturer 1962), International Astronomical Union, Am. Geophysical Union, Brit. Astronomical Association, Phi Beta Kappa, Sigma Xi. Research and numerous publs. on astrometry and astrophysics of comets and minor planets including 79 recoveries of returning periodic comets; visual and spectroscopic binary stars, computation of orbits of comets and minor planets, photog. astrometry.

Office: U Ariz Lunar and Planetary Lab Tucson Arizona 85721

ROGERS, JOHN JAMES WILLIAM, geology educator; born Chicago, June 27, 1930; son of Edward James and Josephine (Dickey) R.; married Barbara Bongard, November 30, 1956; children: Peter, Timothy. Bachelor of Science, California Institute Tech., 1952, Doctor of Philosophy, 1955; Master of Science, University Minnesota, 1952. Lic. geologist, North Carolina. From instructor to professor Rice University, Houston, 1954-75, master Brown College; 1966-71, chairman geological department; 1971-74; W.R. Kenan Junior professor geology University North Carolina, Chapel Hill, 1975—. Co-author: Fundamentals of Geology, 1966, Precambrian Geology of India, 1987; co-editor: Holocene Geology of Galveston Bay, 1969, Precambrian of South India, 1983, Basalts, 1984; regional editor Journal African Earth Scis., 1982—; contributor articles to professional journals. Fellow Geological Society Am., Geological Society India, Geological Society Africa (hon.); member Mineralogical Society Am., Am. Association Petroleum Geologists, Society Econ. Pale-ontologists and Mineralogists. Home: 1816 Rolling Road Chapel Hill North Carolina 27514 Office: U of North Carolina Department Geology CB #3315 Chapel Hill North Carolina 27599-3315

ROMEY, WILLIAM DOWDEN, geologist, educator; born Richmond, Indiana, October 26, 1930; son of William Minter and Grace Warring (Dowden) R.; married Lucretia Alice Leonard, July 16, 1955; children—Catherine Louise, Gretchen Elizabeth, William Leonard. Bachelor of Arts with highest honors, Ind. University, 1952; student, University Paris, 1950-51, 52-53; Doctor of Philosophy, University California at Berkeley, 1962. Assistant professor geology and sci. education Syracuse University, 1962-66, associate professor; 1966-69; executive director earth sci. ednl. program Am. Geological Institute, 1969-72; professor, chairman department geology St. Lawrence University, Canton, New York, 1971-76; professor St. Lawrence University, 1976—, professor, chairman department geography; 1983—; educational consultant, 1962—; National Acad. Sci. visitor Union of the Soviet Socialist Republics Acad. Sci., 1967; visiting geoscientist Am. Geological Institute, 1964-66, 71; earth sci. consultant Compton's Encyclopedia, 1970-71; adj. professor Union Grad. School, 1974—; member board research advisers and readers Walden University, 1981—. Author: (with others) Investigating the Earth, 1967, (with J. Kramer, E. Muller, J. Lewis) Investigations in Geology, 1967, Inquiry Techniques for Teaching Science, 1968, Risk-Trust-Love, 1972, Consciousness and Creativity, 1975, Confluent Education in Science, 1976; co-editor: Geochemical Prospecting for Petroleum, 1959; associate editor: Journal College Science Teaching, 1972-74, Geological Society Am. Bull, 1979-84, Journal Geological Edn, 1980—; editor-in-chief: Ash Lad Press, 1975—; contributor articles on geology, geography and education to professional publications. Board of directors Onondaga Nature Centers, Incorporated, 1966-69. Served to lieutenant United States Naval Reserve, 1953-57; lieutenant commander Reserves. Woodrow Wilson Foundation fellow, 1959-60,

61-62; National Science Foundation sci. faculty fellow University Oslo, 1967-68. Fellow Geological Society Am., American Association for the Advancement of Science; member National Association Geology Teachers (vice president 1971-72), New York Acad. Sciences, National Association Geology Teachers (president 1972-73), Association Am. Geographers, Am. Geophysical Union, Geological Society Norway, Association Educating Teachers of Sci., Can. Association Geographers, Association for Can. Studies in United States, Phi Beta Kappa, Sigma Xi, Phi Delta Kappa. Office: St Lawrence U Department Geography Canton New York 13617

ROOSA, STUART, Apollo astronaut, beverage distributor; born Durango, Colorado, August 16, 1933; son of Dewey R.; married Joan C. Barrett; children: Christopher A., John D., Stuart Allen, Rosemary D. Educated, Oklahoma State University, University Arizona; Bachelor of Science in Aeronautical Engineering, University Colorado; Doctor of Letters, University St. Thomas, 1971. Served as commissioned officer United States Air Force, from 1953; advanced through grades to colonel; formerly experimental test pilot United States Air Force, Edwards Air Force Base, California; named astronaut National Aeronautics and Space Administration, 1966; member support crew (Apollo IX); command module pilot (Apollo XIV), 1971; backup command module pilot (Apollo XVI and XVII); assigned crew training space shuttle until 1976; president Gulf Coast Coors, Incorporated, Gulfport, Mississippi, 1981—. Decorated Distinguished Service medal National Aeronautics and Space Administra-

tion, Air Force Command Pilot Astronaut Wings, USAF Distinguished Service Medal; recipient Arnold Air Soc.'s John F. Kennedy award, 1971, City New York Gold medal, 1971. Office: Gulf Coast Coors Incorporated Post Office Box 2007 Gulfport Mississippi 39503

ROSE, NOEL RICHARD, immunologist, microbiologist, educator; born Stamford, Connecticut, December 3, 1927; son of Samuel Allison and Helen (Richard) R.; married Deborah S. Harber, June 14, 1951; children: Alison, David, Bethany, Jonathan. Bachelor of Science, Yale University, 1948; Master of Arts, University Pennsylvania, 1949, Doctor of Philosophy, 1951; Doctor of Medicine, State University of New York, Buffalo, 1964. From instructor to professor microbiology State University of New York School Medicine, Buffalo, 1951-73; director Center for Immunology State University of New York School Medicine, 1970-73; director Erie County Laboratories; 1964-70; director World Health Organization Collaborating Center for Autoimmune Disorders, Detroit, 1968—; professor immunology and microbiology, chairman department immunology and microbiology Wayne State University School Medicine, 1973—82; professor, chairman department immunology and infectious diseases Johns Hokins University School Hygiene and Pub. Health, 1982—; joint appt. Johns Hopkins University School Medicine, 1982—; consultant in field. Editor: (with others) International Convocation on Immunology, 1969, Methods in Immunodiagnosis, 1973, 3d rev. edition, 1986, The Autoimmune Diseases, 1986, Microbiology, Basic

Principles and Clinical Applications, 1983 Principles of Immunology, 1973, 2d rev. edition, 1979, Specific Receptors of Antibodies, Antigens and Cells, 1973, Manual of Clinical Immunology, 1976, 2d rev. edition, 1980, Genetic Control of Autoimmune Disease, 1978, Immunopathology, 1988—, Recent Advances in Clinical Immunology, 1983; editor-in-chief Clin. Immunology and Immunopathology, 1988—; contributor articles to professional journals. Recipient award Sigma Xi, 1952, award Alpha Omega Alpha, 1976, Lamp award, 1975, Faculty Recognition award Wayne State University Board Govs., 1979, President's award for excellence in teaching, 1979, Distinguished Service award Wayne State University School Medicine, 1982, University Pisa medal, 1986; named to Acad. Scholars Wayne State University, 1981; Josiah Macy fellow, 1979. Fellow Am. Public Health Association, Am. Acad. Allergy and Immunology, Am. Acad. Microbiology (board govs.), member Acad. Clinical Lab. Physicians and Scientists, American Association for the Advancement of Science, Am. Association Immunologists, Am. Association Pathologists, Am. Society Clinical Pathologists, Am. Society Microbiology, Brit. Society Immunology, College Am. Pathologists, Société Française d'Immunologie, Can. Society Immunology, Society Experimental Biology and Medicine Council, Clinical Immunology Society (secretary, treasurer), Sigma Xi (president Johns Hopkins University chapter 1988), Alpha Omega Alpha, Delta Omega. Office: Johns Hopkins U School Hygiene / Pub Health/Dept Immunology 615 N Wolf St Baltimore Maryland 21205

ROSEN, ORA MENDELSOHN, molecular biologist, physician; born New York City, October 26, 1935; daughter of Isaac and Fannie (Soyer) Mendelsohn; married Jerard Hurwitz; children: Gideon Rosen, Isaac Rosen. Bachelor of Arts, Barnard College, 1956; Doctor of Medicine, Columbia University, 1960. Resident in internal medicine 1960-62, postdoctral fellow in molecular biology; 1962-65; assistant professor molecular biology and medicine Albert Einstein College Medicine, New York City, 1965-70, associate professor; 1970-75, professor; 1975-84, chairman department molecular pharmacology; 1976-84; staff Sloan Kettering Institute for Cancer Research, New York City, 1984—; research professor Biochemistry, 1988. Member Am. Cancer Society. Recipient Mather award Columbia University, 1981; Freedberg award New York Acad. Sciences, 1984. Fellow American College of Physicians; member Am. Society Clinical Investigation, Am. Society Biological Chemistry. Office: Sloan Kettering Institute 1275 York Avenue New York New York 10021

ROSENBERG, LEON E., medical educator, geneticist, university dean; born Madison, Wisconsin, March 3, 1933; son of Abraham Joseph and Celia (Mazursky) R.; married Elaine Lewis, August 29, 1954 (divorced November 1971); children—Robert, Diana, David; married Diane Drobnis, July 4, 1979; 1 child, Alexa. Bachelor of Arts, U.Wis-Madison, 1954, Doctor of Medicine, 1957. Assistant professor medicine Yale School Medicine, New Haven, 1965-68, associate professor pediatrics and medicine; 1968-72, professor human genetics, medicine and pediatrics chairman department human genetics; 1972-84, dean School Medicine; 1984—, C.N.H. Long professor; 1980—; member adv. council NIADDK, 1980-83; member committee on infant health Robert Wood Johnson Foundation, 1982—; member panel Institute Medicine, National Institutes of Health, 1983-84; chairman adv. committee scholars program Hartford Foundation, New York City, 1984—. Author: Amino Acid Metabolism and Its Disorders, 1974; editor: Metabolic Control and Disease, 1981. Served to senior surgeon United States Public Health Service, 1959-65. Recipient Distinguished Alumnus citation University Wis.-Madison, 1982. Fellow American Association for the Advancement of Science, Institute Medicine of National Acad. Sciences, Am. Acad. Arts and Sciences, National Acad. Sciences; member Am. Society Clinical Investigation (vice president 1978-79), Am. Society Human Genetics (president 1980-81), Association Am. Physicians, Am. Pediatric Society, Am. Society Biological Chemists. Democrat. Jewish. Avocations: tennis; skiing; jogging. Office: Yale U School Medicine 333 Cedar St New Haven Connecticut 06510

ROSENBERG, SAUL ALLEN, oncologist, educator; born Cleveland, August 2, 1927. Bachelor of Science, Western Reserve University, 1948, Doctor of Medicine, 1953. Diplomate Am. Board Internal Medicine. Intern University Hospital, Cleveland, 1953-54; resident in internal medicine Peter Bent Brigham Hospital, Boston, 1954-61; research assistant toxicology Atomic Energy Commission Medical Research Project, Western Reserve University, 1948-53; assistant professor medicine and radiology

Stanford (California) University, 1961-65, associate professor; 1965-79, chief div. oncology; 1965—, professor; 1970—, Am. Cancer Society professor; chairman board Northern California Cancer Program, 1974-80. Contributor articles to professional journals. Served to lieutenant Medical Corps United States Naval Reserve, 1954-56. Fellow American College of Physicians; member Am. Association Cancer Research, Institute Medicine National Acad. Sci., Am. Association Cancer Education, Am. Federation Clinical Research, Am. Society Clinical Oncology (president 1982-83), Association Am. Physicians, California Acad. Medicine, Radiation Research Society, Western Society Clinical Research, Western Association Physicians. Office: Stanford U School Medicine Div Oncology Stanford California 94305

ROSENBERG, STEVEN AARON, surgeon, medical researcher; born New York City, August 2, 1940; son of Abraham and Harriet (Wendroff) R.; married Alice Ruth O'Connell, September 15, 1968; children—Beth, Rachel, Naomi. Bachelor of Arts, Johns Hopkins University, 1960, Doctor of Medicine, 1963; Doctor of Philosophy, Harvard University, 1968. Resident in surgery Peter Bent Brigham Hospital, Boston, 1963-64, 68-69, 72-74; resident fellow in immunology Harvard University Medical School, Boston, 1969-70; clinical associate immunology branch National Cancer Institute, Bethesda, Maryland, 1970-72; chief surgery National Cancer Institute, 1974—, associate editor Journal; 1974—; member U.S.-USSR Cooperative Immunotherapy Program, 1974—, U.S.-Japan Cooperative Immunotherapy Program, 1975—; clinical associate professor surgery George Washington University Medical Center, 1976—; professor surgery Uniformed Services University Health Sciences. Contributor articles to professional journals. Served with United States Public Health Service, 1970-72. Recipient Meritorious Service medal Pub. Health Service, 1981; co-recipient Armand Hammer Cancer prize, 1985. Member Society University Surgeons, Society Surgical Oncology, Surgical Biology Club II, Halsted Society, Transplantation Society, Am. Association Immunologists, Am. Association Cancer Research, Phi Beta Kappa, Alpha Omega Alpha. Office: National Cancer Institute NIH Building 10 9000 Rockville Pike Bethesda Maryland 20892

ROSENBLUETH, EMILIO, earthquake engineer; born Mexico City, Mexican, April 8, 1926; son of Emilio and Charlotte (Deutsch) R.; married Alicia Laguette, February 20, 1954; children: David, Javier, Pablo, Monica. Civil Engineer, National Autonomous University Mexico, 1947, Ph.Doctor (honorary), 1985; Master of Science in Civil Engineering, University Illinois, 1949, Doctor of Philosophy, 1951; Doctor of Philosophy honorary, University Waterloo, Ontario, Can., 1983. Surveyor and structural engineer 1945-47; soil mechanics assistant Ministry Hydraulic Resources, also University Illinois, 1947-50; structural engineer Federal Electricity Commission, also Ministry Navy, 1951-55; professor engineering National Autonomous University Mexico, 1956-87; professor emeritus National Autonomous University Mexico, 1987—; regent National Autonomous University Mexico, 1972-

81; president DIRAC Group Cons., 1970-77; vice-minister Ministry Education, 1977-82; president Réunion Internationale des Laboratoires d'Essais des Materiaux (RILEM), 1965-66. Co-author: Fundamentals of Earthquake Engineering, 1971; Co-editor: Seismic Risk and Engineering Decisions, 1976; Contributor to professional publications. Trustee Autonomous Metropolitana University, 1974-77; member working group engring. seismology United Nations Educational, Scientific and Cultural Organization, 1965. Recipient M. Hidalgo medal, Mexican, 1985; Prince of Asturias prize for sci. and tech., Spain, 1985; Luis Elizondo prize, 1974; Distinguished Service in Engineering award University Illinois, 1976; professor honoris causa National University Engineering, Peru, 1964, University award for Sci. Research, University Illinois, 1986, Nathan M. Newmark medal, 1987. Member Mexican Acad. Sci. Research (president 1964-65 Sci. award 1963), Mexican Society Earthquake Engineering, Mexican Society Soil Mechanics (trustee), International Association Earthquake Engineering (president 1973-77), Mexican Association Civil Engineers (M.A. Urquijo research prize 1977, N. Carrillo research award 1984), Mexican Math. Society, Mexican Geophysical Union, Seismological Society Am., Society Experimental Stress Analysis, Latin Am. Association Seismology and Earthquake Engineering, Association Computing Machinery, New Zealand Society Earthquake Engineering, Sigma Xi; hon. member Am. Concrete Institute, American Society of Civil Engineers (W.L. Huber Research prize 1965, Moisseiff award 1966, Alfred M.

Freudenthal medal 1976), International Association Earthquake Engineering (president 1972-76); foreign associate National Acad. Arts and Sciences, National Acad. Sciences, National Acad. Engring, 3d World Acad. Sciences (board directors). Office: Institute de Ingenieria, Ciudad University, Mexico City 04510, Mexico

ROSS, IAN MUNRO, electrical engineer; born Southport, England, August 15, 1927; came to United States, 1952, naturalized, 1960; married Christina Leinberg Ross, August 24, 1955; children: Timothy Ian, Nancy Lynn, Stina Marguerite. Bachelor of Arts, Gonville and Caius College, Cambridge (England) University, 1948; Master of Arts in Electrical Engineering, Cambridge University, 1952, Doctor of Philosophy, 1952; Doctor of Science (honorary), New Jersey Institute Tech., 1983; Doctor of Engineering (honorary), Stevens Institute Tech., 1983. With American Telephone and Telegraph Company Bell Laboratories (and affiliates), 1952—, executive director network planning div.; 1971-73, vice president network planning and customer services; 1973-76; executive vice president systems engineering and devel. American Telephone and Telegraph Company Bell Laboratories (and affiliates), Holmdel, New Jersey, 1976-79; president American Telephone and Telegraph Company Bell Laboratories (and affiliates), 1979—; director Thomas & Betts Corp., B.F. Goodrich Company. Patentee in field. Recipient Liebmann Memorial prize Institute of Electrical and Electronic Engineers, 1963, Pub. Service award National Aeronautics and Space Administration, 1969,

Founders medal Institute of Electrical and Electronic Engineers, 1988. Fellow Institute of Electrical and Electronics Engineers (Liebmann Memorial prize 1963, Founders medal 1988), Am. Acad. Arts and Sciences; member National Acad. Engineering. Home: 5 Blackpoint Horseshoe Rumson New Jersey 07760 Office: AT&T Bell Labs Incorporated Crawfords Corner Road Holmdel New Jersey 07733

ROSS, RICHARD FRANCIS, veterinarian, microbiologist, educator; born Washington, Iowa, April 30, 1935; son of Milton Edward and Olive Marie (Berggren) R.; married Karen Mae Paulsen, September 1, 1957; children—Scott, Susan. Doctor of Veterinary Medicine, Iowa State University, 1959, Master of Science, 1961, Doctor of Philosophy, 1965. Research associate Iowa State University, Ames, 1959-61; assistant professor Iowa State University, 1962-65, associate professor; 1966-72, professor; 1972—, prof.-in-charge; 1985—; operating manager Vet. Laboratory Incorporated, Remsen, Iowa, 1961-62; postdoctoral fellow Rocky Mountain Laboratory, NIAID, Hamilton, Montana, 1965-66; senior United States scientist Alexander von Humboldt Foundation, Bonn, Federal Republic Germany, 1975-76; chairman International Research Program on Comparative Mycoplasmology, 1982-86; president Iowa State University Research Foundation, Ames, 1984-86; Howard Dunne memorial lecturer Am. Association Swine Practitioners, 1984. Contributor numerous articles to professional publications, 1963—. Named Distinguished Professor, Iowa State University, 1982, Hon. Master Pork Producer, Iowa Pork Producers

Association, 1985; recipient faculty citation Iowa State University Alumni Association, 1984; Beecham award for research excellence, 1985. Member Am. College Veteran Microbiologists (diplomate, vice chairman 1974-75, sec.-treas. 1977-83), Am. Society Microbiology (chairman division 1985-86), International Organization Mycoplasmology, American Veterinary Medical Association, American Association for the Advancement of Science, Osborn Research Club. Republican. Lutheran. Avocations: fishing; gardening; jogging. Home: 2003 Northwestern Avenue Ames Iowa 50010 Office: Iowa State U Veteran Research Institute Ames Iowa 50011

ROSSI, BRUNO, physicist; born Venice, Italy, April 13, 1905; son of Rino and Lina (Minerbi) R.; married Nora Lombroso, April 10, 1938; children—Florence S., Frank R., Linda L. Student, University Padua, 1923-25, University Bologna, 1925-27; honorary doctorate, University Palermo, 1964, University Durham, England, 1974, University Chicago, 1977. Assistant physics department University Florence, 1928-32; professor physics University Padua, 1932-38; research associate University Manchester, England, 1939; research associate in cosmic rays University Chicago, 1939-40; associate professor physics Cornell University, 1940-43; professor physics Massachusetts Institute Tech., 1946—, Institute professor; 1966-70, Institute professor emeritus; 1970—; Member staff Los Alamos Laboratory; 1943-46, hon. fellow Tata Institute Fundamental Research, Bombay, India, 1971; member physics committee National Aeronautics and Space Administration; hon. professor University Mayor, San Andres, La Paz, Bolivia. Author: Rayons Cosmiques, 1935, (with L. Pincherle) Lezioni di Fisca Sperimentale Elettrologia, 1936, Lezioni di Fisica Sperimentale Ottica, 1937, Ionization Chambers and Counters, 1949, (with Staub), High Energy Particles, 1952, Optics, 1957, Cosmic Rays, 1964, (with S. Olbert) Introduction to the Physics of Space, 1970, Momenti nella vite di uno Scientiato, 1987. Recipient Cresson medal Franklin Institute, 1974, National Medal of Sci., 1983, Wolf award, 1987; decorated Order of Merit (Republic of Italy). Member Am. Acad. Arts and Sciences (Rumford prize 1976), National Acad. Sci. (space sci. board, astronomy survey committee), Deutsche Akademieder Naturforscher Leopoldina, Am. Physical Society, Am. Institute Physics, Accademia dei Lincel (International Feltrinelli award 1971), International Astronomical Union, Am., Royal astronomical socs., Accademia Patavina di Scienze, Letteree Arti, Accademia Ligure di Scienze e Lettere, Bolivian Acad. Sciences (corr.), American Association for the Advancement of Science, Am. Philosophical Society, Italian Physical Society (Gold medal 1970), Inststuto Veneto di Science, Lettere e Arti, Sigma Xi. Home: 221 Mount Auburn St Cambridge Massachusetts 02138 also: Wolf Found /Mr Yaron Gruder, Post Office Box 398, Herzlia Bet 46103, Israel

ROTA, GIAN-CARLO, educator, mathematician; born Vigevano, Italy, April 27, 1932; came to United States, 1950, naturalized, 1961; son of Giovanni and Gina (Facoetti) R.; married Teresa Rondón-Tarchetti, June 23, 1956 (divorced 1979). Bachelor of Arts summa cum laude, Princeton University, 1953; Master of Arts, Yale University, 1954, Doctor of Philosophy, 1956; Doctor h.c., University Strasbourg, 1984, University L'Aguila, 1989. Visiting fellow Courant Institute Math. Sciences, New York University, 1956-57; B. Pierce instructor Harvard University, 1957-59; assistant professor, then associate professor math. Massachusetts Institute of Technology, 1959-65, professor math.; 1967-74, professor applied math. and philosophy; 1975—; professor math. Rockefeller University, 1965-67; visiting professor Courant Institute Math. Sciences, 1964, University Illinois, 1965, Ind. University, 1964, University Paris, 1972, University Mexico, 1973, Scuola Normale Superiore, 1975, 86, University Buenos Aires, 1975, University Strasbourg, 1976, 78, 87, University Southern California, 1985—; Taft lecturer University Cincinnati, 1971; special visiting professor University Colorado, 1969-82; Andre' Aisenstadt visiting professor University Montreal, 1971; Hardy lecturer London Math. Society, 1973; professore linceo, Rome, 1979, University Cagliari, 1989, University Milan, 1989, I.H.E.S., France, 1989; lezioni lincee, Pisa, Italy, 1986; consultant Rand Corp., 1965-71; Sigma Xi national lecturer, 1980-81; fellow Los Alamos Sci. Laboratory, 1966—; consultant Brookhaven National Laboratory, 1969-71. Author: (with G. Birkhoff) Ordinary Differential Equation, 1962, (with H. Crapo) Combinational Geometries, 1970, Finite Operator Calculus, 1975, MAA Survey in Combinatorics, 1978; (with M. Kac and J.T. Schwartz) Discrete Thoughts, 1986, (with K. Baclawski and M. Cerasoli) Introduziome alla probabilita, 1986; also articles

combinatorial theory, differential equations, probability, philosophy.; Editor Journal Combinatorial Theory, 1966—, Journal Math. and Mechanics, 1965-71, Journal Math. Analysis, 1966—, Utilitas Mathematica, 1973—; asso. editor Am. Math. Monthly, 1966-73; Procs. Royal Society Edinburgh, 1976-85; editor-in-chief Advances in Mathematics, 1967—, Advances in Applied Math., 1980—; editor: Bulletin Am. Math. Soc, 1967-73, 79-84, Encyclopedia of Math, 1974—, Mathematicians of our Time, 1982. Sloan fellow, 1962-64. Fellow Am. Acad. Arts and Sciences, Academia Argentina de Ciencias, Institute Math. Statistics, National Academy of Sciences, American Association for the Advancement of Science (chair math. section 1988); member Am. Math. Association (Hedrick lecturer 1967), Am. Math Society (council 1967-72, 83-86), London Math. Society, Heidegger Circle, Husserl Circle, Society Industrial and Applied Math. (vice president 1975), Am. Philosophical Association, Society Phenomenology and Existential Philosophy, American Association of University Women, Unione Mathematica Italiana, Unión Matemática Argentina (life), Phi Beta Kappa (president chapter 1978-80). Roman Catholic. Address: 2-351 Massachusetts Institute of Technology Cambridge Massachusetts 02139

ROTHMAN, FRANK GEORGE, biology educator, biochemical genetics researcher; born Budapest, Hungary, February 2, 1930; came to United States, 1938; son of Stephen and Irene Elizabeth (Manheim) R.; married Joan Therese Kiernan, Aug.22, 1953; children: Michael, Jean,

Stephen, Maria. Bachelor of Arts, University Chicago, 1948, Master of Science, 1951; Doctor of Philosophy, Harvard University, 1955. Postdoctoral fellow National Science Foundation, University Wisconsin, Massachusetts Institute of Technology, 1956-58, Am. Cancer Society, Massachusetts Institute of Technology, Cambridge, 1958-59; postdoctoral associate Massachusetts Institute of Technology, Cambridge, 1957-61; assistant professor Brown University, Providence, 1961-65, associate professor; 1965-70, professor; 1970—, dean of biology; 1984—. Contributor articles to professional journals. Served with United States Army, 1954-56. Special fellow USPHS, University Sussex, England, 1967-68; National Science Foundation grantee, 1961-84. Member Genetics Society Am., Society for Devel. Biology, Gerontological Society Am. Office: Brown University Box G Providence Rhode Island 02912

ROUSE, IRVING, anthropologist, emeritus educator; born Rochester, New York, August 29, 1913; son of Benjamin Irving and Louise Gillespie (Bohachek) R.; married Mary Uta Mikami, June 24, 1939; children: Peter, David. Bachelor of Science, Yale University, 1934, Doctor of Philosophy, 1938. Assistant anthropology Yale Peabody Museum, 1934-38, assistant curator; 1938-47, associate curator; 1947-54, research associate; 1954-62, curator; 1977-85, emeritus curator; 1985—; instructor anthropology Yale University, 1939-43, assistant professor; 1943-48; associate professor Yale, 1948-54; professor Yale University, 1954-69, Charles J. MacCurdy professor anthropology; 1969-84, professor emeritus; 1984—. Author monographs on archaeology of, Florida, Cuba, Haiti, Puerto Rico, Venezuela. Recipient Medalla Commemorativa del Vuelo Panamericano pro Faro de Colon Government Cuba, 1945, A. Cressy Morrison prize in natural sci. New York Acad. Sci., 1951, Viking fund medal Wenner-Gren Foundation, 1960; Guggenheim fellow, 1963-64. Member Am. Anthropological Association (president 1967-68), Eastern States Archeological Federation (president 1946-50), Association Field Archaeology (president 1977-78), Society Am. Archaeology (editor 1946-50, president 1952-53), National Acad. Sciences, Am. Acad. Arts and Sciences, Society Antiquaries (London). Office: Box 2114 Yale Station New Haven Connecticut 06520

ROY, RUSTUM, interdisciplinary materials researcher, educator; born Ranchi, India, July 3, 1924; came to United States, 1945, naturalized, 1961; son of Narendra Kumar and Rajkumari (Mukherjee) R.; married Della M. Martin, June 8, 1948; children: Neill, Ronnen, Jeremy. Bachelor of Science, Patna (India) University, 1942; Master of Science, Patna (India) University, India, 1944; Doctor of Philosophy, Pennsylvania State University, 1948; Doctor of Science (honorary), Tokyo Institute Tech., 1987. Research assistant Pennsylvania State University, 1948-49, member faculty; 1950—, professor geochemistry; 1957—, professor solid state; 1968—, chairman solid state tech. program; 1960-67, chairman sci. tech. and society program; 1977-84, director;

1984—, director materials research laboratory; 1962-85, Evan Pugh professor; 1981—; senior sci. officer National Ceramic Laboratory, India, 1950; member committee mineral sci. tech. National Acad. Sciences, 1967-69, committee survey materials sci. tech.; 1970-74; executive committee chemical div. National Research Council, 1967-70, national materials adv. board; 1970-77, member committee radioactive waste management; 1974-80, chairman panel waste solidification; 1976-80; chairman committee National Research Council, Union of the Soviet Socialist Republics and Eastern Europe, 1976-81; member committee material sci. and engineering National Research Council, 1986—; member Pennsylvania Gov.'s Sci. Adv. Committee; chairman materials adv. panel, 1965—; member adv. committee engineering National Science Foundation, 1968-72, adv. committee to ethical and human value inplications sci. and tech., 1974-76, adv. committee div. materials research, 1974-77; founder Materials Research Society, 1973, president, 1976; Hibbert lecturer University London, 1979; director Kirkridge, Incorporated, Bangor, Pennsylvania; consultant to industry; adv. committee College Engineering, Stanford University, 1984-86. Author: Honest Sex, 1968, Crystal Chemistry of Non-metallic Materials, 1974, Experimenting with Truth, 1981, Radioactive Waste Disposal, Volume 1, the Waste Package, 1983, Lost at the Frontier, 1985; also articles.; editor-in-chief: Materials Research Bull, 1966—, Bulletin Science Tech. and Soc, 1981—. Chairman board Dag Hammarskjold College, 1973-75; chairman ad hoc committee sci., tech. and church National Council Chs., 1966-68. Sci. policy fellow Brookings Institution, 1982-83. Member National Acad. Engineering, Mineralogical Society Am. (award 1957), Am. Chemical Society (Petroleum Research Fund award 1960), American Association for the Advancement of Science (chairman chemistry section 1985), National Association Sci. Tech and Society (president 1988—), Royal Swedish Acad. Engineering Sciences (foreign member), Indian National Acad. Sci. (foreign member), Am. Ceramic Society (Sosman lecturer 1975, Orton lecturer 1984). Home: 528 S Pugh St State College Pennsylvania 16801 Office: 102 Materials Research Lab University Park Pennsylvania 16802

RUBBIA, CARLO, physicist; born Georizia, Italy, March 31, 1934; son of Silvio and Bice (Liceni) R.; married Marisa Rome, June 27, 1960; children—Laura, Andrea. Diploma, Scuola Normale, Pisa, 1958; Master of Arts (honorary), Harvard University, 1970. Research fellow Columbia University, New York City, 1960-61; assistant professor physics University Rome, 1961-62; professor physics Harvard University, Cambridge, Massachusetts, 1960-89; senior research physicist European Organization for Nuclear Research, Geneva, 1962—, director general; 1989—. Recipient Nobel prize in physics, 1984. Member European Physics Society, Am. Physics Society; foreign associate, National Acad. Sciences. Office: CERN, Lab for Particle Physics, 1211 Geneva 23, Switzerland

RUBENSTEIN, ARTHUR HAROLD, physician, educator; born Johannesburg, South Africa, December 28, 1937; came to United States, 1967; son of Montague and Isabel

(Nathanson) R.; married Denise Hack, August 19, 1962; children: Jeffrey Lawrence, Errol Charles. Bachelor of Medicine, Bachelor.Ch., University Witwatersrand, 1960. Diplomate Am. Board Internal Medicine. Fellow in endocrinology Postgrad. Medical School, London, 1965-66; fellow in medicine University Chicago, 1967-68; assistant professor 1968-70, associate professor; 1970-74, professor; 1974—, Lowell T. Coggeshall professor medical sci.; 1981—, associate chairman department medicine; 1975-81, chairman; 1981—; attending physician Mitchell Hospital, University Chicago, 1968—; member study section National Institutes of Health, 1973-77, Hadassah Medical Adv. Board, 1986—, adv. council National Institute Arthritis, Metabolism and Digestive Diseases, 1978-80; chairman National Diabetes Adv. Board, 1982, member, 1981-83. Editorial board: Diabetes, 1973-77, Endocrinology, 1973-77, Journal Clin. Investigation, 1976-81, Am. Journal Medicine, 1978-81, Diabetologia, 1982-86, Diabetes Medicine, 1987—; contributor articles to professional journals. Recipient David Rumbough Memorial award Juvenile Diabetes Foundation, 1978. Fellow American College of Physicians (master), College Physicians (S. Africa), Royal College Physicians (London); member Am. Society for Clinical Investigation, Am. Diabetes Association (Eli Lilly award 1973, Banting medal 1983, Solomon Berson Memorial lecturer 1985, Banting lecturer BDA 1987), Endocrine Society, Am. Federation for Clinical Research, Central Society for Clinical Research (vice president 1988, president 1989), Association Am. Physicians. (treasurer 1984—), Am. Board Internal Medicine , Am. Acad. Arts and Sciences, Institute of Medicine. Home: 5517 S Kimbark Avenue Chicago Illinois 60637 Office: U Chicago Diabetes Research & Training Center 5841 S Maryland Chicago Illinois 60637

RUBIN, GERALD MAYER, molecular biologist, biochemistry educator; born Boston, March 31, 1950; son of Benjamin H. and Edith (Weisberg) R.; married Lynn S. Mastalir, May 7, 1978; 1 child, Alan F. Bachelor of Science, Massachusetts Institute of Technology, 1971; Doctor of Philosophy, Cambridge University, England, 1974. Helen Hay Whitney Foundation fellow Stanford University School Medicine, California, 1974-76; assistant professor biological chemistry Sidney Farber Cancer Inst.-Harvard University Medical School, Boston, 1977-80; staff member Carnegie Institution of Washington, Baltimore, 1980-83; John D. MacArthur professor biochemistry University Calif.-Berkeley, 1983—; investigator Howard Hughes Medical Institute, 1987—. Recipient Young Scientist award Passano Foundation, 1983, U.S. Steel Foundation award National Acad. Sciences, 1985, Eli Lilly award in biochemistry Am. Chemical Society, 1985, Genetics Society Am. medal, 1986. Member National Acad. Sciences. Office: U California Department Biochemistry Berkeley California 94720

RUBIN, GUSTAV, orthopedic surgeon, consultant, researcher; born New York City, May 19, 1913; son of William and Rose (Strongin) R.; married Mildred Synthia Holtzer, July 4, 1946 (deceased December 1964); married Esther Rosenberg Partnow, July 23, 1965; 1 stepchild, Michael Partnow. Bachelor of Science, New York University, 1934; Doctor of

Medicine, SUNY-Downstate Medical Center, 1939. Diplomate Am. Board Orthopedic Surgery. Intern Maimonides Hospital, Brooklyn, 1939-41; resident in orthopedics Hospital for Joint Diseases, New York City, 1941-42, 1946; practice medicine specializing in orthopedics Brooklyn, 1947-56; chief Special Prosthetic Clinic Veteran's Administration Prosthetics Center, New York City, 1956—, director special team for amputations, mobility, prosthetics/orthotics; 1985—, member chief medical director adv. group on prosthetics services, rehabilitation research and devel.; 1985—, orthopedic consultant; 1970—; medical advisor prosthetic research committee New York State Disabled American Veterans, 1970—; lecturer prosthetics New York University, 1972—; clinical professor orthopedics New York College Podiatric Medicine, 1980—. Contributor articles to professional journals. Served to captain United States Army, 1942-46. Recipient National Comdrs. award Disabled American Veterans, 1968, Amvets award for outstanding service, 1969, award for Service to Veterans Allied Veterans Memorial Committee, 1970, Eastern Paralyzed Veterans Association award, 1977, award for Service to Israeli Wounded Israeli Government Department Rehabilitation, 1981, Cert. of Merit, National Amputation Foundation, 1972, Olin E. Teague award Veteran's Administration, 1984, Physician of Year award President's Commn. on Employment of Handicapped, 1984. Fellow Am. Acad. Orthopedic Surgeons, American College of Surgeons, Am. Acad. Neurological and Orthopedic Surgeons; member Alumni Association Hospital Joint Disease, Sigma Xi. Jewish. Avocations: sculpting; oil painting. Home: 15 Circle Dr Post Office Box 572 Moorestown New Jersey 08057 Office: 215 E 27th St New York New York 10016

RUBIN, THEODORE ISAAC, psychiatrist; born Brooklyn, April 11, 1923; son of Nathan and Esther (Marcus) R.; married Eleanor Katz, June 16, 1946; children: Jeffrey, Trudy, Eugene. Bachelor of Arts, Brooklyn College, 1946; Doctor of Medicine, University Lausanne, Switzerland, 1951; graduate, Am. Institute Psychoanalysis, 1964. Resident psychiatrist Los Angeles Veteran's Administration Hospital, 1953, Rockland (New York) State Hospital, 1954, Brooklyn State Hospital, 1955, Kings County (New York) Hospital, 1956; chief psychiatrist Women's House of Detention, New York City, 1957; member faculty Downstate Medical School, New York State University, 1957-59; private practice New York City, 1956—; member medical board Karen Horney Psychoanalytic Clinic, 1964—; also training and supervising psychoanalyst, physician-in-charge of Obesity Clinic; member faculty Am. Institute Psychoanalytic Psychoanalysis, 1962—; also training and supervising psychoanalyst New School Social Research, 1967—. Author: Jordi, 1960, Lisa and David, 1961, Sweet Daddy, 1963, Platzo and the Mexican Pony Rider, 1965, The Thin Book by a Formerly Fat Psychiatrist, 1966, The 29th Summer, 1966, Cat, 1966, Coming Out, 1967, The Winner's Note Book, 1967, The Angry Book, 1969, Forever Thin, 1970, Emergency Room Diary, 1972, Doctor Rubin Please Make Me Happy, 1974, Shrink, 1974, Compassion and Self-Hate, An Alternative to Despair, 1975, Love Me, Love My Fool, 1976,

Reflections in a Goldfish Tank, 1977, Alive and Fat and Thinning in America, 1978, Reconciliations, 1980, Through My Own Eyes, 1982, One to One, Understanding Personal Relationships, 1983, Not to Worry, The American Family Book of Mental Health, 1984, In The Life, 1984, Overcoming Indecisiveness, 1985, Lisa and David, The Story Continues, 1986, Miracle at Bellevue, 1986; member editorial board Am. Journal Psychoanalysis; also articles, columns. President trustees Am. Institute Psychoanalysis, Served as officer United States Naval Reserve, World War II. Recipient Adolf Meyer award Association Improvement Mental Hosps., 1963. Fellow Am. Acad. Psychoanalysis; member New York County Medical Society, Am. Psychiat. Association, Association Advancement Psychoanalysis, Authors Guild. Office: 219 E 62d St New York New York 10021

RUBIN, VERA COOPER, research astronomer; born Philadelphia, July 23, 1928; daughter of Philip and Rose (Applebaum) Cooper; married Robert J. Rubin, June 25, 1948; children: David M., Judith S. Young, Karl C., Allan M. Bachelor of Arts, Vassar College, 1948; Master of Arts, Cornell University, 1951; Doctor of Philosophy, Georgetown University, 1954; Doctor of Science honorary, Creighton University, 1978, Harvard University, 1988. Research associate to assistant professor Georgetown University, Washington, 1955-65; physicist University Calif.-LaJolla, 1963-64; astronomer Carnegie Institutions, Washington, 1965—; Chancellor's Distinguished professor University Calif.-Berkeley, 1981; visiting committee Harvard College Observatory, Cambridge, Mas-

sachusetts, 1976-82. Associate editor: Astrophys. Journal Letters, 1977-82; editorial board: Science Magazine, 1979-87; contributor numerous articles sci. journals; associate editor: Astron. Journal, 1972-77. President's Disting. Visitor, Vassar College, 1987. Member Smithsonian Institution Council, 1979-85; Phi Beta Kappa scholar, 1982-83. Member Am. Astronomical Society (council 1977-80), International Astronomical Union (president Commission on Galaxies 1982-85), Association Univs. Research in Astronomy (director 1973-76), National Acad. Sciences (Space Sci. Board 1974-77, 81, 87—, committee on human rights), Am. Acad. Arts and Sciences, Phi Beta Kappa. Democrat. Jewish.

RUBINOFF, IRA, biologist, research administrator, conservationist; born New York City, December 21, 1938; son of Jacob and Bessie (Rose) R.; married Roberta Wolff, March 19, 1961; 1 son, Jason; married Anabella Guardia, February 10, 1978; children: Andres, Ana. Bachelor of Science, Queens College, 1959; Master of Arts, Harvard University, 1960, Doctor of Philosophy, 1963. Biologist, assistant director marine biology Smithsonian Tropical Research Institute, Balboa, Republic of Panama, 1964-70; assistant director sci. Smithsonian Tropical Research Institute, 1970-73, director; 1973—; associate in ichthyology Harvard University, 1965—; courtesy professor Florida State University, Tallahassee, 1976—; member sci. adv. board Gorgas Memorial Institute, 1964—; trustee Rare Animal Relief Effort, 1976-85; board of directors Charles Darwin Foundation for Galapagos Islands, 1977—; chairman board fellowships and grants Smithsonian Institution, 1978-79; visiting fellow Wolfson College, Oxford (England) University, 1980-81; visiting scientist Mus. Comparative Biology—Harvard University, 1987-88. Author Strategy for Preservation of Moist Tropical Forests; Contributor articles to professional journals. Board of directors International School, Panama, 1983-85; hon. director Instituto Latino americano de Estudios Avanzados . Awarded Order of Vasco Nunez de Balboa of Republic of Panama. Fellow Linnean Society (London), American Association for the Advancement of Science; member Am. Society Naturalists, Society Study of Evolution, New York Acad. Sciences, National Association Conservation of Nature Panama (board directors). Club: Cosmos (Washington). Home: Box 2072, Balboa Republic of Panama Office: Smithsonian Tropical Research Institute APO Miami Florida 34002-0011

RUBINSTEIN, LUCIEN JULES, neuropathologist, educator; born Antwerp, Belgium, October 15, 1924; son of Emile and Diane (Silberfeld) R.; married Dorothea Elizabeth Lunzer, 1950; children: Marion Harriet, Edmund John, Francis Marcel; married Mary Margaret Herman, 1969. L.R.C.P., M.R.C.S., Bachelor of Medicine, Bachelor of Science (honorary) with distinction in medicine and forensic, University London (England), 1948, Doctor of Medicine, 1952. House surgeon, house physician, casualty officer London Hospital, 1948-49, pathology assistant, demonstrator chemical pathology; 1949-52; lecturer, senior lecturer morbid anatomy Medical College London Hospital, 1954-61;

visiting assistant professor neuropathology University Minnesota, 1959-60; visiting scientist National Institutes of Health, 1960; attending neuropathologist Montefiore Hospital, New York City, 1961-64; associate professor neuropathology Columbia, 1961-64; professor pathology (neuropathology) Stanford School Medicine, 1964-81; professor pathology, director div. neuropathology University Virginia School Medicine, Charlottesville, 1981—; adviser World Health Organization, Geneva; adv. consultant National Institute Neurological Diseases and Stroke, National Institutes of Health, Bethesda, Maryland. Author: (with D.S. Russell) Pathology of Tumors of the Nervous System, 1959, 4th edition, 1977, Tumors of the Central Nervous System, 1972; member editorial board: Neuropathology Applied Neurobiology, Acta Neuropathologica, Cancer. Contributor articles to professional journals. Served with Medical Corps Brit. Army, 1952-54. Recipient T.A.M. Ross prize in clinical medicine and pathology London Hospital, 1948, Farber award for brain tumor research, 1982. Member Am. Association Neuropathologists (president 1970-71, council member 1966-74), International Acad. Pathology, Brit. Neuropath. Society, Mexican Association Pathologists (hon.), World Federation Neurology. Home: 303 Rookwood Dr Ednam Forest Charlottesville Virginia 22901 Office: U Va School Medicine Charlottesville Virginia 22908

RUDIN, WALTER, mathematician, educator; born Vienna, Austria, May 2, 1921; came to United States, 1945; son of Robert and Natalie (Adlersberg) R.; married Mary Ellen

Estill, August 19, 1953; children: Catherine, Eleanor, Robert J., Charles M. Bachelor of Arts, Duke University, 1947, Master of Arts, 1947, Doctor of Philosophy, 1949. Instructor Duke University, Durham, North Carolina, 1949-50, Massachusetts Institute of Technology, Cambridge, Massachusetts, 1950-52; assistant professor math. University Rochester, New York, 1952-55, associate professor; 1955-57, professor; 1957-59; professor math. University Wis.-Madison, 1959—. Author: Principles of Mathematical Analysis, 1953, 64, 76, Fourier Analysis on Groups, 1962, Real and Complex Analysis, 1966, 74, 87, Function Theory on Polydiscs, 1969, Functional Analysis, 1973, Function Theory on the Unit Ball of Cn, 1980; foreign language editions; contributor numerous research articles to professional journals. Served as petty officer Royal Navy, 1943-45. Member Am. Math. Society, Math. Association Am. Office: Department Math U Wisconsin Madison Wisconsin 53706

RUSSELL-HUNTER, W(ILLIAM) D(EVIGNE), zoology educator, research biologist, writer; born Rutherglen, Scotland, May 3, 1926; came to United States, 1963, naturalized, 1968; son of Robert R. and Gwladys (Dew) R-H.; married Myra Porter Chapman, March 22, 1951; 1 child, Peregrine D. Bachelor of Science with honors, University Glasgow, 1946, Doctor of Philosophy, 1953, Doctor of Science, 1961. Sci. officer Bisra, Brit. Admiralty, Millport, Scotland, 1946-48; assistant lectr University Glasgow, Scotland, 1948-51, university lecturer in zoology; 1951-63; examiner in biology Pharmaceutical Society Great Britain, Edinburgh, 1957-63; chairman department invertebrate zoology Marine Biological Laboratory, Woods Hole, Massachusetts, 1964-68, trustee; 1967-75, 77—; professor zoology Syracuse University, New York, 1963—; consultant editor McGraw-Hill Encyclopedias, 1977—; board of directors Upstate Freshwater Institute, Syracuse, 1981—. Author: Biology of Lower Invertebrates, 1967, Biology of Higher Invertebrates, 1968, Aquatic Productivity, 1970, A Life of Invertebrates, 1979, The Mollusca: Ecology, 1983; managing editor: Biol. Bulletin Woods Hole, Massachusetts, 1968-80; contributor over 120 articles to sci. journals. William Wasseroton award Syracuse University, 1988; Carnegie and Browne fellow, 1954; research grantee National Institutes of Health, 1964-70, National Science Foundation, 1971-81, U.S. Army C.E., 1985-87; confirmed Scottish armiger, 1967. Fellow Linnean Society London, Royal Society Edinburgh, Institute Biology United Kingdom, American Association for the Advancement of Science; member Ecological Society Am., American Association of University Profs. Avocations: book collecting, small boat sailing, model railroading. Office: Syracuse U 029L Lyman Hall Syracuse New York 13244

RUTAN, ELBERT L. (BURT RUTAN), aircraft designer; born 1943; son of George and Irene R.; married. Student, California State Polytech. College. Civilian stability and control specialist United States Air Force, Edwards Air Force Base, California, 1972-75; aircraft designer J. Bede, Kansas, 1975; founder Rutan Aircraft Factory, Mojave, California, 1975, Scaled Composites, Mojave, California, 1982; vice president Beech Aircraft, 1985—. Designer more than

100 aircraft including VariViggen, Solitaire, Defiant, and other kits; designer Voyager aircraft, first to fly around-the-world without stopping, refueling. Recip. Spirit of St. Louis Medal, Am. Society Mech. Engrs., 1987, Best Design Award, Exptl. Aircraft Association. Office: Scaled Composites Incorporated Mojave Airport Hangar 78 Mojave California 93501

RUTAN, RICHARD GLENN (DICK), aircraft comapny executive; born Loma Linda, California, January 1, 1938; son of George and Irene Rutan. Bachelor of Science, Am. Technological University, 1974; Doctor in Science and Tech. (honorary), Central New England College, 1987. Commissioned 2d lieutenant United States Air Force, 1959, advanced through grades to lieutenant colonel; 1975, retired; 1978; production manager, chief test pilot Rutan Aircraft Factory, 1978-81; co-founder Voyager Aircraft Company, Mojave, California, 1981—. Decorated Silver Star, Distinguished Flying Cross with silver oak leaf cluster, Purple Heart, Air medal (16). Recipient Louis Bleroit medal Federation Aeronautique Internationale, 1982, Collier trophy National Aviation Club, 1986, Presidential Citizen's Medal of Honor, 1986, Godfrey L. Cabot award Aero Club New England, 1987, Patriot of Year award, 1987, Newsmaker of Year award Aviation Writers Am., 1987, Deedalian Dist, Achievement award, 1987, Lindbergh Eagle award San Diego Aerospace Mus., 1987, Ivan P. Kinslow award Society Expl. Test Pilots, 1987, Gold medal Royal Aero Club, Grande Medallion, Medalle de Ville Paris Paris Aero Club, numerous others. World Record for 1st closed circuit, great circle distance around-the-world, non-stop, non-refueled flight. Office: Voyager Aircraft Incorporated Hangar 77 2833 Del Mar Mojave California 93501

RUTTER, WILLIAM J., biochemist, educator; born Malad City, Idaho, August 28, 1928; son of William H. and Cecilia (Dredge) R.; married Jacqueline Waddoups, August 31, 1951 (divorced November 1969); children: William Henry II, Cynthia Susan; married Virginia Alice Bourke, 1972 (divorced 1978). Bachelor of Arts, Harvard University, 1949; Master of Arts, University Utah, 1950; Doctor of Philosophy, University Illinois, 1952. United States Public Health Service postdoctoral fellow University Wisconsin, Madison, 1952-54, Nobel Institute, Stockholm, 1954-55; from assistant professor to professor biochemistry, department chemistry University Illinois, 1955-65; professor biochemistry University Washington, 1965-69; Hertzstein professor biochemistry University California, San Francisco, 1969—, chairman department biochemistry and biophysics; 1969-82, director Hormone Research Institute; 1983—; chairman board of directors Chiron Corp.; member United States Public Health Service Biochemistry and Nutrition Fellowship Panel, 1963-66; consultant physiological chemistry study section National Institutes of Health, 1967-71; member basic sci. adv. executive committee National Cystic Fibrosis Research Foundation, 1969-74, chairman, 1972-74, pres.'s adv. council, 1974-75; executive committee div. biology and agriculture National Research Council, 1969-72; member developmental biology panel National Science Foundation, 1971-

73; member biomed. adv. committee Los Alamos Sci. Laboratory, 1972-75; president Pacific Slope Biochem. Conference, 1972-73; member board sci. counselors National Institute Environmental Health Sciences, 1976—; member adv. committee biology div. Oak Ridge National Laboratory, 1976-80; adv. board Oak Ridge National Laboratory and Martin-Marietta Energy Systems, 1984-87; basic research adv. committee National Foundation, 1976—; board of directors Keystone Life Sci. Study Ctr; sci. adv. board German Center Molecular Biology, University Heidelberg, 1983—; panel sci. advisors International Center Genetic Engineering and Biotechnology, 1984—. Asso. editor: Journal Experimental Zoology, 1968-72; editor: PAABS Revista, 1971-76, Journal Cell Biology, 1976-78, Archives Biochemistry and Biophysics, 1978—, Developmental Genetics, 1979—; editorial board various journals. Served with United States Naval Reserve, 1945. Guggenheim fellow, 1962-63. Member Am. Society Biological Chemists (treasurer 1970-76, member editorial board journal 1970-75), Am Society Cell Biology, Am. Chemical Society (Pfizer award enzyme chemistry 1967), Am. Society Developmental Biology (president 1975-76), National Acad. Sciences. Home: 80 Everson St San Francisco California 94131 Office: U California Hormone Research Institute San Francisco California 94143-0534

RYLANDER, HENRY GRADY, JR., mechanical engineering educator; born Pearsall, Texas, August 23, 1921; married; 4 children. Bachelor of Science, University Texas, 1943, Master of Science, 1952; Doctor of Philosophy in Mechanical Engineering, Georgia Institute Tech., 1965. Design engineer Steam Div., Aviation Gas Turbine Div., Westinghouse Electrical Corp., 1943-47; from assistant to associate professor mechanical engineering University Texas, Austin, 1947-68, research scientist; 1950, professor mechanical engineering; 1968—, Joe J. King professor engineering, adj. assistant professor electrical and biomed. engineering; 1980—; consultant in field. Member American Society of Mechanical Engineers. Am. Society Lubrication Engineers. Office: U Tex College Engring Austin Texas 78712

SABIN, ALBERT BRUCE, physician, scientist, emeritus educator; born Bialystok, Poland, August 26, 1906; son of Jacob and Tillie (Krugman) S.; married Heloisa Dunshee de Abranches, July 28, 1972; children: Deborah, Amy. Bachelor of Science, Doctor of Medicine, New York University, 1931; recipient 31 honorary degress from United States and foreign univs. Research associate New York University College Medicine, 1926-31; house physician Bellevue Hospital, New York City, 1932-33; National Research Council fellow Lister Institute, London, 1934; member sci. staff Rockefeller Institute for Medical Research, New York City, 1935-39; associate professor pediatrics University Cincinnati College Medicine and Children's Hospital Research Foundation, 1939-43, professor research pediatrics; 1946-60, Distinguished Service professor; 1960-71, Emeritus Distinguished Service professor; 1971—; president Weizmann Institute of Sci., Rehovot, Israel, 1970-72; board governors Weizmann Institute of Sci., 1965—; consultant United States Army, 1941-62; member Armed Forces Epidemiological Board, 1963-69; consultant National Institutes of Health, United States Public Health Service, 1947-73; member National Adv. Council National Institute Allergy and Infectious Diseases, 1965-70; Fogarty scholar Fogarty International Center for Advanced Study in Health Sciences, National Institutes of Health, 1973; member adv. committee on medical research Pan Am. Health Organization, 1973-76; expert consultant National Cancer Institute, 1974; member United States Army Medical Research and Devel. Adv. Panel, 1974-79; consultant Surgeon General, United States Army, 1974—; Distinguished Research professor of biomedicine Medical University South Carolina, Charleston, 1974-82, emeritus, 1982—; senior expert consultant Fogarty International Center, National Institutes of Health, 1984-86; consultant to assistant secretary for health Department of Health, Education and Welfare, 1975-77. Author over 300 papers in field. Board governors Hebrew University Jerusalem, 1965—; trustee New York University, 1966-70. Served to lieutenant colonel United States Army, 1943-46. Decorated Legion of Merit.; Recipient Antonio Feltrinelli prize in med. and surg. sci. Accademia Nazionale dei Lincei, Rome, 1964; Albert Lasker clinical medicine research award, 1965; gold medal Royal Society Health, London, 1969; U.S. National Medal of Sci., 1971; Distinguished Civilian Service medal U.S. Army, 1973; Presidential Medal of Freedom, 1986, Medal of Liberty, 1986, Order of Friendhsip Among Peoples, Union of Soviet Socialist Republics, 1986; many other awards. Member National Acad. Sciences, Am. Acad. Arts and Sciences, Association Am. Physicians, Am. Pediatric Society, Infectious Diseases Society Am. (president 1969), numerous other United States and hon. foreign memberships. Research in field of poliomyelitis, human viral diseases, toxoplasmosis and human cancer. Home: Sutton Towers Apartment 1001 3101 New Mexico Avenue Northwest Washington District of Columbia 20016 Office: NIH Building 38A Room B2N13 Bethesda Maryland 20892

SAGAN, CARL EDWARD, astronomer, educator, author; born New York City, November 9, 1934; son of Samuel and Rachel (Gruber) S.; married Ann Druyan, 1 child, Alexandra; children by previous marriages: Dorion Solomon, Jeremy Ethan, Nicholas. Bachelor of Arts with general and special honors, University Chicago, 1954, Bachelor of Science, 1955, Master of Science, 1956, Doctor of Philosophy, 1960; Doctor of Science (honorary), Rensselaer Polytechnic Institute, 1975, Denison University, 1976, Clarkson College Tech., 1977, Whittier College, 1978, Clark University, 1978, Am. University, 1980; Doctor of Hebrew Literature (honorary), Skidmore College, 1976, Lewis and Clark College, 1980, Brooklyn College, City University of New York, 1982; Doctor of Laws (honorary), University Wyoming, 1978. Miller research fellow University Calif.-Berkeley, 1960-62; visiting assistant professor genetics Stanford Medical School, 1962-63; astrophysicist Smithsonian Astrophysical Observatory, Cambridge, Massachusetts, 1962-68; assistant professor Harvard University, 1962-67; member faculty Cornell University,

1968—, professor astronomy and space sciences; 1970—, David Duncan professor; 1976—, director Laboratory Planetary Studies; 1968—, associate director Center for Radiophysics and Space Research; 1972-81; president Carl Sagan Productions (Cosmos TV series), 1977—; nonresident fellow Robotics Institute, Carnegie-Mellon University, 1982—; NSF-Am. Astronomical Society visiting professor various colleges, 1963-67, Condon lecturer, Oregon, 1967-68; Holiday lecturer American Association for the Advancement of Science, 1970; Vanuxem lecturer Princeton University, 1973; Smith lecturer Dartmouth College, 1974, 77; Wagner lecturer University Pennsylvania, 1975; Bronowski lecturer University Toronto, 1975; Philips lecturer Haverford College, 1975; Distinguished scholar Am. University, 1976; Danz lecturer University Washington, 1976; Clark Memorial lecturer University Texas, 1976; Stahl lecturer Bowdoin College, 1977; Christmas lecturer Royal Institution, London, 1977; Menninger Memorial lecturer Am. Psychiat. Association, 1978; Carver Memorial lecturer Tuskegee Institute, 1981; Feinstone lecturer United States Military Acad., 1981; Pal lecturer Motion Picture Acad. Arts and Sciences, 1982; Dodge lecturer University Arizona, 1982; other hon. lectureships; member various adv. groups National Aeronautics and Space Administration and National Acad. Sciences, 1959—; member council Smithsonian Institution, 1975—; vice chairman working group moon and planets, space organization International Council Sci. Unions, 1968-74; lecturer Apollo flight crews National Aeronautics and Space Administra-

tion, 1969-72; chairman United States del. joint conference United States National and Soviet Acads. Sci. on Communication with Extraterrestrial Intelligence, 1971; responsible for Pioneer 10 and 11 and Voyager 1 and 2 interstellar messages; member Voyager Imaging Sci. Team; judge National Book Awards, 1975; member fellowship panel Guggenheim Foundation, 1976—. Author: Atmospheres of Mars and Venus, 1961, Planets, 1966, Intelligent Life in the Universe, 1966, Planetary Exploration, 1970, Mars and the Mind of Man, 1973, The Cosmic Connection, 1973, Other Worlds, 1975, The Dragons of Eden, 1977, Murmurs of Earth: The Voyager Interstellar Record, 1978, Broca's Brain, 1979, Cosmos, 1980, (novel) Contact, 1985, Comet, 1985; also numerous articles; editor: Icarus: International Journal Solar System Studies, 1968-79, Planetary Atmospheres, 1971, Space Research, 1971, UFO's: A Scientific Debate, 1972, Communication with Extraterrestrial Intelligence, 1973; editorial board: Origins of Life, 1974—, Icarus, 1962—, Climatic Change, 1976—, Science 80, 1979-82. Recipient Smith prize Harvard University, 1964; National Aeronautics and Space Administration medal for exceptional sci. achievement, 1972; Prix Galabert, 1973; John W. Campbell Memorial award, 1974; Klumpke-Roberts prize, 1974;Priestley award, 1975; National Aeronautics and Space Administration medal for distinguished pub. service, 1977, 81; Pulitzer prize for lit., 1978; Washburn medal, 1978; Rittenhouse medal, 1980; Peabody award, 1981; Hugo award, 1981; Seaborg prize, 1981; Roe medal, 1981; National Science Foundation fellow, 1955-60;

Sloan research fellow, 1963-67. Fellow American Association for the Advancement of Science (chairman astronomy section 1975), Am. Acad. Arts and Sciences, American Institute of Aeronautics and Astronautics, Am. Geophysical Union (president planetology section 1980-82), Am. Astronautical Society (council 1976-81, Kennedy award 1984), Brit. Interplanetary Society, Explorers Club (75th Anniversary award 1980); member Am. Physical Society, Am. Astronomical Society (councillor, chairman division for planetary scis. 1975-76), Federation Am. Scientists (council 1977-81), Am. Committee on East-West Accord, Society Study of Evolution, Genetics Society Am., International Astronomical Union, International Acad. Astronautics, International Society Study Origin of Life (council 1980—), Planetary Society (president 1979—), Authors Guild, Phi Beta Kappa, Sigma Xi. Research on physics and chemistry of planetary atmospheres and surfaces, origin of life, exobiology, Mariner, Viking and Voyager spacecraft observations of planets. Office: Cornell U Space Sci Building Ithaca New York 14853

SAGE, ANDREW PATRICK, JR., systems information and computer engineering educator, university dean; born Charleston, South Carolina, August 27, 1933; son of Andrew Patrick and Pearl Louise (Britt) S.; married LaVerne Galhouse, March 3, 1962; children: Theresa Annette, Karen Margaret, Philip Andrew. Bachelor of Science in Electrical Engineering, The Citadel, 1955; Master of Science, Massachusetts Institute of Technology, 1956; Doctor of Philosophy, Purdue University, 1960;

Doctor of Engineering (honorary), University Waterloo, Can., 1987. Registered professional engineer, Texas. Instructor electrical engineering Purdue University, 1956-60; associate professor University Arizona, 1960-63; member tech. staff Aerospace Corp., Los Angeles, 1963-64; professor electrical engineering and nuclear engineering sciences University Florida, 1964-67; professor, director Information and Control Sciences Center, Southern Methodist University, Dallas, 1967-74; head electrical engineering department Information and Control Sciences Center, Southern Methodist University, 1973-74; Quarles professor engineering sci. and systems University Virginia, Charlottesville, 1974-84; chairman department chemical engineering University Virginia, 1974-75, chairman department engineering sci. and systems; 1977-84, associate dean; 1974-80; First Am. Bank professor information tech. George Mason University, Fairfax, Virginia, 1984—, associate vice president for acad. affairs; 1984-85; dean School Information Tech. and Engineering George Mason University, 1985—; consultant Martin Marietta, Collins Radio, Atlantic Richfield, Texas Instruments, LTV Aerospace, Battelle Memorial Institute, TRW Systems, National Science Foundation, Institute Def. Analyses, Planning Research Corp., MITRE, Center for Naval Analysis, Engineering Research Associates; general chairman International Conference on Systems, Man and Cybernetics, 1974, 87; member special program panel on system sci. North Atlantic Treaty Organization, 1981-82. Author: Optimum Systems Control, 1968, 2d edition, 1977, Estimation Theory with

Applications to Communications and Control, 1971, System Identification, 1971, An Introduction to Probability and Stochastic Processes, 1973, Methodology for Large Scale Systems, 1977, Systems Engineering: Methodology and Applications, 1977, Linear Systems Control, 1978, Economic Systems Analysis, 1983, System Design for Human Interaction, 1987, Information Processing in Systems and Organizations, 1989, Introduction to Computer Systems Analysis, Design, and Applications, 1989, Software Systems Engineering, 1989; associate editor: IEEE Transactions on Systems Science and Cybernetics, 1968-72; editor: IEEE Transactions on Systems, Man and Cybernetics, 1972—; associate editor: Automatica, 1968-81; editor, 1981—; member editorial board: Systems Engring, 1968-72, IEEE Spectrum, 1972-73, Computers and Electrical Engineering, 1972—, Journal Interdisciplinary Modeling and Simulation, 1976-80, International Journal Intelligent Systems, 1986—; editor Elsevier North Holland textbook series in system sci. and engring., Matrix Press textbook series on circuits and systems, 1976—; co-editor-in-chief: Journal Large Scale Systems: Theory and Applications, 1978-88, Information and Decision Technologies, 1988—; contributor articles on computer sci. and systems engring. to professional journals. Recipient Frederick Emmonds Terman award Am. Society for Engineering Education, 1970; M. Barry Carlton award Institute of Electrical and Electronic Engineers, 1970; also Norbert Wiener award, 1980; Case Centennial scholar, 1980. Fellow Institute of Electrical and Electronics Engineers (Centennial medal 1984, Outstanding Contribution award 1986), American Association for the Advancement of Science (chmn.-elect section M 1989—), Institute of Electrical and Electronics Engineers Systems; member Man and Cybernetics Society (president 1984-85), Institute Management Sciences, Am. Society for Engineering Education, Am. Institute Artificial Intelligence In Ops. Research Society Am., Sigma Xi, Eta Kappa Nu, Tau Beta Pi. Home: 8011 Woodland Hills Lane Fairfax Station Virginia 22039

SALAM, ABDUS, physicist, educator; born Jhang, Pakistan, January 29, 1926. Student, Government College, Lahore, Pakistan, 1938-46, St. John's College, Cambridge (England) University, 1946-49; Bachelor of Arts, Cambridge University, 1949, Doctor of Philosophy, 1952; 20 Doctor of Science honorary degrees including, Panjab University, 1957, University Edinburgh, 1971, Hindu University, University Chittagong, University Bristol, University Maiduguri, 1981, University Khartoum, University Complutense de Madrid, 1983. Professor Government College, Lahore, 1951-54, University Panjab, 1951-54; fellow St. John's College Cambridge, 1951-56; professor theoretical physics Imperial College, London, 1957—; director International Centre for Theoretical Physics, Trieste, Italy, 1964—; member Atomic Energy Commission Pakistan, 1958-74, Pakistan National Sci. Council, 1963-75, South Commission, 1987; hon. sci. adviser President of Pakistan, 1961-74; member sci. and tech. adv. com United Nations, 1964-75; governor International Atomic Energy Agency, Vienna, 1962-63. Author: Symmetry Concepts in Modern Physics, 1965; Aspects of Quantum Mechanics, 1972. Recipient Hopkins prize Cambridge University, 1957, Adams prize, 1958; Maxwell medal and prize London Physical Society, 1961; Hughes medal Royal Society London, 1964; Atoms for Peace prize, 1968; Oppenheimer prize and medal, 1971; Guthrie medal and prize IPPS, 1976; Matteucci medal Accademia Nazionale dei XL, Rome, 1978; John Torrence Tate medal Am. Institute Physics, 1978; Nobel Prize in Physics, 1979; Einstein medal, 1979, Josef Stefan medal, 1980; Peace medal, 1981; Lomonosov gold medal Union of Soviet Socialist Republics Acad. Sciences, 1983; also numerous decorations. Fellow Royal Society London (medal 1978), Royal Swedish Acad. Sciences; foreign associate United States National Acad. Sciences, Accademia dei Lincei (Rome); foreign member Acad. Sciences Union of the Soviet Socialist Republics, International Union Pure and Applied Physics (vice president); member Third World Acad. Sci. (founding, president). Office: Imperial College, Prince Consort Road, London SW7, England also: International Center Theoretical, Physics, Post Office Box 586, I-34100 Trieste Italy

SALANS, LESTER BARRY, physician, scientist, educator; born Chicago Heights, Illinois, January 25, 1936; son of Leon K. and Jean (Rudnick) S.; married Lois Audrey Kapp, December 21, 1958; children: Laurence Eliot, Andrea Eileen. Bachelor of Arts, University Michigan, 1957; Doctor of Medicine with honors, University Illinois, 1961. Internal medicine intern Stanford University Medical Center, 1961, resident; 1962-64; United States Public Health Service postdoctoral and special fellow Rockefeller University, 1964-67, assistant professor; 1967-68, adj. professor; 1984—; assistant professor medicine Dartmouth College, 1968-70, associate professor; 1970-77, adj. professor; 1978-79; associate director diabetes, endocrinology, metabolism, also chief laboratory cellular metabolism and obesity National Institute Arthritis, Metabolism and Digestive Diseases, National Institutes of Health, Bethesda, 1976-81; director National Institute Arthritis, Diabetes, Digestive and Kidney Diseases, National Institutes of Health, 1981-84; vice president preclin. research Sandoz Research Institute, 1985—; dean Mount Sinai School Medicine, 1984, professor internal medicine; 1984-85, associate clinical professor medicine; 1987—; visiting professor University Geneva, Switzerland, 1974-75. Contributor articles on insulin, diabetes mellitus, obesity to professional journals, textbooks. Recipient National Institutes of Health Research Career Devel. award, 1972-76, National Institutes of Health Directors award, 1980, Juvenile Diabetes Fedn Pub. Service award, 1979. Fellow American College of Physicians; Member Am. Society Clinical Investigation, Am. Federal Clinical Research, Am. Diabetes Society, Endocrine Society, Association Am. Physicians, American Association for the Advancement of Science, Harvey Society, Am. Society Clinical Nutrution. Office: Sandoz Research Institute Route 10 Hanover New Jersey 07936

SALK, JONAS EDWARD, physician, scientist; born New York City, October 28, 1914; son of Daniel B. and Dora (Press) S.; married Donna Lindsay, June 8, 1939; children: Peter Lindsay, Darrell John, Jonathan Daniel; married

Francoise Gilot, June 29, 1970. Bachelor of Science, City College of New York, 1934, Doctor of Laws (honorary), 1955; Doctor of Medicine, New York University, 1939, Doctor of Science (honorary), 1955; Doctor of Laws (honorary), University Pittsburgh, 1955; Doctor of Philosophy (honorary), Hebrew University, 1959; Doctor of Laws (honorary), Roosevelt University, 1955; Doctor of Science (honorary), Turin University, 1957, University Leeds, 1959, Hahnemann Medical College, 1959, Franklin and Marshall University, 1960; Doctor of Hebrew Literature (honorary), Yeshiva University, 1959; Doctor of Laws (honorary), Tuskegee Institute, 1964. Fellow in chemistry New York University, 1935-37, fellow in experimental surgery; 1937-38, fellow in bacteriology; 1939-40; Intern Mount Sinai Hospital, New York City, 1940-42; National Research Council fellow School Pub. Health, University Michigan, 1942-43, research fellow epidemiology; 1943-44, research associate; 1944-46, assistant professor epidemiology; 1946-47; associate research professor bacteriology School Medicine, University Pittsburgh, 1947-49, director virus research laboratory; 1947-63, research professor bacteriology; 1949-55, Commonwealth professor preventive medicine; 1955-57, Commonwealth professor experimental medicine; 1957-63; director Salk Institute Biological Studies, 1963-75, resident fellow; 1963-84, founding director; 1976—, distinguished professor international health sciences; 1984—; developed vaccine, preventive of poliomyelitis, 1955, consultant epidemic diseases secretary war, 1944-47, secretary army, 1947-54; member commission on influenza Army Epidemiological Board, 1944-54, acting director commission on influenza, 1944; member expert adv. panel on virus diseases World Health Organization; adj. professor health sciences, departments psychiatry, community medicine and medicine University California, San Diego, 1970—. Author: Man Unfolding, 1972, The Survival of the Wisest, 1973, (with Jonathan Salk) World Population and Human Values: A New Reality, 1981, Anatomy of Reality, 1983; Contributor sci. articles to journals. Decorated chevalier Legion of Honor France, 1955, officer, 1976; recipient Criss award, 1955, Lasker award, 1956, Gold medal of Congress and presidential citation, 1955, Howard Ricketts award, 1957, Robert Koch medal, 1963, Mellon Institute award, 1969; Presidential medal of Freedom, 1977; Jawaharlal Nehru award for international understanding, 1976. Fellow American Association for the Advancement of Science, Am. Pub. Health Association, Am. Acad. Pediatrics (hon., associate); member Am. College Preventive Medicine, Am. Acad. Neurology, Association Am. Physicians., Society Experimental Biology and Medicine, Institute Medicine (senior), Phi Beta Kappa, Alpha Omega Alpha, Delta Omega. Office: Salk Institute Biol Studies Post Office Box 85800 San Diego California 92138

SALMON, WILLIAM COOPER, mechanical engineer, engineering academy executive; born New York City, September 3, 1935; son of Chenery and Mary (Cooper) S.; married Josephine Stone, September 16, 1967; children—William Cooper, Mary Bradford, Pauline Alexandra. Bachelor of Science in Mechanical Engineering, Massachusetts Institute of Technology, 1957, Master of Science in Mechanical Engineering, 1958, Mechanical Engineer, 1959, Master of Science in Management Science, 1969. Registered professional engineer, Massachusetts. Research and teaching assistant Massachusetts Institute of Technology, Cambridge, 1957-59; senior engineer Microtech, Cambridge, 1959-60; assistant sci. advisor United States Department State, Washington, 1961-74, senior advisor for sci. and tech.; 1978-86; counselor for sci. and tech. Am. embassy, Paris, 1974-78; executive officer National Acad. Engineering, Washington, 1986—. Recipient Superior Honor award Department State, 1964; Meritorious Service award President U.S., 1984; Sloan fellow Massachusetts Institute of Technology, 1968. Member American Society of Mechanical Engineers, National Society Professional Engineers. Episcopalian. Club: Cosmos. Lodge: Masons. Home: Arlington Virginia Office: National Acad Engring 2101 Constitution Avenue Northwest Washington District of Columbia 20418

SALPETER, EDWIN ERNEST, physical sciences educator; born Vienna, Austria, December 3, 1924; came to United States, 1949, naturalized, 1953; son of Jakob L. and Frieder (Horn) S.; married Miriam Mark, June 11, 1950; children—Judy Gail, Shelley Ruth. Master of Science, Sydney University, 1946; Doctor of Philosophy, Birmingham (England) University, 1948; Doctor of Science, University Chicago, 1969, Case-Western Reserve University, 1970. Research fellow Birmingham University, 1948-49; faculty Cornell University, Ithaca, New York, 1949—;

now J.G. White professor physical sciences Cornell University; member United States National Sci. Board, 1979-85. Author: Quantum Mechanics, 1957, 77; Editorial board: Astrophys. Jour, 1966-69; asso. editor: Rev. Modern Physics, 1971—; contributor articles to professional journals. Member AURA board, 1970-72. Recipient Gold medal Royal Astronomical Society, 1973, J.R. Oppenheimer Memorial prize University Miami, 1974, C. Bruce medal Astronomical Society Pacific, 1987. Member Am. Astronomical Society (vice president 1971-73), Am. Philosophical Society, National Acad. Sciences, Am. Acad. Arts and Sciences, Deutsche Akademie Leopoldina. Home: 116 Westbourne Lane Ithaca New York 14850

SALTON, GERARD, computer science educator; born Nuremberg, Germany, March 8, 1927; son of Rudolf and Elisabeth (Tuchmann) S.; married Mary Birnbaum, August 31, 1950; children: Mariann, Peter. Bachelor of Arts magna cum laude, Brooklyn College, 1950, Master of Arts, 1952; Doctor of Philosophy, Harvard University, 1958. Member staff computation laboratory Harvard University, 1952-58, instructor, then assistant professor applied math.; 1958-65; professor computer sci. Cornell University, 1965—, chairman department; 1971-77; consultant to industry. Author: Automatic Information Organization and Retrieval, 1968, The Smart System-Experiments in Automatic Document Processing, 1971, Dynamic Information and Library Processing, 1975, Introduction to Modern Information Retrieval, 1983, Automatic Text Processing, 1989; editor-in-chief: Association Computing

Machinery Communications, 1966-68; Editor-in-chief: Association Computing Machinery Journal, 1969-72; editor: Information Systems, 1974—, ACM Transactions on Data Base Systems. Guggenheim fellow, 1963; recipient Alexander von Humboldt award 1988. Fellow American Association for the Advancement of Science; member Association Computing Machinery (council 1972-78, Outstanding Contbn. award 1983), Phi Beta Kappa. Home: 221 Valley Road Ithaca New York 14850 Office: Upson Hall Cornell U Ithaca New York 14853

SAMIOS, NICHOLAS PETER, physicist; born New York City, March 15, 1932; son of Peter and Niki (Vatick) S.; married Mary Linakis, January 12, 1958; children: Peter, Gregory, Alexandra. Bachelor of Arts, Columbia University, 1953, Doctor of Philosophy, 1957. Instructor physics Columbia University, New York City, 1956-59; assistant physicist Brookhaven National Laboratory, Upton, New York, 1959-62; associate physicist Brookhaven National Laboratory, 1962-64, physicist; 1964-68, senior physicist; 1968—, group leader; 1965-75, chairman department physics; 1975-81, deputy director for high energy and nuclear physics; 1981, director; 1982—; adj. professor Stevens Institute Tech., 1969-75, Columbia University, 1970—. Contributor articles in field to professional journals. Recipient E.O. Lawrence Memorial award, 1980; award in physical and math. scis. New York Acad. Sciences, 1980. Fellow Am. Physical Society, Am. Acad. Arts and Sciences; member National Acad. Sciences, Sigma Xi. Expert field of high energy particle and nuclear physics. Office: Brookhaven National Lab Office of Dir Upton New York 11973

SAMUELSSON, BENGT INGEMAR, medical chemist; born Halmstad, Sweden, May 21, 1934; son of Anders and Stina (Nilsson) S.; married Inga Karin Bergstein, August 19, 1958; children: Bo, Elisabet, Astrid. Doctor of Medical Science, Karolinska Institute, Stockholm, 1960, Doctor of Medicine, 1961; Doctor of Science (honorary), University Chgo, 1978, University Illinois, 1983. Assistant professor Karolinska Institute, 1961-66, professor medical and physiological chemistry; 1972—, chairman physiological chemistry department; 1973-83, dean Medical Faculty; 1978-83, president; 1983—; research fellow Harvard University, 1961-62; professor medical chemistry Royal Vet. College, Stockholm, 1967-72; Harvey lecturer, New York City, 1979; member Nobel Committee Physiology and Medicine, 1984-86, chairman committee, 1987—; member research adv. board Swedish Government, 1985—; member National Commission Health Policy, 1987—. Contbr articles to professional journals. Recipient A. Jahres award Oslo University, 1970, Louisa Gross Horwitz award Columbia University, 1975, Albert Lasker basic med. research award, 1977, Ciba-Geigy Drew award in biomed. research, 1980, Lewis S. Rosentiel award in basic med. research Brandeis University, 1981, Gairdner Foundation award, 1981, Heinrich Wieland prize, 1981, Nobel prize in physiology of medicine, 1982, award medicinal chemistry div. Am. Chemical Society, 1982, Waterford Bio-Med. Sci. award, 1982, International Association Allergology and Clinical Immunology award, 1982, Abraham

White sci. achievement award, 1984. Member Royal Swedish Acad. Sciences, Mediterranean Acad.; hon. member Association Am. Physicians, American Association for the Advancement of Science, Swedish Medical Association, Am. Society Biological Chemists, Italian Pharmaceutical Society, Acad. National Medicina de Buenos Aires, International Society Hematology, Foreign Association United States National Acad. Sciences. Office: Karolinska Institute, Solnavagen 1, S-10401 Stockholm Sweden

SANDAGE, ALLAN REX, astronomer; born Iowa City, June 18, 1926; son of Charles Harold and Dorothy (Briggs) S.; married Mary Lois Connelley, June 8, 1959; children—David Allan, John Howard. Bachelor of Arts, University Illinois, 1948, Doctor of Science (honorary), 1967; Doctor of Philosophy, California Institute Tech., 1953; Doctor of Science (honorary), Yale University, 1966, University Chicago, 1967, Miami University, Oxford, Ohio, 1974; Doctor of Laws (honorary), University Southern California, 1971; Doctor of Science (honorary), Graceland College, Iowa, 1985. Astronomer Mount Wilson Observatory, Palomar Observatory, Carnegie Institution, Washington, 1952—; Peyton postdoctoral fellow Princeton University, 1952; assistant astronomer Hale Observatory, Pasadena, California, 1952-56, astronomer; 1956—; senior research astronomer Space Telescope Sci. Institute National Aeronautics and Space Administration, Baltimore, 1986—; Homewood Professor of Physics Johns Hopkins University, Baltimore, 1987-88; visiting lecturer Harvard University, 1957; member

astronomical expedition to South Africa, 1958; consultant National Science Foundation, 1961-64; Sigma Xi national lecturer, 1966; visiting professor Mount Stromlo Observatory, Australian National University, 1968-69, ; visiting research astronomer University Basel, 1985; research astronomer University California, San Diego, 1985-86; visiting astronomer University Hawaii, 1986; Lindsey lecturer National Aeronautics and Space Administration Goddard Space Flight Center, 1988. Served with United States Naval Reserve, 1944-45. Recipient gold medal Royal Astronomical Society, 1967, Pope Pius XI gold medal Pontifical Acad. Sci., 1966, Rittenhouse medal, 1968, National Medal Sci., 1971; Fulbright-Hayes scholar, 1972. Member LinceiAstron. Society, Rome Astronomical Society, Am. Astronomical Society (Helen Warner prize 1960, Russell prize 1973), Royal Astronomical Society (Eddington medal 1963, Gold medal 1967), Astronomical Society Pacific (Gold medal 1975), Franklin Institute (Elliott Cresson medal 1973), Phi Beta Kappa, Sigma Xi. Home: 8319 Josard Road San Gabriel California 91775 Office: 813 Santa Barbara St Pasadena California 91101

SANGER, FREDERICK, retired molecular biologist; born Rendcomb, Gloucestershire, England, August 13, 1918; son of Frederick and Cicely Sanger; married Joan Howe, 1940; children: Robin, Peter Frederick, Sally Joan. Bachelor of Arts, St. John's College, Cambridge University, 1940, Doctor of Philosophy, 1943; Doctor of Science (honorary), Leicester University, 1968, Oxford University, 1970, Strasbourg University, 1970. Beit Memorial Medical Research fellow University Cambridge, 1944-51, research scientist department biochemistry; 1944-61, research scientist, div. head Medical Research Council Laboratory of Molecular Biology; 1962-83. Contributor articles in field to sci. journals. Recipient Nobel prize for chemistry, 1958, 80; Gairdner Foundation annual award, 1971, 79, William Bate Hardy prize Cambridge Philos. Society, 1976, Copley medal Royal Society, 1977; fellow King's College, Cambridge University, 1954. Member Am. Acad. Arts and Sciences (hon. foreign member), Am. Society Biological Chemists (hon.), Foreign Association, National Academy of Sciences. Home: Far Leys, Fen Lane, Swaffham Bulbeck, Cambridge CB5 ONJ, England Office: MRC Lab Molecular Biology, Hills Road, Cambridge CB2 2QH, England

SANGREY, DWIGHT A., civil engineer, educator; born Lancaster, Pennsylvania, May 24, 1940; married 1964; 5 children. Bachelor of Science, Lafayette College, 1962; Master of Science, University Massachusetts, 1964; Doctor of Philosophy in Civil Engineering, Cornell University, 1968. Engineer H.L. Griswold, Cons. Engineers, 1960-64; project engineer Shell Oil Company, Texas, 1964-65; assistant professor civil engineering Queen's University, Ontario, Can., 1967-70, associate professor; 1970-77; professor civil and environmental engineering Cornell University, 1977-79; professor civil and engineering, department chairman Carnegie-Mellon University, Pittsburgh, 1979-85; dean School Engineering Rensselaer Polytechnic Institute, Troy, New York, 1985—. Recipient Research award American Society for Testing and Materials, 1969; teaching awards, Tau Beta Pi, 1972, Chi Epsilon, 1971, 77, American Society of Civil Engineers, 1985. Office: Rensselaer Polytechnic Institute School Engring Troy New York 12181

SANI, ROBERT LEROY, chemical engineering educator; born Antioch, California, April 20, 1935; married Martha Jo Marr, May 28, 1966; children: Cynthia Kay, Elizabeth Ann, Jeffrey Paul. Bachelor of Science, University Calif.-Berkeley, 1958, Master of Science, 1960; Doctor of Philosophy, University Minnesota, 1963. Postdoctoral researcher department math Rensselaer Polytechnic Institute, Troy, New York, 1963-64; assistant professor University Illinois, Urbana, 1964-70, associate professor; 1970-76; professor chemical engineering University Colorado, Boulder, 1976—; co-director Center for Low-g Fluid Mechanics and Transport Phenomena, University Colorado, Boulder, 1986-89; director Center for Fluid Mechanics and Transport Phenomena, University Colorado, Boulder, 1989—; professeur associe Minister Education France, 1982, 84, 86; consultant Lawrence Livermore National Laboratory, California, 1974—. Contbr numerous chapters to professional publications; editorial board: International Journal Numerical Methods in Fluids, 1981—. Guggenheim fellow, 1970. Member Am. Institute Chemical Engineers, Society Applied and Industrial Math. Democrat. Office: U Colorado Department Chem Engring Campus Box 424 Boulder Colorado 80309

SARGENT, WALLACE LESLIE WILLIAM, astronomer, educator; born Elsham, England, February 15, 1935; son of Leslie William and Eleanor

(Dennis) S.; married Anneila Isabel Cassells, August 5, 1964; children: Lindsay Eleanor, Alison Clare. Bachelor of Science, Manchester University, 1956, Master of Science, 1957, Doctor of Philosophy, 1959. Research fellow California Institute Tech., 1959-62; senior research fellow Royal Greenwich Observatory, 1962-64; assistant professor physics University California, San Diego, 1964-66; member faculty department astronomy California Institute Tech., Pasadena, 1966—; professor California Institute Tech., 1971-81, Ira South Bowen professor astronomy; 1981—. Contributor articles to professional journals. Alfred P. Sloan Foundation fellow, 1968-70; recipient Helen B. Warner prize Am. Astronomical Society, 1969. Fellow Am. Acad. Arts and Sciences, Royal Society (London); member Am. Astronomical Society, Royal Astronomical Society (George Darwin lecturer, 1987), International Astronomical Union. Club: Athenaeum (Pasadena). Home: 400 S Berkeley Avenue Pasadena California 91107 Office: California Institute Tech Astronomy Department 105-24 Pasadena California 91125

SATO, HIROSHI, materials science educator; born Matsuzaka, Mie, Japan, August 31, 1918; came to United States, 1954; son of Masayoshi and Fusae (Ohhara) S.; married Kyoko Amemiya, January 10, 1947; children: Norie M., Nobuyuki Albert, Erika Michiko. Bachelor of Science, Hokkaido Imperial University, Sapparo, Japan, 1938, Master of Science, 1941; Doctor of Science, Tokyo University, 1951. Research associate faculty sci. Hokkaido Imperial University, Sapparo, 1941-42,

assistant professor Institute Low Temperature Sci.; 1942-43; research physicist Institute Physical and Chemical Research, Tokyo, 1943-45; professor Tohoku Imperial University, Sendai, Japan, 1945-57; research physicist Westinghouse Research Laboratories, Pittsburgh, 1954-56; principal scientist Sci. Laboratory, Ford Motor Company, Dearborn, Michigan, 1956-74; professor materials engineering Purdue University, West Lafayette, Ind., 1974—, Ross Distinguished professor engineering; 1984—; affiliate professor department materials sci. University Washington, Seattle, 1986—; visiting professor University Grenoble, France, 1967, Tokyo Institute Tech., 1979, Tech. University Hannover, Federal Republic Germany, 1980-81; consultant Oak Ridge (Tennessee) National Laboratory, 1978, 80. Contributor over 200 articles to professional journals, chapters to books. Recipient U.S. Senior Scientist award Alexander v. Humbold Foundation, 1980; fellow John Simon Guggenheim Memorial Foundation, 1966, Japan Society for Promotion Sci., 1979. Fellow Am. Physical Society; member Japan Physical Society, Am. Ceramic Society, Metallurgical Soc.-AIME, Japan Institute Metals (hon., Prize of Merit 1951). Democrat. Congregationalist. Office: Purdue University School of Materials Engring West Lafayette Indiana 47907

SAUL, GEORGE BRANDON, II, biology educator; born Hartford, Connecticut, August 8, 1928; son of George Brandon and Dorothy (Ayers) S.; married Sue Grau Williams, March 28, 1953. Bachelor of Arts, University Pennsylvania, 1949, Master of Arts, 1950, Doctor of Philosophy, 1954.

From instructor to associate professor Dartmouth, 1954-67; professor biology Middlebury (Vermont) College, 1967—, chairman department; 1968-76, vice president acad. affairs; 1976-79; Research associate California Institute Tech., 1964-65; National Science Foundation postdoctoral fellow University Zurich, Switzerland, 1959-60; visiting scientist Boyce Thompson Institute for Plant Research, Yonkers, New York, 1972-73. Author papers in field. Fellow American Association for the Advancement of Science; member Pennsylvania Acad. Sci., Genetics Society Am., Am. Genetics Association, Radiation Research Society, New York Acad. Sciences, Sigma Xi. Club: Lion. Home: Munger St Rural Delivery 3 Middlebury Vermont 05753

SCARPA, ANTONIO, biomedical scientist, educator; born Padua, Italy, July 3, 1942; son of Angelo and Elena (DeRossi) S. Doctor of Medicine cum laude, University Padua, 1966, Doctor of Philosophy in Pathology, 1970; Master of Arts (honorary), University Pennsylvania, 1978. Assistant professor biochemistry, biophysics University Pennsylvania, Philadelphia, 1973-76, associate professor; 1976-80, professor; 1980-86, director biomed. instrumentation group; 1983-86; professor, chairman department physiology Case Western Reserve University, Cleveland, 1986—, director training center, program project; 1983—; consultant study section National Institutes of Health, Bethesda, 1984—, Am. Heart Association, Dallas, 1986—. Editor (books): Frontiers of Biological Energetics, Calcium Transport and Cell Function, Transport ATPases, Membrane Pathology; editor (journals): Archives Biochemistry and Biophysics, Cell Calcium, FASEB Journal; contributor numerous articles to professional journals. Member Am. Society Physiologists, Am. Society Biolog. Chemistry, Biophys. Society (executive council 1980-83), United States Bioenergetics Group (program chairman 1974-75, 82, 83). Avocations: farming, sailing, painting. Office: Case Western Reserve University Department of Physiology Cleveland Ohio 44106

SCHACHMAN, HOWARD KAPNEK, molecular biologist, educator; born Philadelphia, December 5, 1918; son of Morris H. and Rose (Kapnek) S.; married Ethel H. Lazarus, October 20, 1945; children—Marc, David. Bachelor of Science in Chemical Engineering, Massachusetts Institute Tech., 1939; Doctor of Philosophy in Physical Chemistry, Princeton, 1948; Doctor of Science (honorary), Northwestern University, 1974. Fellow National Institutes of Health, 1946-48; instructor, assistant professor University California at Berkeley, 1948-54, associate professor biochemistry; 1954-59, professor biochemistry and molecular biology; 1959—, chairman department molecular biology, director virus laboratory; 1969-76; member sci. council and sci. adv. board Stazione Zoologica, Naples, Italy, 1988—; board sci. consultant Memorial Sloan-Kettering Cancer Center, 1988—. Author: Ultracentrifugation in Biochemistry, 1959. Served from ensign to lieutenant United States Naval Reserve, 1945-47. Guggenheim Memorial fellow, 1956; Recipient John Scott award, 1964, Warren Triennial prize Massachusetts General Hospital, 1965. Member

National Acad. Sci., Am. Chemical Society (recipient award in Chemical Instrumentation 1962, California secretary award 1958), American Association for the Advancement of Science, Am. Society Biological Chemists (president 1987-88, Merck award 1986), Am. Acad. Arts and Sciences, Federation Am. Socs. for Experimental Biology (president 1988-89), Sigma Xi. Office: U California Molecular Biology and Virus Lab Berkeley California 94720

SCHAFER, RONALD WILLIAM, electrical engineering educator; born Tecumseh, Nebraska, February 17, 1938; son of William Henry and Esther Sophia (Rinnie) S.; married Dorothy Margaret Hall, June 2, 1960; children: William R., John C. (deceased), Katherine L., Barbara Anne. Student, Doane College, Crete, Nebraska, 1956-59; Bachelor of Electrical Engineering, University Nebraska, 1961, Master of Electrical Engineering, 1962; Doctor of Philosophy in Electrical Engineering, Massachusetts Institute of Technology, 1968. Member tech. staff Bell Laboratories, Murray Hill, New Jersey, 1968-74; John O. McCarty/Audiochron professor electrical engineering Georgia Institute Tech., Atlanta, 1974—, chairman; 1979—; president Atlanta Signal Processors Incorporated, 1983—. Co-author: Digital Signal Processing, 1974, Digital Processing of Signals, 1979, Speech Analysis, 1979. Recipient Class of 34 Distinguished Professor award Georgia Institute Tech., 1985. Fellow Institute of Electrical and Electronics Engineers (Emanuel R. Piore award 1980, Acoustics Speech and Signal Processing Society award 1982), Acoustical Society Am.; member American Association for the Advancement of Science. Democrat. Methodist. Lodge: Kiwanis. Office: Ga Institute of Tech Department of Elec Engring Atlanta Georgia 30332-0183

SCHALLER, GEORGE BEALS, zoologist; born Berlin, May 26, 1933; son of George Ludwig S. and Bettina (Byrd) Iwersen; married Kay Suzanne Morgan, August 26, 1957; children: Eric, Mark. Bachelor of Science in Zoology, University Alaska, 1955, Bachelor of Arts in Anthropology, 1955; Doctor of Philosophy in Zoology, University Wisconsin, 1962. Research associate Johns Hopkins University, Baltimore, 1963-66; research zoologist New York Zool. Society, Bronx, 1966—, director international conservation program; 1979—; adj. associate professor Rockefeller University, New York City, 1966—; research associate Am. Mus. Natural History. Author: The Mountain Gorilla, 1963 (Wildlife Society 1965), The Year of the Gorilla, 1964, The Deer and the Tiger, 1967, The Serengeti Lion, 1972 (National Bookaward 1973), Golden Shadows, Flying Hooves, 1973, Mountain Monarchs, 1977, Stones of Silence, 1980, The Giant Pandas of Wolong, 1985. Fellow Center Advanced Study in Behavioral Sciences, Stanford University, 1962; fellow Guggenheim Foundation, 1971; decorated Order of Golden Ark Netherlands; recipient Gold medal World Wildlife Fund, 1980; named hon. member Explorers Club, 1984. Office: New York Zool Society Bronx Park Bronx New York 10460

SCHALLY, ANDREW VICTOR, medical research scientist; born Poland, November 30, 1926; came to United States, 1957; son of Casimir Peter and Maria (Lacka) S.; married; children: Karen, Gordon; married Ana

Maria Comaru, August 1976. Bachelor of Science, McGill University, Can., 1955, Doctor of Philosophy in Biochemistry, 1957; 15 honorary doctorates. Research assistant biochemistry National Institute Medical Research, London, 1949-52; department psychiatry McGill University, Montreal, Quebec, 1952-57; research associate, assistant professor physiology and biochemistry College Medicine, Baylor University, Houston, 1957-62; associate professor Tulane University School Medicine, New Orleans, 1962-67, professor; 1967—; chief Endocrine Polypeptide and Cancer Institute Veteran's Administration Medical Center, New Orleans; senior medical investigator Veteran's Administration, 1973—. Author several books; contributor articles to professional journals. Recipient ; Van Meter prize Am. Thyroid Association, 1969; Ayerst-Squibb award Endocrine Society, 1970; William S. Middletown award Veteran's Administration, 1970; Church Mickle award University Toronto, 1974; Gairdner International award, 1974; Borden award Association Am. Medical Colleges and Borden Company Foundation, 1975; Lasker Basic Research award, 1975; co-recipient Nobel prize for medicine, 1977; USPHS sr. research fellow, 1961-62. Member Endocrine Society, Am. Physiological Society, Society Biological Chemists, American Association for the Advancement of Science, Society Experimental Biological Medicine, International Society Research Biology Reprodn., Society Study Reprodn., Society International Brain Research Organization, Mexican Acad. Medicine, Am. Society Animal Sci., National Acad. Sci., National Acad. Medicine Brazil, Acad. Medicine Venezuela, Acad. Sci. Hungary. Home: 5025 Kawanee Avenue Metairie Louisiana 70002 Office: VA Hosp 1601 Perdido St New Orleans Louisiana 70146

SCHARRER, BERTA VOGEL, anatomy and neuroscience educator; born Munich, Federal Republic Germany, December 1, 1906; daughter of Karl and Johanna V.; widowed. Doctor of Philosophy in Zoology, University Munich, 1930; Doctor of Medicine (honorary), University Giessen, Federal Republic Germany, 1976; Doctor of Science (honorary), Northwestern University, 1977, University North Carolina, 1978, Smith College, 1980, Harvard University, 1982, Yeshiva University, 1983, Mount Holyoke College, 1984, State University of New York, 1985; Doctor of Laws, University Calgary, Alberta, Can., 1982. Research associate Research Institute for Psychiatry, Munich, 1931-34, Neurological Institute, Frankfurt-am-Main, 1934-37, University Chicago Department Anatomy, 1937-38, Rockefeller Institute, New York City, 1938-40; instructor, fellow Western Reserve University Department Anatomy, Cleveland, 1940-46; John Guggenheim fellow University Colorado Department Anatomy, Denver, 1947-48, special United States Public Health Service research fellow; 1948-50; assistant professor (research) department anatomy University Colorado School Medicine, Denver, 1950-55; professor anatomy Albert Einstein College Medicine, 1955-77, acting chairman; 1965-67, 76-77, professor emeritus anatomy and neurosci.; 1978—. Recipient Kraepelin Gold medal, 1978, F.C. Koch award Endocrine Society, 1980, National Medal Sci., 1983. Member

National Acad. Sciences, Am. Acad. Arts & Sciences, Deutsche Acad. Naturforscher Leopoldina (Schleiden medal 1983), Am. Association Anatomists (president 1978-79, Henry Gray award 1982), Am. Society Zoologists, Society Neurosci., Endocrine Society (F.C. Koch award 1980, National Medal of Sci. 1983), International Brain Research Organization, Committee on Brain Sciences of National Research Council, Acad. Ind. Scholars. Research in comparative neuroendocrinology, neurosecretion, neuropeptides. Home: 1240 Neill Avenue Bronx New York 10461 Office: Albert Einstein College Medicine/Dept Anatomy 1300 Morris Park Avenue Bronx New York 10461

SCHAWLOW, ARTHUR LEONARD, physicist, educator; born Mount Vernon, New York, May 5, 1921; son of Arthur and Helen (Mason) S.; married Aurelia Keith Townes, May 19, 1951; children: Arthur Keith, Helen Aurelia, Edith Ellen. Bachelor of Arts, University Toronto, 1941, Master of Arts, 1942, Doctor of Philosophy, 1949, Doctor of Laws (honorary), 1970; Doctor of Science (honorary), University Ghent, Belgium, 1968, University Bradford, England, 1970, University Alabama, 1984, Trinity College, Dublin, Ireland, 1986; Doctor.Tech. (honorary), University Lund, Sweden, 1987. Postdoctoral fellow, research associate Columbia, 1949-51; visiting associate professor Columbia University, 1960; research physicist Bell Telephone Laboratories, 1951-61, consultant; 1961-62; professor physics Stanford University, 1961—, now J.G. Jackson-C.J. Wood professor physics, executive head department; 1966-70, acting chairman department; 1973-74. Author: (with

C.H. Townes) Microwave Spectroscopy, 1955; Co-inventor (with C.H. Townes), optical maser or laser, 1958. Recipient Ballantine medal Franklin Institute, 1962, Thomas Young medal and prize Institute Physics and Physical Society, London, 1963, Schawlow medal Laser Institute Am., 1982; Nobel prize in physics, 1981; named California Scientist of Year, 1973, Marconi International fellow, 1977. Fellow Am. Acad. Arts and Sciences, Am. Physical Society (council 1966-70, chairman division electron and atomic physics 1974, president 1981), Optical Society Am. (hon. member 1983, dir.-at-large 1966-68, president 1975, Frederick Ives medal 1976); member National Acad. Sciences, Institute of Electrical and Electronics Engineers (Liebmann prize 1964), American Association for the Advancement of Science (chairman physics section 1979), Am. Philosophical Society. Office: Stanford U Department Physics Stanford California 94305-4060

SCHELL, ALLAN CARTER, electrical engineer; born New Bedford, Massachusetts, April 14, 1934; son of Charles Carter and Elizabeth (Moore) S.; children: Alice Rosalind, Cynthia Anne. Bachelor of Science, Massachusetts Institute of Technology, 1956, Master of Science in Electrical Engineering, 1956, Doctor of Science, 1961; student, Tech. University Delft, Netherlands, 1956-57. Research physicist Air Force Cambridge Research Laboratories, Bedford, Massachusetts, 1956-76; Guenter Loeser Memorial lecturer Air Force Cambridge Research Laboratories, 1965; director electromagnetics directorate Rome Air Devel. Center, Bedford, 1976-87; chief scientist Headquarters United

States Air Force Systems Command, 1987—; director Electro; visiting associate professor Massachusetts Institute of Technology, 1974. Editor: IEEE Press, 1976-79, IEEE Trans. on Antennas and Propagation, 1969-71; contributor articles to professional journals. Served as lieutenant United States Air Force, 1958-60. Recipient Fulbright award, 1956-57; National Science Foundation fellow, 1955-56, 60-61. Fellow Institute of Electrical and Electronics Engineers (director 1981-82); member Institute of Electrical and Electronics Engineers Antennas and Propagation Society (John T. Bolljahn award 1966, president 1978), International Sci. Radio Union (United States national committee), Sigma Xi, Tau Beta Pi. Patentee in field (9). Office: Andrews Air Force Base Maryland 20334

SCHERAGA, HAROLD ABRAHAM, physical chemistry educator; born Brooklyn, October 18, 1921; son of Samuel and Etta (Goldberg) S.; married Miriam Kurnow, June 20, 1943; children: Judith Anne, Deborah Ruth, Daniel Michael. Bachelor of Science, City College of New York, 1941; Master of Arts, Duke University, 1942, Doctor of Philosophy, 1946, Doctor of Science (honorary), 1961. Teaching, research assistant Duke University, 1941-46; fellow Harvard Medical School, 1946-47; instructor chemistry Cornell University, 1947-50, assistant professor; 1950-53, associate professor; 1953-58, professor; 1958—, Todd professor chemistry; 1965—, chairman department; 1960-67; visiting associate biochemist Brookhaven National Laboratory, summers 1950, 51, consultant biology department, 1950-56; visiting lecturer div. protein chemistry Wool Research Laborato-

ries, Melbourne, Australia, 1959; visiting professor Society for Promotion Sci., Japan, Aug. 1977; member tech. adv. panel Xerox Corp., 1969-71, 74-79; Member biochemistry training committee National Institutes of Health, 1963-65; member research career award committee NIGMS, 1967-71; commission molecular biophysics International Union for Pure and Applied Biophysics, 1965-69, member commission macromolecular biophysics, 1969-75, president, 1972-75, member commission subcellular and macromolecular biophysics, 1975-81; adv. panel molecular biology National Science Foundation, 1960-62; Welch Foundation lecturer, 1962, Harvey lecturer, 1968, Gallagher lecturer, 1968, Lemieux lecturer, 1973, Hill lecturer, 1976, Venable lecturer, 1981; co-chairman Gordon Conference on Proteins, 1963; member council Gordon Research Confs., 1969-71. Author: Protein Structure; Theory of Helix-Coil Transitions in Biopolymers; Co-editor: Molecular Biology, 1961-86; member editorial board: Physiological Chemistry and Physics, 1969-75, Mechanochemistry and Motility, 1970-71, Thrombosis Research, 1972-76, Biophys. Jour, 1973-75, Macromolecules, 1973-84, Computers and Chemistry, 1974-84, International Journal Peptide and Protein Research, 1978—, Journal Computational Chemistry, 1980—, Journal Protein Chemistry, 1982—; corr. PAABS Revista, 1971-73; member editorial adv. board Biopolymers, 1963—, Biochemistry, 1969-74, 85—. Member Ithaca Board Education, 1958-59; Board governors Weizmann Institute, Israel, 1970—; member staff Naval Research Lab. Project, Air Force Office of Scientific Research and Development Project,

World War II. Fulbright, Guggenheim fellow Carlsberg Laboratory, Copenhagen, 1956-57, Weizmann Institute, Israel, 1963; National Institutes of Health Special fellow Weizmann Institute, 1970; Fogarty scholar National Institutes of Health, 1984, 86; recipient Townsend Harris medal City College of New York, 1970, Chemistry Alumni Sci. Achievement award, 1977, Kowalski medal International Society Thrombosis and Haemostasis, 1983, LinderstrØm-Lang medal Carlsberg Laboratory, 1983. Fellow American Association for the Advancement of Science; member National Acad. Sciences, Am. Chemical Society (chairman Cornell section 1955-56, member executive committee division biological chemistry 1966-69, vice chairman division biological chemistry 1970, chairman division biological chemistry 1971, Eli Lilly award 1957, Nichols medal 1974, Kendall award 1978, Pauling award 1985), Am. Society Biological Chemists, Biophys. Society (council 1967-70), Am. Acad. Arts and Sciences, New York Acad. Sciences (hon. life), Phi Beta Kappa, Sigma Xi, Phi Lambda Upsilon. Home: 212 Homestead Terrace Ithaca New York 14850

SCHERR, LAWRENCE, physician, educator; born New York City, November 6, 1928; son of Harry and Sophia (Schwartz) S.; married Peggy L. Binenkorb, June 13, 1954; children—Cynthia E., Robert W. Bachelor of Arts, Cornell University, 1950, Doctor of Medicine, 1957. Diplomate Am. Board Internal Medicine (bd. dirs., sec.-treas. 1979-86). Intern Cornell Medical div. Bellevue Hospital and Memorial Center, 1957-58, assistant resident; 1958-59, research fellow cardiorenal laboratory; 1959-60, chief resident; 1960-61, co-director cardiorenal laboratory; 1961-62, assistant visiting physician; 1961-63, associate visiting physician; 1963-65, director cardiology and renal unit; 1963-67, associate director; 1964-67, visiting physician; 1966-68; physician to out-patients New York Hospital, 1961-63, assistant attending physician; 1963-66, associate attending physician; 1966-71, attending physician; 1971—; assistant attending physician Memorial Sloan-Kettering Cancer Center, 1962-71, consultant; 1971—; consultant St. Francis Hospital, 1973—; director department medicine North Shore University Hospital, 1967—, director acad. affairs, 1969—; assistant in medicine Cornell University Medical College, 1958-59; research fellow New York Heart Association, 1959-60, instructor medicine, 1960-63, assistant professor, 1963-66, associate professor, 1966-71, David J. Greene Distinguished professor, 1971—, associate dean, 1969—; career scientist Health Research Council, New York City, 1962-66; teaching scholar Am. Heart Association, 1966-67. Contributor articles to professional journals. President New York State Board Medicine, 1974-75; board of directors National Board Medical Examiners, 1976-80; chairman Accreditation Council for Grad. Medical Education, 1988. Served to lieutenant United States Naval Reserve, 1950-53. Fellow American College of Physicians (chairman and governor Downstate New York region II 1975-80, regent 1980—,chairman board regents 1985-86; national pres.-elect 1986-87, president 1987-88), Am. Heart Association (fellow council on clinical cardiology), member Am. Federation

Clinical Research, Harvey Society, American Medical Association, New York, Nassau County med. socs., Association Am. Medical Colls., Am. Clinical and Climatologic Association. Home: 93 Hendrickson St Haworth New Jersey 07641 Office: North Shore University Hosp Manhasset New York 11030

SCHIFF, JEROME ARNOLD, biologist, educator; born Brooklyn, February 20, 1931; son of Charles K. and Molly (Weinberg) S. Bachelor of Arts in Biology and Chemistry, Brooklyn College (summer scholar invertebrate zoology Woods Hole Marine Biol. Laboratory), 1952; Doctor of Philosophy in Botany and Biochemistry, University Pennsylvania, 1956. Predoctoral fellow United States Public Health Service, 1954-56; fellow Brookhaven National Laboratories, summer 1956; research associate biology Brandeis University, Waltham, Massachusetts, 1956-57; member faculty Brandeis University, 1957—, professor biology; 1966—, chairman department; 1972-75, Abraham and Etta Goodman professor biology; 1974—; director Institute Photobiology of Cells and Organelles, 1975-87; summer instructor Experimental Marine Botany, Woods Hole, Massachusetts, 1971; senior investigator Experimental Marine Botany, 1972-74, director programs; 1974-79; consultant on devel. biology National Science Foundation, 1965-68, consultant on metabolic biology, 1982-86; visiting professor Tel Aviv University, 1972, Hebrew University, 1972, Weizmann Institute, Israel, 1977; member biology grant rev. program U.S.-Israel Binat. Sci. Foundation, 1974—; member corp. Marine Biological Laboratory. Member editorial board Develop-

mental Biology, 1971-74 Plant Science, 1972-78, associate editor, 1978-81, chief co-editor, 1981—; assistant editor Plant Physiology, 1964-69, adv. editor, 1969-79; member editorial com. Annual Rev. Plant Physiology, 1974-80. Carnegie Institution fellow in plant biology, 1962-63; Recipient Distinguished Alumni award Brooklyn College, 1972. Fellow Am. Acad. Arts and Sciences, American Association for the Advancement of Science; member Society Devel. Biology (secretary 1964-66, executive committee), Am. Society Biological Chemists, Am. Society Plant Physiologists (executive committee 1972—), Biophys. Society, Can. Society Plant Physiologists, International Phycol. Society, Phycol. Society Am., Society Cell Biology, Society General Microbiology, Society Protozoologists, Am. Society Microbiology, International Society Developmental Biologists, Brit. Phycol. Society, Am. Society Photobiology, Botanical Society Am., Sigma Xi. Research in metabolism of protista (algae), sulfate reduction by plants and microorganisms, pathway of biosynthesis of chlorophylls, carotenoids and anthocyanins, chloroplast and mitochondrial devel., replication and function particularly in Euglena. Home: 37 Harland Road Waltham Massachusetts 02154 Office: Institute for Photobiology of Cells and Organelles Brandeis University Waltham Massachusetts 02254

SCHIRRA, WALTER MARTY, JR., business consultant, former astronaut; born Hackensack, New Jersey, March 12, 1923; son of Walter Marty and Florence (Leach) S.; married Josephine Cook Fraser, February 23, 1946; children: Walter Marty III,

Suzanne Karen. Student, Newark College Engineering, 1940-42; Bachelor of Science, United States Naval Academy, 1945; Doctor Astronautics (honorary), Lafayette College, University Southern California, New Jersey Institute Tech. Commissioned ensign United States Navy, 1945, advanced through grades to captain; 1965; designated naval aviator 1948; service aboard battle cruiser Alaska, 1945-46; service with 7th Fleet, 1946; assigned Fighter Squadron 71, 1948-51; exchange pilot 154th United States Air Force Fighter Bomber Squadron, 1951; engaged in devel. Sidewinder missile China Lake, California, 1952-54; project pilot F7U-3 Cutlass; also instructor pilot F7U-3 Cutlass and FJ3 Fury, 1954-56; operations officer Fighter Squadron 124, United States Ship Lexington, 1956-57; assigned Naval Air Safety Officer School, 1957, Naval Air Test Center, 1958-59; engaged in suitability devel. work F4H, 1958-59; joined Project Mercury, man-in-space, National Aeronautics and Space Administration, 1959; pilot spacecraft Sigma 7 in 6 orbital flights, October 1962; in charge operations and training Astronaut Office, 1964-69; command pilot Gemini 6 which made rendezvous with target, Gemini 7, December 1965; commander 11 day flight Apollo 7, 1968; retired 1969; president Regency Investors, Incorporated, Denver, 1969-70; chairman, chief executive officer ECCO Corp., Englewood, Colorado, 1970-73; chairman Sernco, Incorporated, 1973-74; with Johns-Manville Corp., Denver, 1974-77; vice president devel. Goodwin Companies, Incorporated, Littleton, Colorado, 1978-79; independent consultant 1979-80; director Kimberly Clark, Finalco, Net Air International.

Decorated Distinguished Flying Cross(3), Air medal (2), Navy Distinguished Service Medal; recipient Distinguished Service medal (2), also; Exceptional Service medal National Aeronautics and Space Administration. Fellow Am. Astronautical Society, Society Experimental Test Pilots. Home and Office: Post Office Box 73 Rancho Santa Fe California 92067

SCHMIDT-NIELSEN, BODIL MIMI (MRS. ROGER G. CHAGNON), physiologist; born Copenhagen, Denmark, November 3, 1918; came to United States, 1946, naturalized, 1952; daughter of August and Marie (Jorgensen) Krogh; married Knut Schmidt-Nielsen, September 20, 1939 (divorced February 1966); children: Astrid, Bent, Bodil; married Roger G. Chagnon, October 1968. Doctor of Dental Surgery, University Copenhagen, 1941, Doctor.Odont., 1946, Doctor of Philosophy, 1955; Doctor of Science (honorary), Bates College, 1983. Faculty Duke, Durham, North Carolina, 1952-64; professor biology Case Western Reserve University, Cleveland, 1964-71, chairman department; 1970-71, adj. professor; 1971-74; trustee Mount Desert Island Biological Laboratory, Maine, research scientist; 1971-86, executive committee; 1978-85, vice president; 1979-81, president; 1981-85; adj. professor Brown University, Providence, 1972-78, department physiology University Florida, Gainesville, 1987—; Member training grant committee NIGMS, 1967-71. Editor: Urea and the Kidney, 1970; asso. editor: Am. Journal Physiology: Regulatory, Integrative and Comparative Physiology, 1978-81. Trustee College of Atlantic, Bar Harbor, Maine, 1972—. Recipient

Career award National Institutes of Health, 1962; John Simon Guggenheim Memorial fellow, 1952-53; Bowditch lecturer, 1958; Jacobaeus lecturer, 1974. Fellow New York Acad. Sciences, American Association for the Advancement of Science (del. council 1977-79), Am. Acad. Arts and Sciences; member Am. Physiological Society (council 1971-77, president 1975-76, Ray G. Daggs award 1989), Society Experimental Biology and Medicine (council 1969-71). Research, publs. on biochemistry of saliva, water metabolism of desert animals, comparative kidney physiology, comparative physiology of excretory organs. Home: 3984 Northwest 23 Circle Gainesville Florida 32605 also: Salsbury Cove Maine 04672 Office: U Fla Department Physiology Gainesville Florida 32605

SCHMIDT-NIELSEN, KNUT, physiologist, educator; born Norway, September 24, 1915; came to United States, 1946, naturalized, 1952; son of Sigval and Signe Torborg (Sturzen-Becker) Schmidt-N. Mag. Scient., University Copenhagen, 1941, Doctor Phil., 1946; Doctor Medical (honorary), University Lund, Sweden, 1985. Research fellow Carlsberg Laboratories, Copenhagen, 1941-44, Carlsberg Laboratories (University Copenhagen), 1944-46; research associate zoology Swarthmore (Pennsylvania) College, 1946-48; docent University Oslo, Norway, 1947-49; research associate physiology Stanford, 1948-49; assistant professor College Medicine, University Cincinnati, 1949-52; professor physiology Duke, Durham, North Carolina, 1952—; James B. Duke professor physiology Duke, 1963—; Harvey Society lecturer 1962; Regents' lecturer University California at Davis, 1963; Brody Memorial lecturer University Missouri, 1962; Hans Gadow lecturer Cambridge (England) University, 1971; visiting Agassiz professor Harvard, 1972; member panel environmental biology National Science Foundation, 1957-61; member sci. adv. committee New England Regional Primate Center, 1962-66; member national adv. board physiological research laboratory Scripps Institution Oceanography, University California at San Diego, 1963-69, chairman, 1968-69; organizing committee 1st International Conference on Comparative Physiology, 1972-80; president International Union Physiol. Sciences, 1980-86, member United States national committee 1966-78, vice chairman United States national committee, 1969-78; member subcom. on environmental physiology United States national committee International Biological Programme, 1965-67; member committee on research utilization uncommon animals, div. biology and agriculture National Acad. Sciences, 1966-68; member animal resources adv. committee National Institutes of Health, 1968; member adv. board Bio-Med. Sciences, Incorporated, 1973-74; chief scientist Scripps Institution Amazon expedition, 1967. Author: Animal Physiology, 3d. edit, 1970, The Physiology of Desert Animals; Physiological Problems of Heat and Water, 1964, How Animals Work, 1972, Animal Physiology; Adaptation and Environment, 1975, 2d edition, 1979, 3d edition, 1983, Scaling: Why is Animal Size so Important?, 1984; sect. editor: Am. Journal Physiology, 1961-64, 70-76; editor: Journal Applied Physiology, 1961-64, 70-76; editorial board: Journal Cellular and Comparative Physiology, 1961-66,

Physiological Zoology, 1959-70, Am. Journal Physiology, 1971-76, Journal Applied Physiology, 1971-76, Journal Experimental Biology, 1975-79, 83-86; cons. editor: Annals of Arid Zone, 1962—; hon. editorial adv. board: Comparative Biochemistry and Physiology, 1962-63; chief editor: News in Physiol Sciss., 1985-88; contributor articles to sci. publications. Guggenheim fellow, 1953-54; grantee Office Naval Research, 1952-54, 58-61; grantee United Nations Educational Scientific and Cultural Organization, 1953-54; grantee Office Q.M. General, 1953-54; grantee Office Surgeon General, 1953-54; grantee National Institutes of Health, 1955-86; grantee National Science Foundation, 1957-61, 59-60, 60-61, 61-63; recipient Research Career award USPHS, 1964-85. Fellow New York Acad. Sci., American Association for the Advancement of Science, Am. Acad. Arts and Sciences; member National Acad. Sciences, North Carolina Acad. Sci. (Poteat award 1957), Am. Physiological Society, Am. Society Zoologists (chairman division comparative physiology 1964), Society Experimental Biology, Harvey Society (hon.), Royal Danish Acad., Académie des Sciences (France) (foreign associate), Royal Norwegian Society Arts and Sci., Norwegian Acad. Sciences, Physiological Society London (associate), Royal Society London (foreign). Office: Department Zoology Duke University Durham North Carolina 27706

SCHMITT, HARRISON HAGAN, former U.S. senator, geologist, astronaut, consultant; born Santa Rita, New Mexico, July 3, 1935; son of Harrison A. and Ethel (Hagan) S. Bachelor of Arts, California Institute Tech., 1957; postgraduate (Fulbright fellow), University Oslo, 1957-58; Doctor of Philosophy (NSF fellow), Harvard University, 1964; honorary degree, Franklin and Marshall College, Colo School Mines, Rensselaer Poly Institute. Geologist U.S Geological Survey, 1964-65; astronaut National Aeronautics and Space Administration, from 1965; lunar module pilot Apollo 17, December 1972, special assistant to administrator; 1974; assistant administrator Apollo 17 (Office Energy Programs), 1974; member United States Senate from New Mexico, 1977-83; consultant 1983—; member President's Foreign Intelligence Adv. Board, 1984-85, Army Sci. Board, 1985—; director Nord Resources, Sunwest Fin. Services, Orbital Sciences Corp. Board of directors Lovelace Medical Foundation. Recipient MSC Superior Achievement award, 1970, Distinguished Service medal National Aeronautics and Space Administration, 1973. Member American Institute of Aeronautics and Astronautics, Geological Society Am., American Association for the Advancement of Science, Am. Geophysical Union, Am. Association Petroleum Geologists. Home: Post Office Box 14338 Albuquerque New Mexico 87191

SCHNEIDER, DAVID MURRAY, educator, anthropologist; born New York City, November 11, 1918. Bachelor of Science, Cornell University, 1940, Master of Arts, 1941; Doctor of Philosophy, Harvard, 1949. Field trips to Yap Island, Trust Terrace Pacific, 1947-48, Mescalero Apache, New Mexico, 1955-58; lecturer London School Economics, 1949-51; assistant professor Harvard, 1951-55; professor anthropology University California at Berkeley, 1956-60;

professor anthropology University Chicago, 1960—, William B. Ogden distinguished service professor anthropology, emeritus, chairman department anthropology; 1963-66; now emeritus professor anthropology University Calif.-Santa Cruz; Cons. behavioral sci. study section National Institutes of Health, 1960-64; member committee personnel Social Sci. Research Council, 1960-62, board of directors, 1971-73; representative Am. Anthropological Association to div. anthropological and psychological NRC-Nat. Acad. Sciences, 1962-64; director Foundations Fund Research Psychiatry, 1963-66; Fellow Center Advanced Study in Behavioral Sciences, 1955-56, 66-67. Author: (with Homans) Marriage, Authority and Final Causes, 1955, (with Gough) Matrilineal Kinship, 1961, American Kinship, 1968, (with Smith) Class Differences and Sex Role in American Kinship and Family Structure, 1973, (with Cottrell) The American Kin Universe, 1975, Critique of the Study of Kinship, 1984. Fellow Am. Anthropology Association (executive board 1968-70), Am. Acad. Arts and Sciences, Royal Anthropological Institute Great Britain (hon.); member Association Social Anthropologists Commonwealth, Society for Cultural Anthropology (president 1984-88).

SCHNEIDERMAN, HOWARD ALLEN, educator, zoologist; born New York City, February 9, 1927; son of Louis and Anna (Center) S.; married Audrey MacLeod, September 16, 1951; children: Anne Mercedes, John Howard. Bachelor of Arts, Swarthmore College, 1948; Master of Arts in Zoology, Harvard University, 1949, Doctor of Philosophy in Physiology, 1952; Doctor of Science (honorary), La Salle College, 1975, Swarthmore College, 1982. Atomic Energy Commission predoctoral fellow Harvard University, 1949-52, University research fellow; 1952-53; assistant professor zoology, then associate professor Cornell University, 1953-61; professor biology, chairman department Case Western Reserve University, Cleveland, 1961-66; Jared Potter Kirtland Distinguished professor biology Case Western Reserve University, 1966-69, co-director devel. biology center; 1961-69; professor biological sci., dean school, director Center Pathobiology, University California, Irvine, 1969-79; chairman department developmental and cell biology Center Pathobiology, University California, 1969-75; senior vice president Research & Development, Monsanto Company, St. Louis, 1979—; member executive management committee Monsanto Company, 1983—; consultant General Medical Sci. Institute, National Institute Child Health and Devel., National Institutes of Health, 1961-79; instructor invertebrate zoology Marine Biological Laboratory, Woods Hole, Massachusetts, 1956-58, trustee, member executive committee, 1966-72; special research, devel., genetics, insect hormones, and insect physiology; board of directors G. D. Searle and Company. Editorial board: Results and Problems of Cell Differentiation; contributor over 200 articles to professional journals. Adv. commissioner Marshall Scholarship Commission, 1973-77, chairman, 1976-77; trustee Missouri Botanical Garden, 1981—. Served with United States Naval Reserve, 1945-46. National Science Foundation sr. fellow Cambridge (England) University, 1959-60. Fellow American Association for the Advancement of

Science, New York Acad. Sciences; member National Acad. Sci. (assembly life scis. 1975—), Am. Acad. Arts and Sciences, Society Experimental Biology (England), Am. Society Zoologists, Entomological Society Am., Lepidopterist Society, Corp. Marine Biol Lab., Am. Society Naturalists, Society Developmental Biology (president 1965-66), International Society Developmental Biology (director 1981—), Genetics Society Am., American Association of University Women, Am. Institute Biological Sciences, Society Chemical Industry, Am. Society Cell Biology, Japanese Society Developmental Biology, National Sci. Board, Phi Beta Kappa, Sigma Xi. Office: Monsanto Company Department Research and Devel 800 N Linderberg Boulevard Saint Louis Missouri 63167

SCHOTTENFELD, DAVID, epidemiologist, educator; born New York City, March 25, 1931; married Rosalie C. Schaeffer; children: Jacqueline, Stephen. Bachelor of Arts, Hamilton College, 1952; Doctor of Medicine, Cornell University, 1956; Master of Science in Pub. Health, Harvard University, 1963. Diplomate Am. Board Internal Medicine, Am. Board Preventive Medicine. Intern in internal medicine Duke University, Durham, North Carolina, 1956-57; resident in internal medicine Memorial Sloan-Kettering Cancer Center, Cornell University Medical College, New York City, 1957-59; Craver fellow medical oncology Memorial Sloan-Kettering Cancer Center, 1961-62; clinical instructor department pub. health Cornell University, New York City, 1963-67, assistant professor department pub. health; 1965-70, associate professor department pub. health; 1970-73, professor depart-

ment pub. health; 1973-86; John G. Searle professor, chairman epidemiology school pub. health University Michigan, Ann Arbor, 1986—, professor internal medicine; 1986—; visiting professor epidemiology University Minnesota, Minneapolis, 1968, 71, 74, 82, 86; W.G. Cosbie lecturer Can. Oncology Society, 1987. Editor: Cancer Epidemiology and Prevention, 1982; author 7 books; contributor over 120 articles to professional journals. Served with United States Public Health Service, 1959-61. Recipient Acad. Career award in Preventive Oncology, National Cancer Institute, 1980-85. Fellow American Association for the Advancement of Science, Am. College Physicians, Am. College Preventive Medicine, Am. College Epidemiology. Office: U of Michigan School Pub Health Department Epidemiology 109 Observatory St Ann Arbor Michigan 48109-2029

SCHRIEFFER, JOHN ROBERT, research institute administrator; born Oak Park, Illinois, May 31, 1931; son of John Henry and Louise (Anderson) S.; married Anne Grete Thomsen, December 30, 1960; children: Anne Bolette, Paul Karsten, Anne Regina. Bachelor of Science, Massachusetts Institute Tech., 1953; Master of Science, University Illinois, 1954, Doctor of Philosophy, 1957, Doctor of Science, 1974; Doctor of Science (honorary), Tech. University, Munich, Germany, 1968, University Geneva, 1968, University Pennsylvania, 1973, University Cincinnati, 1977, University Tel Aviv, 1987. National Science Foundation postdoctoral fellow University Birmingham, England, also; Niels Bohr Institute, Copenhagen, 1957-58;

assistant professor University Chicago, 1958-59; assistant professor, then associate professor University Illinois, 1959-62; professor University Pennsylvania, Philadelphia, 1962-79; Mary Amanda Wood professor physics University Pennsylvania, 1964-79; Andrew D. White professor at large Cornell University, 1969-75; professor University California, Santa Barbara, 1980—, Chancellor's professor; 1984—, director Institute for Theoretical Physics; 1984—; visiting professor Niels Bohr Institute, summer 1960, 67, University Geneva, fall 1963, 67; visiting professor Stanford University, 1978. Author: Theory of Superconductivity, 1964. Guggenheim fellow Copenhagen, 1967; Recipient Comstock prize National Acad. Sci.; Nobel Prize for Physics, 1972; John Ericsson medal Am. Society Swedish Engrs., 1976; Alumni Achievement award University Illinois, 1979; recipient National Medal of Sci., 1984; Exxon faculty fellow, 1979—. Fellow Am. Physical Society (Oliver E. Buckley solid state physics prize 1968), Exxon Faculty, Los Alamos National Lab.; member National Acad. Sci., Am. Acad. Arts & Sciences, Am. Philosophical Society (National Medal Sci. 1985), Royal Danish Acad. Sciences and Letters, Acad. Sci. Union of the Soviet Socialist Republics. Office: U California Institute Theoretical Physics Santa Barbara California 93106

SCHRIESHEIM, ALAN, research administrator; born New York City, March 8, 1930; son of Morton and Frances (Greenberg) S.; married Beatrice D. Brand, June 28, 1953; children: Laura Lynn, Robert Alan. Bachelor of Science in Chemistry, Polytechnic Institute Brooklyn, 1951; Doctor of Philosophy in Physical Organic Chemistry, Pennsylvania State University, 1954. Chemist National Bureau Standards, 1954-56; with Exxon Research & Engineering Company, 1956-83, director corp. research; 1975-79; general manager Exxon engineering, 1979-83; senior deputy laboratory director Argonne National Laboratory, 1983-84, laboratory director; 1984—; Karcher lecturer University Oklahoma, 1977; Hurd lecturer Northwestern University, 1980; Rosensteil lecturer Brandeis University, 1982; Welch Foundation lecturer, 1987; co-chairman board on chemical sciences and tech. National Research Council, 1980-85; member committee to define future role of chemistry, 1983-84; visiting committee chemistry department Massachusetts Institute of Technology, 1978-85; member adv. committee mechanical engineering and aerospace department Princeton (New Jersey) University, 1983-87; member Pure and Applied Chemistry Committee; del. to People's Republic of China, 1978; member United States national committee International Union Pure and Applied Chemistry, 1982-85; member adv. committee process research and devel. National Bureau Standards, 1979-83, member board assessment of programs, 1983-86; member magnetic fusion adv. committee Department Energy, 1983-86; member adv. committee Div. Physical Sciences University Chicago; member DOE Energy Research Adv. Board, 1983-85; member Congressional Adv. Committee on Sci. and Tech., 1985—; member executive committee Gov.'s Sci. Adv. Committee, Illinois, 1989; member committee on advanced fossil energy techs. National Research Council, 1983-85; member visiting committees

Stanford (California) University, University Utah, Texas Agricultural and Mechanical University, Lehigh University; board governors Argonne National Laboratory; member adv. committee on space systems and tech. National Aeronautics and Space Administration, 1987—; member nuclear engineering and engineering physics visiting committee University Wisconsin, Madison; member Council of Great Lakes Governors Regional Economic Devel. Commission, 1987—, rev. board Compact Ignition Tokamak Princeton University, 1988-89; advisor Sears Investment Management Company, 1988-89; board of directors Petroleum Research Fund, ARCH Devel. Corp., HEICO, Valley Industrial Association, Council on Superconductivity for Am. Competitiveness. Board editors: Chemical Tech.; member editorial board Research and Devel., 1988, Superconductor Industry Magazine, 1988—. Member special visiting committee Field Mus. of Natural History, Chicago, 1987—; board of directors LaRabida Children's Hospital and Research Center, Children's Memorial Hospital, Children's Memorial Institute for Education and Research. Fellow New York Acad. Sciences; member Am. Chemical Society (recipient award petroleum chemistry 1969, chairman petroleum division, councilor), Am. Management Association (research and devel. council 1988—), National Conference Advancement Research, Am. Petroleum Institute (committee on refinery equipment), Am. Institute Chemical Engineers, Gas Research Institute (research coordination council), American Association for the Advancement of Science, Am. Nuclear Society, Rohm and Haas (board directors), Sigma Xi, Phi

Lambda Upsilon. Club: Cosmos (Washington); Chicago, Economic, Commercial (Chicago). Patentee in field. Home: 1440 N Lake Shore Dr Apartment 31AC Chicago Illinois 60610 Office: Argonne National Lab 9700 S Cass Avenue Argonne Illinois 60439

SCHUBEL, JERRY ROBERT, marine science educator, scientist, university dean and official; born Bad Axe, Michigan, January 26, 1936; son of Theodore Howard and Laura Alberta (Gobel) S.; married Margaret Ann Hostetler, June 14, 1958; children: Susan Elizabeth, Kathryn Ann. Bachelor of Science, Alma College, 1957; Master of Arts in Teaching, Harvard University, 1959; Doctor of Philosophy, Johns Hopkins University, 1968. Research associate Chesapeake Bay Institute, Johns Hopkins University, Baltimore, 1968-69, research scientist; 1969-74, adj. research professor, associate director; 1973-74; director Marine Sciences Research Center, State University of New York, Stony Brook, 1974-83, dean, leading professor; 1983—, acting vice provost for research and grad. studies; 1985-86, provost; 1986—, acting director Waste Management Institute; 1985-87. Author: The Living Chesapeake, 1981, (with H.A. Neal) Solid Waste Management and the Environment, 1987; senior editor Coastal Ocean Pollution Assessment News, 1981-86; co-editor in chief Estuaries, 1986—; contributor articles to professional journals. Alfred P. Sloan fellow, 1959. Member National Association State University and Land Grant Colls. (board directors marine division, chairman 1986—), Long Island Environmental Council, Long Island Marine Resources Council, Suffolk

County Recycling Commission, (chairman 1987—), Estuarine Research Federation (vice president 1982-83, president 1985-87), Sigma Xi, Phi Sigma Pi. Avocation: photography. Home: 4 Hiawatha Lane Setauket New York 11733 Office: State University of New York at Stony Brook Main Campus Office of the Provost Stony Brook New York 11794

SCHULTES, RICHARD EVANS, botanist, museum executive, educator; born Boston, January 12, 1915; son of Otto Richard and Maude Beatrice (Bagley) S.; married Dorothy Crawford McNeil, March 26, 1959; children: Richard Evans II, Neil Parker and Alexandra Ames (twins). Bachelor of Arts, Harvard University, 1937, Master of Arts, 1938, Doctor of Philosophy, 1941; Master.H. (honorary), Universidad Nacional de Colombia, Bogotá, 1953. Plant explorer, National Research Council fellow Harvard Botanical Mus., Cambridge, Massachusetts, 1941-42; research associate Harvard Botanical Mus., 1942-53; curator Orchid Herbarium of Oakes Ames, 1953-58, curator economic botany; 1958-85, executive director; 1967-70, director; 1970-85; Guggenheim Foundation fellow, collaborator United States Department Agriculture, Amazon of Colombia, 1942-43; plant explorer in South Am. Bureau Plant Industry, 1944-54; professor biology Harvard University, 1970-72, Paul C. Mangelsdorf professor natural sciences; 1973-81, Edward C. Jeffrey professor biology; 1981-85, emeritus professor; 1985—; adj. professor pharmacognosy University Illinois, Chicago, 1975—; Hubert Humphrey visiting professor Macalaster College, 1979; field agent Rubber Devel. Corp. of United States Government, in South America, 1943-44; collaborator Instituto Argronômico Norte, Belem, Brazil, 1948-50; hon. professor Universidad Nacional de Colombia, 1953—, professor economic botany, 1963; botanical consultant Smith, Kline & French Company, Philadelphia, 1957-67; member National Institutes of Health Adv. Panel, 1964; member selection committee for Latin Am. Guggenheim Foundation, 1964-85; chairman on-site visit University Hawaii Natural Products Grant National Institutes of Health, 1966, 67; Laura L. Barnes Annual lecturer Morris Arboretum, Philadelphia, 1969; Koch lecturer Rho Chi Society, Pittsburgh, 1971, Chicago, 1974; visiting professor economic botany, plants in relation to man's progress Jardín Botánico, Medellín, Colombia, 1973; Cecil and Ida H. Green Visiting Lecturer University British Columbia, Vancouver, Can., 1974; member Hugh Ludlow Library, San Francisco, 1974—. Author: (with P. A. Vestal) Economic Botany of the Kiowa Indians, 1941, Native Orchids of Trinidad and Tobago, 1960, (with A. F. Hill) Plants and Human Affairs, 1960, rev. edition, 1968, (with A. S. Pease) Generic Names of Orchids—their Origin and Meaning, 1963, (with A. Hofmann) The Botany and Chemistry of Hallucinogens, 1973, rev. edition, 1980, Plants of the Gods, 1979, Plant Hallucinogens, 1976, (with W.A. Davis) The Glass Flowers at Harvard, 1982; contributing author: En-cyclopedia Biol. Scis, 1961, Encyclopedia Brit, 1966, 83, Encyclopedia Biochemistry, 1967, McGraw-Hill Yearbook Science, Tech, 1971; author numerous Harvard Bot. Mus. leaflets.; Assistant editor: Chronica Botanica, 1947-52; editor: Bot. Mus. Leaflets, 1957-85, Econ.

Botany, 1962-79; member editorial board: Lloydia, 1965-76, Altered States of Consciousness, 1973—, Journal Psychedelic Drugs, 1974—; member adv. board: Horticulture, 1976-78, Journal Ethnopharmacology, 1978—; Contributor numerous articles to professional journals. Member governing board Amazonas 2000, Bogotá; associate in ethnobotany Museo del Oro, Bogota, 1974—; chairman NRC panels, 1974, 75; member NRC Workshops on Natural Products, Sri Lanka, 1975, participant numerous sems., congresses, meetings. Decorated Orden de la Victoria Regia in recognition of work in Amazon Colombian Government, 1969, Cruz de Boyacá Government of Colombia, 1983, Gold medal for conservation Duke of Edinburgh, 1984. Fellow Am. Acad. Arts, Sciences, Am. College Neuropsychopharmacology; member National Acad. Sci., Linnean Society, Am. Acad. Arts & Sciences, Academia Colombiana de Ciencias Exactas, Fisico-Quimicas y Naturales, Instituto Ecuatoriano de Ciencias Naturales, Sociedad Cientifica Antonio Alzate (Mexico), Argentine Acad. Sciences, Am. Orchid Society (life hon.), Pan Am. Society New England (governor), Asociación de Amigos de Jardines Botánicos (life), Society Econ. Botany (organizer annual meeting 1961, Distinguished Botanist of Year award 1979), New England Botanical Club (president 1954-60), International Association Plant Taxonomy, Am. Society Pharmacognosy, Phytochem. Society North America, Socieded Colombiana de Orquideologia, Association Tropical Biology, Sociedad Cubana de Botánica, Sigma Xi (president Harvard chapter 1971-72), Phi Beta Kappa (Harvard chapter), Beta Nu chapter Phi Sigma (first hon.). Unitarian (vestryman Kings Chapel 1974-76, 82-85). Home: 78 Larchmont Road Melrose Massachusetts 02176 Office: Bot Museum Harvard U Cambridge Massachusetts 02138

SCHULTZ, ALBERT BARRY, engineering educator; born Philadelphia, October 10, 1933; son of George D. and Belle (Seidman) S.; married Susan Resnikov, August 25, 1955; children—Carl, Adam, Robin. Bachelor of Science, University Rochester, 1955; Master.Engineering, Yale University, 1959, Doctor of Philosophy, 1962. Assistant professor University Del., Newark, 1962-65; assistant professor University Illinois, Chicago, 1965-66, associate professor; 1966-71, professor; 1971-83; Vennema professor University Michigan, Ann Arbor, 1983—. Contributor numerous articles to professional journals. Served to lieutenant United States Navy, 1955-58. Research Career awardee National Institutes of Health, 1975-80; Javits neurosci. investigator award National Institutes of Health, 1985-92. Member International Society for Study of Lumbar Spine (president 1981-82), American Society of Mechanical Engineers (chairman bioengring. division 1981-82), Am. Society of Biomechanics (president 1982-83), United States National Committee on Biomechanics (chairman 1982-85), Phi Beta Kappa. Office: University Michigan 3112 GG Brown Lab Ann Arbor Michigan 48109

SCHWAN, HERMAN PAUL, educator, research scientist; born Aachen, Germany, August 7, 1915; came to United States, 1947, naturalized, 1952; son of Wilhelm and Meta (Pattberg) S.; married Anne

Marie DelBorello, June 15, 1949; children: Barbara, Margaret, Steven, Carol, Cathryn. Student, University Goettingen, 1934-37; Doctor of Philosophy, University Frankfurt, 1940; Doctor habil. in physics and biophysics, 1946; Doctor of Science (honorary), University Pennsylvania, 1986. Research scientist, professor Kaiser Wilhelm Institute Biophysics, 1937-47, assistant director; 1945-47; research sci. United States Navy, 1947-50; professor electrical engineering, professor electrical engineering in physical medicine, associate professor physical medicine University Pennsylvania, Philadelphia, 1950—, Alfred F. Moore professor; 1983—; director electromed. div. University Pennsylvania, 1952-73, chairman biomed. engineering; 1961-73, program director biomed. engineer training program; 1960-77; visiting professor University Calif.-Berkeley, 1956, University Frankfurt Federal Republic Germany, 1962, University Würzburg, Federal Republic Germany, 1986-87; lecturer Johns Hopkins University, 1962-67; W.W. Clyde visiting professor University Utah, Salt Lake City, 1980; 10th Lauristan Taylor lecturer National Council Radiation, 1986; Foreign sci. member Max Planck Society Adv. Research, Germany, 1962—; consultant National Institutes of Health, 1962—; chairman national and international meetings biomed. engineering and biophysics, 1959, 61, 65; member national adv. council environmental health Department of Health, Education and Welfare, 1969-71; member National Acad. Scis.-NRC committees, 1968-77, National Acad. Engineering, 1975—. Co-author: Advances in Medical and Biological Physics, 1957, Therapeutic Heat, 1958, Physical Techniques in Medicine and Biology, 1963; editor: Biol. Engring, 1969; co-editor: Interactions Between Electromagnetic Fields and Cells, 1985; member editorial board: Environ. Biophysics; contributor articles to professional journals. Recipient Citizenship award Philadelphia, 1952, 1st prize American Institute of Electrical Engineers, 1953, Achievement award Philadelphia Institute Electrical Engineering and Electronics, 1963, Rajewsky prize for biophysics, 1974, U.S. sr. scientist award Alexander von Humboldt Foundation, 1980-81, Biomed. Engineering Education award Am. Society Engineering Education, 1983, d'Arsonval award Bioelectromagnetics Society, 1985. Fellow Institute of Electrical and Electronics Engineers (Morlock award 1967, Edison medal 1983, Centennial award 1984, chairman and vice chairman national professional group biomed. engineering 1955, 62-68), American Association for the Advancement of Science; member Am. Standards Association (chairman committee 1961-64), Biophys. Society (publicity committee, council, constrn. committee), Society for Cryobiology, International Federation Medical, and Biological Engineering, Biomed. Engineering Society (director), Sigma Xi, Eta Kappa Nu. Home: 99 Kynlyn Road Radnor Pennsylvania 19087 also: 162 59th St Avalon New Jersey 08202 Office: Department Bioengring D2 U Pennsylvania Philadelphia Pennsylvania 19104

SCHWARTZ, LYLE H., government official, materials scientist; born Chicago, August 2, 1936; son of Joseph K. Schwartz and Helen (Shefsky) Bernards; married Tanis Paula Haas, March 27, 1957 (divorced 1971); children—Ara, Justin; married

Celesta Sue Jurkovich, September I, 1973. Bachelor of Science in Science Engineering, Northwestern University, 1959, Doctor of Philosophy in Materials Science, 1964. Professor materials sci. Northwestern University, Evanston, Illinois, 1964-84, director Materials Research Center; 1979-84; director Institute for Materials Scl. and Engineering, National Bureau Standards, Department Commerce, Gaithersburg, Maryland, 1984—; consultant Argonne National Laboratories, Illinois, 1965-79; visiting scientist Bell Telephone Laboratories, Murray Hill, New Jersey, 1971-73. Author: (with J.B. Cohen) Diffraction From Materials, 1977, 2d edition, 1987; also numerous articles and papers. National Science Foundation fellow, 1962-63. Fellow Am. Society for Metals; member American Institute of Mining, Metallurgy and Petroleum Engineers, Am. Physical Society, Am. Crystallography Association, American Association for the Advancement of Science, Sigma Xi. Office: National Bur Standards Building 223 Room B310 Gaithersburg Maryland 20899

SCHWARTZ, MELVIN, business executive, physics educator; born New York City, November 2, 1932; son of Harry and Hannah (Shulman) S.; married Marilyn Fenster, November 25, 1953; children: David N., Diane R., Betty Lynn. Bachelor of Arts, Columbia University, 1953, Doctor of Philosophy, 1958. Associate physicist Brookhaven National Laboratory, 1956-58; member faculty Columbia University, New York City, 1958-66; professor physics Columbia University, 1963-66, Stanford University, California, 1966-83; consultant professor Stanford University, 1983—; chairman board of directors Digital Pathways, In-

corporated, Mountain View, California. Board governors Weizmann Institute Sci. Guggenheim fellow, 1968; recipient Nobel prize in physics, 1988. Fellow Am. Physical Society (Hughes award 1964); member National Acad. Sciences. Discoverer muon neutrino, 1962. Home: 770 Funston Avenue San Francisco California 94118 Office: Digital Pathways Incorporated 201 Ravendale Dr Mountain View California 94043

SCHWARZ, RICHARD HOWARD, obstetrician, gynecologist, educator; born Easton, Pennsylvania, January 10, 1931; son of Howard Eugene and Blanche Elizabeth (Smith) S.; married Patricia Marie Lewis, March 11, 1978; children by previous marriage—Martha L., Nancy Schwarz Tedesco, Paul H., Mary Katherine Schwarz Murray. Doctor of Medicine, Jefferson Medical College, 1955; Master of Arts (honorary), University Pennsylvania, Philadelphia, 1971. Diplomate Am. Board Ob-Gyn. Intern, then resident Philadelphia General Hospital, 1955-59; professor University Pennsylvania, Philadelphia, 1963-78; professor, chairman Downstate Medical Center, Brooklyn, 1978—, dean, vice president acad. affairs; 1983-89, provost, vice president clinical affairs; 1988—. Author: Septic Abortion, 1968. Editor: Handbook of Obstetric Emergencies, 1984, member editorial board journal Ob-Gyn., Milwaukee, 1983-87; contributor articles to professional journals. Board of directors March of Dimes, New York City, 1985—. Served to captain United States Air Force, 1959-63. Member Am. College Obstetricians and Gynecologists (chairman district 2 1984-87, vice president 1989—), Am. Board Ob-Gyn (examiner 1977—). Republican.

Presbyterian. Office: State University of New York Health Sci Center at Brooklyn 450 Clarkson Avenue Brooklyn New York 11203

SCHWARZSCHILD, MARTIN, educator, astronomer; born Potsdam, Germany, May 31, 1912; came to United States, 1937, naturalized, 1942; son of Karl and Else (Rosenbach) S.; married Barbara Cherry, August 24, 1945. Doctor of Philosophy, University Goettingen, 1935; Doctor of Science (honorary), Swarthmore College, 1960, Columbia University, 1973. Research fellow Institute Astrophysics, Oslo (Norway) University, 1936-37, Harvard University Observatory, 1937-40; lecturer, later assistant professor Rutherfurd Observatory, Columbia University, 1940-47; professor Princeton University, 1947-50, Higgins professor astronomy; 1950-79. Author: Structure and Evolution of the Stars. Served to 1st lieutenant Army of the United States, 1942-45. Recipient Dannie Heineman prize Akademie der Wissenschaften zu Goettingen, Germany, 1967; Albert A. Michelson award Case Western Res. University, 1967; Newcomb Cleveland prize American Association for the Advancement of Science, 1957; Rittenhouse Silver medal, 1966; Prix Janssen Société astronomique de France, 1970; Medal from l'Assn. Pour le Developpement International de l'Observatoire de Nice. Fellow Am. Acad. Arts and Sciences; member International Astronomical Union (vice president 1964-70), Akademie der Naturforscher Leopoldina, Royal Astronomical Society (associate, Gold medal 1969, Eddington medal 1963), Royal Astronomical Society Can. (hon.), Am. Astronomical Society (president 1970-72), National Acad.

Sciences (Henry Draper medal 1961), Society Royale des Sciences de Liege (corr.), Royal Netherlands Acad. Sci. and Letters (foreign), Royal Danish Acad. Sci. and Letters (foreign), Norwegian Acad. Sci. and Letters, Astronomical Society Pacific (Bruce medal 1965), Am. Philosophical Society, Sigma Xi.

SCHWEICKART, RUSSELL L., government official, astronaut; born Neptune, New Jersey, October 25, 1935; son of George L. Schweickart; married Clare Grantham Whitfield (divorced); children: Vicki Louise, Russell and Randolph (twins), Elin Ashley, Diana Croom. Bachelor of Science in Aeronautical Engineering, Massachusetts Institute Tech., 1956, Master of Science in Aeros. and Astronautics, 1963. Former research scientist Massachusetts Institute Tech. Experimental Astronomy Laboratory; astronaut Johnson Manned Spacecraft Center, Houston, lunar module pilot (Apollo 9, 1969); director user affairs Office of Applications, National Aeronautics and Space Administration; sci. adv. to Governor Edmund G. Brown, Junior State of California, 1977-79; chairman California Energy Commission, 1979-83, commissioner; 1979-85; president Association Space Explorers, 1985—; consultant and lecturer in field. Served as pilot United States Air Force, 1956-60, 61; Captain Massachusetts Air National Guard. Recipient Distinguished Service medal National Aeronautics and Space Administration, 1970, Exceptional Service medal National Aeronautics and Space Administration, 1974, De La Vaulx medal FAI, 1970, Special Trustees award National Acad. TV Arts and Sciences, 1969. Fellow Am. Astronautical

Society; member Society Experimental Test Pilots, American Institute of Aeronautics and Astronautics, Sigma Xi. Club: Explorers. Office: Association Space Explorers 3278 Sacramento St San Francisco California 94115

SCHWINGER, JULIAN, physicist, educator; born New York City, February 12, 1918; son of Benjamin and Belle (Rosenfeld) S.; married Clarice Carrol, 1947. Bachelor of Arts, Columbia University, 1936, Doctor of Philosophy, 1939, Doctor of Science, 1966; Doctor of Science (honorary), Purdue University, 1961, Harvard University, 1962, Brandeis University, 1973, Gustavus Adolphus College, 1975; Doctor of Laws, City College of New York, 1972. National Research Council fellow 1939-40; research associate University Calif.-Berkeley, 1940-41; instructor, then assistant professor Purdue University, 1941-43; staff member Radiation Laboratory, Massachusetts Institute of Technology, 1943-46; staff Metallurgical Laboratory, University Chicago, 1943; associate professor Harvard University, 1945-47, professor; 1947-72, Higgins professor physics; 1966-72; professor physics University of California at Los Angeles, 1972-80, University professor; 1980—; member board sponsors Bulletin Atomic Sci.; sponsor Federation Am. Scientists; J.W. Gibbs hon. lecturer Am. Math. Society, 1960. Author: Particles and Sources, 1969, (with D. Saxon) Discontinuities in Wave Guides, 1968, Particles, Sources and Fields, 1970, Volume II, 1973, Volume III, 1989, Quantum Kinematics and Dynamics, 1970, Einstein's Legacy, 1985; editor: Quantum Electrodynamics, 1958. Recipient C. L. Mayer nature of light

award, 1949, university medal Columbia University, 1951, 1st Einstein prize award, 1951; National Medal of Sci. award for physics, 1964; co-recipient Nobel prize in Physics, 1965; recipient Humboldt award, 1981, Monie A. Fest Sigma Xi award, 1986, Castiglione di Sicilia award, 1986, Am. Acad. of Achievement award, 1987; Guggenheim fellow, 1970. Member American Association for the Advancement of Science, American Civil Liberties Union, National Acad. Sciences, Am. Acad. Arts and Sciences, Am. Physical Society, New York Acad. Sciences. Office: U California Department Physics Los Angeles California 90024

SCLATER, JOHN GEORGE, geophysics educator; born Edinburgh, Scotland, June 17, 1940; son of John George and Margaret Bennett (Glen) S.; married Paula Edwards, July, 1985; children: Iain Andrew, Stuart Michael. Bachelor of Science, Edinburgh University, 1962; Doctor of Philosophy, Cambridge (England) University, 1965. Research geophysicist Scripps Institute Oceanography, La Jolla, California, 1965-72; associate professor M.I.T., 1972-77, professor; 1977-83; director Joint Program Oceanography Woods Hole Oceanographic Institute, 1981-83; Shell Companies chair in geophysics University Tex.-Austin, 1983—; Sweeney lecturer Edinburgh University, 1976. Contributor articles to professional journals. Recipient Rosenstiel award oceanography, 1979, numerous award for publs. Fellow Geological Society Am., Royal Society London, Am. Geophysical Union (Bucher medal 1985); member National Acad. Sciences (member ocean studies board, 1985-88, chair 1988—). Roman Catholic. Home:

2405 Bowman Avenue Austin Texas 78705 Office: Institute For Geophysics 8701 Mopac Boulevard Austin Texas 78751

SCOTT, DAVID R., former astronaut, engineering executive; born San Antonio, June 6, 1932; son of Tom. W. S.; married Ann Lurton Ott; children: Tracy Lee, Douglas William. Student, University Michigan; Bachelor of Science, United States Military Academy, 1954; Master of Science in Aeros. and Astronautics, Massachusetts Institute of Technology, 1962; graduate, Air Force Experimental Test Pilot School, Edwards AFB, California, 1963; Doctor.Astronautical Science (honorary), University Michigan, 1971. Joined United States Air Force, 1954; advanced through grades to colonel; former director National Aeronautics and Space Administration Dryden Flight Research Center United States Air Force, Edwards, California; astronaut on flights of Gemini VIII, March 1966, (Apollo IX,), March 1969, Apollo XV, July 1971; now president Scott Science and Technology, Incorporated (engineering services), Palmdale, California. Decorated Distinguished Flying Cross, Distinguished Service Medal; recipient Distinguished Service medal, Exceptional Service medal National Aeronautics and Space Administration; United Nations Peace medal, 1971; Special Trustees award National Acad. TV Arts and Sciences, 1969; Robert J. Collier award, 1971. Fellow Am. Astronautical Society, American Institute of Aeronautics and Astronautics (Astronautics award 1966); member Society Experimental Test Pilots, Sigma Xi, Tau Beta Pi, Sigma Gamma Tau. Office: Scott Sci

and Tech Incorporated 39441 N 25th St E Palmdale California 93550

SEABORG, GLENN THEODORE, chemistry educator; born Ishpeming, Michigan, April 19, 1912; son of H. Theodore and Selma (Erickson) S.; married Helen Griggs, June 6, 1942; children: Peter, Lynne Seaborg Cobb, David, Stephen, John Eric, Dianne. Bachelor of Arts, University of California at Los Angeles, 1934; Doctor of Philosophy, University Calif.-Berkeley, 1937; numerous honorary degrees; Doctor of Laws, University Michigan, 1958, Rutgers University, 1970; Doctor of Science, Northwestern University, 1954, University Notre Dame, 1961, John Carroll University, Duquesne University, 1968, Ind. State University, 1969, University Utah, 1970, Rockford College, 1975, Kent State University, 1975; Doctor of Humane Letters, Northern Michigan College, 1962; DPS, George Washington University, 1962; DPA, University Puget Sound, 1963; Doctor of Letters, Lafayette College, 1966; Doctor of Engineering, Michigan Technological University, 1970; Doctor of Science, University Bucharest, 1971, Manhattan College, 1976; Doctor of Philosophy, University Pennsylvania, 1983. Research chemist University Calif.-Berkeley, 1937-39, instructor department chemistry; 1939-41, assistant professor; 1941-45, professor; 1945-71, university professor; 1971, leave of absence; 1942-46, 61-71, director nuclear chemical research; 1946-58, 72-75, associate director Lawrence Berkeley Laboratory; 1954-61, 71—; chancellor University (University Calif.-Berkeley), 1958-61, director Lawrence Hall of Sci.; 1982—; section chief metallurgical laboratory University Chicago, 1942-46;

chairman Atomic Energy Commission, 1961-71, general adv. committee; 1946-50; research nuclear chemistry and physics, transuranium elements.; chairman board Kevex Corp., Burlingame, California, 1972—; member President's Sci. Adv. Committee, 1959-61; member national sci. board National Science Foundation, 1960-61; member President's Committee on Equal Employment Opportunity, 1961-65, Federal Radiation Council, 1961-69, National Aeros. and Space Council, 1961-71, Federal Council Sci. and Tech., 1961-71, National Committee Am.'s Goals and Resources, 1962-64, President's Committee Manpower, 1964-69, National Council Marine Resources and Engineering Devel., 1966-71; chairman Chemical Education Material Study, 1959-74, National Programming Council for Pub. TV, 1970-72; director Educational TV and Radio Center, Ann Arbor, Michigan, 1958-64, 67-70; president 4th United Nations International Conference Peaceful Uses Atomic Energy, Geneva, 1971, also chairman United States del., 1964, 71; United States representative 5th-15th general conferences International Atomic Energy Agency, chairman, 1961-71; chairman United States del. to Union of the Soviet Socialist Republics for signing Memorandum Cooperation Field Utilization Atomic Energy Peaceful Purposes, 1963; member United States del. for signing Limited Test Ban Treaty, 1963; member commission on humanities Am. Council Learned Societies, 1962-65; member sci. adv. board Robert A. Welch Foundation, 1957—; member International Organization for Chemical Sciences in Devel., United Nations Educational, Scientific and Cultural Organization, 1980—, chairman, 1981; member National Commission on Excellence in Education, Department Education, 1981—. Author: (with Joseph J. Katz) Chemical Actinide Elements, 1954, 2d ed. (with Joseph J. Katz and Lester R. Morss) Volumes I & II, 1986, The Chemistry of the Actinide Elements, 1957, The Transuranium Elements, 1958, (with E.G. Valens) Elements of the Universe, 1958 (winner Thomas Alva Edison Foundation award), Man-Made Transuranium Elements, 1963, (with D.M. Wilkes) Education and the Atom, 1964, (with E.K. Hyde, I. Perlman) Nuclear Properties of the Heavy Elements, 1964, (with others) Oppenheimer, 1969, (with W.R. Corliss) Man and Atom, 1971, Nuclear Milestones, 1972, (with Ben Loeb) Kennedy, Khruschev and the Test Ban, 1981; editor: Transuranium Elements: Products of Modern Alchemy, 1978; asso. editor: Journal Chemical Physics, 1948-50; editorial adv. board: Journal Inorganic and Nuclear Chemistry, 1954-82, Industrial Research, Inc, 1967-75; adv. board: Chemical and Engring. News, 1957-59; editorial board: Journal Am. Chemical Soc, 1950-59, Encyclopedia Chemical Tech., 1975—, Revs. in Inorganic Chemistry, 1977—; member hon. editorial adv. board: International Encyclopedia Physical Chemistry and Chemical Physics, 1957—; member panel: Golden Picture Encyclopedia for Children, 1957-61; member cons. and adv. board: Funk and Wagnells Universal Standard Ency, 1957-61; member: Am. Heritage Dictionary Panel Usage Cons, 1964—; contributor articles to professional journals. Trustee Pacific Sci. Center Foundation, 1962-77; trustee Sci. Service, 1965—, president, 1966—; trustee Am.-Scandinavian Foundation, 1968—, Educational Broadcasting Corp., 1970-72; board of directors Swedish Council Am., 1976—, chairman board of directors, 1978-82; board of directors World Future Society, 1969—, California Council for Environmental and Economic Balance, 1974—; board governors Am. Swedish Historical Foundation, 1972—. Recipient John Ericsson Gold medal Am. Society Swedish Engrs., 1948; Nobel prize for Chemistry (with E.M. McMillan), 1951; John Scott award and medal City of Philadelphia, 1953; Perkin medal Am. sect. Society Chemical Industry, 1957; U.S. Atomic Energy Commission Enrico Fermi award, 1959; Joseph Priestley Memorial award Dickinson College, 1960; Sci. and Engineering award Federation Engineering Socs., Drexel Institute Tech., Philadelphia, 1962; named Swedish Am. of Year, Vasa Order of Am., 1962; Franklin medal Franklin Institute, 1963; 1st Spirit of St. Louis award, 1964; Leif Erikson Foundation award, 1964; Washington award Western Society Engrs., 1965; Arches of Sci. award Pacific Sci. Center, 1968; International Platform Association award, 1969; Prometheus award National Electrical Mfrs. Association, 1969; Nuclear Pioneer award Society Nuclear Medicine, 1971; Oliver Townsend award Atomic Indsl. Forum, 1971; Distinguished Honor award U.S. Department State, 1971; Golden Plate award Am. Acad. Achievement, 1972; John R. Kuebler award Alpha Chi Sigma, 1978; Founders medal Hebrew University Jerusalem, 1981; Henry DeWolf-Smyth award Am. Nuclear Society, 1982, Great Swedish Heritage award, 1984, Ellis Island Medal of Honor, 1986, Vannevar Bush Award, National Sci. Board, 1988; decorated officier Legion of Honor France; Daniel Webster medal, 1976. Fellow Am. Physical Society, Am. Institute Chemists (Pioneer award 1968, Gold medal award 1973), Chemical Society London (hon.), Royal Society Edinburgh (hon.), Am. Nuclear Society, California, New York, Washington acads. scis., American Association for the Advancement of Science (president 1972, chairman board 1973), Royal Society Arts (England); member Am. Chemical Society (award in pure chemistry 1947, William H. Nichols medal New York section 1948, Charles L. Parsons award 1964, Gibbs medal chgo. section 1966, Madison Marshall award Northern Alabama section 1972, Priestley medal 1979, president 1976), Am. Philosophical Society, Royal Swedish Acad. Engineering Sciences (adv. council 1980), Am. National, Argentine National, Bavarian, Polish, Royal Swedish, Union of the Soviet Socialist Republics acads. scis., Royal Acad. Exact, Physical and Natural Sciences Spain (acad. foreign corr.), Society Nuclear Medicine (hon.), World Association World Federalists (vice president 1980), Federation Am. Scientists (board sponsors 1980), Deutsche Akademie der Naturforscher Leopoldina (East Germany), National Acad. Pub. Administration, International Platform Association (president 1981—), Am. Hiking Society (director 1979—, vice president 1980), Phi Beta Kappa, Sigma Xi, Pi Mu Epsilon, Alpha Chi Sigma (John R. Kuebler award 1978), Phi Lambda Upsilon (hon.); foreign member Royal Society London, Chemical Society Japan, Serbian Acad. Sci. and Arts. Clubs: Bohemian (San Francisco); Chemists (New York City); Cosmos (Washington), University (Washington); Faculty

(Berkeley). Co-discoverer elements 94-102, and 106: plutonium, 1940, americium, 1944-45, curium, 1944, berkelium, 1949, californium, 1950, einsteinium, 1952, fermium, 1953, mendelevium, 1955, nobelium, 1958, element 106, 1974; co-discoverer nuclear energy isotopes Pu-239, U-233, Np-237, other isotopes including I-131, Fe-59, Te-99m, Co-60; originator actinide concept for placing heaviest elements in periodic system. Office: U California Lawrence Berkeley Lab Berkeley California 94720

SEAGRAVE, RICHARD C., chemical engineering educator; born Westerly, Rhode Island, December 31, 1935; married; 1 child. Bachelor of Science, University Rhode Island, 1957; Master of Science, Iowa State University, 1959, Doctor of Philosophy in Chemical Engineering, 1961. Assistant professor chemical engineering University Connecticut, 1961-62; research fellow California Institute Tech., Pasadena, 1962-63, assistant professor; 1963-66; associate professor engineering Iowa State University, Ames, 1966-71, professor chemical engineering; 1971—, Anson Marston Distinguished professor engineering, department chairman. Member Am. Institute Chemical Engineers. Office: Iowa State U Department Chem Engring Ames Iowa 50010

SEAMANS, ROBERT CHANNING, JR., astronautical engineering educator; born Salem, Massachusetts, October 30, 1918; son of Robert Channing and Pauline (Bosson) S.; married Eugenia Merrill, June 13, 1942; children: Katherine (Mrs. Louis Padulo), Robert Channing III, Joseph, May (Seamans Baldwin), Daniel M. Bachelor of Science,

Harvard University, 1939; Master of Science, Massachusetts Institute Tech., 1942, Doctor of Science, 1951; graduate exec. program business administration, Columbia University, 1959; Doctor of Science, Rollins College, 1962, New York University, 1967; Doctor of Engineering, Norwich Academy, 1971, Notre Dame University, 1974, Rensselaer Polytechnic Institute, 1974, University Wyoming, 1975, George Washington University, 1975, Lehigh University, 1976, Thomas College, 1980, Curry College, 1982. Successively instructor department aeronautical engineering, staff engineer instrumentation laboratory, assistant professor, project leader instrumentation laboratory, associate professor Massachusetts Institute Tech., 1941-55; chief engineer Project Meteor, 1950-53, director flight control laboratory; 1953-55; manager airborne systems laboratory, chief systems engineer airborne systems department Radio Corporation of America, 1955-58, chief engineer missile electronics and controls div.; 1958-60; associate administrator National Aeronautics and Space Administration, 1960-65, deputy administrator; 1965-68, consultant; 1968-69; visiting professor Massachusetts Institute of Technology, 1968, Hunsaker professor; 1968-69; secretary air force 1969-73; president National Acad. Engineering, 1973-74; administrator Energy Research and Development Administration, Washington, 1974-77; Henry R. Luce professor environment and pub. policy Massachusetts Institute of Technology, 1977-84, senior lecturer department aeros. and astronautics; 1984—, dean School Engineering; 1978-81; member sci. adv. board United States Air Force,

1957-62, associate adviser, 1963-67. Board overseers Harvard University, 1968-74; trustee Mus. of Sci., Boston, Sea Education Association, National Geog. Society, Carnegie Institute, Washington, Putnam Funds; trustee Woods Hole Oceanographic Instn. Recipient Naval Ordnance Devel. award, 1945; Godfrey L. Cabot award Aero Club New England, 1965; Distinguished Service medal National Aeronautics and Space Administration, 1965, 69; Robert H. Goddard Memorial trophy, 1968; Distinguished Pub. Service medal Department Defense, 1973; Exceptional Civilian Service award Department Air Force, 1973; General Thomas D. White U.S. Air Force Space Trophy, 1973; Ralph Coats Roe medal American Society of Mechanical Engineers, 1977; Achievement award National Society Professional Engrs.; Thomas D. White National Defense award, 1980; Exceptional Service award Department Air Force, 1985. Fellow Am. Acad. Arts and Sciences, Am. Astronomical Society, Institute of Electrical and Electronics Engineers, American Institute of Aeronautics and Astronautics (hon., Lawrence Sperry award 1951); member International Acad. Astronautics, Am. Society Pub. Administration, National Acad. Engineering, American Association for the Advancement of Science, Air Force Acad. Foundation, Foreign Policy Association, Council on Foreign Relations, Sigma Xi. Clubs: Harvard (Boston); Manchester Yacht (Massachusetts); Essex County (Massachusetts); Chevy Chase, Metropolitan (Washington); Cruising of Am. (Boston Sta.). Office: 33-406 Massachusetts Institute of Technology Cambridge Massachusetts 02139

SEARS, ERNEST ROBERT, geneticist, emeritus educator; born Bethel, Oregon, October 15, 1910; son of Jacob Perlonzo and Ada Estella (McKee) S.; married Caroline F. Eichorn, July 5, 1936; 1 son, Michael Allan; married Lotti Maria Steinitz, June 16, 1950; children: John, Barbara, Kathleen. Bachelor of Science, Oregon State Agrl. College, 1932; Master of Arts, Harvard University, 1934, Doctor of Philosophy, 1936; Doctor of Science, Goettingen University. Agent Department Agriculture, 1936-41, geneticist; 1941-80; research associate University Missouri, Columbia, 1937-63; professor University Missouri, 1963-80, professor emeritus; 1980—; Hannaford research fellow, Australia, 1980-81, Einstein research fellow, Israel, 1981, Agricultural Research Council fellow, England, 1982; Michael visiting professor, Israel, 1985; visiting professor University Stellenbosch, South Africa, 1985. Contributor articles to tech. journals. Fulbright research fellow Germany, 1958; Recipient Stevenson award for research in agronomy, 1951, Hoblitzelle award for research in agrl. sci., 1958, Distinguished Service award Oregon State Agrl. College, 1973; National Agr.-Bus. award, 1981; Wolf prize for agrl. sci., 1986; named to Agr. Research Service Hall of Fame U.S. Department Agr., 1987. Fellow Agronomy Society Am., American Association for the Advancement of Science, Indian Society Genetics and Plant Breeding (hon.), Japanese Genetics Society (hon.); member Am. Acad. Arts and Sciences, National Acad. Sciences, Botanical Society Am., Genetics Society Am. (president 1978-79), Am. Society Naturalists, Genetics Society Can. (Excellence award 1977), Am. Institute Biological Sciences, Am. Association Cereal Chemists (hon.), Sigma Xi (chapter research award 1970), Phi Kappa Phi, Alpha Zeta, Gamma Sigma Delta (Distinguished Service award 1958), Alpha Gamma Rho. Home: 2009 Mob Hill Columbia Missouri 65201

SECOR, DONALD TERRY, JR., geologist, educator; born Oil City, Pennsylvania, November 22, 1934; son of Donald Terry and Mary Elizabeth (LaRue) S.; married Dorothy Eisenhart, June 15, 1959; children: Beth Ann, Jane Marie, Carol Lynn. Bachelor of Science, Cornell University, 1957, Master of Science, 1959; Doctor of Philosophy, Stanford University, 1963. Assistant professor geology University South Carolina, Columbia, 1962-66, associate professor; 1966-79, professor; 1979—, chairman department; 1966-68, 77-81. National Science Foundation grantee, 1966-70, 76—; U.S. Geol. Survey grantee, 1979-82. Fellow Geological Society Am.; member Am. Geophysical Union, American Association for the Advancement of Science. Home: Route 1 Box 251 Newberry South Carolina 29108 Office: U South Carolina Department Geological Scis Columbia South Carolina 29208

SEDLIN, ELIAS DAVID, physician, orthopedic researcher, educator; born New York City, January 21, 1932; son of Arnold Boris and Sonia Davidovna (Lipschitz) S.; married Barbara Sue Zidell, July 9, 1960; children—Faith Avril, Adrian. Bachelor of Science in Biology, University Alabama, 1951; Doctor of Medicine, Tulane University, 1955; Doctor.Medical Science, University Gothenburg, Sweden, 1966. Diplomate: Am. Board Orthopedic Surgery. Intern Mobile (Alabama) General Hospital, 1955-56; resident Charity Hospital, New Orleans, 1956-57; chief resident Bronx (New York). Municipal Hospital, 1959-60; senior resident Henry Ford Hospital, Detroit, 1960-61; research associate, emergency room lecturer Henry Ford Hospital, 1961-63, National Institutes of Health fellow; 1963-64; junior attending physician Detroit Receiving Hospital, 1962-63; special National Institutes of Health fellow department orthopedic surgery Sahlgrenska Sjukhuset, Gothenburg, 1964-66; assistant professor department orthopaedic surgery Albert Einstein College Medicine, 1966-69, associate professor; 1969-75, professor, 1975—, director orthopaedic surgery; 1969-79; professor orthopaedic surgery Mount Sinai School Medicine, 1980—; director orthopaedic surgery Elmhurst General Hospital, Queens, New York, 1980—. Contributor to multiple symposia, professional meetings, also articles to professional journals. Served to captain Army of the United States, 1957-59. Fulbright scholar, 1962; National Science Foundation postdoctoral fellow, 1964; recipient P.D. McGehee award Mobile General Hospital, 1956; Ludvic Hektoen gold medal A.M.A., 1963; Nicholas Andry award Association Bone and Joint Surgeons, 1964. Fellow A.C.S., Am. Acad. Orthopaedic Surgeons, A.A.A.S.; member Orthopedic Research Society, Phi Beta Kappa. Office: 5 E 98th St New York New York 10029

SEFTON, MICHAEL VIVIAN, chemical engineering educator; born London, October 20, 1949; emigrated to Canada, 1951; son of Wolf and Edith (Wislicky) S.; married Cynthia Rochelle Cooper, June 12, 1975;

children—Elana Joelle Bracha, Ari Joseph. Bachelor of Arts in Science, University Toronto, 1971; Doctor of Science, Massachusetts Institute of Technology, 1974. Accredited professional engineer, Ontario. Assistant professor chemical engineering University Toronto, 1974-79, associate professor; 1979-85, professor; 1985—, assistant chairman department; 1981-85, associate chairman department; 1985—; director Chemical Engineering Research Cons., Limited, W. Sefton & Associates. Patentee dispensing device for medicaments, microencapsulation of live aminal cells. Member Chemical Institute Can., Can. Biomaterials Society, Society Biomaterials, Am. Society Artificial Internal Organs. Office: University of Toronto, Department of Chem Engring, Toronto, Ontario Canada M58 1A4

SEITZ, FREDERICK, university president emeritus; born San Francisco, July 4, 1911; son of Frederick and Emily Charlotte (Hofman) S.; married Elizabeth K. Marshall, May 18, 1935. Bachelor of Arts, Leland Stanford Junior University, 1932; Doctor of Philosophy, Princeton University, 1934; Doctorate Honorary Causa, University Ghent, 1957; Doctor of Science, University Reading, 1960, Rensselaer Polytechnic Institute, 1961, Marquette University, 1963, Carnegie Institute Tech., 1963, Case Institute Tech., 1964, Princeton University, 1964, Northwestern University, 1965, University Delaware, 1966, Polytechnic Institute Brooklyn, 1967, University Michigan, 1967, University Utah, 1968, Brown University, 1968, Duquesne University, 1968, St. Louis University, 1969, Nebraska Wesleyan University, 1970, University Illinois, 1972, Rockefeller University, 1981; Doctor of Laws, Lehigh University, 1966, University Notre Dame, 1962, Michigan State University, 1965, Illinois Institute Tech., 1968, New York University, 1969; Doctor of Humane Letters, Davis and Elkins College, 1970, Rockefeller University, 1981, University Pennsylvania, 1985. Instructor physics University Rochester, 1935-36, assistant professor; 1936-37; physicist research laboratories General Electric Company, 1937-39; assistant professor Randal Morgan Laboratory Physics, University Pennsylvania, 1939-41, associate professor; 1941-42; professor physics, head department Carnegie Institute Tech., Pittsburgh, 1942-49; professor physics University Illinois, 1949-57, head department; 1957-64, director control systems laboratory; 1951-52, dean Grad. College, vice president research; 1964-65; executive president National Acad. Sciences, 1962-69; president Rockefeller University, New York City, 1968-78; trustee Ogden Corp., 1977—; director training program Clinton Laboratories, Oak Ridge, 1946-47; Chairman Naval Research Adv. Committee, 1960-62; vice chairman Def. Sci. Board, 1961-62, chairman, 1964-68; sci. adviser North Atlantic Treaty Organization, 1959-60; member national advisory committee Marine Biomed. Institute University Texas, Galveston, 1975-77; member adv. group White House Conference Anticipated Advances in Sci. and Tech., 1975-76; member advisory board Desert Research Institute, 1975-79, Center Strategic and International Studies, 1975—; member National Cancer Advisory Board, 1976-82; director Akzona

Incorporated, Texas Instruments Incorporated; chairman sci. and tech. board Republic of China, 1980—. Author: Modern Theory of Solids, 1940, The Physics of Metals, 1943, Solid State Physics, 1955. Trustee Rockefeller Foundation, 1964-77, Princeton University, 1968-72, Lehigh University, 1970-81, Research Corp., 1966-82, Institute International Education, 1971-78, Woodrow Wilson National Fellowship Foundation, 1972—, University Corp. Atmospheric Research, Am. Museum Natural History, 1975—; trustee John Simon Guggenheim Memorial Foundation, 1973-83, chairman board, 1976-83; member Belgian Am. Education Foundation; board of directors Richard Lounsbery Foundation, 1980—. Recipient Franklin medal Franklin Institute Philadelphia, 1965; Hoover medal Stanford University, 1968; National Medal of Sci., 1973; James Madison award Princeton University, 1978; Edward R. Loveland Memorial award American College of Physicians, 1983; Vannevar Bush award National Sci. Board, 1983. Fellow Am. Physical Society (president 1961); member National Acad. Sciences, Am. Acad. Arts and Sciences, American Institute of Mining, Metallurgy and Petroleum Engineers, Am. Philosophical Society, Am. Institute Physics (chairman govorning board 1954-59), Institute for Defense Analysis, Finnish Acad. Sci. and Letters (foreign member), Phi Beta Kappa Assos. Address: Rockefeller U 1230 York Avenue New York New York 10021

SELTSER, RAYMOND, epidemiologist, educator; born Boston, December 17, 1923; son of Israel and Hannah (Littman) S.; married Charlotte Frances Gale, November 16, 1946; children: Barry Jay, Andrew David. Doctor of Medicine, Boston University, 1947; Master of Public Health, Johns Hopkins University, 1957. Diplomate Am. Board Preventive Medicine (trustee, sec.-treas. 1974-77), Am. Board Medical Specialties (mem. exec. com. 1976-77). Assistant chief medical information and intelligence branch United States Department Army, 1953-56; epidemiologist div. internal health United States Public Health Service, 1956-57; from assistant professor to professor epidemiology Johns Hopkins University School Hygiene and Pub. Health, 1957-81, associate dean; 1967-77, deputy director Oncology Center; 1977-81; dean University Pittsburgh Grad. School Pub. Health, 1981-87, professor epidemiology; 1981-88, dean emeritus; 1988—; associate director United States Public Health Service Centers for Disease Control, Rockville, Maryland, 1988—; consultant National Institute of Mental Health, 1958-70, also various governmental health agys., 1958-79; expert consultant President's Commission on Three Mile Island, 1979-80; member Three Mile Island Adv. Panel Health, National Cancer Institute Cancer Control Grant Rev. Committee, Pennsylvania Department Health Preventive Health Service Block Grant Adv. Task Force, Gov.'s VietNam Herbicide Information Commission Pennsylvania; chairman Toxic/Health Effects Adv. Committee, 1985-87. Trustee, member executive committee, chairman professional adv. committee Harmarville Rehabilitation Center, Pittsburgh, 1982-87; board of directors Health Education Center, Media Information Service. Served to captain Army of the United States, 1951-53, Korea.

Decorated Bronze Star; recipient Centennial Alumni citation Boston U.School Medicine, 1973; elected to Johns Hopkins Society of Scholars, 1986. Fellow American Association for the Advancement of Science, Am. Pub. Health Association (member governing council 1975-77, chairman EPI section council 1979-80), Pennsylvania Pub. Health Association (board directors 1985-88, pres.-elect 1986-88), Am. College Peventive Medicine, Am. Heart Association; member Am. Epidemiological Association, International Epidemiological Association, Am. Society Preventive Oncology, Am. Cancer Society (board directors Pennsylvania division 1985-87, member executive committee 1986-87), Association Schs. Pub. Health (executive committee, chairman education committee), Society Medical Cons. Armed Forces, Society Epidemiologic Research, National Council Radiation Protection and Measurements (consociate), Delta Omega, Sigma Xi. Clubs: University (Pittsburgh), Faculty (Pittsburgh). Office: Center for Disease Control Room 18-34 Parklawn Building 5600 Fishers Lane Rockville Maryland 20857

SHAFFER, ROBERT LYNN, mycologist, educator; born Long Beach, California, December 29, 1929; son of Vere Roswell and Alice Veretta (Goodwin) S.; married Jocelyn Gobeille, September 20, 1958; 1 child, Martha Irene. Bachelor of Science, Kansas State University, 1951, Master of Science, 1952; Doctor of Philosophy, Cornell University, 1955. Instructor in botany University Chicago, 1955-59, assistant professor; 1959-60; assistant professor University Michigan, Ann Arbor, 1960-63, associate professor; 1963-70, professor; 1970-81, Wehmeyer professor fungal taxonomy; 1981—, director herbarium; 1975-86, curator of fungi; 1960—; teacher University Center for Adult Education University Michigan, spring 1969, 75, 76, fall 1968, 70-74, 76-79, 81-82, Ann Arbor Learning Network, fall 1983, Friends of Matthaei Botanical Gardens, fall 1984-86; Skinner lecturer Sarett Nature Center, Benton Harbor, Michigan, 1980; senior mycologist Northeastern Mycological Foray, Bennington, Vermont, 1981; member project adv. panel Flora of North America, 1983-86. Author one book; contributor articles to professional journals. Secretary Mack Elementary School PTO, 1967-68, president, 1968-69. National Science Foundation fellow, 1954-55; grantee National Science Foundation, 1964-73, 75-79, 80—. Member North America Mycological Association (trustee 1967—, Contbn. to Amateur Mycology award 1970), Mycological Society Am. (secretary 1968-71, president 1973-74, various other offices and committees), International Association for Plant Taxonomy, Phi Kappa Phi, Sigma Xi, Gamma Sigma Delta. Avocations: gardening, wine making, hiking, bicycling. Home: 501 N 7th St Ann Arbor Michigan 48103 Office: U of Michigan Herbarium Ann Arbor Michigan 48109-1057

SHANK, CHARLES VERNON, science administrator; born Mount Holly, New Jersey, July 12, 1943; son of Augustus Jacob and Lillian (Peterson) S.; married Brenda Shank, June 16, 1969. Bachelor of Science, University California, Berkeley, 1965, Master of Science, Doctor of Philosophy, 1966. Member tech. staff American Telephone and Telegraph

Company Bell Laboratories, Holmdel, New Jersey, 1969-76, head quantum physics and electronics department; 1976-83, director Electronics Research Laboratory; 1983—. Numerous patents in field. Recipient E. Longstreth medal Franklin Institute, Philadelphia, 1982, Morris E. Leeds award Institute of Electrical and Electronic Engineers, 1982, David Sarnoff award Institute of Electrical and Electronic Engineers, 1989. Fellow American Association for the Advancement of Science, Am. Physical Society, Optical Society Am. (R. W. Wood prize 1981); member National Academy of Sciences, National Academy of Engineering, Am. Acad. Arts and Sciences. Home: 3 White Birch Lane Holmdel New Jersey 07733 Office: AT&T Bell Labs Crawford Corners Road Room 4 E436 Holmdel New Jersey 07733

SHANNON, CLAUDE ELWOOD, mathematician, educator; born Gaylord, Michigan, April 30, 1916; son of Claude Elwood and Mabel Catherine (Wolf) S.; married Mary Elizabeth Moore, March 27, 1949; children: Robert James, Andrew Moore, Margarita Catherine. Bachelor of Science, University Michigan, 1936, Doctor of Science, 1961; Master of Science, Doctor of Philosophy in Math., Massachusetts Institute of Technology, 1940; Master of Science (honorary), Yale University, 1954; Doctor of Science, Princeton University, 1962, University Edinburgh, Scotland, 1964, University Pittsburgh, 1964, Northwestern University, Evanston, Illinois, 1970, Oxford (England) University, 1978, East Anglia University, 1982, Carnegie Mellon University, 1984. Staff Carnegie Institution, Washington, 1939, Bowles fellow; 1939-40;

National Research fellow Princeton University, New Jersey, 1940; consultant National Defense Research Committee, 1941; research mathematician Bell Telephone Laboratories, 1941-72; visiting professor electrical communications Massachusetts Institute of Technology, 1956, professor communications sciences and math.; 1957—, Donner professor sci.; 1958-78, professor emeritus; 1978—; visiting fellow All Souls College, Oxford, 1978; Vanuxem lecturer Princeton University, 1958; Steinmetz lecturer, Schenectady, 1962; director Teledyne, Incorporated; Gibbs lecturer Am. Math. Society, 1965; Shannon lecturer Institute of Electrical and Electronics Engineers, 1973; Chichele Lecturer Oxford University, 1978. Author: Mathematical Theory of Communication, 1949; editor: (with J. Mccarthy) Automata Studies, 1956; contributor papers on math. subjects to professional journals. Recipient American Institute of Electrical Engineers award, 1940, Morris Liebmann Memorial award, 1949, Stuart Ballantine medal Franklin Institute Philadelphia, 1955, Research Corp. award, 1956, Mervin J. Kelly award American Institute of Electrical Engineers, 1962, medal of honor Institute of Electrical and Electronic Engineers, 1966, Harvey prize Am. Society for Techion, 1972, medal of honor Rice University, 1962, National Medal Sci., 1966, Golden Plate award, 1967, Jacquard award, 1978, Harold Pender award, 1978, John Fritz award, 1983, Audio Engineering Society Gold medal, 1985, Kyoto prize Basic Sci., 1985, Marquis Achievement award; fellow Center Advanced Study Behavioral Sciences, Stanford, California, 1957-58. Fellow Institute of Electrical and Electronics Engineers;

member Am. Acad. Arts. and Sciences, National Acad. Sciences, Leopoldina Acad., Royal Netherlands Acad. Arts & Sciences, National Acad. Engineering, Am. Philosophical Society, Royal Irish Acad. Tau Beta Pi, Sigma Xi, Phi Kappa Phi. Home: 5 Cambridge St Winchester Massachusetts 01890

SHAPIRO, IRWIN IRA, physicist, educator; born New York City, October 10, 1929; son of Samuel and Esther (Feinberg) S.; married Marian Helen Kaplun, December 20, 1959; children: Steven, Nancy. Bachelor of Arts, Cornell University, 1950; Master of Arts, Harvard University, 1951, Doctor of Philosophy, 1955. Member staff Lincoln Laboratory Massachusetts Institute of Technology, Lexington, 1954-70; Sherman Fairchild Distinguished scholar California Institute Tech., 1974; Morris Loeb lecturer physics Harvard, 1975; professor geophysics and physics Massachusetts Institute of Technology, 1967-80, Schlumberger professor; 1980-84; Paine professor practical astronomy, professor physics Harvard University, 1982—; senior scientist Smithsonian Astrophysical Observatory, 1982—; director Harvard-Smithsonian Center for Astrophysics, 1983—; consultant National Science Foundation. Contributor articles to professional journals. Recipient Albert A. Michelson medal Franklin Institute, 1975, award in physical and math. scis. New York Acad. Sciences, 1982; Guggenheim fellow, 1982. Fellow American Association for the Advancement of Science, Am. Geophysical Union, Am. Physical Society; member Am. Acad. Arts and Sciences, National Acad. Sciences (Benjamin Apthorp Gould prize 1979), Am. Astronomical Society (Dannie Heineman award 1983, Dirk Brouwer award 1987), International Astronomical Union, Phi Beta Kappa, Sigma Xi, Phi Kappa Phi. Home: 17 Lantern Lane Lexington Massachusetts 02173 Office: Harvard U College Obs 60 Garden St Cambridge Massachusetts 02138

SHAPPIRIO, DAVID GORDON, biologist, educator; born Washington, June 18, 1930; son of Sol and Rebecca (Porton) S.; married Elvera May Bamber, July 8, 1953; children: Susan, Mark. Bachelor of Science with distinction in Chemistry, University Michigan, 1951; Master of Arts, Harvard University, 1953, Doctor of Philosophy in Biology, 1955. National Science Foundation postdoctoral fellow in biochemistry Cambridge University, England, 1955-56; research fellow in physiology Am. Cancer Soc.-NRC, University Louvain, Belgium, 1956-57; member faculty University Michigan, Ann Arbor, 1957—; professor zoological and biological sciences University Michigan, 1967—, associate chairman; 1976-83, acting chairman; 1978, 79, 80, 82, 83, coordinator National Science Foundation undergraduate sci. education program; 1962-67, director honors program College Literature Sci. and Arts; 1983—; visiting lecturer Am. Institute Biological Sciences, 1966-68; consultant in field. Author, editor research on biochemistry and physiology growth, devel., dormancy. Lalor Foundation fellow, 1953-55; Danforth Foundation assoc., 1969—; recipient Distinguished Teaching award University Michigan, 1967; Bausch & Lomb Sci. award, 1974; research grantee, cons. National Institutes of Health, National Science

Foundation. Fellow American Association for the Advancement of Science; member Am. Institute Biological Sciences (vis. lecturer 1966-68), Am. Society Cell Biology, Biochem. Society, Entomological Society Am., Royal Entomological Society, Lepidopterists Society., Society Experimental Biology, Society General Physiologists, Association Biological Lab. Education, Phi Beta Kappa. Office: U Michigan LSA Honors Program 1210 Angell Hall Ann Arbor Michigan 48109-1003

SHARP, PHILLIP ALLEN, biologist, educator; born Kentucky, June 6, 1944; son of Joseph Walter and Katherin (Colvin) S.; married Ann Christine Holcombe, August 29, 1964; children: Christine Alynn, Sarah Katherin, Helena Holcombe. Bachelor of Arts, Union College, Barbourville, Kentucky, 1966; Doctor of Philosophy, University Illinois, Urbana, 1969. National Institutes of Health postdoctoral fellow California Institute Tech., 1969-71; senior research investigator Cold Spring Harbor (New York) Laboratory, 1972-74; associate professor Massachusetts Institute of Technology, Cambridge, 1974-79, professor biology; 1979—, director Center Cancer Research; 1985—; Co-founder, member sci. board, director BIOGEN, 1978—; chairman sci. board, 1987—. Editorial board: Cell, Journal Virology, Molecular and Cellular Biology, 1974-81. Recipient awards Am. Cancer Society, 1974-79, awards Eli Lilly, 1980, awards Nat Acad. Sci./U.S. Steel Foundation, 1980, Howard Ricketts award University Chicago, 1985, Alfred P. Sloan Junior prize General Motors Research Foundation, 1986, award Gairdner Foundation International,

1986, award New York Acad. Sciences, 1986, Louisa Horwitz prize, 1988, Albert Lasker Basic Medical Rsch. award, 1988; awarded Class of '41 chair, 1986-87, John D. MacArthur chair, 1987. Fellow American Association for the Advancement of Science; member Am. Chemical Society, Am. Society Microbiology, National Acad. Sciences (councilor 1986), Am. Acad. Arts and Scis, European Molecular Biology Organization (associate). Home: 119 Grasmere St Newton Massachusetts 02158 Office: Massachusetts Institute of Technology 40 Ames St Room E17-529B Cambridge Massachusetts 02139

SHARPE, WILLIAM NORMAN, JR., mechanical engineer, educator; born Chatham County, North Carolina, April 15, 1938; son of William Norman and Margaret Horne (Womble) S.; married Margaret Ellen Strowd, August 21, 1959; children—William N., J. Ashley. Bachelor of Science, North Carolina State University, Raleigh, 1960, Master of Science, 1961; Doctor of Philosophy, Johns Hopkins University, Baltimore, 1966. Registered professional engineer, Michigan, Louisiana, Maryland. Associate professor Michigan State University, East Lansing, 1970-75, professor; 1975-78; professor, chairman department mechanical engineering Louisiana State University, Baton Rouge, 1978-83; professor, department mechanical engineering Johns Hopkins University, Baltimore, 1983—, Decker professor mechanical engineering; 1985—; senior resident research associate Air Force Materials Laboratory, Dayton, Ohio, 1973-74. Fellow American Society of Mechanical Engineers; member Am. Society Engineering

Education, American Society for Testing and Materials, Society Experimental Mechanics (executive board 1979-81, president 1984-85). Home: 220 Ridgewood Road Baltimore Maryland 21210 Office: Johns Hopkins U Department Mech Engring Latrobe Hall Room 127 Baltimore Maryland 21218

SHAW, BREWSTER H., astronaut; born Cass City, Michigan, May 16, 1945; married Kathleen Mueller; 3 children. Bachelor of Science, University Wisconsin, 1968, Master of Science, 1969. United States astronaut National Aeronautics and Space Administration, 1978—; member support crew 3d, 4th Space Shuttle Flights, National Aeronautics and Space Administration; astronaut Space Shuttle's 9th mission, National Aeronautics and Space Administration, 1983. Office: care Lyndon B Johnson Space Center Houston Texas 77058

SHAW, MILTON CLAYTON, mechanical engineering educator; born Philadelphia, May 27, 1915; son of Milton Fredic and Nellie Edith (Clayton) S.; married Mary Jane Greeninger, September 6, 1939; children—Barbara Jane, Milton Stanley. Bachelor of Science in Mechanical Engineering, Drexel Institute Tech., 1938; Master Engring. Science, University Cincinnati, 1940, Doctor of Science, 1942; Doctor h.c., University Louvain, Belgium, 1970. Research engineer Cincinnati Milling Machine Company, 1938-42; chief materials branch National Advisory Committee for Aeronautics, 1942-46; with Massachusetts Institute Tech., 1946-61, professor mechanical engineering; 1953-61, head materials processing div.; 1952-61; professor, head department mechanical engineering Carnegie Institute Tech., Pittsburgh, 1961-75; university professor Carnegie Institute Tech., 1974-77; professor engineering Arizona State University, Tempe, 1978—; Cons. industrial companies; lecturer in, Europe, 1952; president Shaw Smith & Associates, Incorporated, Massachusetts, 1951-61; Lucas professor Birmingham (England) University, 1961; Springer professor University California at Berkeley, 1972; Distinguished guest professor Arizona State University, 1977; member National Materials Adv. Board, 1971-74; board of directors Engineering Foundation, 1976, vice president conference committee, 1976-78. Recipient Outstanding Research award Arizona State University, 1981; Am. Machinist award, 1973; P. McKenna award, 1975; Guggenheim fellow, 1956; Fulbright lecturer Aachen T.H., Germany, 1957; Organization of European Cooperation and Development fellow to Europe, 1964—. Fellow Am. Acad. Arts and Sciences, American Society of Mechanical Engineers (Hersey award 1967, Thurston lecturer 1971, Outstanding Engineering award 1975, meeting theme organizer 1977, Gold medal 1985, hon. 1980), Am. Society Lubrication Engineers, Am. Society Metals (Wilson award 1971); member (National award 1964); member International Society Prodn. Engineering Research (president 1960-61, hon. member 1975), Am. Society for Engineering Education (G. Westinghouse award 1956), Society Manufacturing Engineers (hon., Gold medal 1958, international education award 1980), National Acad. Engineering, Polish Acad. Sci. Home: 326 E Fairmont Dr Tempe Arizona

85282 Address: 1540 Spanish Moss Way Flagstaff Arizona 86001

SHEN, BENJAMIN SHIH-PING, scientist, educator; born Hangzhou, China, September 14, 1931; son of Nai-cheng and Chen-chiu (Sun) S.; married Lucia Simpson, July 31, 1971; children: William Li, Juliet Ming. Bachelor of Arts summa cum laude, Assumption College, Massachusetts, 1954, Doctor of Science (honorary), 1972; Master of Arts in Physics, Clark University, 1956; Doctor of Science d'Etat in Physics, University Paris, 1964; Master of Arts (honorary), University Pennsylvania, 1971. Teacher Assumption Preparatory School, Worcester, Massachusetts, 1954-56; assistant professor physics State University of New York, Albany, 1956-59; associate professor space sci., department aeros. and astronautics Engineering School, New York University, 1964-66; associate professor University Pennsylvania, Philadelphia, 1966-68, professor; 1968-72, Reese W. Flower professor astronomy and as-trophysics; 1972—; founding chairman Roundtable on Sci., Industry and Policy, Wharton School, 1976—, associate university provost, 1979-80, chairman council grad. deans, 1979-81, acting university provost and chief acad. officer, 1980-81, chairman department astronomy and astrophysics, 1973-79, director Flower and Cook Observatory, 1973-79, chairman grad. committee on sci. and tech. policy, 1985—, member Energy Center, 1976—; consultant General Electric Company, 1961-68, Am. Institute Physics, 1965, 72-75, Office of Tech. Assessment, United States Congress, 1977-78; sci. and tech. advisor United States Senate Budget Committee, 1976-77; guest staff member Brookhaven National Laboratory, 1963-64, 65-70; founding chairman Committee on Pub. Understanding of Sci., New York Acad. Sciences, 1972-75. Author: Contribution à l'Etude du Passage des Protons dans des Milieux Condensés, 1964; editor, co-author: High-Energy Nuclear Reactions in Astrophysics, 1967; co-editor, co-author: Spallation Nuclear Reactions and Their Applications, 1976; associate editor: Biosci. Communications, 1974-77; member editorial board: Earth and Extraterrestrial Scis., 1974-78, associate editor, 1978-79, Comments on Astrophysics, 1979-85; contributor articles to professional journals.
Member Hayden Planetarium committee of board trustees Am. Mus. Natural History, New York City, 1978—; member Sci. adv. board Children's TV Workshop, New York City, 1977, 79—; member adv. committee Mount John Observatory, New Zealand, 1978-84; member ABA-AAAS National Conference Board Lawyers and Scientists, 1986—; former board member New York Acad. Scis., University City Sci. Center Research Park (Philadelphia), University Pennsylvania Research Foundation, The Pennsylvania Ballet. Dupont scholar Wesleyan University, 1956; recipient Cottrell grant Research Corp., 1957-59, Vermeil medal for sci. Society d'Encouragement au Progrès, France, 1978. Fellow Am. Physical Society, American Association for the Advancement of Science (committee on sci. engineering and pub. policy 1978-84, chairman subcom on federal research and devel. budget and policy 1978-81), Royal Astronomical Society (United Kingdom), Joint Association for Geophysics (United Kingdom); member International Astronomical

Union. Office: U Pennsylvania David Rittenhouse Lab Philadelphia Pennsylvania 19104-6394

SHEN, TSUNG YING, medicinal chemistry educator; born Beijing, China, September 28, 1924; came to United States, 1950; son of Tsu-Wei and Sien-Wha (Nieu) S.; married Amy T.C. Lin, June 20, 1953; children: Bernard, Hubert, Theodore, Leonard, Evelyn, Andrea. Bachelor of Science, National Central University, Chung King, China, 1946; diploma, Imperial College Science and Tech., London, 1948; Doctor of Philosophy, University Manchester, England, 1950, Doctor of Science, 1978. Research associate Ohio State University, Columbus, 1950-52, Massachusetts Institute of Technology, Cambridge, 1952-56; senior research chemist Merck, Sharp & Dohme Research Laboratories, Rahway, New Jersey, 1956-65, director synthetic chemical research; 1966-76, vice president membrane chemical research; 1976-77, vice president membrane and arthritis research; 1977-86; A. Burger Professor Medicinal Chemistry University Virginia, Charlottesville, 1986—; visiting professor University Calif.-Riverside, 1973, University Calif.-San Francisco, 1985, Harvard Medical School, 1986; adj. professor Stevens Institute Tech., Hoboken, New Jersey, 1982-85. Member editorial board Clinica Europa Journal, 1977, Prostaglandins and Medicine, 1978, Medicinal Research Revs., 1979, Journal Medicinal Chemistry, 1980-83; patentee in field. Recipient Outstanding Patent award New Jersey Research and Devel. Council, 1975, Rene Descartes medal University Paris, 1977, medal of Merit Giornate Mediche Internazionali del Collegium Biologicum Europea, 1977, cert. of merit Spanish Society Therapeutic Chemistry, 1983, achievement award Chinese Institute Engrs.-U.S.A., 1984. Member Am. Chemical Society (1st Alfred Burger award in medicinal chemistry 1980), New York Acad. Sciences, American Association for the Advancement of Science, International Society Immunopharmacology, Acad. Pharmaceutical Sciences (hon.), Am. Association Pharmaceutical Sci. Home: 303 Ednam Dr Charlottesville Virginia 22901 Office: Chem Department U Va Charlottesville Virginia 22901

SHENK, THOMAS EUGENE, molecular biology educator; born Brooklyn, January 1, 1947; son of Eugene Richard and Helen Marie (Deffenbaugh) S.; married Susan Mary Hillman, July 4, 1979; children—Christopher Thomas, Gregory Thomas. Bachelor of Science, University Detroit, 1969; Doctor of Philosophy, Rutgers University, 1973; postgraduate, Stanford University, 1973-75. Assistant professor molecular biology University Conn.-Farmington, 1975-80; professor molecular biology SUNY-Stony Brook, 1980-84, Princeton University, 1984—; research professor Am. Cancer Society, 1986—. Member Am. Society Microbiology (Eli Lilly award 1982). Office: Princeton U Department Molecular Biology Princeton New Jersey 08544

SHEPARD, ALAN BARTLETT, JR., astronaut, real estate developer; born East Derry, New Hampshire, November 18, 1923; son of Alan Bartlett and Renza (Emerson) S.; married Louise Brewer, March 3, 1945; children: Laura, Juliana. Student, Admiral Farragut

Academy, 1940; Bachelor of Science, United States Naval Academy, 1944; graduate, Naval War College, 1958; Master of Science (honorary), Dartmouth College; Doctor of Science (honorary), Miami University. Commissioned ensign United States Navy, 1944, advanced through grades to rear admiral; 1971, designated naval aviator; 1947; assigned destroyer United States Ship Cogswell, Navy Test Pilot School, Pacific, World War II, Fighter Squadron 42, aircraft carriers in Mediterranean, 1947-49; with United States Navy Test Pilot School, 1950-53, 55-57, took part in high altitude tests, experiments in test and devel. in-flight refueling system, carrier suitability trials of F2H3 Banshee; also trials angled carrier deck operations officer Fighter Squadron 193, Moffett Field (California), carrier United States Ship Oriskany, Western Pacific, 1953-55; test pilot for F4D Skyray, 1955, F3H Demon, F8U Crusader, F11F Tigercat, 1956; project test pilot F5D Skylancer, 1956; instructor Naval Test Pilot School, 1957; aircraft readiness officer staff Comdr.-in-Chief, Atlantic Fleet, 1958-59; joined Project Mercury man in space program National Aeronautics and Space Administration, 1959; first Am. in space May 5, 1961, chief of astronaut office; 1965-74, selected to command Apollo 14 Lunar Landing Mission; 1971, became 5th man to walk on moon, hit 1st lunar golf shot, retired; 1974; partner Mariner Interests, Houston, 1974; president Seven Fourteen Enterprises, 1986; partner, chairman Marathon Construction Company, Houston, 1974-77; former president Windward Coors Company, Deer Park, Texas, 1974; appointed by President as del. to 26th General Assembly United Nations, 1971.

Decorated Distinguished Service Medal, Distinguished Flying Cross, Presidential unit citation, National Aeronautics and Space Administration Distinguished Service medal, Congressional Medal of Honor, 1978; recipient Langley medal Smithsonian Institution, 1964. Fellow Society Experimental Test Pilots; member Order Daedlians, Society Colonial Wars, Lions, Kiwanis, Rotary.

SHEPHERD, JOHN THOMPSON, physiologist; born Northern Ireland, May 21, 1919; son of William Frederick and Matilda (Thompson) S.; married Helen Mary Johnston, July 28, 1945; children: Gillian Mary, Roger Frederick John. Student, Campbell College, Belfast, Northern Ireland, 1932-37; Bachelor of Medicine, Bachelor.Ch., Queen's University, Belfast, 1945, Master.Chir., 1948, Doctor of Medicine, 1951, Doctor of Science, 1956, Doctor of Science (honorary), 1979; Doctor of Medicine (honorary), University Bologna, 1984, University Gent, 1985. Lecturer physiology Queen's University, 1948-53, reader physiology; 1954-57; associate professor physiology Mayo Foundation, 1957-62, professor physiology; 1962—, chairman department physiology and biophysics; 1966-74; board governors Mayo Clinic, 1966-80; trustee Mayo Foundation, 1969-81, director research; 1969-77, director for education; 1977-83, chairman board devel.; 1983-88; dean Mayo Medical School, 1977-83. Author: Physiology of the Circulation in Human Limbs in Health and Disease, 1963, Cardiac Function in Health and Disease, 1968, Veins and Their Control, 1975, Human Cardiovascular System, 1979; Editorial board: Hypertension 1973—, Am. Journal Physiology, Am. Heart

Jour, Microvascular Research; cons. editor Circulation Research, 1982. Recipient National Aeronautics and Space Administration Skylab Achievement award, 1974; Brit. Medical Association scholar, 1949-50; Fulbright scholar, 1953-54; Anglo-French Medical exchange bursar, 1957; International Francqui chair, 1978; Einthoven lecturer 1981. Fellow Am. College Cardiology (hon.), Royal College Physicians (London), Royal Acad. Medicine (Belgium); member Am. Physiological Society, Louis Rapkine Association, Central Society Clinical Research, Am. Heart Association (director 1968—, president 1975-76, hon. fellow council clinical cardiology), Physiological Society Great Brit., Medical Research Society London, National Acad. Sciences (space sci. board 1973-74, chairman committee space biology and medicine 1973), Association Am. Physicians, International Union of Angiology (hon.), Sigma Xi. Home: 600 4th St Southwest Rochester Minnesota 55902 Office: Mayo Building 200 1st St Southwest Rochester Minnesota 55901

SHERWOOD, LOUIS MAIER, physician, scientist, executive; born New York City, March 1, 1937; son of Arthur Joseph and Blanche (Burger) S.; married Judith Brimberg, March 27, 1966; children: Jennifer Beth, Arieh David. Bachelor of Arts with honors, Johns Hopkins University, 1957; Doctor of Medicine with honors, Columbia University, 1961. Diplomate Am. Board Internal Medicine, Subsplty. Board in Endocrinology and Metabolism. Intern Presbyn. Hospital, New York City, 1961-62, assistant resident in medicine; 1962-63; clinical associate research fellow National Heart Institute, National Institutes of Health, Bethesda, Maryland, 1963-66; National Institutes of Health trainee endocrinology and metabolism College Physicians and Surgeons, Columbia University, New York City, 1966-68; associate medicine Beth Israel Hospital and Harvard Medical School, Boston, 1968-69; chief endocrinology Beth Israel Hospital, 1968-72; assistant professor medicine Harvard University, 1969-71, associate professor; 1971-72; physician-in-chief, chairman department medicine Michael Reese Hospital and Medical Center, Chicago, 1972-80; professor medicine, div. biological sciences Pritzker School Medicine, University Chicago, 1972-80; Ted and Florence Baumritter professor medicine and biochemistry Albert Einstein College Medicine, 1980—, chairman department medicine; 1981-87; physician-in-chief Montefiore Hospital and Medical Center, New York City, 1981-87; senior vice president medical and sci. affairs Merck, Sharp & Dohme International, 1987 ; board of directors Physicians and Surgeons Corp., Michael Reese Medical Center, 1973-80, Barren Foundation, 1974-80; Josiah Macy Junior Foundation fellow and visiting scientist Weizmann Institute, Israel, 1978-79; associate member board on subcom. endocrinology and metabolism Am. Board Internal Medicine, 1977-83. Editor: Beth Israel seminars New England Journal Medicine, 1968-71; member editorial board Endocrinology, 1969-73; associate editor Metabolism, 1970-85, General Medicine B Study Sect., NIH, 1975-79; editorial board Year in Endocrinology, 1976—, Calcified Tissue International, 1978-80, Internal Medicine Alert, 1979—; contributor numerous articles on endocrinology, protein hormones, calcium metabolism and ectopic proteins to journals. Trustee Michael Reese Medical Center, 1974-77; member visiting council CUNY Medical School, 1986—; member alumni council Columbia College Physicians and Surgeons, 1986—. Served as surgeon United States Public Health Service, 1963-66. Recipient Joseph Mather Smith prize for outstanding alumni research College Physicians and Surgeons, Columbia University, 1972, Senior Class Teaching award University Chicago, 1976, 77; grantee USPHS, 1968—. Fellow American College of Physicians (Outstanding Contbn. to Internal Medicine award 1987); member American Association for the Advancement of Science, AM. Federation Clinical Research, Am. Institute Chemists, Am. Society Biological Chemists, Am. Society Clinical Investigation (pres.-elect 1981-82, president 1982-83), Association Am. Physicians, Endocrine Society, New York Acad. Sci., Massachusetts Medical Society, Central Society Clinical Research, Association Program Directors Internal Medicine (council 1979-85, president 1983-84), Association Profs. Medicine, Chicago Society Internal Medicine, Interurban Clinical Club, Phi Beta Kappa, Alpha Omega Alpha. Research in protein and polypeptide hormones: structure, function and regulation of secretion; molecular studies of hormone biosynthesis. Office: Merck Sharp & Dohme International Post Office Box 2000 Rahway New Jersey 07065

SHIMKIN, DEMITRI BORIS, anthropo-geographer, educator; born Omsk, Siberia, July 4, 1916; came to United States, 1923; son of Boris Michael and Lydia (Serebrova) S.; married Edith Manning, August 19, 1943 (deceased September 1984); children: Alexander (deceased), Eleanor Shimkin Sorock; married Tauby Heller, June 16, 1985. Bachelor of Arts, University Calif.-Berkeley, 1936, Doctor of Philosophy, 1939. Johnson scholar, university and research fellow University Calif.-Berkeley, 1937-41; instructor National War College, 1946-47, Institute for Advanced Study, Princeton, 1947-48; research associate Russian Research Center, Harvard, 1948-53; social sci. analyst, then senior research specialist United States Bureau Census, Washington, 1953-60; professor anthropology, geography and pub. health University Illinois, Urbana, 1960-85, professor emeritus; 1985—; field work in, Wyoming, 1937-39, 66, 75, Alaska, 1949, Illinois, 1963, 77-82, Mississippi, 1966-72, 78, 81-83, India, 1978, Tanzania, 1983, 84, Israel, 1985; visiting professor anthropology Harvard University, 1964-65, summer 1970; member National Research Council, 1964-67, United States national committee International Biological Program, 1965-69; member task force environmental health Department of Health, Education and Welfare, 1968-69; member task force on civil engineering American Society of Civil Engineers, 1975-78. Author: Minerals: A Key to Soviet Power, 1953, (with others) Trends in Economic Growth, 1955, Man's Health and Environment, 1970, The Water's Edge, 1972, The Extended Family in Black Societies, 1978, Anthropology for the Future, 1978, (with Carolyn Sprague) How Midwesterners Cope, 1981; contributing author: Handbook of North American Indians, Volume II, 1986. Colonel Army of the United

States; retired. Decorated Legion of Merit; fellow Center Advanced Study Behavioral Sciences, 1970-71; sr. Fulbright scholar Kemerovo (Union of Soviet Socialist Republics) State University, spring 1984. Fellow American Association for the Advancement of Science, Am. Anthropological Association, Society for Applied Anthropology (chairman 1987 program), Royal Anthropological Institute; member Association Am. Geographers, Phi Beta Kappa, Sigma Xi. Methodist.

SHIRLEY, DAVID ARTHUR, laboratory director; born North Conway, New Hampshire, March 30, 1934; married Virginia Schultz, June 23, 1956; children: David N., Diane, Michael, Eric, Gail. Bachelor of Science, University Maine, 1955, Doctor of Science (honorary), 1978; Doctor of Philosophy in Chemistry, University Calif.-Berkeley, 1959; Doctor honoris causa, Free University Berlin, 1987. With Lawrence Radiation Laboratory (now Lawrence Berkeley Laboratory), University California, Berkeley, 1958—, associate director, head materials and molecular research div.; 1975-80, director; 1980—, lecturer chemistry; 1959-60, assistant professor; 1960-64, associate professor; 1964-67, professor; 1967—, vice chairman department chemistry; 1968-71, chairman department chemistry; 1971-75. Contributor over 300 rsch. articles. National Science Foundation fellow, 1955-58, 66-67, 70; recipient Ernest O. Lawrence award Atomic Energy Commission, 1972, Humboldt award (sr. U.S. scientist), 1988, Dr.rer.national hc. Free University, 1987. Fellow Am. Physical Society; member National Acad. Sciences, Am. Chemical Society, American Association for the Advancement of Science, Am. Acad. Arts and Sciences, Sigma Xi, Tau Beta Pi, Sigma Pi Sigma, Phi Kappa Phi. Listed by Sci. Citation Index as one of the world's 300 most cited scientists for work published during 1965-78, 1982. Office: Lawrence Berkeley lab 1 Cyclotron Road Berkeley California 94720

SHOCKLEY, WILLIAM BRADFORD, physicist, emeritus educator; born London, February 13, 1910; (parent American citizens); son of William Hillman and May (Bradford) S.; married Jean A. Bailey, 1933 (divorced 1955); children: Alison, William Alden, Richard Condit; married Emmy Lanning, 1955. Bachelor of Science, California Institute Tech., 1932; Doctor of Philosophy, Massachusetts Institute of Technology, 1936; Doctor of Science (honorary), Rutgers University, 1956, University Pennsylvania, 1955, Gustavus Adolphus College, Minnesota, 1963. Teaching fellow M.I.T., 1932-36; member tech. staff Bell Telephone Laboratories, 1936-42, 45, became director transistor physics research; 1954; director Shockley Semicondr. Laboratory; president Shockley Transistor Corp., 1958-60; consultant Shockley Transistor unit Clevite Transistor, 1960-65; lecturer Stanford University, 1958-63, Alexander M. Poniatoff professor engineering sci. and applied sci.; 1963-75, professor emeritus; 1975—; executive consultant Bell Telephone Laboratories, 1965-75; deputy director research, weapons systems evaluation group Department Def., 1954-55; expert consultant Office Secretary War, 1944-45; visiting lecturer Princeton University, 1946; visiting professor California Institute

Tech., 1954-55; sci. adv., policy council Joint Research and Devel. Board, 1947-49; senior consultant Army Sci. Adv. Panel.; Director research Anti-submarine Welfare Operations Research Group United States Navy, 1942-44. Author: Electrons and Holes in Semiconductors, 1950, (with W.A. Gong) Mechanics, 1966; editor: Imperfections of Nearly Perfect Crystals, 1952. Recipient medal for Merit; Air Force Association citation of honor, 1951; U.S. Army cert. of appreciation, 1953; co-winner (with John Bardeen and Walter H. Brattain) Nobel Prize in Physics, 1956; Wilhelm Exner medal Oesterreichischer Gewerbeverein Austria, 1963; Holley medal American Society of Mechanical Engineers, 1963; California Institute Tech. Alumni Distinguished Service award, 1966; National Aeronautics and Space Administration cert. of appreciation Apollo 8, 1969; Public Service Group Achievement award National Aeronautics and Space Administration, 1969; named to Inventor's Hall of Fame, 1974, California Inventor's Hall of Fame, 1983, Infomart Info. Processing Hall of Fame, Dallas, 1988. Fellow American Association for the Advancement of Science; member Am. Physical Society (O.E. Buckley prize 1953), National Acad. Sci. (Comstock prize 1954), Institute of Electrical and Electronics Engineers (Morris Liebmann prize 1952, Gold medal, 25th anniversary of transistor 1972, Medal of Honor 1980), Sigma Xi, Tau Beta Pi. Holder over 90 patents. Inventor of junction transistor; research on energy bands of solids, ferromagnetic domains, plastic properties of metals; semicondr. theory applied to devices and device defects such as dislocations; fundamentals of electromagnetic energy and momentum; mental tools for sci. thinking; ops. research on human quality problems. Home: 797 Esplanada Way Stanford California 94305 Office: Stanford U Stanford Electronics Labs Department Elec Engring McC 202 Stanford California 94305

SHOEMAKER, EUGENE MERLE, geologist; born Los Angeles, April 28, 1928; son of George Estel and Muriel May (Scott) S.; married Carolyn Jean Spellmann, August 18, 1951; children: Christine Carol, Patrick Gene, Linda Susan. Bachelor of Science, California Institute Tech., 1947, Master of Science, 1948; Master of Arts, Princeton University, 1954, Doctor of Philosophy, 1960; Doctor of Science, Arizona State College, 1965, Temple University, 1967, University Arizona, 1984. Geologist United States Geological Survey, 1984—, exploration uranium deposits and investigation salt structures Colorado and Utah; 1948-50, regional investigations geochemistry, vulcanology and structure Colorado Plateau; 1951-56, research on structure and mechanics of meteorite impact and nuclear explosion craters; 1957-60, with E.C.T. Chao, discovered coesite, Meteor Crater, Arizona; 1960, investigation structure and history of moon; 1960-73, established lunar geological time scale, methods of geological mapping of moon; 1960, application TV systems to investigation extra-terrestrial geology; 1961—, geology and paleomagnetism, Colorado Plateau; 1969—, systematic search for planet-crossing asteroids and comets; 1973—, geology of satellites of Jupiter, Saturn and Uranus; 1978—, investigating role of large body impacts on evolution of life; 1981—, organized branch of astrogeology; 1961; co-investigator TV experiment Project Ranger, 1961-65; chief scientist, center of astrogeology United States Geological Survey, 1966-68, research geologist; 1976—; principal investigator geological field investigations in Apollo lunar landing 1965-70, also television experiment Project Surveyor; 1963-68; professor geology California Institute Tech., 1969-85, chairman div. geological and planetary sciences; 1969-72.

Recipient (with E.C.T. Chao) Wetherill medal Franklin Institute, 1965; Arthur S. Flemming award, 1966; National Aeronautics and Space Administration medal for exceptional sci. achievement, 1967; honor award for meritorious service U.S. Department Interior, 1973; Distinguished Service award, 1980; Distinguished Alumni award California Institute Tech., 1986. Member National Acad. Sci., Geological Society Am. (Day medal 1982, Gilbert award 1983), Mineral Society Am., Society Econ. Geologists, Geochem. Society, Am. Association Petroleum Geologists, Am. Geophysical Union, Am. Astronomical Society (Kuiper prize 1984), International Astronomical Union, Meteoritical Society (Barringer award 1984, Leonard medal 1985). Home: Post Office Box 984 Flagstaff Arizona 86002 Office: United States Geol Survey 2255 N Gemini Dr Flagstaff Arizona 86001

SHREFFLER, DONALD CECIL, geneticist; born Kankakee County, Illinois, April 29, 1933; son of Cecil LeRay and Laura Belle (Pearman) S.; married Dorothy Ferne Kramer, August 18, 1957; children: Douglas LeRay, David Kenneth. Bachelor of Science, University Illinois, 1954, Master of Science, 1958; Doctor of Philosophy (NSF predoctoral fellow), California Institute Tech., 1962. Research associate human genetics University Michigan, 1961-64, assistant professor; 1964-68, associate professor; 1968-71, professor; 1971-75; professor genetics Washington University, St. Louis, 1975—; James South McDonnell professor, chairman department Washington University, 1977-84. Editorial board 8 sci. journals; contributor numerous articles to sci. journals. Served with United States Army, 1954-56. Recipient Research Career Devel. award USPHS, 1966-75. Member Genetics Society Am., Am. Society Human Genetics, Am. Association Immunologists (president 1987-88), American Association for the Advancement of Science, Institute Medicine, National Acad. Sci. Methodist. Research in immunogenetics and biochem. genetics. Home: 4 Ricardo Lane Saint Louis Missouri 63124 Office: 660 S Euclid St Saint Louis Missouri 63110

SHUGART, HERMAN HENRY, educator, researcher; born Eldorado, Arkansas, January 19, 1944; son of Herman Henry and Katherine Luvois (Rich) S.; married Ramona Jeanne Kozel, August 27, 1966; children: Erika Christine, Stephanie Laurel. Bachelor of Science, University Arkansas, 1966, Master of Science, 1968; Doctor of Philosophy, University Georgia, 1971. Research scientist Oak Ridge (Tennessee) National Laboratory, 1971-84; assistant professor University Tennessee, Knoxville, 1971-75, associate professor; 1975-82, professor; 1982-84; W.W. Corcoran professor University Virginia, Charlottesville, 1984—. Author: Time Series Analysis, 1978, Systems Ecology, 1979, Forest Succession, 1981, A Theory of Forest Dynamics, 1984. Fellow American Association for the Advancement of Science; member Ecological Society Am. (member editorial board 1981-83). Democrat. Unitarian/Universalist. Avocation: gardening. Home: 107 Cannon Place Charlottesville Virginia 22901 Office: University Va Department Environ Sci Charlottesville Virginia 22903

SHUMWAY, NORMAN EDWARD, surgeon, educator; born Kalamazoo, Michigan, 1923. Doctor of Medicine, Vanderbilt University, 1949; Doctor of Philosophy in Surgery, University Minnesota, 1956. Diplomate: Am. Board Surgery, Am. Board Thoracic Surgery. Intern University Minnesota Hospitals, 1949-50, medical fellow surgery; 1950-51, 53-54, National Heart Institute research fellow; 1954-56, National Heart Institute special trainee; 1956-57; member surgical staff Stanford University Hospitals, 1958—, assistant professor surgery; 1959-61, associate professor; 1961-65, professor; 1965—, head div. cardiovascular surgery School Medicine; 1974—; Frances and Charles D. Field professor Stanford University, 1976—. Served to captain United States Air Force, 1951-53. Member American Medical Association, Society University Surgeons, Am. Association Thoracic Surgery, Am. College Cardiology, Transplantation Society, Samson Thoracic Surgical Society, Society for Vascular Surgery, Alpha Omega Alpha. Office: Stanford U Med Center Department Cardiovascular Surgery 300 Pasteur Dr Stanford California 94305

SIBLEY, CHARLES GALD, biologist, educator; born Fresno, California, August 7, 1917; son of Charles Corydon and Ida (Gald) S.; married Frances Louise Kelly, February 7, 1942; children: Barbara Susanne, Dorothy Ellen, Carol Nadine. Bachelor of Arts, University Calif.—Berkeley, 1940, Doctor of Philosophy, 1948; Master of Arts (honorary), Yale University, 1965. Biologist, United States Public Health Service, 1941-42; instructor zoology University Kansas, 1948-49; assistant professor San Jose (California) State College, 1949-53; associate professor ornithology Cornell University, 1953-59, professor zoology; 1959-65; professor biology Yale University, 1965-86, professor emeritus; 1986—, William Robertson Coe professor ornithology; 1967-86, emeritus; 1986—; director div. vertebrate zoology, curator birds Peabody Mus., 1965-86, director mus.; 1970-76; consultant systematic biology, 1963-65; member adv. committee biological medicine National Science Foundation, 1968—; executive committee biological agriculture National Research Council, 1966-70. Contributor professional journals. Served to lieutenant United States Naval Reserve, 1943-45. Guggenheim fellow, 1959-60. Fellow American Association for the Advancement of Science; member Society Study Evolution, National Acad. Sciences, Am. Society Naturalists, Society Systematic Biology, Am. Ornithologists' Union (president 1986—, Brewster Memorial medal 1971), Royal Australian Ornithological Union, Deutsche Ornithological Gesellschaft, International Ornithological Congress (sec.-gen. 1962, 20th president 1986—). Home: 95 Seafirth Road Tiburon California 94920 Office: San Francisco State U Tiburon Center Box 855 Tiburon California 94920

SIEGBAHN, KAI MANNE BÖRJE, physicist, educator; born Lund, Sweden, April 20, 1918; son of Manne and Karin (Hogbom) S.; married Anna-Brita Rhedin, May 23, 1944; children: Per, Hans, Nils. Bachelor of Science, 1939, Licentiate of Philosophy, 1942; Doctor of Philosophy, University Uppsala, 1944; Doctor of Science honoris causa, University Durham, 1972, University Basel, 1980, University Liege, 1980, Upsala College, 1982, University Sussex, 1983. Research associate Nobel Institute Physics, 1942-51; professor physics Royal Institute Tech., Stockholm, 1951-54; professor, head physics department University Uppsala, Sweden, 1954-84. Author: Beta and Gamma-Ray Spectroscopy, 1955; Alpha, Beta and Gamma-Ray Spectroscopy, 1965; ESCA-Atomic, Molecular and Solid State Structure Studies by Means of Electron Spectroscopy, 1967; ESCA Applied to Free Molecules, 1969. Recipient Lindblom Prize, 1945; Bjorken Prize, 1955, 77; Celsius medal, 1962; Sixten Heyman award, 1971; Harrison Howe award, 1973; Maurice F. Hasler award, 1975; Charles Frederick Chandler medal, 1976; Torbern Bergman medal, 1979; Nobel Prize, 1981; Pitts. award spectroscopy, 1982; Röntgen medal, 1985, Fiuggi award, 1986, Humboldt award, 1986. Member Royal Swedish Acad. Sci., Royal Swedish Acad. Engineering Sciences, Royal Society Sci., Royal Acad. Arts and Sci. Uppsala, Royal Physiographical Society Lund, Societas Scientairum Fennica, Norwegian Acad. Sci., Royal Norwegian Society Sciences and Letters, Am. Acad. Arts and Sciences (hon.), Comite des Poids et Mesures, International Union Pure and Applied Physics (president 1981-84), Pontifical Acad. Sciences, National Acad. Sciences (foreign associate).

SIEKEVITZ, PHILIP, biology educator; born Philadelphia, February 25, 1918; son of Joseph and Tillie (Kaplan) S.; married Rebecca Burstein, August 7, 1949; children: Ruth, Miriam. Bachelor of Science in Biology, Philadelphia College Pharmacy and Scis., 1942, Doctor of Philosophy (honorary), 1972; Doctor of Philosophy in Biochemistry, University Calif.-Berkeley, 1949; Doctor of Philosophy (honorary), University Stockholm, 1974. United States Public Health Service fellow Massachusetts General Hospital, 1949-51; fellow oncology McArdle Laboratory, University Wisconsin, 1951-54; member faculty Rockefeller University, 1954-88, professor cell biology.; until 1988, retired; member molecular biology panel National Science Foundation, 1964-67; panel International Cell Research Organization, 1963-79; board of directors, treasurer, chairman Scientists Committee Pub. Information New York, 1962-80; board of directors New York Universities Committee, 1965-70; council Am. Federation Scientists, 1967-68. Author: (with A. Loewy) Cell Structure and Function, 2d edit, 1969; editor: Journal Cell Biology, 1962-65, Journal Cellular Physiology, 1970—, Biosci., Journal Experimental Zoology, 1969-73, Biochim. Biophysica Acta; member editorial board: Journal Cell Science, Journal Molecular Brain Rsch. Served with United States Army Air Force, 1942-45. Member Am. Society Biological Chemists, Am. Society Cell Biology (president 1966-67), Society Neurosci., American Association for the Advancement of Science, Am. Acad. Arts and Sciences, Am. Institute Biological Scientists, New York Acad. Sciences (hon. life, governing board 1973-79, president 1976), National Acad. Sciences, Sigma Xi. Office: Rockefeller U Lab Cell Biology 1230 York Avenue New York New York 10021

SIEVER, RAYMOND, geology educator; born Chicago, September 14, 1923; son of Leo and Lillie (Katz) S.; married Doris Fisher, March 31, 1945; children—Larry Joseph, Michael David. Bachelor of Science, University Chicago, 1943, Master of Science, 1947, Doctor of Philosophy, 1950; Master of Arts (honorary), Harvard University, 1960. With Illinois Geological Survey, 1943-44, 47-56, geologist; 1953-56; research associate, National Science Foundation senior postdoctoral fellow Harvard University, 1956-57, member faculty; 1957—, professor geology; 1965—, chairman department geological sciences; 1968-71, 76-81; associate geology Woods Hole (Massachusetts) Oceanographic Institution, 1957-65; consultant to industry and government, 1957—.
Author: (with others) Geology of Sandstones, 1965, Sand and Sandstone, 1972, 2d edition, 1987, Earth, 4th edit, 1986, Planet Earth, 1974, Energy and Environment, 1978; also numerous articles, papers.
Served with United States Army Air Force, 1944-46. Recipient Best Paper award Society Econ. Paleontologists and Mineralogists, 1957; President's award Am. Association Petroleum

Geologists, 1952. Fellow Am. Acad. Arts and Sciences, American Association for the Advancement of Science, Geological Society Am.; member Geochem. Society (president organic geochemistry group 1965), Am. Geophysical Union. Home: 38 Avon St Cambridge Massachusetts 02138 Office: Hoffman Lab Harvard University Cambridge Massachusetts 02138

SILVEIRA, MILTON ANTHONY, engineer, government official; born Mattapoisett, Massachusetts, May 4, 1929; son of Antone and Carolinda (Avila) S.; married Joan Weninger, December 23, 1983; children by previous marriage—Leland R., Douglas S., Carolyn M., Robert S. Bachelor of Science, University Vermont, 1951, Master of Science, 1961, Doctor of Philosophy (honorary), 1977; postgraduate, University Virginia, Virginia Poly Institute, University Houston.
Research intern Langley Air Force Base, Hampton, Virginia, 1951; chief engineering United States Army, St. Louis, 1951-55; acting head loads branch National Aeronautics and Space Administration, Hampton, 1955-63; project manager Manned Spacecraft Center National Aeronautics and Space Administration, Houston, 1963-67, various engineering positions, deputy manager orbiter project Johnson Space Center; 1967-81; assistant to deputy administrator National Aeronautics and Space Administration, Washington, 1981-83, chief engineer; 1983-86; vice president advance requirements and analysis, Washington operations Ford Aerospace and Communications Corp., Arlington, Virginia, 1987—.
Member American Institute of

Aeronautics and Astronautics. Home: 7213 Evans Mill Road McLean Virginia 22101 Office: Ford Aerospace and Communications Suite 1300 1235 Jefferson Davis Highway Arlington Virginia 22202

SILVERMAN, PAUL HYMAN, zoologist, former university official; born Minneapolis, October 8, 1924; son of Adolph and Libbie (Idlekope) S.; married Nancy Josephs, May 20, 1945; children: Daniel Joseph, Claire. Student, University Minnesota, 1942-43, 46-47; Bachelor of Science, Roosevelt University, 1949; Master of Science in Biology, Northwestern University, 1951; Doctor of Philosophy in Parasitology, University Liverpool, England, 1955, Doctor of Science, 1968. Research fellow Malaria Research Station, Hebrew University, Israel, 1951-53; research fellow department entomology and parasitology School Tropical Medicine, University Liverpool, 1953-56; senior sci. officer department parasitology Moredun Institute, Edinburgh, Scotland, 1956-59; head department immunoparasitology Allen & Hanbury, Limited, Ware, England, 1960-62; professor zoology and veterinary pathology and hygiene University Illinois, Urbana, 1963-72; chairman department zoology University Illinois, 1964-65, head department zoology; 1965-68; senior staff member Center for Zoonoses Research, 1964; professor biology, head div. natural sciences Temple Buell College, Denver, 1970-71; professor biology, chairman department biology, acting vice president research, vice president research and grad. affairs, associate provost for research and acad. services University New Mexico, 1972-77; provost for research and grad. studies State University of New York, Central Administration, Albany, 1977-79; president Research Foundation, State University of New York, Albany, 1979-80, University Maine, Orono, 1980-84; fellow bio. and medical div. Lawrence Berkeley Laboratory, University California Berkeley, 1984-86, acting div. head; 1986-87; adj. professor medical parasitology School Pub. Health University Calif.-Berkeley, 1986, associate laboratory director for life sciences, director Donner Laboratory; 1987—, director Systemwide Biotech. Research and Education Program; 1989—; consultant, examiner Middle States Association Schools and Colleges, Commission Colleges and Universities, North Central Association Colleges and Secondary Schools, 1964—; chairman Commission on Institutions Higher Education, 1974-76; adj. professor University Colorado, Boulder, 1970-72; Fulbright professor zoology Australian National University, Canberra, 1969; adjoint professor biology University Colorado, Boulder, 1970-72; examiner for Western Association Schools and Colleges, Accrediting Commission for Senior Colleges and Universities, California, 1972—; member board National Council on Postsecondary Accreditation, Washington, 1975-77; faculty apointee Sandia Corp., Department Energy, Albuquerque, 1974-81; project director research in malaria immunology and vaccination Agency for International Development, 1965-76; project director research in Helminth immunity United States Public Health Service, National Institutes of Health, 1964-72; senior consultant to Ministry Education and Culture, Brasilia, Brazil, 1975—; consultant to United States Senator George Mitchell, Maine; adv. on malaria immunology World Health Organization, Geneva, 1967; board of directors Inhalation Toxicology Research Institute, Lovelace Biomed. and Environmental Research Institute, Albuquerque, 1977—; member New York State Gov.'s High Tech. Opportunities Task Force; chairman research and rev. committee New York State Sci. and Tech. Foundation; member pres.'s council New England Land Grant Universities; member policies and issues committee National Association State Universities and Land Grant Colleges; board advs. Lovelace-Bataan Medical Center, Albuquerque, 1974-77; adv. committee United States Army Command and General Staff College, Fort Leavenworth, Kansas, 1983-84; corporator Bangor Savings Bank. Contributor articles to professional journals. Board of directors Historic Albany Foundation; chairman Maine Gov.'s Economic Devel. Conference; chairman research rev. committee New York State Sci. and Tech. Foundation. Fellow Royal Society Tropical Medicine, Hygiene, N. Mexican Acad. Sci.; member Am. Society Parasitologists, Am. Society Tropical Medicine and Hygiene, Am. Society Immunologists, Brit. Society Parasitology (council), Brit. Society Immunologists, Society General Microbiology, Society Protozoologists, Am. Society Zoologists, Am. Institute Biological Sciences, American Association for the Advancement of Science, New York Acad. Sciences, New York Society Tropical Medicine, Greater Bangor Chamber of Commerce (director), Sigma Xi, Phi Kappa Phi. Club: B'nai B'rith. Patentee process for prodn. parasitic helminth vaccine. Office: U California Berkeley Donner Lab Lawrence Berkeley Lab Berkeley California 94720

SIMMONS, LEE GUYTON, JR., zoological park director; born Tucson, February 20, 1938; son of Lee Guyton and Dorothy Esther (Taylor) S.; married Marie Annette Geim, September 6, 1959; children: Lee Guyton, Heather, Heidi. Student, Central State College; Doctor of Veterinary Medicine, Oklahoma State University. Resident veterinarian Columbus Zoo, Powell, Ohio, 1963-66, Henry Doorly Zoo, Omaha; research consultant Veteran's Administration Hospital; associate instructor University Nebraska Medical Center, Omaha; adj. associate professor oral biology Creighton University School Dentistry. Author: International Pedigree Book of Snow Leopards, 1982; contributor articles to professional journals. Board of directors Nebraska State Mus., Lincoln. Served with United States Army Reserve. Recipient National Idealism award City of Hope, 1979; named Man of Year, Lions Club, 1978. Fellow American Veterinary Medical Association, Am. Association Zool. Veterinarians (secretary), Am. Association Zool. Parks, Nebraska Veterinary Medical Association (Veterinarian of Year 1979). Lodge: Rotary. Office: Office of the Director Henry Doorly Zoo 10th St & Deerpark Boulevard Omaha NE 68107

SINGER, BURTON HERBERT, statistics educator; born Chicago, June 12, 1938; married; 1 child. Bachelor of Science, Case Institute Tech., 1959, Master of Science, 1961; Doctor of Philosophy in Statistics, Stanford University, 1967. From assistant to associate professor statistics Columbia University, New York City, 1967-77, professor math. statistics; 1977-85, chairman department math. statistics; from 1985; now chairman biostats. Yale University School Medicine, New Haven, Connecticut; statistical consultant Rand Corp., 1971—, Union Carbide Corp., 1971—, United States Atomic Energy Commission, 1972-75; research associate statistician Princeton University, 1972-73. Member American Association for the Advancement of Science, Am. Statistical Association, Psychomet Society. Office: Yale U School Medicine Department Edpidemiology & Pub Health New Haven Connecticut 06510

SINGER, ISADORE MANUEL, mathematician, educator; born Detroit, May 4, 1924; married; 5 children. Bachelor of Science, University Michigan, 1944; Master of Science, University Chicago, 1948, Doctor of Philosophy in Math., 1950. Moore instructor math. Massachusetts Institute of Technology, Cambridge, 1950-52, professor math.; 1956-70, Norbert Wiener professor; 1970-79, John D. MacArthur professor math. (1st holder); 1983—; assistant professor University of California at Los Angeles, 1952-54; visiting professor math University California, Berkeley, 1977-79, professor; 1979-83, Miller professor math.; 1982-83, professor math.; 1977-83; visiting assistant professor math. Columbia University, New York City, 1954-55; member Institute Advanced Study, 1955-56; past steering committee Center for Non-Linear Sciences, Los Alamos National Labs; adv. board Institute Theoretical Physics, University California, Santa Barbara; board of directors Santa Fe Institute; member various organizing committees and editor proceedings for conferences in field. Former editor professional journals. Alfred P. Sloan fellow, 1959-62; Guggenheim fellow, 1968-69, 75-76; recipient National Medal of Sci., 1983. Member National Acad. Sciences (past councillor, former member Commission Math. and Physical Sciences, other committee), Am. Philosophical Society, Am. Acad. Arts and Sciences, Am. Math. Society (vice president 1970-72, past executive committee, Bocher Memorial prize 1969), Am. Physical Society, International Congress Mathematicians (program committee 1986). Office: Massachusetts Institute of Technology Department Math Cambridge Massachusetts 02139

SINGER, MARCUS JOSEPH, educator, biologist; born Pittsburgh, August 28, 1914; son of Benjamin and Rachel (Gershenson) S.; married Leah Horelick, June 8, 1938; children: Robert H., Jon Fredric. Bachelor of Science, University Pittsburgh, 1938; Master of Arts, Harvard University, 1940, Doctor of Philosophy, 1942. Member faculty Harvard Medical School, 1942-51, assistant professor anatomy; until 1951; visiting professor anatomy Long Island College Medicine, 1950; associate professor, then professor zoology and child devel. Cornell University, 1951-61; visiting fellow Dutch Brain Institute, Amsterdam; formerly H.W. Payne professor anatomy, director department Case Western Reserve University School Medicine, Cleveland, now emer. professor; associate director Devel. Biology Center Case Western Reserve University School Medicine, from 1961; visiting professor anatomy Hebrew University, Jerusalem, 1974; Zyskind hon. visiting professor faculty health sciences Ben Gurion University Negev, Beersheba, Israel, 1975-76; visiting professor Gunma University, Japan, 1977; member cell biology study section National Institutes of Health, 1971-74, neurology study section, from 1976. Author: (with P. Yakovlev) Human Brain in Sagittal Section, 1954, Dog Brain in Section, 1962; editor: Journal Morphology, 1965-70, asso. editor, 1970-72, Journal Experimental Zoology, 1963-68, 70-71, editorial board, 1970-74; contributor articles on nervous system, histochemistry regeneration, cytology to professional publications. Guggenheim fellow Rome, 1967; von Humboldt fellow W. Ger., 1980-81. Fellow Am. Acad. Arts and Sciences, Ohio Acad. Sci., American Association for the Advancement of Science; member Am. Neurological Association (associate), Am. Association Anatomists, Society Zoologists, International Brain Research Organization, Association Research Nervous and Mental Diseases, Society Devel. and Growth, Biological Stain Commission, Sigma Xi. Office: Department Anatomy Case Western Reserve U Cleveland Ohio 44106

SINGER, MAXINE FRANK, biochemist; born New York City, February 15, 1931; daughter of Hyman S. and Henrietta (Perlowitz) Frank; married Daniel Morris Singer, June 15, 1952; children: Amy Elizabeth, Ellen Ruth, David Byrd, Stephanie Frank. Bachelor of Arts, Swarthmore College, 1952, Doctor of Science (honorary), 1978; Doctor of Philosophy, Yale University, 1957; Doctor of Science, Wesleyan University, 1977, U.Md.-Baltimore County, 1985, Cedar Crest College, 1986, City University of New York, 1988, Brandeis University, 1988.

United States Public Health Service postdoctoral fellow National Institutes of Health, Bethesda, Maryland, 1956-58; research chemist (biochemistry) National Institutes of Health, 1958-74; head section on nucleic acid enzymology National Cancer Institute, 1974-79; chief Laboratory of Biochemistry, National Cancer Institute, 1979-87, research chemist; 1987-88; president Carnegie Institute Washington, 1988—; Regents visiting lecturer University California, Berkeley, 1981; board of directors Foundation for Advanced Education in Sciences, 1972-78, 85-86; member sci. council International Institute Genetics and Biophysics, Naples, Italy, 1982-86. Member editorial board Journal Biol. Chemistry, 1968-74, Science mag, 1972-82; chairman editorial board Procs. of National Acad. Scis., 1985-88; contributor articles to scholarly journals. Trustee Wesleyan University, Middletown, Connecticut, 1972-75; trustee Yale Corp., New Haven, 1975—; board governors Weizmann Institute Sci., Rehovot, Israel, 1978—; board of directors Whitehead Inst, 1985—. Recipient award for achievement in biological scis. Washington Acad. Sciences, 1969, award for research in biological scis. Yale Sci. and Engineering Association, 1974, Superior Service Honor award Department of Health, Education and Welfare, 1975, Directors award National Institutes of Health, 1977, Distinguished Service medal Department of Health and Human Services, 1983, Presidential Distinguished Executive Rank award, 1987, U.S. Distinguished Executive Rank award, 1987. Fellow Am. Acad. Arts and Sciences; member American Association for the Advancement of Science (Sci. Freedom and

Responsibility award 1982), Am. Society Biological Chemists, Am. Society Microbiologists, Am. Chemical Society, Institute Medicine (National Acad. Sciences), National Acad. Sciences (council 1982-85), Pontifical Acad. of Sciences. Home: 5410 39th St Northwest Washington District of Columbia 20015 Office: Carnegie Institute Washington 1530 P St Northwest Washington District of Columbia 20015

SIRI, WILLIAM EMIL, physicist; born Philadelphia, January 2, 1919; son of Emil Mark and Caroline (Schaedel) S.; married Margaret Jean Brandenburg, December 3, 1949; children: Margaret Lynn, Ann Kathryn. Bachelor of Science, University Chicago, 1942; postgraduate in physics, University Calif.-Berkeley, 1947-50. Licensed professional engineer, California. Research engineer Baldwin-Lima-Hamilton Corp., 1943; physicist Manhattan Project Lawrence-Berkeley Laboratory, University California at Berkeley, 1943-45, principal investigator biophysics and research; 1945-74; manager energy analysis program Lawrence Berkeley Laboratory, 1974-81; senior scientist emeritus University California, 1981—; executive vice president Am. Mount Everest Expedition, Incorporated; Field leader University California Peruvian Expeditions, 1950-52; leader California Himalayan Expedition, 1954; field leader International Physiol. Expedition to Antarctica, 1957; deputy leader Am. Mount Everest Expedition, 1963. Author: Nuclear Radiations and Isotopic Tracers, 1949, papers on energy systems analyses, biophys. research, conservation and mountaineering. President Save San Francisco Bay Association, 1968-88; Board of directors Sierra Club Foundation, 1964-78, Mountain Medicine Institute, 1988—; vice chairman The Bay Institute, 1985—. Served to lieutenant (junior grade) United States Naval Reserve, 1950-59. Co-recipient Hubbard medal National Geog. Society, 1963, Elisa Kent Kane medal Philadelphia Geog. Society, 1963, Sol Feinstone Environmental award, 1977. Member Am. Physical Society, Biophys. Society, Am. Association Physicists in Medicine, Sigma Xi. Democrat. Lutheran. Clubs: Sierra (director 1955-74, president 1964-66, William Colby award 1975), American Alpine (vice president), Explorers (certificate of merit 1964). Home: 1015 Leneve Place El Cerrito California 94530 Office: U California Lawrence Berkeley Lab 1 Cyclotron Road Berkeley California 94720

SJOSTRAND, FRITIOF STIG, biologist, educator; born Stockholm, Sweden, November 5, 1912; son of Nils Johan and Dagmar (Hansen) S.; married Marta Bruhn-Fahraeus, March 24, 1941 (deceased June 1954); 1 child, Rutger; married Ebba Gyllenkrok, March 28, 1955; 1 child, Johan; married Birgitta Petterson, January 23, 1969; 1 child, Peter. Doctor of Medicine, Karolinska Institutet, Stockholm, 1941, Doctor of Philosophy, 1945; Doctor of Philosophy (honorary), University Siena, 1974, North-East Hill University, Chillon, India, 1989. Assistant professor anatomy Karolinska Institutet, 1945-48, associate professor; 1949-59, professor histology; 1960-61; research associate Massachusetts Institute of Technology, 1947-48; visiting professor University of California at Los Angeles, 1959, professor zoology; 1960-82, professor emeritus molecular biology; 1982—. Author: Über die Eigenfluoreszenz Tierischer Gewebe Mit Besonderer Berücksichtigung der Säger tierniere, 1944, Electron Microscopy of Cells and Tissues, Volume I, 1967; also numerous articles. Decorated North Star Orden Sweden; recipient Jubilee award Swedish Medical Society, 1959, Anders Retzius gold medal, 1967; Paul Ehrlich-Ludwig Darmstäedter prize, 1971. Fellow Royal Microscopic Society (hon.; London), Am. Acad. Arts and Sciences; member Japan Electron Microscopy Society (hon.), Scandinavian Electron Microscopy Society (hon.). Devel. technique for high resolution electron microscopy of cells, fluorescence microspectrography; invented ultramicrotome.

SKINNER, BURRHUS FREDERIC, psychologist, educator; born Susquehanna, Pennsylvania, March 20, 1904; son of William Arthur and Grace (Burrhus) S.; married Yvonne Blue, November 1, 1936; children—Julie (Mrs. Ernest Vargas), Deborah (Mrs. Barry Buzan). Bachelor of Arts, Hamilton College, 1926, Doctor of Science, 1951; Master of Arts, Harvard University, 1930, Doctor of Philosophy, 1931, Doctor of Science, 1985; Doctor of Science, North Carolina State University, 1960, University Chicago, 1967, University Missouri, 1968, Alfred University, 1969, University Exeter, England, 1969, Ind. University, 1970, McGill University, 1970, C.W. Post Center Long Island University, 1971, Dickinson College, 1972, Lowell Technological Institute, 1974, Nasson College, 1976, Colby College, 1984; Doctor of Letters (honorary), Ripon College, 1957, Tufts University, 1977, SUNY-Buffalo, 1986; Doctor of Humane Letters, Rockford College, 1971, Framingham (Massachusetts) State College, 1972, University Md.-Balt. County, 1973, New College, Hofstra University, 1974, Experimental College Institute Behavioral Research, 1974, Johns Hopkins University, 1979, State University of New York, Buffalo, 1986; Doctor of Laws, Ohio Wesleyan University, 1971, Hobart and William Smith College, 1972, Western Michigan University, 1976; Doctor.Soc.Science, University Louisville, 1977, Doctor.Laws, Keio University, Tokyo, 1979. Research fellow National Research Council, Harvard, 1931-33; junior fellow Harvard Society Fellows, 1933-36; instructor psychology University Minnesota, Minneapolis, 1936-37; assistant professor University Minnesota, 1937-39, associate professor; 1939-45; conducted war research sponsored by General Mills, Incorporated, 1942-43; professor psychology, chairman department Ind. University, 1945-48; William James lecturer Harvard, 1947, professor psychology; 1948-57, Edgar Pierce professor; 1958-74, professor emeritus; 1974—. Author: Behavior of Organisms, 1938, Walden Two, 1948, Science and Human Behavior, 1953, Verbal Behavior, 1957, (with C.B. Ferster) Schedules of Reinforcement, 1957, Cumulative Record, 1959, rev. 1961, 72, (with J.G. Holland) The Analysis of Behavior, 1961, The Technology of Teaching, 1968, Contingencies of Reinforcement: A Theoretical Analysis, 1969, Beyond Freedom and Dignity, 1971, About Behaviorism, 1974, Particulars of My Life, 1976, Reflections on Behaviorism and Society, 1978, The Shaping of a Behaviorist, 1979, Notebooks, 1980, A Matter of Consequences, 1983, Enjoy Old Age,

1983, Upon Further Reflection, 1986. Recipient distinguished sci. contribution award, 1958, National medal Sci., 1968, Gold medal Am. Psychol. Association, 1971, Joseph P. Kennedy, Junior Foundation award, 1971; award for excellence in psychiatry Albert Einstein School Medicine, 1985; President's award New York Acad. Sciences, 1985; Guggenheim fellow, 1944-45. Fellow Royal Society Arts; member Am. Psychological Association, Swedish Psychological Society, Brit. Psychological Society, Spanish Psychological Society, American Association for the Advancement of Science, National Acad. Sci., Am. Acad. Arts and Sciences, Am. Philosophical Society, Phi Beta Kappa, Sigma Xi. Home: 11 Old Dee Road Cambridge Massachusetts 02138

SKINNER, G(EORGE) WILLIAM, anthropologist, educator; born Oakland, California, February 14, 1925; son of John James and Eunice (Engle) S.; married Carol Bagger, March 25, 1951 (divorced January 1970); children: Geoffrey Crane, James Lauriston, Mark Williamson, Jeremy Burr; married Susan Mann, April 26, 1980; 1 daughter, Alison Jane. Student, Deep Springs (California) College, 1942-43; Bachelor of Arts with distinction in Far Eastern Studies, Cornell University, Ithaca, New York, 1947, Doctor of Philosophy in Cultural Anthropology, 1954. Field director Cornell University Southeast Asia program, also Cornell Research Center, Bangkok, Thailand, 1951-55; research associate in Indonesia, 1956-58; associate professor, then professor anthropology Cornell University, Ithaca, New York, 1960-65; assistant professor sociology Columbia, 1958-60; senior specialist in residence East-West Center Honolulu, 1965-66; professor anthropology Stanford, 1966—; Barbara Kimball Browning professor humanities and sciences 1987—; visiting professor University Pennsylvania, 1977, Duke University, spring, 1978, Keio University, Tokyo, spring 1985, fall 1988, University Calif.-San Diego, fall 1986; field research China, 1949-50, 77, 89, Southeast Asia, 1950-51, Thailand, 1951-53, 54-55, Java and Borneo, 1956-58, Japan, 1985, 88; member joint committee on contemporary China Social Sci. Research Council-Am. Acad. Learned Societies, 1961-65, 80-81, international committee on Chinese studies, 1963-64, member joint committee on Chinese studies, 1981-83; member subcom. research Chinese Society Social Sci. Research Council, 1961-70, chairman, 1963-70; director program on East Asian Local Systems, 1969-71; director Chinese Society Bibliography Project, 1964-73; associate director Cornell China Program, 1961-63; director London-Cornell Project Social Research, 1962-65; member committee on scholarly communication with People's Republic of China, National Acad. Sciences, 1966-70, member social sciences and humanities panel, 1982-83; member adv. committee Center for Chinese Research Materials, Association Research Libraries, 1967-70. Author: Chinese Society in Thailand, 1957, Leadership and Power in the Chinese Community of Thailand, 1958; also articles; Editor: The Social Sciences and Thailand, 1956, Local, Ethnic and National Loyalties in Village Indonesia, 1959, Modern Chinese Society: An Analytical Bibliography, 3 vols, 1973, (with Mark Elvin) The Chinese City

Between Two Worlds, 1974, (with A. Thomas Kirsch) Change and Persistence in Thai Society, 1975, The City in Late Imperial China, 1977, The Study of Chinese Society, 1979. Served to ensign United States Naval Reserve, 1943-46. Fellow Center for Advanced Study in Behavioral Sciences, 1969-70; Guggenheim fellow, 1969; National Institute of Mental Health special fellow, 1970. Fellow Am. Anthropological Association, A.A.A.S., Am. Sociological Association; member Association Asian Studies (board directors 1962-65, chairman nominating committee 1967-68, president 1983-84), Am. Acad. Political and Social Sci., Society for Cultural Anthropology, International Union for Sci. Study of Population, Social Sci. History Association, Am. Ethnological Society, Population Association Am., Siam Society, Society Ch'ing Studies, Society Econ. Anthropology, National Acad. Sciences, Phi Beta Kappa, Sigma Xi. Office: Stanford University Department Anthropology Stanford California 94305

SLAUGHTER, JOHN BROOKS, university administrator; born Topeka, March 16, 1934; son of Reuben Brooks and Dora (Reeves) S.; married Ida Bernice Johnson, August 31, 1956; children: John Brooks, Jacqueline Michelle. Student, Washburn University, 1951-53; Bachelor of Science in Electrical Engineering, Kansas State University, 1956, Doctor of Science (honorary), 1988; Master of Science in Engineering, University of California at Los Angeles, 1961; Doctor of Philosophy in Engineering Scis, University California, San Diego, 1971; Doctor of Engineering (honorary),

Rensselaer Polytechnic Institute, 1981; Doctor of Science (honorary), University Southern California, 1981, Tuskegee Institute, 1981, University Maryland, College Park, 1982, University Notre Dame, 1982; Doctor.Science (honorary), University Miami, 1983, University Massachusells, 1983, Texas Southern University, 1984, University Toledo, 1985, University Illinois, 1986, State University of New York, 1986; Doctor of Humane Letters (honorary), Bowie State College, 1987; Doctor.Science, Morehouse College, 1988, Kansas State University, 1988. Registered professional engineer, Washington (state). Electronics engineer General Dynamics Convair, San Diego, 1956-60; with Naval Electronics Laboratory Center, San Diego, 1960-75, div. head; 1965-71, department head; 1971-75; director applied physics laboratory University Washington, 1975-77; assistant director National Science Foundation, Washington, 1977-79; director National Science Foundation, 1980-82; acad. vice president, provost Washington State University, 1979-80; chancellor University Maryland, College Park, 1982-88; president Occidental College, Los Angeles, 1988—; board of directors, vice chairman San Diego Transit Corp., 1968-75; member committee on minorities in engineering National Research Council, 1976-79; member Commission on Pre-Coll. Edu. in Math., Sci., and Tech. National Sci. Board, 1982-83; board of directors Monsanto Company, Avery International, International Business Machines Corporation, and Union Bank. Editor: Journal Computers and Elec. Engring, 1972—. Board of directors San Diego Urban League, 1962-66, president, 1964-66; member President's

Committee on National Medal Sci., 1979-80; trustee Rensselaer Polytechnical Institute, 1982; chairman President's Committee National Collegiate Athletic Association, 1986-88. Naval Electronics Lab Center fellow, 1969-70; Recipient Engineering Alumnus award UCLA, 1978; Distinguished Service award National Science Foundation, 1979; Recipient Distinguished Service in Engineering award Kansas State University, 1981; recipient UCLA Engineering Distinguished Alumnus of Year, 1978, University Calif.-San Diego Distinguished Alumnus of Year, 1982. Fellow Institute of Electrical and Electronics Engineers (chairman committee on minority affairs 1976-80); member National Academy of Engineering, National Collegiate Athletic Association (chairman president commission), Tau Beta Pi, Eta Kappa Nu, Alpha Phi Alpha. Office: Occidental College 1600 Campus Dr Los Angeles California 90041 also: U Maryland College Park College Park Maryland 20742

SLAYTON, DONALD KENT, astronaut; born Sparta, Wisconsin, March 1, 1924; son of Charles Sherman and Victoria Adelia (Larson) S.; married Marjory Lunney, May 15, 1955 (divorced); 1 son, Kent Sherman; married Bobbie Osborn, October 8, 1983. Bachelor of Aeronautical Engineering, University Minnesota, 1949; Doctor of Science (honorary), Carthage College, 1960; Doctor of Engineering (honorary), Michigan Tech. Institute. Served to captain, pilot United States Army Air Force, 1942-46; engineer Boeing Aircraft Company, 1949-51; commissioned captain United States Air Force, 1951, advanced to major; 1959, resigned; 1963; fighter pilot, maintenance officer Germany, 1952-55; fighter test pilot Edwards Air Force Base, Cal., 1955-59; joined Project Mercury, manned space flight, National Aeronautics and Space Administration, 1959, chief astronaut; 1962-63, director flight crew operations; 1963-74; member crew Apollo-Soyuz pilot docking module, 1975; manager Space Shuttle Approach and Landing Test, 1975-77, Space Shuttle Orbital Flight Test, 1978-82; president Space Services Incorporated, 1982—. Fellow Society Experimental Test Pilots, American Institute of Aeronautics and Astronautics, Am. Astronautical Society; member Order of Daedalians, Am. Fighter Aces. Office: 7015 Gulf Freeway Suite 140 Houston Texas 77087

SLOVITER, HENRY ALLAN, medical educator; born Philadelphia, June 16, 1914; son of Samuel and Rose (Seltzer) S.; married Dolores Korman, April 3, 1969. Bachelor of Arts, Temple University, 1935, Master of Arts, 1936; Doctor of Philosophy, University Pennsylvania, 1942, Doctor of Medicine, 1949. Chemist, United States Naval Base, Philadelphia, 1936-45; intern Hospital University Pennsylvania, 1949-50; research fellow University Pennsylvania School Medicine, 1945-49, assistant professor; 1952-56, associate professor; 1956-68, professor; 1968—; visiting scientist biochemistry department Tokyo University; United States project officer United States Public Health Service Fogarty International Center program Institute for Biology, Belgrade, Yugoslavia, 1971, 74; visiting professor Academia Sinica, China, 1983; research scientist Tokyo Metropolitan Institute Medical Research, 1984. Contributor articles professional journals. Am. Cancer Society fellow National Institute Medical Research, London, England, 1950-52; College de France endocrinology dept. research fellow Paris, 1952; sr. international fellow USPHS Fogarty International Center, St. Mary's Hospital Medical School, London, 1978; recipient Glycerine Research award, 1954; exchange scholar Tokyo University, 1963; exchange scholar Union of Soviet Socialist Republics, 1965, 71, India, 1967. Fellow American Association for the Advancement of Science; member International Society Neurochemistry, Am. Society Biological Chemists, International Society Blood Transfusion, Am. Physiological Society. Home: 310 S Front St Philadelphia Pennsylvania 19106 Office: School Medicine U Pennsylvania Philadelphia Pennsylvania 19104

SMAGORINSKY, JOSEPH, meteorologist; born New York City, January 29, 1924; son of Nathan and Dinah (Azaroff) S.; married Margaret Knoepfel, May 29, 1948; children: Anne, Peter, Teresa, Julia, Frederick. Bachelor of Science, New York University, 1947, Master of Science, 1948, Doctor of Philosophy, 1953; Doctor of Science (honorary), University Munich, 1972. Research assistant, instructor meteorology New York University, 1946-48; with United States Weather Bureau, 1948-50, 53-65, chief general circulation research section; 1955-63; meteorologist Institute Advanced Study, Princeton, New Jersey, 1950-53; acting director Institute Atmospheric Sciences, Environmental Sciences Services Administration, Washington, 1965-66; director Geophysical Fluid Dynamics Laboratory, Environmental Sciences

Services Adminstrn.-NOAA, Washington and Princeton, 1964-83; consultant 1983—; vice chairman United States Committee Global Atmospheric Research Program, National Acad. Sci., 1967-73, 80-87, officer, 1974-77, member climate board, 1978-87, chairman committee on international climate programs, 1979, board international organizations and programs, 1979-83, chairman climate research committee, 1981-87; chairman joint organizing committee Global Atmospheric Research Program, International Council Sci. Unions/World Meteorol. Organization, 1976-80, officer, 1967-80; chairman Joint Sci. Committee World Climate Research Program, 1980-81; chairman climate coordinating forum International Council Sci. Unions, 1980-84; visiting lecturer with rank of professor Princeton University, 1968-83, visiting senior fellow, 1983; Sigmx Xi national lecturer, 1983-85; Brittingham visiting professor University Wisconsin, 1986. Contributor to professional publns. Served to 1st lieutenant United States Army Air Force, 1943-46. Decorated Air medal; recipient Gold medal Department Commerce, 1966; award for sci. research and achievement Environmental Sci. Services Administration, 1970; U.S. Presidential award, 1980; Buys Ballot Gold medal Royal Netherlands Acad. Arts and Sciences, 1973; IMO prize and Gold medal World Meteorol. Organization, 1974. Fellow Am. Acad. Arts and Sciences, Am. Meteorological Society (councilor 1974-77, associate editor journal 1965-74, Meisinger award 1967, Wexler Memorial lecturer 1969, Carl-Gustaf Rossby Research Gold medal 1972, Cleveland Abbe award for distinguished service to atmospheric sci. 1980, president

1986); member Royal Meteorological Society (hon.)(Symons Memorial lecturer 1963, Symons meml gold medal 1981). Home: 21 Duffield Place Princeton New Jersey 08540 Office: Princeton University Department Geol and Geophys Scis Scis Guyot Hall Princeton New Jersey 08544

SMITH, ALBERT CHARLES, biologist, educator; born Springfield, Massachusetts, April 5, 1906; son of Henry Joseph and Jeanette Rose (Machol) S.; married Nina Grönstrand, June 15, 1935; children: Katherine (Mrs. L. J. Campbell), Michael Alexis; married Emma van Ginneken, August 1, 1966. Bachelor of Arts, Columbia University, 1926, Doctor of Philosophy, 1933. Assistant curator New York Botanical Garden, 1928-31, associate curator; 1931-40; curator herbarium Arnold Arboretum of Harvard University, 1940-48; curator div. phanerogams United States National Mus., Smithsonian Institution, 1948-56; program director systematic biology National Science Foundation, 1956-58; director Mus. of Natural History, Smithsonian Institution, 1958-62, assistant secretary; 1962-63; professor botany, director research University Hawaii, Honolulu, 1963-65; Gerrit Parmile Wilder professor botany University Hawaii, 1965-70, professor emeritus; 1970—; Ray Ethan Torrey professor botany University Massachusetts, Amherst, 1970-76; professor emeritus University Massachusetts, 1976—; editorial consultant National Tropical Botanical Garden, Hawaii, 1977—; botanical expeditions, Colombia, Peru, Brazil, Brit. Guiana, Fiji, West Indies, 1926-69; del. International Botanical Congresses, Amsterdam, 1935, Stockholm, 1950; vice president systematic section, Montreal, 1959,

International Zool. Congress, London, 1958. Author: Flora Vitiensis Nova: a New Flora of Fiji, Volume I, 1979, Volume II, 1981, Volume III, 1985, Volume IV, 1988; also tech. articles; Editor: Brittonia, 1935-40, Journal Arnold Arboretum, 1941-48, Sargentia, 1942-48, Allertonia, 1977-88; editorial com.: International Code Botanical Nomenclature, 1954-64. Bishop Museum fellow Yale University, 1933-34; Guggenheim fellow, 1946-47; Robert Allerton award for excellence in tropical botany, 1979. Fellow Am. Acad. Arts and Sciences, Linnean Society London; member Botanical Society Am., Association Tropical Biology (president 1967-68), International Association Plant Taxonomy (vice president 1959-64), National Acad. Sciences, Fiji Society (hon.). Club: Washington Biologists' Field (president 1962-64). Office: University Hawaii Department Botany Honolulu Hawaii 96822

SMITH, HAMILTON OTHANEL, molecular biologist, educator; born New York City, August 23, 1931; son of Bunnie Othanel and Tommie Harkey S.; married Elizabeth Anne Bolton, May 25, 1957; children: Joel, Barry, Dirk, Bryan, Kirsten. Student, University Illinois, 1948-50; Bachelor of Arts in Math, University California, Berkeley, 1952; Doctor of Medicine, Johns Hopkins University, 1956. Intern Barnes Hospital, St. Louis, 1956-57; resident in medicine Henry Ford Hospital, Detroit, 1959-62; United States Public Health Service fellow department human genetics University Michigan, Ann Arbor, 1962-64; research associate University Michigan, 1964-67; assistant professor molecular biology and genetics Johns Hopkins University

School Medicine, Baltimore, 1967-69; associate professor Johns Hopkins University School Medicine, 1969-73, professor; 1973—; associate Institut für Molekularbiologie der University Zurich, Switzerland, 1975-76. Contributor articles to professional journals. Served to lieutenant Medical Corps United States Naval Reserve, 1957-59. Recipient Nobel Prize in medicine, 1978; Guggenheim fellow, 1975-76. Member Am. Society Microbiology, American Association for the Advancement of Science, Am. Society Biological Chemists, National Acad. Sci. Office: Johns Hopkins U School Medicine/Dept Microbiology 725 N Wolfe St Baltimore Maryland 21205

SMITH, HARLAN JAMES, educator, astronomer; born Wheeling, West Virginia, August 25, 1924; son of Paul Elder and Anna Persis (McGregor) S.; married Joan Greene, December 21, 1950; children: Nathaniel, Sarah (deceased), Julia, Theodore, Hannah. Bachelor of Arts, Harvard University, 1949, Master of Arts, 1951, Doctor of Philosophy, 1955; Doctor.Physical Science (honorary), Nicholas Copernicus University, Torun, Poland, 1973; Doctor.Physical Science, Denison University, 1983. Research assistant astronomy, teaching fellow and research fellow Harvard University, Cambridge, Massachusetts, 1946-53; from instructor to associate professor astronomy Yale University, New Haven, 1953-63, professor astronomy, chairman department; 1963-78, Edward Randall Junior Centennial professor astronomy; 1985—; director McDonald Observatory, University Texas, Austin, 1963—; member Space Sci. Board, 1977-79. Co-editor: Astron. Jour,

1960-63. Served as weather observer United States Army Air Force, 1943-46. George R. Agassiz research fellow Harvard Obs., 1952-53. Fellow American Association for the Advancement of Science; Member Am. Astronomical Society (acting secretary 1961-62, chairman planetary division 1974-75, council 1975-78, vice president 1977-79), Royal Astronomical Society, Am. Geophysical Union, Associate Univs. Research in Astronomy (chairman board 1980-82), American Association for the Advancement of Science, International Astronomical Union, Sigma Xi. Home: 2705 Pecos St Austin Texas 78703 Office: U Tex-Austin McDonald Obs Post Office Box 1337 Fort Davis Texas 79734

SMITH, JOE MAUK, chemical engineer, educator; born Sterling, Colorado, February 14, 1916; son of Harold Rockwell and Mary Calista (Mauk) S.; married Essie Johnstone McCutcheon, December 23, 1943; children—Rebecca K., Marsha Mauk. Bachelor of Science, California Institute Tech., 1937; Doctor of Philosophy, Massachusetts Institute Tech., 1943. Chemical engineer Texas Company, Standard Oil Company of California, 1937-41; instructor chemical engineering Massachusetts Institute Tech., 1943; assistant professor chemical engineering University Maryland, 1945; professor chemical engineering Purdue University, 1945-56; dean College Tech., University New Hampshire, 1956-57; professor chemical engineering Northwestern University, 1957-59, Walter P. Murphy professor chemical engineering; 1959-61; professor engineering University California, 1961—, chairman department chemical engineering; 1964-72; hon. professor chemical engineering University Buenos Aires, Argentina, 1964—; Fulbright lecturer, England, Italy, Spain, 1965, and, Argentina, 1963, 65, Ecuador, 1970; Mudaliar Memorial lecturer University Madras, India, 1967; United Nations Educational, Scientific and Cultural Organization consultant, Venezuela, 1972—. Author: Introduction to Chemical Engineering Thermodynamics, 1949, 4th edit, 1986, Chemical Engineering Kinetics, 1956, 3d edition, 1981. Guggenheim research award for study in Holland; also Fulbright award, 1953-54. Member Am. Chemical Society, Am. Institute Chemical Engineers 77 (Walker award 1960, Wilhelm award 1977, Lewis award 1984), National Acad. Engineering, Sigma Xi, Tau Beta Pi.

SMOLUCHOWSKI, ROMAN, physicist, emeritus educator; born Zakopane, Austria, August 31, 1910; came to United States, 1935, naturalized, 1946; son of Marian and Sophia (Baraniecka) S.; married Louise Catherine Riggs, February 3, 1951; children: Peter, Irene. Master of Arts, University Warsaw, 1933; Doctor of Philosophy, University Groningen, Holland, 1935. Member Institute Advanced Study, Princeton, 1935-36, instructor, research associate physics department; 1939-41; professor solid state sciences, head solid state and materials program Princeton University, 1960-78; research associate, head physics section Institute Metals, Warsaw, 1936-39; research physicist General Electric Research Laboratories, Schenectady, 1941-46; associate professor, staff Metals Research Laboratory, Carnegie Institute Tech., 1946-50, professor physics and metallurgical engineering; 1950-56, professor physics; 1956-60; professor astronomy and physics University Texas, Austin, 1978—; visiting professor International School Solid State Physics, Mol, Belgium, 1963, Facultédes Sciences, Paris, 1965-66; lecturer School Planetary Physics, Super-Besse, France, 1972; Fulbright professor University Sorbonne-Paris, 1955-56; lecturer International School Solid State Physics, Varenna, Italy, 1957, University Liege, Belgium, 1956, Faculté des Sciences, Paris, 1965-66; visiting professor National Research Council of Brazil, 1958-59, Tech. University Munich, 1974; member solid state panel Research and Devel. Board, Department Def., 1949, secretary panel, 1950-61; member tech. adv. board Aircraft Nuclear Propulsion, 1950; chmn committee on magnetism Office Naval Research, 1952-56; chairman committee on solids National Research Council, 1950-61, chairman solid state sciences panel, 1961-67, chairman div. physical sciences, 1969-75; member space sci. board National Acad. Sciences, 1969-75, member physics survey, 1963-66, 1969-72; adv. committee metallurgy Oak Ridge National Laboratory, 1960-62, member committee on planetary and lunar exploration, 1980-84. Author: (with Mayer and Weyl) Phase Transformations in Nearly Perfect Crystals, 1952, (with others) Molecular Science and Molecular Engineering, 1959, The Solar System—Sun, Planets and Life, 1983; editor: (with N. Kurti) Monograph Series on Solid State, 1957, (with J. W. Wilkins and E. Burstein) Comments in Condensed Matter Physics, (with M. Glazer) Phase Transitions; (with others) Ices in the Solar System, The Galaxy and the Solar System; editor-in-chief: Crystal

Lattice Defects and Amorphous Materials, Semiconductors and Insulators; asso. editor: Fundamentals of Cosmic Physics; Contributor articles to professional journals. Chairman board trustees Simon's Rock College, 1971-72. Guggenheim Memorial fellow, 1974; fellow Churchill College Cambridge University, England, 1974. Fellow Am. Physical Society (chairman division solid state physics 1944-46), Am. Acad. Arts and Sciences; member American Association for the Advancement of Science, International Astronomical Union, Finnish Acad. Sciences and Letters, Am. Astronomical Society, Mexican Acad. Engineering, Brazilian Acad. Sciences, Sigma Xi, Alpha Sigma Mu, Pi Mu Epsilon. Home: 1401 Ethridge Avenue Austin Texas 78703 Office: U Tex Department Physics and Astronomy Austin Texas 78712

SMULLIN, LOUIS DIJOUR, electrical engineer, educator; born Detroit, February 5, 1916; married; 4 children. Bachelor of Science in Engineering, University Michigan, 1936; Master of Science, Massachusetts Institute of Technology, 1939. Draftsman Swift Electrical Welder Company, Michigan, 1936; engineer Ohio Brass Company, 1936-38, Farnsworth TV Corp., 1939-40, Scintilla Magneto div. Bendix Aviation Corp., 1940-51; section head radiation laboratory Massachusetts Institute of Technology, Cambridge, 1941-46; head microwave tube laboratory Federal Telecommunications Laboratories div. International Telephone and Telegraph Corp., New Jersey, 1946-48; head tube laboratory Research Laboratory Electronics, 1948-50; div. head Lincoln Laboratory, 1950-55; from associate to professor Massachusetts Institute of Technology, Cambridge, 1955-76, Dugald Caleb Jackson professor electrical engineering; 1976—, chairman department electrical engineering; 1967—; member steering committee Kanpur Indo-Am. Program, 1961-65; visiting professor Indian Institute Tech., Kanpur, 1965-66; National Science Foundation working group sci. and engineering instruction, India; board governors Israel Institute Tech. Fellow Institute of Electrical and Electronics Engineers, Am. Acad. Arts and Sciences; member National Acad. Engineering (telecommunications committee), Am. Physical Society. Office: Massachusetts Institute of Technology Department Elec Engring Cambridge Massachusetts 02139

SNELL, GEORGE DAVIS, geneticist; born Bradford, Massachusetts, December 19, 1903; son of Cullen Bryant and Katharine (Davis) S.; married Rhoda Carson, July 28, 1937; children: Thomas Carleton, Roy Carson, Peter Garland. Bachelor of Science, Dartmouth College, 1926; Master of Science, Harvard University, 1928, Doctor of Science, 1930; Doctor of Medicine (honorary), Charles University, Prague, 1967; Doctor of Laws (honorary), Colby College, 1982; Doctor of Science (honorary), Dartmouth College, 1974, Gustavus Adolphus College, 1981, University Maine, 1981, Bates College, 1982, Ohio State University, 1984. Instructor zoology Dartmouth College, 1929-30, Brown University, 1930-31; assistant professor Washington University, St. Louis, 1933-34; research associate Jackson Laboratory, 1935-56, senior staff scientist; 1957—, emeritus; 1969—, sci. administrator; 1949-50. Co-author: Histocompatibility, 1976; also sci. papers in field; editor: The Biology of the Laboratory Mouse, 1941. Recipient Bertner Foundation award in field cancer research, 1962; Griffin award Animal Care Panel, 1962; career award National Cancer Institute, 1964-68; Gregor Mendel medal Czechoslovak Acad. Sciences, 1967; International award Gairdner Foundation, 1976; Wolf Foundation prize in medicine, 1978; award National Institute Arthritis and Infectious Disease-Nat. Cancer Institute, 1978; Nobel prize in medicine (with Dausset and Benacerraf), 1980; National Research Council fellow University Texas, 1931-33; National Institutes of Health health research grantee for study genetics and immunology of tissue transplantation, 1950-73 (allergy and immunology study sect. 1958-62); Guggenheim fellow, 1953-54. Member National Acad. Sciences, Transplantation Society, Am. Acad. Arts and Sci., French Acad. Sciences (foreign associate), Am. Philosophical Society, Brit. Transplantation Society (hon.), Phi Beta Kappa. Home: 21 Atlantic Avenue Bar Harbor Maine 04609

SNYDER, SOLOMON HALBERT, psychiatrist, pharmacologist; born Washington, December 26, 1938; son of Samuel Simon and Patricia (Yakerson) S.; married Elaine Borko, June 10, 1962; children: Judith Rhea, Deborah Lynn. Doctor of Medicine cum laude, Georgetown University, 1962, Doctor of Science (honorary), 1986; Doctor of Science (honorary), Northwestern University, 1981. Intern Kaiser Foundation Hospital, San Francisco, 1962-63; research associate National Institute of Mental Health, Bethesda, Maryland, 1963-65; resident psychiatry Johns Hopkins Hospital, Baltimore, 1965-68; associate professor psychiatry and pharmacology Johns Hopkins Medical School, 1968-70, professor; 1970-77, distinguished Service professor psychiatry and pharmacology; 1977-80, distinguished Service professor neurosci., psychiatry, and pharmacology; 1980—, director department neurosci.; 1980—; National Institutes of Health lecturer, 1979. Author: Uses of Marijuana, 1971, Madness and the Brain, 1973, Opiate Receptor Mechanisms, 1975, The Troubled Mind, 1976, Biologic Aspects of Mental Disorder, 1980, Drugs and the Brain, 1986, Brainstorming, 1989; editor Perspectives in Neuropharmacology, 1971, Frontiers in Catecholamine Research, 1973, Handbook of Psychopharmacology, 1974; contributor articles to professional journals. Served with United States Public Health Service, 1963-65. Recipient Outstanding Scientist award Maryland Acad. Sciences, 1969; John Jacob Abel award Am. Pharmacology Society, 1970; A.E. Bennett award Society Biological Psychiatry, 1970; Gaddum award Brit. Pharm. Society, 1974; F.O. Schmitt award in neuroscis. Massachusetts Institute of Technology, 1974; Nicholas Giarman lecture award Yale University, 1975; Rennebohm award University Wisconsin, 1976; Salmon award, 1977; Stanley Dean award Am. College Psychiatrists, 1978; Harvey Lecture award, 1978; Lasker award, 1978; Wolf prize, 1983; Dickson prize, 1983; Sci. Achievement award American Medical Association, 1985; Ciba-Geigy-Drew award, 1985; Strecker prize, 1986; Edward Sachar Memorial award Columbia University, 1986; Paul K. Smith Memorial lecture award George Washington University,

1986; Sense of Smell award Fragrance Research Foundation, 1987; Julius Axelrod lecture award CUNY, 1988; John Flynn Memorial lecture award Yale University, 1988. Fellow Am. College Neuropsychopharmacology (Daniel Efron award 1974), Am. Psychiat. Association (Hofheimer award 1972, Distinguished Sbvc. award 1989), Am. Acad. Arts and Sciences; member Psychiat. Research Society, National Acad. Sciences, Society for Neuroscis. (president 1979-80), Am. Society Biological Chemists, Am. Pharmacology Society, Institute Medicine. Home: 2300 W Rogers Avenue Baltimore Maryland 21209

SNYDERMAN, RALPH, medical educator, physician; born Brooklyn, March 13, 1940; married Judith Ann Krebs, November 18, 1967; 1 child, Theodore Benjamin. Bachelor of Science, Washington College, Chestertown, Maryland, 1961; Doctor of Medicine, SUNY-Bklyn., 1965. Diplomate Am. Board Internal Medicine, Am. Board Allergy and Immunology. Medical intern Duke University Hospital, Durham, North Carolina, 1965-66, medical resident; 1966-67, assistant professor medicine and immunology; 1972-74, associate professor; 1974-77, chief, div. rheumatology and immunology; 1975-87, professor medicine and immunology; 1980-84, Frederic M. Hanes professor medicine, professor immunology; 1984-87; surgeon United States Public Health Service, National Institutes of Health, Bethesda, Maryland, 1967-69; senior staff fellow National Institute Dental Research, National Institutes of Health, Bethesda, Maryland, 1969-70, senior investigator immunology section laboratory microbiology and

immunology; 1970-72; chief, div. rheumatology Durham Veteran's Administration Hospital, Bethesda, Maryland, 1972-75; vice president medical research and devel. Genentech, Incorporated, South San Francisco, California, 1987-88, senior vice president medical research and devel.; 1988—; adj. assistant professor oral biology University North Carolina School Dental Medicine, Chapel Hill, 1974-75; director Lab Immune Effector Function, Howard Hughes Medical Institute, Durham, 1977—; adj. professor medicine University California, San Francisco, 1987—. Editor: Contemporary Topics in Immunobiology, 1984, Medical Clinics of North American, 1985, Inflammation: Basic Concepts and Clinical Correlates, 1988; contributor articles to professional journals. Recipient Alexander von Humboldt award Federal Republic Germany, 1985. Member Association Am. Physicians, Am. Association Immunologists, Am. Society Clinical Investigation, Am. Acad. Allergy, Am. Association Cancer Research, Am. Society Experimental Pathology, Am. Federation Clinical Research, Am. Association Pathologists, Reticuloendothelial Society, Am. Rheumatism Association, Sigma Xi. Office: Genentech Incorporated VP Med Research & Devel 460 Point San Bruno Boulevard South San Francisco California 94080

SOKOLOFF, LOUIS, physiologist, neurochemist; born Philadelphia, October 14, 1921; (married); 2 children. Bachelor of Arts, University Pennsylvania, 1943, Doctor of Medicine, 1946. Intern Philadelphia General Hospital, 1946-47; research fellow in physiology University Pennsylvania Grad. School Medicine,

1949-51, instructor, then associate; 1951-56; associate chief, then chief section cerebral metabolism National Institute of Mental Health, Bethesda, Maryland, 1953-68; chief laboratory cerebral metabolism National Institute of Mental Health, 1968—. Chief editor: Journal Neurochemistry, 1974-78. Served to captain Medical Corps United States Army, 1947-49. Recipient F.O. Schmitt medal in neurosci., 1980, Albert Lasker clinical med. research award, 1981, Karl Spencer Lashley award, 1987, Distinguished Graduate award University Pennsylvania, 1987, National Acad. Sciences award in Neurosci., 1988, Georg Charles de Hevesy Nuclear Medicine Pioneer award, 1988, Mihara award, 1988. Member Am. Physiological Society, Association Research Nervous and Mental Diseases, Am. Biophys. Society, Am. Acad. Neurology, Am. Neurological Association, Am. Society Biological Chemists, Am. Society Neurochemistry, United States National Acad. Sciences. Office: NIMH Building 36 Room 1A-05 Bethesda Maryland 20892

SOLOMON, DAVID HARRIS, educator, physician; born Cambridge, Massachusetts, March 7, 1923; son of Frank and Rose (Roud) S.; married Ronda L. Markson, June 23, 1946; children: Patricia Jean (Mrs. Richard E. Sinaiko), Nancy Ellen. Bachelor of Arts, Brown University, 1944; Doctor of Medicine, Harvard University, 1946. Intern Peter Bent Brigham Hospital, Boston, 1946-47; resident Peter Bent Brigham Hospital, 1947-48, 50-51; fellow endocrinology New England Center Hospital, Boston, 1951-52; faculty University of California at Los Angeles School Medicine, 1952—, professor medicine; 1966—, vice chairman department medicine; 1968-71, chairman department; 1971-81, associate director, geriatrics; 1982—; chief medical service Harbor General Hospital, Torrance, California, 1966-71; consultant Wadsworth Veteran's Administration Hospital, Los Angeles, 1952—, Sepulveda Veteran's Administration Hospital, 1971—; consultant metabolism training committee United States Public Health Service, 1960-64, endocrinology study section, 1970-73; member dean's committee Wadsworth, Sepulveda Veteran's Administration hospitals. Editor: Journal Am. Geriatric Society, 1988—; contributor numerous articles to professional journals. Recipient Mayo Soley award, 1986. em. Association Am. Physicians, Am. Society Clinical Investigation, Am. Federation Clinical Research, Western Society Clinical Research (councillor 1963-65), Endocrine Society (Robert H. Williams award 1989), Am. Thyroid Association (president 1973-74, Distinguished Service award 1986), Society Experimental Biology and Medicine, American College of Physicians (master), Los Angeles Society Internal Medicine (executive council 1960-62), Institute Medicine National Acad. Sciences, American Association for the Advancement of Science, Association Profs. Medicine (president 1980-81), Western Association Physicians (councillor 1972-75, president 1983-84), Am. Geriatrics Society (board directors 1985—), Phi Beta Kappa, Sigma Xi, Alpha Omega Alpha. Home: 863 Woodacres Road Santa Monica California 90402 Office: University of California at Los Angeles School Medicine Department Medicine Los Angeles California 90024

SOMASUNDARAN, PONISSERIL, engineering and applied science educator, consultant, researcher; born Pazhookara, Kerala, India, June 28, 1939; came to United States, 1961; son of Kumara Moolayil and Lakshmikutty (Amma) Pillai; married Usha N., May 25, 1966; 1 child, Tamara. Bachelor of Science, Kerala University, Trivandrum, India, 1958; Bachelor of Education, Indian Institute Science, Bangalore, 1961; Master of Science, University Calif.-Berkeley, 1962, Doctor of Philosophy, 1964. Research engineer University Calif.-Berkeley, 1964; research engineer International Minerals & Chemical Corp., Skokie, Illinois, 1965-67; research chemist R.J. Reynolds Industries, Incorporated, Winston-Salem, North Carolina, 1967-70; associate professor Columbia University, New York City, 1970-78; professor mineral engineering Columbia University, 1973-83, La Von Duddleson Krumb professor; 1983—; chairman Henry Krumb School Mines Columbia University, 1988—, director Langmuir Center for Colloids and Interfaces, 1987—; consultant numerous agys., companies, including National Institutes of Health, 1974, B.F. Goodrich, 1974, National Science Foundation, 1974, Alcan, 1981, United Nations Educational, Scientific and Cultural Organization, 1982, Sohio, 1984-85, International Business Machines Corporation, 1984; member panel National Research Council; chairman numerous international symposia and National Science Foundation workshops; member adv. panel Bureau Mines Generic Centers, 1983—; Henry Krumb lecturer American Institute of Mining, Metallurgy, and Petroleum Engineers, 1988; keynote and plenary lecturer international meetings. Editor books, including: Fine Particles Processing, 1980 (Publication Board award 1980); editor-in-chief Colloids and Surfaces, 1980—; Henry Krumb lecturer AIME, 1988; contributor numerous articles to professional publications Patentee in field. President Keralasamajam of Greater New York, New York City, 1974-75; board of directors Federation Indian Associates, New York City, 1974—, Vols. in Service to Education in India, Hartford, Connecticut, 1974—. Recipient Distinguished Achievement in Engineering award, AINA, 1980, Antoine M. Gaudin award Society Mining Engrs.-AIME, 1983, Achievements in Applied Sci. award 2d World Malayalam Conference, 1985, Robert H. Richards award, American Institute of Mining, Metallurgy and Petroleum Engineers, 1986, Arthur F. Taggart award Society Mining Engrs.-AIME, 1987, honor award Association Ind. in Am., 1988, honor award American Institute of Architects, 1988; named Mill Man of Distinction, Society Mining Engrs.-AIME, 1983. Fellow Institution Mining and Metallurgy (United Kingdom); member Society Mining Engineers (board directors 1982-85, distinguished member, various awards), Engineering Foundation (vice chairman conference committee 1983-85, chairman conference committee 1985-88, board executive committee 1985-88), National Acad. Engineering, Am. Chemical Society, New York Acad. Sciences, Am. Institute Chemical Engineers, Society Petroleum Engineers, International Association Colloid and Surface Scientists, Sigma Xi. Office: Columbia U 911 Southwest Mudd Building New York New York 10027

SOMLYO, ANDREW PAUL, physician, scientist, university administrator; born Budapest, Hungary, February 25, 1930; son of Anton and Clara Maria (Kiss) S.; married Avril V. Russell, May 25, 1961; 1 child, Andrew Paul. Bachelor of Science, University Illinois, 1954, Master of Science, 1956, Doctor of Medicine, 1956; Master of Science, Drexel Institute Tech., Philadelphia, 1963; Master of Arts (honorary), University Pennsylvania, Philadelphia, 1981. Assistant physician Columbia-Presbyn. Medical Center, New York City, 1960-61; research associate Presbyn. Hospital, Philadelphia, 1961-67; assistant professor pathology University Pennsylvania, Philadelphia, 1964-67, associate professor; 1967-71, professor; 1971-88, professor physiology and pathology; 1973-88, director Pennsylvania Muscle Institute; 1973-88; chairman, Charles Slaughter professor department physiology, professor cardiology University Virginia, Charlottesville, 1988—; consultant National Institutes of Health. Author (with others): Vascular Neuroeffector Systems, 1971, The Handbook of Physiology, Vascular Smooth Muscle, 1981, Microprobe Analysis of Biological Systems, 1981, Magnesium: Experimental and Clinical Research, Recent Advantages in Light and Optical Imaging in Biology and Medicine, 1986; contributor numerous articles to Journal Biol. Chemistry, Journal Physiology, Am. Heart Journal, Journal Pediatrics, Journal Cell Biology, others; member editorial board: Blood Vessels, Am. Journal Physiology, 1979-83, Journal Applied Physiology, 1973-76, Journal Histochemistry and Cytochemistry, 1978-81, Journal Cardiovascular Pharmacology, 1977-87, Cell Calcium,

1979—, Circulation Research, 1978-86, Motility, 1979-85, Journal Ultrastructure Research, 1979—, Journal Electron Microscopy Techniques; editor Journal Muscle Research and Cell Motility, 1988—; editor: Regulation and Contraction of Smooth Muscle, 1987. Member American Association for the Advancement of Science, Society General Physiologists, Am. Physiological Society, Biophys. Society, Microbeam Analysis Society, Am. Society for Cell Biology, Alpha Omega Alpha. Office: U Va School Medicine Department Physiology Jordan Hall Charlottesville Virginia 22908

SONNERUP, BENGT ULF-STEN, engineering sciences educator; born Malmö, Sweden, July 7, 1931; married; 3 children. BME, Chalmers Institute Tech., 1953; MAE, Cornell University, 1960, Doctor of Philosophy in Fluid Mechanics, 1961. Project engineer Stal-Laval Steam Turbine Company, Sweden, 1954-56, Bofors Company, Sweden, 1956-58; fellow Center Radiophys. & Space Research, Cornell University, 1961-62; fellow Institute Plasma Physics, Roayl Institute Tech., Sweden, 1962-64, associate professor; 1964-70, professor; 1970-81; Sydney East Junkins professor engineering sciences Dartmouth College, Hanover, New Hampshire, 1981—; lecturer Uppsala University, 1963; fellow European Space Research Organization, European Space Research Institute, Italy, 1970-71; visiting scientist Max Planck Institute Extraterrestrial Physics, Garching, Federal Republic Germany, 1978-79. Editor: Journal Geophysical Research, 1982-85. Member American Association for the

Advancement of Science, Am. Geophysical Union, American Institute of Aeronautics and Astronautics. Research in plasma physics and magnetohydrodynamics applied to problems in space physics, particularly the structure of the magnetopause current layer; magnetosphere and the nature of magnetic field merging. Office: Dartmouth College Radiophysics Lab Hanover New Hampshire 03755

SOREN, DAVID, archaeology educator and administrator; born Philadelphia, October 7, 1946; son of Harry Friedman and Erma Elizabeth (Salamon) Soren; married Noelle Louise Schattyn, December 22, 1967. Bachelor of Arts, Dartmouth College, 1968; Master of Arts, Harvard University, 1972, Doctor of Philosophy, 1973. Cert. Rome Classics Center Curator of coins Fogg Art Mus., Cambridge, Massachusetts, 1972; assistant professor University Missouri, Columbia, 1972-76, associate professor, department head; 1976-81; professor archaeology University Arizona, Tucson, 1982-83, department head; 1984—; guest curator, lecturer Am. Mus. Natural History, New York City, 1983—; adj. professor art University Arizona, Tucson, 1983—, creator, director Kourion excavations, Cyprus, 1982—, Portugal, 1983—; pot consultant, field director Tunisia Excavations Chicago Oriental Inst./Smithsonian Institution, 1973-78; creator/dir. Am. Excavations at Lugnano, Italy, 1988. Author: Kourion: Search for a Lost Roman City, 1988; co-author: Corpus des Mosaiques de Tunisie, 1972, 76, 80, monograph on Cyprus, Carthage: A Mosaic of Ancient Tunisia, 1987; author 2 books on film: Unreal Reality, 1978, Rise and Fall of Fantasy Film, 1980; producer film A Mosaic of Ancient Tunisia, 1987; editor: Excavations at Kourion I, 1987; contributor articles to professional journals. National Endowment for the Humanities research grantee, 1979; featured articles on his work, Newsweek, Conoisseur, National Geographic, others. Fulbright grantee, Lisbon, 1983; recipient Cine Golden Eagle, 1980, Angenieux Film award, Indsl. Photog. Magazine, 1980, Outstanding American Under 40 award C. Johns Hopkins/Britain's Royal Institute International Affairs, 1985; named Outstanding American Under 40 Esquire magazine, 1985. Member Archaeol. Institute Tucson (president 1983—), Am. School Oriental Research (dept. representative 1981—), National Geog. Society (project director 1983-84), Luso-Am. Commission (citation 1983-84). Subject of National Geographic spl. Archeological Detectives, 1985. Office: U Ariz Department Classics 371 MLB Tucson Arizona 85721

SOUTHWICK, CHARLES HENRY, zoologist, educator; born Wooster, Ohio, August 28, 1928; son of Arthur F. and Faye (Motz) S.; married Heather Milne Beck, July 12, 1952; children: Steven, Karen. Bachelor of Arts, College Wooster, 1949; Master of Science, University Wisconsin, 1951, Doctor of Philosophy, 1953. National Institutes of Health fellow 1951-53; assistant professor biology Hamilton College, 1953-54; National Science Foundation fellow Oxford (England) University, 1954-55; faculty Ohio University, 1955-61; associate professor pathobiology Johns Hopkins School Hygiene and Pub. Health, Baltimore, 1961-68; professor Johns Hopkins School Hygiene and Pub. Health, 1968-79; associate director Johns Hopkins International Center for Medical Research and Training, Calcutta, India, 1964-65; chairman department environmental, population and organismic biology University Colorado, Boulder, 1979-82, professor biology; 1979—; member primate adv. committee National Acad. Sci.-NRC, 1963-75, committee primate conservation, 1974-75; member Gov.'s Sci. Adv. Committee State of Maryland, 1975-78; member committee on research and exploration National Geog. Society, 1979—. Editor: Primate Social Behavior, 1963, Animal Aggression, 1970, Nonhuman Primates in Biomedical Research, 1975, Ecology and the Quality of Our Environment, 1976, Global Ecology, 1985; Ecology and Behavior of Food-Enhanced Primate Groups, 1988. Recipient Fulbright Rsch. award India, 1959-60. Fellow American Association for the Advancement of Science, Acad. Zoology, Animal Behavior Society; member Am. Society Zoologists, Ecological Society Am., Am. Society Mammalogists, Am. Society Primatology, International Primatology Society, International Society Study Aggression. Rsch., publs. on animal social behavior and population dynamics, influences animal social behavior on demographic characteristic mammal populations, primate ecology and behavior, estuarine ecology and environmental quality.

SPARKS, ROBERT EDWARD, chemical engineering educator; born Marshall, Missouri, September 25, 1930; married; 3 children. Bachelor of Science, University Missouri, 1952; Doctor Engineering, Johns Hopkins University, 1960. Research engineer Esso Research & Engineering Company, 1960-62, senior engineer; 1962-63; from assistant professor to professor chemical engineering Case Western Reserve University, 1963-72; Stanley and Lucy Lapata professor chemical engineering Washington University, St. Louis, 1972—, also director biological transportation laboratory, chemical engineering department; consultant National Institute Arthritis and Metabolic Disease, 1965-74, Goodyear Tire & Rubber Company, 1966-74. Member American Association for the Advancement of Science, Am. Institute Chemical Engineers, Am. Society Artificial Internal Orgns. Research in med. engring.; design of the artificial kidney, membrane transport, emulsion breaking, velocity profile control, mass transfer and fluid mechanics in chemical reactors, microencapsulation, controlled drug release, inventive reasoning. Office: Washington University Department of Chem Engring Urbauer Hall Saint Louis Missouri 63130

SPERRY, ROGER WOLCOTT, neurobiologist, educator; born Hartford, Connecticut, August 20, 1913; son of Francis B. and Florence (Kraemer) S.; married Norma G. Deupree, December 28, 1949; children: Glenn Tad, Janeth Hope. Bachelor of Arts, Oberlin College, 1935, Master of Arts, 1937, Doctor of Science (honorary), 1982; Doctor of Philosophy, University Chicago, 1941, Doctor of Science (honorary), 1977; Doctor of Science (honorary), Cambridge University, 1972, Kenyon College, 1979, Rockefeller University, 1980. Research fellow Harvard and Yerkes Laboratories, 1941-46; assistant professor anatomy University Chicago, 1946-52, section chief

National Institute Neurological Diseases of National Institutes of Health, also associate professor psychology; 1952-53; Hixon professor psychobiology California Institute Tech., 1954-84, Trustee professor Emeritus; 1984—; research brain organization and neural mechanism. Contributor articles to professional journals, chapters to books.; Editorial board: Behavioral Biology. Recipient Oberlin College Alumni citation, 1954; Howard Crosby Warren medal Society Exptl. Psychologists, 1969; California Scientist of Year award California Mus. Sci. and Industry, 1972; award Passano Foundation, 1973; Albert Lasker Basic Medical Research award, 1979; co-recipient William Thomas Wakeman Research award National Paraplegia Foundation, 1972, Claude Bernard sci. journalism award, 1975, Distinguished research award International Visual Literacy Association, 1979; Wolf Foundation prize in medicine, 1979; Nobel prize in physiology or medicine, 1981, Realia award Institute for Advanced Philos. Research, 1986. Fellow American Association for the Advancement of Science, Am. Acad. Arts and Sciences, Am. Psychological Association (recipient Distinguished Sci. Contbn. award 1971); member Royal Acad. (foreign member), National Acad. Sciences, Am. Physiological Society, Am. Association Anatomists, International Brain Research Organization, Society for Study of Devel. and Growth, Psychonomic Society, Am. Society Naturalists, Am. Zool. Society, Society Developmental Biology, Am. Philosophical Society (Lashley prize 1976), Am. Neurological Association (hon.), Society for Neurosci., International Society Devel. Biologists, American Association of

University Profs., Pontifical Acad. Sciences, Institute for Advanced Philosophical Research (Realia award 1986), Sigma Xi. Office: California Institute Tech 1201 E California St Pasadena California 91125

SPIEGEL, MELVIN, educator, biologist; born New York City, December 10, 1925; son of Philip Edward and Sadie (Friedman) S.; married Evelyn Sclufer, April 16, 1955; children: Judith Ellen, Rebecca Ann. Bachelor of Science, University Illinois, 1948; Doctor of Philosophy, University Rochester, 1952; Master of Arts (honorary), Dartmouth College, 1967. Research fellow University Rochester, 1952-53, California Institute Tech., 1953-55, 64-65; assistant professor Colby College, 1955-59; member faculty Dartmouth College, 1959—, professor biology; 1966—, chairman department biological sciences; 1972-74; summer investigator Marine Biological Laboratory, Woods Hole, Massachusetts, 1954—; senior research biologist University Calif.-San Diego, 1970-71; visiting professor biochemistry National Institute Medical Research, Mill Hill, London, 1971; visiting professor Biocenter, University Basel, 1979-82, 85; Wilson Memorial lecturer University North Carolina, 1975; program director developmental biology National Science Foundation, 1975-76; member cell biology study section National Institutes of Health, 1966-70. Editorial board: Biol. Bulletin, 1966-70, 71-75, Cell Differentiation, 1979-88 ; contributor articles to professional journals. Trustee Marine Biol. Lab. Corp.; member executive committee, trustee Marine Biol. Lab., 1976-80. Served with Army of the United States, 1943-46, European Theatre of

Operations. Decorated Purple Heart with 2 oak leaf clusters, Combat Inf. badge. Fellow American Association for the Advancement of Science; member Am. Society Zoologists, Am. Society Cell Biology, Am. Society Developmental Biology, International Society Developmental Biologists (sec.-treas. 1977-81, board directors 1981-85), Sigma Xi. Home: 15 Barrymore Road Hanover New Hampshire 03755

SPINRAD, HYRON, astronomer; born New York City, February 17, 1934; son of Emanuel B. and Ida (Silverman) S.; married Bette L. Abrams, August 17, 1958; children—Michael, Robert, Tracy. Bachelor of Arts, University California at Berkeley, 1955, Master of Arts, 1959, Doctor of Philosophy (Lick Obs. fellow), 1961. Studied galaxies University California at Berkeley, 1960-61; planetary atmospheres work Jet Propulsion Laboratory, Pasadena, California, 1961-63; investigation atmospheres of coolest stars University California at Berkeley, 1964-70. Member Am. Astronomical Society, Astronomical Society Pacific. Spl. research water vapor on Mars, molecular hydrogen on Jupiter, Saturn, Uranus and Neptune, temperature measurements on Venus atmosphere, spectra of galaxies and near-infrared observations, 71-72, location of faint radio galaxies, redshifts of galaxies, galaxy evolution and cosmology, 1973, spectroscopic observations of volatile gases in comets. Home: 7 Ketelsen Dr Moraga California 94556 Office: Department Astronomy University California Berkeley California 94720

SPIRO, MELFORD ELLIOT, anthropology educator; born Cleveland, April 26, 1920; son of Wilbert I. and Sophie (Goodman) S.;

married Audrey Goldman, May 27, 1950; children: Michael, Jonathan. Bachelor of Arts, University Minnesota, 1941; Doctor of Philosophy, Northwestern University, 1950. Member faculty Washington University, St. Louis, 1948-52, University Connecticut, 1952-57, University Washington, 1957-64; professor anthropology University Chicago, 1964-68; professor, chairman department anthropology University California, San Diego, 1968—; Board directors Social Sci. Research Council, 1960-62. Author: (with E.G. Burrows) An Atoll Culture, 1953, Kibbutz: Venture in Utopia, 1955, Children of Kibbutz, 1958, Burmese Supernaturalism, 1967, Buddhism and Society: A Great Tradition and Its Burmese Vicissitudes, 1971, Kinship and Marriage in Burma, 1977, Gender and Culture: Kibbutz Women Revisited, 1979; editor: Context and Meaning in Culture Anthropology, 1965, Oedipus in the Trobriands, 1982. Fellow Am. Acad. Arts and Sciences, National Acad. Sciences; member Am. Anthropological Association, Am. Ethnological Society (president 1967-68), American Association for the Advancement of Science, Society for Psychological Anthropology (president 1979-80).

SPITZER, LYMAN, JR., astronomer; born Toledo, June 26, 1914; son of Lyman and Blanche C. (Brumback) S.; married Doreen D. Canaday, June 29, 1940; children: Nicholas, Dionis, Lutetia, Lydia. Bachelor of Arts, Yale University, 1935, Doctor of Science, 1958; Henry Fellow, Cambridge (England) University, 1935-36; Doctor of Philosophy, Princeton University, 1938; National Research fellow, Harvard University, 1938-39; Doctor of

Science, Case Institute Tech., 1961, Harvard University, 1975, Princeton University, 1984; Doctor of Laws, Toledo University, 1963. Instructor physics and astronomy Yale University, 1939-42; scientist Special Studies Group, Columbia University Div. War Research, 1942-44; director Sonar Analysis Group, 1944-46; associate professor astrophysics Yale University, 1946-47; professor astronomy, chairman department and director obs. Princeton University, 1947-79, Charles A. Young professor astronomy; 1952-82, chairman research board; 1967-72, director project Matterhorn; 1953-61, chairman executive committee Plasma Physics Laboratory; 1961-66, senior research astromoner; 1982—; trustee Woods Hole Oceanographic Institute, 1946-51; member Committee on Undersea Warfare, National Research Council, 1948-51; member Yale University Council, 1948-51; chairman Scientists Committee on Loyalty Problems, 1948-51; chairman Space Telescope Institute Council, AURA, 1981—; foreign corr. Royal Society Sciences, Liège, 1961—. Author: monograph Physics of Fully Ionized Gases, 1956, rev., 1962; Diffuse Matter in Space, 1968, Physical Processes in the Interstellar Medium, 1978, Searching Between The Stars, 1982, Dynamical Evolution of Globular Clusters, 1987; editor: Physics of Sound in the Sea, 1946; contributor articles to Astrophysical Journal, Physics of Fluids, Physical Rev., others. Recipient Rittenhouse medal, 1957; Exceptional Sci. Achievement medal National Aeronautics and Space Administration, 1972; Bruce Gold medal, 1973; Henry Draper Gold medal, 1974; James C. Maxwell prize, 1975; Distinguished Pub. Service medal National Aeronautics and Space Administration, 1976; Gold medal Royal Astronomical Society, 1978; National medal sci., 1980; Janssen medal, 1980; Franklin medal, 1980; Crafoord prize Royal Swedish Acad. Sciences, 1985; Madison medal Princeton University, 1989. Fellow Am. Physical Society; member National Acad. Sci., Am. Acad. Arts and Sciences, Am. Philosophical Society, Am. Astronomical Society (past president), Royal Astronomical Society (associate), Astronomical Society Pacific, Am. Alpine Club, Alpine Club (London). Unitarian. Research on interstellar matter, space astronomy, stellar dynamics, stellar atmospheres, broadening of spectral lines, conductivity of ionized gases, controlled release of thermonuclear energy.

SPOCK, BENJAMIN MCLANE, physician, educator; born New Haven, May 2, 1903; son of Benjamin Ives and Mildred Louise (Stoughton) S.; married Jane Davenport Cheney, June 25, 1927 (divorced 1976); children: Michael, John Cheney; married Mary Morgan Councille, October 24, 1976. Bachelor of Arts, Yale University, 1925, student Medical School, 1925-27; Doctor of Medicine, Columbia University, 1929. Intern in medicine Presbyn. Hospital, New York City, 1929-31; in pediatrics New York Nursery and Child's Hospital, 1931-32; in psychiatry New York Hospital, 1932-33; practice pediatrics New York City, 1933-44, 46-47; instructor pediatrics Cornell Medical College, 1933-47; assistant attending pediatrician New York Hospital, 1933-47; consultant in pediatric psychiatry New York City Health Department, 1942-47; consultant psychiatry Mayo Clinic and Rochester Child Health Project,

Rochester, Minnesota; associate professor psychiatry Mayo Foundation, University Minnesota, 1947-51; professor child devel. University Pittsburgh, 1951-55, Western Reserve University, 1955-67. Author: Baby and Child Care, 1946, (with J. Reinhart and W. Miller) A Baby's First Year, 1954, (with M. Lowenberg) Feeding Your Baby and Child, 1955, Dr. Spock Talks with Mothers, 1961, Problems of Parents, 1962, (with M. Lerrigo) Caring for Your Disabled Child, 1965, (with Mitchell Zimmerman) Dr. Spock on Vietnam, 1968, Decent and Indecent, 1970, A Teenagers Guide to Life and Love, 1970, Raising Children in a Difficult Time, 1974, Spock on Parenting, 1988. Presidential candidate Peoples Party, 1972, advocator National Committee for a Sane Nuclear Policy (SANE), co-chairman, 1962 . Served to lieutenant commander Medical Corps, United States Naval Reserve, 1944-46. Home: Post Office Box 1890 Saint Thomas Virgin Islands 00803-1890 also: Post Office Box N Rogers AR 72756

STACHEL, JOHN JAY, physicist, educator; born New York City, March 29, 1928; son of Jacob Abraham and Bertha S.; married Eveleyn Lenore Wassermann, February 8, 1953; children: Robert, Laura, Deborah. Bachelor of Science, City College of New York, 1956; Master of Science, Stevens Institute Tech., 1959, Doctor of Philosophy, 1962. Instructor physics Lehigh University, Bethlehem, Pennsylvania, 1959-61; instructor physics University Pittsburgh, 1961-62, research associate; 1962-64; assistant professor physics Boston University, 1964-69, associate professor; 1969-72, professor; 1972—; director Center for Einstein Studies, Boston University, 1985—; visiting research associate Institute Theoretical Physics, Warsaw, 1962; visiting professor King's College, University London, 1970-71; visiting senior research fellow Department Physics, Princeton University, 1977-84. Editor: Selected Papers Leon Rosenfeld, 1979, Foundations of Space-Time Theories, 1977, Collection Papers of Albert Einstein, Princeton University Press, 1977—. National Science Foundation, National Endowment for the Humanities grantee, 1984—. Member Federation Am. Scientists, American Association of University Profs. Office: Einstein Papers 745 Commonwealth Avenue Boston Massachusetts 02215

STADTMAN, EARL REECE, biochemist; born Carrizozo, New Mexico, November 15, 1919; son of Walter William and Minnie Ethyl (Reece) S.; married Thressa Campbell, October 19, 1943. Bachelor of Science, University California, Berkeley, 1942, Ph.Doctor, 1949. With Alcan Highway survey Public Rds. Administration, 1942-43; research assistant University California, Berkeley, 1938-49; senior laboratory technican University California, 1949; Atomic Energy Commission fellow Massachusetts General Hospital, Boston, 1949-50; chemist laboratory cellular physiology National Heart Institute, 1950-58, chief enzyme section; 1958-62, chief laboratory biochemistry; 1962—; Biochemist Max Planck Institute, Munich, Germany, Pasteur Institute, Paris, 1959-60; faculty department microbiology University Maryland; professor biochemistry grad. program department biology Johns Hopkins University; adv. committee Life

Sciences Research Office, Am. Federation Biological Sci., 1974-77; Board directors Foundation Advanced Education Sciences, 1966-70, chairman department biochemistry, 1966-68; biochem. study section research grants National Institutes of Health, 1959-63. Editor: Journal Biol. Chemistry, 1960-65, Current Topics in Cellular Regulation, 1968—, Circulation Research, 1968-70; executive editor: Archives Biochemistry and Biophysics, 1960—, Life Scis, 1973-75, Procs. National Acad. Sci, 1975-81, Trends in Biochem. Research, 1975-78; editorial adv. board: Biochemistry, 1969-76, 81—. Recipient medallion Society de Chemie Biologique, 1955, medallion University Pisa, 1966, Presidential rank award as Distinguished Senior Executive, 1981. Member Am. Chemical Society (Paul Lewis Lab. award in enzyme chemistry 1952, executive committee biological division 1959-64, chairman division 1963-64, Hillebrand award 1969), Am. Society Biological Chemists (publs. committee 1966-70, council 1974-77, 82-84, president 1983—, Merck award 1983), National Acad. Sciences (award in microbiology 1970), Am. Acad. Arts and Sciences, Am. Society Microbiology, Washington Acad. Sciences (award biological chemistry 1957, national medal sci. 1979, meritorious executive award 1980). Office: National Heart and Lung Institute Bethesda Maryland 20014

STAFFORD, THOMAS PATTEN, retired military officer, former astronaut; born Weatherford, Oklahoma, September 17, 1930; married Faye Laverne Shoemaker; children: Dionne, Karin. Bachelor of Science, United States Naval Academy, 1952; student, United States Air Force Experimental Flight Test School, 1958-59; Doctor of Science (honorary), Oklahoma City University, 1967; Doctor of Laws (honorary), Western State University College Law, 1969; Doctor.Communications (honorary), Emerson College, 1969; Doctor.Aeronautical Engineering (honorary), Embry-Riddle Aeronautical Institute, 1970. Commissioned 2d lieutenant United States Air Force, 1952; advanced through grades to lieutenant general; chief performance branch Aerospace Research Pilot School, Edwards Air Force Base, California; with National Aeronautics and Space Administration, Houston, 1962-75; assigned Project Gemini, pilot Gemini VI, command pilot Gemini IX, commander Apollo X, chief astronaut office; 1969-71; deputy director flight crew operations, commander Apollo-Soyuz flight, 1975; commander Air Force Flight Test Center, Edwards Air Force Base; deputy chief staff Research, Devel. and Aquisition, 1979; retired 1979; chairman board Omega Watch Company Am. Co-author: Handbook for Performance Flight Testing. Decorated Distinguished Flying Cross with oak leaf cluster; 3 D.S.M.s Air Force; recipient 2 National Aeronautics and Space Administration Distinguished Service medals, 2 National Aeronautics and Space Administration Exceptional Service medals, Air Force Command Pilot Astronuat Wings; Chanute Flight award American Institute of Aeronautics and Astronautics, 1976; Veterans of Foreign Wars National Space award, 1976; General Thomas D. White USAF Space trophy National Geog. Society, 1976; Gold Space medal Federation Aeronautique Internationale, 1976; co-recipient American Institute of Aeronautics and

Astronautics, 1966, Harmon International Aviation trophy, 1966, National Acad. Television Arts and Sciences special Trustees award, 1969. Fellow Am. Astronautical Society, Society Experimental Test Pilots; member American Federation of TV and Radio Artists (hon. life). Address: 1006 Cameron St Alexandria Virginia 22314

STAHL, PHILIP DAMIEN, physiology and cell biology educator; born Wheeling, West Virginia, October 4, 1941; married; 3 children. Bachelor of Science, West Liberty State College, 1964; Doctor of Philosophy in Pharmacology, West Virginia University, 1967. From assistant to associate professor Washington University Medical School, St. Louis, 1971-81, professor physiology; from 1982—, head department; 1984—, now Edward Mallinckrodt Junior professor cell biology and physiology; fellow Space Sci. Research Center, University Missouri, 1967; Arthritis Foundation fellow molecular biology, Vanderbilt University, 1968-70. Member Brit. Biochem. Society, Am. Chemical Society, Am. Physiological Society, Am. Society Biological Chemists. Research in Lysosomes. Office: Washington University Department Cell Biology & Physiology Saint Louis Missouri 63130

STAMLER, JEREMIAH, physician, educator; born New York City, October 27, 1919; son of George and Rose (Baras) S.; married Rose Steinberg, 1942; 1 son, Paul J. Bachelor of Arts, Columbia University, 1940; Doctor of Medicine, State University of New York, Brooklyn, 1943. Certified specialist in clin. nutrition. Intern Long Island College Medicine div. Kings County Hospital, Brooklyn, 1944, fellow pathology; 1947; research fellow cardiovascular department Medical Research Institute, Michael Reese Hospital, Chicago, 1948, research associate; 1949-55, assistant director department; 1955-58; established investigator Am. Heart Association, 1952-58; director heart disease control program Chicago Board Health, 1958-74, director chronic disease control div.; 1961-63, director div. adult health and aging; 1963-74; associate department medicine Medical School, Northwestern University, Evanston, Illinois, 1958-59, assistant professor; 1959-65, associate professor; 1965-71, professor, chairman department community health and preventive medicine; 1972-86, Harry W. Dingman professor cardiology; 1973—; attending physician Northwestern Memorial Hospital, 1973—; executive director Chicago Health Research Foundation, 1963-72, board of directors; 1972—; consultant medicine St. Joseph Hospital, Chicago, 1964—, Presbyn.-St. Luke's Hospital, Chicago, 1966—; professorial lecturer department medicine Pritzker School Medicine, University Chicago, 1970—; visiting professor internal medicine Rush. Presbyn.-St. Luke's Medical Center, 1972—. Author: (with L. N. Katz) Experimental Atheroscleroses, 1953, (with others) Nutrition and Atherosclerosis, 1958, (with A. Blakeslee) Your Heart Has Nine Lives-Nine Steps to Heart Health, 1963, (with others) Epidemiology of Hypertension, 1967, Lectures on Preventive Cardiology, 1967, (with A. Blakeslee) Four Keys to a Healthy Heart, 1976; foreign cons., editoral cons.: Heartbeat. Served to captain Army of the United States, 1944-46. Recipient award for outstanding efforts in heart research Am. Heart Association, 1964, Howard W. Blakeslee award, 1964, award of merit, 1967; Albert and Mary Lasker Medical Journalism award, 1965, Conrad Elvehjem award Wisconsin Medical Society, 1967, (with others) Albert Lasker Special Service award, 1980, others. Fellow Am. College Cardiology (Distinguished Service award 1985), Am. Pub. Health Association (John M. Snow award 1986), American Association for the Advancement of Science; member Am. Federation Clinical Research, Am. Heart Association (board directors, past vice-chmn. executive committee, fellow council arteriosclerosis, chairman council on epidemiology 1979—), Am. Physiological Society, Am. Society Clinical Investigation, Am. Society Clinical Nutrition, Am. Society Study Arteriosclerosis (past board directors, past chairman program committee, past sec.-treas.), Am., Chicago diabetes associations, Association Teachers Preventive Medicine, Am. Society Clinical Nutrition, Association Clinical Scientists, Middle States Pub. Health Association, Central Society Clinical Research, Chicago Heart Association (Coeur d'Or award 1979), Am. Heart Association (Research Achievement award 1981), Illinois Pub. Health Association (member executive committee), Illinois Acad. Sciences, Diabetes Association Greater Chicago (director), Society Experimental Biology and Medicine (secretary Illinois chapter), Am. Institute Nutrition, Chicago Nutrition Association, Chicago Acad. Sciences, International Society and Federation Cardiology (chairman sci. board, council on epidemiology and prevention), Institute Medicine Chicago, Phi Beta Kappa. Office: 303 E Chicago Avenue Chicago Illinois 60611

STARR, CHAUNCEY, research institute executive; born Newark, April 14, 1912; son of Rubin and Rose (Dropkin) S.; married Doris Evelyn Debel, March 20, 1938; children: Ross M., Ariel E. Electrical Engineer, Rensselaer Polytechnic Institute, 1932, Doctor of Philosophy, 1935, Doctor of Engineering (honorary), 1964; Doctor of Engineering (honorary), Swiss ETH, 1980; Doctor Science (honorary), Tulane University, 1986—. Research fellow physics Harvard, 1935-37; research associate Massachusetts Institute Tech., 1938-41; research physicist D.W. Taylor Model Basin, Bureau Ships, 1941-42; staff radiation laboratory University California, 1942-43, Tennessee Eastman Corp., Oak Ridge, 1943-46, Tennessee Eastman Corp. (Clinton Laboratories), 1946; chief special research North Am. Aviation, Incorporated, Downey, California, 1946-49; director atomic energy research department North Am. Aviation, Incorporated, 1949-55, vice president; 1955-66; general manager North Am. Aviation, Incorporated (Atomics International div.), 1955-60, president div.; 1960-66; dean engineering University California at Los Angeles, 1966-73; consultant professor Stanford, 1974—; president Electric Power Research Institute, 1973-78, vice chairman; 1978-87, president emeritus; 1987—; Director Atomic Industrial Forum. Contributor sci. articles to professional journals. Decorated Legion of Honor France).; recipient Henry D. Smyth award Atomic Indsl. Forum, 1983. Fellow Am. Nuclear Society (past president), Am. Physical Society, American Association for the Advancement of

Science (director); member American Institute of Aeronautics and Astronautics (senior), Am. Power Conference, National Acad. Engineering, Am. Society Engineering Education, Royal Swedish Acad. for Engineering Sciences, Eta Kappa Nu, Sigma Xi. Home: 95 Stern Lane Atherton California 94025

STARR, RICHARD CAWTHON, botany educator; born Greensboro, Georgia, August 24, 1924; son of Richard Neal and Ida Wynn (Cawthon) S. Bachelor of Science in Secondary Edn, Georgia Southern College, 1944; Master of Arts, George Peabody College, 1947; postgraduate (Fulbright scholar), Cambridge (England) University, 1950-51; Doctor of Philosophy, Vanderbilt University, 1952. Faculty, Ind. University 1952—, professor botany; 1960-76, founder, head culture collection algae; 1953-76; professor botany University Texas at Austin, 1976-78; Head course marine botany Marine Biological Laboratory, Woods Hole, Massachusetts, 1959-63. Algae sect. editor: Biol. Abstracts, 1959—; editorial board: Journal Phycology, 1965-68, 76—, Archiv für Protistenkunde; asso. editor: Phycologia, 1963-69; Contributor articles to professional journals. Trustee Am. Type Culture Collection, 1962-68, 80-85. Guggenheim fellow, 1959; sr. fellow Alexander von Humboldt-Stiftung, 1972-73; recipient Distinguished Texas Scientist award Texas Acad. Sci., 1987. Fellow American Association for the Advancement of Science, Ind. Acad. Sci.; member National Acad. Sciences (Gilbert Morgan Smith Award 1985), Am. Institute Biological Sciences (governing board 1976-77, executive committee 1980), Botanical Society Am. (secretary 1965-69, vice president 1970, president 1971, Darbaker prize 1955), Phycological Society Am. (past president, vice president, treasurer), Society Protozoologists, International Phycological Society (secretary 1964-68), Brit. Phycological Society, Akademie Wissenschaft zu Göttingen (corr.). Sigma Xi. Office: Department Botany University Texas Austin Texas 78712

STARZL, THOMAS EARL, physician, educator; born Le Mars, Iowa, March 11, 1926; son of Roman F. and Anna Laura (Fitzgerald) S.; married Barbara Brothers, November 27, 1954 (divorced); children: Timothy, Rebecca, Thomas; married Joy D. Conger, August 1, 1981. Bachelor of Arts, Westminster College, 1947, Doctor of Science (honorary), 1965; Master of Arts, Northwestern University, 1950, Doctor of Medicine, Doctor of Philosophy, 1952; Doctor of Science (honorary), New York Medical College, 1970, Westmar College, 1974, Medical College Wisconsin, 1981, Northwestern University, 1982, Bucknell University, 1985, Muhlenberg College, 1985, Mount Sinai School Medicine, 1988; DMed (honorary), University Louvain, Belgium, 1985, University Genova, 1988, University Rennes, 1988; Doctor of Laws (honorary), University Wyoming, 1971; Doctor of Hebrew Literature (honorary), LaRoche College, 1988. Member faculty Northwestern University Medical School, Evanston, Illinois, 1958-61; member faculty University Colorado Medical School, Denver, 1962-80, professor surgery; 1964-80, chairman department surgery; 1972-80; professor University Pittsburgh, 1981—; member staff Presbyterian Hospital, University Hospital,

Children's Hospital of Pittsburgh, Pittsburgh Veteran's Administration Hospital. Author: Experience in Renal Transplantation, 1964, Experience in Hepatic Transplantation, 1969; contributor articles to professional journals. Recipient award Westminster College, 1965, Achievement award Lund University, 1965, Eppinger award Society International de Chirurgie, 1965, Eppinger prize, Freiburg, 1970, William S. Middleton award for outstanding research in Veteran's Administration system, 1968, Merit award Northwestern University, 1969, Distinguished Achievement award Modern Medicine, 1969, Creative Council award University Colorado, 1971, Colorado Man of Year award, 1967, Brookdale award American Medical Association, 1974, David Hume Memorial award National Kidney Foundation, 1978, Pitts. Man of Year award, 1981; Markle scholar, 1958. Fellow American College of Surgeons (Sheen award 1982), Am. Acad. Arts and Sciences; member Society University Surgeons, Society Vascular Surgery, Am. Surgical Association, Transplantation Society, Deutsche Gesellschaft für Chirurgie, numerous others. Office: U Pittsburgh School Medicine Department Surgery Pittsburgh Pennsylvania 15261

STAVITSKY, ABRAM BENJAMIN, immunologist, educator; born Newark, May 14, 1919; son of Nathan and Ida (Novak) S.; married Ruth Bernice Okney, December 6, 1942; children: Ellen Barbara, Gail Beth. Bachelor of Arts, University Michigan, 1939, Master of Science, 1940; Doctor of Philosophy, University Minnesota, 1943; V.Doctor of Medicine, University Pennsylvania, 1946. Research fellow California Institute Tech., 1946-47;

faculty Case Western Reserve University, 1947—, professor microbiology; 1962—, professor molecular biology; 1983—; Member expert committee immunochemistry World Health Organization, 1963-83; member microbiology fellowship committee National Institutes of Health, 1963-66; member microbiology test committee National Board Medical Examiners, 1970-73; chairman microbiology test committee National Board Podiatry Examiners, 1978-82. Member editorial board Journal Immunological Methods, 1979—, Immunopharmacology, 1983—. Vice president Ludlow Community Association, 1964-66. Fellow American Association for the Advancement of Science; member Am. Association Immunologists, Am. Society Microbioloby, Am. Society Tropical Medicine Hygiene, Sigma Xi. Home: 14604 Onaway Road Shaker Heights Ohio 44120 Office: 2119 Abington Road Cleveland Ohio 44106

STEBBINS, GEORGE LEDYARD, retired educator, research botanist; born Lawrence, New York, January 6, 1906; son of George Ledyard and Edith Alden (Candler) S.; married Margaret Goldsborough Chamberlaine, June 14, 1931; children: Edith Candler Paxman, Robert Lloyd, George Ledyard (deceased); married Barbara Jean Brumley, July 27, 1958. Bachelor of Arts, Harvard University, 1928, Master of Arts, 1929, Doctor of Philosophy, 1931; Doctor of Science (honorary), University Paris, 1962; Doctor of Science (honorary), Carleton College, 1983, Ohio State University, 1983. Instructor biology Colgate University, Hamilton, New York, 1931-35; junior geneticist University California, Berkeley, 1935-39, assistant professor; 1939-41, associate professor; 1941-47, professor genetics; 1947-50; professor genetics University California, Davis, 1950-73, professor emeritus; 1973—; visiting exchange professor University Chile, Santiago, 1973, visiting professor Carleton College, Northfield, Minnesota, 1977, 86, San Francisco State University, 1977-78, Ohio State University, Columbus, 1978-79. Author: (with C.W. Young) The Human Organism and the World of Life, 1983; author: Variation and Evolution in Plants, 1950, Processes of Organic Evolution, 1966, 2 edition, 1971, 3 edition, 1977, The Basis of Progressive Evolution, 1969, Higher Plant Evolution Above the Species Level, 1974, Darwin to DNA: Molecules to Humanity, 1982. Guggenheim Foundation research fellow, Algeria, Europe, 1954, 60-61, Australian Am. Exchange fellow, Canberra, Australia, 1974-75, Center for Advanced Behavioral Studies fellow, Palo Alto, California, 1968-69; named Distinguished Vis. Scientist, Smithsonian Institution, Washington, 1981-82. Member National Acad. Sciences, Am. Philosophical Society (Lewis prize 1959), Am. Acad. Arts and Sciences, Botanical Society Am. (president 1962), Society for Study of Evolution (president 1959), Am. Society Naturalists (president 1969). Democrat. Unitarian. Avocations: hiking, mountain climbing, music listening. Home: 1135 Euclid Avenue Berkeley California 94708 Office: University of California Department of Genetics Davis California 95616

STEELE, JOHN HYSLOP, marine scientist, oceanographic institute administrator; born Edinburgh, United Kingdom, November 15, 1926; son of Adam and Annie H.; married Margaret Evelyn Travis, March 2, 1956; 1 son, Hugh. Bachelor of Science, University College, London University, 1946, Doctor of Science, 1964. Marine scientist Marine Laboratory, Aberdeen, Scotland, 1951-66; senior principal sci. officer Marine Laboratory, 1966-73, deputy director; 1973-77; director Woods Hole Oceanographic Institution, Massachusetts, 1977—, president; 1986—; visiting research fellow Woods Hole Oceanographic Institution, 1958, lecturer marine biological laboratory; 1967; visiting professor University Miami, 1961; member National Science Foundation panel for international Decade of Ocean Exploration, 1972-73, Council Marine Biological Association of United Kingdom, 1974-76, Council Scottish Marine Biological Association, 1974-78; member board ocean studies and board polar research National Research Council; corp. member Marine Biological Laboratory, Woods Hole, Massachusetts; member committee for research and exploration National Geog. Society. Author: The Structure of Marine Ecosystems, 1974; Contributor articles to professional journals. Served with Brit. Royal Air Force, 1947-49. Recipient Alexander Agassiz medal National Acad. Sci., 1973. Fellow American Association for the Advancement of Science, Royal Society Edinburgh, Royal Society London, Am. Acad. Arts and Sciences. Home: Meteor House Woods Hole Massachusetts 02543 Office: Woods Hole Oceanographic Instn Woods Hole Massachusetts 02543

STEFFY, JOHN RICHARD, nautical archaeologist, educator; born Lancaster, Pennsylvania, May 1,

1924; son of Milton Grill and Zoe Minerva (Fry) S.; married Esther Lucille Koch, October 20, 1951; children: David Alan, Loren Craig. Student, Pennsylvania Area College, Lancaster, 1946-47, Milwaukee School Engineering, 1947-49. Partner M.G. Steffy & Sons, Denver, Pennsylvania, 1950-72; ship reconstructor Kyrenia Ship Project, Cyprus, 1972-73, Institute Nautical Archaeology, College Station, Texas, 1973—; associate professor anthropology, Texas Agricultural and Mechanical University, College Station, 1976—; lecturer on ship construction. Contributor articles to professional publications. Secretary Denver Borough Authority, Pennsylvania, 1962-72. Served with United States Navy, 1942-45. MacArthur Foundation fellow, 1985. Member Archaeol. Institute Am., Society Nautical Research, North America Society Oceanic History. Republican. Methodist. Lodge: Lions. Office: Institute Nautical Archaeology Post Office Drawer AU College Station Texas 77840

STEINBERG, DANIEL, preventive medicine physician, educator; born Windsor, Ontario, Canada, July 21, 1922; came to United States, 1922; son of Maxwell Robert and Bess (Krupp) S.; married Sara Murdock, November 30, 1946 (deceased July 1986); children—Jonathan Henry, Ann Ballard, David Ethan. Bachelor of Science with highest distinction, Wayne State University, 1941, Doctor of Medicine with highest distinction, 1944; Doctor of Philosophy with distinction (fellow Am. Cancer Society 1950-51), Harvard University, 1951. Intern Boston City Hospital, 1944-45; physician Detroit Receiving Hospital, 1945-46; instructor physiology Boston University School Medicine, 1947-48; joined United States Public Health Service, 1951, medical director; 1959; research staff laboratory cellular physiology and metabolism National Heart Institute, 1951-53, chief section metabolism; 1956-61, chief of laboratory metabolism; 1962-68; lecturer grad. program National Institutes of Health, 1955, member sci. adv. committee ednl. activities; 1955-61, committee chairman; 1955-60; member metabolism study section United States Public Health Service, 1959-61; chairman heart and lung research rev. committee B National Heart, Lung and Blood Institute, 1977-79; visiting scientist Carlsberg Laboratories, Copenhagen, 1952-53, National Institute Medical Research, London, 1960-61, Rockefeller University, 1981; president Lipid Research Incorporated, 1961-64, adv. board; 1964-73; professor medicine, head div. metabolic disease School Medicine, University California, San Diego and La Jolla; also program director basic sciences medicine School Medicine, University California, 1968—. Former editor Journal Lipid Research; member editorial board Jour Clin. Investigation, 1969-74, Journal Biol. Chemistry, 1980-84, Arteriosclerosis, 1980—; executive editor Analytical Biochemistry, 1978-80; contributor articles to professional journals. Board of directors Foundation Advanced Education in Scis., 1959-68, president, 1956-62, 65-67. Served to captain Medical Corps Army of the United States, World War II. Member National Acad. Sciences, American Association for the Advancement of Science, Am. Heart Association (member executive committee council on arterioscler-osis 1960-63, 65-73, chairman council arteriosclerosis 1967-69), Federation

Am. Scientists (executive committee 1957-58), Am. Society Biological Chemists, Am. Society Clinical Investigation, Association Am. Physicians, Am. Federation Clinical Research, American Medical Association, European Atherosclerosis Discussion Group, Am. Physiological Society, Alpha Omega Alpha.

STEINBERGER, JACK, physicist, educator; born Bad Kissingen, Federal Republic Germany, May 25, 1921; came to United States, 1935; son of Ludwig Lazarus and Berta (May) S.; married Joan Beauregard, November 17, 1964, (divorced 1964); children: Joseph, Richard Ned; married Cynthia Eva Alff; children: Julia Karen, John Paul. Bachelor of Science in Chemistry, University Chicago, 1942, Doctor of Philosophy in Physics, 1948. Member Institute for Advanced Study, Princeton, New Jersey, 1948-49; assistant University California, Berkeley, 1949-50; professor Columbia University, New York City, 1950-71, Higgins professor; 1967-71; staff member European Organization for Nuclear Research, Geneva, 1968-86, director; 1969-72; professor Scuola Normale, Pisa, Italy, 1986—. Fellow Guggenheim Foundation, Sloan Foundation; recipient National Medal of Sci., 1988, Nobel prize in physics, 1988. Member National Acad. Sciences, Am. Acad. Arts and Sciences, Heidelberg Acad. Sciences. Home: 25 Chemin des Merles, Onex CH 1213, Switzerland Office: European Center for, Nuclear Research, 1211 Geneva 23, Switzerland

STEINER, DONALD FREDERICK, biochemist, physician, educator; born Lima, Ohio, July 15, 1930; son of Willis A. and Katherine (Hoegner) S. Bachelor of Science in Chemistry and Zoology, University Cincinnati, 1952; Master of Science in Biochemistry, University Chicago, 1956, Doctor of Medicine, 1956; Doctor Medical Science (honorary), University Umea, 1973, University Illinois, 1984. Intern, King County Hospital, Seattle, 1956-57; United States Public Health Service postdoctoral research fellow, assistant medicine University Washington Medical School, 1957-60; member faculty University Chicago Medical School, 1960—, A.N. Pritzker professor biochemistry and medicine; 1985—, chairman department biochemistry; 1973-79; Jacobaeus lecturer, Oslo, 1970; Luft lecturer, Stockholm, 1984; senior investigator Howard Hughes Medical Institute, University Chicago, 1986—. Co-editor: The Endocrine Pancreas, 1972, discoverer proinsulin. Recipient Gairdner award Toronto, 1971; Hans Christian Hagedorn medal Steensen Memorial Hospital, Copenhagen, 1970; Lilly award, 1969; Ernst Oppenheimer award, 1970; Diaz-Cristobal award International Diabetes Federation, 1973; Banting medal Am. Diabetes Association, 1976; Banting medal Brit. Diabetes Association, 1981; Passano award, 1979; Wolf prize in medicine, 1985. Member National Acad. Sciences, Am. Society Biochemists and Molecular Biologists, American Association for the Advancement of Science, Am. Diabetes Association (50th Anniversary medallion 1972), European Association Study Diabetes, Am. Acad. Arts and Sciences, Sigma Xi, Alpha Omega Alpha. Home: 2626 N Lakeview Avenue Apartment 2508 Chicago Illinois 60614

STEINFINK, HUGO, chemical engineering educator; born Vienna, Austria, May 22, 1924; son of Mendel and Malwina (Fiderer) S.; married Cele Intrator, March 21, 1948; children: Dan E., Susan D. Bachelor of Science, City College of New York, 1947; Master of Science, Columbia University, 1948; Doctor of Philosophy, Brooklyn Polytechnic Institute, 1954. Research chemist Shell Devel. Company, Houston, 1948-51, 53-60; Jewel McAlister Smith professor chemical engineering University Texas, Austin, 1960—. Contributor articles to professional journals. Served with Army of the United States, 1944-46. Fellow Am. Mineral Society; member Am. Chemical Society, Am. Crystallographic Society, Am. Institute Chemical Engineers, Materials Research Society, Phi Beta Kappa, Sigma Xi, Phi Lambda Epsilon. Home: 3811 Walnut Clay Austin Texas 78731 Office: U Tex College Engring Austin Texas 78712

STEITZ, JOAN ARGETSINGER, biophysics educator; born Minneapolis, January 26, 1941; daughter of Glenn D. and Elaine (Magnusson) Argetsinger; married Thomas A. Steitz, August 20, 1966; 1 child, Jonathan Glenn. Bachelor of Science, Antioch College, 1963; Doctor of Philosophy, Harvard University, 1967; Doctor of Science (honorary), Lawrence University, Appleton, Wisconsin, 1982, Rochester University School Medicine, 1984. Postdoctoral fellow MRC Laboratory Molecular Biology, Cambridge, England, 1967-70; assistant professor molecular biophysics and biochemistry Yale University, New Haven, 1970-74; associate professor Yale University, 1974-78, professor molecular biophysics and biochemistry; 1978—. Recipient Young Scientist award Passano Foundation, 1975, Eli Lilly award in biological chemistry, 1976, U.S. Steel Foundation award in molecular biology, 1982, Lee Hawley, Senior award for arthritis research, 1984, National Medal of Sci., 1986. Fellow American Association for the Advancement of Science; member Am. Acad. Arts and Sci., National Acad. Arts and Sci. Home: 45 Prospect Hill Road Stony Creek Branford Connecticut 06405 Office: Yale U School Medicine 333 Cedar St Post Office Box 3333 New Haven Connecticut 06510

STENT, GUNTHER SIEGMUND, molecular biologist, educator; born Berlin, Germany, March 28, 1924; came to United States, 1940, naturalized, 1945; son of George and Elizabeth (Karfunkelstein) S.; married Inga Loftsdottir, October 27, 1951; 1 son, Stefan Loftur. Bachelor of Science, University Illinois, 1945, Doctor of Philosophy, 1948; (honorary) Doctor of Science, York University, Toronto, Ontario, Can., 1984. Research assistant University Illinois, 1945-48; research fellow California Institute Tech., 1948-50, University Copenhagen, Denmark, 1950-51, Pasteur Institute, Paris, France, 1951-52; assistant research biochemist University California, Berkeley, 1952-56; faculty University California, 1956—, professor molecular biology; 1959—, professor arts and sciences; 1967-68, chairman molecular biology; 1980-86, director virus laboratory; 1980-86; document analyst United States Field Intelligence Agency Tech., 1946-47; member genetics panel National Institutes of Health, 1959-64, National

Science Foundation, 1965-68; fellow Institute Advanced Studies, Berlin, 1985—. Author: Papers On Bacterial Viruses, 2d edit, 1966, Molecular Biology of Bacterial Viruses, 1963, Phage and the Origin of Molecular Biology, 1966, The Coming of the Golden Age, 1969, Function and Formation of Neural Systems, 1977, Morality as a Biological Phenomenon, 1978, Paradoxes of Progress, 1978, Molecular Genetics, 2d edit, 1978; member editorial board: Journal Molecular Biology, 1965-68, Genetics, 1963-68, Zeitschrift für Vererbungslehre, 1962-68, Annual Revs. Genetics, 1965-69, Annual Revs. Microbiology, 1966-70; contributor numerous sci. papers to professional lit. Merck fellow National Research Council, 1948-54; sr. fellow National Science Foundation, 1960-61; Guggenheim fellow, 1969-70. Member Am. Acad. Arts and Sciences, Society Neurosci., National Acad. Sciences, Am. Philosophical Society. Home: 145 Purdue Avenue Berkeley California 94708

STEPHANOPOULOS, GREGORY, chemical engineering educator, consultant, researcher; born Kalamata, Greece, March 10, 1950; came to United States, 1973; son of Nicholas and Elizabeth (Bitsanis) S.; married Maria Flytzani; children—Nicholas-Odysseas, Alexander. Bachelor of Science, National Tech. University, Athens, Greece, 1973; Master of Science, University Florida, Gainesville, 1975; Doctor of Philosophy, University Minnesota, Minneapolis, 1978. Registered professional engineer, Greece. Assistant professor chemical engineering California Institute Tech., Pasadena, 1978-83, associate professor chemical engineering;

1983-85; professor chemical engineering Massachusetts Institute of Technology, Cambridge, 1985—. Editor: Kinetics and Thermodynamics of Biological Systems, 1983. Member editorial board Mathematical Biosciences, 1984—, Biotech. Progress, 1984—. Contributor articles to professional journals. Dreyfus Teacher scholar Camille and Henry Dreyfus Foundation, 1982; recipient President Young Investigator award National Science Foundation, 1984; National Science Foundation grantee, 1980—. Member Am. Institute Chemical Engineers (programming coordinator 1983), Am. Chemical Society. Greek Orthodox. Avocations: chess; music; travel. Office: Mass Institute Tech Department Chem Engring 66-552 Cambridge Massachusetts 02139

STEVENS, HAROLD RUSSELL, physician, anesthesiologist; born Detroit, November 18, 1930; son of Harold Russell and Etheleen Mae (Stone) S.; married Karen Lee Leathers; children—Kirk Russell, Martha Lee, Kori Lynn, Kelly Lou. Bachelor of Arts, Albion College, 1952; Doctor of Medicine, University Michigan, 1955. Diplomate Am. Board Anesthesiology. Resident in anesthesiology Toledo Hospital, Ohio, 1960-62, research associate Institute Medical Research; 1965-70, director respiratory team; 1967—, chairman anesthesiology; 1983-86, director intensive care; 1975-88, director cardiac surgery; 1981-84; health councilor Community Planning Council Northwestern Ohio, 1970-71; co-director respiratory therapy Mercy Hospital, Toledo, 1969-83, director anesthesiology, 1968-79; adj. professor University Toledo, 1971—; assistant clinical professor Medical

College Ohio, Toledo, 1971—. Contributor articles to Anesthesiology, Journal Asthma Research, LANCET, International Anesthesiology Clinics. Trustee Maumee Valley Foundation, Toledo, 1971-73; site examiner Joint Reverend Committee for Respiratory Theraphy Education, 1977—. Served to captain MC, United States Air Force, 1957-59. DeVilbiss Fund grantee, 1965. Fellow Am. College Anesthesiology; member Acad. Medicine Toledo and Lucas County (councilor 1970-71), Ohio Society Anesthesiology (president 1982-83), Ohio State Medical Association (del. 1983—), Am. Society Anesthesiologists (alternate del. 1980), American Medical Association, Am. Heart Association (trustee Northwestern Ohio 1980—), Lung Association Northwestern Ohio (trustee 1977-80). Republican. Episcopalian. Clubs: Inverness, Toledo. Lodges: Masons, Shriners. Home: 4204 Northmoor Road Toledo Ohio 43606 Office: 3939 Monroe St Suite 116 Toledo Ohio 43606

STEWART, HARRIS BATES, JR., oceanographer; born Auburn, New York, September 19, 1922; son of Harris B. and Mildred (Woodruff) S.; married Elise Bennett Cunningham, February 21, 1959; children: Dorothy Cunningham, Harry Hasburgh; 2d married Louise Conant Thompson, December 22, 1988. Graduate, Phillips Exeter Academy, 1941; Bachelor of Arts, Princeton, 1948; Master of Science, Scripps Institution Oceanography, University California, 1952, Doctor of Philosophy, 1956. Hydrographic engineer United States Navy Hydrographic Office expedition to, Persian Gulf, 1948-49; instructor Hotchkiss School, 1949-51; research assistant Scripps Institution Oceanography, 1951-56; diving geologist, project manager Geological Diving Cons., Incorporated, San Diego, 1953-57; chief oceanographer United States Coast & Geodetic Survey, 1957-65, department assistant director; 1962-65; director Institute Oceanography, Environmental Sci. Services Administration, United States Department Commerce, 1965-69; director Atlantic Oceanographic and Meteorol. Laboratories, National Oceanographic and Atmospheric Administration, 1969-78, consultant; 1978-80; professor marine sci., director Center for Marine Studies, Old Dominion University, Norfolk, Virginia, 1980-85; adj. professor department oceanography Old Dominion University, 1986—; director Southeast Bank of Dadeland; chairman Florida Commission Marine Sci. and Tech.; member executive committee, earth sciences div. National Acad. Sciences; chairman adv. board National Oceanographic Data Center, 1965-66; chairman survey panel interagy. committee oceanography Federal Council Sci. and Tech., 1959-67; chairman adv. committee underseas features United States Board Geog. Names, 1964-67; member sci. party Northern Holiday Expedition, 1951; Capricorn Expedition, 1952-53; chief scientist Explorer Oceanographic Expedition, 1960, Pioneer Indian Ocean Expedition, 1964, Discoverer Expedition, 1968, NOAA-Carib Expedition, 1972, Researcher Expedition, 1975; member United States delegation Intergovtl. Oceanographic Commission, 1961-65; member Governor California Adv. Commission Marine Resources; chairman adv. council Department Geological and Geophysical Sciences Princeton; vice president Dade Marine

Institute, 1976-77, president, 1977-79; trustee, member executive committee Associate Marine Institutes; member Fisheries Management Adv. Council Virginia Marine Resources Commission, 1984-85; vice chairman adv. council University National Oceanographic Laboratory System, 1983-85. Author: The Global Sea, 1963, Deep Challenge, 1966, The Id of the Squid, 1970, Challenger Sketchbook, 1972, No Dinosaurs on the Ark, 1988. Board of directors Vanguard School, Miami, 1974-76. Served as pilot United States Army Air Force, 1942-46, PTO. Decorated comendador Almirante Padilla, Colombia).; Recipient Meritorious award Department Commerce, 1960, Exceptional Service award, 1965. Fellow American Association for the Advancement of Science, Geological Society Am., Marine Tech. Society (vice president); member Florida Acad. Sciences (president 1978-79), Virginia Acad. Sci., Am. Geophysical Union, International Oceanographic Foundation (vice president 1974-80), Zool. Society Florida (president 1970-73), Marine Historical Association, Cape Ann Historical Association. Presbyterian. Clubs: Cosmos (Washington); Explorers (New York City). Home (summer): 11 Atlantic Dr Scarborough Maine 04074 Home (winter): 644 Alhambra Circle Coral Gables Florida 33134

STEWART, ROBERT LEE, army officer, astronaut; born Washington, August 13, 1942; son of Lee Olin and Mildred Kathleen (Wann) S.; married Mary Jane Murphy; children—Ragon Annette, Jennifer Lee. Bachelor of Science in Math., University Southern Mississippi, 1964; Master of Science in Aerospace Engineering, University Texas, 1972; graduate, United States Army Air Def. School. Commissioned 2d lieutenant United States Army, 1964, advanced through grades to brigadier general; 1986, fire team leader armed helicopter platoon 101st Aviation Battalion, instructor pilot Primary Helicopter School; battalion operations officer, battalion executive officer 309th Aviation Battalion, United States Army, Seoul, Korea, 1972-73; experimental test pilot Aviation Engineering Flight Activity, United States Army, Edwards Air Force Base, California; astronaut candidate National Aeronautics and Space Administration, 1978, mission specialist Space Shuttle Mission 41-B; 1984-85; mission specialist STS-SIJ 1985-86; deputy commander United States Army Strategic Defense Command, Huntsville, Alabama, 1987—. Recipient National Aeronautics and Space Administration Space Flight medal, 1984, 85; named Army Aviator of Year, 1984; decorated Distinguished Service Medal, Legion of Merit, Distinguished Flying Cross with 3 clusters, Bronze Star, Meritorious Service medal, Air medal with 32 clusters, Army Commendation medal with oak leaf cluster and V device, 2 Purple Hearts, National Defense Service medal, Vietnamese Cross of Gallantry, others. Member Society Experimental Test Pilots, Association United States Army, Army Aviation Association Am. Avocations: photography; woodworking. Home: 20 Ripley Lane Redstone Arsenal Alabama 35808 Office: USASDC Huntsville Alabama 35807

STILLINGER, FRANK HENRY, chemist, educator; born Boston, August 15, 1934; son of Frank Henry and Gertrude (Metcalf) S.; married Dorothea Anne Keller, August 18, 1956; children—Constance Anne,

Andrew Metcalf. Bachelor of Science, University Rochester, 1955; Doctor of Philosophy, Yale University, 1958. National Science Foundation postdoctoral fellow Yale University, 1958-59; with Bell Telephone Laboratories, Murray Hill, New Jersey, 1959—; head chemical physics department Bell Telephone Laboratories, 1976-79; member evaluation panel National Bureau Standards, 1975-78; member adv. committee for chemistry National Science Foundation, 1980-83, member adv. committee for advanced scientific computing, 1984-86; distinguished lecturer in chemistry University Maryland, 1981; Karcher lecturer University Oklahoma, 1984; Trumbull lecturer Yale University, 1984; Washburn Memorial lecturer University Nebraska, 1986l Gucker lecturer University Ind., 1987; W.A. Noyes lecturer University Texas, 1988. Associate editor Physical Rev. Contributor articles to professional journals. Recipient Elliott Cresson medal Franklin Institute, 1978, Hildebrand award Am. Chemical Society, 1986; Welch Foundation fellow, 1974. Fellow Am. Physical Society (Langmur award 1989); member American Association for the Advancement of Science, National Acad. Sciences. Club: Early Am. Coppers Inc. Home: 216 Noe Avenue Chatham New Jersey 07928 Office: 600 Mountain Avenue Murray Hill New Jersey 07974

STOKOE, KENNETH H., II, civil engineer, educator. BSCE, University Michigan, 1966, MSCE, 1967, Doctor of Philosophy, 1972. Brunswick-Abernathy Regents professor soil dynamics and geotech. engineering University Texas, Austin, 1985—.

Office: U Tex Department Civil Engring Austin Texas 78712

STONE, WILLIAM HAROLD, geneticist, educator; born Boston, December 15, 1924; son of Robert and Rita (Scheinberg) S.; married Elaine Morein, November 24, 1947; children: Susan Joy, Debra M.; married Carmen Maqueda, December 22, 1971; 1 son, Alexander R.M. Bachelor of Arts, Brown University, 1948; Master of Science, University Maine, 1949; Doctor of Philosophy, University Wisconsin, 1953; Doctor of Science (honorary), University Cordoba, Spain, 1984. Research assistant Jackson Memorial Laboratory, Bar Harbor, Maine, 1947-48; faculty department genetics University Wisconsin, Madison, 1949-83; professor University Wisconsin, 1961-83, professor medical genetics; 1964-83; Cowles Distinguished professor department biology Trinity University, San Antonio, 1983—; staff scientist Southwest Foundation for Biomed. Research, San Antonio, 1983—; member panel blood group experts Food and Agriculture Organization (of the United Nations), 1962-67, program director immunogenetics research, Spain, 1971-74; adj. professor University Texas Health Sci. Center, 1985—; member Community Health Services Research Adv. Committee, 1987—, Council Institute Laboratory Animal Resources, National Research Council; member competitive research grants panel USDA; board of directors Southern Texas Regional Bloodbank, 1986—, Texas Research and Tech. Foundation, 1986—, Mind Sci. Foundation, 1988—, Winston School, 1989—, Institute Laboratory Animal Sci., 1977-89. Author: Immunogenetics, 1967; Contributor articles to professional journals. Recipient I.I. Ivanov medal Union of Soviet Socialist Republics, 1974; California Institute Tech. National Institutes of Health fellow, 1960-61. Member Am. Institute Biological Sciences, National Research Council, Assembly Life Sciences, National Acad. Sciences, American Association for the Advancement of Science, Am. Society Immunologists, Am. Genetics Association, Am. Aging Society, Genetics Society, Am. Society Human Genetics, Research Society Am., International Society Transplant, Am. Society Animal Sci., International Primatological Society, Federation Am. Society Experimental Biology (member pub. affairs committee), Sigma Xi, Gamma Alpha., Beta Beta Beta. Office: Department Biology Trinity U San Antonio Texas 78284

STOOKEY, STANLEY DONALD, chemist; born Hay Springs, Neb., May 23, 1915; son of Stanley Clarke and Hermie Lucille (Knapp) S.; married Ruth Margaret Watterson, December 26, 1940; children—Robert Alan, Margaret Ann, Donald Bruce. Bachelor of Arts, Coe College, 1936, Doctor of Laws, 1959; Master of Science, Lafayette College, 1937; Doctor of Philosophy in Physical Chemistry, Massachusetts Institute of Technology, 1940. With Corning Glass Works Research, New York, 1940-79, director fundamental chemical research; 1970-79. Contributor articles to professional journals; patentee field of photosensitive glasses, glass ceramics, photochromatic and polychromatic glasses. Recipient National Medal of Tech., 1986. Fellow Am. Ceramic Society; member National Acad. Engineering, Am. Chemical Society (Inventor of Year award 1971), Sigma Xi. Republican. Methodist. Home: 12 Timber Lane Painted Post New York 14870

STORK, GILBERT (JOSSE), chemistry educator and investigator; born Brussels, Belgium, December 31, 1921; son of Jacques and Simone (Weil) S.; married Winifred Stewart, June 9, 1944; children: Diana, Linda, Janet, Philip. Bachelor of Science, University Florida, 1942; Doctor of Philosophy, University Wisconsin, 1945; Doctor of Science (honorary), Lawrence College, 1961, University Paris, 1979, University Rochester, 1982, Emory University, 1988. Senior research chemist Lakeside Laboratories, 1945-46; instructor chemistry Harvard University, 1946-48, assistant professor; 1948-53; associate professor Columbia University, 1953-55, professor; 1955-67, Eugene Higgins professor; 1967—, chairman department; 1973-76; plenary lecturer numerous international symposia, named Lectureships in United States and abroad; consultant Syntex, International Flavors and Fragrances; chairman Gordon Steroid Conference, 1958-59; board editors Journal Organic Chemistry, 1955-61. Hon. adv. editor: Tetrahedron Letters, Nouveau Journal de Chimie, Tetrahedron, Heterocycles; Editorial board: Accounts of Chemical Research, 1968-71. Recipient Baekeland medal, 1961, Harrison Howe award, 1962, Edward Curtis Franklin Memorial award Stanford, 1966, Gold medal Synthetic Chems. Mfrs. Association, 1971, Nebraska award, 1973, Roussel prize in steroid chemistry, 1978, Edgar Fahs Smith award, 1982, Willard Gibbs medal, 1982, National Medal of Science,

1982, Linus Pauling award, 1983, Tetrahedron prize, 1985, Remsen award, 1986, Cliff S. Hamilton award 1986, Mony Ferst award, Sigma Xi, 1987; Guggenheim fellow, 1959. Fellow Am. Acad. Arts and Sciences, National Acad. Sciences (award in chem scis. 1982); member Chemist Club (hon.), Am. Chemical Society (award in pure chemistry 1957, award for creative work in synthetic organic chemistry 1967, Nichols medal 1980, Arthur C. Cope award 1980, chairman organic chemistry division 1967), Royal Society Chemistry (hon., London), Pharmaceutical Society Japan (hon.). Home: 459 Next Day Hill Englewood New Jersey 07631 Office: Columbia U New York New York 10027

STRANGWAY, DAVID WILLIAM, geologist, university president; born Canada, June 7, 1934. Bachelor of Arts in Physics and Geology, University Toronto, 1956, Master of Arts in Physics, 1958, Doctor of Philosophy, 1960. Senior geophysicist Dominion Gulf Company Limited, Toronto, 1956; chief geophysicist Ventures Limited, 1956-57, senior geophysicist; summer 1958; research geophysicist Kennecott Copper Corp., Denver, 1960-61; assistant professor University Colorado, Boulder, 1961-64, M.I.T., 1965-68; member faculty University Toronto, 1968-85, professor physics; 1971-85, chairman department geology; 1972-80, vice president, provost; 1980-83, president; 1983-84; president University British Columbia, 1985—; chief geophysics branch Johnson Space Center, National Aeronautics and Space Administration, Houston, 1970-72, chief physics branch, 1972-73, acting chief planetary and earth sci. div., 1973;

visiting professor geology University Houston, 1971-73; interim director Lunar Sci. Institute, Houston, 1973; visiting committee geological sciences Brown University, 1974-76, Memorial University, St. John's, Newfoundland, 1974-79, Princeton University, 1980-86. vice president Can. Geosci. Council, 1977; chairman proposal evaluating team Universities Space Research Associates, 1977-78, Ontario Geosci. Research Fund, 1978-81; Pahlavi lecturer Government of Iran, 1978; consultant to government and industry, member numerous government and sci. adv. and investigative panels. Author numerous papers, reports in field. Member Premier's Council Sci. and Tech. Recipient National Aeronautics and Space Administration Exceptional Sci. Achievement medal, 1972; hon. member Can. Society Exploration Geophysicists. Fellow Royal Astronomical Society, Royal Society Can.; member Society Exploration Geophysicists (Virgil Kauffman Gold medal 1974), Geological Association Can. (president 1978-79, Logan medal), Can. Geophysical Union (chairman 1977-79, J. Tuzo Wilson medal 1987), Am. Geophysical Union (section planetology section 1978-81), European Association Exploration Geophysicists, Society Geomagnetism and Geoelectricity Japan, Can. Geosci. Council (president 1980), American Association for the Advancement of Science, Can. Exploration Geophysicists, Society Experimental Geophysics (hon.), Business Council of British Columbia.

STRITTMATTER, PETER ALBERT, astronomer, educator; born London, England, September 12, 1939; came to United States, 1970.; son of Albert and Rosa S.; married Janet Hubbard Parkhurst, March 18, 1967; children—Catherine D., Robert P. Bachelor of Arts, Cambridge University, England, 1961, Master of Arts, 1963, Doctor of Philosophy, 1967. Staff scientist Institute for Astronomy, Cambridge, England, 1967-70; staff scientist department physics University Calif.-San Diego, La Jolla, California, 1970-71; associate professor department astronomy University Arizona, Tucson, 1971-74, professor department astronomy; 1974—; director Steward Observatory, Tucson, 1975—; member staff Max Planck Institute Radioastronomy, Bonn, W. Germany, 1981—. Contributor articles to professional journals. Recipient Senior award Humboldt Foundation, 1979-80. Fellow Royal Astronomical Society; member Am. Astronomical Society, Astronomische Gesellschaft. Office: U Ariz Steward Obs Tucson Arizona 85721

STROHBEHN, JOHN WALTER, engineering science educator; born San Diego, November 21, 1936; son of Walter William and Gertrude (Powell) S.; children from previous marriage: Jo, Kris, Carolyn; married Barbara Ann Brungard, August 30, 1980. Bachelor of Science, Stanford University, 1958, Master of Science, 1959, Doctor of Philosophy, 1964. Associate professor engineering sci. Dartmouth College, Hanover, New Hampshire, 1968-73, professor; 1973—, associate dean; 1976-81, adj. professor medicine; 1979—, Sherman Fairchild professor; 1983—; acting provost Dartmouth College, 1987; distinguished lecturer Institute of Electrical and Electronics Engineers Antennas and Propagation Society, 1979-82. Editor: Laser Propagation in

the Clear Atmosphere, 1978; associate editor Trans. Ant and Propagation, 1969-71, Trans. Biomed. Engring., 1981—; contributor articles to professional journals. Scoutmaster Boy Scouts Am., Norwich, Vermont, 1971-73; board of directors Norwich Recreation and Conservation Council. Fellow Optical Society Am., American Association for the Advancement of Science; member Radiation Research Society, Bioelectromagnetics Society (board directors 1982-85), North America Hyperthermia Group (president 1986), American Association for the Advancement of Science. Avocations: jogging; hiking; skiing. Home: 5 Weatherby Road Hanover New Hampshire 03755 Office: Dartmouth College Thayer School Engring Tuck Dr Hanover New Hampshire 03755

SU, KENDALL LING-CHIAO, engineering educator; born Fujian, Peoples Republic China, July 10, 1926; came to United States, 1948; son of Ru-chen and Sui-hsiong (Wang) S.; married Jennifer Geetsone Chang, September 10, 1960; children: Adrienne, Jonathan. Bachelor of Electrical Engineering, Xiamen University, Peoples Republic China, 1947; Master of Electrical Engineering, Georgia Institute Tech, 1949; Doctor of Philosophy, Georgia Tech. University, 1954. Junior engineer Taiwan Power Company, Taipei, Republic China, 1947-48; assistant professor Georgia Institute Tech, Atlanta, 1954-59, associate professor; 1959-65, professor; 1965-70, Regents professor; 1970—; member tech. staff Bell Laboratories, Murray Hill, New Jersey, 1957. Author: Active Network Synthesis, 1965, Time-Domain Synthesis of Linear Networks, 1969,

Fundamentals of Circuits, Electronics, and Signal Analysis, 1978; mem sci. adv. com. Newton Graphic Science magazine, 1987—. Fellow Institute of Electrical and Electronics Engineers; member Chinese Language Computer Society, Phi Kappa Phi, Sigma Xi (president Georgia Institute Tech chapter 1968-69, 72-73, Faculty Research award 1957), Eta Kappa Nu. Methodist. Office: Ga Institute of Tech School of Elec Engring Atlanta Georgia 30332-0250

SUPPES, PATRICK, educator; born Tulsa, March 17, 1922; son of George Biddle and Ann (Costello) S.; married Joan Farmer, April 16, 1946 (divorced 1970); children: Patricia, Deborah, John Biddle; married Joan Sieber, March 29, 1970 (divorced 1973); married Christine Johnson, May 26, 1979; children: Alexandra Christine, Michael Patrick. Bachelor of Science, University Chicago, 1943; Doctor of Philosophy (Wendell T. Bush fellow), Columbia University, 1950; Doctor of Laws, University Nijmegen, Netherlands, 1979; Dr.h.c., Académie de Paris, University Paris V, 1982. Instructor, Stanford University, 1950-52; assistant professor Stanford, 1952-55, associate professor; 1955-59, professor philosophy, statistics, education and psychology; 1959—; founder, chief executive officer Computer Curriculum Corp., 1967—. Author: Introduction to Logic, 1957, Axiomatic Set Theory, 1960, Sets and Numbers, books 1-6, 1966, Studies in the Methodology and Foundations of Science, 1969, A Probabilistic Theory of Causality, 1970, Logique du Probable, 1981, Probabilistic Metaphysics, 1984, Estudios de Filosofia y Metodologí de la Ciencia, 1988, (with Davidson and Siegel) Decision Making, 1957, (with Richard C. Atkinson) Markov Learning Models for Multiperson Interactions, 1960, (with Shirley Hill) First Course in Mathematical Logic, 1964, (with Edward J. Crothers) Experiments on Second-Language Learning, 1967, (with Max Jerman and Dow Brian) Computer-assisted Instruction, 1965-66, Stanford Arithmetic Program, 1968, (with D. Krantz, R.D. Luce and A. Tversky) Foundations of Measurement, Volume 1, 1971, (with M. Morningstar) Computer-Assisted Instruction at Stanford, 1966-68, 1972, (with B. Searle and J. Friend) The Radio Mathematics Project: Nicaragua, 1974-75, 1976. Served to captain United States Army Air Force, 1942-46. Recipient Nicholas Murray Butler Silver medal Columbia, 1965, Distinguished Sci. Contbr. award Am. Psychol. Association, 1972, Teachers College medal for distinguished service, 1978; Center for Advanced Study Behavioral Sciences fellow, 1955-56; National Science Foundation fellow, 1957-58. Fellow Am. Psychological Association, American Association for the Advancement of Science, Am. Acad. Arts and Sciences; member Math Association Am., Psychometric Society, Am. Philosophical Association, Association Symbolic Logic, Am. Math Society, Académie Internationale de Philosophie des Sciences (titular), National Acad. Education (president 1973-77), National Acad. Sciences, Am. Psychological Association, International Institute Philosophy, Finnish Acad. Sci. and Letters, International Union History and Philosophy of Sci. (division logic, methodology and philosophy of sci., president 1975-79), Am. Educational Research Association (president 1973-74), Sigma Xi.

SUTHERLAND, ROBERT LOUIS, engineering company executive, educator; born Fellsmere, Florida, May 15, 1916; son of John Alexander and Georgia Myrtle (Legg) S.; married Mary-Alice Reed, May 18, 1945; children—Robert Hynes, Wayne Muzzy, Connie Anne, Nancy Lee, John Gary. Bachelor of Science, University Illinois, 1939, Master of Science, 1948. Registered professional engineer, Illinois, Iowa, Wyoming. Devel. engineer Firestone Tire & Rubber Company, Akron, Ohio, 1939-41; research engineer Borg & Beck div. Borg-Warner Corp., Chgo, 1941; test engineer Buick Motor Div. General Motors Corp., Melrose Park, Illinois, 1942-43; senior engineer research department Aeronca Aircraft Corp., Middletown, Ohio, 1943-45; research associate College Engineering, University Illinois, 1945-48; assistant, then associate professor mechanical engineering State University Iowa, Iowa City, 1948-58; city engineer Coralville, Iowa, 1950-53; professor mechanical engineering University Wyoming, Laramie, 1958-80; professor emeritus University Wyoming, 1980—, head department; 1960-70; president Skyline Engineering Company Incorporated, Laramie, 1972—; research engineer Collins Radio Company, Cedar Rapids, Iowa, summer 1954, consultant engineer, 1950-56; staff engineer Environmental Test Laboratory, Martin Company, Denver, summer 1960; director Hunter Manufacturing Company, Iowa City, 1955-58, secretary board, 1956-58. Author: Engineering Systems Analysis, 1958; Contributor articles to professional journals. Business adviser mfg. group Junior Achievement, Middletown, 1943-44; member Iowa City School Study Council, 1956-58; Member Civil Air Patrol, Chicago, 1941-43; legis. fellow to National Conference State Legislatures, 1982-84. Co-recipient Richard L. Templin award American Society for Testing and Materials, 1952. Fellow American Society of Mechanical Engineers (life, regional vice president 1965-67); member Society Automotive Engineers, Sigma Xi, Sigma Tau, Pi Tau Sigma, Tau Beta Pi. Methodist (steward, chmn. ofcl. board 1964-65, trustee 1966-69, president board 1967-69, lay leader 1969-72, chmn. council ministries 1973-75, chmn. finance com. 1975-79). Club: Kiwanian (director Laramie chpt. 1963-65, 79-82, president 1966, div. lt. gov. 1970-71, life mem. 1978). Home: 1420 Sanders St Laramie Wyoming 82070

SUTNICK, ALTON IVAN, medical school dean, physician; born Trenton, New Jersey, July 6, 1928; son of Michael and Rose (Horwitz) S.; married Mona Reidenberg, August 17, 1958; children: Amy, Gary. Bachelor of Arts, University Pennsylvania, 1950, Doctor of Medicine, 1954; postgraduate studies in biomed. math., Drexel Institute Tech., 1961-62; postgraduate studies in biometrics, Temple University, 1969-70. Diplomate Am. Board Internal Medicine. Rotating intern Hospital University Pennsylvania, 1954-55, resident in anesthesiology; 1955-56, resident in medicine; 1956, United States Public Health Service postdoctoral research fellow; 1956-57; assistant instructor anesthesiology, then assistant instructor medicine University Pennsylvania School Medicine, 1955-57; resident in medicine Wishard Memorial Hospital, Indianapolis, 1957-58; chief resident in medicine Wishard Memorial Hospital, 1960-61; resident instructor medicine Ind. University School Medicine, Indianapolis, 1957-58; United States Public Health Service postdoctoral research fellow Temple University Hospital, 1961-63; instructor, then associate in medicine Temple University School Medicine, 1962-65; member faculty University Pennsylvania School Medicine, 1965-75, associate professor medicine; 1971-75; clinical assistant physician Pennsylvania Hospital, 1966-71; research physician, then associate director Institute Cancer Research, Philadelphia, 1965-75; visiting professor medicine Medical College Pennsylvania, Philadelphia, 1971-74; professor medicine, dean Medical College Pennsylvania, 1975—, dean; 1975-89, senior vice president; 1976-89, vice president ednl. committee for foreign medical grads.; 1989—; director clinical devel. Am. Oncologic Hospital, Philadelphia, 1973-75; attending physician Philadelphia Veteran's Administration Hospital, 1967—, Hospital Medical College Pennsylvania, 1971—; consultant in field. Member United States national committee International Union Against Cancer, 1969-72; member National Conference Cancer Prevention and Detection, 1973, National Workshop Professional Education in High Blood Pressure, 1973, National Cancer Control Planning Conference, 1973; vice chairman Governor Pennsylvania Task Force Cancer Control, 1974-76, chairman committee cancer detection, 1974-76; member health research adv. board State of Pennsylvania, 1976-78; member diagnostic research adv. group National Cancer Institute, 1974-78; chairman coordinating committee, comprehensive cancer center program Fox Chase Cancer Center, University Pennsylvania Cancer Center, 1975; consultant World Health Organization, Government of India, 1979, Government of Indonesia, 1980, entire Southeast Asia region, 1981; member National Conference on Medical Education. Author numerous articles in field.; Assistant editor: Annals Internal Medicine, 1972-75; editorial board other medical journals. Board of directors Philadelphia Council International Visitors, 1972-77, Israel Cancer Research Fund, 1975—, Am. Associates Ben Gurion University, 1986— ; board trustees Educational Comm. Foreign Medical Grads., 1987-89; adv. commission International Participation Philadelphia '76, 1973-76. Served to captain Medical Corps Army of the United States, 1958-60. Recipient Arnold and Marie Schwartz award in medicine American Medical Association, 1976; Torch of Learning award Am. Friends of Hebrew University, 1981. Fellow American College of Physicians, College Physicians Philadelphia (censor 1977-86 , councillor 1977-86); member Am. Federation Clinical Research (president Temple University chapter 1964-65), Am. Association Cancer Research, Am. Society Clinical Oncology, Association Am. Cancer Insts., Association Am. Medical Colls., Northeast Consortium on Medical Education (treasurer 1983-89, chairman 1986-87), Council of Deans of Private Free-Standing Medical Schs. (co-founder, chairman 1983-85), Pennsylvania Council Deans (chairman 1987-89), Am. Cancer Society (vice chairman service committee Philadelphia division 196, board directors 1974-80, chairman awards committee 1976), Am. Lung Association, American Medical Association, American Association for the Advancement of Science, Am.

Heart Association, Pan Am. Medical Association, Philadelphia Cooperative Cancer Association, New York Acad. Sciences, Pennsylvania Heart Association, Heart Association Southeastern Pennsylvania, Pennsylvania Medical Society, Philadelphia County Medical Society (chairman committee international med. affairs 1964-72), Pennsylvania Lung Association, Philadelphia Association for Clinical Trials (board directors 1980-81), Health Systoms Agency Southeastern Pennsylvania (governor board, executive committee 1983-87, secretary 1985-87), Am. Association Ben Gurion University (board directors 1986—), Society des Medecins Militaires Français, International Medical School Affiliates Consortium (co-founder, vice chairman 1985-87), Phi Beta Kappa, Sigma Xi, Alpha Omega Alpha (councillor 1963-65). Discovered assn. of hepatitis B surface antigen with hepatitis; performed 1st studies of pulmonary Surfactant in adult human lung disease; developed cancer screening system based on risk status. Home: 2135 St James Place Philadelphia Pennsylvania 19103

SWETS, JOHN ARTHUR, scientist; born Grand Rapids, Michigan, June 19, 1928; son of John A. and Sara Henrietta (Heyns) S.; married Maxine Ruth Crawford, July 16, 1949; children—Stephen Arthur, Joel Brian. Bachelor of Arts, University Michigan, Ann Arbor, 1950, Master of Arts, 1953, Doctor of Philosophy, 1954. Instructor psychology University Michigan, Ann Arbor, 1954-56; assistant professor psychology M.I.T., Cambridge, 1956-60, associate professor psychology; 1960-63; vice president Bolt Beranek & Newman Incorporated, Cambridge, 1964-69,

senior vice president; 1969-74, general manager research, devel. and consultant, director; 1971-74; chief scientist BBN Laboratories, Cambridge, 1975—; lecturer department clinical epidemiology Harvard Medical School, 1985-88, department health care policy, 1988—; member corp. Education Devel. Center, Newton, Massachusetts, 1971-75; visiting research fellow Philips Laboratories, Netherlands, 1958; Regents' professor University California, 1969; advisor vision committee, committee on hearing and bioacoustics National Acad. Sci.-NRC, 1960—; advisor, consultant, lecturer numerous governmental and professional organizations in science. Co-author: (with D.M. Green) Signal Detection Theory and Psychophysics, 1966; (with R.M. Pickett) Evaluation of Diagnostic Systems: Methods From Signal Detection Theory, 1982; editor: Signal Detection and Recognition by Human Observers, 1964; (with L.L. Flliott) Psychology and the Handicapped Child, 1974; (with D. Druckman) Enhancing Human Performance, 1988; contributor articles to professional journals; member editorial board Medical Decision Making, 1980-85, Psychological Science, 1989—. Past member numerous civic organizations; member corp. Winchester Hospital, Massachusetts, 1981-84. Fellow Acoustical Society Am., Am. Psychological Association, American Association for the Advancement of Science, Society Experimental Psychologists (Howard Crosby Warren medal 1985); member Psychonomic Society, Psychometric Society, Society Math. Psychology, Evaluation Research Society, Sigma Xi, Sigma Alpha Epsilon.

Congregationalist (moderator). Clubs: Winchester Country, Cosmos. Office: Bolt Beranek & Newman Incorporated 10 Fawcett St Cambridge Massachusetts 02238

SWIFT, HEWSON HOYT, educator, biologist; born Auburn, New York, November 8, 1920; son of Arthur L., Jr. and Hildegarde (Hoyt) S.; married Joan Woodcock, June 6, 1942; children: Deirdre Anne, Barbara Jean. Bachelor of Arts, Swarthmore College, 1942; Master of Science, State University Iowa, 1945; Doctor of Philosophy, Columbia University, 1950. Curator spiders United States National Museum, Washington, 1945-46; lecturer zoology Columbia, 1948-49; member faculty University Chicago, 1949—, professor zoology; 1958-70, Distinguished Service professor biology and pathology; 1971-77, chairman department biology; 1972-77, George Wells Beadle Distinguished Service professor biology and pathology; 1977-84, George Wells Beadle Distinguished Service professor department molecular genetics and cell biology and department pathology; 1984—; visiting professor Harvard University, 1970-71; visiting senior scientist CSIRO, Canberra, Australia, 1977-78; member cell biology study section National Institutes of Health, 1958-62; member devel. adv. panel National Science Foundation, 1962-65; adv. panel etiology of cancer Am. Cancer Society, 1965-70; member adv. panel National Cancer Institute, 1972-75. Recipient Quantrell award for excellence in teaching University Chicago, 1977; E.B. Wilson award for outstanding contributions to cell biology, 1985. Fellow American Association for the Advancement of

Science, Am. Acad. Arts and Sciences, National Acad. Sciences (chairman section on cellular and developmental biology 1974-77); member Am. Society Cell Biology (president 1964, editorial board of Jour.), Histochem. Society (president 1973, editorial board journal), Electron Microscope Society Am., Genetics Society Am.

SYNGE, RICHARD LAURENCE MILLINGTON, biochemist; born Liverpool, England, October 28, 1914; son of Laurence M. and Katharine (Swan) S.; married Ann Stephen, 1943; 3 sons, 4 daughters. Doctor of Philosophy; educated, Winchester College, Trinity College, Cambridge (England) University; Doctor of Science (honorary), University East Anglia, 1977, University Aberdeen, 1987; Doctor of Philosophy (honorary), University Uppsala, 1980. Biochemist Wool Industries Research Association, Leeds, England, 1941-43; staff biochemist Lister Institute Preventive Medicine, London, 1943-48; head department protein chemistry Rowett Research Institute, Aberdeen, Scotland, 1948-67; biochemist Food Research Institute, Norwich, England, 1967-76; hon. professor School Biological Sciences, University East Anglia, 1968-84; visiting biochemist Ruakura Animal Research Station, Hamilton, New Zealand, 1958-59. Member editorial board Biochem. Journal, 1949-55. Recipient (with A.J.P. Martin) Nobel prize for chemistry, 1952; John Price Wetherill medal Franklin Institute, 1959; named hon. fellow Trinity College, Cambridge University, 1972. Fellow Royal Society Chemistry, Royal Society; hon. member Royal Irish Acad., Royal Society New Zealand, Am. Society Biological

Chemists. Home: 19 Meadow Rise Road, Norwich NR2 3QE, England

SZASZ, THOMAS STEPHEN, psychiatrist, educator, writer; born Budapest, Hungary, April 15, 1920; came to United States, 1938, naturalized, 1944; son of Julius and Lily (Wellisch) S.; married Rosine Loshkajian, October 19, 1951 (divorced 1970); children: Margot Claire, Susan Marie. Bachelor of Arts, University Cincinnati, 1941, Doctor of Medicine, 1944; Doctor of Science (honorary), Allegheny College, 1975, University Francisco Marroquin, Guatemala, 1979. Diplomate: Nat. Board Medical Examiners, Am. Board Psychiatry and Neurology. Intern 4th Medical Service Harvard, Boston City Hospital, 1944-45; assistant resident medicine Cincinnati General Hospital, 1945-46, assistant clinician internal medicine div. out-patient dispensary; 1946; assistant resident psychiatry University Chicago Clinics, 1946-47; training research fellow Institute Psychoanalysis, Chicago, 1947-48; research assistant Institute Psychoanalysis, 1949-50, staff member; 1951-56; practice medicine, specializing in psychiatry, psychoanalysis Chicago, 1949-54, Bethesda, Maryland, 1954-56, Syracuse, New York, 1956—; professor psychiatry State University New York, Syracuse, 1956—; visiting professor department psychiatry University Wisconsin, Madison, 1962, Marquette University School Medicine, Milwaukee, 1968, University New Mexico, 1981; holder numerous lectureships, including C.P. Snow lecturer Ithaca College, 1970; E.South Meyer Memorial lecturer University Queensland Medical School; Lambie-Dew orator Sydney University, 1977;

Member national adv. committee board Tort and Medical Yearbook; consultant committee mental hygiene New York State Bar Association; member research adv. panel Institute Study Drug Addiction; adv. board Corp. Economic Education, 1977—. Author: Pain and Pleasure, 1957, The Myth of Mental Illness, 1961, Law, Liberty and Psychiatry, 1963, Psychiatric Justice, 1965, The Ethics of Psychoanalysis, 1965, Ideology and Insanity, 1970, The Manufacture of Madness, 1970, The Second Sin, 1973, Ceremonial Chemistry, 1974, Heresies, 1976, Karl Kraus and the Soul-Doctors, 1976, Schizophrenia: The Sacred Symbol of Psychiatry, 1976, Psychiatric Slavery, 1977, The Theology of Medicine, 1977, The Myth of Psychotherapy, 1978, Sex by Prescription, 1980, The Therapeutic State, 1984, Insanity: The Idea and its Consequences, 1987; editor: The Age of Madness, 1973; cons. editor of psychiatry and psychology: Stedman's Medical Dictionary, 22d edit, 1973; contributing editor: Reason, 1974—, Libertarian Rev., 1986—; editorial board: Psychoanalytic Rev, 1965—, Journal Contemporary Psychotherapy, 1968—, Law and Human Behavior, 1977—, Journal Libertarian Studies, 1977—, Children and Youth Services Rev, 1978—, Am. Journal Forensic Psychiatry, 1980—, Free Inquiry, 1980—. Served to commander, Medical Corps United States Naval Reserve, 1954-56. Recipient Stella Feiss Hofheimer award University Cincinnati, 1944, Holmes-Munsterberg award International Acad. Forensic Psychology, 1969; Wisdom award honor, 1970; Acad. prize Institutum atque Academia Auctorum Internationalis, Andorra, 1972; Distinguished Service award Am.

Institute Pub. Service, 1974; Martin Buber award Midway Counseling Center, 1974; others; named Humanist of Year Am. Humanist Association, 1973; Hon. fellow Postgrad. Center for Mental Health, 1961, Mencken award, 1981, Humanist Laureate, 1984, Statue of Liberty-Ellis Island Foundation Archives Roster, 1986. Life fellow Am. Psychiat. Association, Am. Psychoanalytic Association, International and Western New York psychoanalytic socs. Home: 4739 Limberlost Lane Manlius New York 13104 Office: 750 E Adams St Syracuse New York 13210

SZEGO, CLARA MARIAN, physiologist, educator; born Budapest, Hungary, March 23, 1916; came to United States, 1921, naturalized, 1927; daughter of Paul S. and Helen (Elek) S.; married Sidney Roberts, September 14, 1943. Bachelor of Arts, Hunter College, 1937; Master of Science (Garvan fellow), University Minnesota, 1939, Doctor of Philosophy, 1942. Instructor physiology University Minnesota, 1942-43; Minnesota Cancer Research Institute fellow 1943-44; research associate Office of Scientific Research and Development, National Bureau Standards, 1944-45, Worcester Foundation Experimental Biology, 1945-47; research instructor physiological chemistry Yale University School Medicine, 1947-48; member faculty University of California at Los Angeles, 1948—, professor biology; 1960—. Named Woman of Year in Sci. Los Angeles Times, 1957-58; Guggenheim fellow, 1956; named to Hunter College Hall of Fame, 1987. Fellow A.A.A.S.; member Am. Physiological Society, Am. Society Cell Biology, Endocrine Society (CIBA award 1953), Society for Endocrinology (Great Britain), Biochem. Society (Great Britain), International Society Research Reprodn., Phi Beta Kappa (president University of California at Los Angeles chapter 1973-74), Sigma Xi (president University of California at Los Angeles chapter 1976-77). Research and numerous publs. on steroid protein interactions, mechanisms of hormone action and lysosome participation in normal cell function. Home: 1371 Marinette Road Pacific Palisades California 90272 Office: U California Department Biology Los Angeles California 90024

SZEKELY, JULIAN, materials engineering educator; born Budapest, Hungary, November 23, 1934; came to United States, 1966, naturalized, 1975; son of Gyula and Ilona (Nemeth) S.; married Elizabeth Joy Pearn, March 2, 1963; children: Richard J., Martin T., Rebecca J., Mathew T., David A. Bachelor of Science, Imperial College, London, 1959; Doctor of Philosophy, D.I.C., 1961; Doctor of Science, D.I.C., England, 1972. Lecturer metallurgy Imperial College, 1962-66; associate professor chemical engineering State University New York at Buffalo, 1966-68, professor; 1968-76; director Center for Process Metallurgy, 1970-76; professor materials engineering Massachusetts Institute Tech., Cambridge, 1976—; consultant to government and industry. Author: (with New Jersey Themelis) Rate Phenomena in Process Metallurgy, 1971, (with W.H. Ray) Process Optimization, 1973, (with J.W. Evans and H.Y. Sohn) Gas-Solid Reactions, 1976, Fluid Flow Aspects of Metals Processing, 1979; (with J.W. Evans and J.K. Brimocombe) Mathematical Modelling of Metals Processing Operations; Editor: Ironmaking Technology, 1972, The Steel Industry and the Environment, The Steel Industry and The Energy Crisis, 1975, The Future of the World's Steel Industry, 1976, Alternative Energy Sources for the Steel Industry, 1977; Contributor articles to professional journals. Recipient Junior Moulton medal Brit. Institute Chemical Engrs., 1964; Extractive Metallurgy Div. Sci. award Am. Institute Mining and Metall. Engrs., 1973; also Mathewson Gold medal, 1973; Howe Memorial lecturer, 1979, Extractive Metall. lecturer, 1987 ; Sir George Beilby Gold medal Brit. Institute Chemical Engrs.-Soc. Chemical Industry-Inst. Metals, 1973; Curtis McGraw research award Am. Society Engineering Education, 1974; Professional Progress award Am. Institute Chemical Engrs., 1974; Charles H. Jennings Memorial award Am. Welding Society, 1983; John Simon Guggenheim fellow, 1974. Member National Acad. Engineering. Office: Room 4-117 Department Materials Sci and Engring Mass Institute Tech Cambridge Massachusetts 02139

TALMAGE, DAVID WILSON, physician, medical educator, former university administrator; born Kwangju, Korea, September 15, 1919; son of John Van Neste and Eliza (Emerson) T.; married LaVeryn Marie Hunicke, June 23, 1944; children: Janet, Marilyn, David, Mark, Carol. Student, Maryville (Tennessee) College, 1937-38; Bachelor of Science, Davidson (North Carolina) College, 1941; Doctor of Medicine, Washington University, St. Louis, 1944. Intern Georgia Baptist Hospital, 1944-45; resident medicine Barnes Hospital, St. Louis, 1948-50; fellow medicine Barnes Hospital, 1950-51; assistant professor pathology University Pittsburgh, 1951-52; assistant professor, then associate professor medicine University Chicago, 1952-59; professor medicine University Colorado, 1959—, professor microbiology; 1960-86, distinguished professor; 1986—, chairman department; 1963-65, associate dean; 1966-68, dean; 1969-71; director Webb-Waring Lung Institute, 1973-83, associate dean for research; 1983-86; member national council National Institute Allergy and Infectious Diseases, National Institutes of Health, 1963-66, 73-77. Author: (with John Cann) Chemistry of Immunity in Health and Disease; editor: Journal Allergy, 1963-67, (with M. Samter) Immunological Diseases. Served with Medical Corps Army of the United States, 1945-48. Markle scholar, 1955-60. Member A.O.A., Am. Acad. Allergy (president), Am. Association Immunologists (president), National Acad. Sciences, Institute Medicine, Phi Beta Kappa. Office: U Colorado School Medicine Denver Colorado 80262

TARJAN, ROBERT ENDRE, computer scientist; born Pomona, California, April 30, 1948; son of George and Helen Emma (Blome) T.; married Gail Maria Zawacki, April 22, 1978; children—Alice Marisha, Zosia Emma Zawacki, Lily Maxine. Bachelor of Science, California Institute Tech., 1969; Master of Science, Stanford University, 1971, Doctor of Philosophy, 1972. Assistant professor Cornell University, Ithaca, New York, 1972-73; Miller fellow University Calif.-Berkeley, 1973-75; assistant professor Stanford University, Palo Alto, California, 1975-

77, associate professor; 1977-80; member tech. staff American Telephone and Telegraph Company Bell Laboratories, Murray Hill, New Jersey, 1980—; adj. professor New York University, New York City, 1981-85; James South McDonnell distinguished university professor Princeton University, 1985—. Author: Data Structures and Network Algorithms, 1983; (with G. Polya and D. Woods) Notes on Introductory Combinatorics, 1983. Guggenheim fellow, 1978; recipient Nevanlinna prize International Math. Union, 1983. Fellow Am. Acad. Arts and Sciences; member National Acad. Sciences, National Acad. Engineering, Association Computing Machinery (A.M. Turing award 1986), Society Industrial and Applied Math., American Association for the Advancement of Science. Office: Princeton U Department Computer Sci Princeton New Jersey 08544

TASKER, JOHN BAKER, veterinary medical educator, college dean; born Concord, New Hampshire, August 28, 1933; son of John Baker and Catherine Mabel (Baker) T.; married Grace Ellen Elliott, June 17, 1961; children—Sybil Alice, Sarah Catherine, Sophia Ethel. Doctor of Veterinary Medicine, Cornell University, 1957, Doctor of Philosophy, 1963. Instructor Cornell University, Ithaca, New York, 1960-61; from associate professor to professor Cornell University, 1967-78; from assistant professor to associate professor Colorado State University, Fort Collins, 1963-67; professor vet. clinical pathology, associate dean Louisiana State University, 1978-84; professor vet. pathology, dean College Vet. Medicine, Michigan State University, East Lansing, 1984—;

consultant Ralston-Purina Company, St. Louis, 1978, Universidad Nacional P. Urena, Dominican Republic, 1980, University Nebraska, Lincoln, 1982-83. Editor: Veterinary Clinics of North America, 1976. Served to lst lieutenant United States Army, 1958-60. Recipient Outstanding Instructor award Colorado State University Vet. College, 1967; Norden Teaching award Cornell University Vet. College, 1977. Member American Veterinary Medical Association, Michigan Veterinary Medical Association, Am. College Veterinary Pathologists (diplomate; examiner 1972-74), Am. Society Veterinary Clinical Pathology (president 1971-72), Association Am. Veterinary Medical Colls. (executive committee 1986—). Avocations: reading; traveling. Home: 3519 Apple Valley Road Okemos Michigan 48864 Office: Michigan State U College Veterinary Medicine A-133 E Fee Hall East Lansing Michigan 48824

TAUBE, HENRY, chemistry educator; born Saskatchewan, Canada, November 30, 1915; came to United States, 1937, naturalized, 1942; son of Samuel and Albertina (Tiledetski) T.; married Mary Alice Wesche, November 27, 1952; children: Linda, Marianna, Heinrich, Karl. Bachelor of Science, University Saskatchewan, 1935, Master of Science, 1937, Doctor of Laws, 1973; Doctor of Philosophy, University California, 1940; Doctor of Philosophy (honorary), Hebrew University of Jerusalem, 1979; Doctor of Science (honorary), University Chicago, 1983, Polytechnic Institute, New York, 1984, State University of New York, 1985, University Guelph, 1987; Doctor of Science honoris causa, Seton Hall University, 1988, Seton Hall University, Debrecen, Hungary, 1988. Instructor University

California, 1940-41; instructor, assistant professor Cornell University, 1941-46; faculty University Chicago, 1946-62, professor; 1952-62, chairman department chemistry; 1955-59; professor chemistry Stanford University, 1962—, Marguerite Blake Wilbur professor; 1976, chairman department; 1971-74; Baker lecturer Cornell University, 1965. Hon. member Hungarian Acad., Scis., 1988. Recipient Harrison Howe award, 1961; Chandler medal Columbia University, 1964; F.P. Dwyer medal University N.S.W., Australia, 1973; National medal of Sci., 1976, 77; Allied Chemical award for Excellence in Graduate Teaching and Innovative Sci., 1979; Nobel Prize in Chemistry, 1983; Bailar medal University Illinois, 1983; Robert A. Welch Foundation Award in chemistry, 1983; Distinguished Achievement award International Precious Metals Institute, 1986; Guggenheim fellow, 1949, 55. Member Am. Acad. Arts and Sciences, National Acad. Sciences (award in chemical scis. 1983), Am. Chemical Society (Kirkwood award New Haven section 1965, award for nuclear applications in chemistry 1955, Nichols medal New York section 1971, Willard Gibbs medal Chicago section 1971, Distinguished Service in Advancement Inorganic Chemistry award 1967, T.W. Richards medal NE section 1980, Monsanto Company award in inorganic chemistry 1981, Linus Pauling award Puget Sound section 1981, Priestley medal 1985, Oesper award Cincinnati section 1986), Royal Physiographical Society of Lund (foreign member), Am. Philosophical Society, Finnish Acad. Sci. and Letters, Royal Danish Acad. Sciences and Letters, College Chemists of Catalonia and Beleares (hon.), Can. Society Chemistry (hon.), Hungarian Acad. Sciences (hon. member), Royal Society (foreign member), Phi Beta Kappa, Sigma Xi, Phi Lambda Upsilon (hon.). Office: Stanford U Department Chemistry Stanford California 94305

TAUBMAN, MARTIN ARNOLD, immunologist; born New York City, July 10, 1940; son of Herman and Betty (Berger) T.; married Joan Petra Mikelbank, May 30, 1965; children: Benjamin Abby, Joel David. Bachelor of Science, Brooklyn College, 1961; Doctor of Dental Surgery, Columbia University, 1965; Doctor of Philosophy, State University of New York, Buffalo, 1970. Assistant member staff Forsyth Dental Center, Boston, 1970—; head immunology department Forsyth Dental Center, 1972—, associate member staff; 1974-80, senior staff member; 1980—; assistant clinical professor oral biology and pathophysiology Harvard University School Dental Medicine, 1976-79, associate clinical professor; 1979—; member oral biology and medicine study section National Institutes of Health, 1980-84. Author articles, chapters in books. Fellow USPHS, 1962-63; postdoctoral fellow, 1966-70; recipient Research Career Devel. award, 1971-76, Fred Birnberg Alumni award for distinguished dental research Columbia University Association Dental Alumni. Member American Association for the Advancement of Science, International Association Dental Research, Am. Association Immunologists, Am. Association Dental Research (vice president 1987—, president elect 1988, president 1989). Office: Forsyth Dental Center 140 Fenway Boston Massachusetts 02115

TAUC, JAN, physics educator; born Pardubice, Czechoslovakia, April 15, 1922; came to United States, 1969, naturalized, 1978; son of Jan and Josefa (Semonska) T.; married Vera Koubelova, October 18, 1947; children: Elena (Mrs. Milan Kokta), January. Ing.Doctor in Electrical Engineering, Tech. University Prague, 1949; RNDr., Charles University, 1956; Dr.Sc. in Physics, Czechoslovak Academy Scis., 1956. Scientist microwave research Sci. and Tech. Research Institute, Tanvald and Prague, 1949-52; head semiconductor department Institute Solid State Physics, Czechoslovak Acad. Sciences, 1953-69; professor experimental physics Charles University, 1964-69, director Institute Physics; 1968-69; member tech. staff Bell Telephone Laboratories, Murray Hill, New Jersey, 1969-70; professor engineering and physics Brown University, 1970—, L. Herbert Ballou professor engineering and physics; 1983—, director material research laboratory; 1983-88; director East Fermi Summer School, Varenna, Italy, 1965; visiting professor University Paris, 1969, Stanford University, 1977, Max Planck Institute Solid State Research, Stuttgart, Germany, 1982; United Nations Educational, Scientific and Cultural Organization fellow, Harvard, 1961-62. Author: Photo and Thermoelectric Effects in Semiconductors, 1962, also numerous articles.; Editor: The Optical Properties of Solids, 1966, Amorphous and Liquid Semiconductors, 1974; co-editor: Solid State Communications, 1963—. Recipient National prize Czechoslovak Government, 1955, 69; Senior U.S. Scientist award Humboldt Foundation, 1981. Fellow Am. Physical Society (Frank Isakson prize 1982), American Association for the Advancement of Science; founding member European Physical Society; corr. member Czechoslovak Acad. Sciences, 1963-71. Office: Div Engring Brown University Providence Rhode Island 02912

TAX, SOL, educator, anthropologist; born Chicago, October 30, 1907; son of Morris Paul and Kate (Hanwit) T.; married Gertrude Jospe Katz, July 4, 1933; children: Susan Margaret, Marianna. Bachelor of Philosophy, University Wisconsin, 1931, Doctor of Hebrew Literature (honorary), 1969; Doctor of Philosophy, University Chicago, 1935; Doctor of Laws (honorary), Wilmington College, 1974; Doctor of Science (honorary), University Del Valle De Guatemala, 1974, Beloit College, 1975. Member Logan Mus. North Africa Expedition, 1930; member field party Laboratory Anthropology Mescalero Apache, 1931; research among Fox Indians, 1932-34; ethnologist Carnegie Institution, Washington, 1934-48; field research Indians, Guatemala, 1934-41, Chiapas, Mexico, 1942-46; visiting professor National Institute Anthropology and History, Mexico, 1942-43; research associate University Chicago, 1940-44, associate professor; 1944-48, professor; 1948—, associate dean div. social sciences; 1948-53, chairman department anthropology; 1955-58, dean university extension; 1963-68; director Fox Indian Project, 1948-62; research associate Wenner-Gren Foundation Anthropological Research, 1957—; co-ordinator Am. Indian Chicago Conference, University Chicago, 1961, Carnegie Cross-Cultural Education Program, 1962-67; member executive committee United States National Commission United

Nations Educational, Scientific and Cultural Organization, 1963-65; member committee international relations anthropology National Research Council, 1956-66, committee international relations behavioral sciences, 1966—; special adv. anthropology to secretary Smithsonian Institution, 1965—; director Center Study Man; consultant United States Office Education, 1965—; member Community Activities and Continuing Education Council Illinois, 1965-67; secretary Illinois Mus. Board, 1958-70; board of directors Council Study Mankind, executive committee, 1965—; board advs. Council International Communications, 1966—; board of directors Am. Indian Devel., Incorporated; trustee Native Am. Educational Services College. Author: Heritage of Conquest: The Ethnology of Middle America, 1952, Penny Capitalism: A Guatemalan Indian Economy, 1953; editor: Civilization of Ancient America, 1951, Acculturation in the Americas, 1952, Indian Tribes of Aboriginal America, 1952, An Appraisal of Anthropology Today, 1953, 29th International Congress Americanists, 1949-52, Evolution after Darwin, 3 volumes, 1960, Anthropology Today-Selections, 1962, Horizons of Anthropology, 1964, Viking Fund Publications in Anthropology, 1960-68, The People versus The System: A Dialogue in Urban Conflict; associate editor Am. Anthropologist, 1948-53, editor, 1953-56; contributing editor Handbook Latin Am. Studies, 1947-52; founder, editor Current Anthropology-A World Journal of Scis. of Man; general editor World Anthropology, 91 volumes, 1975-79. President Hyde Park Community Council, 1952-53. Viking medalist, 1961-65; fellow Center Advanced Study Behavioral Sciences, 1969-70; decorated Government Czechoslovakia, 1969. Fellow Am. Anthropological Association (president 1958-59, Distinguished Service award 1977), American Association for the Advancement of Science, Am. Folklore Society, Society Applied Anthropology (Bronislaw Malinowski award 1977); hon. member Zlovakian Anthropological Society Ziovak Acad. Sciences, Royal Anthropological Institute Great Britain, Hungarian Anthropological Institute, Chilean Anthropological Institute; member Mexican Anthropological Society, National Research Council, International Union Anthropological and Ethnological Sciences (president 1968-73), Sigma Xi. Club: Quadrangle. Home: 1700 E 56th St Chicago Illinois 60637

TAYLOR, EDWARD CURTIS, chemistry educator; born Springfield, Massachusetts, August 3, 1923; son of Edward Curtis and Margaret Louise (Anderson) T.; married Virginia Dion Crouse, June 29, 1946; children: Edward Newton, Susan Raines. Student, Hamilton College, 1942-44, Doctor of Science (honorary), 1969; Bachelor of Arts, Cornell University, 1946, Doctor of Philosophy, 1949. Postdoctoral fellow National Acad. Sciences, Zurich, Switzerland, 1949-50; DuPont postdoctoral fellow chemistry University Illinois, 1950-51, faculty; 1951-54, assistant professor organic chemistry; 1952-54; faculty Princeton University, 1954—, professor chemistry; 1964—, A. Barton Hepburn professor organic chemistry; 1966—, chairman department chemistry; 1974-79; visiting professor Technische Hochschule, Stuttgart, Germany, 1960, University East

Anglia, 1969, 71; Distinguished visiting professor University Buffalo, 1968, University Wyoming, 1977; Backer lecturer University Groningen, Holland, 1969; member chemistry adv. committee Office Sci. Research, United States Air Force, 1962-73, Cancer Chemotherapy National Service Center, 1958-62; consultant research divs. Procter & Gamble, 1953—, Eastman Kodak Company, 1965-83, Tennessee Eastman Company, 1968-83, Eli Lilly & Company, 1970—, Burroughs Wellcome Company, 1983-87, E.I. duPont de Nemours & Company, 1986—, Polaroid Corp., 1986—. Author: (with McKillop) Chemistry of Cyclic Enaminonitriles and o-Aminonitriles, 1970, Principles of Heterocyclic Chemistry; film course, 1974; editor: (with Raphael, Wynberg) Advances in Organic Chemistry, volumes I-V, 1960-65, (with Wynberg) volume VI, 1969, volumes VII-IX, 1970-79, (with W. Pfleiderer) Pteridine Chemistry, 1964, (with A. Weissberger) The Chemistry of Heterocyclic Compounds, 1968—, General Heterocyclic Chemistry, 1968—; organic chemistry editorial adviser, Intersci. Pubs., 1968—; member editorial adv. board: Journal Medicinal Chemistry, 1962-66, Journal Organic Chemistry, 1971-75, Synthetic Communications, 1971—, Heterocycles, 1973—, Chemical Substructure Index, 1971—, Advances in Heterocylic Chemistry, 1983—. . Recipient research awards Smith Kline & French Foundation, 1955, research awards Hoffmann-LaRoche Foundation, 1964, 65, research awards Ciba Foundation, 1971; sr. faculty fellow Harvard University, 1959; Recipient Distinguished Hamilton award, 1977; Guggenheim fellow, 1979-80;

recipient U.S. sr. scientist prize Alexander von Humboldt Foundation, 1983. Fellow New York Acad. Sciences, Am. Institute Chemists; member Am. Chemical Society (award for creative work in synthetic organic chemistry, 1974, chairman organic chemistry division 1976-77), German Chemical Society, Chemical Society London, Phi Beta Kappa, Sigma Xi, Phi Kappa Phi. Home: 288 Western Way Princeton New Jersey 08540

TAYLOR, J(AMES) HERBERT, cell biology educator; born Corsicana, Texas, January 14, 1916; son of Charles Aaron and Delia May (McCain) T.; married Shirley Catherine Hoover, May 1, 1946; children: Lynne Sue, Lucy Delia, Michael Wesley. Bachelor of Science, Southern Oklahoma State University, 1939; Master of Science, University Oklahoma, 1941; Doctor of Philosophy, University Virginia, 1944. Assistant professor bacteriology and botany University Oklahoma, Norman, 1946-47; associate professor botany University Tennessee, Knoxville, 1948-51; assistant professor botany Columbia University, New York City, 1951-54; associate professor Columbia University, 1954-58, professor cell biology; 1958-64; professor biological sci. Florida State University, Tallahassee, 1964-83, Robert O. Lawton distinguished professor biological sci.; 1983—; associate director Institute Molecular Biophysics, Florida State University, 1970-79; director Institute Molecular Biophysics, 1980-85; consultant Oak Ridge National Laboratory, 1949-51; research collaborator Brookhaven National Laboratory, 1951-58; national lecturer Sigma Xi Research Society. Author: Molecular Genetics, Volume 1, 1963, Volume 2, 1965,

Volume 3, 1979; DNA Methylation and Cellular Differentiation, 1983; also papers on molecular genetics; contributor over 100 articles in field to professional journals. President Unitarian Church Tallahassee, 1968-70. Served with Medical Corps United States Army, 1944-46, PTO. Recipient Meritorious Research award Michigan State University, 1960; Guggenheim fellow California Institute Tech., 1958-59. Member National Acad. Sciences, American Association for the Advancement of Science, Am. Institute Biological Sci., Am. Society Cell Biologists (president 1969-70), Biophysics Society, Genetics Society Am. Democrat. Office: Institute Molecular Biophysics Fla State U Tallahassee Florida 32306

TAYLOR, ROY LEWIS, botanist; born Olds, Alberta, Canada, April 12, 1932; son of Martin Gilbert and Crystal (Thomas) T. Bachelor of Science, Sir George Williams University, Montreal, Quebec, Can., 1957; Doctor of Philosophy, University California at Berkeley, 1962. Pub. school teacher Olds School Div., 1949-52; junior high school teacher Calgary School Board, Alberta, 1953-55; chief taxonomy section, research branch Can. Agricultural Department, Ottawa, Ontario, 1962-68; director Botanical Garden, professor botany, professor plant sciences University British Columbia, Vancouver, 1968-85; president, chief executive officer Chicago Horticultural Society, 1985—; director Chicago Botanical Garden, Glencoe, Illinois, 1985—; President Western Botanical Services Limited. Author: The Evolution of Canada's Flora, 1966, Flora of the Queen Charlotte Islands, Volumes I and II, 1968, Vascular Plants of British Columbia: A Descriptive Resource

Inventory, 1977; The Rare Plants of British Columbia, 1985. Recipient George White Medal of Honor, Massachusetts Hort. Society, 1986. Fellow Linnean Society London; member Canadian Botanical Association (president 1967-68), Biological Council Can. (president 1973-74), Am. Association Mus.'s (accreditation committee 1980-85, chairman 1985-88), Am. Association Botanical Gardens and Arboreta (president 1976, 77, Award of Merit, 1987), Ottawa Valley Curling Association (president 1968-69), British Columbia Society Landscape Architects (hon.), British Columbia Botanical Garden (hon.). Club: Governor-General's Curling of Canada (life); University (Chicago). Office: Chicago Botanic Garden Post Office Box 400 Glencoe Illinois 60022

TAYLOR, SAMUEL JAMES, mathematics educator; born Carrickferbus, Northern Ireland, December 13, 1929; came to United States, 1984; son of Robert James and Janie (Catherwood) T.; married; children—Richard, Charles, Jonathan, Helen. Bachelor of Science, Queen's University, Belfast, Northern Ireland, 1950; Doctor of Philosophy, Cambridge University, 1954. Bye fellow Peterhouse, Cambridge University, England, 1953-55; lecturer Birmingham University, England, 1955-62; professor London University, 1962-75, Liverpool University, England, 1975-83; visiting professor University British Columbia, Vancouver, Can., 1983-84; Whyburn professor math. University Virginia, Charlottesville, 1984—, chairman department; 1986—. Author: Introduction to Measure and Probability, 1966, Exploring Mathematical Thought, 1970,

Introduction to Measure and Integration, 1973; editor: Decomposition of Probability Distributions, 1964. Procter vis. fellow Princeton University, New Jersey 1952. Fellow Cambridge Philosophical Society, Institute Math. Statistics; member London Math. Society (secretary 1962-65, 68-71, editor 1980-83), Am. Math. Society. Presbyterian. Office: U Va Department Math Math and Astronomy Building Charlottesville Virginia 22903

TEDLOCK, DENNIS, anthropology educator; born St. Joseph, Missouri, June 19, 1939. Bachelor of Arts, University New Mexico, 1961; Doctor of Philosophy in Anthropology, Tulane University, 1968. Assistant professor anthropology Iowa State University, 1966-67; assistant professor rhetoric University California, Berkeley, 1967-69; research associate School Am. Research, 1969-70; assistant professor anthropology Brooklyn College, 1970-71; assistant professor Yale University, 1972-73; associate University professor, anthropology and religion Boston University, 1973-82, University professor, anthropology and religion; 1982-87; professor, department English, State University of New York, Buffalo, 1987—; visiting assistant professor Wesleyan University, 1971-72; adj. professor University New Mexico, 1980-81. Author: Finding the Center: Narrative Poetry of the Zuni Indians, 1972; co-editor: Teachings from the American Earth, 1975; also translator, contributor articles to professional journals. Recipient Poets, Playwrights, Editors, Essayists and Novelists translation prize for Popol Vuhi: The Mayan Book of Creation, 1986. Office: State University of New York Buffalo Department English Buffalo New York 14260

TEICH, MALVIN CARL, electrical engineering educator; born New York City, May 4, 1939; son of Sidney R. and Loretta K. Teich. Bachelor of Science in Physics, Massachusetts Institute of Technology, 1961; Master of Science in Electrical Engineering, Stanford University, 1962; Doctor of Philosophy in Quantum Electronics, Cornell University, 1966. Research scientist Massachusetts Institute of Technology Lincoln Laboratory, Lexington, Massachusetts, 1966-67; professor engineering sci. Columbia University, New York City, 1967—, chairman department electrical engineering; 1978-80. Contributor articles to professional journals; patentee. Recipient Citation Classic award Institute for Sci. Info., 1981; Guggenheim Memorial Foundation fellow, 1973. Fellow Optical Society Am. (optics letters editorial adv. panel 1977-79); member Institute of Electrical and Electronics Engineers (Browder J. Thompson Memorial prize 1969), Am. Physical Society, Acoustical Society Am., Sigma Xi. Office: Columbia U Department Elec Engring New York New York 10027

TELLER, EDWARD, physicist; born Budapest, Hungary, January 15, 1908; naturalized, 1941; son of Max and Ilona (Deutch) T.; married Augusta Harkanyi, February 26, 1934; children: Paul, Susan Wendy. Student, Institute Tech., Karlsruhe, Germany, 1926-28, University Munich, 1928; Doctor of Philosophy, University Leipzig, Germany, 1930; Doctor of Science (honorary), Yale University, 1954, University Alaska, 1959, Fordham University, 1960, George Washington University, 1960, University Southern California, 1960,

St. Louis University, 1960, Rochester Institute Tech., 1962, PMC Colls., 1963, University Detroit, 1964, Clemson University, 1966, Clarkson College, 1969; Doctor of Laws, Boston College, 1961, Seattle University, 1961, University Cincinnati, 1962, University Pittsburgh, 1963, Pepperdine University, 1974, University Maryland at Heidelberg, 1977; Doctor of Science, Doctor of Humane Letters, Mount Mary College, 1964; Doctor of Philosophy, Tel Aviv University, 1972; Doctor.Natural Science, DeLaSalle University, Manila, 1981; Doctor Medical Science (n.c.), Medical University South Carolina, 1983. Research associate Leipzig, 1929-31, Goettingen, Germany, 1931-33; Rockefeller fellow Copenhagen, 1934; lecturer University London, 1934-35; professor physics George Washington University, Washington, 1935-41, Columbia, 1941-42; physicist University Chicago, 1942-43, Manhattan Engineer District, 1942-46, Los Alamos Sci. Laboratory, 1943-46; professor physics University Chicago, 1946-52; professor physics University California, 1953-60, professor physics-at-large; 1960-70, University professor; 1970-75; professor emeritus, chairman department applied sci. University California, Davis and Livermore, 1963-66; assistant director Los Alamos Sci. Laboratory, 1949-52; consultant Livermore branch University California Radiation Laboratory, 1952-53; associate director Lawrence Livermore Laboratory, University California, 1954-58, 60-75; director Lawrence Livermore Radiation Laboratory, University California, 1958-60; now director emeritus, consultant; concerned with planning and prediction function atomic bomb and hydrogen bomb Lawrence Livermore Radiation Laboratory, University California, Manhattan District of Columbia, 1942-46; also Metallurgical and Laboratory of Argonne National Laboratory, University Chicago, 1942-43, 46-52, and Los Alamos, New Mexico, 1943-46; also Radiation Laboratory, Livermore, California, 1952-75; senior research fellow Hoover Institution War, Revolution and Peace, Stanford University, 1975—; member sci. adv. board United States Air Force; member White House Sci. Council; member adv. board Federal Emergency Management Agency; board of directors Association to Unite the Democracies; past member general adv. committee Atomic Energy Commission; former member President's Foreign Intelligence Adv. Board. Author: (with Francis Owen Rice) The Structure of Matter, 1949, (with A.L. Latter) Our Nuclear Future, 1958, (with Allen Brown) The Legacy of Hiroshima, 1962, The Reluctant Revolutionary, 1964, (with G.W. Johnson, W.K. Talley, G.H. Higgins) The Constructive Uses of Nuclear Explosives, 1968, (with Segre, Kaplan and Schiff) Great Men of Physics, 1969, The Miracle of Freedom, 1972, Energy: A Plan for Action, 1975, Nuclear Energy in the Developing World, 1977, Energy from Heaven and The Earth, 1979, The Pursuit of Simplicity, 1980, Better a Shield than a Sword, 1987. Past board of directors Def. Intelligence School, Naval War College; board of directors Federal Union, Hertz Foundation, Am. Friends of Tel Aviv University; sponsor Atlantic Union, Atlantic Council United States, University Centers for Rational Alternatives; member Committee to Unite Am., Incorporated; board governors Am. Acad. Achievement.

Recipient Joseph Priestley Memorial award Dickinson College, 1957, Harrison medal Am. Ordnance Association, 1955; Albert Einstein award, 1958; General Donovan Memorial award, 1959; Midwest Research Institute award, 1960; Research Institute Am. Living History award, 1960; Golden Plate award Am. Acad. Achievement, 1961; Gold medal Am. Acad. Achievement, 1982; Thomas E. White and Enrico Fermi awards, 1962; Robins award of Am., 1963; Leslie R. Groves Gold medal, 1974; Harvey prize in sci. and tech. Technion Institute, 1975; Semmelweiss medal, 1977; Albert Einstein award Technion Institute, 1977; Henry T. Heald award Illinois Institute Tech., 1978; Gold medal Am. College Nuclear Medicine, 1980; A.C. Eringen award, 1980; named ARCS Man of Year, 1980, Distinguished Scientist, National Sci. Devel. Board, 1981; Paul Harris award Rotary Foundation, 1980; Distinguished Scientist Phil-Am. Acad. Sci. and Engineering, 1981; Lloyd Freeman Hunt Citizenship award, 1982; National medal of Sci., 1983; Joseph Handleman prize, 1983, Sylvanus Thayer Medal, 1986. Fellow Am. Nuclear Society, Am. Physical Society, Am. Acad. Arts and Sciences, Hudson Institute (hon.); member National Acad. Sciences, Am. Geophysical Union, Society Engineering Sciences, International Platform Association. Research on chem., molecular and nuclear physics, quantum mechanics, thermonuclear reactions, applications of nuclear energy, astrophysics, spectroscopy of polyatomic molecules, theory of atomic nuclei. Office: Hoover Instn Stanford California 94305 also: Post Office Box 808 Livermore California 94550

TEMIN, HOWARD MARTIN, scientist, educator; born Philadelphia, December 10, 1934; son of Henry and Annette (Lehman) T.; married Rayla Greenberg, May 27, 1962; children: Sarah Beth, Miriam Judith. Bachelor of Arts, Swarthmore College, 1955, Doctor of Science (honorary), 1972; Doctor of Philosophy, California Institute Tech., 1959; Doctor of Science (honorary), New York Medical College, 1972, University Pennsylvania, 1976, Hahnemann Medical College, 1976, Lawrence University, 1976, Temple University, 1979, Medical College Wisconsin, 1981, Colorado State University, 1987, PM Curie, Paris, 1988. Postdoctoral fellow California Institute Tech., 1959-60; assistant professor oncology University Wisconsin, 1960-64, associate professor; 1964-69, professor; 1969—, Wisconsin Alumni Research Foundation professor cancer research; 1971-80, Am. Cancer Society professor viral oncology and cell biology; 1974—, H.P. Rusch professor cancer research; 1980—, Steenbock professor biological sciences; 1982—; member research policy adv. committee University Wisconsin Medical School, 1979—; member International Committee Virus Nomenclature Study Group for RNA Tumor Viruses, 1973-75, subcoms. HTLV and Acquired Immune Deficiency Syndrome viruses, 1985; member virology study section National Institutes of Health, 1971-74, member dir.'s adv. committee, 1979-83; consultant working group on human gene therapy NIH/RAC, 1984—, member National Cancer Adv. Board, 1987—; member NAS/IOM Committee for a National Strategy for Acquired Immune Deficiency Syndrome, 1986, NAS/

IOM Acquired Immune Deficiency Syndrome activities oversight committee, 1987—; member National Academy of Sciences Report Review Committee, 1988—, National Cancer Institute (special virus cancer program tumor virus detection segment working group), 1972-73; sponsor Federation Am. Scientists, 1976—; sci. adv. Stehlin Foundation, Houston, 1972—; member Waksman award committee National Acad. Sci., 1976-81; member United States Steel award Committee, 1980-83, chairman, 1982; district lecturer Hermann University, Connecticut, 1988, Ochoa lecture lut. Cong. Biochem., Prague, 1988, Muller lecture lut. Cong., General, Toronto, 1988. Associate editor: Journal Cellular Physiology, 1966-77, Cancer Research, 1971-74; executive editor Molecular Carcinogenesis, 1987; member editorial board: Journal Virology, 1971—, Intervirology, 1972-75, Proc. National Acad. Scis, 1975-80, Archives of Virology, 1975-77, Annual Rev. General, 1983, Molecular Biology and Evolution, 1983—, Oncogene Research, 1987—, J./AIDS, 1988—. Co-recipient Warren Triennial prize Massachusetts General Hospital, 1971, Gairdner Foundation International award, 1974, Nobel Prize in medicine, 1975; recipient Medical Society Wisconsin Special commendation, 1971, Papanicolaou Institute PAP award, 1972, M.D. Anderson Hospital and Tumor Institute Bertner award, 1972, U.S. Steel Foundation award in Molecular Biology, 1972, Theobald Smith Society Waksman award, 1972, Am. Chemical Society award in Enzyme Chemistry, 1973, Modern Medicine award for Distinguished Achievement, 1973, Harry Shay Memorial lecturer Fels Research Institute, 1973; Griffuel prize Association Devel. Recherche Cancer, Villejuif, 1972, New Horizons lecturer award Radiol. Society N.Am., 1968, G.H.A. Clowes lecturer award Association Cancer Research, 1974, National Institutes of Health Dyer lecturer award, 1974, Harvey lecturer award, 1974, Charlton lecturer award Tufts University, 1976, Hoffman-LaRoche lecturer award Rutgers University, 1979, Yoder hon. lecturer award St. Joseph Hospital, Tacoma, 1983, Cetus lecturer award University California, Berkeley, 1984; DuPont lecturer award Harvard University, 1985, Japanese Foundation for Promotion Cancer Research lecturer award, 1985, Herz Memorial lecturer award Tel-Aviv University, 1985, Amoros. Memorial lecturer award University West Indies, 1986, Albert Lasker award in basic med. sci., 1974, Lucy Wortham James award Society Surg. Oncologists, 1976, Gruber award Am. Acad. Dermatology, 1981; named to Central High School Hall of Fame, Philadelphia, 1976; recipient Pub. Health Service Research Career Devel. award National Cancer Institute, 1964-74, 1st Hilldale award in Biolog. Sci. University Wisconsin, 1986, Braund Distinguished vis. professor award University Tennessee, 1987, Eisenstark lecturer award University Missouri, 1987, 1st Wilmot vis. professor award University Rochester, 1987. Fellow Am. Acad. Arts and Sciences, Wisconsin Acad. Sci. Arts and Letters; member National Acad. Sciences, Am. Philosophical Society, Tissue Culture Association (hon. 1987), Royal Society. Office: U Wisconsin McArdle Lab 450 N Randall St Madison Wisconsin 53706

TENNEY, STEPHEN MARSH, physiologist, educator; born

Bloomington, Illinois, October 22, 1922; son of Harry Houser and Caroline (Marsh) T.; married Carolyn Cartwright, October 18, 1947; children: Joyce B., Karen M., Stephen M. Bachelor of Arts, Dartmouth; Doctor of Medicine, Cornell University; Doctor of Science (honorary), University Rochester. From instructor to associate professor of medicine and physiology University Rochester School Medicine, 1951-56; professor physiology Dartmouth Medical School, Hanover, New Hampshire, 1956—; dean Dartmouth Medical School, 1960-62, acting dean; 1966, 73—, director medical sciences; 1957-59, chairman department physiology; 1956-77, Nathan Smith professor physiology; 1974—; medical director Parker B. Francis Foundation, 1975-83, executive vice president; 1984—; Chairman physiology study section National Institutes of Health, 1962-65; training committee National Heart Institute, 1968-71; member executive committee National Research Council; member physiology panel National Institutes of Health study Office Sci. and Tech.; member regulatory biology panel National Science Foundation, 1971-75; chairman board sci. counselors National Heart and Lung Institute, 1974-78; chairman Commission Respiratory Physiology International Union Physiol. Sciences. Asso. editor: Journal Applied Physiology, 1976—, Handbook of Physiology; editorial board: Am. Journal Physiology, Circulation Research, Physiological Revs; Contributor articles to sci. journals. Served with United States Naval Reserve, 1947-49; senior medical officer Shanghai. Markle scholar in med. sci., 1954-59. Fellow Am. Acad. Arts and Sciences, American Association for the Advancement of Science; member Institute Medicine of National Acad. Sciences, Am. Physiological Society, Am. Society Clinical Investigation, New York Acad. Sciences, Gerontological Society, Am. Heart Association, Association Am. Medical Colls., Sigma Xi.

TERRY, ROBERT DAVIS, educator, neuropathologist; born Hartford, Connecticut, January 13, 1924; married Patricia Ann Blech, June 27, 1952; 1 son, Nicolas Saul. Bachelor of Arts, Williams College, 1946; Doctor of Medicine, Albany (New York) Medical College, 1950. Diplomate: Am. Board Pathology, Am. Board Neuropathology. Postdoctoral training St. Francis Hospital, Hartford, 1950, Bellevue Hospital, New York City, 1951, Montefiore Hospital, New York City, 1952-53, 54-55, Institute Recherches sur le Cancer, Paris, France, 1953-54; senior postdoctoral fellow Institute Recherches sur le Cancer, 1965-66; assistant pathologist Montefiore Hospital, 1955-59; associate professor department pathology Einstein College Medicine, Bronx, New York, 1959-64; professor Einstein College Medicine, 1964-84, acting chairman department pathology; 1969-70, chairman; 1970-84; professor departments neuroscis. and pathology University Calif.-San Diego, 1984—; member study section pathology National Institutes of Health, 1964-68; study sections National Multiple Sclerosis Society, 1964-72, 74-78; member board sci. counselors National Institute Neurological and Communicative Disorders and Stroke, National Institutes of Health, 1976-80, chairman, 1977-80; member national sci. council Huntington's Disease Association, 1978-81; member medical and sci. adv. board Alzheimer's Disease Society, Incorporated, 1978-88. Editorial adv. board: Journal Neuropathology and Experimental Neurology, 1963-83, 85-88, Lab. Investigation, 1967-77, Revue Neurologique, 1977-87, Annals of Neurology, 1978-82, Ultrastructural Pathology, 1978-86, Am. Journal Pathology, 1985—. Served with Army of the United States, 1943-46. Recipient Potamkin prize for Alzheimer Research, 1988. Member Am. Association Neuropathologists (president 1969-70), New York Pathological Society (vice president 1969-71, president 1971-73), Am. Society Experimental Pathology, Am. Neurological Association, Am. Acad. Neurologists. Research, publs. on Alzheimer's disease and Tay Sachs disease.

TESAR, DELBERT, machine systems and robotics educator, researcher, manufacturing consultant; born Beaver Crossing, Nebraska, September 2, 1935; son of Louis and Clara (Capek) T.; married Rogene Kresak, February 1, 1957; children: Vim Lee, Aleta Anne, Landon Grady, Allison Jeanne. Bachelor of Science in Mechanical Engineering, University Nebraska, 1958, Master of Science, 1959; Doctor of Philosophy, Georgia Tech. University, 1964. Associate professor University Florida, Gainesville, 1965-71, professor; 1972-83, grad. research professor; 1983-84, director, founder Center Intelligent Machines and Robotics; 1978-84; Curran chair in engineering University Texas, Austin, 1985—; lecturer in field., board of directors Robotics International, 1982—; member rev. panel National Bureau Standards, Gaithersburg, Maryland, 1982-88; member sci. adv. board to Air Force, 1982-86, numerous others. Author: (with others) Cam System Design, 1975. Patentee in field. Contributor articles to professional journals. Expert witness house sci. and tech. committee United States House of Representatives, 1978-84. Member Florida Engineering Society (Outstanding Tech. Achievement award 1982), American Society of Mechanical Engineers. Avocations: antiques; art; travel. Home: 8005 Two Coves Dr Austin Texas 78730 Office: U Tex Department Mech Engring ETC 4.146 Austin Texas 78712

THAGARD, NORMAN E., astronaut; born Florida, 1943; married Rex Kirby Johnson. Bachelor of Science, Florida State University, Master of Science; Doctor of Medicine, University Texas, 1977. Astronaut National Aeronautics and Space Administration, 1978—, mission specialist Challenger Flight 2, mission specialist Space Lab 3. Contributor (articles to professional journals). Served with United States Military Corps, 1969-70, Vietnam. Office: Lyndon B Johnson Space Center NASA Houston Texas 77058

THIER, SAMUEL OSIAH, physician, educator; born Brooklyn, June 23, 1937; son of Sidney and May Henrietta (Kanner) T.; married Paula Dell Finkelstein, June 28, 1958; children: Audrey Lauren, Stephanie Ellen, Sara Leslie. Student, Cornell University, 1953-56; Doctor of Medicine, State University New York, Syracuse, 1960. Diplomate: Am. Board Internal Medicine (dir. 1977-85, exec. com. 1981-85, chmn. 1984-85). Intern Massachusetts General Hospital, Boston, 1960-61; assistant resident Massachusetts General Hospital, 1961-62, senior resident; 1964-65, clinical and research fellow;

1965, chief resident; 1966; clinical associate National Institute Arthritis and Metabolic Diseases, 1962-64; from instructor to assistant professor medicine Harvard University Medical School, 1967-69; assistant in medicine, chief renal unit Massachusetts General Hospital, Boston, 1967-69; associate professor, then professor medicine University Pennsylvania Medical School, 1969-72, vice chairman department; 1971-74; associate director medical services Hospital University Pennsylvania, 1969-74; David Paige Smith professor internal medicine 1978-81, Sterling professor medicine; 1981-85; chairman department Yale University School Medicine, 1975-85; chief medicine Yale-New Haven Hospital, 1975-85, board of directors, 1978-85; president Institute Medicine, National Acad. Sciences, 1986—; board of directors Hospice, Incorporated, 1976-82. Member editorial board: New England Journal Medicine, 1978-81; Contributor articles to medical journals. Member adv. committee to the director National Institute of Health, 1980-85. Served with United States Public Health Service, 1962-64. Recipient Christian R. and Mary F. Lindback Foundation Distinguished Teaching award, 1971. Fellow American College of Physicians (board regents 1982-85); member Association Am. Medical Colls. (adminstrv. board council acad. socs.), John Morgan Society, Am. Federation Clinical Research (president 1976-77), Am. Society Nephrology, Am. Physiological Society, Institute Medicine, National Acad. Sciences, International Society Nephrology, Association Profs. Medicine, Association Am. Physicians, Interurban Clinical Club; Alpha Omega Alpha. Home: 4319 Westover Place Northwest Washington District of Columbia 20016 Office: National Acad Scis Institute of Medicine 2101 Constitution Avenue Washington District of Columbia 20418

THOMAS, EDWARD DONNALL, physician, educator; born Mart, Texas, March 15, 1920; son of Edward E. and Angie (Hill) T.; married Dorothy Martin, December 20, 1942; children: Edward Donnall, Jeffery A., Elaine. Bachelor of Arts, University Texas, 1941, Master of Arts, 1943; Doctor of Medicine, Harvard University, 1946. Diplomate: Am. Board Internal Medicine. National Research Council fellow medicine department biology Massachusetts Institute of Technology, 1950-51; instructor medicine Harvard Medical School, Boston; also hematologist Peter Bent Brigham Hospital, 1953-55; research associate Cancer Research Foundation, Children Medical Center, Boston, 1953-55; physician in chief Mary Imogene Bassett Hospital, also associate clinical professor medicine College Physicians and Surgeons, Columbia University, 1955-63; professor University Washington School Medicine, Seattle, 1963—. Member National Acad. Sciences, Am. Society Clinical Investigation, Association Am. Physicians, Am. Society Hematology, Am. Federation Clinical Research, International Society Hematology, Am. Association Cancer Research, Western Association Physicians, Am. Society Clinical Oncology, Transplantation Society. Research and numerous publs. on hematology, marrow transplantation, biochemistry and irradiation biology. Office: Fred Hutchingson Cancer Research Center

1124 Columbia St Seattle Washington 98104

THOMAS, GARETH, metallurgy educator; born Maesteg, United Kingdom, August 9, 1932; came to United States, 1960, naturalized, 1977; son of David Bassett and Edith May (Gregory) T.; married Elizabeth Virginia Cawdry, January 5, 1960; 1 son, Julian Guy David. Bachelor of Science, University Wales, 1952; Doctor of Philosophy, Cambridge University, 1955, Doctor of Science, 1969. I.C.I. fellow Cambridge University, 1956-59; assistant professor University California, Berkeley, 1960-63; associate professor University California, 1963-67, professor metallurgy; 1967—, associate dean grad. div.; 1968-69, assistant chancellor, acting vice chancellor for acad. affairs; 1969-72; sci. director National Center Electron Microscopy, 1982—; consultant to industry. Author: Transmission Electron Microscopy of Metals, 1962, Electron Micoscopy and Strength of Crystals, 1963, (with O. Johari) Stereographic Projection and Applications, 1969, Transmission Electron Microscopy of Materials, 1980; contributor articles to professional journals. Recipient Curtis McGraw Research award Am. Society Engineering Education, 1966; E.O. Lawrence award Department Energy, 1978; Guggenheim fellow, 1972. Fellow Am. Society Metals (Bradley Stoughton Young Teachers award 1965, Grossman Publ. award 1966), Am. Institute Mining, Metallurgical and Petroleum Engineers; member Electron Microscopy Society Am. (prize 1965, president 1976), Am. Physical Society, National Acad. Sciences, National Acad. Engineering, Brit. Institute Metals (Rosenheim medal 1977), International Federation Electron Microscopy Socs. (secretary general 1974-82), Brit. Iron and Steel Institute. Club: Marylebone Cricket (England). Patentee in field. Office: Lawrence Berkeley Lab National Center Electron Microscopy 1 Cyclotron Road Berkeley California 94720

THOMAS, LEO J., manufacturing company executive; born Grand Rapids, Michigan, October 30, 1936; son of Leo John and Christal (Dietrich) T.; married Joanne Juliani, December 27, 1958; children: Christopher, Gregory, Cynthia, Jeffrey. Student, College St. Thomas, 1954-56; Bachelor of Science, University Minnesota, 1958; Master of Science, University Illinois, 1960, Doctor of Philosophy, 1961. Research chemist Research Laboratories, Rochester, New York, 1961-67, head; 1967-70, assistant div. head color photography div.; 1970-72, tech. assistant to director; 1972-75, assistant director; 1975-77, vice president, director; 1977-78, senior vice president, director; 1978-84, 1984-85; general manager Life Sciences, Rochester, New York, 1984-85, senior vice president, general manager; 1985—; board of directors Rochester Telephone Corp., Norstar Bank, John Wiley and Sons Incorporated, New York City; vice-chairman Sterling Drug Incorporated, chairman, 1988—. Member National Acad. Engineering, Am. Institute Chemical Engineers, American Association for the Advancement of Science, National Research Council (board cooperative sci. and tech.), Rochester Chamber of Commerce. Office: 90 Park Avenue New York New York 10016 also: Sterling Drug Incorporated 90 Park Avenue New York New York 10016

THOMAS, LEWIS, physician, educator, former medical administrator; born Flushing, New York, November 25, 1913; son of Joseph S. and Grace Emma (Peck) T.; married Beryl Dawson, January 1, 1941; children: Abigail, Judith, Eliza. Bachelor of Science, Princeton University, 1933, Doctor of Science (honorary), 1976; Doctor of Medicine, Harvard University, 1937, Doctor of Science (honorary), 1986; Master of Arts, Yale University, 1969; Doctor of Science (honorary), University Rochester, 1974, University of Toledo, 1976, Columbia University, 1978, Memorial University Newfoundland, 1978, University North Carolina, 1979, Worcester Foundation, 1979, Williams College, 1982, Connecticut College, 1983, University Wales, 1983, University Arizona, 1985, Long Island University, 1987; Doctor of Laws (honorary), Johns Hopkins University, 1976, Trinity College, 1980; Doctor of Humane Letters (honorary), Duke University, 1976, Reed College, 1978; Doctor of Letters (honorary), Dickinson College, 1980, Ursinus College, 1981, SUNY-Stony Brook, 1983; Doctor of Music. (honorary), New England Conservatory Music, 1982; Doctor of Humane Letters (honorary), New York University School Medicine, 1983; Doctor of Letters (honorary), Drew University, 1983; Doctor of Philosophy, Weizmann Institute, 1984; Doctor of Science (honorary), Rockefeller University, 1989. Intern Boston City Hospital, 1937-39, Neurological Institute, New York City, 1939-41; Tilney Memorial fellow Thorndike Laboratory, Boston City Hospital, 1941-42; visiting investigator Rockefeller Institute, 1942-46; assistant professor pediatrics Medical School Johns Hopkins University, Baltimore, 1946-48; associate professor medicine Medical School Tulane University, New Orleans, 1948-50; professor medicine Medical School Tulane University, 1950; professor pediatrics and medicine, director pediatric research laboratories Heart Hospital, University Minnesota, Minneapolis, 1950-54; professor, chairman department pathology New York University School Medicine, 1954-58, professor, chairman department medicine; 1958-66, dean; 1966-69; professor, chairman department pathology Yale University, New Haven, 1969-72, dean, School Medicine; 1972-73; professor medicine, pathology Medical School Cornell University, New York City, 1973—, professor biology Sloan Kettering Institute div.; 1973—; adj. professor Rockefeller University, New York City, 1975—; president, chief executive officer Memorial Sloan-Kettering Cancer Center, New York City, 1973-80, chancellor; 1980-83; president emeritus Memorial Sloan-Kettering Cancer Center, New York City, 1984—; professor SUNY-Stony Brook Health Sciences Center, 1984—; scholar-in-residence Cornell University Medical College, 1988—; scholar-in-residence, Cornell University Medical College, 1988—; director 3d and 4th medical divs. Bellevue Hospital, 1958-66, president medical board, 1963-66; consultant Manhattan Veteran's Administration Hospital, 1954-69; consultant to Surgeon General Department Army, Surgeon General United States Public Health Service; member pathology study section National Institutes of Health, 1955-59, national adv. health council, 1960-64, national adv. child health and human devel. council, 1964-68; member commission on streptococcal disease Armed Forces Epidemiological Board, 1950-62; member President's Sci. Adv. Committee, 1967-70, Institute Medicine, 1971, National Acad. Sciences, 1972—, member council and governing board, 1979—; chairman overview cluster subcom. President's Biomed. Research Panel, 1975-76; member Tech. Assessment Adv. Council, 1980—; board of directors, trustee Squibb Corp. Member New York City Board Health, 1956-69; member board sci. consultant Sloan-Kettering Institute Cancer Research, 1966-72; member Sloan-Kettering Institute, 1973-83; board of directors Josiah Macy Junior Foundation, 1975-84; board sci. advisors Massachusetts General Hospital, 1970-73, Scripps Clinic and Research Foundation, 1969-78; board of directors, research councilth Research Institute of City New York, 1964-69; board overseers Harvard College, 1976-82; member sci. adv. committee Sidney Farber Cancer Institute, 1978—; member council Grad. School Business and Pub. Administration, Cornell University, 1978-82; member awards assembly General Motors Cancer Research Foundation, 1978-83; associate fellow Ezra Stiles College Yale University. Author: Lives of a Cell, 1974, Medusa and the Snail, 1979, The Youngest Science, 1983, Late Night Thoughts on Listening to Mahler's Ninth Symphony, 1983; member editorial board Daedalus, Cellular Immunology, Am. Journal Pathology. Trustee N.Y.C.-Rand Institute, 1967-71, The Rockefeller University, 1975—, Draper Lab., 1975-81, John Simon Guggenheim Memorial Foundation, 1975-85, Mount Sinai School Medicine, 1979-85, Educational Broadcasting Company, 1977-83, Menninger Foundation, 1980—; board of directors Lounsbery Foundation, 1982—; chairman board Monell Chem. Senses Center, 1982—; board advisors Kennedy Institute Ethics, Georgetown University, 1982—; trustee National Hospice, 1978—; member board overseers University Pennsylvania School Nursing, 1983—; adv. council Program in History of Sci. Princeton University, 1982—; board of directors Am. Friends Cambridge University, 1984—; member adv. committee Aaron Diamond Foundation, 1985—; director Commonwealth Fund Book Program, 1982—. Served to lieutenant commander Medical Corps United States Naval Reserve, 1941-46. Recipient Distinguished Achievement award Modern Medicine, 1975; National Book award for Arts and Letters, 1975; Honor award Am. Medical Writers Association, 1978; Medical Education award American Medical Association, 1979; Bard award in medicine and sci. Bard College, 1979; Am. Book award, 1981; St. Davids Society award, 1980; Recipient Woodrow Wilson award Princeton University, 1980, award Cosmos Club, Washington, 1982; Richard Hopper Day award Philadelphia Acad. Natural Sciences, 1985; Lewis Thomas award for communications American College of Physicians, 1986; Milton Helpern Memorial award, 1986; Encyclopaedia Brit. award, 1986; Alfred P. Sloan Junior Memorial award, 1987; William B. Coley award Cancer Research Institute, 1987, Gold-Headed Cane award Am. Association Pathologists, 1988. Fellow Am. Acad. Arts and Sciences, Am. Rheumatism Association; member National Acad. Sciences, Am. Acad. and Institute Arts and Letters, Am. Philosophical Association, Am. Society Experimental Pathology, Practitioners Society, Am. Acad. Microbiology, Peripatetic Clinical Society, Am. Society Clinical Investigation, Am. Association Immunologists, Society Am. Bacteriologists, Association Am. Physicians (Kober medal 1983), Am. Pediatric Society, New York Acad. Sciences (pres.-elect 1988), Harvey Society (councillor), Scientists' Institute for Pub. Info (chairman board 1982— award for excellence in sci. communication), American Association of University Profs., Society Experimental Biology and Medicine, Am. Society Clinical Oncology, Friends of History of Sci. Society (council 1982—), Council on Foreign Relations, Interurban Clinical Club, Phi Beta Kappa, Alpha Omega Alpha. Club: Century Association. Office: Cornell University Med College 1300 York Avenue New York New York 10021

THOMPSON, JAMES BURLEIGH, JR., geologist, educator; born Calais, Maine, November 20, 1921; son of James Burleigh and Edith (Peabody) T.; married Eleanora Mairs, August 3, 1957; 1 son, Michael A. Bachelor of Arts, Dartmouth, 1942, Doctor of Science (honorary), 1975; Doctor of Philosophy, Massachusetts Institute Tech., 1950. Instructor geology Dartmouth, 1942; research assistant Massachusetts Institute Tech., 1946-47, instructor; 1947-49; instructor petrology Harvard, 1949-50, assistant professor; 1950-55, associate professor mineralogy; 1955-60, professor; 1960-77, Sturgis Hooper professor geology; 1977—; guest professor Swiss Federal Institute Tech., 1977-78. Served to 1st lieutenant United States Army Air Force, 1942-46. Guggenheim fellow, 1963; Sherman Fairchild distinguished

scholar California Institute Tech., 1976. Fellow Mineralogical Society Am. (president 1967-68, recipient Roebling medal 1978), Geological Society Am. (A.L. Day medal 1964), Am. Acad. Arts and Sciences; member American Association for the Advancement of Science, Am. Geophysical Union, National Acad. Sciences, Geochem. Society (president 1968-69, Goldschmidt medal 1985), Sigma Xi. Office: Harvard U Cambridge Massachusetts 02138

THOMPSON, MILTON ORVILLE, aeronautical engineer; born Crookston, Minnesota, May 4, 1926; son of Peter and Alma Teresa (Evenson) T.; married Therese Mary Beytebiere, June 25, 1949; children—Eric P., Milton Orville, Brett, Peter K., Kye C. Bachelor of Science in Engineering, University Washington, 1953; postgraduate, University Southern California, 1956-59. Associate engineer Boeing Company, Seattle, 1953-55; research pilot National Aeronautics and Space Administration (formerly National Advisory Committee for Aeronautics), Edwards, California, 1956-66; assistant director research National Aeronautics and Space Administration (formerly National Advisory Committee for Aeronautics), 1967-72, director research projects; 1972-74, chief engineer; 1974-78; associate director National Aeronautics and Space Administration Dryden Flight Research Center, 1978—. Contributor articles to tech. journals X-15 rocket air plane pilot. Served with United States Naval Reserve, 1944-49. Recipient Octave Chanute award Am. Institute Aeros. and Astronautics, 1967; Distinguished Service medal National Aeronautics and Space

Administration, 1978; Exceptional Service medal, 1981. Fellow Explorers Club; member Society Experimental Test Pilots (Ivan C. Kinchloe award 1966). First to fly lifting body entry vehicle. Home: 1640 W Avenue L-12 Lancaster California 93534 Office: NASA-Dryden Flight Research Center Post Office Box 273 Edwards Air Force Base California 93523

THOMPSON, RAYMOND HARRIS, educator, anthropologist; born Portland, Me., May 10, 1924; son of Raymond and Eloise (MacIntyre) T.; married Molly Kendall, September 9, 1948; children: Margaret Kelsey, Thompson Luchetta, Mary Frances. Bachelor of Science, Tufts University, 1947; Master of Arts, Harvard University, 1950, Doctor of Philosophy, 1955. Fellow div. historical research Carnegie Institution, Washington, 1950-52; assistant professor anthropology, curator Mus. Anthropology, University Kentucky, 1952-56; faculty University Arizona, 1956—, professor anthropology; 1964—, Riecker Distinguished professor; 1980—, head department; 1964-80; director Arizona State Mus., from 1964; member adv. panel program in anthropology National Science Foundation, 1963-64, member mus. collections program; member National Science Foundation grad. fellowship panel National Acad. Scis.-NRC, 1964-66; member research in nursing in patient care rev. committee United States Public Health Service, 1967-69; committee on social sci. commission education in agriculture and natural resources National Acad. Sciences, 1968-69; member anthropology committee examiners Grad. Record Exam., 1967-70, chairman, 1969-70; member committee recovery archaeol. remains, 1972-77, chairman, 1973-77; collaborator National Park Service, 1972-76; member Arizona Historical Adv. Commission, 1966—, chairman, 1971-74, chairman historical sites rev. committee, 1971-83; chairman Arizona Humanities Council, 1973-77, member, 1979—; member research review panel for archaeology National Endowment for Humanities, 1976-77, member rev. panel for museums, 1978; consultant task force on archaeology Adv. Council on Historic Preservation, 1978. Author: Modern Yucatecan Maya Pottery Making, 1958; editor: Migrations in New World Culture History, 1958; editorial board: Science, 1972-77. Trustee Mus. Northern Arizona, 1969—; board of directors Tucson Mus. Art, 1974-77. Served with United States Naval Reserve, 1944-45, PTO. Fellow American Association for the Advancement of Science (chairman section H 1977-78), Tree-Ring Society, Am. Anthropological Association (Distinguished Service award 1980); member Society Am. Archaeology (editor 1958-62, member executive committee 1963-64, president 1976-77); member Am. Society Conservation Archaeology (Conservation award 1980), Seminario de Cultura Maya, Am. Association Museums, International Council Museums (associate), Council Museum Anthropology (director 1978-79, president 1980-83), Association Sci. Mus. Directors (sec.-treas. 1978—), Arizona Acad. Sci., Arizona Archaeol. and Historical Society, Arizona Mus. Association (president 1983, 84), Phi Beta Kappa, Sigma Xi. Office: University Ariz Department Anthropology Tucson Arizona 85721

THOMPSON, RICHARD FREDERICK, psychologist, educator; born Portland, Oregon, 1930; son of Frederick Albert and Margaret St. Clair (Marr) T.; married Judith K. Pedersen, May 22, 1960; children: Kathryn M., Elizabeth K., Virginia St. C. Bachelor of Arts, Reed College, 1952; Master of Science, University Wisconsin, 1953, Doctor of Philosophy, 1956. Assistant professor medical psychology Medical School University Oregon, Portland, 1959-63, associate professor; 1963-65, professor; 1965-67; professor psychobiology University California, Irvine, 1967-73, 75-80; professor psychology Harvard University, Cambridge, Massachusetts, 1973-74; Lashley chair professor Harvard University, Cambridge, 1973; professor psychology, Bing professor human biology Stanford University, Palo Alto, California, 1980-87; Keok professor psychology and human biology University Southern California, Los Angeles, 1987—. Author: Foundations of Physiological Psychology, 1967, (with others) Psychology, 1971, Introduction to Physiological Psychology, 1975; Psychology editor (with others), W.H. Freeman & Company publications, chief editor, Behavioral Neurosci., 1983—; editor: Journal Comparative and Physiological Psychology, 1981-83, Behavioral Scis., 1983—; regional editor: (with others) Physiology and Behavior; contributor (with others) articles to professional journals.
Fellow American Association for the Advancement of Science, Am. Psychological Association (Distinguished Sci. Contbn. award 1974, governing council 1974—), Society Neunosci. (councilor 1972-76); member International Brain Research Organization, Psychonomic Society (governor 1972-77, chairman 1976),

National Acad. Sciences, Society Experimental Psychology. Office: University of Southern California Department of Psychology University Park Los Angeles California 94305

THOMPSON, ROBERT LEE, agriculturist, economist, educator; born Canton, New York, April 25, 1945; son of Robert M. and Esther Louise (Weatherup) T.; married Karen Hansen, August 9, 1968; children—Kristina Marie, Eric Robert. Bachelor of Science, Cornell University, Ithaca, New York, 1967; Master of Science, Purdue University, West Lafayette, Ind., 1969, Doctor of Philosophy, 1974. Volunteer agriculturalist International Volunteer Service, Pakse and Vientiane, Laos, 1968-70; visiting professor Federal University Vicosa, Brazil, 1972-73; professor Purdue University, West Lafayette, Ind., 1974—; research scholar International Institute for Applied Systems Analysis, Laxenburg, Austria, 1983; senior staff economist Council Economic Advisers, Washington, 1983-85; assistant secretary economics United States Department Agriculture, Washington, 1985-87; dean agriculture Purdue University, West Lafayette, Ind., 1987—; director National Cooperative Bank, Washington, NCB Capital Corp., Commodity Credit Corp., Washington, USDA Grad. School, Washington; consultant Southern Regional Council, Inter-Am. Devel. Bank, USAID, Agriculture Can., Ford Foundation, Brazilian Agriculture Ministry, Food and Agriculture Organization (of the United Nations), International Food Policy Research Institute, International Maize and Wheat Improvement Center. Contributor numerous articles to professional publications Author monographs, book chapters. Recipient Agrl. Research award Purdue University, 1983. Member Am. Agricultural Economics Association (member editorial council 1983-85, recipient Quality of Communication award 1979), Am. Economics Association, International Association Agricultural Economists, Sigma Xi, Gamma Sigma Delta. Republican. Avocation: foreign language study. Home: 9932 Coffer Woods Road Burke Virginia 22015 Office: USDA 22E Administration Building Room 114 Washington District of Columbia 20250 also: Purdue U School Agriculture West Lafayette Indiana 47907

THORNE, KIP STEPHEN, physicist, educator; born Logan, Utah, June 1, 1940; son of David Wynne and Alison (Comish) T.; married Linda Jeanne Peterson, September 12, 1960 (divorced 1977); children: Kares Anne, Bret Carter; married Carolee Joyce Winstein, July 7, 1984. Bachelor of Science in Physics, California Institute Tech., 1962; Master of Arts in Physics (Woodrow Wilson fellow, Danforth Foundation fellow), Princeton University, 1963, Doctor of Philosophy in Physics (Danforth Foundation fellow, NSF fellow), 1965, postgraduate (NSF postdoctoral fellow), 1965-66; Doctor of Science (honorary), Illinois College, 1979; Dr.h.c., Moscow University, 1981. Research fellow California Institute Tech., 1966-67, associate professor theoretical physics; 1967-70, professor; 1970—, William R. Kenan, Junior professor; 1981—; Fulbright lecturer, France, 1966; visiting associate professor University Chicago, 1968; visiting professor Moscow University, 1969, 75, 78, 82, 83, 86; visiting senior research associate Cornell University, 1977; adj. professor University Utah, 1971—; A.D. White prof.-at-large Cornell University, 1986—; member International Committee on General Relativity and Gravitation, 1971-80, Committee on U.S.-USSR Cooperative in Physics, 1978-79, Space Sci. Board, National Aeronautics and Space Administration, 1980-83. Co-author: Gravitation Theory and Gravitational Collapse, 1965, Gravitation, 1973, Black Holes: The Membrane Paradigm, 1986. Alfred P. Sloan Foundation Research fellow, 1966-68; John Simon Guggenheim fellow, 1967; recipient Sci. Writing award in physics and astronomy Am. Institute Physics-U.S. Steel Foundation, 1969. Member National Acad. Sciences, Am. Acad. Arts and Sciences, Am. Astronomical Society, Am. Physical Society, International Astronomical Union, American Association for the Advancement of Science, Sigma Xi, Tau Beta Pi. Research in theoretical physics and astrophysics. Office: 130-33 California Institute Tech Pasadena California 91125

THORNTON, WILLIAM E., astronaut; born Faison, North Carolina, April 29, 1929; married Elizabeth Jennifer Fowler; 2 sons. Bachelor of Science, University North Carolina, 1952, Doctor of Medicine, 1963. Director electronics div. Del Mar Engineering Laboratories, Los Angeles, 1956-62; instructor University North Carolina Medical School, 1963-64; intern Wilford Hall, United States Air Force Hospital, Lackland Air Force Base, San Antonio, 1964-65; with aerospace medical div. Brooks Air Force Base, San Antonio, 1965-67; scientist-astronaut National Aeronautics and Space Administration, 1967—;

instructor department medicine University Texas Medical Branch, from 1977; member Shuttle flight, 1983, member Spacelab flight, 1985. Patentee in field. Decorated Legion of Merit; recipient Exceptional Service, Exceptional Sci. Achievement awards National Aeronautics and Space Administration. Member crew, investigator space medicine problems Challenger space shuttle, 1983, 85. Office: NASA Astronaut DFC Johnson Spacecraft Center Houston Texas 77058

TIEN, CHANG LIN, mechanical engineering educator; born Wuhan, China, July 24, 1935; came to United States, 1956, naturalized, 1969; son of Yun Chien and Yun Di (Lee) T.; married Di Hwa Liu, July 25, 1959; children: Norman Chihnan, Phyllis Chihping, Christine Chihyih. Bachelor of Science, National Taiwan University, 1955; Master of Mechanical Engineering, University Louisville, 1957; Master of Arts, Doctor of Philosophy, Princeton University, 1959. Acting assistant professor department mechanical engineering University Calif.—Berkeley, Berkeley, 1959-60; assistant professor University Calif.—Berkeley, 1960-64, associate professor; 1964-68, professor; 1968-87, A. Martin Berlin professor; 1987—, department chairman; 1974-81, also vice chancellor for research; 1983-85; tech. consultant Lockheed Missiles & Space Company, General Electric Company. Contributor articles to profl journals. Guggenheim fellow, 1965. Fellow American Society of Mechanical Engineers (Max Jakob Heml. award ASME—Am. Institute Chemical Engineers 1981, Heat Transfer Memorial award 1974, Larson Memorial award 1975),

American Institute of Aeronautics and Astronautics (Thermophysics award 1977); member National Acad. Engineering. Home: 1451 Olympus Avenue Berkeley California 94708 Office: Department Mech Engring U California Berkeley California 94720

TIGER, LIONEL, social scientist, anthropology consultant; born Montreal, Quebec, Canada, February 5, 1937; son of Martin and Lillian (Schneider) T.; married Virginia Conner, August 19, 1964; 1 child, Sebastian Benjamin. Bachelor of Arts, McGill University, 1957, Master of Arts, 1959; Doctor of Philosophy, University London, 1963. Instructor anthropology University Ghana, Accra, 1960; assistant professor department anthropology and sociology University British Columbia, Vancouver, 1963-68; associate professor anthropology Rutgers University, New Brunswick, New Jersey, 1969-74, professor anthropology; 1974—; consultant, research director Harry F. Guggenheim Foundation, New York City, 1972-84; chairman board social scientists United States News and World Report, 1986—. Author: Men in Groups, 1969, (with Robin Fox) The Imperial Animal, 1971, (with Joseph Shepher) Women in the Kibbutz, 1975, Optimism: The Biology of Hope, 1979, China's Food, 1985, The Manufacture of Evil: Ethics, Evolution, and the Industrial System, 1987; editor: Female Hierarchies, 1978; member editorial board: Social Science Information, Ethology and Sociobiology journal. Recipient West Indies Susman award for excellence in teaching, 1985, McNaughton prize for creative writing; ASDA Foundation rsch. fellow, 1985; fellow Can. Council Research, Ford Foundation Foreign

Area Tng. fellow, Can. Council-Killam fellow for interdisciplinary research, Rockefeller fellow Aspen Institute, 1979, H.F. Guggenheim Foundation, 1988. Fellow Royal Anthropological Institute (Great Britain); member Am. Anthropological Association, Can. Anthropological Association, Am. Sociological Association, Society for Study Evolution, Poets, Playwrights, Essayists and Novelists (executive board, treasurer 1988). Home: 248 W 23d St 4th Floor New York New York 10011 also: Rural Delivery 2 Millbrook New York 12545 Office: Rutgers U George St Douglass Campus New Brunswick New Jersey 08903

TIMMERHAUS, KLAUS DIETER, chemical engineering educator; born Minneapolis, September 10, 1924; son of Paul P. and Elsa L. (Bever) T.; married Jean L. Mevis, August 3, 1952; 1 daughter, Carol Jane. Bachelor of Science in Chemical Engineering, University Illinois, 1948, Master of Science, 1949, Doctor of Philosophy, 1951. Registered professional engineer, Colorado. Process design engineer California Research Corp., Richmond, 1952-53; extension lecturer University California, Berkeley, 1952; member faculty University Colorado, 1953—, professor chemical engineering; 1961—, associate dean engineering; 1963-86, director engineering research center college engineering; 1963-86, chairman aerospace department; 1979-80, chairman chemical engineering department; 1986—; chemical engineer cryogenics laboratory National Bureau Standards, Boulder, summers 1955,57,59,61; lecturer University California at Los Angeles, 1961-62; section head engineering div. National Science Foundation, 1972-73; consultant in field. Board directors Colorado Engineering Experiment Station, Incorporated, Engineering Measurements Company, both Boulder. Editor: Advances in Cryogenic Engineering, volumes 1-25, 1954-80; co-editor: International Cryogenic Monograph Series, 1965—. Served with United States Naval Reserve, 1944-46. Recipient Distinguished Service award Department Commerce, 1957; Samuel C. Collins award outstanding contributions to cryogenic tech., 1967; George Westinghouse award, 1968; Alpha Chi Sigma award for chemical engineering rsch., 1968; Meritorious Service award Cryogenic Engineering Conference, 1967; R.L. Stearns Professional Achievement award University Colorado, 1981; Distinguished Pub. Service award National Science Foundation, 1984. Fellow American Association for the Advancement of Science; member National Acad. Engineering, Am. Astronomical Society, Am. Institute Chemical Engineers (vice president 1975, president 1976, Founders award 1978, Eminent Chemical Engineer award 1983, W. K. Lewis award 1987), Am. Society for Engineering Education (board directors 1986-88, 3M Chem Engineering division award 1980), International Institute Refrigeration (vice president 1979-87, president 1987—, United States national commission 1983—, president 1983-86, W.T. Pentzer award 1989), Austrian Acad. Sci., Cryogenic Engineering Conference (chairman 1956-67, board directors 1956—), Sigma Xi (vice president 1986-87, president 1987-88, board directors 1981-89), Sigma Tau, Tau Beta Pi, Phi Lambda Upsilon. Home: 905 Brooklawn Dr Boulder Colorado 80303

TING, SAMUEL CHAO CHUNG, physicist, educator; born Ann Arbor, Michigan, January 27, 1936; son of Kuan H. and Jeanne (Wong) T.; married Kay Louise Kuhne, November 23, 1960; children: Jeanne Min, Amy Min; married Susan Carol Marks, April 28, 1985; 1 child, Christopher M. Bachelor of Science in Engineering, University Michigan, 1959, Master of Science, 1960, Doctor of Philosophy, 1962, Doctor of Science (honorary), 1978; Doctor of Science (honorary), Chinese University Hong Kong, 1987. Ford Foundation fellow European Organization of Nuclear Research (European Organization Nuclear Research), Geneva, 1963; instructor physics Columbia University, 1964, assistant professor; 1965-67; group leader Deutsches Elektronen-Synchrotron, Hamburg, Federal Republic of Germany, 1966; associate professor physics M.I.T., Cambridge, 1967-68; professor M.I.T., 1969—, Thomas Dudley Cabot Institute professor; 1977—; program consultant Div. Particles and Fields, Am. Physical Society, 1970, Beijing Normal College, 1987, Chinese University Hong Kong, 1987, Jiatong University, Shanghai, Peoples Republic China, 1987; hon. professor Beijing Normal College, China, 1987, Jiatong University, Shanghai, 1987. Associate editor: Nuclear Physics B, 1970; contributor articles in field to professional journals; editorial board: Nuclear Instruments and Methods; advisor Journal Modern Physics A. Recipient Nobel prize in Physics, 1976, De Gasperi prize in Sci., Italian Republic, 1988; Am. Acad. Sci. and Arts fellow, 1975; Ernest Orlando Lawrence award U.S. Government, 1976; Eringen medal Society Engineering Sci., 1977. Member National Acad. Sci., Pakistani Acad. Sci. (foreign member), Academia Sinica (foreign member). Office: Massachusetts Institute of Technology Department Physics 51 Vassar St Cambridge Massachusetts 02139

TODARO, GEORGE JOSEPH, pathologist; born New York City, July 1, 1937; son of George J. and Antoinette (Piccinni) T.; married Jane Lehv, August 12, 1962; children: Wendy C., Thomas M., Anthony A. Bachelor of Science, Swarthmore College, 1958; Doctor of Medicine, New York University, 1963. Intern New York University School Medicine, New York City, 1963-64, fellow in pathology; 1964-65, assistant professor pathology; 1965-67; staff associate Viral Carcinogenesis branch National Cancer Institute, Bethesda, Maryland, 1967-70, head molecular biology section; 1969-70; chief Viral Carcinogenesis branch National Cancer Institute (Laboratory Viral Carcinogenesis), 1970-83; sci. director, president Oncogen, Seattle, 1987—; faculty member Genetics Program, George Washington University; affiliate professor pathology University Washington, Seattle, 1983—. Editor: Cancer Research, 1973-86, Archives of Virology, 1976—, Journal Biol. Chemistry, 1979—; contributor articles to professional journals. Served as medical officer United States Public Health Service, 1967-69. Recipient Borden Undergrad. Research award, 1963, USPHS Career Devel. award, 1967, Department of Health, Education and Welfare Superior Service award, 1971, Gustav Stern award for virology, 1972, Parke-Davis award in exptl. pathology, 1975; Walter Hubert lecturer Brit. Cancer Society, 1977. Member National Acad. Sciences, Am. Society Microbiology, Am. Association Cancer Research, Society Experimental Biology and Medicine, Am. Society Biological Chemists, Am. Society Clinical Investigation. Home: 1940 15th Avenue E Seattle Washington 98112 Office: Oncogen 3005 1st Avenue Seattle Washington 98121

TODD, ALEXANDER ROBERTUS (BARON TODD OF TRUMP-INGTON), educator; born Glasgow, Scotland, October 2, 1907; son of Alexander and Jane (Lowrie) T.; married Alison Sarah Dale, January 30, 1937 (deceased 1987); children: Alexander Henry, Helen Todd Brown, Hilary Alison. Bachelor of Science (Carnegie Research scholar 1928-29), University Glasgow, 1928, Doctor of Science, 1938; Dr.phil.national, University Frankfurt am Main, 1931; Doctor of Philosophy, Oxford University, England, 1933; Master of Arts, University Cambridge, England, 1944; Doctor of Laws (honorary), univs. of Glasgow, Melbourne, Edinburg, California, Manchester, Hokkaido; Dr.rer.national (honorary), University Kiel; Doctor of Literature (honorary), University Sydney; Doctor of Science (honorary), univs. of London, Exeter, Warwick, Sheffield, Liverpool, Oxford, Leicester, Durham, England, University of Wales, University Madrid, Spain, University Aligarh, India, University Strasbourg, France, Harvard University, Yale University,University Michigan, University Paris, University Adelaide, Australia, University Strathclyde, Scotland, Australian National University, University Cambridge, University Philippines, Tufts University, Chinese University Hong Kong, Hong Kong University. Member staff Lister Institute Preventive Medicine, London, 1936-38; reader biochemistry University London, 1937-38; professor, director chemical laboratories University Manchester, England, 1938-44; professor organic chemistry University Cambridge, England, 1944-71, fellow Christ's College; 1944—, master; 1963-78; chancellor University Strathclyde, 1963—; director Fisons Limited, London, 1963-78, National Research Devel. Corp., London, 1968-76; visiting professor California Institute Tech., 1938, University Chicago, 1948, University Sydney, 1950, Massachusetts Institute of Technology, Cambridge, 1954, University California, 1970, Texas Christian University, 1980; chairman adv. Council Sci. Policy, 1952-64, Royal Commission Medical Education, 1965-68. Contributor articles to professional journals. Chairman Nuffield Foundation, London, 1936-80; chairman governors United Cambridge Hosps., 1969-74; chairman trustees Croucher Foundation, Hong Kong, 1980-87, 88—. Created knight, 1954, baron (life peer), 1962; Order of Merit (United Kingdom); Order Rising Sun (Japan); recipient Nobel prize for chemistry, 1957; Pour le Merite (W. Germany), 1966; Lomonosov medal U.S.S.R. Acad. Sci., 1978; medals various chemical socs., sci. orgns., including Royal Copley medals Royal Society, 1949; named master Salter's Company, 1961. Fellow Royal Society (president 1975-80), Australian Chemical Institute (hon.), Manchester College Tech. (hon.), Royal Society Edinburgh (hon.), Royal College Physicians London (hon.), Royal College Physicians, Sure, Glasgow; member French, German, Spanish,

Belgian, Swiss, Japanese chemical socs. (all hon.), Australian, Austrian, Ghana, Polish acads. sci., Acad. Natural Philosophy Halle (Germany), Am. Philosophical Society, New York Acad. Sci., National Acad. Sciences (United States of America), American Association for the Advancement of Science (all foreign member), Chemical Society (president 1960-62), International Union Pure and Applied Chemistry (president 1963-65), Society Chemical Industry. Office: Christ's College, Cambridge CB2 3BU, England

TOMASI, THOMAS B., cell biologist, adminstrator; born May 24, 1927; son of Thomas B. and Ivis (Ratazzi) T.; children—Barbara, Theodore, Anne. Bachelor of Arts, Dartmouth College, Hanover, New Hampshire, 1950; Doctor of Medicine, University Vermont, Burlington, 1954; Doctor of Philosophy, Rockefeller University, 1965. Intern, resident, chief resident Columbia Presbyn. Hospital, New York City, 1954-58, instructor medicine; 1958-60; professor, chairman div. experimental medicine University Vermont, Burlington, 1960-65; professor medicine, director immunology State University of New York, Buffalo, 1965-73; professor, chairman immunology department Mayo Medical School, Rochester, Minnesota, 1973-81; director Cancer Center, Distinguished University professor, chairman department cell biology University North Mexico, Albuquerque, 1981-86; director Roswell Park Memorial Institute, Buffalo, 1986—, chairman molecular medicine and immunology department. Author: The Immune System of Secretions, 1976; contributor over 200 articles to professional journals. Served with United States Navy, 1945-

46. Member Am. Society Cell Biology, Am. Association Immunologists, Am. Association Cancer Research, Am. Society Clinical Investigation, Am. Federation Clinical Research, Association Am. Physicians. Roman Catholic. Avocations: skiing, tennis, hunting, fishing, gardening. Home: 7980 E Quaker Road Orchard Park New York 14127 Office: Roswell Park Memorial Institute 666 Elm St Buffalo New York 14263

TOMBAUGH, CLYDE WILLIAM, educator, astronomer; born Streator, Illinois, February 4, 1906; son of Muron D. and Adella Pearl (Chritton) T.; married Patricia Irene Edson, June 7, 1934; children: Annette Roberta, Alden Clyde. Bachelor of Arts, University Kansas, 1936, Master of Arts, 1939; Doctor of Science (honorary), Arizona State University, 1960. Assistant Lowell Observatory, Flagstaff, Arizona, 1929, assistant astronomer; 1938; instructor sci. Arizona State College, Flagstaff, 1943-45; visiting assistant professor astronomy University of California at Los Angeles, 1945-46; astronomer Aberdeen Ballistics Laboratories Annex/White Sands Missile Range, Las Cruces, New Mexico, 1946—, chief optical measurement section; 1948, chief research and evaluation branch planning department Flight Determination div.; 1948-53, chief investigator search for natural satellites project; 1953-58, planetary astrophysical researcher; 1958—; research associate professor astronomy New Mexico State University, 1955-59, professor; 1965-73, professor emeritus; 1973—, with planetary astrophysics research program; 1959—; discoverer planet Pluto, 1930, 1 globular star cluster, 1932, 6 galactic star clusters, variable stars, asteroids, clusters of nubulae; extensive search for distant planets and natural earth's satellites, studies in apparent distribution extragalactic nebulae, geological studies Mars' and Moon's surface features, production telescope mirrors; member expedition extension satellite research project, Quito, Ecuador, 1956-58. Author: Out of the Darkness: the Planet Pluto, 1980; contributor articles to professional journals. Edward Emory Slosson scholar in sci. University Kansas, 1932-36; recipient Jackson-Guilt medal and gift Royal Astronomical Society England, 1931, Fairbanks award Society Photog. Instrument Engrs., 1968, Bruce Blair award, 1965, Distinguished Service citation University Kansas, 1966. Fellow Society for Research on Meteorites, American Institute of Aeronautics and Astronautics; member Am. Astronomical Society, International Astronomical Union, Astronomical Society Pacific, Sigma Xi. Member Unitarian Church. Avocations: grinding telescope mirrors, designing small telescopes. Home: Post Office Box 306 Mesilla Park New Mexico 88047 Office: New Mexico State U Department Astronomy Post Office Box 4500 Las Cruces New Mexico 88003

TONEGAWA, SUSUMU, biology educator; born Nagoya, Japan, September 5, 1939; came to United States, 1963; son of Tsutomu and Miyoko (Masuko) T.; married Mayumi Yoshinari, September 28, 1985; 1 child, Hidde Tonegawa. Bachelor of Science, Kyoto University, Japan, 1963; Doctor of Philosophy, University Calif.-San Diego, 1968. Research assistant University Calif.-San Diego, 1963-64, teaching assistant; 1964-68; member Basel Institute Immunology, Switzerland, 1971-81; professor biology Massachusetts Institute of Technology, Cambridge, 1981—. Editorial board Journal Molecular and Cellular Immunology. Decorated Order of Culture, Emperor of Japan; recipient Cloetta prize, 1978, Avery Landsteiner prize Gesselschaft für Immunologie, 1981, Louisa Gross Horwitz prize Columbia University, 1982, award Gardiner Foundation International, Toronto, Can., 1983, Robert Koch Foundation prize, Bonn. Rep. of West Germany, 1986, co-recipient Albert Lasker Medical Research award, 1987, Nobel prize in Physiology or Medicine, 1987; named Person with Cultural Merit Japanese Government, 1983. Member National Academy of Sciences (foreign associate), Am. Association Immunologists (hon.), Scandinavian Society Immunology (hon.). Office: Massachusetts Institute of Technology 77 Massachusetts Avenue Cambridge Massachusetts 02139

TOP, FRANKLIN HENRY, JR., physician, researcher; born Detroit, March 1, 1936; son of Franklin Henry Sr. and Mary (Madden) T.; married Lois Elizabeth Fritzell, September 23, 1961; children: Franklin H. III, Brian N., Andrew M. Bachelor of Science, Yale University, 1957, Doctor of Medicine cum laude, 1961. Diplomate Am. Board Pediatrics. Intern, resident, infectious diseases fellow University Minnesota Hospitals, Minneapolis, 1961-66; commissioned officer United States Army, advanced through grades to colonel; medical officer, department virus diseases Walter Reed Army Institute Research, Washington, 1966-70, chief department virus diseases; 1973-76, director div. communicative diseases and immunology; 1976-79, deputy director; 1979-81, director and commandant; 1983-87; chief department virology Seato Medical Research Laboratory, Bangkok, 1970-73; commander United States of America Medical Research Institute of Chemical Defense, Aberdeen Proving Ground, Maryland, 1981-83; retired United States Army, 1987; senior vice president Praxis Biologics Incorporated, Rochester, New York, 1987—. Contributor over 40 articles to medical journals. Decorated Legion of Merit with 2 Oak Leaf Clusters. Fellow Am. Acad. Pediatrics, Infectious Diseases of Am.; member American Medical Association, Am. Association Immunologists, Alpha Omega Alpha. Avocation: ornithology. Office: Praxis Biologics Incorporated 30 Corporate Woods Suite 300 Rochester New York 14623

TOWNES, CHARLES HARD, physics educator; born Greenville, South Carolina, July 28, 1915; son of Henry Keith and Ellen Sumter (Hard) T.; married Frances H. Brown, May 4, 1941; children: Linda Lewis, Ellen Screven, Carla Keith, Holly Robinson. Bachelor of Arts, Bachelor of Science, Furman University, 1935; Master of Arts, Duke University, 1937; Doctor of Philosophy, California Institute Tech., 1939. Member tech. staff Bell Telephone Laboratory, 1939-47; associate professor physics Columbia University, 1948-50, professor physics; 1950-61; executive director Columbia Radiation Laboratory, 1950-52, chairman physics department; 1952-55; provost and professor physics Massachusetts Institute of Technology, 1961-66, Institute professor; 1966-67; vice president, director research Institute Defense Analyses, Washington, 1959-61; professor physics University California at Berkeley, 1967-86, professor physics emeritus; 1986—; Guggenheim fellow, 1955-56; Fulbright lecturer University Paris, 1955-56, University Tokyo, 1956; lecturer, 1955, 60; director Enrico Fermi International School Physics, 1963; Richtmeyer lecturer Am. Physical Society, 1959; Scott lecturer University Cambridge, 1963; Centennial lecturer University Toronto, 1967; Lincoln lecturer, 1972-73, Halley lecturer, 1976; director General Motors Corp.; member President's Sci. Adv. Committee, 1966-69, vice chairman, 1967-69; chairman sci. and tech. adv. committee for manned space flight National Aeronautics and Space Administration, 1964-69; member President's Committee on Sci. and Tech., 1976. Author: (with A.L. Schawlow) Microwave Spectroscopy, 1955; author, co-editor: Quantum Electronics, 1960, Quantum Electronics and Coherent Light, 1964; editorial board: (with A.L. Schawlow) Rev. Science Instrument, 1950-52, Physical Rev, 1951-53; board: (with A.L. Schawlow) Physical, Rev, 1951-53, Journal Molecular Spectroscopy, 1957-60, Procs. National Acad. Scis, 1978—; contributor articles to sci. publications. Trustee California Institute Tech., Carnegie Instn. of Washington, Pacific School Religion; member corp. Woods Hole Oceanographic Instn. Recipient numerous hon. degrees and awards, including; Nobel prize for physics, 1964; Stuart Ballantine medal Franklin Institute, 1959, 62; Thomas Young medal and prize Institute Physics and Physical Society, England, 1963; Distinguished Public Service medal National Aeronautics and Space Administration, 1969; Wilhelm Exner award Austria, 1970; Niels Bohr International Gold medal, 1979; National Sci. medal, 1983, Berkeley citation University California, 1986; named to National Inventors Hall of Fame, 1976, Engineering and Sci. Hall of Fame, 1983. Fellow Am. Physical Society (council 1959-62, 65-71, president 1967, Plyler prize 1977), Optical Society Am. (hon., Mees medal 1968), Institute of Electrical and Electronics Engineers (medal of honor 1967), California Acad. Sciences; member Am. Philosophical Society, Am. Astronomical Society, Am. Acad. Arts and Sciences, National Acad. Sciences (council 1969-72, 78-81, chairman space sci. board 1970-73, Comstock award 1959), Société Française de Physique (council 1956-58), Royal Society (foreign), Pontifical Acad. Sciences, Max-Planck Institute for Physics and Astrophysics (foreign member). Patentee masers and lasers; research nuclear and molecular structure, quantum electronics, interstellar molecules, radio and infrared astrophysics. Office: University California at Berkeley Department of Physics Berkeley California 94720

TOWNSEND, JOHN WILLIAM, JR., physicist, aerospace company executive; born Washington, March 19, 1924; son of John William and Elenore (Eby) T.; married Mary Irene Lewis, February 7, 1948; children: Bruce Alan, Nancy Dewitt, John William III, Megan Lewis. Bachelor of Arts, Williams College, 1947, Master of Arts, 1949, Doctor of Science, 1961. With Naval Research Laboratory, 1949-55, branch head; 1955-58; with National Aeronautics and Space Administration, 1958-68, deputy director Goddard Space Flight Center; 1965-68; deputy administra-

tion Environmental Sciences Services Administration, 1968-70; associate administrator National Oceanic and Atmospheric Administration, 1970-77; president Fairchild Space and Electronics Company, 1977-82; vice president Fairchild Industries, 1979-85; president Fairchild Space Company, 1983-85; senior vice president Fairchild Industries, 1985-87, executive vice president; 1987; director National Aeronautics and Space Administration Goddard Space Flight Center, 1987—; Member United States Rocket, Satellite Research Panel, 1950—; chairman management board Am. Satellite Company, 1985—; chairman space applications board National Research Council, 1985—. Author numerous papers, reports in field. President town council, Forest Heights, Maryland, 1951-55. Served with United States Army Air Force, 1943-46. Recipient Professional Achievement award Engrs. and Architects Day, 1957; Meritorious Civilian Service award Navy Department, 1957; Outstanding Leadership medal National Aeronautics and Space Administration, 1962; Distinguished Service medal, 1971; recipient Arthur S. Fleming award Federal Government, 1963. Fellow Am. Meteorological Society, American Institute of Aeronautics and Astronautics, American Association for the Advancement of Science; member Am. Physical Society, National Acad. Engineering, Am. Geophysical Union. International Astronautical Federation (member, trustee international, acad. astronautics), Sigma Xi. Home: 15810 Comus Road Clarksburg Maryland 20871

TOWNSEND, MILES AVERILL, mechanical and aerospace

engineering educator; born Buffalo, New York, April 16, 1935; son of Francis Devere and Sylvia (Wolpa) T.; children: Kathleen Townsend Hastings, Melissa, Stephen, Joel, Philip. Bachelor of Arts, Stanford University, 1955; Bachelor of Science MechE, University Michigan, 1958; advanced certificate, University Illinois, 1963, Master of Science in Theoretical and Applied Mechanics, 1967; Doctor of Philosophy, University Wisconsin, 1971. Registered professional engineer, Illinois, Wisconsin, Tennessee, Ontario. Project engineer Sundstrand, Rockford, Illinois, 1959-63, Twin Disc Incorporated, Rockford, 1963-65, 67-68; senior engineer Westinghouse Electric Corp., Sunnyvale, California, 1965-67; instructor, fellow University Wisconsin, Madison, 1968-71; associate professor University Toronto, Ontario, Can., 1971-74; professor mechanical engineering Vanderbilt University, Nashville, 1974-81; Wilson professor mechanical and aerospace engineering, chairman department University Virginia, Charlottesville, 1982—; partner, vice president Endev Limited, Can. and United States, 1972—; consultant in field. Contributor numerous articles to professional journals; 7 patents in field. Recipient numerous research grants and contracts. Fellow American Society of Mechanical Engineers (member council on engineering, productivity committee); member American Association for the Advancement of Science, New York Acad. Sciences, Sigma Xi. Avocations: running, reading, music. Home: 222 Harvest Dr Charlottesville Virginia 22901 Office: University Va/ Dept Mech and Aerospace Engring Thornton Hall McCormick Road Charlottesville Virginia 22903

TRAIN, RUSSELL ERROL, environmentalist; born Jamestown, Rhode Island, June 4, 1920; son of Charles R. and Errol C. (Brown) T.; married Aileen Bowdoin, May 27, 1954; children—Nancy, Emily, Bowdoin, Errol. Bachelor of Arts, Princeton University, 1941, Doctor of Laws (honorary), 1970; Bachelor of Laws, Columbia University, 1948, Doctor of Laws (honorary), 1970; Doctor of Laws (honorary), Bates College, 1970, Drexel University, 1970; Doctor.E. (honorary), Worcester Polytechnic Institute, 1970; Doctor of Science (honorary), St. Mary's College, 1970, Clarkson College Tech., 1973, Salem College, 1975, Southwestern University, 1976, Michigan State University, 1976; Doctor of Civil Law (honorary), University of South, 1973. Bar: District of Columbia bar 1949. Attorney staff joint committee on internal revenue taxation United States Congress, 1949-53; chief counsel Ways and Means Committee, United States House of Representatives, 1953-54, minority adviser; 1955-56; assistant to secretary, head legal adv. staff Treasury Department, 1956-57; judge United States Tax Court, 1957-65; president Conservation Foundation, 1965-69; also trustee; undersec. Department Interior, 1969-70; chairman Council on Environmental Quality, 1970-73; administrator Environmental Protection Agency, Washington, 1973-77; senior associate Conservation Foundation, 1977; president, chief executive officer World Wildlife Fund-U.South, Washington, 1978-85, chairman board; 1985—; chairman board Conservation Foundation, 1985—; co-chairman Year 2000 Committee; chief executive Washington National Monument Association; member

National Water Commission, 1968; chief negotiator United Nations Conference Human Environment, 1972; representative International Whaling Commission, 1972, other international conferences; director Union Carbide Corp., Applies Energy Services Incorporated. Trustee World Wildlife Fund International, Switzerland; trustee emeritus African Wildlife Foundation, Elizabeth Haub Foundation; board director Alliance To Save Energy, Am. Conservation Association, Scientists Institute for Pub. Information, Rockefeller Brothers Fund, Citizens for Ocean Law, World Resource Institute, board of directors, chairman Clean Sites Incorporated Served to major, Field Artillery Army of the United States, 1941-46. Recipient Albert Schweitzer medal Animal Welfare Institute, 1972; Aldo Leopold medal Wildlife Society, 1975; Conservationist of Year award National Wildlife Federation, 1974; John and Alice Tyler Ecology award, 1978; Freese award American Society of Civil Engineers, 1978; Public Welfare award National Acad. Sciences, 1981; Elizabeth Haub prize in international environmental law, 1981, Lindbergh award, 1985, Environmental Law Institute award, 1986. Member Council Foreign Relations, Washington Institute Foreign Affairs, North Atlantic Council, Adv. Committee on Pollution of the Sea (United States vice president). Office: World Wildlife Fund-US 1250 24th St Northwest Washington District of Columbia 20037-3444

TRAUB, J(OSEPH) F(REDERICK), computer scientist, educator; born June 24, 1932; married Pamela Ann McCorduck, December 6, 1969; children: Claudia Renee, Hillary Anne. Bachelor of Science, City College of New York, 1954; Doctor of Philosophy, Columbia University, 1959. Member tech. staff Bell Laboratories, Murray Hill, New Jersey, 1959-70; professor computer sci. and math., head department computer sci. Carnegie-Mellon University, Pittsburgh, 1971-79; Edwin Howard Armstrong professor computer sci., chairman department, professor math. Columbia University, 1979-86; professor computer sci. Princeton (New Jersey) University, 1986-87; president John Von Neumann National Supercomputer Center, Consortium for Sci. Computing, Princeton, 1986-87; Edwin Howard Armstrong professor, chairman department computer sci., professor math. Columbia University, New York City, 1987—; director New York State Center Computers and Information Systems, 1982—; distinguished lecturer Massachusetts Institute of Technology, 1977; visiting Mackay professor University California, Berkeley, 1978-79; consultant Hewlett-Packard, 1982, International Business Machines Corporation, 1984, Schlumberger, 1986; Member pres.'s adv. committee computer sci. Stanford University, 1972-75, chairman, 1975-76; member adv. committee Federal Judicial Center; member sci. council I.R.I.A., Paris, 1976-80; member central steering committee, computing sci. and engineering research study National Science Foundation, also liaison to panel on theoretical computer sci. and panel on numerical comp., 1974-80; member adv. committee Carnegie-Mellon Institute Research, 1978-79; member applied math. div. rev. committee Argonne National Laboratory, 1973-75; member adv. committee math. and computer sci. National Science Foundation, 1978-

80; chairman computer sci. and tech. board National Research Council, 1986—; trustee Columbia University Press, 1983-85. Author: Iterative Methods for the Solution of Equations, 1964; (with H. Wozniakowski) A General Theory of Optimal Algorithms, 1980; (with G. Wasilkowski and H. Wozniakowski) Information, Uncertainty, Complexity, 1983, Information-Based Complexity, 1988; editor: Complexity of Sequential and Parallel Numerical Algorithms, 1973, Analytical Computational Complexity, 1976, Algorithms and Complexity: New Directions and Recent Results, 1976, Journal Association Computing Machinery, 1970-76, Transactions on Math. Software, 1974-76, Journal Computer and System Scis, 1973-86, International Journal on Computers and Math. with Applications, 1974—; founding editor Journal Complexity, 1985—, Annual Rev. Computer Science, 1986—. Fellow American Association for the Advancement of Science (council 1971-74); member Conference Board Math. Sciences (council 1971-74), Association Computing Machinery (chairman awards committee 1974-76, member committee on fellows), Society Industrial and Applied Math., Institute of Electrical and Electronics Engineers, Am. Math Society, National Acad. Engineering (membership committee for computer sci., electrical engineering and control 1986—). Home: 96 Battle Road Princeton New Jersey 08540 Office: Columbia U Department Computer Sci Computer Sci Building New York New York 10027

TRIVELPIECE, ALVIN WILLIAM, physicist, aerospace executive; born Stockton, California, March 15, 1931; son of Alvin Stevens and Mae (Hughes) T.; married Shirley Ann Ross, March 23, 1953; children: Craig Evan, Steve Edward, Keith Eric. Bachelor of Science, California Polytechnic College, San Luis Obispo, 1953; Master of Science, California Institute Tech., 1955, Doctor of Philosophy, 1958. Fulbright scholar Delft (Netherlands) University, 1958-59; assistant professor, then associate professor University California at Berkeley, 1959-66; professor physics University Maryland, 1966-76; on leave as assistant director for research div. controlled thermonuclear research Atomic Energy Commission, Washington, 1973-75; vice president Maxwell Laboratories Incorporated, San Diego, 1976-78; corp. vice president Sci. Applications, Incorporated, La Jolla, California, 1978-81; director Office of Energy Research, United States Department Energy, Washington, 1981-87; executive officer American Association for the Advancement of Science, Washington, 1987-88; director Oak Ridge (Tennessee) National Laboratory, 1988—; vice president Martin Marietta Energy Systems. Author: Slow Wave Propagation in Plasma Wave Guides, 1966, (with N.A. Krall) Principles of Plasma Physics, 1973; also articles. Named Distinguished Alumnus California Polytechnic State University, 1978, Distinguished Alumnus California Institute Tech., Pasadena, California, 1987; recipient U.S. Sec. of Energy's Gold medal for Distinguished Service, 1986; Guggenheim fellow, 1966. Fellow Am. Physical Society, American Association for the Advancement of Science, Institute of Electrical and Electronics Engineers; member Am. Nuclear Society, American

Association of University Profs., New York Acad. Sciences, Am. Association Physics Teachers, Sigma Xi. Clubs: Cosmos, Capital Hill, National Press. Patentee in field. Home: 8 Rivers Run Way Oak Ridge Tennessee 37830 Office: Oak Ridge National Lab Office of Dir Post Office Box 2008 Oak Ridge Tennessee 37831

TRULY, RICHARD H., astronaut; born Fayette, Mississippi, November 12, 1937; son of James B. Truly; married Colleen Hanner; children: Richard, Michael, Daniel, Bennett, Lee Margaret. Bachelor of Aeronautical Engineering, Georgia Institute Tech., 1959. Commissioned ensign United States Navy, 1959, advanced through grades, rear admiral, assigned Fighter Squadron 33; 1960-63, served in United States Ship Intrepid; served in United States Ship Intrepid United States Ship Enterprise, 1960-63; astronaut Manned Orbiting Laboratory Program United States Air Force, 1965-69; astronaut National Aeronautics and Space Administration, 1969—, commander Columbia Flight 2; 1981; commander Columbia Flight 2 Challenger Flight 3, 1983; director Space Shuttle program 1986—. Office: Lyndon B Johnson Space Center NASA Houston Texas 77058 also: NASA Space Flight 600 Independence Avenue Southwest Washington District of Columbia 20546

TRYON, ROLLA MILTON, JR., botanist, educator; born Chicago, August 26, 1916. Bachelor of Science, University Chicago, 1937; Master of Philosophy, University Wisconsin, 1938; Master of Science, Harvard University, 1940, Doctor of Philosophy in Botany, 1941. Laboratory technician Chemical Warfare Service Massachusetts Institute of Technology, 1942; instructor botany Dartmouth Coll, 1942, laboratory technician; 1943-44; instructor botany University Wisconsin, 1944-45; assistant professor University Minnesota, 1945-48; associate professor Washington University, St. Louis, 1948-57; curator herbarium and ferns Gray Herbarium Harvard University, Cambridge, Massachusetts, 1958—; professor biology Harvard University, 1972—; curator Herbarium, Minneapolis, 1946-48; assistant curator herbarium Missouri Botanical Garden, 1948-57. Member Am. Society Plant Taxon, Am. Fern Society, Botanical Society Am. Office: Gray Herbarium Harvard University 22 Divinity Avenue Cambridge Massachusetts 02138

TUCKER, RICHARD LEE, civil engineer, educator; born Wichita Falls, Texas, July 19, 1935; son of Floyd Alfred and Zula Florence (Morris) T.; married Shirley Sue Tucker, September 1, 1956; children: Brian Alfred, Karen Leigh. Bachelor of Civil Engineering, University Texas, 1958, Master of Civil Engineering, 1960, Doctor of Philosophy in Civil Engineering, 1963. Registered professional engineer, Texas. Instructor civil engineering University Texas, 1960-62; from assistant professor to professor University Texas, Arlington, 1962-74, associate dean engineering; 1963-74; v.p Luther Hill & Associate, Incorporated, Dallas, 1974-76; C.T. Wells professor project management University Texas, Austin, from 1976, director Construction Industry Institute; from 1983, director Construction Engineering and Project Management Program; president Tucker and Tucker Cons., Incorporated, Austin, 1976—.

Contributor numerous articles and papers to professional journals. Named Outstanding Young Engineer, Texas Society Professional Engrs., 1965, Outstanding Young Man, City of Arlington, 1967. Fellow American Society of Civil Engineers (R.L. Peurifoy award 1986); member Society Am. Military Engineers, National Research Council, MOLES (hon.). Baptist. Office: University Tex at Austin Constrn Industry Institute 3208 Red River Suite 300 Austin Texas 78705

TUKEY, JOHN WILDER, statistics educator, researcher; born New Bedford, Massachusetts, June 16, 1915; son of Ralph H. and Adah M. (Tasker) T.; married Elizabeth L. Rapp, July 19, 1950. Bachelor of Science, Brown University, 1936, Sc.Master, 1937, Doctor of Science, 1965; Master of Arts, Princeton University, 1938, Doctor of Philosophy, 1939; Doctor of Science (honorary), Case Institute Tech., 1962, Yale University, 1968, University Chicago, 1969. Member math. faculty Princeton University, 1939-65, professor; 1950-65, professor statistics; 1965—, Donner professor sci.; 1976—, chairman department statistics; 1965-70, research associate fire control research office; 1941-45; Hitchcock professor University Calif.-Berkeley, 1975; member tech. staff Bell Laboratories, 1945—, assistant director research communication prins.; 1958-62, associate executive director research; from 1961; member National Research Council, 1951-60, President's Sci. Adv. Committee, 1960-63, President's Air Quality Adv. Board, 1968-71; member United States del. United Nations Conference on Human Environmental, Stockholm, 1972; member National Adv.

Committee Oceans and Atmosphere, 1975—. Author: Denumerability and Convergence in Topology, 1940; Statistical Problems of the Kinsey Report (with Cochran and Mosteller), 1954; (with R.B. Blackman), The Measurement of Power Spectra from the Point of View of Communications Engineering, 1958; also sci. articles. Board fellows, member corp. Brown University, 1974—. Guggenheim fellow, 1949-50; Center Advanced Study in Behavioral Sciences fellow, 1957-58; recipient National Medal of Sci., 1973. Fellow American Association for the Advancement of Science, Am. Statistical Association, Am. Society Quality Control, Institute Math. Statistics, New York Acad. Sci., Ops. Research Society Am., Royal Statistical Society (hon.); member Am. Math. Society, Association Computing Machinery, Biometric Society, Math. Association Am., National Acad. Sciences, Am. Philosophical Society, Am. Acad. Arts and Sciences, International Statistical Institute, Sigma Xi. Club: Cosmos (Washington). Office: Princeton U Department Stats Princeton New Jersey 08540

TURRO, NICHOLAS JOHN, chemistry educator; born Middletown, Connecticut, May 18, 1938; son of Nicholas John and Philomena (Russo) T.; married Sandra Jean Misenti, August 6, 1960; children—Cynthia Suzanne, Claire Melinda. Bachelor of Arts, Wesleyan University, 1960, Doctor.Science (honorary), 1984; Doctor of Philosophy, California Institute Tech., 1963. Instructor Columbia University, New York City, 1964-65, assistant professor; 1965-67, associate professor; 1967-69, professor chemistry; 1969—, William P. Schweitzer professor chemistry;

1982—, chairman chemistry department; 1981-84; Cons. E.I. duPont de Nemours and Company, Incorporated. Author: Molecular Photochemistry, 1965, (with G.S. Hammond, J.N. Pitts, D.H. Valentine) Survey of Photochemistry, volume 1, 1968, volume 2, 1970, volume 3, 1971, (with A.A. Lamola) Energy Transfer and Organic Photochemistry, 1971, Modern Molecular Photochemistry, 1978; Editorial board: (with A.A. Lamola) Journal Organic Chemistry, 1974—, Nouveau J. de Chimie, Spectroscopy Letters, Encyclopedia of Physical Science and Tech., Journal of Reactive Intermediates. National Science Foundation fellow; Alfred P. Sloan Foundation fellow.; Recipient Eastman Kodak award for excellence in grad. research, award for pure chemistry, 1973; U.S. Department Energy E.O. Lawrence award, 1983; Urey award Columbia University, 1983; Guggenheim fellow Oxford University, 1985; Fairchild scholar California Institute Tech., 1984-85. wem. National Acad. Sci., Am. Chemical Society (editorial board journal 1984—, Harrison Howe award, Rochester, New York section 1986, Arthur C. Cope award 1986), Am. Acad. Arts and Sciences, Am. Chemical Society (Fresenius award 1973, award for pure chemistry 1974, James Flack Norris award 1987), Chemical Society (London), New York Acad. Sciences (Freda and Gregory Halpern award in photochemistry 1977), Am. Society Photochemistry and Photobiology, International Solar Energy Society, European Photo-Chem. Association; Phi Beta Kappa, Sigma Xi. Home: 125 Downey Dr Tenafly New Jersey 07670

TYLER, CARL WALTER, JR., physician, health research adminis-trator; born Washington, August 22, 1933; son of Carl Walter and Elva Louise (Harlan) T.; married Elma Hermione Matthias, June 23, 1956; children—Virginia Louise, Laureen, Jeffrey Alan, Cynthia Kay. Bachelor of Arts, Oberlin College, 1955; Doctor of Medicine, Western Reserve University, 1959. Diplomate Am. Board Ob-Gyn. Rotating intern University Hospitals of Cleveland, 1959-60, resident in ob-gyn; 1960-64; medical officer United States Public Health Service, 1964; obstetrician-gynecologist United States Public Health Service Indian Health Service, Tahlequah, Oklahoma, 1964-66; epidemic intelligence service officer Bureau Epidemiology, Centers for Disease Control, Atlanta, 1966-67; director family planning evaluation div. Bureau Epidemiology, Centers for Disease Control, 1967-80, assistant director for sci.; 1980-82, acting director Center for Health Promotion and Education; 1982, director epidemiology program office; 1982—; clinical assistant professor ob-gyn Emory University School Medicine, Atlanta, 1966-80, clinical associate professor, 1980—, also clinical associate professor preventive medicine and community health, adj. associate professor sociology College Arts and Sciences, 1977—; member adv. committee on oral contrapection World Health Organization, Geneva, 1974-77, member adv. committee maternal and child health, 1982—; lecturer in field. Editor: (monograph) Venereal Infections; contributor articles to professional journals. Chairman Dekalb County Schools committee on instruction programs, subcom. on health, physical education and safety, (Georgia), 1967-68; active Georgia State Soccer Coaches Association, Atlanta, 1973-79, DeKalb

County Young Men's Christian Association. Josiah Macy Foundation fellow, 1956-58; National Institutes of Health grantee, 1961-64; recipient Meritorious Service medal USPHS, 1984, Superior Service award, 1974; Carl S. Shultz Population award APHA, 1976, medal of Excellence Ctrs. for Disease Control, 1984. Fellow Am. College Ob-Gyn (chairman community health committee 1974-77), Am. College Preventive Medicine, Am. College Epidemiological; member Am. Epidemiologic Society, International Epidemiologic Association, Am. Pub. Health Association (governing council 1976-78), Association Planned Parenthood Professionals, Population Association Am., Sierra Club. Club: Briarcliff Woods Beach (Dekalb County, Georgia). Avocations: photography; camping; canoeing; volleyball. Office: Department of Health & Human Services Ctrs for Disease Control 1600 Clifton Road NE Atlanta Georgia 30333

UHLENBECK, KAREN KESKULLA, mathematician, educator; born Cleveland, August 24, 1942; daughter of Arnold Edward and Carolyn Elizabeth (Windeler) Keskulla; married Olke Cornelis, June 12, 1965 (divorced). Bachelor of Science in Math., University Michigan, 1964; Doctor of Philosophy in Math., Brandeis University, 1968. Instructor math. Massachusetts Institute of Technology, Cambridge, 1968-69; lecturer University Calif.-Berkeley, 1969-71; assistant professor University Ill.-Urbana, 1971-78; associate professor, then professor University Ill.-Urbana, Chicago, 1977-83; professor University Chicago, 1983-88; Sid Richardson Centennial Chair in Math. University Texas,

1988—. Author: Instantons and Four Manifolds, 1984. Contributor articles to professional journals. Fellow Sloan Foundation, 1974-76, MacArthur Foundation, 1983; grad. fellow National Science Foundation, 1964-68. Member National Acad. Sciences, Alumni Association University Michigan (Alumnae of Year 1984), Am. Math. Society, Am. Women in Math., Phi Beta Kappa. Avocations: gardening; canoeing. Office: U Tex Department Math Austin Texas 78712

UHLIR, ARTHUR, JR., electrical engineer, university adminstrator; born Chicago, February 2, 1926; son of Arthur and Helene (Houghteling) U.; married Ingeborg Williams, July 24, 1954; children—Steven, Donald, David. Bachelor of Science, Illinois Institute Tech., 1945, Master of Science in Chemical Engineering, 1948; Master of Science in Physics, University Chicago, 1950, Doctor of Philosophy in Physics, 1952. Process analyst Douglas Aircraft, Chicago, 1945; assistant engineer Armour Research Foundation, Chicago, 1945-48; member tech. staff Bell Telephone Laboratories, Murray Hill, New Jersey, 1951-58; director semi- conductor research and devel., manager semicondr. div., group vice president engineering Microwave Associates, Incorporated, Burlington, Massachusetts, 1958-69; director research Computer Metrics, Rochelle Park, New Jersey, 1969-73; professor electrical engineering Tufts University, Medford, Massachusetts, 1970—; chairman department electrical engineering Tufts University, 1970-75, dean of engineering; 1973-80. Atomic Energy Commission fellow, 1949-51. Fellow Institute of Electrical and Electronics Engineers; member Am. Physical Society, American

Association for the Advancement of Science, Sigma Xi. Home: 45 Kendal Common Road Weston Massachusetts 02193 Office: Elec Engring Department Tufts University Medford Massachusetts 02155

ULTMANN, JOHN ERNEST, physician, educator; born Vienna, Austria, January 6, 1925; came to United States, 1938, naturalized, 1943; son of Oskar and Hedwig (Schechter) U.; married Ruth E. Layton, May 25, 1952; children: Monica, Michelle, Barry. Student, Brooklyn College, 1946, Oberlin College, 1946-48; Doctor of Medicine, Columbia University, 1952; Doctor h.c., Heidelberg University, Federal Republic Germany, 1986. Diplomate: Nat. Board Medical Examiners, Am. Board Internal Medicine. Intern New York Hosp.-Cornell Medical Center, New York City, 1952-53; resident New York Hospital, 1953-55; Am. Cancer Society fellow in hematology Columbia, 1955-56; practice medicine specializing in internal medicine New York City, 1956-68, Chicago, 1968—; member staff Francis Delafield Hospital, 1955-68, Presbyterian Hospital, 1956-68, Bellevue Hospital, 1961-68; career scientist Health Research Council City New York, 1959-68; consultant Harlem Hospital, New York City, 1966-68; director clinical oncology Franklin McLean Memorial Research Institute, 1968—; professor medicine School Medicine University Chicago, 1970—; also director Cancer Research Center and dean for research and devel.; chairman board sci. counselors div. cancer treatment National Cancer Institute, 1976-80, member board sci. counselors div. cancer prevention and control, 1985-88; member Adv. Board Cancer Control to Governor of Illinois, 1976—, chairman, 1985—. Asso. editor: Cancer Research, 1974-78; editorial board: Annals Internal Medicine, 1974-81, Blood, 1975-77; cons. editor: Am. Journal Medicine, 1975—; Contributor articles to professional journals. Board of directors Association Am. Cancer Insts., 1974-75, pres.-elect, 1983-84, president, 1984-85, chairman board, 1985-86; board of directors at-large Illinois div. Am. Cancer Society, 1976-79; trustee Illinois Cancer Council, 1976—; chairman National Coalition for Cancer Research, 1985—. Served with Army of the United States, 1943-46. Fellow A.C.P., Institute Medicine Chicago; member Am. Federation Clinical Investigation, Society Study Blood, Am. Association Cancer Research, International, Am. socs. hematology, American Association of University Profs., American Association for the Advancement of Science, Harvey Society, Am. Society Clinical Oncology (director 1978—, pres.-elect 1980-81, president 1981-82, past president 1982-83), Chicago Society Internal Medicine, Central Society Clinical Research, Sociedad Chilena de Cancerologia, Sociedad Chilena de Hematologia, Phi Beta Kappa, Alpha Omega Alpha. Home: 5632 S Harper Avenue Chicago Illinois 60637 Office: U Chicago Cancer Research Center 5841 S Maryland Avenue Chicago Illinois 60637

UMBREIT, WAYNE WILLIAM, bacteriologist, educator; born Markesan, Wisconsin, May 1, 1913; son of William Traugott and Augusta (Abendroth) U.; married Doris McQuade, July 31, 1937; children: Dorayne Loreda, Jay Nicholas, Thomas Hayden. Bachelor of Arts, University Wisconsin, 1934, Master of Science, 1936, Doctor of Philosophy,

1939. Instructor soil microbiology Rutgers University, 1937-38; faculty University Wisconsin, Madison, 1938-44; assistant professor bacteriology and chemistry University Wisconsin, 1941-44; faculty Cornell University, 1944-47, professor bacteriology; 1946-47; head department enzyme chemistry Merck Institute, Rahway, New Jersey, 1947-58; associate director 1958; chairman department bacteriology Rutgers University, New Brunswick, New Jersey, 1958-75; professor microbiology, director grad. programs Rutgers University, 1969-83, professor emeritus microbiology; 1983—; director laboratories Southern Branch Watershed Association, 1983—. Author: (with Burris, Stauffer) Manometric Techniques, 1945, 5th edition, 1972, (with Oginsky) An Introduction to Bacterial Physiology, 1954, Metabolic Maps, 1960, Modern Microbiology, 1962, Essentials of Bacterial Physiology, 1976; Editor: Advances in Applied Microbiology, volumes 1-10, 1959-68; Contributor articles to professional journals. Recipient Biochem. Congress Symposium medal Paris, France, 1952. Fellow Am. Acad. Microbiology, New York Acad. Sci., A.A.A.S.; member Am. Society for Microbiology (Eli Lilly award in bacteriology 1947, Carski Foundation award for distinguished teaching 1968), Society Biological Chemists, Am. Chemical Society, Theobald Smith Society (Waksman award in microbiology 1957, past president), American Association of University Profs., Sigma Xi. Home: 498 Route 2 Flemington New Jersey 08822

UNKLESBAY, ATHEL GLYDE, geologist, educator; born Byesville, Ohio, February 11, 1914; son of Howard Ray and Madaline (Archer) U.; married Wanda Eileen Strauch, September 14, 1940 (deceased 1971); children: Kenneth, Marjorie, Carolyn, Allen; married Mary Wheeler Myhre, June 8, 1973 (deceased 1980). Bachelor of Arts, Marietta College, 1938, Doctor of Science (honorary), 1977; Master of Arts, State University Iowa, 1940, Doctor of Philosophy, 1942. Geologist United States Geological Survey, 1942-45, Iowa Geological Survey, 1945-46; assistant professor Colgate, 1946-47; member faculty University Missouri, Columbia, 1947—; professor geology University Missouri, 1954—, chairman department; 1959-67, vice president administration; 1967-79; executive director Am. Geological Institute, 1979-85; consultant in field. Author: Geology of Boone County, 1952, Common Fossils of Missouri, 1955, Pennsylvanian Cephalopods of Oklahoma, 1962; also articles. Member Columbia Board Education, 1954-70, Columbia Parks and Recreation Commission, 1954-57. Wilton Park fellow, 1968, 72, 76. Member Am. Association Petroleum Geologists, Paleontological Society Am., Geological Society Am., Econ. Paleontologists and Mineralogists, National Association Geology Teachers, Sigma Xi. Methodist. Club: Cosmos. Home: 37 G Broadway Village Dr Columbia Missouri 65201

VALIANT, LESLIE GABRIEL, computer scientist; born March 28, 1949; son of Leslie and Eva Julia (Ujlaki) V.; married Gayle Lynne Dyckoff, July 2, 1977; children—Paul A., Gregory J. Master of Arts, Kings College, Cambridge, United Kingdom, 1970; D.I.C., Imperial College, London, 1971; Doctor of Philosophy, University Warwick, United Kingdom,

1973. Visiting assistant professor Carnegie-Mellon University, Pittsburgh, 1973-74; lecturer University Leeds, England, 1974-76; lecturer, reader University Edinburgh, Scotland, 1976-82; visiting professor Harvard University, 1982, Gordon McKay professor computer sci. and applied math.; 1982—. Guggenheim fellow, 1985-86; recipient Nevanlinna prize, 1986. Office: Harvard University 33 Oxford St Cambridge Massachusetts 02138

VALLEE, BERT LESTER, biochemist, physician, educator; born Hemer, Westphalia, Germany, June 1, 1919; came to United States, 1938, naturalized, 1948; son of Joseph and Rosa (Kronenberger) V.; married Natalie T. Kugris, May 29, 1947. Bachelor of Science, University Berne, Switzerland, 1938; Doctor of Medicine, New York University College Medicine, 1943; Master of Arts (honorary), Harvard, 1960; Doctor of Medicine (honoris causa), Karolinska Institutet, Stockholm, Sweden, 1987. Research fellow Harvard Medical School, Boston, 1946-49; research associate Harvard Medical School, 1949-51, associate; 1951-56, assistant professor medicine; 1956-60, associate professor; 1960-64, professor biological chemistry; 1964-65, Paul C. Cabot professor biological chemistry; 1965-80, Paul C. Cabot professor biochem. sciences; 1980—; research associate department biology Massachusetts Institute Tech., Cambridge, 1948—; physician Peter Bent Brigham Hospital, Boston, 1961-80; biochemist-in-chief Brigham & Women's Hospital, Boston, 1980—; sci. director Biophysics Research Laboratory, Harvard Medical School, Peter Bent Brigham Hospital, 1954-80; head Center for Biochem. and Biophys. Sciences and Medicine, Harvard Medical School and Brigham & Women's Hospital, 1980—. Author 1 book.; contributor articles and chapters to sci. publications. Founder, trustee Boston Biophysics Research Foundation, 1957—; founder, president Endowment for Research in Human Biology, Incorporated, 1980—. Recipient Warner-Chelcott award, 1969, Buchman Memorial award California Institute Tech., 1976; Linderstrøm-Lang award and gold medal, 1980; Willard Gibbs Medal award, 1981, William C. Rose award in biochemistry, 1982. Fellow American Association for the Advancement of Science, National Acad. Sciences, Am. Acad. Arts and Sciences, New York Acad. Sciences; member Am. Society Biological Chemists, Am. Chemical Society (Willard Gibbs gold medal 1981), Optical Society Am., Biophys. Society, Swiss Biochem. Society (hon. foreign member), Royal Danish Acad. Sciences and Letters, Alpha Omega Alpha. Home: 56 Browne St Brookline Massachusetts 02146

VAN ALLEN, JAMES ALFRED, physicist, educator; born Mount Pleasant, Iowa, September 7, 1914; son of Alfred Morris and Alma E. (Olney) Van A.; married Abigail Fithian Halsey, October 13, 1945; children: Cynthia Olney Van Allen Schaffner, Margot Isham, Sarah Halsey, Thomas Halsey, Peter Cornelius. Bachelor of Science, Iowa Wesleyan College, 1935; Master of Science, University Iowa, 1936, Doctor of Philosophy, 1939; Doctor of Science (honorary), Iowa Wesleyan College, 1951, Grinnell College, 1957, Coe College, 1958, Cornell College, Mount Vernon, Iowa, 1959, University Dubuque, 1960,

University Michigan, 1961, Northwestern University, 1961, Illinois College, 1963, Butler University, 1966, Boston College, 1966, Southampton College, 1967, Augustana College, 1969, St. Ambrose College, 1982, University Bridgeport, 1987. Research fellow, physicist department terrestial magnetism Carnegie Institution, Washington, 1939-42; physicist, group and unit supervisor applied physics laboratory Johns Hopkins University, Baltimore, 1942, 46-50; organizer, leader sci. expeditions study cosmic radiation Peru, 1949, Gulf of Alaska, 1950, Greenland, 1952, 57, Antartica, 1957; Carver professor physics, head department University Iowa, Iowa City, 1951—; Regents fellow Smithsonian Institution, 1981; research associate Princeton, New Jersey, 1953-54; member devel. group radio proximity fuse National Def. Research Council, Office of Scientific Research and Development; pioneer high altitude research with rockets, satellites and space probes; board of directors Iowa Electric Light and Power Company, 1st National Bank Iowa City. Author: Origins of Magnetospheric Physics, 1983; contributing author: Physics and Medical of Upper Atmosphere, 1952, Rocket Exploration of the Upper Atmosphere; editor: Scientific Uses of Earth Satellites, 1956; associate editor Journal Geophysical Research, 1959-64, Physics of Fluids, 1958-62; contributor numerous articles to sci. journals. Served to lieutenant commander United States Navy, 1942-46, ordnance and gunnery specialist, combat observer. Received Physics award Washington Acad. Sci., 1949, Space Flight award Am. Astronautical Society, 1958, Louis W. Hill Space Transp. award Institute Aeronautical Sciences, 1959, Elliot Cresson medal Franklin Institute, 1961, Golden Omega award Electrical Insulation Conference, 1963, Iowa Broadcasters Association award, 1964, Fellows award of merit Am. Cons. Engrs. Council, 1978, Crafoord prize Royal Acad. Sciences, Sweden, 1989; Guggenheim Foundation research fellow, 1951; named commander Order du Merit Pour la Recherche et l'Invention, 1964. Fellow Am. Rocket Society (C.N. Hickman medal for devel. Aerobee rocket 1949), Institute of Electrical and Electronics Engineers, Am. Physical Society, Am. Geophysical Union (president 1982-84, John A. Fleming award 1963, 64, William Bowie medal); member Iowa Acad. Sci., National Acad. Sciences, International Acad. Astronautics (founding), Am. Philosophical Society, Am. Astronomical Society, Royal Astronomical Society United Kingdom (gold medal 1978), Am. Acad. Arts and Sciences, Sigma Xi, Gamma Alpha. Presybterian. Club: Cosmos (Washington). Discovered radiation belts around earth. Office: University Iowa 203 Physics Building Iowa City Iowa 52242

VAN ANDEL, TJEERD HENDRIK, geologist; born Rotterdam, The Netherlands, February 15, 1923; married 1962; 6 children. BSc, State University Groningen, 1946, Master of Science, 1948, Doctor of Philosophy in Geology, 1950. Assistant professor geology State Agriculture University, Wageningen, The Netherlands, 1948-50; sedimentologist Royal Dutch Shell Research Laboratory, 1950-53; senior sedimentologist Cia Shell de Venezuela, 1953-56; associate research geologist Scripps Institute Oceanography, University California, 1957-64, research geologist; 1964-68, lecturer geology; 1957-68; professor geology School Oceanography Oregon State University, 1968-76; Wayne Loel professor earth sci. department geology Stanford (California) University, 1976—; visiting professor University California, Berkeley, 1963; senior fellow Woods Hole Oceanography Institute, 1963; sci. adv. committee Deep Sea Drilling Project, 1964-68; research associate geology Scripps Institute Oceanography, 1968-72; member geodynamics committee National Acad. Sci., 1970-75; managing consultant Institute Ocean Exploration, National Science Foundation, 1971-72; visiting professor geophysics Stanford University, 1974-75; group chairman sci. committee ocean research Unesco, 1975-78, co-edn. World Ocean Atlas Commission. Recipient F.P. Shepard medal, 1978, New Brunswick Watkins award, 1980, Waterschoot Van der Gracht medal, 1984. Fellow Royal Netherlands Acad Sci.; member American Association for the Advancement of Science, Society Field Archaeologists, Society Econ. Paleontology and Mineral, Geology Society Am., Am. Geophysics Union. Office: Stanford U Department of Geology Stanford California 94305

VAN DEN BERGH, SIDNEY, astronomer; born Wassenaar, Netherlands, May 20, 1929; emigrated to United States, 1948; son of Sidney J. and Mieke (van den Berg) vandenB.; married Gretchen Krause (deceased); children by previous marriage: Peter, Mieke, Sabine. Student, Leiden (Netherlands) University, 1947-48; Bachelor of Arts, Princeton University, 1950; Master of Science, Ohio State University, 1952; Doctor rer. national, Goettingen University, 1956.

Assistant professor Perkins Observatory, Ohio State University, Columbus, 1956-58; research associate Mount Wilson Observatory, Palomar Observatory, Pasadena, California, 1968-69; professor astronomy David Dunlap Observatory, University Toronto, Ontario, Can., 1958-77; director Dominion Astrophysical Observatory, Victoria, British Columbia, 1977-86. Fellow Royal Society London, Royal Society Can.; member Am., Royal Astronomical Society. Home: 418 Lands End Road, Sidney, British Columbia Canada V8L 4R4 Office: Dominion Astrophysic, Observatory, Victoria, British Columbia Canada V8X 4M6

VAN DER MEER, SIMON, accelerator physicist; born The Hague, The Netherlands, November 24, 1925; son of Pieter and Jetske (Groeneveld) van der M.; married Catharina M. Koopman, April 26, 1966; children: Esther, Mathijs. Engineering degree in physics, Polytechnic University, Delft, The Netherlands, 1952; Doctor (honorary), University Geneva, 1983, University Amsterdam, The Netherlands, 1984, University Genoa, Italy, 1985. Research engineer Philips Physics Laboratory, Eihdhoven, The Netherlands, 1952-55; senior engineer European Organization of Nuclear Research European Organization Nuclear Research, Geneva, 1956—. Co-recipient Nobel prize for physics, 1984. Member Royal Netherlands Acad. Sciences (corr.), (foreign hon.) American Association for the Advancement of Science. Office: European Orgn Nuclear Research, 1211 Geneva 23 Switzerland

VAN DYKE, MILTON DENMAN, aeronautical engineering educator;

born Chicago, August 1, 1922; son of James Richard and Ruth (Barr) Van D.; married Sylvia Jean Agard Adams, June 16, 1962; children: Russell B., Eric J., Nina A., Brooke A. and Byron J. and Christopher M. (triplets). Bachelor of Science, Harvard University, 1943; Master of Science, California Institute Tech., 1947, Doctor of Philosophy, 1949. Research engineer National Advisory Committee for Aeronautics, 1943-46, 50-54, 55-58; visiting professor University Paris, France, 1958- 59; professor aeronautical Stanford, 1959—; consultant aerospace industry, 1949—; president Parabolic Press. Author: Perturbation Methods in Fluid Mechanics, 1964, An Album of Fluid Motion, 1982. Trustee Society For Promotion of Sci. and Scholarship, Incorporated Served with United States Naval Reserve, 1944-46. Guggenheim and Fulbright fellow, 1954-55. Member Am. Acad. Arts and Sciences, National Acad. Engineering, Am. Physical Society, Phi Beta Kappa, Sigma Xi, Sierra Club. Office: Div Applied Mechanics Stanford University Stanford California 94305

VANE, JOHN ROBERT, pharmacologist; born Worcestershire, England, March 29, 1927; son of Maurice and Frances Florence V.; married Elizabeth Daphne Page, April 4, 1948; children: Nicola, Miranda. Bachelor of Science in Chemistry, University Birmingham, 1946; Bachelor of Science in Pharmacology, Oxford University, 1949, Doctor of Philosophy, 1953, Doctor of Science, 1970; Doctor.Medical (honorary), University Cracow, Poland, 1977, Copernicus Academy Medicine, Cracow; Doctor (honorary), Rene Descartes University, Paris, 1978; Doctor of Science (honorary), City University of New York, 1980, Aberdeen University, 1983, New York Medical College, Birmingham University, University Surrey, 1984, Camerino University, Italy, 1984. Fellow Therapeutic Research Council, Oxford University, 1946-48; researcher worker Sheffield University, 1948-49, Nuffield Institute Medical Research, Oxford University, 1949-51; Stothert research fellow Royal Society, 1951-53; instructor, then assistant professor pharmacology Yale University Medical School, 1953-55; member faculty Institute Basic Medical Sciences, Royal College Surgeons England, 1955-73, professor experimental pharmacology; 1966-73; group research and devel. director Wellcome Foundation Limited, Beckenham, Kent, 1973-85; board of directors William Harvey Research Institute, St. Bartholomew's Hospital Medical College Wellcome Foundation Limited, London, 1986—. Co-editor: Adrenergic Mechanisms, 1960; Prostaglandin Synthetase Inhibitors, 1974; Metabolic Functions of the Lung, Volume 4, 1977; Handbook of Experimental Pharmacology, 1978; Prostacyclin, 1979; Interactions Between Platelets and Vessel Walls, 1981; contributor numerous articles to professional journals. Decorated knight bachelor; recipient Baly medal Royal College Physicians; Albert Lasker Basic Medical Research award; Peter Debye prize; Nuffield Gold medal; Ciba Geigy Drew award Drew University; Feldberg Foundation prize; Dale medal Society for Endocrinology, 1981; Nobel prize in medicine, 1982; Galen Medal Worshipful Society Apothecaries, 1983; Louis Pasteur Foundation prize, Santa Monica, California, 1984. Fellow American College of

Physicians (hon.), Institute Biology, Royal Society, Brit. Pharmaceutical Society; member Polish Pharmaceutical Society (hon.), Physiological Society, Royal Acad. Medicine Belgium, Royal Netherlands Acad. Arts and Sciences, Polish Acad. Sciences (foreign), Am. Acad. Arts and Sciences (foreign hon.), Society Drug Research, National Acad. Sciences (foreign associate). Home: White Angles, 7 Beech Dell, Keston BR2 6EP Kent, England Office: William Harvey Research Institute, St Bartholomew's Hosp Med College, London EC1M 6BQ, England

VAN HOFTEN, JAMES DOUGAL ADRIANUS, executive, former astronaut; born Fresno, California, June 11, 1944; son of Adriaan and Beverly (McCurdy) van H.; married Vallarie Davis, May 31, 1975; children—Jennifer Lyn, Jamie Juliana, VictoriaJane. Bachelor of Science, University Calif.-Berkeley, 1966; Master of Science, Colorado State University, 1968, Doctor of Philosophy, 1976. Assistant professor University Houston, 1976-78; astronaut National Aeronautics and Space Administration, Houston, 1978-86; manager space programs Bechtel National, Incorporated, San Francisco, 1986—. Served with United States Navy, 1969-74; lieutenant colonel Air National Guard 1984—. Recipient Distinguished Service award Colorado State University, 1984; Distinguished Citizen award Fresno Council Boy Scouts Am., 1984; Distinguished Achievement award Pi Kappa Alpha, 1984. Associate fellow American Institute of Aeronautics and Astronautics; member American Society of Civil Engineers (Aerospace Sci. and Tech. Application award 1984). Republican.

Home: 1014 Regio Court Lafayette California 94549 Office: Bechtel National Incorporated 50 Beale St San Francisco California 94119

VAN LOPIK, JACK RICHARD, geologist, educator; born Holland, Michigan, February 25, 1929; son of Guy M. and Minnie (Grunst) Van L.; 1 son, Charles Robert (deceased). Bachelor of Science, Michigan State University, 1950; Master of Science, Louisiana State University, 1953, Doctor of Philosophy, 1955. Geologist, section chief, assistant chief, chief geology branch United States Army Corps of Engineers, Waterways Experiment Station, Vicksburg, Mississippi, 1954-61; chief area evaluation section, tech. director, manager Space and Environmental Sci. Programs, tech. requirements director geosciences operations Texas Instruments, Incorporated, Dallas, 1961-68; chairman department marine sci. Texas Instruments, Incorporated, 1968-74; professor department marine sci., director sea grant devel., dean Center for Wetland Resources, Louisiana State University, Baton Rouge, 1968—; chairman Coastal Resources Directorate of United States National Committee for Man and Biosphere, United States National Commission for United Nations Educational, Scientific and Cultural Organization, 1975-82; director Gulf South Research Institute, 1974—; member National Adv. Committee Oceans and Atmosphere, 1978-84; member adv. council National Coastal Resources Research and Devel. Institute, 1985—; ofcl. del. XX Congreso Internacional, Mexico City, 1956, XII Gen Assembly International Union Geodesy and Geophysics, Helsinki, 1960; chairman panel on geography and land use National Acad. Scis.-NRC, committee on remote sensing programs for earth resources surveys, 1969-77. Fellow Geological Society Am., A.A.A.S.; member Am. Astronautical Society (director Southwest section 1967-68), Am. Society Photogrammetry (director 1969-72, chairman photo interpretation committee 1960, 65, representative earth scis. division National Research Council 1968-71), Am. Geophysical Union, Am. Association Petroleum Geologists (acad. adv. committee 1973-78), Association Am. Geographers, Society Econ. Paleontologists and Mineralogists (member research committee 1962-65), Am. Management Association, Society Research Administrators, Marine Tech. Society, National Association Corp. Directors, Am. Water Resources Association, Society Am. Military Engineers, Sea Grant Association (executive board 1972-74, 80-82), National Ocean Industries Association (adv. council 1973—), Sigma Xi. Home: 9 Rue Sorbonne Baton Rouge Louisiana 70808 Office: Center for Wetland Resources Louisiana State U Baton Rouge Louisiana 70803

VAN VALKENBURG, MAC ELWYN, engineering educator; born Union, Utah, October 5, 1921; son of Charles Mac and Nora (Walker) Van V.; married Evelyn J. Pate, August 27, 1943; children: Charles Mac II, JoLynne, Kaye, David R., Nancy J., Susan L. Bachelor of Science in Electrical Engineering, University Utah, 1943; Master of Science, Massachusetts Institute Tech., 1946; Doctor of Philosophy, Stanford, 1952. With Radiation Laboratory, Massachusetts Institute Tech., 1943-45, Research Laboratory Electronics,

1945-46; member faculty University Utah, 1946-55, University Illinois, 1955-66; professor electrical engineering Princeton, 1966-74, chairman department; 1966-72; professor electrical engineering University Illinois, Urbana, 1974—, acting dean College Engineering; 1984-85, dean College Engineering; 1985-88, dean emeritus; 1988—; visiting professor Stanford, University Colorado, University California, Berkeley, University Hawaii, Manoa, 1978-79, University Arizona, 1982-83. Author: Network Analysis, 3d edit, 1974, Introduction to Modern Network Synthesis, 1960, Introductory Signals and Circuits, 1967, Signals in Linear Circuits, 1974, Circuit Theory: Foundations and Classical Contributions, 1974, Linear Circuits, 1982, Analog Filter Design, 1982; editor-in-chief: IEEE Press, 1983-86. Fellow Institute of Electrical and Electronics Engineers (vice president, board directors 1969-73, editor transactions 1960-63, proc. 1966-69, Education medal 1972, Cirs. medal 1987); member Am. Society Engineering Education (George Westinghouse award 1963, Benjamin Garver Lamme award 1978, Guillemin prize 1978), National Acad. Engineering, Sigma Xi, Tau Beta Pi, Phi Kappa Phi. Home: 209 W Vermont Avenue Urbana Illinois 61801 Office: U Illinois 155 Everitt Lab 1406 W Green St Urbana Illinois 61801-2991

VARMUS, HAROLD ELIOT, microbiologist, educator; born Oceanside, New York, December 18, 1939; son of Frank and Beatrice (Barasch) V.; married Constance Louise Casey, October 25, 1969; children: Jacob Carey, Christopher Isaac. Bachelor of Arts, Amherst College, 1961, Doctor of Science (honorary), 1984; Master of Arts, Harvard University, 1962; Doctor of Medicine, Columbia University, 1966. Lic. physician, California. Intern, resident Presbyterian Hospital, N.Y.C ., 1966-68; clinical associate National Institutes of Health, Bethesda, Maryland, 1968-70; lecturer department microbiology University Calif.-San Francisco, 1970-72; assistant professor University California, San Francisco, 1972-74; associate professor University California, San Franisco, 1974-79; professor University California, San Francisco, 1979—, Am. Cancer Society research professor; 1984—; consultant Chiron Corp., Emoryville, California. Editor: Molecular Biology of Tumor Viruses, 1982, 85; Readings in Tumor Virology, 1983, Molecular and Cell Biology Journal; associate editor: Cell Journal; member editorial board: Cancer Surveys. Named California Acad. Sci. Scientist of Year, 1982; co-recipient Lasker Foundation award, 1982; Passano Foundation award, 1983; Armand Hammer Cancer prize, 1984; General Motors Alfred Sloan award, Shubitz Cancer prize National Acad. Sciences 1984. Member Am. Society Virology, Am. Society Microbiology, American Association for the Advancement of Science. Democrat. Home: 956 Ashbury St San Francisco California 94117 Office: U California Med School Department Microbiology Parnassus Avenue San Francisco California 94143

VILLARREAL, CARLOS CAS-TANEDA, engineer; born Brownsville, Texas, November 9, 1924; son of Jesus Jose and Elisa L. (Castaneda) V.; married Doris Ann Akers, September 10, 1948; children: Timothy Hill, David Akers. Bachelor of Science, United States Naval Academy, 1948; Master of Science, United States Navy Postgrad. School, 1950; Doctor of Laws (honorary), St. Mary's University, 1972. Registered professional engineer. Commissioned ensign United States Navy, 1948, advanced through grades to lieutenant; 1956; commanding officer United States Ship Rhea, 1951, United States Ship Osprey, 1952; commander Mine Div. 31, 1953; resigned 1956; manager marine and industrial operation General Electric Company, 1956-66; vice president marketing and administration Marquardt Corp., 1966-69; head Urban Mass Transit Administration, Department Transportation, Washington, 1969-73; commissioner Postal Rate Commission, 1973-79, vice chairman; 1975-79; vice president Washington operations Wilbur Smith and Associates, engineering design and consultant firm, 1979-84, senior vice president; 1984-86, executive vice president; 1987—, also board of directors; lecturer in field; member industry sector adv. committee Department Commerce; member section 15 adv. committee Department Transportation, 1983-86. Contributor to professional journals. Member devel. committee Wolftrap Farm Park for the Performing Arts, 1973-78; member council St. Elizabeth Church, 1982-86, chairman fin. committee; member board education St. Elizabeth School; board of directors Associate Catholic Charities, 1983-86; member fin. committee Catholic Charities, U.S.A. Decorated knight Sovereign Mil. Hospitaller Order St. John of Jerusalem of Rhodes and Malta, 1981; recipient award outstanding achievement Department Transp. Member Am. Pub. Transit Association,

Institute of Electrical and Electronics Engineers, Society Naval Architects and Marine Engineers, Society Am. Military Engineers, Am. Rds. and Transportation Builders Association (chairman pub. transp. adv. council), Transportation Research Board, Am. Cons. Engineers Council (vice chairman international committee), American Society of Civil Engineers, NSPE (president District of Columbia Society 1986-87), Washington Society Engineers, International Bridge, Tunnel and Turnpike Association. Republican. Roman Catholic. Clubs: University (Washington), Army- Navy (Washington); University (Cincinnati). Office: 1100 Connecticut Avenue Northwest Suite 750 Washington District of Columbia 20036

VISOTSKY, HAROLD MERYLE, psychiatrist, educator; born Chicago, May 25, 1924; son of Joseph and Rose (Steinberg) V.; married Gladys Mavrich, December 18, 1955; children: Jeffrey, Robin. Student, Herzl College, Chicago, 1943-44, Baylor University, 1944-45, Sorbonne, 1945-46; Bachelor of Science, University Illinois, 1947, Doctor of Medicine magna cum laude, 1951. Intern Cincinnati General Hospital, 1951-52; resident University Illinois, Illinois Research and Educational Hospital, also Neuropsychiat. Institute, Chicago, 1952-55; assistant professor University Illinois College Medicine, 1957-61, associate professor psychiatry; 1965-69, director psychiatric residency training and education; 1955-59; professor, chairman department psychiatry and behavioral sciences Northwestern University Medical School, Chicago, 1969—; director Psychiat. Institute, chairman department psychiatry Northwestern Memorial Hospital;

senior attending physician Evanston (Illinois) Hospital; Polio respiratory center psychiatric consultant National Foundation Infantile Paralysis, University Illinois, 1955-59; director mental health Chicago Board Health div. mental health services, 1959-63; director Illinois Department Mental Health, 1962-69; examiner Am. Board Psychiatry and Neurology, 1964—; director Center Mental Health and Psychiat. Services, Am. Hospital Association, 1979—; member 1st United States mission on mental health to Union of the Soviet Socialist Republics State Department Mission, 1967; chairman task force V Joint Commission on Mental Health of Children, 1967-69; member adv. committee on community mental health service National Institute Mental Health, 1965—; member professional adv. committee Jerusalem Mental Health Center; professional adv. group Am. Health Services, Incorporated; adv. committee Joint Commission Accreditation Hospitals, Council Psychiat. Facilities; member special panel mental illness for board of directors American Civil Liberties Union; rector Lincoln Acad. of Illinois Faculty Social Service; member select committee psychiatric care and evaluation Department of Health, Education and Welfare; member faculty Practising Law Institute; board overseers Spertus College Judaica, Chicago, 1981—. Contributor articles to psychiatric journals, chapters psychiatric textbooks. Trustee Erikson Institute Early Education, Illinois Hospital Association, Mental Health Law Project, Washington. Served with Army of the United States, 1942-46. Decorated D.S.C., Purple Heart, Bronze Star; recipient Edward A. Strecker award

Institute Pennsylvania Hospital, 1969; Medical Alumnus of Year award University Illinois, 1976; Distinguished Service award Chicago chapter Anti-Defamation League; Distinguished Service award B'nai B'rith, 1978. Fellow Am. Orthopsychiat. Association (director vice president 1970-71, president 1976-77, Leadership in Community Health Programs award 1986), Am. Psychiat. Association (chairman council on mental health services 1967—, vice president 1973-74, board trustees, 1973-83, secretary 1981-83, chairman council national affairs 1975-78, committee on abuse of psychiatry and psychiatrists, chairman council international affairs 1984—, E.B. Bowis award 1981, Adminstrv. Psychiatry award 1985, Simon Bolivar award 1983, Special Presidential Commendation award 1988), American Association for the Advancement of Science, Am. College Psychiatrists (charter, board regents 1976-79, vice president 1980, president 1983-84, E.B. Bowis award 1981, Gold medal Distinguished service award 1988), Chicago Institute Medicine, Am. College Mental Health Administrators (founding fellow); member Am. Association Chairman Department Psychiatry (president elect 1987—, president 1987—), Am. Association Social Psychiatry (vice president 1976, pres.-elect 1987, president 1988-89), Council Medical Specialty Socs., American Medical Association, Illinois Psychiat. Society (president 1965-66), Am. College Psychoanalysts, Mental Health Law Project (board trustees 1973—)World Association Social Psychiatry (councilor, executive council 1984—), World Psychiatric Association (rev. committee 1985—), Alpha Omega Alpha. Home: 1128 Ridge Avenue Evanston Illinois 60202 Office:

Northwestern Memorial Hosp Superior St & Fairbanks Court Chicago Illinois 60611

VITERBI, ANDREW JAMES, electrical engineering and computer science educator, business executive; born Bergamo, Italy, March 9, 1935; came to United States, 1939, naturalized, 1945; son of Achille and Maria (Luria) V.; married Erna Finci, June 15, 1958; children: Audrey, Alan, Alexander. Bachelor of Science, Massachusetts Institute of Technology, 1957, Master of Science, 1957; Doctor of Philosophy, University Southern California, 1962. Research group supervisor C.I.T. Jet Propulsion Laboratory, 1957-63; member faculty School Engineering and Applied Sci., University of California at Los Angeles, 1963-73, associate professor; 1965-69, professor; 1969-73; executive vice president Linkabit Corp., 1973-82; president M/A-Com Linkabit, Incorporated, 1982-84; chief scientist, senior vice president M/A-Com. Incorporated, 1985; professor electrical engineering and computer sci. University California, San Diego, 1985—; vice chairman, chief tech. officer Qualcomm Incorporated, 1985—; chairman United States Commission C, URSI, 1982-85; visiting committee department elec. engineering and computer sci. Massachusetts Institute of Technology, 1984—. Author: Principles of Coherent Communication, 1966, (with J.K. Omura) Principles of Digital Communication and Coding, 1979; board editors: Proc. IEEE, 1968-77; member board editors: Information and Control, 1967, Transactions on Information Theory, 1972-75. Recipient award for valuable contributions to telemetry, space electronics and telemetry group

Institute of Radio Engineers, 1962; best original paper award National Electronics Conference, 1963; outstanding paper award, info. theory group Institute of Electrical and Electronic Engineers, 1968; Christopher Columbus International Communications award, 1975; Aerospace Communication award American Institute of Aeronautics and Astronautics, 1980; Outstanding Engineering Graduate award University Southern California, 1986. Fellow Institute of Electrical and Electronics Engineers (past chairman info. theory group, Alexander Graham Bell medal, 1984); member National Acad. Engineering. Office: Qualcomm Incorporated 10555 Sorrento Valley San Diego California 92121

VOLPE, ERMINIO PETER, educator, biologist; born New York City, April 7, 1927; son of Rocco and Rose (Ciano) V.; children—Laura Elizabeth, Lisa Lawton, John Peter. Bachelor of Science, City College New York, 1948; Master of Arts, Columbia, 1949, Doctor of Philosophy (Newberry award 1952), 1952. Member faculty Newcomb College, 1952-60, professor zoology; 1960-64; professor biology Tulane University, New Orleans, 1964-81; W.R. Irby distinguished professor biology Tulane University, 1979-81, chairman department; 1964-66, 69-79, asso dean grad. school; 1967-69; professor basic medical sciences (genetics) Mercer University School Medicine, Macon, Georgia, 1981—; consultant National Commission Undergrad. Education in Biological Sciences, 1964-71; member steering committee Biological Sciences Curriculum Study, 1966-70; panelist National Research Council, 1967-70; member United States National Commission for United Nations Educational, Scientific and Cultural Organization, 1968-72; regional lecturer Sigma Xi, 1970-72; chairman Advanced Placement Test in Biology, Educational Testing Service, 1975—. Author: (textbook) Understanding Evolution, 1985, Human Heredity and Birth Defects, 1971, Patterns and Experiments in Developmental Biology, 1973, Man, Nature, and Society, 1975, The Amphibian Embryo in Transplantation Immunity, 1980, Biology and Human Concerns, 1983, Patient in the Womb, 1984, Test-Tube Conception: A Blend of Love and Science, 1987; member editorial board journal Copeia, 1962-63; asso. editor Journal Experimental Zoology, 1968-76, 84-85; editor (journal) Am. Zoologist, 1975-80; contributor articles to professional journals. Served with United States Naval Reserve, 1945-46. Fellow American Association for the Advancement of Science; member Genetics Society Am., Am. Society Zoologists (president 1981), Am. Society Naturalists, Society Devel. Biology, Society Study Evolution, Am. Society for Cell Biology, Am. Society Human Genetics, Phi Beta Kappa (vice president Tulane University chapter 1962), Sigma Xi (president Tulane University chapter 1964, faculty award 1972.). Office: Mercer University School Medicine Box 134 Macon Georgia 31207

WAGNER, ROBERT RODERICK, scientist, educator, physician; born New York City, January 5, 1923; son of Nathan and Mary (Mendelsohn) W.; married Mary Elizabeth Burke, March 23, 1967. Bachelor of Arts, Columbia University, 1943; Doctor of Medicine, Yale University, 1946. Intern, assistant resident physician Yale-New Haven Medical Center, 1946-47, 49-

50; research fellow National Institute Medical Research, London, England, 1950-51; instructor, then assistant professor medicine Yale University, 1951-55; assistant, then associate professor medicine Johns Hopkins University, 1956-59, associate professor microbiology; 1959-64, assistant, then associate dean medical faculty; 1957-63, professor microbiology; 1964-67; visiting fellow, member Common Room All Souls College Oxford University, 1967, 76; professor, chairman department microbiology University Virginia, 1967—, Marion McNulty Weaver and Malvin Weaver professor oncology, director Cancer Center; 1984—; visiting scientist Chinese Acad. Medical Sciences, 1982; visiting professor Universities Giessen and Wuerzburg (W. Ger.), 1983; Cons. Am. Cancer Society Member committees; United States Public Health Service, National Science Foundation, Association Am. Medical Colleges, American Medical Association, National Board Medical Examiners.; board of directors W. Alton Jones Cell Sci. Center, Lake Placid, New York, 1982—. Editor-in-chief: Journal Virology, 1966-82. Served to lieutenant United States Naval Reserve, 1947-49. Rockefeller Foundation resident scholar Villa Serbelloni, Bellagio, Italy, 1976; Macy Foundation Faculty scholar Oxford University, 1976; recipient Distinguished U.S. Scientist award Alexander von Humboldt Foundation, 1983. Fellow American Association for the Advancement of Science (councillor); member Association Am. Physicians, Am. Society Clinical Investigation, Am. Society Biological Chemists, Am. Association Immunologists, Am. Society for Microbiology (councillor), Association Medical School Microbiology Chairman (president 1974), Am. Society Virology (president 1984). Office: Department Microbiology U Va Charlottesville Virginia 22908

WAGNER, ROY, anthropology educator, researcher; born Cleveland, October 2, 1938; son of Richard Robert and Florence Helen (Mueller) W.; married Brenda Sue Geilhausen, June 14, 1968; children: Erika Susan, Jonathan Richard. Bachelor of Arts, Harvard University, 1961; Master of Arts, University Chicago, 1962, Doctor of Philosophy, 1966. Assistant professor anthropology Southern Illinois University, Carbondale, 1966-68; associate professor Northwestern University, Evanston, Illinois, 1969-74; professor University Virginia, Charlottesville, 1974—, chairman department; 1974-79; member cultural anthropology panel National Science Foundation, Washington, 1981-82. Author: Habu, 1972, The Invention of Culture, 1975, Lethal Speech, 1978, Symbols That Stand for Themselves, 1986. Social Sci. Research Council faculty research grantee, 1968; National Science Foundation postdoctoral research grantee, 1979. Fellow Am. Anthropol. Association. Avocation: student hot-air balloon pilot. Home: Rt 2 Box 132 Ruckersville Virginia 22968 Office: University Va Department Anthropology Charlottesville Virginia 22903

WAGNER, WARREN HERBERT, JR., educator, botanist; born Washington, August 29, 1920; son of Warren Herbert and Harriet Lavinia (Claflin) W.; married Florence Signaigo, July 16, 1948; children: Warren Charles, Margaret Frances. Bachelor of Arts, University Pennsylvania, 1942; Doctor of Philosophy, University California at Berkeley, 1950; special student,

Harvard, 1950-51. Instructor Harvard, summer 1951; faculty University Michigan at Ann Arbor, 1951—, professor botany; 1962—, curator pteridophytes; 1961—, director Botanical Gardens; 1966-71, chairman department botany; 1975-77, distinguished senior faculty lecturer; 1985; special research higher plants, origin and evolution ferns, methods accurate deduction phylogenetic relationships fossil and living plants. Panelist syst National Science Foundation, 1962-65, principal investigator project evolutionary characters ferns; 1960—, monograph grapeferns; 1980—; director botanical research aeroallergens National Institutes of Health, 1957-64; chairman Michigan Natural Areas Council, 1958-59; member Smithsonian Council, 1967-72, hon. member, 1972—; consultant member Survival Service Commission, International Union for Conservation of Nature and Natural Resources, 1971-75. Trustee Cranbrook Institute Scis. Recipient Distinguished Faculty Achievement award University Michigan, 1975, Amoco Outstanding Teacher award, 1980. Fellow American Association for the Advancement of Science (secretary section botanical scis., vice president section 1968); member National Acad. Sciences, Am. Fern Society (secretary 1952-54, curator, librarian 1957-77, president 1970, 71, hon. member 1978), Am. Society Plant Taxonomists (council 1958-65, president 1966), Society for Study Evolution (vice president 1965-66, council member 1967-69, president 1972), Am. Society Naturalists, International Association Pteridologists (vice president 1981-87, president 1987—), Botanical Society Am. (president 1977, merit award 1978), Michigan Botanical Club (president 1967-71), Torrey Botanical Club, New England Botanical Club, International Society Plant Morphologists, International Association Plant Taxonomy, Sigma Xi, Phi Kappa Tau. Club: Explorers. Home: 2111 Melrose Avenue Ann Arbor Michigan 48104

WAINWRIGHT, STEPHEN A., zoology educator, design consultant; born Indianapolis, October 9, 1931; son of Guy A. and Jeannette (Harvey) W.; married M. Ruth Wainwright, July 25, 1956; children: Peter C., Ian P., Archer T., Jennifer S. Bachelor of Science in Zoology, Duke University, 1953; Bachelor of Arts in Zoology, Cambridge University, England, 1958; Doctor of Philosophy, University California, Berkeley, 1962; Master of Arts, Cambridge University, 1963. Associate professor zoology Duke University, Durham, North Carolina, 1964-76, professor; 1976-85, J.B. Duke professor; 1985—; adj. professor design school North Carolina State University, Raleigh, 1983—. Author: (with others) Mechanical Design in Organisms, 1976, Axis and Circumference, 1988. Served as corporal United States Army, 1953-55. National Science Foundation postdoctoral fellow, 1962-64. Fellow American Association for the Advancement of Science; member Marine Biological Association United Kingdom, Am. Society Zoologists (president 1988), Am. Society Biomechanics (president 1981). Avocation: sculpture. Office: Duke U Department Zoology Durham North Carolina 27706

WAIT, JAMES RICHARD, electrical engineering educator, scientist; born Ottawa, Ontario, Canada, January 23, 1924; came to United States, 1955, naturalized, 1960; son of George Enoch and Doris Lillian (Browne) W.; married Gertrude Laura Harriat, June 16, 1951; children—Laura, George. Bachelor of Arts in Science, University Toronto, Ontario, 1948; Master of Arts in Science, 1949, Doctor of Philosophy in Electromagnetic Theory, 1951. Research engineer Newmont Exploration, Limited, New York City, 1948-51; section leader Defense Research Telecommunications Establishment, Ottawa, 1952-55, senior scientist; 1970-71; scientist United States Department Commerce Laboratories, Boulder, Colorado, 1955-80; adj. professor electrical engineering University Colorado, Boulder, 1961-80; professor electrical engineering, geosci. University Arizona, Tucson, 1980—, Regents professor; 1988—; fellow Cooperative Institute Research Environmental Sciences, 1968-80; senior scientist Office of Director Environmental Research Laboratories, Boulder, 1967-70, 72-80; Visiting research fellow laboratory electromagnetic theory University Denmark, Copenhagen, 1961; visiting professor Harvard, 1966-67, Catholic University, Rio de Janeiro, Brazil, 1971; mem.-at-large United States national committee International Sci. Radio Union, 1963-65, 69-72, del. general assemblies, Boulder, 1957, London, 1960, Tokyo, 1963, Ottawa, 1969, Warsaw, Poland, 1972, Lima, Peru, 1975, Helsinki, Finland, 1978; secretary United States national committee, 1976-78. Founder Journal Radio Sci, 1959, editor, 1959-68; editor: Pure and Applied Geophysics, 1964-75; editor international series monographs on electromagnetic waves Pergamon Press, 1961-73, Institution Elec. Engrs, London,

1974—. Served with Canadian Army, 1942-45. Recipient Gold medal Department Commerce, 1958; Samuel Wesley Stratton award National Bureau Standards, 1962; Arthur S. Flemming award Washington Chamber of Commerce, 1964; Outstanding Publ. award Office Telecommunications, Washington, 1972; Research and Achievement award National Oceanic and Atmospheric Administration, 1973; Van der Pol gold medal, 1978. Fellow Institute of Electrical and Electronics Engineers (member adminstrv. committee on antennas and propagation 1966-73, Harry Diamond award 1964, Centennial medal 1984), Institute of Electrical and Electronics Engineers Geosci. Society (achievement award 1985), Institution Electrical Engineers (Great Britain), Sci. Research Society Am. (Boulder Scientist award 1960), American Association for the Advancement of Science; member National Acad. Engineering. Office: U Ariz Department Elec and Computer Engring Tucson Arizona 85721

WALD, GEORGE, biochemist, educator; born New York City, November 18, 1906; son of Isaac and Ernestine (Rosenmann) W.; married Frances Kingsley, May 15, 1931 (divorced); children: Michael, David; married Ruth Hubbard, 1958; children: Elijah, Deborah. Bachelor of Science, New York University, 1927, Doctor of Science (honorary), 1965; Master of Arts, Columbia University, 1928, Doctor of Philosophy, 1932; Doctor of Medicine (honorary), University Berne, 1957; Doctor of Science, Yale University, 1958, Wesleyan University, 1962, McGill University, 1966, Amherst College, 1968, University Rennes, 1970, University Utah, 1971,

Gustavus Adolphus University, 1972; Doctor of Hebrew Literature, Kalamazoo College, 1984, University Leon, Nicaragua, 1984. National Research Council fellow at Kaiser Wilhelm Institute Berlin and Heidelberg, University Zurich, University Chicago, 1932-34; tutor biochem. sciences Harvard University, 1934-35, instructor biology; 1935-39, faculty instructor; 1939-44, associate professor biology; 1944-48, professor; 1948—, Higgins professor biology; 1968-77, professor emeritus; 1977—; visiting professor biochemistry University California, Berkeley, summer 1956; National Sigma Xi lecturer, 1952; chairman divisional committee biology and medical sciences National Science Foundation, 1954-56; Guggenheim fellow, 1963-64; Overseas fellow Churchill College, Cambridge University, 1963-64; participant U.S.-Japan Eminent Scholar Exchange, 1973; guest China Association Friendship with Foreign Peoples, 1972; vice president Permanent Peoples' Tribunal, Rome, 1980—. Co-author: General Education in a Free Society, 1945, Twenty Six Afternoons of Biology, 1962, 66, also sci. papers on vision and biochem. evolution. Recipient Eli Lilly prize Am. Chemical Society, 1939; Lasker award Am. Pub. Health Association, 1953; Proctor medal Association Research in Ophthalmology, 1955; Rumford medal Am. Acad.; Arts and Sciences, 1959; Ives medal Optical Society Am., 1966; Paul Karrer medal in chemistry University Zurich, 1967; co-recipient Nobel prize for physiology, 1967; T. Duckett Jones award Helen Hay Whitney Foundation, 1967; Bradford Washburn medal Boston Mus. Sci., 1968; Max Berg award, 1969; Priestley medal Dickinson College, 1970.

Fellow National Acad. Sci., Am. Acad. Arts and Sciences, Am. Philosophical Society. Home: 21 Lakeview Avenue Cambridge Massachusetts 02138 Office: Harvard U Biol Labs Cambridge Massachusetts 02138

WALKER, CHARLES ALLEN, chemical engineer, educator; born Wise County, Texas, June 18, 1914; son of Jackson Lamar and Eula (Hamilton) W.; married Bernice Rolf, December 24, 1942; children: Allen Rolf, John Lamar, Laurence Gordon. Bachelor of Science, University Texas, 1938, Master of Science, 1940; Doctor of Engineering, Yale University, 1948. Faculty Yale University, 1942-84, professor chemical engineering; 1956-84, master Berkeley College; 1959-69, chairman department engineering and applied sci.; 1974-76, Raymond John Wean professor; 1979-84, professor emeritus; 1984—, chairman department chemical engineering; 1981-84; member staff Yale Institution for Social and Policy Studies, 1970-84; consultant chemical engineer, 1942—. Board of directors Connecticut Fund for the Environmental, 1978-86. Fellow American Association for the Advancement of Science; member Sci. Research Society Am. (past national director, treas 1968-73), Am. Chemical Society (petroleum research fund adv. board 1970-81, chairman 1972-81), Am. Institute Chemical Engineers, Am. Society Engineering Education, Connecticut Acad. Sci. and Engineering, Phi Beta Kappa (hon.), Sigma Xi (director 1976-78), Tau Beta Pi, Phi Lambda Upsilon. Club: Yale (New Haven). Home: 29 Meadow Brook Road Hamden Connecticut 06517

WALKER, ERIC ARTHUR, consulting engineer, institute executive; born Long Eaton, England, April 29, 1910; came to United States, 1923, naturalized, 1937; son of Arthur and Violet Elizabeth (Haywood) W.; married L. Josephine Schmeiser, December 20, 1937; children: Gail (Mrs. Peter Hearn), Brian. Bachelor of Science, Harvard University, 1932, Master of Science, 1933, Doctor of Science, 1935; Doctor of Laws, Temple University, 1957, Lehigh University, 1957, Hofstra College, 1960, Lafayette College, 1960, University Pennsylvania, 1960, University Rhode Island, 1962; Doctor of Humane Letters, Elizabethtown College, 1958; Doctor of Literature, Jefferson Medical College, 1960; Doctor of Science, Wayne State University, 1965, Thiel College, 1966, University Notre Dame, 1968, University Pittsburgh, 1970. Registered professional engineer, Pennsylvania. Instructor math. Tufts College, 1933-34, assistant professor, associate professor electrical engineering; 1935-38, head electrical engineering department; 1935-40; head electrical engineering department University Connecticut, 1940-43; associate director Harvard University Underwater Sound Laboratory, 1942-45; director Ordnance Research Laboratory, Pennsylvania State University, 1945-52, head electrical engineering department; 1945-51; dean School Engineering Pennsylvania State University, 1951-56, vice president university; 1956, president; 1956-70; vice president sci. and tech. Aluminum Company Am., 1970-76; member and past chairman board Institute for Def. Analysis, 1978—; executive secretary Research and Devel. Board, 1950-51; consultant National Research Council, 1949-50; member and past chairman committee on undersea warfare; chairman President's Committee on Tech. and Distribution Research for Benefit of Small Business, 1957; member national sci. board National Science Foundation, 1962-68, chairman national sci. board, 1966-68; chairman Naval Research Adv. Committee, 1963-65, 71-73, Army Sci. Adv. Panel, 1956-58; vice chairman President's Committee Scientists and Engineers, 1956-58; adv. panel on engineering and tech. manpower President's Sci. Adv. Committee; member Gov.'s Committee of 100 for Better Education, 1960-61; board of directors Engineering Foundation; chairman board Institute for Def. Analyses. Contributor to tech. magazines. United board visitors United States Naval Acad., 1958-60, United States Mil. Acad., 1962-64. Recipient Horatio Alger award, 1959, Tasker H. Bliss award Am. Society Mil. Engrs., 1959; Golden Omega award Am. Institute E.E and National Electrical Mfg. Association, 1962; DoD Pub. Service medal, 1970; Presidential citation, 1970. Fellow Institute of Electrical and Electronics Engineers, Am. Acoustical Society, Am. Institute E.E., Am. Physical Society; member Am. Institute Physics, Am. Society Engineering Education (Lamme award 1965, president 1956-57), Pennsylvania Association Colls. and Univs. (president 1950- 60), Middle States Association Colls. and Secondary Schs. (commission higher education 1958-61), Engineers Joint Council (president 1962-63), National Association State Univs. and Land-Grant Colls. (executive committee 1958-62), National Acad. Engineering (president 1966-70), Am. Acad. Arts and Sciences, Newcomen Society,

Royal Society Arts, Sigma Xi, Tau Beta Pi, Phi Kappa Phi. Clubs: Duquesne, Cosmos. Home: 904 Outer Dr State College Pennsylvania 16801

WALLACE, CRAIG KESTING, research director; born Woodbury, New Jersey, December 4, 1928; son of Howard Kesting and Geneva Moore (Dilkes) W.; married Nancy Jane Bijur, June 30, 1960; children—Gebre Egzeabher, Craig Kesting, Pamela Jane. Bachelor of Arts cum laude, Princeton University, 1950; Doctor of Medicine, New York Medical College, 1955. Rotating intern Jefferson Medical College Hospital, Philadelphia, 1955-56, resident in medicine; 1956-59, chief resident in medicine; 1959-60; associate professor medicine and pathobiology Johns Hopkins University, Baltimore, 1964-72; associate director international research National Institutes of Health, Bethesda, Maryland, 1984—; director Fogarty International Center, Bethesda, 1984-87. Member editorial board Ethiopian Medical Journal, 1974-76, chairman, 1975-76, corr. editor, 1983—contributor articles to professional journals. Served to captain Medical Corps, United States Navy, 1960-63, 72-82. Decorated Meritorious Service medal with gold star, Navy Commendation medal. Fellow Royal Society Tropical Medicine and Hygiene, Infectious Diseases Society Am., American College of Physicians; member Am. Society Tropical Medicine and Hygiene. Republican. Episcopalian. Club: Princeton (New York City). Office: NIH Building 1 Room 238 Bethesda Maryland 20892

WALLACE, ROBERT EARL, geologist; born New York City, July 16, 1916; son of Clarence Earl and Harriet (Wheeler) W.; married Gertrude Kivela, March 19, 1945; 1 child: Alan R. Bachelor of Science, Northwestern University, 1938; Master of Science, California Institute Tech., 1940, Doctor of Philosophy, 1946. Registered geologist, California, engineering geologist, California. Geologist United States Geological Survey, various locations, 1942—; regional geologist United States Geological Survey, Menlo Park, California, 1970-74; chief scientist Office of Earthquakes, Volcanoes and Engineering United States Geological Survey, Menlo Park, 1974-87; assistant and associate professor Washington State College, Pullman, 1946-51; member adv. panel National Earthquake Prediction Evaluation Council, 1980—, Stanford University School Earth Sci., 1972-82; chairman engineering criteria rev. board San Francisco Bay Conservation and Devel. Commission. Contributor articles to professional journals. Recipient Meritorious Service award U.S. Department Interior, 1978, Distinguished Service award U.S. Department Interior, 1978; Japanese Indsl. Tech. Association fellow, 1984. Fellow American Association for the Advancement of Science, Geological Society Am. (chair cordillidan section 1967-68), Earthquake Engineering Research Institute, member Seismological Society Am. (medalist 1988). Avocations: bird watching, ham radio, water color painting. Office: United States Geol Survey 345 Middlefield Road Menlo Park California 94025

WALSER, RODGER M., electrical engineering educator. Bachelor of Electrical Engineering, University Michigan, 1959, Master of Electrical Engineering, 1961, Doctor of Philosophy, 1967. Professor, now J.H.

Herring Centennial professor engring University Texas, Austin. Member Institute of Electrical and Electronics Engineers. Office: Department Elec & Computer England U Tex/Austin Austin Texas 78712

WALSH, LEO MARCELLUS, agricultural college administrator; born Moorland, Iowa, January 16, 1931; married, 1958. Bachelor of Science, Iowa State University, 1952; Master of Science, University Wisconsin, 1957, Doctor of Philosophy in Soils, 1959. Assistant professor, extension specialist University Wisconsin, Madison, 1959-64, associate professor; 1964-68, professor soils; 1968—, chairman department; 1972-79, dean College Agricultural and Life Sciences; 1979—. Fellow American Association for the Advancement of Science, Am. Society Agronomy, Soil Sci. Society Am. (former president). Office: College Agrl & Life Scis U Wisconsin 140 Agrl Hall Madison Wisconsin 53706

WALTON, CHARLES MICHAEL, civil engineering educator; born Hickory, North Carolina, July 28, 1941; son of Charles O. and Virginia Ruth (Hart) W.; married Betty Grey Hughes; children: Susan, Camila, Michael, Gantt. Bachelor of Science, Virginia Military Institute, 1963; Master of Civil Engineering, North Carolina State University, 1969, Doctor of Philosophy, 1971. Research assistant North Carolina State University, Raleigh, 1967-71; transportation planning engineer North Carolina Highway Commission, Raleigh, 1970-71; assistant professor civil engineering University Texas, Austin, 1971-76, associate professor; 1976-83, professor; 1983-87, Bess Harris Jones Centennial professor natural resource policy studies; 1987—;

transportation consultant, 1970—; associate director Center for Transportation Research, University Texas, 1980—. Contributor articles to professional journals. Member Austin plan Steering Committee; chairman Urban Transportation Commission, Austin, Urban Design Task Force, Austin. Member American Society of Civil Engineers (Harland Bartholomew award 1987, Frank M. Masters engineering award 1987), Transportation Research Board, Institute Transportation Engineers, Society Am. Military Engineers, Ops. Research Society Am., Austin Chamber of Commerce (Leadership Austin Program). Democrat. Methodist. Home: 3404 River Road Austin Texas 78703 Office: U Tex/Austin Department Civil Engring Austin Texas 78712

WALTON, ERNEST THOMAS SINTON, physicist; born Dungarvan, County Waterford, Ireland, October 6, 1903; son of J.A. Walton; married Winifred Isabel Wilson, 1934; 4 children. Master of Arts, Methodist College, Belfast; Master of Science, Trinity College, Dublin; Doctor of Philosophy, Cambridge University; Doctor of Science (honorary), Queen's University, Belfast, Ireland, Gustavus Adolphus College, Minnesota, University Ulster, Minnesota. Erasmus Smith's professor natural and experimental philosophy Trinity College, Dublin, 1947-74, fellow emeritus; 1974—. Recipient Overseas Research scholar, 1927-30, Senior Research award, dept. sci. and indsl. research, 1930-34, Clerk Maxwell scholar, 1932-34, Hughes medal, Royal Society, 1938, Nobel prize for physics, 1951. Home: 26 St Kevin's Park, Dartry Road, Dublin 6 Ireland Office: Trinity

College, Department Physics, Dublin Ireland

WANG, AN, office automation systems company executive; born Shanghai, China, February 7, 1920; came to United States, 1945, naturalized, 1955; son of Yin Lu and Zen Wan (Chien) W.; married Lorraine Chiu, July 10, 1949; children: Frederick A., Courtney S., Juliette L. Bachelor of Science, Chiao Tung University, 1940; Master of Science, Harvard University, 1946, Doctor of Philosophy, 1948; Doctor of Science (honorary), Lowell Institute Tech, 1971; Doctor.Commercial Science (honorary), Suffolk University, 1980; Doctor of Science (honorary), Southeastern Massachusetts University, 1981; Doctor of Engineering (honorary), Poly Institute New York, 1982; Doctor of Science (honorary), Syracuse University, 1982; Doctor of Laws (honorary), Emmanuel College, 1982; Doctor of Science in Business Administration (honorary), Bryant College, 1982; Doctor of Humane Letters (honorary), Fairleigh Dickinson University, 1982; Doctor.Business Economics (honorary), Tufts University, 1982; Doctor of Science (honorary), University Hartford, 1983; Doctor of Laws (honorary), Boston College, 1983; Doctor of University (honorary), University Stirling, Scotland, 1983; Doctor of Science (honorary), Northeastern University, 1984; Doctor of Engineering Science, Merrimack College, 1984; Doctor of Science (honorary), Brown University, 1985; Doctor of Science, University Massachusetts, Amherst, 1986; Doctor of Engineering (honorary), Worcester Polytechnic Institute, 1987; LL.Doctor, Harvard University, 1987; Doctor of Science (honorary), Boston University, 1988; Doctor Engineering (honorary), Rensselaer Polytechnic Institute, 1988; Doctor of Humanities (honorary), Northeast School Law, 1988; Doctor of Science (honorary), Williams College, 1988, Chiao Tung University, 1988. Teacher Chiao-Tung University, China, 1940-41; engineer Central Radio Works, China, 1941-45, Chinese Government Supply Agency, Ottawa, Ontario, Can., 1946-47; research fellow Harvard, 1948-51; owner Wang Laboratories, Cambridge, Massachusetts, 1951-55; chairman board, chief executive officer, director Wang Laboratories, Incorporated, Lowell, Massachusetts, 1955—. Patentee in field. Trustee Northeastern University, Mus. Sci. Fellow Institute of Electrical and Electronics Engineers, Am. Acad. Arts and Sciences; member National Acad. Engineering, Sigma Xi. Office: Wang Labs Incorporated 1 Industrial Avenue Lowell Massachusetts 01851

WANG, CHAO-CHENG, mathematician, philosopher; born Peoples Republic of China, July 20, 1938; came to United States, 1961; son of N.S. and V.T. Wang; married Sophia C.L. Wang; children: Ferdinand, Edward. Bachelor of Science, National Taiwan University, 1959; Doctor of Philosophy, Johns Hopkins University, 1965. Assistant professor Johns Hopkins University, Baltimore, 1966-68, associate professor; 1968-69; professor Rice University, Houston, 1968-79, Noah Harding professor; 1979—, chairman math. sci. department; 1983—. Author numerous books in field; contributor articles to professional journals. Named Distinguished Young Scientist Maryland Acad. Sci., 1968. Member Society Natural Philosophy (treasurer 1985-86). Office: Rice

University Department of Math Sciences Houston Texas 77251

WASSERBURG, GERALD JOSEPH, geology and geophysics educator; born New Brunswick, New Jersey, March 25, 1927; son of Charles and Sarah (Levine) W.; married Naomi Z. Orlick, December 21, 1951; children: Charles David, Daniel Morris. Student, Rutgers University; Bachelor of Science in Physics, University Chicago, 1951, Master of Science in Geology, 1952, Doctor of Philosophy, 1954; Doctor Honorary Causa, Brussels University, 1985, University Paris, 1986; Doctor of Science (honorary), Arizona State University, 1987. Research associate Institute Nuclear Studies, University Chicago, 1954-55; assistant professor California Institute Tech., Pasadena, 1955-59, associate professor; 1959-62, professor geology and geophysics; 1962-82, John D. MacArthur professor geology and geophysics; 1982—; Served on Juneau Ice Field Research Project, 1950; consultant Argonne National Laboratory, Lamont, Illinois, 1952-55; former member United States National Committee for Geochem., committee for Planetary Exploration Study, National Research Council, adv. council Petroleum Research Fund, Am. Chemical Society; member lunar sample analysis planning team (LSAPT) Manned Spacecraft Center, National Aeronautics and Space Administration, Houston , 1968-71, chairman,1970; lunar sample rev. board 1970-72; member Facilities Working Group LSAPT, Johnson Space Center, 1972—; member sci. working panel for Apollo missions, Johnson Space Center, 1971-73; advisor National Aeronautics and Space Administration, 1968—, physical sciences committee, 1971-75, member lunar base steering committee, 1984; chairman committee for planetary and lunar exploration, member space sci. board National Acad. Sciences, 1975-78; chairman div. Geological and Planetary Sciences, California Institute Tech.; visiting professor University Kiel, Republic of Germany, 1960, Harvard University, 1962, University Bern, Switzerland, 1966, Swiss Federal Tech. Institute, 1967, Max Planck Institute, Mainz and Heidelberg, Republic of Germany, 1985; invited lecturer, Vinton Hayes Senior Fellow, Harvard University, 1980, Jaeger-Hales Lecture, Australian National University, 1980, Harold Jeffreys Lecture, Royal Astronomical Society, 1981, Ernst Cloos Lecturer, Johns Hopkins University, 1984, H.L. Welsh Disitng. Lecturer, University Toronto, Can. 1986.; Green visiting professor University British Columbia 1982; 60th Anniversary Symposium speaker, Hebrew University, Jerusalem, 1985. Recipient Group Achievement award, National Aeronautics and Space Administration, 1969, Exceptional Sci. Acheivement award, National Aeronautics and Space Administration, 1970, Distinguished Pub. Service medal, National Aeronautics and Space Administration, 1973, J.F. Kemp medal Columbia University, 1973, Professional Achievement award University Chicago Alumni Association, 1978, Distinguished Pub. Service medal with cluster, National Aeronautics and Space Administration, 1978, Wollaston medal Geol. Society London, 1985, Senior Scientist award, Alexander von Humboldt-Stiftung, 1985, Crafoord prize Royal Swedish Acad. Sciences, 1986; named Hon. Foreign Fellow

European Union Geoscis., 1983, recipient Holmes medal 1987; Rgents fellow Smithsonian Institute. Fellow American Association for the Advancement of Science, Am. Geophysical Union (planetology section, Harry H. Hess medal 1985), Geological Society Am. (life, Arthur L. Day medal 1970), Meteoritical Society (president 1987-88, Leonard medal 1975); member Geochem. Society (Goldschmidt medal 1978), National Acad. Sciences (Arthur L. Day prize and lectureship 1981, J. Lawrence Smith medal 1985), Norwegian Acad. Sci. and Letters, Am. Phil. Society. Research interests include geochemistry and geophysics and the application of the methods of chemical physics to problems in the earth scis. Major researches have been the determination of the time scales of nucleosynthesis, connections between the interstellar medium and solar material, the time of the formation of the solar system, the chronology and evolun of the earth, moon and meteorites, the establishment of dating methods using long-lived natural radio-activities, the study of geologic and lunar processes using nuclear and isotopic effects as a tracer in nature, the origin of natural gases, and the application of thermodynamic methods of geologic systems. Home: 2100 Pinecrest Dr Altadena California 91001 Office: California Institute of Tech Div of Geol & Planetary Scis Pasadena California 91125

WASSERMAN, ROBERT HAROLD, biology educator; born Schenectady, February 11, 1926; son of Joseph and Sylvia (Rosenberg) W.; married Marilyn Mintz, June 11, 1950; children: Diane Jean, Arlene Lee, Judith Rose. Bachelor of Science, Cornell University, 1949, Doctor of Philosophy, 1953; Master of Science, Michigan State University, 1951. Research associate Atomic Energy Commission project University Tennessee, Oak Ridge, 1953-55; senior scientist medical div. Oak Ridge Institute Nuclear Studies, 1955-57; associate professor department physical biology New York State Vet. College, Cornell University, 1957-63, professor; 1963—, acting head physical biology department; 1963-64, 71, 75—, chairman department /sect. physiology; 1983—, member executive committee div. biological sci.; 1983—; visiting fellow Institute Biological Chemistry, Copenhagen, 1964-65; chairman Conference on Calcium Transport, 1962; co-chairman Conference on Cell Mechanisms for Calcium Transfer and Homeostasis, 1970; chairman Symposium Calcium-Binding Proteins, 1977; member food and nutrition board National Research Council; consultant National Institutes of Health, Oak Ridge Institute Nuclear Studies; member pub. affairs committee Federation Am. Societies Experimental Biology, 1974-77 ; chairman committee MPI, National Research Council. Board editors: Calcified Tissue Research, 1977-80, Procs. Society Experimental Biol. Medicine, 1970-76, Cornell Veterinarian, Journal Nutrition; contributor: articles to professional journals. Served with United States Army, 1944-45. Recipient Mead Johnson award, 1969, Andre Lichtwitz prize INSERM, 1982; Guggenheim fellow, 1964-65, 72; NSF-OECD fellow, 1964-65. Member Am. Physiological Society, Society Experimental Biology and Medicine, Am. Institute Nutrition, American Association for the Advancement of Science, National Acad. Sciences,

Sigma Xi, Phi Kappa Phi, Phi Zeta. Home: 207 Texas Lane Ithaca New York 14850

WATSON, JAMES DEWEY, molecular biologist, educator; born Chicago, April 6, 1928; son of James Dewey and Jean (Mitchell) W.; married Elizabeth Lewis, 1968; children: Rufus Robert, Duncan James. Bachelor of Science, University Chicago, 1947, Doctor of Science, 1961; Doctor of Philosophy, Ind. University, 1950; Doctor of Science, 1963; Doctor of Laws, University Notre Dame, 1965; Doctor of Science, Long Island University, 1970, Adelphi University, 1972, Brandeis University, 1973, Albert Einstein College Medicine, 1974, Hofstra University, 1976, Harvard University, 1978, Rockefeller University, 1980, Clarkson College, 1981, State University of New York, 1983; Doctor of Science (honorary), University Buenos Aires, Argentina, 1986, Rutgers University, 1988. Research fellow National Research Council, University Copenhagen, 1950-51; National Foundation Infantile Paralysis fellow Cavendish Laboratory, Cambridge University, 1951-53; senior research fellow biology California Institute Tech., 1953-55; assistant professor biology Harvard, 1955-58, associate professor; 1958-61, professor; 1961-76; director Cold Spring Harbor Laboratory, 1968—. Author: Molecular Biology of the Gene, 1965, 2d edition, 1970, 3d edition, 1976, 4th edition, 1986, The Double Helix, 1968, (with John Tooze) The DNA Story, 1981; (with others) The Molecular Biology of the Cell, 1983; (with John Tooze and David Kurtz) Recombinant DNA: A Short Course, 1983. Hon. fellow Clare College, Cambridge University; Recipient (with F. H. C. Crick) John Collins Warren prize Massachusetts General Hospital, 1959; Eli Lilly award in biochemistry Am. Chemical Society, 1959; Albert Lasker prize Am. Pub. Health Association, 1960; with F.H.C. Crick Research Corp. prize, 1962; with F.H.C. Crick and M.H.F. Wilkins Nobel prize in medicine, 1962; Presidential medal of freedom, 1977. Member Royal Society (London), National Acad. Sciences (Carty medal 1971), Am. Philosophical Society, Danish Acad. Arts and Sciences, Am. Association Cancer Research, Am. Acad. Arts and Sci., Am. Society Biological Chemists. Home: Bungtown Road Cold Spring Harbor New York 11724 Office: Cold Spring Harbor Lab Post Office Box 100 Cold Spring Harbor New York 11724

WEBB, ROGER PAUL, electrical engineer, educator; born Cedar City, Utah, December 28, 1936; married, 1957. Bachelor of Electrical Engineering, University Utah, 1957; Master of Electrical Engineering, University Southern California, 1959; Doctor of Philosophy in Electrical Engineering, Georgia Institute Tech., 1964. Engineer Douglas Aircraft Corp., 1957-59; project engineer Sperry Phoenix Company, 1959-60; from assistant to associate professor Georgia Institute Tech., 1963-77, associate director, GA Power professor Electrical Engineering; 1978—; consultant Lockheed-Ga. Company, 1966—. Member Institute of Electrical and Electronics Engineers. Research in automatic control systems. Office: Ga Institute Tech Department Elec Engring Atlanta Georgia 30332-0183

WEDEPOHL, LEONHARD M., engineering educator; born Pretoria, Republic of South Africa, January 26,

1933; son of Martin Willie and Liselotte B.M. (Franz) W.; children: Martin, Graham. Bachelor of Science (England), Rand University, 1953; Doctor of Philosophy, University Manchester, England, 1957. Registered professional engineer, British Columbia. Planning engineer Escom, Johannesburg, Republic of South Africa, 1957-61; manager L.M. Erricson, Pretoria, Republic of South Africa, 1961-62; section leader Reyrolle, Newcastle, England, 1962-64; professor, head department Manchester University, 1964-74; dean engineering University Manitoba, Winnipeg, Can., 1974-79; dean applied sci. University British Columbia, Vancouver, Can., 1979-85, professor electrical engineering; 1985—; member Sci. Research Council, London, 1968-74; director Manitoba Hydro, Winipeg, 1965-69, British Columbia Hydro, Vancouver, 1980-84, British Columbia Sci. Council, 1981-84; vice president Quantic Laboratories, Winnipeg, 1986—; consultant Horizon Robotics, Saskatoon, 1986—; chairman implementation team Sci. Place Can., 1985. Contributor articles to sci. journals; patentee in field. Named Hon. Citizen City of Winnipeg, 1979. Fellow Institution Electrical Engineers (premium 1967); member Association Professional Engineers Manitoba, Association Professional Engineers British Columbia. Avocations: music; cross-country skiing; hiking. Office: U British Columbia, 2324 Main Hall, Vancouver, British Columbia Canada V6T 1W5

WEEKS, ROBERT ANDREW, materials science researcher, educator; born Birmingham, Alabama, August 23, 1924; son of William Andrew and Annie Bell (Hammond) W.; married Jane Sutherland, March 20, 1948; children—Kevin Dale, Robin Dee, Loren Hammond, Kerry Andrew. Bachelor of Science, Birmingham-So. University, 1947; Master of Science, University Tennessee, 1951; Doctor of Philosophy, Brown College, 1966. Senior physicist Union Carbide Corp., Oak Ridge, Tennessee, 1951-84; research professor material sci. Vanderbilt University, 1984—; distinguished visiting professor Am. University in Cairo, 1970-71; invited professor Ecole Polytechnic Federale de Lausanne, Switzerland, 1981; visiting professor Catholic University, Leuven, Belgium, 1983; consultant numerous private corporations and federal agys. Co-editor: Effects of Modes of Formation on Structure of Glass, 1985, 88; associate editor Journal Geophysical Research, 1968-74; editor Journal Non-Crystalline Solids, 1988—; contributor numerous articles to professional journals. Served with United States Army, 1943-46. Union Carbide fellow, 1964; Fulbright lecturer, 1980; research fellow Reading University, 1971. Fellow Am. Ceramic Society; member Am. Physical Society, Am. Ceramic Society (editorial committee journal 1968—), American Association for the Advancement of Science, Materials Research Society. Avocation: photography. Home: 2104 Tooles Bend Road Knoxville Tennessee 37922 Office: Vanderbilt U Post Office Box 1678 Nashville Tennessee 37235

WEERTMAN, JOHANNES, materials science educator; born Fairfield, Alabama, May 11, 1925; son of Roelof and Christina (van Vlaardingen) W.; married Julia Ann Randall, February 10, 1950; children: Julia Ann, Bruce Randall. Student, Pennsylvania State

College, 1943-44; Bachelor of Science, Carnegie Institute Tech. (now Carnegie Mellon University), 1948, Doctor of Science, 1951; postgraduate, Ecole Normale Superieure, Paris, France, 1951-52. Solid State physicist United States Naval Research Laboratory, Washington, 1952-58; consultant United States Naval Research Laboratory, 1960-67; sci. liaison officer United States Office Naval Research, Am. Embassy, London, England, 1958-59; faculty Northwestern University, Evanston, Illinois, 1959—; professor materials sci. department Northwestern University, 1961-68, chairman department; 1964-68, professor geological sciences department; 1963—, Walter P. Murphy professor materials sci.; 1968—; visiting professor geophysics California Institute Tech., 1964, Scott Polar Research Institute, Cambridge (England) University, 1970-71, Swiss Federal Institute Reactor Research, Switzerland, 1986; consultant United States Army Cold Regions Research and Engineering Laboratory, 1960-75, Oak Ridge National Laboratory, 1963-67, Los Alamos Sci. Laboratory, 1967—; co-editor materials sci. books MacMillan Company, 1962-76. Author: (with wife) Elementary Dislocation Theory, 1964; editorial board (with wife) Metal. Trans, 1967-75, Journal Glaciology, 1972—; asso. editor: (with wife) Journal Geophysical Research, 1973-75; contributor (with wife) articles to professional journals. Served with United States Military Corps, 1943-46. Honored with naming of Weertman Island in Antarctica.; Fulbright fellow, 1951-52; recipient Acta Metallurgica gold medal, 1980; Guggenheim fellow, 1970-71. Fellow Am. Society Metals, Am. Physical Society, Geological Society Am., Am. Geophysical Union (Horton award 1962); member National Acad. Engineering, Am. Geophysical Union, Am. Institute Mining, Metallurgical and Petroleum Engineers (Mathewson gold medal 1977), Am. Institute Physics, International Glaciological Society (Seligman Crystal award 1983), American Association for the Advancement of Science, Arctic Institute, Am. Quaternary Association, Explorers Club, Sigma Xi, Tau Beta Pi, Phi Kappa Phi, Alpha Sigma Mu, Pi Mu Epsilon. Club: Evanston Running. Home: 834 Lincoln St Evanston Illinois 60201

WEIMER, PAUL K(ESSLER), electrical engineer; born Wabash, Indiana, November 5, 1914; son of Claude W. and Eva V. (Kessler) W.; married Katherine E. Mounce, July 18, 1942; children: Katherine Weimer Lasslob, Barbara Weimer Blackwell, Patricia Weimer Hess. Bachelor of Arts, Manchester College, 1936, Doctor of Science (honorary), 1968; Master of Arts in Physics, University Kansas, 1938; Doctor of Philosophy in Physics, Ohio State University, 1942. Professor physical sci. Tabor College, 1937-39; research engineer David Sarnoff Research Center, Radio Corporation of America Laboratories, Princeton, New Jersey, 1942-65; fellow tech. staff David Sarnoff Research Center, Radio Corporation of America Laboratories, 1965-81, consultant; 1981—. Recipient TV Broadcasters award, 1946; Zworykin TV prize Institute Radio Engrs., 1959, Sarnoff award in sci. Radio Corporation of America, 1963, Outstanding Paper award Solid State Circuits Conference, 1963, 65, Kulturpreis award German Photographic Society, 1986, Albert Rose Electronic Imager of Year award, 1987. Fellow Institute of Electrical and Electronics Engineers (Morris Liebmann prize 1966); member National Acad. Engineering. Holder 88 patents in field; active in initial devel. of TV camera tubes, solid state devices. Home and Office: 112 Random Road Princeton New Jersey 08540

WEINBERG, ROBERT ALLAN, biochemist, educator; born Pittsburgh, November 11, 1942; son of Fritz E. and Lore (Reichhardt) W.; married Amy Shulman, November 19, 1976; children—Aron, Leah Rosa. Bachelor of Science, Massachusetts Institute of Technology, 1964, Ph.Doctor, 1969; Doctor of Philosophy (honorary), Northwestern University, 1984. Instructor Stillman College, Tuscaloosa, Alabama, 1965-66; research fellow Weizmann Institute, Rehovoth, Israel, 1969-70, Salk Institute, LaJolla, California, 1970-72; from assistant professor to professor biochemistry Massachusetts Institute of Technology, Cambridge, 1973—; member Whitehead Institute, Cambridge, 1984—. Contributor articles to professional journals. Recipient Bristol Myers award, 1984, Armand Hammer award, 1984. Member National Acad. Sci. (sci. award 1984). Avocations: genealogy; house building. Office: Whitehead Institute 9 Cambridge Center Cambridge Massachusetts 02142

WEINBERG, STEVEN, physicist, educator; born New York City, May 3, 1933; son of Fred and Eva (Israel) W.; married Louise Goldwasser, July 6, 1954; 1 child, Elizabeth. Bachelor of Arts, Cornell University, 1954; postgraduate, Copenhagen Institute Theoretical Physics, 1954-55; Doctor of Philosophy, Princeton University, 1957; Master of Arts (honorary), Harvard University, 1973; Doctor of Science (honorary), Knox College, 1978, University Chicago, 1978, University Rochester, 1979, Yale University, 1979, City University of New York, 1980, Clark University, 1982, Dartmouth College, 1984; Doctor of Philosophy (honorary), Weizmann Institute, 1985; Doctor of Literature (honorary), Washington College, 1985. Research associate, instructor Columbia University, 1957-59; research physicist Lawrence Radiation Laboratory, Berkeley, California, 1959-60; member faculty University Calif.-Berkeley, 1960-69, professor physics; 1964-69; visiting professor Massachusetts Institute of Technology, 1967-69, professor physics; 1969-73; Higgins professor physics Harvard University, 1973-83; senior scientist Smithsonian Astrophysical laboratory, 1973-83; Josey professor sci. University Tex.-Austin, 1982—; senior consultant Smithsonian Astrophysical Observatory, 1983—; consultant Institute Def. Analyses, Washington, 1960-73, Arms Control and Disarmament Agency, 1973; member President's Committee on National Medal of Sci., 1979-82, Council of Scholars, Library of Congress, 1983-85; senior adv. La Jolla Institute; chair in physics Collège de France, 1971; member National Research Council Committee on International Security and Arms Control, 1981; director Jerusalem Winter School Theoretical Physics, 1983—; member adv. council Texas SSC High Energy Research Facility, 1987, National Acad. Sciences Supercolliders Site Eval. committee, 1987-88; Silliman lecturer Yale University, 1977; Richtmeyer lecturer, 1974; Scott lecturer Cavendish Laboratory, 1975; Lauritsen Memorial lecturer California Institute Tech., 1979; Bethe lecturer Cornell University, 1979; de Shalit lecturer Weizman Institute, 1979; Einstein lecturer Israel Acad. Arts and Sciences, 1984; Sloan fellow, 1961-65; Loeb lecturer in physics Harvard University, 1966-67; Cherwell-Simon lecturer Oxford University, 1983; Bampton lecturer Columbia University, 1983; Morris Loeb visiting professor physics Harvard University, 1983—; Hilldale lecturer University Wisconsin, 1985; Clark lecturer University Tex.-Dallas, 1986; Dirac lecturer University Cambridge, 1986. Author: Gravitation and Cosmology: Principles and Applications of the General Theory of Relativity, 1972, The First Three Minutes: A Modern View of the Origin of the Universe, 1977, The Discovery of Subatomic Particles, 1982; co-author (with R. Feynman) Elementary Particles and the Laws of Physics, 1987; research and publications on elementary particles, quantum field theory, cosmology; co-editor, Cambridge University Press, monographs on math. physics; editorial board, Progress in Science Culture, University Chicago Press, series on theoretical astrophysics; member sci. book com. Sloan Foundation, 1985—; adv. board Issues in Science and Tech., 1984-87; member editorial board Journal Math. Physics, 1986—; board associate editors Nuclear Physics B. Board overseers SSC Accelerator, 1984-86; board advisers Santa Barbara Institute Theoretical Physics, 1983-86. Recipient J. Robert Oppenheimer memorial prize, 1973, recipient Dannie Heineman prize in math. physics, 1977, Am. Institute Physics-U.S. Steel Foundation sci. writing award, 1977, Nobel prize in physics, 1979, Elliott Cresson medal Franklin Institute, 1979. Member Am. Acad. Arts and Sciences (council), Am. Physical Society (past councilor at large, panel on faculty positions committee on status of women in physics), National Acad. Sci. (supercollider site evaluation committee 1987—), Einstein Archives (adv. board 19888—), International Astronomical Union, Council Foreign Relations, Am. Philosophical Socity, Royal Society London (foreign member), Am. Mediaeval Acad., History of Sci. Society, Philosophical Society Texas. Clubs: Saturday (Boston); Headliners, Tuesday (Austin); Cambridge Sci. Society.

WEINSTEIN, GEORGE WILLIAM, ophthalmology educator; born East Orange, New Jersey, January 26, 1935; son of Henry J. and Irma C. (Klein) W.; married Sheila Valerie Wohlreich, June 20, 1957; children: Bruce David, Elizabeth Joyce, Rachel Andrea. Bachelor of Arts, University Pennsylvania, 1955; Doctor of Medicine, State University of New York, Brooklyn, 1959. Diplomate Am. Board Ophthalmology (bd. dirs. 1981—). Intern then resident in ophthalmology Kings County Hospital, Brooklyn, 1959-63; assistant professor ophthalmology Johns Hopkins University, Baltimore, 1967-70; head ophthalmology department University Texas, San Antonio, 1970-80; professor, Jane McDermott Shott chairman West Virginia University, Morgantown, 1980—; chairman Long Range Planning committee, 1986—. Author: Key Facts in Ophthalmology, 1984; editor: Open Angle Glaucoma, 1986; editor Ophthalmic Surgery journal, 1971-81, Current Opinion in Opthalmology journal, 1988—; contributor articles to professional journals. Served to lieutenant commander United States Public Health Service, 1963-65. Senior International fellow Fogarty International Center National Institutes of Health, 1987. Member American College of Surgeons (board govs. 1983-85, board regents 1987—), Association University Profs. of Ophthalmology (president 1986-87), Am. Acad. Ophthalmology (board directors 1980—, pub. and professional secretary 1981—, Honor award, Senior Honor award), Alpha Omega Alpha (faculty 1987). Jewish. Avocations: music, photography, tennis, basketball. Home: 28 Lakeview Dr Morgantown West Virginia 26505 Office: W Va U College Medicine Department Ophthalmology Morgantown West Virginia 26506

WEINSTEIN, GERALD D., dermatology educator; born New York City, October 13, 1936; married Marcia Z. Weinstein; children: Jeff, Jon, Debbie. Bachelor of Arts, University Pennsylvania, 1957, Doctor of Medicine, 1961. Diplomate Am. Board Dermatology. Intern Los Angeles County General Hospital, 1961-62; clinical associate dermatology branch National Cancer Institution National Institutes of Health, Bethesda, Maryland, 1962-64; resident Department Dermatology University Miami, Florida, 1964-65, assistant professor; 1966-71, associate professor; 1971-74, professor; 1975-79; professor University California, Irvine, 1979—, acting dean College Medicine; 1985-87; attending staff Veteran's Administration Medical Center, Long Beach, California, 1979—, UCI Medical Center, Orange, California, 1979—, St. Joseph Hospital, Orange, 1980—; consultant Naval Regional Medical Center, San Diego, 1980—. Contributor articles to professional journals, chapters to books. Special postdoctoral fellow National Institutes of Health, 1965-67; co-recipient Award for Psoriasis Research Taub International Memorial, 1971. Member Am. Acad. Dermatology (chairman task force on psoriasis 1986—, board directors 1984—). Office: University of California Irvine California College of Medicine Office of the Dean Irvine California 92717

WEISFELDT, MYRON LEE, physician, educator; born Milwaukee, April 25, 1940; son of Simon Charles and Sophia (Price) W.; married Linda Nan Zaremski, December 29, 1963; children—Ellyn Joy, Lisa Janel, Sara Michelle. Bachelor of Arts, Johns Hopkins University, 1962, Doctor of Medicine, 1965. Intern and resident Columbia-Presbyn. Medical Center, New York City, 1965-67; fellow in cardiology Massachusetts General Hospital, Boston, 1970-72; assistant professor medicine Johns Hopkins University, Baltimore, 1972-78, professor medicine; 1978—, Robert L. Levy professor cardiology; 1979—; director cardiology Johns Hopkins Medical Institute, Baltimore, 1975—, Peter Belfer Laboratory for Johns Hopkins, Ischemic Heart Disease Special Center Research, 1977—; board of directors Am. Heart Association, 1984—, pres.-elect, 1988-89; cardiology adv. committee National Heart, Lung and Blood Institute, 1986—, chairman 1988—. Editor: The Aging Heart, 1980; editorial board Journal Clin. Investigation, 1984-88, Circulation, 1980-86, 1988—, Journal Am. College Cardiology, 1987—, Journal Molecular and Cellular Cardiology, 1975-80, 1986—, Circulation Research, 1988—. Served with United States

Public Health Service, 1967-69. Grantee National Institutes of Health, 1977—. Member Association University Cardiologists, Am. Society Clinical Investigation, Association Am. Physicians, Phi Beta Kappa, Alpha Omega Alpha. Jewish. Club: Interurban Clin. Home: 2112 Webb Lane Baltimore Maryland 21209 Office: Johns Hopkins Hosp Blalock 536 Baltimore Maryland 21205

WEISSKOPF, VICTOR FREDERICK, physicist; born Vienna, Austria, September 19, 1908; came to United States, 1937, naturalized, 1942; son of Emil and Martha (Gut) W.; married Ellen Tvede, September 5, 1934; children: Thomas Emil, Karen Louise. Doctor of Philosophy, University Goettingen, Germany, 1931. Research associate University Copenhagen, Denmark, 1932-34, Institute of Tech., Zûrich, Switzerland, 1934-37; assistant professor physics University Rochester, New York, 1937-43; with Manhattan Project, Los Alamos, N.M., 1943-46; professor physics Massachusetts Institute Tech., 1946-60; director general European Organization for Nuclear Research, Geneva, Switzerland, 1961-65; Institute professor Massachusetts Institute Tech., 1965—; chairman high energy physics adv. panel Atomic Energy Commission, 1967-73. Author: (with J. Blatt) Theoretical Nuclear Physics, 1952, Knowledge and Wonder, 1962, Physics in the Twentieth Century, 1972; (with K. Gottfried) Concepts of Particle Physics, 1984; articles on nuclear physics, quantum theory, radiation theory, etc. in science journals. Recipient Max Planck medal Germany, 1956, Hi Majorana award, 1970, G. Gamov award, 1971, Boris Pregel award, 1971, Prix Mondial Cino

del Duca France, 1972, L. Boltzmann prize Austria, 1977, National Medal of Sci. U.S., 1980, Wolf prize, Jerusalem, 1982, Enrico Fermi Award, U.S. Department of Energy, 1988. Fellow Am. Physical Society (president 1960); member National Acad. Sciences, Am. Acad. Arts and Sciences (president 1975-79), French Academie des Sciences (corr.), Austrian Acad. Sci. (corr.), Danish Acad. Sci. (corr.), Bavarian Acad. Sci. (corr.), Scottish Acad. Sci. (corr.), Soviet Acad. Sci. (corr., Pontifical Acad. Sci.), Spanish Acad. Sci. (corr.), German Acad. Sci. Home: 36 Arlington St Cambridge Massachusetts 02140

WELBER, IRWIN, research laboratory executive; born 1927; married. Bachelor of Science, Union College, 1948; Master of Electrical Engineering, Rensselaer Polytechnic Institute, 1950. With American Telephone and Telegraph Company Bell Laboratories, Murray Hill, New Jersey, 1950-86, vice president transmission systems; 1981; president Sandia National Laboratories, Albuquerque, 1986—, also board of directors. Office: Sandia National Labs Office President Albuquerque New Mexico 87185

WELCH, ASHLEY JAMES, engineering educator; born Fort Worth, May 3, 1933; married, 1952; 3 children. Bachelor of Science, Texas Tech University, 1955; Master of Science, Southern Methodist University, 1959; Doctor of Philosophy in Electrical Engineering, Rice University, 1964. Aerophys. engineer General Dynamics, Fort Worth, 1957-60; instructor electrical engineering Rice University, 1960-64, from assistant to associate professor; 1964-74, director engineering computing facility; 1970-71, director biomed. engineering program; 1971-75; professor electrical and biomed. engineering University Texas, Austin, 1975—, Marion East Forsman Centennial professor engineering; 1985—. Member Institute of Electrical and Electronics Engineers, Association Research Vision and Opthalmology. Research in laser-tissue interaction, application of lasers in medicine. Office: University of Texas at Austin Department of Elec and Computer Engring Austin Texas 78712

WELLER, THOMAS HUCKLE, physician, emeritus educator; born Ann Arbor, Michigan, June 15, 1915; son of Carl V. and Elsie A. (Huckle) W.; married Kathleen R. Fahey, August 18, 1945; children: Peter Fahey, Nancy Kathleen, Robert Andrew, Janet Louise. Bachelor of Arts, University Michigan, 1936; Master of Science, 1937, Doctor of Laws (honorary), 1956; Doctor of Medicine, Harvard, 1940; Doctor of Science, Gustavus Adolphus University, 1975, University Massachusetts, 1985; Doctor of Humane Letters, Lowell University, 1977. Diplomate Am. Board Pediatrics. Teaching fellow bacteriology Harvard Medical School, 1940-41, research fellow tropical medicine, pediatrics; 1947-48, instructor comparative pathology, tropical medicine; 1948-49, assistant professor tropical pub. health School Pub. Health; 1949-50, associate professor; 1950-54, Richard Pearson Strong professor tropical pub. health; 1954-85, professor emeritus; 1985—, head department; 1954-81; intern bacteriology and pathology Children's Hospital, Boston, 1941; intern medicine Children's Hospital, 1942, assistant resident medicine; 1946,

assistant director research div. infectious diseases; 1949-55; member commission parasitic diseases Armed Forces Epidemiological Board, 1953-72, director; 1953-59; charge parasitology, bacteriology, virology sections Antilles Department Medical Laboratory, Puerto Rico. Author sci. papers. Served to major Medical Corps Army of the United States, 1942-46. Recipient E. Mead Johnson award for development tissue culture procedures in study virus diseases Am. Acad. Pediatrics, 1953; Kimble Methodology award, 1954; Nobel prize in physiology and medicine, 1954; George Ledlie prize, 1963; Weinstein Cerebral Palsy award, 1973; Stern Symposium honoree, 1972; Bristol award Infectious Diseases Society Am., 1980; Gold medal and diploma of honor University Costa Rica, 1984. Fellow Am. Acad. Arts and Sciences; member Harvey Society, American Medical Association, Am. Society Parasitologists, Am., Royal socs. tropical medicine and hygiene, Am. Pub. Health Association, American Association for the Advancement of Science, Am. Epidemiological Society, National Acad. Sciences, Am. Pediatric Society, Association Am. Physicians, Society Experimental Biology and Medicine, Am. Association Immunologists. Society Pediatric Research, Phi Beta Kappa., Sigma Xi, Alpha Omega Alpha. Home and Office: 56 Winding River Road Needham Massachusetts 02192

WESCOTT, ROGER WILLIAMS, anthropology educator; born Philadelphia, April 28, 1925; son of Ralph Wesley and Marion (Sturges-Jones) W.; married Hilja J. Brigadier, April 11, 1964; children: Walter, Wayne. Graduate, Phillips Exeter

Academy, 1942; Bachelor of Arts summa cum laude, Princeton University, 1945, Master of Arts, 1947, Doctor of Philosophy, 1948; Master of Literature, Oxford University, 1952. Assistant professor history and human relations Boston University and Massachusetts Institute Tech., 1953-57; associate professor English and social sci., also director African language program Michigan State University, 1957-62; professor anthropology and history Southern Connecticut State College, 1962-66; professor, chairman anthropology and linguistics Drew University, Madison, New Jersey, 1966—; Presidential professor Colorado School Mines, 1980-81; first holder endowed Chair of Excellence in Humanities University Tennessee, 1988-89; foreign language consultant United States Office Education, 1961; president School Living, Brookville, Ohio, 1962-65; executive director Institute Exploratory Education, New York City, 1963-66; Korzybski lecturer Institute General Semantics, New York City, 1976; forensic linguist New Jersey State Cts., 1982-83; host Other Views, New Jersey Cable TV, Trenton, 1985—. Author: A Comparative Grammar of Albanian, 1955, Introductory Ibo, 1961, A Bini Grammar, 1963, An Outline of Anthropology, 1965, The Divine Animal, 1969, Language Origins, 1974, Visions, 1975, Sound and Sense, 1980, also poems and articles. Rhodes scholar, 1948-50; Ford fellow, 1955-56; Am. Council Learned Socs. scholar, 1951-52. Fellow Am. Anthropological Association, American Association for the Advancement of Science, African Studies Association; member Association for Poetry Therapy, International Society Comparative Study of Civilizations (co-founder, 1st vice president), Linguistic Association Can. and United States (president 1976-77), International Linguistic Association, Committee for the Future, Phi Beta Kappa. Home: 11 Green Hill Road Madison New Jersey 07940

WESSELLS, NORMAN KEITH, biologist, educator, university administrator; born Jersey City, May 11, 1932; son of Norman Wesley and Grace Mahan Wessells; married Catherine Pyne Briggs; children: Christopher, Stephen, Philip, Colin. Bachelor of Science, Yale University, 1954, Doctor of Philosophy, 1960. Assistant professor biology Stanford (California) University, 1962-65, associate professor; 1965-70, professor; 1971—, chairman biological sci.; 1972-78; acting director Hopkins Marine Station, 1972-75, associate dean humanities and sciences; 1977-81, dean; 1981-88; professor biology, provost, vice president acad. affairs University Oregon, Eugene, 1988—. Author: (with F. Wilt) Methods in Developmental Biology, 1965, Vertebrates: Adaptations, 1970, Vertebrates: A Laboratory Text, 1976, 81, Tissue Interactions and Development, 1977, Vertebrates; Adaptations; Vertebrates: Physiology, 1979, (with S. Subtelny) The Cell Surface, 1980, (with J. Hopson) Biology, 1988. Served with United States Naval Reserve, 1954-56. Am. Cancer Society postdoctoral fellow, 1960-62; Am. Cancer Society scholar cancer research, 1966-69; Guggenheim fellow, 1976-77. Member Society Devel. Biology (president 1979-80), Am. Society Zoologist. Office: U Oregon Office of Provost Johnson Hall Eugene Oregon 97403

WEST, ROBERT CULBERTSON, chemistry educator; born Glen Ridge, New Jersey, March 18, 1928; son of Robert C. and Constance (MacKinnon) W.; children: David Russell, Arthur Scott, Derek. Bachelor of Arts, Cornell University, 1950; Master of Arts, Harvard University, 1952, Doctor of Philosophy, 1954. Assistant professor Lehigh University, 1954-56; member faculty University Wis.-Madison, 1956—, professor chemistry; 1963—, Eugene G. Rochow professor; 1980; adj. professor Southern Oregon State College, 1984—; industrial and government consultant, 1961—; Abbott lecturer University North Dakota, 1964; Fulbright lecturer Kyoto University, 1964-65; visiting professor University Würzburg, 1968-69, Haile Selassie I University, 1972, University Calif.-Santa Cruz, 1977, University Utah, 1981, Institute Chemical Physics Chinese Acad. Sci., 1984, Justus Liebigs University, Giessen, Federal Republic of Germany; Jean Day Memorial lecturer Rutgers University, 1973; Japan Society for Promotion Sci. visiting professor Tohoku University, 1976, Gunma University, 1987; Lady Davis visiting professor Hebrew University, 1979; Cecil and Ida Green honors professor Texas Christian University, 1983; Karcher lecturer University Oklahoma, 1986; Broberg lecturer North Dakota State University, 1986; Xerox lecturer University British Columbia, 1986. Co-editor: Advances in Organometallic Chemistry, Volumes I-XXIX, 1964—, Organometallic Chemistry—A Monograph Series, 1968—; contributor articles to professional journals. President Madison Community School, 1970-71; board of directors Women's Medical Fund, 1971—, Zero Population Growth, 1980—; board of directors, vice president Protect Abortion Rights Incorporated, 1980; lay minister Prairie Unitarian Universalist Society, 1982. Recipient F.S. Kipping award, 1970; Amoco Distinguished Teaching award, 1974; Outstanding Sci. Innovator award Sci. Digest, 1985; Chemical Pioneering award Am. Institute Chemists, 1988. Member Am. Chemical Society, Chemical Society (London), Japan Chemical Society, American Association for the Advancement of Science, Wisconsin Acad. Sci. Home: 305 Nautilus Dr Madison Wisconsin 53705

WESTHEIMER, FRANK HENRY, chemist, educator; born Baltimore, January 15, 1912; son of Henry Ferdinand and Carrie (Burgunder) W.; married Jeanne Friedmann, August 31, 1937; children: Ruth Susan, Ellen. Bachelor of Arts, Dartmouth College, 1932, Doctor of Science (honorary), 1961; Master of Arts, Harvard University, 1933, Doctor of Philosophy, 1935; Doctor of Science (honorary), University Chicago, 1973, University Cincinnati, 1976, Tufts University, 1978, University North Carolina, 1983, Bard College, 1983, Weizmann Institute, 1987, University Illinois at Chicago, 1988. Instructor chemistry University Chicago, 1936-41, assistant professor; 1941-44, associate professor; 1946-48, professor chemistry; 1948-53; visiting professor Harvard, 1953-54, professor chemistry; 1954—, chairman department; 1959-62; Overseas fellow Churchill College, University Cambridge, England, 1962-63; member President's Sci. Adv. Committee, 1967-70; research supervisor Explosives Research Laboratory, National Def. Research Committee, 1944-45; chairman committee survey chemistry National Acad. Sciences, 1964-65. Associate editor Journal Chemical Physics, 1942-44, 52-54; editorial board Journal Am. Chemical Soc, 1960-69, Procs. National Acad. Scis., 1983—; contributor articles to professional journals. Recipient Naval Ordnance Development award, 1946, Army-Navy cert. of appreciation, 1948, James Flack Norris award in phys.-organic chemistry, 1970, Willard Gibbs medal, 1970, Theodore W. Richards medal, 1976; award in chemical scis. National Acad. Sci., 1980, Richard Kokes award, 1980, Charles Frederick Chandler medal, 1980, Rosenstiel award, 1981, Nichols medal, 1982, Robert A. Welch award, 1982, Ingold medal, 1983, Cope award, 1982, National Medal of Sci., 1986, Paracelsus medal, 1988, Priestley medal, 1988; fellow Columbia University National Research Council, 1935-36, Guggenheim Foundation, 1962-63, Fulbright-Hays Foundation, 1974. Member National Acad. Sci. (council 1971-75, 76-79), Am. Philosophical Society (council 1981-84), Am. Acad. Arts and Sciences (secretary 1985—), Royal Society (foreign member). Home: 3 Berkeley St Cambridge Massachusetts 02138

WETHERILL, GEORGE WEST, geophysicist; born Philadelphia, August 12, 1925; son of George West and Leah Victoria (Hardwick) W.; married Phyllis May Steiss, June 17, 1950; children: Rachel, George, Sarah. Bachelor of Philosophy, University Chicago, 1948, Bachelor of Science in Physics, 1949, Master of Science, 1951, Doctor of Philosophy in Physics, 1953. Member staff department terrestrial magnetism Carnegie Institute, Washington, 1953-60; professor geophysics and geology University of California at Los Angeles, 1960-75, chairman department planetary and space sci.; 1968-72; director department terrestrial magnetism Carnegie Institute, Washington, 1975—; consultant National Aeronautics and Space Administration, National Science Foundation, National Acad. Sci. Contributor articles to professional journals. Served with United States Navy, 1943-46. Recipient G.K. Gilbert award Geol. Society Am., 1984, Professional Achievement Citation University Chicago Alumni Association, 1985. Fellow Am. Acad. Arts and Sciences, Am. Geophysical Union (president planetology section 1970-72), Meteoritical Society (vice president 1971-74, 81-83, president 1983-85, Leonard medal 1981); member Geochem. Society (vice president 1973-74, president 1974-75), International Association Geochem. and Cosmochemistry (president 1977-80), International Astronomical Union, Am. Astronomical Society Div. Planetary Sciences and Div. Dynamic Astronomy (G.P. Kuiper prize 1986), National Acad. Sciences, Society Free Quakers, International Society for Study of Origin of Life. Episcopalian. Office: 5241 Broad Branch Road Northwest Washington District of Columbia 20015

WETHINGTON, JOHN ABNER, JR., educator; born Tallahassee, April 18, 1921; son of John Abner and Mary McQueen (Hale) W.; married Kathryn Kemp Greene, August 19, 1943; 1 son, John Abner III. Bachelor of Arts, Emory University, 1942, Master of Arts, 1943; Doctor of Philosophy, Northwestern University, 1950. Visiting research assistant Princeton, 1943-44; chemist Fercleve Corp., Oak

Ridge, 1944-46; chemist to senior chemist Oak Ridge National Laboratory, 1949-53; assistant professor to professor nuclear engineering University Florida, 1953-85, professor emeritus; 1985—; on leave as fellow Lawrence Livermore Laboratory, California, 1971-72; visiting scientist Puerto Rico Nuclear Center, 1962-63, Oak Ridge National Laboratory, 1979-80; United States del. to Radiation Congress, Haregate, England, 1963, 2d International Conference Peaceful Uses of Atomic Energy, Switzerland, 1958; faculty participant Oak Ridge School Reactor Tech., 1957-58. Contributor articles to professional journals. Fellow American Association for the Advancement of Science; member Am. Chemical Society, Am. Nuclear Society, Phi Beta Kappa, Sigma Xi, Alpha Chi Sigma. Democrat. Methodist. Home: 109 Northwest 22d Dr Gainesville Florida 32605

WETZEL, ROBERT GEORGE, botanist; born Ann Arbor, Michigan, August 16, 1936; son of Wilhelm and Eugenia (Wagner) W.; married Carol Ann Andree, August 9, 1959; children: Paul Robert, Pamela Jeanette, Timothy Mark, Kristina Marie. Bachelor of Science, University Michigan, 1958, Master of Science, 1959; Doctor of Philosophy, University California at Davis, 1962; Doctor of Philosophy (honorary), University Uppsala (Sweden), 1984. Research associate Ind. University, Bloomington, 1962-65; assistant professor botany Michigan State University, Hickory Corners, 1965-68; associate professor Michigan State University, 1968-71, professor; 1971-86; professor University Michigan, Ann Arbor, 1986—; consultant International Biological Program,

London, 1967-75; chairman International Seagrass Commission, 1974-75; founding member International Lake Environment Committee, 1986—. Author: Limnology, 1975, 2d rev. edition, 1983, Limnological Analyses, 1979, To Quench Our Thirst: Present and Future Freshwater Resources of the United States, 1983; editor: Periphyton of Freshwater Ecosystems, 1983; contributor numerous articles on ecology and freshwater biol. systems to professional journals; member editorial board: Aquatic Botany, 1975—. Served with United States Naval Reserve, 1954-62. Recipient First T. Erlander National professorship Swedish National Research Council and University Uppsala, 1982-83; Atomic Energy Commission grantee, 1965-75; National Science Foundation grantee, 1962—; Energy Research and Development Administration grantee, 1975-77; Department Energy grantee, 1978—. Fellow American Association for the Advancement of Science; member Royal Danish Acad. Sciences (elected foreign member 1986), Am. Institute Biological Sciences, Am. Society Limnology and Oceanography (editorial board 1971-74, vice president 1979-80, president 1980-81), Aquatic Plant Management Society, Ecological Society Am., International Association Ecology, Freshwater Biological Association United Kingdom, International Association Theoretical and Applied Limnology (general secretary, treasurer 1968—), International Phycological Society, Michigan Acad. Sciences, North America Benthological Society, Phycological Society Am., International Association Great Lakes Research, Japanese Society Limnology, Michigan Botanical

Society, International Association Aquatic Vascular Plant Biologists (founder, president 1979—), Sigma Xi, Phi Sigma. Home: 5661 Tanglewood Dr Ann Arbor Michigan 48105 Office: U Michigan Department Biology Ann Arbor Michigan 48109

WEYMANN, RAY J., astronomy educator; born Los Angeles, December 2, 1934; son of August Charles and Lucile (Rausch) W.; married Barbara Lee McDermott, June 16, 1956; children—Lynn Elizabeth, Catherine Ann, Steven Christopher. Bachelor of Science, California Institute Tech., Pasadena, 1956; Doctor of Philosophy, Princeton University, 1959. Postdoctoral fellow California Institute Tech., Pasadena, 1959-61; assistant professor University Arizona, Tucson, 1961-63, associate professor; 1964-67, professor astronomy; 1967—, director Steward Observatory; 1970-75; professor astronomy University Arizona, Tuscon, 1975-86; assistant professor University of California at Los Angeles, 1963-64; director Mount Wilson and Las Campanas Observatories, 1986—. Contributor articles to professional journals. Member Am. Astronomical Society (vice president 1981-83), Astronomical Society Pacific (president 1973-75), Am. Acad. Arts and Sci., National Acad. Sciences. Office: Carnegie Institute Washington Mt Wilson & Las Campanas Obs 813 Santa Barbara St Pasadena California 91101

WHEELER, JOHN ARCHIBALD, scientist; born Jacksonville, Florida, July 9, 1911; son of Joseph Lewis and Mabel (Archibald) W.; married Janette Hegner, June 10, 1935; children: Isabel Letitia Wheeler Ufford, James English, Alison Christie Wheeler Lahnston. Doctor of Philosophy, Johns Hopkins University, 1933, Doctor of Laws (honorary), 1977; Doctor of Science (honorary), Western Reserve University, 1958, University North Carolina, 1959, University Pennsylvania, 1968, Middlebury College, 1969, Rutgers University, 1969, Yeshiva University, 1973, Yale University, 1974, University Uppsala, 1975, University Maryland, 1977, Gustavus Adolphus University, 1981, Catholic University Am., 1982, University Newcastle-upon-Tyne, 1983, Princeton University, 1986; Doctor of Letters (honorary), Drexel University, 1987. National Research Council fellow New York, Copenhagen, 1933-35; assistant professor physics University North Carolina, 1935-38; assistant professor physics Princeton University, 1938-42, associate professor; 1945-47, professor; 1947-76, Joseph Henry professor physics; 1966-76, Joseph Henry professor physics emeritus; 1976—; professor physics, director Center for Theoretical Physics University Texas, Austin, 1976-86, Ashbel Smith professor; 1979-86, Blumberg professor; 1981-86, Smith and Blumberg professor emeritus; 1986—; consultant and physicist on atomic energy projects Princeton University, 1939-42, University Chicago, 1942, E.I. duPont de Nemours & Company, Wilmington, Del., and Richland, Washington, 1943-45, Los Alamos, 1950-53; director project Matterhorn Princeton University, 1951-53; Guggenheim fellow, Paris and Copenhagen, 1949-50; summer lecturer University Michigan, University Chicago, Columbia University; Lorentz professor University Leiden, 1956; Fulbright professor Kyoto University, 1962; 1st visiting fellow Clare College

Cambridge University, 1964; Ritchie lecturer Edinburgh, 1958; visiting professor University Calif.-Berkeley, 1960; Battelle professor University Washington, 1975; sci. adviser United States Senate del. to 3d annual conference North Atlantic Treaty Organization Parliamentarians, Paris, 1957; member adv. committee Oak Ridge National Laboratory, 1957-65, University California, Los Alamos and Livermore, 1972-77; vice president International Union Physics, 1951-54; chairman joint committee Am. Physical Society and Am. Philosophical Society on history theoretical physics in 20th Century, 1960-72; sci. adv. board United States Air Force, 1961, 62; chairman Department Def. Advanced Research Projects Agency Project 137, 1958; member United States General Adv. Committee Arms Control and Disarmament, 1969-72, 74-77. Author or co-author: Geometrodynamics, 1962, Gravitation Theory and Gravitational Collapse, 1965, Spacetime Physics, 1966, Einsteins Vision, 1968, Gravitation, 1973, Black Holes, Gravitational Waves and Cosmology, 1974, Frontiers of Time, 1979, (with W. Zurek) Quantum Theory and Measurement, 1983; contributor 328 articles to professional journals. Trustee Battelle Memorial Institute, 1959—. Recipient A. Cressy Morrison prize New York Acad. Sci. for work on nuclear physics, 1947; Albert Einstein prize Strauss Foundation, 1965; Enrico Fermi award Atomic Energy Commission, 1968; Franklin medal Franklin Institute, 1969; National medal of Sci., 1971; Herzfeld award, 1975; Outstanding Graduate Teaching award University Texas, 1981; Niels Bohr International Gold medal, 1982; Oersted medal Am. Association Physics Teachers, 1983,

J. Robert Oppenheimer memorial prize, 1984. Fellow American Association for the Advancement of Science (director 1965-68), Am. Physical Society (president 1966); member Am. Math Society, International Astronomical Union, Am. Acad. Arts and Sciences, National Academy of Sciences, Am. Philosophical Society (councillor 1963-66, 76-79, vice president 1971-73), Royal Danish Acad. Sciences, Royal Acad. Sci. (Uppsala, Sweden), l'Académie Internationale de Philosophie des Sciences (vice president 1987—), International Union Physics (vice president 1951-54), Phi Beta Kappa, Sigma Xi. Unitarian (trustee 1965). Office: Princeton U Princeton New Jersey 08544

WHINNERY, JOHN ROY, electrical engineering educator; born Read, Colorado, July 26, 1916; son of Ralph V. and Edith Mable (Bent) W.; married Patricia Barry, September 17, 1944; children—Carol Joanne, Catherine, Barbara. Bachelor of Science in Electrical Engineering, University California at Berkeley, 1937, Doctor of Philosophy, 1948. With General Electric Company, 1937-46; part-time lecturer Union College, Schenectady, 1945-46; associate professor electrical engineering University Calif.-Berkeley, 1946-52, professor, vice chairman div. electrical engineering; 1952-56, chairman; 1956-59; dean College Engineering University Calif-Berkeley, 1959-63, professor electrical engineering; 1963-80, University professor College Engineering; 1980—; visiting member tech. staff. Bell Telephone Laboratories, 1963-64; research sci. electron tubes Hughes Aircraft Company, Culver City, 1951-52. Author: (with Simon Ramo) Fields and

Waves in Modern Radio, 1944, 2d edition (with Ramo and Van Duzer), 1985, (with D. O. Pederson and J. J. Studer) Introduction to Electronic Systems, Circuits and Devices; also tech. articles. Chairman Commission Engring. Education, 1966-68; member sci. and tech. committee Manned Space Flight, National Aeronautics and Space Administration, 1963-69; member President's Committee on National Sci. Medal, 1970-73, 79-80; standing committee controlled thermonuclear research Atomic Energy Commission, 1970-73.

Recipient Education medal Institute of Electrical and Electronic Engineers, 1967, Lamme medal Am. Society Engineering Education, 1975; Microwave Career award Institute of Electrical and Electronic Engineers Microwave Theory and Techniques Society, 1977; Engring Alumni award University California at Berkeley, 1980; named to Hall of Fame Modesto High School (California), 1983; Guggenheim fellow, 1959. Fellow I.R.E. (director 1956-59), Optical Society Am., Am. Acad. Arts and Sciences; member National Acad. Engineering (Founders award 1986), National Acad. Sciences, Institute of Electrical and Electronics Engineers (life member, director 1969-71, secretary 1971, Centennial medal 1984, Medal of Honor 1985), Phi Beta Kappa, Sigma Xi, Tau Beta Pi, Eta Kappa Nu. Congregationalist. Home: One Daphne Court Orinda California 94563 Office: U California Berkeley California 94720

WHIPPLE, FRED LAWRENCE, astronomer; born Red Oak, Iowa, November 5, 1906; son of Harry Lawrence and Celestia (MacFarl) W.; married Dorothy Woods, 1928 (divorced 1935); 1 son, Earle Raymond; married Babette F. Samelson, August 20, 1946; children: Dorothy Sandra, Laura. Student, Occidental College, 1923-24; Bachelor of Arts, University of California at Los Angeles, 1927, Doctor of Philosophy, at Berkeley, 1931; Master of Arts (honorary), Harvard, 1945; Doctor of Science, Am. International College, 1958; Doctor of Literature (honorary), Northeastern University, 1961; Doctor of Science (honorary), Temple University, 1961, University Arizona, 1979; Doctor of Laws (honorary), C.W. Post College, Long Island University, 1962. Teaching fellow University California at Berkeley, 1927-29; Lick Observatory fellow 1930-31; instructor Stanford, summer 1929, University California, summer 1931; staff member Harvard Observatory, 1931—; instructor Harvard, 1932-38, lecturer; 1938-45; research associate Radio Research Laboratory, 1942-45, associate professor astronomy; 1945-50, professor astronomy; 1950—, chairman department; 1949-56, Phillips professor astronomy; 1968-77; director Smithsonian Astrophysical Observatory, 1955-73, senior scientist, 1973—; member Rocket Research Panel United States, 1946-57; United States subcom National Aeronautics and Space Administration, 1946-52, United States Research and Devel. Board Panel, 1947-52; chairman Tech. Panel on Rocketry; member Tech. Panel on Earth Satellite Program; other committees International Geophysical Year, 1955-59; member, past officer International Astronomical Union; consultant missions to United Kingdom and Mediterranean Theatre of Operation, 1944; del. Inter-Am. Astrophysical Congress, Mexico, 1942; active leader project on Upper-Atmospheric Research via Meteor Photog. sponsored by Bureau Ordnance, United States Navy, 1946-51; by Bureau Ordnance, United States Navy (Office Naval Research), 1951-57, United States Air Force, 1948-62; member committee meteorology, space sci. board, committee on atmospheric sics. National Acad. Scis.-NRC, 1958-65; project director Harvard Radio Meteor Project, 1958—; adviser Sci. Adv. Board, United States Air Force, 1963-67; special consultant committee Sci. and Astronautics United States House Representatives, 1960-73; chairman Gordon Research Confs., 1963; director Optical Satellite Tracking Project, National Aeronautics and Space Administration, 1958-73; project director Orbiting Astronomical Observatory, 1958-72; director Meteorite Photography and Recovery Program, 1962-73, consultant planetary atmospheres, 1962-69; member space sciences working group on Orbiting Astronomical Observatories, 1959-70; chairman sci. council geodetic uses artifical satellites Committee Space Research, 1965—. Author: Earth, Moon and Planets, rev. edit, 1968, Orbiting The Sun: Planets and Satellites of The Solar System; co-author: Survey of the Universe; Contributor: sci. papers on astron. and upper atmosphere to Encyclopedia Brit; magazines, other publications; Asso. editor: Astronomical Jour, 1954-56, 64—; editor: Smithsonian Contributions to Astrophysics, 1956-73, Planetary and Space Science, 1958—, Science Revs, 1961—; editorial board: Earth and Planetary Science Letters; inventor tanometer, meteor bumper; a developer window as radar countermeasure, 1944. Decorated commander Order of Merit for research and invention, Esnault-Pelterie award France; recipient Donohue medals for ind. discovery of 6 new comets; Presidential Cert. of Merit for sci. work during World War II; J. Lawrence Smith medal National Acad. Sciences for research on meteors, 1949; medal for astronomical research University Liege, 1960; Space Flight award Am. Astronautical Society, 1961; Distinguished Federal Civilian Service award, 1963; Space Pioneers medallion for contributions to federal space program, 1968; Public Service award for contributions to OAO2 development National Aeronautics and Space Administration, 1969; Leonard medal Meteoritical Society, 1970; Kepler medal American Association for the Advancement of Science, 1971; Career Service award National Civil Service League, 1972; Henry medal Smithsonian Institution, 1973; Alumnus of Year Achievement award UCLA, 1976; Golden Plate award Am. Acad. Achievement, 1981; Gold medal Royal Astronomical Society, 1983; Bruce Medal, Astronomical Society Pacific, 1986; Benjamin Franklin fellow Royal Society Arts, London, 1968—; depicted on postal stamp of Mauritania, 1986. Fellow Am. Astronomical Society (vice president 1962-64, 1987 Russell lecturer), Am. Rocket Society, Am. Geophysical Union; associate Royal Astronomical Society; member National Acad. Sciences, American Institute of Aeronautics and Astronautics Astronautics (aerospace tech. panel space physics 1960-63), Astronautical Society Pacific, Solar Assos., International Sci. Radio Union (United States of America national committee 1949-61), Am. Meteoritical Society,

Am. Standards Association, Am. Acad. Arts and Sciences, Am. Philosophical Society (councillor section astronomy and earth scis. 1966—), Royal Society Sciences Belgium (corr.), International Acad. Astronautics (sci. advisory committee 1962—), International Astronautical Federation, American Association for the Advancement of Science, Am. Meteorological Society, Royal Astronomical Society (associate), Phi Beta Kappa, Sigma Xi, Pi Mu Epsilon. Clubs: Examiner (Boston); Cosmos (Washington). Office: 60 Garden St Cambridge Massachusetts 02138

WHITE, ROBERT EDWARD, chemical engineering educator; born Jersey City, August 31, 1917; son of Frank Armour and Frances (deGeorge) W.; married Gloria Elizabeth Ingersoll, June 12, 1943; children: Jeffrey R., Donna L., Barbara J., Linda L., Thomas F. Bachelor of Chemical Engineering, Polytechnic Institute Brooklyn, 1938, Master of Chemical Engineering, 1940, Doctor of Chemical Engineering (Foster Wheeler graduate fellow), 1942. Junior engineer Vulcan Engineering, Cincinnati, 1939, 40; research engineer York Corp., Pennsylvania, 1942-47; assistant professor chemical engineering Bucknell University, 1947-49; associate professor chemical engineering Villanova (Pennsylvania) University, 1949-51, professor; 1951-86, professor emeritus; 1986—, chairman department; 1949-83; Cons. chemical engineer petroleum, paper industries, water treatment. Contributor articles to professional journals. Chairman board Newtown (Pennsylvania) Municipal Authority, 1969—; founder, chairman Citizens for Better Government, 1966-68. Recipient Centennial Achievement award Polytechnic Institute Brooklyn, 1956; Distinguished Award in Chemistry Am. Institute Chemists, 1979; Lindback award for outstanding teaching, 1980. Fellow Am. Institute Chemical Engineers (director 1970-72), Am. Society Engineering Education (chairman Middle-Atlantic section 1963-64), Technical Association of the Pulp and Paper Industry, Sigma Xi, Tau Beta Pi, Phi Lambda Upsilon, Alpha Chi Sigma. Patentee in field. Office: Villanova U Department Chem Engring Villanova Pennsylvania 19085

WHITE, ROBERT MAYER, meteorologist; born Boston, February 13, 1923; son of David and Mary (Winkeller) W.; married Mavis Seagle, April 18, 1948; children—Richard Harry, Edwina Janet. Bachelor of Arts, Harvard, 1944; Master of Science, Massachusetts Institute Tech., 1949, Doctor of Science, 1950; Doctor of Science (honorary), Long Island University, 1976, Rensselaer Polytechnic Institute, 1977, University Wisconsin, Milwaukee, 1978; Doctor of Science (honorary), University Bridgeport, 1984, University Rhode Island, 1986; Doctor of Philosophy (honorary), Johns Hopkins University, 1982, Drexel University, 1985. Project scientist Air Force Cambridge Research Center, 1950-58, chief meteorol. devel. laboratory; 1958-59; associate director research department Travelers Ins. Company, 1959-60; president Travelers Research Center, Incorporated, 1960-63; chief United States Weather Bureau, 1963-65; administrator Environmental Sci. Services Administration, 1965-70, National Oceanographic and Atmospheric Administration, 1970-77; president Joint Oceanographic Institute,

Incorporated, 1977-79; chairman Climate Research Board, executive officer National Acad. Sciences, 1977-79; administrator National Research Council, 1979-80; president University Corp. Atmospheric Research, 1980-83; chairman commission natural resources National Acad. Sciences, 1980-83; president National Acad. Engineering, Washington, 1983—; permanent United States representative, member executive committee World Meteorol. Organization, 1963-77; United States commissioner International Whaling Commission, 1973-77; chairman Marine Fisheries Adv. Committee, 1970-77, World Climate Conference, 1979; member National Adv. Committee Oceans and Atmosphere, 1979—; board of directors Charles Stark Draper Laboratory Incorporated, National Sci. Center Communications and Electronics Foundation, 1985—; member national adv. committee Government and Pub. Affairs University Illinois, 1987—. Author articles in field; member editorial board Am. Society Engring. Education journal. Board overseers Harvard University, 1977—; visiting committee meteorology and planetary sci. Massachusetts Institute Tech.; Member visiting committee Kennedy School Government, Harvard University; board of directors Resources for Future, 1980—. Served to captain United States Army Air Force, World War II. Decorated Legion of Honor France; recipient Jesse L. Rosenberger medal University Chicago, 1971; Cleveland Abbe award Am. Meteorol. Society, 1969; Godfrey L. Cabot award Aero Club Boston, 1966; Rockefeller Pub. Service award, 1974; David B. Stone award New England Aquarium, 1975; Neptune award Am. Oceanic Organization, 1977; Matthew Fontaine Maury award Smithsonian Institution, 1976; International Conservation award National Wildlife Federation, 1976; International Meteorol. Organization prize, 1980. Fellow Am. Meterol. Society (council 1965-67, 77—, Charles Franklin Brooks award 1978), Am. Geophysical Union; member National Acad. Engineering (council 1977), Marine Tech. Society, Council Foreign Relations, National Action Council Minorities in Engineering Incorporated. Club: Cosmos. Home: 8306 Melody Court Bethesda Maryland 20187 Office: 2101 Constitution Avenue Northwest Washington District of Columbia 20418

WIDNALL, SHEILA EVANS, aeronautics educator; born Tacoma, Washington, July 13, 1938; daughter of Rolland John and Genievieve Alice (Krause) Evans; married William Soule Widnall, June 11, 1960; children—William, Ann. Bachelor of Science, Massachusetts Institute of Technology, 1960, Master of Science, 1961, Doctor of Philosophy, 1964; Doctor of Philosophy (honorary), New England College, 1975, Lawrence University, 1987, Cedar Crest College, 1988. Assistant professor Massachusetts Institute of Technology, Cambridge, 1964-70, assistant professor; 1970-74, professor aeronautics; 1974—; director university research United States D.O.T., Washington, 1974-75; director Chemfab Incorporated, Bennington, Vermont, Aerospace Corp., Los Angeles, Draper Laboratories, Cambridge, Massachusetts, ANSER, Arlington, Virginia; board trustees Carnegie Corp., 1984—. Contributor articles to professional journals; patentee in field; associate editor AIAA Journal Aircraft, 1972-75, Physics of Fluids, 1981—, Journal Applied Mechanics, 1983-87; member editorial board Science '85, 1984-86. Chairman faculty Massachusetts Institute of Technology, Cambridge, 1970-81, committee on undergrad. admission and fin. aid, 1982-84; board visitors United States Air Force Acad., Colorado Springs, Colorado, 1978-83. Fellow American Association for the Advancement of Science (board directors 1982—, president elect 1986-87, president 1987-88, chairman 1988—), Am. Physical Society (executive committee 1979-82), American Institute of Aeronautics and Astronautics (board directors 1975-77, Lawrence Spery award 1972), Am. Acad. Arts and Sciences; member Society Women Engineers (Outstanding Achievement award 1975), American Society of Mechanical Engineers, National Acad. Engineering, Am. Acad. Arts and Sciences. Club: Seattle Mountaineers. Office: Massachusetts Institute of Technology 77 Massachusetts Avenue Cambridge Massachusetts 02139

WIEGENSTEIN, JOHN GERALD, physician; born Fredericktown, Missouri, June 22, 1930; son of John Joseph and Dorothy Faye (Mulkey) W.; married Dorothy Iris Scifers, December 27, 1952; children: Mark, Barbara, Paula, Cynthia. Bachelor of Science, University Michigan, 1956, Doctor of Medicine, 1960. Intern United States Tripler Army General Hospital, Honolulu, 1960-61; general practice Lansing, Michigan, 1963-67; practice emergency medicine St. Lawrence Hospital, Lansing, 1967-75; director department emergency medicine Ingham Medical Center,

Lansing, 1975—; professor, chief section emergency medicine Michigan State University, 1982—; founder International Research Institute for Emergency Medicine, president; 1983-85; president Am. Board Emergency Medicine, 1982-83. Served with United States Air Force, 1951-53; Medical Corps United States Army, 1960-63. Member American Medical Association, Am. College Emergency Physicians (president, chairman board 1968-71, board directors 1968-76), Michigan State Medical Society (award 1971), Ingham County Medical Society, Galens Hon. Medical Society, University Association Emergency Medicine, Society Teachers Emergency Medicine. Office: Ingham Med Center Department of Emergency Medicine 401 W Greenlawn Lansing Michigan 48910

WIESEL, TORSTEN NILS, neurobiologist, educator; born Upsala, Sweden, June 3, 1924; came to United States, 1955; son of Fritz Samuel and Anna-Lisa Elisabet (Bentzer) W.; 1 daughter, Sara Elisabet. Doctor of Medicine, Karolinska Institute, Stockholm, 1954; Master of Arts (honorary), Harvard University, 1967. Instructor physiology Karolinska Institute, 1954-55; assistant department child psychiatry Karolinska Hospital, 1954-55; fellow in ophthalmology Johns Hopkins University, 1955-58, assistant professor ophthalmic physiology; 1958-59; associate in neurophysiology and neuropharmacology Harvard University Medical School, Boston, 1959-60; assistant professor neurophysiology and neuropharmacology Harvard University Medical School, 1960-64, assistant professor neurophysiology, department psychiatry; 1964-67, professor physiology; 1967-68, professor neurobiology; 1968-74, Robert Winthrop professor neurobiology; 1974-83, chairman department neurobiology; 1973-82; professor neurobiology Rockefeller University, New York City, 1983—; Ferrier lecturer Royal Society London, 1972; National Institutes of Health lecturer, 1975; Grass lecturer Society Neurosci., 1976; lecturer College de France, 1977; Hitchcock professor University Calif.-Berkeley, 1980; Sharpey-Schafer lecturer Physical Society London; George Cotzias lecturer Am. Acad. Neurology, 1983. Contributor numerous articles to professional journals. Recipient Jules Stein award Trustees for Prevention Blindness, 1971, Lewis S. Rosenstiel prize Brandeis University, 1972, Friedenwald award Trustees of Association for Research in Vision and Ophthalmology, 1975, Karl Spencer Lashley prize Am. Philos. Society, 1977, Louisa Gross Horwitz prize Columbia University, 1978, Dickson prize University Pitts., 1979, Nobel prize in Physiology/Medicine, 1981. Member Am. Physiological Society, Am. Philosophical Society, American Association for the Advancement of Science, Am. Acad. Arts and Sciences, National Acad. Arts and Sciences, Swedish Physiological Society, Society Neurosci. (president 1978-79), Royal Society (foreign member), Physiological Society (England) (hon. member). Office: Rockefeller U York Avenue & 66th St New York New York 10021

WIESNER, JEROME BERT, engineering educator, researcher; born Detroit, May 30, 1915; son of Joseph and Ida (Friedman) W.; married Laya Wainger, September 1, 1940; children: Stephen Jay, Zachary Kurt, Elizabeth Ann, Joshua A. Bachelor of Science, University Michigan, 1937, Master of Science, 1938, Doctor of Philosophy, 1950. Associate director University Michigan Broadcasting Service, 1937-40; chief engineer Acoustical Record Laboratory, Library of Congress, 1940-42; staff Massachusetts Institute of Technology Radiation Laboratory, Cambridge, Massachusetts, 1942-45, University of California Los Alamos Laboratory, 1945-46; member faculty Massachusetts Institute of Technology, Cambridge, 1946-71, director research laboratory of electronics; 1952-61, head department electrical engineering; 1959-60, dean of sci.; 1964-66, provost; 1966-71, president; 1971-80, Institute researcher and professor; 1980—; life member Massachusetts Institute of Technology Corp., Cambridge; special assistant to President on sci. and tech., 1961-64; chairman President's Sci. Adv. Committee, 1961-64; chairman tech. assessment adv. council Office Tech. Assessment, United States Congress, 1976-79; Director Automatix, Damon Biotech., Cons. for Management Incorporated, The Faxon Company. Author: Where Science and Politics Meet, 1965, ABM—An Evaluation, 1969. Board governors Weizmann Institute Sci., MacArthur Foundation; trustee Woods Hole Oceanographic Institute, Kennedy Memorial Trust; board of overseers Harvard University, 1987—. Fellow Institute of Electrical and Electronics Engineers, Am. Acad. Arts and Sciences; member Am. Philosophical Society, American Association of University Profs., Am. Geophysical Union, Acoustical Society Am., National Acad. Engineering, National Acad. Sciences,

Massachusetts Institute of Technology Corp. (life), Sigma Xi, Phi Kappa Phi, Eta Kappa Nu, Tau Beta Pi. Home: 61 Shattuck Road Watertown Massachusetts 02172 Office: Massachusetts Institute of Technology 20 Ames St E15-207 Cambridge Massachusetts 02139

WIGLER, MICHAEL, molecular biologist; born 1948. With Cold Spring Harbor Laboratory, New York. Recipient Pfizer Biomed. Research award, 1986. Office: Cold Spring Harbor Lab Mammalian Cell Genetics Section Cold Spring Harbor New York 11724

WIGNER, EUGENE PAUL, physicist, educator; born Budapest, Hungary, November 17, 1902; came to United States, 1930, naturalized, 1937; son of Anthony and Elisabeth (Einhorn) W.; married Amelia Z. Frank, December 23, 1936 (deceased 1937); married Mary Annette Wheeler, June 4, 1941 (deceased November 1977); married Eileen C.P. Hamilton, December 29, 1979. Chemical Engineer and Doctor Engineering, Technische Hochschule, Berlin, 1925; honorary Doctor of Science, University Wisconsin, 1949, Washington University, 1950, Case Institute Tech., 1956, University Chicago, 1957, Colby College, 1959, University Pennsylvania, 1961, Thiel College, 1964, University Notre Dame, 1965, Technische Universität Berlin, 1966, Swarthmore College, 1966, Université de Louvain, Belgium, 1967; Dr.Junior, University Alberta, 1957; Doctor of Humane Letters, Yeshiva University, 1963; honorary degrees, University Liège, 1967, University Illinois, 1968, Seton Hall University, 1969, Catholic University, 1969, Rockefeller University, 1970, Israel Institute Tech., 1973, Lowell University, 1976, Princeton University, 1976, University Texas, 1978, Clarkson College, 1979, Allegheny College, 1979, Gustav Adolphus College, 1981, Stevens Institute Tech., 1982, State University of New York, 1982, Louisiana State University, 1985. Assistant Technische Hochschule, Berlin, 1926-27, assistant professor; 1928-33; assistant University Göttingen, 1927-28; lecturer Princeton University, 1930, part-time professor math. physics; 1931-36; professor physics University Wisconsin, 1936-38; Thomas D. Jones professor theoretical physics Princeton University, 1938-71; on leave of absence 1942-45; with Metallurgical Laboratory, University Chicago, 1946-47; as director research and devel. Clinton Laboratories; director Civil Defense Research Project, Oak Ridge, 1964-65; Lorentz lecturer Institute Lorentz, Leiden, 1957; consultant professor Louisiana State University, 1971-85, retired; 1985; member general adv. committee Atomic Energy Commission, 1952-57, 59-64; member math. panel National Research Council, 1952-54; physics panel National Science Foundation, 1953-56; visiting committee National Bureau Standards, 1947-51. Author: (with L. Eisenbud) Nuclear Structure, 1958, The Physical Theory of Neutron Chain Reactors (with A.M. Weinberg), 1958, Group Theory and its Applications to the Quantum Mechanics of Atomic Spectra, 1931, English translation, 1959, Symmetries and Reflections, 1967, Survival and the Bomb, 1969. Decorated medal of Merit, 1946; recipient Franklin medal Franklin Institute, 1950, citation New Jersey Teachers Association, 1951, Enrico Fermi award Atomic Energy Commission, 1958, Atoms for Peace award, 1960, Max Planck medal

German Physical Society, 1961, Nobel prize for physics, 1963, George Washington award Am. Hungarian Studies Foundation, 1964, Semmelweiss medal Am. Hungarian Medical Association, 1965, National Sci. medal, 1969, Pfizer award, 1971, Albert Einstein award, 1972, Golden Plate medal Am. Acad. Achievement, 1974, Distinguished Achievement award Louisiana State University, 1977, Wigner medal, 1978, Founders medal International Cultural Foundation, 1982, Medal of the Hungarian Central Research Institute, Medal of the Autonomous University Barcelona, Am. Preparedness award, 1985; named Nuclear Pioneer Society Nuclear Medicine, 1977, Colonel Gov. of Louisiana, 1983. Member Royal Society England (foreign), Royal Netherlands Acad. Sci. and Letters, Am. Nuclear Society, Am. Physical Society (vice president 1955, president 1956), Am. Math. Society, Am. Association Physics Teachers, Am. Acad. Arts and Sciences, Am. Philosophical Society, National Acad. Sciences, New York Acad. Sciences (hon. life member), Austrian Acad. Sciences, German Physical Society, Franklin Institute, American Association for the Advancement of Science, Sigma Xi, Acad. Sci., Gottingen, Germany (corr.), Hungarian Acad. Sci. (hon.), Austrian Acad. Sciences (hon.), Hungarian L. Eötvös Physical Society (hon.). Office: Princeton U Jadwin Hall Princeton New Jersey 08540

WILEY, WILLIAM RODNEY, microbiologist, administrator; born Oxford, Mississippi, September 5, 1931; son of William Russell and Edna Alberta (Threlkeld) W.; married Myrtle Louise Smith, November 10, 1952; 1 child: Johari. Bachelor of Science, Tougaloo College, Mississippi, 1954; Master of Science, University Illinois, Urbana, 1960; Doctor of Philosophy, Washington State University, Pullman, 1965. Instructor electronics and radar repair Keesler AFB-U.South Air Force, 1956-58; Rockefeller Foundation fellow University Illinois, 1958-59; research associate Washington State University, Pullman, 1960-65; research scientist department biology Battelle-Pacific Northwest Laboratories, 1965-69, manager cellular and molecular biology section department biology; 1969-72, institute coordinator, life sciences program, associate manager department biology; 1972-74, manager department biology; 1974-79, director research; 1979-84; director Pacific Northwest div. Battelle Memorial Institute, Richland, Washington, 1984—; adj. associate professor microbiology Washington State University, Pullman, 1968—; consultant and lecturer in field. Contributor chapters to books, articles to professional journals Co-author book in microbiology. Member Washington Tech. Center, 1984—, sci. adv. panel Washington Tech. Center, 1984—; member adv. committee University Washington School Medicine, 1976-79; trustee Gonzaga University, 1981—; board of directors MESA program University Washington, Seattle, 1984—, United Way of Benton & Franklin Counties, Washington, 1984—, Tri-City Industrial Devel. Council, 1984—; member Washington Council Tech. Advancement, 1984-85 ; board of directors Economic Devel. Partnership for Washington, 1984—, Northwest College and University Association for Sci., 1985—; member Tri-City University Center Citizens Adv. Council, 1985—; appointed Washington State Higher Education

Coordinating Board, 1986—, Washington State Foundation, 1986—; member Washington State University board Regents, 1989—. Served with United States Army, 1954-56. Member Am. Society Biological Chemists, Am. Society Microbiology, American Association for the Advancement of Science, Society Experimental Biology and Medicine, Sigma Xi. Office: Battelle Memorial Institute Pacific Northwest Div Battelle Boulevard Richland Washington 99352

WILKINS, MAURICE HUGH FREDERICK, biophysicist; born Pongaroa, New Zealand, December 15, 1916; son of Edgar Henry and Eveline (Whittaker) W.; married Patricia Ann Chidgey, March 12, 1959; children: Sarah Fenella, George Hugh, Emily Lucy Una, William Henry. Doctor of Philosophy, St. John's College, Cambridge, 1940; Doctor of Laws, University Glasgow, 1972. Research with Manhattan Project, University California, Berkeley, 1944; lecturer St. Andrews University, 1945; member faculty Kings College, London, 1946—, deputy director biophysics unit Medical Research Council; 1955-70, director biophysics unit; 1970-72, director neurobiology unit; 1972-74, professor molecular biology; 1962-70, professor biophysics; 1970-81, also director MRC cell biophysics unit (formerly Medical Research Council neurobiology unit); 1974-80. Decorated commander Brit. Empire; recipient Albert Lasker award Am. Pub. Health Association, 1960, Nobel prize for physiology and medicine (with F.H.C. Crick and J.D. Watson), 1962; fellow King's College, 1973—. Fellow Royal Society, 1959; member Brit. Biophys. Society (past chairman),

Am. Society Biological Chemists (hon.), Brit. Society for Social Responsibility in Sci. (president 1969), Am. Acad. Arts and Sciences (foreign hon.). Research, publs. on structure of nerve membranes and X-ray diffraction analysis of structure of DNA; devel. of electron trap theory of phosphorescence and thermoluminescence; light microscopy techniques for cyto-chem. research, including use of interference microscope for dry mass determination in cells.

WILKINSON, GEOFFREY, chemist, educator; born Todmorden, England, July 14, 1921; son of Henry and Ruth (Crowther) W.; married Lise Schou, July 17, 1951; children: Anne Marie, Pernille Jane. BSc, Imperial College, London, 1941, Doctor of Philosophy, 1946; Doctor of Science (honorary), University Edinburgh, University Granada, 1977, Columbia University, 1979, University Bath, 1980. With National Research Council, Can., 1943-46; staff Radiation Laboratory, University California, Berkeley, Can., 1946-50; member faculty Massachusetts Institute of Technology, Can., 1950-51; faculty chemistry department Harvard University, Can., 1951-55; faculty Imperial College Sci. and Tech., University London, Can., 1955—, professor emritus; 1955—; Falk-Plaut visiting lecturer Columbia, 1961; Arthur D. Little visiting professor Massachusetts Institute of Technology, 1967; Hawkins Memorial lecturer University Chicago, 1968; 1st Mond lecturer Royal Society Chemistry, 1981; Chini lecturer Italian Chemical Society, 1981. Author: (with F.A. Cotton) Advanced Inorganic Chemistry: A Comprehensive Text, 5th edition, 1988; Basic Inorganic Chemistry, 2d edition, 1987. John

Simon Guggenheim fellow, 1954; recipient award inorganic chemistry Am. Chemical Society, 1966, Centennial Foreign fellow, 1976, Royal Society Chemistry transition metal chemistry, 1972; Lavoisier medal French Chemical Society, 1968; Nobel prize in chemistry, 1973; Hiroshima University medal, 1978; Royal medal, 1981; Galileo medal University Pisa, 1983. Fellow Royal Society; foreign member Royal Danish Acad. Sci., Am. Acad. Arts and Sciences, National Acad. Sciences, Spanish Sci. Research Council. Office: Imperial College Sci & Tech, Department Chemistry, London SW7 2AY, England

WILLEY, GORDON RANDOLPH, retired anthropologist, archaeologist, educator; born Chariton, Ia., March 7, 1913; son of Frank and Agnes Caroline (Wilson) W.; married Katharine W. Whaley, September 17, 1938; children—Alexandra, Winston. Bachelor of Arts, University Arizona, 1935, Master of Arts, 1936, Doctor of Letters (honorary), 1981; Doctor of Philosophy, Columbia University, 1942; Master of Arts honoris causa, Harvard University, 1950; Doctor of Letters honoris causa, Cambridge University, 1977, University New Mexico, 1984. Archaeol. assistant National Park Service, Macon, Georgia, 1936-38; archaeologist Louisiana State University, 1938-39; archaeol. field supervisor Peru, 1941-42; instructor anthropology Columbia University, 1942-43; anthropologist Bureau Am. Ethnology, Smithsonian Institution, 1943-50; Bowditch professor archaeology Harvard University, 1950-83, senior professor anthropology; 1983-87, chairman department anthropology; 1954-57; visiting professor Am. archaeology Cambridge (England) University, 1962-63; member expeditions to Peru, Panama, 1941-52, Brit. Honduras, 1953-56, Guatemala, 1958, 60, 62, 64, 65, 66, 67, 68, Nicaragua, 1959, 61, Honduras, 1973, 75-77. Author: Excavations in the Chancay Valley, Peru, 1943, Archaeology of the Florida Gulf Coast, 1949, Prehistoric Settlement Patterns in the Viru Valley, Peru, 1953, Introduction to American Archaeology, 2 vols, 1966-71, The Artifacts of Altar de Sacrificios, 1972, Excavations of Altarde Sacrificious, Guatemala, 1973, Das Alte Amerika, 1974, The Artifacts of Seibal, Guatemala, 1978, Essays in Maya Archaeology, 1987; co-author: Early Ancon and Early Supe Cultures, 1954, The Monagrillo Culture of Panama, 1954, Method and Theory in American Archaelogy, 1958, Prehistoric Maya Settlements in the Belize Valley, 1965, The Ruins of Altar de Sacrificios, Department of Peten, Guatemala: An Introduction, 1969, the Maya Collapse: An Appraisal, 1973, A History of American Archaeology, 1974, 2d edition, 1980, The Origins of Maya Civilization, 1977, Lowland Maya Settlement Patterns: A Summary View, 1981; co-editor: Courses Toward Urban Life, 1962, Precolumbian Archaeology, 1980, A Consideration of the Early Classic Period in the Maya Lowlands, 1985; editor: Prehistoric Settlement Patterns of the New World, 1956, Archaeological Researches in Retrospect, 1974. Overseas fellow Churchill College, Cambridge University, 1968-69; decorated Order of Quetzal Guatemala; recipient Viking Fund medal, 1953; Gold medal Archaeol. Institute Am., 1973; Alfred V. Kidder medal for achievement in Am. Archacology, 1974; Huxley medal

Royal Anthrop. Institute, London, 1979; Walker prize Boston Mus. Sci., 1981; Drexel medal for archaeology University Mus., Philadelphia, 1981, Golden PLate award Am. Acad. Achievement, 1987. Fellow Am. Anthropological Association (president 1961), Am. Acad. Sci., London Society Antiquaries, Society Am. Archaeology (president 1968, Distinguished Service award 1980); member National Acad. Sci., Am. Philosophical Society, Royal Anthropological Institute Great Britain and Ireland, Phi Beta Kappa; corr. member Brit. Acad. Clubs: Cosmos (Washington); Tavern (Boston).

WILLIAMS, CARROLL MILTON, biologist, educator; born Richmond, Virginia, December 2, 1916; son of George Leslie and Jessie Ann (Hendricks) W.; married Muriel Anne Voter, June 26, 1941; children: John Leslie (deceased), Wesley Conant, Peter Glenn (deceased), Roger Lee. Bachelor of Science, University Richmond, 1937, Doctor of Science (honorary), 1960; Master of Arts, Harvard University, 1938, Doctor of Philosophy, 1941, Doctor of Medicine summa cum laude, 1946. Assistant professor Harvard University, 1946-48, associate professor zoology; 1948-53, professor; 1953-66, Benjamin Bussey professor biology; 1966-87, Bussey professor emeritus; 1987—, chairman department; 1959-62; chief scientist phase C of Alpha Helix Expedition to Upper Amazon 1967. Trustee Radcliffe College, 1961-64. Recipient Newcomb Cleveland prize American Association for the Advancement of Science, 1950, Boylston prize and medal Harvard Medical School, 1961, George Ledlie prize Harvard University, 1967, Howard Taylor Ricketts award University Chicago, 1969; Guggenheim fellow, 1955-56. Fellow Am. Acad. Arts and Sciences (council 1954-57, 1973-77), Entomological Society Am., American Association for the Advancement of Science (council 1952-54); member National Acad. Sci. (chairman section zoology 1970-73, council 1973-76, 85-88, chairman biological sci. 1982-85), Institute Medicine, Am. Society Zoologists, Am. Physiological Society, Am. Philosophical Society, Society Devel. Biology, Harvey Society, Lepidopterists Society, Signet Society, Cambridge Entomological Club, Cambridge Sci. Club, Examiner Club, Phi Beta Kappa, Sigma Xi. Research on juvenile hormones in insects. Home: 27 Eliot Road Lexington Massachusetts 02173

WILLIAMS, JACK MARVIN, chemist; born Delta, Colorado, September 26, 1938; son of John Davis and Ruth Emma (Gallup) W.; married Joan Marlene Davis, March 7, 1958; 3 children. Bachelor of Science with honors, Lewis and Clark College, 1960; Master of Science, Washington State University, 1964, Doctor of Philosophy, 1966. Postdoctoral fellow Argonne (Illinois), National Laboratory, 1966-68, assistant chemist; 1968-70, associate chemist; 1970-72, chemist; 1972-77, senior chemist, group leader; 1977—; visiting guest professor University Missouri, Columbia, 1980, 81, 82, University Copenhagen, 1980, 83, 85. Board editors Inorganic Chemistry, 1979—, associate editor, 1982—. Crown-Zellerbach scholar, 1959-60; NDEA fellow, 1960-63; recipient Distinguished Performance at Argonne National Labs. award University Chicago, 1987. Member Am. Crystallographic Association, Am.

Chemical Society (treasurer inorganic division 1982-84), Am. Physical Society, American Association for the Advancement of Science. Office: Chemistry Div 9700 S Cass Avenue Argonne Illinois 60439

WILLIAMS, LUTHER STEWARD, biologist, consultant, federal agency administrator; born Sawyerville, Alabama, August 19, 1940; son of Roosevelt and Mattie B. (Wallace) W.; married Constance Marie Marion, August 23, 1963; children: Mark Steward, Monique Marie. Bachelor of Arts magna cum laude, Miles College, 1961; Master of Science, Atlanta University, 1963; Doctor of Philosophy, Purdue University, 1968, Doctor of Science (honorary), 1987. National Science Foundation laboratory assistant Spelman College, 1961-62; National Science Foundation laboratory assistant Atlanta University, 1962-63, instructor biology, faculty research grantee; 1963-64, assistant professor biology; 1969-70, president; 1984-87; grad. teaching assistant Purdue University, West Lafayette, Ind., 1964-65, grad. research assistant; 1965-66, assistant professor biology; 1970-73, associate professor; 1973-79, professor; 1979-80, National Institutes of Health Career Devel. awardee; 1971-75, assistant provost; 1976-80; dean Grad. School, professor biology Washington University, St. Louis, 1980-83; vice president acad. affairs, dean Grad. School University Colorado, Boulder, 1983-84; Am. Cancer Society postdoctoral fellow SUNY-Stony Brook, 1968-69; associate professor biology Massachusetts Institute of Technology, 1973-74; now special assistant to director National Institute General Medical Sciences, National Institutes of Health, Bethesda, Maryland; chairman rev. committee MARC Program, National Institute General Medical Sciences, National Institutes of Health, 1972-76; grant reviewer National Institutes of Health, 1971-73, 76, National Science Foundation, 1973, 76-80, Medical Research Council of New Zealand, 1976; member life sciences sreening committee recombinant DNA adv. committee Department of Health, Education and Welfare, 1979-81; member national adv. general medical sci. council National Institutes of Health, 1980-85; member adv. committee Office Tech. Assessment, Washington, 1984-87; chairman fellowship adv. committee National Research Council Ford Foundation, 1984-85; mem.-at-large Grad. Record Exam. Board, 1981-85, chairman minority grad. education committee, 1983-85; member health, safety and environmental affairs. committee National Laboratories, University Calif, 1981-87; member adv. panel Office Tech. Assessment, United States Congress, 1985-86; member federal task force on women, minorities and the handicapped in sci. and tech., 1987—; member adv. panel to director sci. and tech. centers devel. National Science Foundation, 1987—; member national adv. committee White House Initiative on Historically Black Colleges and Universities on Sci. and Tech., 1986—; numerous other adv. boards and committees. Contributor sci. articles to professional journals. Vice chairman board advisors Atlanta Neighborhood Justice Center, 1984-87; board of directors Metropolitan Atlanta United Way, 1986-87, Butler St. Young Men's Christian Association, Atlanta, 1985-87; trustee Atlanta Zool. Association, 1985-87, Miles College, 1984-87, Atlanta

University, 1983-87. National Institutes of Health fellow Purdue University, 1966-68. Member Am. Society Microbiology, Am. Chemical Society, Am. Society Biological Chemists (member educational affairs committee 1979-82, committee on equal opportunities for minorities 1972-84), American Association for the Advancement of Science, New York Acad. Sciences. Office: NIH National Institute of Gen Med Scis 5333 Westbard Avenue Bethesda Maryland 20892

WILLIAMS, MARTIN, editor, writer, educator; born Richmond, Virginia, August 9, 1924; son of John Bell and Rebecca (Yancey) W.; children from former marriage: Charles, Frederick, Frank. Bachelor of Arts, University Virginia, 1948; Master of Arts, University Pennsylvania, 1950. Lecturer, instructor Columbia University, New York City, 1952-56; editor Macmillan Company, New York City, 1955; free-lance writer New York City, 1956-71; editor Americana, New York City, 1959-60; director Jazz Program, New York City, 1971—; editor Smithsonian Press, New York City; lecturer numerous educational institutions. Author numerous books. Address: 2101 Shenandoah Road Alexandria Virginia 22308

WILLIAMS, THOMAS FRANKLIN, physician, educator; born Belmont, North Carolina, November 26, 1921; son of T.F. and Mary L. (Deaton) W.; married Catharine Carter Catlett, December 15, 1951; children: Mary Wright, Thomas Nelson. Bachelor of Science, University North Carolina, 1942; Master of Arts, Columbia University, 1943; Doctor of Medicine, Harvard University, 1950. Diplomate: Am. Board Internal Medicine. Intern Johns Hopkins, Baltimore, 1950-51; assistant resident physician Johns Hopkins, 1951-53; resident physician Boston Veteran's Administration Hospital, 1953-54; research fellow University North Carolina, Chapel Hill, 1954-56; instructor department medicine and preventive medicine University North Carolina, 1956-57, assistant professor; 1957-61, associate professor; 1961-68, professor; 1968; attending physician Strong Memorial Hospital, Rochester, New York, 1968—; consultant physician Genesee Hospital, Rochester, New York, 1973—, St. Mary's Hospital, Rochester, New York, 1974-83, Highland Hospital, Rochester, New York, 1973; professor medicine, preventive medicine and community health University Rochester, 1968-83, also professor radiation biology and biophysics; 1968-82, on leave; 1983—; member adv. board University Rochester (School Medicine and Dentistry), 1968-83; clinical professor medicine University Virginia, 1983—; lecturer medicine Johns Hopkins University, 1983—; clinical professor depts family medicine and medicine Georgetown University, 1983—; director National Institute on Aging National Institutes of Health, 1983—; medical director Monroe Community Hospital, Rochester, 1968-83; member rev. committees National Center for Health Services Research; member adv. board St. Ann's Home; member governing board National Research Council, 1981-83. Contributor articles on endocrine disorders, diabetes, health care delivery in chronic illness and aging to professional publications. Served with United States Naval Reserve, 1943-46. USPHS fellow, 1966-67; Markle scholar, 1957-61. Fellow Am. Pub. Health Association, A.C.P.; member New York State,

Monroe County med. socs., Institute Medicine, National Acad. Sciences (council 1980-83), Am. Diabetes Association (director 1974-80), American Association for the Advancement of Science, Am. Federation Clinical Research, Society Experimental Biology and Medicine, Am. Geriatrics Society, Am. Gerontological Society, Rochester Regional Diabetes Association (president 1977-79), North Carolina Council for Human Relations (chairman 1963-66). Episcopalian. Home: 5202 W Cedar Lane Bethesda Maryland 20814 Office: NIH Building 31 Room 2C-02 Bethesda Maryland 20892

WILLIAMSON, THOMAS GARNETT, nuclear engineering and engineering physics educator; born Quincy, Massachusetts, January 27, 1934; son of Robert Burwell and Elizabeth B. (McNeer) W.; married Kaye Darlan Love, August 16, 1961; children: Allen, Sarah, David. Bachelor of Science, Virginia Military Institute, 1955; Master of Science, Rensselaer Polytechnic Institute, 1957; Doctor of Philosophy, University Virginia, 1960. Assistant professor nuclear engineering and engineering physics department University Virginia, Charlottesville, 1960-62, associate professor; 1962-69, professor; 1969—, chairman department; 1977—; with General Atomic (California), 1965, Combustion Engineering, Windsor, Connecticut, 1970-71, Los Alamos Sci. Laboratory, 1969, National Bureau Standards, Gaithersburg, Maryland, 1984-85; consultant Philippine Atomic Energy Commission, 1963, Virginia Power Company, 1975—, Babcock & Wilcox, Lynchburg, Virginia, 1975—. Vestryman Church of Our Savior, Charlottesville. Fellow Am. Nuclear Society; member American Association for the Advancement of Science, Am. Society Engineering Education, Sigma Xi, Tau Beta Pi. Episcopalian. Home: 225 Rivanwood Dr Charlottesville Virginia 22901 Office: University of Va Reactor Facility Charlottesville Virginia 22901

WILSON, ALLAN CHARLES, biochemistry educator; born Ngaruawahia, New Zealand, October 18, 1934; came to United States, 1955; son of Charles and Eunice Boyce (Wood) W.; married Leona Greenbaum, September 13, 1958; children: Ruth, David. Bachelor of Science, University Otago, New Zealand, 1955, Doctor of Science (honorary), 1989; Master of Science, Washington State University, 1957; Doctor of Philosophy, University California, Berkeley, 1961. Postdoctoral fellow Brandeis University, Waltham, Massachusetts, 1961-64; assistant professor University California, Berkeley, 1964-68, associate professor; 1968-72, professor biochemistry; 1972—. Contributor numerous articles to professional journals and books. Fellow Guggenheim Memorial Foundation, 1972-73, 79-80, Am. Acad. Arts and Sciences, 1983, Royal Society, 1986, MacArthur Foundation, 1986—. Member Am. Society Biological Chemists. Office: University of California 401 Barker Hall Berkeley California 94720

WILSON, EDWARD OSBORNE, biologist, educator; born Birmingham, Alabama, June 10, 1929; son of Edward Osborne and Inez (Freeman) W.; married Irene Kelley, October 30, 1955; 1 daughter, Catherine Irene. Bachelor of Science, University Alabama, 1949, Master of Science, 1950; Doctor of Philosophy,

Harvard University, 1955; Doctor of Science (honorary), Duke University, Grinnell College, Lawrence University, University West Florida; Doctor Phil., Uppsala University; Doctor of Humane Letters, University Alabama, Hofstra University; Doctor of Laws, Simon Fraser University. Junior fellow Society Fellows, Harvard University, 1953-56, member faculty; 1956—, Baird professor sci.; 1976—, curator entomology; 1971—; fellow Guggenheim Foundation, 1978, member selection committee, 1982—; board of directors World Wildlife Fund, 1983—, Organization Tropical Studies, 1984—. Author: The Insect Societies, 1971, Sociobiology: The New Synthesis, 1975, On Human Nature, 1978, Promethean Fire, 1983, Biophilia, 1984, others. Recipient Cleve.-AAAS research prize, 1967; National Medal Sci., 1976; Pulitzer prize for nonfiction, 1979; Leidy medal Acad. Natural Sci., Philadelphia, 1979; Distinguished Service award Am. Institute Biological Sciences, 1976; Mercer award Ecol. Society Am., 1971; Founders Memorial award and L.O. Howard award Entomol. Society Am., 1972, 85; Archie Carr medal University Florida, 1978; Distinguished Service award Am. Humanist Society, 1982; Tyler ecology prize, 1984; Silver medal National Zool. Park; German Ecol. Institute prize, 1987; others. Fellow Am. Acad. Arts and Sciences, Am. Phil. Society, Deutsche Akad. Naturforsch.; member National Acad. Sci., Am. Genetics Association (hon. life), Brit. Ecological Society (hon. life), Entomological Society Am. (hon. life). Home: 9 Foster Road Lexington Massachusetts 02173 Office: Harvard University Mus Comparative Zoology Cambridge Massachusetts 02138

WILSON, KENNETH GEDDES, physics research administrator, educator; born Waltham, Massachusetts, June 8, 1936; son of E. Bright and Emily Fisher (Buckingham) W.; married Alison Brown, 1982. Bachelor of Arts, Harvard University, 1956, Doctor of Science honorary, 1981; Doctor of Philosophy, California Tech. Institute, 1961; Doctor of Philosophy (honorary), University Chicago, 1976. Assistant professor, then professor physics Cornell University, Ithaca, New York, 1963—, James A. Weeks chairman in physical sci.; 1974—. Recipient Nobel prize in physics, 1982, Dannie Heinemann Prize, 1973, Boltzmann medal, 1975, Wolf Prize, 1980, A.C. Eringen medal, 1984, Franklin medal, 1983, Distinguished alumni award California Institute Tech., 1981. Member National Acad. Sciences, Am. Philosophical Society, Am. Acad. Arts and Sciences.

WILSON, ROBERT WOODROW, radio astronomer; born Houston, January 10, 1936; son of Ralph Woodrow and Fannie May (Willis) W.; married Elizabeth Rhoads Sawin, September 4, 1958; children—Philip Garrett, Suzanne Katherine, Randal Woodrow. Bachelor of Arts with honors in Physics, Rice University, 1957; Doctor of Philosophy, California Institute Tech., 1962. Research fellow California Institute Tech., Pasadena, 1962-63; member tech. staff American Telephone and Telegraph Company Bell Laboratories, Holmdel, New Jersey, 1963-76; head radio physics research department American Telephone and Telegraph Company Bell Laboratories, 1976—. Recipient Henry Draper medal Royal Astronomical Society, London, 1977, Herschel medal National Acad.

Sciences, 1977; Nobel prize in physics, 1978; National Science Foundation fellow, 1958-61; Cole fellow, 1957-58. Member Am. Astronomical Society, International Astronomical Union, Am. Physical Society, International Sci. Radio Union, National Acad. Sciences, Phi Beta Kappa, Sigma Xi. Discoverer of 3 deg. k Microwave Backgraound Radiation, 1965; discoverer of CO and other molecules in interstellar space using their millimeter wavelength radiation. Home: 9 Valley Point Dr Holmdel New Jersey 07733 Office: AT&T Bell Labs HOH L239 Holmdel New Jersey 07733

WINCHESTER, ALBERT MCCOMBS, biology educator, author; born Waco, Texas, April 20, 1908; son of Robert Stevenson and Mamie Katherine (Moore) W.; married Josephine Milam Walker, December 23, 1934; 1 daughter, Betty Jo. Bachelor of Arts, Baylor University, 1929; Master of Arts, University Texas, 1931, Doctor of Philosophy, 1934; postgraduate, University Chicago, 1940, Harvard, 1952, University Michigan, 1959, University Munich, 1960. Head biological department Oklahoma Baptist University, Shawnee, Oklahoma, 1935-42; professor biology Baylor University, 1942-46; head biology department Stetson University, DeLand, Florida, 1946-61; professor biology University Northern Colorado, Greeley, 1962—; specialist in human heredity and biological photography. University Northern Colorado. Author: Zoology-the Science of Animal Life, 1947, rev. 1961, Biology and its Relation to Mankind, 1949. rev. 1957, 69, 75, Genetics, A Survey of the Principles of Heredity, 1951, rev. 1958, 71, 76,

Hebrew transl., 1974, Spanish transl., 1977, Chinese transl., 1977, Heredity and Your Life, 1957, rev. 1960, 1966, Spanish transl., 1974, Genetics Laboratory Manual, 1958, 77, Heredity, 1962, rev., 1975, Modern Biological Principles, 1965, rev. edition, 1970, Russian transl., 1976, Human Development and Inheritance, 1968, Concepts of Zoology, 1970, Human Heredity, 1971, rev., 1975, 78, 83, The Nature of Human Sexuality, 1973, Heredity, Evolution and Humankind, 1975, Genetics, the Human Approach, 1983; also sects. on biology Encyclopedia Science; sects. on genetics Encyclopedia Brit., World Book, Am. People's Encyclopedia. Member Colorado Board Examiners in Basic Scis. Named Outstanding Scholar of Year University Northern Colorado, 1972. Fellow American Association for the Advancement of Science; member Am. Society Human Genetics, Genetics Society Am., Eugenics Society Am., Sigma Xi., Elk, Lion. Home: 2316 15th St Apartment 411 Greeley Colorado 80631

WINFREE, ARTHUR TAYLOR, biologist, educator; born St. Petersburg, Florida, May 15, 1942; son of Charles Van and Dorothy Rose (Scheb) W.; married Ji-Yun Yang, June 18, 1983; children—Rachael, Erik. Bachelor of Engineering. in Physics, Cornell University, 1965; Doctor of Philosophy in Biology, Princeton University, 1970. Lic. private pilot. Assistant professor theoretical biology University Chicago, 1969-72; associate professor biology Purdue University, West Lafayette, Ind., 1972-79; professor Purdue University, 1979-86; professor ecology and evolutionary biology University Arizona, Tucson, 1986—;

president, director research Institute Natural Philosophy, Incorporated, 1979—. Author: The Geometry of Biological Time, 1980, When Time Breaks Down, 1986, The Timing of Biological Clocks, 1987. Recipient Career Devel. award National Institutes of Health, 1973-78; National Science Foundation grantee, 1966—; MacArthur fellow, 1984-89. Home: 1210 Placita de Graciela Tucson Arizona 85718 Office: University Ariz 326 BSW Tucson Arizona 85721

WINKLER, ROBERT LEWIS, statistics educator, researcher, author, consultant; born Chicago, February 12, 1943; son of Roy Henry and Catherine Pauline (Fleming) W.; married Dorothy Marie Hespen, June 13, 1964; children: Kevin Mark, Kristin Lynne. Bachelor of Science, University Illinois, 1963; Doctor of Philosophy, University Chicago, 1966. Assistant professor Ind. University, Bloomington, 1966-69, associate professor; 1969-72, professor; 1972-80, distinguished professor quantitative business analysis; 1980-84; visiting associate professor University Washington, Seattle, 1970-71; visiting scientist National Center Atmospheric Research, Boulder, Colorado, 1972; research scientist international Institute Applied Systems Analysis, Laxenburg, Austria, 1973-74; visiting professor Stanford University, 1974, Institut Européen d'Administration des Affaires, Fontainebleau, France, 1980-81; International Business Machines Corporation research professor Duke University, 1984-85, Calvin Bryce Hoover professor, 1985—consultant in field, 1970—. Author: Statistics, 1970, Introduction to Bayesian Inference and Decision, 1972; contributor numerous articles to professional journals; departmental editor: Management Science, 1981—; associate editor 7 professional journals, 1970—. Fellow Am. Institute Decision Sciences, Am. Statistical Association; member Institute Management Sci. (vice president publs. 1982-85), International Institute Forecasters. Home: 225 Huntington Drive Chapel Hill North Carolina 27514 Office: Duke U Fuqua School Business Durham North Carolina 27706

WINOGRAD, SHMUEL, mathematician; born Tel Aviv, January 4, 1936; came to United States, 1956, naturalized, 1965; son of Pinchas Mordechai and Rachel Winograd; married Elaine Ruth Tates, Jan 5, 1958; children: Danny H., Sharon A. Bachelor of Science in Electrical Engineering, Massachusetts Institute of Technology, MSEE; Doctor of Philosophy in Math., New York University, 1968. Member research staff International Business Machines Corporation, Yorktown Heights, New York, 1961-70, director math. sci. department; 1970-74, 81—; International Business Machines Corporation fellow 1972—; permanent visiting professor Technion, Israel. Author: (with J.D. Cowan) Reliable Computations in the Presence of Noise; research on complexity of computations and algorithms for signal processing. Fellow Institute of Electrical and Electronics Engineers (W. Wallace McDowell award 1974); member Am. Math. Society, Math. Association Am., Association Computing Machines, National Acad. Sciences, Society Industrial and Applied Math., Am. Acad. Arts and Sciences. Home: 235 Glendale Road Scarsdale New York 10483 Office: International Business Machines

Corporation Research Post Office Box 218 Yorktown Heights New York 10598

WINOGRAD, TERRY ALLEN, computer science educator; born Takoma Park, Maryland, February 24, 1946; married Carol Hutner; children: Shoshana, Avra. Bachelor of Arts In Math., Colorado College, 1966, Doctor of Science (honorary), 1986; postgraduate, University College, London, 1967; Doctor of Philosophy in Applied Math., Massachusetts Institute of Technology, 1970. Instructor math. Massachusetts Institute of Technology, 1970-71, assistant professor electrical engring; 1971-74; visiting assistant professor computer sci. and linguistics Stanford (California) University, 1973-74, from assistant professor to associate professor; 1974-86, associate professor computer sci.; 1986—; consultant Xerox Palo Alto (California) Research Center, 1972-85, Hermenet Incorporated, San Francisco, 1981-83, Action Techs., 1983—, Logonet Incorporated, San Francisco, 1986—; lecturer in field; member adv. board Center for Teaching and Learning Stanford University, 1979-83, member acad. council committee on information tech., 1981-83, member undergrad. council School Engineering, 1985—; adviser State of California, 1983. Board of directors Live Oak Institute, Berkeley, California, 1980—, president, 1984—. Grantee Advanced Research Project Agys., 1969-75, National Science Foundation, 1975-77, 82-85, Xerox, 1975-80, System Devel. Foundation, 1982-83; Hon. Woodrow Wilson fellow, 1966, Hon. National Science Foundation fellow, 1966, Fulbright fellow, 1966-67, Danforth fellow, 1967-70, Mellon Junior Faculty fellow, 1977. Member Computer Professionals for Social Responsibility (member national executive committee 1983—, member national board directors 1984—, president 1987—), Association Computational Linguistics (member editorial board journal 1974-77), Am. Association Artificial Intelligence, Union of Concerned Scientists, Association for Computing Machinery. Home: 746 Esplanada Way Stanford California 94305 Office: Stanford U Department Computer Science Stanford California 94305-2140

WITTWER, SYLVAN HAROLD, former university dean, plant scientist, lecturer, writer; born Hurricane, Utah, January 17, 1917; son of Joseph and Mary Ellen (Stucki) W.; married Maurine Cottle, July 27, 1938; children: La Ree Wittwer Farrar, Alice Wittwer Sowards, Arthur John, Carl Thomas. Bachelor of Science, Utah State College, 1939; Doctor of Philosophy, University Missouri, 1943; Doctor of Science honorary, Utah State University, 1982. Instructor horticulture University Missouri, 1943-46; assistant professor horticulture Michigan State University, East Lansing, 1964-68, associate professor; 1948-50, professor; 1950—, associate dean College Agriculture and Natural Resources; 1965-83, director Agricultural Experiment Station; agriculture management consultant Government of Belize, Belmopan, 1987—. Co-author: Feeding a Billion, 1987; contributor articles to professional journals. Recipient Distinguished Faculty award Michigan State University, 1965; recipient Benjamin Duggar award in plant physiology Auburn University, 1967, Chevron Chemical Agrl. Spokesman of Year award, 1975, Distinguished Service award in Agr. Michigan Farm Bureau, 1976, James E. Talmadge Sci. Achievement award Brigham Young University, 1977, Citation of Merit College Agr., University Missouri Master Farmer award Michigan Vegetable Council, Incorporated, 1983, Hon. Alumnus award Michigan State University, 1983, Distinguished Faculty award Michigan Association Gov. Board Colleges and Universities, 1983, Distinguished Service award Am. Farm Bureau Federation, 1984, Outstanding Educator award Religious Heritage Am., 1985, MI Sci. Trailblazer award as pioneer in world agr., food and nutrition research, 1986. Member Am. Society Horticultural Sci., American Association for the Advancement of Science, Am. Society Plant Physiologists, Botanical Society Am., Society Devel. Biology, Virgin Islands Lenin All Union Acad. Agricultural Sciences (Union of the Soviet Socialist Republics), International Horticultural Society, Scandinavian Society Plant Physiologists, Sigma Xi. Office: Post Office Box 73, 1088 Rose Apple, Belmopan Belize

WOLFE, CHARLES MORGAN, electrical engineering educator; born Morgantown, West Virginia, December 21, 1935; son of Slidell Brown and Mae Louise (Maness) W.; children—David Morgan, Diana Michele. Bachelor of Science in Electrical Engineering, West Virginia University, Morgantown, 1961, Master of Science in Electrical Engineering, 1962; Doctor of Philosophy, University Illinois, 1965. Research associate University Illinois, Urbana, 1965; member staff Massachusetts Institute of Technology Lincoln Laboratory, Lexington, Massachusetts, 1965-75;

professor electrical engring Washington University, St. Louis, 1975—, director semicondr. research laboratory; 1979—, Samuel C. Sachs professor; 1982; consultant Massachusetts Institute of Technology Lincoln Laboratory, 1975-76, Fairchild Semicondr., Palo Alto, California, 1975-76, Air Force Avionics Laboratory, Dayton, Ohio, 1976-79, University Illinois, 1983—. Editor: Gallium Arsenide and Related Compounds, 1979; contributor articles to professional journals, chapters to books. Served as sergeant United States Military Corps, 1955-58. Fellow Institute of Electrical and Electronics Engineers (field awards committee 1984-87); member Electrochemical Society (Electronics Div. award 1978), Am. Physical Society, American Association for the Advancement of Science. Office: Washington U Box 1127 Saint Louis Missouri 63130

WOLFF, SIDNEY CARNE, astronomer, observatory administrator; born Sioux City, Iowa, June 6, 1941; daughter of George Albert and Ethel (Smith) Carne; married Richard J. Wolff, August 29, 1962. Bachelor of Arts, Carleton College, 1962, Doctor of Science (honorary), 1985; Doctor of Philosophy, University California, Berkeley, 1966. Postgrad. research fellow Lick Obs, Santa Cruz, California, 1969; assistant astronomer University Hawaii, Honolulu, 1967-71, associate astronomer; 1971-76; astronomer, associate director Institute Astronomy, Honolulu, 1976-83, acting director; 1983-84; director Kitt Peak National Observatory, Tucson, 1984-87, National Optical Atronomy Observatories, 1987—. Author: The A-Type Stars—Problems and Perspectives, 1983; (with others) Exploration of the Universe, 1987,

Realm of the Universe, 1988; contributor articles to professional journals. Research fellow Lick Obs. Santa Cruz, California, 1967. Member Astronomical Society Pacific (president 1984-86, board directors 1979-85), Am. Astronomical Society (council 1983-86), International Astronomical Union. Office: Kitt Peak National Obs 950 N Cherry Avenue Post Office Box 26732 Tucson Arizona 85726

WOOD, FRANK BRADSHAW, astronomer, educator; born Jackson, Tennessee, December 21, 1915; son of Thomas Frank and Mary (Bradshaw) W.; married Elizabeth Hoar Pepper, October 5, 1945; children—Ellen, Eunice, Mary, Stephen. Bachelor of Science, University Florida, 1936; postgraduate, University Arizona, 1938-39; Master of Arts, Princeton, 1940, Doctor of Philosophy, 1941. Research associate Princeton, 1946; National Research Council fellow Steward Observatory, University Arizona, also Lick Observatory, University California, 1946-47; assistant professor University Arizona, 1947-50; associate professor University Pennsylvania, 1950, professor astronomy; 1954-68, chairman department; 1954-57, 58-68; executive director Flower and Cook Observatory, 1950-54, director; 1954-68, Flower professor; 1958-68; professor astronomy, director optical astronomical observatories University Florida, Gainesville, 1968—; associate chairman department University Florida, 1971-77; established South Pole obs. station, University Florida, 1985—. Author: (with J. Sahade) Interacting Binary Stars, 1978; Editor: Astronomical Photoelectric Photometry, 1953,

Present and Future of Telescope of Moderate Size, 1958, Photoelectric Astronomy for Amateurs, 1963; Contributor articles to professional journals. Colonel, aide de camp, gov.'s staff, State of Tennessee; served with United States Naval Reserve, 1941-46. Decorated Air medal; Fulbright fellow Australian National University, 1957-58; NATO sr. fellow in sci. University Canterbury, Christchurch, New Zealand, 1973; Fulbright fellow Instituto de Astronomia y Fisica del Espacio, Buenos Aires, 1977; recipient Plaque of Appreciation, Government South Korea, 1988. Member Am. Astronomical Society (council 1958-61), Royal Astronomical Society New Zealand (hon.), International Astronomical Union (president commission 42 1967-70, vice president commission 38 1979-82, president 1982-85), Royal Astronomical Society, Florida Acad. Sci. (chairman phys. scis. section 1974-75, president 1983-84), Astronomical Society Can., Astronomical Society Pacific, Explorers Club, Retired Officers Association, Institute Amateur and Professional Photoelectric Photometry, Navy League. Episcopalian. Clubs: Torch, Kiwanis, Troa. Home: 714 Northwest 89th St Gainesville Florida 32607 Office: Department Astronomy U Fla Gainesville Florida

WOOD, WILLIAM BARRY, III, biologist, educator; born Baltimore, February 19, 1938; son of William Barry, Jr. and Mary Lee (Hutchins) W.; married Marie-Elisabeth Renate Hartisch, June 30, 1961; children: Oliver Hartisch, Christopher Barry. Bachelor of Arts, Harvard University, 1959; Doctor of Philosophy, Stanford University, 1963.

Assistant professor biology California Institute Tech., Pasadena, 1965-68; associate professor California Institute Tech., 1968-69, professor biology; 1970-77; professor molecular, cellular and developmental biology University Colorado, Boulder, 1977—; chairman department University Colorado, 1978-83; member panel for developmental biology National Science Foundation, 1970-72; physiological chemistry study section National Institutes of Health, 1974-78; member committee on sci. and public policy National Acad. Sciences, 1979-80; member National Institutes of Health Cellular and Molecular Basis of Disease Rev. Committee, 1984—. Author: (with J.H. Wilson, R.M. Benbow, L.E. Hood) Biochemistry: A Problems Approach, 2d edit, 1981, (with L.E. Hood and J.H. Wilson) Molecular Biology of Eucaryotic Cells, 1975, (with L.E. Hood and I.L. Weissman) Immunology, 1978, (with L.E. Hood, I.L. Weissman, and J.H. Wilson) Immunology, 2d edition, 1984, (with L.E. Hood and I.L. Weissman) Concepts in Immunology, 1978; editorial rev. board Science, 1984—; member editorial board Cell, 1984-87; contributor articles to professional journals. Recipient U.S. Steel Molecular Biology award, 1969; National Institutes of Health research grantee, 1965—; Guggenheim fellow, 1975-76. Member National Acad. Sciences, Am. Acad. Arts and Sciences, Am. Society Biological Chemists, Genetics Society Am., Society for Developmental Biology, Society Nematology, Am. Society Microbiologists, American Association for the Advancement of Science. Office: Department MCD Biology Box 347 U Colorado Boulder Colorado 80309

WOODBURY, MAX ATKIN, biomathematician, educator; born St. George, Utah, April 30, 1917; son of Angus Munn and Grace (Atkin) W.; married Lida Gottsch, May 30, 1947; children—Carolyn, Max Ten Eyck, Christopher, Gregory. Bachelor of Science, University Utah, 1939; Master of Science, University Michigan, 1941, Doctor of Philosophy, 1948; Master of Public Health, University North Carolina, Chapel Hill, 1977. Faculty University Michigan, 1947-49, Princeton, 1950-52, University Pennsylvania, 1952-54; member Institute Advanced Study, Princeton, 1949-50; principal investigator logistics research project Office Naval Research, George Washington University, 1954-56; faculty New York University, 1956-65; professor computer sci. · Duke University, professor biomath. Medical Center; 1966—, senior fellow Center for Study of Aging and Human Devel.; 1975—, senior fellow Center Demographic Studies; 1985—; president Biomed. Information-processing Organization, 1961-62, Institute for Biomed. Computer Research, 1961-71; consultant World Health Organization, UNIVAC, CBS on computer election forecasts, 1952-62, sci. organizations, universities, government agys., corporations. Contributor articles to professional journals. Served with United States Army Air Force, 1941-46, Mediterranean Theatre of Operations. USPHS, National Institutes of Health grantee, also other government agys., 1947—; recipient MERIT award National Institute on Aging, National Institutes of Health, June 1, 1988-May 30, 1998. Fellow American Association for the Advancement of Science, Am. Statistical Association, Institute Math. Statistics; member numerous sci., professional socs., Phi Beta Kappa, Sigma Xi, Phi Kappa Phi. Home: 4008 Bristol Road Durham North Carolina 27707 Office: Duke U 2117 Campus Dr Durham North Carolina 27706

WOODSON, HERBERT HORACE, electrical engineering educator; born Stamford, Texas, April 5, 1925; son of Herbert Viven and Floy (Tunnell) W.; married Blanche Elizabeth Sears, August 17, 1951; children: William Sears, Robert Sears, Bradford Sears. Bachelor of Science, Master of Science, Massachusetts Institute of Technology, 1952, Doctor of Science in Electrical Engineering, 1956. Registered professional engineer, Texas, Massachusetts. Instructor electrical engineering, also project leader magnetics div. Naval Ordnance Laboratory, 1952-54; member faculty M.I.T., 1956-71, professor electrical engineering; 1965-71, Philip Sporn professor energy processing; 1967-71; professor electrical engineering, chairman department University Texas, Austin, 1971-81, Alcoa Foundation professor; 1972-75, Texas Atomic Energy Research Foundation professor engineering; 1980-82, Ernest H. Cockrell Centennial professor engineering; 1982—, director Center for Energy Studies; 1973—, associate dean devel. and planning College Engineering; 1986-87, acting dean; 1987-88, dean; 1988—; staff engineer elec. engineering div. AEP Service Corp., New York City, 1965-66; consultant to industry, 1956—. Author: (with others) Electromechanical Dynamics, parts I, II, III. Served with United States Naval Reserve, 1943-46. Fellow Institute of Electrical and Electronics Engineers (president Power Engineering Society 1978-80); member Am. Society Engineering Education, National Acad. Engineering, American Association for the Advancement of Science. Patentee in field. Home: 7603 Rustling Road Austin Texas 78731 Office: College Engring U Tex Austin Texas 78731

WOODWELL, GEORGE MASTERS, ecologist, educator, author, lecturer; born Cambridge, Massachusetts, October 23, 1928; son of Philip McIntire and Virginia (Sellers) W.; married Alice Katharine Rondthaler, June 23, 1955; children: Caroline Alice, Marjorie Virginia, Jane Katharine, John Christopher. Bachelor of Arts, Dartmouth College, 1950; Master of Arts, Duke University, 1956, Doctor of Philosophy, 1958; Doctor of Science (honorary), Williams College, 1977, Miami University, 1984, Carleton College, 1988. Member faculty University Maine, 1957-61, associate professor botany; 1960-61; visiting assistant ecologist, biology department Brookhaven National Laboratory, Upton, New York, 1961-62; ecologist Brookhaven National Laboratory, 1965-67, senior ecologist; 1967-75; founder, director Ecosystems Center, 1975-85; deputy and assistant director Marine Biological Laboratory, Woods Hole, Massachusetts, 1975-76; founder, director Woods Hole Research Center, 1985—; lecturer Yale School Forestry, 1967—, president; 1988—; chairman Conference on Long Term Biological Consequences of Nuclear War, 1982-83. Editor: Ecological Effects of Nuclear War, 1965, Diversity and Stability in Ecological Systems, 1969, (with E.V. Pecan) Carbon and the Biosphere, 1973, The Role of Terrestrial Vegetation in the Global Carbon Cycle: Measurement by

Remote Sensing, 1984. Founding trustee Environmental Def. Fund, 1967; founding trustee Natural Resources Def. Council, 1970, vice chairman, 1974—; founding trustee World Resources Institute, 1982—; board of directors World Wildlife Fund, 1970-84, chairman, 1980-84; board of directors Conservation Foundation, 1975-77, Ruth Mott Fund, 1984—; adv. committee TMI Pub. Health Fund., 1980—. Fellow American Association for the Advancement of Science, Am. Acad. Arts and Sciences; member Brit. Ecological Society, Ecological Society Am. (vice president 1966-67, president 1977-78), Sea Education Association (board directors 1980-85), Sigma Xi. Research, pub. on structure and function of natural communities, biotic impoverishment, especially ecological effects of ionizing radiation, effects of persistent toxins, world carbon cycle. Office: Woods Hole Research Center Box 296 Fisher House 13 Church St Woods Hole Massachusetts 02543

WOOLDRIDGE, DEAN EVERETT, scientist, executive; born Chickasha, Oklahoma, May 30, 1913; son of Auttie Noonan and Irene Amanda (Kerr) W.; married Helene Detweiler, September 1936; children—Dean Edgar, Anna Lou, James Allan. Bachelor of Arts, University Oklahoma, 1932, Master of Science, 1933; Doctor of Philosophy, California Institute Tech., 1936. Member tech. staff Bell Telephone Laboratories, New York City, 1936-46; co-director research and devel. labs Hughes Aircraft Company, Culver City, California, 1946-52, vice president research and devel.; 1952-53; president, director Ramo-Wooldridge Corp., Los Angeles, 1953-58, Thompson Ramo Wooldridge,

Incorporated, Los Angeles, also Cleveland, 1958-62; research associate California Institute Tech., 1962-79. Author: The Machinery of the Brain, 1963, The Machinery of Life, 1966, Mechanical Man, 1968, Sensory Processing in the Brain, 1979, also articles. Recipient citation of Honor Air Force Association, 1950, Raymond E. Hackett award, 1955, Westinghouse Sci. Writing award American Association for the Advancement of Science, 1963. Fellow American Association for the Advancement of Science, Am. Acad. Arts and Sci., Am. Physical Society, Institute of Electrical and Electronics Engineers, American Institute of Aeronautics and Astronautics; member National Acad. Sciences, National Acad. Engineering, California Institute Assos., Am. Institute Physics, Phi Beta Kappa, Sigma Xi, Tau Beta Pi, Phi Eta Sigma, Eta Kappa Nu. Address: 4545 Via Esperanza Santa Barbara California 93110

WOOLLEY, GEORGE WALTER, biologist, educator; born Osborne, Kansas, November 9, 1904; son of George Aitcheson and Nora Belle (Jackson) W.; married Anne Geneva Collins, November 2, 1936; children: George Aitcheson, Margaret Anne, Lawrence Jackson. Bachelor of Science, Iowa State University, 1930; Master of Science, University Wisconsin, 1931, Doctor of Philosophy, 1935. Fellow University Wisconsin, 1935-36; member staff Jackson Memorial Laboratory, Bar Harbor, Maine, 1936-49; board of directors Jackson Memorial Laboratory, 1937-49, vice president board; 1943-47, assistant director and sci. administrator; 1947-49, visiting research associate; 1949—; member chief div. steroid biology Sloan-

Kettering Institute, New York City, 1949-58, professor biology; 1949-58; professor biology Sloan-Kettering Institute div. Cornell University Medical College, Ithaca, New York, 1951—, chief div. human tumor experimental chemotherapy; 1958-61, chief div. tumor biology; 1961-66; associate scientist Sloan-Kettering Institute Cancer Research, 1966—; health sci. administrator, program coordinator, head biological sciences section National Institute General Medical Sciences, National Institutes of Health, 1966-85; consultant National Education Service United States, Washington, 1961—; special consultant to National Cancer Institute, National Institutes of Health, 1956—; Member Expert Panel on Carcinogenicity, unio intern. contra cancerum, 1962—; member panel committee on growth National Research Council, 1945-51; member several international medical congresses. Author chapters in medical books.; Member editorial board: Journal National Cancer Inst, 1947-50. Trustee Dalton Schools.
Fellow American Association for the Advancement of Science, New York Acad. Sci.; member Am. Mus. Natural History, National Sci. Teachers Association (cons. 1961—), Am. Association Cancer Research (director 1951-54), Am. Society Human Genetics, Mount Desert Island Biological Lab., Society Experimental Biology and Medicine, Am. Institute Biological Sciences, Am. Association Anatomists, Am. Genetic Association, Wisconsin Acad. Arts Sci. and Letters, Jackson Lab. Association, Genetics Society Am., Environmental Mutagen Society, Sigma Xi. Clubs: Bar Harbor, Bar Harbor (Maine) Yacht. Home: Apartment 336 Kenwood Place 5301 Westbard Circle Bethesda Maryland 20816 Office: 5333 Westbard Avenue Bethesda Maryland 20016

WOYCZYNSKI, WOJBOR ANDRZEJ, mathematician, educator; born Czestochowa, Poland, October 24, 1943; came to United States, 1970; son of Eugeniusz and Otylia Sabina (Borkiewicz) W.; divorced; 1 child, Martin Wojbor. MSEE, Wroclaw (Poland) Polytech., 1966; Doctor of Philosophy in Math., Wroclaw University, 1968. Assistant professor Institute Math. Wroclaw University, 1968-72, associate professor; 1972-77; professor, department math. Cleveland State University, Cleveland, 1977-82; professor, chairman department math. and statistics Case Western Reserve University, Cleveland, 1982—; research fellow Institute Math. Polish Acad. Sciences, Warsaw, 1969-76; post-doctoral fellow Carnegie-Mellon University, Pittsburgh, 1970-72; visiting associate professor Northwestern University, Evanston, Illinois, 1976-77; visiting professor Aarhus University, Denmark, 1972, University Paris, 1973, University Wic., Madison, 1976, University South Carolina, 1979, University North Carolina, Chapel Hill, 1983, 84, Gottingen University, Federal Republic Germany, 1985.
Dep. editor-in-chief: Annals of the Polish Math. Society, 1973-77; associate editor: Chemometrics Journal, 1987—, Probability and Mathematical Statistics, 1988—; co-editor: Martingale Theory and Harmonic Analysis in Banach Spaces, 1982, Probablility Theory and Harmonic Analysis, 1986; author: (monograph) Martingales and Geometry in Banach Spaces I, 1975, part II, 1978. Recipient Great prize of the Polish Math. Society, Warsaw, 1972, research grants National

Science Foundation, Washington, 1970,71, 76, 77, 81, 87—, Office of Naval Research, Washington, 1985-88. Fellow: Institute of Math. Statistics; member Am. Math. Society, Polish Math. Society, Polish Institute Arts and Sciences. Roman Catholic. Club: Park East Racquet (Beachwood, Ohio). Avocations: tennis, music, skiing, sailing. Home: 18417 Scottsdale Boulevard Shaker Heights Ohio 44122 Office: Case Western Reserve U Department of Math Cleveland Ohio 44106

WRIGHT, HERBERT E(DGAR), JR., geologist; born Malden, Massachusetts, September 13, 1917; son of Herbert E. and Annie M. (Richardson) W.; married Rhea Jane Hahn, June 21, 1943; children—Richard, Jonathan, Stephen, Andrew, Jeffrey. Bachelor of Arts, Harvard University, 1939; Master of Arts, 1941, Doctor of Philosophy, 1943; Doctor of Science (honorary), Trinity College, Dublin, Ireland, 1966; Doctor of Philosophy (honorary), Lund University, Sweden, 1987. Instructor Brown University, 1946-47; assistant professor geology University Minnesota, Minneapolis, 1947-51; associate professor University Minnesota, 1951-59, professor; 1959-74, Regents' professor geology, ecology and botany; 1974—; director Limnological Research Center, 1963—. Served to major United States Army Air Force, 1942-45. Decorated Distinguished Flying Cross, Air medal with 6 oak leaf clusters; Guggenheim fellow, 1954-55; Wenner-Gren fellow, 1954-55. Fellow Geological Society Am., American Association for the Advancement of Science, Scientists Institute Pub. Information; member Ecological Society Am., Am. Society Limnology, Oceanography, Am. Quaternary Association, Arctic Institute, Brit. Ecological Society. Research on Quaternary geology, paleoecology, paleolimnology and environ. archaeology in Minnesota, Wyoming, Sweden, Yukon, Labrador, Peru, eastern Mediterranean. Home: 1426 Hythe St Saint Paul Minnesota 55108 Office: 221 Pillsbury Hall U of Minnesota 310 Pillsbury Dr Southeast Minneapolis Minnesota 55455

WRIGHT, RICHARD NEWPORT, III, civil engineer, government official; born Syracuse, New York, May 17, 1932; son of Richard Newport and Carolyn (Baker) W.; married Teresa Rios, August 23, 1959; children—John Stannard, Carolyn Maria, Elizabeth Rebecca, Edward Newport. Bachelor of Civil Engineering, Syracuse University, 1953, Master of Civil Engineering (Parcel fellow), 1955; Doctor of Philosophy, University Illinois, 1962. Junior engineer Pennsylvania Railroad, Philadelphia, 1953-55; instructor civil engineering University Illinois, Urbana, 1957-62; assistant professor University Illinois, 1962-65, associate professor; 1965-70, professor; 1970-74, adj. professor; 1974-79; chief structures section building Research div. United States Bureau Standards, Washington, 1971-72; president International Council for building Research, Studies and Documentation, 1983-86; deputy director tech. Center building Tech., 1972-73, director, 1974—. Contributor articles to professional journals. Vice president Montgomery Village Foundation, 1988—, board of directors, 1985—. Served with Army of the United States, 1955-57. Named Federal Engineer of Year National Society Professional Engrs., 1988. Fellow American Society of Civil

Engineers. Home: 20081 Doolittle St Montgomery Village Maryland 20879 Office: Center Building Technology National Bureau Standards Gaithersburg Maryland 20899

WRIGHT, STEPHEN GAILORD, civil engineering educator, consultant; born San Diego, August 13, 1943; son of Homer Angelo and Elizabeth Videlle (Ward) W.; married Ouida Jo Kennedy; children: Michelle, Richard. BSCE, University California, Berkeley, 1966, MSCE, 1967, Doctor of Philosophy Civil Engineer, 1969. Professor civil engineering University Texas, Austin, 1969—. Contributor numerous tech. papers & research reports, 1969—. Member American Society of Civil Engineers. Republican. Presbyterian. Home: 3406 Shinoak Dr Austin Texas 78731 Office: U Tex Department Civil Engring Austin Texas 78712

WU, THEODORE YAO-TSU, engineer; born Changchow, Kiangsu, China, March 20, 1924; came to United States, 1948, naturalized, 1962; son of Ren Fu and Gee-Ing (Shu) W.; married Chin-Hua Shih, June 17, 1950; children: Fonda Bai-yueh, Melba Bai-chin. Bachelor of Science, Chiano-Tung University, 1946; Master of Science, Iowa State University, 1948; Doctor of Philosophy, California Institute Tech., 1952. Member faculty California Institute Tech., Pasadena, 1952—; associate professor California Institute Tech., 1957-61, professor engineering sci.; 1961—; visiting professor Hamburg (Germany) University, 1964-65; consultant numerous industrial firms. Editorial board: Advances in Applied Mechanics series, 1970; Contributor professional journals. Guggenheim fellow, 1964-65. Fellow Am. Physical Society, American Institute of Aeronautics and Astronautics

(associate); member Sigma Xi, National Acad. Engineering, Phi Tau Phi. Office: California Institute Tech Pasadena California 91125

WYLIE, CLARENCE RAYMOND, JR., educator; born Cincinnati, September 9, 1911; son of Clarence Raymond and Elizabeth M. (Shaw) W.; married Sikri M. Aho, June 27, 1935 (deceased 1956); children: Chris Raymond (deceased), Charles Victor; married Ellen F. Rasor, June 25, 1958. Bachelor of Science, Wayne State University, 1931, Bachelor of Arts, 1931; Master of Science, Cornell University, 1932, Doctor of Philosophy, 1934. Instructor Ohio State University, 1934-40, assistant professor; 1940-46; consultant mathematican Propeller Laboratory, Wright Field, Dayton, Ohio, 1943-46; chairman department math. and acting dean College of Engineering, Air Institute Tech., Wright Field, Dayton, 1946-48; professor math. University Utah, Salt Lake City, 1948-69; chairman department University Utah, 1948-67; professor math. Furman University, Greenville, South Carolina, 1969—; William R. Kenan, Junior professor math. Furman University, 1971-78, Kenan professor emeritus; 1978—, chairman department math.; 1970-76; part-time consultant math. General Electric Company, Schenectady, Briggs Manufacturing Company, Detroit, Aero Products div. General Motors Corp., Dayton; Humble lecturer in sci. Humble Oil Company, 1955; distinguished visitor Westminster College, Salt Lake City, 1981; consultant mathematician Holloman Air Base, New Mexico, 1955, 56. Author: 101 Puzzles in Thought and Logic, 1958, Advanced Engineering Mathematics, 5th edit, 1982,

Introduction to Projective Geometry, 1969, Differential Equations, 1979; other books, also papers, articles, pub. in math. journals Strange Havoc; poems, 1956, The World of Eric Lim; limericks, 1987, also miscellaneous poetry. Recipient Distinguished Alumni award Wayne State University, 1956, Distinguished Engineering Alumni Achievement award, 1985, named to Engineering College Hall of Fame, 1985; Algernon Sydney Sullivan award Furman University, 1982; Bell Tower award Furman University, 1986. Fellow American Association for the Advancement of Science; member Math. Association Am. (chairman Rocky Mountain section 1955-56, board govs. 1957-60, section lecturer Southeastern section 1983), Am. Math. Society, Am. Society Engineering Education (chairman math. division 1949-50, 1957-58), Utah Acad. Sci. Arts and Letters, South Carolina Acad. Sci., Phi Beta Kappa, Sigma Xi, Pi Mu Epsilon, Sigma Pi Sigma, Pi Kappa Delta, Delta Sigma Rho, Sigma Delta Psi, Sigma Rho Tau, Phi Kappa Phi, Tau Kappa Alpha. Methodist.

WYNGAARDEN, JAMES BARNES, physician; born East Grand Rapids, Michigan, October 19, 1924; son of Martin Jacob and Johanna (Kempers) W.; married Ethel Vredevoogd, June 20, 1946 (divorced 1977); children: Patricia Wyngaarden Fitzpatrick, Joanna Wyngaarden Gandy, Martha Wyngaarden Krauss, Lisa Wyngaarden Rolland, James Barnes Jr. Student, Calvin College, 1942-43, Western Michigan University, 1943-44; Doctor of Medicine, University Michigan, 1948; Doctor of Science (honorary), University Michigan and Medical College of Ohio, 1984, Tel Aviv University, 1987; Doctor of Philosophy (honorary), University Illinois, Chicago, 1985; Doctor of Science (honorary), George Washington University, 1985. Diplomate: Am. Board Internal Medicine. Intern Massachusetts General Hospital, Boston, 1948-49; resident Massachusetts General Hospital, 1949-51; visiting investigator Pub. Health Research Institute, New York City, 1952-53; investigator National Institutes of Health, United States Public Health Service, Bethesda, Maryland, 1953-56; associate professor medicine and biochemistry Duke Medical School, 1956-61, professor; 1961-65; visiting scientist Institute de Biologie-Physiochemique, Paris, 1963-64; professor, chairman University Pennsylvania Medical School, 1965-67; physician-in-chief Medical Service Hospital University PA., Philadelphia, 1965-67; Frederic M. Hanes professor, chairman department medicine Duke Medical School, 1967-82; physician-in-chief Medical Service Duke University Hospital, Durham, North Carolina, 1967-82; chief of staff Duke University Hospital, Durham, 1981-82; director National Institutes of Health, Bethesda, MD, 1982-89; member staff Duke, Veteran's Administration, Durham County hospitals; consultant Office Sci. and Tech. Executive Office of President, 1966-72; Member President's Sci. Adv. Committee, 1972-73; member President's Committee for National Medal of Sci., 1977-80; member adv. committee biology and medicine Atomic Energy Commission, 1966-68; member board sci. counselors National Institutes of Health, 1971-74; member adv. board Howard Hughes Medical Institute, 1969-82; member adv. council Life Insurance Medical Research Fund, 1967-70; adv. board

Sci. Year, 1977-81; vice chairman Committee on Study National Needs for Biomed. and Behavioral Research Personnel, National Research Council, 1977-81. Author: (with W.N. Kelley) Gout and Hyperuricemia, 1976; (with J.B. Stanbury) The Metabolic Bases of Inherited Disease, 1966; (with O. Sperling, A. DeVries) Purine Metabolism in Man, 1974; editor: (with L.H. Smith Junior) Cecil Textbook of Medicine, 1982, 85; Member editorial board: Journal Biol. Chemistry, 1971-74, Arthritis and Rheumatism, 1959-66, Journal Clinical Investigation, 1962-66, Annual Internal Medicine, 1964-74, Medicine, 1963— ; editor: (with J.B. Stanbury, D.S. Fredrickson) The Metabolic Basis of Inherited Disease, 1960, 66, 72, 78, 83, (with O. Sperling and A. DeVries) Purine Metabolism in Man, 1974, (with L.H. Smith, Junior) Cecil Textbook of Medicine, 16th edit, 1982, 17th edition, 1985, 18th edition, 1988 (with L.H. Smith Junior) Rev. of General Internal Medicine: A Self-Assessment Guide, 2d edition, 1982, 3d edition, 1985. Board of directors Royal Society Medicine Foundation, 1971-76, The Robert Wood Johnson Foundation Clin. Scholar Program., 1973-78. Served with United States Naval Reserve, 1943-46; senior surgeon United States Public Health Service, 1951-56, rear admiral United States Public Health Service, 1982—. Recipient Borden Undergrad. Research award University Michigan, 1948, North Carolina Governor's award for sci., 1974, Distinguished Alumnus award Western Michigan University, 1984, Robert Williams award Association Profs. Medicine, 1985; Dalton scholar in medicine Massachusetts General Hospital, 1950; Royal College Physicians fellow, 1984. Member Am. Rheumatism Association, Am. Federation Clinical Research, Southern Society Clinical Investigation (president 1974, founder's medal 1978), American College of Physians (John Phillips Memorial award 1980), Am. Society Clinical Investigation, American Association for the Advancement of Science, Am. Society Biological Chemists, Association Am. Physicians (councillor 1973-77, president 1978), Endocrine Society, National Acad. Sciences, Royal Acad. Sciences Sweden, Am. Acad. Arts and Sci., Institute Medicine, Sigma Xi. Democrat. Presbyterian. Club: Interurban Clinical (Baltimore). Avocations: tennis, skiing, painting. Office: National Institute of Health Building 1 Room 124 Bethesda Maryland 20892

WYSS, ORVILLE, microbiology educator; born Medford, Wisconsin, September 10, 1912; son of John and Gertrude (Walther) W.; married Margaret Bedell, May 31, 1941; children: Ann, Jane, Patti Bess. Bachelor of Science, University Wisconsin, 1937; Master of Science, 1938, Doctor of Philosophy, 1941. Industrial research Wallace and Tiernan Company, Belleville, New Jersey, 1941-45; faculty University Texas, 1945—, professor microbiology; 1948—, chairman department microbiology; 1959-69, 75-76. Author: Elementary Microbiology, 1964, Principles of Biology, 1964, Microorganisms and Man, 1971; also articles microbial physiology.; Asso. editor: Bacteriological Revs, 1960-66. Antarctic research fellow McMurdo Sound, 1961; Exchange scholar Union of Soviet Socialist Republics, 1965; Fulbright fellow Sydney, Australia, 1970; Fulbright fellow Kathmandu, Nepal, 1978; Bose lecturer Calcutta

University, 1971. Charter fellow Am. Acad. Microbiology (board govs.); fellow American Association for the Advancement of Science; member Am. Society Biological Chemists, Am. Society Microbiology (president 1964-65), Texas Acad. Sci., Am. Chemical Society, Brit. Society General Microbiology, Sigma Xi (past president Texas), Phi Kappa Phi (past president Texas). Democrat. Unitarian. Club: Headliner's. Home: 4606 Madrona Dr Austin Texas 78731

YALOW, ROSALYN SUSSMAN, medical physicist; born New York City, July 19, 1921; daughter of Simon and Clara (Zipper) Sussman; married A. Aaron Yalow, June 6, 1943; children: Benjamin, Elanna. Bachelor of Arts, Hunter College, 1941; Master of Science, University Illinois, Urbana, 1942, Doctor of Philosophy, 1945; Doctor of Science (honorary), University Illinois, Chicago, 1974, Philadelphia College Pharmacy and Science, 1976, New York Medical College, 1976, Medical College Wisconsin, Milwaukee, 1977, Yeshiva University, 1977, Southampton (New York) College, 1978, Bucknell University, 1978, Princeton University, 1978, Jersey City State College, 1979, Medical College Pennsylvania, 1979, Manhattan College, 1979, University Vermont, 1980, University Hartford, 1980, Rutgers University, 1980, Rensselaer Polytechnic Institute, 1980, Colgate University, 1981, University Southern California, 1981, Clarkson College, 1982, University Miami, 1983, Washington University, St. Louis, 1983, Adelphi University, 1983, University Alberta (Can.), 1983, Columbia University, 1984, State University of New York, 1984, Tel Aviv University, 1985, Claremont (California) University, 1986, Mills College, Oakland, California, 1986, Cedar Crest College, Allentown, Pennsylvania, 1988, Drew University, Madison, New Jersey, 1988, Lehigh University, 1988; Doctor of Humane Letters (honorary), Hunter College, 1978, Sacred Heart University, Connecticut, 1978, St. Michael's College, Winooski Park, Vermont, 1979, Johns Hopkins University, 1979, College St. Rose, 1988; Doctor honoris causa, University Rosario, Argentina, 1980, University Ghent, Belgium, 1984; Doctor Humanities and Letters (honorary), Columbia University, 1984; Doctor of Philosophy honoris causa, Bar-Ilan University, Israel, 1987. Diplomate: Am. Board Scis. Lecturer, assistant professor physics Hunter College, 1946-50; physicist, assistant chief radiosotope service Veteran's Administration Hospital, Bronx, New York, 1950-70, chief nuclear medicine; 1970-80, acting chief radioisotope service; 1968-70; research professor Mount Sinai School Medicine, City University of New York, 1968-74, Distinguished Service professor; 1974-79, Solomon A. Berson Distinguished prof.-at-large; 1986—; Distinguished prof.-at-large Albert Einstein College Medicine, Yeshiva University, 1979-85, professor emeritus; 1986—; chairman department clinical sciences Montefiore Medical Center, Bronx, 1980-85; consultant Lenox Hill Hospital, New York City, 1956-62, World Health Organization, Bombay, 1978; secretary United States National Committee on Medical Physics, 1963-67; member national committee Radiation Protection, Subcom. 13, 1957; member President's Study Group on Careers for Women, 1966-72; senior medical investigator Veteran's Administration, 1972—; director Solomon A. Berson

Research Laboratory, Veteran's Administration Hospital, Bronx, New York, 1973—. Co-editor: Hormone and Metabolic Research, 1973-79; editorial adv. council: Acta Diabetologica Latina, 1975-77, Encyclopedia Universalis, 1978—; editorial board: Mount Sinai Journal Medicine, 1976-79, Diabetes, 1976, Endocrinology, 1967-72; contributor numerous articles to professional journals. Board of directors New York Diabetes Association, 1974.

Recipient Veteran's Administration William S. Middleton Medical Research award, 1960; Eli Lilly award Am. Diabetes Association, 1961; Van Slyke award New York met. sect. Am. Association Clinical Chemists, 1968; award A.C.P., 1971; Dickson prize University Pitts., 1971; Howard Taylor Ricketts award University Chicago, 1971; Gairdner Foundation International award, 1971; Commemorative medallion Am. Diabetes Association, 1972; Bernstein award Medical Society State New York, 1974; Boehringer-Mannheim Corp. award Am. Association Clinical Chemists, 1975; Sci. Achievement award American Medical Association, 1975; Exceptional Service award Veteran's Administration, 1975; A. Cressy Morrison award New York Acad. Sciences, 1975; sustaining membership award Association Mil. Surgeons, 1975; Distinguished Achievement award Modern Medicine, 1976; Albert Lasker Basic Medical Research award, 1976; La Madonnina International prize Milan, 1977; Golden Plate award Am. Acad. Achievement, 1977; Nobel prize for physiology medicine, 1977; citation of esteem St. John's University, 1979; G. von Hevesy medal, 1978; Rosalyn S. Yalow Research and Devel. award established Am. Diabetes Associa-tion, 1978; Banting medal, 1978; Torch of Learning award Am. Friends Hebrew University, 1978; Virchow gold medal Virchow-Pirquet Medical Society, 1978; Gratum Genus Humanum gold medal World Federation Nuclear Medicine or Biology, 1978; Jacobi medallion Asso. Alumni Mount Sinai School Medicine, 1978; Jubilee medal College of New Rochelle, 1978; Veteran's Administration Exceptional Service award, 1978; Federal Woman's award, 1961; Harvey lecturer, 1966; Am. Gastroenterol. Association Memorial lecturer, 1972; Joslin lecturer New England Diabetes Association, 1972; Franklin I. Harris Memorial lecturer, 1973; 1st Hagedorn Memorial lecturer Acta Endocrinologica Congress, 1973; Sarasota Medical award for achievement and excellence, 1979; gold medal Phi Lambda Kappa, 1980; Achievement in Life award Encyclopaedia Brit., 1980; Theobald Smith award, 1982; President's Cabinet award University Detroit, 1982; John and Samuel Bard award in medicine and sci. Bard College, 1982; Distinguished Research award Dallas Association Retarded Citizens, 1982, National Medal Sci., 1988; numerous others. Fellow New York Acad. Sciences (chairman biophysics division 1964-65), Am. College Radiology (associate in physics), Clinical Society New York Diabetes Association; member National Acad. Sciences, Am. Acad. Arts and Sciences, Am. Physical Society, Radiation Research Society, Am. Association Physicists in Medicine, Biophys. Society, Society Nuclear Medicine, Endocrine Society (Koch award 1972, president 1978), Am. Physiological Society, (hon.) Harvey Society, (hon.) Medical Association Argentina, (hon.) Diabetes Society

Argentina, (hon.) Am. College Nuclear Physicians, (hon.) The New York Acad. Medicine, (hon.) Am. Gastroentorological Association, (hon.) New York Roentgen Society, (hon.) Society Nuclear Medicine, Phi Beta Kappa, Sigma Xi, Sigma Pi Sigma, Pi Mu Epsilon, Sigma Delta Epsilon. Office: Virginia Med Center 130 W Kingsbridge Road Bronx New York 10468

YANDERS, ARMON FREDERICK, research administrator; born Lincoln, Nebraska, April 12, 1928; son of Fred W. and Beatrice (Pate) Y.; married Evelyn Louise Gatz, August 1, 1948; children: Mark Frederick, Kent Michael. Bachelor of Arts, Nebraska State College, Peru, 1948; Master of Science, University Nebraska, 1950, Doctor of Philosophy, 1953. Research associate Oak Ridge National Laboratory and Northwestern University, 1953-54; biophysicist United States Naval Radiological Defense Laboratory, San Francisco, 1955-58; associate geneticist Argonne (Illinois) National Laboratory, 1958-59; with department zoology Michigan State University, 1959-69; professor, assistant dean Michigan State University (College Natural Sci.), 1963-69; professor biological sciences University Missouri, Columbia, 1969—, dean College Arts and Sciences; 1969-82, research professor, director Environmental Trace Substances Research Center; 1983—; research professor, director Environmental Trace Substances Research Center and Sinclair Comparative Medicine Research Farm, Columbia, 1984—; Trustee Argonne Universities Association, 1965-77, vice president, 1969-73, president, 1973, 76-77, chairman board, 1973-75; board of directors

Council of Colleges of Arts and Sciences, 1981-82; member adv. committee environmental hazards Veteran's Administration, Washington, 1985—. Contributor articles to professional journals. Served from ensign to lieutenant United States Naval Reserve, 1954-58. Fellow American Association for the Advancement of Science; member American Association of University Profs. (Robert W. Martin acad. freedom award 1971), Am. Institute Biological Sci., Environmental Mutagen Society, Genetics Society Am., Radiation Research Society, Society Environmental Toxicology and Chemistry. Home: 2405 Ridgefield Road Columbia Missouri 65203 Office: U Missouri Environ Trace Substances Research Ctr/Sinclair Comparative Medicine Research Farm Route 3 Columbia Missouri 65203

YANG, CHEN NING, physicist, educator; born Hofei, Anhwei, People's Republic of China, September 22, 1922; naturalized, 1964; son of Ke Chuan and Meng Hwa Lo; married Chih Li Tu, August 26, 1950; children: Franklin, Gilbert, Eulee. Bachelor of Science, National Southwest Associate University, China, 1942; Doctor of Philosophy, University Chicago, 1948; Doctor of Science (honorary), Princeton University, 1958, Brooklyn Polytechnic Institute, 1965, University Wroclaw, Poland, 1974, Gustavus Adolphus College, 1975, University Maryland, 1979, University Durham, England, 1979, Fudan University, 1984, Eldg. Technische Hochschule, Switzerland, 1987. Instructor, University Chicago, 1948-49; member Institute Advanced Study, Princeton University, 1949-55, professor; 1955-66; Albert Einstein professor State University of New

York, Stony Brook, 1966—; director State University of New York (Institute Theoretical Physics), 1966—. Trustee Rockefeller University, 1970-76, Salk Institute, 1978—, Ben Gurion University, 1980—. Recipient Albert Einstein Commemorative award in sci., 1957, Nobel prize for physics, 1957, Rumford prize, 1980, National medal of sci., 1986, Liberty award, 1986. Member Am. Physical Society, National Acad. Sciences, Brazilian Acad. Sciences, Venezuelan Acad. Sciences, Royal Spanish Acad. Sciences, Am. Philosophical Society, American Association for the Advancement of Science (board directors 1975-79), Sigma Xi. Office: State University of New York Department Physics Stony Brook New York 11794

YARDLEY, JOHN FINLEY, aerospace engineer; born St. Louis, February 1, 1925; son of Finley Abna and Johnnie (Patterson) Y.; married Phyllis Steele, July 25, 1946; children: Kathryn, Robert, Mary, Elizabeth, Susan. Bachelor of Science, Iowa State College, 1944; Master of Science, Washington University, St. Louis, 1950. Structral and aeronautical engineer McDonnell Aircraft Corp., St. Louis, 1946-55; chief strength engineer McDonnell Aircraft Corp., ` 1956-57; project engineer Mercury spacecraft design, 1958-60; launch operations manager Mercury and Gemini spacecraft, Cape Canaveral, Florida, 1960-64; Gemini tech. director Mercury and Gemini spacecraft, 1964-67; vice president, deputy general manager Eastern div. McDonnell Douglas Astronautics, 1968-72, vice president, general manager; 1973-74, president; 1981—; associate administrator for manned space flight National Aeronautics and Space Administration, Washington, 1974-81. Served to ensign United States Naval Reserve, 1943-46. Recipient Achievement award St. Louis sect. Institute Aerospace Sciences, 1961, John J. Montgomery award, 1963, Pub. Service award National Aeronautics and Space Administration, 1963, 66 ; professional achievement citation Iowa State College, 1970, Spirit of St. Louis medal, 1973, Alumni citation Washington University, 1975, Distinguished Achievement citation Iowa State University, 1976, Presidential citation as meritorious executive Senior Executive Service, 1980, National Aeronautics and Space Administration Distinguished Service medal, 1981, Goddard Memorial trophy, 1983, Achievement award Washington University Engineering Alumni, 1983, Elmer A. Sperry award, 1986; named Engineer of Year National Aeronautics and Space Administration, 1982; Von Karman Astronautics Lectureship award, 1988. Fellow American Institute of Aeronautics and Astronautics (Goddard award 1982), Am. Astronautical Society (Space Flight award 1978); member International Acad. Astronautics, National Aeronautics and Space Administration Alumni League (board directors), National Acad. Engineering, St. Louis Counts (associate), National Space Club (board govs.), Tau Beta Pi, Phi Kappa Phi, Phi Eta Sigma, Phi Mu Epsilon. Presbyterian. Home: 14319 Cross Timbers Court Chesterfield Missouri 63017

YARIV, AMNON, scientist, educator; born Tel Aviv, Israel, April 13, 1930; came to United States, 1951, naturalized, 1964; son of Shraga and

Henya (Davidson) Y.; married Frances Pokras, April 10, 1972; children: Elizabeth, Dana, Gabriela. Bachelor of Science, University California, Berkeley, 1954, Master of Science, 1956, Doctor of Philosophy, 1958. Member tech. staff Bell Telephone Laboratories, 1959-63; director laser research Watkins-Johnson Company, 1963-64; member faculty California Institute Tech., 1964—, Thomas G. Myers professor electrical engineering and applied physics; 1966—; chairman board ORTEL Incorporated; consultant in field. Author: Quantum Electronics, 1967, 75, Introduction to Optical Electronics, 1971, 77, Theory and Applications of Quantum Mechanics, Propagation of Light in Crystals. Served with Israeli Army, 1948-50. Recipient Pender award University Pennsylvania. Fellow Institute of Electrical and Electronics Engineers, Am. Optical Society (Ives medal 1986), Am. Acad. Arts and Sciences; member Am. Physical Society, National Acad. Engineering. Office: 1201 California Avenue Pasadena California 91125

YEAGER, CHARLES ELWOOD, retired air force officer; born Myra, West Virginia, February 13, 1923; son of Albert Hal and Susie May (Sizemore) Y.; married Gennis Faye Dickhouse, February 26, 1945; children: Sharon Yeager Flick, Susan F., Donald C., Michael D. Graduate, Air Command and Staff School, 1952, Air War College, 1961; Doctor of Science (honorary), West Virginia University, 1948, Marshall University, Huntington, West Virginia, 1969; Doctor in Aeronautical Science, Salem College, West Virginia, 1975. Enlisted in United States Army Air Force, 1941; advanced through grades to brigadier general United States Air Force, 1969, fighter pilot, European Theatre of Operations; 1943-46, experimental flight test pilot; 1945-54; various command assignments United States Air Force, United States, Germany, France and Spain, 1954-62; commander 405th Fighter Wing, Seymour Johnson Air Force Base, North Carolina, 1968-69; vice commander 17th Air Force, Ramstein Air Base, Federal Republic Germany, 1969-71; United States defense representative to Pakistan 1971-73; special assistant to commander Air Force Inspection and Safety Center, Norton Air Force Base, California, 1973, director aerospace safety; 1973-75; retired 1975. Author: (with Leo Janos) Yeager: An Autobiography, 1985, (with Charles Leerhsen) Press On!, 1988. Decorated Distinguished Service Medal with oak leaf cluster, Silver Star with oak leaf cluster, Legion of merit with oak leaf cluster, Distinguished Flying Cross with 2 oak leaf clusters, Bronze star with V device, Air medal with 10 oak leaf clusters, Air Force Commendation medal, Purple Heart. First man to fly faster than speed of sound. Home: Post Office Box 128 Cedar Ridge California 95924

YOCHELSON, ELLIS L(EON), paleontologist; born Washington, November 14, 1928; son of Morris Wolf and Fannie (Botkin) Y.; married Sally Witt, June 10, 1950; children: Jeffrey, Abby, Charles. Bachelor of Science, University Kansas, 1949, Master of Science, 1950; Doctor of Philosophy, Columbia University, 1955. Paleontologist, United States Geological Survey, 1952-85; biostratigrapher, specializing on Paleozoic gastropods and minor classes of extinct mollusks; lecturer night school George Washington

University, 1962-65; lecturer University College, University Maryland, 1966-74, University Del., 1981; visiting professor University Maryland, 1986-87; organizer North America Paleontological Convention, 1969, editor proceedings; 1970-71; member National Research Council, 1959-68; member organizing committee International Congress Systematic and Evolutionary Biology, Boulder, Colorado, 1972; research associate department paleobiology United States National Mus. Natural History; sec.-gen. IX International Congress Carboniferous Stratigraphy and Geology, 1979; member centennial committee United States Geological Survey, 1979. Co-editor: Essays in Paleontology and Stratigraphy, 1967; editor: Scientific Ideas of G.K. Gilbert, 1980; contributor numerous articles to professional journals. Fellow American Association for the Advancement of Science (chairman section E 1971); member Society Systematic Zoology (secretary 1961-66, councilor 1973), International Palaeontol. Association (treasurer 1972-76), Paleontological Society (president 1976), History of Earth Sciences Society (sec.-treas. 1982-85, secretary 1986-87, pres.-elect 1988, president 1989), Paleontological Association, Sigma Xi. Office: Smithsonian Instn E-317 Mus Natural History Washington District of Columbia 20560

YOUNG, JOHN WATTS, astronaut; born San Francisco, September 24, 1930; son of William H. Y.; married Susy Feldman; children by previous marriage: Sandra, John. Bachelor of Science in Aeronautical Engineering, Georgia Institute Tech., 1952; Doctor Applied Science (honorary), Florida

Doctor of Laws (honorary), Western State University, 1969. Joined United States Navy, 1952, advanced through grades to captain; test pilot, program manager F4 weapons systems projects; 1959-62; then maintenance officer (Fighter Squadron 143, Naval Air Station), Miramar, California; chief astronaut office Flight Operations Directorate 1975—, participant 54-hour, 36-orbit maiden flight of Shuttle Columbia; 1981; member Presdl. Commission on the Space Shuttle, 1986. Recipient National Aeronautics and Space Administration Distinguished Service medal (3), National Aeronautics and Space Administration Exceptional Service medal (2); decorated Distinguished Flying Cross, Distinguished Service Medal; named Distinguished Young Alumnus Georgia Tech. Institute, 1965, Distinguished Alumni Service award, 1972. Fellow Am. Astronautical Society (Flight Achievement award 1972), Society Experimental Test Pilots (Iven Kincheloe award 1972); member Am. Institute Aeros. and Astronautics (Haley Astronautics award 1973), Sigma Chi. Astronaut NASA, made 1st two-man 3 orbit flight, Gemini 3, March 1965, Gemini 10 flight, 1966, Apollo 10 8-day flight lunar landing dress rehearsal, 1969, Apollo 16, 1972; dir. space shuttle br., astronaut office, 1973-75. Office: NASA Manned Spacecraft Center Houston Texas 77058

YOUNG, ROY ALTON, university administrator, educator; born McAlister, New Mexico, March 1, 1921; son of John Arthur and Etta Julia (Sprinkle) Y.; married Marilyn Ruth Sandman, May 22, 1950; children: Janet Elizabeth, Randall Owen. Bachelor of Science, New

College, 1941; Master of Science, Iowa State University, 1942, Doctor of Philosophy, 1948; Doctor of Laws (honorary), New Mexico State University, 1978. Teaching fellow Iowa State University, 1941-42, instructor; 1946-47, Industrial fellow; 1947-48; assistant professor Oregon State University, 1948-50, associate professor; 1950-53, professor; 1953—, head department botany and plant pathology; 1958-66, dean research; 1966-70, acting president; 1969-70, vice president for research and grad. studies; 1970-76, director Office for Natural Resources Policy; 1986—; chancellor University Nebraska, Lincoln, 1976-80; managing director, president Boyce Thompson Institute Plant Research, Cornell University, Ithaca, New York, 1980-86; board of directors Pacific Power and Light, PacifiCorp; member Commission on Undergrad. Education in Biological Sciences, 1963-68, Gov.'s Sci. Council, 1987—; consultant State Experiment Stations div. USDA; chairman subcom. plant pathogens, agriculture board National Acad. Scis.-NRC, 1965-68, member executive committee study on problems of pest control, 1972-75; member executive committee National Govs.' Council on Sci. and Tech., 1970-74; member United States committee man and biosphere United Nations Educational, Scientific and Cultural Organization, 1973-82; member committee to rev. United States component International Biological Program, National Acad. Sciences, 1974-76; member adv. panel on post-doctoral fellowships in environmental sci. Rockefeller Foundation, 1974-78; board of directors Boyce Thompson Institute for Plant Research, 1975—; member adv. committee Directorate for Engineering and Applied Sci., National Science Foundation, 1977-81, member sea grant adv. panel, 1978-80; member policy adv. committee Office of Grants, USDA, 1985-86. Board of directors Boyce Thompson Southwestern Arboretum, 1981—, Am. Phytopath. Society Foundation, 1986—, Oregon Grad. Center, 1987—; trustee Ithaca College, 1982—. Served to lieutenant United States Naval Reserve, 1943-46. Fellow American Association for the Advancement of Science (executive committee Pacific division 1963-67, president division 1971), Am. Phytopath. Society (president Pacific division 1957, chairman special committee to develop plans for endowment 1984-86); member Oregon Acad. Sci., National Association State Univs. and Land Grant Colls. (chairman council for research policy and adminstrn. 1970, chairman standing committee on environment and energy 1974-82, chairman committee on environment 1984-86), Sigma Xi, Phi Kappa Phi, Phi Sigma, Sigma Alpha Epsilon. Home: 3605 Northwest Van Buren St Corvallis Oregon 97330 Office: Oregon State U Natural Resources Policy Snell Hall Corvallis Oregon 97331-1651

YUEN, PAUL C(HAN), electrical engineer; born Hilo, Hawaii, June 7, 1928. Bachelor of Science, University Chicago, 1952; Master of Science, Illinois Institute Tech., 1955, Doctor of Philosophy in Electrical Engineering, 1960. Cyclotron technician University Chicago, 1950-52; engineer Standard Coil Productions, 1953-54; associate research engineer Armour Research Foundation, Chicago, 1954-57; research engineer Illinois Institute

Tech., Chicago, 1957-60; assistant professor electrical engineering Illinois Institute Tech., 1960-61; associate professor electrical engineering University Hawaii, Manoa, 1961-65, professor electrical engineering; 1965—; acting dean College Engineering University Hawaii, Manoa, 1969, 77-78, associate dean; 1970-79, assistant to chancellor; 1971-72; acting director Center Engineering Research University Hawaii, Manoa, 1976-77; director Hawaii Natural Energy Institute, 1977-81; dean College Engineering University Hawaii, Manoa, 1981—; acting president Pacific International Center High Technological Research, 1983—. Member Institute of Electrical and Electronics Engineers (Centennial medal 1984), Am. Geophysical Union, Am. Society Engineering Education, International Union Radio Sci. Office: University of Hawaii-Manoa Department of Engring Honolulu Hawaii 96822

YUNIS, JORGE JOSE, geneticist, pathologist, educator; born Sincelejo, Colombia; married Mary Brogmus. Doctor of Medicine, Central University, Madrid, Spain, 1956. General practice medicine Barranquilla, Colombia, 1957-59; resident in clinical pathology University Minnesota, Minneapolis, 1959-62, resident in anatomical pathology; 1962-64, member faculty; 1965—, professor; 1969—, director grad. studies of laboratory medicine; 1969-74, director grad. studies of pathology; 1972-74, chairman human genetics committee for health sciences; 1972-77; visiting professor numerous universities. Author: Human Chromosome Method, 1965, 75, Biochemical Methods in Red Cell Genetics, 1969, Molecular Pathology, 1975, New Chromosomal Syndromes, 1977, Molecular Structure of Human Chromosomes, 1977; contributor more than 200 articles to professional journals. Named Clinical Professor of Year, Harvard Medical School, 1987; honored by Colombian Parliament, Bogota, 1986. Member Leukemia Society Am. (trustee 1983-88), Colombian Acad. Medicine. Office: University Minnesota Hosps Med School Box 198 Minneapolis Minnesota 55455

ZARE, RICHARD NEIL, chemistry educator; born Cleveland, November 19, 1939; son of Milton and Dorothy (Amdur) Z.; married Susan Leigh Shively, April 20, 1963; children—Bethany Jean, Bonnie Sue, Rachel Amdur. Bachelor of Arts, Harvard, 1961; postgraduate, University California at Berkeley, 1961-63; Doctor of Philosophy (NSF predoctoral fellow), Harvard, 1964. Postdoctoral fellow Harvard, 1964; postdoctoral research associate Joint Institute for Laboratory Astrophysics, 1964-65; assistant professor chemistry Massachusetts Institute Tech., 1965-66; assistant professor department physics and astrophysics University Colorado, 1966-68, associate professor physics and astrophysics, associate professor chemistry; 1968-69; professor chemistry Columbia, 1969-77, Higgins professor natural sci.; 1975-77; professor Stanford University, 1977—, Shell Distinguished professor chemistry; 1980-85, Marguerite Blake Wilbur professor chemistry; 1987—; consultant Aeronomy Laboratory, National Oceanographic and Atmospheric Administration, 1966-77, radio standards physics div. National Bureau Standards, 1968-77,

Lawrence Livermore Laboratory, University California, 1974—, Stanford Research Institute, 1974—, Los Alamos Sci. Laboratory, University California, 1975—; fellow adjoint, Joint Institute Laboratory Astrophysics, University Colorado; member International Business Machines Corporation Sci. Advisory Committee, 1977—. editor Chemical Physics Letters, 1982-85. Recipient Fresenius award Phi Lambda Upsilon, 1974; Michael Polanyi medal, 1979; National Medal Sci., 1985 award Spectroscopy Society Pitts., 1983, Michelson-Morley award, Case Institute Tech./Case Western Res. University, 1986; nonresident fellow Joint Institute for Laboratory Astrophysics, 1970—; Alfred P. Sloan fellow, 1967-69; Christensen fellow St. Catherine's College, Oxford University, 1982; Stanford University fellow, 1984-86. Fellow American Association for the Advancement of Science; member National Acad. Sci., Am. Acad. Arts and Sciences, Am. Physical Society (Earle K. Plyler prize 1981, Irving Langmuir prize 1985), Am. Chemical Society (Harrison Howe award Rochester section 1985, Remsen award Maryland section 1985, Kirkwood award, Yale University, New Haven section 1986), Chemical Society London, Phi Beta Kappa. Research and publs. on laser chemistry and chem. physics. Office: Stanford U Department Chemistry Stanford California 94305

ZEN, E-AN, research geologist; born Peking, China, May 31, 1928; came to United States, 1946, naturalized, 1963; son of Hung-chun and Heng-chi'h (Chen) Z. Bachelor of Arts, Cornell University, 1951; Master of Arts, Harvard University, 1952, Doctor of Philosophy, 1955. Research fellow Woods Hole Oceanographic Institute, 1955-56, research associate; 1956-58; assistant professor University North Carolina, 1958-59; geologist United States Geological Survey, 1959-80, research geologist; 1981—; visiting associate professor California Institute Tech., 1962; Crosby visiting professor M.I.T., 1973; Harry H. Hess senior visiting fellow Princeton University, 1981; counselor 28th International Geological Congress. 1986—. Contributor articles to professional journals. Fellow Geological Society Am. (councillor 1985-88), American Association for the Advancement of Science, Am. Acad. Arts and Sciences, Mineralogical Society Am. (council 1975-77, president 1975-76); member Geological Society Washington (president 1973), National Acad. Sciences, Mineralogical Association Can. Office: Mail Stop 959 United States Geol Survey National Center Reston Virginia 22092

ZETLIN, LEV, civil engineer, educator; born Namangan, Russia, July 14, 1918; son of Mark and Alexandra (Senelnikoff) Z.; married Eve Shmueli, January 24, 1946; children: Alexandra, Thalia, Michael Steven. Diploma, Higher Tech. Institute, Palestine, 1939; Master of Civil Engineering, Cornell University, 1951, Doctor of Philosophy, 1953. Research associate, assistant professor civil engineering Cornell University, 1951-55; distinguished professor civil engineering Pratt Institute, New York City, 1956—; visiting professor civil engineering Manhattan College, New York City, 1957-59; guest lecturer Columbia, University Minnesota, University Virginia, 1955-63; University professor engineering and architecture University Virginia, 1967;

consultant engineer; president Zetlin-Argo Liaison & Guidance Corp., Lev Zetlin Cons., Special Structural Systems, Incorporated; member Internal Board Engineering; Cons. to James Bay Energy Corp., Can., Montreal Olympics Stadium.; Member Concrete Industry Board New York City; former member adv. panel General Services Administration, housing tech. joint panel Department Commerce-Dept. Housing and Urban Devel.; member planning committee building research adv. board National Acad. Sciences; past president International Tech. Cooperation Centre. Member editorial adv. board Building: Constrn. Mag, 1962—; Author: Reinforced Concrete Design, Standard Handbook for Engineers, 1968, Suspension Structures, Structural Engineering Handbook, 1968; Contributor articles to professional journals; chapter on stadiums Encyclopedia Brit. Trustee, chairman consultor committee Manhattan College Sacred Heart, New York; member New York State Council on Arts, 1978. Decorated Knight of honour Mil. and Hospitaler Order St. John of Jerusalem, Knight of Malta; recipient Prestressed Concrete Institute award for New York State Observation Towers New York Worlds Fair, 1964; Gold medal Société Arts, Sciences, Lettres, 1969; named to Professional and Executive Hall of Fame. Fellow American Society of Civil Engineers; member Society Am. Military Engineers, International Association Bridge and Structural Engineers, Institute Structural Engineers (England), New York Acad. Sciences, Am. Concrete Institute, Sigma Xi, Phi Kappa Phi, Chi Epsilon. Inventor prestressed runways, light gage airplane hangars, cable suspension structures, systems

bldgs.; cons. Montreal Olympics Stadium, investigator major structural collapses such as Hayatt Regency, Kansas City, Missouri, Mianus Bridge, Connecticut, L'Ambique Place, Bridgeport, Connecticut. Home: 45 E 80th St New York New York 10021 Office: Zetlin-Argo The Harbor Towers 3901 S Flagler Dr West Palm Beach Florida 33405

ZEWAIL, AHMED HASSAN, chemistry and chemical engineering educator, editor, consultant; born Damanhour, Egypt, February 26, 1946; came to United States, 1969, naturalized, 1982.; son of Hassan A. Zewail and Rawhia Dar; children—Maha, Amani. Bachelor of Science, Alexandria University, Egypt, 1967, Master of Science, 1969; Doctor of Philosophy, University Pennsylvania, 1974. Teaching assistant University Pennsylvania, Philadelphia, 1969-70; International Business Machines Corporation fellow University Calif.-Berkeley, 1974-76; assistant professor chemistry and chemical engineering California Institute Tech., Pasadena, 1976-78, associate professor; 1978-82, professor; 1982—; consultant Xerox Corp., Webster, New York, 1977-80, ARCO Solar, Incorporated, California, 1978-81. Editor Laser Chemistry journal, 1981-85, Photochemistry and Photobiology, volumes I and II, Advances in Laser Chemistry, Advances in Laser Spectroscopy. Contributor more than 150 articles on research and devel. in lasers and applications to sci. journals; patentee solar energy field. Tchr.-scholar award Dreyfus Foundation, 1979-85; Sloan Foundation research fellow, 1978-82; recipient Alexander von Humboldt award for sr. U.S. scientists, 1983; John Simon Guggenheim

Memorial Foundation award, 1987. Buck-Whitney medal, 1985. Fellow Am. Physical Society; member Am. Chemical Society. Office: California Institute Tech Chem 127 72 Pasadena California 91125

ZIMMERMAN, EARL ABRAM, physician, scientist, educator, neuroendocrinology researcher; born Harrisburg, Pennsylvania, May 5, 1937; son of Earl Beckley and Hazel Marie (Myers) Z.; married Diane Leenheer, September 14, 1960 (divorced August 1982); m Poppy Ann Warren, September 5, 1982. Bachelor of Science in Chemistry, Franklin and Marshall College, 1959; Doctor of Medicine, University Pennsylvania, 1963. Diplomate Am. Board Psychiatry and Neurology, Am. Board Internal Medicine. Intern Presbyn. Hospital, New York City, 1963-64, resident; 1964-65; resident Neurological Institute CPMC, New York City, 1965-68, research fellow endocrinology; 1970-72; assistant professor to professor neurology Columbia University, New York City, 1972-85; professor, chairman department neurology Oregon Health Sci. University, Portland, 1985—; director neurology Helen Hayes Hospital, Haverstraw, New York, 1982-83. Member editorial board: Journal Histochem. Cytochemistry, 1980-85, 87, Neuroendocrinology, 1985-88, Annals of Neurology, 1985; contributor numerous articles to professional journals. Served to major United States Air Force, 1968-70. Recipient research award National Institutes of Health, 1977-85. Member Am. Neurological Association (program chairman 1980-82), Am. Acad. Neurology (Wartenber lecturer 1985), Endocrine Society. Democrat.

Member United Church of Christ. Avocations: woodworking; gardening; theatre; music; art; skiing; tennis. Home: 2347 Northwest Flanders Portland Oregon 97210 Office: Oregon Health Sci U Department Neurology 3181 Southwest Sam Jackson Park Road Portland Oregon 97201

ZINDER, NORTON DAVID, geneticist, educator; born New York City, November 7, 1928; son of Harry Jean and (Gottesman) Z.; married Marilyn Estreicher, December 24, 1949; children—Stephen, Michael. Bachelor of Arts, Columbia University, 1947; Master of Science, University Wisconsin, 1949, Doctor of Philosophy, 1952. Assistant Rockefeller University, New York City, 1952-56; associate Rockefeller University, 1956-58, associate professor genetics; 1958-64, professor; 1964—, John D. Rockefeller Junior professor; 1977—; consultant genetic-biology National Science Foundation, 1962-66, Office Tech. Assessment, Washington, 1979-81, Chas. Pfizer & Company, 1963-67; chairman ad hoc committee to rev. viral cancer program National Cancer Institute, 1973-74; member visiting committee department biology Harvard University, 1975—, section virology Yale University, 1975—, department biochemistry Princeton University, 1975-86; member sci. adv. board Carter-Wallace Incorporated, 1982-85, Genetic Systems Corp., 1981-86; mem.adv. committee Alliance International Health Care Trust, 1984— ; trustee Cold Spring Harbor Laboratory, 1967-85, secretary to board, 1980-85; other affiliations. Associate editor: Virology; sect. editor Intervirology, 1973—. Recipient Eli Lilly award in microbiology and immunology, 1962, U.S. Steel Foundation award in molecular biology, 1966, medal of excellence Columbia University, 1969, award in sci. freedom & responsibility American Association for the Advancement of Science, 1982; Am. Cancer Society scholar, 1955-58. Fellow Am. Acad. Arts and Sciences (council 1984-87); member National Acad. Sciences (executive committee Assembly of Life Sciences 1975—, board army sci. and tech. 1981, council 1988—), Society Am. Biological Chemists, Genetics Society Am., Am. Society for Microbiology, Council Foreign Relations, Harvey Society, Sigma Xi. Spl. research in microbial genetics. Home: 450 E 63d St New York New York 10021 Office: Rockefeller U 66th St and York Avenue New York New York 10021

ZWANZIG, ROBERT WALTER, physical science educator; born Brooklyn, April 9, 1928; son of Walter and Bertha (Weil) Z.; married H. Frances Ryder, June 6, 1953; children: Elizabeth Ann, Carl Philip. Bachelor of Science, Polytechnic Institute Brooklyn, 1948; Master of Science, University Southern California, 1950; Doctor of Philosophy, California Institute Tech., 1952. Research associate Yale, 1951-54; assistant professor Johns Hopkins, 1954-58; physical chemist National Bureau Standards, 1958-66; research professor University Maryland, College Park, 1966—; Distinguished professor physical sci. University Maryland, 1980—. Asso. editor: Journal of Chemical Physics, 1965-67, Journal of Math. Physics, 1968-70, Transport Theory and Statistical Physics, 1970, Collective Phenomena, 1972—, Chemical Physics, 1973—; Contributor articles

professional journals. Department Commerce Silver medal, 1965. Fellow Am. Physical Society, Am. Acad. Arts and Sciences, American Association for the Advancement of Science; member National Acad. Sciences, Am. Chemical Society (Peter Debye award in phys. chemistry 1976; Irving Langmuir award 1984). Home: 5314 Sangamore Road Bethesda Maryland 20816 Office: U Maryland Institute for Physical Sciences and Tech College Park Maryland 20742

ZWOYER, EUGENE MILTON, consulting engineer; born Plainfield, New Jersey, September 8, 1926; son of Paul Ellsworth and Marie Susan (Britt) Z.; married Dorothy Lucille Seward, February 23, 1946; children: Gregory, Jeffrey, Douglas. Student, University Notre Dame, 1944, Missouri Valley College, 1944-45; Bachelor of Science, University New Mexico, 1947; Master of Science, Illinois Institute Tech., 1949; Doctor of Philosophy, University Illinois, 1953. Member faculty University New Mexico, Albuquerque, 1948-71, professor civil engineering, director Eric Wang Civil Engineering Research Facility; 1961-70; research associate University Illinois, Urbana, 1951-53; owner, consultant engineer Eugene Zwoyer & Associates, Albuquerque, 1954-72; executive director, secretary American Society of Civil Engineers, New York City, 1972-82; president Am. Association Engineering Societies, New York City, 1982-84; executive vice president T.Y. Lin International, San Francisco, 1984-86; president; 1986—. Trustee Small Business Research Corp., 1976-80; trustee Engring. Information, Incorporated, 1981-84; international trustee People-to-People International 1974-86; vice president World

Federation Engring. Orgns., 1982-85. Served to lieutenant (junior grade) United States Navy, 1944-46. Named Outstanding Engineer of Year Albuquerque chapter N.Mex Society Professional Engrs., 1969, One Who Served the Best Interests of the Constrn. Industry, Engineering News Record, 1980; recipient Distinguished Alumnus award the Civil Engineering Alumni Association at University Illinois, 1979, Distinguished Alumnus award Engineering College Alumni Association, University New Mexico, 1982, Can.-Am. Civil Engineering Amity award Am. Society Civil Engrs., 1988, Award for Outstanding Professional Contbns. and Leadership College Engineering University New Mexico, 1989. Member American Society of Civil Engineers (district director 1968-71), NSPE, Am. Concrete Institute, Am. Society Engring Education, American Association for the Advancement of Science, National Acad. Code Administration (trustee, member executive committee 1973-79), Engineers Joint Council (director 1978-79), Engineering Society Commission on Energy (director 1977-82), Sigma Xi, Sigma Tau, Chi Epsilon. Home: 6363 Christie Avenue Apartment 1326 Emeryville California 94608 Office: T Y Lin International 315 Bay Street San Francisco California 94133

ZYGMUND, ANTONI, mathematician, educator; born Warsaw, Poland, December 26, 1900; son of Wincenty and Antonina (Perkowska) Z.; married Irena Parnowska, 1925; 1 child. Student, University Warsaw; Doctor h.c., Washington University, St. Louis, University Torun, Poland, University Uppsala, Paris-Sud. Instructor Polytechnic School, Warsaw, 1922-29; docent University Warsaw, 1926-30; professor University Wilno, Poland, 1930-39, Mount Holyoke College, South Hadley, Massachusetts, 1940-45, University Pennsylvania, Philadelphia, 1945-47; professor math. University Chicago, 1947—, professor emeritus. Author: Trigonometric Series, 1935, 59, 77; (with S. Saks) Analytic Functions, 1938, 56. Recipient National Medal of Sci., 1986. Member National Acad. Sciences, Polish Acad. Sci., Spanish Acad. Sci., London Math. Society (hon.), Italian Acad. Sci., Argentine Acad. Sci. Office: University Chicago Department Math Chicago Illinois 60637